Our Nation's Archive

THE HISTORY OF THE UNITED STATES IN DOCUMENTS

Our Nation's Archive

THE HISTORY OF THE UNITED STATES IN DOCUMENTS

EDITED BY ERIK BRUUN AND JAY CROSBY

BLACK DOG
& LEVENTHAL
PUBLISHERS
NEW YORK

Copyright © 1999 by Black Dog & Leventhal Publishers, Inc.

Published by Black Dog & Leventhal Publishers, Inc.
151 West 19th Street, New York, NY 10011

Distributed by Workman Publishing Company
708 Broadway, New York, NY 10003

Printed in the United States of America

Designed by Dutton & Sherman

ISBN 1-57912-067-9

h g f e d c b a
Library of Congress Cataloging-in-Publication Data
Our national archive : key documents, opinions, speeches, letters, and songs that shaped our nation /
    edited by Erik Bruun and Jay Crosby.
      p. cm.
    Includes index
    ISBN 1-57912-067-9
    1. United States--History Sources. I. Bruun, Erik A., 1961- . II. Crosby, Jay
  E173.077 1999   99-29451
  973--dc21   CIP

pp.853 constitutes a continuation of this copyright page

ACKNOWLEDGMENTS

As in any publishing endeavor, this book would not be what it is without the invaluable contribution of several hard-working, intelligent people. Copy editor Lydia Ogden proved to be a finely screened biblio-filter for the many, many errors that crept into the original manuscript. Michael Driscoll, an all-around swell person, toiled to secure dozens of permissions and tackle any and all editorial assignments sent his way. Designers Debbie Dutton and Joseph Sherman crafted a handsome layout for the text, and polished William Kiester's jacket idea. Christine Kelly did yeoman's work inputting many of the documents. Anna Bromley's steady hand as production manager made the complicated and tedious seem simple and graceful.

Several friends and relatives offered helpful suggestions and materials for documents. Contributing their advice and insights were Christian Bruun, Philip Deely, Kit Crosby, Eleanor Tillinghast, Robin Getzen, Robert Harrison, Maude Hennessey, Bertel Bruun, and Lelia Bruun. In addition, valuable assistance in collecting materials was provided by the staffs of the New York Public Library, Columbia University Library, New York University Library, Simon's Rock College Library, and one of the great thriving independent small-town bookstores, The Bookloft in Great Barrington, Massachusetts.

Finally, special acknowledgement should be made to J.P. Leventhal who conceived of the book and our super-capable editor Jessica MacMurray whose encouragement helped nourish our flagging morale and direction proved right on the mark. All of these people helped elevate the quality of this book far beyond our own capacity. For that and their kindness, we are very grateful.

CONTENTS

1763–1789: THE CREATION OF A REPUBLIC

Contents

1861-1865: CIVIL WAR AND A NEW BIRTH OF FREEDOM

1941-1960: WAR, PROSPERITY AND AN UNEASY PEACE

INTRODUCTION

Primary sources bring life and relevancy to the past. We feel the chill of persecution when we read the transcript of a Salem witch trial, the brutality of war becomes all too real in recollections of a GI on Omaha Beach and a Lowell woman's account of working in a 19th-century mill lends a human, everyday insight into a culture that set the stage for where we are today. The personal anguish of the civil rights movement is impossible to ignore when Martin Luther King, Jr., from a jail cell in Birmingham, describes the poignancy of telling his daughter why she cannot go to Funtown like the white children do. With 20-20 hindsight, read Defense Secretary Robert McNamara's recommendation to expand the United States forces in Vietnam, mindful of the consequences for the young men who would fight and die as a result of those words. It may or may not be important to know that Benjamin Franklin signed the Treaty of Paris, but his "Advice to a Young Tradesman" contains lessons today that the hottest entrepreneur on Wall Street would be wise to consider.

From the struggles of the earliest colonists to eke out a living and devise a method for self-government, to the United States' present status as the world's only superpower, Americans have blazed an extraordinary trail.

Unfortunately, the path has not only been marked by glory. American history claims more than its share of disgraces. European settlers took the country, often by violence, from Native Americans, virtually wiping out a people in the process and stripping the survivors of their land and dignity. An entire population was enslaved and then institutionally repressed. While unfettered capitalism in the 1800s helped build a wealthy industrial power, it did so on the backs of children and workers. And, despite being a nation of immigrants, the United States' treatment of them is not cloaked with honor. Today, as we look back at the positive strides, we must also accept responsibility for the missteps.

As the American narrative unfolds in documents from the people who witnessed it, themes of history emerge. Step by step, women have elevated their political and economic rights. The shameful schism between European settlers and their African slaves dating back to 1619 has been narrowed, but is yet to be fully bridged. The virtues of thrift and hard work were necessities in the colonies when survival was at stake, and remain in place today. The basic principles of liberty, freedom and equality continue to serve as the nation's basic goals, even if there are different interpretations of what they mean and opposing views about the best way to achieve them.

For better or worse, history is treated as a story line of events, dates, and prominent individuals. This approach makes for a simple, easy-to-tell account of our past, but at the same time, it strips away the contributions of those who did not make the historian's cut and sidesteps the diverse perspectives of those whose ideas faded with the passage of time. It is easy to forget that each of us has an impact on the course of our nation's history; we all contribute to our individual and collective heritage.

No matter how important George Washington and Abraham Lincoln were— and they were fantastically influential—none of what they accomplished could have happened without tens of thousands of others to advance their causes. Had Washington spent the winter by himself at Valley Forge, the Americans would not have won the war. Lincoln could have railed against the expansion of slavery all he wanted, but if a majority of the electors in 1860 had not chosen him as president, he would have been a footnote in the history books.

One of the purposes of this book is to not only record the "important" documents of American history, but also to acknowledge the millions of individuals who shaped events and forged a successful democracy of the people, for the people. Farm boys who trained muskets on redcoats. Mothers who sacrificed their children for the Union's cause. Tough, hard-bitten men and women built this country. Their perspectives are important. They are the central ingredients in United States history.

CHAPTER ONE

Pre-Columbus–1763

A New World

🍂 How the World Was Made

CHEROKEE NATION

When Columbus arrived in America in 1492 the continent was already populated by as many as 40 million people from six hundred or more Native American tribes. Approximately 15,000 to 20,000 years earlier, the first humans are believed to have walked to North America via a land bridge in what is now the Bering Straits and then dispersed throughout North and South America. The densest populations were along the coasts and major rivers, around the Great Lakes, and in Mexico, Florida, California and the Caribbean islands. Each nation had a distinct language and culture, some of which were very sophisticated and complex. Within those distinct cultures, different legends evolved of how the world was made. The Cherokee originally occupied what is now south-eastern United States but were forcibly removed in the early nineteenth century. Like many native origin stories, the Cherokee creation myth places a close spiritual bond between people, animals and nature.

The earth is a great island floating in a sea of water, and suspended at each of the four cardinal points by a cord hanging down from the sky vault, which is of solid rock. When the world grows old and worn out, the people will die and the cords will break and let the earth sink down into the ocean, and all will be water again. The Indians are afraid of this.

When all was water, the animals were above Galunlati, beyond the arch; but it was very much crowded, and they were wanting more room. They wondered what was below the water, and at last Dayunisi, "Beaver's Grandchild," the little Water-beetle, offered to go and see if it could learn. It darted in every direction over the surface of the water, but could find no firm place to rest. Then it dived to the bottom and came up with some soft mud, which began to grow and spread on every side until it became the island which we call the earth. It was afterward fastened to the sky with four cords, but no one remembers who did this.

At first the earth was flat and very soft and wet. The animals were anxious to get down, and sent out different birds to see if it was yet dry, but they found no place to alight and came back again to Galunlati. At last it seemed to be time, and they sent out the Buzzard, the father of all the buzzards we see now. He flew all over the earth, low down near the ground, and it was still soft. When he reached the Cherokee country, he was very tired,

and his wings began to flap and strike the ground, and wherever they struck the earth there was a valley, and where they turned up again there was a mountain. When the animals above saw this, they were afraid that the whole world would be mountains, so they called him back, but the Cherokee country remains full of mountains to this day.

When the earth was dry and the animals came down, it was still dark, so they got the sun and set it in a track to go every day across the island from east to west, just overhead. It was too hot this way, and Tsiskagili, the Red Crawfish, had his shell scorched a bright red, so that his meat was spoiled, and the Cherokee do not eat it: but was still too hot. They raised it another time, and another, until it was seven hand-breadths high and just under the sky arch. Then it was right, and they left it so. This is why the conjurers call the highest place Gulkwagine Digalunlatiyn, "The Seventh Height," because it is seven hand-breadths above the earth. Every day the sun goes along under this arch, and returns at night on the upper side to the starting place.

There is another world under this, and it is like ours in everything—animals, plants, and people—save that the seasons are different. The streams that come down from the mountains are the trails by which we reach this underworld, and the springs at their head are the doorways by which we enter it, but to do this one must fast and go to water and have one of the underground people for a guide. We know that the seasons in the underworld are different from ours, because the water in the springs is always warmer in winter and cooler in summer than the outer air.

When the animals and plants were first made— we do not know by whom—they were told to watch and keep awake for seven nights, just as young men now fast and keep awake when they pray to their medicine. They tried to do this, and nearly all were awake through the first night, but the next night several dropped off to sleep, and the third night others were asleep, and then others, until on the seventh night, of all the animals only the owl, the panther, and one or two more were still awake. To these were given the power to see and to go about in the dark, and to make prey of the birds and animals which must sleep at night. Of the trees only the cedar, the pine, the spruce, the holly, and the laurel were awake to the end, and to them it was given to be always green and to be greatest for medicine, but to the others it was said: "Because you have not endured to the end you shall lose your hair every winter."

Men came after the animals and plants. At first there were only a brother and a sister until he struck her with a fish and told her to multiply, and so it was. In seven days a child was born to her, and thereafter every seven days another, and they increased very fast until there was danger that the world could not keep them. Then it was made that a woman should have only one child in a year, and it has been so ever since.

✿ "This is the wisdom of the great spirit"

IROQUOIS FEDERATION CONSTITUTION

The five nations of the Iroquois (Mohawks, Oneidas, Onondagas, Cayugas, and Senecas) lived together for centuries in a large territory in what is now upstate New York. The tribes were divided into clans who formed tight-knit communities. At a certain point in their history, however, the clans and tribes feuded fiercely with each other—this conflict led to a downward spiral of increasing violence. To stop the cycle, according to legend, a Huron elder named Deganawida appeared in the five nations to bring peace and preach thirteen laws, each of which carried a moral overtone, by which the nations could live in unity and peace. He spoke with Hiawatha, an Onondaga tribe member, who became the chief spokesman for the new laws. Deganawida and Hiawatha convinced the chiefs of all five tribes to abide by the new law and create the Hodenosaunee, or Iroquois, Confederacy.

To administer the law, a new structure of governance was created in which members of all five tribes had to work together in common councils to make decisions. The structure described here allowed the different nations to live in harmony under one law. It was a form of democracy and self-government that influenced enlightened European philosophers and European settlers. The structure of the league directly influenced Benjamin Franklin's 1754 Albany Plan of Union and played an indirect role in the ultimate formation of the United States government.

This is wisdom and justice on the part of the Great Spirit to create and raise chiefs, give and establish unchangable laws, rules and customs between the Five Nation Indians, the Mohawks, Oneidas, Onondagas, Cayugas and Senecas and the other nations of Indians here in North America. The object of these laws is to establish peace between the numerous nations of Indians, hostility will be done away with, for the preservation and protection of life, property and liberty.

And the number of chiefs in this confederation of the five Nation Indians are fifty in number, no more and no less. They are the ones to arrange, to legislate and to look after the affairs of their people.

And the Mohawks, an Indian Nation, forms a party of the body of this Five Nation Indians confederation, and their representatives in this confederation is nine chiefs.

And the Oneidas, an Indian Nation, forms a party of the body of this Five Nation Indians confederation, and their representatives in this confederation is nine chiefs.

And the Onondagas, an Indian Nation, forms a party of the body of this Five Nation Indians confederation, and their representatives in this confederation is fourteen chiefs.

And the Cayugas, an Indian Nation, forms a party of the body of this Five Nation Indians confederation, and their representatives in this confederation is ten chiefs.

And the Senecas, an Indian Nation, forms a party of the body of this Five Nation Indians confederation, and their representatives in this confederation is eight chiefs.

And when the Five Nation Indians confederation chiefs assemble to hold a council, the council shall be duly opened and closed by the Onondaga chiefs, the Firekeepers. They will offer thanks to the Great Spirit that dwells in heaven above: the source and ruler of our lives, our daily wants and daily health, and they will then declare the council open for the transaction of business, and give decisions of all that is done in the council.

And there are three totems or castes of the Mohawk nation, the Tortoise, the Wolf and the Bear; each has three head chiefs, nine in all. The chiefs of the Tortoise and Wolf castes are the council by themselves, and the chiefs of the Bear castes are to listen and watch the progress of the council or discussion of the two castes; and if they see any error they are to correct them, and explain, where they are wrong; and when they decide with the sanction of the Bear castes then their speaker will refer the matter to the other side of the council fire, to the second combination chiefs, the Oneidas and Cayugas.

And the council of the five Nations shall not be opened until all of the three castes of the Mohawk chiefs are present; and if they are not all present it shall be legal for them to transact the business of the council if all the three totems have one or more representatives present, and if not it shall not be legal except in small matters; for all the three castes of the Mohawk chiefs must be present to be called a full council.

🍂 *"With fifty men all can be kept in subjection"*

CHRISTOPHER COLUMBUS

Christopher Columbus set sail for Japan in the summer of 1492. He landed in the Caribbean Islands on October 12, thinking he was in Asia. Thus, Europe "discovered" America and the natives who lived there.

Although the initial meeting between the two peoples was peaceful, the seeds of conflict were immediately apparent, as Columbus's diary entry makes clear. Columbus not only planned to bring several of the natives back to Spain with him, but also imagined converting entire nations to Christianity and subjecting them to Spanish rule.

Columbus returned to America three more times. Despite his world-shaking discovery, Columbus proved to be a terrible administrator and he was eventually thrown in jail by his own men. Within 20 years, most of the Caribbean natives who had greeted Columbus and his fellow explorers died of disease or were killed by the Spanish explorers.

In order to win the friendship and affection of that people, and because I was convinced that their conversion to our Holy Faith would be better promoted through love than through force; I presented some of them with red caps and some strings of glass beads which they placed around their necks, and with other trifles of insignificant worth that delighted them and by which we have got a wonderful hold on their affections. They afterwards came to the boats of the vessels swimming, bringing us parrots, cotton thread in balls, and spears, and many other things, which they bartered for others we gave them, as glass beads and little bells. Finally they received everything and gave whatever they had with good will. But I thought them to be a very poor people....

I saw some scars on their bodies, and to my signs asking them what these meant, they answered in the same manner, that people from neighboring islands wanted to capture them, and they had defended themselves; and I did believe, and do believe, that they came from the mainland to take them prisoners.

They must be good servants and very intelligent, because I see that they repeat very quickly what I told them, and it is my conviction that they would easily become Christians, for they seem not to have any sect.

If it pleases our Lord, I will take six of them from here to your Highnesses on my departure, that they may learn to speak. The people are totally unacquainted with arms, as your Highnesses will see by observing the seven which I have caused to be taken in. With fifty men all can be kept in subjection, and made to do whatever you desire.

🍂 *Spanish explorers in Florida*

ALVER NUNEZ CABEZA DE VACA

Panfilo de Narvaez led a disastrous Spanish expedition to Florida in 1528. Hostile natives attacked the explorers and the Florida wilderness wreaked havoc on their journey. Starting three hundred men strong, they were forced to abort the trip and head for home, but were shipwrecked off modern-day Texas. Eight years later four surviving members of the journey arrived in Mexico City.

The character of the country
The country where we came on shore to this town and region of Apalachen is for the most part level, the ground of sand and stiff earth. Throughout are immense trees and open woods, in which are walnut, laurel, and another tree called liquid-amber, cedars, savins, evergreen oaks, pines, red-oaks, and palmitos like those of Spain. There are many lakes, great and small, over every part of it; some troublesome of fording, on account of depth and the great number of trees lying throughout them. Their beds are sand. The lakes in the country of Apalachen are much larger than those we found before coming there.

In this province are many maize fields; and the houses scattered as are those of the Gelves. There are deer of three kinds, rabbits, hares, bears, lions, and other wild beasts. Among them we saw an animal [the opossum] with a pocket on its belly, in which it carries its young until they know how to seek food, and if it happen that they should be out feeding and any one come near, the mother will not run until she has gathered them in together. The country is very cold. It has fine pastures for herds. Birds are of various kinds. Geese in great numbers. Ducks, mallards, royal-ducks, fly-catchers, night-herons and partridges abound. We saw many falcons, gerfalcons, sparrow-hawks, merlins and numerous other fowl.

Two hours after our arrival at Apalachen, the Indians who had fled from there came in peace to us, asking for their women and children, whom we released; but the detention of a cacique [chief] by the Governor produced great excitement, in consequence of which they returned for battle early the next day, and attacked us with such promptness and alacrity that they succeeded in setting fire to the houses in which we were. As we sallied they fled to the lakes near by, because of which and the large maize fields we could do then no injury, save in the single instance of one Indian, whom we killed. The day following, others came against us as the first had done, escaping in the same way, except one who was also slain.

We were in the town twenty-five days, in which time we made three incursions, and found the country very thinly peopled and difficult to travel for the bad passages, the woods and lakes. We inquired of the cacique we kept and the natives we brought with us, who were the neighbors and enemies of these Indians, as to the nature of the country, the character and condition of the inhabitants, of the food and all other matters concerning it. Each answered apart from the rest, that the largest town in all that region was Apalachen; the people beyond were less numerous and poorer, the land little occupied, and the inhabitants much scattered; that thenceforward were great lakes, dense forests, immense deserts and solitudes. We then asked touching the region towards the south, as to the towns and subsistence in it. They said that in keeping such a direction, journeying nine days, there was a town called Aute, the inhabitants whereof had much maize, beans, and pumpkins, and being near the sea they had fish, and that those people were their friends.

In view of the poverty of the land, the unfavorable accounts of the population and of everything else we heard, the Indians making continual war upon us, wounding our people and horses at the places where they went to drink, shooting from the lakes with such safety to themselves that we could not retaliate, killing a lord of Tesuco, named Don Pedro, whom the commissary brought with him, we determined to leave that place and go in quest of the sea, and the town of Aute of which we were told.

At the termination of the twenty-five days after our arrival we departed, and on the first day got through those lakes and passages without seeing any one, and on the second day we came to a lake difficult of crossing, the water reaching to the paps, and in it were numerous logs. On reaching the middle of it we were attacked by many Indians from behind trees, who thus covered themselves that we might not get sight of them, and others were on the fallen timbers. They drove their arrows with such effect they wounded many men and horses, and before we got through the lake they took our guide. They now followed, endeavoring to contest the passage; but our coming out afforded no relief, nor gave us any better position; for when we wished to fight them they retired immediately into the lake, whence they continued to wound our men and beasts. The Governor, seeing this, commanded the cavalry to dismount and charge the Indians on foot. Accordingly the comptroller alighting with the rest, attacked them, when they all turned and ran into the lake at hand, and thus the passage was gained.

Some of our men were wounded in this conflict, for whom the good armor they wore did not avail. There were those this day who swore that they had seen two red oaks, each the thickness of the lower part of the leg, pierced through from side to side by arrows; and this is not so much to be wondered at, considering the power and skill with which the Indians are able to protect themselves. I myself saw an arrow that had entered the butt of an elm to the depth of a span.

The Indians we had so far seen in Florida are all archen. They go naked, are large of body, and appear at a distance like giants. They are of admirable proportions, very spare and of great activity and strength. The bows they use are as thick as the arm, of eleven or twelve palms in length, which they will discharge at two hundred paces with so great precision that they miss nothing.

Having got through this passage, at the end of a league we arrived at another of the same character, but worse, as it was longer, being half a league in extent. This we crossed freely, without interruption from the Indians, who, as they had spent on the former occasion their store of arrows, had nought with which they dared venture to engage us. Going through a similar passage the next day, I discovered the trail of persons ahead, of which I gave notice to the Governor, who was in the rear-guard, so that though the Indians came upon us, as we were prepared they did no harm. After emerging upon the plain they followed us, and we went back on them in two directions. Two we killed, and they wounded me and two or three others. Coming to woods we could do them no more injury, nor make them further trouble.

In this manner we travelled eight days. After that occurrence we were not again beset until within a league of the place to which I have said we were going. There, while on our way, the Indians came about us without our suspicion, and fell upon the rear-guard. A hidalgo, named Avellaneda, hearing the cries of his serving boy, went back to give assistance, when he was struck by an arrow near the edge of his cuirass and so severe was the wound, the shaft having passed almost entirely through his neck, that he presently died. The corpse was carried to Aute, where we arrived at the end of nine days' travel from Apalache. We found all the inhabitants gone and the houses burned. Maize, beans, and pumpkins were in great plenty, all beginning to be fit for gathering. Having rested two days, the Governor begged me to go and look for the sea, as the Indians said it was near; and we had before discovered it, while on the way, from a very large stream, to which we had given the name of River of the Magdalena [St. Mark's River].

Accordingly, I set out the next day after, in company with the commissary, Captain Castillo, Andres Dorantes, seven more on horseback, and fifty on foot. We travelled until the hour of vespers, when we arrived at a road or entrance of the sea. Oysters were abundant, over which the men rejoiced, and we gave thanks to God that he had brought us there. The following morning I sent twenty men to explore the coast and ascertain its direction. They returned the night after, reporting that those creeks and bays were large, and lay so far inland as made it difficult to examine them agreeably to our desires, and that the sea shore was very distant.

These tidings obtained, seeing our slender means and condition for exploring the coast, I went back to the Governor. On our arrival we found him and many others sick. The Indians had assaulted them the night before, and because of the malady that had come upon them, they had been pushed to extremity. One of the horses had been killed. I gave a report of what I had done, and of the embarrassing nature of the country. We remained there that day.

We go from Aute

The next morning we left Aute, and travelled all day before coming to the place I had visited. The journey was extremely arduous. There were not horses enough to carry the sick, who went on increasing in numbers day by day, and we knew of no cure. It was piteous and painful to witness our perplexity and distress. We saw on our arrival how small were the means for advancing farther. There was not anywhere to go; and if there had been, the people were unable to move forward, the greater part being ill, and those were few who could be on duty. I cease here to relate more of this, because any one may suppose what would occur in a country so remote and malign, so destitute of all resource, whereby either to live in it or go out of it; but most certain assistance is in God, our Lord, on whom we never failed to place reliance. One thing occurred, more afflicting to us than all the rest, which was, that of the persons mounted, the greater part commenced secretly to plot, hoping to secure a better fate for themselves by abandoning the Governor and the sick, who were in a state of weakness and prostration. But, as among them were many hidalgos and persons of gentle condition, they would not permit this to go on, without informing the Governor and the officers of your Majesty; and as we showed them the deformity of their purpose, and placed before them the moment when they should desert their captain, and those who were ill and feeble, and above all the disobedience to the orders of your Majesty, they determined to remain, and that whatever might happen to one should be the lot of all, without forsaking the rest.

❧ De Orbe Novo

PETER MARTYR AND RICHARD EDEN

In what may be the first written celebration of diversity in America, the Italian Peter Martyr, who traveled with the first

Spanish explorers, describes the wonder of God in creating different colored people in his 1516 book *De Orbe Novo*. His writings were later translated and amplified for English readers by Richard Eden.

One of the marvellous things that God useth in the composition of man is colour, which doubtless can not be considered without great admiration in beholding one to be white, and another black, being colours utterly contrary. Some likewise to be yellow, which is between black and white, and other of other colours, as it were of divers liveries. And as these colours are to be marvelled at, even so is it to be considered how they differ from another as it were by degrees, forasmuch as some men are white after divers sorts of whiteness, yellow after divers manners of yellow, and black after divers sorts of blackness; and how from white they go to yellow by discolouring to brown and red, and to black by ash colour, and murrey somewhat lighter than black; and tawny like unto the West Indians which are altogether in general either purple or tawny like unto sod quinces, or of the colour of chestnuts or olives—which colour is to them natural and not by their going naked, as many have thought, albeit their nakedness have somewhat helped them thereunto. Therefore in like manner and with such diversity as men are commonly white in Europe and black in Africa, even with like variety are they tawny in these Indies, with divers degrees diversely inclining more or less to black or white. No less marvel is to consider that men are white in Europe and black in Africa, even with like variety are they tawny in these Indies, with divers degrees diversely inclining more or less to black or white. No less marvel is it to consider that men are white in Seville, and black at the cape of Buena Speranza, and of chestnut colour at the river of Plata, being all in equal degrees from the equinoctial line. Likewise that the men of Africa and Asia that live under the burnt line (called Zona Torida) are black, and not they that live beneath or on this side the same line as in Mexico, Yucatan, Quauhtema, Lian, Nicaragua, Panama, Santo Domingo, Paria, Cape, Saint Augustine, Lima, Quito and the other lands of Peru which touch in the same equinoctial.... It may seem that such variety of colours proceedeth of man, and not of the earth, which may well be although we be all born of Adam and Eve, and know not the cause why God hath ordained it, otherwise than to consider that his divine majesty hath

done this as infinite other to declare his omnipotence and wisdom in such diversity of colours as appear not only in the nature of man, but the like also in beasts, birds and flowers, where diverse and contrary colours are seen in one little feather, or the leaves growing out of one little stalk. Another thing is also to be noted as touching these Indians, and this is that their hair is not curled as is the Moors' and Ethiopians' that inhabit the same clime; neither are they bald except very seldom, and that but little. All which things may give further occasion to philosophers to search the secrets of nature and complexions of men with the novelties of the new world.

"*The seven cities are seven little villages*"

FRANCISCO VAZQUEZ DE CORONADO

Spain had great success in exploring and conquering the riches of Mexico in the early 1500s, sacking the Aztec Empire and looting its wealth. In 1540, Spain hoped to expand on its conquests and sent an expedition northward, led by Francisco Vazquez de Coronado, in search of the fabled Seven Cities of Cibola. Coronado traveled for more than a thousand miles in what is today Arizona, New Mexico, Texas and Kansas, in vain. Instead of cities of gold, he found mud villages.

The disappointments and small discoveries of the journey are reflected in this excerpt from a lengthy narrative Coronado wrote about halfway into the journey. Wandering from village to village, he pursues flimsy leads on a fool's errand. Native Americans skirt his efforts at converting them to Christianity and offer little assistance in finding golden cities that didn't exist.

Coronado returned to Mexico City in 1542. He was considered incompetent. Plans to conquer and settle the region were drastically scaled back.

It now remains for me to tell about this city and kingdom and province, of which the Father Provincial gave Your Lordship an account. In brief, I can assure you that in reality he had not told the truth in a single thing that he said, but everything is the reverse of what he said, except the name of the city and the large stone houses. For, although they are not decorated with turquoises, nor made of lime nor of good bricks, nevertheless they are very good houses, with three and four and five stories, where there are very good apartments and good rooms with corridors, and some very good rooms under ground and paved, which are made for winter, and are something like a sort of hot baths. The ladders which they have for their houses are all movable and portable, which are taken up and placed wherever they please. They are made of two pieces of wood, with rounds like ours.

The Seven Cities are seven little villages, all having the kind of houses I have described. They are all within a radius of 5 leagues. They are all called the kingdom of Cevola, and each has its own name and no single one is called Cevola, but all together are called Cevola. This one which I have called a city I have named Granada, partly because it has some similarity to it, as well as out of regard for Your Lordship. In this place where I am now lodged there are perhaps 200 houses, all surrounded by a wall, and it seems to me that with the other houses, which are not so surrounded, there might be altogether 500 families. There is another town near by, which is one of the seven, but somewhat larger than this, and another of the same size as this, and the other four are somewhat smaller. I send them all to Your Lordship, painted with the route. The skin on which the painting is made was found here with other skins.

The people of the towns seem to me to be of ordinary size and intelligent, although I do not think that they have the judgment and intelligence which they ought to have to build these houses in the way in which they have, for most of them are entirely naked except the covering of their privy parts, and they have painted mantles like the one which I send to Your Lordship. They do not raise cotton, because the country is very cold, but they wear mantles, as may be seen by the exhibit which I send. It is also true that some cotton thread was found in their houses. They wear the hair on their heads like the Mexicans. They all have good figures, and are well bred. I think that they have a quantity of turquoises, which they had removed with the rest of their goods, except the corn, when I arrived, because I did not find any women here nor any men under 15 years or over 60, except two or three old men who remain in command of all the other men and the warriors. Two points of emerald and some little broken stones which approach the color of rather poor garnets were found in a paper, besides other stone crystals, which I gave to one of my ser-

vants to keep until they could be sent to Your Lordship. He has lost them, as they tell me. We found fowls, but only a few, and yet there are some. The Indians tell me that they do not eat these in any of the seven villages, but that they keep them merely for the sake of procuring the feathers. I do not believe this, because they are very good, and better than those of Mexico.

The climate of this country and the temperature of the air is almost like that of Mexico, because it is sometimes hot and sometimes it rains. I have not yet seen it rain, however, except once when there fell a little shower with wind, such as often falls in Spain. The snow and the cold are usually very great, according to what the natives of the country all say. This may very probably be so, both because of the nature of the country and the sort of houses they build and the skins and other things which these people have to protect them from the cold. There are no kinds of fruit or fruit trees. The country is all level, and is nowhere shut in by high mountains, although there are some hills and rough passages. There are not many birds, probably because of the cold, and because there are no trees fit for firewood here, because they can bring enough for their needs from a clump of very small cedars 4 leagues distant. Very good grass is found a quarter of a league away, where there is pasturage for our horses as well as mowing for hay, of which we had great need, because our horses were so weak and feeble when they arrived.

The food which they eat in this country is corn, of which they have a great abundance, and beans and venison, which they probably eat (although they say that they do not), because we found many skins of deer and hares and rabbits. They make the best corn cakes I have ever seen anywhere, and this is what everybody ordinarily eats. They have the very best arrangement and machinery for grinding that was ever seen. One of these Indian women here will grind as much as four of the Mexicans. They have very good salt in crystals, which they bring from a lake a day's journey distant from here. No information can be obtained among them about the North sea or that on the west, nor do I know how to tell Your Lordship which we are nearest to. I should judge that it is nearer to the western, and 150 leagues is the nearest that it seems to me it can be thither. The North sea ought to be much farther away. Your Lordship may thus see how very wide the country is. They have many animals—bears, tigers, lions, porcupines, and some sheep as big as a horse, with very large horns and little tails. I have seen some of their horns the size of which was something to marvel at. There are also wild goats, whose heads I have seen, and the paws of the bears and the skins of the wild boars. For game they have deer. Leopards, and very large deer, and every one thinks that some of them are larger than that animal which Your Lordship favored me with, which belonged to Juan Melaz. They inhabit some plains eight days' journey toward the north. They have some of their skins here very well dressed and they prepare and paint them where they kill the cows, according to what they tell me.

These Indians say that the kingdom of Totonteac, which the Father Provincial praised so much, saying that it was something marvelous, and of such a very great size, and that cloth was made there, is a hot lake, on the edge of which there are five or six houses. There used to be some others, but these have been destroyed by war. The kingdom of Marata can not be found, nor do these Indians know anything about it. The kingdom of Acus is a single small city, where they raise cotton, and this is called Acucu. I say that this is the country, because Acus, with or without the aspiration, is not a word in this region; and because it seems to me that Acucu may be derived from Acus, I say that it is this town which has been converted into the kingdom of Acus. They tell me that there are some other smaller ones not far from this settlement, which are situated on a river which I have seen and of which the Indians have told me. God knows that I wish I had better news to write to Your Lordship, but I must give you the truth, as I wrote you from Culiacan, I must advise you of the good as well as of the bad. But you may be assured that if there had been all the riches and all the treasures of the world, I could not have done more in His Majesty's service and in that of Your Lordship than I have done, in coming here where you commanded me to go, carrying, both my companions and myself, our food on our backs for 300 leagues, and traveling on foot many days, making our way over hills and rough mountains, besides other labors which I refrain from mentioning. Nor do I think of stopping until my death, if it serves His Majesty or Your Lordship to have it so.

Three days after I captured this city, some of the Indians who lived here came to offer to make peace. They brought me some turquoises and poor mantles, and I received them in His Majesty's name with as good a speech as I could, making them understand the purpose of my coming to this country, which is, in the name of His Majesty and by the commands of Your Lordship, that they and all others in this province should become Christians and should know the true God for their Lord, and His Majesty for their king and earthly lord. After this they returned to their houses and suddenly, the next day, they packed up their goods and property, their women and children, and fled to the hills, leaving their towns deserted, with only some few remaining in them. Seeing this, I went to the town which I said was larger than this, eight or ten days later, when I recovered from my wounds. I found a few of them there, whom I told that they ought not to feel any fear, and I asked them to summon their lord to me. By what I can find out or observe, however, none of these towns have any, since I have not seen any principal house by which any superiority over others could be shown. Afterward, an old man, who said he was their lord, came with a mantle made of many pieces, with whom I argued as long as he stayed with me. He said that he would come to see me with the rest of the chiefs of the country, three days later, in order to arrange the relations which should exist between us. He did so, and they brought me some little ragged mantles and some turquoises. I said that they ought to come down from their strongholds and return to their houses with their wives and children, and that they should become Christians, and recognize His Majesty as their king and lord. But they still remain in their strongholds, with their wives and all their property.

I commanded them to have a cloth painted for me, with all the animals that they know in that country and although they are poor painters, they quickly painted two for me, one of the animals and the other of the birds and fishes. They say that they will bring their children so that our priests may instruct them, and that they desire to know our law. They declare that it was foretold among them more than fifty years ago that a people such as we are should come, and the direction they should come from and that the whole country would be conquered. So far as I can find out, the water is what these Indians worship, because they say that it makes the corn grow and sustains their life, and that the only other reason they know is because their ancestors did so. I have tried in every way to find out from the natives of these settlements whether they know of any other peoples or provinces or cities. They tell me about seven cities which are at a considerable distance, which are like these, except that the houses there are not like these, but are made of earth, and small, and that they raise much cotton there. The first of these four places about which they know is called, they say, Tucano. They could not tell me much about the others. I do not believe that they tell me the truth, because they think that I shall soon have to depart from them and return home. But they will quickly find that they are deceived in this. I sent Don Pedro de Tobar there with his company and some other horsemen, to see it. I would not have dispatched this packet to Your Lordship until I had learned what he found there, if I thought that I should have any news from him within twelve or fifteen days. However, as he will remain away at least thirty, and, considering that this information is of little importance and that the cold and the rains are approaching, it seemed to me that I ought to do as Your Lordship commanded me in your instructions, which is, that as soon as I arrived here, I should advise you thereof, and this I do, by sending you this plain narrative of what I have seen, which is bad enough, as you may perceive. I have determined to send throughout all the surrounding regions, in order to find out whether there is anything, and to suffer every extremity before I give up this enterprise, and to serve His Majesty, if I can find any way in which to do it, and not to lack in diligence until Your Lordship directs me as to what I ought to do....

As far as I can judge, it does not appear to me that there is any hope of getting gold or silver, but I trust in God that, if there is any, we shall get our share of it, and it shall not escape us through any lack of diligence in the search. I am unable to give Your Lordship any certain information about the dress of the women, because the Indians keep them guarded so carefully that I have not seen any, except two old women. These had on two long skirts reaching down to their feet and open in front, and a girdle, and they are tied together with some cotton strings. I asked the Indians to give me one of those which they wore, to send to you, since they were not willing to show me the women. They brought me two mantles, which are these that I send, almost painted over. They have two tassels, like the women

of Spain, which hang somewhat over their shoulders.

The death of the negro is perfectly certain, because many of the things which he wore have been found, and the Indians say that they killed him here because the Indians of Chichilticale said that he was a bad man, and not like the Christians, because the Christians never kill women, and he killed them, and because he assaulted their women, whom the Indians love better than themselves. Therefore they determined to kill him, but they did not do it in the way that was reported, because they did not kill any of the others who came with him, nor did they kill the lad from the province of Petatlan, who was with him, but they took him and kept him in safe custody until now. When I tried to secure him, they made excuses for not giving him to me, for two or three days, saying that he was dead, and at other times that the Indians of Acucu had taken him away. But when I finally told them that should be very angry if they did not give him to me, they gave him to me. He is an interpretor; for although he can not talk much, he understands very well.

Some gold and silver has been found in this place, which those who know about minerals say is not bad. I have not yet been able to learn from these people where they got it. I perceive that they refuse to tell me the truth in everything, because they think that I shall have to depart from here in a short time, as I have said. But trust in god that they will not be able to avoid answering much longer. I beg Your Lordship to make a report of the success of this expedition to His Majesty, because there is nothing more than what I have already said. I shall not do so until it shall please God to grant that we find what we desire. Our Lord God protect and keep your most illustrious Lordship. From the province of Cevola, and this city of Granada, the 3r of August, 1540. Francisco Vazquez de Coronado kisses the hand of your most illustrious Lordship.

❧ Francis Drake stakes a claim for California

FRANCIS FLETCHER

The British adventurer Sir Francis Drake discovered northern California and claimed it as part of the British kingdom in

1579, while on his round-the-world journey. He was the first Englishman to sail around Cape Horn and to the west coast of North America. Despite Drake's claim, the Spanish settled northern California as one of its own American colonies.

This country our general named Albion, and that for two causes; the one in respect of the white banks and cliffs, which lie toward the sea; the other, that it might have some affinity, even in name also, with our own country, which was sometime so called.

Before we went from there, our general caused to be set up a monument of our being there; as also of her majesties, and successors right and title to that kingdom, namely a plate of brass, fast nailed to a great and firm post; whereon is engraven her graces name, and the day and year of our arrival there, and of the free giving up, of the province and kingdom, both by the king and people, into her majesties hands; together with her highness' picture, and arms in a piece of sixpence current English money, showing itself by a hole made of purpose through the plate: underneath was likewise engraven the name of our general &c.

The Spaniards never had any dealing, or so much as set a foot in this country; the utmost of their discoveries, reaching only to many degrees Southward of this place.

❧ *"We give grant to our trustie"*

CHARTER TO SIR WALTER RALEIGH

Sir Walter Raleigh of England established the first colony in British America. Having worked with his half-brother Sir Humphrey Gilbert on two aborted colonization efforts, Raleigh took on the task himself when Gilbert died in 1583. On March 25, 1584, Queen Elizabeth granted Raleigh a charter to found a colony.

Raleigh sponsored five expeditions to the New World costing more than forty thousand pounds. The first expedition established a settlement at Roanoke Island, North Carolina, in 1585. A year later, Sir Francis Drake returned surviving colonists back to England.

A second settlement was established on the island in 1587. Virginia Dare was the first child of English parents born in the colony. Relief expeditions were delayed because of the Spanish Armada invasion in 1588. When ships finally returned to Roanoke in 1590, the colony was gone leaving no trace or clue of its demise.

Elizabeth, by the Grace of God of England, Fraunce and Ireland Queene, defender of the faith, &c. To all people to whome these presents shall come, greeting.

Knowe yee that of our especial grace, certain science, and meere motion, we give graunt to our trustie and welbeloved servant Walter Ralegh, Esquire, and to his heires assignes for ever, free libertie and license from time to time, and at all times for ever hereafter, to discover, search, finde out, and view such remote, heathen and barbarous lands, countries, and territories, not actually posssessed of any Christian Prince, nor inhabited by Christian People, as to him, shall seeme good, and the same to have, holde occupie and enjoy to him, for ever, with all perogatives, thereto or thereabouts both by sea and land, whatsoever we by out letters patent may graunt…and the said Walter Ralegh, his heirs and assignes,… shall goe to travaile thither to inhabite or remaine, there to build and fortifie, at the discretion of the said Walter Ralegh.

And we do likewise give and graunt full authoritie, libertie and power to the said Walter Ralegh, that he shall have, take, and leade in the saide voyage, and travaile thitherward, or to inhabit there with him, or them, and every or any of them, such and so many of our subjects as shall willingly accompanie him or them.…

And further that the said Walter Ralegh, shall have all the soile of all such lands, territories, and Countreis, so to bee discovered and possessed as aforesaide, and of all such Cities, castles, townes, villages, and places in the same, with the right, royalties, franchises, and jurisdictions, as well marine as other within the saide landes, or Countreis, or the seas thereunto adjoining, to be had, or used, with full power to dispose thereof, and of every part in fee-simple or otherwise, according to the order of the lawes of England,…. reserving always to us our heires, and successors, for all services, duties, and demaundes, the fift part of all the oare of golde and silver, that from time to time, and at all times shal be there gotten and obtained.…

And moreover, we doe give and graunt license to the said Walter Ralegh, that he, shall and may for his and their defence, encounter and expulse, repell and resist all as without the especiall liking and license of the said Walter Ralegh, shall attempt to inhabite within the said Countreis, or within the space of two hundred leagues neere to the place or places within such Countreis, where the saide Walter Ralegh, shall within six yeeres make their dwellings. And for uniting in more perfect league and amitie, of such Countreis, landes, and territories so to bee possessed and inhabited as aforesaide with our Realmes of Englande and Ireland, and the better incouragement of men to these enterprises: we do declare that all such Countreis, so hereafter to be possessed and inhabited as is aforesaide, from thenceforth shall bee of the allegiance of us, our heires and successours. And wee doe graunt to the saide Walter Ralegh, and to all and every of them, that they being either borne within our saide Realms of Englande, shall and may have all the priviledges of free Denizens, and persons native of England.

And we do give and graunt to the said Walter Ralegh, that he shall, within the said mentioned remote landes have full and meere power and authoritie to correct, punish, pardon, governe, and rule by their and every or any of their good discretions and pollicies, as well in causes capital, or ciminall, as civil, all such our subjects as shall from time to time adventure themselves in the said journies or voyages, or that shall at any time hereafter inhabite any such landes, countreis, or territories as aforesaide, according to such statutes, lawes and ordinances, as shall bee by him the saide Walter Ralegh devised, or established, for the better government of the said people as aforesaid. So always as the said statutes, lawes, and ordinances may be as neere as conveniently may be agreeable to the forme of the lawes, statutes, government, or pollicie of England....

Provided alwayes, and our will and pleasure is, and wee do hereby declare to all Christian kings, princes and states, that if the saide Walter Ralegh, his heires or assignes, or any of them, or any other by their licence or appointment, shall at any time or times hereafter, robbe or spoile by sea or by lande, or do any acte of unjust or unlawful hostilitie, to any of the subjects of us, our heires or successors, or to any of the subjects of any the kings, princes, rulers, governors, or estates, being them in perfect league and amitie with us, our heires and successors, and that upon such injury, or upon such injury, or upon just complaint of any such prince, ruler, governor, or estate, or their subjects, wee, our heires, and successours, shall make open proclamation within any the portes of our Realme of England, that the saide Walter Raleghe, his heirs and assignes, and adherents, or any to whome these our letters patents may estende, shall within the termes to be limitted, by such proclamation, make full restitution, and satisfaction of all such injuries done, so as both we and the said princes, or other so complayning, may holde us and themselves fully contented. And that if the saide Walter Raleigh, his heires and assignes, shall not make or cause to be made satisfaction accordingly, within such time so to be limited, that then it shall be lawfull to us our heires and successors, to put the saide Walter Ralegh, his heires and assignes and adherents, and all the inhabitants of the said places to be discovered (as is aforesaide) or any of them out of our allegiance and protection, and that from and after such time of putting out of protection the said Walter Ralegh, his heires, assignes and adherents, and others so to be put out, and the said places within their habitation, possession and rule, shal be out of our allegeance and protection, and free for all princes and others, to pursue with hostilitie, as being not our subjects, nor by us any way to be avouched, maintained or defended, not to be holden as any of ours, nor to our protection or dominion, or allegiance any way belonging, for that expresse mention of the cleer yeerely value of the certaintie of the premises, or any part thereof, or of any other gift, or grant by us, or any our progenitors, or predecessors to the said Walter Ralegh, before this time made in these presents be not expressed, or any other grant, ordinance, provision, proclamation, or restraint to the contrarye thereof, before this time given, ordained, or provided, or any other thing, cause, or matter whatsoever, in any wise notwithstanding. In witness whereof, we have caused these our letters to be made patents. Witnesse our selves, at Westminster, the 25th day of March, in the sixe and twentieth yeere our Raigne.

🍂 Struggling to settle Jamestown

JOHN SMITH

An intrepid explorer and entrepreneur, John Smith played an instrumental role in settling the first permanent English settlement in North America at Jamestown and encouraging the Pilgrims to locate in New England. Smith accompanied the initial settlers of Jamestown who arrived at the Virginia colony in the spring of 1607. The 105 colonists quickly succumbed to disease—almost half were dead by September. The gracious intervention of nearby Native Americans and Smith's vigorous leadership rescued the colony from disaster.

Relations with local tribes, however, did not always go smoothly. Conflicts emerged. In a now-legendary moment, Smith was captured by the Native Americans in 1608 and was about to be executed when the young princess Pocahontas intervened on his behalf. Smith returned to England after being injured in an accidental explosion and actively promoted the new colony. He sailed back to America to explore New England in 1614 and subsequently wrote two books about the experience.

Although historians question whether the Pocahontas incident actually occurred, Smith undoubtedly played a major role in saving the disorganized and despondent Jamestown colony from annihilation, ignited widespread interest in America through his writings, and played a direct role in the settling of Massachusetts. The following two excerpts describe the deplorable status of Jamestown in its first few months and then Smith's account of the Pocahontas incident, which he did not include in his original writings about his role in Jamestown.

After many crosses in The Downs by tempests, we arrived safely upon the southwest part of the great Canaries; within four or five days after we set sail for Domineca, the 26th of April. The first land we made, we fell with Cape Henry, the very mouth of the Bay of Chesapeake, which at the present we little expected having by a cruel storm been put to the northward. Anchoring in this bay, twenty or thirty went ashore with the Captain, and in coming aboard they were assaulted with certain Indians which charged them within pistolshot, in which conflict Captain Archer and Mathew Morton were shot. Whereupon Captain Newport, seconding them, made a shot at them which the Indians little respected, but having spent their arrows retired without harm. And in that place was the box opened wherein the Council for Virginia was nominated. And arriving at the place where we are now seated, the Council was sworn and the president elected…where was made choice for our situation and a very fit place for the erecting of a great city. All our provision was brought ashore, and with as much speed as might be went about fortification….

Captain Newport, having set things in order, set sail for England the 22d of June, leaving provision for thirteen or fourteen weeks. The day before the ship's departure, the king of Pamaunkee sent the Indian that had met us before, in our discovery, to assure us of peace. Our fort being then palisaded round, and all our men in good health and comfort,

albeit that through some discontented humors it did not so long continue. God (being angry with us) plagued us with such famine and sickness that the living were scarce able to bury the dead—our want of sufficient good victuals, with continual watching, four or five each night at three bulwarks, being the chief cause. Only of sturgeon had we great store, whereon our men would so greedily surfeit as it cost many lives…. Shortly after it pleased God, in our extremity, to move the Indians to bring us corn, ere it was half ripe, to refresh us when we rather expected they would destroy us. About the 10th of September there were about forty-six of our men dead….

Our provisions being now within twenty days spent, the Indians brought us great store both of corn and bread ready-made, and also there came such abundance of fowls into the rivers as greatly refreshed our weak estates, whereupon many of our weak men were presently able to go abroad. As yet we had no houses to cover us, our tents were rotten, and our cabins worse than nought. Our best commodity was iron, which we made into little chisels. The president and Captain Martin's sickness constrained me to be cape merchant, and yet to spare no pains in making houses for the company, who, notwithstanding our misery, little ceased their malice, grudging and muttering.

As at this time most of our chiefest men were either sick or discontented, the rest being in such despair as they would rather starve and rot with idleness than be persuaded to do anything for their own relief without constraint, our victuals being now within eighteen days spent, and the Indian trade decreasing, I was sent to the mouth of the river, to Kegquouhtan and Indian town, to trade for corn and try the river for fish; but our fishing we could not effect by reason of the stormy weather. With fish, oysters, bread, and deer they kindly traded with me and my men.

II

And now, the winter approaching, the rivers became so filled with swans, geese, ducks, and cranes, that we daily feasted with good bread, Virginia peas, pumpkins, and putchamins fish, fowl, and divers sorts of wild beasts as fat as we could eat them: so that none of tuftaffety humorists desired to go for England.

But our comedies never endured long without a

tragedy; some idle exceptions being muttered against Captain Smith for not discovering the head of the Chickahamania River, and taxed by the Council to be too slow in so worthy an attempt. The next voyage he preceeded so far that with much labor by cutting of trees asunder he made his passage; but when his barge could pass no farther, he left her in a broad bay out of danger of shot, commanding none should go ashore till his return: himself with two English and two savages went up higher in a canoe; but he was not long absent but his men went ashore, whose want of government gave both occasion and opportunity to the savages to surprise one George Cassen, whom they slew, and much failed not to have cut off the boat and all the rest.

Smith, little dreaming of that accident, being go to the marshes at the river's head, twenty miles in the desert, had his two men slain, as is supposed, sleeping by the canoe, whilst himself by fowling sought them victual: finding he was beset with 200 savages; two of them he slew, still defending himself with the aid of a savage his guide, whom he bound to his arm with his garters, and used him as a buckler, yet he was shot in his thigh a little, and had many arrows stuck in his clothes; but no great hurt, till at last they took him prisoner. When this news came to Jamestown, much was their sorrow for his loss, few expecting what ensued.

Six or seven weeks those barbarians kept him prisoner, many strange triumphs and conjurations they made of him, yet he so demeaned himself amongst them, as he not only diverted them from surprising the fort but procured his own liberty, and got himself and his company such estimation amongst them those savages admired him more than their own Quiyouckosucks.

The manner how they used and delivered him is as follows....

He demanding for their captain, they showed him Opechankanough, king of Pamaunkee, to whom he gave a round ivory double compass dial. Much they marveled at the playing of the fly and needle, which they could see so plainly and yet not touch it because of the glass that covered them. But when he demonstrated by that globe-like jewel the roundness of the earth and skies, the sphere of the sun, moon, and stars, and how the sun did chase the night round about the world continually; the greatness of the land and sea, the diversity of nations, variety of complex-

ions, and how we were to them antipodes, and many other such like matters, they all stood as amazed with admiration. Notwithstanding, within an hour after they tied him to a tree, and as many as could stand about him prepared to shoot him: but the king holding up the compass in his hand, they all laid down their bows and arrows, and in a triumphant manner led him to Orapaks, where he was after their manner kindly feasted, and well used.

At last they brought him to Werowocomoco, where was Powhatan, their emperor. Here more than two hundred of those grim courtiers stood wondering at him, as he had been a monster; till Powhatan and his train had put themselves in their greatest braveries. Before a fire upon a seat like a bedstead, he sat covered with a great robe, made of raccoon skins, and all the tails hanging by. On either hand did sit a young wench of sixteen or eighteen years, and along on each side the house, two rows of men, and behind them as many women, with all their heads and shoulders painted red, many of their heads bedecked with the white down of birds, but every one with something, and a great chain of white beads about their necks. At his entrance before the king, all the people gave a great shout. The queen of Appamatuck was appointed to bring him water to wash his hands, and another brought him a bunch of feathers, instead of a towel to dry them. Having feasted him after their best barbarous manner they could, a long consultation was held, but the conclusion was, two great stones were brought before Powhatan: then as many as could laid hands on him, dragged him to them, and thereon laids his head, and being ready with their clubs to beat out his brains, Pocahontas, the king's dearest daughter, when no entreaty could prevail, got his head in her arms, and laid her own upon his to save his from death: whereat the emperor was contented he should live to make him hatchets, and her bells, beads, and copper; for they thought him as well as all occupations as themselves. For the king himself will make his own robes, shoes, bows, arrows, pots; plant, hunt, or do anything as well as the rest.

Two days after, Powhatan having disguised himself in the most fearfulest manner he could, caused Captain Smith to be brought forth to a great house in the woods, and there upon a mat by the fire to be left alone. Not long after, from behind a mat that divided the house was made the most dolefulest noise he ever heard; then Powhatan, more like a devil than a man, with some two hundred more as black as himself, came unto him and told him now they were friends, and presently he should go to Jamestown, to send him two great guns, and a grindstone, for which he would give him the county of Capahowosick, and for ever esteem him as his son Nantaquoud.

❧ "What can you get by war?"

CHIEF POWHATAN

Chief Powhatan ruled over the Algonquin tribes in Virginia when Jamestown was settled. He was the chief who presided over John Smith's capture and Pocahontas' father. Powhatan gave this speech, as reported by John Smith, in 1609 warning of likely future problems between the colonists and his people. After Powhatan died, the Algonquin waged war on the white settlers.

Why will you take by force what you may obtain by love? Why will you destroy us who supply you with food? What can you get by war? We are unarmed, and willing to give you what you ask, if you come in a friendly manner.

I am not so simple as not to know it is better to eat good meat, sleep comfortably, live quietly with my women and children, laugh and be merry with the English, and being their friend, trade for their copper and hatchets, than to run away from them.

Take away your guns and swords, the cause of all our jealousy, or you may die in the same manner.

❧ Lost in the Woods

SAMUEL DE CHAMPLAIN

Samuel de Champlain was a Frenchman who explored the Saint Lawrence River, founded Quebec in 1608 on behalf of France and was the first European to discover Lake Champlain. He also charted much of the New England and Canadian coast. In 1609, he participated in a raid against the Iroquois Indians, marking the first time the Iroquois were attacked with muskets. The event bred a longstanding hatred of the French in the Iroquois, who would serve as valuable allies to the British for the next 150 years. This episode took place in Canadian America when Champlain was exploring

with a band of Huron Indians. Getting lost represented a major risk in the largely unexplored New World.

When they first went out hunting, I lost my way in the woods, having followed a certain bird that seemed to me peculiar. It had a beak like that of a parrot, and was of the size of a hen. It was entirely yellow, except the head which was red, and the wings which were blue, and it flew by intervals like a partridge. The desire to kill it led me to pursue it from tree to tree for a very long time, until it flew away in good earnest. Thus losing all hope, I desired to retrace my steps, but found none of our hunters, who had been constantly getting ahead, and had reached the enclosure. While trying to overtake them, and going, as it seemed to me, straight to where the enclosure was, I found myself lost in the woods, going now on this side now on that, without being able to recognize my position. The night coming on, I was obliged to spend it at the foot of a great tree, and in the morning set out and walked until three o'clock in the afternoon, when I came to a little pond of still water. Here I noticed some game, which I pursued, killing three or four birds, which were very acceptable, since I had had nothing to eat. Unfortunately for me there had been no sunshine for three days, nothing but rain and cloudy weather, which increased my trouble. Tired and exhausted I prepared to rest myself and cook the birds in order to alleviate the hunger which I began painfully to feel, and which by God's favor was appeased.

When I had made my repast I began to consider what I should do, and to pray God to give me the will and courage to sustain patiently my misfortune if I should be obliged to remain abandoned in this forest without counsel or consolation except the Divine goodness and mercy, and at the same time to exert myself to return to our hunters. Thus committing all to His mercy I gathered up renewed courage, going here and there all day, without perceiving any foot-print or path, except those of wild beasts, of which I generally saw a good number. I was obliged to pass here this night also. Unfortunately I had forgotten to bring with me a small compass which would have put me on the right road, or nearly so. At the dawn of day, after a brief repast, I set out in order to find, if possible, some brook and follow it, thinking that it must of necessity flow into the river on the border of which our hunters were encamped. Having resolved upon this plan, I carried it out so well that at noon I found myself on the border of a little lake, about a league and a half in extent, where I killed some game, which was very timely for my wants; I had likewise remaining some eight or ten charges of powder, which was a great satisfaction.

I proceeded along the border of this lake to see where it discharged, and found a large brook, which I followed until five o'clock in the evening, when I heard a great noise, but on carefully listening failed to perceive clearly what it was. On hearing the noise, however, more distinctly, I concluded that it was a fall of water in the river which I was searching for. I proceeded nearer, and saw an opening, approaching which I found myself in a great and far-reaching meadow, where there was a large number of wild beasts, and looking to my right I perceived the river, broad and long. I looked to see if I could not recognize the place, and walking along on the meadow I noticed a little path where the savages carried their canoes. Finally, after careful observation, I recognized it as the same river, and that I had gone that way before.

I passed the night in better spirits than the previous ones, supping on the little I had. In the morning I re-examined the place where I was, and concluded from certain mountains on the border of the river that I had not been deceived, and that our hunters must be lower down by four or five good leagues. This distance I walked at my leisure along the border of the river, until I perceived the smoke of our hunters, where I arrived to the great pleasure not only of myself but of them, who were still searching for me, but had about given up all hopes of seeing me again. They told me not to stray off from them any more, or never to forget to carry with me my compass, and they added: "If you had not come, and we had not succeeded in finding you, we should never have gone again to the French, for fear of their accusing us of having killed you." After this he was very careful of me when I went hunting, always giving me a savage as companion, who knew how to find again the place from which he started so well that it was something very remarkable.

Coercing children to Virginia

SIR EDWIN SANDYS

Emigrating to Jamestown was a perilous enterprise. Disease, non-existent sanitation, violence and shockingly inadequate planning created a mortality rate of well over 50 percent for the first several years of the colony's existence. To literally keep the colony alive, the Virginia Company needed to re-supply it with people. In 1619, 100 children from London aged 12 and older were transported to Jamestown and apprenticed by the Company. Officials then wanted another hundred "superfluous" London children for the same purpose. Some of the children, however, did not want to go. This letter from the Virginia Company in 1620 requested permission from the City of London to send the children against their will, which the city granted.

Right Honorable:

Being unable to give my personal attendance upon the Lords, I have presumed to address my suit in these few lines unto your Honor. The City of London have by act of their Common Council, appointed one hundred children out of their superfluous multitude to be transported to Virginia; there to be bound apprentices for certain years, and afterward with very beneficial conditions for the children. And have granted moreover a levy of five hundred pounds among themselves for the appareling of those children, and toward their charges of transportation. Now it falleth out that among those children, sundry being ill disposed, and fitter for any remote place than for this City, declare their unwillingness to go to Virginia, of whom the City is especially desirous to be disburdened, and in Virginia under severe masters they may be brought to goodness. But this City wanting authority to deliver, and the Virginia Company to transport, these persons against their wills, the burden is laid upon me, by humble suit unto the Lords to procure higher authority for the warranting thereof. May it please your Honor therefore, to vouchsafe unto us of the Company here, and to the whole plantation in Virginia, that noble favor, as to be a means unto their Lordships out of their accustomed goodness, and by their higher authority, to discharge both the City and our Company of this difficulty, as their Lordship.

"Wives for the people of Virginia"

VIRGINIA COMPANY

In addition to children, the all-male Jamestown colony soon needed other residents: women. Here, the Virginia Company notifies the colony in 1621 that it has arranged for the transportation of 12 women to serve as wives. The presence of women changed the character of Jamestown into a more settled colony with a long-term future. Discontent was reduced and prospects for settlers were enhanced.

We send you in this ship one widow and eleven maids for wives for the people in Virginia. There hath been especial care had in the choice of them; for there hath not any one of them been received but upon good commendations, as by a note herewith sent you may perceive. We pray you all therefore in general to take them into your care; and more especially we recommend them to you Master Pountis, that at their first landing they may be housed, lodged and provided for of diet till they be married, for such was the haste of sending them away, as that straitened with time we had no means to put provisions aboard, which defect shall be supplied by the magazine ship. And in case they cannot be presently married, we desire they may be put to several householders that have wives till they can be provided of husbands. There are near fifty more which are shortly to come, are sent by our most honorable Lord and Treasurer the Earl of Southampton and certain worthy gentlemen, who taking into their consideration that the Plantation can never flourish till families be planted and the respect of wives and children fix the people on the soil, therefore have given this fair beginning, for the reimbursing of whose charges it is ordered that every man that marries them give 120 lbs. weight of the best leaf tobacco for each of them, and in case any of them die, that proportion must be advanced to make it up upon those that survive.... And though we are desirous that marriage be free according to the law of nature, yet would we not have these maids deceived and married to servants, but only to freemen or tenants as have means to maintain them. We pray you therefore to be fathers to them in this business, not enforcing them to marry against their wills; neither send we them to be servants, save in case of extremity, for we would have their condition so much bettered as multitudes may be allured thereby to come unto you. And you may

assure such men as marry those women that the first servants sent over by the Company shall be consigned to them, it being our intent to preserve families and to prefer married men before single persons. The tobacco that shall be due upon the marriage of these maids we desire Master Pountis to receive and to return by the first.... To conclude, the Company, for some weighty reasons too long to relate, have ordered that no man marrying these women expect the proportion of land usually allotted for every head, which to avoid clamor or trouble hereafter, you shall do well to give them notice of.

"Combine ourselves into a civil Body Politick"

THE MAYFLOWER COMPACT

Written and signed on the *Mayflower* as the famous ship approached New England, the Mayflower Compact committed the settlers of the new colony to live under a rule of law based on the consent of its people. This became the fundamental tenet of American civil government.

The settlers agreed to the compact for several reasons. One was that the settlers were landing farther north than planned and were thus outside of the jurisdiction of the Virginia Company under whose authority they expected to fall and had made the appropriate arrangements prior to leaving. They needed to forge a compact for self-rule.

Secondly, several "strangers" who were not part of the separatist Puritan congregation that initiated the journey threatened to do as they pleased when they arrived on shore. A formal agreement among all the settlers made prior to the landing would provide a stronger bond for self-government than the now dubious company patent.

Finally, it was common practice for separatist religious groups to engage in compacts or covenants pledging loyalty among themselves, devotion to the New Testament and submission to elders selected by the congregation. Shortly after agreeing to the compact, the settlers elected John Carver as governor. Of the 41 men who signed the compact in November, only 20 survived the coming winter.

In the name of God Amen. We whose names are underwritten, the loyall subjects of our dread sovereigne Lord King James by the grace of God, of great Britaine, Franc, & Ireland kind, defender of the faith, &c.

Having undertaken for the Glory of God, and Advancement of the Christian Faith, and the Honour of our King and Country, a voyage to plant the first colony in the northern Parts of Virginia;

do by these Presents, solemnly and mutually in the Presence of God and of one another, convenant and combine ourselves together into a civil Body Politick, for our better Ordering and Preservation, and Furtherance of the Ends aforesaid; And by Virtue hereof to enact, constitute, and frame, such just and equal Laws, Ordinances, Acts, Constitutions and Offices, from time to time, as shall be thought most meet and convenient for the General good of the Colony; unto which we promise all due Submission and Obedience.

In witnes whereof we have hereunder sub-scribed our names at Cap-Codd the 11 of November , in the year of the raigne of our soveraigne Lord King James of England, France, & Ireland the eighteenth and of Scotland the fiftie fourth. An: Com. 1620

🌿 *Of Plymouth Plantation*

WILLIAM BRADFORD

William Bradford was one of the original settlers of Plymouth and would serve as governor of the colony for 31 years. He recorded the Puritan's perilous journey to the New World and the hardships they encountered in their first few years. Having arrived in Plymouth in the early winter with inade-quate provisions, the settlers struggled mightily to survive.

Septe. 6. These troubles being blown over, and now all being compact together in one ship, they put to sea again with a prosperous wind, which continued divers days together, which was some encourage-ment unto them, yet according to the usual manner many were afflicted with sea-sickness. And I may not omit here a special work of God's providence. There was a proud and very profane young man, one of the sea-men, of a lusty, able body, which made him the more haughty; he would always be contemning the poor people in their sickness, and cursing them daily with grievous execrations, and did not let to tell them, that he hoped to help to cast half of them overboard before they came to their journeys end, and to make merry with what they had; and if he were by any gently reproved, he would curse and swear most bitterly. But it pleased God before they came half seas over, to smite this young man with a grievous disease, of which he died in a desperate manner, and so was himself the first that was thrown overboard. Thus his curses

light on his own head; and it was an astonishment to all his fellows, for they noted it to be the just hand of God upon him.

After they had enjoyed fair winds and weather for a season, they were encountered many times with cross winds, and met with many fierce storms, with which the ship was shrewdly shaken, and her upper works made very leaky; and one of the main beams in the mid ships was bowed and cracked, which put them in some fear that the ship could not be able to perform the voyage. So some of the chief of the company, perceiving the mariners to fear the sufficiency of the ship, as appeared by their mutterings, they entered into serious consultation with the master and other officers of the ship, to consider in time of the danger; and rather to return than to cast themselves into a desperate and inevitable peril. And truly there was great distrac-tion and difference of opinion amongst the mariners themselves; fain would they do what could be done for their wages' sake, (being now half the sea over,) and on the other hand they were loath to hazard their lives too desperately. But in examining of all opinions, the master and others affirmed they knew the ship to be strong and firm under water; and for the buckling of the main beam, there was a great iron screw the passengers brought out of Holland, which would raise the beam into his place; the which being done, the car-penter and the master affirmed that with a post put under it, set firm in the lower deck, and otherways bound, he would make it sufficient. And as for the decks and upper works they would caulk them as well as they could, and thought with the working of the ship they would not long keep staunch [watertight] yet there would otherwise be no great danger, if they did not overpress her with sails. So they committed themselves to the will of God, and resolved to proceed....

But to omit other things (that I may be brief,) after long beating at sea they fell with that land which is called Cape Cod; the which being made and certainly known to be it, they were not a little joyful. After some deliberation had amongst them-selves and with the master of the ship, they tacked about and resolved to stand for the southward (the wind and weather being fair) to find some place about Hudson's River for their habitation. But after they had sailed the course about half the day, they fell amongst dangerous shoals and roaring breakers, and they were so far entangled therewith as they conceived themselves in great danger; and the wind shrinking upon them withal, they resolved to bear up again for the Cape, and thought themselves happy to get out of those dangers before night overtook them, as by God's providence they did. And the next day they got into the Cape-harbor where they rid in safety....

Being thus arrived in good harbor and brought safe to land, they fell upon their knees and blessed the God of heaven, who had brought them over the vast and furious ocean, and delivered them from all the perils and miseries thereof, again to set their feet on the firm and stable earth, their proper element. And no marvel if they were thus joyful, seeing wise Seneca was so affected with sailing a few miles on the coast of his own Italy; as he affirmed, that he had rather remain twenty years on his way by land, than pass by sea to any place in a short time; so tedious and dreadful was the same unto him.

But here I cannot but stay and make a pause, and stand half amazed at this poor peoples present condition; and so I think will the reader too, when he well considers the same. Being thus past the vast ocean, and a sea of troubles before in their preparation (as may be remembered by the which went before), they had now no friends to welcome them, nor inns to entertain or refresh their weather-beaten bodies, no houses or much less towns to repair to, to seek for succor. It is recorded in Scripture as a mercy to the apostle and his shipwrecked company, that the barbarians shewed them no small kindness in refreshing them, but these savage barbarians, when they met with them (as after will appear) were readier to fill their sides full of arrows than otherwise. And for the season it was winter, and they that know the winters of that country know them to be sharp and violent, and subject to cruel and fierce storms, dangerous to travel to known places, much more to search an unknown coast. Besides, what could they see but a hideous and desolate wilderness, full of wild beasts and wild men? And what multitudes there might be of them they knew not. Nether could they, as it were, go up to the top of Pisgah, to view from this wilderness a more goodly country to feed their hopes; for which way soever they turned their eyes (save upward to the heavens) they could have little solace or content in respect of any outward objects. For summer being done, all things stand upon them with a weather-beaten face; and the whole country, full of woods and thickets, represented a wild and savage hue. If they looked behind them, there was the mighty ocean which they had passed, and was now as a main bar and gulf to separate them from all the civil parts of the world. If it be said they had a ship to succor them, it is true; but what heard they daily from the master and company? But that with speed they should look out a lace with their shallop, where they would be at some near distance; for the season was such as he would not stir from thence till a safe harbor was discovered by them, where they could be, and he might go without danger; and that victuals consumed apace, but he must and would keep sufficient for themselves and their return. Yea, it was uttered by some, that if they got not a place in time, they would turn them and their goods ashore and leave them. Let it also be considered what weak hopes of supply and succor they left behind them, that might bear up their minds in this sad condition and trial they were under; and they could not but be very small. It is true, indeed, the affection and love of their brethren at Leyden was cordial and entire towards them, but they had little power to help them, or themselves; and how the case stood between them and the merchants at their coming away, hath already been declared. What could now sustain them but the spirit of God and his grace? May not and ought not the children of these fathers rightly say: "Our fathers were Englishmen which came over this great ocean, and were ready to perish in this wilderness; but they cried unto the Lord, and he heard their voice, and looked on their adversity, etc." "Let them therefore praise the Lord, because he is good, and his mercies endure forever. Yea, let them which have been redeemed of the Lord, show how he has delivered them from the hand of the oppressor. When they wandered in the desert wilderness out of the way, and found no city to dwell in, both hungry, and thirsty, their soul was overwhelmed in them. Let them confess before the Lord his loving-kindness, and his wonderful works before the sons of men."...

Starving Time
In these hard and difficult beginnings they found some discontents and murmurings arise amongst

some, and mutinous speeches and carriages in others; but they were soon quelled and overcome by the wisdom, patience, and just and equal carriage of things by the Governor [John Carver] and better part, which clove faithfully together in the main. But that which was most sad and lamentable was, that in 2 or 3 months' time half of their company died, especially in January: and February, being the depth of winter, and wanting houses and other comforts; being infected with the scurvy and other diseases, which this long voyage and their inaccommodate condition had brought upon them; so as there died some times 2 or 3 of a day, in the foresaid time; that of 100 and odd persons, scarce 50 remained. And of these in the time of most distress, there was but 6 or 7 persons, who, to their great commendations be it spoken, spared no pains, night nor day, but with abundance of toil and hazard of their own health, fetched them wood, made them fires, dressed them meat, made their beds, washed their loathsome clothes, clothed and unclothed them; in a word, did all the homely and necessary offices for them which dainty and queasy stomachs cannot endure to hear named; and all this willingly and cheerfully, without any grudging in the least, showing herein their true love unto their friends and brethren. A rare example and worthy to be remembered. Two of these 7 were Mr. William Brewster, their reverend Elder, and Myles Standish, their Captain and military commander, unto whom myself and many others, were much beholden in our low and sick condition. And yet the Lord so upheld these persons, as in this general calamity they were not at all infected with sickness or lameness. And what I have said of these, I may say of many others who died in this general visitation, and others yet living, that whilst they had health, yea, or any strength continuing, they were not wanting to any that had need of them. And I doubt not but their recompense is with the Lord....

Indian Relations

All this while the Indians came skulking about them, and would sometimes show themselves aloof off, but when any approached near them, they would run away. And once they stole away their tools where they had been at work, and were gone to dinner. But about the 16th of March a certain Indian came boldly amongst them, and spoke to them in broken English, which they could well understand, but marveled at it. At length they understood by discourse with him, that he was not of these parts, but belonged to the eastern parts, where some English ships came to fish, with whom he was acquainted, and could name sundry of them by their names, amongst whom he had got his language. He became profitable to them in acquainting them with many things concerning the state of the country in the east parts where he lived, which was afterwards profitable unto them; as also of the people here, of their names, number, and strength; of their situation and distance from this place, and who was chief amongst them. His name was Samaset; he told them also of another Indian whose name was Squanto, a native of this place, who had been in England and could speak better English than himself. Being, after some time of entertainment and gifts, dismissed, a while after he came again, and 5 more with him, and they brought again all the tools that were stolen away before, and made way for the coming of their great Sachem, called Massasoyt; who, about 4 or 5 days after, came with the chief of his friends and other attendance, with the aforesaid Squanto. With whom, after friendly entertainment, and some gifts given him, they made a peace with him (which hath now continued this 24 years) in these terms:

1. That neither he nor any of his should injure or do hurt to any of their people.
2. That if any of his did any hurt to any of theirs, he would send the offender, that they might punish him.
3. That if anything were taken away from any of theirs, he should cause it to be restored; and they should do the like to his.
4. If any did unjustly war against him, they would aid him; if any did war against them, he should aid them.
5. He should send to his neighbors confederates, to certify them of this, that they might not wrong them, but might be likewise comprised in the conditions of peace.
6. That when their men came to them, they should leave their bows and arrows behind them.

After these things he returned to his place called Sowams, some 40 mile from this place, but Squanto continued with them, and was their interpreter, and was a special instrument sent of God for their good beyond their expectation. He directed them how to set their corn, where to take fish, and to procure other commodities, and was also their pilot to bring them to unknown places for their profit, and never left them till he died. He was a native of this place, and scarce any left alive besides himself. He was carried away with divers others by one Hunt, a master of a ship, who thought to sell them for slaves in Spain; but he got away for England, and was entertained by a merchant in London, and employed to Newfoundland and other parts, and lastly brought hither into these parts by one Mr. Derruer, a gentleman employed by Sir Ferdinando Gorges and others, for discovery, and other designs in these parts....

❧ *"Liberty is the proper end and object of authority"*

JOHN WINTHROP

As a 12-term governor of the Massachusetts Bay Colony, John Winthrop helped establish the theocracy that ruled the Puritan settlement. In a sermon aboard the *Arbella* in 1630, he famously stated: "For we must consider that we shall be a city upon a hill. The eyes of all people are upon us, so that if we shall deal falsely with our God in this work we have undertaken, and so cause Him to withdraw his present help from us, we shall be made a story and a byword through the world."

Fifteen years later, Winthrop delivered this speech on the nature of liberty and authority.

...We account him who breaks not his covenant. The covenant between you and us is the oath you have taken of us, which is to this purpose, that we shall govern you and judge your causes by the rules of God's laws and our own, according to our best skill. When you agree with a workman to build you a ship or house, etc., he undertakes as well for his skill as for his faithfulness, for it is his profession, and you pay him for both. But when you call one to be a magistrate, he doth not profess nor undertake to have sufficient skill for that office, nor can you furnish him with gifts, etc.; therefore you must run the hazard of his skill and ability. But if he fails in faithfulness, which by his oath he is bound unto, that he must answer for....

There is a twofold liberty—natural (I mean as our nature is not corrupt) and civil or federal. The first is common to man with beasts and other creatures. By this, man, as he stands in relation to man simply, hath liberty to what he lists; it is a liberty to evil as well as to good. This liberty is incompatible and inconsistent with authority, and cannot endure the least restraint of the most just authority. The exercise and maintaining of this liberty makes men grow more evil, and in time to be worse than brute beasts: omens sumus licentia deteriores. This is that great enemy of truth and peace, that wild beast, which all the ordinances of God are bent against, to restrain and subdue it.

The other kind of liberty I call civil or federal; it may also be termed moral, in reference to the covenant between God and man, in the moral, in reference of the covenant between God and man, in the moral law, and the politic covenants and constitutions, amongst men themselves. This liberty is the proper end and object of authority, and cannot subsist without it; and it is a liberty to that only which is good, just, and honest. This liberty you are to stand for, with the hazard (not only of your good, but) of your lives, if need be. Whatsoever crosseth this is not authority but a distemper thereof. This liberty maintained and exercised in a way of subjection to authority; it is of the same kind of liberty wherewith Christ hath made us free. The women's own choice makes such a man her husband; yet, being so chosen, he is her lord, and she is subject to him, yet in a way of liberty, not of bondage; and a true wife accounts her subjection her honor and her freedom, and would not think her condition safe and free but in her subjection to her husband's authority. Such is the liberty of the church under the authority of Christ, her king and husband; his yoke is so easy and sweet to her as a bride's ornaments; and if through forwardness or wantonness etc. she shake it off, at any time, she is at no rest in her spirit until she take it up again; and whether her lord smiles upon her, and embraceth her in his arms, or whether he frowns, or rebukes, or smites her, she apprehends the sweetness of his love in all, and is refreshed, supported, and instructed by every such dispensation of his authority over her.

On the other side, ye know who they are that complain of this yoke and say, let us break their bands etc. We will not have this man to rule over us. Even so, brethren, it will be between you and your magistrates. If you stand for your natural corrupt liberties, and will do what is good in your own eyes, you will not endure the least weight of authority but will murmur, and oppose, and be always striving to shake off that yoke; but if you will be satisfied to enjoy such civil and lawful liberties, such as Christ allows you, then will you quietly and cheerfully submit unto that authority which is set over you, in all the administrations of it, for your good. Wherein, if we fail at any time, we hope we shall be willing (by God's assistance) to hearken to good advice from any of you, or in any other way of god; so shall your liberties be preserved, in upholding the honor and power of authority amongst you.

❧ *"Patroon Charter of New Netherlands"*

DUTCH EAST INDIA COMPANY

The Charter of Freedoms and Exemptions to Patroons established the patron system of land tenure on Manhattan in the Dutch colony of New Netherlands in 1629. The colony would be annexed by the British in 1664, but the system would remain largely in place.

The charter gave the patrons vast authority over land that they settled. They would eventually hold estates as large as a million acres and be among the wealthiest colonists in America. Patrons were given tax relief and other assistance for the settlement of the new colony, although certain activities such as producing textiles were prohibited.

III. All such shall be acknowledged Patroons of New Netherland who shall, within the space of four years next after they have given notice to any of the Chambers of the Company here, or to the Commander or Council there, undertake to plant a Colonie there of fifty souls, upwards of fifteen years old; one-fourth part within one year, and within three years after the sending of the first, making together four years, the remainder, to the full number of fifty persons; but it is to be observed that the Company reserve the Island of the Manhattes to themselves.

IV. They shall, from the time they make known the situation of the places where they propose to settle Colonies, have the preference to all others of the absolute property of such lands as they have there chosen; but in case the situation should not afterwards please them, or they should have been mistaken as to the quality of the land, they may, after remonstrating concerning the same to the Commander and Council there, be at liberty to choose another place.

V. The Patroons, by virtue of their power, shall and may be permitted, at such places as they shall settle their Colonies, to extend their limits four leagues along the shore, that is, on one side of a navigable river, or two leagues on each side of a river, and so far into the country as the situation of the occupiers will permit; provided and conditioned that the Company keep to themselves the lands lying and remaining between the limits of Colonies to dispose thereof, when at such time as they shall think proper, in such manner that no person shall be allowed to come within seven or eight leagues of them without their consent, unless the situation of the land thereabout be such that the Commander and Council, for good reasons, should order otherwise....

VI. They shall forever possess and enjoy all the lands lying within the aforesaid limits, together with the fruits, rights, minerals, rivers and fountains thereof; as also the chief command and lower jurisdictions, fishing, fowling and grinding, to the exclusion of all others, to be holden from the Company as a perpetual inheritance, without it ever devolving again to the Company, and in case it should devolve, to be redeemed and repossessed with twenty guilders per Colonie, to be paid to this Company, at the Chamber here or to their Commander there, within a year and six weeks after the same occurs, each at the Chamber where he originally sailed from; and further, no person or persons whatsoever shall be privileged to fish and hunt but the patroons and such shall permit. And in case any one should in time prosper so much as to found one or more cities, he shall have power and authority to establish officers and magistrates there, and to make use of the title of his Colonie, according to his pleasure and to the quality of the persons....

X. The Patroons and colonists shall be privileged to send their people and effects thither, in ships belonging to the Company, provided they take the oath, and pay to the Company for bringing over the people, as mentioned in the first article....

XII. Inasmuch as it is intended to people the Island of the Manhattas first, all fruits and wares that are produced on the lands situate on the North river, and lying thereabout, shall, for the present, be brought there before being sent else-where....

XIII. All the patroons of Colonies in New Netherland, and of Colonies on the Island of Manhattes, shall be at liberty to sail and traffic all along the coast, from Florida to Terra Neuf, provid-ed that they do again return with all such goods as they shall get in trade to the Island of Manhattes, and pay five per cent duty to the Company, in order, if possible, that, after the necessary inventory of the goods shipped be taken, the same may be sent hither....

XV. It shall be also free for the aforesaid Patroons to traffic and trade all along the coast of New Netherland and places circumjacent, with such goods as are consumed there, and receive in return for them all sorts of merchandise that may be had there, except beavers, otters, minks, and all sorts of peltry, which trade the Company reserve to them-selves. But the same shall be permitted at such places where the Company have no factories, condi-tioned that such traders shall be obliged to bring all the peltry they can procure to the Island of Manhattes, in case it may be, at any rate, practica-ble, and there deliver to the Director, to be by him shipped hither with the ships and goods; or, if they should come here without going there, then to give notice thereof to the Company, that a proper account thereof may be taken, in order that they may pay to the Company one guilder for each mer-chantable beaver and otter skin; the property, risk and all other charges remaining on account of the Patroons or owners.

XVI. All coarse wares that the Colonists of the Patroons there shall consume, such as pitch, tar, weed-ashes, wood, grain, fish, salt, hearthstone and such like things shall be conveyed in the Company's ships, at the rate of eighteen guilders per last....

XVIII. The Company promises the colonists of the Patroons that they shall be free from customs, taxes, excise, imposts for many years; and after the expiration of the said ten years, at the highest, such customs as the goods pay here for the present....

XX. From all judgments given by the Courts of the Patroons for upwards of fifty guilders, there may be an appeal to the Company's Commander and Council in New Netherland.

XXI. In regard to such private persons as on their own account,... shall be inclined to go thith-er and settle, they shall, with the approbation of the Director and Council there, be at liberty to take up and take possession of as much land as they shall be able properly to improve....

XXIII. Whosoever, whether colonists of Patroons for their Patroons, or free persons for themselves, or others for their masters, shall discov-er any shores, bays or other fit places for erecting fisheries, or the making of salt ponds, they may take possession thereof, and begin to work on them as their own absolute property, to the exclusion of all others. And it is consented to that the patroons of colonists may send ships along the coast of New Netherland, on the cod fishery....

XXVI. Whoever shall settle any Colonie out of the limits of the Manhattes Island, shall be obliged to satisfy the Indians for the land they shall settle upon, and they may extend or enlarge the limits of their Colonies if they settle a proportionate number of colonists thereon.

XXVII. The Patroons and colonists shall in particular, and in the speediest manner, endeavor to find out ways and means whereby they may sup-port a Minister and Schoolmaster, that thus the service of God and zeal for religion may not grow cool and be neglected among them, and they shall, for the first procure a Comforter of the sick there....

XXIX. The Colonists shall not be permitted to make any woolen, linen or cotton cloth, nor weave any other stuffs there, on pain of being banished, and as perjurers, to be arbitrarily punished.

XXX. The company will use their endeavors to supply the colonists with as many Blacks as they conveniently can, on the conditions hereafter to be made, in such manner, however, that they shall not be bound to do it for a longer time than they shall think proper.

XXXI. The Company promise to finish the fort on the Island of Manhattes, and to put it in a pos-ture of defence without delay.

🌿 "A shelter for the poor and persecuted"

ROGER WILLIAMS

Tolerance ran shallow in Puritan Plymouth and

Massachusetts Bay. It did not take long for religious factions to emerge. Roger Williams questioned the church's authority to mediate between an individual and God. As a result, the young minister was expelled from Massachusetts. Setting a trend that would last for almost 300 years, Williams headed west. He founded Rhode Island as a new colony in 1636 as a sanctuary for religious toleration. He recalled the experience many years later.

Rhode Island's 1636 charter would later state that no person would be persecuted for his or her religious beliefs. As a result, Rhode Island would become a destination for Jews and Quakers. The first Baptist Church in America was in Providence and the first American synagogue was in Newport.

When I was unkindly and unchristianly, as I believe, driven from my house and land and wife and children (in the midst of New England winter, now about 35 years past) at Salem, that ever-honored Governor Mr. Winthrop privately wrote to me to steer my course to Nahigonset-Bay and Indians for many high and heavenly and public ends, encouraging me [because of] the freeness of the place and from any English claims or patents. I took his prudent motion as a hint and voice from God and waving all other thoughts and motions, I steered my course from Salem (though in winter snow which I fell yet) unto these parts, wherein I may say I have seen the face of God.

I first pitched, and begun to build and plant at Sekonk, now Rehoboth, but I received a letter from my ancient friend Mr. Winslow, then Governour of Plymouth, professing his own and others love and respect to me, yet lovingly advising me, since I was fallen into the edge of their bounds and they were loath to displease the Bay, to remove but to the other side of the water and then he said I had the country free before me and might be as free as themselves and we should be loving neighbors together. These were the joint understandings of these two eminently wise and Christian Governors and others, in their day, together with their council and advice as to the freedom and vacancy of this place, which in this respect and many other Providences of the most holy and only wise, I called Providence.

Sometime after Plymouth, great Sachim Ousamagquin [Wampanoag chief Massasoit], upon occasion affirming that Providence was his land and therefore Plymouth's land and some resenting it, the then prudent and godly Governor Mr. Bradford and others of his godly council, answered that if after due examination it should be found true what the bar-

barian said, yet having, to my loss of a harvest that year, been now (though by their gentle advice) as good as banished from Plymouth as from the Massachusetts; and I had quietly and patiently departed from them, at their motion, to the place where now I was, I should not be molested and tossed up and down again while they had breath in their bodies; and surely between those my friends of the Bay and Plymouth, I was sorely tossed for fourteen weeks, in a bitter winter season, not knowing what bread or bed did mean; beside the yearly loss of no small matter in my trading with English and natives, being debarred from Boston, the chief mart and port of New England....

Upon frequent exceptions against Providence men that we had no authority for civil government, I went purposely to England and upon my report and petition, the Parliament granted us a charter of government for these parts, so judged vacant on all hands.

Here all over this colony, a great number of weak and distressed souls, scattered are flying hither from Old and New England, the Most High, and only wise hath in his infinite wisdom provided this country and this corner as a shelter for the poor and persecuted, according to their several persuasions....

We must part with lands and lives before we part with such a jewel.

❧ "What breach of law is that Sir?"

EXAMINATION OF MRS. ANN HUTCHINSON

Ann Hutchinson followed Roger Williams into exile to Rhode Island. She had arrived in Massachusetts Bay Colony in 1634 and quickly come into conflict with the authorities when she held weekly meetings with other women to discuss religious matters. The colony's theocratic government objected to her actions and her belief that salvation could be gained through faith rather than obedience to the laws of the church and state.

Clear-headed and brave, she held her ground during the trial which lasted several days. This exchange between Hutchinson and Massachusetts Governor John Winthrop reflected the determination of both perspectives. Hutchinson was banished in 1637. After living in Rhode Island, she and her family later moved to New York where she and all of her family save one member were killed in an Indian raid.

GOVERNOR WINTHROP. Mrs. Hutchinson, you are called here as one of those that have troubled the peace of the commonwealth and the churches here; you are known to be a woman that hath had a great share in the promoting and divulging of those opinions that are causes of this trouble, and to be nearly joined not only in affinity and affection with some of those the court had taken notice of and passed censure upon, but you have spoken divers things as we have been informed very prejudicial to the honour of the churches and ministers thereof, and you have maintained a meeting and an assembly in your house that hath been condemned by the general assembly as a thing not tolerable nor comely in the sight of God nor fitting for your sex, and notwithstanding that was cried down you have continued the same, therefore we have thought good to send for you to understand how things are, that if you be in an erroneous way we may reduce you that so you may become a profitable member here among us, otherwise if you be obstinate in your course that then the court may take such course that you may trouble us no further, therefore I would intreat you to express whether you do not assent and hold in practice to those opinions and factions that have been handled in court already, that is to say, whether you do not justify Mr. Wheelwright's sermon and the petition.

MRS. HUTCHINSON. I am called here to answer before you but I hear no things laid to my charge.

WINTHROP. I have told you some already and more I can tell you.

HUTCHINSON. Name one, Sir.

WINTHROP. Have I not named some already?

HUTCHINSON. What have I said or done?

WINTHROP. Why for your doings, this you did harbour and countenance those that are parties in this faction that you have heard of.

HUTCHINSON. That's a matter of conscience, Sir.

WINTHROP. Your conscience you must keep or it must be kept for you.

HUTCHINSON. Must not I then entertain the saints because I must keep my conscience?

WINTHROP. Say that one brother should commit felony or treason and come to his brother's house, if he knows him guilty and conceals him he is guilty of the same. It is his conscience to entertain him, but if his conscience comes into act in giving countenance and entertainment to him that hath broken the law he is guilty too. So if you do countenance those that are transgressors of the law you are in the same fact.

HUTCHINSON. What law do they transgress?

WINTHROP. The law of God and of the state.

HUTCHINSON. In what particular?

WINTHROP. Why in this among the rest, whereas the Lord doth say honour thy father and thy mother.

HUTCHINSON. Ey Sir in the Lord.

WINTHROP. This honour you have broke in giving countenance to them.

HUTCHINSON. In entertaining those did I entertain them against any act (for there is the thing) or what God hath appointed?

WINTHROP. Why the fifth commandment.

HUTCHINSON. I deny that for he saith in the Lord.

WINTHROP. You have joined with them in the faction.

HUTCHINSON. In what faction have I joined with them?

WINTHROP. In presenting the petition.

HUTCHINSON. Suppose I had set my hand to the petition what then?

WINTHROP. You saw that case tried before.

HUTCHINSON. But I had not my hand to the petition.

WINTHROP. You have councelled them.

HUTCHINSON. Wherein?

WINTHROP. Why in entertaining them.

HUTCHINSON. What breach of law is that Sir?

WINTHROP. Why dishonoring of parents.

HUTCHINSON. But put the case Sir that I do fear the Lord and my parents, may not I entertain them that fear the Lord because my parents will not give me leave?

WINTHROP. If they be the fathers of the commonwealth, and they of another religion, if you entertain them then you dishonor your parents and are justly punishable.

HUTCHINSON. If I entertain them, as they have dishonoured their parents I do.

WINTHROP. No but you by countenancing them above others put honor upon them.

HUTCHINSON. I may put honor upon them as the children of God and as they do honor the Lord.

WINTHROP. We do not mean to discourse with those of your sex but only this; you do adhere unto them and do endeavor to set forward this faction and so you do dishonour us.

HUTCHINSON. I do acknowledge no such thing neither do I think that I ever put any dishonour upon you.

WINTHROP. Why do you keep such a meeting at your house as you do every week upon a set day?

HUTCHINSON. It is lawful for me so to do, as it is all your practices and can you find a warrant for yourself and condemn me for the same thing? The ground of my taking it up was, when I first came to this land because I did not go to such meetings as those were, it was presently reported that I did not allow of such meetings but held them unlawful and therefore in that regard they said I was proud and did despise all ordinances, upon that a friend came unto me and told me of it and I to prevent such aspersions took it up, but it was in practice before I came therefore I was not the first.

WINTHROP. For this, that you appeal to our practice you need no confutation. If your meeting had answered to the former it had not been offensive, but I will say that there was no meeting of women alone, but your meeting is of another sort for there are sometimes men among you.

HUTCHINSON. There was never any man with us.

WINTHROP. Well, admit there was no man at your meeting and that you were sorry for it, there is no warrant for your doings, and by what warrant do you continue such a course?

HUTCHINSON. I conceive there lyes a clear rule in Titus, that the elder women should instruct the younger and then I must have a time wherein I must do it.

WINTHROP. All this I grant you, I grant you a time for it, but what is this to the purpose that you Mrs. Hutchinson must call a company together from their callings to come to be taught of you?

HUTCHINSON. Will it please you answer me this and to give me a rule for them, I will willingly submit to any truth. If any come to my house to be instructed in the ways of God what rule have I to put them away?

WINTHROP. But suppose that a hundred men come unto you to be instructed will you forbear to instruct them?

HUTCHINSON. As far as I conceive I cross a rule in it.

WINTHROP. Very well and do you not so here?

HUTCHINSON. No Sir for my ground is they are men.

WINTHROP. Men and women all are one for that, but suppose that a man should come and say Mrs. Hutchinson I hear that you are a woman that God hath given his grace unto and you have knowledge in the word of God. I pray instruct me a little, ought you not to instruct this man?

HUTCHINSON. I think I may. Do you think it not lawful for me to teach women and why do you call me to teach the court?

WINTHROP. We do not call you to teach the court but to lay open yourself.

HUTCHINSON. I desire you that you would then set down a rule by which I may put them away that come unto me and so have peace in so doing.

WINTHROP. You must shew your rule to receive them.

HUTCHINSON. I have done it.

WINTHROP. I deny it because I have brought more arguments than you have.

HUTCHINSON. I say, to me it is a rule.

❧ *"That old deluder Satan"*

FIRST MASSACHUSETTS SCHOOL LAW

When colonists first arrived in America they relied on parents and apprentice masters to teach the young how to read and write. However, this was not always a reliable method of learning. Massachusetts was the first colony to impose educational requirements. Leaders were concerned that illiteracy and infidelity were overtaking the colony. In 1642, the colony required parents and masters to take responsibility for teaching their charges to read and write. Five years later Massachusetts passed the first law requiring communities to establish schools for the instruction of reading and writing.

It being one chief project of that old deluder Satan to keep men from the knowledge of the Scriptures, as in former times by keeping them in an unknown tongue, so in these latter times by persuading from the use of tongues, that so at least the true sense and meaning of the original might be clouded by false glosses of saint-seeming deceivers, that learning may not be buried in the grave of our fathers in the church and commonwealth, the Lord assisting our endeavors.

It is therefore ordered, that every township in this jurisdiction, after the Lord hath increased them to the number of fifty householders, shall then forth-with appoint one within their town to teach all such children as shall resort to him to write and read, whose wages shall be paid either by the parents or masters of such children, or by the inhabitants in general by way of supply, as the major part of those that order the prudentials of the town shall appoint. Provided, those that send their children be not oppressed by paying much more than they can have them taught for in other towns. And it is further ordered, that where any town shall increase to the number of 100 families or householders, they shall set up a grammar school, the master thereof being able to instruct youth so far as they may be fitted for the university. Provided, that if any town neglect the performance hereof above one year, that every such town shall pay five pounds to the next school till they shall perform this order.

❧ Maryland Act of Toleration

MARYLAND ASSEMBLY

Maryland was settled in 1634 under a grant to the Catholic Calvert family, the Lords Baltimore, as a Catholic refuge. It became the only English colony in North America with a large Catholic minority. In 1649, the second Lord Baltimore feared neighboring Puritans in Virginia would be emboldened by the Puritan victory in the English Civil War. The Maryland Assembly passed the Act of Toleration, a major step in the principle of freedom of religion in America.

The act, however, was highly qualified, allowing freedom of religion only for those who believed in Jesus Christ: Blasphemers were subject to capital punishment, Jews were not allowed to hold public office for almost two centuries, and believing in God was a requirement for holding public office until 1961. Nevertheless, the concept of freedom of religion was established and resulted in relatively harmonious relations between the religious sects. The success of religious toleration in Maryland served as a model for the nation a century later.

Be it therefore enacted That whatsoever person or persons within this Province shall from henceforth blaspheme god, or shall deny our Saviour Jesus Christ to bee the sonne of God, or shall deny the holy Trinity the father sonne and holy Ghost, or the Godhead of any of the said Three persons of the trinity or the Unity of the Godhead shall be punished with death and confiscation or forfeiture of all his or her lands....

Be it Therefore enacted (except as in this present Act is before Declared and sett forth) that noe person or persons whatsoever within this Province, or the Islands, Ports, Harbors, Creekes, or havens thereunto belonging professing to believe in Jesus Christ, shall from henceforth bee any waies troubled, Molested or discountenanced for or in respect of his or religion nor in the free exercise thereof within this Province or the Islands thereunto belonging nor any way compelled to the beleife or exercise of any other religion against his or her consent, soe as they may be not unfaithful to the Lord Proprietary, or molest or conspire against the civil Government established or to bee established in this Province under him or his heires.

❧ "Said persons shall enjoy exemptions"

TAX RELIEF FOR CHILDREN IN NEW NETHERLANDS

New colonies such as the Dutch New Netherlands (which would soon become British New York) needed to sustain themselves for the long term. They frequently took measures to encourage existing settlers to have children themselves and potential colonists to bring children with them. In 1650, New Netherlands offered to relieve residents one-year's taxation for every child brought or beget to the colony.

On the arrival of the aforesaid persons in New Netherland, they shall be allowed and granted the privilege of choosing and taking up, under quit rent or as a fief, such parcels of land as they shall in any way be able to cultivate for the production of all sorts of fruits and crops of those parts, on condition that they shall be bound to commence the same within the year, on pain of being again deprived of said lands.

Said persons shall enjoy Exemption from tenths of all aforesaid fruits and crops of the term of years, and thenceforth one additional year's Exemption for every legitimate child they shall convey thither or get there.

❧ "This indenture made"

A TYPICAL INDENTURE CONTRACT

The most common way for prospective colonists to pay their way for the cross-Atlantic journey to America in the 17th century was to become an indentured servant. In exchange for passage, the shipowner would "sell" the passenger to a master for a certain number of years, or the would-be passenger could make the arrangements himself. At the conclusion of the contract, the servant would be free. Often the servant would have also gained knowledge of a trade and receive a payment. Most indentured servants were under 19 years old, with average being between 16 and 18. The following is a standard contract between a servant and his master outlining their mutual obligations, including moral responsibilities on the part of the servant.

This indenture made the 6th day of June in the year of our Lord Christ 1659, witnesseth, that Bartholomew Clarke the sone of John Clarke of the City of Canterbury, sadler, of his own liking and with the consent of Francis Plumer of the City of Canterbury, brewer, hath put himself apprentice unto Edward Rowzie of Virginia, planter, as an apprentice with him to dwell from the day of the date above mentioned unto the full term of four years from thence next ensuing fully to be complete and ended, all which said term the said Bartholemew Clarke well and faithfully the said Edward Rowzie as his master shall serve, his secrets keep, his commands most just and lawful he shall observe, and fornication he shall not commit, nor contract matrimony with any woman during the said term; he shall not do hurt unto his master nor consent to the doing of any, but to his power shall hinder and prevent the doing of any; at cards, dice or any unlawful games he shall not play; he shall not waste the goods of his said master nor lend them to anybody without his master's consent; he shall not absent himself from his said master's service day or night, but as a true and faithful servant, shall demean himself. And the said Edward Rowzie in the mystery, art, and occupation of a planter…the said Bartholomew shall teach or cause to be taught, and also during said term shall find and allow his apprentice competent meat, drink, apparel, washing, lodging with all other things fitting for his degree, and in the end thereof, fifty acres of land to be laid out for him, and all other things which according to the custom of the country is or ought to be done.

❧ The Execution of Mary Dyer

MASSACHUSETTS COURT RECORDS

With the English Revolution of 1649 and the ascent of a Puritan government in England, Quakers were targeted for persecution. Many sought refuge in America. Puritan New England did not welcome them. The first Quakers to arrive in Boston were forced back on their ship bound for England. Two years later, Massachusetts Bay banished Quakers entirely from their settlement upon pain of death.

In 1660, the government made good on its pledge and condemned four Quakers to death by hanging. One of them was a woman named Mary Dyer, as recorded in this excerpt from the Massachusetts Court Records. Public anger at the hangings led to the repeal of the death penalty. The only colony that accepted Quakers at the time was Rhode Island.

The whole Court mett together sent for Mary Dyer, who rebelliously, after sentence of death past against hir, returned into this jurisdiction. Being come before the Court, she acknowledged hirself to be Mary Dyer, the person, & was condemned by this Court to death. Being asked what she had to say why the sentence should not be executed, she gave no answer but that she denied our lawe, came to beare witness against it, & could not choose but come & doe as formerly. The whole Court mett together voted, that the said Mary Dyer, for hir rebelliously returning into this jurisdiction, (notwithstanding the favor of this court towards hir,) shall be, by the marshall generall, on the first day of June, about nine of the clocke in the morning, carried to the place of execution, and according to the sentence of the Generall Court in october last, be put to death; that the secretary issue out warrant accordingly; which sentence the Governor declared to hir in open Court; & warrant issued out accordingly to Edward Michelson, marshall generall, & to Captain James Oliver, & his order, as formerly.

❧ Massachusetts Declaration of Liberties

MASSACHUSETTS GENERAL COURT

When Massachusetts was first chartered there was an implicit belief that the colony was not necessarily bound by the laws of English Parliament. Puritan leaders reaffirmed that belief many times. In 1661, that understanding was made explicit with the Declaration of Liberties by the Massachusetts General Courts. Massachusetts declared that the colony could set its own laws, provided they were "not repugnant" to British law.

Concerning our liberties

1. Wee conceive the pattent (under God) to be the first and maine foundation of our civil politye, by a Gouvernor & Company, according as in therein exprest.
2. The Gouvernor & Company are, by the pattent, a body politicke, in fact & name.
3. This body politicke is vested with power to make freemen....
6. The Gouvernor, Deputy Gouvernor, Assistants, & select representatives or deputies have full power and authoritie, both legislative & executive, for the gouvernment of all the people heere, whither inhabitants or straingers, both concerning eclesiasticks & in civils, without appeale, excepting lawe or lawes repugnant to the lawes of England....
8. Wee conceive any imposition prejudicial to the country contrary to any just law of ours, not repugnant to the lawes of England to be an infringement of our right.

❧ God's Controversy with New England

MICHAEL WIGGLESWORTH

Michael Wigglesworth was a popular writer and minister in Puritan New England. His sermon "The Day of Doom," a 224-stanza poem on good and evil, was the first American bestseller. The following 1662 poem was written at about the same time. While celebrating New England's religious calling and the fortitude of the original settlers, he bemoans the deteriorating standards of his contemporaries and denounces the present conditions of the once-noble colony.

"Beyond the great Atlantick flood"
There is a region vast,
A country where no English foot
In former ages past:
A waste and howling wilderness,
Where none inhabited
But hellish fiends, and brutish men
That Devils worshiped.

This region was in darkness plac't
Far off from heavens light,
Amidst the shaddows of grim death
And of eternal night.
For there the sun of righteousness
Had never made to shine
The light of his sweet countenance,
And grace which is divine:

Until the time drew nigh wherein
The glorious Lord of hostes
Was pleasd to lead his armies forth
Into those forrein coastes.
At whose approach the darkness sad
Soon vanished away,
And all the shaddows of the night
Were turnd to lightsome day.

The stubborn he in pieces brake,
Like vessels made of clay:
And those that sought his peoples hurt
He turned to decay.
Those curst Amalekites, that first
Lift up their hand on high
To fight against Gods Israel,
Were ruin'd fearfully.

Thy terrours on the Heathen folk,
O Great Jehovah, fell:
The fame of thy great acts, o Lord,
Did all the nations quell.
Some hid themselves for fear of thee
In forrests wide and great:
Some to thy people croutching came,
For favour to entreat.

Some were desirous to be taught
The knowledge of thy wayes,
And being taught, did soon accord
Therein to spend their dayes.
Thus were the fierce and barbarous

Brought to civility,
And those that liv'd like beasts (or worse)
To live religiously.

O happiest of dayes wherein
The blind received sight,
And those that had no eyes before
Were made to see the light.
The wilderness hereat rejoyc't,
The woods for joy did sing,
The vallys and the little hills
Thy praises echoing.

Our temp'rall blessings did abound:
But spiritual good things
Much more abounded, to the praise
Of that great King of Kings.
Gods throne was here set up; here was
His tabernacle pight.
This was the place, and these the folk
In whom he took delight.

Our morning starrs shone all day long:
Their beams gave forth such light,
As did the noon-day sun abash,
And 's glory dazle quite.
Our day continued many years,
And had no night at all:
Yea many thought the light would last,
And be perpetuall.

Such, o New-England, was they first,
Such was thy best estate:
But, Loe! A strange and sudden change
My courage did amate.
The brightest of our morning starrs
Did wholly disappeare:
And those that tarried behind
With sack-cloth covered were.

Moreover, I beheld and saw
Our welken overkest,
And dismal clouds for sun-shine late
O'respread from east to west.
The air became tempestuous;
The wilderness gan quake:
And from above with awfull voice
Th' Almight thundring spake.

Are these the men that erst at my command
Forsook their ancient seats and native soile,
To follow me into a desart land,
Contemning all the trayell and the toile,
Whose love was such to purest ordinances

As made them set at nought their fair inheritances?

Are these the men that prized libertee
To walk with God according to their light,
To be as good as he would have them bee,
To serve and worship him with all their might,
Before the pleasures which a fruitful field,
And country flowing-full of all good things, could
    yield?

Are these the folk whom from the british Iles,
Through the stern billows of the watry main,
I safely led so many thousand miles,
As if their journey had been through a plain?
Whom having from all enemies protected,
And through so many deaths and dangers well
    directed,

I brought and planted on the western shore,
Where nought but bruits and salvage wights did
    swarm
(Untaught, untrain'd, untam'd by vertue's lore)
that sought their blood, yet could not do them
    harm?
My fury's flaile them thresht, my fatall broom
Did sweep them hence, to make my people Elbow-
    room.

Are these the men whose gates with peace I
    crown'd,
To whom for bulwarks I salvation gave,
Whilst all things else with rattling tumults sound,
And mortall frayes send thousands to the grave?
Whilest their own brethren bloody hands
    embrewed
In brothers blood, and Fields with carcases
    bestrewed?

Is this the people blest with bounteous store,
By land and sea full richly clad and fed,
Whom plenty's self stands waiting still before,
And powreth out their cups well tempered?
For whose dear sake an howling wilderness
I lately turned into a fruitful paradeis?

Are these the people in whose hemisphere
Such bright-beam'd, glis'tring, sun-like starrs I
    placed,
As by their influence did all things cheere,
As by their light blind ignorance defaced,
As errours into lurking holes did fray,
As turn'd the late dark night into a lightsome day?
Are these the folks to whom I milked out
And sweetnes stream'd from consolations brest;

Whose soules I fed and strengthened throughout
With finest spirituall food most finely drest?
On whom I rained living bread from Heaven
Withouten Errour's bane, or Superstition's leaven?

With whom I made a Covenant of peace,
And unto whom I did most firmly plight
My faithfulness, If whilst I live I cease
To be their Guide, their God, their full delight;
Since them with cords of love to me I drew,
Enwrapping in my grace such as should then ensew.

Are these the men, that now mine eyes behold,
Concerning whom I thought, and whilome spake,
First Heaven shall pass away together scrold,
Ere they my lawes and righteous wayes forsake,
Or that they slack to runn their heavenly race?
Are these the same? Or are some others come in
    place?
If these be they, how is that I find
In stead of holiness Carnality,
In stead of heavenly frames an Earthly mind,
For burning zeal luke-warm Indifferency,
For flaming Love, key-cold Dead-heartedness,
For temperance (in meat, and drinke, and cloaths)
    excess?

Whence cometh it, that Pride, and Luxurie
Debate, Deceit, Contention and Strife,
False-dealing, Covetousness, Hypocrisie
(With such like Crimes) amongst them are so rife,
That one of them doth over-reach another?
And that an honest man can hardly trust his
    Brother?
How is it, that Security, and Sloth,
Amongst the best are Common to be found?
That grosser sinns, in stead of Graces Growth,
Amongst the many more and more abound?
I hate dissembling shews of Holiness.
Or practise as you talk, or never more profess.

Judge not, vain world, that all are hypocrites
That do profess more holiness then thou:
All foster not dissembling, guilefull spirites,
Nor love their lusts, though very many do.
Some sin through want of care and constant watch,
Some with the sick converse, till they the sickness
    catch.

Some, that maintain a reall root of grace,

Are overgrown with many noysome weeds,
Whose heart, that those no longer may take place,
The benefit of due correction needs.
And such as these however gone astray
I shall by stripes reduce into a better way.

Moreover some there be that still retain
Their ancient vigour and sincerity;
Whom both their own, and others sins, constrain
To sigh, and mourn, and weep, and wail, and cry:
And for their sakes I have forborn to powre
My wrath upon Revolters to this present houre.

To praying Saints I always have respect,
And tender love, and pittifull regard:
Nor will I now in any wise neglect
Their love and faithful service to reward;
Although I deal with others for their folly,
And turn their mirth to tears that have been too
    too jolly.

For think not, O Backsliders, in your heart,
That I shall still your evill manners beare:
Your sinns me press as sheaves do load a cart,
And therefore I will plague you for this geare
Except you seriously, and soon, repent,
Ile not delay your pain and heavy punishment.

And who be those themselves that yonder shew?
The seed of such as name my dreadful Name!
On whom whilere compassions skirt I threw
Whilest in their blood they were, to hide their
    shame!
Whom my preventing love did neer me take!
Whom for mine own I mark't, lest they should me
    forsake!

I look't that such as these to vertue's Lore
(Though none but they) would have Enclin'd their
    ear:
That they at least mine image should have bore,
And sanctify'd my name with awfull fear.
Let pagan's Bratts pursue their lusts, whose meed
Is Death: For christians children are an holy seed.

But hear O Heavens! Let Earth amazed stand;
Ye Mountaines melt, and Hills come flowing down:
Let horror seize upon both Sea and Land;
Let Natures self be cast into a stown.
I children nourisht, nurtur'd and upheld:

But they against a tender Father have rebell'd.

What could have been by me performed more?
Or wherein fell I short of your desire?
Had you but askt, I would have op't my store,
And given what lawfull wishes could require.
For all this bounteous cost I lookt to see
Heaven-reaching-hearts, and thoughts, Meekness,
    Humility.
But lo, a sensuall Heart all void of grace,
An Iron neck, a proud presumptuous Hand;
A self-conceited, stiff, stout, stubborn Race,
That fears no threats, submits to no command:
Self-will'd, perverse, such as can beare no yoke;
A Generation even ripe for vengeance stroke.

Ah dear New-England! Dearest land to me;
Which unto God hast hitherto been dear,
And mayst be still more dear than formerlie,
If to his voice thou wilt incline thine ear.

Consider wel and wisely what the rod,
Wherewith thou art from yeer to yeer chastized,
Instructeth thee. Repent, and turn to God,
Who will not have his nurture despized.

Thou still hast in thee many praying saints,
Of great account, and precious with the Lord,
Who dayly powre out unto him their plaints,
And strive to please him both in deed and
    word.

Cheer on, sweet souls, my heart is with you all,
And shall be with you, maugre sathan's might:
And whereso'ere this body be a Thrall,
Still in New-England shall be my delight.

🍂 An Act Concerning Negroes and Other Slaves

MARYLAND GENERAL ASSEMBLY

The first black Africans brought to the New World as "servants" arrived in Jamestown in 1619. Initially, blacks had a similar status as white indentured servants with the same ability to gain emancipation after a period of work. In most cases, whites preferred white laborers as it was a relationship they were used to from their European experiences.

Gradually, however, the desperate need for laborers led to a shift in policy in which white settlers subjugated both native populations and black Africans as permanent slaves. Throughout the second half of the seventeenth century, the bondage of Africans became part of most colonies' criminal and civil law. The following act was passed by the General Assembly of Maryland in 1664. It made all existing black servants permanent slaves. In addition, any white woman who was married to a black slave became a slave herself.

Be it enacted by the Right Honorable the Lord Proprietary by the advise and consent of the upper and lower house of this present Generall Assembly, that all Negroes or other slaves already within the province, and all Negroes and other slaves to be hereafter imported into the province, shall serve durante vita. And all children born of any Negro or other slave shall be slaves as their fathers were, for the term of their lives. And forasmuch as divers freeborn English women, forgetful of their free condition and to the disgrace of our nation, marry Negro slaves, by which also divers suits may arise touching the issue of such women, and a great damage befalls the masters of such Negroes for prevention whereof, for deterring such freeborn women from such shameful matches. Be it further enacted by the authority, advice, and consent aforesaid, that whatsoever freeborn woman shall marry any slave from and after the last day of this present Assembly shall serve the master of such slave during the life of her husband. And that all the issue of such freeborn women so married shall be slaves as their fathers were. And be it further enacted, that all the issues of English or other freeborn women that have already married Negroes shall serve the masters of their parents till they be thirty years of age and no longer.

🍂 "Thus we were butchered"

MARY ROWLANDSON

King Philip's War devastated the British settlements in New England. The Native American Metacom, chief of the Wampanoags who had initially greeted the pilgrims with welcome arms, led an alliance of Indian tribes in the brutal war. Metacom, who was known as King Philip by the settlers, reacted against the rapidly growing settlements that were infringing on Indian lands.

Lasting from early 1675 to the summer of 1676 when Metacom was killed, the war set back English colonization in New England by 30 years. Half the region's towns and cities were attacked. Eight percent of the adult male white population was killed. The native tribes suffered similar casualties.

Mary Rowlandson's account of the early-morning winter attack on the Lancaster settlement and her ensuing 11-week trial as a prisoner of the Indians was perhaps the most popular book about the war. Her description reflected the violence of frontier life and the brutality of the Indian wars.

On the 10th of February, 1675, came the Indians with great numbers upon Lancaster. Their first coming was about sunrising.

Hearing the noise of some guns, we looked out; several houses were burning, and the smoke ascending to heaven. There were five persons taken in one house; the father and the mother and a suckling child they knocked on the head; the other two they took and carried away alive. There were two others, who, being out of their garrison upon some occasion, were set upon; one was knocked on the head, the other escaped. Another there was who, running along, was shot and wounded, and fell down; he begged of them his life, promising them money (as they told me), but they would not hearken to him, but knocked him in the head, and stripped him naked, and split open his bowels. Another seeing many of the Indians about his barn ventured and went out, but was quickly shot down. There were three others belonging to the same garrison who were killed; the Indians, getting upon the roof of the barn, had advantage to shoot down upon them over their fortification. Thus these murderous wretches went on burning and destroying before them.

At length they came and beset our own house, and quickly it was the dolefullest day that ever mine eyes saw. The house stood upon the edge of a hill; some of the Indians got behind the hill, others into the barn, and others behind anything that could shelter them; from all which places they shot against the house; so that the bullets seemed to fly like hail, and quickly they wounded one man among us, then another, and then a third. About two hours (according to my observation in that amazing time) they had been about the house before they prevailed to fire it; they fired it once, and one ventured out and quenched it, but they quickly fired it again, and that took. Now is the dreadful hour come that I have often heard of, but

now mine eyes see it. Some in our house were fighting for their lives, others wallowing in their blood, the house on fire over our heads, and the bloody heathen ready to knock us on the head if we stirred out. Now might we hear mothers and children crying out for themselves and one another, "Lord, what shall we do?" Then I took my children (and one of my sisters hers) to go forth and leave the house, but, as soon as we came to the door and appeared, the Indians shot so thick that the bullets rattled against the house as if one had taken a handful of stones and threw them, so that we were forced to give back. We had six stout dogs belonging to our garrison, but none of them would stir, though another time if any Indian had come to the door, they were ready to fly upon him and tear him down. The Lord hereby would make us the more to acknowledge His hand, and to see that our help is always in Him. But out we must go, the fire increasing, and coming along behind us roaring, and the Indians gaping before us with their guns, spears, and hatchets to devour us.

No sooner were we out of the house but my brother-in-law (being before wounded in defending the house, in or near the throat) fell down dead, whereat the Indians scornfully shouted and hallooed, and were presently upon him, stripping off his clothes. The bullets flying thick, one went through my side, and the same (as would seem) through the bowels and hand of my dear child in my arms. One of my elder sister's children (named William) had then his leg broke, which the Indians perceiving they knocked him on the head. Thus were we butchered by those merciless heathen, standing amazed, with the blood running down to our heels. My eldest sister being yet in the house, and seeing those woeful sights, the infidels hauling mothers one way and children another, and some wallowing in their blood; and her elder son telling her that her son William was dead, and myself wounded, she said, "And, Lord, let me die with them"; which was no sooner said, but she was struck with a bullet, and fell down dead over the threshold. I hope she is reaping the fruit of her good labors, being faithful to the services of God in her place.

I had often before this said, that if the Indians should come, I should chose rather to be killed by them than taken alive, but when it came to the trial, my mind changed; their glittering weapons so daunted my spirit, that I chose rather to go along with those (as I may say) ravenous bears, than that moment to end my days.

❧ "Adversity doth still our joyes attend"

ANNE BRADSTREET

Anne Bradstreet arrived in the Massachusetts Bay Colony in 1630 with her husband and parents. Only 18 years old, she initially did not enjoy her new primitive lifestyle, but eventually reconciled herself to it as part of God's will. She eventually moved to Ipswich where she raised a family and wrote several poems.

Unbeknownst to her, in 1650, a brother-in-law took some of the poems back to England and published them in a book entitled *The Tenth Muse Lately Sprung Up in America,* making it the first book of poetry by an American writer. Embarrassed by the publication of her poems, she wrote a subsequent poem entitled "The Author of Her Book" about the experience. This and several other poems were later published in 1678, six years after her death.

"The Author of Her Book"
Thou ill-form'd offspring of my feeble brain,
Who after birth did'st by my side remain,
Till snatcht from thence by friends, less wise than
    true
Who thee abroad, expos'd to publick view,
Made thee in raggs, halting to th' press to trudge,
Where errors were not lessened (all may judge)
At thy return my blushing was not small,
My rambling brat (in print) should mother call,
I cast thee by as one unfit for light,
Thy Visage was so irksome in my sight;
Yet being mine own, at length affection would
Thy blemishes amend, if so I could:
I wash'd they face, but more defects I saw,
And rubbing off a spot, still made a flaw.
I stretcht thy joynts to make thee even feet,
Yet still thou run'st more hobling then is meet;
In better dress to trim thee was my mind,
But nought save home-spun Cloth, i'th' house I
    find
In this array, 'mongst Vulgars mayst thou roam
In Critick's hands, beware thou dost not come;
And take they way where yet thou art not known,
If for thy Farther askt, say, thou hadst none:
And for they Mother, she alas is poor,
Which caus'd her thus to send thee out of door.

"Before the Birth of One of Her Children"
All things within this fading world hath end,
Adversity doth still our joyes attend;
No tyes so strong, no friends so dear and sweet,
But with deaths parting blow is sure to meet.
The sentence past is most irrevocable,
A common thing, yet oh inevitable;
How soon, my Dear, death may my steps attend,
How soon't may be they Lot to lose thy friend,
We both are ignorant, yet love bids me
These farewell lines to recommend to thee,
That when that knot's unty'd that made us one,
I may seem thine, who in effect am none.
And if I see not have my dayes that's due,
What nature would, God grant to yours and you;
The many faults that well you know I have,
Let be interr'd in my oblivion's grave;
If any worth or virtue were in me
Let that live freshly in they memory
And when thou feel'st no grief, as I no harms,
Yet love thy dead, who long lay in thine arms:
And when thy loss shall be repaid with gains
Loot to my little babes my dear remains.
And if thou love thy self, or loved'st me
These O protect from step Dames injury.
And if chance to thine eyes shall bring this verse,
With some sad sighs honour my absent
    Herse;
And kiss this paper for they love's dear sake,
Who with salt tears this last Farewell did take.

❧ "We may always live together as neighbors and friends"

WILLIAM PENN

William Penn, a Quaker, was granted a land charter in the New World by Charles II in 1681 as repayment of a family debt. The king, who dubbed the land Pennsylvania, intended it as a haven for Quakers, who were unwelcome in most of America. Penn accepted the lands along the west bank of the Delaware River. He threw himself into the enterprise.

The colony proved to be unlike any other colony in its acceptance of other religions, principles of self-government, and relations with the native population. Unlike the warlike posturing of the original Virginia and Massachusetts settlers, Penn was determined to establish relations with Native Americans as equals. In 1681, Penn wrote a letter expressing that sentiment in forging a new, longstanding relationship with the native populations. The contrast between Penn's approach and the much harsher one of the Jamestown settlers and New England Puritans toward native peoples set the framework for two fundamentally different approaches to Native Americans that persisted for three centuries.

My Friends:

There is one great God and power that hath made the world and all things therein, to whom you and I and all people owe their being and well-being, and to whom you and I must one day give an account, for all that we do in the world; this great God hath written His law in our hearts, by which we are taught and commanded to love and help, and do good to one another, and not to do harm and mischief one unto another. Now this great God hath been pleased to make me concerned in your parts of the world, and the King of the country where I live hath given unto me a great province therein; but I desire to enjoy it with your love and consent, that we may always live together as neighbors and friends, else what would the great God say to us, who hath made us not to devour and destroy one another, but live soberly and kindly together in the world? Now I would have you will observe, that I am very sensible of the unkindness and injustice that hath been too much exercised toward you by the people of these parts of the world, who have sought themselves, and to make great advantages by you, rather than be examples of justice and goodness unto you, which I hear, hath been matter of trouble to you, and cause great grudgings and animosities, sometimes to the shedding of blood, which hath made the great God angry. But I am not such a man, as is well known in my own country, I have great love and regard towards you, and I desire to win and gain your love and friendship by a kind, just and peaceable life, and the people I send are of the same mind, and shall in all things behave themselves accordingly; and if any thing shall offend you or your people, you shall have a full and speedy satisfaction for the same, by an equal number of just men on both sides, that by no means you may have just occasion of being offended against them. I shall shortly come to you myself, at what time we may more largely and freely confer and discourse of these matters; in the meantime, I have sent my commissioners to treat with you about land, and a firm league of peace; let me desire you to be kind to them and the people, and receive these presents and tokens which I have sent to you, as a testimony of my good will to you, and my resolution to live justly, peaceably and friendly with you.

I am your loving friend,
William Penn

🍂 France claims Louisiana

JACQUES DE LA METAIRIE

In 1682, more than 140 years after the Spanish explorer Hernando de Soto claimed the Mississippi River on behalf of Spain, the French explorer Robert Cavelier, Sieur de la Salle, sailed down the Mississippi and proclaimed it as belonging to France. He named the great waterway the River Colbert in honor of the French Minister of Finance.

The French claim stuck. French outposts were erected and settlers arrived. French claims in America also included the area north of New England, the Great Lakes region and much of the Mississippi basin, which became known as the Louisiana Territory. After the French and Indian War in 1763, the British took the Great Lakes region. Napoleon sold Louisiana to the United States at the outset of the 19th century.

We continued our voyage till the 6th, when we discovered three channels by which the River Colbert discharges itself into the sea. On the 8th, we reascended the river, a little above its confluence with the sea, to find a dry place, beyond the reach of inundations. Here we prepared a column and a cross, and to the said column were affixed the arms of France, with this inscription:

Louis le Grand, Roi de France et de Navarre, Regne le Neuvieme, Avril, 1682

The whole party, under arms, chanted the Te Deum, the Exaudiat, the Domine salvum fac Regem; and then, after a salute of firearms and cries of Vive le Roi, the column was erected by M. De la Salle, who, standing near it, said with a loud voice, in French: "In the name of the most high, mighty, invincible, and victorious Prince, Louis the Great, by the Grace of God, King of France and of Navarre, Fourteenth of that name, this ninth day of April, one thousand six hundred and eighty-two, I do now take, in the name of his Majesty, possession of this country of Louisiana, the seas, harbours, ports, bays, adjacent straits; and all the nations, people, provinces, cities, towns, villages, mines, minerals, fisheries, streams, and rivers, comprised in the extent of the said Louisiana, from the mouth of the great river St. Louis on the eastern side, otherwise called Ohio, Alighin [Allegheny], Chikachas [Chickasaws], and this with the consent of the Chaouanons [Shawnee], Chikachas, and the other people dwelling therein, with whom we have made alliance; as also along the River Colbert, or Mississippi, from its source…as far as its mouth at the sea, or the Gulf of Mexico, upon the assurance which we have received from all these [Indian] nations, that we are the first Europeans who have descended or ascended the said River Colbert….

To which the whole assembly responded with shouts of Vive le Roi, and with salutes of firearms. Moreover, the Sieur de la Salle caused to be buried at the foot of the tree, to which the cross was attached, a leaden plate, on one side of which were engraved the arms of France.

❧ "We are against this traffic of men"

RESOLUTIONS OF GERMANTOWN MENNONITES

By the end of the 17th century, black slavery was rising rapidly in the American colony as a source of labor. Few protested. Quakers and Mennonites, however, who were largely outcasts of the more mainstream colonists, objected. On February 18, 1688, Mennonites in Germantown, Pennsylvania, issued the first protest against slavery.

This is to the monthly meeting held at Richard Worrell's:

These are the reasons why we are against the traffic of men-body, as followeth: Is there any that would be done or handled at this manner? Viz., to be sold or made a slave for all the time of his life? How fearful and faint-hearted are many at sea, when they see a strange vessel, being afraid it should be a Turk, and they should be taken, and sold for slaves into Turkey. Now, what is this better done, than Turks do? Yea, rather it is worse for them, which say they are Christians; for we hear that the most part of such negers are brought hither against their will and consent, and that many of

them are stolen. Now, though they are black, we cannot conceive there is more liberty to have them slaves, as it is to have other white ones. There is a saying, that we should do to all men like as we will be done ourselves; making no difference of what generation, descent, or colour they are. And those who steal or rob men, and those who buy or purchase them, are they not all alike? Here is liberty of conscience, which is right and reasonable; here ought to be likewise liberty of the body, except of evil-doers, which is another case. But to bring men hither, or to roll and sell them against their will, we stand against. In Europe there are many oppressed for conscience-sake; and here there are those oppressed which are of a black colour. And we who know that men must not commit adultery—some do commit adultery in others, separating wives from their husbands, and giving them to others: and some sell the children of these poor creatures to other men. Ah! Do consider well this thing, you who do it, if you would be done at this manner— and if it is done according to Christianity! You surpass Holland and Germany in this thing. This makes an ill report in all those countries of Europe, where they hear of [it], that the Quakers do here handel men as they handel there the cattle. And for that reason some have no mind or inclination to come hither. And who shall maintain this your cause, or plead for it? Truly, we cannot do so, except you shall inform us better hereof, viz.: that Christians have liberty to practice these things. Pray, what thing in the world can be done worse towards us, than if men should rob or steal us away, and sell us for slaves to strange countries; separating husbands from their wives and children. Being now this is not done in the manner we would be done at; therefore, we contradict, and are against this traffic of men-body. And we who profess that it is not lawful to steal, must, likewise, avoid to purchase such things as are stolen, but rather help to stop this robbing and stealing, if possible. And such men ought to be delivered out of the hands of the robbers, and set free as in Europe. Then is Pennsylvania to have a good report, instead, it hath now a bad one, for this sake, in other countries; Especially whereas the Europeans are desirous to know in what manner the Quakers do rule in their province; and most of them do look upon us with an envious eye. But if this is done well, what shall we say is done evil?

If once these slaves (which they say are so

wicked and stubborn men,) should join themselves—fight for their freedom, and handel their masters and mistresses, as they did handel them before; will these masters and mistresses take the sword at hand and war against these poor slaves, like, as we are able to believe, some will not refuse to do? Or, have these poor negers not as much right to fight for their freedom, as you have to keep them slaves?

Now consider well this thing, if it is good or bad. And in case you find it to be good to handel these blacks in that manner, we desire and require you hereby lovingly, that you may inform us herein, which at this time never was done, viz., that Christians have such a liberty to do so. To the end we shall be satisfied on this point, and satisfy likewise our good friends and acquaintances in our native country, to whom it is a terror, or fearful thing, that men should be handled so in Pennsylvania.

This is from our meeting at Germantown held the 18th of the 2d month, 1688, delivered to the monthly meeting at Richard Worrell's.

Plan of Union

WILLIAM PENN

Throughout the 17th century, the colonies in British America were scattered and diverse. Although they shared a language, their mother country and confronted many of the same obstacles, they also embraced different religions, ethos and means of commerce. People rarely thought beyond the interests of their own settlements, much less their colonies. Communication did not travel faster than a ship.

But as the new century approached, William Penn made the first proposal for union among the British colonies to consider and act on matters of common interest. The plan did not become a reality but reflected a burgeoning sense of unity among the colonies.

A brief and plain scheme how the English colonies in the North parts of America—viz., Boston, Connecticut, Rhode Island, New York, New Jersey, Pennsylvania, Maryland, Virginia and Carolina—may be made more useful to the crown and one another's peace and safety with an universal concurrence.

That the several colonies before mentioned do meet once a year, and oftener if need be during the war, and at least once in two years in times of peace, by their stated and appointed deputies, to debate and resolve of such measures as are most advisable for their better understanding and the public tranquillity and safety.

That, in order to it, two persons, well qualified for sense, sobriety, and substance, be appointed by each province as their representatives of deputies, which in the whole make the congress to consist of twenty persons.

That the king's commissioner, for that purpose specially appointed, shall have the chair and preside in the said congress.

That they shall meet as near as conveniently may be to the most central colony for ease of the deputies.

Since that may in all probability be New York, both because it is near the centre of the colonies and for that it is a frontier and in the king's nomination, the governor of that colony may therefore also be the king's high commissioner during the session, after the manner of Scotland.

That their business shall be to hear and adjust all matters of complaint or difference between province and province. As, 1st, where persons quit their own province and go to another, that they may avoid their just debts, though they be able to pay them; 2nd, where offenders fly justice, or justice cannot well be had upon such offenders in the provinces that entertain them; 3rd, to prevent or cure injuries in point of commerce; 4th, to consider the ways and means to support the union and safety of these provinces against the public enemies. In which congress the quotas of men and charges will be much easier and more equally, set than it is possible for any establishment made here to do; for the provinces, knowing their own condition and one another's, can debate that matter with more freedom and satisfaction, and better adjust and balance their affairs in all respects for their common safety.

That, in times of war, the king's high commissioner shall be general or chief commander of the several quotas upon service against the common enemy, as he shall be advised, for the good and benefit of the whole.

🍂 "I will honour my Father & Mother"

THE NEW ENGLAND PRIMER

First published in 1690, *The New England Primer* remained popular well into the 18th century as an educational tool for children with which to learn to read and write. It also had heavy overtones of religious and patriotic messages.

Now the Child being entred in his Letters and Spelling, let him learn these and such like Sentences by Heart, whereby he will be both instructed in his Duty, and encouraged in his Learning.

The Dutiful Child's Promises,
I will fear God, and honour the King.
I will honour my Father & Mother.
I will Obey my Superiours.
I will Submit to my Elders.
I will love my Friends.
I will hate no Man.
I will forgive my Enemies, and pray to God, and obey the Holy Commandments.
I will learn my Catechism.
I will keep the Lord's Day Holy.
I will Reverence God's Sanctuary,
For our God is a consuming Fire.

An Alphabet of Lessons for Youth

A wise Son makes a glad Father, but a foolish Son is the heaviness of his Mother.

Better is a little with the fear of the Lord, than great treasure and trouble therewith.

Come unto Christ all ye that labour and are heavy laden, and He will give you rest.

Do not the abominable thing which I hate, saith the Lord.

Except a Man be born again, he cannot see the Kingdom of God.

Foolishness is bound up in the heart of a Child, but the rod of Correction shall drive it far from him.

Grieve not the Holy Spirit.

Holiness becomes God's House for ever.

It is good for me to draw near unto God.

Keep thy Heart with all Diligence, for out of it are the issues of Life.

Liars shall have their part in the lake which burns with fire and brimstone.

Many are the Afflictions of the Righteous, but the Lord delivers them out of them all.

Now is the accepted time, now is the day of salvation.

Out of the abundance of the heart the mouth speaketh.

Pray to thy Father which is in secret, and thy Father sees in secret, shall reward thee openly.

Quit you like Men, be strong, stand fast in the Faith.

Remember thy Creator in the days of thy Youth.

Salvation belongeth to the Lord.

Trust in God at all times ye people pour out your hearts before him.

Upon the wicked shall rain an horrible Tempest.

Woe to the wicked, it shall be ill with him, for the reward of his hands shall be given him.

Exhort one another daily while it is called to day, lest any of you be hardened through the deceitfulness of Sin.

Young Men ye have overcome the wicked one.

Zeal hath consumed me, because thy enemies have forgotten the words of God.

🍂 Indictment v. George Jacobs, Sr.

A SALEM WITCH TRIAL

Seventeenth-century America and Europe witnessed many witch trials, but none matched the mania of the Salem witch trials of 1692. Nineteen men and women and two dogs were hanged or pressed to death after being convicted of witchcraft. Most of the evidence was based on the testimony of a handful of witnesses, largely teenage girls, who later confessed to having fabricated the stories.

The witch trials emerged out of the dogmatism of Puritan New England and an insecure insistence by religious leaders to preserve the colony's perceived deterioration of moral and ethical values. Cotton Mather, a leading minister, helped publicize and heighten anxiety of witches by publishing descriptions of cases he knew.

The following excerpts are from the trial of George Jacobs, Sr., who was targeted as a witch. Three hundred years later, the trial reads like a tragic farce. It illustrates the impossible situation he and the other accused were in, the ludicrousness of the evidence, and the presumption of guilt that prevailed.

Indictment v. George Jacobs, Sr.

That George Jacobs, Sr., of Salem in the county of Essex, the 11th day of May in the fourth year of the reign of our Sovereign Lord and Lady William and Mary, by the grace of God of England, Scotland, France, and Ireland King and Queen, Defenders of the Faith, etc., and divers other days and times as well before as after, certain detestable arts called witchcrafts and sorceries wickedly and feloniously hath used, practiced, and exercised at and within the township of Salem in the county of Essex aforesaid, in upon and against one Mercy Lewis of Salem village, single woman, by which said wicked arts the said Mercy Lewis the 11th day of May in the fourth year abovesaid, and divers other days and times as well before as after, was and is tortured, afflicted, pinned, consumed, wasted, and tormented; and also for sundry other acts of witchcraft by said George Jacobs committed and done before and since that time against the peace of our Sovereign Lord and Lady the King and Queen, their crown and dignity, and against the form of the statutes in that case made and provided.

Witnesses: Mercy Lewis, Elizabeth Hubbard, Mary Walcott and Sarah Churchill

Examination of George Jacobs, Sr.

JUDGE: Here are them that accuse you of acts of witchcraft.

JACOBS: Well, let us hear who are they and what are they.

JUDGE: Abigail Williams—(Jacobs laughed.)

JACOBS: Because I am falsely accused. Your worship, all of you, do you think this is true?

JUDGE: Nay, what do you think?

JACOBS: I never did it.

JUDGE: Who did it?

JACOBS: Don't ask me.

JUDGE: Why should we not ask you? Sarah Churchill accuseth you; there she is.

JACOBS: I am as innocent as the child born tonight. I have lived 33 years here in Salem.

JUDGE: What then?

JACOBS: If you can prove I am guilty, I will lie under it.

JUDGE: Sarah Churchill said, "Last night I was afflicted at Deacon Ingersall's," and Mary Walcott said, "It was a man with two staves; it was my master."

JACOBS: Pray do not accuse me; I am as clear as your worships. You must do right judgments.

JUDGE: What book did he bring you, Sarah?

SARAH: The same the other woman brought.

JACOBS: The devil can go in any shape.

JUDGE: Did he not…appear on the other side of the river and hurt you? Did not you see him?

SARAH: Yes, he did.

JUDGE: Look there, she accuseth you to your face; she chargeth you that you hurt her twice. Is it not true?

JACOBS: What would you have me bsay? I never wrong no man in word nor deed.

JUDGE: Here are three evidences [i.e. Abigail, Sarah and Mary].

JACOBS: You tax me for a wizard; you may as well tax me for a buzzard. I have done no harm.

JUDGE: It is no harm to afflict these?

JACOBS: I never did it.

JUDGE: But how comes it to be in your appearance?

JACOBS: The devil can take any likeness.

JUDGE: Not without their consent.

JACOBS: Please your worship, it is untrue; I never showed the book. I am silly about these things as the child born last night.

JUDGE: That is your saying. You argue you have lived so long, but then Cain might [have] lived long before he killed Abel, and you might live long before the devil had so prevailed on you.

JACOBS: Christ hath suffered three times for me.

JUDGE: What three times?

JACOBS: He suffered the Cross and jail—

"You had as good confess," said Sarah Churchill, "if you are guilty."

JACOBS: Have you heard that I have any witchcraft?

SARAH: I know you live a wicked life.

JACOBS: Let her make it out.

JUDGE: Doth he ever pray in his family?

SARAH: Not unless by himself.

JUDGE: Why do you not pray in your family?

JACOBS: I cannot read.

JUDGE: Well, but you may pray for all that. Can you say the Lord's prayer. Let us hear you.

SARAH: He might in several parts of it, and could not repeat it right after Mary Mialls.

JUDGE: Sarah Churchill, when you wrote in the book, you was showed your master's name, you said.

SARAH: Yes, sir.

JACOBS: If she say so, if you do not know it, what will you say?

JUDGE: But she saw you or your likeness tempt her to write.

JACOBS: One in my likeness; the devil may present my likeness.

JUDGE: Were you not frighted, Sarah Churchill, when the representation of your master came to you?

SARAH: Yes.

JACOBS: Well! Burn me or hang me, I will stand in the truth of Christ; I know nothing of it.

JUDGE: Do you know nothing of getting your son George and his daughter to sign?

JACOBS: No, nothing at all.

The Second Examination of said George

Jacobs, 11 May 1692

The bewitched fell into most grievous fits and screechings when he came in.

JUDGE: Is this the man that hurts you?

Abigail Williams cried out, "This is the man," and fell into a violent fit.

Ann Putnam said, "This is the man," and he hurts her and brings the book to her and would have her write in the book, and she should be as well as his granddaughter.

JUDGE: Mercy Lewis, is this the man?

MERCY: This is the man; (after much interruptions by fits) he almost kills me.

Elizabeth Hubbard said the man never hurt her till today he came upon the table.

JUDGE: Mary Walcott, is this the man.

After much interruptions by fits she said, "This is the man"; he used to come with two staves and beat her with one of them.

JUDGE: What do you say, are you not a witch?

JACOBS: No, I know it not, if I were to die presently.

Mercy Lewis went to come near him but fell into great fits. Mercy Lewis's testimony read.

JUDGE: What do you say to this?

JACOBS: Why, it is false; I know not of it any more than the child that was born tonight.

Ann Putnam said, "Yes, you told me so, that you had been so this 40 years."

Ann Putnam and Abigail Williams had each of them a pin stuck in their hands and they said it was

this old Jacobs. Abigail Williams' testimony read.

JUDGE: Are you the man that made disturbance at a lecture in Salem?

JACOBS: No great disturbances. Do you think I use witchcraft?

JUDGE: Yes indeed.

JACOBS: No, I use none of them.

Testimonies

The testimony of George Herrick, aged thirty-four years or thereabouts, testifieth and saith: some time in May last, by order of their Majesties justices, I went to the prison in Salem to search George Jacobs, Sr.—and likewise William Dounton, the jail keeper, and Joseph Neal, constable, was in presence and concerned with me in the search—where under the said Jacobs his right shoulder we found a teat about a quarter of an inch long or better, with a sharp point drooping downwards, so that I took a pin from said Dounton and run it through the said teat, but there was neither water, blood, nor corruption, nor any other matter, and so we make return.

William Dounton testifieth the above written; and we farther testify and say that said Jacobs was not in the least sensible in what we had done, for after I had made return to the magistrates and returned, I told the said Jacobs, and he knew nothing before.

Sworn in Court, August 4, 1692.

Mary Warren affirmed before the jury of inquest that George Jacobs, Sr., has afflicted her, said Warren, and beat her with his staff, he or his apparition. Said Warren says she has seen said Jacobs or apparition afflict Mary Walcott and beat her with his staff. She said also that said Jacobs has afflict Ann Putnam. Said Warren verily thinks said George Jacobs is a wizard. August, 1692, upon her oath. Jurat in curia.

Mercy Lewis v. George Jacobs, Sr.

The deposition of Mercy Lewis, who testifieth and saith that on 20th April 1692 at or about midnight there appeared to me the apparition of an old, very gray-headed man and told me that his name was George Jacobs, and that he had had two wives; and he did torture me and beat me with a stick which he had in his hand, and urged me to write in his book, which I refused to do. And so he hath continued ever since by times, coming sometimes with two sticks in his hands to afflict me, still tempting me to write in his book, but most dreadful he fell upon me and did torture me to write in his book, but most dreadful he fell upon me and did torture me on the 9th of May at evening, after I came home from the examination of his maid, threating to kill me that night if I would not write in his book, because I did witness against his maid and persuaded her to confess. But because I would not yield to his hellish temptations, he did torture me most cruelly by beating me with the two sticks which he had in his hands and almost ready to put all my bones out of joint till my strength and heart was ready to fail. But being upheld by an Almighty hand and encouraged by them that stood by, I endured his tortures that night. The 10th May he again set upon me and afflicted me most grievously a great many times in the day, still urging me to write in his book, but at evening he again tortured me most grievously by pinching me and beating me black and blue and threatening to kill me if I would not write in his book. But I told him I would not write in his book, if he would give all the world. Then again he did torture me most grievously but at last went away from me. Also on the 15th May 1692, being the day of the examination of George Jacobs, then I saw that it was that very man that told me his name was George Jacobs, and he did also most dreadfully torment me, almost ready to kill me, and I verily believe in my heart that George Jacobs is a most dreadful wizard and that he hath very often afflicted and tormented me by his acts of witchcraft.

❧ "An Act for the Encouragement of the Importation of White Servants"

SOUTH CAROLINA

By the end of the 17h century South Carolina had started to prosper as a colony centered around Ashley River. South Carolina, however, relied heavily on black slave labor, in part because whites suffered much higher mortality rates in the low country sections. Black slaves outnumbered white colonists, prompting fears of slave rebellion.

To mitigate this danger, the colony decided in 1698 to pay incoming ships to bring young white men to the colony and to require slave owners to accept them as indentured servants.

Whereas, the great number of Negroes which of late have been imported into this Colony may endanger the safety thereof if speedy care be not taken and encouragement given for the importation of white servants,

Be it enacted…that every merchant, owner or master of any ship or vessel, or any other person not intending to settle and plant here, which shall bring any white male servants, Irish only excepted, into Ashley river, above sixteen years of age and under forty, and the same shall deliver to the Receiver General, shall receive and be paid by the said Receiver…the sum of thirteen pounds for every servant delivered, and for every boy of twelve years and under sixteen, imported and delivered to the Receiver as aforesaid; Provided, that every servant, as aforesaid, hath not less than four years to serve from and after the day of his arrival in Ashley River, and every boy aforesaid, not less than seven years. And if any person shall deliver to the Receiver aforesaid, any servant or boy, as aforesaid, which hath less time to serve than the respective times before appointed, the Receiver shall pay such person proportionably to the rates and times aforesaid, for so long time as such servant or boy hath to serve.

Every owner of every plantation to which doth belong six men Negro slaves above sixteen years old, shall take from the Receiver one servant, when it shall happen to be his lot to have one, and shall within three months pay the said Receiver so much money for the said servant as the Receiver gave to the person from whom he received the same; and the owner of every plantation to which doth belong twelve Negro men, as aforesaid, shall when it shall be his lot, take two servants as aforesaid; and every master of every plantation proportionably.

❧ "Help Lord"

COTTON MATHER

Disease was a scourge of colonial American life. Epidemics swept through communities, striking adults and especially children. Infant mortality was high. In 1713 a measles epidemic struck Boston. In less than two weeks, the renowned minister Cotton Mather lost his wife and three children to measles. With Job-like endurance, Mather recorded the epidemic's impact on his family. Mather had fifteen children, but only two survived to become adults.

October 18, 1713. The Measles coming into the Town, it is likely to be a Time of Sickness, and much Trouble in the Families of the Neighbourhood. I would by my public Sermons and Prayers, endeavour to prepare the Neighbours for the Trouble which their Families are likely to meet withal.

The Apprehension of a very deep Share, that my Family may expect in the common Calamity of the spreading Measles, will oblige me to be much in pleading the Great Family-Sacrifice, that so the wrath of heaven may inflict no sad Thing on my Family; and to quicken and augment the Expressions of Piety, in the daily Sacrifices of my Family; and to lay hold on the Occasion to awaken Piety, and Preparation for Death, in the Souls of the children.

November 4, 1713. In my poor Family, now, first, Wife has the Measles appearing on her; we know not yett how she will be handled.

My Daughter Nancy is also full of them; not in such uneasy Circumstances as her predecessors.

My Daughter Lizzy is likewise full of them; yett somewhat easily circumstanced.

My Daughter Jerusha, droops and seems to have them appearing.

My Servant-maid, lies very full and ill of them.

Help Lord; and look mercifully on my poor, sad, sinful Family, for the Sake of the Great Sacrifice!

November 7, 1713. I sett apart this Day, as I had much Cause, and it was high Time, to do, for Prayer with Fasting before the Lord. Not only are my Children, with a Servant, lying sick, but also my Consort is in a dangerous Condition, and can gett no Rest; Either Death, or Distraction, is much feared for her. It is also an Hour of much Distress in my Neighbourhood. So, I humbled myself before the Lord, for my own Sins, and the Sins of my Family; and I presented before Him the great Sacrifice of my Saviour, that His wrath may be turned away from me, and from my Family; and that the Destroyer might not have a Commission to inflict any deadly Stroke upon us.

November 8, 9, 1713. This Day, I entertained my Neighbourhood, with a Discourse, on Job.

XVIII. II. *The Cup which my Father has given me shall not I drink it?* And, lo, this Day, my Father is giving me a grievous and bitter Cup, which I hop'd, had passed from me.

For these many Months, and ever since I heard of the venemous Measles invading the Countrey sixty Miles to the Southward of us, I have had a strong Distress on my Mind, that it will bring on my poor Family, a Calamity, which is now going to be inflicted. I have often, often express'd my Fear unto my Friends concerning it. And now, the Thing that I greatly feared is coming upon me!

When I saw my Consort safely delivered, and very easy, and the Measles appearing with favourable Symptoms upon her, and the Physician apprehending all to look very comfortably, I flattered myself, that my Fear was all over.

But this Day we are astonished, at the surprising Symptoms of Death upon her; after an extreme Want of Rest by Sleep, for diverse whole Dayes and Nights together.

To part with so desireable, so agreeable a Companion, a Dove from such a Nest of young ones too! Oh! The sad Cup, which my Father has appointed me! I now see the Meaning and the Reason of it, that I have never yett been able to make any Work of it, that I have never yett been able to make any Work of it, in Prayers and Cries to God, that such a Cup as this might pass from me. My Supplications have all along had, a most unaccountable Death and Damp upon them!

Tho' my dear Consort, had been so long without Sleep, yett she retain'd her Understanding.

I had and us'd my Opportunities as well as I could, continually to be assisting her, with Discourses that might support her in this time, and prepare her for what was now before us.

It comforted her to see that her [step] children…were as fond of her, as her own could be!

God made her willing to Dy. God extinguished in her the Fear of Death. God enabled her to committ herself into the Hands of a great and good Saviour; yea, and to cast her Orphans there too, and to believe that He had merciful and wonderful Things to do for them.

I pray'd with her many Times, and left nothing undone, that I could find myself able to do for Consolation.

On Munday between three and four in the Afternoon, my dear, dear, dear Friend expired.

Whereupon, with another Prayer in the melancholy Chamber, I endeavoured the Resignation to which I am now called, and cried to Heaven for the grace that might be suitable to the calamitous Occasion, and carried my poor Orphans unto the Lord.

It comforts me to see how extremely Beloved, and lamented a Gentlewoman, I now find her to be in the Neighbourhood.

Much weakness continues on some of my other Children. Especially the Eldest. And the poor Maid in the Family, is very like to dy.

2. G. D. Oh! The Prayers for my poor Children, oh! The Counsils to them, now called for!

The particular Scriptures, I shall direct them to read! And the Sentences thereof to be gotten by heart.

3. G. D. My Relatives, especially those of my deceased Consort, I will entertain with Books of Piety, that shall have in them a Memorial of her.

November 14, 1713. This Morning, the first Thing that entertains me, after my rising, is, the Death of my Maid-servant, whose Measles passed into a malignant Feaver, which has proved mortal to her.

Tis a Satisfaction to me, that tho' she had been a wild, vain, airy Girl, yett since her coming into my Family, she became disposed unto serious Religion; was awakened unto secret and fervent Supplications; gave herself to God in His Covenant: (upon which, a few Weeks ago, I baptised her: and my poor Instructions, were the means that God blessed for such happy Purposes.)

And now, as I am called still unto more Assiduities in my Preparations for my own Death, and unto more exquisite projections and Contrivances, how a Family visited with so much Death, may become an Example of uncommon Piety: So, I must have my Repentance for my Miscarriages in my Behaviour towards my Servants, very much excited and promoted.

Oh! The Trial, which I this Day called unto in the threatning, the dying Circusmtances of my dear little Jerusha! The Resignation with which I am to offer up that Sacrifice! Father, Lett that Cup pass from me. Nevertheless—

The two Newborns, are languishing in the Arms of Death.

November 15, 1713. Tis a Time of much calamity in my Neighbourhood, and a time of much Mortality seems coming on. My Public Prayers and Sermons must be exceedingly adapted for such a Time.

I am this day called unto a great Sacrifice; for so I feel my little Jerusha. The dear little Creature lies in dying Circumstances. Tho' I pray and cry to the Lord, for the Cup to pass from me, yett the glorious One carries me thro' the required Resignation. I freely give her up. Lord, she is thine! Thy will be done!

November 16, 1713. Little Jerusha begins a little to revive.

November 17-18. About Midnight, little Eleazer died.

November 20, 1713. Little Martha died, about ten o'clock, a.m.

I am again called unto the Sacrifice of my dear, dear, Jerusha.

I begg'd, I begg'd, that such a bitter Cup, as the Death of that lovely child, might pass from me. Nevertheless!—My glorious Lord, brought me to glorify Him, with the most submissive Resignation.

November 21, 1713. This Day, I attended the Funeral, of my two: Eleazar and Martha.

Betwist 9 h. and 10 h. at Night, my lovely Jerusha Expired. She was two years, and about seven Months, old. Just before she died, she asked me to pray with her; which I did, with a distressed, but resigning Soul; and I gave her up unto the Lord. The Minute that she died, she said, That she would go to Jesus Christ. She had lain speechless, many Hours. But in her last Moments, her speech returned a little to her.

Lord, I am oppressed; undertake for me!

November 22, 1713. It will be a great Service unto my Flock, for me to exemplify, a patient Submission to the Will of god, under many and heavy Trials, and a most fruitful Improvement of my Crosses…

My poor Family is now left without any Infant in it, or any under seven Years of Age. I must now apply myself with most exquisite Contrivance, and all the Assiduity imaginable, to cultivate my Children, with a most excellent Education. I have now singular Opportunities for it. Wherefore I must in the first Place, earnestly look up to the glorious Lord, who gives Wisdome, for Direction.

❧ Smallpox inoculation

ZABDIEL BOYLSTON

Though willing to submit to the will of God, Cotton Mather was eager to find ways to prevent unnecessary deaths. In 1721, he convinced Dr. Zabdiel Boylston to experiment with inoculations during a severe smallpox epidemic in Boston. Boylston inoculated both Mather's children and his own. The experiment worked, but it would be many years before smallpox inoculation became an acceptable practice. Many people objected to it on medical and theological grounds. Boylston wrote about the experiment in his 1726 treatise *An Historical Account of the Smallpox Inoculated in New England, Upon All Sorts of Persons, Whites, Blacks, and of All Ages and Constitutions.*

I began the practice indeed from a short consideration thereof; for my children, whose lives were very dear to me, were daily in danger of taking the infection, by my visiting the sick in the natural way; and although there arose such a cloud of opposers at the beginning, yet finding my account in the success, and easy circumstances of my patients (with the encouragement of the good ministers), I resolved to carry it on for the saving of lives, not regarding any, or all the menaces, and opposition that were made against it.

I have not, in this practice, left room for anyone to cavil, and say, that my experiments have not been fair, and full proofs, that inoculating the smallpox is a certain means of moderating the distemper, to the greatest demonstration. This, the warmest opposers of that practice, who have seen any fair trials made, are convinced of; and the only difficulty of convincing all mankind, is how to make them eye-witnesses to a number of sick of the smallpox in both ways of infection; and this would do it at once, and very much to their satisfaction in, and approbation of this method. And here it should be considered how rashly our patients, even whole families together, rushed into this practice....

I have not used this practice only to the healthful and strong, but to the weak and diseased, the aged and the young. Not only to the rich, but have carried it into the houses of the poor, and laid down whole families; and though through my own hurry in business, and their living out of town, I have been forced to leave them to the management of unexperienced nurses, yet they all did well.

We met with no...terrible effects (save that death is terrible in all its shapes) from the smallpox inoculated, as was common amongst us in the natural way, viz. purple spots, convulsion fits, bloody urine, violent inflammations in the eyes, throat, and other parts, scarred faces, some who had lost both eyes, and as it has been thought, near an hundred one eye, with many more melancholy symptoms too tedious here to enumerate; not to mention parents being left childless, children without parents, and sometimes parents and children's being both carried off, and many families broken up by the destruction the smallpox made in the natural way. Indeed, we had some resemblance of those effects; but in none where it was not evident, that they were infected in the natural way before; and though we met with but five or six cases that bordered on, or resembled more or less those symptoms, yet it would not have been strange had there been six times that number; for in Boston, and in the middle of Roxbury, no one knew who were, or who were not infected before inoculated. And this reason I can give for everyone whom I inoculated, and that had not been exposed to an infected air, and which were above one hundred, not any of them had the least shadow of such symptoms upon them, through the whole course of their distemper. However, I do not recommend this practice to be carried on and managed by old women and nurses; no, I would have it carried on and managed by good physicians and surgeons, where they are to be had; but rather than the people should be left a prey to the smallpox in the natural way, let it be managed by nurses, for I cannot help thinking that even in their heads, many less would die of the smallpox by inoculation, than there does in the natural way, though in the best of hands, and under the best of care.

I do not call upon or exhort the physicians and surgeons who are already in the practice, and have used their endeavors to promote it, nor do I pretend to inform or instruct them. My design is only to stir up those who have not yet come into and used this method, and to lay before the people a fair state of the distemper in both ways of infection, that they may be apprized of the danger in the one, and the reasonable expectation they have of doing well in the other. My reasonings and opinions I submit to those of better judgment, but as we are rational creatures, we do, or should delight in acting upon principles of reason; and those who consider this method, and make use of it, I think may be said so to act.

I hope the reader will excuse me for troubling him with some of the difficulties that I met with. I have been basely used and treated by some who were enemies to this method, and have suffered much in my reputation and in my business too, from the odiums and reflections cast upon me for beginning and carrying on this practice in New England; which ill usage I think justly entitles me to make the necessary reflections, and relate matters of fact in my own justification, and to recommend and do justice to the method, which was so exposed and condemned by their misrepresentations, which have been spread abroad in the world; and to set things in a good light, that the world may impartially judge between the parties (if I may be allowed the term) which of the two have acted most like men and Christians, viz. whether those who have opposed and exclaimed against this method without due consideration of, or knowing scarce anything about it; or those who have considered well, been in the practice of, and have proved by their own experience, or that have seen the good effects and benefit of it, and from such reasons have recommended it to others?

Indeed I can easily forgive and pity those who through tenderness, or in point of conscience, have refused the offered mercy, and that have gently appeared against it. Such, with the assistance of a divine, together with the exercise of their own reason upon it, may easily get through their difficulties. But for those who out of private piques, or views, have exclaimed and railed against it, and who have trumpt up the groundless ill consequences that would attend or follow it. Such I leave to sweat it out with just reflection and due repentance. As for my own part, I know of no better way of judging between moral and immoral methods of medical practice, than for the good or ill success that does, or may attend them.

🍃 *The School of Good Manners*

ELEAZER MOODY

Originally written in England, Eleazar Moody's *The School of Good Manners: Composed for the Help of Parents in Teaching their Children How to carry it in their Places during their Minority* was first published in America in 1715. It describes the appropriate behavior for children and reflected the expectations of a society that had little time to accommodate children's rambunctious inclinations.

In Their Discourse

1. Among superiors speak not till thou art spoken to, and bid to speak.
2. Hold not thine hand, nor any thing else, before thy mouth when thou speakest.
3. Come not over-near to the person thou speakest to.
4. If thy superior speak to thee while thou sittest, stand up before thou givest any answer.
5. Sit down till thy superior bid thee.
6. Speak neither very loud, nor too low.
7. Speak clear, not stammering, stumbling nor drawling.
8. Answer not one that is speaking to thee until he hath done.
9. Loll not when thou art speaking to a superior or spoken to by him.
10. Speak not without, Sir, or some other title of respect.
11. Strive not with superiors in argument or discourse; but easily submit thine opinion to their assertions.
12. If thy superior speak any thing wherein thou knowest he is mistaken, correct not nor contradict him, nor grin at the hearing of it; but pass over the error without notice or interruption.
13. Mention not frivolous or little things among grave persons or superiors.
14. If thy superior drawl or hesitate in his words, pretend not to help him out, or to prompt him.
15. Come not too near two that are whispering or speaking in secret, much less may'st thou ask about what they confer.
16. When thy parent or master speak to any person, speak not thou, nor hearken to them.
17. If thy superior be relating a story, say not, "I have heard it before," but attend to it as though it were altogether new. Seem not to question the truth of it. If he tell it not right, snigger not, nor endeavor to help him out, or add to his relation.
18. If any immodest or obscene thing be spoken in thy hearing, smile not, but settle thy countenance as though thou did'st not hear it.
19. Boast not in discourse of thine own wit or doings.

20. Beware thou utter not any thing hard to be believed.
21. Interrupt not any one that speaks, though thou be his familiar.
22. Coming into company, whilst any topic is disoursed on, ask not what was the preceding talk but hearken to the remainder.
23. Speaking of any distant person, it is rude and unmannerly to point at him.
24. Laugh not in, or at thy own story, wit or jest.
25. Use not any contemptuous or reproachful language to any person, though very mean or inferior.
26. Be not over earnest in talking to justify and avouch thy own sayings.
27. Let thy words be modest about those things which only concern thee.
28. Repeat not over again the words of a superior that asketh the a question or talketh to thee.

❧ "A few lines behind me"

WILLIAM BATTIN

America was a land of second chances. Many convicts from England were simply sent to America and sold as indentured servants with the opportunity to begin their lives anew. Here, William Battin regrets that he has wasted his life in crime just before he is about to be hanged in 1722 in Pennsylvania. Instead of the English authorities dispatching him to America, Battin's father did.

I, William Battin, Son of William Battin of White-Parish in Wiltshire in Great Britain, do think it necessary to leave a few lines behind me, that the World may in some Measure know something of my past Life, and what ill Use I have made of the time that God was pleased to bestow upon me in this World.

I had my Education under my Parents, and their Care was much over me; but I dishonoured and rebelled against them, and regarded not their Care for me; and through the Insinuation of the Enemy I neglected their Business, by wandering abroad. So without due Regard to that which is good, I gave up my self to serve the Devil, and to obey his Voice by yielding to his Temptations; which were Lying and picking and Stealing other Men's Goods. I shall briefly mention some of the gross Actions which I have committed before and after the time of my running away from my Parents; which was chiefly stealing of other Men's Goods.

The first thing that I stole was, to the best of my remembrance, a Whalebone Whip from one Henry Whites, next a Cane from my Uncle John Battin, next a Knife and Fork from one Lawrence Tuch, a Great Coat from a Man in White-Parish, and several other Things which were found out by my Parents: For which I was severely chastized by them.

The next Thing I stole was a Silver Watch, of the Value of Five Pounds, from one that I intended to serve an Apprenticeship with, and about an hour after I had Stolen it, I sold it to a Man for an English Half Crown; when my intended Master came to understand that I had stolen the Watch, he put me into Prison, and after three Days he took me out again and whipped me very severely: But I took no Warning, and soon found an Opportunity to make my Escape, taking with me a Beaver Hat, a Suit of Clothes and a Shirt; since which he never saw me.

This was the Course of Life which I followed whilst I was in England.

My Father seeing that there was not any Good like to come of use, ordered me to be brought over a Servant into this Province of Pennsylvania. About 7 or 8 Days after the Ship, which brought me over, was safely arrived here, I was sold to John Hannam of Concord in Chester County. I had scarcely lived with him three Months before I fell again into my old Practice of Stealing and running away; for which Cause, after I had lived with the said Hannam about one Year, he sold me to Joseph Pyle of Bethel in the said County, with whom I continued in the old Practice of stealing.

❧ The Thirteen Virtues

BENJAMIN FRANKLIN

Blending morality with edicts for worldly prosperity, Benjamin Franklin reflected the opportunities of America. In his autobiography, Franklin recalls how he set out to perfect himself. This famous list of 13 virtues addresses personal morality. However, it also coincides with the rules of material success.

In pursuing his own personal and ethical advancement, he was also contributing to the growing prosperity of the new, struggling settlements. Thus, the heavy emphasis Americans placed on a strong work ethic and virtuous conduct was not simply a matter of morality, but also survival in a new and sometimes dangerous world.

It was about this time that I conceiv'd the bold and arduous Project of arriving at moral Perfection. I wish'd to live without committing any Fault at any time; I would conquer all that either Natural Inclination, Custom, or Company might lead me into. As I knew, or thought I knew, what was right and wrong, I did not see why I might not always do the one and avoid the other. But I soon found I had undertaken a Task of more difficulty than I had imagined. While my Attention was taken up in guarding against one Fault, I was often surpriz'd by another. Habit took the Advantage of Inattention. Inclination was sometimes too strong for Reason. I concluded at length, that the mere speculative Conviction that it was our Interest to be completely virtuous, was not sufficient to prevent our Slipping, and that the contrary habits must be broken and good ones acquired and established, before we can have and Dependance on a steady uniform Rectitude of Conduct. For this purpose I therefore contriv'd the following method.

In the various Enumerations of the moral Virtues I had met with in my Reading, I found the Catalogue more or less numerous, as different Writers included more or fewer Ideas under the same Name. Temperance, for Example, was by some confin'd to Eating and Drinking, while by others it was extended to mean the moderating every other Pleasure, Appetite, Inclination or Passion, bodily or mental, even to our Avarice and Ambition. I propos'd to myself, for the sake of Clearness, to use rather more Names with fewer Ideas annex'd to each, than a few Names with more Ideas; and I included under Thirteen Names of Virtues all that at that time occurr'd to me as necessary or desirable, and annex'd to each a short Precept, which fully express'd the Extent I gave to its Meaning.

These Names of Virtues with their Precepts were

1. Temperance: Eat not to dullness. Drink not to elevation.
2. Silence: Speak not but what may benefit others or yourself. Avoid trifling conversation.
3. Order: Let all your things have their places. Let each part of your business have its time.
4. Resolution: Resolve to perform what you ought. Perform without fail what you resolve.
5. Frugality: Make no expense but to do good to others or yourself, i.e., waste nothing.
6. Industry: Lose no time. Be always employed in something useful. Cut off all unnecessary actions.
7. Sincerity: Use no hurtful deceit. Think innocently and justly; if you speak, speak accordingly.
8. Justice: Wrong none by doing injuries or omitting the benefits that are your duty.
9. Moderation: Avoid extremes. Forbear resenting injuries so much as you think they deserve.
10. Cleanliness: Tolerate no uncleanliness in body, clothes, or habitation.
11. Tranquility: Be not disturbed at trifles or at accidents common or unavoidable.
12. Chastity: Rarely use venery but for health or offspring—never to dullness, weakness, or the injury of your own or another's peace or reputation.
13. Humility: Imitate Jesus and Socrates.

Let no Pleasure tempt thee, no Profit allure thee, no Ambition corrupt thee, no Example sway thee, no Persuasion move thee, to do anything which thou knowest to be evil; so shalt thou always live jollily; for a good Conscience is a continual Christmas. Adieu.

✒ Advice to a Young Tradesman

BENJAMIN FRANKLIN

A printer, inventor, philosopher, scientist and writer, Benjamin Franklin first reached a wide audience of American's with his publication *Poor Richard's Almanack*. It was an immensely popular journal that offered advice and pithy wisdom, as well as the news.

Franklin was also a very successful businessman and would become one of the wealthier men in America. He was entirely self-made. Here, he offers some advice to a prospective tradesman that was published in *Poor Richard's Almanack*. Although more than two centuries old, the advice continues to reflect some of the basic values of American enterprise.

To my Friend, A. B.: As you have desired it of me, I write the following hints, which have been of service to me, and may, if observed, be so to you.

Remember that time is money. He that can earn ten shillings a day by his labor and goes abroad or sits idle one-half of that day, though he spends but sixpence during his diversion or idleness, ought not to reckon that the only expense; he has really spent, or rather thrown away, five shillings besides.

Remember that credit is money. If a man lets his money lie in my hands after it is due, he gives me the interest, or so much as I can make of it during that time. This amounts to a considerable sum where a man has good and large credit and makes good use of it.

Remember that money is of the prolific generating nature. Money can beget money, and its offspring can beget more, and so on. Five shillings turned is six; turned again it is seven and threepence, and so on till it becomes a hundred pounds. The more there is of it the more it produces every turning, so that the profits rise quicker and quicker. He that kills a breeding sow destroys all her offspring to the thousandth generation. He that murders a crown destroys all that might have produced even scores of pounds.

Remember that six pounds a year is but a groat a day. For this little sum (which may be daily wasted either in time or expense unperceived) a man of credit may, on his own security, have the constant possession and use of a hundred pounds. So much in stock briskly turned by an industrious man produces great advantage.

Remember this saying, "Thy good paymaster is lord of another man's purse." He that is known to pay punctually and exactly to the time he promises may at any time and on any occasion raise all the money his friends can spare. This is sometimes of great use. After industry and frugality, nothing contributes more to the raising of a young man in the world than punctuality and justice in all his dealings; therefore never keep borrowed money an hour beyond the time you promised, lest a disappointment shut up your friend's purse for ever.

The most trifling actions that affect a man's credit are to be regarded. The sound of your hammer at five in the morning or nine at night heard by a creditor makes him easy six months longer, but if he sees you at a billiard-table or hears your voice at a tavern, when you should be at work, he sends for his money the next day; demands it, before he can receive it, in a lump.

It shows, besides, that you are mindful of what you owe; it makes you appear a careful as well as an honest man, and that still increases your credit.

Beware of thinking all your own that you possess and of living accordingly. It is a mistake that many people who have credit fall into. To prevent this, keep an exact account for some time, both of your expenses and your income. If you take the pains at first to mention particulars, it will have this good effect; you will discover how wonderfully small, trifling expenses mount up to large sums, and will discern what might have been and may for the future be saved without occasionally any great inconvenience.

In short, the way to wealth, if you desire it, is as plain as the way to the market. It depends chiefly on two words, industry and frugality; that is, waste neither time nor money, but make the best use of both. Without industry and frugality nothing will do, and with them everything. He that gets all he can honestly and saves all he gets (necessary expenses excepted), will certainly become rich, if that Being who governs the world, to whom all should look for a blessing on their honest endeavors, doth not, in His wise providence, otherwise determine.

An Old Tradesman

❧ "Dangerous upon several political accounts, especially self-preservation."

A VIRGINIA CLERGYMAN

Starting in 1701, the English Society for the Propagation of the Gospel in Foreign Parts sent missionaries and teachers to the middle and southern American colonies to teach and gain converts to the Church of England. In addition to reaching white colonists, the Society sought American Natives and black slaves, prompting controversy.

Masters were anxious that baptized slaves might claim their freedom. This concern was settled by the British government which formally declared that slaves could be baptized. Teaching slaves how to read and write, however, was out of the question, as this anonymous clergyman reported to the Society in 1724.

As for baptizing Indians and Negroes, several of the

people disapprove of it; because they say it often makes them proud, and not so good servants: But these, and such objections are easily refuted, if the persons be sensible, good, and understand English, and have been taught (or are willing to learn) the principles of Christianity, and if they be kept to the observance of it afterwards; for Christianity encourages and orders them to become more humble and better servants, and not worse, than when they were heathens.

But as for baptizing wild Indians and new Negroes, who have not the least knowledge nor inclination to know and mind our religion, language and customs, but will obstinately persist in their own barbarous ways; I question whether baptism of such (till they be a little weaned of their savage barbarity) be not a prostitute of a thing so sacred.

But as for the Children of Negroes and Indians, that are to live among Christians, undoubtedly they ought all to be baptized; since it is not out of the power of their masters to take care that they have a Christian education, learn their prayers and catechism, and go to church, and not accustom themselves to lie, swear and steal, though such (as the poorer sort in England) be not taught to read and write; which as yet has been found to be dangerous upon several political accounts, especially self-preservation.

❧ "A harmless little beast"

WILLIAM BYRD

William Byrd was one of the great chroniclers of the colonial South. A leading Virginia planter, he wrote four books that helped reveal the wonders of America to Europeans and his colonial contemporaries. The title of one book, *A Journey to the Land of Eden,* reflected the optimism and hopes that America offered.

This excerpt from *The History of the Dividing Line in the Year 1728* describes the ubiquitous possum. An object of marvel for first-time visitors, the possum's appearance and habits were other-worldly. The book was written as an account of his adventures in marking Virginia's southern boundary.

In the evening one of the men knocked down an oppossum, which is a harmless little beast, that will seldom go out of your way, and if take hold of it, will only grin, and hardly ever bite. The flesh was well tasted and tender, approaching nearest to pig, which it also resembles in bigness. The color of its fur was a goose gray, with a swine's snout, and a tail like a rat's, but at least a foot long. By twisting this tail about the arm of a tree, it will hang with all its weight, and swing to anything it wants to take hold of. It has five claws on the forefeet of equal length, but the hinder feet have only four claws, and a sort of thumb standing off at a proper distance. Their feet being thus formed, qualify them for climbing up trees to catch little birds, which they are very fond of. But the greatest particularity of this creature, and which distinguishes it from most others that we are acquainted with, is the false belly of the female, into which her young retreat in time of danger. She can draw the slit, which is the inlet into this pouch, so close, that you must look narrowly to find it, especially if she happens to be a virgin. Within the false belly may be seen seven or eight teats, on which the young ones grow from their first formation till they are big enough to fall off, like ripe fruit from a tree. This is so odd a method of generation, that I should not have believed it without the testimony of mine own eyes. Besides a knowing and credible person has assured me he has more than once observed the embryo opposums growing to the teat before they were completely shaped, and afterwards watched their daily growth till they were big enough for birth. And all this he could the more easily pry into, because the dame was so perfectly gentle and harmless, that he could handle her just as he pleased. I could hardly persuade myself to publish a thing so contrary to course that nature takes in the production of other animals, unless it were a matter commonly believed in all countries where that creature is produced, and has been often observed by persons of undoubted credit and understanding.

Bering explores Alaska for Russia

GEORG STELLAR

The Russian explorer Vitus Bering discovered the Bering Straits in 1730. Eleven years later he returned to the Russian Far West to explore America. The German botanist and naturalist Georg Stellar accompanied Bering and recorded the crew's findings on the Alaskan coast. Stellar's observation would prove correct.

On the return journey the crew was shipwrecked and was forced to stay on an Alaskan island for the winter. Bering died of scurvy. Nevertheless, the survivors returned to Russia with stories of otters, sea lions, sea cows, and seals that led to a bustling Russian fur trade along the Alaskan coast. The Russian settlements, however, never penetrated inland.

We saw land as early as July 15…the mountains, observed extending inland, were so lofty that we could see them quite plainly at sea at a distance of sixteen Dutch miles. I cannot recall having seen higher mountains anywhere in Siberia and Kamchatka. The coast was everywhere much indented and therefore provided with numerous bays and inlets close to the mainland.

It can easily be imagined how happy every one was when land was finally sighted; nobody failed to congratulate Captain Commander, whom the glory for the discovery mostly concerned. He, however, received it all not only very indifferently and without particular pleasure, but in the presence of all he even shrugged his shoulders while looking at the land…. the good Captain Commander was much superior to his officers in looking into the future, and in the cabin he expressed himself to me and Mr. Plenisner as follows: "We think now we have accomplished everything, and many go about greatly inflated, but they do not consider where we have reached land, how far we are from home, and what may yet happen, who knows but that perhaps trade winds may arise, which may prevent us from returning? We do not know this country; nor are we provided with supplied for a wintering."

On Monday the 20th we came to anchor among numerous islands… I struck out in the direction of the mainland in the hopes of finding human beings and habitations. I had not gone more than a verst [two-thirds of a mile] along the beach before I came across signs of people and their doings.

Under a tree I found an old piece of a log hollowed out in the shape of a trough, in which, a couple of hours before, the savages, for lack of pots and vessels, had cooked their meat by means of red-hot stones, just as Kamchadals did formerly…. There were also strewn about the remains of yukola, or pieces of dried fish, which, as in Kamchatka, has to serve the purpose of bread at all meals. There were also great numbers of very large scallops over eight inches across, also blue mussels similar to those found in Kamchatka and, no doubt, eaten raw as the custom is there. In various shells, as on dishes, I found sweet grass completely prepared in Kamchadal fashion, on which water seemed to have been poured in order to extract the sweetness. I discovered further, not far from the fireplace, beside the tree, on which there still were the live coals, a wooden apparatus for making fire, of the same nature as those used in Kamchatka….

From all this I think I may conclude that the inhabitants of this American coast are of the same origin as the Kamchadals, with them they agree completely in such peculiar customs and utensils, particularly in the preparation of sweet grass, which have not been communicated even to the Siberian natives nearest to Kamchatka, for instance the Tunguses and Koryaks.

But if this is so, then it may also be conjectured that America extends farther westward and, opposite Kamchatka, is much nearer in the north, since in view of such a great distance as we traveled of at least 500 miles, it is not credible that the Kamchadals would have been able to get there in their miserable craft….

These, then, are all our achievements and observations, and these not even from the mainland, on which none of us set foot, but only from an island which seemed to be three miles long a half mile wide and the nearest to the mainland (which here forms a large bay studded with many islands) and separated from it by a channel less than half a mile wide. The only reason why we did not attempt to land on the mainland is a sluggish obstinacy and a dull fear…. The time here spent in investigation bears an arithmetical ratio to the time used in fitting out: ten years of preparations for this great undertaking lasted, and ten hours were devoted to the work itself. Of the mainland we have a sketch on paper; of the country itself an imperfect idea, based upon what could be discovered on the island and upon conjectures.

… The animals occurring there and supplying natives with their meat for food and with their skins for clothing are, so far as I had opportunity to observe, hair seals, large and small sharks, whales, and plenty of sea otters…. Of birds I saw only two familiar species, the raven and the magpie; however, of strange and unknown ones I noted more than ten different kinds, all of which were easily distinguished from the European and Siberian [species] by their very particularly bright coloring. Good luck, thanks to my huntsman, placed in my hands a single specimen, of which I remember to have seen a likeness painted in lively colors and described in the newest account of the birds and plants of the Carolinas published in French and English, the name of the author of which, however, does not occur to me now. This bird proved to me that we were really in America. [The bird was a blue jay.]

🐦 "Be upon our guard against power"

JOHN PETER ZENGER

The trial of John Peter Zenger in 1734 established the principle of freedom of the press in America. A New York editor and printer, Zenger founded the *New York Weekly Journal* to oppose Governor William Cosby. Zenger criticized Cosby's actions in print and was consequently thrown in jail for his remarks, which happened to be true.

In particular, Zenger wrote: "We see men's deeds destroyed, judges arbitrarily displaced, new courts erected, without consent of the legislature, by which it seems to me, trials by jury are taken away when a governor pleases." Zenger was held in prison for ten months without a trial. Issuing instructions to his wife and servants, however, he oversaw the continued publication of the *Journal*.

Zenger's initial lawyers were disbarred for attempting to defend him. Nevertheless, Andrew Hamilton—the most prominent lawyer in America—secretly took on the case and arrived in court without warning to Cosby's hand-picked judge, James De Lancey. Zenger went over the head of the judge and the law to appeal to the jury's sense of liberty. Zenger was found not guilty.

ATTORNEY GENERAL BRADLEY: The case before the Court is, whether Mr. Zenger is guilty of libelling his Excellency the Governor of New York, and indeed the whole Administration of the Government. Mr. Hamilton has confessed the printing and publishing, and I think nothing is plainer, than that the words in the information are scandalous, and tend to sedition, and to disquiet the minds of the people of this province. And if such papers are not libels, I think it may be said, there can be no such thing as a libel.

ANDREW HAMILTON: May it please your Honour; I cannot agree with Mr. Attorney. For tho' I freely acknowledge, that there are such things as libels, yet I must insist at the same time, that what my client is charged with is not a libel; and I observed just now, that Mr. Attorney in defining a libel, made use of the words scandalous, seditious, and tend to disquiet the people; but (whether with design or not I will not say) he omitted the word "false."…

CHIEF JUSTICE: You cannot be admitted, Mr. Hamilton, to give the truth of a libel in evidence. A libel is not to be justified; for it is nevertheless a libel that it is true.

HAMILTON: I am sorry the Court has so soon resolved upon that piece of law; I expected first to have been heard to that point. I have not in all my reading met with an authority that says, we cannot be admitted to give the truth in evidence, upon an information for a libel.

CHIEF JUSTICE: The law is clear, That you cannot justify a libel….

HAMILTON: I thank your Honour. Then, gentlemen of the jury, it is to you we must now appeal, for witnesses, to the truth of the facts we have offered, and are denied the liberty to prove; and let it not seem strange, that I apply myself to you in this manner, I am warranted so to do both by law and reason. The last supposes you to be summoned, out of the neighbourhood where the fact is alleged to be committed; and the reason of your being taken out of the neighbourhood is, because you supposed to have the best knowledge of the fact that is to be tried. And were you to find a verdict against my client, you must take upon you to say, the papers referred to in the information, and which we acknowledge we printed and published, are false, scandalous and seditious; but of this I can have no apprehension. You are citizens of New York; you are really what the law supposes you to be, honest and lawful men; and, according to my brief, the facts which we offer to prove were not committed in a corner; they are notoriously known to be true; and therefore in your justice lies our safety. And as we are denied the liberty of giving evidence, to prove the truth of what we have published, I will beg leave to lay it down as a standing rule in such cases, that the suppressing of evidence ought always to be taken for the strongest evidence; and I hope it will have that weight with you....

It is true in times past it was a crime to speak truth, and in that terrible Court of Star-Chamber, many worthy and brave men suffered for so doing; and yet even in that court, and in those bad times, a great and good man dared to say, what I hope will not be taken amiss of me to say in this place, to wit, the practice of informations for libels is a sword in the hands of a wicked King, and an arrant coward to cut down and destroy the innocent; the one cannot, because of his high station, and the other dares not, because of his want of courage, revenge himself in another manner.

BRADLEY: Pray Mr. Hamilton, have a care what you say, don't go too far neither, I don't like those liberties.

HAMILTON: I hope to be pardon'd, Sir, for my zeal upon this occasion: It is an old and wise caution, that when our neighbors house is on fire, we ought to take care of our own. For tho' blessed be God, I live in a government where liberty is well understood, and freely enjoy'd; yet experience has shown us all (I'm sure it has to me) that a bad precedent in one government, is soon set up for an authority in another; and therefore I cannot but think it mine, and every honest man's duty, that (while we pay all due obedience to men in authority) we ought at the same time to be upon our guard against power, wherever we apprehend that it may affect ourselves or our fellow-subjects....

I should think it my duty, if required, to go to the utmost part of the land, where my service could be of any use in assisting to quench the flame of prosecutions upon informations, set on foot by the government, to deprive a people of the right of remonstrating (and complaining too) of the arbitrary attempts of men in power. Men who injure and oppress the people under their administration provoke them to dry out and complain; and then make that very complaint the foundation of new oppressions and prosecutions. I wish I could say there were no instances of this kind. But to conclude; the question before the court and you, gentlemen of the jury,

is not of small nor private concern, it is not the cause of a poor printer, nor of New York alone, which you are now trying; No! It may in its consequence, affect every freeman that lives under a British government on the main of America. It is the best cause. It is the cause of liberty; and I make no doubt but your upright conduct, this day, will not only entitle you to the love and esteem of your fellow-citizens; but every man, who prefers freedom to a life of slavery, will bless and honour you, as men who have baffled the attempt of tyranny; and by an impartial and uncorrupt verdict, have laid a noble foundation for securing to ourselves, our posterity, and our neighbours, that to which nature and the laws of our country have given us a right—the liberty—both of exposing and opposing arbitrary power (in these parts of the world, at least) by speaking and writing the truth....

CHIEF JUSTICE: Gentlemen of the jury. The great pains Mr. Hamilton has taken, to show how little regard juries are to pay to the opinions of judges; and his insisting so much upon the conduct of some judges in trials of this kind; is done, no doubt, with a design that you should take but very little notice of what I may say upon this occasion. I shall therefore only observe to you that, as the facts or words in the information are confessed: the only thing that can come in question before you is, whether the words, as set forth in the information, make a libel. And that is a matter of law, no doubt, and which you may leave to the court....

The Jury withdrew, and in a small time returned, and being asked by the clerk, whether they were agreed of their verdict, and whether John Peter Zenger was guilty of printing and publishing the libels in the information mentioned? They answered by Thomas Bunt, their Foreman, Not Guilty. Upon which there were three Huzzas in the hall which was crowded with people, and the next day I was discharged from my imprisonment.

"Sinners in the Hands of an Angry God"

JONATHAN EDWARDS

Jonathan Edwards' sermon "Sinners in the Hands of an Angry God" was typical of the Great Awakening religious revival movement that swept British America in the 1730s and '40s. Given at Enfield, Connecticut, in 1741, the sermon evokes stark images of the individual man's puny and fragile place in God's world.

Edwards was the leading theologian of the Great Awakening—regarded by many to be the most important religious thinker in American history. Bringing passion and originality to the pulpit, he called for a renewed faith in God, advocated orthodox Calvinism and defended the role of experience and feeling in religious life.

The God that holds you over the pit of hell much as one holds a spider or some loathsome insect over the fire abhors you, and is dreadfully provoked; his wrath towards you burns like fire; he looks upon you as worthy of nothing else but to be cast into the fire; he is of purer eyes than to bear you in his sight; you are ten thousand times as abominable in his eyes as the most hateful venomous serpent is in ours. You have offended him infinitely more than ever a stubborn rebel did his prince, and yet it is nothing but his hand that holds you from falling into the fire every moment; it is ascribed to nothing else that you did not go to hell the last night that you were suffered to awake again in this world, after you closed your eyes to sleep; and there is no other reason to be given why you have not dropped into hell since you arose in the morning, but that God's hand has held you up; there is no other reason to be given why you have not gone to hell, since you have sat here in the house of God provoking his pure eye by your sinful, wicked manner of attending his solemn worship; yea; there is nothing else that is to be given as a reason why you do not this very moment drop down into hell.

O sinner, consider the fearful danger you are in; it is a great furnace of wrath, a wide and bottomless pit, full of the fire of wrath that you are held over in the hands of that God whose wrath is provoked and incensed as much against you as against many of the damned in hell; you hang by a slender thread, with the flames of divine wrath flashing about it, and ready every moment to singe it and burn it asunder, and you have no interest in any mediator, and nothing to lay hold of to save yourself, nothing to keep off the flames of wrath, nothing of your own, nothing that you have ever done, nothing that you can do to induce God to spare you one moment....

It would be dreadful to suffer this fierceness and wrath of Almighty God one moment; but you must suffer it to all eternity: there will be no end to this exquisite, horrible misery: when you look forward, you shall see along forever a boundless duration before you, which will swallow up your thoughts, and amaze your soul; and you will absolutely despair of ever having any deliverance, any end, any mitigation, any rest at all; you will know certainly that you must wear out long ages, millions of millions of ages in wrestling and conflicting with this almighty, merciless vengeance; and then when you have so done, when so many ages have actually been spent by you in this manner, you will know that all is but a point to what remains, so that your punishment will be indeed be infinite. Oh, who can express what the state of a soul in such circumstances is! All that we can possibly say about it gives but a very feeble, faint representation of it; it is inexpressible and inconceivable: for "who knows the power of God's anger!"

How dreadful is the state of those that are daily and hourly in danger of this great wrath and infinite misery! But this is the dismal case of every soul in this congregation that has not been born again, however, moral and strict, sober and religious, they may otherwise be. Oh, that you would consider it, whether you be young or old! There is reason to think that there are many in this congregation now hearing this discourse that will actually be the subjects of this very misery to all eternity. We know not who they are, or in what seats they sit, or what thoughts they now have—it may be they are now at ease, and hear all these things without much disturbance, and are now flattering themselves that they shall escape. If we knew that there was one person, and but one, in the whole congregation, that was to be the subject of this misery, what awful thing it would be to think of! If we knew who it was, what an awful sight it would be to see such a person! How might all the rest of the congregation lift up a lamentable and bitter cry over him! But, alas, instead of one, how many is it likely will remember this discourse in hell! And it would be a wonder, if some that are now present should not be in hell in a very short time, before this year is out. And it would be no wonder if some persons that now sit here in some seats of this meetinghouse, in health, and quiet and secure, should be there before tomorrow morning!...

Therefore let everyone that is out of Christ now awake and fly from the wrath to come. The wrath of Almighty God is now undoubtedly hanging over a great part of this congregation. Let everyone fly out of Sodom. "Haste and escape for your lives, look not behind you, escape to the mountain, lest ye be consumed."

❧ "We are not well used"

CHIEF CANNASSATEGO

As the colonies prospered, European settlers pressed inland and put more and more pressure on Native Americans to relinquish their land either by force or payment. As this 1742 speech by Iroquois Chief Cannassatego makes clear, European terms were less than adequate and respect for treaties was scanty. Native Americans were suffering from the white influence.

We received from the Proprietors yesterday, some goods in consideration of our release of the lands on the west side of the Susquehanna. It is true, we have the full quantity according to agreement; but if the Proprietor had been here himself, we think, in regard of our numbers and poverty, he would have made an addition to them. If the goods were only to be divided amongst the Indians present, a single person would have but a small portion; but if you consider what numbers are left behind, equally entitled with us to a share, there will be extremely little. We therefore desire, if you have the keys of the Proprietor's chest, you will open it, and take out a little more for us.

We know our lands are now become more valuable: the white people think we do not know their value; but we are sensible that the land is everlasting, and the few goods we receive for it are soon worn out and gone. For the future we will sell no lands but when Brother Onas is in the country; and we will know beforehand the quantity of the goods we are to receive. Besides, we are not well used with respect to the lands still unsold by us. Your people daily settle on these lands, and spoil our hunting. We must insist on your removing them, as you know they have no right to settle to the northward of Kittochtinny-Hills. In particular, we renew our complaints against some people who are settled at Juniata, a branch of Susquehanna, and all along the banks of that river, as far as Mahaniay; and desire they may be forthwith made to go off the land; for they do great damage to our cousins the Delawares.

We have further to observe, with respect to the lands lying on the west side of Susquehanna, that though Brother Onas has paid us for what his people possess, yet some parts of that country have been taken up by persons whose place of residence is to the south of this province, from whom we have never received any consideration. This affair was recommended to you by our chiefs at our last treaty; and you then, at our earnest desire, promised to write a letter to that person who has the authority over those people, and to procure us his answer: as we have never heard from you on this head, we want to know what you have done in it. If you have not done anything, we now renew our request, and desire you will inform the person whose people are seated on our lands, that that country belongs to us, in right of conquest; we having bought it with our blood, and taken it from our enemies in fair war; and we expect, as owners of that land, to receive such a consideration for it as the land is worth. We desire you will press him to send us a positive answer: let him say Yes or No: if he says Yes, we will treat with him; if No, we are able to do ourselves justice; and we will do it, by going to take payment ourselves.

It is customary with us to make a present of skins whenever we renew our treaties. We are ashamed to offer our brethren so few; but your horses and cows have eat the grass our deer used to feed on. This has made them scarce, and will, we hope, plead in excuse for our not bringing a larger quantity: if we could have spared more we would have given more; but we are really poor; and desire you'll not consider the quantity, but, few as they are, accept them in testimony of our regard.

❧ Invading Florida

EDWARD KIMBER

Georgia was the last of the thirteen British American colonies. It was created in 1732 by an act of Parliament and settled under the leadership of James Oglethorpe. One of the main purposes of the new colony was to serve as a buffer to Spanish Florida. The British colonies and the Spanish settlers were frequently at war.

In 1740, Oglethorpe invaded Florida and tried to capture Saint Augustine, the oldest permanent settlement in North America. The attack failed and was followed by a Spanish counterinvasion in 1742. Oglethorpe repulsed the Spanish at the Battle of Bloody Marsh. He then attempted a second invasion of Florida.

Edward Kimber took part in the second British onslaught (which also failed) and kept a journal. Here he describes the Native American allies that accompanied Oglethorpe with an equal measure of contempt and fascination.

Friday, March 11. The drums beat to arms at nine, and we remain'd in that posture till twelve at noon, expecting immediately to march; but had, then, orders to retire to our huts. The General's policy was, and is, very observable, in the frequent alarms his people receive, and the frequent motions he obliges them to make; knowing very well, that the rust of inactivity and idleness too soon corrupts the minds, and enervates the body of the soldier. To this are, perhaps, owing, the many different fatigues, his regiment goes thro' in Georgia, which he is always promoting; as, clearing roads, draining swamps, marshes, etc. which so harden'd and strengthen'd the Roman Legions, who have left, from the time of Caesar to the declension of their Empire, eternal monuments of industry and labour, in all the countries they subdu'd. At two o'clock, a hard rain (accompanied with repeated lightnings, and thunder-claps, that are common in these southern climates, and are wonderfully severe; the whole element seeming to be kindled into a livid flame, and all nature meeting with a general dissolution) set in, and continued till we were thoroughly soak'd, and our arms had received considerable damage. At four o'clock, the Cowhati Indians, who went to Augustine, after so long expectations, and divers conjectures about their long stay, return'd; bringing with them five scalps, one hand, which was cut off with the glove on, several arms, clothes, and two or three spades; which they had the boldness to bring away, after having attack'd a boat with upwards of forty men in it, under the very walls of the castle, killing about twenty of them, and over-setting the rest; who also had met with death, but for the continu'd fire of their great guns. It seems, that they were pioneers, and were going, under an officer, to dig clay for the King's works. We heard them long before they came in sight, by the melancholy notes of their warlike death-houp. For the Spaniards having kill'd one of their people, they, as usual with them in that case, gave no quarter, and therefore brought his Excellency no prisoner; which was what he earnestly desir'd. To give you a lively idea of what occurs here, of these sons of

the earth, I premise some description of their figure, manners, and method of making war. As to their figure, 'tis generally of the largest size, well proportion'd, and robust, as you can imagine persons nurs'd up in manly exercises can be. Their colour is a swarthy, copper hue, their hair generally black, and shaven, or pluck'd off by the roots, all round their foreheads and temples. They paint their faces and bodies, with black, red, or other colours, in a truly diabolic manner; or, to speak more rationally, much like the former uncultivated inhabitants of Britain, whom Tacitus mentions. Their dress is a skin or blanket, tied, or loosely cast, over their shoulders; a shirt which they never wash, and which is consequently greasy and black to the last degree; a flap, before and behind, to cover their privities, of red or blue bays, hanging by a girdle of the same; boots about their legs, of bays also; and what they call morgissons, or pumps of deer or buffalo skin, upon their feet. Their arms, and ammunition, a common trading-gun; a pouch with shot and powder; a tomahawk, or diminutive of a hatchet, by their side; a scalping-knife, pistol, etc. But, however, you'll see their dress, by those the General has carry'd to England. As to their manners, tho' they are fraught with the greatest cunning in life, you observe little in their common behaviour, above the brute creation, in their expeditions they hunt for their provision, and, when boiled or barbecu'd, tear it to pieces promiscuously with their fists, and devour it with a remarkable greediness. Their drink is Weetuxee, or water, on these occasions; but, at other times, any thing weaker than wine or brandy, is nauseous to them; and they'll express their great abhorrence by spitting it out, and seeming to spew at it: All which is owing to the loss of their native virtues, since the Europeans have enter'd into all measures for trading with them; for, view them without prejudice, you will perceive some remains of an ancient roughness and simplicity, common to all the first inhabitants of the earth; even to our own dear ancestors, who, I believe, were much upon a level with these Indian hunting warriors, whom his Excellency has so tam'd, since his being in America, and made so subservient to the benefit of the English nation.

When they make an incursion into an enemy's country, they decline the open roads and paths, and only scout along the defiles and woods, ready to pop on any prey that shall appear in the open country; whom they attack with terrible and mournful cries, that astonish even more than their arms. If none of their own party is kill'd, they take prisoners all they can lay hands on; but if on the contrary, they give no quarter. Before they go to war, they undergo the ceremony of physicking, which is done very privately in the recesses of some hoary wood, remote from the eyes of any white person; and generally employs a day or two: Then performing the ceremony of their War-dance, they are ready to begin their work. These two last mention'd ceremonies seem to be a mixture of the religious and the political. Their medicine is a kind of red paste, etc. etc. but of what made, the Lord above knows.

So much will serve for the purpose of this relation; and for a full account of the religious and civil affairs, etc. of these natural sons of America, a farther account of their manners, and other entertaining and curious articles, I refer you to the many good accounts that have formerly been given, by many creditable authors....

Imagine to your self a body of sixty or seventy of these creatures, marching in rank and file, (and by their martial figure, and size, forming, or extending a front equal to that of two hundred men,) with the mournful howls and cries, usual on the occasion, and every now and then popping their pieces off, which was answer'd by the main-guard, as they pass'd, in a continually resum'd fire. His Excellency was seated, to receive them, under some neighbouring trees, on a buffalo's skin, surrounded by his officers; when every one approaching him, he shook them by the hand, welcom'd them home, in the Indian tongue, and thank'd them for the service they had done him. The war captains, or old men, he retain'd; who being seated, had three hogs, fish, oysters, bread, beer, and divers other refreshments given them; when they inform'd his Excellency, there was no camp at Diego: And then his Excellency propos'd their marching again to Augustine, with him and his people; but, whether they had been handled more severely than they represented, or, whether they were terrify'd with the great guns, etc. they seem'd not much inclin'd to it; and seeing that the General used a few persuasions for that end, they objected to his small number, told him, they could shift well enough, but were not pleas'd with the white mens method of going to war. They knew, as they express'd it in

their tongue, that his men were angry and full of blood; but their red passion would drive them into many dangers, etc. They retir'd and made themselves drunk, that evening, and thought no more of their losses or exploits. The General sitting among them, and acquiescing with their manners, in their cups, they promis'd to march with him; but what they said, seem'd forc'd, and he declin'd their aid....

Sunday, March 20. Two more boats arrive from Frederica, with Cherokee Indians; and soon after a schooner, with the Upper-Creeks, Cussitaes, Ocuni's, and Cowhati's; part of whom left us, and return'd to Frederica, as before related; and some of the Talpooses, Tuckabahhe and Savannee nations, who came to assist the General, making in all seventy. Various conjectures are pass'd of his Excellency's intentions, and the men seem to be uneasy for want of action. Our present post, if the Spaniards have any souls, must be very dangerous, and all precautions are taken to receive them in a proper manner. An Indian conjurer prophesies they will be down upon us this night; and therefore, to humour those people's superstition, a double-watch is kept; and another advanc'd-guard mounted under Ensign Chambedaine, as far off as the Horse-Guards ....

Friday, March 25. Fifty Indians set out on another incursion to Augustine, after physicking, and performing the war-dance, with more ceremony than I ever saw them.

Saturday, March 26. At noon his Excellency embark'd in the Walker, with forty soldiers, besides the ship's crew, and forty-six Indians, who were resolv'd to go on this sea-expedition with him; which was an extraordinary offer from them, and show'd their value for the General, whom they call their father. Captain Cart was left, with his scout-boats, to wait for those Indians who went by land. The remainder of the detachment embark'd in the other boats. The rude manners of the Indians on board, who without ceremony took up the cabin and all the conveniences, for lodging, and their arms, and lumber, were somewhat irksome, especially considering their nastiness; however, as his Excellency himself was pleased with lying roughly on the desk, all the voyage, no body else had the least reason to complain.

"An Account Shewing the Progress of the Colony of Georgia"

TRUSTEES OF GEORGIA

Georgia was the only colony to prohibit slavery at its founding. As described below, the Trustees of Georgia charged with supervising the colony had a lengthy list of reasons why they opposed slavery—none had to do with morality or natural law. This anonymously written account attributes the reasons to the security of the colony to avoid rebellion, the proximity to Saint Augustine which barred slavery, the demoralizing effect on other laborers, the costs and the lack of necessity.

The Trustees were induced to prohibit the Use of Negroes within Georgia; the Intention of his Majesty's Charter being to provide for poor People incapable of subsisting themselves at home, and to settle a Frontier for South Carolina, which was much exposed by the small Number of its white Inhabitants. It was impossible that the Poor, who should be sent from hence, and the Foreign persecuted Protestants, who must go in a manner naked into the Colony, could be able to purchase or subsist them, if they had them; and it would be a Charge too great for the Trustees to undertake; and they would be thereby disabled from sending white People. The first Cost of a Negro is about Thirty Pounds; and this Thirty Pounds would pay the Passage over, provide Tools and other Necessaries, and defray the Charge of Subsistence of a white Man for a Year; in which Time it might be hoped that the Planter's own Labour would gain him some Subsistence; consequently the Purchase-money of every Negro, (abstracting the Expence of subsisting him, as well as his Master) by being applied that way, would prevent the sending over a white Man, who would be of Security to the Province; whereas the Negro would render that Security precarious.

It was thought, that the white Man, by having a Negro Slave, would be less disposed to labour himself; and that his whole Time must be employed in keeping the Negro to Work, and in watching against any Danger he or his Family might apprehend from the Slave; and that the Planter's Wife and Children would by the Death, or even the Absence of the Planter, be in a manner at the Mercy of the Negro.

It was also apprehended, that the Spaniards at St. Augustine would be continually inticing away the Negroes, or encouraging them to Insurrections; that the first might easily be accomplished, since a single Negro could run away thither without Companions, and would only have a River or two to swim over; and this Opinion has been confirmed and justified by the Practices of the Spaniards, even in Time of profound Peace, amongst the Negroes in South Carolina; where, tho' at a greater Distance from Augustine, some have fled in Perriaguas and little Boats to the Spaniards, and been protected, and others in large Bodies have been incited to Insurrections, to the great Terror, and even endangering the Loss of that Province; which, though it has been established above Seventy Years, has scarce white People enough to secure her against her own Slaves.

It was also considered, that the Produces designed to be raised in the Colony would not require such Labour as to make Negroes necessary for carrying them on; for the Province of Carolina produces chiefly Rice, which is a Work of Hardship proper for Negroes; whereas the Silk and other Produces which the Trustees proposed to have the People employed on in Georgia, were such as Women and Children might be of as much Use in as Negroes. It was likewise apprehended, that if the Persons who should go over to Georgia at their own Expence, should be permitted the Use of Negroes, it would dispirit and ruin the poor Planters who could not get them, and who by their Numbers were designed to be the Strength of the Province; it would make them clamorous to have Negroes given them; and on the Refusal, would drive them from the Province, or at least make them negligent of their Plantations; where they would be unwilling, nay would certainly disdain to work like Negroes; and would rather let themselves out to the wealthy Planters as Overseers of their Negroes.

It was further thought, That upon the Admission of Negroes the wealthy Planters would, as in all other Colonies, be more induced to absent themselves, and live in other Places, leaving the Care of their Plantations and their Negroes to Overseers.

It was likewise thought, that the poor Planter sent on Charity from his Desire to have Negroes, as well as the Planter who should settle at his own

Expence, would (if he had Leave to alienate) mortgage his Land to the Negro Merchant for them, or at least become a Debtor for the Purchase of such Negroes; and under these Weights and Discouragements would be induced to sell his Slaves again upon any Necessity, and would leave the Province and his Lot to the Negro Merchant; in Consequence of which, all the small Properties would be swallowed up, as they have been in other Places, by the more wealthy Planters.

It was likewise considered, that the admitting of Negroes in Georgia would naturally facilitate the Desertion of the Carolina Negroes, thro' the Province of Georgia; and consequently this Colony, instead of proving a Frontier, and adding a Strength to the Province of South Carolina, would be a Means of drawing off the Slaves of Carolina, and adding thereby a Strength to Augustine.

From these several Considerations, as the Produces to be raised in the Colony did not make Negro Slaves necessary, as the Introduction of them so near to a Garrison of the Spaniards would weaken rather than strengthen the Barrier, and as they would introduce with them a greater Propensity to Idleness among the poor Planters, and too great an Inequality among the People, it was thought proper to make the Prohibition of them a Fundamental of the Constitution.

❧ A Questionnaire on Carolina and Georgia

JOHANN MARTIN BLOZIUS

The prohibition of slavery in Georgia did not last. A group of colonists known as the Malcontents lobbied hard for its introduction, saying that African slaves were better suited for certain types of work and that competing colonies had an unfair advantage over Georgia. The Malcontents prevailed and in 1750 slavery was permitted.

The following document by Pastor Johann Martin Blozius is a series of responses to questions about the migration of Germans to South Carolina and Georgia. He offers an accounting of the tasks, costs and practicalities in establishing a slave plantation in the southern colonies. It provides an excellent account of the yearly routines of southern plantations.

10th Question. How many acres of rice can a Negro man cultivate in one year?

Answer. If it is new land, a Negro man or woman can plant and cultivate 5 acres in one year. But if the field is old and grassy, not more than 3 acres.

11th Question. How much can a Negro cultivate in other crops per year?

Answer. A good slave may plant and cultivate 10 acres of corn and potatoes, if the land is new and good. But if it is old and grassy, not more than 6 acres. N.B. It is customary that each diligent slave must plant and cultivate 3 acres of rice and 4 acres of grain a year, apart from some potatoes, where the land is not too grassy.

12th Question. What is the day's work of each Negro woman?

Answer. A good Negro woman has the same day's work as the man in the planting and cultivating of the fields. The men fall the trees, and the women cut the bushes and carry them together, and thus they share their work, the man doing the hardest and the woman the easiest.

13th Question. What work do the children of male and female sex have?

Answer. The children are used for various small jobs according to their age, such as hoeing the potatoes, feeding the chickens, shooing the birds from the rice and grain.

14th Question. What is the daily work of the Negroes on a plantation throughout the year?

Answer. If one wants to establish a plantation on previously uncultivated land, one orders the Negroes to clear a piece of land of trees and bushes first of all, so as to build the necessary huts on it at once. 2) Until March one has as much land cleared of trees and bushes and prepared for planting as possible. 3) The land which is to be cultivated must be fenced with split poles 2 to 3 feet long and nearly 4 inches thick. Every Negro must split 100 of such poles per day from oaks or firs. Others carry them together, and several make the fence. In this men and women are kept busy. 4) In the evening all the Negroes must occupy themselves with burning the cut bushes and the branches. N.B. When the land is prepared for planting, the bushes must be cut down first and piled on heaps, and afterwards the trees must be felled. The Negroes must hack the branches off the trees, and also pile them in heaps. Now when one observes that all branches and bushes are quite dry, one puts fire to them and lets them burn up. Since the land is full of dry leaves, the fire spreads far and wide and burns grass and everything it finds. One lets the felled trees lie on the field until they rot, for it would be a loss of time if one wanted to split and burn them. N.B. One looks after the best building timber as well as possible. The white oaks are used for barrel staves, and the young white oaks and nut trees are used for hoops.

The order of planting is the following. 1) The Negroes plant potatoes at the end of March unless the weather is too cold. This keeps all Negroes busy, and they have to loosen the earth as much as they can. The potatoes are cut into several pieces and put into long dug furrows, or mounds, which are better than the former. When the leaves have grown 2 or 3 feet long (which is usually the case at the end of May or early June), one piles these leaves on long hills so that both ends project and are not covered. 2) As soon as one is through with the potatoes, one plants Indian corn. A good Negro man or woman must plant half an acre a day. Holes are merely made in the earth 6 feet from one another, and 5 or 6 kernels put into each hole. 3) After the corn the Negroes make furrows for rice planting. A Negro man or woman must account for a quarter acre daily. On the following day the Negroes sow and cover the rice in the furrows, and half an acre is the daily task of a Negro. 4) Now the Negroes start to clean the corn of the grass, and a day's work is half an acre, be he man or woman, unless the ground is too full of roots. 5) When they are through with that, they plant beans together among the corn. At this time the children must weed out the grass in the potato patches. 6) Thereupon they start for the first time to cultivate (behauen) the rice and to clean it of grass. A Negro must complete ∫ acre daily. 7) Now the corn must be cleaned of the grass for the second time, and a little earth put around the stalks like little hills. Some young corn is pulled out, and only 3 or 4 stalks remain. A little earth is also laid on the roots of the beans, all of which the Negroes do at the same time. Their day's task in this work is half an acre for each. 8) As soon as they are through with the corn, they cultivate (hauen) the rice a second time. The quality of the land determines their day's work in this. 9) Corn and rice are cultivated (hauen) for the third and last time. A Negro can take care of an acre and more in this work, and ∫ an acre of rice. Now the work on rice,

corn, and beans is done. As soon as the corn is ripe it is bent down so that the ears hang down towards the earth, so that no water collects in them or the birds damage them. Afterwards the Negroes are used for all kinds of house work, until the rice is white and ripe for cutting, and the beans are gathered, which grow much more strongly when the corn has been bent down. The rice is cut at the end of August or in September, some of it also early in October. The pumpkins, which are also planted among the corn, are now ripening too. White beets are sown in good fertilized soil in July and August, and during the full moon. Towards the middle of August all Negro men of 16 to 60 years must work on the public roads, to start new ones or to improve them, namely for 4 or 5 days, or according to what the government requires, and one has to send along a white man with a rifle or go oneself. At the time when the rice is cut and harvested, the beans are collected too, which task is divided among the Negroes. They gather the rice, thresh it, grind it in wooden mills, and stamp it mornings and evenings. The corn is harvested last. During the 12 days after Christmas they plant peas, garden beans, transplant or prune trees, and plant cabbage. Afterwards the fences are repaired, and new land is prepared for cultivating.

15th Question. What is permitted to Negroes after they have done their required day's work?

Answer. They are given as much land as they can handle. On it they plant for themselves corn, potatoes, tobacco, peanuts, water and sugar melons, pumpkins, bottle pumpkins (sweet ones and stinking ones which are used as milk and drink vessels and for other things). They plant for themselves also on Sundays. For if they do not work they make mischief and do damage. (Sed datur tertium, idque maxime necessarium, namely one should instruct them in the Christian religion to Abraham's example, Genesis 18: 19.) They sell their own crops and buy some necessary things.

16th Question. How much meat, fish, bread, and butter do they receive weekly?

Answer. Their food is nothing but Indian corn, beans, pounded rice, potatoes, pumpkins. If the master wishes, he gives them a little meat when he slaughters. They have nothing but water to drink.

❧ "I have the business of three plantations to transact"

ELIZA LUCAS PINCKNEY

Eliza Lucas Pinckney was one of the most remarkable and accomplished women in 18th century America. At the age of 16, her father made her responsible for the management of three South Carolina plantations. She became the first person to successfully raise indigo in the colony, creating a new cash crop that saved many plantations from 1741-1746 when the rice market collapsed.

Two of her sons, Charles and Thomas, later became national political leaders in the early years of the United States government. Charles would run for president and vice president; Thomas for vice president. Both were Federalists.

This letter was written in 1740 when she was a teenager and reflects the extraordinary opportunities America afforded the young and energetic.

To my good friend Mrs. Boddicot
Dear Madam,

I flatter myself it will be a satisfaction to you to hear I like this part of the world, as my lott has fallen here—which I really do. I prefer England to it, 'tis true, but think Carolina greatly preferable to the West Indias, and was my Papa here I should be very happy.

We have a very good acquaintance from whom we have received much friendship and civility. Charles Town, the principal one in this province, is a polite, agreeable place. The people live very gentile and very much in the English taste. The country is in general fertile and abounds with venison and wild fowl; the venison is much higher flavoured than in England but 'tis seldom fatt.

My Papa and Mama's great indulgence to me leaves it to me to choose our place of residence either in town or country, but I think it more prudent as well as most agreeable to my Mama and self to be in the country during my Father's absence. We are 17 miles by land and 6 by water from Charles town—where we have about 6 agreeable families around us with whom we live in great harmony.

I have a little library well furnished (for my papa has left me most of his books) in which I spend part of my time. My musick and the garden, which I am very fond of, take up the rest of my that is not imployed in business, of which my father has

left me a pretty good share—and indeed, 'twas inavoidable as my Mama's bad state of health prevents her going through any fatigue.

I have the business of 3 plantations to transact, which requires much writing and more business and fatigue of other sorts than you can imagine. But least you should imagine it too burthensom to a girl at my early time of life, give me leave to answer you: I assure you I think myself happy that I can be useful to so good a father, and by rising very early I find I can go through much business. But least you should think I shall be quite moaped with this way of life I am to inform you there is two worthy ladies in Charles town, Mrs. Pickney and Mrs. Cleland, who are partial enough to me to be always pleased to have me with them, and insist upon my making their houses my home when in town and press me to relax a little much oftener than 'tis in my honor to accept of their obliging intreaties. But I some times am with one or the other for 3 weeks or a month at a time, and then enjoy all the pleasures Charles Town affords, but nothing gives me more than subscribing my self.

Your most affectionet and most obliged Servt.

❧ Prohibiting education to slaves

SOUTH CAROLINA

South Carolina was the first colony to make it illegal to teach slaves to write. This law was passed in 1740.

And whereas, the having of slaves taught to write, or suffering them to be employed in writing, may be attended with great inconveniences; Be it therefore enacted...that all and every person and persons whatsoever, who shall hereafter teach, or cause any slave or slaves to be taught, to write, or shall use or employ any slave as a scribe in any manner of writing whatsoever, hereafter taught to write, every such person and persons, shall, for every such offence, forfeit the sum of one hundred pounds current money.

"A new refinement in cruelty"

OLAUDAH ESQUIANO

Olaudah Esquiano was a black slave who learned how to write. As a ten-year-old child, he was captured in Nigeria and sold to English slave traders who carried him to America in 1755. He worked on a Virginia plantation and was subsequently sold to a British naval officer who brought him to London. In 1766, he repurchased his freedom.

Equiano wrote about his experiences as a slave in his autobiography. This account describes the bewilderment of being kidnapped and the horrific conditions of the sea passage to America.

The first object which saluted my eyes when I arrived on the coast was the sea, and a slave-ship, which was then riding at anchor, and waiting for its cargo. These filled me with astonishment, which was soon converted into terror, which I am yet at a loss to describe, nor the then feelings of my mind. When I was carried on board I was immediately handled, and tossed up, to see if I were sound, by some of the crew; and I was now persuaded that I had gotten into a world of bad spirits, and that they were going to kill me. Their complexions too differing so much from ours, their long hair, and the language they spoke, which was very different from any I had ever heard, united to confirm me in this belief. Indeed, such were the horrors of my views and fears at the moment, that, if ten thousand worlds had been my own, I would have freely parted with them all to have exchanged my condition with that of the meanest slave in my own country.

When I looked round the ship too, and saw a large furnace of copper boiling, and a multitude of black people of every description chained together, every one of their countenances expressing dejection and sorrow, I no longer doubted of my fate, and, quite overpowered with horror and anguish, I fell motionless on the deck and fainted. When I recovered a little, I found some black people about me, who I believed were some of those who brought me on board, and had been receiving their pay; they talked to me in order to cheer me, but all in vain. I asked them if we were not to be eaten by those white men with horrible looks, red faces and long hair? They told me I was not; and one of the crew brought me a small portion of spirituous liquor in a wine glass; but, being afraid of him, I would not take

it out of his hand. One of the blacks therefore took it from him and gave it to me, and I took a little down my palate, which, instead of reviving me, as they thought it would, threw me into the greatest consternation at the strange feeling it produced, having never tasted any such liquor before.

Soon after this, the blacks who brought me on board went off, and left me abandoned to despair. I now saw myself deprived of all chance or returning to my native country, or even the least glimpse of hope of gaining the shore, which I now considered as friendly: and I even wished from my former slavery in preference to my present situation, which was filled with horrors of every kind, still heightened by my ignorance of what I was to undergo. I was not long suffered to indulge my grief; I was soon put down under the decks, and there I received such a salutation in my nostrils as I had never experienced in my life; so that with the loathsomeness of the stench, and crying together, I became so sick and low that I was not able to eat, nor had I the least desire to taste any thing. I now wished for the last friend, Death, to relieve me; but soon, to my grief, two of the white men ordered me eatables; and, on my refusing to eat, one of them held me fast by the hands, and laid me across, I think, the windlass, and tied my feet, while the other flogged me severely.

I had never experienced anything of this kind before; and although, not being used to the water, I naturally feared that element the first time I saw it; yet, nevertheless, could I have got over the nettings, I would have jumped over the side, but I could not; and, besides, the crew used to watch us very closely who were not chained down to the decks, lest we should leap into the water; and I have seen some of these poor African prisoners most severely cut for attempting to do so, and hourly whipped for not eating. This indeed was often the case with myself. In a little time after, amongst the poor chained men, I found some of my own nation, which in a small degree gave ease to my mind. I inquired of these what was to be done with us? They gave me to understand we were to be carried to these white people's country to work for them. I then was a little revived, and thought, if it were no worse than working, my situation was not so desperate: but still I feared I should be put to death, the white people looked and acted, as I thought, in so savage a manner; for

I had never seen among any people such instances of brutal cruelty; and this not only shewn towards us blacks, but also to some of the whites themselves.

One white man in particular I saw, when we were permitted to be on deck, flogged so unmercifully with a large rope near the foremast, that he died in consequence of it; and they tossed him over the side as they would have done a brute. This made me fear these people the more; and I expected nothing less than to be treated in the same manner. I could not help expressing my fears and apprehensions to some of my countrymen: I asked them if these people had no country, but lived in this hollow place the ship? They told me they did not, but came from a distant one. "Then," said I, "how comes it in all our country we never heard of them?" They told me, because they lived so very far off. I then asked where were their women? Had they any like themselves! I was told they had: "And why," said I, "do we not see them?" they answered, because they were left behind. I asked how the vessel could go? They told me they could not tell; but that there were cloths put upon the masts by the help of the ropes I saw, and then the vessel went on; and the white men had some spell or magic they put in the water they liked in order to stop the vessel. I was exceedingly amazed at this account, and really thought they were spirits. I therefore wished much to be from amongst them, for I expected they would sacrifice me: but my wishes were in vain; for we were so quartered that it was impossible for any of us to make our escape.

While we staid on the coast I was mostly on deck; and one day, to my great astonishment, I saw one of these vessels coming in with the sails up. As soon as the whites saw it, they gave a great shout, at which we were amazed; and the more so as the vessel appeared larger by approaching nearer. At last she came to an anchor in my sight, and when the anchor was let go, I and my countrymen who saw it were lost in astonishment to observe the vessel stop; and were now convinced it was done by magic. Soon after this the other ship got her boats out, and they came on board of us, and the people of both ships seemed very glad to see each other. Several of the strangers also shook hands with us black people, and made motions with their hands, signifying, I suppose, we were to go to their country; but we did not understand them.

At last, when the ship we were in had got in all her cargo, they made ready with many fearful noises, and we were all put under deck, so that we could not see how they managed the vessel. But this disappointment was the least of my sorrow. The stench of the hold while we were on the coast was so intolerably loathsome, that it was dangerous to remain there for any time, and some of us had been permitted to stay on deck for the fresh air; but now that the whole ship's cargo were confined together, it became absolutely pestilential. The closeness of the place, and the heat of the climate, added to the number in the ship, which was so crowded that each had scarcely room to turn himself, almost suffocated us. This produced copious perspirations, so that the air became unfit for respiration, from a variety of loathsome smells, and brought on a sickness among the slaves, of which many died, thus falling victims to the improvident avarice, as I may call it, of their purchasers. This wretched situation was again aggravated by the galling chains, now become insupportable; and the filth of the necessary tubs, into which children often fell, and were almost suffocated. The shrieks of the women, and the groans of the dying, rendered the whole a scene of horror almost inconceivable.

Happily perhaps for myself I was soon reduced so low here that it was thought necessary to keep me almost always on deck; and from my extreme youth I was not put in fetters. In this situation I expected every hour to share the fate of my companions, some of whom were almost daily brought upon deck at the point of death, which I began to hope would soon put an end to my miseries. Often did I think many of the inhabitants of the deep much more happy than myself; I envied them the freedom they enjoyed, and as often wished I could change my condition for theirs. Every circumstance I met with served only to render my state more painful, and heighten my apprehensions, and my opinion of the cruelty of the whites. One day they had taken a number of fishes; and when they had killed and satisfied themselves with as many as they thought fit, to our astonishment who were on the deck, rather than give any of them to us to eat, as we expected, they tossed the remaining fish into the sea again, although we begged and prayed for some as well as we could, but in vain; and some of my countrymen, being pressed by hunger, took an opportunity, when they thought no one saw them, of trying to get a little privately; but they were discovered, and the attempt procured them some very severe floggings.

One day, when we had a smooth sea and moderate wind, two of my wearied countrymen, who were chained together (I was near them at the time), preferring death to such a life of misery, somehow made through the nettings and jumped into the sea: immediately another quite dejected fellow, who, on account of his illness, was suffered to be out of irons, also followed their example; and I believe many more would very soon have done the same, if they had not been prevented by the ship's crew, who were instantly alarmed. Those of us that were the most active were, in a moment, put down under the deck; and there was such a noise and confusion amongst the people of the ship as I never heard before, to stop her, and get the boat out to go after the slaves. However, two of the wretches were drowned, but they got the other, and afterwards flogged him unmercifully, for thus attempting to prefer death to slavery.

In this manner we continued to undergo more hardships than I can now relate; hardships which are inseparable from this accursed trade. Many a time we were near suffocation, from the want of fresh air, which we were often without for whole days together. This, and the stench of the necessary tubs, carried off many. During our passage I first saw flying fishes, which surprised me very much: they used frequently to fly across the ship, and many of them fell on the deck. I also now first saw the use of the quadrant. I had often with astonishment seen the mariners make observations with it, and I could not think what it meant. They at last took notice of my surprise; and one of them, willing to increase it, as well as to gratify my curiosity, made me one day look through it. The clouds appeared to me to be land, which disappeared as they passed along. This heightened my wonder: and I was no more persuaded than ever that I was in another world, and that every thing about me was magic.

At last we came in sight of the island of Barbados, at which the whites on board gave a great shout, and made many signs of joy to us. We did not know what to think of this; but as the vessel drew nearer we plainly saw the harbour, and other ships of different kinds and sizes: and we soon anchored amongst them off Bridge Town. Many

merchants and planters now came on board, though it was in the evening. They put us in separate parcels, and examined us attentively. They also made us jump, and pointed to the land, signifying we were to go there. We thought by this we should be eaten by these ugly men, as they appeared to us; and, when soon after we were all put down under the deck again, there was much dread and trembling among us, and nothing but bitter cries to be heard all the night from these apprehensions, insomuch that at last the white people got some old slaves from the land to pacify us. They told us we were not to be eaten, but to work, and were soon to go on land, where we should see many of our country people. This report eased us much; and sure enough, soon after we were landed, there came to us Africans of all languages.

We were conducted immediately to the merchant's yard, where we were all pent up together like so many sheep in a fold, without regard to sex or age. As every object was new to me, every thing I saw filled me with surprise. What struck me first was, that the houses were built with bricks, in stories, and in every other respect different from those I have seen in Africa: but I was still more astonished on seeing people on horseback. I did not know what this could mean; and indeed I though these people were full of nothing but magical arts....

We were not many days in the merchant's custody before we were sold after their usual manner, which is this: On a signal given (as the beat of a drum), the buyers rush at once into the yard where the slaves are confined, and make choice of that parcel they like best. The noise and clamour with which this is attended, and the eagerness visible in the countenances of the buyers, serve not a little to increase the apprehensions of the terrified Africans, who may well be supposed to consider them as the ministers of that destruction to which they think themselves devoted. In this manner, without scruple, are relations and friends separated, most of them never to see each other again. I remember in the vessel in which I was brought over, in the men's apartment, there were several brothers, who, in the sale, were sold in different lots; and it was very moving on this occasion to see and hear their cries at parting. O, ye nominal Christians! Might not an African ask you, learned you this from your God? Who says to you, Do unto all men as you would men should do unto you? Is it not enough that we are torn from our country and friends to toil for your luxury and lust of gain? Must every tender feeling be likewise sacrificed to your avarice? Are the dearest friends and relations, now rendered more dear by their separation from their kindred, still to be parted from each other, and thus prevented from cheering the gloom of slavery with the small comfort of being together and mingling their sufferings and sorrows? Why are parents to lose their children, brothers their sisters, or husbands their wives? Surely this is a new refinement in cruelty, which, while it has no advantages to atone for it, thus aggravates distress, and adds fresh horrors even to the wretchedness of slavery.

❧ *"Punishing their secret plots"*

VIRGINIA ASSEMBLY

More than two million African slaves were imported to the British American colonies and the West Indies in the pre-Revolutionary era. Not surprisingly, the brutality of their condition sparked isolated slave revolts. There were at least 30 slave ship revolts in the 18th century. In 1739, a group of Angolan slaves attacked an armory in Stono, South Carolina, killing 30 whites. This was followed by two other revolts. In New York City, thirty African-Americans were executed for arson.

Whites greatly feared the revolts and enacted legislation to squash it. This 1748 act by the Virginia Assembly was typical. It makes the "consulting, plotting, or conspiring" of insurrection punishable by death for all slaves and free blacks.

I. Whereas it is absolutely necessary that effectual Provision should be made for the better ordering and governing of Slaves, free Negroes, Mulattoes, and Indians, and detecting and punishing their secret Plots and dangerous Combinations, and for the speedy Trial of such of them as commit capital Crimes:

II. Be it therefore enacted, by the Lieutenant Governor, Council, and Burgesses of this present General Assembly, and it is hereby enacted, by the Authority of the same, that if any Negro, or other Slaves, shall at any Time consult, advise or conspire to rebel to make Insurrection, or shall plot or con-spire the Murder of any Person or Persons whatsoever, every such consulting, plotting, or conspiring, shall be ajudged and deemed Felony, and the Slave or Slaves convicted thereof, in Manner herein after directed, shall suffer Death, and be utterly excluded all Benefit of Clergy.

III. And whereas many Negroes, under Pretence of practicing Physick, have prepared and exhibited poisonous medicines, by which many Persons have been murdered, and others have languished under long and tedious Indispositions, and it will be difficult to detect such pernicious and dangerous Practices if they should be permitted to exhibit any Sort of Medicine, Be it therefore further enacted, that if any Negro or other Slave, shall prepare, exhibit, or administer, any Medicine whatsoever, he or she so offending shall be judged guilty of Felony, and suffer Death without Benefit of Clergy.

IV. Provided always, that if it shall appear to the Court, before which such Slave shall be tried, that the Medicine was not prepared, exhibited, or administered, with an ill Intent, not attended with any bad Consequences, such Slave shall have the Benefit of Clergy.

V. Provided also, that nothing herein contained shall be construed to extend to any Slave or Slaves administering Medicines by his or her Master's or Mistress's Order, in his or her Family, or the Family of another, with the mutual Consent of the Owner of such Slave, and the Master or Mistress of such Family.

VI. And be it further enacted, by the Authority aforesaid, that every Slave committing such Offence as by Laws is punishable with Death, or Loss of Member, shall be forthwith committed to the common Gaol of the County wherein such Offence shall be done, there to be safely kept, and upon such Commitment the Sheriff of such County shall certify the same, with the Cause thereof, to the Governour or Commander in Chief of this Dominion for the Time being, who is thereupon desired and empowered to issue a Commission of Oyer and Terminer to such Persons as he shall think fit, which persons, forthwith after Receipt of such Commission, are empowered and required to cause the Offender to be publickly arraigned and tried at the Courthouse of the said County, and to take for Evidence the Concession of the Offender, the Oath of one or more credible Witnesses, or such Testimony of Negroes, Mulattoes, or Indians, bond or free, with pregnant Circumstances, as to them shall seem convincing, without the Solemnity of a Jury; and the Offender being by them found guilty, to pass such Judgment upon such Offender as the Law directs for the like Crimes, and on such Judgment to award Execution.

VII. Provided always, that if at such Trial the Court be divided in Opinion whether the accused be guilty or not guilty, in that Case he, she, or they, shall be acquitted: Provided also, that when Judgment of Death shall be passed upon any such Offender there shall be ten Days at least between the time of passing Judgment and the Day of Execution, except in Cases of Conspiracy, Insurrection, or Rebellion.

❧ "Rulers have no authority from God to do mischief"

JONATHAN MAYHEW

As minister of Boston's West Church, Jonathan Mayhew advocated the theories of the British philosopher John Locke. Loyal to England, he nevertheless questioned the divine rights of a king. Secular authority, he believed, was derived from the people.

Speaking in 1750 on the anniversary of the death of Charles I, Mayhew affirmed the right of people to overthrow a tyrannical government. He speaks here to the duty of individual citizens to preserve their rights in the face of despotic rulers. "It is universally better to obey God than Man when the laws of God and Man clash and interfere with one another," he said in an earlier sermon.

Although this sermon came more than a decade before relations between the colonies and England started to deteriorate in earnest, the principles he describes foretell the basis of the American Revolution.

Rulers have no authority from God to do mischief.... It is blasphemy to call tyrants and oppressors God's ministers. They are more properly "the messengers of Satan to buffet us." No rulers are properly God's ministers but such as are "just, ruling in the fear of God." When once magistrates act contrary to their office, and the end of their institution—when they rob and ruin the public, instead of being guardians of its peace and welfare—they immediately cease to be the ordinance and minis-

ters of God, and no more deserve that glorious character than common pirates and highwaymen.

If magistrates are unrighteous,... the main end of civil government will be frustrated. And what reason is there for submitting to that government which does by no means answer the design of government? "Wherefore ye must needs be subject not only for wrath, but also for conscience' sake." Here the apostle [Paul] argues the duty of a cheerful and conscientious submission to civil government from the nature and end of magistracy, as he had before laid it down; i.e., as the design of it was to punish evil-doers, and to support and encourage such as do well;...if the motive and argument for submission to government be taken from the apparent usefulness of civil authority—it follows, that when no such good end can be answered by submission, there remains no argument or motive to enforce it;...And therefore, in such cases, a regard to the public welfare ought to make us withhold from our rulers that obedience and submission which it would otherwise be our duty to render to them. If it be our duty, for example, to obey our king merely for this reason, that he rules for the public welfare (which is the only argument the apostle makes use of), it follows, by a parity of reason, that when he turns tyrant, and makes his subjects his prey to devour and destroy, instead of his charge to defend and cherish, we are bound to throw off our allegiance to him, and to resist; and that according to the tenor of the apostle's argument in this passage. Not to discontinue our allegiance in this case would be to join with the sovereign in promoting the slavery and misery of that society, the welfare of which we ourselves, as well as our sovereign, are indispensably obliged to secure and promote, as far as in us lies. It is true the apostle puts no case of such a tyrannical prince; but, by his grounding his argument for submission wholly upon the good of civil society, it is plain he implicitly authorizes, and even requires us to make resistance, whenever this shall be necessary to the public safety and happiness....

But, then, if unlimited submission and passive obedience to the higher powers, in all possible cases, be not a duty, it will be asked, "How far are we obliged to submit? If we may innocently disobey and resist in some cases, why not in all? Where shall we stop? What is the measure of our duty? This doctrine tends to the total dissolution of civil government, and to introduce such scenes of wild anarchy and confusion as are more fatal to society than the worst of tyranny."

But... similar difficulties may be raised with respect to almost every duty of natural and revealed religion. To instance only in two, both of which are near akin, and indeed exactly parallel to the case before us: It is unquestionably the duty of children to submit to their parents, and of servants to their masters; but no one asserts that it is their duty to obey and submit to them in all supposable cases, or universally a sin to resist them. Now, does this tend to subvert the just authority of parents and masters, or to introduce confusion and anarchy into private families? No. How, then, does the same principle tend to unhinge the government of that larger family the body politic?... Now, there is at least as much difficulty in stating the measure of duty in these two cases as in the case of rulers and subjects; so that this is really no objection—at least, no reasonable one-against resistance to the higher powers. Or, if it is one, it will hold equally against resistance in the other cases mentioned.

We may very safely assert these two things in general, without undermining government: One is, that no civil rulers are to be obeyed when they enjoin things that are inconsistent with the commands of God. All such disobedience is lawful and glorious;...All commands running counter to the declared will of the Supreme Legislator of heaven and earth null and void, and therefore disobedience to duty, not a crime. Another thing that may be asserted with equal truth and safety is, that no law is to be submitted to at the expense of; which is the sole end of all government—the good and safety of society....

Now, as all men are fallible, it cannot be supposed affairs of any state should be always in the best manner possible, even by greatest wisdom and integrity. Nor is it sufficient to legitimate disobedience to the higher powers that they are not so administered, or that they are in some instances very ill-managed; for, upon this principle, it is scarcely supposable that any government at all could be supported, or subsist. Such a principle manifestly tends to the dissolution of government, and to throw all things into confusion and anarchy. But it is equally evident, that those in authority may abuse their and power to such a degree, that

neither the law of reason nor of religion requires that any obedience or submission should be paid to them; but, on the contrary, that they should be totally discarded, the authority which they were before vested transferred to others, who may exercise it to those good purposes for which it is given. Nor is this principle, that resistance to the higher powers is in some extraordinary cases justifiable, so liable to abuse as many persons seem to apprehend it.... Mankind in general have a disposition to be as submissive and passive and tame under government as they ought to be.... While those who govern do it with any tolerable degree of moderation and justice, and in any good measure act up to their office and character by being public benefactors, the people will generally be easy and peaceable, and be rather inclined to flatter and adore than to insult and resist them.... [P]eople know for what end they set up and maintain their governors, and they are the proper judges when they execute their trust as they ought to do it.... Till people find themselves greatly abused and oppressed by their governors, they are not apt to complain; and whenever they do, in fact, find themselves thus abused and oppressed, they must be stupid not to complain. To say that subjects in general are not proper judges when their governors oppress them and play the tyrant, and when they defend their rights, administer justice impartially, and promote the public welfare, is as great treason as ever man uttered. 'T is treason, not against one single man, but the state-against the whole body politic; 't is treason against mankind, 't is treason against common sense, 't is treason against God....

🌺 "I cannot say it without tears"

FRAY CARLOS JOSE DELGADO

By the 1700s, the Spanish had established a significant presence in what is now New Mexico. Spain's interest in the New World had always been two-fold: mercantile and religious. In addition to wanting to make money, the Catholic nation also sought to save souls by converting Native Americans to Christianity.

Conflicts, however, often emerged over these two goals. In this 1750 letter, the priest Fray Carlos Jose Delgado describes the brutal treatment of Native Americans in New Mexico by civil authorities.

Very Reverend Father and our Minister Provincial: I, Fray Carlos Jose Delgado, preacher general, commissary, notary and censor of the Holy Office, apostolic notary, and missionary in the custodian of the conversion of San Pablo of this province of El Santo Evangelio in the kingdom of New Mexico, appear before your reverence only for the purpose of lamenting before your paternal love the grave extortions that we, the ministers of these missions, are suffering, at the hands of the governors and *alcaldes* of that kingdom. I declare, that of the eleven governors and many *alcaldes mayores* whom I have known in the long period of forty years that I have served at the mission called San Augustin de la Isleta, most of them have hated, and do hate to the death, and insult and persecute the missionary religious, causing them all the troubles and annoyances that their passion dictates, without any other reason or fault than the opposition of the religious to the very serious injustices which the said governors and alcaldes inflict upon the helpless Indians recently received into the faith, so that the said converts shall not forsake our holy law and flee to the heathen, to take up anew their former idolatries. This is experienced every day, not without grave sorrow and heartfelt tears on the part of those evangelical sowers, who, on seeing that their work is wasted and that the fecund seed of their preaching to those souls is lost and bears no fruit, cry out to heaven and sorrowfully ask a remedy for this great evil. In order that your reverence's exalted understanding may regard as just the reasons which support the said missionaries in their opposition to the aforesaid extortions, even though it should be at the cost of their lives, and also in order that you may come to their aid with the measures best fitted for the total abolition of the said injuries' and injustices, I shall specify them in the following manner:

The first annoyance with which the persons mentioned molest the Indians is to send agents every year (contrary to the royal ordinances, and especially to a decree of the most excellent senior, Don Francisco Fernandez de la Cueva Henriquez, Duke of Albuquerque, and viceroy of New Spain, issued in this City of Mexico on May 18, 1709, whose content I present, the original being kept in the archive of the *custodia* mentioned) at the time of the harvest, to all the pueblos of the kingdom, under the pretext of buying maize for the support of their households, though most of it is really to be sold in the nearest villages. The said agents take from all the pueblos and missions eight hundred or a thousand fanegas, and compel the Indians to transport them to the place where the governor lives. Besides not paying them anything for the said transportation, they do not pay them for the maize at once, and when the date arrives which they have designated for the payment, if the maize is worth two pesos a fanega they give them only one. Even this amount is not in coin or in any article that can be useful to the Indians, but in baubles, such as *chuchumater*, which are glass beads, ill-made knives, relics, awls, and a few handfuls of common tobacco, the value of which does not amount even to a tenth part of what the maize is worth which they extract from them by force, and this even though as has been said, they pay them only half the proper price that is charged throughout the kingdom. From this manifest injustice two very serious evils result: first, the unhappy Indians are left without anything to eat for the greater part of the year; and second, in order not to perish of hunger they are forced to go to the mountains and hunt for game or to serve on the ranches or farms for their food alone, leaving the missions abandoned.

The second oppression that the Indians frequently suffer at the hands of the governors is being compelled arbitrarily and by force, for the small price of an awl or other similar trifle, to work on the buildings that they need, whatever they may be and whether they require little or much time. The Indians also are required to drive cattle as far as the villa of Chihuahua which is more than two hundred leagues distant from the place where the governors live. They receive in payment for this service only a little ground corn, which they call *pinole*, and the Indian cattle drivers are compelled to pay for those [animals] that are lost or die for want of care or by any other accident. A pernicious evil arises from this cattle driving, for the Indians must abandon their families and leave their lands uncultivated, and, as a consequence, be dying of hunger during the greater part of the year.

The third oppression, and the most grievous and pernicious, from which originate innumerable evils and sins against God, and manifest injuries against the missionaries and Indians, is the wicked dissimulation of the governors in regard to the acts of the *alcaldes mayores*, for it is publicly known throughout the realm that when they give them their *varas*, or wands of office, they tell and advise them to make the Indians work without pity.

With such express license, your reverence can imagine how many disturbances will be caused by men who usually take the employment of alcaldes mayore, solely for the purpose of advancing their own interests and acquiring property with which to make presents to the governors, so that the latter will countenance their unjust proceedings, even though they be denounced before them, and perhaps will even promote them in office. Every year they make the Indians weave four hundred blankets, or as many woolen sheets; they take from all the pueblos squads of thirty or forty Indians and work them the greater part of the year in planting maize and wheat, which they care for until it is placed in the granaries; they send them among the heathen Indians to trade indigo, knives, tobacco, and *chuchumates,* for cattle and for deer hides. Not even the women are exempt from this tyranny, for if the officials cannot make use of their work in any other way they compel them to spin almost all the wool needed for the said sheets and blankets. And the most lamentable thing about all this is that they recompense them for these tasks with only a handful of tobacco, which is divided among eighteen or twenty.

The most grievous thing for the heathen Indians is that the alcaldes and even some of the governors, mix with their wives and daughters, often violating them, and this so openly that with a very little effort the violation of their consorts comes to the knowledge of the husbands, and as a result it often happens that they repudiate their wives and will not receive them until the missionary fathers labor to persuade them. The shameless way in which the officials conduct themselves in this particular is proved by an occasion when a certain governor was in conversation with some missionaries, and an Indian woman came into their presence to charge him with the rape of her daughter, and he, without changing countenance, ordered that she should be paid by merely giving her a buffalo skin that he had at hand.

Yet all that I have hitherto related does not drive the Indians to the limits of desperation or cause them to fall away from our holy faith so much as when the said alcaldes compel them to deliver to them a quantity of deer skins, lard, sheaves [of grain], chickens, and other things that their desires dictate, saying that they are for the governors, who ask for them. The Indian has to submit to this injustice, for they either take it from him without asking, or, if he does not have what the alcaldes ask for or does not give it promptly enough when he has it, he suffers either spoliation or punishment.

These punishments are so cruel and inhuman that sometimes for a slight offence, sometimes because the Indian resists the outrages that they inflict upon him, or sometimes because they are slow in doing what the alcaldes order, they are put in jail for many days, are confined in the stocks, or—and I cannot say it without tears—the officials flog them so pitilessly that, their wrath not being appeased by seeing them shed their blood, they inflict such deep scars upon them that they remain for many years. It is a proof of this second point that when I went among the heathens to reduce the apostates there were among them some who, with an aggrieved air, showed me their scars, thus giving me to understand that the reason why they fled and did not return to the pale of the church was their fear of these cruel punishments.

A further distressing proof of this practice is what was done in the past year at El Paso by a captain to a Catholic Indian of the Zuma nation, sacristan of the mission of El Real. A servant of the captain of El Paso had hidden three ears of corn which he had stolen from his master. The sacristan took them from him, and, without any more proof or reason than having found him with them in his hands, and because the said servant, to escape punishment, said that the innocent Indian often stole corn from the granaries, the said captain became so angered that, in violation of all natural and divine laws, he ordered six soldiers to take the Indian out and kill him in the fields.

They carried out the order, and when the unfortunate Zuma cried aloud for confession they did not yield to his entreaties, but gave him a violent death, perhaps being fearful that the missionary religious, whose duty it was to administer the holy sacrament to him, would prevent the execution of that unjust order, even though it might be at the cost of his life.

The outrage did not stop here, for when the Zuma Indians of the mission of El Real learned of the death of their countryman, they began to rise up, all crying out: "Why, since we are Christians, do they not permit us to confess at the hour of death? Let us flee to the mountains!" They did not flee, our father, either because the soldiers restrained them or because the fathers appealed to them. A still greater injury, however, arose from the remedy, for the governor having ordered a large troop of Zumas of both sexes to come to this city, simply because an Indian woman and two men were not able to travel as fast as the others, having crippled feet, the corporal who was leading them ordered them to be beheaded at a place called El Gallego, where he left the bodies unburied, to the intense grief of their companions and relatives, whose sorrow was not lessened on seeing that the said corporal and the rest of the escort robbed them of their little children in order to sell them as slaves in various places along the road.

Nor is it only the said *alcaldes* and governors that ill-treat the Indians in the manner described, but even the judges who enter to conduct the residencias of the *alcaldes* and governors who have completed their terms of offices, inflict upon the Indians as much injury and hardship as may conduce to the advancement of their own interests and the success of their ambitious desires. It is public knowledge throughout the kingdom that such persons seek to conduct these residencias more for what they gain by unjust and violent spoliation of the Indians than for what they receive from the office that they exercise.

Finally, to such an extreme do the iniquities reach that are practiced against the Indians by governors and alcaldes mayores, as well as by the judges of residencia, that, losing patience and possessed by fear, they turn their backs to our holy mother, the Church, abandon their pueblos and missions, and flee to the heathen, there to worship the devil, and, most lamentable of all, to confirm in idolatries those who have never been illumined by the light of our holy faith, so that they will never give ear or credit to the preaching of the gospel. Because of all this, every day new conversions become more difficult, and the zealous missionaries who in the service of both Majesties are anxiously seeking the propagation of the gospel, most often see their work wasted and do [not] accomplish the purpose of their extended wanderings.

Although it cannot be denied that those barbarous nations are stiffnecked, yet there have been many instances where thousands of them have entered joyfully through the requisite door of the holy sacrament of baptism, and most of the apostates would return to the bosom of the Church if they did not fear, with such good reason, the punishments and extortions that I have already spoken of. They have told me this on most of the occasions when I have entered in fulfillment of my obligation to reduce apostates and convert the heathen. In the year 1742, when, at the cost of indescribable labor and hardships, I reduced four hundred and forty odd among apostates and heathen in the province of Moqui, innumerable souls would have come to the bosom of our holy Church had they not been deterred by the reason that I have stated.

Although the missionary religious ought to oppose themselves to these grave injuries and their pernicious consequences, they often do not do it; first, because they never succeed in attaining their purpose, but on the contrary are insulted, disrespected, and held to be disturbers of the peace; second, because the governors and alcaldes impute and charge them with crimes that they have never committed, which they proceed to prove with false witnesses whom they have suborned before the father custodian, and compel the latter to proceed against the religious whom they calumnate. And although the said custodians know very well that the denunciations are born of hatred, they proceed against the missionaries, changing them from one mission to another, in order to prevent the said governors from committing the excess of using their power to expel the missionaries from the kingdom, as has often happened; and also because, when the custodians do not agree to what the governors ask, the latter refuse to certify the allowance for the administration of the religious, which certification is necessary in order that the most excellent senior viceroy may issue the honorariums that his Majesty (whom may God preserve) assigns for the maintenance of the missionary religious. It has seemed to me that all that I have said ought to be presented before the charitable zeal of your reverence, so that, having it before you as father of those faithful sons, your apostolic missionaries, you may put into execution the means that your discretion may decide upon, with the purpose of ending this great abuse, of redeeming all those helpless people, and consoling your sorrowing sons. It is indisputable that whatever I have said is public, notorious, certain and true, as I swear in *verbo sacerclotis tacto pectore*, at this hospice of Santa Barbara of the pueblo of Tlatelolco, 4 of March 27, 1750. Our very reverend father, your humblest subject, Fray CARLOS

JOSE DELGADO, who venerates you, places himself at your feet.

🍂 *Plan of Union*

BENJAMIN FRANKLIN

When the French and Indian War broke out in 1754, delegates from seven colonies met in Albany, New York, to forge a defensive alliance. Sparked by the idea of colonial unity, Benjamin Franklin drew up a "Plan of Union" to establish a more permanent self-governing relationship, still subject to England's rule.

Observing that "Six Nations of ignorant savages" were able to form a union, Franklin reasoned that the colonies could do likewise. Although the Albany Congress voted in favor of the proposal, the colonial legislatures and the English government rejected the proposal, which threatened their respective authorities. Nevertheless, the idea of a union between colonies was actively discussed among the leadership class for the first time.

It is proposed that humble application be made for an act of parliament of Great Britain, by virtue of which one general government may be formed in America, including all the said colonies, within and under which government each colony may retain its present constitution, except in the particulars wherein a change may be directed by the said act, as hereafter follows.

1. That the said general government be administered by a President-general, to be appointed and supported by the crown; and a Grand Council, to be chosen by the representatives of the people of the several Colonies met in their respective assemblies.
2. That within__months after the passing such act, the House of Representatives that happens to be sitting within that time, or that shall be especially for that purpose convened, may and shall chose members for the Grand Council, in the following proportion, that is to say,

Massachusetts Bay	7
New Hampshire	2
Connecticut	5
Rhode Island	2
New York	4
New Jersey	3
Pennsylvania	6
Maryland	4
Virginia	7
North Carolina	4
South Carolina	4
	48

That after the first three years, when the proportion of money arising out of each Colony to the general treasury can be known, the number of members to be chosen for each Colony shall, from time to time, in all ensuing elections, be regulated by that proportion, yet so as that the number to be chosen by any one Province be not more than seven, nor less than two.

That the Grand Council shall meet once in every year, and oftener if occasion require, at such time and place as they shall adjourn to at the last preceding meeting, or as they shall be called to meet at by the president-General on any emergency; he having first obtained in writing the consent of seven of the members to such call, and sent duly and timely notice to the whole.

That the President-General, with the advice of the Grand council, hold or direct all Indian treaties, in which the general interest of the Colonies may be concerned; and make peace or declare war with Indian nations.

That they make such laws as they judge necessary for regulating all Indian trade.

That they make all purchases from Indians, for the crown, of lands not now within the bounds of particular Colonies, or that shall not be within their bounds when some of them are reduced to more convenient dimensions.

That they raise and pay soldiers and build forts for the defence of any of the Colonies, and equip vessels of force to guard the coasts and protect the trade on the ocean, lakes, or great rivers; but they shall not impress men in any Colony, without the consent of the Legislature.

That for these purposes they have power to make laws, and lay and levy such general duties, imposts, or taxes, as to them shall appear most equal and just (considering the ability and other circumstances of the inhabitants in the several Colonies), and such as may be collected with the least inconvenience to the people; rather discouraging luxury, than loading industry with unnecessary burdens.

That the general accounts shall be yearly set-tled and reported to the several Assemblies.

That the laws shall not be repugnant, but, as near as may be, agreeable to the laws of England and shall be transmitted to the King in council for approbation, as soon as may be after their passing; and if not disapproved within three years after pre-sentation, to remain in force.

That the particular military as well as civil establishments in each Colony remain in their pre-sent state, the general constitution notwithstand-ing; and that on sudden emergencies any Colony may defend itself, and lay the accounts of expense thence arising before the President-General and General Council, who may allow and order pay-ment of the same, as far as they judge such accounts just and reasonable.

"Sorrow was again my lot"

ELIZABETH ASHBRIDGE

Thrice married over the course of her life, Elizabeth Ashbridge was raised in England as an Anglican and first wed at the age of fourteen. Widowed within five years, she sailed to America at the age of twenty to become an indentured ser-vant. She married a man named Sullivan to get away from her master. The following excerpt from her autobiography describes that marriage, which coincided with her shift to the Quaker religion.

Sullivan—like many colonists—objected to Quakers and abused his wife over her conversion and other matters. Elizabeth's description, which was written with help from her third husband, Aaron Ashbridge, many years later, provides a compelling description of the status of Quakers and gender relations in colonial America.

When meeting-time came, I longed to go, but dared not to ask my husband's leave. As the Friends were getting ready themselves, they asked him if he would accompany them, observing, that they know those who were to be his employers, and, if they were at meeting, would speak to them. He consent-ed. The woman Friend then said. "And wilt thou let thy wife go too;" which request he denied; but she answered his objections so prudently that he could not be angry, and at last consented. I went with joy, and a heavenly meeting it was. My spirit did rejoice in the God of my salvation. May I ever, in humility, preserve the remembrance of his tender mercies to me.

By the end of the week, we got settled in our new situation. We took a room, in a friend's house, one mile from each school, and eight from the meeting-house. I now deemed it proper to let my husband see I was determined to join with friends. When first day came, I directed myself to him in this manner: "My dear, art thou willing to let me go to meeting?" He flew into a rage, and replied "No you shan't." Speaking firmly, I told him, "That, as a dutiful wife, I was ready to obey all his lawful com-mands; but, when they imposed upon my con-science, I could not obey him. I had already wronged myself, in having done it too long; and though he was near to me, and, as a wife ought, I loved him, yet God, who was nearer than all the world to me, had made me sensible that this was the way in which I ought to go. I added, that this was no small cross to my own will; but I had given up my heart, and I trusted that He who called for it would enable me, for the remainder of my life, to keep it steadily devoted to his service; and I hoped I should not, on this account, make the worse wife." I spoke, however, to no purpose; he contin-ued inflexible.

I had now put my hand to the plough, and resolved not to draw back; I therefore went without leave. I expected he would immediately follow and force me back, but he did not. I called at the house of one of the neighbours, and getting a girl to show me the way, I went on rejoicing, and praising God in my heart.

Thus, for some time, I had to go eight miles on foot to meeting, which I never thought hard. My husband had a horse, but he would not suffer me to ride on it; nor when my shoes were worn out, would he let me have a new pair; but, though he hoped, on this account, to keep me from meeting, it did not hinder me: I have tied them round with strings to keep them on.

Finding that all the means he had yet used could not alter my resolutions, he several times struck me with severe blows. I endeavoured to bear all with patience, believing that the time would come when he would see I was in the right. Once he came up to me, took out his penknife, and said, "If you could to go to meeting tomorrow, with this knife I'll cripple you, for you shall not be a Quaker." I made him no answer. In the morning, I set out as usual; he did not attempt to harm me. Having despaired of recovering me himself, he fled, for help, to the priest, whom he told, that I had been a very religious woman, in the way of the Church of England, of which I was a member, and had a good certificate from Long Island; that I was now bewitched, and had turned Quaker, which almost broke his heart; and, therefore, he desired that, as he was one who had the care of souls, he would come and pay me a visit, and use his endeavours to reclaim me, which he hoped, by the blessing of God, would be done. The priest consented, and fixed the time for his coming, which was that day two weeks, as he said he could not come sooner. My husband came home extremely pleased, and told me of it. I replied, with a smile, I trusted I should be enabled to give a reason for the hope within me; yet I believed, at the same time, that the priest would never trouble himself about me, which proved to be the case. Before the day he appointed came, it was required of me, in a more public manner, to confess to the world what I was. I felt myself called to up to prayer in meeting. I trembled, and would freely have given up my life to be excused. What rendered the required service harder on me was, that I was not yet taken under the care of friends; and was kept from requesting to be so, for fear I should bring a scandal on the society. I begged to be excused till I had joined, and then I would give up freely. The answer was, "I am a covenant-keeping God, and the word that I spake to thee, when I found thee in distress, even that I would never forsake thee, if thou wouldst be obedient to what I should make known unto thee, I will assuredly make good. If thou refusest, my spirit shall not always strive. Fear not, I will make way for thee through all thy difficulties, which shall be many, for my name's sake; but, be faithful, and I will give thee a crown of life." To this language I answered "thy will, O God, be done; I am in thy hand, do with me according to thy word;" and I then prayed.

This day, as usual, I had gone to meeting on foot. While my husband (as he afterwards told me) was lying on the bed, these words crossed his mind: "Lord, where shall I fly to shun thee," &c. upon which he arose, and, seeing it rain, got the horse and set off to fetch me, arriving just as the meeting broke up. I got on horseback as quickly as possible, lest he should hear I had been speaking; he did hear of it nevertheless, and, as soon as we were in

the woods, began with saying, "Why do you mean thus to make my life unhappy? What, could you not be a Quaker, without turning fool in this manner?" I answered in tears, "My dear, look on me with pity, if thou hast any; canst thou think that I, in the bloom of my days, would bear all that thou knowest of, and much that thou knowest not of, if I did not feel it my duty." These words touched him, and, he said, "Well, I'll e'en give you up; I see it wont avail to strive; if it be of God I cannot overthrow it; and, if of yourself, it will soon fall." I saw the tears stand in his eyes, at which I was overcome with joy, and began already to reap the fruits of my obedience. But my trials were not yet over. The time appointed for the priest to visit me arrived, but no priest appeared. My husband went to fetch him, but he refused, saying he was busy, which so displeased my husband that he never went to hear him again, and, for some time, went to no place of worship.

My faith was now assaulted in another way, so strongly, that all my former trials were but trifling to it. This exercise came upon me unexpectedly, by hearing a woman speak of a book she had read, in which it was asserted that Christ was not the Son of God. A voice within me seemed to answer "No more he is, it's all a fancy, and the contrivance of men." Thus again was I filled with inexpressible trouble, which continued three weeks; and again did I seek desolate places, where I might make my moan. I have lain whole nights without sleep. I thought myself deserted of god, but did not let go my trust in him. I kept alive a hope that He who had delivered me as it were out of the paw of the bear, and the jaws of the lion, would in his own good time, deliver me from this temptation also. This was, at length, my experience; and I found the truth of his words, that all things shall work together for the good of those who love and fear him. My present exercises were to prepare me for further services in his cause; and it is necessary for his ministers to experience all conditions, that they may thereby be abler to speak to them.

This happened just after my first appearance as a minister, and friends had not been to talk with me. They did not well know what to do, till I had appeared again, which was not for some time, when the Monthly Meeting appointed four friends to pay me a visit. They left me well satisfied with the conference, and I joined the society. My husband still went to no place of worship. One day he said to me, "I would go to meeting, only I'm afraid I shall hear you clack, which I cannot bear." I used no persuasions. When meeting-time came, he got the horse, took me behind him, and went. For several months, if he saw me offer to rise, he went out; till, one day, I rose before he was aware and then, as he afterwards owned, he was ashamed to do it.

From this time, he left off the practice, and never hindered me from going to meeting. Though he did not take up the cross, yet his judgment was convinced; and, sometimes, melting into tears, he would say to me, "My dear, I have seen the beauty there is in the truth, and that thou has followed the right way, in which I pray God to preserve thee." I told him that I hoped He who had given me strength would also favour him, "O," said he, "I cannot bear the reproach thou dost, to be called turn-coat, and become a laughing-stock to the world, but I'll no longer hinder thee." This I considered a favour, and a little hope remained that my prayers, on his account, would be heard.

We lived in a small house by ourselves, which, though mean, and though we had little to put in it, our bed being no better than chaff, I was truly content. The only desires I had were for my own preservation, and to be blessed with the reformation of my husband. He was connected with a set of men whom he feared would make game of him, which indeed they already did; asking him when he designed to commence preacher, for they saw he intended to turn Quaker, and seemed to love his wife better since she became one than before. They used to come to our house, and provoked him to sit up and drink with them, sometimes till near day, while I have been sorrowing in a stable. Once, as I sat in this condition, I heard him say to his company, "I can't bear any longer to afflict my poor wife in this manner; for, whatever you may think of her, I do believe she's a good woman." He then came to me and said, "come in, my dear, god has given thee a deal of patience: I'll put an end to this practice." This was the last time they sat up at night.

My husband now thought that if he was in any place where it was not known he had been so bitter against friends, he could do better. I object to this, fearing it would not be for his benefit. Frequently, in a broken and affectionate manner, he condemned his ill usage of me. I answered, that I hoped it had been for my good, and therefore desired he would

not be afflicted on that account. According to the measure of grace received, I did what I could, both by example and precept, for his good. My advice was for him to stay where he was, as I was afraid he would grow weaker in his good resolutions, of he removed.

All I could say would not avail. Hearing of a place at Bordentown, he went thither, but was not suited. He next removed to Mount Holly, where he settled. We had each of us a good school; we soon got our house pretty well furnished, and might have done very well. Nothing seemed wanting to complete my happiness, except the reformation of my husband, which I had much reason to doubt I should not see soon. It fell out according to my fears. He addicted himself much to drinking, and grew worse than before. Sorrow was again my lot, I prayed for patience to bear my afflictions, and to submit to the dispensations of Providence. I murmured not; nor do I recollect that I ever uttered any harsh expressions except on one occasion. My husband coming home a little intoxicated, (a state in which he was very fractious,) and finding me at work by a candle, he put it out, fetching me, at the same time, a box on the ear, and saying, "You don't earn your light." At this unkind usage, which I had not been used to for the last two years, I was somewhat angry, and said, "Thou art a vile man." He struck me again; but my anger had cooled, and I received the blow without so much as a word in return. This also displeased him, and he went on in a distracted like manner, uttering such expressions of despair as, he believed he was predestined to damnation, and did not care how soon God struck him dead. I said very little, till, at length, in the bitterness of my soul, I broke out into these expressions: "Lord, look down on my afflictions, and deliver me by some means or other." My prayer was granted, but in such a manner that I thought it would have killed me. He went to Burlington, where he got drunk, and inlisted to go as a common soldier to Cuba, in the year 1740. I had drunk my bitter cups, but this seemed the bitterest of them all. A thousand times I blamed myself for making such a request, which I was afraid had displeased God, who had, in displeasure, granted it for my punishment.

I have since had cause to believe that he was benefited by his rash act, as, in the army, he did what he could not at home; he suffered for the testimony of truth. When they came to prepare for an engagement, he refused to fight; he was whipt, and brought before the general, who asked him, why he inlisted if he would not fight. "I did it," said he, in "in a drunken frolic, when the devil had the better of me; but now my judgment is convinced I ought not to fight, neither will I, whatever I suffer. I have but one life, and you may take that if you please, for I'll never take up arms." He was adhered to this resolution. By their cruel usage of him in consequence, he was so much disabled that the general sent him to Chelsea Hospital, near London. Within nine months afterwards, he died at this place, and I hope made a good end.

Having been obliged to say much of his ill usage to me, I have thought it my duty to say what I could in his favour. Although he was so bad, I never thought him the worst of men. If he had suffered religion to have had its perfect work, I should have been happy in the lowest situation of life. I have had cause to bless god, for enabling me, in the station of a wife, to do my duty, and now that I am a widow, I submit to his will. May I still be preserved by the arm of Divine Power; may I never forget the tender mercies of my God, the remembrance of which often boweth my soul in humility before his throne, and I cry, "Lord! What was I, that thou shouldst have revealed to my soul the knowledge of thy truth, and have done so much for one who deserved thy displeasure? Mayst thou, O God, be glorified, and I abased. It is thy own works that praise thee; and, of a truth, to the humble soul, thou makest every bitter thing sweet."

❧ "A man's house is his castle"

JAMES OTIS

James Otis was one of the leading lawyers in America. In 1761, he was engaged by some Boston merchants to defend them against the exchequer of England. Otis questioned the constitutionality of a writ of assistance allowing authorities to search homes and businesses without cause.

Otis's speech against the writs of assistance became a famous case and served as a basis for the Constitution's Bill of Rights' 4th Amendment prohibiting illegal search and seizure. No official record of Otis' speech was made. The following, however, are notes of the remarks taken by John Adams who heard Otis speak.

l. Otis. This writ is against the fundamental principles of law. The privilege of the House. A man who is quiet, is as secure in his house, as a prince in his castle—notwithstanding all his debts and civil processes in kind. But—

For flagrant crimes and in cases of great necessity, the privilege may be infringed on. For felonies an officer may break an oath, that is, by a special warrant to search such a house, sworn to be suspected, and good grounds of suspicion appearing.

Make oath coram Lord Treasurer, or Exchequer in England, or a magistrate here, and get a special warrant for the public good, to infringe the privilege of house.

General warrant to search for felonies. Hawkins, Pleas of the Crown. Every petty officer, from the highest to the lowest; and if some of them are common, others are uncommon.

Government justices used to issue such perpetual edicts. (Q. With what particular reference.) But one precedent, and that in the reign of Charles II., when star chamber powers and all powers but lawful and useful powers, were pushed to extremity.

The authority of this modern practice of the Court of Exchequer. It has an Imprimatur. But what may not have? It may be owing to some ignorant Clerk of the Exchequer. But all precedents, and this among the rest, are under the control of the principles of law. Lord Talbot. Better to observe the known principles of law than any one precedent, though in the House of Lords.

As to Acts of Parliament. An act against the Constitution is void; an act against natural equity is void; and if an act of Parliament should be made, in the very words of this petition it would be void. The executive Courts must pass such acts into disuse.

8 Rep. 118 from Viner. Reason of the common law to control an act of Parliament. Iron manufacture. Noble Lord's proposal, that we should send our horses to England to be shod. If an officer will justify under a writ, he must return it. 12. Mod. 396, perpetual writ. Statute Charles II. We have all as good right to inform as customhouse officers, and every man may have a general irreturnable commission to break houses.

By 12 of Charles, on oath before Lord Treasurer, Barons of Exchequer, or Chief Magistrate, to break, with an officer. 14 C. to issue a warrant requiring sheriffs, &c. to assist the officers to search for goods not entered or prohibited. 7 & 8. W. & M. gives officers in plantations same powers with officers in England.

Continuance of writs and processes proves no more, nor so much, as I grant a special writ of assistance on special oath for special purpose.

Pew indorsed warrant to Ware. Justice Walley searched House. Province Law. p. 114.

Bill in chancery. This Court confined their chancery power to revenue, &c.

2 .... In the first place, may it please your Honors, I will admit that writs of one kind may be legal; that is, special writs, directed to special officers, and to search certain houses, &c. specially set forth in the writ, may be granted by the Court of Exchequer at home, upon oath made before the Lord Treasurer by the person who asks it, that he suspects such goods to be concealed in those very places he desires to search. The act of 14 Charles II, which Mr. Gridley mentions, proves this. And in this light the writ appears like a warrant from a Justice of the Peace to search for stolen goods. Your Honors will find in the old books concerning the office of a Justice of the Peace, precedents of general warrants to search suspected houses. But in more modern books you will find only special warrants to search such and such houses specially named, in which the complainant has before sworn that he suspects his goods are concealed; and you will find it adjudged that special warrants only are legal. In the same manner I rely on it, that the writ prayed for in this petition, being general, is illegal. It is a power, that places the liberty of every man in the hands of every petty officer. I say I admit that special writs of assistance, to search special places, may be granted to certain persons on oath; but I deny that the writ now prayed for can be granted, for I beg leave to make some observations on the writ itself, before I proceed to other acts of Parliament. In the first place, the writ is universal, being directed "to all and singular Justices, Sheriffs, Constables, and other officers and subjects;" so, that, in short, it is directed to every subject in the King's dominions. Every one with this writ may be a tyrant; if this commission be legal, a tyrant in a legal manner also may control, imprison, or murder any one within the realm. In the next place, it is perpetual; there is no return. A man is accountable to no person for his doings. Every man may reign secure in his petty tyranny, and spread terror and desolation around him. In the third place, a person with this writ, in the day time, may enter all houses, shops, &c. at will, and command all to assist him. Fourthly, by this writ not only deputies &c. but even their menial servants, are allowed to lord it over us. Now one of the most essential branches of English liberty is the freedom of one's house. A man's house is his castle; and whilst he is quiet, he is as well guarded as a prince in his castle. This writ, if it should be declared legal, would totally annihilate this privilege. Custom-house officers may enter our houses, when they please; we are commanded to permit their entry. Their menial servants may enter, may break locks, bars, and every thing in their way; and whether they break through malice or revenge, no man, no court, can inquire. Bare suspicion without oath is sufficient. This wanton exercise of his power is not chimerical suggestion of a heated brain. I will mention some facts. Mr. Pew had one of these writs, and when Mr. Ware succeeded him, he endorsed this writ over to Mr. Ware; so that these writs are negotiable from one officer to another; and so your Honors have no opportunity of judging the persons to whom this vast power is delegated Another instance is this: Mr. Justice Walley had called this same Mr. Ware before him by a constable, to answer for a breach of Sabbath-day acts, or that of profane swearing. As soon as he had finished, Mr. Ware asked him if he had done. He replied, Yes/ Well then, said Mr. Ware, I will show you a little of my power. I command you to permit me to search your house for uncustomed goods. And went on to search his house from the garret to the cellar; and then served the constable in the same manner. But to show another absurdity in this writ; if: it should be established, I insist upon it, every person by the 14 Charles II. Has this power as well as custom-house officers. The Words are, "It shall be lawful for any person-or persons authorized," &c. What a scene does this open! Every man, prompted by revenge, ill humor, or wantonness, to inspect the inside of his neighbor's house, may get a writ of assistance. Others will ask it from self-defence; one arbitrary exertion will provoke another, until society be involved in tumult and in blood.

Again, these writs are not returned. Writs in their nature are temporary things. When the purposes for which they are issued are answered, they exist no more; but these live forever; no one can be called to account. Thus reason and the constitution are both against this writ. Let us see what authority there is for it. Not more than one instance can be found of it in all our law-books; and that was in the zenith of arbitrary power, namely, in the reign of Charles II, when star-chamber powers were pushed to extremity by some ignorant clerk of the exchequer. But had this writ been in any book whatever, it would have been illegal. All precedents are under the control of the principles of law. Lord Talbot says it is better to observe these than any precedents, though in the House of Lords, the last resort of the subject. No Acts of Parliament can establish such a writ; though it should be made in 'the very words of the petition, it would be void. An act against the constitution is void. (vid. Viner.) But these prove no more than what I before observed, that special writs may be granted on oath and probable suspicion. The act of 7 & 8 William III. That the officers of the plantation shall have the same powers, &c., is confined to this sense; that an officer should show probable ground; should take his oath of it; should do this before a magistrate; and that such magistrate, if he thinks proper, should issue a special warrant to a constable to search the places. That of 6 Anne can prove no more.

CHAPTER TWO

1763–1789

Creation of a Republic

A course in midwifery

PENNSYLVANIA GAZETTE

In early 1765, Dr. William Shippen, Jr., initiated and taught a course in midwifery in Philadelphia to help reduce the number of botched and fatal births that plagued the colony and the entire seaboard. His first class was held in the Pennsylvania Hospital. The class grew into the Medical School of the College of Philadelphia later that year, which in turn became the University of Pennsylvania in 1791. This article from the January 31, 1765, *Pennsylvania Gazette* further describes the reasons for holding the class.

Dr. Shippen Jr., having been lately called to the assistance of a number of women in the country, in difficult labors, most of which was made so by the unskillful old women about them, the poor women having suffered extremely, and their innocent little ones being entirely destroyed, whose lives might have been easily saved by proper management, and being informed of several desperate cases in the different neighborhoods which had proved fatal to the mothers as to their infants, and were attended with the most painful circumstances too dismal to be related, he thought it his duty immediately to begin his intended courses in Midwifery, and has prepared a proper apparatus for that purpose, in order to instruct those women who have virtue enough to own their ignorance and apply for instructions, as well as those young gentlemen now engaged in the study of that useful and necessary branch of surgery, who are taking pains to qualify themselves to practice in different parts of the country with safety and advantage to their fellow citizens.

The Doctor proposes to begin his first course as soon as a number of pupils sufficient to defray necessary expence shall apply....

In order to make the course more perfect, a convenient lodging is provided for the accommodation of a few poor women, who otherwise might suffer for want of the common necessaries on those occasions, to be under the care of a sober honest matron, well acquainted with lying-in women, employed by the Doctor for that purpose.

"The two parties were fixed upon each other"

REBELLION IN NEW YORK

The Hudson Valley was largely owned and ruled by a handful of families of Dutch descent in an almost feudal arrangement. The families appointed magistrates and representatives to the New York assembly and held criminal jurisdiction over their massive estates. Tenants were compelled to pay rent in kind and deeply resented the arrangement.

In June 1766, violence broke out when the Albany sheriff attempted to evict settlers on John Van Renselear's land. Almost 2000 armed settlers revolted, closed the courts, and opened the local jails. This account of the confrontation between the two sides was published in the *Boston Gazetteer*.

The inhabitants of a place called Nobletown and a place called Spencertown lying west of Sheffield, Great Barrington, and Stockbridge, who has purchased of the Stockbridge Indians the lands they now possess; by virtue of an order of the General Court of this province, and settled about two hundred families; John Van Renselear Esq., pretending a right to said lands, had treated the inhabitants very cruelly, because they would not submit to him as tenants, he claiming a right to said lands by virtue of a patent from the Government of New York; that said Van Renselear some years ago raised a number of men and came upon the poor people, imprisoned others, and has been constantly vexing and injuring the people. That on the 26th of last month said Renselear came down with between two and three hundred men, all armed with guns, pistols and swords; that upon intelligence that 500 men armed were coming against them, about forty or fifty of the inhabitants went out unarmed, except with sticks, and proceeded to a fence between them and the assailants, in order to compromise the matter between them. That the assailants came up to the fence, and Hermanus Schuyler the Sheriff of the County of Albany, fired his pistol down...upon them and three other fired their guns over them. The inhabitants thereupon desired to talk with them, and they would not harken; but the Sheriff, it was said by some who knew him, ordered the men to fire, who thereupon fired, and killed one of their own men, who had got over the fence and one of the inhabitants likewise within the fence. Upon this the chief of the inhabitants, unarmed as aforesaid, retreated most of them into the woods, but twelve betook themselves to the house from whence they set out and there defended themselves with six small arms and some ammunition that where therein. The two parties here fired upon each other. The assailants killed one man in the house, and the inhabitants wounded several of them, whom the rest carried off and retreated, to the number of seven, none of whom at the last accounts were dead. That the Sheriff shewed no paper, not attempted to execute any warrant, and the inhabitants never offered any provocation at the fence, excepting their continuing there, nor had any one of them a gun, pistol or sword, till they retreated to the house. At the action at the fence one of the inhabitants had a leg broke, whereupon the assailants attempted to seize him and carry him off. He therefore begged that they would consider the misery that he was in, declaring that he would rather die than be carried off, whereupon one of the assailants said "you shall die then" and discharging his pistol upon him as he lay on the ground, shot him to the body, as the wounded man told the informant; that the said wounded man was alive when he left him, but not like to continue long. The affray happened about sixteen miles distant from Hudson's River. It is feared the Dutch will pursue these poor people for thus defending themselves, as murderers; and keep them in great consternation.

✤ "Poverty is almost an entire stranger"

BY AN IMPARTIAL HAND

For much of American history, publications and brochures have been written to encourage or induce Europeans to emigrate to America. In the 1760s, a wave of about 20,000 disaffected Scottish Highlanders crossed the Atlantic to live in the southern colonies. They came to represent a significant part of Southern society, populating both the backcountry yeoman and the Cotton Belt's slaveholders in the nineteenth century.

Here a promotional brochure written "by an Impartial Hand" provides information about North Carolina, citing several reasons why it would behoove Highlanders to leave the Old World in favor of the promise, opportunity and freedom of the southern American colonies.

Migrations to America from many parts of Britain, particularly to the province of North Carolina, from the Highlands and isles of Scotland, have, of

late, become very frequent and numerous, and are likely to continue so. Whatever this may be owing to, the matter is serious, and, to some, the consequences are very alarming. The natives of the Highlands and isles have always been remarkable for the strongest attachment to the place of their nativity, and for the highest respect towards their masters and superiors. In these, they were wont to find kind patrons and protectors, and cherishing, indulgent fathers to themselves and families. This endeared to them a soil and climate to which nature has not been very liberal of its favours, in somuch, that they have ever shewn the utmost aversion at leaving their country, or removing to happier regions, and more indulgent climates. That this is true of the Highlanders in general, will be acknowledged by those who are in the least acquainted with them. The cause, then, that could induce a people of this cast, to forsake their native lands, in such numbers, and make them seek for habitations in countries far distant and unknown, must, doubtless, be very cogent and powerful. And, here, let the present land-holders and proprietors consider, whether of late, they are not greatly to blame? whether they have not begun to shake the iron rod of oppression too much over them? Let proprietors of the largest estates among them, such whose fortunes enables them to figure it away in life, ask themselves, if they have not used every means to estrange the affections of the Highlanders from them? whether they have not contributed all in their power, and, in a manner, exerted themselves to make their home intolerable and disagreeable to them, and lessen their once strong attachment towards their beloved, though poor country, so as to make them forget their native prejudices, surmount every apparent difficulty, and become emigrants and adventurers to other climes and regions far remote....

...[I]s there any wonder, if, under their present discouraging circumstances, and considering the dark and gloomy prospects they have before them at home, that the Highlanders should seek for refuge in some happier land, on some more hospitable shore, where freedom reigns, and where, unmolested by Egyptian taskmasters, they may reap the produce of their own labour and industry. For this purpose, where can they better betake themselves than to the large continent of America, to that part of it especially, to which some of their countrymen went sometime ago, where their posterity still live well and independently, and to which, of late, numbers have gone, who shew no inclination to return; but, on the contrary, send the most favourable accounts to their friends and acquaintance in the Highlands, and the most pressing invitations for them to follow after them across the Atlantic....

In the following pages, I mean to give my countrymen a short sketch of the Carolina, with regard to its climate, soil, produce, and man of settling there, founded upon unquestionable evidence, as well as personal observation, by which it will appear how little credit is due to the ridiculous and discouraging accounts given in the public papers, at the desire of some of the landholders, by which also will be shewn, that of all our colonies it is the most proper for Highlanders of any degree to remove to, if they want to live in a state ease, and independence. No circumstance shall be exaggerated, as it is to deceive or mislead any person; the simple truth shall be told, and judged of as they really are....

This colony is but in a manner in its infancy, and newly settled in respect to its neighbouring ones. There is a great coincidence between the soil, produce, and face of the country with those of Virginia; but, in the fertility of nature, Carolina has the advantage. In a word, the northern parts of it produce the same things with the southern parts of Virginia, and in greater perfection. The southern parts of it produce the same things with which the northern parts of South Carolina abounds; and, as in the back parts it skirts or runs along a great part of South Carolina, the produce is much the same as in that country and is conveyed by rivers or land carriage to Charlestoun, and other ports of that province for sale. Its commodities and general produce are very valuable, consisting of rice, indico, hemp, tobacco, fir, deer skins, turpentine, pitch, tar, raw hides, tanned leather, flower, flax-seed, cotton, corn, pease, pottatoes, honey, bees-wax, Indian corn, barrelled beef and pork, tallow, butter, rosin, square timber of different sorts, deals [unfinished lumber], staves, and all kind of lumber. This short description will not admit of entering into the manner in which the above commodities are cultivated, but the late settlers there from the Highlands are assiduous in their employments; and this, joined with the hospitality, friendship and harmony, that subsists among them in general, from whatever country, cannot fail, in a short time, of making the province flourish, and of rewarding their labour with independence and wealth, the offspring of ingenuity and industry....

The land in Carolina is easily cleared, as there is little or no under-wood, and the woods mostly consist of tall trees, at a considerable distance; and, by the different species of these, the quality of the soil is easily known. The grounds which bear the oak, the walnut, and the hickory, are reckoned the best; they are of a dark sand intermixed with loam. The pine barren is worst, being almost all sand; yet it bears the pine tree, and some useful plants, naturally yielding good profit in pitch, tar, and turpentine. When this sort of land is cleared, which is done very easily, it produces for two or three years together, very good crops of Indian corn and pease; and, when it lies low, and is flooded, it answers for rice. Their low rich swampy grounds bear rice, which is one of their staple commodities. It is, as before observed, that on the sides of the rivers, all the good timber, and large useful trees, are found in abundance; behind these stretches of good land, the country is covered with pines and firs, from which tar, turpentine, and rosin are made, and for which articles there is a fund inexhaustible for many years. In the forests, the trees are far separate, as I observed, and free of shrubs and underwood; they are lofty, and very straight, so that a person may ride through them, in any direction, without danger or inconveniency. I have seen the inhabitants hunting foxes, bears, and deer, through the woods, galloping very hard. Nothing surprises an European more, at first sight, than the size of the trees here, and in other American colonies. Their trunks are often from 50 to 70 feet high, without a limb or branch, and frequently above 30 feet in circumference, of which the natives and Indians make canoes, some of them so large, that they will carry 30 to 40 barrels of pitch, though formed of one entire piece of timber. Curious pleasure-boats are likewise made of these. Vegetation is amazingly quick in this province; the soil, in general, will produce most things; the climate has something so kindly, that the soil, when left to itself, throws out an immense quantity of flowers and flowering shrubs. All kinds of European grain grow there, such as barley, wheat, oats and rye, clover and lucern grass. Plants from Europe arrive at perfection here, beyond what they do in their native country. Wine and silks with proper culture, might be had here. For variety of roots and herbs, I believe, it rivals any country. The sassafras, sarsaparilla, the China root, the Indian pink, the golden rod, the horoun [horehound], and the snake root of various sorts, are natives here, and found scattered through the woods, together with other medicinal and aromatic herbs. There is a kind of tree, from which runs an oil of an extraordinary virtue for curing of wounds, and another that yields a balm thought to be little inferior to that of Mecca. Besides these, there are other trees that yield gums, liquorice, rhubarb; and other physical roots are found to thrive extremely well. The power of vegetation has been found so great, that a peach tree will bear in three years after putting of the stone into the ground. The fig-tree will bear two crops in the year, of large and luscious fruit. Melons, the Canada peach, and the white common peach, grow well and large, as do grapes, and all kinds of fruit, (except currants, goose-berries, and the red cherry) from the small cherry to the large melon, nothing can be more luscious. The fruit here has such a delicious flavour, that they who once taste of it, will despise the watery taste of that in Britain, where fruit-trees are not natural to the soil. Prodigious quantities of honey are found here, of which they make excellent spirits, and mead [a fermented honey beverage] as good as Malaga sack. It is incredible to think what plenty of fish is taken both in their salt and fresh water rivers, which fisher-men sell for a trifle. The fish most admired are the whiting, the angel fish, the king fish, the fat-back, the forgey, the fresh water trout, and the rock fish. Neither herring, turbot, or salmon, can exceed these in richness and delicious taste. Oysters too of a fine flavor are got in the rivers, and on the coast. With all these kinds of fish the market at Wilmington abounds. Here, one may buy all kinds of meats, from the squirrel and opposum to the bullock, and all very good, nothing in England coming up to their pork. Beef and pork is sold from 1d. to 2d. a pound, their fattest pullets at 6d. a piece, chickens at 3s. a dozen, geese at ld., turkeys at 18d. a piece. But fish and wild fowl are still cheaper in their seasons; and deer are sold from 5 to 10s. a piece. Merchants in the town, and considerable planters in the country, are now beginning to have a taste for living, and some gay equipages may be

seen; they are generous, well bred, and dress much; are polite, humane, and hospitable; and never tired of rendering strangers all the service in their power: nor is this mere pageantry and shew; their behavior at home is consistent with their appearance abroad. Their houses are elegant, their tables always plentifully covered and their entertainment sumptuous. They are fond of company, living very sociable and neighbourly, visiting one another often. Poverty is almost an entire stranger among them, as the settlers are the most hospitable and charitable people that can be met with to all strangers, and especially to such as by accident or misfortunes are rendered incapable to provide for themselves....

Besides the Highlanders that are settled in Cumberland county, some late emigrants have betaken themselves to Anson county, which abounds in good ground. In these counties, former settlers dispose of plantations, with some open ground upon them, to new-comers, and retire farther back into the country. Plantations of about 3 quarters of a mile square, have been sold for between 40 and 50£. which produce indico, tobacco, cotton, rice, wheat, Indian corn, barley, rye, and oats without ever being dunged; for, as all the land abounds with nitre, it is a long time before it is exhausted, and they use no manure. I have been informed, that if a settler can keep three servants or negroes clearing his grounds for two years, he may sell 700 bushels of wheat, and 5,000 weight of tobacco for every year afterwards, besides many other articles. Two men and four horses will work a large plantation in their best land, after cleared. They often plow with one horse. Wheat is sown in October and November, and some in March. They plant Indian corn and tobacco between April and May. Some lands give three crops in the year....

❧ "Rules of Civility"

GEORGE WASHINGTON

Even before he became commander of the Continental Army in the American Revolution, George Washington held a national reputation. Besides distinguishing himself as a soldier in the French and Indian War, Washington commanded respect simply through his conduct. A Virginia planter and surveyor, he actively sought to live a good life. Although the story of his admitting to chopping down a tree as a child may have been a myth, it captured Washington's essence. As a young man he wrote a list of "Rules of Civility" that he derived from a French book of etiquette. Washington memorized the list and attempted to live by its rules to control his temper and passions.

1. Every action in company ought to be with some sign of respect to those present.

2. In the presence of others sing not to yourself with a humming voice, nor drum with your fingers or feet.

3. Speak not when others speak, sit not when others stand, and walk not when others stop.

4. Turn not your back to others, especially in speaking; jog not the table or desk on which another reads or writes; lean not on anyone.

5. Be no flatterer, neither play with anyone that delights nor be played with.

6. Read no letters, books, or papers in company; but when there is a necessity for doing it, you must ask leave. Come not near the books or writings of anyone so as to read them unasked; also look not nigh when another is writing a letter.

7. Let you countenance be pleasant, but in serious matters somewhat grave.

8. Show yourself not glad at the misfortune of another, though he were your enemy.

9. They that are in dignity or office have in all places precedency, but whilst they are young, they ought to respect those that are their equals in birth or other qualities, though they have no public charge.

10. It is good manners to prefer them to whom we speak before ourselves, especially if they be above us, with whom in no sort we ought to begin.

11. Let your discourse with men of business be short and comprehensive.

12. In visiting the sick do not presently play the physician if you be not knowing therein.

13. In writing or speaking give to every person his due title according to his degree and the custom of the place.

14. Strive not with your superiors in argument, but always submit your judgment to others with modesty.

15. Undertake not to teach your equal in the art he himself professes; it savors of arrogancy.

16. When a man does all he can, though it succeeds not well, blame not him that did it.

17. Being to advise or reprehend anyone, consider whether it ought to be in public or in private, presently or at some other time, also in what terms to do it; and in reproving show no signs of choler, but do it with sweetness and mildness.

18. Mock not nor jest at anything of importance; break no jests that are sharp or biting; and if you deliver anything witty or pleasant, abstain from laughing thereat yourself.

19. Wherein you reprove another be unblamable yourself, for example is more prevalent than precept.

20. Use no reproachful language against anyone, neither curses nor revilings.

21. Be not hasty to believe flying reports to the disparagement of anyone.

22. In your apparel be modest, and endeavor to accommodate nature rather than procure admiration. Keep to the fashion of your equals, such as are civil and orderly with respect to time and place.

23. Play not the peacock, looking everywhere about you to see if you be well decked, if your shoes fit well, if your stockings set neatly and clothes handsomely.

24. Associate yourself with men of good quality if you esteem your reputation, for it is better to be alone than in bad company.

25. Let your conversation be without malice or envy, for it is a sign of tractable and commendable nature; and in all causes of passion admit reason to govern.

26. Be not immodest in urging your friend to discover a secret.

27. Utter not base and frivolous things amongst grown and learned men, nor very difficult questions or subjects amongst the ignorant, nor things hard to be believed.

28. Speak not of doleful things in time of mirth nor at the table; speak not of melancholy things, as death and wounds; and if others mention them, change, if you can, the discourse. Tell not your dreams but to your intimate friends.

29. Break not a jest when none take pleasure in mirth. Laugh not aloud, nor at all without occasion. Deride no man's misfortunes, though there seem to be some cause.

30. Speak not injurious words, neither in jest or

earnest. Scoff at none, although they give occasion.

31. Be not forward, but friendly and courteous, the first to salute, hear and answer, and be not pensive when it is time to converse.

32. Detract not from others, but neither be excessive in commending.

33. Go not thither where you know not whether you shall be welcome or not. Give not advice without being asked; and when desired, do it briefly.

34. If two contend together, take not the part of either unconstrained, and be not obstinate in your opinion; in things indifferent be of the major side.

35. Reprehend not the imperfection of others, for that belongs to parents, masters, and superiors.

36. Gaze not on the marks or blemishes of others, and ask not how they came. What you may speak in secret to your friend deliver not before others.

37. Speak not in an unknown tongue in company, but in your own language; and that as those of quality do, and not as the vulgar. Sublime matter treat seriously.

38. Think before you speak; pronounce not imperfectly, nor bring out your words too hastily, but orderly and distinctly.

39. When another speaks, be attentive yourself, and disturb not the audience. If any hesitate in his words, help him not, nor prompt him without being desired; interrupt him not, nor answer him till his speech be ended.

40. Treat with men at fit times about business, and whisper not in the company of others.

41. Make no comparisons; and if any of the company be commended for any act of virtue, commend not another for the same.

42. Be not apt to relate news if you know not the truth thereof. In discoursing of things you have heard, name not your author always. A secret discover not.

43. Be not curious to know the affairs of others, neither approach to those that speak in private.

44. Undertake not what you cannot perform; but be careful to keep your promise.

45. When you deliver a matter, do it without passion and indiscretion, however mean the person may be you do it to.

46. When your superiors talk to anybody, hear them; neither speak nor laugh.

47. In disputes be not so desirous to overcome as not to give liberty to each one to deliver his opinion, and submit to the judgment of the major part, especially if they are judges of the dispute.

48. Be not tedious in discourse, make not many digressions, nor repeat often the same matter of discourse.

49. Speak no evil of the absent, for it is unjust.

50. Be not angry at table, whatever happens; and if you have reason to be show it not; put on a cheerful countenance, especially if there be strangers, for good humor makes one dish a feast.

51. Set not yourself at the upper end of the table; but if it be your due, or the master of the house will have it so, contend not, lest you should trouble the company.

52. When you speak of God or his attributes, let it be seriously, in reverence and honor, and obey your natural parents.

53. Let your recreations be manful, not sinful.

54. Labor to keep alive in your breaks that little spark of celestial fire called conscience.

❧ Taxation without representation

THE STAMP ACT

At the conclusion of the French and Indian War in 1763, the costs of maintaining the American colonies outweighed the financial benefits for the mother country. To try to bridge the difference, English Parliament passed a multitude of new acts pertaining to its colonies over the next two years. These included: the Sugar Act imposing duties on American imports; the Currency Act prohibiting the colonies from printing their own money; the Quartering Act requiring colonists to provide food and shelter to British troops; and most notably the Stamp Act, requiring that printed documents be issued solely on special stamped paper.

Angered by these actions taken by Parliament across the Atlantic Ocean with no input from Americans, colonists issued resolutions, called for assemblies of protest and imposed boycotts. In 1765, delegates from nine colonies met in New York City specifically to protest the Stamp Act, the first direct tax on the colonies. They voted on a 14-point resolution protesting the tax. Mobs rioted in the streets. Stamp collectors were forced to resign. A widespread boycott made the tax ineffective. The Stamp Tax was repealed in 1766.

The Congress met according to adjournment, and resumed, etc., upon mature deliberation agreed to the following declarations of the rights and grievances of the colonists, in America, which were ordered to be inserted…. the present and impending misfortunes of the British colonies on this continent, having considered as maturely as time will permit the circumstances of the said colonies, esteem it our indispensable duty to make the following declarations of our humble opinion, respecting the most essential rights and liberties of the colonists, and of the grievances under which they labor, by reason of several late acts of Parliament.

1. That His Majesty's subjects in these colonies owe the same allegiance to the Crown of Great Britain that is owing from his subjects born within the Realm, and all due subordination to that august body, the parliament of Great Britain.

2. That His Majesty's liege subjects in these colonies are entitled to all the inherent rights and liberties of his natural-born subjects within the Kingdom of Great Britain.

3. That it is inseparably essential to the freedom of a people, and the undoubted right of Englishmen, that no taxes be imposed on them but with their own consent, given personally or by their representatives.

4. That the people of these colonies are not, and, from their local circumstances, cannot be represented in the House of Commons in Great Britain.

5. That the only representatives of the people of these colonies are persons chosen therein by themselves, and that no taxes ever have been or can be constitutionally imposed on them but by their respective legislature.

6. That all supplies to the Crown being free gifts of the people, it is unreasonable and inconsistent with the principles and spirit of the British constitution for the people of Great Britain to grant to His Majesty the property of the colonists.

7. That trial by jury is the inherent and invaluable right of every British subject in these colonies.

8. That the late act of Parliament entitled "An act for granting and applying certain stamp duties, and other duties, in the British colonies and plantations in America, etc.," by imposing taxes on the inhabitants of these colonies, and the said act and several other acts by extending the jurisdiction of the Courts of Admiralty beyond its ancient limits, have a manifest tendency to subvert the rights and liberties of the colonists.

9. That the duties imposed by several late acts of Parliament, from the peculiar circumstances of these colonies, will be extremely burdensome and grievous; and from the scarcity of specie, the payment of them absolutely impracticable.

10. That as the profits of the trade of these colonies ultimately center in Great Britain to pay for the manufactures which they are obliged to take from thence, they eventually contribute very largely to all supplies granted there to the Crown.

11. That the restrictions imposed by several late acts of Parliament on the trade of these colonies will render them unable to purchase the manufactures of Great Britain.

12. That the increase, prosperity, and happiness of these colonies depend on the full and free enjoyment of their rights and liberties, and an intercourse with Great Britain mutually affectionate and advantageous.

13. That it is the right of the British subjects in these colonies to petition the King or either house of Parliament.

Lastly. That it is the indispensable duty of these colonies, to the best of sovereigns, to the mother country, and to themselves, to endeavor by a loyal and dutiful address to His Majesty and humble applications to both houses of Parliament, to procure the repeal of the act of granting and applying certain stamp duties, of all clauses of any other acts of parliament whereby the jurisdiction of the Admiralty is extended as aforesaid, and the other late acts for the restriction of American commerce.

The Liberty Song

JOHN DICKINSON

Believed to be the first patriotic American ballad, "The Liberty Song" was immensely popular in America at this time. John Dickinson wrote the song in 1768 after he had already gained a national reputation as the author of "Letters from a Farmer in Pennsylvania," a series of twelve letters directed against the Townshend Acts.

Dickinson would later serve in the militia in the American Revolution, although he opposed the Declaration of Independence. Nevertheless, he also served in the Continental Congress and helped draft the Articles of Confederation and the Constitution.

"The Liberty Song"

Come join hand in hand, brave Americans all,
And rouse your bold hearts at fair Liberty's call;
No tyrannous acts shall suppress your just claim,
Or stain with dishonor America's name.
In freedom we're born, and in freedom we'll live,
Our purses are ready,
Steady, friends, steady,
Not as slaves, but as freemen our money
    we'll give.
Our worthy forefathers—let's give them a cheer—
To climates unknown did courageously steer;
Thro' oceans to deserts for freedom they came,
And dying bequeth'd us their freedom and fame.
Their generous bosoms all dangers despis'd
So highly, so wisely, their birthrights they priz'd;
We'll keep what they gave, we will piously keep,
Nor frustrate their toils on the land and the deep.
The tree their own hands had to liberty rear'd
They live to behold growing strong and rever'd;
With transport then cried, "Now our wishes
    we gain,
For our children shall gather the fruits of our pain."
Swarms of placeman and pensioners soon will
    appear
Like locusts deforming the charms of the year;
Suns vainly will rise, showers vainly descend,
If we are to drudge for what others shall spend.
Then join in hand, brave Americans all,
By uniting we stand, by dividing we fall;
In so righteous a cause let us hope to succeed,
For heaven approves of each generous deed.
All ages shall speak with amaze and applause,
Of the courage we'll show in support of our laws;
To die we can bear—but to serve we disdain,
For shame is to freedom more dreadful than pain.
This bumper I crown for our Sovereign's health,
And this for Britannia's glory and wealth;
That wealth and that glory immortal may be,
If she is but just—and if we are but Free.

❧ The Regulators of North Carolina

PETITION OF THE INHABITANTS OF ANSON COUNTY, NORTH CAROLINA

Sectionalism divided British American colonies even as many of them started to unify in their opposition to British policies. This was especially the case in the southern colonies of Virginia and North and South Carolina, where backcountry non-slaveholding farmers frequently found themselves at odds with the more established seaboard communities.

In the fall of 1769, the tension erupted into open conflict in the Carolinas. Known as the Regulators, they formed bands to intimidate courts and interfere in the collection of rents. These frontiersmen objected to being underrepresented in politics, unfairly taxed and wrongly persecuted for their religious differences. This petition, issued in 1769, outlines their specific complaints to the North Carolina Assembly.

Like in the Hudson Valley, where internal rife split the region, it was no surprise that a large portion of the population in the western frontier of the Carolinas remained loyal to England during the American Revolution.

Mr. Speaker and Gentlemen of the Assembly

The Petition of the Inhabitants of Anson County, being part of the Remonstrance of the Province of North Carolina,

Humbly sheweth, That the Province in general labour under general grievances, and the Western part thereof under particular ones; which we not only see but very sensibly feel, being crouch'd beneath our sufferings: and, notwithstanding our sacred priviledges, have too long yielded ourselves slaves to remorseless oppression. Permit us to conceive it to be our inviolable right to make known our grievances, and to petition for redress; as appears in the Bill of Rights pass'd in the reign of King Charles the first as well as the act of Settlement of the Crown of the Revolution. We therefore beg leave to lay before you a specimen thereof, that your compassionate endeavours may tend to the relief of your injured Constituents, whose distressed condition calls aloud for aid. The alarming cries of the oppressed possibly may reach your Ears; but without your zeal how shall they ascend the throne. How relentless is the breast without sympathy, the heart that cannot bleed on a View of our calamity; to see tenderness removed, cruelty stepping in; and all our liberties and priviledges in, invaded and abridg'd by (as it were) domesticks who are conscious of their guilt and void of remorse. O how daring! how relentless! whilst impending Judgments loudly threaten and gaze upon them, with every emblem of merited destruction.

A few of the many grievances are as follows, viz.,

1. That the poor Inhabitants in general are much oppress'd by reason of disproportionate Taxes, and those of the western Counties in particular; as they are generally in mean circumstances.

2. That no method is prescribed by Law for the payment of the Taxes of the Western counties in produce (in lieu of a Currency); as is in other Counties within this Province to the Peoples great oppression.

3. That Lawyers, Clerks, and other petitioners, in place of being obsequious Servants for the Country's use, are become a nuisance, as the business of the people is often transacted without the least degree of fairness, the intention of the law evaded, exorbitant fees extorted, and the sufferers left to mourn under their oppressions.

4. That an Attorney should have it in his power, either for the sake of ease or interest or to gratify their malevolence and spite, to commence suits to what Courts he pleases, however inconvenient it may be to the Defendant: is a very great oppression.

5. That all unlawful fees taken on Indictment, where the Defendant is acquitted by his Country (however customary it may be) is an oppression.

6. That Lawyers, Clerks, and others extorting more fees than is intended by law; is also an oppression.

7. That the violation of the King's Instructions to his delegates, their artfulness in concealing the same from him; and the great Injury the People thereby sustains: is a manifest oppression.

And for remedy whereof, we take the freedom to recommend the following mode of redress, not doubting audience and acceptance; which will not only tend to our relief, but command prayers as a duty from your humble Petitioners.

1. That at all elections each suffrage be given by Ticket & Ballot.

2. That the mode of Taxation be altered, and each person to pay in proportion to the profits arising from his Estate.

3. That no future tax be laid in Money, until a currency is made.

4. That there may be established a Western as well as a Northern and Southern District, and a Treasurer for the same.

5. That when a currency is made it may be let out by a Loan office on Land security, and not to be call'd in by a Tax.

6. That all debts above 40 shillings and under 10 pounds be tried and determined without Lawyers, by a jury of six freeholders impanneled by a Justice, and that their verdict be enter'd by the said Justice, and be a final judgment.

7. That the Chief Justice have no perquisites, but a Sallary only.

8. That Clerks be restricted in respect to fees, costs, and other things within the course of their office.

9. That Lawyers be effectually Barr'd from exacting and extorting fees.

10. That all doubts may be removed in respect to the payment of fees and costs on Indictments where the Defendant is not found guilty by the jury, and therefore acquitted.

11. That the Assembly make known by Remonstrance to the King, the conduct of the cruel and oppressive Receiver of the Quit Rents, for omitting the customary easie and effectual method of collecting by distress, and pursuing the expensive mode of commencing suits in the most distant Courts.

12. That the Assembly in like manner make known that the Governor and Council do frequently grant Lands to as many as they think proper without regard to head rights, notwithstanding the contrariety of His Majesties Instructions; by which means immense sums has been collected and numerous. Patents granted, for much of the most fertile lands in this Province, that is yet uninhabited and uncultivated, environed by great numbers of poor people who are necessitated to toil in the cultivation of bad Lands whereon they hardly can subsist, who are thereby deprived of His Majesties liberality and Bounty: nor is there the least regard paid to the cultivation clause

in said Patent mentioned, as many of the said Council as well as their friends and favorites enjoy large Quantities of Lands under the above-mentioned circumstances.

13. That the Assembly communicates in like manner the Violation of His Majesties Instructions respecting the Land Office by the Governor and Council, and of their own rules, customs and orders; if it be sufficiently proved that after they had granted Warrants for many Tracts of Land, and that the same was in due time survey'd and return'd, and the Patent fees timely paid into the said office; and that if a private Council was called on purpose to avoid spectators, and peremptory orders made that Patents should not be granted; and Warrants by their orders arbitrarily to have issued in the names of other Persons for the same Lands, and if when intreated by a solicitor they refus'd to render so much as a reason for their so doing, or to refund any part of the money by them extorted.

14. That some method may be pointed out that every improvement on Lands in any of the Proprietor's part be proved when begun, by whom, and every sale made, that the eldest may have the preference of at least 300 Acres.

15. That all taxes in the following counties be paid as in other Counties in the Province, (i. e.) in the produce of the Country and that ware Houses be erected as follows, (viz.) in Anson County, at Isom Haley's ferry landing on Pe Dee river; Rowan and Orange,…Cumberland… Mecklenburg… and in Tryon County ….

16. That every denomination of People may marry according to their respective Mode, Ceremony, and custom, after due publication or Licence.

17. That Doctor Benjamin Franklin or some other known patriot be appointed Agent, to represent the unhappy state of this Province to His Majesty, and to solicit several Boards in England.

❧ "I heard the word 'fire'"

THE BOSTON MASSACRE

The repeal of the Stamp Act in 1766 relieved tensions, but they were soon reignited when Parliament passed the Townshend Acts in 1767. This series of acts imposed import duties on all glass, lead, paints and tea sent from England to the colonies. Customs boards and courts were established to collect and enforce the duties. Boston and other American ports were determined not to obey and they set up nonimportation associations. The Massachusetts House of Representatives called for colonial resistance to the Townshend Acts. In response, the British sent five regiments to Boston.

A crowd of Bostonians attacked a group of these British sentries on March 5, 1770, with snowballs and rocks. The British soldiers fired into the crowd, killing three people on the spot and fatally wounding two others. Seven of the soldiers, including the commanding officer Captain Thomas Preston, were arrested and tried for murder. Future revolutionary leaders John Adams and Josiah Quincy defended them. Preston and four of the soldiers were acquitted. Two soldiers were found guilty of manslaughter.

The Boston Massacre led to the repeal of the Townshend Acts, with the exception of the tea tax.

I, Richard Palmes, of Boston, of lawful age, testify and say, that between the hours of nine and ten o'clock of the fifth instant, I heard one of the bells ring, which I supposed was occasioned by fire, and enquiring where the fire was, was answered that the soldiers were abusing the inhabitants; I asked where, was first answered at Murray's barracks. I went there and spoke to some officers that were standing at the door, I told them I was surprised they suffered the soldiers to go out of the barracks after eight o'clock; I was answered by one of the officers, pray do you mean to teach us our duty; I answered I did not, only to remind them of it. One of them then said, you see that the soldiers are all in their barracks, and why do you not go to your homes. Mr. James Lamb and I said, Gentlemen, let us go home, and were answered by some, home, home. Accordingly I asked Mr. William Hickling if he was going home, he said he was; I walked with him as far as the post-office, upon my stopping to talk with two or three people, Mr. Hickling left me: I then saw Mr. Pool Spear going towards the town-house, he asked me if I was going home, I told him I was; I asked him where he was going that way, he said he was going to his brother David's. But when I got to the town-pump, we were told there was a rumpus at the Custom-house door; Mr. Spear said to me you had better not go, I told him I would go and try to make peace. I immediately went there and saw Capt. Preston at the head of six or eight soldiers in a circular form, with guns breast high and bayonets fixed; the said Captain stood almost to the end of their guns. I went immediately to

Capt. Preston (as soon as Mr. Bliss had left him), and asked him if their guns were loaded, his answer was they are loaded with powder and ball; I then said to him, I hope you do not intend they shall fire upon the inhabitants, his reply was, by no means. When I was asking him these questions, my left hand was on his right shoulder; Mr. John Hickling had that instant taken his hand off my shoulder, and stepped to my left, then instantly I saw a piece of snow or ice fall among the soldiers on which the soldier at the officer's right hand stepped back and discharged his gun at the space of some seconds the soldier at his lift fired next, and the others one after the other. After the first gun was fired, I heard the word "fire," but who said it I know not. After the first gun was fired, the said officer had full time to forbid the other soldiers not to fire, but I did not hear him speak to them at all; then turning myself to the left I saw one man dead, distant about six feet; I having a stick in my hand made a stroke at the soldier who fired, and struck the gun out of his hand. I then made a stroke at the officer, my right foot slipped, that brought me on my knee, the blow falling short; he says I hit his arm; when I was recovering myself from the fall, I saw the soldier that fired the first gun endeavoring to push me through with his bayonet, on which I threw my stick at his head, the soldier starting back, gave me an opportunity to jump from him into Exchange lane, or I must been inevitably run through my body. I looked back and saw three persons laying on the ground, and perceiving a soldier stepping round the corner as I thought to shoot me, I ran down Exchange lane, and so up to the next into King Street, and followed Mr. Gridley with several other persons with the body of Capt. Morton's apprentice, up to the prison house, and saw he had a ball shot through his breast; at my return I found that the officers and soldiers were gone to the main guard. To my best observation there were not seventy people in King street at the time of their firing, and them very scattering; but in a few minutes after the firing there were upwards of a thousand....

🍂 "Rally, Mohawks! Bring out your axes"

BOSTON TEA PARTY

In 1773, the British Parliament gave the East Indian Company a virtual monopoly on selling tea in the American colonies with a three percent tax. Enraged American merchants and consumers reacted angrily to the act. Philadelphia and New York refused to accept ships bearing the tea. In Boston, the Dartmouth arrived in late November bearing a shipment of tea. Two other ships soon followed.

Mass meetings were held by Boston citizens. A formal motion that "the people of Boston should not suffer the tea to land" was passed on December 16. That night a band of scantily disguised "Indians" boarded the three ships and tossed hundreds of tea chests into Boston Harbor.

Rally, Mohawks! Bring out your axes,
And tell King George we'll pay no taxes
On his foreign tea;
His threats are vain, and vain to think
To force our girls and wives to drink
His vile Bohea!
Ten rally, boys, and hasten on
To meet our chiefs at the Green Dragon.

Our Warren's there and bold Revere,
With hands to do, and words to cheer,
For liberty and laws;
Our country's "braves" and firm defenders
Shall ne'er be left by true North-Enders
Fighting Freedom's cause!
Then rally, boys, and hasten on
To meet our chiefs at the Green Dragon.

🍂 "Every American are sharers in the insult"

RESOLUTIONS ON THE BOSTON PORT ACT

Celebrated by many American colonists, the Boston Tea Party infuriated British Parliament. The British government passed a series of laws in rapid order known as the Intolerable Acts (including the Boston Port Act) closing the Boston port and forcibly occupying the rebellious city with British troops. But rather than bending Bostonians to their British will, the acts heightened colonialist's anger at their mother country. And not just in Boston. Many colonialists came to the defiant city's defense. These two proclamations came from Farmington, Connecticut and Philadelphia, Pennsylvania.

Proceedings of Farmington, Connecticut

May 19, 1774

Early in the morning was found the following handbill, posted up in various parts of town: "To pass through the fire at six o'clock this evening, in honour to the immortal goddess of Liberty, the late infamous Act of the British Parliament for farther distressing the American Colonies; the place of execution will be the public parade, where all Sons of Liberty are desired to attend."

Accordingly, a very numerous and respectable body were assembled of near one thousand people, when a huge pole, just forty-five feet high, was erected and consecrated to the shrine of liberty; after which the Act of Parliament for blocking up the Boston harbour was read aloud, sentenced to the flames and executed by the hands of the common hangman; then the following resolves were passed:

1st. That it is the greatest dignity, interest and happiness of every American to be united with our parent State, while our liberties are duly secured, maintained and supported by our rightful Sovereign, whose person we greatly revere; whose government, while duly administered, we are ready with our lives and properties to support.

2nd. That the present ministry, being instigated by the devil and led on by their wicked and corrupt hearts, have a design to take away our liberties and properties to enslave us forever.

3rd. That the late Act which their malice hath caused to be passed in parliament, for blocking up the port of Boston, is unjust, illegal and oppressive; and that we and every American are sharers in the insult offered to the town of Boston.

4th. That those pimps and parasites who dared to advise their masters to such detestable measures be held in utter abhorrence by us and every American and their names loaded with the curses of all succeeding generations.

5th. That we scorn the chains of slavery; we despise every attempt to rivet them upon us; we are the sons of freedom and resolved that, till time shall be no more, godlike virtue shall blazon our hemisphere.

Pennsylvania Resolutions

At a very large and respectable meeting of the freeholders and freemen of the city and county of Philadelphia, on June 18, 1774. Thomas Willing, John Dickinson, chairmen.

I. Resolved, That the act of parliament for shutting up the port of Boston is unconstitutional, oppressive to the inhabitants of that town, dangerous to the liberties of the British colonies, and therefore, considering our brethren at Boston as suffering in the common cause of America:

II. That a congress of deputies from the several colonies in North America is the most probably and proper mode of procuring relief for our suffering brethren, obtaining redress of American grievances, securing our rights and liberties, and re-establishing peace and harmony between Great Britain and these colonies, on a constitutional foundation.

III. That a large and respectable committee be immediately appointed for the city and county of Philadelphia, to correspond with the sister colonies and with the several counties in this province, in order that all may unite in promoting and endeavoring to attain the great and valuable ends mentioned in the foregoing resolution.

IV. That the committee nominated by this meeting shall consult together, and on mature deliberation determine what is the most proper mode of collecting the sense of this province, and appointing deputies for the same, to attend a general congress, and having determined thereupon, shall take such measures as by them shall be judged most expedient, for procuring this province to be represented at the said congress in the best manner that can be devised for promoting the public welfare.

V. That the committee be instructed immediately to set on foot a subscription for the relief of such poor inhabitants of the town of Boston as may be deprived of their means of subsistence....

❧ "An attack on one colony is an attack on all"

VIRGINIA CALLS FOR CONTINENTAL CONGRESS

Taking a step further than mere condemnation, on May 27, 1774, a delegation of Virginians, including George Washington, Thomas Jefferson and Patrick Henry, called for a general congress of all colonies to meet. One month later, Massachusetts set the date and place: September 1 in Philadelphia.

…We are further clearly of opinion, that an attack, made on one of our sister colonies, to compel submission to arbitrary taxes, is an attack made on all British America, and threatens ruin to the rights of all, unless the united wisdom of the whole be applied. And for this purpose it is recommended to the committee of correspondence, that they communicate, with their several corresponding committees, on the expediency of appointing deputies from the several colonies of British America, to meet in general Congress, at such place annually as shall be thought most convenient; there to deliberate on those general measures which the united interests of America may from time to time require.

❧ "Life, liberty, and property"

DECLARATION AND RESOLVES OF THE FIRST CONGRESS

Fifty-five delegates met in Philadelphia to form the first Contintental Congress. They represented both the radical and moderate elements of the 13 colonies. After six weeks of intense debate and maneuvering, the radical voices of discontent prevailed. Members included John and Sam Adams, Roger Sherman, John Jay, John Dickinson, Joseph Galloway (who would later join the Loyalists), George Washington, Richard Henry Lee, Patrick Henry and Peyton Randolph, who was chosen as president of Congress.

On October 14, 1774, Congress issued its Declaration and Resolves, including a declaration of rights of the colonies. Congress subsequently formed the Association, a governing body between the states that called for a cutting off of trade with Great Britain and a ban on the slave trade. Congress also passed a series of acts and petitions directed at the people of Great Britain, King George III and Quebec. Over the next several months conventions, assemblies and town or county meetings from 11 colonies approved the proceedings of Congress. Only the New York Assembly rejected it and Georgia never acted on it.

That the inhabitants of the English Colonies in North America, by the immutable laws of nature, the principles of the English constitution, and the several charters or compacts, have the following Rights:

Resolved,

That they are entitled to life, liberty, and property, and they have never ceded to any sovereign power whatever, a right to dispose of either without their consent.

That our ancestors, who first settled these colonies, were at the time of their emigration from the mother country, entitled to all the rights, liberties, and immunities of free and natural-born subjects within the realm of England.

That by such emigration they by no means forfeited, surrendered, or lost any of those rights, but that they were, and their descendants now are entitled to the exercise and enjoyment of all such of them, as their local and other circumstances enable them to exercise and enjoy.

That the foundation of English liberty, and of all free government, is a right in the people to participate in their legislative council: and as the English colonists are not represented in the British parliament, they are entitled to a free and exclusive power of legislation in their several provincial legislatures, where their right of representation can alone be preserved, in all cases of taxation and internal polity, subject only to the negative of their sovereign, in such manner as has been heretofore used and accustomed. But, from the necessity of the case, and a regard to the mutual interest of both countries, we cheerfully consent to the operation of such acts of the British parliament, as are bona fide restrained to the regulation of our external commerce, for the purpose of securing the commercial advantages of the whole empire to the mother country, and the commercial benefits of its respective members excluding every idea of taxation, internal or external, for raising a revenue on the subjects in America without consent.

That the respective colonies are entitled to the common law of England, and more especially to the great and inestimable privilege of being tried by their peers of the vicinage, according to the course of that law.

That they are entitled to the benefit of such of the English statutes, as existed at the time of their colonization; and which they have, by experience, respectively found to be applicable to their several local and other circumstances.

That these, his majesty's colonies, are likewise entitled to all the immunities and privileges granted and confirmed to them by royal charters, or secured by their several codes of provincial laws.

That they have a right to peaceably assemble, consider of their grievances, and petition the King; and that all prosecutions, prohibitory proclamations, and commitments for the same, are illegal.

That the keeping of a standing army in these colonies, in times of peace, without the consent of the legislature of that colony in which such army is kept, is against the law.

It is indispensably necessary to good government, and rendered essential by the English constitution, that the constituent branches of the legislature be independent of each other; that, therefore, the exercise of legislative power in several colonies, by a council appointed during pleasure, by the crown, is unconstitutional, dangerous, and destructive to the freedom of American legislation.

🍂 "Who is there to mourn for Logan? Not one"

CHIEF LOGAN

White atrocities committed against a peaceful Iroquois tribe known as the "Mingoes" provoked an Indian war of retaliation. In 1774, whites sought to end the war with Chief Logan. When Logan met with the white negotiators he explained his reasons for launching the war and expressed his eagerness for peace. Thomas Jefferson praised the speech as one of the most eloquent in history.

I appeal to any white man to say, if ever he entered Logan's cabin hungry, and he gave him not meat; if ever he came cold and naked, and he clothed him not. During the course of the last long and bloody war, Logan remained idle in his cabin, an advocate for peace. Such was my love for the whites that my countrymen pointed as they passed, and said, "Logan is the friend of the white man." I had even thought to have lived with you, but for the injuries of one

man, Colonel Cressap, who last spring, in cold blood and unprovoked, murdered all the relations of Logan, not even sparing my women and children. There runs not a drop of my blood in the veins of any living creature. This called on me for revenge. I have sought it; I have killed many; I have fully glutted my vengeance. For my countrymen I rejoice at the beams of peace. But do not harbor a thought that mine is the joy of fear. Logan never felt fear! He will not turn on his heel to save his life. Who is there to mourn for Logan? Not one.

🍂 "Give me liberty or give me death"

PATRICK HENRY

By the spring of 1775, America was ripe for violence. The British remained encamped in Boston while militia units openly trained in surrounding towns, preparing for violence. The Continental Congress's call for an end to importing goods from Great Britain had a dramatic impact, cutting trade with British merchants by as much as 99 percent. Both sides became increasingly recalcitrant to give in to the other.

In Virginia, colonists strengthened their militia and debated how to respond to British actions in Boston. In March, Virginian delegates met in Richmond to consider the Continental Congress's resolutions. Initially tame in spirit, Patrick Henry famously gave a rousing speech to enflame the delegation to support the declarations. The actual words of the speech as recalled by William Wirt are subject to some historical doubt, but it has become embedded in American legend.

Alarmed by the convention's defiance, the British dissolved the Virginia House of Burgess, seized the gunpowder in Williamsburg and attempted to incite a slave rebellion. All of which had the combined effect of pushing the relatively moderate colony firmly on the side of the radicals in New England.

Mr. President: No man thinks more highly than I do of the patriotism, as well as abilities, of the very worthy gentlemen who have just addressed the House. But different men often see the same subjects in different lights; and therefore, I hope that it will not be thought disrespectful to those gentlemen, if, entertaining as I do, opinions of a character very opposite to theirs, I shall speak forth my sentiments freely and without reserve. This is no time for ceremony. The question before the House is one of awful moment to this country. For my own part I consider it as nothing less than a question of freedom or slavery, and in proportion to the magnitude of the subject ought to be the freedom of the debate. It is only in this way that we can hope to arrive at truth and fulfill the great responsibility which we hold to God and our country. Should I keep back my opinions at such a time, through fear of giving offense, I should consider myself as guilty of treason toward my country and of an act of disloyalty toward the majesty of heaven, which I revere above all earthly kings.

Mr. President, it is natural to man to indulge in the illusions of hope. We are apt to shut our eyes against a painful truth and listen to the song of that siren, till she transforms us into beasts. Is this the part of wise men, engaged in a great and arduous struggle for liberty? Are we disposed to be of the number of those who, having eyes, see not, and having ears, hear not, the things which so nearly concern their temporal salvation? For my part, whatever anguish of spirit it may cost, I am willing to know the whole truth, to know the worst and to provide for it.

I have but one lamp by which my feet are guided, and that is the lamp of experience. I know of no way of judging of the future but by the past. And judging by the past, I wish to know what there has been in the conduct of the British ministry for the last ten years to justify those hopes with which gentlemen have been pleased to solace themselves and the House? Is it that insidious smile with which our petition has been lately received? Trust it not, sir; it will prove a snare to your feet. Suffer not yourselves to be betrayed with a kiss. Ask yourselves how this gracious reception of our petition comports with these warlike preparations which cover our waters and darken our land. Are fleets and armies necessary to a work of love and reconciliation? Have we shown ourselves unwilling to be reconciled that force must be called in to win back our love? Let us not deceive ourselves, sir. These are the implements of war and subjugation, the last arguments to which kings resort. I ask gentlemen, sire, what means this martial array, if its purpose be not to force us to submission? Can gentlemen assign any other possible motives for it? Has Great Britain any enemy, in this quarter of the world, to call for all this accumulation of navies and armies? No, sir, she has none. They are meant for us; they can be meant for no other. They are sent over to bind and rivet upon us those chains which the British ministry have been so long forging. And what have we to oppose them? Shall we try argument? Sir, we have been trying that for the last ten years. Have we anything new to offer on the subject? Nothing. We have held the subject up in every light of which it is capable, but it has been all in vain. Shall we resort to entreaty and humble supplication? What terms shall we find which have not been already exhausted? Let us not, I beseech you, sir, deceive ourselves longer. Sir, we have done everything that could be done to avert the storm which is now coming on. We have petitioned; we have remonstrated; we have supplicated; we have prostrated ourselves before the tyrannical hands of the ministry and parliament. Our petitions have been slighted; our remonstrances have produced additional violence and insult; our supplications have been disregarded; and we have been spurned, with contempt, from the foot of the throne. In vain, after these things, may we indulge the fond hope of peace and reconciliation. There is no longer any room for hope. If we wish to be free—if we mean to preserve inviolate those inestimable privileges for which we have been so long contending—if we mean not basely to abandon the noble struggle in which we have been so long engaged, and which we have pledged ourselves never to abandon until the glorious object of our contest shall be obtained, we must fight! I repeat it, sir, we must fight! An appeal to arms and to the God of Hosts is all that is left us.

They tell us, sir, that we are weak, unable to cope with so formidable an adversary. But when shall we be stronger? Will it be the next week, or the next year? Will it be when we are totally disarmed, and when a British guard shall be stationed in every house? Shall we gather strength by irresolution and inaction? Shall we acquire the means of effectual resistance by lying supinely on our backs and hugging the delusive phantom of hope, until our enemies shall have bound us hand and foot? Sir, we are not weak, if we make a proper use of the means which the God of nature hath placed in our power. Three millions of people, armed in the holy cause of liberty, and in such a country as that which we possess, are invincible by any force which our enemy can send against us. Besides, sir, we shall not fight our battles alone. There is a just God who presides over the destinies of nations, and who will raise friends to fight our battles for us. The battle, sire, is not to the strong alone; it is to the vigilant, the active, the brave. Besides, sir, we have no election. If we were base enough to desire it, it is now too late to retire from the contest. There is no retreat but in submission and slavery. Our chains are forged. Their clanking may be heard on the plains of Boston. The war is inevitable—and let it come. I repeat it, sir, let it come.

It is in vain, sir, to extenuate the matter. Gentlemen may cry peace, peace!—but there is no peace. The war is actually begun. The next gale that sweeps from the north will bring to our ears the clash of resounding arms. Our brethren are already in the field. Why stay we here idle? What is it that gentlemen wish? What would they have? Is life so dear, or peace so sweet, as to be purchased at the price of chains and slavery? Forbid it, Almighty God. I know not what course others may take, but as for me: give me liberty, or give me death!

"Fire! By God, fire!"

THE REVEREND JONAS CLARK

Concerned about the growing number of American militia groups surrounding Boston in the spring of 1775, the British decided to seize a store of guns and ammunition in the town of Concord on the outskirts of Boston. A column of British soldiers set out on the evening of April 18. Warned by messengers, including Paul Revere, American militiamen gathered to confront the British troops.

One of these units was in Lexington, a village on the road to Concord. Ironically, the militia unit was in the midst of breaking up when the British troops arrived. Although accounts differ as to who fired the first shot, the British routed the militiamen, killing eight. This account comes from a sermon relating the incident by the Reverend Jonas Clark, pastor of the church in Lexington.

The skirmish marked the beginning of the American Revolution. It was the first violent conflict between the two sides.

British soldiers marched on to Concord, discarding token resistance and destroying the arsenal of weapons. On the return trip, however, the British were overwhelmed by swarming militia units that held Concord's North Bridge and drove the redcoats into a headlong retreat to Boston. The British suffered 250 casualties.

Between the hours of twelve and one, on the morning of the nineteenth of April, we received intelligence, by express, from the Honorable Joseph Warren, Esq., at Boston, "that a large body of the king's troops (supposed to be a brigade of about 12 or 1,500) were embarked in boats from Boston, and gone over to land on Lechmere's Point (so called) in Cambridge; and that it was shrewdly suspected that they were ordered to seize and destroy the stores belonging to the colony, then deposited at Concord."…

Upon this intelligence, as also upon information of the conduct of the officers as above-mentioned, the militia of this town were alarmed and ordered to meet on the usual place of parade; not with any design of commencing hostilities upon the king's troops, but to consult what might be done for our own and the people's safety; and also to be ready for whatever service providence might call us out to, upon this alarming occasion, in case overt acts of violence or open hostilities should be committed by this mercenary band of armed and blood-thirsty oppressors.…

The militia met according to order and waited the return of the messengers, that they might order their measures as occasion should require. Between 3 and 4 o'clock, one of the expressed returned, informing that there was no appearance of the troops on the roads either from Cambridge or Charlestown; and that it was supposed that the movements in the army the evening before were only a feint to alarm the people. Upon this, therefore, the militia company were dismissed for the present, but with orders to be within call of the drum—waiting the return of the other messenger, who was expected in about an hour, or sooner, if any discovery should be made of the motions of the troops. But he was prevented by their silent and sudden arrival at the place where he was waiting for intelligence. So that, after all this precaution, we had no notice of their approach till the brigade was actually in the town and upon a quick march within about a mile and a quarter of the meeting house and place of parade.

However, the commanding officer thought best to call the company together, not with any design of opposing so superior a force, much less of commencing hostilities, but only with a view to determine what to do, when and where to meet, and to dismiss and disperse.

Accordingly, about half an hour after four o'clock, alarm guns were fired and the drums beat to arms, and the militia were collecting together. Some, to the number of about 50 or 60, or possibly more, were on the parade, others were coming towards it. In the mean time, the troops having thus stolen a march upon us and, to prevent any intelligence of their approach, having seized and held prisoners several persons whom they met unarmed upon the road, seemed to come determined for murder and bloodshed—and that whether provoked to it or not! When within about half a quarter of a mile of the meeting-house, they halted, and the command was given to prime and load which being done, they marched on till they came up to the east end of said meeting-house, in sight of our militia (collecting as aforesaid) who were about 12 or 13 rods distant.

Immediately upon their appearing so suddenly and so nigh, Capt. Parker, who commanded the militia company, ordered the men to disperse and take care of themselves, and not to fire. Upon this, our men dispersed—but many of them not so speedily as they might have done, not having the most distant idea of such brutal barbarity and more than savage cruelty from the troops of a British king, as they immediately experienced! For, no sooner did they come in sight of our company, but one of them, supposed to be an officer of rank, was heard to say to the troops, "Damn them! We will have them!" Upon which the troops shouted aloud, huzza'd, and rushed furiously towards our men.

About the same time, three officers (supposed to be Col. Smith, Major Pitcairn and another officer) advanced on horse back to the front of the body, and coming within 5 or 6 rods of the militia, one of them cried out, "Ye villains, ye Rebels, disperse! Damn you, disperse!"—or words to this effect. One of them (whether the same or not is not easily determined) said "Lay down your arms! Damn you, why don't you lay down your arms?" The second of these officers, about this time, fired a pistol towards the militia as they were dispersing. The foremost, who was within a few yards of our men, brandishing his sword and then pointing towards them, with a loud voice said to the troops, "Fire! By God, fire!"—which was instantly followed by a discharge of arms from the said troops, succeeded by a very heavy and close fire upon our party, dispersing, so long as any of them were with-

in reach. Eight were left dead upon the ground! Ten were wounded. The rest of the company, through divine goodness, were (to a miracle) preserved unhurt in this murderous action!...

One circumstance more before the brigade quitted Lexington, I beg leave to mention, as what may give a further specimen of the spirit and character of the officers and men of this body of troops. After the militia company were dispersed and the firing ceased, the troops drew up and formed in a body on the common, fired a volley and gave three huzzas, by way of triumph and as expressive of the joy of victory and glory of conquest! Of this transaction, I was a witness, having, at that time, a fair view of their motions and being at the distance of not more than 70 or 80 rods from them.

"The Day on which the fate of America depends"

JABIGAIL ADAMS

Having driven the British back to Boston, American units laid siege to the encamped city. In June, Colonel Prescott occupied Breeds Hill overlooking Charlestown in Boston Harbor. The British stormed the position on June 17 in what became known as the Battle of Bunker Hill. It was the first pitched battle of the war. Although the British took the position, they suffered extraordinary casualties. Of the 2,500 British troops engaged, there were 1,150 casualties. The Americans lost 400 out of 1,500 men. Further, the American line held fast against greater numbers of professional soldiers, heightening American resolve to fight.

Nevertheless, the battle showed the cost of revolution. Abigail Adams wrote to her husband John Adams of the battle and the loss of a friend in the conflict.

Boston, Sunday, 18 June 1775
Dearest Friend,

The day—perhaps the decisive day—is come, on which the fate of America depends. My bursting heart must find vent at my pen. I have just heard that our dear friend, Dr. Warren, is no more, but fell gloriously fighting for his country; saying, Better to die honorably in the field, than ignominiously hang upon the gallows. Great is our loss. He has distinguished himself in every engagement, by his courage and fortitude, by animating the soldiers and leading them on by his own example. A particular account of these dreadful, but I hope glorious days, will be transmitted you, no doubt, in the exactest manner.

"The race is not to the swift, nor the battle to the strong; but the God of Israel is He that giveth strength and power unto his people. Trust in him at all times, ye people, pour out your hearts before him; God is a refuge for us." Charlestown is laid in ashes. The battle began upon our intrenchments upon Bunker's Hill, Saturday morning about three o'clock, and has not ceased yet, and it is now three o'clock Sabbath afternoon.

It is expected they will come out over the Neck tonight, and a dreadful battle must ensue. Almighty God, cover the heads of our countrymen, and be a shield to our dear friends! How many have fallen, we know not. The constant roar of the cannon is so distressing that we cannot eat, drink or sleep. May we be supported and sustained in the dreadful conflict. I shall tarry here till it is thought unsafe by my friends, and then I have secured myself a retreat at your brother's, who has kindly offered me part of his house. I cannot compose myself to write any further at present. I will add more as I hear further.

Tuesday afternoon

I have been so much agitated, that I have not been able to write since Sabbath day. When I say that ten thousand reports are passing, vague and uncertain as the wind, I believe I speak the truth. I am not able to give you any authentic account of last Saturday, but you will not be destitute of intelligence. Colonel Palmer has just sent me word that he has an opportunity of conveyance. Incorrect as this scrawl will be, it shall go. I ardently pray that you may be supported through the arduous task you have before you. I wish I could contradict the report of the Dr's death; but it is a lamentable truth, and tears of the multitude pay tribute to his memory; those favorite lines of Collins continually sound in my ears: "How sleep the brave" etc.

I must close…. I have not pretended to be particular with regard to what I have heard because I know you will collect better intelligence. The spirits of the people are very good; the loss of Charlestown affects them no more than a drop in the bucket.

I am, most sincerely, yours,
Portia

"I do not think myself equal to the command"

GEORGE WASHINGTON

In May 1775, the Second Continental Congress met and was confronted with the task of forging a national army. One of the first steps was to name a commander. George Washington was the obvious choice. A military hero in the French and Indian War with a sterling reputation, Washington was a moderate but steadfast patriot to the cause. As a Virginian, he could help unite the colonies in the revolution, which had largely been a New England affair. No other candidates were nominated or considered for the position and he was selected by a unanimous vote.

Washington accepted the position reluctantly, as the following response to Congress and letter to his wife Martha reflected. He commanded the Revolutionary Army for the next eight years. Although he suffered several military defeats and hardships, Washington's extraordinary strength of character helped carry the army to success. Even John Adams, who was known for sharp criticisms of others, described Washington to his wife Abigail as modest, virtuous, amiable, generous and brave.

June 16, 1775

Mr. President: Tho' I am truly sensible of the high Honour done me in this Appointment, yet I feel great distress from a consciousness that my important trust: However as the Congress desires I will enter upon the momentous duty, and exert every power I Possess In their Service for the Support of the glorious Cause: I beg they will accept my most cordial thanks for this distinguished testimony of the Approbation.

But lest some unlucky event should happen unfavourable to my reputation, I beg it may be remembered by every Gentleman in the room, that

I this day declare with the utmost sincerity, I do not think myself equal to the Command I am honoured with.

As to pay, Sir I beg leave to Assure the Congress that as no pecuniary consideration could have tempted me to have accepted this Arduous employment, (at the expence of my domestic ease and happiness) I do not wish to make any proffit from it: I will keep an exact Account of my expences; those I doubt not they will discharge and that is all I desire.

Philadelphia, June 18, 1775

My Dearest,

I am now set down to write to you on a subject which fills me with inexpressible concern, and this concern is greatly aggravated and increased, when I reflect upon the uneasiness I know it will give you. It has been determined in Congress, that the whole army raised for the defence of the American cause shall be put under my care, and that it is necessary for me to proceed immediately to Boston to take upon me the command of it.

You may believe me, my dear patsy, when I assure you, in the most solemn manner that, so far from seeking this appointment, I have used every endeavor in my power to avoid it, not only from my unwillingness to part with you and the family, but from a consciousness of its being a trust too great for my capacity, and that I should enjoy more real happiness in one month with you at home, than I have the most distant prospect of finding abroad, if my stay were to be seven times seven years. But as it has been a kind of destiny, that has thrown me upon this service, I shall hope that my undertaking it is designed to answer some good purpose. You might, and I suppose did perceive, from the tenor of my letters, that I was apprehensive I could not avoid this appointment, as I did not pretend to intimate when I should return. That was the case. It was utterly out of my power to refuse this appointment, without exposing my character to such censures, as would have reflected dishonor upon myself, and given pain to my friends. This, I am sure, could not, and ought not, to be pleasing to you, and must have lessened me considerably in my own esteem. I shall rely, therefore, confidently on that providence, which has heretofore preserved and been bountiful to me, not doubting but that I shall return safe to you in the fall. I shall feel no pain from the toil or the danger of the campaign; my unhappiness will flow from the uneasiness I know you will feel from being left alone. I therefore beg, that you will summon your whole fortitude, and pass your time as agreeably as possible. Nothing will give me so much sincere satisfaction as to hear this, and to hear it from your own pen. My earnest and ardent desire is, that you would pursue any plan that is most likely to produce content, and a tolerable degree of tranquility; as it must add greatly to my uneasy feelings to hear, that you are dissatisfied or complaining at what I really could not avoid.

As life is always uncertain, and common prudence dictates to every man the necessity of settling his temporal concerns, while it is in his power, and while the mind is calm and undisturbed, I have, since I came to this place (for I had not time to do it before I left home) got Colonel Pendleton to draft a will for me, by the directions I gave him, which will I now enclose. The provision made for you in case of my death will, I hope, be agreeable.

I shall add nothing more, as I have several letters to write, but to desire that you will remember me to your friends, and to assure you that I am with the most unfeigned regard, my dear patsy, your affectionate, &c.

"I was great and you were little"

STOCKBRIDGE INDIAN

George Washington was not the only person confronted with an uncomfortable decision. Men and women throughout the colonies were forced to choose sides. Perhaps no group had a more ambiguous decision to make than the Native Americans. Fearful of the Americans' westward ambitions, many tribes were lured into the conflict on the British side by promises of future benefits. Others, however, had grown comfortable with the white settlers and embraced their cause. The following speech was given to the Massachusetts congress by a member of the Stockbridge tribe in Western Massachusetts in 1775.

Brothers!

You remember, when you first came over the great waters, I was great and you were little—very small. I then took you in for a friend, and kept you under my arms, so that no one might injure you. Since that time we have ever been true friends: there has never been any quarrel between us. But now our conditions are changed. You are become great and tall. You reach to the clouds. You are seen all around the world. I am become small—very little. I am not so high as your knee. Now you take care of me; and I look to you for protection.

Brothers! I am sorry to hear of this great quarrel between you and old England. It appears that blood must soon be shed to end this quarrel. We never till this day understood the foundation of this quarrel between you and the country you came from. Brothers! Whenever I see your blood running, you will soon find me about to revenge my brothers' blood. Although I am low and very small, I will grip hold of your enemy's heel, that he cannot run so fast, and so light, as if he had nothing at his heels.

Brothers! You know I am not so wise as you are; therefore I ask your advice in what I am now going to say. I have been thinking, before you come to action, to take a run to the westward and feel the mind of my Indian brethren, the Six Nations, and know how they stand—whether they are on your side or for your enemies. If I find they are against you, I will try to turn their minds. I think they will listen to me, for they have always looked this way for advice, concerning all important news that comes from the rising sun. If they hearken to me, you will not be afraid of any danger from behind you. However their minds are affected, you shall soon know by me. I think I can do you more service in this way than by marching off immediately to Boston and staying there. It may be a great while before blood runs. Now, as I said, you are wiser than I; I leave this for your consideration, whether I come down immediately or wait till I hear some blood is spilled.

Brothers! I would not have you think by this that we are falling back from our engagements. We are ready to do anything for your relief, and should be guided by your counsel.

Brothers! One thing I ask you, if you send for me to fight: that you will let me fight in my own way. I am not used to fight English fashion; there-fore you must not expect I can train like your men. Only point out to me where your enemies keep, and that is all I shall want to know.

❧ Common Sense

THOMAS PAINE

Although many Americans by the beginning of 1776 were convinced that the colonies should become independent of Great Britain, a large portion of the population remained unconvinced. The colonies had been under British rule for more than 150 years. As clumsy and oppressive as its actions had been for the previous twelve years, separation was a big step. Many paused before taking the leap.

Published on January 9, 1776, Thomas Paine's *Common Sense* stirred the nation to revolution. Within three months, more than 100,000 copies were in circulation—an unbelievable number considering there were only three million people in all 13 British colonies. Written in plain language, Paine tore down the notion of monarchical rule, American dependence on Britain for economic prosperity and British benevolence.

The pamphlet struck a cord, helping to inspire widespread calls for independence which would culminate half a year later with the Declaration of Independence.

Some writers have so confounded society with government as to leave little or no distinction between them; whereas they are not only different, but have different origins. Society is produced by our wants and government by our wickedness; the former promotes our happiness positively by uniting our affections, the latter negatively by restraining our vices. The one encourages intercourse, the other creates distinctions. The first is a patron, the last a punisher.

Society in every state is a blessing, but government, even in its best state, is but a necessary evil; in its worst state an intolerable one; for when we suffer or are exposed to the same miseries by a government, which we might expect in a country without government, our calamity is heightened by reflecting that we furnish the means by which we suffer. Government, like dress, is the badge of lost innocence; the palaces of kings are built upon the ruins of the bowers of paradise. For were the impulses of conscience clear, uniform, and irresistibly obeyed, man would need no other lawgiver; but that not being the case, he finds it necessary to surrender up a part of his property to furnish means for the protection of the rest; and this he is induced to do by the same prudence which in every other case advises him out of two evils to choose the least. Wherefore, security being the true design and end of government, it unanswerably follows that whatever form thereof appears most likely to ensure it to us, with the least expense and greatest benefit, is preferable to all others....

But there is another greater distinction for which no truly natural or religious reason can be assigned, and that is the distinction of men into kings and subjects. Male and females are the distinctions of nature, good and bad the distinctions of heaven; but how a race of men came into the world so exalted above the rest, and distinguished like some new species, is worth inquiring into, and whether they are the means of happiness or of misery to mankind.

In the early ages of the world, according to the Scripture chronology there were no kings; the consequence of which was there were no wars; it is the pride of kings which throws mankind into confusion. Holland without a king hath enjoyed more peace for this last century than any of the monarchical government in Europe. Antiquity favors the same remark; for the quiet and rural lives of the first patriarchs have a happy something in them, which vanishes when we come to the history of Jewish royalty.

Government by kings was first introduced into the world by the heathens from whom the children of Israel copied the custom. It was the most prosperous invention the Devil ever set on foot for the promotion of idolatry. The heathens paid divine honors to their deceased kings, and the Christian world has improved on the plan by doing the same to their living ones. How impious is the title of sacred Majesty applied to a worm, who in the midst of his splendor is crumbling into dust!

As the exalting of one man so greatly above the rest cannot be justified on the equal rights of nature, so neither can it be defended on the authority of Scripture; for the will of the Almighty, as declared by Gideon and the prophet Samuel, expressly disapproves of government by kings....

To the evil of monarchy we have added that of hereditary succession; and as the first is a degradation and a lessening of ourselves, so the second, claimed as a matter of right, is an insult and imposition on posterity. For all men being originally equals, no one by birth could have a right to set up

his own family in perpetual preference to all others forever, and though himself might deserve some decent degree of honors of his contemporaries, yet his descendants might be far too unworthy to inherit them. One of the strongest natural proofs of the folly of hereditary right in kings, is that nature disapproves it, otherwise she would not so frequently turn it into ridicule by giving mankind an ass for a lion.

... Most wise men in their private sentiments have ever treated hereditary right with contempt; yet it is one of those evils which when once established is not easily removed; many submit from fear, others from superstition, and the most powerful part shares with the king the plunder of the rest.

This is supposing the present race of kings in the world to have had an honorable origin; whereas it is more than probable that, could we take off the first of them nothing better than the principal ruffian of some restless gang, whose savage manners of pre-eminence in subtility obtained him the title of chief among the plunderers; and who by increasing in power, and extending his depredations, overawed the quiet and defenseless to purchase their safety by frequent contributions. Yet his electors could have no idea of giving hereditary right to his descendents, because such a perpetual exclusion of themselves was incompatible with the free and unrestrained principles they professed to live by. Wherefore, hereditary succession in early ages of monarchy could not take place as a matter of claim, but as something casual or complemental; but as few or no records were extant in those days, and traditionary history stuffed with fables, it was very easy, after the lapse of a few generations, to trump up some superstitious tale conveniently timed, Mahomet-like, to cram hereditary right down the throats of the vulgar. Perhaps the disorders which threatened, or seemed to threaten, on the decease of a leader and the choice of a new one (for elections among ruffians could not be very orderly) induced many at first to favor hereditary pretensions; by which means it happened, as it hath happened since, that what at first was submitted to as a convenience was afterward claimed as a right.

England, since the conquest, hath known some few good monarchs, but groaned beneath a much larger number of bad ones; yet no man in his senses can say that their claim under William theConqueror is a very honorable one. A French bastard, landing with an armed banditti and establishing himself king of England against the consent of the natives, is in plain terms a very paltry rascally original. It certainly hath no divinity in it. However it is needless to spend much time exposing the folly of hereditary right; if there are any so weak as to believe it, let them promiscuously worship the Ass and the Lion, and welcome. I shall neither copy their humility, nor disturb their devotion....

The nearer any government approaches to a republic, the less business there is for a king. It is somewhat difficult to find a proper name for the government of England. Sir William Meredith calls it a republic; but in its present state it is unworthy of the name, because the corrupt influence of the crown, by having all the places in its disposal, hath so effectually swallowed up the power, and eaten out the virtue of the House of Commons (the republican part in the constitution) that the government of England is nearly as monarchical as that of France or Spain. Men fall out with names without understanding them. For 'tis the republican and not the monarchical part of the constitution of England which Englishmen glory in, viz. The liberty of choosing a house of commons from out of their own body—and it is easy to see that when republican virtues fail, slavery ensues. Why is the constitution of England sickly but because monarchy hath poisoned the republic, the crown has engrossed the commons?

In England a king hath little more to do than to make war and give away places; which in plain terms is to impoverish the nation and set it together by the ears. A pretty business indeed for a man to be allowed eight hundred thousand sterling a year for, and worshipped into the bargain! Of more worth is one honest man to society, and in the sight of God, than all the crowned ruffians that ever lived....

The sun never shined on a cause of greater worth. 'Tis not the affair of a city, a county, a province, or a kingdom; but of a continent—of at least one-eight part of the habitable globe. 'Tis not the concern of a day, a year, or an age; posterity are virtually involved in the contest, and will be more or less affected even to the end of time by the proceedings now. Now is the seed-time of continental union, faith, and honor. The least fracture now will be like a name engraved with the point of a pin in the tender rind of a young oak; the wound would enlarge with the tree, and posterity read it in full grown characters.

By referring the matter from argument to arms, a new era for politics is struck—a new method of thinking has arisen. All plans, proposals, etc. prior to the nineteenth of April, i.e. to the commencement of hostilities, are like the almanacks of the last year; which though proper then, are superseded and useless now. Whatever was advanced by the advocates on either side of the question then, terminated in one and the same point, viz. a union with Great Britain; the only difference between the parties was the method of effecting it; the one proposing force, the other friendship; but it has so far happened that the first has failed, and the second has withdrawn her influence.

As much has been said of the advantages of reconciliation, which, like an agreeable dream, has passed away and left us as we were, it is but right that we should examine the contrary side of the argument, and inquire into some of the many material injuries which these colonies sustain, and always will sustain, by being connected with and dependent on Great Britain. To examine that connection and dependence on the principles of nature and common sense; to see what we have to trust to, if separated, and what we are to expect, if dependent.

I have heard it asserted by some, that as America has flourished under her former connection with Great Britain, the same connection is necessary towards her future happiness, and will always have the same effect. Nothing can be more fallacious than this kind of argument. We may as well assert that because a child has thrived upon milk, it is never to have meat, or that the first twenty years of our lives is to become the precedent for the next twenty. But even this is admitting more than is true; for I answer roundly that America would have flourished as much, and probably much more, had no European power taken any notice of her. The commerce by which she hath enriched herself are necessaries of life, and will always have a market while eating is the custom of Europe....

But Britain is the parent country, say some. Then the more shame upon her conduct. Even brutes do not devour their young, nor savages make war upon their families; wherefore, the assertion, if true, turns to her reproach; but it happens not to be true, or only partly so, and the phrase parent or mother country hath been jesuitically adopted by the king and his parasites, with a low papistical design of gaining an unfair bias on the credulous weakness of our minds. Europe, and not England, is the parent country of America. This new world hath been the asylum for the persecuted lovers of civil and religious liberty from every part of Europe. Hither have they fled, not from the tender embraces of the mother, but from the cruelty of the monster; and it is so far true of England, that the same tyranny which drove the first emigrants from home pursues their descendants still....

I challenge the warmed advocate for reconciliation to show a single advantage that this continent can reap by being connected with Great Britain. I repeat the challenge, not a single advantage is derived. Our corn will fetch its price in any market in Europe, and our imported goods must be paid for, buy them where we will.

But the injuries and disadvantages which we sustain by that connection are without number; and our duty to mankind at large, as well as to ourselves, instruct us to renounce the alliance: because any submission to, or dependence on, Great Britain, tends directly to involve this continent in European wars and quarrels, and set us at variance with nations who would otherwise seek our friendship, and against whom we have neither anger nor complaint. As Europe is our market for trade, we ought to form no partial connection with any part of it. 'Tis the true interest of America to steer clear of European contentions, which she never can do while by her dependence on Britain she is made the makeweight in the scale of British politics.

Europe is too thickly planted with kingdoms to be long at peace, and whenever a war breaks out between England and any foreign power, the trade of America goes to ruin, because of her connection with Britain. The next war may not turn out like the last, and should it not, the advocates for reconciliation now will be wishing for separation then, because neutrality in that case would be a safer convoy than a man of war. Everything that is right or reasonable pleads for separation. The blood of the slain, the weeping voice of nature cries, 'Tis time to part. Even the distance at which the Almighty hath placed England and America is a strong and natural proof that the authority of the one over the other was never the design of heaven....

It is repugnant to reason, to the universal order of things, to all examples from former ages, to suppose that this continent can long remain subject to any external power. The most sanguine in Britain does not think so. The utmost stretch of human wisdom cannot, at this time, compass a plan, short of separation, which can promise the continent even a year's security. Reconciliation is now a fallacious dream. Nature has deserted the connection, and art cannot supply her place. For, as Milton wisely expressed, "Never can true reconcilement grow where wounds of deadly hate have pierced so deep."...

As to government matters, it is not in the power of Britain to do this continent justice: the business of it will soon be too weighty and intricate to be managed with any tolerable degree of convenience by a power so distant from us, and so very ignorant of us; for if they cannot conquer us they cannot govern us. To be always running three or four thousand miles with a tale or a petition, waiting four or five months for an answer, which, when obtained, requires five or six more to explain it in, will in a few years be looked upon as folly and childishness. There was a time when it was proper, and there is a proper time for it to cease.

Small islands not capable of protecting themselves are the proper objects for government to take under their care; but there is something absurd in supposing a continent to be perpetually governed by an island. In no instance hath nature made the satellite larger than its primary planet; and as England and America, with respect to each other, reverse the common order of nature, it is evident that they belong to different systems. England to Europe: America to itself.

I am not induced by motives of pride, party, or resentment to espouse the doctrine of separation and independence; I am clearly, positively, and conscientiously persuaded that 'tis the true interest of this continent to be so; that everything short of that is mere patchwork, that it can afford no lasting felicity—that it is leaving the sword to our children, and shrinking back at a time when a little more, a little further, would have rendered this continent the glory of the earth....

To talk of friendship with those in whom our

reason forbids us to have faith, and our affections wounded through a thousand pores instruct us to detest, is madness and folly. Every day wears out the little remains of kindred between us and them; and can there be any reason to hope that as the relationship expires the affection will increase, or that we shall agree better when we have ten times more and greater concerns to quarrel over then ever?

Ye that tell us of harmony and reconciliation, can ye restore to us the time that is past? Can ye give to prostitution its former innocence? Neither can ye reconcile Britain and America. The last cord is now broken, the people of England are presenting addresses against us. There are injuries which nature cannot forgive; she would cease to be nature if she did. As well can the lover forgive the ravisher of his mistress, as the continent forgive the murderers of Britain. The Almighty hath implanted in us these inextinguishable feelings for good and wise purposes. They are the guardians of his image in our hearts. They distinguish us from the herd of common animals. The social compact would dissolve, and justice extirpated from the earth, or have only a casual existence, were we callous to the touches of affection. The robber and the murderer would often escape unpunished, did not injuries which out tempers sustain, provoke us into justice.

O ye that love mankind! Ye that dare oppose not only the tyranny but the tyrant, stand forth! Every spot of the old world is overrun with oppression. Freedom hath been hunted round the globe. Asia and Africa have long expelled her. Europe regards her like a stranger, and England hath given her warning to depart. O receive the fugitive, and prepare in time an asylum for mankind!

❧ "All men are by nature equally free and independent"

VIRGINIA DECLARATION

As independence was becoming more and more of a foregone conclusion, states started to write constitutions for themselves. Having been familiar with bills of rights for more than a century in the American colonies, the new constitutions included a listing of citizens' fundamental rights and privileges.

The most influential and famous bill of rights was Virginia's. Drafted by George Mason, this document served as a model for many other American states and was widely admired in France. The declaration was approved on May 15, 1776.

A declaration of rights made by the representatives of the good people of Virginia, assembled in full and free convention; which rights do pertain to them and their posterity, as the basis and foundation of government.

1. That all men are by nature equally free and independent, and have certain inherent rights, of which, when they enter into a state of society, they cannot by any compact deprive or divest their posterity; namely, the enjoyment of life and liberty, with the means of acquiring and possessing property, and pursuing and obtaining happiness and safety.

2. That all power is vested in, and consequently derived from, the people; that magistrates are their trustees and servants, and at all times amenable to them.

3. That government is or ought to be instituted for the common benefit, protection, and security of the people, nation, or community; of all the various modes and forms of government, that is best which is capable of producing the greatest degree of happiness and safety, and is most effectually secured against the danger of maladministration; and that when any government shall be found inadequate or contrary to these purposes, a majority of the community hath an indubitable, unalienable and indefeasible right to reform, alter or abolish it, in such manner as shall be judged most conducive to the public weal.

4. That no man, or set of men, are entitled to exclusive or separate emoluments or privileges from the community, but in consideration of publick services; which, not being descendible, neither ought the offices of magistrate, legislator or judge to be hereditary.

5. That the legislative and executive powers of the state should be separate and distinct from the judiciary; and that the members of the two first may be restrained from oppression, by feeling and participating the burthens of the people, they should, at fixed periods, be reduced to a private station, return into that body from which they were originally taken, and the vacancies be supplied by frequent, certain, and regular actions, in

which all, or any part of the former members to be again eligible or ineligible, as the laws shall direct.

6. That elections of members to serve as representatives of the people in assembly, ought to be free; and that all men having sufficient evidence of permanent common interest with, and attachment to the community, have the right of suffrage, and cannot be taxed or deprived of their property for publick uses, without their own consent, or that of their representatives so elected, nor bound by any law to which they have not, in like manner, assented for the public good.

7. That all power of suspending laws, or the execution of laws, by any authority without consent of the representatives of the people, is injurious to their rights, and ought not to be exercised.

8. That in all capital or criminal prosecutions a man hath a right to demand the cause and nature of his accusation, to be confronted with the accusers and witnesses, to call for evidence in his favour, and to a speedy trial by an impartial jury of his vicinage, without whose unanimous consent he cannot be found guilty; nor can he be compelled to give evidence against himself; that no man be deprived of his liberty, except by the law of the land or the judgment of his peers.

9. That excessive bail ought not to be required, nor excessive fines imposed, nor cruel and unusual punishments inflicted.

10. That general warrants, whereby an officer or messenger may be commanded to search suspected places without evidence of a fact committed, or to seize any person or persons not named, or whose offence is not particularly described and supported by evidence, are grievous and oppressive, and ought not to be granted.

11. That in controversies respecting property, and in suits between man and man, the ancient trial by jury is preferable to any other, and ought to be held sacred.

12. That the freedom of press is one of the great bulwarks of liberty, and can never be restrained but by despotick governments.

13. That a well-regulated militia, composed of the body of the people trained to arms, is the proper, natural and safe defence of a free state; that standing armies in time of peace should be avoided as dangerous to liberty; and that in all cases the military should be under strict subordination to, and governed by, the civil power.

14. That the people have a right to uniform government; and therefore, that no government separate from, or independent of the government of Virginia, ought to be erected or established within the limits thereof.

15. That no free government, or the blessings of liberty, can be preserved to any people, but by a firm adherence to justice, moderation, temperance, frugality and virtue,
and by frequent recurrence to fundamental principles.

16. That religion, or the duty which we owe to our Creator, and the manner of discharging it, can be directed only by reason and conviction, not by force or violence; and therefore all men are equally entitled to the free exercise of religion, according to the dictates of conscience; and that it is the mutual duty of all to practise Christian forbearance, love, and charity towards each other.

🌿 "All inhabitants shall be entitled to vote"

NEW JERSEY CONSTITUTION

Days before the Continental Congress declared independence, New Jersey approved a new constitution giving all inhabitants with minimal property qualifications the right to vote. For the next 30 years, women and blacks participated in New Jersey elections. But in 1807 the Maryland Legislature, alleging fraudulent voting practices by "aliens, females, and persons of color," passed a new law limiting voting rights to "free, white, male" citizens.

Whereas all the constitutional authority ever possessed by the Kings of Great Britain over these Colonies, or their other dominions, was, by compact, derived from the people, and held of them, for the common interest of the whole society; allegiance and protection are, in the nature of things, reciprocal ties, each equally depended upon the other, and liable to be dissolved by the others being refused or withdrawn. And whereas George the Third, King of Great Britain, has refused protection to the good people of these Colonies; and, by assenting to sundry acts of the British Parliament, attempting to subject them to the absolute dominion of that body; and has also made war upon them, in the most cruel and unnatural manner, for no other cause, than asserting their just rights—all civil authority under him is necessarily at an end, and a dissolution of government in each Colony has consequently taken place.

And whereas, in the present deplorable situation of these Colonies, exposed to the fury of a cruel and relentless enemy, some form of government is absolutely necessary, not only for the preservation of good order, but also the more effectually to unite the people, and enable them to exert their whole force in their own necessary defence: and as the honorable the Continental Congress, the supreme council of the American Colonies, has advised such of the Colonies as have not yet gone into measures, to adopt for themselves, respectively, such government as shall best conduce to their own happiness and safety, and the well-being of America in general: We, the representatives of the Colony of New Jersey, having been elected by all the Counties, in the freest manner, and in congress assembled, have, after mature deliberations, agreed upon a set of charter rights and the form of a Constitution, in manner following,…

That all inhabitants of this Colony, of full age, who are worth fifty pounds proclamation money, clear estate in the same, and have resided within the County in which they claim a vote for twelve months immediately preceding the election, shall be entitled to vote for Representatives in Council and Assembly; and also for all other public officers, that shall be elected by the people of the County at large.

❧ "When in the course of human events"

THE DECLARATION OF INDEPENDENCE

In the spring of 1776, with Washington's forces fighting British troops outside of New York, the Second Continental Congress began to consider declaring independence. On June 7, Richard Henry Lee of Virginia introduced a resolution calling for a declaration of independence. While a majority of the delegates favored the motion, the Middle States were not ready to break with the mother country.

A committee consisting of Thomas Jefferson, John Adams, Benjamin Franklin, Robert Livingstone, and Roger Sherman was appointed to draft the declaration. Jefferson was charged with the actual writing of the document. In the meantime, several of the moderates swung their votes. In New Jersey the loyalist governor was ousted from power and a new delegation was sent to Congress authorized to vote for independence. Maryland, too, changed its position.

On July 1, four states still would not vote for independence. South Carolina and Pennsylvania voted against it, Delaware's delegation was divided, and New York was paralyzed by indecision. But over the next twenty-four hours, Delaware delegate Caesar Rodney traveled to Philadelphia to break his state's stalemate, the South Carolina and Pennsylvania delegations changed their minds and New York decided to abstain from voting. On July 2, Congress voted unanimously for independence. After making several changes to Jefferson's original draft, Congress again voted unanimously to adopt the Declaration of Independence. 55 delegates from all 13 states signed the declaration.

In CONGRESS, July 4, 1776

The unanimous Declaration of the thirteen united States of America,

When in the Course of human events, it becomes necessary for one people to dissolve the political bands which have connected them with another, and to assume among the powers of the earth, the separate and equal station to which the Laws of Nature and of Nature's God entitle them, a decent respect to the opinions of mankind requires that they should declare the causes which impel them to the separation.

We hold these truths to be self-evident, that all men are created equal, that they are endowed by their Creator with certain unalienable Rights, that among these are Life, Liberty, and the pursuit of Happiness. That to secure these rights, Governments are instituted among Men, deriving their just powers from the consent of the governed. That whenever any Form of Government becomes destructive of these ends, it is the Right of the People to alter or to abolish it, and to institute new Government, laying its foundation on such principles and organizing its powers in such form, as to them shall seem most likely to effect their Safety and Happiness.

Prudence, indeed, will dictate that Governments long established should not be changed for light and transient causes; and accordingly all experience hath shewn, that mankind are more disposed to suffer, while evils are sufferable, than to right themselves by abolishing the forms to which they are accustomed.

But when a long train of abuses and usurpations, pursuing invariably the same object evinces a design to reduce them under absolute Despotism, it is their right, it is their duty, to throw off such Government, and to provide new Guards for their future security.

Such has been the patient sufferance of these Colonies; and such is now the necessity which constrains them to alter their former Systems of Government. The history of the present King of Great Britain [George III] is a history of repeated injuries and usurpations, all having in direct object the establishment of an absolute Tyranny over these States. To prove this, let Facts be submitted to a candid world.

He has refused his Assent to Laws, the most wholesome and necessary for the public good.

He has forbidden his Governors to pass Laws of immediate and pressing importance, unless suspended in their operation till his Assent should be obtained, and when so suspended, he has utterly neglected to attend to them.

He has refused to pass other Laws for the accommodation of large districts of people, unless those people would relinquish the right of Representation in the Legislature, a right inestimable to them and formidable to tyrants only.

He has called together legislative bodies at places unusual, uncomfortable, and distant from the depository of their public Records, for the sole purpose of fatiguing them into compliance with his measures.

He has dissolved Representative Houses repeatedly, for opposing with manly firmness his invasions on the rights of the people.

He has refused for a long time, after such dissolutions, to cause others to be elected; whereby the Legislative powers, incapable of Annihilation, have returned to the People at large for their exercise; the State remaining in the meantime exposed to all the dangers of invasion from without, and convulsions within.

He has endeavoured to prevent the population of these States; for that purpose obstructing the Laws for Naturalization of Foreigners; refusing to pass others to encourage their migrations hither, and raising the conditions of new Appropriations of Lands.

He has obstructed the Administration of Justice, by refusing his Assent to Laws for establishing Judiciary powers.

He has made Judges dependent on his Will alone, for the tenure of their offices, and the amount and payment of their salaries.

He has erected a multitude of New Offices, and sent hither swarms of Officers to harass our people, and eat out their substance.

He has kept among us, in times of peace, Standing Armies, without the consent of our legislatures.

He has affected to render the Military independent of and superior to the Civil power.

He has combined with others to subject us to a jurisdiction foreign to our constitution and unacknowledged by our laws; giving his Assent to their Acts of pretended Legislation:

For protecting them by a mock Trial from punishment for any Murders which they should commit on the Inhabitants of these States:

For cutting off our Trade with all parts of the world:

For imposing Taxes on us without our Consent:

For depriving us in many cases of the benefits of Trial by Jury:

For transporting us beyond Seas to be tried for pretended offences:

For abolishing the free System of English Laws in a neighbouring Province, establishing therein an Arbitrary government, and enlarging its Boundaries so as to render it at once an example and fit instrument for introducing the same absolute rule into these Colonies:

For taking away our Charters, abolishing our most valuable Laws and altering fundamentally the Forms of our Governments:

For suspending our own Legislatures, and declaring themselves invested with power to legislate for us in all cases whatsoever.

He has abdicated Government here by declaring us out of his Protection and waging War against us.

He has plundered our seas, ravaged our Coasts, burnt our towns, and destroyed the lives of our people.

He is at this time transporting large Armies of foreign Mercenaries to complete the works of death, desolation and tyranny, already begun with circumstances of cruelty and perfidy scarcely paralleled in the most barbarous ages, and totally unworthy of the Head of a civilized nation.

He has constrained our fellow Citizens taken Captive on the high Seas to bear Arms against their Country, to become the executioners of their friends and Brethren, or to fall themselves by their Hands.

He has excited domestic insurrections amongst us, and has endeavoured to bring on the inhabitants of our frontiers, the merciless Indian Savages, whose known rule of warfare is an undistinguished destruction of all ages, sexes and conditions.

In every stage of these Oppressions We have Petitioned for Redress in the most humble terms. Our repeated Petitions have been answered only by repeated injury. A Prince, whose character is thus marked by every act which may define a Tyrant, is unfit to be the ruler of a free people.

Nor have We been wanting in attentions to our British brethren.

We have warned them from time to time of attempts by their legislature to extend an unwarrantable jurisdiction over us.

We have reminded them of the circumstances of our emigration and settlement here.

We have appealed to their native justice and magnanimity, and we have conjured them by the ties of our common kindred to disavow these usurpations, which would inevitably interrupt our connections and correspondence.

They too have been deaf to the voice of justice and of consanguinity. We must, therefore, acquiesce in the necessity, which denounces our Separation, and hold them, as we hold the rest of mankind, Enemies in War, in Peace Friends.

We, therefore, the Representatives of the United States of America, in General Congress, Assembled, appealing to the Supreme Judge of the world for the rectitude of our intentions, do, in the Name, and by the authority of the good People of these Colonies, solemnly publish and declare:

That these United Colonies are, and of Right ought to be Free and Independent States; that they are Absolved from all Allegiance to the British Crown, and that all political connection between them and the State of Great Britain is and ought to be totally dissolved; and that as Free and Independent States, they have full Power to levy War, conclude Peace, contract Alliances, establish Commerce, and to do all other Acts and Things which Independent States may of right do.

And for the support of this Declaration, with a firm reliance on the protection of Divine Providence, we mutually pledge to each other our Lives, our Fortunes, and our sacred Honor.

"I can see the rays of ravishing light and glory"

JOHN ADAMS TO ABIGAIL ADAMS

Americans rejoiced at the declaration, perhaps none so much as John Adams of Massachusetts. A firebrand patriot, Adams had been a principal engineer for the independence movement and exulted in the triumph in this letter to his wife, Abigail. Although he was correct that independence would be celebrated with parades for generations to come, he ascribed the wrong date. Although the actual vote for independence took place July 2, history would place the date for independence on the day the formal declaration was adopted.

The second day of July 1776, will be the most memorable epocha in the history of America. I am apt to believe that it will be celebrated by succeeding generations as the great anniversary festival. It ought to be commemorated as the day of deliverance, by solemn acts of devotion to God Almighty. It ought to be solemnized with pomp and parade, with shows, games, sports, guns, bells, bonfires and illuminations, from one end of this continent to the other, from this time forward, forevermore.

You will think me transported with enthusiasm, but I am not. I am well aware of the toil, and blood, and treasure, that it will cost us to maintain this declaration, and support and defend these States. Yet, through all the gloom, I can see the rays of ravishing light and glory. I can see that the end is more than worth all the means, and that posterity will triumph in that day's transaction, even though we should rue it, which I trust in God we shall not.

❧ "Remember the ladies"

ABIGAIL ADAMS

Abigail Adams was more than the wife of John Adams. Intelligent and forthright, she is one of the leading female voices of the 18th century and was in a position to express her views to influential ears. She maintained a lengthy correspondence with her husband and served as his informal advisor and confidante. Here she offers some advice from two letters on the role of women in American affairs.

I long to hear that you have declared an independency—and by the way in the New Code of Laws which I suppose it will be necessary for you to make I desire you would Remember the ladies, and be more generous and favorable to them than your ancestors. Do not put such unlimited power into the hands of the Husbands. Remember all Men would be tyrants if they could. If particular care and attention is not paid to the Ladies we are determined to foment a Rebellion, and will not hold ourselves bound by any laws in which we have no voice, or Representation.

That your Sex are Naturally Tyrannical is a Truth so thoroughly established as to admit of no dispute, but such of you as wish to be happy willingly give up the harsh title of Master for the more tender and endearing one of Friend. Why, then, not put it out of the power of the vicious and the Lawless to use us with cruelty and indignity without impunity. Men of Sense in all Ages abhor those customs which treat us only as the vassals of your Sex. Regard us then as Beings placed by providence under your protection and in imitation of the Supreme Being make use of that power only for our happiness.

Patriotism in the female sex is the most disinterested of virtues. Excluded from honors and from office, we cannot attach ourselves to the State or Government from having held a place of eminence. Even in the freest countries our property is subject to the control and disposal of partners, to whom the laws have given a sovereign authority. Deprived of a voice in legislation, obliged to submit to those laws which are imposed upon us, is it not sufficient to make us indifferent to the public welfare? Yet all history and every age exhibit instances of patriotic virtue in the female sex; which considering our situation equals the most heroic of yours.

❧ "I only regret that I have but one life to lose for my country"

NATHAN HALE

Captain Nathan Hale was captured by British troops on Long Island in September 1776. He had volunteered to go behind enemy lines to scout out their troop movements. An American officer with the British, perhaps his own cousin, recognized Hale and betrayed him. Hale was taken to Manhattan and summarily hanged as a spy.

His famous last words and the bearing in which he spoke them made him a legend. Even the British officers who witnessed the execution admired his courage. This account was given by William Hull, an officer in the American army.

In a few days an officer came to our camp, under a flag of truce, and informed Hamilton, then a captain of artillery, but afterwards the aid to General Washington, that Captain Hale had been arrested within the British lines, condemned as a spy and executed that morning.

I learned the melancholy particulars from this officer, who was present at his execution and seemed touched by the circumstances attending it.

He said that Captain Hale had passed through their army, both of Long Island and York Island. That he had procured sketches of the fortifications, and made memoranda of their number and different positions. When apprehended, he was taken before Sir William Howe, and these papers, found concealed upon his person, betrayed his intentions. He at once declared his name, his rank in the American army, and his object in coming within the British lines.

Sir William Howe, without the form of a trial, gave orders for his execution the following morning. He was placed in the custody of the provost marshal, who was a refugee and hardened to human suffering and every softening statement of the heart. Captain Hale, alone, without sympathy or support, save from that above, on the near approach of death asked for a clergyman to attend him. It was refused. He then requested a Bible; that too was refused by his inhuman jailer.

"On the morning of his execution," continued the officer, "my station was near the fatal spot, and I requested the Provost Marshal to permit the prisoner sit in my marquee, while he was making the necessary preparations. Captain Hale entered: he was calm, and bore himself with gentle dignity, in the consciousness of rectitude and high intentions. He asked for writing materials, which I furnished him: he wrote two letters, one to his mother and one to a brother officer." He was shortly after summoned to the gallows. But a few persons were around him, yet his characteristic dying words were remembered. He said, "I only regret that I have but one life to lose for my country."

❧ *Betty Zane*
THOMAS DUNN ENGLISH

The American Revolution in the western frontier was a bitter, brutal affair, pitting frontiersmen against British troops and their Native American allies. Most of the fighting took place around a handful of scattered settlements such as Fort Henry. In 1777, British soldiers and Native Americans attacked the fort. Low on powder, Betty Zane volunteered to leave the fort to get more ammunition in the face of enemy fire. Her action helped save the fort. A century later, poet Thomas Dunn English celebrated the event in the following poem.

Women are timid, cower and shrink
At show of danger, some folk think;
But men there are who for their lives
Dare not so far asperse their wives.
We let that pass—so much is clear,
Though little perils they may fear,
When greater perils men environ,
Then women show a front of iron;
And, gentle in their manner, they
Do bold things in a quiet way,
And so our wondering praise obtain,
As on a time did Betty Zane.

A century since, out in the West,
A block-house was by Girty pressed—
Girty, the renegade, the dread
Of all that border, fiercely led
Five hundred Wyandots, to gain
Plunder and scalp-locks from the slain;
And in this hold—Fort Henry then,
But Wheeling now—twelve boys and men
Guarded with watchful ward and care
Women and prattling children there,
Against their rude and savage foes,
And Betty Zane was one of those....

Now Betty's brothers and her sire
Were with her in this ring of fire,
And she was ready, in her way,
To aid their labor day by day,
In all a quiet maiden might.
To mould the bullets for the fight,
And, quick to note and so report,
Watch every act outside the fort;
Or, peering through the loopholes, see
Each phase of savage strategy—
These were her tasks, and thus the maid
The toil-worn garrison could aid.

Still, drearily the fight went on
Until a week had nearly gone,
When it was told—a whisper first,
And then in loud alarm it burst—
Their power scarce was growing; they
Knew where a keg unopened lay
Outside the fort at Zane's—what now?
Their leader stood with anxious brow.
It must be had at any cost,
Or toil and fort and lives were lost.
Some one must do that work of fear;
What man of men would volunteer?

Two offered, and so earnest they,
Neither his purpose would give way;
And Shephard, who commanded, dare
Not pick or choose between the pair.
But ere they settled on the one
By whom the errand should be done,
Young Betty interposed, and said,
"Let me essay the task instead.
Small matter 'twere if Betty Zane,
A useless woman, should be slain;
But death, if dealt on one of those,
Gives too much vantage to our foes."

Her father smiled with pleasure grim—
Her pluck gave painful pride to him;
And while her brothers clamored "No!"
He uttered, "Boys, let Betty go!
She'll do it at less risk than you;
But keep her steady in your view,
And be your rifles shields for her,
If yonder foe make step or stir,
Pick off each wretch who draws a bead,
And so you'll serve her in her need.

Now I recover from surprise,
I think our Betty's purpose wise."

The gate was opened, on she sped;
The foe, astonished gazed, 'tis said,
And wondered at her purpose, till
She gained that log-hut by the ill.
But when, in apron wrapped, the cask
She backward bore, to close her task,
The foemen saw her aim at last,
And poured their fire upon her fast.
Bullet on bullet near her fell,
While rang the Indians' angry yell;
But safely through that whirring rain,
Powder in arms, came Betty Zane.

They filled their horns, both boys and men
And so began the fight again.
Girty, who there so long had stayed,
By this new feat of feats dismayed,
Fired houses round and cattle slew,
And moved away—the fray was through.
But when the story was told
How they maintained the leaguered hold,
It was agreed, though fame was due
To all who in that fight were true,
The highest meed of praise, 'twas plain,
Fell to the share of Betty Zane....

✆ *"Further depreciations must ensue"*

ROBERT MORRIS

The American Revolution wreaked havoc on the American economy. Congress did not have the money to pay its army nor the credit to acquire loans for the task. Faced with little other choice, the fledgling government simply printed money to purchase supplies and pay wages. Rampant inflation ensued, particularly when many states followed suit and printed their own local currencies.

From 1776 to 1781, the value of paper currency dropped to 1/150th of its original value. Robert Morris identified the potential for this problem early on in this December 21, 1776 letter to the American commissioners in France who were desperately seeking French financial assistance.

Morris, who five years later as Superintendent of Finance would personally help pay for expenses in the Yorktown campaign and use his personal credit to secure loans for the military, established the Bank of North America in 1782 to help reaffirm the nation's financial footing. Nevertheless, he could not compel states to contribute to the national treasury, nor stop rampant profiteering. The government remained bankrupt throughout the revolution and for many years afterward.

Gentlemen:…I must add to this gloomy picture one circumstance, more distressing than all the rest, because it threatens instant and total ruin to the American cause, unless some radical cure is applied, and that speedily; I mean the depreciation of the Continental currency. The enormous pay of our Army, the immense expense at which they are supplied with provisions, clothing and other necessaries, and in short, the extravagance that has prevailed in most departments of the publick service, have called forth prodigious emissions of paper money, both Continental and Colonial. Our internal enemies, who, Alas! Are numerous and rich, have always been undermining its value by various artifices, and now that our distresses are wrought to a pitch by the success and near approach of the enemy, they speak plainer and many peremptorily refuse to take it at any rate. Those that do receive it, do it with fear and trembling; and you may judge of its value, even amongst those, when I tell you that 250 pounds continental money, or 666 2-3 dollars, is given for a bill of exchange of 100 pounds sterling, sixteen dollars for a half-johannas, two paper dollars for one of silver, three dollars for a pair of shoes, twelve dollars for a hat, and so on; a common labourer asks for two dollars a day for his work and idles half his time.

All this amounts to a real depreciation of the money. The war must be carried on at an expense proportioned to this value, which must inevitably call for immense emissions, and, of course, still further depreciations must ensue. This can only be prevented by borrowing in the money now in circulation. The attempt is made, and I hope will succeed by loan or lottery. The present interrupt those measures here, and as yet I am not informed how they go in other States, but something more is necessary; force must be inevitably employed, and I fear to see that day. We have already calamities sufficient for any country, and the measure will be full when one part of the American people is obliged to dragoon another, at the same time that they are opposing a most powerful external foe.

🌿 *"These are the times that try men's souls"*

THOMAS PAINE

Thomas Paine's second great pamphlet of the American Revolution was *The American Crisis*. A rousing patriotic work, it was published in December 1776. Washington's army had been in constant retreat for much of the year in the disastrous Long Island and New York campaigns. The army was defeated and dejected. Help from abroad was not materializing. And the nation was growing tired of the costs of rebellion.

Paine speaks to the problems, cites historic low points in other successful ventures, reaffirms the rightness of the cause and reminds readers of the poor alternatives to continuing the fight. Paine's words would once again help rally the nation. Although Paine was America's most popular writer, he refused royalties to keep the cost of his pamphlets low and accessible to as many people as possible.

These are the times that try men's souls. The summer soldier and the sunshine patriot will, in this crisis, shrink from the service of his country; but he that stands it NOW, deserves the love and thanks of man and woman. Tyranny, like hell, is not easily conquered; yet we have this consolation with us, that the harder the conflict, the more glorious the triumph. What we obtain too cheap, we esteem too lightly; 'tis dearness only that gives every thing its value. Heaven knows how to put a proper price upon its goods; and it would be strange indeed, if so celestial an article as FREEDOM should not be highly rated. Britain, with an army to enforce her tyranny, has declared that she has a right (not only to TAX) but "to BIND us in ALL CASES WHATSOEVER," and if being bound in that manner, is not slavery, then is there no such a thing as slavery upon earth. Even the expression is impious, for so unlimited a power can belong only to God....

I have as little superstition in me as any man living, but my secret opinion has ever been, and still is, that God Almighty will not give up a people to military destruction, or leave them unsupportedly to perish, who have so earnestly and so repeatedly sought to avoid the calamities of war, by every decent method which wisdom could invent. Neither have I so much of the infidel in me, as to suppose that He has relinquished the government of the world, and given us up to the care of devils; and as I do not, I cannot see on what grounds the king of Britain can look up to Heaven for help against us: a common murderer, a highwayman, or a housebreaker, has as good a pretence as he.

'Tis surprising to see how rapidly a panic will sometimes run through a country. All nations and ages have been subject to them: Britain has trembled like an ague at the report of a French fleet of flat bottomed boats; and in the fourteenth century the whole English army, after ravaging the kingdom of France, was driven back like men petrified with fear; and this brave exploit was performed by a few broken forces collected and headed by a woman, Joan of Arc. Would that heaven might inspire some Jersey maid to spirit up her countrymen, and save her fair fellow sufferers from ravage and ravishment!...

I call not upon a few, but upon all: not on this state or that state, but on every state; up and help us; lay your shoulders to the wheel; better have too much force than too little, when so great an object is at stake. Let it be told to the future world, that in the depth of winter, when nothing but hope and virtue could survive, that the city and the country, alarmed at one common danger, came forth to meet and to repulse it. Say not that thousands are gone, turn out your tens of thousands; throw not the burden of the day upon Providence, but "show your faith by your works" that God may bless you. It matters not where you live, or what rank of life you hold, the evil or the blessing will reach you all. The far and the near, the home counties and the back, the rich and the poor, will suffer or rejoice alike. The heart that feels not now, is dead: the blood of his children will curse his cowardice, who shrinks back at a time when a little might have saved the whole, and made them happy. I love the man that can smile in trouble, that can gather strength from distress, and grow brave by reflection. 'Tis the business of little minds to shrink; but he whose heart is firm, and whose conscience approves his conduct, will pursue his principles unto death. My own line of reasoning is to myself as straight and clear as a ray of light. Not all the treasures of the world, so far as I believe, could have induced me to support an offensive war, for I think it murder; but if a thief breaks into my house, burns and destroys my property, and kills or threatens to kill me, or those that are in it, and to "bind me in all cases whatsoever," to his absolute will, am I to suffer it? What signifies it to me, whether he who does it is a king or a common man; my countryman or not my countryman: whether it be done by an individual villain, or an army of them? If we reason to the root of things we shall find no difference; neither can any just cause be assigned why we should punish in the one case and pardon in the other. Let them call me rebel, and welcome, I feel no concern from it; but I should suffer the misery of devils, were I to make a whore of my soul by swearing allegiance to one whose character is that of a sottish, stupid, stubborn, worthless, brutish man. I conceive likewise a horrid idea in receiving mercy from a being, who at the last day shall be shrieking to the rocks and mountains to cover him, and fleeing with terror from the orphan, the widow, and the slain of America.

There are cases which cannot be overdone by language, and this is one. There are persons too who see not the full extent of the evil which threatens them, they solace themselves with hopes that the enemy, if they succeed, will be merciful. It is the madness of folly, to expect mercy from those who have refused to do justice; and even mercy, where conquest is the object, is only a trick of war; the cunning of the fox is as murderous as the violence of the wolf; and we ought to guard equally against both....

I thank God that I fear not. I see no real cause for fear. I know our situation well, and can see the way out of it.... By perseverance and fortitude we have the prospect of a glorious issue; by cowardice and submission, the sad choice of a variety of evils—a ravaged country—a depopulated city—habitants without safety, and slavery without hope—our homes turned into barracks and bawdy-houses for Hessians, and a future race to provide for, whose fathers we shall doubt of. Look on this picture and weep over it! And if there yet remains one thoughtless wretch who believes it not, let him suffer it unlamented....

❧ *Yankee Doodle*

TRADITIONAL FOLK SONG

The most famous song to come out of the American Revolution was "Yankee Doodle." Ironically, historians believe the song pre-dated the revolution and was originated by British soldiers who mocked the simple ways of American colonials. "Yankee" was a condescending term for a backward New Englander and "doodle" referred to a fool. Nevertheless, Americans spun the insult on its head and eagerly adopted the song as their own and devised hundreds of variations.

Yankee Doodle went to town,
A-ridin' on a pony,
Stuck a feather in his cap
And called it Macaroni.

CHORUS:
Yankee Doodle, keep it up,
Yankee Doodle Dandy,
Mind the music and the step
And with the girls be handy.

Father and I went down to camp
Along with Captain Gooding,
And there we see the men and boys
As thick as hasty pudding.

And there we see a thousand men,
As rich as 'Squire David,
And what they wasted every day,
I wish it could be saved.

The 'lasses they eat every day
Would keep a house a winter.
They have as much that I'll be bound,
They eat it when they're a mind to.

And there we see a swamping gun,
Big as a log of maple,
Upon a deuced little cart,
A load for Father's cattle.

And every time they shoot it off
It takes a horn of powder,
And makes a noise like Father's gun,
Only a nation louder.

I went as night to one myself
As Siah's underpinning,
And Father went as nigh again—
I thought the deuce was in him.

Cousin Simon grew so bold
I thought he would have cock't it;
It scared me so, I shrinked it off
And hung by Father's pocket.

And Captain Davis had a gun,
He kind of clapt his hand on't;
And stuck a crooked stabbing iron
Upon the little end on't.

And there I see a pumpkin shell
As big as Mother's bason,
And every time they touched it off
They scampered like the nation.

I see a little barrel too,
The heads were made of leather,
They knocked upon't with little clubs,
And called the folks together.

And there was Captain Washington,
And gentlefolks about him.
They say he's grown so tarnal proud
He will not go without 'em.

He got him on his meeting clothes,
Upon a slapping stallion.
He set the world along in rows,
In hundreds and millions.

The blaming ribbons in his hat,
They look'd so tearing fine ah,
I wanted pockily to get
To give to my Jemimah.

I see another snarl of men
A-digging graves, they told me,
So tarnal long, so tarnal deep,
They 'tended they should hold me—

It scared me so I hooked it off,
Nor stopt as I remember,
Nor turned about till I got home
Locked up in Mother's chamber.

🍃 "Let tyrants shake their iron rod"

WILLIAM BILLINGS

Credited by some as the father of American music, William Billings was a self-taught musician who wrote several books of songs. One of his most popular Revolutionary songs was "Chester", a hymn-like song extolling young American patriots who confound veteran British generals.

Let tyrants shake their iron rod,
And slavery clank her galling chains;
We fear them not, we trust in God—
New England's God for ever reigns.

Howe and Burgoyne, and Clinton, too,
With Prescott and Cornwallis joined;
Together plot our overthrow,
In one infernal league combined.

When God inspired us for the fight,
Their ranks were broke, their lines were forced;
Their ships were shattered in our sight,
Or swiftly driven from our coast.

The foe comes on with haughty stride;
Our troops advance with martial noise;
Their veterans flee before our youth,
And generals yield to beardless boys.

What grateful offering shall we bring?
What shall we render to the Lord?
Lord hallelujahs let us sing,
And praise his name on every chord.

🍃 The Rebels

CAPTAIN SMYTH

Loyalist American troops, too, had their own patriotic songs—only they were to King George III. Captain Smyth of the Simcoe's Queen's Rangers wrote "The Rebels" in 1778, a song praising Americans brave enough to stand up to their neighbors in support of the king, and sharply criticizing the rebels. Loyalists saw the revolutionaries as restricting liberty and destroying the country and economy.

Ye brave, honest subjects, who dare to be loyal

And have stood the brunt of every trial
Of hunting-shirts and rifle-guns:
Come listen awhile, and I'll sing you a song;
I'll show you those Yankees are all in the wrong,
Who, with blustering look and most awkward gait,
'Gainst their lawful sovereign dare for to prate,
With their hunting-shirts and rifle-guns.

The arch-rebels, barefooted tatterdemallions,
In baseness exceed all other rebellions,
With their hunting-shirts and rifle-guns.
To rend the empire, the most infamous lies
Their mock-patriot Congress do always devise;
Independence, like the first of rebels, they claim,
But their plots will be damned in the annals
    of fame,
With their hunting-shirts and rifle-guns.

Forgetting the mercies of Great Britain's king,
Who saved their forefathers' necks from the
    string;
With their hunting-shirts and rifle-guns.
They renounce allegiance and take up their arms,
Assemble together like hornets in swarms.
So dirty their backs and so wretched their show
That carrion-crow follows wherever they go,
With their hunting-shirts and rifle-guns.

With loud peals of laughter, your sides, sirs, would
    crack
To see General Convict and Colonel Shoe-black,
With their hunting-shirts and rifle-guns.
See cobblers and quacks, rebel priests and the like,
Pettifoggers and barbers, with sword and with pike,
All strutting, the standard of Stan beside,
And honest names, using, their black deeds to hide.
With their hunting-shirts and rifle-guns.

This perjured banditti now ruin this land,
And o'er its poor people claim lawless command,
With their hunting-shirts and rifle-guns.
Their pasteboard dollars prove a common curse;
They don't chink like silver and gold in our purse.
With nothing their leaders have paid their
    debts off;
Their honor's dishonor, and justice they scoff,
With their hunting-shirts and rifle-guns.

For one lawful ruler, many tyrants we've got,
Who force young and old to their wars, to be shot,

With their hunting-shirts and rifle-guns.
Our good king, God speed him! Never used
    men so;
We then could speak, act, and like freemen could
    go;
But committees enslave us, our Liberty's gone,
Our trade and church murdered, our country's
    undone,
With their hunting-shirts and rifle-guns.

Come take up your glasses, each true loyal heart,
And may every rebel meet his due desert,
With their hunting-shirts and rifle-guns.
May Congress, Conventions, those damn'd inquisi-
    tions,
Be fed with hot sulphur, from Lucifer's kitchens,
May commerce and peace again be restored,
And Americans own their true sovereign lord!
Then oblivion to shirts and rifle-guns.
God save the King!

❧ "Perpetual union between the states"

ARTICLES OF CONFEDERATION

The Second Continental Congress resolved on June 11, 1776 to draw up a formal confederation between the colonies. John Dickinson of Pennsylvania provided the basis for the plan that was eventually adopted on November 15, 1777. Representatives of the states signed the document in 1778 and 1779. Only Maryland refused to sign.

The agreement called for a league of friendship between the newfound states in a loose union. The document lacked many essential components for the new nation, such as a judicial system, meaningful authority and the ability to levy taxes. Nevertheless, it provided a basis for union on common issues such as diplomacy, defense and commerce.

Although the deficiencies of the Articles of Confederation would help lead to disorder in the 1780s, as a whole, the Articles provided a foundation that was strong enough to keep the country united through the American Revolution. The document later served as a jumping off point from which to build a stronger, more permanent national government as determined by the Constitution.

To all to whom these presents shall come, we the undersigned delegates of the states affixed to our names send greeting. Whereas, The delegates of the United States of America in Congress assembled did on the fifteenth day of November in the year of Our Lord one thousand seven hundred and seventy-seven, and in the second year of the independence of America, agree to certain articles of confederation and perpetual union between the states of New Hampshire, Massachusetts Bay, Rhode Island and Providence Plantations, Connecticut, New York, New Jersey, Pennsylvania, Delaware, Maryland, Virginia, North Carolina, South Carolina, and Georgia in the words following, viz., "Articles of perpetual union between the states of New Hampshire, Massachusetts Bay, Rhode Island and Providence Plantations, Connecticut, New York, New Jersey, Pennsylvania, Delaware, Maryland, Virginia, North Carolina, South Carolina, and Georgia."

Article I

The style of this confederacy shall be "The United States of America."

Article II

Each retains its sovereignty, freedom, and independence, and every power, jurisdiction, and right, which is not by this confederation expressly delegated to the United States, in Congress assembled.

Article III

The said states hereby severally enter into a firm league of friendship with each other for their common defense, the security of their liberties, and their mutual and general welfare, binding themselves to assist each other against all force offered to, or attacks made upon them, or any of them, on account of religion, sovereignty, trade, or any other pretense whatever.

Article IV

The better to secure and perpetuate mutual friendship and intercourse among the people of the different states in this union, the free inhabitants of each of these states—paupers, vagabonds, and fugitives from justice excepted—shall be entitled to all privileges and immunities of free citizens in the several states; and all the people of each state shall have free ingress and regress to and from any other state, and shall enjoy therein all the privileges of trade and commerce, subject to the same duties, impositions, and restrictions as the inhabitants thereof respectively, provided that such restriction shall not extend so far as to prevent the removal of property imported into any state, to any other state of which the owner is an inhabitant; provided also that no imposition, duties and restriction shall be laid by any state on the property of the United States, or either of them.

If any person guilty of, or charged with treason, felony, or other high misdemeanor in any state shall flee from justice, and be found in any of the United States, he shall upon demand of the governor or executive power of the state from which he fled be delivered up and removed to the state having jurisdiction of his offense.

Full faith and credit shall be given in each of these states to the records, acts, and judicial proceedings of the courts and magistrates of every other state.

Article V

For the more convenient management of the general interests of the United States, delegates shall be annually appointed in such manner as the legislature of each state shall direct, to meet in Congress on the first Monday in November, in every year, with a power reserved to each state to recall its delegates, or any of them, at any time within the year, and to send others in their stead for the remainder of the year.

No state shall be represented in Congress by less than two, nor more than seven members; and no person shall be capable of being a delegate for more than three years in any term of six years; nor shall any person, being a delegate, be capable of holding any office under the United States for which he, or another of his benefit, receives any salary, fees, or emolument of any kind.

Each state shall maintain its own delegates in a meeting of the states, and while they act as members of the committee of the states.

In determining questions in the United States in Congress assembled, each state shall have one vote.

Freedom of speech and debate in Congress shall not be impeached or questioned in any court, or place out of Congress, and the members of Congress shall be protected in their persons from arrests and imprisonments during the time of their going to and from, and attendance on Congress, except for treason, felony, or breach of the peace.

Article VI

No state without the consent of the United States in Congress assembled shall send any embassy to, or receive any embassy from, or enter into any conference, agreement, or alliance or treaty with any king, prince, or state; nor shall any person holding any office or profit or trust under the United States, or any of them, accept of any present, emolument, office, or title of any kind whatever from any king, prince, or foreign state; nor shall the United States in Congress assembled, or any of them, grant any title of nobility.

No two or more states shall enter into any treaty, confederation, or alliance whatever between them without the consent of the United States in Congress assembled, specifying accurately the purposes for which the same is to be entered into, and how long it shall continue.

No state shall lay any imposts or duties which may interfere with any stipulations in treaties entered into by the United States in Congress assembled, with king, prince, or state, in pursuance of any treaties already proposed by congress to the courts of France and Spain.

No vessels of war shall be kept up in time of peace by any state, except such number only as shall be deemed necessary by the United States in Congress assembled, for the defense of such state, or its trade; nor shall any body of forces be kept up by any state in time of peace, except such numbers only as in the judgment of the United States, in Congress assembled, shall be deemed requisite to garrison the forts necessary for the defense of such state; but every state shall always keep up a well-regulated and disciplined militia, sufficiently armed and accoutered, and shall provide and constantly have ready for use, in public stores, a due number of field pieces and tents, and a proper quantity of arms, ammunition, and camp equipage.

No state shall engage in any war without the consent of the United States of Congress assembled, unless such state be actually invaded by enemies, or shall have received certain advice of a resolution being formed by some nation of Indians to invade such state, and the danger is so imminent as not to admit of a delay till the United States in Congress assembled can be consulted....

Article VII

When land forces are raised by any state for the common defense, all officers of or under the rank of colonel shall be appointed by the legislature of each state respectively by whom such forces shall be raised, or in such manner as such state shall direct, and all vacancies shall be filled up by the state which first made the appointment.

Article VIII

All charges of war, and all other expenses that shall be incurred for the common defense or general welfare, and allowed by the United States in Congress assembled, shall be defrayed out of a common treasury, which shall be supplied by the several states in proportion to the value of all land within each state, granted to or surveyed for any person, as such land and the buildings and improvements thereon shall be estimated according to such mode as the United States in Congress assembled shall from time to time direct and appoint....

Article IX

The United States in Congress assembled shall have the sole and exclusive right and power of determining on peace and war, except in the cases mentioned in the sixth article—of sending and receiving ambassadors—entering into treaties and alliances, provided that no treaty of commerce shall be made whereby the legislative power of the respective states shall be restrained from imposing such imposts and duties on foreigners, as their own people are subjected to, or from prohibiting the exportation or importation of any species of goods or commodities whatsoever—of establishing rules for deciding in all cases, what captures on land or water shall be legal, and in what manner prizes taken by land or naval forces in the service of the United States shall be divided or appropriated—of granting letters or marque and reprisal in times of peace—appointing courts for the trial of piracies and felonies committed on the high seas and establishing courts for receiving and determining finally appeals in all cases of captures, provided that no member of Congress shall be appointed a judge of any of the said courts.

The United States in Congress assembled shall also be the last resort on appeal in all disputes and differences now subsisting or that hereafter may arise between two or more states concerning boundary, jurisdiction, or any other cause whatsoever....

All controversies concerning the private right of soil claimed under different grants of two or more states, whose jurisdiction as they may respect such lands, and the states which passed such grants are adjusted, the said grants or either of them being at the same time claimed to have originated antecedent to such settlement of jurisdiction, shall on the petition of either party to the Congress of the United States be finally determined as near as may be in the same manner as is before prescribed for deciding disputes respecting territorial jurisdiction between different states.

The United States in Congress assembled shall also have the sole and exclusive right and power of regulating the alloy and value of coin struck by their own authority, or by that of the respective states—fixing the standard of weights and measures throughout the United States—regulating the trade and managing all affairs with the Indians, not members of any state within its own limits be not infringed or violated—establishing and regulating post offices from one state to another throughout all the United States, and exacting such postage on the papers passing through the same as may be requisite to defray the expenses of the said office—appointing all officers of the land forces in the service of the United States, excepting regimental officers—appointing all the officers of the naval forces, and commissioning all officers whatever in the service of the United States—making rules for the government and regulation of the said land and naval forces, and directing the operations.

The United States in Congress assembled shall have authority to appoint a committee to sit in the recess of Congress, to be denominated a Committee of the States, and to consist of one delegate from each state; and to appoint such other committees and civil officers as may be necessary for managing the general affairs of the United States under their direction—to appoint one of their number to preside, provided that no person be allowed to serve in the office of president more than one year in any term of three years; to ascertain the necessary sums of money to be raised for the service of the United States, and to appropriate and apply the same for defraying the public expenses—or borrow money or emit bills on the credit of the United States, transmitting every half-year to the respective states an account of the sums of

money so borrowed or emmitted—to build and equip a navy—to agree upon the number of land forces, and to make requisitions from each state for its quota in proportion to the number of white inhabitants in each state; which requisition shall be binding, and thereupon the legislature of each state shall appoint the regimental officers, raise the men, and clothe, arm, and equip them in a soldierlike manner at the expense of the United States, and the officers and men so clothed, armed, and equipped shall march to the place appointed, and within the time agreed on by the United States in Congress assembled....

The United States in Congress assembled shall never engage in a war, nor grant letters of marque and reprisal in time of peace, nor enter into any treaties or alliances, nor coin money, nor regulate the value thereof, nor ascertain the sums and expenses necessary for the defense and welfare of the United States, or any of them, nor emit bills, nor borrow money on the credit of the United States, nor appropriate money, nor agree upon the number of vessels of war to be built or purchased, nor the number of land or sea forces to be raised, nor appoint a commander in chief of the army or navy, unless nine states assent to the same: nor shall a question on any other point, except for adjourning from day to day, be determined unless by the votes of a majority of the United States in Congress assembled.

The Congress of the United States shall have the power to adjourn to any time within the year, and to any place within the United States, so that no period of adjournment be for a longer duration than the space of six months, and shall publish the journal of their proceedings monthly, except such parts thereof relating to treaties, alliances, or military operations, as in their judgment require secrecy; and the yeas and nays of the delegates of each state on any question shall be entered on the journal when it is desired by any delegate; and the delegates of a state, or any of them, at his or their request shall be furnished with a transcript of the said journal, except such parts as are above excepted, to lay before the legislatures of the several states.

Article X
The Committee of the States, or any nine of them, shall be authorized to execute, in the recess of

Congress, such of the powers of Congress as the United States in Congress assembled, by the consent of nine states, shall from time to time think expedient to vest them with; provided that no power be delegated to the said committee for the exercise of which, by the Articles of Confederation, the voice of nine states in the Congress of the United States assembled is requisite.

Article XI

Canada acceding to this confederation, and joining in the measures of the United States, shall be admitted into, and entitled to all the advantages of this union: but no other colony shall be admitted into the same unless such admission be agreed upon by nine states.

Article XII

All bills of credit emitted, monies borrowed, and debts contracted by, or under the authority of Congress, before the assembling of the United States, in pursuance of the present confederation, shall be deemed and considered as a charge against the United States, for payment and satisfaction whereof the said United States and the public faith are hereby solemnly pledged.

Article XIII

Every state shall abide by the determinations of the United States in Congress assembled on all questions which, by this confederation, are submitted to them. And the articles of this confederation shall be inviolably observed by every state, and the union shall be perpetual; nor shall any alteration at any time hereafter be made in any of them, unless such alteration be agreed to in a Congress of the United States, and be afterward confirmed by the legislatures of every state.

And Whereas, It hath pleased the Great Governor of the World to incline the hearts of the legislatures we respectively represent in congress to approve of, and to authorize us to ratify, the said Articles of Confederation and perpetual union: Know Ye, That we the undersigned delegates, by virtue of the power and authority to us given for that purpose, do by these presents, in the name and in behalf of our respective constituents, fully and entirely ratify and confirm each and every of the said Articles of Confederation and perpetual union, and all and singular the matters and things therein

contained: and we do further solemnly plight and engage the faith of our respective constituents, that they shall abide by the determinations of the United States in Congress assembled on all questions which, by the said confederation, are submitted to them. And that the articles thereof shall be inviolably observed by the states we respectively represent, and that the union shall be perpetual. In witness whereof we have hereunto set our hands in Congress.

Done at Philadelphia in the state of Pennsylvania the ninth day of July in the year of Our Lord one thousand seven hundred and seventy-eight, and in the third year of the independence of America.

"Nothing but virtue has kept our army together"

COLONEL JOHN BROOKS FROM VALLEY FORGE

Sick, ill-clad and starving, Washington's army spent the winter of 1778 in Valley Forge. The previous year had been a disappointing one for Washington, whose forces were pushed about by a larger British army, despite an important American victory at Saratoga, New York.

By the time the American troops settled in at Valley Forge in Pennsylvania in December their situation was already desperate. Mismanagement and graft deprived the soldiers of clothing, food, wages and supplies. The bravery and disinterested patriotism of these American soldiers over the next several months became a legend.

And when the brutal encampment ended, despite the loss of more than 2,000 men to starvation, fever and cold, the army was a stronger, better-trained military unit. A new discipline had emerged, in part due to the new drilling from the Prussian Baron Friedrich von Steuben.

Colonel John Brooks of Massachusetts wrote of the plight in January 1778 to a friend. His words reflect the hardships, determination and nagging bitterness that marked the army's condition.

You make me smile when you observe that you are so sanguine about matters in this quarter at present as you were. My dear friend, what ever made you sanguine? Could How's marching through a vast extent of country—a country very well formed for defence; could the action at Brandywine, at which time Genl. Washington's army was entirely routed for that day, with as great loss, at least, as ever was published; could the Germantown affair, in which our army were again broke, dispersed, and persued for more than ten miles from the place of the first attack, with the loss of more than one thousand men; in short, could a large superiority of numbers on the side of Mr. How through the whole campaign, and in consequence thereof his being able to go to what point he pleased—I ask could any of these make you sanguine? Even now, since the northern troops have joined, How's army is the largest, which is now some ten thousand, ours not eight thousand.

With respect to the clothing, etc., etc., of our army, believe it, Sir, to be bad enough. Ever since our march from Albany our men have been suffering all the inconveniences of an inclement season and a want of cloathing. For a week past we have had snow, and as cold weather as I almost ever knew at home. To see our poor brave fellows living in tents, bare-footed, bare-legged, bare-breeched, etc., etc., in snow, in rain, on marches, in camp, and on duty, without being able to supply their wants is really distressing. Where the fault is I know not, but am rather inclined to think our General Court has not done everything that might be expected of them. If it be for want of foresight in our rulers, the Lord pity us! But if it be through negligence or design, "is there not some chosen curse" reserved for those who are cause of so much misery?

Another thing which has been the occasion of much complaint is the unequal distribution and scanty allowance for provisions. For the former of these the Commissary's are accountable. The cursed Quakers and other inhabitants are the cause of the latter. But those difficulties are at an end. Large supplies of provisions from N. England (which on account of the critical situation of affairs has been stopped till now) are now coming into camp. Another ground of uneasiness among our troops (the northern) is the want of money. Our regiment has never received but two months pay for twelve months past. This difficulty I hope will soon be over.

I have mentioned these particulars not to sink your spirits, but just to give you a small idea of a soldier's life. Under all those disadvantages no men ever shew more spirit or prudence than ours. In my opinion nothing but virtue has kept our army together through this campaign. There has been that great principle, the love of our country, which first called us into the field, and that only to influence us.

But this will not last always: Some other motives must cooperate with this in order to keep an army together any length of time. Upon the same principle that we love our country we love ourselves. It must be for private interest of officers, at least, to continue in the service any considerable time: and without having an experienced army you cannot have a respectable army; and without a respectable army you cannot have a good army. I know of no reason why one part of the community should sacrifice their all for the good of it, while the rest are filling their coffers. We have this consolation, however, that it cannot be said that we are bought or bribed into service. Those officers who can keep out of debt, especially who have considerable families, this year may with propriety be called good husbands.

The above intelligence with respect to How's and the American army will help you to account for the loss of Philadelphia, the forts on the Delaware, etc., etc. I assure you those events have not been lost for want of spirit, but numbers. As to my observations with respect to the situation of the army at present, and their future prospects, I have made them at your desire and for your speculation. As to another campaign, I can form no judgment about it. How Congress will augment their force is not public. By the inactivity of the States it seems as if they chose to prolong the war.

The States of Pennsylvania and Maryland do not seem to have any more idea of liberty than a savage has of civilization. In general they have not been able to feel themselves interested in this controversey. They have ever supposed (till woefull experience taught them otherwise) that the King's troops were as kind, merciful and just as they represented themselves to be. But now the tone is altering fast. Even some of the Thees and Thous, who have had their wives ravished, housed plundered and burned, are now ready, on any party's making a sally from the city, to take their arms and oppose them. Last winter How made the Jersey's the best of Whigs. I hope all will be converted in these States this [winter]; and that next summer the whole continent will feel their importance and exert that small part of her strength which, when duly applied, will be sufficient to hurl all the How's in the universe into atoms.

What would have been the situation of New England at this moment had they shown the same disposition towards Genl. Burgoyne which the cringing, non-resisting, ass-like fools of this State have done towards How? The chains of British slavery would have been unalterably fixed: and instead of adressing you at this time as a freeman, I should have expressed my friendship to a slave. Oh! Horrid thought! To be a slave! Oh! Base idea first conceived in hell!

"Do thou, great Liberty! Inspire our souls,
And make our lives in thy possession happy,
Or our deaths glorious in thy just defence!"

✒ "I have not yet begun to fight!"

CAPTAIN JOHN PAUL JONES

Although the British Navy had unquestioned dominance of the sea, America was able to mount a significant navy to pester British trade and shipping routes. Far and away the most daring and successful naval officer was Captain John Paul Jones. Early in the war, he led raids into Canada capturing ships and destroying fisheries.

When France joined the American cause, Benjamin Franklin arranged for Jones to use France as the base for attacks on Great Britain itself. His squadron struck the British and Irish coasts. On September 23, 1779, Jones who was in command of the *Bon Homme Richard* (named in honor of Franklin's *Poor Richard's Almanac*) encountered a 40-ship convoy of merchant ships escorted by the British warships *Serapis* and *Countess of Scarborough.* Even though the *Serapis* outgunned his ship 44 to 40, Jones attacked the British vessel.

At the outset of the battle, Jones was at a disadvantage and when asked to surrender ("strike down") he replied with the memorable words, "I have not yet begun to fight." The three-hour battle, which took place in plain view of nearby shore, ended in American victory. This account of the outset of the battle comes from Lieutenant Richard Dale who served on the *Bon Homme Richard.*

On the 23rd of September, 1779, being below, was roused by an unusual noise upon deck. This induced me to go upon deck when I found the men were swaying up the royal yards, preparatory to making sail for a large fleet under our lee. I asked the coasting pilot what fleet it was?

He answered, "The Baltic fleet under convoy of the *Serapis* of 44 guns and the *Countess of Scarborough* of 20 guns."

A general chase commenced of the *Bon Homme Richard*, the *Venegeance*, the *Pallas* and the *Alliance*, the latter ship being then in sight after a separation from the squadron of nearly three weeks,

but which ship, as usual disregarded the private signals of the Commodore. At this time our fleet headed to the northward with a light breeze, Flamborough head being about two leagues distant. At 7 p.m. it was evident the Baltic fleet perceived we were in chace from the signal of the *Serapis* to the merchantment to stand in shore. At the same time the *Serapis* and *Countess of Scarborough* tacked ship and stood off shore, with the intention of drawing off our attention from the convoy. When these ships had separated from the convoy about two miles, they again tacked and stood in shore after the merchantmen.

At about eight, being within hail, the *Serapis* demanded, "What ship is that?"

He was answered, "I can't hear what you say."

Immediately after, the *Serapis* hailed again, "What ship is that? Answer immediately, or I shall be under the necessity of firing into you."

At this moment I received orders from Commodore Jones to commence the action with a broadside, which indeed appeared to be simultaneous on board both ships. Our position being to windward of the *Serapis* we passed ahead of her, and the *Serapis* coming up on our larboard quarter, the action commenced abreast of each other. The *Serapis* soon passed ahead of the *Bon Homme Richard*, and when he thought he had gained a distance sufficient to go down athwart the fore foot to rake us, found he had not enough distance, and that the *Bon Homme Richard* would be aboard him, put his helm a-lee, which brought the two ships on a line, and the *Bon Homme Richard*, having head way, ran her bows into the stern of the *Serapis.*

We had remained in this situation but a few minutes when we were again hailed by the *Serapis*, "Has your ship struck?"

To which Captain Jones answered, "I have not yet begun to fight!"

✒ "One more step to universal civilization"

EMANCIPATION IN PENNSYLVANIA

When Thomas Jefferson wrote that "all men are created equal" he meant white men. Cynical observers of the American Revolutionary cause were quick to point out that freedom and liberty were peculiar ambitions for a country of slaveholders. Many Americans saw the hypocrisy and acted on it.

In the north, where slavery was allowed but not nearly as common as the southern states, slavery was abolished. Rhode Island was the first in 1774 to declare all slaves in its colony free. The Massachusetts Supreme Court struck down slavery. The following preamble was to an act providing for gradual emancipation in Pennsylvania.

The situation was not as simple in the south where there were hundreds of thousands of slaves that provided the foundation for the entire region's economy. Nonetheless, some of the states outlawed or imposed restrictions on the slave trade. Many of the leaders in the Revolution privately condemned slavery even as they owned slaves themselves. Patrick Henry described it as a "lamentable evil." He wrote: "Would anyone believe I am the master of slaves of my own purchase! I am drawn along by the general inconvenience of living here without them. I will not, I cannot justify it."

Preamble to the act passed by the Pennsylvania Assembly

When we contemplate our abhorrence of that condition to which the arms and tyranny of Great Britain were exerted to reduce us, when we look back on the variety of dangers to which we have been exposed, and how miraculously our wants in many instances have been supplied, and our deliverances wrought, when even hope and human fortitude have become unequal to the conflict, we are unavoidably led to a serious and grateful sense of the manifold blessings which we have undeservedly received from the hand of that Being from whom every good and perfect gift cometh.

Impressed with these ideas, we conceive that it is our duty, and we rejoice that it is in our power, to extend a portion of that freedom to others which has been extended to us, and release them from the state of thralldom to which we ourselves were tyrannically doomed, and from which we have now every prospect of being delivered. It is not for us to inquire why, in the creation of mankind, the inhabitants of the several parts of the earth were distinguished by differences in feature or complexion. It is sufficient to know that all are the work of the Almighty hand. We find in the distribution of the human species, that the most fertile as well as the most barren parts of the earth are inhabited by men of complexions different from ours, and from each other; from whence we may reasonably as well as religiously infer that He who placed them in their various situations has extended equally his care and

protection to all, and that it becomes not us to counteract His mercies.

We esteem it a peculiar blessing granted to us that we are enabled this day to add one more step to universal civilization by removing, as much as possible, the sorrows of those who have lived in undeserved bondage, and from which, by the assumed authority of the kings of Great Britain, no effectual legal relief can be obtained. Weaned, by a long curse of experience, from those narrow prejudices and partialities we had imbibed, we find our hearts enlarged with kindness and benevolence toward men of all conditions and nations, and we conceive ourselves at this particular period particularly called upon by the blessings which we have received, to manifest the sincerity of our profession, and to give a substantial proof of our gratitude.

❧ "This is to us a most glorious day"

CORNWALLIS SURRENDERS AT YORKTOWN

After six years of constant warfare, the bulk of the British army found itself trapped in Yorktown on Virginia's coastal peninsula by a combined force of American and French troops in the fall of 1781. For the first time in the war, Washington's forces outnumbered the British, and by a two to one margin.

Led by General Charles Cornwallis, the only hope for the British was that a major relief squadron from New York City would arrive. But the British were slow to depart and a French fleet commanded by Comte de Grasse sealed Cornwallis' from reinforcements or escape.

Trapped, Cornwallis surrendered his 7,500-man army, effectively ending hostilities of the American Revolution. Having negotiated generous terms, the British laid down their arms October 19. The following account of the formal capitulation was written by Dr. James Thacher.

This is to us a most glorious day, but to the English one of bitter chagrin and disappointment. Preparations are now making to receive as captives that vindictive, haughty commander and that victorious army, who, by their robberies and murders, have so long been a scourge to our brethren of the Southern states. Being on horseback, I anticipate a full share of satisfaction in viewing the various movements in the interesting scene.

The stipulated terms of capitulation are similar

to those granted to General Lincoln at Charleston the last year. The captive troops are to march out with shouldered arms, colors cased and drums beating a British or German march, and to ground their arms at a place assigned for the purpose. The officers are allowed their side-arms and private property, and the generals and such officers as desire it are to go on parole to England or New York. The marines and seamen of the king's ships are prisoners of war to the navy of France; and the land forces to the United States. All military and artillery stores to be delivered up unimpaired. The royal prisoners to be sent into the interior of Virginia, Maryland and Pennsylvania in regiments, to have rations allowed them equal to the American soldiers, and to have their officers near them. Lord Cornwallis to man and despatch the *Bonetta* sloop-of-war with despatches to Sir Henry Clinton at New York without being searched, the vessel to be returned and the hands accounted for.

At about twelve o'clock, the combined army was arranged and drawn up in two lines extending more than a mile in length. The Americans were drawn up in a line on the right side of the road, and the French occupied the left. At the head of the former, the great American commander, mounted on his noble courser, took his station, attended by his aid. At the head of the latter was posted the excellent Count Rochambeau and his suite. The French troops, in complete uniform, displaying a martial and noble appearance; their bans of music, of which the timbrel formed a part, is a delightful novelty and produced while marching to the ground a most enchanting effect. The Americans, though not all in uniform, nor their dress so neat, yet exhibited an erect, soldierly air, and every countenance beamed with satisfaction and joy. The concourse of spectators from the country was prodigious, in point of numbers was probably equal to the military, but universal silence and order prevailed.

It was about two o'clock when the captive army advanced through the line formed for their reception. Every eye was prepared to gaze on Lord Cornwallis, the object of peculiar interest and solicitude; but he disappointed our anxious expectations; pretending indisposition, he made General O'Hara his substitute as the leader of his army. This officer was followed by the conquered troops in a slow and solemn step, with shouldered arms, colors

cased and drums beating a British march. Having arrived at the head of the line, General O'Hara, elegantly mounted, advanced to his excellency the commander-in-chief, taking off his hat, and apologized to his excellency for the non-appearance of Earl Cornwallis. With his usual dignity and politeness, his excellency pointed to Major-General Lincoln for directions, by whom the British army was conducted into a spacious field, where it was intended they should ground their arms.

The royal troops, while marching through the line formed by the allied army, exhibited a decent and neat appearance, as respects arms and clothing, for their commander opened his store and directed every soldier to be furnished with a new suit complete, prior to the capitulation. But in their line of march we remarked a disorderly and unsoldierly conduct, their step was irregular, and their ranks frequently broken.

But it was in the field, when they came to the last act of the drama, that the spirit and pride of the British soldier was put to the severest test: here their mortification could not be concealed. Some of the platoon officers appeared to be exceedingly chagrined when giving the word "ground arms," and I am a witness that they performed this duty in a very unofficer-like manner; and that many of the soldiers manifested a sullen temper, throwing their arms on the pile with violence, as if determined to render them useless. This irregularity, however, was checked by the authority of General Lincoln. After having grounded their arms and divested themselves of their accoutrements, the captive troops were conducted back to Yorktown and guarded by our troops till they could be removed to the place of their destination.

The British troops that were stationed at Gloucester surrendered at the same time and in the same manner to the command of the Duke de Luzerne.

This must be a very interesting and gratifying transaction to General Lincoln, who, having himself been obliged to surrender an army to a haughty foe the last year, has now assigned him the pleasing duty of giving laws to a conquered army in return, and of reflecting that the terms which were imposed on him are adopted as a basis of the surrender in the present instance. It is a very gratifying circumstance that every degree of harmony, confidence and friendly intercourse subsisted between the American and French troops during the campaign—no contest, except an emulous spirit to excel in exploits and enterprise against the common enemy, and a desire to be celebrated in the annals of history for an ardent love of great and heroic actions.

We are not to be surprised that the pride of the British officers is humbled on this occasion, as they have always entertained an exalted opinion of their own military prowess and affected to view the Americans as a contemptible, undisciplined rabble. But there is no display of magnanimity when a great commander shrinks from the inevitable misfortunes of war; and when it is considered that Lord Cornwallis has frequently appeared in splendid triumph at the head of his army, by which he is almost adored, we conceive it incumbent on him cheerfully to participate in their misfortunes and degradations, however humiliating; but it is said he gives himself up entirely to vexation and despair.

❧ *What Is an American?*

J. HECTOR ST. JOHN DE CRÈVECOEUR

J. Hector St. John de Crèvecoeur came to America during the French and Indian War as a soldier. When peace came, he stayed to explore the Great Lakes region before settling in New York State as a farmer. He left America during the American Revolution divided in his loyalties and in 1782 published a famous book *Letter from an American Farmer* that described the new country and the character of its people. He returned to America at the conclusion of the war only to discover his farm destroyed and family scattered or dead.

His answer to the question "What is an American?" has stood the test of time, reflecting the diverse origin of its citizens but common bounds in the forging of a new nation peopled by citizens from many different parts of the world.

The next wish of this traveler will be to know whence came all these people. They are a mixture of English, Scottish, Irish, French, Dutch, Germans, and Swedes. From this promiscuous breed, that race now called Americans have arisen. The eastern provinces must indeed be excepted as being the unmixed descendants of Englishmen. I have heard many wish that they had been more intermixed also; for my part, I am no wisher and think it much better as it has happened. They exhibit a most conspicuous figure in this great and

variegated picture; they too enter for a great share in the pleasing perspective displayed in these thirteen provinces. I know it is fashionable to reflect on them, but I respect them for what they have done; for the accuracy and wisdom with which they have settled their territory; for the decency of their manners; for their early love of letters; their ancient college, the first in this hemisphere; for their industry, which to me who am but a farmer is the creation of everything. There never was a people, situated as they are, who with so ungrateful a soil have done more in so short a time. Do you think that the monarchical ingredients have purged them from all foul stains? Their histories assert the contrary.

In this great American asylum, the poor of Europe have by some means met together, and in consequence of various causes; to what purpose should they ask one another what countrymen they are? Alas, two thirds of them had no country. Can a wretch who wanders about, who works and starves, whose life is a continual scene of sore affliction or pinching penury—can that man call England or any other kingdom his country? A country that had no bread for him, whose fields procured him no harvest, who met with nothing but the frowns of the rich, the severity of the laws, with jails and punishments, who owned not a single foot of extensive surface of this planet? No! Urged by a variety of motives, here they came. Everything has tended to regenerate them: new laws, a new mode of living, a new social system; here they are become men: in Europe they were as so many useless plants, wanting vegetative mould and refreshing showers; they withered, and were mowed down by want, hunger, and war; but now, by the power of transplantation, like all other plants they have taken root and flourished! Formerly they were not numbered in any civil lists of their country, except in those of the poor; here they rank as citizens. By what invisible power hath this surprising metamorphosis been performed? By that of the laws and that of their industry. The laws, the indulgent laws, protect them as they arrive, stamping on them the symbol of adoption; they receive ample rewards for their labors; these accumulated rewards procure them lands; those land confer on them the title of freemen, and to that title every benefit is affixed which men can possibly acquire. This is the great operation daily performed by our laws. Whence proceed these laws? From our government. Whence that government? It is derived from the original genius and strong desire of the people ratified and confirmed by the crown. This is the great chain which links us all, this is the picture which every province exhibits, Nova Scotia excepted. There the crown has done all; either there were no people who had genius or it was not much attended to; the consequence is that the province is very thinly inhabited indeed; the power of the crown in conjunction with the muskets has prevented men from settling there. Yet some parts of it flourished once, and it contained a mild, harmless set of people. But for the fault of a few leaders, the whole was banished. The greatest political error the crown ever committed in America was to cut off men from a country which wanted nothing but men!

What attachment can a poor European emigrant have for a country where he had nothing? The knowledge of the language, the love of a few kindred as poor as himself, were the only cords that tied him; his country is now which gives him his land, bread, protection, and consequence; Ubi panis ibi patria is the motto of all emigrants. What, then, is the American, this new man? He is either a European or the descendant of a European; hence that strange mixture of blood, which you will find in no other country. I could point out to you a family whose grandfather was an Englishman, whose wife was Dutch, whose son married a French woman, and whose present four sons have now four wives of different nations. He is an American, who, leaving behind him all his ancient prejudices and manners, receives new ones from the new mode of life he has embraced, the new government he obeys, and the new rank he holds. He becomes an American by being received in the broad lap of our great Alma Mater. Here individuals of all nations are melted into a new race of men, whose labors and posterity will one day cause great changes in the world. Americans are the western pilgrims who are carrying along with them that great mass of arts, sciences, vigor, and industry which began long since in the East; they will finish the great circle. The Americans were once scattered all over Europe; here they are incorporated into one of the finest systems of population which has ever appeared, and which will hereafter become distinct by the power of the different climates they inhabit. The American ought to love this country much better than that wherein either he or his forefathers were born. Here the rewards of his industry follow with equal steps the progress of his labor; his labor is founded on the basis of nature, self-interest; can it want a stronger allurement? Wives and children, who before in vain demanded of him a morsel of bread, now, fat and frolicsome, gladly help their father to clear those fields whence exuberant crops are to arise to feed and clothe them all, without any part being claimed, either by a despotic prince, a rich abbot, or a mighty lord. Here religion demands but little of him: a small voluntary salary to the minister and gratitude to God; can he refuse these? The American is a new man, who acts upon new principles; he must therefore entertain new ideas and form new opinions. From involuntary idleness, servile dependence, penury, and useless labor, he has passed to toils of a very different nature, rewarded by ample subsistence. This is an American.

❧ "One more distinguished proof of unexampled patriotism"

GEORGE WASHINGTON

Having defeated their common enemy on the battlefield, Americans had to learn how to live with each other. In January 1783, the new nation faced the real possibility of a military coup. Their pay in arrears, food and clothing payments ignored, and a pledge to institute a pension stalled in Congress, American officers were ready to turn against their civilian government. Congress added salt to the wounds when in February it rejected a proposal for officers to exchange their pensions for six years' pay.

Major John Armstrong distributed two anonymous letters stating the officers' grievances and calling for action. The second letter announced a meeting of officers to be held at March 15 and implied that the meeting had Washington's backing. But it did not. Unexpectedly, Washington appeared at the meeting and talked the potentially mutinous officers out of acting upon their frustrations.

Major Samuel Shaw recorded the event and Washington's speech. He noted that Washington's conduct had as much impact as his words. After reading the first paragraph, Washington paused, reached for his spectacles "observing at the same time that he had grown gray in their services, and now found himself growing blind," Shaw wrote. "There was something so natural, so unaffected, in this appeal as rendered it superior to the most studied oratory. It forces its way to the heart, and you might see sensibility moisten every eye."

"On other occasions," Shaw continued, Washington "had been supported by the exertions of an Army and the countenance of his friends; but in this he stood single and alone.... he appeared, not at the head of his troops, but as it were in opposition to them; and for a dreadful moment the interests of the Army and its General seemed to be in competition! He spoke—every doubt was dispelled, and the tide of patriotism rolled again in its wonted course."

Gentlemen: By an anonymous summons, an attempt has been made to convene you together; how inconsistent with the rules of propriety! How unmilitary! And how subversive of all order and discipline, let the good sense of the Army decide.

In the moment of this Summons, another anonymous production was sent into circulation, addressed more to the feelings and passions, than to the reason and judgment of the Army.... That the Address is drawn with great Art, and is designed to answer the most insidious purposes. That it is calculated to impress the mind, with an idea of premeditated injustice in the Sovereign power of the United States, and rouse all those resentments which must unavoidably flow from such a belief. That the secret mover of this Scheme (whoever he may be) intended to take advantage of the passions, while they were warmed by the recollection of past distresses, without giving time for cool, deliberative thinking, and that composure of Mind which is so necessary to give dignity and stability to measure is rendered too obvious, by the mode of conducting the business, to need other proof than a reference to the proceeding....

It can scarcely be supposed, at this late state of the War, that I am indifferent to its interests. But, how are they to be promoted? The way is plain, says the anonymous Addresser. If War continues, remove into the unsettled Country; there establish yourselves, and leave an ungrateful Country to defend itself.... This dreadful alternative, of either deserting our Country in the extremest hour of her distress, or turning our Arms against it, (which is the apparent object, unless Congress can be compelled into instant compliance) has something so shocking in it, that humanity revolts at the idea. My God! What can this writer have in view, by recommending such measures? Can he be a friend to the Army? Can he be a friend to this Country?

Rather, is he not an insidious Foe? Some Emissary, perhaps, from New York, plotting the ruin of both, by sowing the seeds of discord and separation between the Civil and Military powers of the Continent?...

For myself...a grateful sence of the confidence you have ever placed in me, a recollection of the cheerful assistance, and prompt obedience I have experienced from you, under every vicissitude of fortune, and the sincere affection I feel for an Army, I have so long had the honor to Command, will oblige me to declare, in this public and solemn manner, that in the attainment of compleat justice for all your toils and dangers, and in the gratification of every wish, so far as may be done consistently with the great duty I owe my Country, and those powers we are bound to respect, you may freely command my Services to the utmost of my abilities.

While I give you these assurances, and pledge myself in the most unequivocal manner, to exert whatever ability I am possessed of, in your favor, let me entreat you, Gentlemen, on your part, not to take any measures, which, viewed in the calm light of reason, will lessen the dignity, and sully the glory you have hitherto maintained; let me request you to rely on the plighted faith of your Country, and place a full confidence in the purity of the intentions of Congress; that, previous to your dissolution as an Army they will cause all your Accts. to be fairly liquidated....

And let me conjure you, in the name of our common Country, as you value your own sacred honor, as you respect the rights of humanity, and as you regard the Military and National character of America, to express your utmost horror and detestation of the Man who wished, under any specious pretences, to overturn the liberties of our Country, and who wickedly attempts to open the flood Gates of Civil discord, and deluge our rising Empire in Blood. By thus determining, and thus acting, you will pursue the plain and direct road to the attainment of your wishes. You will defeat the insidious design of our Enemies, who are compelled to resort from open force to secret artifice. You will give one more distinguished proof of unexampled patriotism and patient virtue, raising superior to the pressure of the most complicated sufferings; and you will, by the dignity of your Conduct, afford occasion for Posterity to say, when speaking of the glorious example you have exhibited to Mankind, "had this day been wanting, the World had never seen the last stage of perfection to which human nature is capable of attaining."

❧ *"Free, sovereign, and independent States"*

THE PARIS PEACE TREATY

Almost two years after the British defeat at the Battle of Yorktown concluded significant hostilities in the American Revolution, the British signed the Paris Peace Treaty acknowledging the independence of the United States.

Article I. His Britannic Majesty acknowledges the said United States, viz. New Hampshire, Massachusetts Bay, Rhode Island, and Providence Plantations, Connecticut, New York, New Jersey, Pennsylvania, Delaware, Maryland, Virginia, North Carolina, and Georgia, to be free, sovereign and independent States; that he treats with them as such, and for himself, his heirs and successors, relinquishes all claims to the Government, proprietary and territorial rights of the same, and every part thereof....

Article III. It is agreed that the people of the United States shall continue to enjoy unmolested the right to take fish of every kind on the Grand Bank, and on all the other banks of Newfoundland; also in the Gulph of Saint Lawrence, and at all other places in the sea where the inhabitants of both countries used at any time heretofore to fish. And also that the inhabitants of the United States shall have liberty to take fish of every kind on such part of the coast of Newfoundland as British fishermen shall use (but not to dry or cure the same on that island) and also on the coasts, bays and creeks of all other of His Britannic Majesty's dominions in America; and that the American fishermen shall have liberty to dry and cure fish in any of the unsettled bays, harbours and creeks of Nova Scotia, Magdalen Islands, and Labrador, so long as the same or either of them shall be settled, it shall not be lawful for the said fishermen to dry or cure fish at such settlements, without previous agreement for that purpose with the inhabitants, proprietors or possessors of the ground.

Article IV. It is agreed that creditors on either side shall meet with no lawful impediment to the recovery of the full value in sterling money, of all bona fide debts heretofore contracted.

Article V. It is agreed that the Congress shall earnestly recommend it to the legislatures of the respective States, to provide for the restitution of all estates, rights and properties which have been confiscated, belonging to real British subjects, and also of the estates, rights and properties of persons resident in districts in the possession of His Majesty's arms, and who have not borne arms against the said United States. And that persons of any other description shall have free liberty to go to any part or parts of any of the thirteen United States, and therein to remain twelve months, unmolested in their endeavours to obtain the restitution of such of their estates, rights and properties as may have been confiscated; and that Congress shall also earnestly recommend to the several States a reconsideration and revision of all acts or laws regarding the premises, so as to render the said laws or acts perfectly consistent, not only with justice and equity, but with that spirit of conciliation which, on the return of the blessings of peace, should universally prevail. And that congress shall also earnestly recommend to the several States, that the estates, rights and properties of such last mentioned persons, shall be restored to them, they refunding to any persons who may be now in possession, the bona fide price (where any has been given) which such persons may have paid on purchasing any of the said lands, rights or properties, since the confiscation. And it is agreed, that all persons who have any interest in confiscated lands, either by debts, marriage settlements or otherwise, shall meet with no lawful impediment in the prosecution of their just rights.

Article VI. That there shall be no future confiscations made, nor any prosecutions commenced against any person or persons for, or by reason of the part which he or they may have taken in the present war; and that no person shall, on that account, suffer any future loss or damage, either in his person, liberty, or property; and that those who may be in confinement on such charges, at the time of the ratification of the treaty in America, shall be immediately set at liberty, and the prosecutions so commenced be discontinued.

Article VII. There shall be a firm and perpetual peace between His Britannic Majesty and the said States, and between the subjects of the one and the citizens of the other, wherefore all hostilities, both by sea and land, shall from henceforth cease. All prisoners on both sides shall be set at liberty, and His Britannic Majesty shall, with all convenient speed, and without causing any destruction, or carrying away any negroes or other property of the American inhabitants, withdraw all his armies, garrisons and fleets from the said United States, and from every post, place and harbour within the same; leaving in all fortifications the American artillery that may be therein; And shall also order and cause all archives, records, deeds and papers, belonging to any of the said States, or their citizens, which, in the course of the war, may have fallen into the hands of his officers, to be forthwith restored and deliver'd to the proper States and persons to whom they belong.

Article VIII. The navigation of the river Mississippi, from its source to the ocean, shall forever remain free and open to the subjects of Great Britain, and the citizens of the United States.

Article IX. In case it should so happen that any place or territory belonging to the United States, should have been conquer'd by the arms of either from the other, before the arrival of the said provisional articles in America, it is agreed, that the same shall be restored without difficulty, and without requiring any compensation....

❧ *"There never was a good war or a bad peace"*

BENJAMIN FRANKLIN

Benjamin Franklin led the American negotiators for the peace treaty. In July 1783 when negotiations for the peace treaty were concluded and final approval a formality, Franklin wrote to Joseph Banks about his relief that the war had ended. After eight years of war, he, like the new nation, was ready for peace and the opportunity to apply their industry to more productive purpose.

I join with you most cordially in rejoicing at the return of peace. I hope it will be lasting, and that mankind will at length, as they call themselves reasonable creatures, have reason and sense enough to settle their differences without cutting throat; for, in my opinion, there never was a good war or a bad peace. What vast additions to the conveniences and comforts of living might mankind have acquired, if the money spent in wars had been employed in works of public utility! What an extension of agriculture, even to the tops of our mountains; what rivers rendered navigable or joined by canals; what bridges, aqueducts, new roads and other public works, edifices and improvements, rendering England a complete paradise, might have been obtained by spending those millions in doing good which in the last war have been spent in doing mischief; in bringing misery into thousands of families, and destroying the lives of so many thousands of working people, who might have performed useful labor!

❧ *On Religion*

THOMAS JEFFERSON

Thomas Jefferson wrote *Notes on Virginia* in 1781 after he had resigned as governor of Virginia to recuperate from an injury resulting from fall off a horse. Despite Jefferson's lofty standing as an American writer, it was his only full-length book. He wrote it in response to an inquiry from the Marquis de Barbe-Marbois, Secretary of the French Legation in Philadelphia, about Virginia. Gathering materials he had accumulated over the previous twenty years, he wrote at length on a wide variety of subjects in Virginia, including its wildlife, politics and geography. It was subsequently published in a limited edition in France in 1784. The book was very influential in French political circles, and represent a major contribution to the American scientific community.

The following excerpt discusses his and the state's tolerant view of religion. Virginia's early history was not marked by religious tolerance. The Virginia Assembly passed several laws in the 1600s reflecting the Anglican Church's prejudices against Quakers and requiring all children to be baptized. By the time of the American Revolution, however, Virginia—having seen the benefits of religious tolerance in neighboring colonies—declared freedom of religion as natural right in its Declaration of Rights. Here, Jefferson expounds upon the benefits of religious diversity.

The legitimate powers of government extend to such acts only as are injurious to others. But it does me no injury for my neighbor to say there are twenty gods, or no God. It neither picks my pocket nor breaks my leg. If it be said, his testimony in a court of justice cannot be relied on, reject it then, and be the stigma on him. Constraint may make him worse by making him a hypocrite, but it will never make him a truer man. It may fix him obstinately in his errors, but will not cure them. Reason and free inquiry are the only effectual agents against error. Give a loose to them, they will support the true religion by bringing every false one to their tribunal, to the test of their investigation. They are the natural enemies of error and of error only. Had not the Roman government permitted free inquiry, Christianity could never have been introduced. Had not free inquiry been indulged at the era of the Reformation, the corruptions of Christianity could not have been purged away. If it be restrained now, the present corruptions will be protected, and new ones encouraged.

Was the government to prescribe to us our medicine and diet, our bodies would be in such keeping as our souls are now. Thus in France the emetic was once forbidden as a medicine, and the potato as an article of food. Government is just as infallible, too, when it fixed systems in physics. Galileo was sent to the Inquisition for affirming that the earth was a sphere; the government had declared it to be as flat as a trencher, and Galileo was obliged to abjure his error. This error, however, at length prevailed, the earth became a globe, and Descartes declared it was whirled round its axis by a vortex. The government in which he lived was wise enough to see that this was no question of civil jurisdiction, or we should all have been involved by authority in vortices. In fact, the vortices have been exploded, and the Newtonian principle of gravitation is now more firmly established, on the basis of reason, than it would be were the government to step in, and to make it an article of necessary faith.

Reason and experiment have been indulged, and error has fled before them. It is error alone which needs the support of government. Truth can stand by itself. Subject opinion to coercion: whom will you make your inquisitors? Fallible men; men governed by bad passions, by private as well as public reasons. And why subject it to coercion? To produce uniformity. But is uniformity of opinion desirable? No more than of face and stature. Introduce the bed of Procustes then, and as there is danger that the large men may beat the small, make us all of a size, by lopping the former and stretching the latter. Difference of opinion is advantageous to religion. The several sects perform the office of a censor morum over such other. Is uniformity attainable? Millions of innocent men, women, and children, since the introduction of Christianity, have been burnt, tortured, fined, imprisoned; yet we have not advanced one inch toward uniformity. What has been the effect of coercion? To make one-half the world fools, and the other half hypocrites, to support roguery and error all over the earth. Let us reflect that it is inhabited by a thousand millions of people. That these profess probably a thousand different systems of religion. That ours is but one of that thousand. That if there be but one right, and ours that one, we should wish to see the 999 wandering sects gathered into the fold of truth. But against such a majority we cannot effect this by force. Reason and persuasion are the only practicable instruments. To make way for these, free inquiry must be indulged; and how can we wish others to indulge it while we refuse it ourselves. No two, say I, have established the same. Is this a proof of the infallibility of establishments? Our sister states of Pennsylvania and New York, however, have long subsisted without any establishment at all. The experiment was new and doubtful when they made it. It has answered beyond conception. They flourished infinitely. Religion is well supported to preserve peace and order; or if a sect arises, whose tenets should subvert morals, good sense has fair play, and reasons and laughs it out of doors, without suffering the state to be troubled with it. They do not hang more malefactors than we do. They are not more disturbed with religious dissensions. On the contrary, their harmony is unparalleled, and can be ascribed to nothing but their unbounded tolerance, because there is no other circumstance in which they differ from every nation on earth. They have made the happy discovery that the way to silence religious disputes is to take no notice of them.

❧ An Act for Establishing Religious Freedom

THOMAS JEFFERSON

Jefferson wrote a bill proposing that Virginia formally establish religious freedom in 1779, but it was not enacted by the Virginia Assembly in 1786. The act provided the formal protection of religious freedom and officially articulates the concept that would serve as a central pillar of American freedom throughout the country's history.

Well aware that the opinions and belief of men depend not on their own will, but follow involuntarily the evidence proposed to their minds; that Almighty God hath created the mind free, and manifested his supreme will that free it shall remain by making it altogether insusceptible of restraint; that all attempts to influence it by temporal punishments, or burthens, or by civil incapacitations, tend only to beget habits of hypocrisy and meanness, and are a departure from the plan of the holy author of our religion, who being lord both of body and mind, yet chose not to propagate it by coercions on either, as was in his Almighty power to do, but to extend it by its influence on reason alone; that the impious presumption of legislators and rulers, civil as well as ecclesiastical, who, being themselves but fallible and uninspired men, have assumed dominion over the faith of others, setting up their own opinions and modes of thinking as the only true and infallible, and as such endeavoring to impose them on others, hath established and maintained false religions over the greatest part of the world and through all time: That to compel a man to furnish contributions of money for the propagation of opinions which he disbelieves and abhors, is sinful and tyrannical; that even forcing him to support this or that teacher of his own religious persuasion, is depriving him of the comfortable liberty of giving his contributions to the particular pastor whose morals he would make his pattern, and whose power he feels most persuasive to righteousness; and is withdrawing from the ministry those temporary rewards, which proceeding from an approbation of their personal conduct, are an additional incitement to earnest and unremitting labors for the instruction of mankind; that our civil rights have no dependence on our religious opinions, any more than our opinions in physics or geometry; that therefore the proscribing of any citizen as unworthy of public confidence by laying upon him an incapacity of being called to offices of trust and emolument, unless he profess or renounce this or that religious opinion, is depriving him injuriously of those privileges and advantages to which, in common with his fellow citizens, he has a natural right; that it tends also to corrupt the principles of that very religion it is meant to encourage, by brib-

ing, with a monopoly of worldly honors and emoluments, those who will externally profess and conform to it; that though indeed these are criminal who do not withstand such temptation, yet neither are those innocent who lay the bait in their way; that the opinions of men are not the object of civil government, nor under its jurisdiction; that to suffer the civil magistrate to intrude his powers into the field of opinion and to restrain the profession of propagation of principles on supposition of their ill tendency is a dangerous fallacy, which at once destroys all religious liberty, because he being of course judge of that tendency will make his opinions the rule of judgment, and approve or condemn the sentiments of others only as they shall square with or differ from his own; that is time enough for the rightful purposes of civil government for its officers to interfere when principles break out into overt acts against peace and good order; and finally, that truth is great and will prevail if left to herself; that she is the proper and sufficient antagonist to error, and has nothing to fear from conflict unless by human interposition disarmed of her natural weapons, free argument and debate; errors ceasing to be dangerous when it is permitted freely to contradict them.

We the General Assembly of Virginia do enact that no man shall be compelled to frequent or support any religious worship, place, or ministry whatsoever, nor shall be enforced, restrained, molested, or burthened in his body or goods, nor shall otherwise suffer, on account of his religious opinions or belief; but that all men shall be free to profess, and by argument to maintain, their opinions in matters of religion, and that the same shall in no wise diminish, enlarge, or affect their civil capacities.

And though we well know that this assembly, elected by the people for the ordinary purposes of legislation only, have no power to restrain the acts of succeeding Assemblies, constituted with powers equal to our own, and that therefore to declare this act irrevocable would be of no effect in law; yet we are free to declare, and do declare, that the rights hereby asserted are of the natural rights of mankind, and that if any act shall be hereafter passed to repeal the present or to narrow its operation, such act will be an infringement of natural right.

🌿 "There are important defects in the system"

THE ANNAPOLIS CONVENTION

Squabbling states, restive farmers and a deteriorating order marked the United States in the 1780s. United in their desire to leave the British Empire, the newborn states simply could not get along after their common enemy left the scene. Inflation ran rampant, the economy was collapsing, former soldiers were unpaid for their services, and the weakness of the federal government were just some of the problems that confronted the nation.

Concerned by the failings of the new nation, Virginia issued an invitation to all states to meet and discuss ways to repair the situation. Although nine accepted, only five (New York, New Jersey, Pennsylvania, Delaware and Virginia) attended the September 1786 gathering in Annapolis, Maryland. Determined to confront the issues by forming a stronger federal government, the convention approved a resolution written by Alexander Hamilton stating the need to reconstitute the federal government and issuing an invitation to attend a convention in May 1787 in Philadelphia. Unanimously approved, the Annapolis Convention set the stage from which to build a new constitution.

To the Honorable, the legislatures of Virginia, Delaware, Pennsylvania, New Jersey, and New York, the commissioners from the said states, respectively assembled at Annapolis, humbly beg leave to report:

That, pursuant to their several appointments, they met at Annapolis in the state of Maryland on the 11th day of September instant, and having proceeded to a communication of their powers, they found that the states of New York, Pennsylvania, and Virginia had, in substance and nearly in the same terms, authorized their respective commissioners to meet such other commissioners as were, or might be, appointed by the other states in the Union, at such time and place as should be agreed upon by the said commissioners, to take into consideration the trade and commerce of the United States, to consider how far a uniform system in their commercial intercourse and regulations might be necessary to their common interest and permanent harmony, and to report to the several states such an act, relative to this great object, as when unanimously ratified by them would enable the United States in Congress assembled effectually to provide for the same....

Deeply impressed, however, with the magni-

tude and importance of the object confided to them on this occasion, your commissioners cannot forbear to indulge an expression of their earnest and unanimous wish that speedy measures be taken to effect a general meeting of the states in a future convention, for the same and such other purposes as the situation of public affairs may be found to require.

If, in expressing this wish, or in intimating any other sentiment, your commissioners should seem to exceed the strict bounds of their appointment, they entertain a full confidence that a conduct, dictated by an anxiety for the welfare of the United States, will not fail to receive an indulgent construction.

In this persuasion, your commissioners submit an opinion that the idea of extending the powers of their deputies to other objects than those of commerce, which has been adopted by the state of New Jersey, was an improvement on the original plan, and will deserve to be incorporated into that of a future convention. They are the more naturally led to this conclusion as in the course of their reflections on the subject they have been induced to think that the power of regulating trade is of such comprehensive extent, and will enter so far into the general system of the federal government, that to give it efficacy and to obviate questions and doubts concerning its precise nature and limits may require a correspondent adjustment of other parts of the federal system.

That there are important defects in the system of the federal government is acknowledged by the acts of all those states which have concurred in the present meeting; that the defects, upon a closer examination, may be found greater and more numerous than even these acts imply is at least so far probably, from the embarrassments which characterize the present state of our national affairs, foreign and domestic, as may reasonably be supposed to merit a deliberate and candid discussion, in some mode, which will unite the sentiments and councils of all the states. In the choice of the mode, your commissioners are of opinion that a convention of deputies from the different states, for the special and sole purpose of entering into this investigation and digesting a plan for supplying such defects as may be discovered to exist, will be entitled to a preference from considerations which will occur without being particularized.

Your commissioners decline an enumeration of

those national circumstances on which their opinion respecting the propriety of a future convention, with more enlarged powers, is founded; as it would be a useless intrusion of facts and observations, most of which have been frequently the subject of public discussion, and none of which can have escaped the penetration of those to whom they would in this instance be addressed. They are, however, of a nature so serious as, in the view of your commissioners, to render the situation of the United States delicate and critical, calling for an exertion of the united virtue and wisdom of all the members of the Confederacy.

Under this impression, your commissioners, with the most respectful deference, beg leave to suggest their unanimous conviction that it may essentially tend to advance the interests of the Union if the states, by whom they have been respectively delegated, would themselves concur and use their endeavors to procure the concurrence of the other states in the appointment of commissioners, to meet at Philadelphia on the second Monday in May next, to take into consideration the situation of the United States, to devise such further provisions as shall appear to them necessary to render the Constitution of the federal government adequate to the exigencies of purpose to the United States in Congress assembled, as when agreed to by them, and afterward confirmed by the legislatures of every state, will effectually provide for the same.

Though your commissioners could not with propriety address these observations and sentiments to any but the states they have the honor to represent, they have nevertheless concluded from motives of respect to transmit copies of this report to the United States Congress assembled, and to the executives of the other states.

❧ "The late rising of the people"

SHAYS' REBELLION

In western Massachusetts, economic depression, corruption and a wave of farm foreclosures for non-payment of taxes sparked Shays' Rebellion. Thousands of farmers and former soldiers (Shays was an officer in the American Revolution) rebelled against the Massachusetts government. Here, one of the leaders of the rebellion, Daniel Gray, outlines the reasons for the revolt to an audience in Hampshire County.

A state militia put down the rebellion, but within two years all participants had been pardoned and most of the complaints resolved. Shays' Rebellion heightened national concern about the rapid deterioration of the fledgling country and helped create a renewed sense of urgency to revamp the central government.

Gentlemen,

We have thought proper to inform you of some of the principal causes of the late risings of the people, and also of their present movement, viz.

1st. The present expensive mode of collecting debts, which by reason of the great scarcity of cash, will of necessity fill our gaols with unhappy debtors; and thereby a reputable body of people rendered incapable of being serviceable either to themselves or the community.

2nd. The monies raised by impost and excise being appropriated to discharge the interest of governmental securities, and not the foreign debt, when these securities are not subject to taxation.

3rd. A suspension of the writ of Habeas Corpus, by which those persons who have stepped forth to assert and maintain the rights of the people, are liable to be taken and conveyed even to the most distant part of the Commonwealth, and thereby subjected to an unjust punishment.

4th. The unlimited power granted to Justices of the Peace and Sheriffs, Deputy Sheriffs, and Constables, by the Riot Act, indemnifying them to prosecution thereof; when perhaps, wholly actuated from a principle of revenge, hatred, and envy.

Furthermore, Be assured, that this body, now at arms, despise the idea of being instigated by British emissaries, which is so strenuously propagated by the enemies of our liberties: And also wish the most proper and speedy measures may be taken, to discharge both our foreign and domestic debt.

Per Order,
Daniel Gray, Chairman of the Committee

The Northwest Ordinance

CONGRESS

The Confederation Congress passed in 1787 the Northwest Ordinance setting the terms for the federal territory northwest of the Ohio River. Individual states had handed over their claims for the largely unsettled land to the United States government. The Northwest Ordinance imposed federal authority in the territory and set forth the terms for the creation of new states (there would be five and part of a sixth) in it. The act, which was the most important legislation approved by the Confederate Congress, provided an orderly procedure for the conveyance of land into the public domain the acceptance of new states into the republic. It banned slavery in the territory, pledged to honor the rights of Native Americans, and encouraged "religion, morality and knowledge." The Northwest Ordinance was the first piece of federal legislation guaranteeing freedom of religion, speech, and press, and determined that a territory can become eligible for statehood when it has 60,000 adult males.

BE IT ORDAINED by the United States in Congress assembled, That the said territory, for the purposes of temporary government, be one district, subject, however, to be divided into two districts, as future circumstances may, in the opinion of Congress, make it expedient ....

Be it ordained by the authority aforesaid, That there shall be appointed from time to time by Congress, a governor, whose commission shall continue in force for the term of three years, unless sooner revoked by Congress; he shall reside in the district, and have a freehold estate therein in 1,000 acres of land, while in the exercise of his office.

There shall be appointed from time to time by Congress, a secretary, whose commission shall continue in force for four years unless sooner revoked; he shall reside in the district, and have a freehold estate therein in 5oo acres of land, while in the exercise of his office. It shall be his duty to keep and preserve the acts and laws passed by the legislature, and the public records of the district, and the proceedings of the governor in his executive department, and transmit authentic copies of such acts and proceedings, every six months, to the Secretary of Congress: There shall also be appointed a court to consist of three judges, any two of whom to form a court, who shall have a common law jurisdiction, and reside in the district, and have each therein a freehold estate in 500 acres of land while in the exercise of their offices, and their commissions shall continue in force during good behavior.

The governor and judges, or a majority of them, shall adopt and publish in the district such laws of the original States, criminal and civil, as may be necessary and best suited to the circumstances of the district, and report them to Congress from time to time: which laws shall be in force in the district until the organization of the General Assembly therein, unless disapproved of by Congress; but afterwards the Legislature shall have authority to alter them as they shall think fit.

The governor, for the time being, shall be commander-in-chief of the militia, appoint and commission all officers in the same below the rank of general officers; all general officers shall be appointed and commissioned by Congress.

Previous to the organization of the general assembly, the governor shall appoint such magistrates and other civil officers in each county or township, as he shall find necessary for the preservation of the peace and good order in the same: After the general assembly shall be organized, the powers and duties of the magistrates and other civil officers shall be regulated and defined by the said assembly; but all magistrates and other civil officers not herein otherwise directed, shall, during the continuance of this temporary government, be appointed by the governor.

For the prevention of crimes and injuries, the laws to be adopted or made shall have force in all parts of the district, and for the execution of process, criminal and civil, the governor shall make proper divisions thereof; and he shall proceed from time to time as circumstances may require, to lay out the parts of the district in which the Indian titles shall have been extinguished, into counties and townships, subject however to such alterations as may thereafter be made by the legislature.

So soon as there shall be five thousand free male inhabitants of full age in the district, upon giving proof thereof to the governor, they shall receive authority, with time and place, to elect representatives from their counties or townships to represent them in the general assembly: Provided, That, for every five hundred free male inhabitants, there shall be one representative, and so on progressively with the number of free male inhabitants shall the right of representation increase, until the number of representatives shall amount to twenty-five; after which, the number and proportion of representatives shall be regulated by the legislature: Provided, That no person be eligible or qualified to act as a representative unless he shall have been a citizen of one of the United States three years, and be a resident in the district, or unless he shall have resided in the district three years; and, in either case, shall likewise hold in his own right, in fee simple, two hundred acres of land within the same: Provided, also, That a freehold in fifty acres of land in the district, having been a citizen of one of the states, and being resident in the district, or the like freehold and two years residence in the district, shall be necessary to qualify a man as an elector of a representative.

The representatives thus elected, shall serve for the term of two years; and, in case of the death of a representative, or removal from office, the governor shall issue a writ to the county or township for which he was a member, to elect another in his stead, to serve for the residue of the term.

The general assembly or legislature shall consist of the governor, legislative council, and a house of representatives. The Legislative Council shall consist of five members, to continue in office five years, unless sooner removed by Congress; any three of whom to be a quorum: and the members of the Council shall be nominated and appointed in the following manner, to wit: As soon as representatives shall be elected, the Governor shall appoint a time and place for them to meet together; and, when met, they shall nominate ten persons, residents in the district, and each possessed of a freehold in five hundred acres of land, and return their names to Congress; five of whom Congress shall appoint and commission to serve as aforesaid; and, whenever a vacancy shall happen in the council, by death or removal from office, the house of representatives shall nominate two persons, qualified as aforesaid, for each vacancy, and return their names to Congress; one of whom Congress shall appoint and commission for the residue of the term. And every five years, four months at least before the expiration of the time of service of the members of council, the said house shall nominate ten persons, qualified as aforesaid, and return their names to Congress; five of whom Congress shall appoint and commission to serve as members of the council five years, unless sooner removed. And the governor,

legislative council, and house of representatives, shall have authority to make laws in all cases, for the good government of the district, not repugnant to the principles and articles in this ordinance established and declared. And all bills, having passed by a majority in the house, and by a majority in the council, shall be referred to the governor for his assent; but no bill, or legislative act whatever, shall be of any force without his assent. The governor shall have power to convene, prorogue, and dissolve the general assembly, when, in his opinion, it shall be expedient.

The governor, judges, legislative council, secretary, and such other officers as Congress shall appoint in the district, shall take an oath or affirmation of fidelity and of office; the governor before the president of congress, and all other officers before the Governor. As soon as a legislature shall be formed in the district, the council and house assembled in one room, shall have authority, by joint ballot, to elect a delegate to Congress, who shall have a seat in Congress, with a right of debating but not of voting during this temporary government.

And, for extending the fundamental principles of civil and religious liberty, which form the basis whereon these republics, their laws and constitutions are erected; to fix and establish those principles as the basis of all laws, constitutions, and governments, which forever hereafter shall be formed in the said territory: to provide also for the establishment of States, and permanent government therein, and for their admission to a share in the federal councils on an equal footing with the original States, at as early periods as may be consistent with the general interest:

It is hereby ordained and declared by the authority aforesaid, That the following articles shall be considered as articles of compact between the original States and the people and States in the said territory and forever remain unalterable, unless by common consent, to wit:

ART. 1. No person, demeaning himself in a peaceable and orderly manner, shall ever be molested on account of his mode of worship or religious sentiments, in the said territory.

ART. 2. The inhabitants of the said territory shall always be entitled to the benefits of the writ of habeas corpus, and of the trial by jury; of a proportionate representation of the people in the legislature; and of judicial proceedings according to the course of the common law. All persons shall be bailable, unless for capital offences, where the proof shall be evident or the presumption great. All fines shall be moderate; and no cruel or unusual punishments shall be inflicted. No man shall be deprived of his liberty or property, but by the judgment of his peers or the law of the land; and, should the public exigencies make it necessary, for the common preservation, to take any person's property, or to demand his particular services, full compensation shall be made for the same. And, in the just preservation of rights and property, it is understood and declared, that no law ought ever to be made, or have force ill the said territory, that shall, in any manner whatever, interfere with or affect private contracts or engagements, bona fide, and without fraud, previously formed.

ART. 3. Religion, morality, and knowledge, being necessary to good government and the happiness of mankind, schools and the means of education shall forever be encouraged. The utmost good faith shall always be observed towards the Indians; their lands and property shall never be taken from them without their consent; and, in their property, rights, and liberty, they shall never be invaded or disturbed, unless in just and lawful wars authorized by Congress; but laws founded in justice and humanity, shall from time to time be made for preventing wrongs being done to them, and for preserving peace and friendship with them.

ART. 4. The said territory, and the States which may be formed therein, shall forever remain a part of this Confederacy of the United States of America, subject to the Articles of Confederation, and to such alterations therein as shall be constitutionally made; and to all the acts and ordinances of the United States in Congress assembled, conformable thereto. The inhabitants and settlers in the said territory shall be subject to pay a part of the federal debts contracted or to be contracted, and a proportional part of the expenses of government, to be apportioned on them by Congress according to the same common rule and measure by which apportionments thereof shall be made on the other States; and the taxes for paying their proportion shall be laid and levied by the authority and direction of the legislatures of the district or districts, or new States, as in the original States, within the time agreed upon by the United States

in Congress assembled. The legislatures of those districts or new States, shall never interfere with the primary disposal of the soil by the United States in Congress assembled, nor with any regulations Congress may find necessary for securing the title in such soil to the bona fide purchasers. No tax shall be imposed on lands the property of the United States; and, in no case, shall non-resident proprietors be taxed higher than residents. The navigable waters leading into the Mississippi and St. Lawrence, and the carrying places between the same, shall be common highways and forever free, as well to the inhabitants of the said territory as to the citizens of the United States, and those of any other States that may be admitted into the confederacy, without any tax, impost, or duty therefore.

ART. 5. There shall be formed in the said territory, not less than three nor more than five States; and the boundaries of the States, as soon as Virginia shall alter her act of cession, and consent to the same, shall become fixed and established as follows, to wit: The western State in the said territory, shall be bounded by the Mississippi, the Ohio, and Wabash Rivers; a direct line drawn from the Wabash and Post Vincents, due North, to the territorial line between the United States and Canada; and, by the said territorial line, to the Lake of the Woods and Mississippi. The middle State shall be bounded by the said direct line, the Wabash from Post Vincents to the Ohio, by the Ohio, by a direct line, drawn due north from the mouth of the Great Miami, to the said territorial line, and by the said territorial line. The eastern State shall be bounded by the last mentioned direct line, the Ohio, Pennsylvania, and the said territorial line: Provided, however, and it is further understood and declared, that the boundaries of these three States shall be subject so far to be altered, that, if Congress shall hereafter find it expedient, they shall have authority to form one or two States in that part of the said territory which lies north of an east and west line drawn through the southerly bend or extreme of lake Michigan. And, whenever any of the said States shall have sixty thousand free inhabitants therein, such State shall be admitted, by its delegates, into the Congress of the United States, on an equal footing with the original States in all respects whatever, and shall be at liberty to form a permanent constitution and State government: Provided, the constitution and government so to be formed, shall be republican, and in conformity to the principles contained in these articles; and, so far as it can be consistent with the general interest of the confederacy, such admission shall be allowed at an earlier period, and when there may be a less number of free inhabitants in the State than sixty thousand.

ART. 6. There shall be neither slavery nor involuntary servitude in the said territory, otherwise than in the punishment of crimes whereof the party shall have been duly convicted: Provided, always, That any person escaping into the same, from whom labor or service is lawfully claimed in any one of the original States, such fugitive may be lawfully reclaimed and conveyed to the person claiming his or her labor or service as aforesaid.

Be it ordained by the authority aforesaid, That the resolutions of the 3rd of April 1784, relative to the subject of this ordinance, be, and the same are hereby repealed and declared null and void.

❧ "We the People"

THE CONSTITUTION

In May 1787, forty-two delegates from twelve states (Rhode Island refused to participate) converged in Philadelphia to try to hammer out a constitution for a new, stronger federal government. For four months in sweltering heat and through impassioned debates, the many and diverse perspectives of the delegates clashed and sought compromise to find common ground to achieve the common goal of preserving the nation. States' rights, slavery, the authority of an executive, concerns about small states being dominated by large states, westward expansion, liberty, and many other issues were all touched upon and addressed in the final document.

Some of the leading figures of the Revolution, including George Washington and Benjamin Franklin, participated, as well as the leading young political thinkers James Madison, James Wilson, and Alexander Hamilton. The convention was held in secret, with sentries at the door. Washington—who would later call the gathering a "miracle"—was unanimously selected as president of the convention.

In the end, not every delegate was satisfied nor every issue fully resolved, but a document that delegates from all twelve states could support was completed and put forward to the nation for approval. On March 4, 1789, the day which had been fixed for starting operations of a national government under the new Constitution, eleven states had ratified the Constitution. North Carolina ratified it in November 1789 and Rhode Island in May 1790. In 1791, responding to widespread concerns that provisions protecting individual liberties be included, Congress added the Bill of Rights. Although many people expected the Constitution to be a temporary fix for the struggling country, it has withstood the test of time and provided the foundation for American government for more than two centuries and served as a model for countries across the globe.

We the People of the United States, in Order to form a more perfect Union, establish Justice, insure domestic Tranquility, provide for the common defence, promote the general Welfare, and secure the Blessings of Liberty to ourselves and our Posterity, do ordain and establish this Constitution for the United States of America.

Article. I.

Section 1. All legislative Powers herein granted shall be vested in a Congress of the United States, which shall consist of a Senate and House of Representatives.

Section. 2. The House of Representatives shall be composed of Members chosen every second Year by the People of the several States, and the Electors in each State shall have the Qualifications requisite for Electors of the most numerous Branch of the State Legislature.

No Person shall be a Representative who shall not have attained to the Age of twenty five Years, and been seven Years a Citizen of the United States, and who shall not, when elected, be an Inhabitant of that State in which he shall be chosen.

Representatives and direct Taxes shall be apportioned among the several States which may be included within this Union, according to their respective numbers, which shall be determined by adding to the whole Number of free Persons, including those bound to Service for a Term of Years, and excluding Indians not taxed, three fifths of all other Persons. The actual Enumeration shall be made within three Years after the first Meeting of the Congress of the United States, and within every subsequent Term of ten Years, in such Manner as they shall by Law direct. The Number of Representatives shall not exceed one for every thirty Thousand, but each State shall have at Least one Representative; and until such enumeration shall be made, the State of New Hampshire shall be entitled to chuse three, Massachusetts eight, Rhode-Island and Providence Plantations one, Connecticut five, New-York six, New Jersey four, Pennsylvania eight, Delaware one, Maryland six,

Virginia ten, North Carolina five, South Carolina five, and Georgia three.

When vacancies happen in the Representation from any State, the Executive Authority thereof shall issue Writs of Election to fill such Vacancies.

The House of Representatives shall chuse their Speaker and other Officers; and shall have the sole Power of Impeachment.

Section. 3. The Senate of the United States shall be composed of two Senators from each State, chosen by the Legislature thereof, for six Years; and each Senator shall have one Vote.

Immediately after they shall be assembled in Consequence of the first Election, they shall be divided as equally as may be into three Classes. The Seats of the Senators of the first Class shall be vacated at the Expiration of the second Year, of the second Class at the Expiration of the fourth Year, and of the third Class at the Expiration of the sixth Year, so that one third may be chosen every second Year; and if Vacancies happen by Resignation, or otherwise, during the Recess of the Legislature of any State, the Executive thereof may make temporary Appointments until the next Meeting of the Legislature, which shall then fill such Vacancies.

No Person shall be a Senator who shall not have attained to the Age of thirty Years, and been nine Years a Citizen of the United States, and who shall not, when elected, be an Inhabitant of that State for which he shall be chosen.

The Vice President of the United States shall be President of the Senate, but shall have no Vote, unless they be equally divided.

The Senate shall chuse their other Officers, and also a President pro tempore, in the Absence of the Vice President, or when he shall exercise the Office of President of the United States.

The Senate shall have the sole Power to try all Impeachments. When sitting for that Purpose, they shall be on Oath or Affirmation. When the President of the United States is tried, the Chief Justice shall preside: And no Person shall be convicted without the Concurrence of two thirds of the Members present.

Judgment in Cases of Impeachment shall not extend further than to removal from Office, and disqualification to hold and enjoy any Office of honor, Trust or Profit under the United States: but the Party convicted shall nevertheless be liable and subject to Indictment, Trial, Judgment and Punishment, according to Law.

Section. 4. The Times, Places and Manner of holding Elections for Senators and Representatives, shall be prescribed in each State by the Legislature thereof; but the Congress may at any time by Law make or alter such Regulations, except as to the Places of chusing Senators.

The Congress shall assemble at least once in every Year, and such Meeting shall be on the first Monday in December, unless they shall by Law appoint a different Day.

Section. 5. Each House shall be the Judge of the Elections, Returns and Qualifications of its own Members, and a Majority of each shall constitute a Quorum to do Business; but a smaller Number may adjourn from day to day, and may be authorized to compel the Attendance of absent Members, in such Manner, and under such Penalties as each House may provide.

Each House may determine the Rules of its Proceedings, punish its Members for disorderly Behaviour, and, with the Concurrence of two thirds, expel a Member.

Each House shall keep a Journal of its Proceedings, and from time to time publish the same, excepting such Parts as may in their Judgment require Secrecy; and the Yeas and Nays of the Members of either House on any question shall, at the Desire of one fifth of those Present, be entered on the Journal.

Neither House, during the Session of Congress, shall, without the Consent of the other, adjourn for more than three days, nor to any other Place than that in which the two Houses shall be sitting.

Section. 6. The Senators and Representatives shall receive a Compensation for their Services, to be ascertained by Law, and paid out of the Treasury of the United States. They shall in all Cases, except Treason, Felony and Breach of the Peace, be privileged from Arrest during their Attendance at the Session of their respective Houses, and in going to and returning from the same; and for any Speech or Debate in either House, they shall not be questioned in any other Place.

No Senator or Representative shall, during the Time for which he was elected, be appointed to any civil Office under the Authority of the United States, which shall have been created, or the Emoluments whereof shall have been encreased during such time; and no Person holding any Office under the United States, shall be a Member of either House during his Continuance in Office.

Section. 7. All Bills for raising Revenue shall originate in the House of Representatives; but the Senate may propose or concur with Amendments as on other Bills.

Every Bill which shall have passed the House of Representatives and the Senate, shall, before it become a Law, be presented to the President of the United States; If he approve he shall sign it, but if not he shall return it, with his Objections to that House in which it shall have originated, who shall enter the Objections at large on their Journal, and proceed to reconsider it. If after such Reconsideration two thirds of that House shall agree to pass the Bill, it shall be sent, together with the Objections, to the other House, by which it shall likewise be reconsidered, and if approved by two thirds of that House, it shall become a Law. But in all such Cases the Votes of both Houses shall be determined by yeas and Nays, and the Names of the Persons voting for and against the Bill shall be entered on the Journal of each House respectively. If any Bill shall not be returned by the President within ten Days (Sundays excepted) after it shall have been presented to him, the Same shall be a Law, in like Manner as if he had signed it, unless the Congress by their Adjournment prevent its Return, in which Case it shall not be a Law.

Every Order, Resolution, or Vote to which the Concurrence of the Senate and House of Representatives may be necessary (except on a question of Adjournment) shall be presented to the President of the United States; and before the Same shall take Effect, shall be approved by him, or being disapproved by him, shall be repassed by two thirds of the Senate and House of Representatives, according to the Rules and Limitations prescribed in the Case of a Bill.

Section. 8. The Congress shall have Power To lay and collect Taxes, Duties, Imposts and Excises, to pay the Debts and provide for the common Defence and general Welfare of the United States; but all Duties, Imposts and Excises shall be uniform throughout the United States;

To borrow Money on the credit of the United States;

To regulate Commerce with foreign Nations, and among the several States, and with the Indian Tribes;

To establish an uniform Rule of Naturalization, and uniform Laws on the subject of Bankruptcies throughout the United States;

To coin Money, regulate the Value thereof, and of foreign Coin, and fix the Standard of Weights and Measures;

To provide for the Punishment of counterfeiting the Securities and current Coin of the United States;

To establish Post Offices and post Roads;

To promote the Progress of Science and useful Arts, by securing for limited Times to Authors and Inventors the exclusive Right to their respective Writings and Discoveries;

To constitute Tribunals inferior to the supreme Court;

To define and punish Piracies and Felonies committed on the high Seas, and Offences against the Law of Nations;

To declare War, grant Letters of Marque and Reprisal, and make Rules concerning Captures on Land and Water;

To raise and support Armies, but no Appropriation of Money to that Use shall be for a longer Term than two Years;

To provide and maintain a Navy;

To make Rules for the Government and Regulation of the land and naval Forces;

To provide for calling forth the Militia to execute the Laws of the Union, suppress Insurrections and repel Invasions;

To provide for organizing, arming, and disciplining, the Militia, and for governing such Part of them as may be employed in the Service of the United States, reserving to the States respectively, the Appointment of the Officers, and the Authority of training the Militia according to the discipline prescribed by Congress;

To exercise exclusive Legislation in all Cases whatsoever, over such District (not exceeding ten Miles square) as may, by Cession of particular States, and the Acceptance of Congress, become the Seat of the Government of the United States, and to exercise like Authority over all Places purchased by the Consent of the Legislature of the State in which the Same shall be, for the Erection of Forts, Magazines, Arsenals, dock-Yards, and other needful Buildings;—And

To make all Laws which shall be necessary and proper for carrying into Execution the foregoing

Powers, and all other Powers vested by this Constitution in the Government of the United States, or in any Department or Officer thereof.

Section. 9. The Migration or Importation of such Persons as any of the States now existing shall think proper to admit, shall not be prohibited by the Congress prior to the Year one thousand eight hundred and eight, but a Tax or duty may be imposed on such Importation, not exceeding ten dollars for each Person.

The Privilege of the Writ of Habeas Corpus shall not be suspended, unless when in Cases of Rebellion or Invasion the public Safety may require it.

No Bill of Attainder or ex post facto Law shall be passed.

No Capitation, or other direct, Tax shall be laid, unless in Proportion to the Census or Enumeration herein before directed to be taken.

No Tax or Duty shall be laid on Articles exported from any State.

No Preference shall be given by any Regulation of Commerce or Revenue to the Ports of one State over those of another: nor shall Vessels bound to, or from, one State, be obliged to enter, clear, or pay Duties in another.

No Money shall be drawn from the Treasury, but in Consequence of Appropriations made by Law; and a regular Statement and Account of the Receipts and Expenditures of all public Money shall be published from time to time.

No Title of Nobility shall be granted by the United States: And no Person holding any Office of Profit or Trust under them, shall, without the Consent of the Congress, accept of any present, Emolument, Office, or Title, of any kind whatever, from any King, Prince, or foreign State.

Section. 10. No State shall enter into any Treaty, Alliance, or Confederation; grant Letters of Marque and Reprisal; coin Money; emit Bills of Credit; make any Thing but gold and silver Coin a Tender in Payment of Debts; pass any Bill of Attainder, ex post facto Law, or Law impairing the Obligation of Contracts, or grant any Title of Nobility.

No State shall, without the Consent of the Congress, lay any Imposts or Duties on Imports or Exports, except what may be absolutely necessary for executing it's inspection Laws: and the net Produce of all Duties and Imposts, laid by any State on Imports or Exports, shall be for the Use of the Treasury of the United States; and all such Laws shall be subject to the Revision and Controul of the Congress.

No State shall, without the Consent of Congress, lay any Duty of Tonnage, keep Troops, or Ships of War in time of Peace, enter into any Agreement or Compact with another State, or with a foreign Power, or engage in War, unless actually invaded, or in such imminent Danger as will not admit of delay.

Article. II.
Section. 1. The executive Power shall be vested in a President of the United States of America. He shall hold his Office during the Term of four Years, and, together with the Vice President, chosen for the same Term, be elected, as follows

Each State shall appoint, in such Manner as the Legislature thereof may direct, a Number of Electors, equal to the whole Number of Senators and Representatives to which the State may be entitled in the Congress: but no Senator or Representative, or Person holding an Office of Trust or Profit under the United States, shall be appointed an Elector.

The Electors shall meet in their respective States, and vote by Ballot for two Persons, of whom one at least shall not be an Inhabitant of the same State with themselves. And they shall make a List of all the Persons voted for, and of the Number of Votes for each; which List they shall sign and certify, and transmit sealed to the Seat of the Government of the United States, directed to the President of the Senate. The President of the Senate shall, in the Presence of the Senate and House of Representatives, open all the Certificates, and the Votes shall then be counted. The Person having the greatest Number of Votes shall be the President, if such Number be a Majority of the whole Number of Electors appointed; and if there be more than one who have such Majority, and have an equal Number of Votes, then the House of Representatives shall immediately chuse by Ballot one of them for President; and if no Person have a Majority, then from the five highest on the List the said House shall in like Manner chuse the President. But in chusing the President, the Votes shall be taken by States, the Representation from each State having one Vote; A quorum for this

Purpose shall consist of a Member or Members from two thirds of the States, and a Majority of all the States shall be necessary to a Choice. In every Case, after the Choice of the President, the Person having the greatest Number of Votes of the Electors shall be the Vice President. But if there should remain two or more who have equal Votes, the Senate shall chuse from them by Ballot the Vice President.

The Congress may determine the Time of chusing the Electors, and the Day on which they shall give their Votes; which Day shall be the same throughout the United States.

No Person except a natural born Citizen, or a Citizen of the United States, at the time of the Adoption of this Constitution, shall be eligible to the Office of President; neither shall any Person be eligible to that Office who shall not have attained to the Age of thirty five Years, and been fourteen Years a Resident within the United States.

In Case of the Removal of the President from Office, or of his Death, Resignation, or Inability to discharge the Powers and Duties of the said Office, the Same shall devolve on the Vice President, and the Congress may by Law provide for the Case of Removal, Death, Resignation or Inability, both of the President and Vice President, declaring what Officer shall then act as President, and such Officer shall act accordingly, until the Disability be removed, or a President shall be elected.

The President shall, at stated Times, receive for his Services, a Compensation, which shall neither be encreased nor diminished during the Period for which he shall have been elected, and he shall not receive within that Period any other Emolument from the United States, or any of them.

Before he enter on the Execution of his Office, he shall take the following Oath or Affirmation:—"I do solemnly swear (or affirm) that I will faithfully execute the Office of President of the United States, and will to the best of my Ability, preserve, protect and defend the Constitution of the United States."

Section. 2. The President shall be Commander in Chief of the Army and Navy of the United States, and of the Militia of the several States, when called into the actual Service of the United States; he may require the Opinion, in writing, of the principal Officer in each of the executive Departments, upon any Subject relating to the Duties of their respective Offices, and he shall have Power to grant Reprieves and Pardons for Offences against the United States, except in Cases of Impeachment.

He shall have Power, by and with the Advice and Consent of the Senate, to make Treaties, provided two thirds of the Senators present concur; and he shall nominate, and by and with the Advice and Consent of the Senate, shall appoint Ambassadors, other public Ministers and Consuls, Judges of the supreme Court, and all other Officers of the United States, whose Appointments are not herein otherwise provided for, and which shall be established by Law: but the Congress may by Law vest the Appointment of such inferior Officers, as they think proper, in the President alone, in the Courts of Law, or in the Heads of Departments.

The President shall have Power to fill up all Vacancies that may happen during the Recess of the Senate, by granting Commissions which shall expire at the End of their next Session.

Section. 3. He shall from time to time give to the Congress Information of the State of the Union, and recommend to their Consideration such Measures as he shall judge necessary and expedient; he may, on extraordinary Occasions, convene both Houses, or either of them, and in Case of Disagreement between them, with Respect to the Time of Adjournment, he may adjourn them to such Time as he shall think proper; he shall receive Ambassadors and other public Ministers; he shall take Care that the Laws be faithfully executed, and shall Commission all the Officers of the United States.

Section. 4. The President, Vice President and all civil Officers of the United States, shall be removed from Office on Impeachment for, and Conviction of, Treason, Bribery, or
other high Crimes and Misdemeanors.

Article. III.
Section. 1. The judicial Power of the United States, shall be vested in one supreme Court, and in such inferior Courts as the Congress may from time to time ordain and establish. The Judges, both of the supreme and inferior Courts, shall hold their Offices during good Behaviour, and shall, at stated Times, receive for their Services, a Compensation, which shall not be diminished during their

Continuance in Office.

Section. 2. The judicial Power shall extend to all Cases, in Law and Equity, arising under this Constitution, the Laws of the United States, and Treaties made, or which shall be made, under their Authority;—to all Cases affecting Ambassadors, other public Ministers and Consuls;—to all Cases of admiralty and maritime Jurisdiction;—to Controversies to which the United States shall be a Party;—to Controversies between two or more States;—between a State and Citizens of another State;—between Citizens of different States, — between Citizens of the same State claiming Lands under Grants of different States, and between a State, or the Citizens thereof, and foreign States, Citizens or Subjects.

In all Cases affecting Ambassadors, other public Ministers and Consuls, and those in which a State shall be Party, the supreme Court shall have original Jurisdiction. In all the other Cases before mentioned, the supreme Court shall have appellate Jurisdiction, both as to Law and Fact, with such Exceptions, and under such Regulations as the Congress shall make.

The Trial of all Crimes, except in Cases of Impeachment, shall be by Jury; and such Trial shall be held in the State where the said Crimes shall have been committed; but when not committed within any State, the Trial shall be at such Place or Places as the Congress may by Law have directed.

Section. 3. Treason against the United States, shall consist only in levying War against them, or in adhering to their Enemies, giving them Aid and Comfort. No Person shall be convicted of Treason unless on the Testimony of two Witnesses to the same overt Act, or on Confession in open Court.

The Congress shall have Power to declare the Punishment of Treason, but no Attainder of Treason shall work Corruption of Blood, or Forfeiture except during the Life of the Person attainted.

Article. IV.

Section. 1. Full Faith and Credit shall be given in each State to the public Acts, Records, and judicial Proceedings of every other State. And the Congress may by general Laws prescribe the Manner in which such Acts, Records and Proceedings shall be proved, and the Effect thereof.

Section. 2. The Citizens of each State shall be entitled to all Privileges and Immunities of Citizens in the several States.

A Person charged in any State with Treason, Felony, or other Crime, who shall flee from Justice, and be found in another State, shall on Demand of the executive Authority of the State from which he fled, be delivered up, to be removed to the State having Jurisdiction of the Crime.

No Person held to Service or Labour in one State, under the Laws thereof, escaping into another, shall, in Consequence of any Law or Regulation therein, be discharged from such Service or Labour, but shall be delivered up on Claim of the Party to whom such Service or Labour may be due.

Section. 3. New States may be admitted by the Congress into this Union; but no new State shall be formed or erected within the Jurisdiction of any other State; nor any State be formed by the Junction of two or more States, or Parts of States, without the Consent of the Legislatures of the States concerned as well as of the Congress.

The Congress shall have Power to dispose of and make all needful Rules and Regulations respecting the Territory or other Property belonging to the United States; and nothing in this Constitution shall be so construed as to Prejudice any Claims of the United States, or of any particular State.

Section. 4. The United States shall guarantee to every State in this Union a Republican Form of Government, and shall protect each of them against Invasion; and on Application of the Legislature, or of the Executive (when the Legislature cannot be convened) against domestic Violence.

Article. V.

The Congress, whenever two thirds of both Houses shall deem it necessary, shall propose Amendments to this Constitution, or, on the Application of the Legislatures of two thirds of the several States, shall call a Convention for proposing Amendments, which, in either Case, shall be valid to all Intents and Purposes, as Part of this Constitution, when ratified by the Legislatures of three fourths of the several States, or by Conventions in three fourths thereof, as the one or the other Mode of Ratification may be proposed by the Congress; Provided that no Amendment which may be made prior to the Year One thousand eight hundred and eight shall in any Manner affect the first and fourth Clauses in the Ninth Section of the first Article; and that no State, without its Consent, shall be deprived of its equal Suffrage in the Senate.

Article. VI.

All Debts contracted and Engagements entered into, before the Adoption of this Constitution, shall be as valid against the United States under this Constitution, as under the Confederation.

This Constitution, and the Laws of the United States which shall be made in Pursuance thereof; and all Treaties made, or which shall be made, under the Authority of the United States, shall be the supreme Law of the Land; and the Judges in every State shall be bound thereby, any Thing in the Constitution or Laws of any State to the Contrary notwithstanding.

The Senators and Representatives before mentioned, and the Members of the several State Legislatures, and all executive and judicial Officers, both of the United States and of the several States, shall be bound by Oath or Affirmation, to support this Constitution; but no religious Test shall ever be required as a Qualification to any Office or public Trust under the United States.

Article. VII.

The Ratification of the Conventions of nine States, shall be sufficient for the Establishment of this Constitution between the States so ratifying the Same.

Done in Convention by the Unanimous Consent of the States present the Seventeenth Day of September in the Year of our Lord one thousand seven hundred and Eighty seven and of the Independence of the United States of America the Twelfth In witness whereof We have hereunto subscribed our Names,

George Washington, President and deputy from Virginia

New Hampshire
John Langdon
Nicholas Gilman
Massachusetts
Nathaniel Gorham
Rufus King
Connecticut
William Samuel Johnson
Roger Sherman

New York
Alexander Hamilton
New Jersey
William Livingston
David Brearley
William Paterson
Jonathan Dayton
Pennsylvania
Benjamin Franklin
Thomas Mifflin
Robert Morris
George Clymer
Thomas FitzSimons
Jared Ingersoll
James Wilson
Gouvernor Morris
Delaware
George Read
Gunning Bedford Jun
John Dickinson
Richard Bassett
Jacob Broom
Maryland
James McHenry
Dan of St. Thomas Jenifer
Daniel Carroll
Virginia
John Blair
James Madison Jr.
North Carolina
William Blount
Richard Dobbs Spaight
Hu Williamson
South Carolina
J. Rutledge
Charles Cotesworth Pinckney
Charles Pinckney
Pierce Butler
Georgia
William Few
Abraham Baldwin
Attest
William Jackson, Secretary

Address in Favor of the Constitution

BENJAMIN FRANKLIN

By 1787, Benjamin Franklin was considered the wisest man in America. Franklin, 82, had been dispensing wisdom as "Poor Richard" for decades. He had discovered and captured lightning. Franklin was one of the first to call for national union. He had convinced France to come to the aid of America in the Revolution, and he negotiated the Treaty of Paris forcing England to recognize American sovereignty. Aside from George Washington, nobody commanded the same respect.

He participated throughout the Constitutional Convention, though he was twenty years older than the next oldest delegate, and more than twice as old as most of the delegates. Many of Franklin's pet ideas—a unicameral legislature and unpaid officers—were rejected and he was on the losing side of several issues. Nevertheless, Franklin supported the Constitution. Upon the conclusion of the convention on September 17, he rose to speak in favor of the document. His speech embodied the spirit of compromise and conciliation that he saw was necessary to forge a democratic nation. The speech was widely circulated throughout America and very influential in swaying public opinion in favor of the Constitution. His articulation of the spirit of compromise marked an indispensable feature of American government.

Mr. President, I confess that I do not entirely approve of this Constitution at present, but Sir, I am not sure I shall never approve it: For having lived long, I have experienced many Instances of being oblig'd, by better Information or fuller Consideration, to change Opinions even on important Subjects, which I once thought right, but found to be otherwise. It is therefore that the older I grow the more apt I am to doubt my own Judgment, and to pay more Respect to the Judgment of others. Most Men indeed, as well as most Sects in Religion, think themselves in Possession of all Truth, and that wherever others differ from them it is far Error. Steele, a Protestant in a Dedication, tells the Pope, that the only Difference between our two Churches, in their Opinions of the Certainty of their Doctrine, is, the Romish Church is infallible, and the Church of England is never in the Wrong. But tho' many private Persons think almost as highly of their own infallibility, as of that of their Sect, few express it so naturally as a certain French Lady, who, in a little Dispute with her Sister, said, I don't know how it happens, Sister, but I meet with nobody but myself that's always in the right. Il n'y a que moi qui a toujours raison.

In these Sentiments, Sir, I agree to this Constitution, with all its Faults, if they are such; because I think a General Government necessary for us, and there is no Form of Government but what may be a Blessing to the People if well administered; and I believe farther that this is likely to be well administered for a Course of Years, and can only end in Despotism as other Forms have done before it when the People shall become so corrupted as to need Despotic Government, being incapable of any other. I doubt too whether any other Convention we can obtain may be able to make a better Constitution: For when you assemble a Number of Men to have the Advantage of their joint Wisdom, you inevitably assemble with those Men all their Prejudices, their Passions, their Errors of Opinion, their local Interests, and their selfish Views. From such an Assembly can a perfect Production be expected? It therefore astonishes me, Sir, to find this System approaching so near to Perfection as it does; and I think it will astonish our Enemies, who are waiting with Confidence to hear that our Councils are confounded, like those of the Builders of Babel, and that our States are on the Point of Separation, only to meet hereafter for the Purpose of cutting one another's Throats. Thus I consent, Sir, to this Constitution because I expect no better, and because I am sure that it is not the best. The Opinions I have had of its Errors, I sacrifice to the Public Good. I have never whisper'd a Syllable of them abroad. Within these Walls they were born, and here they shall die. If every one of us in returning to our Constituents were to report the Objections he has had to it, and use his Influence to gain partizans in support of them, we might prevent its being generally received, and thereby lose all the salutary Effects and great Advantages resulting naturally in our favor among foreign Nations, as well as among ourselves, from our real or apparent Unanimity. Much of the Strength and Efficiency of any Government, in procuring and securing Happiness to the People, depends on Opinion, on the general Opinion of the Goodness of that Government as well as of the Wisdom and Integrity of its Governors. I hope therefore that for our own Sakes, as a part of the People, and for the sake of our Posterity, we shall act heartily and unanimously in recommending this Constitution, wherever our Influence may extend, and turn our future Thoughts and Endeavours to the Means of having it well administered.

On the whole, Sir, I cannot help expressing a Wish, that every Member of the Convention, who may still have Objections to it, would with me on this Occasion doubt a little of his own Infallibility, and to make manifest our Unanimity, put his Name to this Instrument.

"The tree of liberty must be refreshed"

THOMAS JEFFERSON

Not everyone agreed with Franklin's perspective. The publication of the proposed Constitution came as a surprise to many who were not even aware that a completely new form of government was in the works. Initial reactions were mixed. Thomas Jefferson, who was in Paris at the time of the convention, had decidedly mixed views of the Constitution. In this November 13, 1787, letter to William Stephens Smith he expresses his reaction and questions the need for a new Constitution.

Dear Sir,

...I do not know whether it is to yourself or Mr. Adams I am to give my thanks for the copy of the new constitution. I beg leave through you to place them where due. It will be yet three weeks before I shall receive them from America. There are very good articles in it: and very bad. I do not know which preponderate. What we have lately read in the history of Holland, in the chapter on Stadholder, would have sufficed to set me against a Chief magistrate eligible for a long duration, if I had ever been disposed towards one: and what we have always read of the elections of Polish kings should have forever excluded the idea of one continuable for life. Wonderful is the effect of impudent and persevering lying. The British ministry have so long hired their gazetteers to repeat and model into every form lies about our being in anarchy, that the world has at length believed them, the English nation has believed them, the ministers themselves have come to believe them, and what is more wonderful, we have believed them ourselves. Yet where does this anarchy exist? Where did it ever exist, except in the single instance of Massachusetts? And can history produce an instance of a rebellion so honourably conducted? I say nothing of its motives. They were founded in ignorance, not wickedness. God forbid we should

ever by 20 years without such a rebellion. The people can not be all, and always, well informed. The part which is wrong will be discontented in proportion to the importance of the facts they misconceive. If they remain quiet under such misconceptions it is a lethargy, the forerunner of death to the public liberty. We have had 13 states independent 11 years. There has been one rebellion. That comes to one rebellion in a century and a half for each state. What country before ever existed a century and half without rebellion? And what country can preserve it's liberties if the rulers are not warned from time to time that their people preserve the spirit of resistance? Let them take arms. The remedy is to set them right as to facts, pardon and pacify them. What signify a few lives lost in a century or two? The tree of liberty must be refreshed from time to time with the blood of patriots and tyrants. It is it's natural manure. Our Convention has been too much impressed by the insurrection of Massachusetts: and in the spur of the moment they are setting up a kite to keep the hen yard in order. I hope in god this article will be rectified before the new constitution is accepted.

Debating the need for a Bill of Rights

JAMES WILSON AND JOHN SMILIE

One of the major points of contention in the debates over the Constitution was a Bill of Rights guaranteeing citizens certain liberties. Pennsylvania held a convention in November to consider ratifying the Constitution. Almost immediately, one of the major points of contention was the lack of a declaration of rights guaranteeing certain liberties to citizens, as this November 28, 1787, exchange between James Wilson, who signed the Constitution, and John Smilie shows. Pennsylvania ratified the Constitution on December 12, five days after Delaware was the first state to do so.

JAMES WILSON: Mr. President, we are repeatedly called upon to give some reason why a bill of rights has not been annexed to the proposed plan. I not only think that enquiry is at this time unnecessary and out of order, but I expect, at least, that those who desire us to shew why it was omitted, will furnish some arguments to shew that it ought to have been inserted; for the proof of the affirmative naturally falls upon them. But the truth is, Sir, that this circumstance, which has since occasioned so much clamour and debate, never struck the mind of any member in the late convention 'till, I believe, within three days of the dissolution of that body, and even then, of so little account was the idea, that it passed off in a short conversation, without introducing a formal debate, or assuming the shape of a motion. For, Sir, the attempt to have thrown into the national scale an instrument in order to evince that any power not mentioned in the constitution was reserved, would have been spurned as an insult to the common understanding of mankind. In civil government it is certain, that bills of right are unnecessary and useless, not can I conceive whence the contrary notion has arisen. Virginia has no bill of rights, and will it be said that her constitution was less free?

JOHN SMILIE: I beg leave to observe, Mr. President, that although it has not been inserted in the printed volume of state constitutions, yet I have been assured by Mr. Mason, that Virginia has a bill of rights.

WILSON: I do not rely upon the information of Mr. Mason, or of any other gentleman on a question of this kind, but I refer to the authenticity of the volume which contains the state constitutions, and in that Virginia has no bill of rights. But, Sir, has South Carolina no security for her liberties? That state has no bill of rights. Are the citizens of the Eastern shore of Delaware more secured in their freedom, or more enlightened on the subject of government than the citizens of the western shore? New Jersey has no bill of rights; New York has none. Thus, Sir, it appears from the example of other states, as well as from principle, that a bill of rights is neither an essential nor a necessary instrument in framing a system of government, since liberty may exist and be as well secured without it. But it was not only unnecessary, but on this occasion, it was found impracticable; for who will be bold enough to undertake to enumerate all the rights of the people? And when the attempt to enumerate them is made, it must be remembered that if the enumeration is not complete, every thing not expressly mentioned will be presumed to be purposefully omitted. So it must be with a bill of rights, and an omission in stating the powers granted to the government, is not so dangerous as an omission recapitulating the rights reserved by the

people. We have already seen the origin of magna charta, and tracing the subject still further we find the petition of rights claiming the liberties of the people, according to the laws and statutes of the realm, of which the great charter was the most material; so that here again recourse is had to the old source from which their liberties are derived, the grant of the king. It was not 'till the revolution that the subject was placed upon a different footing, and even then the people did not claim their liberties as an inherent right, but as the result of an original contract between them and the sovereign. Thus, Mr. President, an attention to the situation of England, will shew that the conduct of that country in respect to bills of rights, cannot furnish an example to the inhabitants of the United States, who by the revolution have regained all their natural rights, and possess their liberty neither by grant nor contract. In short, Sir, I have said that a bill of rights would have been improperly annexed to the federal plan, and for this plain reason, that it would imply that whatever is not expressed given, which is not the principle of the proposed constitution.

SMILIE: The arguments which have been urged, Mr. President, have not in my opinion, satisfactorily shewn that a bill of rights would have been an improper, nay, that it is not a necessary appendage to the proposed system. As it has been denied that Virginia possesses a bill of rights, I shall on that subject only observe, that Mr. Mason, a gentleman certainly of great information and integrity, has assured me that such a thing does exist, and I am persuaded, I shall be able to a future period to lay it before the convention. But, Sir, the state of Delaware has a bill of rights, and I believe one of the honorable members who now contests the necessity and propriety of that instrument, took a very conspicuous part in the formation of the Delaware government. It seems however that the members of the federal convention were themselves convinced, in some degree, of the expediency and propriety of a bill of rights, for we find them expressly declaring the writ of Habeas Corpus and the trial by jury in criminal cases shall not be suspended or infringed. How does this indeed agree with the maxim that whatever is not given is reserved? Does it not rather appear from the reservation of these two articles that every thing else, which is not specified is included in the powers delegated to the government? This, sir, must prove the necessity of a full and explicit declaration of rights; and when we further consider the extensive, the undefined powers vested in the administrators of this system, when we consider the system itself as a great political compact between the governors and the governed, a plain, strong, and accurate, criterion by which the people might at once determine when, and in what instance, their rights were violated, is a preliminary, without which this plan ought no to be adopted. So loosely, so inaccurately are the powers which are enumerated in this constitution defined, that it will be impossible, without a test of that kind, to ascertain the limits of authority, and to declare when government has degenerated into oppression. In that event the contest will arise between the people and the rulers: "You have exceeded the powers of your office, you have oppressed us," will be the language of the suffering citizens. The answer of the government will be short—"We have not exceeded our power: you have no text by which you can prove it." Hence, Sir, it will be impracticable to stop the progress of tyranny, for there will be no check but the people, and their exertions must be futile and uncertain; since it will be difficult indeed, to communicate to them, the violation that has been committed, and their proceedings will be neither systematical nor unanimous. It is said, however, that the difficulty of framing a bill of rights was insurmountable: but, Mr. President, I can not agree in this opinion. Our experience, and the numerous precedents before us, would have furnished a very sufficient guide. At present there is no security, even for the rights of conscience, and under the sweeping force of the sixth article, every principle of a bill of rights, every stipulation for the most sacred and invaluable privileges of man, are left to the mercy of government.

❧ Federalist I: On the Purpose of the Writer

ALEXANDER HAMILTON

To encourage public support for the Constitution, James Madison of Virginia and Alexander Hamilton and John Jay wrote a series of letters explaining the advantages of the Constitution and debunking criticisms of it. Collectively, the eighty-five essays became known as The Federalist Papers. They were initially published in a series of New York publications—*The Independent Journal, Packet and Daily Advertiser*—in 1787 and 1788. Hamilton wrote fifty-one essays, Madison fifteen, and Jay five. The balance were written by Hamilton or Madison or the two together. All of the articles were signed "Publius." The first article was published in *The Independent Journal* on October 27, 1787.

Although Hamilton had argued for a stronger executive than the Constitution allowed, he became one of the document's most forceful advocates. He was the only New York delegate to sign the Constitution while the other two state representatives refused to endorse the proposal. New York's approval of the Constitution was critical to the success of the new nation. Although the Constitution was ratified by the required nine states by the time New York met to consider the Constitution, the failure of New York to participate would have literally split the new country in two and deprived it of a major commercial center. The Federalist Papers heavily influenced the state's decision to ratify the Constitution on July 26, 1788. In a larger sense, The Federalist Papers constituted an extraordinary articulation of the principles of self-government. Thomas Jefferson described them as "the best commentary on the principles of government which was ever written."

After an unequivocal experience of the inefficacy of the subsisting Federal Government, you are called upon to deliberate on a new Constitution for the United States of America. The subject speaks its own importance; comprehending in its consequences, nothing less than the existence of the UNION, the safety and welfare of the parts of which it is composed, the fate of an empire, in many respects, the most interesting in the world. It has been frequently remarked, that it seems to have been reserved to the people of this country, by their conduct and example, to decide the important question, whether societies of men are capable or not, of establishing good government from reflection and choice, or whether they are forever destined to depend, for their political constitutions, on accident and force. If there be any truth in the remark, the crisis, at which we are arrived, may with propriety be regarded as the era in which that decision is to be made; and a wrong election of the part we shall act, may, in this view, deserve to be considered as the general misfortune of mankind.

This idea will add the inducements of philanthropy to those of patriotism to heighten the solicitude, which all considerate and good men must feel for the event. Happy will it be if our choice should be decided by a judicious estimate of our true interests, unperplexed and unbiassed by considerations not connected with the public good. But this is a thing more ardently to be wished, than seriously to be expected. The plan offered to our deliberations affects too many particular interests, innovates upon too many local institutions, not to involve in its discussion a variety of objects foreign to its merits, and of views, passions, and prejudices little favorable to the discovery of truth.

Among the most formidable of the obstacles which the new Constitution will have to encounter, may readily be distinguished the obvious interest of a certain class of men in every State to resist all changes which may hazard a diminution of the power, emolument, and consequence of the offices they hold under the State establishments—and the perverted ambition of another class of men, who will either hope to aggrandize themselves by the confusions of their country or will flatter themselves with fairer prospects of elevation from the subdivision of the empire into several partial confederacies, than from its union under one government.

It is not, however, my design to dwell upon observations of this nature. I am well aware that it would be disingenuous to resolve indiscriminately the opposition of any set of men (merely because their situations might subject them to suspicion) into interested or ambitious views: Candor will oblige us to admit, that even such men may be actuated by upright intentions; and cannot be doubted that much of the opposition which has made its appearance, or may hereafter make its appearance, will spring from sources blameless at least, if not respectable; the honest errors of minds led astray by preconceived jealousies and fears. So numerous, indeed, and so powerful are the causes which serve to give a false bias to the judgment, that we, upon many occasions, see wise and good men on the wrong as well as on the right side of questions of the first magnitude to society. This circumstance, if duly attended to, would furnish a lesson of moderation to those who are ever so much persuaded of their being in the right in any controversy. And a further reason for caution in this respect might be drawn from the reflection that we are not always sure that those who advocate the truth are influenced by purer principles than their antagonists. Ambition, avarice, person-

al animosity, party opposition, and many other motives not more laudable than these, are apt to operate as well upon those who support, as upon those who oppose, the right side of a question. Were there not even these inducements to moderation, nothing could be more ill-judged than that intolerant spirit, which has at all times characterized political parties. For, in politics as in religion, it is equally absurd to aim at making proselytes by fire and sword. Heresies in either can rarely be cured by persecution.

And yet however just these sentiments will be allowed to be, we have already sufficient indications that it will happen in this as in all former cases of great national discussion. A torrent of angry and malignant passions will be let loose. To judge from the conduct of the opposite parties, we shall be led to conclude that they will mutually hope to evince the justness of their opinions and to increase the number of their converts by the loudness of their declamations and the bitterness of their invectives. An enlightened zeal for the energy and efficiency of government will be stigmatized, as the offspring of a temper fond of despotic power, and hostile to the principles of liberty. An over-scrupulous jealousy of danger to the rights of the people, which is more commonly the fault of the head than of the heart, will be represented as mere pretence and artifice; the stale bait for popularity at the expense of public good. It will be forgotten, on the one hand, that jealousy is the usual concomitant of violent love, and that the noble enthusiasm of liberty is too apt to be infected with a spirit of narrow and illiberal distrust. On the other hand, it will be equally forgotten that the vigor of government is essential to the security of liberty; that in the contemplation of a sound and well-informed judgment their interests can never be separated; and that a dangerous ambition more often lurks behind the specious mask of zeal for the rights of the people than under the forbidding appearance of zeal for the firmness and efficiency of government. History will teach us that the former has been found a much more certain road to the introduction of despotism than the latter; and that of those men who have overturned the liberties of republics the greatest number have begun their career by paying an obsequious court to the people; commencing demagogues, and ending tyrants.

In the course of the preceding observations I have had an eye, my fellow-citizens, to putting you upon your guard against all attempts, from whatever quarter, to influence your decision in a matter of the utmost moment to your welfare by impressions other than those which may result from the evidence of truth. You will, no doubt, at the same time, have collected from the general scope of them that they proceed from a course not unfriendly to the new Constitution. Yes, my countrymen, I own to you that after having given it an attentive consideration I am clearly of the opinion it is in your interest to adopt it. I am convinced that this is the safest course for your liberty, your dignity, and your happiness. I affect not reserves, which I do not feel. I will not amuse you with an appearance of deliberation, when I have decided. I frankly acknowledge to you my convictions, and I will freely lay before you the reasons on which they are founded. The consciousness of good intentions disdains ambiguity. I shall not, however, multiply professions on this head. My motives must remain in the depository of my own breast; my arguments will be open to all, and may be judged of by all. They shall at least be offered in a spirit which will not disgrace the cause of truth.

I propose, in a series of paper, to discuss the following interesting particulars: The utility of the UNION to your political prosperity; the insufficiency of the present confederation to preserve that Union; the necessity of a government at least equally energetic with the one proposed, to the attainment of this object; the conformity of the proposed Constitution to the true principles of republican government; its analogy to your own State Constitution; and, lastly, the additional security, which its adoption will afford to the preservation of that species of government, to liberty and to property.

In the progress of this discussion I shall endeavor to give a satisfactory answer to all the objections which shall have made their appearance, that may seem to have any claim to your attention.

It may, perhaps, be thought superfluous to offer arguments to prove the utility of UNION, a point, no doubt, deeply engraved on the hearts of the great body of the people in every State, and one which, it may be imagined, has no adversaries. But the fact is that we already hear it whispered in the private circles of those who oppose the new Constitution, that the Thirteen States are of too great extent for any general system, and that we must of necessity resort to separate confederacies of distinct portions of the whole. This doctrine will, in all probability, be gradually propogated, till it has votaries enough to countenance an open avowal of it. For nothing can be more evident, to those who are able to take an enlarged view of the subject, than the alternative of an adoption of the new Constitution or a dismemberment of the Union. It will, therefore, be of use to begin by examining the advantages of that Union, the certain evils, and the probable dangers, to which every State will be exposed from its dissolution. This shall accordingly constitute the subject of my next address.

Publius

Federalist LI: On the Safety of Multiple Interests

JAMES MADISON

Known as "The Father of the Constitution," James Madison served as the secretary of the Constitutional Convention and was a prime mover in the decision to completely change the government instead of simply amending the Articles of Confederation. He kept copious notes of the convention, which were published after his death. In The Federalist Papers, Madison wrote extensively on the balance of power and the role of faction in democracy. Rather than trying to snuff different interests, he sought to control them through a system of checks and balances in the governmental framework. Like all of the framers of the Constitution, Madison brought a scholarly knowledge of political science and practical experience in establishing and operating democratic governments in their fledgling states. The blend of theory and practice helped lead to the success of the Constitution and its ultimate ratification. Madison would later be the fourth President of the United States and would oversee the War of 1812. This article was published on February 6, 1788, in *The Independent Journal* and was addressed to the people of New York.

...It is of great importance, not only to guard the society against the oppression of its rulers; but to guard one part of the society against the injustice of the other part. Different interests necessarily exist in different classes of citizens. If a majority be united by a common interest, the rights of the minority will be insecure. There are but two methods of providing against this evil: The one by creating a will in the community independent of the majority, that is, of the society itself; the other by comprehending in the society so many separate descriptions of citizens as will render an unjust combination of a majority of the whole, very improbable, if not impracticable. The first method prevails in all governments possessing an hereditary or self-appointed authority. This at best is but a precarious security; because a power independent of the society may as well espouse the unjust views of the major, as the rightful interests of the minor party, and may possibly be turned against both parties. The second method will be exemplified in the federal republic of the United States. Whilst all authority in it will be derived from and dependent on the society, the society itself will be broken into so many parts, interests and classes of citizens, that the rights of individuals, or of the minority, will be in little danger from interested combinations of the majority. In a free government, the security of civil rights must be the same as that for religious rights. It consists in the one case in the multiplicity of sects. The degree of security in both cases will depend on the number of interests and sects; and this may be presumed to depend on the extent of country and number of people comprehended under the same government. This view of the subject must particularly recommend a proper federal system to all the sincere and considerate friends of republican government: Since it shows that in exact proportion as the territory of the union may be formed into more circumscribed confederacies or states, oppressive combinations of a majority will be facilitated, the best security under the republican form, for the rights of every class of citizens, will be diminished; and consequently, the stability and independence of some members of the government, the only other security, must be proportionally increased. Justice is the end of government. It is the end of civil society. It ever has been, and ever will be pursued, until it be obtained, or until liberty be lost in the pursuit. In a society under the forms of which the stronger faction can readily unite and oppress the weaker, anarchy may as truly be said to reign, as in a state of nature where the weaker individual is not secured against the violence of the stronger: And as in the latter state even the stronger individuals are prompted by the uncertainty of their condition, to submit to a gov-

ernment which may protect the weak as well as themselves: So in the former state, will the more powerful factions or parties be gradually induced by a like motive, to wish for a government which will protect all parties, the weaker as well as the more powerful? It can be little doubted, that if the state of Rhode Island was separated from the confederacy, and left to itself, the insecurity of rights, under the popular form of government within such narrow limits, would be displayed by such reiterated oppressions of factious majorities, that some power altogether independent of the people would soon be called for by the voice of the very factions whose misrule had proved the necessity of it. In the extended republic of the United States, and among the great variety of interests, parties, and sects which it embraces, a coalition of a majority of the whole society could seldom take place on any other principles than those of justice and the general good; and there being thus less danger to a minor from the will of the major party, there must be less pretext, also, to provide for the security of the former by introducing into the government a will not dependent on the latter; or, in other words, a will independent of the society itself. It is no less certain than it is important, notwithstanding the contrary opinions which have been entertained, that the larger the society, provided it lie within a practicable sphere, the more duly capable it will be of self government. And happily for the republican cause, the practicable sphere may be carried to a very great extent by a judicious modification and mixture of the federal principle.

Observations on the Constitution

JOHN DICKINSON

Critics of the Constitution decried it as putting too much authority in the hands of a central government that could infringe on individual liberties. John Dickinson, however, argues in this article on the necessity of sacrificing separate rights for the good of all. He argues that the preservation of liberty requires some sacrifice of freedom. It is a theme that has resonated throughout American history in a delicate balance. Dickinson's article appeared in the *Pennsylvania Mercury and Universal Advertiser* on April 17, 1788. A Philadelphia lawyer, Dickinson helped write the Articles of Confederation, so in arguing for the Constitution, he was in effect lobbying against his own creation.

The Writer of this Address hopes that he will now be thought so disengaged from the objections against the part of the principle assumed, concerning the power of the people, that he may be excused for recurring to his assertion, that the power of the people pervading the proposed system, together with the strong confederation of the states, will form an adequate security against every danger that has been apprehended.

It is a mournful, but may be a useful truth, that the liberty of single republics has generally been destroyed by some of the citizens, and of confederated republics, by some of the associated states.

It is more pleasing, and may be more profitable to reflect, that their tranquillity and prosperity have commonly been promoted, in proportion to the strength of their government for protecting the worthy against the licentious.

As in forming a political society, each individual contributes some of his rights, in order that he may, from a common stock of rights, derive greater benefits than he could from merely his own; so, in forming a confederation, each political society should contribute such a share of their rights as will, from a common stock of rights, produce the largest quantity of benefits for them.

But, what is that share? and, how to be managed? Momentous questions! Here, flattery is treason; and error, destruction.

Are they unanswerable? No. Our most gracious Creator does not condemn us to sigh for unattainable blessedness: But one thing he demands—that we should seek for it in his way, and not in our own.

Humility and benevolence must take place of pride and overweening selfishness. Reason, then rising above these mists, will discover to us, that we cannot be true to ourselves, without being true to others—that to be solitary, is to be wretched—that to love our neighbors as ourselves is to love ourselves in the best manner—that to give is to gain—and, that we never consult our own happiness more effectually than when we most endeavor to correspond with the Divine designs, by communicating happiness, as much as we can, to our fellow-creatures. inestimable truth! sufficient, if they do not barely ask what it is, to melt tyrants into men, and to sooth the inflamed minds of a multitude into

mildness—sufficient to overflow this earth with unknown felicity—inestimable truth! which our Maker, in his providence, enables us not only to talk and write about, but to adopt in practice of vast extent, and of instructive example.

Let us now enquire, if there be not some principle, simple as the laws of nature in other instances, from which, as from a source, the many benefits of society are deduced.

We may with reverence say, that our Creator designed men for society, because otherwise they cannot be happy. They cannot be happy without freedom; nor free without security; that is, without the absence of fear; nor thus secure, without society. The conclusion is strictly syllogistic—that men cannot be free without society, which freedom produces the greatest happiness.

As these premises are invincible, we have advanced a considerable way in our inquiry upon this deeply interesting subject. If we can determine what share of his rights every individual must contribute to the common stock of rights in forming a society, for obtaining equal freedom, we determine at the same time, what share of their rights each political society must contribute to the common stock of rights in forming a confederation, which is only a larger society, for obtaining equal freedom: For, if the deposit be not proportioned to the magnitude of the association in the latter case, it will generate the same mischief among the component parts of it, from their inequality, that would result from a defective contribution to association in the former case, among the component parts of it, from their inequality.

Each individual then must contribute such a share of his rights as is necessary for attaining that security that is essential freedom; and he is bound to make this contribution by the law of his nature; that is, by the command of his creator; therefore, he must submit his will, in what concerns all, to the will of the whole society. What does he lose by this submission? The power of doing injuries to others—the dread of suffering injuries from them—and the incommodities of mental or bodily weakness. What does he gain by it? The aid of those associated with him—protection against injuries from them or others—a capacity of enjoying his undelegated rights to the best advantage—a repeal of his fears—and tranquillity of mind—or, in other words, that perfect liberty better described in the

Holy Scriptures, than any where else, in these expressions—"When every man shall sit under his vine, and under his fig tree, and none shall make him afraid."

The like submission, with a correspondent expansion and accommodation, must be made between states, for the like benefits in a confederation....

If, as some persons seem to think, a bill of rights is the best security of rights, the sovereignties of the several states have this best security, for they are not barely declared to be rights, but are taken into it as component parts for their perpetual preservation by themselves. In short, the government of each state is, and is to be, sovereign and supreme in all matters that relate to each state only. It is to be subordinate barely in those matters that relate to the whole; and it will be their own faults, if the several states suffer the federal sovereignty to interfere in things of their respective jurisdictions. An instance of such interference with regard to any single state will be a dangerous precedent as to all, and therefore will be guarded against by all, as the trustees or servants of the several states will not dare, if they retain their senses, so to violate the independent sovereignty of their respective states, that justly darling object of American affections, to which they are responsible, besides being endeared by all the charities of life.

The common sense of mankind agrees to the devolution of individual wills in society; and if it has not been as universally assented to in confederation, the reasons are evident, and worthy of being retained in remembrance by Americans....

How beautifully and forcibly does the inspired Apostle Saint Paul, argue upon a sublimer subject, with a train of reasoning strictly applicable to the present? His words are—"If the foot shall say, because I am not the hand, I am not of the body; is it therefore not of the body? and if the ear shall say, because I am not the eye, I am not of the body; is it therefore not of the body?" As plainly inferring, as could be done in that allegorical manner, the strongest censure of such partial discontents, especially, as his meaning is enforced by his description of the benefits of union in these expressions—"But, now they are many members, yet but one body: and the eye cannot say to the hand, I have no need of thee again; nor again, the head to the feet, I have no need of you."

❧ *"There is no alternative"*

GEORGE WASHINGTON

Like many of the signers of the Constitution, George Washington had mixed feelings about the particulars of the document. However, as this 1788 letter to the Marquis de Lafayette makes clear, Washington was willing to overlook the details for the sake of the most pressing issues. For Washington these were limiting the powers of government to as little as possible and dividing government into branches that would prevent the rise of any single individual or class. The alternative to the Constitution, he believed, was anarchy.

You appear to be, as might be expected from a real friend to this Country, anxiously concerned about its present political situation. So far as I am able I shall be happy in gratifying that friendly solicitude. As to my sentiments with respect to the merits of the new Constitution, I will disclose them without reserve (although by passing through the Post offices they should become known to the world) for, in truth, I have nothing to conceal on that subject. It appears to me, then little short of a miracle, that the Delegates from so many different States (which States you know are also different from each other in their manners, circumstances and prejudices) should unite in forming a system of national Government, so little liable to well founded objections. Nor am I yet such an enthusiastic, partial or undiscriminating admirer of it, as not to perceive it is tinctured with some real (though not radical) defects. The limits of a letter would not suffer me to go fully into an examination of them; nor would the discussion be entertaining or profitable, I therefore forebear to touch upon it. With regard to the two great points (the pivots on which the whole machine must move) my Creed is simple:

1st—That the general Government is not invested with more Powers than are indispensably necessary to perform the functions of a good Government; and, consequently, that no objection ought to be made against the quantity of Power delegated to it:

2ly—That these Powers (as the appointment of all Rulers will forever arise from, and , at short stated intervals, recur to the free suffrage of the People) are so distributed among the legislative, Executive, and Judicial Branches, into which the general Government is arranged, that it can never be in danger of degenerating into a monarchy, an

Oligarchy, an Aristocracy, or any other despotic or oppressive form; so long as there shall remain any virtue in the body of the People.

I would not be understood my dear marquis to speak of consequences which may be produced, in the revolution of ages, by corruptions of morals, profligacy of manners, and listlessness for the preservation of the natural and unalienable rights of mankind; nor of the successful usurpations that may be established at such an unpropitious juncture, upon the ruins of liberty, however, providently guarded and secured, as these are contingencies against which no human prudence can effectually provide. It will at least be a recommendation to the proposed Constitution that it is provided with more checks and barriers against the introduction of tyranny, & those of a nature less liable to be surmounted, than any government hitherto instituted among mortals, hath possessed. We are not to expect perfection in this world: but mankind, in modern times, have apparently made some progress in the science of Government. Should that which is now offered to the People of America, be found on experiment less perfect than it can be made—a Constitutional door is left open for its amelioration. Some respectable characters have wished that the States, after having pointed out whatever alterations and amendments may be judged necessary, would appoint another federal Convention to modify it upon those documents. For myself I have wondered that sensible men should not see the impracticability of the scheme. The members would go fortified with such Instructions that nothing but discordant ideas could prevail. Had I but slightly suspected (at the time when the late Convention was in session) that another Convention would not be likely to agree upon a better form of Government, I should now be confirmed in the fixed belief that they would not be able to agree upon any System whatever: So many, I may add, such contradictory, and, in my opinion, unfounded objections have been urged against the System in contemplation; many of which would operate equally against every efficient Government that might be proposed. I will only add, as a farther opinion founded on the maturest deliberation, that there is no alternative—no hope of alteration—no immediate resting place—between the adoption of this and a recurrence to an unqualified state of Anarchy, with all its deplorable consequences.

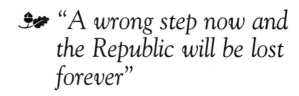

"A wrong step now and the Republic will be lost forever"

PATRICK HENRY

The legendary revolutionary Patrick Henry was one of the staunchest opponents of the Constitution, which he feared would squash individual liberties. Saying he represented the voice of the people, he described his misgivings at the outset of the Virginia Constitutional Convention. Despite Henry's objections, which were widespread, Virginia ratified the Constitution on June 25, 1788.

Mr. Chairman. The public mind, as well as my own, is extremely uneasy at the proposed change of Government. Give me leave to form one of the number of those who wish to be thoroughly acquainted with the reasons of this perilous and uneasy situation—and why we are brought hither to decide on this great national question. I consider myself as the servant of the people of this Commonwealth, as a centinel over their rights, liberty, and happiness. I represent their feelings when I say, that they are exceedingly uneasy, being brought from that state of full security, which they enjoyed, to the present delusive appearance of things. A year ago the minds of our citizens were at perfect repose. Before the meeting of the late Federal Convention at Philadelphia, a general peace, and an universal tranquility prevailed in this country; but since that period they are exceedingly uneasy and disquieted. When I wished for an appointment to this Convention, my mind was extremely agitated for the situation of public affairs. I conceive the republic to be in extreme danger. If our situation be thus uneasy, whence has arisen this fearful jeopardy? It arises from this fatal system—it arises from a proposal to change our government: A proposal that goes to the utter annihilation of the most solemn engagements of the States. A proposal of establishing 9 States into a confederacy, to the eventual exclusion of 4 States. It goes to the annihilation of those solemn treaties we have formed with foreign nations. The present circumstances of France—the good offices rendered us by that kingdom, require our most faithful and most punctual adherence to our treaty with her. We are in alliance with the Spaniards, the Dutch, the Prussians: Those treaties bound us as thirteen

States, confederated together—Yet, here is a proposal to sever that confederacy. Is it possible that we shall abandon all our treaties and national engagements? And for what? I expected to have heard the reasons of an event so unexpected to my mind, and many others. Was our civil polity, or public justice, endangered or sapped? Was the real existence of the country threatened—or was this preceded by a mournful progression of events? This proposal of altering our Federal Government is of a most alarming nature: make the best of this new Government—say it is composed by any thing but inspiration—you ought to be extremely cautious, watchful, jealous of your liberty; for instead of securing your rights you may lose them forever. If a wrong step be now made, the republic may be lost forever. If this new government will not come up to the expectation of the people, and they should be disappointed—their liberty will be lost, and tyranny must and will arise. I repeat it again, and I beg Gentlemen to consider, that a wrong step made now will plunge us into misery, and our Republic will be lost. It will be necessary for the Convention to have a faithful historical detail of the facts, that preceded the session of the Federal Convention, and the reasons that actuated its members in proposing an entire alteration of Government— and to demonstrate the dangers that awaited us. If they were of such awful magnitude, as to warrant a proposal so extremely perilous as this, I must assert, that this Convention has an absolute right to a thorough discovery of every circumstance relative to this great event. And here I would make this enquiry of those worthy characters who composed a part of the late Federal convention. I am sure they were fully impressed with the necessity of forming a great consolidated Government, instead of a confederation. That this is a consolidated government is demonstrably clear, and the danger of such a Government, is, to my mind very striking. I have the highest veneration for these Gentlemen, but, Sir, give me leave to demand, what right had they to say, We, the People. My political curiosity, exclusive of my anxious solicitude for the public welfare, leads me to ask, who authorised them to speak the language of, We, the People, instead of We, the States? States are the characteristics, and the soul of a confederation. If the States be not the agents of this compact, it must be one great consol-idated National Government of the people of all the States. I have the highest respect for those Gentlemen who formed the Convention, and were some of them not here, I would express some testimonial of my esteem for them. America had on a former occasion put the utmost confidence in them: A confidence which was well placed: And aim sure, Sir, I would give up any thing to them; I would chearfully confide in them as my Representatives. But, Sir, on this great occasion, I would demand the cause of their conduct. Even from that illustrious man, who saved us by his valor, I would have a reason for his conduct—that liberty which he has given us by his valor, tells me to ask this reason, and sure I am, were he here, he would give us that reason: but there are other Gentlemen here, who can give us this information. The people gave them no power to use their name. That they exceeded their power is perfectly clear. It is not mere curiosity that actuates me—I wish to hear the real actual existing danger, which should lead us to take these so dangerous in my conception. Disorders have arisen in other parts of America, but here, Sir, no dangers, no insurrection or tumult, has happened—every thing has been calm and tranquil. But notwithstanding this, we are wandering on the great ocean of human affairs. I see no landmark to guide us. We are running we know not whither. Difference in opinion has gone to a degree of inflammatory resentment in different parts of the country—which has been occasioned by this perilous innovation. The Federal Convention ought to have amended the old system—for this purpose they were solely delegated: The object of their mission extended to no other consideration. You must therefore forgive the solicitation of one unworthy member, to know what danger could have arisen under the present confederation, and what are the causes of this proposal to change our Government.

❧ The Raising: A New Song for Federal Mechanics

FRANCIS HOPKINSON

Francis Hopkinson published this Federalist song in the *Pennsylvania Gazette* in 1788 to support and celebrate the Constitution. It captures the essential principles that the Federalists advocated—a firm federal government and free citizens—by comparing the founding of the new government to the construction of a strong house. The song represented the spirit with which the new country embarked upon becoming a new nation in a sometimes hostile world.

i.

Come muster, my Lads, your mechanical Tools,
Your Saws and your Axes, your Hammers
    and Rules;
Bring your Mallets and Planes, your Level and
    Line,
And Plenty of Pins of American Pine;
For our roof we will raise, and our Song still
    shall be—
A government firm and our Citizens free.

ii.

Come, up with Plates, lay them firm on the Wall,
Like the People at large, they're the Ground-work
    of;
Examine them well, and see that they're sound,
Let no rotten Parts in our Building be found;
For our Roof we will raise, and our Song still shall
    be—
Our Government firm, and our Citizens free.

iii.

Now hand up the Girders, lay each in his Place,
Between them the Joists must divide all the Space;
Like Assembly-men, these should lye level along,
Like Girders, our Senate prove loyal and strong;
For our Roof we will raise, and our Song still shall
    be—
A government firm, over Citizens free.

iv.

The Rafters now frame—your King-Posts and
    Braces,
And drive your Pins home, to keep all in their
    Places;
Let Wisdom and Strength in the Fabric combine,
And your Pins be all made of American Pine;
For our Roof we will raise, and our Song still shall
    be—
A government firm, over Citizens free.

v.

Our King-Posts are Judges—How upright
    they stand,
Supporting the Braces, the Laws of the Land—
The Laws of the Land, which divide Right
    from Wrong,
And strengthen the Weak, by weak'ning the
    Strong;
For our Roof we will raise, and our Song still shall
    be—
Laws equal and just, for a People that's free.

vi.

Up! Up with the Rafters—each Frame is a State!
How nobly they rise! their Span, too, how great!
From the North to the South, o'er the Whole they
    extend,
And rest on the Walls, while the Walls they
    defend!
For our Roof we will raise, and our Song still shall
    be—
Combined in Strength, yet as Citizens free.

vii.

Now enter the Purlins, and drive your Pins
    through,
And see that your Joints are drawn home, and
    all true;
The Purlins will bind all the Rafters together,
The strength of the Whole shall defy Wind and
    Weather;
For our Roof we will raise, and our Song still shall
    be—
United as States, but as Citizens free.

viii.

Come, raise up the Turret—our Glory and Pride—
In the Centre it stands, o'er the Whole to preside;
The Sons of Columbia shall view with Delight
Its Pillars, and Arches, and Towering Height;
Our Roof is now rais'd, and our Song still
    shall be—
A Federal Hearth, o'er a People still free.

ix.

Huzza! my brave Boys, our Work is complete,
The World shall admire Columbia's fair
    Seat;
It's strength against Tempest and Time shall
    be Proof,

And Thousands shall come to dwell under our roof.
Whilst we drain the deep Bowl, our Toast
    still shall be—
Our government firm, and our Citizens free.

CHAPTER THREE

1789–1836

The New Nation

❧ First Inaugural Address

GEORGE WASHINGTON

After the Constitution was ratified, an election was held in early 1789. To the surprise of nobody, George Washington was elected as the first president. Many of the framers of the Constitution envisioned Washington as the president while they were drafting the job description. On April 6, 1789, Washington was formally named as president with John Adams as vice president. On April 30, Washington delivered the nation's first inaugural address.

Fellow Citizens of the Senate and of the House of Representatives:

Among the vicissitudes incident to life no event could have filled me with greater anxieties than that of which notification was transmitted by you, and received on the 14th day of the present month. On the one hand, I was summoned by my country, whose voice I can never hear but with veneration and love, from a retreat which I had chosen with the fondest predilection, and, in my flattering hopes, with an immutable decision, as the asylum of my declining years—a retreat which was rendered every day more necessary as well as more dear to me by the addition of habit to inclination, and of frequent interruptions in my health to the gradual waste committed on it by time. On the other hand, the magnitude and difficulty of the trust to which the voice of my country called me, being sufficient to awaken in the wisest and most experienced of her citizens a distrustful scrutiny into his qualifications, could not but overwhelm with despondence of one who (inheriting inferior endowments from nature and unpracticed in the duties of civil administration) ought to be peculiarly conscious of his own deficiencies. In this conflict of emotions all I dare aver is that it has been my faithful study to collect my duty from a just appreciation of every circumstance by which it might be affected. All I dare hope is that if, in executing this task, I have been too much swayed by a grateful remembrance of former instances, or by an affectionate sensibility to this transcendent proof of the confidence of my fellow-citizens, and have thence too little consulted my incapacity as well as disinclination for the weighty and untried cares before me, my error will be palliated by the motives which mislead me, and its consequences be judged by my country with some share of the partiality in which they originated.

Such being the impressions under which I have, in obedience to the public summons, repaired to the present station, it would be peculiarly improper to omit in this first official act my fervent supplications to that Almighty Being who rules over the universe, who presides in the councils of nations, and whose sides in the councils of nations, and whose providential aids can supply every human defect, that His benediction may consecrate to the liberties and happiness of the people of the United States a Government instituted by themselves for these essential purposes, and may enable every instrument employed in its administration to execute with success the functions allotted to his charge.... No people can be bound to acknowledge and adore the Invisible Hand which conducts the affairs of men more than those of the United States. Every step by which they have advanced to the character of an independent nation seems to have been distinguished by some token of providential agency; and in the important revolution just accomplished in the system of their united government the tranquil deliberations and voluntary consent of so many distinct communities from which the event has resulted can not be compared with the means by which most governments have been established without some return of pious gratitude, along with an humble anticipation of the future blessings which the past seems to presage....

By the article establishing the executive department it is made the duty of the President "to recommend to your consideration such measures as he shall judge necessary and expedient." The circumstances under which I now meet you will acquit men from entering into that subject further than to refer to the great constitutional charter under which you are assembled, and which, in defining your powers, designates the objects to which your attention is to be given. It will be more consistent with those circumstances, and far more congenial with the feelings which actuate me, to substitute, in place of a recommendation of particular measures, the tribute that is due to the talents, the rectitude, and the patriotism which adorn the characters selected to devise and adopt them. In these honorable qualifications I behold the surest pledges that as on one side no local prejudices or attachments, no separate views nor party animosities, will misdirect the comprehensive and equal eye which ought to watch over this great assemblage of communities and interests, so, on another, that the foundation of our national policy will be laid in the pure and immutable principles of private morality, and the preeminence of free government be exemplified by all the attributes which can win the affections of its citizens and command the respect of the world. I dwell on this prospect with every satisfaction which an ardent love for my country can inspire, since there is no truth more thoroughly established than that there exists in the economy and course of nature an indissoluble union between virtue and happiness; between duty and advantage; between the genuine maxims of an honest and magnanimous policy and the solid rewards of public prosperity and felicity; since we ought to be no less persuaded that the propitious smiles of Heaven can never be expected on a nation that disregards the eternal rules of order and right which heaven itself has ordained; and since the preservation of the sacred fire of liberty and the destiny of the republican model of government are justly considered, perhaps, as deeply, as finally, staked on the experiment intrusted to the hands of the American people.

Besides the ordinary objects submitted to your care, it will remain with your judgment to decide how far an exercise of the occasional power delegated by the fifth article of the Constitution is rendered expedient at the present juncture by the nature of objections which have been urged against the system, or by the degree of inquietude which has given birth to them....

To the foregoing observations I have one to add, which will be most properly addressed to the House of Representatives. It concerns myself, and will therefore be as brief as possible. When I was first honored with a call into the service of my country, then on the eve of an arduous struggle for its liberties, the light in which I contemplated my duty required that I should renounce every pecuniary compensation. From this resolution I have in no instance departed; and being still under the impressions which produced it, I must decline as inapplicable to myself any share in the personal emoluments which may be indispensably included in a permanent provision for the executive department, and must accordingly pray that the pecuniary estimates for the station in which I am placed may during my continuance in it be limited to such

actual expenditures as the public good may be thought to require.

Having thus impaired to you my sentiments as they have been awakened by the occasion which brings us together, I shall take my present leave; but not without resorting once more to the benign parent of the Human Race in humble supplication that, since He has been pleased to favor the American people with opportunities for deliberating in perfect tranquility, and dispositions for deciding with unparalleled unanimity on a form of government for the security of their union and the advancement of their happiness, so His divine blessing may be equally conspicuous in the enlarged views, the temperate consultations, and the wise measures on which the success of this Government must depend.

❧ The Judiciary Act of 1789

CONGRESS

One of the first tasks Congress undertook was organizing the judiciary. Article Three of the Constitution simply created a Supreme Court and referred the establishment of other courts to Congress. The Judiciary Act of 1789 created the framework for the American judicial system, thus providing a national institution that would play an important role in binding the states as a single nation. The act established federal district and circuit courts, made the Supreme Court as the final appellate court and created the position of Attorney General.

Section 1. Be it enacted, That the supreme courts of the United States shall consist of a chief justice and five associate justices, any four of whom shall be a quorum, and shall hold annually at the seat of government two sessions, the once commencing the first Monday of February, and the other the first Monday of August. That the associate justices shall have precedence according to the date of their commissions, or when the commissions of two or more of them bear date on the same day, according to their respective ages.

Section 2. That the United States shall be, and they hereby are, divided into thirteen districts, to be limited and called as follows,...

Section 3. That there be a court called a District Court in each of the aforementioned districts, to consist of one judge, who shall reside in the district for which he is appointed, and shall be called a District Judge, and shall hold annually four sessions,...

Section 9. That the district courts shall have, exclusively of the courts of the several States, cognizance of all crimes and offences that shall be cognizable under the authority of the United States, committed within their respective districts, or upon the high seas; where no other punishment than whipping, not exceeding thirty stripes, a fine not exceeding one hundred dollars, or a term of imprisonment not exceeding six months, is to be inflicted; and shall have exclusive original cognizance of all civil cases of admiralty and maritime jurisdiction, including all seizures under laws of impost, navigation, or trade of the United States.... And shall also have cognizance, concurrent with the courts of the several States, or the circuit courts, as the case may be, of all causes where an alien sues for a tort only in violation of the law of nations or a treaty of the United States. And shall also have cognizance, concurrent as last mentioned, of all suits at common law where the United States sue, and the matter in dispute amounts, exclusive of costs to the sum or value of one hundred dollars. And shall also have jurisdiction exclusively of the courts of the several States, of all suits against counsuls of vice-counsuls, except for offences above the description aforesaid. And the trial of issues in fact, in the district courts, in all cases except civil causes of admiralty and maritime jurisdiction, shall be by jury....

Section 11. That the circuit courts shall have original cognizance, concurrent with the courts of the several States, of all suits of a civil nature at common law or in equity, where the matter in dispute exceeds, exclusive of costs, the sum or value of five hundred dollars, and the United States are plaintiffs or petitioners; or an alien is a party, or the suit is between a citizen of the State where the suit is between a citizen of the State where the suit is brought and a citizen of another State. And shall have exclusive cognizance of all crimes and offences cognizable under the authority of the United States, except where this act otherwise provides, or the laws of the United States shall otherwise direct, and concurrent jurisdiction with the district courts of the crimes and offences cognizable therein.... And the circuit courts shall also have appellate jurisdic-

tion from the district courts under the regulations and restrictions hereinafter provided....

Section 13. That the Supreme Court shall have exclusive jurisdiction of all controversies of a civil nature, where a state is a party, except between a state and its citizens; and except also between a state and citizens of other states, or aliens, in which latter case it shall have original but not exclusive jurisdiction. And shall have exclusively all such jurisdiction of suits or proceedings against ambassadors or other public ministers, or their domestics, or domestic servants, as a court of law can have or exercise consistently with the law of nations; and original, but not exclusive jurisdiction of all suits brought by ambassadors or other public ministers, or in which a consul or vice consul shall be a party. And the trial of issues in fact in the Supreme Court in all actions at law against citizens of the United States shall be by jury. The Supreme Court shall also have appellate jurisdiction from the circuit courts and courts of the several states in the cases hereinafter specially provided for; and shall have power to issue writs of prohibition to the district courts, when proceedings as courts of admiralty and maritime jurisdiction, and writs of mandamus, in cases warranted by the principle and usage of law, to any courts appointed, or persons holding office under the authority of the United States....

Section 35.... And there shall also be appointed a meet person learned in the law to act as attorney-general of the United States, who shall be sworn or affirmed to a faithful execution of his office; whose duty it shall be to prosecute and conduct all suits in the Supreme Court in which the United States shall be concerned, and to give his advice and opinion upon questions of law when required by the President of the United States, or when requested by the heads of any of the departments, touching any matters that may concern their departments, and shall receive such compensation for this services as shall by law be provided.

❧ On Public Credit

ALEXANDER HAMILTON

One of the most controversial and difficult issues that confronted the new federal government was the national and individual states' war debts. Fearing that the debts would not be paid, many debt holders sold their notes at deeply discounted prices to speculators. The new federal government assumed the debts, although some people suggested that the government not pay the full obligations.

Treasury Secretary Alexander Hamilton delivered a report on public credit calling for the full payment of the debts. Hamilton argued that the government needed to establish its credibility and solidify financial markets to help foster the national economy. This position, along with his advocacy for a national bank and federal excise tax, led to sharp criticisms of Hamilton for trying to create a privileged class of wealthy at the expense of the general public. Hamilton, however, prevailed, thus creating a sound environment for the issuing of bank loans to fuel the young nation's economy and establishing a federal tax system to pay off outstanding war debts.

States, like individuals, who observe their engagements, are respected and trusted; while the reverse is the fate of those, who pursue an opposite conduct.

Every breach of the public engagements, whether from choice or necessity, is in different degrees hurtful to public credit. When such a necessity does truly exist, the evils of it are only to be palliated by a scrupulous attention, on the part of the government, to carry the violation no farther than the necessity absolutely requires, and to manifest, if the nature of the case admits of it, a sincere deposition to make reparation, whenever circumstances permit. But with every possible mitigation, credit must suffer, and numerous mischiefs ensue. It is therefore highly important, when an appearance of necessity seems to press upon the public councils, that they should examine well its reality, and be perfectly assured, that there is no method of escaping from it, before they yield to its suggestions…. Those who are most commonly creditors of a nation, are, generally speaking, enlightened men; and there are signal examples to warrant a conclusion, that when a candid and fair appeal is made to them, they will understand their true interest too well to refuse their concurrence in such modifications of their claims, as any real necessity may demand.

While the observance of that good faith, which is the basis of public credit, is recommended by the strongest inducements of political expediency, it is enforced by considerations of still greater authority. There are arguments for it, which rest on the immutable principles of moral obligation. And in proportion as the mind is disposed to contemplate, in order of Providence, an intimate connection between public virtue and public happiness, will be its repugnancy to a violation of those principles.

This reflection derives additional strength from the nature of the debt of the United States. It was the price of liberty. The faith of America has been repeatedly pledged for it, and with solemnities, that give peculiar force to the obligation….

To justify and preserve their confidence; to promote the increasing respectability of the American name; to answer the calls of justice; to restore landed property to its due value; to furnish new resources both to agriculture and commerce; to cement more closely the union of the states; to add to their security against foreign attack; to establish public order on the basis of an upright and liberal policy. These are the great and invaluable ends to be secured, by a proper and adequate provision, at the present period, for the support of public credit….

It will procure to every class of the community some important advantages, and remove some no less important disadvantages.

The advantage to the public creditors from the increased value of that part of their property which constitutes the public debt, needs no explanation.

But there is a consequence of this, less obvious, though not less true, in which every other citizen is interested. It is a well known fact that in countries in which the national debt is properly funded, an object of established confidence, it answers most of the purposes of money. Transfers of stock or public debt are there equivalent payments in specie; or in other words, stock, in the principal transaction of business, passes current as specie. The same thing would, in all probability happen here, under the like circumstances.

The benefits of this are various and obvious.

Trade is extended by it; because there is a larger capital to carry it on….

The proprietors of lands would not only feel the benefit of this increase in the value of their property, and of a more prompt and better sale, when they had occasion to sell; but the necessity of selling would be, itself, greatly diminished….

It is agreed on all hands, that that part of the debt which has been contracted abroad, and is denominated the foreign debt, ought to be provided for, according to the precise terms of the contracts relating to it. The discussions, which can arise, therefore, will have reference essentially to the domestic part of it, or to that which has been contracted at home. It is to be regretted, that there is not the same unanimity of sentiment on this part as on the other.

The Secretary has too much deference for the opinions of every part of the community, not to have observed one, which has, more than once, made its appearance in the public prints, and which is occasionally to be met with in conversation. It involves this question, whether a discrimination are for making possessors, by purchase. Those who advocate a discrimination are for making a full provision for the securities of the former, at their nominal value; but contend, that the latter ought to receive no more than the cost to them, and the interest: And the idea is sometimes suggested of making good the difference to the primitive possessor....

The Secretary, after the most mature reflection on the force of this argument, is induced to reject the doctrine it contains, as equally unjust and impolitic, as highly injurious, even to the original holders of public securities; as ruinous to public credit.

It is inconsistent with justice, because in the first place, it is a breach of contract; in violation of the rights of a fair purchaser.

The nature of the contract in its origin, is, that the public will pay the sum expressed in the security, to the first holder, or his assignee. The intent, in making the security assignable, is, that the proprietor may be able to make use of his property, by selling it for as much as it may be worth in the market, and that the buyer may be safe in the purchase.

Every buyer therefore stands exactly in the place of the seller, has the same right with him to the identical sum expressed in the security, and having acquired that right, by fair purchase, and in conformity to the original agreement and intention of the government, his claim cannot be disputed, without manifest injustice.

That he is to be considered as a fair purchaser, results from this: Whatever necessity the seller may have been under, was occasioned by the government, in not making a proper provision for its debts. The buyer had no agency in it, and therefore ought not to suffer. He is not even chargeable with having taken an undue advantage. He paid what the commodity was worth in the market, and took the risks of reim-

bursement upon himself. He of course gave a fair equivalent, and ought to reap the benefit of his hazard; a hazard which was far from inconsiderable, and which, perhaps, turned on little less than a revolution in government.

❧ On the Equality of the Sexes

JUDITH SARGENT MURRAY

Judith Sargent Murray moved to the United States from England in 1770 with her husband John Murray, who preached the doctrine of Universalism. She wrote two popular plays and the novel *The Story of Margaretta.* Murray explored numerous topics of the day including education, creating a national theater, liberty and patriotism. She became one of the first American citizens to extend the notion of equality to women. The following is a poem Murray wrote as introduction to her 1790 essay "On the Equality of the Sexes."

That minds are not alike, full well I know,
This truth each day's experience will show;
To heights surprising some great spirits soar,
With inborn strength mysterious depths explore;
Their eager gaze surveys the path of light,
Confest it stood to Newton's piercing sight.
Deep science, like a bashful maid retires,
And but the ardent breast her worth inspires;
By perseverance the coy fair is won.
And Genius, led by Study, wears the crown.
But some there are who wish not to improve,
Who never can the path of knowledge love,
Whose souls almost with the dull body one,
With anxious care each mental pleasure shun;
Weak is the level'd, enervated mind,
And but while here to vegetate design'd.
The torpid spirit mingling with its clod,
Can scarcely boast its origin from God;
Stupidly dull—they move progressing on—
They eat, and drink, and all their work is done.
While others, emulous of sweet applause,
Industrious seek for each event a cause,
Tracing the hidden springs whence knowledge
    flows,
Which nature all in beauteous order shows.
Yet cannot I their sentiments imbibe,
Who this distinction to the sex ascribe,
As if a woman's form must needs enroll,

A weak, servile, an inferiour soul;
And that the guise of man must still proclaim,
Greatness of mind, and him, to be the same:
Yet as the hours revolve fair proofs arise,
Which the bright wreath of growing fame supplies;
And in past times some men have sunk so low,
That female records nothing less can show.
But imbecility is still confin'd,
And by the lordly sex to us consign'd;
They rob us of the power t' improve,
And then declare we only trifles love;
Yet haste the era, when the world shall know,
That such distinctions only dwell below;
The soul unfetter'd, to no sex confin'd,
Was for the abodes of cloudless day design'd.
Mean time we emulate their manly fires,
Through erudition all their thoughts inspires,
Yet nature with equality imparts,
And *noble passions*, swell e'en *female hearts*.

❧ *"The right of the people"*

THE BILL OF RIGHTS

Responding to widespread objections that the Constitution did not include specified guarantees of liberties and rights, James Madison proposed several amendments to the First Congress in 1789. Within two years ten amendments known as the Bill of Rights were approved. These additions have provided the foundation for the protection of fundamental liberties in the United States. They include freedom of speech and religion, the right to bear arms, protection against unreasonable searches and seizures, the guarantee of legal due process, the right to a public trial, legal counsel and a judgement by a jury and several other basic protections.

AMENDMENT I

Congress shall make no law respecting an establishment of religion, or prohibiting the free exercise thereof; or abridging the freedom of speech, or of the press; or the right of the people to peaceably assemble, and to petition the Government for a redress of grievances.

AMENDMENT II

A well-regulated Militia, being necessary to the security of a free State, the right of the people to keep and bear Arms shall not be infringed.

AMENDMENT III

No soldier shall, in time of peace, be quartered in any house, without the consent of the Owner, nor in time of war, but in a manner prescribed by law.

AMENDMENT IV

The right of the people to be secure in their persons, houses, papers, and effects against unreasonable searches and seizures, shall not be violated, and no Warrants shall issue, but upon probable cause, supported by Oath or affirmation, and particularly describing the place to be searched, and the persons or things to be seized.

AMENDMENT V

No person shall be held to answer for a capital, or otherwise infamous crime, unless on a presentment or indictment of a Grand Jury, except in cases arising in the land or naval forces, or in the Militia, when in actual service in time of War or public danger; nor shall any person be subject for the same offence to be twice put in jeopardy of life or limb; nor shall be compelled in any criminal case to be a witness against himself, nor be deprived of life, liberty, or property, without due process of law; nor shall private property be taken for public use, without just compensation.

AMENDMENT VI

In all criminal prosecutions, the accused shall enjoy the right to a speedy and public trial, by an impartial jury of the State and district wherein the crime shall have been committed, which district shall have been previously ascertained by law, and to be informed of the nature and cause of the accusation; to be confronted with the witnesses against him; to have compulsory process for obtaining witnesses in his favor, and to have the Assistance of Counsel for his defense.

AMENDMENT VII

In suits at common law, where the value in controversy shall exceed twenty dollars, the right of trial by jury shall be preserved, and no fact tried by a jury, shall be otherwise reexamined in any Court of the United States, than according to the rules of the common law.

AMENDMENT VIII

Excessive bail shall not be required, nor excessive

fines imposed, nor cruel and unusual punishments inflicted.

AMENDMENT IX

The enumeration in the Constitution, of certain rights, shall not be construed to deny or disparage others retained by the people.

AMENDMENT X

The powers not delegated to the United States by the Constitution, nor prohibited by it to the States, are reserved to the States respectively, or to the people.

The Hasty Pudding

JOEL BARLOW

Joel Barlow's mock-heroic 1793 poem "The Hasty Pudding" celebrated the simple values of America. The sentiments of the poem were triggered when the writer gets a whiff of cornmeal in a Swiss Alpine inn, reminding the author of his native hasty pudding. In mocking and sentimental verses, Barlow punctures European pretensions in favor of ordinary American ways.

…Dear Hasty Pudding, what unpromised joy
Expand my heart, to meet thee in Savoy!
Doomed o'er the world through devious paths to
    roam,
Each clime is my country, and each house my
    home,
My soul is soothed, my cares have found an end,
I greet my long-lost, unforgotten friend.
For thee through Paris, that corrupted town,
How long in vain I wandered up and down,
Where shameless Bacchus, with his drenching
    hoard,
Cold from his cave usurps the morning board.
London is lost in smoke and steeped in tea;
No Yankee there can lisp the name of thee;
The uncouth word, a libel on the town,
Would call a proclamation from the crown.
For climes oblique, that fear the sun's full rays,
Chilled in their fogs, exclude the generous
    maize;
A grain whose rich luxuriant growth requires
Short gentle showers, and bright ethereal fires.
But here, though distant from our native shore,
With mutual glee we meet and laugh once more.

The same! I know thee by that yellow face,
That strong complexion of true Indian race,
Which time can never change, nor soil impair,
Nor alpine snows, nor turkey's morbid air;
For endless years, through every mild domain,
Where grows the maize, there thou art sure to
    reign.
But man, more fickle, the bold incense claims,
In different realms to give thee different names.
Thee the soft nations round the warm Levant
Polenta call, the French of course polenta;
Ev'n in thy native regions, how I blush
To hear the Pennsylvanians call thee mush!
On Hudson's banks, while men of Belgic spawn
Insult and eat thee by the name suppawn.
All spurious appellations, void of truth;
I've better known thee from my earliest youth,
Thy name is hasty Pudding! Thus our sires
Were wont to greet thee fuming from their
    fires;
And while they argued in thy just defense
With logic clear, they thus explained the sense:
"In haste and boiling cauldron, o'er the blaze,
Receives and cooks the ready-powered maize;
In haste 'tis served, and then in equal haste,
With cooling milk, we make the sweet repast.
No carving to be done, no knife to grate
The tender ear, and wound the stony plate;
But the smooth spoon, just fitted to the lip,
And taught with art the yielding mass to dip,
By frequent journeys to the bowl well stored,
Performs the hasty honors of the board."
Such is thy name, significant and clear,
A name, a sound to every Yankee dear,
But most to me, whose heart and palate chaste
Preserve my pure hereditary taste….
My song resounding in its grateful glee,
No merit claims; I praise myself in thee.
My father loved thee through his length of days;
For thee his fields were shaded o'er with maize;
From thee what health, what vigor he
    possessed,
Ten sturdy freemen from his loins attest;
Thy constellation ruled my natal morn,
And all my bones were made of Indian corn.
Delicious grain! whatever form it take,
To roast or boil, to smother or to bake,
In every dish 'tis welcome still to me,
But most, my Hasty Pudding, most in thee….

❧ Charlotte Temple

SUSANNA HASWELL ROWSON

First published in the United States in 1793, Susanna Haswell Rowson's *Charlotte Temple* was America's best-selling book until the publication of *Uncle Tom's Cabin* 60 years later. Rowson's novel told the tale of a young woman who fell in love with a man and was betrayed by him. The book was one of several popular novels in the "women's fiction" genre that attracted large audiences. The following excerpt is from the book's preface.

For the perusal of the young and thoughtless of the fair sex, this Tale of truth is designed; and I could wish my fair readers to consider it as not merely the effusion of Fancy, but as a reality. The circumstances on which I have founded this novel were related to me some little time since by an old lady who had personally known Charlotte, though she concealed the real names of the characters, and likewise the place where the unfortunate scenes were acted: yet as it was impossible to offer a relation to the public in such an imperfect state, I have thrown over the while a slight veil of fiction, and substituted names and places according to my own fancy. The principal characters in this little tale are now consigned to the silent tomb: it can therefore hurt the feelings of no one; and may, I flatter myself, be of service to some who are so unfortunate as to have neither friends to advise, or understanding to direct them, through the various and unexpected evils that attend a young and unprotected woman in her first entrance into life.

While the tear of compassion still trembled in my eye for the fate of the unhappy Charlotte, I may have children of my own, said I, to whom this recital may be of use, and if to your own children, said Benevolence, why not the many daughters of Misfortune who, deprived of natural friends, or spoilt by a mistaken education, are thrown on an unfeeling world without the least power to defend themselves from the snares not only of the other sex, but from the more dangerous arts of the profligate of their own.

Sensible as I am that a novel writer, at a time when such a variety of works are ushered into the world under that name stands but a poor chance for fame in the annals of literature, but conscious that I wrote with a mind anxious for the happiness of that sex whose morals and conduct have so powerful an influence on mankind in general; and convinced that I have not wrote a line that conveys a wrong idea to the head or a corrupt wish to the heart, I shall rest satisfied in the purity of my own intentions, and if I merit not applause, I feel that I dread not censure.

If the following tale should save one hapless fair one from the error which ruined poor Charlotte, or rescue from impending misery the heart of one anxious parent, I shall feel a much higher gratification in reflecting on this trifling performance, than could possibly result from the applause which might attend the most elegant finished piece of literature whose tendency might deprave the heart or mislead the understanding.

❧ Whiskey Rebellion

WILLIAM FINDLEY

In 1791 the federal government created an excise tax on distilled spirits and stills. The levy fell particularly hard on farmers in western Pennsylvania and Virginia who converted their corn crops into whiskey because of the high cost to transport corn to eastern markets. Often unable to pay the excise tax because of a shortage of currency in the local economies, which often relied heavily on bartering, many farmers refused to pay the tax in what became known as the "Whiskey Rebellion" of 1794. Washington sent troops to compel the payment of taxes. William Findley, a "country democrat," wrote this account of the farmers' plight two years after the "rebellion," which only had sporadic bouts of violence.

If the numerous difficulties encountered and hardships sustained, by the people inhabiting the western counties of Pennsylvania, were to be minutely related, their behavior under them fairly stated, their conduct generally would be entitled to a much greater proportion of approbation than blame, and their sufferings would have a powerful claim on the sympathy of their fellow citizens....

The people in the western counties anticipated their experiencing peculiar hardships from the excise. Without money, or the means of procuring it, and consuming their whiskey only in their families or using it as an article of barter, which, though it in some respects answered the place of money, yet would not be received in pay for the excise tax, they thought it hard to pay as much tax on what sold with them but from two shillings, to two shillings and six pence, as they did where it brought double that price. These, and such like arguments, were not new. I found them in use against the state excise when I went to reside in that county. They arose from their situation, and the simplest person feeling their force, know how to use them.

Some talked of laying aside their still altogether, till they would have time to observe the effects of the law on other places, and have time to reflect on the subject; and this method was advised, in preference to a more violent mode of opposition, by some who were apprehensive of outrages being committed. But though several peaceable men laid aside their stills or sold them, yet there never was any associations or resolutions among the inhabitants to that purpose....

The great error among the people was an opinion, that an immortal law might be opposed and yet the government respected and all the other laws obeyed, and they firmly believed that the excise law was an immoral one. This theory become with many a religious principle, in defence of which they reasoned with considerable address. In endeavoring to restore order, and submission to the laws, the most arduous talk with people otherwise of good morals was to convince them of the error of this principle. As no riots that I knew of were attempted in the county where I reside, or by the people of it previous to the insurrection, and as I had never heard any person threaten any other kind of opposition than laying aside their stills, I consequently knew nothing of this principle being entertained till the insurrection took place; but then I found it to be one of the greatest obstacles to people even of good understanding signing such assurances as might imply an approbation of the law. Indeed I despair that people, residing in situations where excises, applying directly to agriculture, demand two or three times the quantum of tax in proportion to the price in the market for the produce of their farm, that the farmers in more favorable situations have to pay, can ever be brought to approve of such a law by any methods in the power of government. Their objections are obvious and easily comprehended, and address themselves powerfully to their interests; whereas the arguments arising from the unequal pressure of imposts on the inhabitants of towns, and people generally who manufacture little themselves, and consequently consume much of foreign manufactures or luxuries, not coming under their observation, are not understood nor admitted in abatement of their own complaints; consequently the citizens in situations remote from market are advocates for direct taxes, proportioned to the value of property, and always pay them without complaint. To explain the operation of other taxes, which tended to an abatement of the pressure of the excise tax, and the inequality which would arise from apportioning direct taxes according to the constitutional rule, was the great object of those who endeavored to reconcile the people to the excise law. There were circumstances however which could be accommodated to the principles of justice. These were balanced with political considerations.

❧ Modern Chivalry

HUGH HENRY BRACKENRIDGE

Hugh Henry Brackenridge's six-volume satirical novel *Modern Chivalry* (1792-1815) probed the shortcomings of American democracy. Similar to Don Quixote, the main character, Captain Farrago, wandered the countryside with an Irish servant, Teague O'Regan. The plot line gave Brackenridge—an unsuccessful politician himself—an opportunity to spoof different regions, but also explore the complex problems that American democracy raised. In this excerpt he delves into the subtle dilemmas that equal opportunity raised at election time.

A democracy is beyond all question the freest government: because under this, every man is equally protected by the laws, and has equally a voice in making them. But I do not say an equal voice; because some men have stronger lungs than others, and can express more forcibly their opinions of public affairs. Others, though they may not speak very loud, yet have a faculty of saying more in a short time; and even in case of others, who speak little or none at all, yet what they do say containing good sense, comes with greater weight; so that all things considered, every citizen, has not, in this sense of the word, an equal voice. But the right being equal, what great harm if it is unequally exercised? Is it necessary that every man should become a statesmen? No more than that every man should become a poet or a painter. The sciences are open to all; but let him only who has taste and genius pursue them. If any man covets the office of a bishop, says St.

Paul, he covets a good work. But again, he adds this caution, Ordain not a novice, lest being lifted up with pride, he falls into the condemnation of the devil. It is indeed making a devil of a man to lift him up to a state to which he is not suited. A ditcher is a respectable character, with his overalls on, and a spade in his hand; but put the same man to those offices which require the head, whereas he has been accustomed to impress with his foot, and there appears a contrast between the man and the occupation.

There are individuals in society, who prefer honor to wealth; or cultivate political studies as a branch of literary pursuits; and offer themselves to serve public bodies, in order to have an opportunity of discovering their knowledge, and exercising their judgment. It must be chagrining to these, and hurtful to the public, to see those who have no talent this way, and ought to have no taste, preposterously obtrude themselves upon the government. It is the same as if a bricklayer should usurp the office of tailor, and come with his square and perpendicular, to take the measure of a pair of breeches.

It is proper that those who cultivate oratory, should go to the house of orators. But for an Ay and No man to be ambitious of that place, is to sacrifice his credit to his vanity.

I would not mean to insinuate that legislators are to be selected from the more wealthy of the citizens, yet a man's circumstances ought to be such as afford him leisure for study and reflection. There is often without taste or talent. I have no idea, that because a man lives in a great house, and has a cluster of bricks or stones about his backside, that he is therefore fit for a legislator. There is so much pride and arrogance with those who consider themselves the first in a government, that it deserves to be checked by the populace, and the evil most usually commences on this side. Men associate with their own persons, the adventitious circumstances of birth and fortune: So that a fellow blowing with fat and repletion, conceives himself superior to the poor lean man, that lodges in an inferior mansion. But as in all cases, so in this, there is a medium. Genius and virtue are independent, but the man of ability and integrity that ought to be called forth to serve his country: and while, on the one hand, the aristocratic part of the government, arrogates a right to represent; on the other hand, the democratic contends the point; and from this conjunction and opposition of forces, there

is produced a compound resolution, which carries the object in an intermediate direction. When we see, therefore, a Teague O'Regan lifted up, the philosopher will reflect, that it is to balance some purse-proud fellow, equally as ignorant, that comes down from the sphere of the aristocratic interest.

But every man ought to consider for himself, whether it is his use to be this drawback, on either side. For as when good liquor is to be distilled, you throw in some material useless in itself to correct the effervescence of the spirit; so it may be his part to act as a sedative. For though we commend the effect, yet still the material retains but its original value.

But as the nature of things is such, let no man, who means well to the commonwealth, and offers to serve it, be hurt in his mind when someone of meaner talents is preferred. The people are a sovereign, and greatly despotic; but, in the main, just.

I have a great mind, in order to elevate the composition, to make quotations from the Greek and Roman history. And I am conscious to myself, that I have read over the writers on the government of Italy and Greece, in ancient, as well as modern times. But I have drawn a great deal more from reflection on the nature of things; than from all the writings I have ever read. Nay, the history of the election, which I have just given, will afford a better lesson to the American mind, than all that is to be found in other examples. We have seen here, a weaver a favored candidate, and in the next instance, a bog-trotter superseding him. Now it may be said, that this is fiction; but fiction, or no fiction, the nature of the thing will make it a reality. But I return to the adventure of the Captain, whom I have upon my hands; and who, as far as I can yet discover, is a good honest man; and means what is benevolent and useful; though his ideas may not comport with the ordinary manner of thinking, in every particular.

❧ *American Cooking*

AMELIA SIMMONS

Mrs. Amelia Simmons published at her own expense the first cookbook of American recipes. Written in 1796, the 47-page book was entitled: *American Cookery, or the art of dressing viands, fish, poultry and vegetables, and the best modes of making pastes, puffs, pies, tarts, puddings, custards and preserves, and all kinds of cakes, from the imperial plum to plain cake; adapted to this country and all grades of life.*

Some historians have described it as the "Declaration of American Independence in Cooking." Simmons recited for the first time American meals made of distinctly American ingredients—pumpkins, squash, cranberries, gingerbread and other indigenous foods. Although Simmons acknowledged borrowing a few English recipes, *American Cookery* helped define the new country as being distinct from Europe—even in the kitchen, challenging the imported collections of recipes that had previously prevailed in American kitchens. The book was enormously popular, with reprintings and new editions being done well into the 1830s.

A tasty Indian Pudding

No. 1. Three pints scalded milk, seven spoons fine Indian meal, stir well together while hot, let stand till cooled: add four eggs, half pound butter, spice and sugar; bake four hours.

No. 2. Three pints scalded milk to one pint meal salted; cool, add two eggs, four ounces butter, sugar or molasses, and spice sufficient; it will require two and a half hours baking.

No. 3. Salt a pint meal, wet with one quart milk, sweeten and put into a strong cloth, brass or bell metal vessel, stone or earthen pot, secure from wet and boil twelve hours.

A crookneck, or winter squash pudding.

Core, boil and skin a good squash, and bruise it well; take six large apples, pared, cored and stewed tender, mix together; add six or seven spoonfuls of dry bread or biscuit, rendered fine as meal, one pint milk or cream, two spoons rose water, two of wine, five or six eggs beaten and strained, nutmeg, salt and sugar to your taste, one spoon flour, beat all smartly together, bake one hour.

The above is a good recipe for pumpkins, potatoes, or yams, adding more moistening, or milk and rose-water, and to the two latter a few black or Lisbon currants, or dry whortleberries scattered in will make it better.

Pumpkin.

No. 1. One quart stewed and strained, three pints milk, six beaten eggs, sugar, mace, nutmeg and ginger, laid into paste no. 7, or 3, cross and chequer it, and bake in dishes three quarters of an hour.

No. 2. One quart of milk, one pint pumpkin, four eggs, molasses, alspice, and ginger in a crust, bake one hour.

Apple Pie.

Stew and strain the apples, to every three pints, grate the peal of a fresh lemon, add rose-water and sugar to your taste, and bake in paste No. 3.

Every species of fruit, such as pears, raspberries, blackberries, may be only sweetened, without spice, and bake in No. 3.

Molasses Gingerbread.

One table spoon of cinnamon, one spoonful ginger, some coriander or alspice, put to four tea spoons pearlash, dissolved in half pint of water, four pound flour, one quart molasses, six ounces butter, (if in summer rub in the butter, if in the winter, warm the butter and molasses, and pour to the spiced flour) knead well till stiff, the more the better, the lighter and whiter it will be; bake brisk fifteen minutes; don't scorch; before it is put in, wash it with whites and sugar beat together.

"An Anglican monarchical aristocratical party has sprung up"

THOMAS JEFFERSON

Almost from the beginning of Washington's term as president, Thomas Jefferson objected to the government's economic policies. Jefferson served as the Secretary of State from 1789 to 1794 in Washington's cabinet and found himself constantly at odds with Treasury Secretary Alexander Hamilton. Jefferson strongly objected to the imposition of excise taxes, full payment of federal debt and the creation of a national bank. When Jefferson resigned his position in 1794, he wrote Washington that he had been "duped" into supporting policies he did not endorse. As this April 24, 1796, letter to Phillip Mazzei makes clear, Jefferson believed that Washington and the federal government had abandoned the principles of the Revolution for the sake of convenience and money.

The aspects of our politics has wonderfully changed since you left us. In place of that noble love of liberty and republican government which carried us triumphantly through the war, an Anglican monarchical aristocratical party has sprung up, whose avowed object is to draw over us the substance, as they have already done the forms, of the British government. The main body of our citizens, however, remain true to their republican principles; the whole landed interest is republican, and so is a great mass of talents. Against us are the Executive, the Judiciary, two out of three branches of the Legislature, all the officers of the government, all who want to be officers, all timid men who prefer the calm of despotism to the boisterous sea of liberty, British merchants and Americans trading on British capital, speculators and holders in the banks and public funds, a contrivance invented for the purposes of corruption, and for assimilating us in all things to the rotten as well as the sound parts of the English model. It would give you a fever were I to name to you the apostates who have gone over to these heresies, men who were Samsons in the field and Solomons in the council, but who have had their heads shorn by the harlot England. In short, we are likely to preserve the liberty we have obtained only by unremitting labors and perils. But we shall preserve it; and our mass of weight and wealth on the good side is so great, as to leave no danger that force will ever be attempted against us. We have only to awake and snap the Lilliputian cords with which they have been entangling us during the first sleep which succeeded our labors.

❧ *"Counsels of an old and affectionate friend"*

WASHINGTON'S FAREWELL ADDRESS

Having considered retiring in 1792 near the end of his first term as president, Washington was determined to not serve a third term in 1796. He announced his decision to retire to his Cabinet on September 15, 1796, in what has become known as his farewell address. Washington took the opportunity to offer some parting advice, much of which was followed.

The retiring president warned against factional divisiveness which he feared—rightly, as it turned out—might pull the new nation apart and expressed his concerns about political parties undermining the government. His most important statement, however, concerned foreign affairs. He strongly encouraged the United States to "steer clear of permanent alliances with any portion of the foreign world." Washington's "Great Rule" served as the nation's guiding foreign policy until America's entry into World War I.

The period for a new election of a citizen to administer the Executive Government of the United States being not far distant, and the time actually arrived when your thoughts must be employed in designating the person who is to be clothed with that important trust, it appears to me proper, especially as it may conduce to a more distinct expression of the public voice, that I should now apprise you of the resolution I have formed to decline being considered among the number of those out of whom a choice is to be made....

The impressions with which I first undertook the arduous trust were explained on the proper occasion. In the discharge of this trust I will only say that I have, with good intentions, contributed toward the organization and administration of the Government the best exertions of which a very fallible judgment was capable. Not unconscious in the outset of the inferiority of my qualifications, experience in my own eyes, perhaps still more in the eyes of others, has strengthened the motives to diffidence of myself; and every day the increasing weight of years admonishes me more and more that the shade of retirement is as necessary to me as it will be welcome. Satisfied that if any circumstances have given peculiar value to my services they were temporary, I have the consolation to believe that, while choice and prudence invite me to quit the political scene, patriotism does not forbid it....

Here, perhaps, I ought to stop. But a solicitude for your welfare which can not end with my life, and the apprehension of danger natural to that solicitude, urge me on an occasion like the present to offer to your solemn contemplation and to recommend to your frequent review some sentiments which are the result of much reflection, of no inconsiderable observation, and which appear to me all important to the permanency of your felicity as a people ....

The unity of government which constitutes you one people is also now dear to you. It is justly so, for it is a main pillar in the edifice of your real independence, the support of your tranquillity at home, your peace abroad, of your safety, of your prosperity, of that very liberty which you so highly prize. But as it is easy to foresee that from different causes and from different quarters much pains will be taken, many artifices employed, to weaken in your minds the conviction of this truth, as this is the point in your political fortress against which the batteries of internal and external enemies will be most constantly and actively (though often covertly and insidiously) directed, it is of infinite moment that you should properly estimate the immense value of your national union to your collective and individual happiness; that you should cherish a cordial, habitual, and immovable attachment to it; accustoming yourselves to think and speak of it as of the palladium of your political safety and prosperity; watching for its preservation with jealous anxiety; discountenancing whatever may suggest even a suspicion that it can in any event be abandoned, and indignantly frowning upon the first dawning of every attempt to alienate any portion of our country from the rest or to enfeeble the sacred ties which now link together the various parts.

The name of American, which belongs to you in your national capacity, must always exalt that just pride of patriotism more than any appellation derived from local discriminations. With slight shades of difference, you have the same religion, manners, habits, and political principles. You have in common cause fought and triumphed together. The independence and liberty you possess are the work of joint councils and joint efforts, of common dangers, sufferings, and successes.

But these considerations, however powerfully they address themselves to your sensibility, are greatly outweighed by those which apply more immediately to your interest. Here every portion of our country finds the most commanding motives for carefully guarding and preserving the union of the whole.

The North, in an unrestrained intercourse with the South, protected by the equal laws of a common government, finds in the productions of the latter great additional resources of maritime and commercial enterprise and precious materials of manufacturing industry. The South, in the same intercourse, benefiting by the same agency of the North, sees its agriculture grow and its commerce expand. Turning partly into its own channels the seamen of the North, it finds its particular navigation invigorated; and while it contributes in different ways to nourish and increase the general mass of the national navigation, it looks forward to the protection of a maritime strength to which itself is unequally adapted. The East, in a like intercourse with the West, already finds, and in the progressive improvement of interior communications by land

and water will more and more find, a valuable vent for the commodities which it brings from abroad or manufactures at home. The West derives from the East supplies requisite to its growth and comfort, and what is perhaps of still greater consequence, it must of necessity owe the secure enjoyment of indispensable outlets for its own productions to the weight, influence, and the future maritime strength of the Atlantic side of the Union, directed by an indissoluble community of interest as one nation. Any other tenure by which the West can hold this essential advantage, whether derived from its own separate strength or from an apostate and unnatural connection with any foreign power, must be intrinsically precarious....

Is there a doubt whether a common government can embrace so large a sphere? Let experience solve it. To listen to mere speculation in such a case were criminal. It is well worth a fair and full experiment. With such powerful and obvious motives to union affecting all parts of our country, while experience shall not have demonstrated its impracticability, there will always be reason to distrust the patriotism of those who in any quarter may endeavor to weaken its bonds....

To the efficacy and permanency of your union a government for the whole is indispensable. No alliances, however strict, between the parts can be an adequate substitute. They must inevitably experience the infractions and interruptions which all alliances in all times have experienced. Sensible of this momentous truth, you have improved upon your first essay by the adoption of a Constitution of Government better calculated than your former for an intimate union and for the efficacious management of your common concerns. This Government, the offspring of our own choice, uninfluenced and unawed, adopted upon full investigation and mature deliberation, completely free in its principles, in the distribution of its powers, uniting security with energy, and containing within itself a provision for its own amendment, has a just claim to your confidence and your support. Respect for its authority, compliance with its laws, acquiescence in its measures, are duties enjoined by the fundamental maxims of true liberty. The basis of our political systems is the right of the people to make and to alter their constitutions of government. But the constitution which at any time exists till changed by an explicit and authentic act of the whole people is sacredly obligatory upon all. The very idea of the power and the right of the people to establish government presupposes the duty of every individual to obey the established government....

Toward the preservation of your Government and the permanency of your present happy state, it is requisite not only that you steadily discountenance irregular oppositions to its acknowledged authority, but also that you resist with care the spirit of innovation upon its principles, however specious the pretexts. One method of assault may be to effect in the forms of the Constitution alterations which will impair the energy of the system, and thus to undermine what can not be directly overthrown. In all the changes to which you may be invited remember that time and habit are at least as necessary to fix the true character of governments as of other human institutions; that experience is the surest standard by which to test the real tendency of the existing constitution of a country; that facility in changes upon the credit of mere hypothesis and opinion exposes to perpetual change, from the endless variety of hypothesis and opinion; and remember especially that for the efficient management of your common interests in a country so extensive as ours a government of as much vigor as is consistent with the perfect security of liberty is indispensable. Liberty itself will find in such a government, with powers properly distributed and adjusted, its surest guardian. It is, indeed, little else than a name where the government is too feeble to withstand the enterprises of faction, to confine each member of the society within the limits prescribed by the laws, and to maintain all in the secure and tranquil enjoyment of the rights of person and property.

I have already intimated to you the danger of parties in the State, with particular reference to the founding of them on geographical discriminations. Let me now take a more comprehensive view, and warn you in the most solemn manner against the baneful effects of the spirit of parry generally.

This spirit, unfortunately, is inseparable from our nature, having its root in the strongest passions of the human mind. It exists under different shapes in all governments, more or less stifled, controlled, or repressed; but in those of the popular form it is seen in its greatest rankness and is truly their worst enemy....

It serves always to distract the public councils

and enfeeble the public administration. It agitates the community with ill-founded jealousies and false alarms; kindles the animosity of one part against another: foments occasionally riot and insurrection. It opens the door to foreign influence and corruption, which find a facilitated access to the government itself through the channels of parry passion. Thus the policy and the will of one country are subjected to the policy and will of another....

It is important, likewise, that the habits of thinking in a free country should inspire caution in those intrusted with its administration to confine themselves within their respective constitutional spheres, avoiding in the exercise of the powers of one department to encroach upon another. The spirit of encroachment tends to consolidate the powers of all the departments in one, and thus to create, whatever the form of government, a real despotism.... If in the opinion of the people the distribution or modification of the constitutional powers be in any particular wrong, let it be corrected by an amendment in the way which the Constitution designates. But let there be no change by usurpation; for though this in one instance may be the instrument of good, it is the customary weapon by which free governments are destroyed. The precedent must always greatly overbalance in permanent evil any partial or transient benefit which the use can at any time yield.

Of all the dispositions and habits which lead to political prosperity, religion and morality are indispensable supports. In vain would that man claim the tribute of patriotism who should labor to subvert these great pillars of human happiness—these firmest props of the duties of men and citizens. The mere politician, equally with the pious man, ought to respect and to cherish them. A volume could not trace all their connections with private and public felicity. Let it simply be asked, Where is the security for property, for reputation, for life, if the sense of religious obligation desert the oaths which are the instruments of investigation in courts of justice? And let us with caution indulge the supposition that morality can be maintained without religion. Whatever may be conceded to the influence of refined education on minds of peculiar structure, reason and experience both forbid us to expect that national morality can prevail in exclusion of religious principle.

It is substantially true that virtue or morality is a

necessary spring of popular government. The rule indeed extends with more or less force to every species of free government. Who that is a sincere friend to it can look with indifference upon attempts to shake the foundation of the fabric? Promote, then, as an object of primary importance, institutions for the general diffusion of knowledge. In proportion as the structure of a government gives force to public opinion, it is essential that public opinion should be enlightened.

As a very important source of strength and security, cherish public credit. One method of preserving it is to use it as sparingly as possible, avoiding occasions of expense by cultivating peace, but remembering also that timely disbursements to prepare for danger frequently prevent much greater disbursements to repel it; avoiding likewise the accumulation of debt, not only by shunning occasions of expense, but by vigorous exertions in time of peace to discharge the debts which unavoidable wars have occasioned, not ungenerously throwing upon posterity the burden which we ourselves ought to bear....

Observe good faith and justice toward all nations. Cultivate peace and harmony with all. Religion and morality enjoin this conduct. And can it be that good policy does not equally enjoin it? It will be worthy of a free, enlightened, and at no distant period a great nation to give to mankind the magnanimous and too novel example of a people always guided by an exalted justice and benevolence. Who can doubt that in the course of time and things the fruits of such a plan would richly repay any temporary advantages which might be lost by a steady adherence to it? Can it be that Providence has not connected the permanent felicity of a nation with its virtue? The experiment, at least, is recommended by every sentiment which ennobles human nature. Alas! is it rendered impossible by its vices?...

Against the insidious wiles of foreign influence (I conjure you to believe me, fellow citizens) the jealousy or a free people ought to be constantly awake, since history and experience prove that foreign influence is one of the most baneful foes of republican government. But that jealousy, to be useful, must be impartial, else it becomes the instrument of the very influence to be avoided, instead of a defense against it. Excessive partiality for one foreign nation and excessive dislike of another cause those whom they actuate to see danger only on one side, and serve to veil and even second the arts of influence on the other. Real patriots who may resist the intrigues of the favorite are liable to become suspected and odious, while its tools and dupes usurp the applause and confidence of the people to surrender their interests....

It is our true policy to steer clear of permanent alliances with any portion of the foreign world, so far, I mean, as we are now at liberty to do it; for let me not be understood as capable of patronizing infidelity to existing engagements. I hold the maxim no less applicable to public than to private affairs that honesty is always the best policy. I repeat, therefore, let those engagements be observed in their genuine sense. But in my opinion it is unnecessary and would be unwise to extend them.

Taking care always to keep ourselves by suitable establishments on a respectable defensive posture, we may safely trust to temporary alliances for extraordinary emergencies.

Harmony, liberal intercourse with all nations are recommended by policy, humanity, and interest. But even our commercial policy should hold an equal and impartial hand neither seeking nor granting exclusive favors or preferences; consulting the natural course of things; diffusing and diversifying by gentle means the streams of commerce, but forcing nothing; establishing with powers so disposed, in order to give trade a stable course to define the rights of our merchants, and to enable the Government to support them, conventional rules of intercourse, the best that present circumstances and mutual opinion will permit, but temporary and liable to be from time to time abandoned or varied as experience and circumstances shall dictate; constantly keeping in view that it is folly in one nation to look for disinterested favors from another; that it must pay with a portion of its independence for whatever it may accept under that character; that by such acceptance it may place itself in the condition of having given equivalents for nominal favors, and yet of being reproached with ingratitude for not giving more. There can be no greater error than to expect or calculate upon real favors from nation to nation. It is an illusion which experience must cure, which a just pride ought to discard ....

Relying on its kindness in this as in other things, and actuated by that fervent love toward it which is so natural to a man who views in it the native soil of himself and his progenitors for several generations, I anticipate with pleasing expectation that retreat in which I promise myself to realize without alloy the sweet enjoyment of partaking in the midst of my fellow-citizens the benign influence of good laws under a free government—the ever-favorite object of my heart, and the happy reward, as I trust, of our mutual cares, labors, and dangers.

❦ Hail, Columbia

JOSEPH HOPKINSON

Originally titled "The Favorite New Federal Song, Adapted to the President's March," "Hail, Columbia" was introduced in 1798 in Philadelphia to repeated ovations. Although anti-Federalists derided the song, "Hail, Columbia" was enormously popular. Throughout the 19th century, "Hail, Columbia" was considered as an unofficial national anthem, along with "The Star-Spangled Banner."

Hail! Columbia happy land
Hail! ye Heroes heav'n born band
Who fought and bled in freedom's cause
Who fought and bled in freedom's cause
And when the storm of war was gone
Enjoy'd the peace your valor won
Let Independence be our boast
Ever mindful what it cost
Ever grateful for the prize
Let its Altar reach the Skies
Firm united let us be
Rallying round our Liberty
As a band of Brothers join'd
Peace and safety we shall find.

Immortal Patriots rise once more
Defend your rights—defend your shore
Let no rude foe with impious hand
Let no rude foe with impious hand
Invade the shrine where sacred lies
Of toil and blood the well earned prize
While off'ring peace, sincere and just
In heav'n we place a manly trust
That truth and justice may prevail
And ev'ry scheme of bondage fail.

Sound sound the trump of fame
Let Washington's great name

Ring thro the world with loud applause,
Ring thro the world with loud applause,
Let ev'ry clime to Freedom dear
Listen with a joyful ear—
With equal skill with godlike pow'r
He governs in the fearful hour
Of horrid war or guides with ease
The happier times of honest peace.

Behold the Chief who now commands
Once more to serve his Country stands
The rock on which the storm will beat
The rock on which the storm will beat
But arm'd in virtue firm and true
His hopes are fixed on Heav'n and you—
When hope was sinking in dismay
When glooms obscur'd Columbia's day
His steady mind from changes free
Resolv'd on Death or Liberty.

❦ Alien and Sedition Acts

CONGRESS

In the spring of 1798 three documents were published showing that French agents demanded bribes from U.S. envoys. Known as the XYZ Affair, the incident sparked a wave of anti-foreign sentiments. John Adams and the Federalist Party reacted with a series of four acts known as the Alien and Sedition Acts giving the government widespread authority to arrest and exile foreigners from the United States.

The legislation extended the residency requirements for citizenship, authorized the president to deport aliens considered dangerous to public safety and authorized the government to arrest, jail and remove aliens during wartime. The Alien Acts were never enforced but prompted many foreign residents to either flee the country or go into hiding. Twenty-five people were arrested under the Sedition Act, often for writing or publishing articles that criticized Federalist policies.

The legislation and prosecutions were sharply criticized by Jefferson, Madison and other political opponents of the Federalists as being unconstitutional and a betrayal to the principles of the American Revolution. Jefferson later pardoned those convicted under the Sedition Act. Two of the four acts follow.

The Alien Act

Section 1. Be it enacted, That it shall be lawful for the President of the United States at any time during the continuance of this act, to order all such aliens as he shall judge dangerous to the peace and safety of the United States, or shall have reasonable grounds to suspect are concerned in any treasonable or secret machinations against the government thereof, to depart out of the territory of the United States, within such time as shall be expressed in such order, which order shall be served on such alien by delivering him a copy thereof, or leaving the same as his usual abode, and returned to the office of the Secretary of State, by the marshal or other person to whom the same shall be directed. And in case any alien, so ordered to depart, shall be found at large within the United States after the time limited in such order for his departure, and not having obtained a license from the President to reside therein, or having obtained such license shall not have conformed thereto, every such alien shall, on conviction thereof, be imprisoned for a term not exceeding three years, and shall never after be admitted to become a citizen of the United States. Provided always, and be it further enacted, that if any alien so ordered to depart shall prove to the satisfaction of the President, by evidence to be taken before such person or persons as the President shall direct, who are for that purpose hereby authorized to administer oaths, that no injury or danger to the United States will arise from suffering such alien to reside therein, the president may grant a license to such alien to remain within the United States for such time as he shall judge proper, and at such place as he may designate. And the President may also require of such alien to enter into a bond to the United States, in such penal sum as he may direct, with one or more sufficient sureties to the satisfaction of the person authorized by the president to take the same, conditioned for the good behavior of such alien during his residence in the United States, and not violating his license, which license the President may revoke, whenever he shall think proper.

Section 2. And be it further enacted, that it shall be lawful for the President of the United States, whenever he may deem it necessary for the public safety, to order to be removed out of the territory thereof, any alien who may or shall be in prison in pursuance of this act; and to cause to be arrested and sent out of the United States such of those aliens as shall have been ordered to depart therefrom and shall not have obtained a license as aforesaid, in all cases where, in the opinion of the President, the public safety requires a speedy removal. And if any alien so removed or sent out of the United States by the President shall voluntarily return thereto, unless by permission of the President of the United States, such alien on conviction thereof, shall be imprisoned so long as, in the opinion of the President, the public safety may requires....

Section 6. And be it further enacted, That this act shall continue and be in force for and during the term of two years from the passing thereof.

The Sedition Act

Section 1. Be it enacted ... that if any persons shall unlawfully combine or conspire together, with intent to oppose any measure or measures of the government of the United States, which are or shall be directed by proper authority, or to impede the operation of any law of the United States, or to intimidate or prevent any person holding a place or office in or under the government of the United States, from undertaking, performing or executing his trust or duty; and if any person or persons, with intent as aforesaid, shall counsel, advise, or attempt to procure any insurrection, riot, unlawful assembly, or combination, whether such conspiracy, threatening, counsel, advice, or attempt shall have the proposed effect or not, he or they shall be deemed guilty of a high misdemeanor, and on conviction, before any court of the United States having jurisdiction thereof, shall be punished by a fine not exceeding five thousand dollars, and by imprisonment during a term not less than six months nor exceeding five years; and further, at the discretion of the court may be holder, to find sureties for his good behaviour in such sum, and for such time, as the said court may direct.

Section 2. That if any person shall write, print, utter, or publish, or shall cause or procure to be written, printed, uttered or published, or shall knowingly and willingly assist or aid in writing, printing, uttering or publishing any false, scandalous and malicious writing or writings against the government of the United States, or the President of the United States, with intent to defame the said government, or either house of the said Congress, or the said President, or to bring them, or either of them, into contempt or disrepute; or to excite against them, or either or any of them, the hatred of the good people of the United States, or to stir up sedition within the United States, or to excite any unlawful combinations therein, for opposing or resisting any law of the United States, or any act of the President of the United States, done in pursuance of any such law, or of the powers in him vested by the constitution of the United States, or to resist, oppose, or defeat any such law or act, or to aid, encourage or abet any hostile designs of any foreign nation against the United States, their people or government, then such person, being thereof convicted before any court of the United States having jurisdiction thereof, shall be punished by a fine not exceeding two thousand dollars, and by imprisonment not exceeding two years.

Section 3. That if any person shall be prosecuted under this act, for the writing or publishing any libel aforesaid, it shall be lawful for the defendant, upon the trial of the cause, to give in evidence in his defence, the truth of the matter contained in the publication charged as libel. And the jury who shall try the cause, shall have a right to determine the law and the fact, under the direction of the court, as in other cases.

Section 4. That this act shall continue to be in force until March 3, 1801, and no longer....

🍃 "First in the hearts of his countrymen"

HENRY LEE

When Washington died in 1799 the United States lost a hero of national proportion. For eight difficult years, Washington lead American forces in the Revolution in spite of constant military defeats, malnutrition and discontent within the ranks and being outnumbered by a larger, richer army. He restrained himself from the temptations of seizing personal power and exercised his standing to check military coups. As the first president, he set forth a standard of personal conduct and public policies that continued through the 20th century.

General Henry Lee (who served with Washington and was the father of Robert E. Lee) delivered this famous tribute at Washington's funeral summing up Washington's record. Stories of Washington's honesty and courage soon became part of American folklore. Although much of it was made up, the ideals that Washington represented served as a model for Americans to aspire.

First in war—first in peace—and first in the hearts of his countrymen, he was second to none in the humble and endearing scenes of private life; pious, just, humane, temperate and sincere; uniform, dignified and commanding, his example was as edifying to all around him, as were the effects of that example lasting.

To his equals he was condescending, to his inferiors kind and to the dear object of his affections exemplarily tender; correct throughout, vice shuddered in his presence, and virtue always felt his fostering hand; the purity of his private character gave effulgence to his public virtues.

His last scene comported with the whole tenor of his life—although in extreme pain, not a sigh, not a groan escaped him; and with undisturbed serenity he closed his well-spent life. Such was the man America has lost—such was the man for whom our nation mourns.

Methinks I see his august image, and I hear falling from his venerable lips these deep-sinking words:

"Cease, Sons of America, lamenting our separation: go on, and confirm by your wisdom the fruits of our joint councils, joint efforts, and common dangers; reverence religion, diffuse knowledge throughout your land, patronize the arts and sciences; let Liberty and Order be inseparable companions. Control party spirit, the bane of free governments; observe good faith to, and cultivate peace with all nations, shut up every avenue to foreign influence, contract rather than extend national connection, rely on yourselves only: be Americans in thought, word, and deed;—thus will you give immortality to that union which was the constant object of my terrestrial labors; thus will you preserve undisturbed to the latest posterity the felicity of a people to me most dear, and thus will you supply (if my happiness is now aught to you) the only vacancy in the round of pure bliss high Heaven bestows."

🍃 Inaugural Address

THOMAS JEFFERSON

Thomas Jefferson's first inaugural address took place in the context of bitter partisanship. Jefferson, a Republican, had defeated the Federalist candidate Aaron Burr in a tight, heated election. Jefferson's victory marked the first time there was a transfer of political power and took place only a few years after the Alien and Sedition Acts were directed at political opponents of the Federalists. Jefferson's assertion of the rights of the minority and his defense of the Bill of Rights—which had been placed in danger by the Alien and Sedition Acts—set a precedent. With the exception of the Civil War, the transfer of power from one political party to another has never been questioned since Jefferson.

Called upon to undertake the duties of the first executive office of our country, I avail myself of the presence of that portion of my fellow citizens which is here assembled to express my grateful thanks for the favor with which they have been pleased to look toward me, to declare a sincere consciousness that the task is above my talents, and that I approach it with those anxious and awful presentiments which the greatness of the charge and the weakness of my powers so justly inspire. A rising nation, spread over a wide and fruitful land, traversing all the seas with the rich productions of their industry, engaged in commerce with nations who feel power and forget right, advancing rapidly to destinies beyond the reach of mortal eye—when I contemplate these transcendent objects, and see the honor, the happiness, and the hopes of this beloved country committed to the issue and the auspices of this day, I shrink from the contemplation, and humble myself before the magnitude of the undertaking. Utterly indeed should I despair did not the presence of many whom I here see remind me that in the other high authorities provided by our Constitution I shall find resources of wisdom, of virtue, and of zeal on which to rely under all difficulties. To you then, gentlemen, who are charged with the sovereign functions of legislation, and to those associated with you, O look with encouragement for that guidance and support which may enable us to steer with safety the vessel in which we are all embarked amidst the conflicting elements of a troubled world.

During the contest of opinion through which we have past the animation of discussions and of exertions has sometimes worn an aspect which might impose on strangers unused to think freely and to speak and to write what they think. But this being now decided by the voice of the nation, enounced according to the rules of the constitution, all will of course arrange themselves under the will of the law, and united in common efforts for the common good. All too will bear in mind this sacred principle, that though the will of the majority is in all cases to prevail, that will, to be rightful, must be reasonable; that the minority possess their equal rights, which equal laws must protect, and to violate would be oppression. Let us then, fellow citizens, unite with one heart and one mind; let us restore to social intercourse that harmony and affection without which liberty and even life itself are but dreary things. And let us reflect that, having banished from our land that religious intolerance under which mankind so long bled and suffered, we have yet gained little, if we countenance a political intolerance, as despotic, as wicked, and as capable of bitter and bloody persecutions. During the throes and convulsions of the ancient world, during the agonizing spasms of infuriated man, seeking through blood and slaughter his long-lost liberty, it was not wonderful that the agitation of the billows should reach even this distant and peaceful shore; that this should be more felt and feared by some, and less by others, and should divide opinions as to measures of safety; but every difference of opinion is not a difference of principle. We have called by different names brethren of the same principle. We are all Republicans; we are all Federalists. If there be any among us who wish to dissolve this Union, or to change its republican form, let them stand undisturbed as monuments of the safety with which error of opinion may be tolerated, where reason is left free to combat it. I know, indeed, that some honest men fear that a republican government cannot be strong, that this government is not strong enough. But would the honest patriot, in the full tide of successful experiment, abandon a government which has so far kept us free and firm, on the theoretic and visionary fear, that this government, the world's best hope, may, by possibility, want energy to preserve itself? I trust not. I believe this, on the contrary, the strongest government on earth. I believe it the only one where every man, at the call of the law, would fly to the standard of the law, and would meet invasion of the public order as his own personal concern. Sometimes it is said that man cannot be trusted with the government of himself. Can he, then, be trusted with the government of others? Or have we found angels, in the form of kings, to govern him? Let history answer this question.

Let us, then, with courage and confidence, pursue our own federal and republican principles, our attachment to union and representative government. Kindly separated by nature and a wide ocean from the exterminating havoc of one quarter of the globe; too high-minded to endure the degradation of the others, possessing a chosen country, with room enough for our descendants to the thousandth and thousandth generation, entertaining a due sense of our equal right to the use of our own facilities, to the acquisition of our own industry, to honor and confidence from our fellow citizens, resulting not from birth but from our actions and their sense of them, enlightened by a benign religion, professed in deed and practiced in various forms, yet all of them inculcating honesty, truth, temperance, gratitude, and the love of man, acknowledging and adorning an overruling Providence, which, by all its dispensations, proves that it delights in the happiness of man here, and his greater happiness hereafter—with all these blessings, what more is necessary to make us a happy and prosperous people? Still one thing more, fellow citizens, a wise and frugal government, which shall restrain men from injuring one another, shall leave them otherwise free to regulate their own pursuits of industry and improvement, and shall not take from the mouth of labor the bread it has earned. This is the sum of good government; and this is necessary to close the circle of our felicities.

About to enter, fellow citizens, on the exercises of duties which comprehend everything dear and valuable to you, it is proper you should understand what I deem the essential principles of this government, and consequently those which ought to shape its administration. I will compress them in the narrowest compass they will bear, stating the general principle, but all its limitations. Equal and exact justice to all men, of whatever state or persuasion, religious or political; peace, commerce, and honest friendship with all nations, entangling alliances with none; the support of the state governments in all their rights, as the most competent administrations for our domestic concerns and the surest bulwarks against anti-republican tendencies; the preservation of the general government in its whole constitutional vigor, as the sheet anchor of our peace at home and safety abroad; a jealous care of the right of election by the people, a mild and safe corrective of abuses which are lopped by the sword of revolution where peaceable remedies are unprovided; absolute acquiescence in the decisions of the majority, the vital principle and immediate parent of despotism; a well disciplined militia, our best reliance in peace and for the first moments of war, till regulars may relieve them; the supremacy of the civil over the military authority; economy in the public expence, that labor may be lightly burthened; the honest payment of our debts and sacred preservation of the public faith; encouragement of agriculture, and of commerce as its handmaid; the diffusion of information and arraignment of all abuses at the bar of the public reason; freedom of religion; freedom of the press, and freedom of person under the protection of habeus corpus, and trial by juries impartially selected. These principles form the bright constellation which has gone before us and guided our steps through an age of revolution and reformation. The wisdom of our sages and blood of our heroes have been devoted to their attainment. They should be the creed of our political faith, the text of civic instruction, the touchstone by which to try the services of those we trust; and should we wander from them in moments of alarm, let us hasten to retrace our steps and to regain the road which alone leads to peace, liberty, and safety.

I repair, then, fellow-citizens, to the post you have assigned me. With experience enough in subordinate stations to know the difficulties of this the greatest of all, I have learnt to expect that it will rarely fall to the lot of imperfect men to retire from this station with the reputation and the favor which bring him into it. Without pretensions to that high confidence you reposed in our first and greatest revolutionary character, whose preeminent services had entitled him to the first place in his country's love and destined for him the fairest page in the volume of faithful history, I ask so much confidence only as may give firmness and effect to the legal administration of your affairs. I shall often go wrong through defect of judgment. When right, I shall often be thought wrong by those whose positions will not common a view of the whole ground. I ask your indulgences for my own errors, which will never be intentional, and your support against the errors of others, who may condemn what they would not if seen in all its parts. The approbation implied by your suffrage is a great consolation to me for the past, and my future solicitude will be to retain the good opinion of those who have bestowed it in advance, to conciliate that of others by doing them all the good in my power, and to be instrumental to the happiness and freedom of all.

Relying, then, on the patronage of your good

will, I advance with obedience to the work, ready to retire from it whenever you become sensible how much better choices it is in your power to make. And may that infinite power which rules the destinies of the universe lead our councils to what is best, and give them a favorable issue for your peace and prosperity.

❧ "A contemptible hypocrite"

ALEXANDER HAMILTON

Despite the unquestionably dynamic impact Thomas Jefferson had in shaping American ideals and crafting a vision for the new democratic nation, Jefferson was not universally admired in his day. Long-time political adversary Alexander Hamilton observed in an 1801 letter to James Bayard, that Jefferson was "crafty," "a contemptible hypocrite" and overly concerned about his popularity. Two hundred years later, Jefferson's legacy remains clouded. While he penned the Declaration of Independence articulating man's right to liberty, Jefferson owned slaves. Before becoming president, he strongly supported a frugal budget, but as president he oversaw the Louisiana Purchase and aggressive westward expansion.

[I]t is too late for me to become [Jefferson's] apologist. Nor can I have any disposition to do it. I admit that his politics are tinctured with fanaticism, that he is too much in earnest in his democracy, that he has been a mischievous enemy to the principal measures of our past administration, that he is crafty and persevering in his objects, that he is not scrupulous about the means of success, nor very mindful of truth, and that he is a contemptible hypocrite. But it is not true as is alleged that he is an enemy to the power of the Executive, or that he is for confounding the powers in the House of Rs. It is a fact which I have frequently mentioned that while we were in the administration together he was generally for a large construction of the Executive authority, and not backward to act upon it in cases which coincided with his views. Let it be added, that in his theoretic Ideas he has considered as improper the participations of the Senate in the Executive Authority. I have more than once made the reflection that viewing himself as the reversioner, he was solicitous to come into possession of a Good Estate. Nor is it true that Jefferson is zealot enough to do anything in pursuance of his principles which will contravene his popularity, or his interest. He is as likely as any man I know to temporize—to calculate what will be likely to promote his own reputation and advantage; and the probable result of such a temper is the preservation of systems, though originally opposed, which being once established, could not be overturned without danger to the person who did it. To my mind a true estimate of Mr. J.'s character warrants the expectation of a temporizing rather than a violent system. That Jefferson has manifested a culpable predilection for France is certainly true; but I think it a question whether it did not proceed quite as much from her popularity among us, as from sentiment, and in proportion as that popularity is diminished his zeal will cool. Add to this that there is no fair reason to suppose him capable of being corrupted, which is a security that he will not go beyond certain limits. It is not at all improbable that under the change of circumstances Jefferson's Gallicism has considerably abated.

❧ Madison v. Marbury: "It is…the duty of the judicial department to say what the law is"

SUPREME COURT CHIEF JUSTICE JOHN MARSHALL

Supreme Court Chief Justice John Marshall's 1803 decision in *Marbury v. Madison* established the Supreme Court's authority to declare an act of Congress void if it deems it to be unconstitutional. Although the Supreme Court did not void another Congressional act until the Dred Scott decision in 1857, *Marbury v. Madison* was a crucial case in affirming the balance of governmental powers set forth in the Constitution. The particular issues in the case involved a provision in the Judiciary Act of 1789 giving the Supreme Court authority to issue a writ of mandamus and the president's authority—or rather lack of authority—to withhold the commission of William Marbury as justice of the peace.

The question, whether an act, repugnant to the constitution, can become the law of the land, is a question deeply interesting to the United States; but, happily, not of an intricacy proportionate to its interest. It seems only necessary to recognize certain principles, supposed to have been long and well established, to decide it. That the people have an original right to establish, for their future government, such principles as, in their opinion, shall most conduce to their own happiness, is the basis on which the whole American fabric has been erected. The exercise of this original right is a very great exertion; nor can it, nor ought it, to be frequently repeated. The principles, therefore, so established, are deemed fundamental: and as the authority from which they proceed is supreme, and can seldom act, they are designed to be permanent. This original and supreme will organizes the government, and assigns to different departments their respective powers. It may either stop here, or establish certain limits not to be transcended by those departments. The government of the United States is of the latter description. The powers of the legislature are defined and limited; and those limits may not be mistaken or forgotten, the constitution is written. To what purpose are powers limited, and to what purpose is that limitation committed to writing, if these limits may, at any time, be passed by those intended to be restrained? The distinction between a government with limited and unlimited powers is abolished, if those limits do not confine the persons on whom they are imposed, and if acts prohibited and acts allowed, are of equal obligation. It is a proposition too plain to be contested, that the constitution controls any legislative act repugnant to it; or that the legislature may later alter the constitution by an ordinary act.

Between these alternatives, there is no middle ground. The constitution is either superior paramount law, unchangeable by ordinary means, or it is on a level with ordinary legislative acts, and, like other acts, is alterable when the legislature shall please to alter it. If the former part of the alternative be true, then a legislative act, contrary to the Constitution, is not law: if the latter part be true, then written constitutions are absurd attempts, on the part of the people, to limit a power, in its own nature, illimitable.

Certainly, all those who have framed written constitutions contemplate them as forming the fundamental and paramount law of the nation, and consequently, the theory of every such government must be, that an act of the legislature, repugnant to the constitution, is void. This theory is essentially attached to a written constitution, and is, consequently to be considered, by this court, as one of the fundamental principles of our society. It is not, therefore, to be lost sight of, in the further consideration of this subject.

If an act of the legislature, repugnant to the constitution, is void, does it, notwithstanding its invalidity, bind the courts, and oblige them to give it effect? Or, in other words, though it be not law, does it constitute a rule as operative as if it was a law? This would be to overthrow, in fact, what was established in theory; and would seem, at first view, an absurdity too gross to be insisted on. It shall, however, receive a more attentive consideration.

It is, emphatically, the province and duty of the judicial department, to say what the law is. Those who apply the rule to particular cases, must of necessity expound and interpret that rule. If two laws conflict with each other, the courts must decide on the operation of each. So, if a law be in opposition to the constitution; if both the law and the constitution apply to a particular case, so that the court must either decide that case, conformable to the law, disregarding the constitution; or conformable to the constitution, disregarding the law; the court must determine which of these conflicting rules governs the case: this is of the very essence of judicial duty. If then, the courts are to regard the constitution, and the constitution is the superior to any ordinary act of the legislature, the constitution, and not such ordinary act, must govern the case to which they both apply.

Those, then, who controvert the principle, that the constitution is to be considered, in court, as a paramount law, are reduced to the necessity of maintaining that courts must close their eyes on the constitution, and see only the law. This doctrine would subvert the very foundation of all written constitutions. It would declare that an act which, according to the principles and theory of our government, is entirely void, is yet, in practice, completely obligatory. It would declare, that if the legislature shall do what is expressly forbidden, such act, notwithstanding the express prohibition, is in reality effectual. It would be giving to the legislature a practical and real omnipotence, with the same breath which professes to restrict their powers within narrow limits. It is prescribing limits, and declaring that those limits may be passed at pleasure. That it thus reduces to nothing, what we have deemed the greatest improvement on political institutions, a written constitution, would, of itself, be sufficient, in America, where written constitutions have been viewed with so much reverence, for rejecting the construction. But the peculiar expressions of the constitution of the United States furnish additional arguments in favor of its rejection. The judicial power of the United States is extended to all cases arising under the constitution. Could it be the intention of those who gave this power, to say, that in using it, the constitution should not be looked into? That a case arising under the constitution should be decided, without examining the instrument under which it arises? This is too extravagant to be maintained. In some cases, then, the constitution must be looked into by the judges. And if they can open it at all, what part of it are they forbidden to read or to obey?

There are many other parts of the constitution which serve to illustrate this subject....

[The phraseology] of the constitution of the United States confirms and strengthens the principle, supposed to be essential to all written constitutions, that a law repugnant to the constitution is void; and that courts, as well as other departments, are bound by that instrument.

❧ "The French Republic... doth hereby cede"

THE LOUISIANA PURCHASE

Jefferson approached Napoleon Bonaparte of France in 1803 with an offer to purchase a small portion of Louisiana and a coastal section of the Florida Territories, which France had recently taken from Spain. Napoleon shocked the United States envoy with a counteroffer to sell the entire Louisiana Territory, a massive 888,000-square mile expanse that would almost double the size of the United States. Immersed in European affairs, Napoleon saw little reason to keep the territory and preferred to sell it to the United States rather than allow Great Britain to gain control over it.

Jefferson seized the opportunity and quickly secured a deal acquiring the territory, which encompassed most of the watershed of the massive Mississippi River, for $15 million. Largely unoccupied at the time, the Louisiana Purchase included what would become Arkansas, Iowa, Missouri, Nebraska, North Dakota and South Dakota, as well as parts of Colorado, Kansas, Minnesota, Montana, Oklahoma and Wyoming. The acquisition also secured the Mississippi River as a critical trade route for the Northwest Territory.

The President of the United States of America, and

the First Consul of the French Republic, in the name of the French people, desiring to remove all source of misunderstanding relative to objects of discussion mentioned in the second and fifth articles of the convention of the 8th Vendemiaire, an 9 (30th September, 1800) relative to the rights claimed by the United States, in virtue of the treaty concluded at Madrid, the 27th of October, 1795, between his Catholic Majesty and the said United States, and willing to strengthen the union and friendship which at the time of the said convention was happily reestablished between the two nations, have respectively named their Plenipotentiaries, to wit: the President of the United States, by and with the advice and consent of the Senate of the said States, Robert R. Livingston, Minister Plenipotentiary of the United States, and James Monroe, Minister Plenipotentiary and Envoy Extraordinary of the said States, near the Government of the French Republic; and the First Consul, in the name of the French people, Citizen Francis Barbe Marbols, Minister of the Public Treasury; who, after having respectively exchanged their full powers, have agreed to the following articles:

Article I. Whereas by the article the third of the treaty concluded at St. Idelfonso, the 9th Vendemiaire, an 9 (1st October, 1800,) between the First Consul of the French Republic and His Catholic Majesty, it was agreed as follows: "His Catholic Majesty promises and engages on his part, to cede to the French Republic, six months after the full and entire execution of the conditions and stipulations herein relative to His Royal Highness the Duke of Parma, the colony or province of Louisiana, with the same extent that it now has in the hands of Spain, and that it had when France possessed it, and such as it should be after the treaties subsequently entered into between Spain and other States." And whereas, in pursuance of the treaty, and particularly of the third article, the French Republic has an incontestable title to the domain and to the possession of the said territory: The First Consul of the French Republic desiring to give to the United States a strong proof of his friendship, doth hereby cede to the said United States, in the name of the French Republic, forever and in full sovereignty, the said territory, with all its rights and appurtenances, as fully and in the same manner as they have been acquired by the French Republic, in virtue of the abovementioned treaty, concluded with His

Catholic Majesty.

Article II. In the cession made by the preceding article are included the adjacent islands belonging to Louisiana, all public lots and squares, vacant lands, and all public buildings, fortifications, barracks, and other edifices which are not private property. The archives, papers, and documents, relative to the domain and sovereignty of Louisiana and its dependences, will be left in the possession of the commissaries of the United States, and copies will be afterwards given in due form to the magistrates and municipal officers of such of the said papers and documents as may be necessary to them.

Article III. The inhabitants of the ceded territory shall be incorporated in the Union of the United States, and admitted as soon as possible, according to the principles of the Federal constitution, to the enjoyment of all the rights, advantages, and immunities of citizens of the United States; and in the mean time they shall be maintained and protected in the free enjoyment of their liberty, property, and the religion which they profess.

Article IV. There shall be sent by the Government of France a commissary to Louisiana, to the end that he do every act necessary, as well to receive from the officers of His Catholic Majesty the said country and its dependences, in the name of the French Republic, if it has not been already done, as to transmit it in the name of the French Republic to the commissary or agent of the United States.

Article V. Immediately after the ratification of the present treaty by the President of the United States, and in case that of the First Consul shall have been previously obtained, the commissary of the French Republic shall remit all military posts of New Orleans, and other parts of the ceded territory, to the commissary or commissaries named by the President to take possession; the troops, whether of France or Spain, who may be there, shall cease to occupy any military post from the time of taking possession, and shall be embarked as soon as possible, in the course of three months after the ratification of this treaty.

Article VI. The United States promise to execute such treaties and articles as may have been agreed between Spain and the tribes and nations of Indians, until, by mutual consent of the United States and the said tribes or nations, other suitable articles shall have been agreed upon.

Article VII. As it is reciprocally advantageous to the commerce of France and the United States to encourage the communication of both nations for a limited time in the country ceded by the present treaty, until general arrangements relative to the commerce of both nations may be agreed on; it has been agreed between the contracting parties, that the French ships coming directly from France or any of her colonies, loaded only with the produce and manufactures of France or her said colonies: and the ships of Spain coming directly from Spain or any of her colonies, loaded only with the produce or manufactures of Spain or her colonies, shall be admitted during the space of twelve years in the port of New Orleans, and in all other legal ports of entry within the ceded territory, in the same manner as the ships of the United States coming directly from France or Spain, or any of their colonies, without being subject to any other or greater duty on merchandise, or other or greater tonnage than that paid by the citizens of the United States.

During the space of time above mentioned, no other nation shall have a right to the same privileges in the ports of the ceded territory; the twelve years shall commence three months after the exchange of ratifications, if it shall take place in France, or three months after it shall have been notified at Paris to the French Government, if it shall take place in the United States; it is however well understood that the object of the above article is to favor the manufactures, commerce, freight, and navigation of France and of Spain, so far as relates to the importations that the French and Spanish shall make into the said ports of the United States, without in any sort affecting the regulations that the United States may make concerning the exportation of the produce and merchandise of the United States, or any right they may have to make such regulations.

Article VIII. In future and forever after the expiration of the twelve years, the ships of France shall be treated upon the footing of the most favored nations in the ports above mentioned.

Article IX. The particular convention signed this day by the respective ministers, having for its object to provide for the payment of debts due to the citizens of the United States by the French Republic prior to the 30th Septr., 1800, (8th Vendemiaire, an 9,) is approved, and to have its execution in the same manner as if it had been inserted in this present treaty; and it shall be ratified in the same form and in the same time, so that the one shall not be ratified distinct from the other.

Another particular convention signed at the same date as the present treaty relative to a definitive rule between the contracting parties is in the like manner approved, and will be ratified in the same form, and in the same time, and jointly.

Article X. The present treaty shall be ratified in good and due form and the ratifications shall be exchanged in the space of six months after the date of the signature by the Ministers Plenipotentiary, or sooner if possible.

In faith whereof, the respective Plenipotentiaries have signed these articles in the French and English languages; declaring nevertheless that the present treaty was originally agreed to in the French language; and have thereunto affixed their seals.

✌ "His information fell far short of my expectation or wishes"

MERIWETHER LEWIS

Having acquired the Louisiana Territory, Jefferson commissioned his secretary, Meriwether Lewis, and William Clark to explore the newly purchased lands and to find "the most direct and practical water communication across the continent for purposes of commerce." Jefferson also charged them with gathering scientific information, investigating commercial opportunities and fostering friendly relations with local Native American tribes on the journey. Most people believed at the time that it was a relatively short distance from the western headwaters of the Missouri River to the eastern source of the Columbia River, which would take them to Oregon and the Pacific Ocean.

Lewis, Clark and their thirty-two men, however, were disappointed to discover that the Rocky Mountains lay in the way of this overland link. Led by their Shoshone guide Sacajawea, they persevered and were able to communicate with Native American tribes who showed them where and how to traverse the Rocky Mountains. In this excerpt from Lewis's diary, he describes how they learned of a specific overland route that would take them over the Continental Divide to the Columbia River and identified the Nez Perce to lead them on this leg of the journey.

Tuesday, August 20th 1805

I walked down the river about 3/4 of a mile and selected a place near the river bank unperceived by the Indians for a cash [cache], which I set three men to make, and directed the centinel to discharge his gun if he perceived any of the Indians going down in that direction which was to be the signal for the men at work on the cash to desist and seperate, least these people should discover our deposit and rob us of the baggage we intend leaving here. by evening the cash was completed unperceived by the Indians, and all our packages made up. the Pack-saddles and harnes is not yet complete, in this operation we find ourselves at a loss for nails and boards; for the first we substitute throngs of raw hide which answer verry well, and for the last [had] to cut off the blades of our oars and use the plank of some boxes which have heretofore held other articles and put those articles into sacks of raw hide which I have had made for the purpose, by this means I have obtained as many boards as will make 20 saddles which I suppose will be sufficient for our present exegencies. I made up a small assortment of medicines, together with the specemines of plants, minerals, seeds etc, which, I have collected betwen this place and the falls of the Missouri which I shall deposit here.

I now prevailed on the Chief to instruct me with rispect to the geography of his country, this he undertook very cheerfully, by delienating the rivers on the ground, but I soon found that his information fell far short of my expectation or wishes, he drew the river on which we now are [the Lemhi] to which he placed two branches just above us, which he shewed me from the openings of the mountains were in view; he next made it discharge itself into a large river which flowed from the S.W. about ten miles below us

[the Salmon], then continued this joint stream in the same direction of this valley or N.W. for one days march and then enclined it to the West for 2 more days march, here he placed a number of heaps of sand on each side which he informed me represented the vast mountains of rock eternally covered with snow through which the river passed, that the perpendicular and even juting rocks so closely hemned in the river that there was no possibil[it]y of passing along the shore; that the bed of the river was obstructed by sharp pointed rocks and the rapidity of the stream such that the whole surface of the river was beat into perfect foam as far as the eye could reach, that the mountains were also inaccessible to man or horse, he said that this being the state of the country in that direction that himself nor none of his nation had ever been further down the river than these mountains.

I then enquired the state of the country on either side of the river but he could not inform me. he said there was an old man of his nation a days march below who could probably give me some information of the country to the N.W. and refered me to an old man then present for that to the S.W. the Chief further informed me that he had understood from the persed nosed [Nez Perce] Indians who inhabit this river below the rocky mountains that it ran a great way toward the seting sun and finally lost itself in a great lake of water which was illy taisted, and where the white men lived. I next commenced my enquiries of the old man to whom I had been refered for information relative the country SW. of us. this he depicted with horrors and obstructions scarcely inferior to that just mentioned. he informed me that the band of this nation to which he belonged resided at the distance of 20 days march from hence not far from the white people with whom they traded for horses mules cloth metal beads and the shells which they woar as orniment being those of a species of periloister, that the course to his relations was a little to the West of South. that in order to get to his relations the first seven days we should be obliged to climb over steep and rocky mountains where we could find no game to kill nor anything but roots such as a ferce and warlike nation lived on whom he called the broken mockcrsons or mockersons with holes, and said inhabited those mountains and lived like the bear of other countries among the rocks and fed on roots or the flesh of such horses as they could take or steel from those who passed through their country, that in passing this country the feet of our horses would be so much wounded with the stones many of them would give out. the next part of the rout was about 10 days through a dry and parched sandy desert in which [there is] no food at this season for either man or horse, and in which we must suffer if not perish for the want of water. that the sun had now dryed up the little pools of water which exist through this desert plain in the spring season and had also scorched all the grass, that no animal inhabited this plain on which we could hope to subsist, that about the center of

this plain a large river passed from S.E. to N.W. which was navigable but afforded neither Salmon nor timber, that beyond this plain th[r]ee or four days march his relations lived in a country tolerable fertile and partially covered with timber on another large river which ran in the same direction of the former, that this last discharged itself into a large river on which many numerous nations lived with whom his relations were at war but whether this last discharged itself into the great lake or not he did not know. that from his relations it was yet a great distance to the great or stinking lake as they call the Ocean. that the way which such of his nation as had been to the Stinking lake traveled was up the river on which they lived and over to that on which the white people lived which last they knew discharged itself into the Ocean, and that this was the way which he would advise me to travel if I was determined to proceed to the Ocean but would advise me to put off the journey untill the next spring when he would conduct me. I thanked him for his information and advise and gave him a knife with which he appeared to be much gratifyed.

from this narrative I was convinced that the streams of which he had spoken as runing through the plains and that on which his relations lived were southern branches of the Columbia, heading with the rivers Apostles and Collorado, and that the rout he had pointed out was to the Vermillion Sea or gulph of Callifornia. I therefore told him that this rout was more to the South than I wished to travel, and requested to know if there was no rout on the left of this river on which we now are, by means of which, I could intercept it below the mountains through which it passes; but he could not inform me of any except that of the barren plain which he said joined the mountain on that side and through which it was impossible for us to pass at this season even if we were fortunate enough to escape from the broken mockerson Indians. I now asked Cameahwait by what rout the Pierced nosed indians, who he informed me inhabited this river below the mountains, came over to the Missouri; this he informed me was to the north, but added that the road was a very bad one as he had been informed by them and that they had suffered excessively with hunger on the rout being obliged to subsist for many days on berries alone as there was no game in that part of the mountains which were broken rockey and so thickly covered with timber that they could scarcely pass. however knowing that Indians had passed, and did pass, at this season on that side of this river to the same below the mountains, my rout was instantly settled in my own mind, p[r]ovided the account of this river should prove true on an investigation of it, which I was determined should be made before we would undertake the rout by land in any direction. I felt perfectly satisfyed, that if the Indians could pass these mountains with their women and Children, that we could also pass them; and that if the nations on this river below the mountains were as numerous as they were stated to be that they must have some means of subsistence which it would be equally in our power to procure in thc same country, they informed me that there was no buffaloe on the West side of these mountains; that the game consisted of a few Elk deer and Antelopes, and that the natives subsisted on fish and roots principally.

in this manner I spent the day smoking with them and acquiring what information I could with respect to their country, they informed me that they could pass to the Spaniards by the way of the yellowstone river in 10 days. I can discover that these people are by no means friendly to the Spaniards. their complaint is, that the Spaniards will not let them have fire arms and amunition, that they put them off by telling them that if they suffer them to have guns they will kill each other, thus leaving them defenceless and an easy prey to their bloodthirsty neighbours to the East of them, who being in possession of fire arms hunt them up and murder them without rispect to sex or age and plunder them of their horses on all occasions, they told me that to avoid their enemies who were eternally harrassing them that they were obliged to remain in the interior of these mountains at least two thirds of the year where the[y] suffered as we then saw great heardships for the want of food sometimes living for weeks without meat and only a little fish roots and berries, but this added Clameahwait, with his ferce eyes and lank jaws grown meager for the want of food, would not be the case if we had guns, we could then live in the country of buffaloe and eat as our enimies do and not be compelled to hide ourselves in these mountains and live on roots and berries as the bear do. we do not fear our enimies when placed on an equal footing with them. I told them that the

Minnetares Mandans & recares of the Missouri had promised us to desist from making war on them & that we would indevour to find the means of making the Minnetares of fort d[e] Prarie or as they call them Pahkees desist from waging war against them also. that after our finally returning to our homes towards the rising sun whitemen would come to them with an abundance of guns and every other article necessary to their defence and comfort, and that they would be enabled to supply themselves with these articles on reasonable terms in exchange for the skins of the beaver Otter and Ermin so abundant in their country, they expressed great pleasure at this information and said they had been long anxious to see the whitemen that traded guns; and that we might rest assured of their friendship and that they would do whatever we wished them.

🍃 "Jerks cannot be easily described"

BARTON WARREN STONE

Religious activity after the American Revolution dropped sharply as church memberships declined to less than ten percent. But starting in the late 1790s a renewed interest in Christianity blossomed during the Second Great Awakening. The movement was marked by great camp meetings where participants danced in ecstasy, jerked uncontrollably and barked like dogs.

Barton Warren Stone was one of many circuit-riding ministers who traveled the West and South to start new evangelical churches in the early 1800s. He participated in the great 1801 camp meeting at Cane Ridge, Kentucky, and took part in numerous revival meetings. In his 1843 autobiography he describes the bizarre jerking behavior that overtook attendants.

The bodily agitations or exercises, attending the excitement in the beginning of this century, were various, and called by various names;—as the falling exercise—the jerks—the dancing exercise—the barking exercise—the laughing and singing exercise, &c.—The falling exercise was very common among all classes, the saints and sinners of every age and of every grade, from the philosopher to the clown. The subject of this exercise would, generally, with a piercing scream, fall like a log on the floor, earth, or mud, and appear as dead. Of thousands of similar cases, I will mention one. At a meeting, two gay young ladies, sisters, were standing together attending to the exercises and preaching at the time. Instantly they both fell, with a shriek of distress, and lay for more than an hour apparently in a lifeless state. Their mother, a pious Baptist, was in great distress, fearing they would not revive. At length they began to exhibit symptoms of life, by crying fervently for mercy, and then relapsed into the same death-like state, with an awful gloom on their countenances. After awhile, the gloom on the face of one was succeeded by a heavenly smile, and she cried out, precious Jesus, and rose up and spoke of the love of God—the preciousness of Jesus, and of the glory of the gospel, to the surrounding crowd, in language almost superhuman, and pathetically exhorted all to repentance. In a little while after, the other sister was similarly exercised. From that time they became remarkably pious members of the church.

I have seen very many pious persons fall in the same way, from a sense of the danger of their unconverted children, brothers, or sisters—from a sense of the danger of their neighbors, and of the sinful world. I have heard them agonizing in tears and strong crying for mercy to be shown to sinners, and speaking like angels to all around.

The jerks cannot be so easily described. Sometimes the subject of the jerks would be affected in some one member of the body, and sometimes in the whole system. When the head alone was affected, it would be jerked backward and forward, or from side to side, so quickly that the features of the face could not be distinguished. When the whole system was affected, I have seen the person stand in one place, and jerk backward and forward in quick succession, their head nearly touching the floor behind and before. All classes, saints and sinners, the strong as well as the weak, were thus affected. I have inquired of those thus affected. They could not account for it; but some have told me that those were among the happiest seasons of their lives. I have seen some wicked persons thus affected, and all the time cursing the jerks, while they were thrown to the earth with violence. Though so awful to behold, I do not remember that any one of the thousands I have seen ever sustained an injury in body. This was as strange as the exercise itself.

The dancing exercise. This generally began with the jerks, and was peculiar to professors of religion. The subject, after jerking awhile, began to dance, and then the jerks would cease. Such dancing was indeed

heavenly to the spectators; there was nothing in it like levity, nor calculated to excite levity in the beholders. The smile of heaven shone on the countenance of the subject, and assimilated to angels appeared the whole person. Sometimes the motion was quick and sometimes slow. Thus they continued to move forward and backward in the same track or alley till nature seemed exhausted, and they would fall prostrate on the floor or earth, unless caught by those standing by. While thus exercised, I have heard their solemn praises and prayers ascending to God.

The barking exercise, (as opposers contemptuously called it,) was nothing but the jerks. A person affected with the jerks, especially in his head, would often make a grunt, or bark, if you please, from the suddenness of the jerk. This name of barking seems to have had its origin from an old Presbyterian preacher of East Tennessee. He had gone into the woods for private devotion, and was seized with the jerks. Standing near a sapling, he caught hold of it, to prevent his falling, and as his head jerked back, he uttered a grunt or kind of noise similar to a bark, his face being turned upwards. Some wag discovered him in this position, and reported that he found him barking up a tree.

The laughing exercise was frequent, confined solely with the religious. It was a loud, hearty laughter, but one sui generis; it excited laughter in none else. The subject appeared rapturously solemn, and his laughter excited solemnity in saints and sinners. It is truly indescribable.

The running exercise was nothing more than, that persons feeling something of these bodily agitations, through fear, attempted to run away, and thus escape from them; but it commonly happened that they ran not far, before they fell, or became so greatly agitated that they could proceed no farther. I knew a young physician of a celebrated family, who came some distance to a big meeting to see the strange things he had heard of. He and a young lady had sportively agreed to watch over, and take care of each other, if either should fall. At length the physician felt something very uncommon, and started from the congregation to run into the woods; he was discovered running as for life, but did not proceed far till he fell down, and there lay till he submitted to the Lord, and afterwards became a zealous member of the church. Such cases were common.

I shall close this chapter with the singing exercise. This is more unaccountable than any thing else I ever saw. The subject in a very happy state of mind would sing most melodiously, not from the mouth or nose, but entirely in the breast, the sounds issuing thence. Such music silenced every thing, and attracted the attention of all. It was most heavenly. None could ever be tired of hearing it. Doctor J. P. Campbell and myself were together at a meeting, and were attending to a pious lady thus exercised, and concluded it to be something surpassing any thing we had known in nature.

Thus have I given a brief account of the wonderful things that appeared in the great excitement in the beginning of this century. That there were many eccentricities, and much fanaticism in this excitement, was acknowledged by its warmest advocates; indeed it would have been a wonder, if such things had not appeared, in the circumstances of that time. Yet the good effects were seen and acknowledged in every neighborhood, and among the different sects it silenced contention, and promoted unity for awhile; and these blessed effects would have continued, had not men put forth their unhallowed hands to hold up their tottering ark, mistaking it for the ark of God.

❧ "We also have a religion"

CHIEF RED JACKET

Christian missionaries approached the Seneca Native American tribe in 1805 seeking converts. The Seneca Chief Sagaoyeatha, who was known as Red Jacket, rose to speak in defense of their native religion.

Red Jacket, who was given the name for a red coat the British gave him when he agreed to fight with them against the Americans during the Revolution, consistently struggled to maintain his tribe's native traditions. Nevertheless, he sought peace with the American government and had friendly relations with George Washington. In the War of 1812, he convinced his tribe to not join the British as allies, although many other Native American tribes did.

There was a time when our forefathers owned this great island. Their seats extended from the rising to the setting sun. The Great Spirit had made it for the use of Indians. He had created the buffalo, the deer, and other animals for food. He had made the bear and the beaver. Their skins served us for clothing. He had scattered them over the country and taught us how to take them. He had caused the earth to produce corn for bread. All this He had done for His red children because He loved them. If we had some disputes about our hunting-ground they were generally settled without the shedding of much blood.

But an evil day came upon us. Your forefathers crossed the great water and landed on this island. Their numbers were small. They found friends and not enemies. They told us they had fled from their own country for fear of wicked men and had come here to enjoy their religion. They asked for a small seat. We took pity on them, granted their request, and they sat down among us. We gave them corn and meat; they gave us poison in return.

The white people, brother, had now found our country. Tidings were carried back and more came among us. Yet we did not fear them. We took them to be friends. They called us brothers. We believed them and gave them a larger seat. At length their numbers had greatly increased. They wanted more land; they wanted our country. Our eyes were opened and our minds became uneasy. Wars took place. Indians were hired to fight against Indians, and many of our people were destroyed. They also brought strong liquor among us. It was strong and powerful, and has slain thousands.

Brother, our seats were once large and yours were small. You have now become a great people, and we have scarcely a place left to spread our blankets. You have got your country, but are not satisfied; you want to force your religion upon us.

Brother, continue to listen.
You say that you are sent to instruct us how to worship the Great Spirit agreeably to his mind; and, if we do not take hold of the religion which you white people teach, we shall be unhappy hereafter. You say that you are right and we are lost. How do we know this to be true?

We understand that your religion is written in a book. If it was intended for us, as well as you, why has not the Great Spirit given it to us, and not only to us, but why did he not give to our forefathers the knowledge of that book, with the means of understanding it rightly. We only know what you tell us about it. How shall we know when to believe, being so often deceived by the white people?

Brother, you say there is but one way to worship the Great Spirit. If there is but one religion, why do you white people differ so much about it? Why do not all agree, as you can all read the book?

Brother, we do not understand these things. We are told that your religion was given to your forefathers and has been handed down from father to son. We also have a religion which was given to our forefathers and has been handed down to us, their children. We worship in that way. It teaches us to be thankful for all the favors we receive, to love each other, and to be united. We never quarrel about religion.

Brother, we do not wish to destroy your religion and take it from you. We only want to enjoy our own.

✺ *The Burr Conspiracy*

THOMAS JEFFERSON

When Aaron Burr lost the presidential election to Jefferson in 1800, as the runner-up in the contest the Federalist candidate became Jefferson's vice president. In 1804, Burr shot and killed his personal and political enemy Alexander Hamilton in a duel. Burr's political career ended on the spot. But in January 1807, Jefferson (whose vice president was now George Clinton) accused Burr of being involved in a plot to carve a new country out of the Southwest. After a highly partisan trial, Burr was acquitted.

Agreeably to the request of the House of Representatives communicated in their resolution of the 16th instant, I proceed to state, under the reserve therein expressed, information received touching an illegal combination of private individuals against the peace and safety of the Union, and a military expedition planned by them against the territories of a power in amity with the united States, with the measures I have pursued for suppressing the same....

Some time in the latter part of September I received intimations that designs were in agitation in the Western country unlawful and unfriendly to the peace of the Union, and that the prime mover in these was Aaron Burr, heretofore distinguished by the favor of his country....

[I]t was known that many boats were under preparation, stores of provisions collecting, and an unusual number of suspicious characters in motion on the Ohio and its waters. Besides dispatching the confidential agent to that quarter, orders were at the time sent to the governors of the Orleans and Mississippi territories and to the commanders of the land and naval forces there to be on their guard against surprise and in constant readiness to resist any enterprise which might be attempted on the vessels, posts, or other objects under their care; and on the 8th November instructions were forwarded to General Wilkinson to hasten an accommodation with the Spanish commandant on the Sabine, and as soon as that was effected to fall back with his principal force to the hither bank of the Mississippi for the defense of the interesting points on that river. By a letter received from that officer on the 25th of November, we learnt that a confidential agent of Aaron Burr had been deputed to him with communications, partly written in cipher and partly oral, explaining his designs, exaggerating his resources, and making such offers of emolument and command to engage him and the army in his unlawful enterprise as he had flattered himself would be successful. The General,... immediately dispatched a trusty officer to me with information of what had passed....

The General's letter ... and some other information received a few days earlier, when brought together developed Burr's general design.... It appeared that he contemplated two distinct objects, which might be carried on either jointly or separately, and either the one or the other first, as circumstances should direct. One of these was the severance of the Union of these States by the Alleghany Mountains; the other attack on Mexico....

He found at once that the attachment of the Western country to the present Union was not to be shaken; that its dissolution could not be effected with the consent of its inhabitants, and that his resources were inadequate as yet to effect it by force. He took his course then at once, determined to seize on New Orleans, plunder the bank there, possess himself of the military and naval stores, and proceed on his expedition to Mexico, and to this object all his means and preparations were now directed. He collected from all the quarters where himself or his agents possessed influence all the ardent, restless, desperate, and disaffected persons who were ready for any enterprise analogous to their characters. He seduced good and well-meaning citizens, some by assurances that he possessed the confidence of the Government and was acting under its secret patronage, a pretense which procured some credit from the state of our difference with Spain, and others by offers of land in Bastrop's claim on the Washita....

Surmises have been hazarded that this enterprise is to receive aid from certain foreign powers; but these surmises are without proof or probability....

By letters from General Wilkinson ... I received the important affidavit [by which] it will be seen that of three of the principal emissaries of Mr. Burr whom the General had caused to be apprehended, one had been liberated by habeas corpus, and two others ... have been embarked by him for ports in the Atlantic states.... As soon as these persons shall arrive they will be delivered to the custody of the law and left to such course of trial, both as to place and process, as the functionaries of the law may direct.

❧ "An embargo on all ships and vessels"

THE EMBARGO ACT

Despite the United States' desire to insulate itself from European affairs, the Napoleonic Wars pulled the United States into a trade war with England and France. Starting in 1805, English ships captured American vessels engaged in trade with the French West Indies. Similarly, the French intervened in American trade with the British. Hoping to resolve the matter, Jefferson signed the Embargo Act of 1807 forbidding all trade with foreign nations.

Intended to bring England and France to terms, the Embargo Act stunted American commerce and was difficult to enforce. Congress and President James Madison withdrew the Embargo Act in 1809 with the Non-Intercourse Act, giving the President the authority to allow trade with selected foreign powers. Trade relations between the nations proved very difficult, however, and in 1810 resulted with Madison authorizing trade with France, but not England.

An Act laying an Embargo on all ships and vessels in the ports and harbors of the United States.

Be it enacted, That an embargo be, and hereby is laid on all ships and vessels in the ports and places within the limits or jurisdiction of the United States, cleared or not cleared, bound to any

foreign port or place; and that no clearance be furnished to any ship or vessel bound to such foreign port or place, except vessels under the immediate direction of the President of the United States: and that the President be authorized to give such instructions to the officers of the revenue, and of the navy and revenue cutters of the United States, as shall appear best adapted for carrying the same into full effect: Provided, that nothing herein contained shall be construed to prevent the departure of any foreign ship or vessel, either in ballast, or with the goods, wares and merchandise on board of such foreign ship or vessel, when notified of this act.

Section 2. That during the continuance of this act, no registered, or sea letter vessel, having on board goods, wares and merchandise, shall be allowed to depart from one port of the United States to any other within the same, unless the master, owner, consignee or factor of such vessel shall first give bond, with one or more sureties to the collector of the district from which she is bound to depart, in a sum of double the value of the vessel and cargo, that the said goods, wares, or merchandise shall be relanded in some port of the United States, dangers of the seas excepted, which bond, and also a certificate from the collector where the same may be relanded, shall by the collector respectively be transmitted to the Secretary of the Treasury. All armed vessels possessing public commissions from any foreign power, are not to be considered as liable to the embargo laid by this act.

❧ "I prefer war to submission"

FELIX GRUNDY

By 1811 the long-simmering tensions between the United States and Great Britain were at a fevered pitch. Americans were outraged at the British Navy's practice of impressing American sailors into involuntary service. On the Western Frontier, the British were accused of inciting Native American attacks on white settlers.

A clique of "War Hawks" emerged calling for American military action against the British intrusions on the young nation's sovereignty. These included Representative Felix Grundy of Tennessee who delivered the following speech to Congress in 1811, as well as future national leaders Henry Clay of Kentucky and John C. Calhoun of South Carolina.

New England, however, opposed war, fearing it would stifle the region's economy.

On June 1, 1812, President John Madison asked Congress to declare war on Great Britain. The formal declaration was made on July 18, 1812.

What, Mr. Speaker, are we now called on to decide? It is, whether we will resist by force the attempt, made by [the British] Government, to subject our maritime rights to the arbitrary and capricious rule of her will; for my part I am not prepared to say that this country shall submit to have her commerce interdicted or regulated, by any foreign nation. Sir, I prefer war to submission.

Over and above these unjust pretensions of the British Government, for many years past they have been in the practice of impressing our seamen, from merchant vessels; this unjust and lawless invasion of personal liberty, calls loudly for the interposition of this Government. To those better acquainted with the facts in relation to, I leave it fill up the picture. My mind is irresistibly drawn to the West.

... It cannot be believed by any man who will reflect, that the savage tribes, uninfluenced by other Powers, would think of making war on the United States. They understand too well their own weakness, and our strength. They have already felt the weight of our arms; they know they hold the very soil on which they live as tenants at sufferance. How, then, sir, are we to account for their late conduct? In one way only; some powerful nation must have intrigued with them, and turned their peaceful disposition towards us into hostilities. Great Britain alone has intercourse with those Northern tribes; I therefore infer, that if British gold has not been employed, their baubles and trinkets, and the promise of support and a place of refuge if necessary, have had their effect....

This war, if carried on successfully, will have its advantages. We shall drive the British from our continent—they will no longer have an opportunity of intriguing with our Indian neighbors, and setting on the ruthless savage to tomahawk our women and children. That nation will lose her Canadian trade, and, by having no resting place in this country, her means of annoying us will be diminished.... I am willing to receive the Canadians as adopted brethren; it will have beneficial political effects; it will preserve the equilibrium of the Government. When Louisiana shall be fully peopled, the Northern States will lose their power; they will be at the dis-

cretion of others; they can be depressed at pleasure, and then this Union might be endangered—I therefore feel anxious not only to add the Floridas to the South, but the Canadas to the North of this empire....

🌿 *The Star-Spangled Banner*

FRANCIS SCOTT KEY

While negotiating for the freedom of a friend captured by the British, Francis Scott Key witnessed the British bombardment of Fort McHenry near Baltimore on the night of September 13-14, 1814, as a huge American flag waved above the fort. The next morning when the bombing had ended, Key looked to see that flag was still there.

Inspired by the experience, he wrote a poem and set it to the tune of "To Anacreon in Heaven." Key's song was first performed on October 19, 1814, in Baltimore. It was instantly popular and remained a favorite of American troops throughout the 1800s. In 1904, all military posts were required to perform it during morning and evening colors. Congress formally adopted "The Star-Spangled Banner" as the national anthem in 1931.

Oh, say, can you see by the dawn's early light,
What so proudly we hailed at the twilight's last
gleaming?
Whose broad stripes and bright stars, through the
perilous fight,
O'er the ramparts we watched were so gallantly
streaming?
And the rockets' red glare, the bombs bursting in
air,
Gave proof through the night that our flag was still
there.
Oh, say, does that star-spangled banner yet wave
O'er the land of the free and the home of the
brave!

On the shore, dimly seen thro' the mists of the
deep,
Where the foe's haughty host in dread silence
reposes,
What is that which the breeze o'er the towering
steep,
As it fitfully blows, half conceals, half discloses?
Now it catches the gleam of the morning's first
beam,

In full glory reflected, now shines on the stream.
'Tis the star-spangled banner; on, long may it wave
O'er the land of the free, and the home of the
    brave!

And where is that band who so vauntingly swore
That the havoc of war and the battle's confusion
A home and a country should leave us no more?
Their blood has washed out their foul footsteps'
    pollution.
No refuge could save the hireling and slave
From the terror of flight, or the gloom of the grave:
And the star-spangled banner in triumph doth
    wave
O'er the land of the free, and the home of the
    brave!
Oh, thus be it ever when freemen shall stand
Between their loved homes and the war's
    desolation;
Blest with victory and peace, may the heaven res-
    cued land
Praise the power that hath made and preserved us a
    nation!
Then conquer we must, when our cause it is just,
And this be our motto: "In God is our trust!"
And the star-spangled banner in triumph doth
    wave,
O'er the land of the free, and the home of the
    brave!

❧ Acting on behalf of the children

PENNSYLVANIA SUPREME COURT

American society in the early 1800s assigned a high value on children. European travelers frequently wrote in disapproving terms about the freedoms American children enjoyed in their relations with their parents. Similarly, courts in the United States increasingly looked to the interests of children over parents regarding custody, illegitimacy and conflicts between parents and children.

In 1813, the Pennsylvania Supreme Court set an important precedent in *Commonwealth v. Addicks* when it established that the interests of the children in a divorce were paramount in determining custody.

The Court, upon the application of Joseph Lee, granted a habeas corpus to the defendants, to bring up two female children, his daughters, in their custody; and they were accordingly brought into Court, under the care of their mother, Barbara Addicks, with whom, as was stated in the return, they had lived ever since their birth.

One of the children was ten, the other about seven years old.

J. R. Ingersoll for the father, read to the Court the proceedings in the Common pleas, upon a libel for divorce by Lee against Barbara, at present the wife of Addicks, by which it appeared, that about the beginning of the present year, she had had a child by Addicks, and for some time before, and constantly since, had lived with him. Lee was divorced from *a vinculo*, for this cause, on the 12th of June 1813; and since that time, the wife and Addicks were married.… He contended that the father, as the natural guardian of the children, had a right to their custody, and that the nature of the intercourse between their mother and Addicks, rendered it highly improper to permit them to remain under her care.

Hopkinson contra, replied, that it was entirely in the Court's discretion to interfere or not, as there was no illegal restraint of the children; and for the purpose of enabling the Court to exercise a sound discretion upon the subject, he gave them an outline of the mother's history, her marriage with Lee, his conduct to her and his family, and their circumstances under which acquaintences with Addicks and her subsequent indiscretion had originated. From the whole it appeared, that she was at least as unfortunate, as she was culpable; that for four years prior to the divorce, from the embarrassments of Lee, and other causes, he had made no provision for either his wife or these children, although he had been applied to for this purpose. That during period, the mother had kept a boarding house, and had educated the children herself, having applied in this manner the accomplishments she had acquired in the course of an excellent education in Canada. That the marriage with Addicks had taken place without a knowledge of the legal impediment, and that in no respect had her intercourse with him, interfered with the attention that was due to the children, whose sex as well as age, particularly required the care of a mother.

J. R. Ingersoll on the other hand, made a statement to exculpate the husband, and to shew that his pecuniary circumstances, which at one time prevented him to educate and maintain the daughters, as he did a son of the same marriage, who had always been under his care.

One fact was not disputed, that the children were well treated and educated by the mother, and had hitherto in no respect suffered under her care.

After holding the case under advisement for a day, the Chief Justice now delivered the Court's opinion.

Tilgham, C. J. we have considered the law, and are of opinion, that although we are bound to free the person from all illegal restraints, we are not bound to decide who is entitled to the guardianship, or to deliver infants to the custody of any particular person. But we may in our discretion do so, if we think that, under the circumstances of the case, it ought to be done…. The present case is attended with peculiar and unfortunate circumstances. We cannot avoid expressing our disapprobation of the mother's conduct, although so far as regards her treatment of the children, she is in no fault. They appear to have been well taken care of in all respects. It is to them, that our anxiety is principally directed; and it appears to us, that considering their tender age, they stand in need of that kind of assistance, which can be afforded by none so well as a mother. It is on their account, therefore, that exercising the discretion with which the law has invested us, we think it best, at present, not to take them from her. At the same time, we desire it to be distinctly understood, that the father is not to be prevented from seeing them. If he does not choose to go to the house of their mother, she ought to send them to him, when he desires it, taking it for granted that he will not wish to carry them abroad, so much as to interfere with their education.

❧ *Report and Resolution of the Hartford Convention*

HARTFORD CONVENTION

Federalist delegates from five New England states met at the Hartford Convention in the December of 1814. They were frustrated with Republican President James Madison's administration and dissatisfied with the results of the War of 1812. Although the United States had won several battles in the Great Lakes and against menacing Native American tribes, the British had captured Washington, D. C., sacked the White House and imposed a punishing penalty on New England trade which had ground to a virtual halt

The Convention objected to several actions taken by Madison and the decreasing influence of the more populous North on federal policy. Ironically, like the South 30 years hence, New England feared the dilution of its authority that came about from accepting western states into the union.

The convention settled on a series of proposed constitutional amendments and brought them to the Capitol to present to the federal government. The delegates arrived, however, just as the Treaty of Ghent ending the War of 1812 was signed and news of the American victory at the Battle of New Orleans reached Washington. Chagrined, delegates abandoned the resolutions and the Federalist Party suffered a major blow from which it never recovered.

…To investigate and explain the means whereby this fatal reverse has been effected, would require a voluminous discussion. Nothing more can be attempted in this report than a general allusion to the principle outlines of the policy which has produced this vicissitude. Among these may be enumerated—

First. A deliberate and extensive system for effecting a combination among certain states, by exciting local jealousies and ambition, so as to secure to popular leaders in one section of the Union the controul of public affairs in perpetual succession. To which primary object most other characteristics of the system may be reconciled.

Secondly. The political intolerance displayed and avowed in excluding from office men of unexceptionable merit, for want of adherence to the executive creed.

Thirdly. The infraction of the judiciary authority and rights, by depriving judges of their offices in violation of the constitution.

Fourthly. The abolition of existing taxes, requisite to prepare the country for those changes to which nations are always exposed, with a view to the acquisition of popular favour.

Fifthly. The influence of patronage in the distribution of offices, which in these states has been almost invariably made among men the least entitled to such distinction, and who have sold themselves as ready instruments for distracting public opinion, and encouraging administration to hold in contempt the wishes and remonstrances of a people thus apparently divided.

Sixthly. The admission of new states into the

Union formed at pleasure in the western region, has destroyed the balance of power which existed among the original States, and deeply affected their interest.

Seventhly. The easy admission of naturalized foreigners, to places of trust, honor, or profit, operating as an inducement to the malcontent subjects of the old world to come to these States, in quest of executive patronage, and to repay it by an abject devotion to executive measures.

Eighthly. Hostility to Great Britain, and partiality to the late government of France, adopted as coincident with popular prejudice, and subservient to the main object, party power. Connected with these must be ranked erroneous and distorted estimates of the power and resources of those nations, of the probable results of their controversies, and of our political relations to them respectively.

Lastly and principally. A visionary and superficial theory in regard to commerce, accompanied by a real hatred but a feigned regard to its interests, and a ruinous perseverance in efforts to render it an instrument of coercion and war.

But it is not conceivable that the obliquity of any administration could, in so short a period, have so nearly consummated the work of national ruin, unless favoured by defects in the constitution.

To enumerate all the improvement of which that instrument is susceptible, and to propose such amendments as might render it in all respects perfect, would be a task which this convention has not thought proper to assume. They have confined their attention to such as experience has demonstrated to be essential, and even among these, some are considered entitled to a more serious attention than others. They are suggested without any intentional disrespect to other states, and are meant to be such as all shall find an interest in promoting. Their object is to strengthen, and if possible to perpetuate, the union of the states, by removing the grounds of existing jealousies, and providing for a fair and equal representation, and a limitation of powers, which have been misused....

Therefore resolved,

That it be and hereby is recommended to the legislatures of the several states represented in this Convention, to adopt all such measures as may be necessary effectually to protect the citizens of said states from the operation and effects of all acts which have been or may be passed by the Congress of the United States, which shall contain provisions, subjecting the militia or other citizens to forcible drafts, conscriptions, or impressments, not authorised by the constitution of the United States.

Resolved, That it be and hereby is recommended to the said Legislatures, to authorize an immediate and earnest application to be made to the government of the United States, requesting their consent to some arrangement whereby the said states may, assume upon themselves the defence of their territory against the enemy; and a reasonable portion of the taxes, collected within said States, may be paid into the respective treasuries thereof, and appropriated to the payment of the balance due said states, and to the future defence of the same. The amount so paid into the said treasuries to be credited, and the disbursements made as aforesaid to be charged to the United States.

Resolved, That it be, and hereby is, recommended to the legislatures of the aforesaid states, to pass laws (where it has not already been done) authorizing the governors or commanders-in-chief of their militia to make detachments from the same, or to form voluntary corps, as shall be most convenient and conformable to their constitutions, and to cause the same to be well armed, equipped, and disciplined, and held in readiness for service; and upon the request of the governor of either of the other states to employ the whole of such detachment or corps, as well as the regular forces of the state, or such part thereof as may be required and can be spared consistently with the safety of the state, in assisting the state, making such request to repel any invasion thereof which shall be made or attempted by the public enemy.

Resolved, That the following amendments of the constitution of the United States be recommended to the states represented as aforesaid, to be proposed by them for adoption by the state legislatures, and in such cases as may be deemed expedient by a convention chosen by the people of each state.

And it is further recommended, that the said states shall persevere in their efforts to obtain such amendments, until the same shall be effected.

First. Representatives and direct taxes shall be apportioned among the several states which may be included within this Union, according to their respective numbers of free persons, including those bound to serve for a number of years, and excluding Indians not taxed, and all other persons.

Second. No new state shall be admitted into the Union by Congress, in virtue of the power granted by the constitution, without the concurrence of two thirds of both houses.

Third. Congress shall not have power to lay any embargo on the ships or vessels of the citizens of the United States, in the ports or harbours thereof, for more than sixty days.

Fourth. Congress shall not have power, without concurrence of two thirds of both houses, to interdict the commercial intercourse between the United States and any foreign nation, or the dependencies thereof.

Fifth. Congress shall not make or declare war, or authorize acts of hostility against any foreign nation, without the concurrence of two thirds of both houses, except such acts of hostility be in defence of the territories of the United States when actually invaded.

Sixth. No person who shall hereafter be naturalized, shall be eligible as a member of the senate or house of representatives of the United States, nor capable of holding any civil office under the authority of the United States.

Seventh. The same person shall not be elected president of the United States a second time; nor shall the president be elected from the same state two terms in succession.

Resolved, That if the application of these states to the government of the United States, recommended in a foregoing resolution, should be unsuccessful and peace should not be concluded, and the defence of these states should be neglected, as it has since the commencement of the war, it will, in the opinion of this convention, be expedient for the legislatures of the several states to appoint delegates to another convention, to meet at Boston…with such powers and instructions as the exigency of a crisis so momentous may require.

"The Hunters of Kentucky"

CELEBRATING THE BATTLE OF NEW ORLEANS

Two war heroes emerged out the War of 1812 who would become future presidents. William Henry Harrison, the governor of the Indiana Territory, defeated the Shawnee leader Tecumsah's confederacy of tribes first at the Battle of Tippecanoe prior to the war and then finally at the Battle of the Thames in 1813.

Even more famously, Andrew Jackson defeated Creek warriors at the Battle of Horseshoe Bend and the British in the one-sided Battle of New Orleans in January 1815, two weeks after the Treaty of Ghent had been signed. Jackson later enhanced his fighting reputation with his victories over the Seminoles in the Spanish Floridas in 1817-18. The popular song "The Hunters of Kentucky, or the Battle of New Orleans" celebrated "Old Hickory" Jackson's victory at New Orleans.

Ye gentlemen and ladies fair
Who grace this famous city
Just listen, if you've time to spare,
While I rehearse a ditty;
And for the opportunity,
Conceive yourselves quite lucky,
For 'tis not often here you see
A hunter from Kentucky.
Oh, Kentucky,
The Hunters of Kentucky
Oh, Kentucky,
The Hunters of Kentucky.

We are a hardy, free born race,
Each man to fear a stranger,
Whae'er the game we join chase,
Despising toil and danger.
And if a daring foe annoys,
Whate'er his strength or forces,
We'll show them that Kentucky boys
Are alligators—horses.

I 'spose you've read it in the prints,
How Packenham attempted
To make Old Hickory Jackson wince,
But soon his scheme repented;
For we with rifles cock'd,
Thought such occasion lucky,
And soon around the general flock'd

The Hunters of Kentucky.

You've heard, I 'spose how New Orleans
Is famed for wealth and beauty;
There's girls of every hue, it seems,
From snowy white to sooty,
So Packenham he made his brags,
If he in fight was lucky,
He'd have their girls and cotton bags,
In spite of old Kentucky.
But Jackson he was wide awake,
And wasn't scar'd at trifles,
For well he knew what aim we take
With our Kentucky rifles.
So he led us up to a Cyprus swamp,
The ground was low and mucky,
There stood John Bull in martial pomp,
And here was old Kentucky.

A bank was raised to hide our breast,
Not that we thought of dying,
But that we always take a rest,
Unless the game is flying.
Behind it stood our little force,
None wish'd it to be greater,
For every man was half a horse,
And half an alligator.

They did not let their patience tire,
Before they show'd their faces,
We did not choose to waste our fire,
So snugly kept our places.
But when so near we saw them wink,
We thought it time to stop 'em,
And it would have done you good, I think,
To see Kentuckians drop 'em.

They found, at last, 'twas vain to fight,
Where lead was their booty,
And so they wisely took to fight,
And left us all the beauty.
And now if danger e'er annoys,
Remember what our trade is,
Just send for us Kentucky boys,
And we'll protect ye ladies.

McCulloch v. Maryland: "The constitution and the laws made in pursuance thereof are supreme"

SUPREME COURT CHIEF JUSTICE JOHN MARSHALL

McCulloch v. Maryland was one of the great landmark cases of the Supreme Court, establishing the supremacy of federal sovereignty and setting the parameters of states' authority. The case centered around an act passed by Maryland applying burdensome taxes on bank notes not issued by Maryland, including federal notes.

Marshall's decision determined that the national bank was constitutional and that states could not attempt to impede the federal government's authority. Although several states condemned the ruling, the unanimous opinion offered a justification for the supremacy of federal over states' rights which would serve as the legal foundation for the permanent relationship between states and the federal government.

In the case now to be determined, the defendant, a sovereign State, denies the obligation of a law enacted by the legislature of the Union, and the plaintiff, on his part, contests the validity of an act which has been passed by the legislature of that State. The constitution of our country, in its most interesting and vital parts, is to be considered; the conflicting powers of the government of the Union and of its members, as marked in that constitution, are to be discussed; and an opinion given, which may essentially influence the great operations of the government. No tribunal can approach such a question without a deep sense of its importance, and of the awful responsibility involved in its decision. But it must be decided peacefully, or remain a source of hostile legislation, perhaps of hostility of a still more serious nature; and if it is to be so decided, by this tribunal alone can the decision be made. On the Supreme Court of the United States has the constitution of our country devolved this important duty all their powers to the State sovereignties, and had nothing more to give. But, surely, the question whether they may resume and modify the powers granted to government does not remain to be settled in this country. Much more might the legitimacy of the general government be doubted, had it been created by the States. The powers delegated to the State sovereignties were to be exercised by themselves, not by a distinct and independent sovereignty, created by themselves. To the formation of a league, such as was the confederation, the State sovereignties were certainly competent. But when, "in order to form a more perfect union," it was deemed necessary to change this alliance into an effective government, possessing great and sovereign powers, and acting directly on the people, the necessity of referring it to the people, and of deriving its powers directly from them, was felt and acknowledged by all.

The government of the Union, then, (whatever may be the influence of this fact on the case,) is, emphatically, and truly, a government of the people. In form and in substance it emanates from them. Its powers are granted by them, and are to be exercised directly on them, and for their benefit.

This government is acknowledged by all to be one of enumerated powers. The principle, that it can exercise only the powers granted to it, would seem too apparent to have required to be enforced by all those arguments which its enlightened friends, while it was depending before the people, found it necessary to urge. That principle is now universally admitted. But the question respecting the extent of the powers actually granted, is perpetually arising, and will probably continue to arise, as long as our system shall exist.

In discussing these questions, the conflicting powers of the general and State governments must be brought into view, and the supremacy of their respective laws, when they are in opposition, must be settled.

If any one proposition could command the universal assent of mankind, we might expect it would be this—that the government of the Union, though limited in its powers, is supreme within its sphere of action. This would seem to result necessarily from its nature. It is the government of all; its powers are delegated by all; it represents all, and acts for all. Though any one State may be willing to control its operations, no State is willing to allow others to control them. The nation, on those subjects on which it can act, must necessarily bind its component parts. But this question is not left to mere reason: the people have, in express terms, decided it, by saying, "this constitution, and the laws of the United States, which shall be made in pursuance thereof,"

"shall be the supreme law of the land," and by requiring that the members of the State legislatures, and the officers of the executive and judicial departments of the States, shall take the oath of fidelity to it.

The government of the United States, then, though limited in its powers, is supreme; and its laws, when made in pursuance of the constitution, form the supreme law of the land, "any thing in the constitution or laws of any State to the contrary notwithstanding."

Among the enumerated powers, we do not find that of establishing a bank or creating a corporation. But there is no phrase in the instrument which, like the articles of confederation, excludes incidental or implied powers; and which requires that every thing granted shall be expressly and minutely described. Even the 10th amendment, which was framed for the purpose of quieting the excessive jealousies which had been excited, omits the word "expressly," and declares only that the powers "not delegated to the United States, nor prohibited to the States, are reserved to the States or to the people;" thus leaving the question, whether the particular power which may become the subject of contest has been delegated to the one government, or prohibited to the other, to depend, on a fair construction of the whole instrument. The men who drew and adopted this amendment had experienced the embarrassments resulting from the insertion of this word in the articles of confederation, and probably omitted it to avoid those embarrassments. A constitution, to contain an accurate detail of all the subdivisions of which its great powers will admit, and of all the means by which they may be carried into execution, would partake of the prolixity of a legal code, and could scarcely be embraced by the human mind. It would probably never be understood by the public. Its nature, therefore, requires, that only its great outlines should be marked, its important objects designated, and the minor ingredients which compose those objects be deduced from the nature of the objects themselves....

In considering this question, then, we must never forget, that it is a constitution we are expounding. Although, among the enumerated powers of government, we do not find the word "bank" or "incorporation," we find the great powers to lay and collect taxes; to borrow money; to regulate commerce; to declare and conduct a war; and to raise and support armies and navies. The sword and the purse, all the external relations, and no inconsiderable portion of the industry of the nation, are entrusted to its government. It can never be pretended that these vast powers draw after them others of inferior importance, merely because they are inferior. Such an idea can never be advanced. But it may with great reason be contended, that a government, entrusted with such ample powers, on the due execution of which the happiness and prosperity of the nation so vitally depends, must also be entrusted with ample means for their execution. The power being given, it is the interest of the nation to facilitate its execution. It can never be their interest, and cannot be presumed to have been their intention, to clog and embarrass its execution by withholding the most appropriate means. Throughout this vast republic, from the St. Croix to the Gulph of Mexico, from the Atlantic to the Pacific, revenue is to be collected and expended, armies are to be marched and supported. The exigencies of the nation may require that the treasure raised in the north should be transported to the south, that raised in the east conveyed to the west, or that this order should be reversed....

The power of creating a corporation, though appertaining to sovereignty, is not, like the power of making war, or levying taxes, or of regulating commerce, a great substantive and independent power, which cannot be implied as incidental to other powers, or used as a means of executing them. It is never the end for which other powers are exercised, but a means by which other objects are accomplished.... The power of creating a corporation is never used for its own sake, but for the purpose of effecting something else. No sufficient reason is, therefore, perceived, why it may not pass as incidental to those powers which are expressly given, if it be a direct mode of executing them.

But the constitution of the United States has not left the right of Congress to employ the necessary means, for the execution of the powers conferred on the government, to general reasoning. To its enumeration of powers is added that of making "all laws which shall be necessary and proper, for carrying into execution the foregoing powers, and all other powers vested by this constitution, in the government of the United States, or in any department thereof."...

We admit, as all must admit, that the powers of the government are limited, and that its limits are not to be transcended. But we think the sound construction of the constitution must allow to the national legislature that discretion, with respect to the means by which the powers it confers are to be carried into execution, which will enable that body to perform the high duties assigned to it, in the manner most beneficial to the people. Let the end be legitimate, let it be within the scope of the constitution, and all means which are appropriate, which are plainly adapted to that end, which are not prohibited, but consist with the letter and spirit of the constitution, are constitutional.

If a corporation may be employed indiscriminately with other means to carry into execution the powers of the government, no particular reason can be assigned for excluding the use of a bank, if required for its fiscal operations. To use one, must be within the discretion of Congress, if it be an appropriate mode of executing the powers of government. That it is a convenient, a useful, and essential instrument in the prosecution of its fiscal operations, is not now a subject of controversy.... The time has passed away when it can be necessary to enter into any discussion in order to prove the importance of this instrument, as a means to effect the legitimate objects of the government.

But, were its necessity less apparent, none can deny its being an appropriate measure; and if it is, the degree of its necessity, as has been very justly observed, is to be discussed in another place. Should Congress, in the execution of its powers, adopt measures which are prohibited by the constitution; or should Congress, under the pretext of executing its powers, pass laws for the accomplishment of objects not entrusted to the government; it would become the painful duty of this tribunal, should a case requiring such a decision come before it, to say that such an act was not the law of the land. But where the law is not prohibited, and is really calculated to effect any of the objects entrusted to the government, to undertake here to inquire into the degree of its necessity, would be to pass the line which circumscribes the judicial department, and to tread on legislative ground. This court disclaims all pretensions to such a power.

... After the most deliberate consideration, it is the unanimous and decided opinion of this

Court, that the act to incorporate the Bank of the United States is a law made in pursuance of the constitution, and is a part of the supreme law of the land.

It being the opinion of the Court, that the act incorporating the bank is constitutional; and that the power of establishing a branch in the State of Maryland might be properly exercised by the bank itself, we proceed to inquire...whether the State of Maryland may, without violating the constitution, tax that branch?

That the power of taxation is one of vital importance; that it is retained by the States; that it is not abridged by the grant of a similar power to the government of the Union; that it is to be concurrently exercised by the two governments: are truths which have never been denied. But, such is the paramount character of the constitution, that its capacity to withdraw any subject from the action of even this power, is admitted. The States are expressly forbidden to lay any duties on imports or exports, except what may be absolutely necessary for executing their inspection laws. If the obligation of this prohibition must be conceded—if it may restrain a State from the exercise of its taxing power on imports and exports; the same paramount character would seem to restrain, as it certainly may restrain, a State from such other exercise of this power, as is in its nature incompatible with, and repugnant to, the constitutional laws of the Union. A law, absolutely repugnant to another, as entirely repeals that other as if express terms of repeal were used.

On this ground the counsel for the bank place its claim to be exempted from the power of a State to tax its operations. There is no express provision for the case, but the claim has been sustained on a principle which so entirely pervades the constitution, is so intermixed with the materials which compose it, so interwoven with its web, so blended with its texture, as to be incapable of being separated from it, without rending it into shreds.

This great principle is, that the constitution and the laws made in pursuance thereof are supreme; that they control the constitution and laws of the respective States, and cannot be controlled by them. From this, which may be almost termed an axiom, other propositions are deduced as corollaries, on the truth or error of which, and on their application to this case, the cause has been

supposed to depend. These are, 1st. that a power to create implies a power to preserve. 2nd. That a power to destroy, if wielded by a different hand, is hostile to, and incompatible with these powers to create and to preserve. 3d. That where this repugnancy exists, that authority which is supreme must control, not yield to that over which it is supreme.

These propositions, as abstract truths, would, perhaps, never be controverted. Their application to this case, however, has been denied; and, both in maintaining the affirmative and the negative, a splendor of eloquence, and strength of argument, seldom, if ever, surpassed, have been displayed.

The power of Congress to create, and of course to continue, the bank, was the subject of the preceding part of this opinion; and is no longer to be considered as questionable.

That the power of taxing it by the States may be exercised so as to destroy it, is too obvious to be denied. But taxation is said to be an absolute power, which acknowledges no other limits than those expressly prescribed in the constitution, and like sovereign power of every other description, is trusted to the discretion of those who use it....

The argument on the part of the State of Maryland, is, not that the States may directly resist a law of Congress, but that they may exercise their acknowledged powers upon it, and that the constitution leaves them this right in the confidence that they will not abuse it.

That the power to tax involves the power to destroy; that the power to destroy may defeat and render useless the power to create; that there is a plain repugnance, in conferring on one government a power to control the constitutional measures of another, which other, with respect to those very measures, is declared to be supreme over that which exerts the control, are propositions not to be denied. But all inconsistencies are to be reconciled by the magic of the word CONFIDENCE. Taxation, it is said, does not necessarily and unavoidably destroy. To carry it to the excess of destruction would be an abuse, to presume which, would banish that confidence which is essential to all government.

But is this a case of confidence? Would the people of any one Slate trust those of another with a power to control the most insignificant operations of their State government? We know they would not. Why, then, should we suppose that the people of any one State should be willing to trust those of another with a power to control the operations of a government to which they have confided their most important and most valuable interests? In the legislature of the Union alone, are all represented. The legislature of the Union alone, therefore, can be trusted by the people with the power of controlling measures which concern all, in the confidence that it will not be abused. This, then, is not a case of confidence, and we must consider it as it really is.

If we apply the principle for which the State of Maryland contends, to the constitution generally, we shall find it capable of changing totally the character of that instrument. We shall find it capable of arresting all the measures of the government, and of prostrating it at the foot of the States. The American people have declared their constitution, and the laws made in pursuance thereof, to be supreme; but this principle would transfer the supremacy, in fact, to the States.

If the States may tax one instrument, employed by the government in the execution of its powers, they may tax any and every other instrument. They may tax the mail; they may tax the mint; they may tax patent rights; they may tax the papers of the custom-house; they may tax judicial process; they may tax all the means employed by the government, to an excess which would defeat all the ends of government. This was not intended by the American people. They did not design to make their government dependent on the States.

… It has also been insisted, that, as the power of taxation in the general and State governments is acknowledged to be concurrent, every argument which would sustain the right of the general government to tax banks chartered by the States, will equally sustain the right of the States to tax banks chartered by the general government.

But the two cases are not on the same reason. The people of all the States have created the general government, and have conferred upon it the general power of taxation. The people of all the States, and the States themselves, are represented in Congress, and, by their representatives, exercise this power. When they tax the chartered institutions of the States, they tax their constituents; and these taxes must be uniform. But, when a State taxes the operations of the government of the United States, it acts upon institutions created, not by their own constituents, but by people over whom they claim no control. It acts upon the measures of a government created by others as well as themselves, for the benefit of others in common with themselves. The difference is that which always exists, and always must exist, between the action of the whole on a part, and the action of a part on the whole between the laws of a government declared to be supreme, and those of a government which, when in opposition to those laws, is not supreme.

The Court has bestowed on this subject its most deliberate consideration. The result is a conviction that the States have no power, by taxation or otherwise, to retard, impede, burden, or in any manner control, the operations of the constitutional laws enacted by Congress to carry into execution the powers vested in the general government. This is, we think, the unavoidable consequence of that supremacy which the constitution has declared.

We are unanimously of opinion, that the law passed by the legislature of Maryland, imposing a tax on the Bank of the United States, is unconstitutional.

⚓ *Treaty of Ghent*

CONGRESS

The Treaty of Ghent ending the War of 1812 meant that Native American tribes could no longer turn to European nations in alliances against the United States. Although fighting would continue for many years, the eventual subjugation of Native Americans had become all but a foregone conclusion.

The government thus turned its emphasis in 1819 from military action against Native Americans to a "civilization policy" in which Native Americans would be taught basic education, religious training and farming methods consistent with white, Christian principles. The government allocated a relatively paltry $10,000 per year for this purpose, which was largely used for Christian missionary training.

Most tribes did not embrace the civilization policy. One exception was the Cherokee nation in the Southeast which cleared fields, established villages, learned trades, and went to schools and churches in significant numbers. Ironically, the success of the Cherokees contributed to their demise. Eager to confiscate their fertile farms, President Andrew Jackson removed the Cherokees in the 1830s in a forced march westward.

Be it enacted, etc., That, for the purpose of providing against the further decline and final extinction of the Indian tribes, adjoining to the frontier settlements of the United States, and for introducing among them the habits and arts of civilization, the President of the United States shall be, and he is hereby, authorized, in every case where he shall judge improvements in the habits and condition of such Indians practicable, and that the means of instruction can be introduced with their own consent, to employ capable persons, of good moral character, to instruct them in the mode of agriculture suited to their situation; and for teaching their children in reading, writing, and arithmetic, and for performing such other duties as may be enjoined, according to such instruction and rules as the President may give and prescribe for the regulation of their conduct, in the discharge of their duties.

And be it further enacted, That the annual sum of ten thousand dollars be, and the same is hereby, appropriated, for the purpose of carrying into effect the provisions of this act; and an account of the expenditure of the money and proceedings, in execution of the foregoing provisions, shall be laid annually before Congress.

❧ *Florida Treaty*

CONGRESS

Spain ceded Florida to the United States with the signing of the Adams-Onis Treaty on February 2, 1819. Negotiated by Secretary of State John Quincy Adams, the treaty also defined the western boundary between the United States and Mexico. The definition excluded Texas, prompting widespread criticism of Adams. Spain's decision to sell Florida for $5 million coincided with Andrew Jackson's invasion into the Spanish territory and capture of Pensacola while fighting the First Seminole War against the Seminole Indians.

Article II. His Catholic Majesty cedes to the United States, in full property and sovereignty, all territories which belonged to him, situated to the eastward of the Mississippi, known by the name of East and West Florida. The adjacent islands dependent on said provinces, all public lots and squares, vacant lands, public edifices, fortifications, barracks, and other buildings, which are not private property, archives and documents, which relate directly to the property and sovereignty of said provinces, are included in this article....

Article V. the inhabitants of the ceded territories shall be secured in the free exercise of their religion, without any restriction....

Article VI. the inhabitants of the territories

which His Catholic Majesty cedes to the United States, by this treaty, shall be incorporated in the Union of the United States, as soon as may be consistent with the principles of the Federal Constitution, and admitted to the enjoyment of all the privileges, rights, and immunities of the citizens of the United States....

Article XI. The United States, exonerating Spain from all demands in future, on account of the claims of their citizens to which the renunciations herein contained extend, and considering them entirely cancelled, undertake to make satisfaction for the same, to an amount not exceeding five millions of dollars. To ascertain the full amount and validity of those claims, a commission, to consist of three Commissioners, citizens of the United States, shall be appointed by the President, by and with the advice and consent of the Senate....

Article XV. Spanish vessels, laden only with productions of Spanish growth or manufacture, coming directly from Spain, or her colonies, shall be admitted, for the term of twelve years, to the ports of Pensacola and St. Augustine, without paying other or higher duties on their cargoes, or of tonnage, than will be paid by the vessels of the United States. During the said term no other nation shall enjoy the same privileges within the ceded territories....

❧ *The Missouri Compromise*

CONGRESS

The acquisition of the Louisiana Territory applied renewed strain on the relations between slave and non-slave states over the question of whether slaves would be allowed in new states. Southern slave states were concerned that they would lose their political influence in government. In the North, sentiment against slavery was starting to rise. Although few people were calling for a national abolition of slavery, many people were opposed to extending it westward.
In 1820, Kentucky Senator Henry Clay forged a compromise. In exchange for admitting Missouri as a slave state, Maine would be accepted as a free state to maintain the precarious balance in the U.S. Senate. Further, slavery in the Louisiana Territory would be banned north of the 36°30′ boundary.

Be it enacted by the Senate and House of Representatives of the United States of America, in Congress assembled, That the inhabitants of that portion of the Missouri territory included within the boundaries hereinafter designated, be, and they are hereby, authorized to form for themselves a constitution and state government, and to assume such name as they shall deem proper; and the said state, when formed, shall be admitted into the Union, upon an equal footing with the original states, in all respects whatsoever.

Section 2. And be it further enacted, That the said state shall consist of all the territory included within the following boundaries, to wit: Beginning in the middle of the Mississippi river, on the parallel of thirty-six degrees of north latitude; thence west, along that parallel of latitude, to the St. Francois river; thence up, and following the course of that river, in the middle of the main channel thereof, to the parallel of latitude of thirty-six degrees and thirty minutes; thence west, along the same, to a point where the said parallel is intersected by a meridian line passing through the middle of the mouth of the Kansas river, where the same empties into the Missouri river, thence, from the point aforesaid north, along the said meridian line, to the intersection of the parallel of latitude which passes through the rapids of the river Des Moines, making the said line to correspond with the Indian boundary line; thence east, from the point of intersection last aforesaid, along the said parallel of latitude, to the middle of the channel of the main fork of the said river Des Moines; thence down and along the middle of the main channel of the said river Des Moines, to the mouth of the same, where it empties into the Mississippi river; thence, due east, to the middle of the main channel of the Mississippi river; thence down, and following the course of the Mississippi river, in the middle of the main channel thereof, to the place of beginning: Provided, The said state shall ratify the boundaries aforesaid; And Provided also, That the said state shall have concurrent jurisdiction on the river Mississippi, and every other river bordering on the said state, so far as the said rivers shall form a common boundary to the said state; and any other state or states, now or hereafter to be formed and bounded by the same, such rivers to be common to both; and that the river Mississippi, and the navigable rivers and waters leading into the same, shall be common highways, and for ever free, as well to the inhabitants of the said state as to other citizens of the United States, without any tax, duty, impost, or toll, therefor, imposed by the said state....

Section 4. And be it further enacted, That the members of the convention thus duly elected, shall be, and they are hereby authorized to meet at the seat of government of said territory on the second Monday of the month of June next; and the said convention, when so assembled, shall have power and authority to adjourn to any other place in the said territory, which to them shall seem best for the convenient transaction of their business; and which convention, when so met, shall first determine by a majority of the whole number elected, whether it be, or be not, expedient at that time to form a constitution and state government for the people within the said territory, as included within the boundaries above designated....

Section 5. And be it further enacted, That until the next general census shall be taken, the said state shall be entitled to one representative in the House of Representatives of the United States.

Second. That all salt springs, not exceeding twelve in number, with six sections of land adjoining to each, shall be granted to the said state for the use of said state....

Fifth. That thirty-six sections, or one entire township, which shall be designated by the President of the United States, together with the other lands heretofore reserved for that purpose, shall be reserved for the use of a seminary of learning, and vested in the legislature of said state, to be appropriated solely to the use of such seminary by the said legislature....

Section 8. And be it further enacted, That in all that territory ceded by France to the United States, under the name of Louisiana, which lies north of thirty-six degrees and thirty minutes north latitude, not included within the limits of the state, contemplated by this act, slavery and involuntary servitude, otherwise than in the punishment of crimes, whereof the parties shall have been duly convicted, shall be, and is hereby, forever prohibited: Provided always, That any person escaping into the same, from whom labour or service is lawfully claimed, in any state or territory of the United States, such fugitive may be lawfully reclaimed and conveyed to the person claiming his or her labour or service as aforesaid.

❧ The Monroe Doctrine

JAMES MONROE

Prompted by concerns that France might try to acquire for-mer Spanish colonies in Latin America such as Mexico, President James Monroe asserted in his 1823 annual mes-sage to Congress that the Western Hemisphere was not sub-ject to European colonization. Any attempts by European powers to exercise undue influence in Latin America, Monroe said, would be considered as a threat to the United States. In return, Monroe pledged that the United States would not intervene in European affairs.

The Monroe Doctrine, which was in large part conceived by Secretary of State John Quincy Adams, formed the basis of American policy until World War I. Even today, the United States exercises the spirit of the doctrine in its approach to Latin American affairs.

At the proposal of the Russian Imperial govern-ment, made through the minister of the Emperor residing here, full power and instructions have been transmitted to the minister of the United States at St. Petersburg to arrange by amicable negotiation the respective rights and interests of the two nations on the northwest coast of this continent. A similar proposal had been made by His Imperial Majesty to the Government of Great Britain, which has likewise been acceded to. The govern-ment of the United States has been desirous by this friendly proceeding of manifesting the great value which they have invariably attached to the friend-ship of the Emperor and their solicitude to culti-vate the best understanding with his government. In the discussions to which this interest has given rise and in the arrangements by which they may terminate the occasion has been judged proper for asserting, as a principle in which the rights and interests of the United States are involved, that the American continents, by the free and independent condition which they have assumed and maintain, are henceforth not to be considered subjects for future colonization by any European powers....

It was stated at the commencement of the last session that a great effort was then making in Spain and Portugal to improve the condition of the peo-ple of those countries, and that it appeared to be conducted with extraordinary moderation. It need scarcely be remarked that the result has been so far very different from what was then anticipated. Of events in that quarter of the globe, with which we have so much intercourse and from which we derive our origin, we have always been anxious and interested spectators. The citizens of the United States cherish sentiments the most friendly in favor of the liberty and happiness of their fellow-men on that side of the Atlantic. In the wars of the European powers in matters relating to themselves we have never taken any part nor does it comport with our policy so to do. It is only when our rights are invaded or seriously menaced that we resent injuries or make preparation for our defense. With the movements in this hemisphere we are of neces-sity more immediately connected, and by causes which must be obvious to all enlightened and impartial observers. The political system of allied powers is essentially different in this respect from that of America. This difference proceeds from that which exists in their respective Governments; and to the defense of our own, which has been achieved by the loss of so much blood and treasure, matured by the wisdom of their most enlightened citizens, and under which we have enjoyed unex-ampled felicity, this whole nation is devoted. We owe it, therefore, to candor and to the amicable relations existing between the United States and those powers to declare that we should consider any attempt on their part to extend their system to any portion of this hemisphere as dangerous to our peace and safety. With the existing colonies or dependencies of any European power we have not interfered and shall not interfere. But with the Governments who have declared their indepen-dence and maintained it, and whose independence we have, on great consideration and on just princi-ples, acknowledged, we could not view any interpo-sition for the purpose of oppressing them, or con-trolling in any other manner their destiny, by any European power in any other light than as the manifestation of an unfriendly disposition toward the United States. In the war between those new Governments and Spain we declared our neutrality at the time of their recognition, and to this we have adhered, and shall continue to adhere, provid-ed no change shall occur which, in the judgment of the competent authorities of this Government, shall make a corresponding change on the part of the United States indispensable to their security.

The late events in Spain and Portugal show that Europe is still unsettled. Of this important fact no stronger proof can be adduced than that the allied powers should have thought it proper, on any principle satisfactory to themselves, to have interposed by force in the internal concerns of Spain. To what extent such interposition may be carried, on the same principle, is a question in which all independent powers whose governments differ from theirs are interested, even those most remote, and surely none more so than the United States. Our policy in regard to Europe, which was adopted at an early stage of the wars which have so long agitated that quarter of the globe, nevertheless remains the same, which is, not to interfere in the internal concerns of its powers; to consider the government de facto as the legitimate government for us; to cultivate friendly relations with it, and to preserve those relations by a frank, firm, and manly policy, meeting in all instances the just claims of every power, submitting to injuries from none. But in regard to those continents circumstances are eminently and conspicuously different. It is impossible that the allied powers should extend their political system to any portion of either continent without endangering our peace and happiness; nor can anyone believe that our southern brethren, if left to themselves, would adopt it of their own accord. It is equally impossible, therefore, that we should behold such interposition in any form with indifference. If we look to the comparative strength and resources of Spain and those new Governments, and their distance from each other, it must be obvious that she can never subdue them. It is still the true policy of the United States to leave the parties to themselves, in the hope that other powers will pursue the same course.

❧ "This was all burlesque on me"

DAVY CROCKETT

Known for his folksy humor, Davy Crockett was one of the more colorful characters on the American frontier. He served in the Tennessee legislature and was elected to one term in the U.S. Congress. His autobiography described his experiences on the frontier and in politics and made him a national legend, although some scholars question the authorship. Crockett went to Texas to help fight for the region's independence. He was killed at the Alamo, making him a hero to both Texas and the United States. In this excerpt of his 1834 autobiography Crockett describes how he stumbled into politics.

I had on hand a great many skins, and so, in the month of February, I packed a horse with them, and taking my eldest son along with me, cut out for a little town called Jackson, situated about forty miles off. We got there well enough, and I sold my skins, and bought me some coffee, and sugar, powder, lead, and salt. I packed them all up in readiness for a start, which I intended to make early next morning. Morning came, but I concluded, before I started, I would go and take a horn with some of my old fellow-soldiers that I had met with at Jackson.

I did so; and while we were engaged in this, I met with three candidates for the Legislature; a Doctor Butler, who was, by marriage, a nephew to General Jackson, a Major Lynn, and a Mr. McEver, all first-rate men. We all took a horn together, and some person present said to me, "Crockett, you must offer for the Legislature." I told him I lived at least forty miles from any white settlement, and had no thought of becoming a candidate at that time. So we all parted and I and my little boy went on home.

It was about a week or two after this, that a man came to my house and told me I was a candidate. I told him not so. But he took out a newspaper from his pocket, and show'd me where I was announced. I said to my wife that this was all a burlesque on me, but I was determined to make it cost the man who had put it there at least the value of the printing, and of the fun he wanted at my expense. So I hired a young man to work in my place on my farm, and turned out myself electioneering. I hadn't been out long, before I found the people began to talk very much about the bear hunter, the man from the cane; and the three gentlemen, who I have already named, soon found it necessary to enter into an agreement to have a sort of caucus at their March court, to determine which of them was the strongest, and the other two was to withdraw and support him. As the court came on, each one of them spread himself, to secure the nomination; but it fell on Dr. Butler, and the rest backed out. The doctor was a clever fellow, and I have often said he was the most talented man I ever run against for any office. His being related to Gen'l. Jackson also helped him on very much; but I was in for it, and I was determined to push ahead and go through, or stick. Their meeting was held in Madison county, which was the strongest in the representative district, which was composed of eleven counties, and they seemed bent on having the member from there.

At this time Col. Alexander was a candidate for Congress, and attending one of his public meetings one day, I walked to where he was treating the people, and he gave me an introduction to several of his acquaintances, and informed them that I was out electioneering. In a little time my competitor, Doctor Butler, came along; he passed by without noticing me, and I suppose, indeed, he did not recognise me. But I hailed him, as I was for all sorts of fun; and when he turned to me, I said to him, "Well, doctor, I suppose they have weighed you out to me; but I should like to know why they fixed your election for March instead of August? This is," said I, "a branfire new way of doing business, if a caucus is to make a representative for the people!" He now discovered who I was, and cried out, "D--n it, Crockett, is that you?"—"Be sure it is," said I, "but I don't want it understood that I have come electioneering. I have just crept out of the cane, to see what discoveries I could make among the white folks." I told him that when I set out electioneering, I would go prepared to put every man on as good footing when I left him as I found him on. I would therefore have me a large buckskin hunting-shirt made, with a couple of pockets holding about a peck each; and that in one I would carry a great big twist of tobacco, and in the other my bottle of liquor; for I knowed when I met a man and offered him a dram, he would throw out his quid of tobacco to take one, and after he had taken his horn, I would out with my twist and give him another chaw. And in this way he would not be worse off than when I found him; and I would be sure to leave him in a first-rate humour. He said I could beat him electioneering all hollow. I told him I would give him better evidence of that before August, notwithstanding he had many advantages over me, and particularly in the way of money; but I told him that I would go on the products of the country; that I had industrious children, and the best of coon dogs, and they would hunt every night till midnight to support my election; and when the coon fur wa'n't good, I would myself go a wolfing, and shoot down a wolf, and skin his head, and his scalp would be good to me for three dollars, in our state treasury money; and in this way I would get along on the big string. He stood like he was both

amused and astonished, and the whole crowd was in a roar of laughter. From this place I returned home, leaving the people in a first-rate way; and I was sure I would do a good business among them. At any rate, I was determined to stand up to my lick-log, salt or no salt.

In a short time there came out two other candidates, a Mr. Shaw and a Mr. Brown. We all ran the race through; and when the election was over, it turned out that I beat them all by a majority of two hundred and forty-seven votes, and was again returned as a member to the Legislature from a new region of the country, without losing a session. This reminded me of the old saying—"A fool for luck, and a poor man for children."

I now served two years in that body from my new district, which was the years 1823 and '24. At the session of 1823, I had a small trial of my independence, and whether I would forsake principle for party, or for the purpose of following after big men. The term of Col. John Williams had expired, who was a senator in Congress from the state of Tennessee. He was a candidate for another election, and was opposed by Pleasant M. Miller, Esq., who, it was believed, would not be able to beat the colonel. Some two or three others were spoken of, but it was at last concluded that the only man who could beat him was the present "government," General Jackson. So, a few days before the election was to come on, he was sent for to come and run for the senate. He was then in nomination for the presidency; but sure enough he came, and did run as the opponent of Colonel Williams, and beat him too, but not by my vote. The vote was, for Jackson, thirty-five; for Williams, twenty-five. I thought the colonel had honestly discharged his duty, and even the mighty name of Jackson couldn't make me vote against him.

But voting against the old chief was found a mighty uphill business to all of them except myself. I never would, nor never did, acknowledge I had voted wrong; and I am more certain now that I was right than ever.

I told the people it was the best vote I ever gave; that I had supported the public interest, and cleared my conscience in giving it, instead of gratifying the private ambition of a man.

I let the people know as early as then, that I wouldn't take a collar around my neck with the letters engraved on it,

MY DOG.
ANDREW JACKSON.

During these two sessions of the Legislature, nothing else turned up which I think it worth while to mention; and, indeed, I am fearful that I am too particular about many small matters; but if so, my apology is, that I want the world to understand my true history, and how I worked along to rise from a cane-brake to my present station in life.

Col. Alexander was the representative in Congress of the district I lived in, and his vote on the tariff law of 1824 gave a mighty heap of dissatisfaction to his people. They therefore began to talk pretty strong of running me for Congress against him. At last I was called on by a good many to be a candidate. I told the people that I couldn't stand that; it was a step above my knowledge, and I know'd nothing about Congress matters.

However, I was obliged to agree to run, and myself and two other gentlemen came out. But Providence was a little against two of us this hunt, for it was the year that cotton brought twenty-five dollars a hundred; and so Colonel Alexander would get up and tell the people, it was all the good effect of this tariff law; that it had raised the price of their cotton, and that it would raise the price of everything else they made to sell. I might as well have sung psalms over a dead horse, as to try to make the people believe otherwise; for they knowed their cotton had raised, sure enough, and if the colonel hadn't done it, they didn't know what had. So he rather made a mash of me this time as he beat me exactly two votes, as they counted the polls, though I have always believed that many other things had been as fairly done as that same count.

He went on, and served out his term, and at the end of it cotton was down to six or eight dollars a hundred again; and I concluded I would try him once more, and see how it would go with cotton at the common price, and so I became a candidate.

"The greatest inland trade ever witnessed"

DE WITT CLINTON

The Erie Canal opened in 1825. The canal connected the Hudson River at Albany to Lake Erie at Buffalo, thus providing a critical transportation route from the port of New York to the Midwest. As Governor De Witt Clinton describes, the canal assured New York City's position as a world commercial center and opened the way for an economic explosion in the Midwest. The opening of the canal sparked the economies of Buffalo, Rochester, Cleveland, Columbus, Detroit, Chicago and Syracuse.

On the 4th of July, 1817, the work was commenced. The Champlain and the greater part of the Erie canal are now in a navigable state, and in less than a year the whole, comprising an extent of about four hundred and twenty-five miles, will be finished. Every year's experience will enhance the results in the public estimation, and benefits will be unfolded which we can now hardly venture to anticipate. As a bond of union between the Atlantic and western states, it may prevent the dismemberment of the American empire. As an organ of communication between the Hudson, the Mississippi, the St. Lawrence, the great lakes of the north and west, and their tributary rivers, it will create the greatest inland trade ever witnessed. The most fertile and extensive regions of America will avail themselves of its facilities for a market. All their surplus productions, whether of the soil, the forest, the mines, or the water, their fabrics of art and their supplies of foreign commodities will concentrate in the city of New York, for transportation abroad or consumption at home. Agriculture, manufactures, commerce, trade, navigation, and the arts, will receive a correspondent encouragement. That city will, in course of time become the granary of the world, the emporium of commerce, the seat of manufactures, the focus of great moneyed operations, and the concentrating point of vast, disposable, and accumulating capitals, which will stimulate, enliven, extend, and reward the exertions of human labour and ingenuity, in all their processes and exhibitions. And, before the revolution of a century, the whole island of Manhattan, covered with habitations and replenished with a dense population, will constitute one vast city.

☙ Internal improvements

JOHN QUINCY ADAMS

Projects such as the Erie Canal highlighted the role government could play in fostering the American economy. President John Quincy Adams embraced the policy of internal improvements and encouraged the government's participation in education and scientific endeavor. In his first annual message to Congress in 1825 Adams urged Congress to support a series of projects pertaining to the exploration of the west, establishing a standard for scales and weights and building the first astronomical observatory, marking the start of the government's involvement in observing and ultimately exploring space.

In assuming her station among the civilized nations of the earth it would seem that our country had contracted the engagement to contribute her share of mind, of labor, and of expense to the improvement of those and of expense to the improvement of those parts of knowledge which lie beyond the reach of individual acquisition, and particularly to geographical and astronomical science. Looking back to the history only of the half century since the declaration of our independence, and observing the generous emulation with which the Governments of France, Great Britain, and Russia have devoted the genius, the intelligence, the treasures of their respective nations to the common improvement of the species in these branches of science, is it not incumbent upon us to inquire whether we are not bound by obligations of a high and honorable character to contribute our portion of energy and exertion to the common stock? The voyages of discovery prosecuted in the course of that time at the expense of those nations have not only redounded to their glory, but to the improvement of human knowledge. We have been partakers of that improvement and owe for it a sacred debt, not only of gratitude, but of equal or proportional exertion in the same common cause. Of the cost of these undertakings, if the mere expenditures of outfit, equipment, and completion of the expeditions were to be considered the only charges, it would be unworthy of a great and generous nation to take a second thought. One hundred expeditions of circumnavigation like those of Cook and La Perouse would not burden the exchequer of the nation fitting them out so much as the ways and means of defraying a single campaign in war. But if we take into account the lives of those benefactors of mankind of which their services in the cause of their species were the purchase, how shall the cost of those heroic enterprises be estimated, and what compensation can be made to them or to their countries for them? Is it not by bearing them in affectionate remembrance? Is it not still more by imitating their example—by enabling countrymen of our own to pursue the same career and to hazard their lives in the same cause?

In inviting the attention of Congress to the subject of internal improvements upon a view thus enlarged it is not my design to recommend the equipment of an expedition for circumnavigating the globe for purposes of scientific research and inquiry. We have objects of useful investigation nearer home, and to which our cares may be more beneficially applied. The interior of our own territories has been imperfectly explored. Our coasts along many degrees of latitude upon the shores of the Pacific ocean, though much frequented by our spirited commercial navigators, have been barely visited by our public ships. The River of the West, first fully discovered and navigated by a countryman of our own, still bears the name of the ship in which he ascended its waters, and claims the protection of our armed national flag at its mouth. With the establishment of a military post there or at some other point of that coast, recommended by my predecessor and already matured in the deliberations of the last Congress, I would suggest the expediency of connecting the equipment of a public ship for the exploration of the whole northwest coast of this continent.

The establishment of an uniform standard of weights and measures was one of the specific objects contemplated in the formation of our Constitution, and to fix that standard was one of the powers delegated by express terms in that instrument to Congress. The Governments of Great Britain and France have scarcely ceased to be occupied with inquiries and speculations on the same subject since the existence of our Constitution, and with them it has expanded into profound, laborious, and expensive researches into the figure of the earth and comparative length of the pendulum vibrating seconds in various latitudes from the equator to the pole. These researches have resulted in the composition and publication of several works highly interesting to the cause of science. The experiments are yet in the process of performance. Some of them have recently been made on our own shores, within the walls of one of our own fellow-citizens. It would be honorable to our country if the sequel of the same experiments should be countenanced by the patronage of our Government, as they have hitherto been by those of France and Britain.

Connected with the establishment of an university, or separate from it, might be undertaken the erection of an astronomical observatory, with provision for the support of an astronomer, to be in constant attendance of observation upon the phenomena of the heavens, and for the periodical publication of his observations. It is with no feeling of pride as an American that the remark may be made that on the comparatively small territorial surface of Europe there are existing upward of 130 of these light-houses of the skies, while throughout the whole of American hemisphere there is not one. If we reflect a moment upon the discoveries which in the last four centuries have been made in the physical constitution of the universe by the means of these buildings and of observers stationed in them, shall we doubt of their usefulness to every nation? And while scarcely a year passes over our heads without bringing some new astronomical discovery to light, which we must fain receive at second hand from Europe, are we not cutting ourselves off from the means of returning light for light while we have neither observatory nor observer upon our half of the globe and the earth revolves in perpetual darkness to our unsearching eyes?

✿ "The palladium of human liberty"

FRANCES WRIGHT

Frances Wright immigrated to the United States from Scotland in 1824 and quickly become one of the nation's leading reformers. She lived in the utopian community New Harmony, Indiana, helped found Nashoba (an unsuccessful colony for emancipated blacks in Tennessee), and led the Workingmen's Party in New York. Energetic and eloquent, she was a passionate advocate for abolition, universal education and equal rights for women. Wright's impact was so great that leading newspaper editor William Cullen Bryant wrote an ode to her:

"Thou wonder of the age, from whom

Religion waits her final doom,
Her quiet death, her euthanasia,
Thou in whose eloquence and bloom
The age beholds a new Aspasia!"

On July 4, 1828, Wright delivered an Independence Day address at New Harmony in which she urged Americans to embrace patriotism as a love of liberty and human improvement—not the narrower definition of country.

Our hearts should expand on this day, which calls to memory the conquest achieved by knowledge over ignorance, willing cooperation over blind obedience, opinion over prejudice, new ways over old ways—when, fifty-two years ago, America declared her national independence, and associated it with her republic federation. Reasonable is it to rejoice on this day, and useful to reflect thereon; so that we rejoice for the real, and not any imaginary, good; and reflect on the positive advantages obtained, and on those which it is ours farther to acquire.

Dating, as we justly may, a new era in the history of man from the Fourth of July, 1776, it would be well—that is, it would be useful—if on each anniversary we examined the progress made by our species in just knowledge and just practice. Each Fourth of July would then stand as a tidemark in the flood of time by which to ascertain the advance of the human intellect, by which to note the rise and fall of each successive error, the discovery of each important truth, the gradual melioration in our public institutions, social arrangements, and, above all, in our moral feelings and mental views....

In continental Europe, of late years, the words "patriotism" and "patriot" have been used in a more enlarged sense than it is usual here to attribute them, or than is attached to them in Great Britain. Since the political struggles of France, Italy, Spain, and Greece, the word "patriotism" has been employed, throughout continental Europe, to express a love of the public good; a preference for the interests of the many to those of the few; a desire for the emancipation of the human race in general than that felt for any country, or inhabitants of a country, in particular. And "patriot," in like manner, is employed to signify a lover of human liberty and human improvement rather than a mere lover of the country in which he lives, or the tribe to which he belongs.

Used in this sense, patriotism is a virtue, and a

patriot a virtuous man. With such an interpretation, a patriot is a useful member of society, capable
of enlarging all minds and bettering all hearts with
which he comes in contact; a useful member of the
human family, capable of establishing fundamental
principles and of merging his own interest, those of
his associates, and those of his nation in the interests of the human race. Laurels and statues are vain
things and mischievous as they are childish; but
could we imagine them of use, on such a patriot
alone could they be with any reason bestowed....

If such a patriotism as we have last considered
should seem likely to obtain in any country, it
should be certainly in this. In this which is truly
the home of all nations and in the veins of whose
citizens flows the blood of every people on the
globe. Patriotism, in the exclusive meaning, is surely not made for America. Mischievous everywhere,
it were for her both mischievous and absurd. The
very origin of the people is opposed to it. The institutions, in their principle, militate against it. The
day we are celebrating protests against it.

It is for Americans, more especially, to nourish
a nobler sentiment, one more consistent with their
origin, and more conducive to their future
improvement. It is for them more especially to
know why they love their country; and to feel that
they love it, not because it is their country, but
because it is the palladium of human liberty—the
favored scene of human improvement. It is for
them, more especially, to examine their institutions, because they have the means of improving
them; to examine their laws, because at their will
they can alter them. It is for them to lay aside luxury whose wealth is in industry; idle parade whose
strength is in knowledge; ambitious distinctions
whose principle is equality. It is for them not to
rest, satisfied with words, who can seize upon
things; and to remember that equality means, not
the mere equality of political rights, however valuable, but equality of instruction and equality of
virtue; and that liberty means, not the mere voting
at elections, but the free and fearless exercise of the
mental faculties and that self-possession which
springs out of well-reasoned opinions and consistent practice. It is for them to honor principles
rather than men—to commemorate events rather
than days; when they rejoice, to know for what
they rejoice only for what has brought and what
brings peace and happiness to men.

The event we commemorate this day has procured much of both, and shall procure in the
onward course of human improvement more than
we can now conceive of. For this—for the good
obtained and yet in store for human beings rather
than as Americans—as reasoning beings, not as
ignorants. So shall we rejoice to good purpose and
in good feeling; so shall we improve the victory
once on this day achieved, until all mankind hold
with us the Jubilee of Independence.

"What is the profession of a Woman?"

CATHERINE BEECHER

Although there was widespread instruction for girls at the
elementary school level and some instruction at the sec-
ondary level, there was no higher education for women.
Along with Emma Willard in Troy, New York, Catherine
Beecher pioneered the introduction of higher education for
women. A champion of instructing women teachers,
Catherine Beecher founded the Hartford (Connecticut) Female
Seminary in 1823 for that purpose. The following is an
excerpt from a report she wrote in 1829 entitled
"Suggestions Respecting Improvements in Education,
Presented to the Trustees of the Hartford Female Seminary."

It is to mothers, and to teachers, that the world is
to look for the character which is to be enstamped
on each succeeding generation, for it is to them
that the great business of education is almost exclusively committed. And will it not appear by examination that neither mothers nor teachers have ever
been properly educated for their profession. What
is the profession of a Woman? Is it not to form
immortal minds, and to watch, to nurse, and to rear
the bodily system, so fearfully and wonderfully
made, and upon the order and regulation of which,
the health and well-being of the mind so greatly
depends?

But let most of our sex upon whom these arduous duties devolve, be asked; have you ever devoted
any time and study, in the course of your education,
to any preparation for these duties? Have you been
taught any thing of the structure, the nature, and
the laws of the body, which you inhabit? Were you
ever taught to understand the operation of diet, air,
exercise and modes of dress upon the human frame?
Have the causes which are continually operating:

to prevent good health, and the modes by which it might be perfected and preserved ever been made the subject of any instruction? Perhaps almost every voice would respond, no; we have attended to almost every thing more than to this; we have been taught more concerning the structure of the earth; the laws of the heavenly bodies; the habits and formation of plants; the philosophy of languages; more of almost any thing, than the structure of the human frame and the laws of health and reason. But is it not the business, the profession of a woman to guard the health and form the physical habits of the young? And is not the cradle of infancy and the chamber of sickness sacred to woman alone? And ought she not to know at least some of the general principles of that perfect and wonderful piece of mechanism committed to her preservation and care?

The restoration of health is the physician's profession, but the preservation of it falls to other hands, and it is believed that the time will come, when woman will be taught to understand something respecting the construction of the human frame; the physiological results which will naturally follow from restricted exercise, unhealthy modes of dress, improper diet, and many other causes, which are continually operating to destroy the health and life of the young.

Again let our sex be asked respecting the instruction they have received in the course of their education, on that still more arduous and difficult department of their profession, which relates to the intellect and the moral susceptibilities. Have you been taught the powers and faculties of the human mind, and the laws by which it is regulated? Have you studied how to direct its several faculties; how to restore those that are overgrown, and strengthen and mature those that are deficient? Have you been taught the best modes of communicating knowledge as well as of acquiring it? Have you learned the best mode of correcting bad moral habits and forming good ones? Have you made it an object to find how a selfish disposition may be made generous; how a reserved temper may be made open and frank; how pettishness and ill humor may be changed to cheerfulness and kindness? Has any Woman studied her profession in this respect? It is feared the same answer must be returned, if not from all, at least from most of our sex. No; we have acquired wisdom from the obser-

vation and experience of others, on almost all other subjects, but the philosophy of the direction and Control of the human mind has not been an object of thought or study. And thus it appears that tho' it is Woman's express business to rear the body, and form the mind, there is scarcely anything to which her attention has been less directed....

If all females were not only well educated themselves, but were prepared to communicate in an easy manner their stores of knowledge to others; if they not only knew how to regulate their own minds, tempers and habits, but how to effect improvements in those around them, the face of society would speedily be changed. The time may come when the world will look back with wonder to behold how much time and effort have been given to the mere cultivation of the memory, and how little mankind have been aware of what every teacher, parent, and friend could accomplish in forming the social, intellectual and moral character of those by whom are surrounded.

Appeals to the Colored Citizens of the World

DAVID WALKER

With his words practically leaping off the page in seething indignation, David Walker wrote his essay "Appeals to the Colored Citizens of the World" in 1829 from Boston. A free African-American who was born in the South, Walker called for slaves to fight against slavery. He bluntly accused whites of hypocrisy. Walker's pamphlet spurred the abolitionist movement in the North. In the South, the pamphlet was outlawed. One year after the essay was published Walker died mysteriously.

...[W]e, (colored people of these United States of America) are the most wretched, degraded and abject set of beings that ever lived since the world began, and that the white Americans having reduced us to the wretched state of slavery, treat us in that condition more cruel (they being an enlighted and Christian people,) than any heathen nation did any people whom it had reduced to our condition. These affirmations are so well confirmed in the minds of all unprejudiced men, who have taken the trouble to read histories, that they need no elucidation from me. [T]hose enemies who have for hundreds of years stolen our rights, and kept us ignorant of Him and His divine worship; he will remove. Millions of whom, are this day, so ignorant and avaricious, that they cannot conceive how God can have an attribute of justice, and show mercy to us because it pleased Him to make us black—which colour, Mr. Jefferson calls unfortunate!!!!!! As though we are not as thankful to our God, for having made us as it pleased himself, as they (the whites,) are for having made them white. They think because they hold us in their infernal chains of slavery, that we wish to be white, or of their color—but they are dreadfully deceived—we wish to be just as it pleased our Creator to have made us, and no avaricious and unmerciful wretches, have any business to make slaves of, or hold us in slavery. How would they like for us to make slaves of, and hold them in cruel slavery, and murder them as they do us?--But is Mr. Jefferson's assertions true? viz. "that it is unfortunate for us that our Creator has been pleased to make us black." We will not take his say so, for the fact. The world will have an opportunity to see whether it is unfortunate for us, that our Creator has made us darker than the whites.

Fear not the number and education of our enemies, against whom we shall have to contend for our lawful right; guaranteed to us by our Maker; for why should we be afraid, when God is, and will continue, (if we continue humble) to be on our side?

The man who would not fight under our Lord and Master Jesus Christ, in the glorious and heavenly cause of freedom and of God—to be delivered from the most wretched, abject and servile slavery, that ever a people was afflicted with since the foundation of the world, to the present day—ought to be kept with all of his children or family, in slavery, or in chains, to be butchered by his cruel enemies ....

Here let me ask Mr. Jefferson, (but he is gone to answer at the bar of God, for the deeds done in his body while living,) I therefore ask the whole American people, had I not rather die, or be put to death, than to be a slave to any tyrant, who takes not only my own, but my wife and children's lives by the inches? Yea, would I meet death with avidity far! far!! in preference to such servile submission to the murderous hands of tyrants. Mr. Jefferson's very severe remarks on us have been so extensively

argued upon by men whose attainments in literature, I shall never be able to reach, that I would not have meddled with it, were it not to solicit each of my brethren, who has the spirit of a man, to buy a copy of Mr. Jefferson's "Notes on Virginia," and put it in the hand of his son. For let no one of us suppose that the refutations which have been written by our white friends are enough—they are whites—we are blacks.

We, and the world wish to see the charges of Mr. Jefferson refuted by the blacks themselves, according to their chance; for we must remember that what the whites have written respecting this subject, is other men's labours, and did not emanate from the blacks. I know well, that there are some talents and learning among the coloured people of this country, which we have not a chance to develop, in consequence of oppression; but our oppression ought not to hinder us from acquiring all we can. For we will have a chance to develop them by and by. God will not suffer us, always to be oppressed. Our sufferings will come to an end, in spite of all the Americans this side of eternity. Then we will want all the learning and talents among ourselves, and perhaps more, to govern ourselves. "Every dog must have its day," the American's is coming to an end ....

[A]t the close of the first Revolution in this country, with Great Britain, there were but thirteen States in the Union, now there are twenty-four, most of which are slave-holding States, and the whites are dragging us around in chains and in handcuffs, to their new States and Territories to work their mines and farms, to enrich them and their children and millions of them believing firmly that we being a little darker than they, were made by our Creator to be an inheritance to them and their children for ever the same as a parcel of brutes.

Are we MEN!! I ask you, O my brethren! are we MEN? Did our Creator make us to be slaves to dust and ashes like ourselves? Are they not dying worms as well as we? Have they not to make their appearance before the tribunal of Heaven, to answer for the deeds done in the body, as well as we? Have we any other Master but Jesus Christ alone? Is he not their Master as well as ours? What right then, have we to obey and call any other Master, but Himself? How we could be so submissive to a gang of men, whom we cannot tell whether they are as good as ourselves or not, I never could conceive. However, this is shut up with the Lord, and we cannot precisely tell but I declare, we judge men by their works ....

Americans! notwithstanding you have and do continue to treat us more cruel than any heathen nation ever did a people it had subjected to the same condition that you have us. Now let us reason—I mean you of the United States, whom I believe God designs to save from destruction, if you will hear. For I declare to you, whether you believe it or not, that there are some on the continent of America, who will never be able to repent. God will surely destroy them, to show you his disapprobation of the murders they and you have inflicted on us. I say, let us reason; had you not better take our body, while you have it in your power, and while we are yet ignorant and wretched, not knowing but a little, give us education, and teach us the pure religion of our Lord and Master, which is calculated to make the lion lay down in peace with the lamb, and which millions of you have beaten us nearly to death for trying to obtain since we have been among you, and thus at once, gain our affection while we are ignorant? Remember Americans, that we must and shall be free and enlightened as you are, will you wait until we shall, under God, obtain our liberty by the crushing arm of power? Will it not be dreadful for you? I speak Americans for your good. We must and shall be free I say, in spite of you. You may do your best to keep us in wretchedness and misery, to enrich you and your children, but God will deliver us from under you. And wo, wo, will be to you if we have to obtain our freedom by fighting. Throw away your fears and prejudices then, and enlighten us and treat us like men, and we will like you more than we do now hate you, and tell us now no more about colonization, for America is as much our country, as it is yours.

Treat us like men, and there is no danger but we will all live in peace and happiness together. For we are not like you, hard hearted, unmerciful, and unforgiving. What a happy country this will be, if the whites will listen. What nation under heaven, will be able to do any thing with us, unless God gives us up into its hand? But Americans, I declare to you, while you keep us and our children in bondage, and treat us like brutes, to make us support you and your families, we cannot be your

friends. You do not look for it, do you? Treat us then like men, and we will be your friends. And there is not a doubt in my mind, but that the whole of the past will be sunk into oblivion, and we yet, under God, will become a united and happy people. The whites may say it is impossible, but remember that nothing is impossible with God ....

If any are anxious to ascertain who I am, know the world, that I am one of the oppressed, degraded and wretched sons of Africa, rendered so by the avaricious and unmerciful, among the whites. If any wish to plunge me into the wretched incapacity of a slave, or murder me for the truth, know ye, that I am in the hand of God, and at your disposal. I count my life not dear unto me, but I am ready to be offered at any moment. For what is the use of living, when in fact I am dead. But remember, Americans, that as miserable, wretched, degraded and abject as you have made us in preceding, and in this generation, to support you and your families, that some of you, (whites) on the continent of America, will yet curse the day that you ever were born. You want slaves, and want us for your slaves!!! My colour will yet, root some of you out of the very face of the earth!!!!!!...

See your Declaration Americans!!! Do you understand your own language? Hear your language, proclaimed to the world, July 4th, 1776—

We hold these truths to be self evident--that ALL men are created EQUAL!! that they are endowed by their creator with certain unalienable rights; that among these are life, liberty, and the pursuit of happiness!!

Compare your own language above, extracted from your Declaration of Independence, with your cruelties and murders inflicted by your cruel and unmerciful fathers and yourselves on our fathers and on us—men who have never given your fathers or you the least provocation!!!!!!

Hear your language further!

But when a long train of abuses and usurpation, pursuing invariably the same object, evinces a design to reduce them under absolute despotism, it is their right, it is their duty, to throw off such government, and to provide new guards for their future security.

Now, Americans! I ask you candidly, was your sufferings under Great Britain, one hundredth part as cruel and tyrannical as you have rendered ours under you? Some of you, no doubt, believe that we will never throw off your murderous government and "provide new guards for our future security." If Satan has made you believe it, will he not deceive you? Do the whites say, I being a black man, ought to be humble, which I readily admit? I ask them, ought they not to be as humble as I? Or do they think that they can measure arms with Jehovah? Will not the Lord yet humble them? Or will not these very coloured people whom they now treat worse than brutes, yet under God, humble them low down enough? Some of the whites are ignorant enough to tell us, that we ought to be submissive to them that they may keep their feet on our throats. And if we do not submit to be beaten to death by them, we are bad creatures and of course must be damned, &c.

If any man wishes to hear this doctrine openly preached to us by the American preachers, let him go into the Southern and Western sections of this country I do not speak from hear say—what I have written, is what I have seen and heard myself. No man may think that my book is made up of conjecture—I have travelled and observed nearly the whole of those things myself, and what little I did not get by my own observation, I received from those among the whites and blacks, in whom the greatest confidence may be placed.

The Americans may be as vigilant as they please, but they cannot be vigilant enough for the Lord, neither can they hide themselves, where he will not find and bring them out....

❧ Woodman, Spare That Tree

GEORGE PERKINS MORRIS

As industrialism swept through urban New England, pastoral scenes were being replaced with new, gritty factories that spoiled the surrounding environment. George Perkins Morris's famous poem "Woodman, Spare That Tree" published in 1830 reminded readers of nature's values. The poem was instantly popular and has served as an inspiration for protectors of the environment ever since.

Woodman, spare that tree!
Touch not a single bough!
In youth it sheltered me,
And I'll protect it now.
'Twas my forefather's hand
That placed it near his cot;

There, woodman, let it stand,
Thy axe shall harm it not!

That old familiar tree,
Whose glory and renown
Are spread o'er land and sea,
And wouldst thou hew it down?
Woodman, forbear thy stroke!
Cut not its earth-bound ties;
O, spare that aged oak,
Now towering to the skies!

When but an idle boy
I sought its graceful shade;
In all their gushing joy
Here too my sisters played.
My mother kissed me here;
My father pressed my hand—
Forgive this foolish tear,
But let that old oak stand!

My heart-strings round thee cling,
Close as thy bark, old friend!
Here shall the wild-bird sing,
And still thy branches bend.
Old tree! The storm still brave!
And, woodman, leave the spot;
While I've a hand to save,
Thy axe shall hurt it not.

❧ "I will be heard"

WILLIAM LLOYD GARRISON

Walker's indictment of slavery helped generate a greater sense of urgency to the abolitionist movement. In 1831, William Lloyd Garrison began publishing *The Liberator,* an abolitionist newspaper demanding the end of slavery. He published *The Liberator* for thirty-four years, all the while pressing for abolition and expanding to embrace other reform movements such as womens' suffrage, prohibition and more humane treatment of Native Americans.

Garrison helped galvanize the abolitionist movement and became its leading spokesman. In 1833, he founded the American Anti-Slavery Society. He incensed Southern resentment. A $5,000 reward was offered by the state of Georgia for his arrest and conviction. But true to his inaugural issue, Garrison would not relent in his criticisms of slavery.

To THE PUBLIC.
In the month of August, I issued proposals for

publishing "THE LIBERATOR" in Washington city; but the enterprise, though hailed in different sections of the country, was palsied by public indifference. Since that time, the removal of the Genius of Universal Emancipation to the Seat of Government has rendered less imperious the establishment of a similar periodical in that quarter.

During my recent tour for the purpose of exciting the minds of the people by a series of discourses on the subject of slavery, every place that I visited gave fresh evidence of the fact, that a greater revolution in public sentiment was to be effected in the free states—and particularly in New England—than at the south. I found contempt more bitter, opposition more active, detraction more relentless, prejudice more stubborn, and apathy more frozen, than among slave owners themselves. Of course, there were individual exceptions to the contrary. This state of things afflicted, but did not dishearten me. I determined, at every hazard, to lift up the standard of emancipation in the eyes of the nation, within sight of Bunker Hill and in the birth place of liberty. That standard is now unfurled; and long may it float, unhurt by the spoliations of time or the missiles of a desperate foe—yea, till every chain be broken, and every bondman set free! Let southern oppressors tremble—let their secret abettors tremble—let their northern apologists tremble—let all the enemies of the persecuted blacks tremble.

I deem the publication of my original Prospectus unnecessary, as it has obtained a wide circulation. The principles therein inculcated will be steadily pursued in this paper, excepting that I shall not array myself as the political partisan of any man. In defending the great cause of human rights, I wish to derive the assistance of all religions and of all parties.

Assenting to the "self-evident truth" maintained in the American Declaration of Independence, "that all men are created equal, and endowed by their Creator with certain inalienable rights—among which are life, liberty and the pursuit of happiness," I shall strenuously contend for the immediate enfranchisement of our slave population. In Park-street Church, on the Fourth of July, 1829, in an address on slavery, I unreflectingly assented to the popular but pernicious doctrine of gradual abolition. I seize this opportunity to make a full and unequivocal recantation, and thus publicly to ask pardon of my God, of my country, and of my brethren the poor slaves, for having uttered a sentiment so full of timidity, injustice and absurdity. A similar recantation, from my pen, was published in the Genius of Universal Emancipation at Baltimore, in September, 1829. My conscience is now satisfied.

I am aware, that many object to the severity of my language; but is there not cause for severity? I will be as harsh as truth, and as uncompromising as justice. On this subject, I do not wish to think, or speak, or write, with moderation. No! no! Tell a man whose house is on fire, to give a moderate alarm; tell him to moderately rescue his wife from the hands of the ravisher; tell the mother to gradually extricate her babe from the fire into which it has fallen—but urge me not to use moderation in a cause like the present. I am in earnest—I will not equivocate—I will not excuse—I will not retreat a single inch—AND I WILL BE HEARD. The apathy of the people is enough to make every statue leap from its pedestal, and to hasten the resurrection of the dead.

It is pretended, that I am retarding the cause of emancipation by the coarseness of my invective, and the precipitancy of my measures. The charge is not true. On this question my influence—humble as it is—is felt at this moment to a considerable extent, and shall be felt in coming years—not perniciously, but beneficially—not as a curse, but as a blessing; and posterity will bear testimony that I was right. I desire to thank God, that he enables me to disregard "the fear of man which bringeth a snare," and to speak his truth in its simplicity and power.

And here I close with this fresh dedication:

"Oppression! I have seen thee, face to face,
And met thy cruel eye and cloudy brow;
But thy soul-withering glance I fear not now—
For dread to prouder feelings doth give place
Of deep abhorrence! Scorning the disgrace
Of slavish knees that at thy footstool bow,
I also kneel—but with far other bow
Do hail thee and thy herd of hirelings base:
I swear, while life-blood warms my throbbing veins,
Still to oppose and thwart, with heart and hand,
Thy brutalizing sway—till Africa's chains
Are burst, and Freedom rules the rescued land,
Trampling Oppression and his iron rod:
Such is the vow I take so HELP ME GOD!"

❧ "To live in comfort"

GJERT GREGORIUSSEN HOVLAND

Like thousands of European immigrants, Gjert Gregoriussen Hovland of Norway found opportunity in the United States. Having moved to western New York in 1831, he wrote back to his home country about the wisdom of the decision and the wonders of the new country. From 1790 to 1830 fewer than 400,000 Europeans moved to Europe. Over the next 30 years, however, the pace increased ten-fold—largely due to letters such as this, combined with famine in Ireland and political unrest in Germany.

I must take this opportunity to let you know that we are in the best of health, and that we—both my wife and I—find ourselves exceedingly well satisfied. Our son attends the English school and talks English as well as the native-born. Nothing has made me more happy and contented than the fact that we left Norway and journeyed to this country. We have gained more since our arrival here than I did during all the time that I lived in Norway, and I have every prospect of earning a livelihood here for myself and my family—even if my family were larger, so long as God gives me good health.

Such excellent plans have been developed here that, even though one be infirm, no one need suffer want. Competent men are elected whose duty it is to see that no needy persons, either in the cities or in the country, shall have to beg for their living. If a man dies and is survived by a widow and children who are unable to support themselves— they have the privilege of petitioning these officials. To each one will then be given every year as much as is needed of clothes and food, and no discrimination will be shown between the native-born and those from foreign countries. These things I have learned through daily observation, and I do not believe there can be better laws and arrangements for the benefit and happiness of the common man in the whole world.

No, everyone must work for his living here, and it makes no difference whether he is of low or of high estate. It would heartily please me if I could learn that everyone of you who are in need and have little chance of gaining support for yourselves and your families would make up your mind to leave Norway and to come to America, for, even if many more were to come, there would still be room

here for all. For all those who are willing to work there is no lack of employment and business here. It is possible for all to live in comfort and without suffering want.

❧ "The last should be first"

CONFESSIONS OF NAT TURNER

A charismatic slave minister, Nat Turner led a slave uprising in southeastern Virginia in 1831. The rebellion started with a band of five slaves that marched through the countryside murdering whites and attracting more than 75 followers. Sixty whites were killed before the rebellion was put down by the local militia. Nevertheless, the brutality of the uprising struck fear into the hearts of the South. Regional resolve to tighten control over slaves was bolstered. Turner and his followers were executed, but not before Thomas R. Gray interviewed Turner.

TURNER: And on the 12th of May, 1828, I heard a loud noise in the heavens, and the Spirit instantly appeared to me and said the Serpent was loosened, and Christ had laid down the yoke he had borne for the sins of men, and that I should take it on and fight against the Serpent, for the time was fast approaching when the first should be last and the last should be first.

GRAY: Do you not find yourself mistaken now?

TURNER: Was not Christ crucified? And by signs in the heavens that it would be made known to me when I should commence the great work—and until the first sign appeared, I should conceal it from the knowledge of men—And on the appearance of the sign (the eclipse of the sun last February), I should arise and prepare myself, and slay my enemies with their own weapons. And immediately on the sign appearing in the heavens, the seal was removed from my lips, and I communicated the great work laid out before me to do, to four in whom I had the greatest confidence (Henry, Hark, Nelson, and Sam)—It was intended by us to have begun the work of death on the 4th of July last—Many were the plans formed and rejected by us, and it affected my mind to such a degree, that I fell sick, and the time passed without our coming to any determination how to commence—Still forming new schemes and rejecting them, when the sign appeared again, which determined me not to wait longer.

Since the commencement of 1830, I had been

living with Mr. Joseph Travis, who was to me a kind master, and placed the greatest confidence in me: in fact, I had no cause to complain of his treatment of me. On Saturday evening, the 20th of August, it was agreed between Henry, Hark and myself, to prepare a dinner the next day for the men we expected, and then to concert a plan, as we had not yet determined on any. Hark, on the following morning, brought a pig, and Henry brandy, and being joined by Sam, Nelson, Will, and Jack, they prepared in the woods a dinner, where, about three o'clock, I joined them....

I saluted them on coming up, and asked Will how came he there, he answered, his life was worth no more than others, and his liberty as dear to him. I asked him if he thought to obtain it? He said he would, or lose his life. This was enough to put him in full confidence. Jack, I knew, was only a tool in the hands of Hark, it was quickly agreed we should commence at home (Mr. J. Travis') on that night, and until we had armed and equipped ourselves, and gathered sufficient force, neither age nor sex was to be spared (which was invariably adhered to). We remained at the feast, until about two hours in the night, when we went to the house and found Austin; they all went to the cider press and drank, except myself. On returning to the house Hark went to the door with an axe, for the purpose of breaking it open, as we knew we were strong enough to murder the family, if they were awakened by the noise; but reflecting that it might create an alarm in the neighborhood, we determined to enter the house secretly, and murder them whilst sleeping. Hark got a ladder and set it against the chimney, on which I ascended, and hoisting a window, entered and came down stairs, unbarred the door, and removed the guns from their places. It was then observed that I must spill the first blood. On which, armed with a hatchet, and accompanied by Will, I entered my master's chamber, it being dark, I could not give the death blow, the hatchet glanced from his head, he sprang from the bed and called his wife, it was his last word, Will laid him dead, with a blow of his axe, and Mrs. Travis shared the same fate, as she lay in bed. The murder of this family, five in number, was the work of a moment, not one of them awoke; there was a little infant sleeping in a cradle, that was forgotten, until we had left the house and gone some distance, when Henry and Will returned and killed it; we got here four guns that would shoot, and several old muskets, with a pound or two of powder. We remained some time at the barn, where we paraded; I formed them in a line as soldiers, and … carrying them through all the manoeuvres I was master of.

❧ The Free Enquirer

NEW HARMONY GAZETTE

The rise of industrialization in America requiring unskilled labor, combined with a shortage of labor led to the widespread use of child labor. Children 12 years old and younger worked 12 to 14 hour days. The abuse of children prompted sharp criticism, including from the pro-slavery South which noted the hypocrisy of Northern abolitionists.

This poem, entitled "The Free Enquirer," was published in *New Harmony Gazette* in 1832. It expressed the plight of young factory workers. Starting in 1837, states began passing child labor legislation setting minimum ages and hours for child labor in manufacturing industries.

I often think how once we used in summer fields to
    play,
And run about and breathe the air that made us
    glad and gay;
We used to gather buttercups and chase the
    butterfly;
I loved to feel the light breeze lift my hair as it
    went by!

Do you still play in those bright fields? And are the
    flowers still there?
There are no fields where I live now—no flowers
    any where!
But day by day I go and turn a dull and tedious
    wheel;
You cannot think how sad, and tired, and faint I
    often feel.

I hurry home to snatch the meal my mother can
    supply,
Then back I hasten to the task—that not to hate I
    try.
At night my mother kisses me, when she has
    combed my hair,
And laid me in my little bed, but—I'm not happy
    there:

I dream about the factory, the fines that on us
    wait—

I start and ask my father if—I have not lain too
    late?
And once I heard him sob and say—"Oh, better
    were a grave,
Than such a life as this for thee, thou little sinless
    slave!"

I wonder if I ever shall obtain a holiday?
Oh, if I do, I'll go to you and spend it all in play!
And then I'd bring some flowers home, if you will
    give me some,
And at my work I'll think of them and holidays to
    come!

America

SAMUEL SMITH

Set to the music of the British national anthem "God Save
the King," the song "America" was introduced in Boston on
July 4, 1832. The Reverend Samuel F. Smith had written it.
He later said he had no intentions or expectations for it to
become a national hymn for the United States. But he was
wrong. "America" was and remains a popular patriotic song.

My country 'tis of thee
Sweet land of liberty:
Of thee I sing.
Land where my fathers died
Land of the pilgrims' pride
From every mountainside
Let freedom ring.
My native country—thee
Land of the noble free
Thy name I love;
I love thy rocks and rills
Thy woods and templed hills
My heart with rapture thrills
Like that above.
Let music swell the breeze
And ring from all the trees
Sweet freedom's song
Let all that breathe partake
Let mortal tongues awake
Let rocks their silence break
The sound prolong.
Our fathers' God to thee
Author of liberty
To thee we sing
Long may our land be bright

With freedom's holy light
Protect us by thy might
Great God, our King.

Reply to Jackson's bank veto

DANIEL WEBSTER

On July 10, 1832, President Andrew Jackson vetoed
Congress's attempt to renew the charter of the Second Bank
of the United States. Jackson objected to the government's
participation in a bank that enriched a handful of shareholders, included foreign participation and indebted western
farmers to the eastern business establishment. He declared
the national bank undemocratic and unconstitutional.

While Jackson's tough stance against money interests
engendered popular support, it enraged bank proponents
such as Massachusetts Senator Daniel Webster who delivered this stinging reply to Jackson's veto message the next
day in Congress. Webster argued that a national bank was
critical to the country's economic prosperity, predicting economic doom and the disintegration of the Constitution.

Jackson's veto prevailed. He transferred government funds
from the national institution to state banks. The head of the
Second Bank of the United States responded by calling in commercial loans, triggering a financial panic that plunged the country into recession, thus fulfilling half of Webster's prophecy.

I will not conceal my opinion that the affairs of the
country are approaching an important and dangerous crisis. At the very moment of almost unparalleled general prosperity, there appears an unaccountable disposition to destroy the most useful
and most approved institutions of the government.
Indeed, it seems to be in the midst of all this
national happiness that some are found openly to
question the advantages of the Constitution itself;
and many more ready to embarrass the exercise of
its just power, weaken its authority, and undermine
its foundations. How far these notions may be carried, it is impossible to say. We have before us the
practical result of one of them. The bank has fall-
en, or is to fall....
    The responsibility justly lies with [the
President], and there it ought to remain. A great
majority of the people are satisfied with the bank as
it is, and desirous that it should be continued. They
wished no change. The strength of this public sentiment has carried the bill through Congress,
against all the influence of the administration, and

all the power of organized party. But the President has undertaken, on his own responsibility, to arrest the measure, by refusing his assent to the bill. He is answerable for the consequences, therefore, which necessarily follow the change which the expiration of the bank charter may produce; and if these consequences shall prove disastrous, they can fairly be ascribed to his policy only, and the policy of his administration.

The bill was not passed for the purpose of benefiting the present stockholders. Their benefit, if any, is incidental and collateral. Nor was it passed on any idea that they had a right to a renewed charter, although the message argues against such right, as if it had been somewhere set up and asserted. No such right has been asserted by any body. Congress passed the bill, not as a bounty or a favor to the present stockholders, nor to comply with any demand of right on their part; but to promote great public interests, for great public objects. Every bank must have some stockholders, unless it be such a bank as the President has recommended, and in regard to which he seems not likely to find much concurrence of other men's opinions; and if the stockholders, whoever they may be, conduct the affairs of the bank prudently, the expectation is always, of course, that they will make it profitable to themselves, as well as useful to the public. If a bank charter is not to be granted, because, to some extent, it may be profitable to the stockholders, no charters can be granted. The objection lies against all banks.

Sir, the object aimed at by such institutions is to connect the public safety and convenience with private interests. It has been found by experience, that banks are safest under private management, and that government banks are among the most dangerous of all inventions. Now, Sir, the whole drift of the message is to reverse the settled judgment of all the civilized world, and to set up government banks, independent of private interest or private control. For this purpose the message labors, even beyond the measure of all its other labors, to create jealousies and prejudices, on the ground of the alleged benefit which individuals will derive from the renewal of this charter. Much less effort is made to show that government, or the public, will be injured by the bill, than that individuals will profit by it....

The President is as much bound by the law as any private citizen, and can nor more contest its validity than any private citizen. He may refuse to obey the law, and so may a private citizen; but both do it at their own peril, and neither of them can settle the question of its validity. The President may say a law is unconstitutional, but he is not the judge. Who is to decide that question? The judiciary alone possesses this unquestionable and hitherto unquestioned right. The judiciary is the constitutional tribunal of appeal for the citizens, against both Congress and the executive, in regard to the constitutionality of laws. It has this jurisdiction expressly conferred upon it, and when it has decided the question, its judgment must, from the very nature of all judgments that are final, and from which there is no appeal, be conclusive....

[We] have arrived at a new epoch. We are entering on experiments, with the government and the Constitution of the country, hitherto untried, and of fearful and appalling aspect. This message calls us to the contemplation of a future which little resembles the past.... It appeals to every prejudice which may betray men into a mistaken view of their own interests, and to every passion which may lead them to disobey the impulses of their understanding. It urges all the specious topics of State rights and national encroachment against that which a great majority of the States have affirmed to be rightful, and in which all of them have acquiesced. It sows, in an unsparing manner, the seeds of jealousy and ill-will against that government of which its author is the official head. It raises a cry, that liberty is in danger, at the very moment when it puts forth claims to powers heretofore unknown and unheard of. It affects alarm for the public freedom, when nothing endangers that freedom so much as its own unparalleled pretences. This, even, is not all. It manifestly seeks to inflame the poor against the rich; it wantonly attacks whole classes of the people, for the purpose of turning against them the prejudices and the resentment of other classes. It is a state paper which finds no topic too exciting for its use, no passion too inflammable for its address and its solicitation.

Such is this message. It remains now for the people of the United States to choose between the principles here avowed and their government. These cannot subsist together. The one or the other must be rejected. If the sentiments of the message shall receive general approbation, the Constitution will have perished even earlier than the moment which its enemies originally allowed for the termination of its existence. It will not have survived to its fiftieth year.

❧ "Compared to disunion all other evils are light"

ANDREW JACKSON

In July 1832 Congress passed a tariff aimed at protecting northern manufacturers from foreign competition. The effect on the South was to increase the cost of domestic products and stifle trade. On November 24 the South Carolina Legislature issued an "Ordinance of Nullification" declaring the tariffs of 1828 and 1832 null and void in South Carolina. The ordinance made it illegal for anyone in South Carolina to execute the provisions of the tariff and defied the federal government to impose the tariff in South Carolina.

President Andrew Jackson, who was born in South Carolina and sympathized with the Southern perspective, responded to the ordinance with his own "Proclamation to the People of South Carolina" stating that the tariff would be imposed and that states did not have the right to defy federal laws. After outlining the fundamental constitutional issues involved in his decision, he then advised South Carolina that it would have more to gain as part of the United States then as a separate sovereignty, despite the inequity of the tariff.

South Carolina continued its defiance, yielding only after a compromise bill was passed by Congress in spring of 1833. However, the strains of conflict between South and North were becoming more and more apparent. The needs of the divergent economies of the manufacturing North and the agricultural, commodity-based South would continue to clash, culminating in the Civil War.

Whereas the said ordinance prescribes to the people of South Carolina a course of conduct in direct violation of their duty as citizens of the United States, contrary to the laws of their country, subversive of its Constitution, and having for its object the destruction of the Union—that Union which, coeval with our political existence, led our fathers, without any other ties to unite them than those of patriotism and a common cause, through a sanguinary struggle to a glorious independence; that sacred Union, hitherto inviolate, which, perfected by our happy Constitution, has brought us, by the favor of heaven, to a state of prosperity at home and high consideration abroad rarely, if ever, equaled in the history of nations:

To preserve this bond of our political existence from destruction, to maintain inviolate this state of national honor and prosperity, and to justify the confidence my fellow-citizens have reposed in me, I, Andrew Jackson, President of the United States, have thought proper to issue this my proclamation, stating my views of the Constitution and laws applicable to the measures adopted by the convention of South Carolina and to the reasons they have put forth to sustain them, declaring the course which duty will require me to pursue, and, appealing to the understanding and patriotism of the people, warn them of the consequences that must inevitably result from an observance of the dictates of the convention.

The ordinance is founded, not on the indefensible right of resisting acts which are plainly unconstitutional and too oppressive to be endured, but on the strange position that any one State may not only declare an act of Congress void, but prohibit its execution; that they may do this consistently with the Constitution. That the true construction of that instrument permits a state to retain its place in the Union and yet be bound by no other of its laws than those it may choose to consider as constitutional. It is true, they add, that to justify this abrogation of a law it must be palpably contrary to the Constitution; but it is evident that to give the right of resisting laws of that description, coupled with the uncontrolled right to decide what laws deserve that character, is to give the power of resisting all laws; for as by the theory there is no appeal, the reasons alleged by the State, good or bad, must prevail....

If this doctrine had been established at an earlier day, the Union would have been dissolved in its infancy. The excise law in Pennsylvania, the embargo and nonintercourse law in the Eastern States, the carriage tax in Virginia, were all deemed unconstitutional, and were more unequal in their operation than any of the laws now complained of; but, fortunately, none of those States discovered that they had the right now claimed by South Carolina. The war into which we were forced to support the dignity of the nation and the rights of our citizens might have ended in defeat and disgrace, instead of victory and honor, if the States who supposed it a ruinous and unconstitutional measure had thought they possessed the right of nullifying the act by which it was declared and denying supplies for its prosecution. Hardly and unequally as those measures bore upon several members of the Union, to the legislatures of none did this efficient and peaceable remedy, as it is called, suggest itself. The discovery of this important feature in our Constitution was reserved to the present day. To the statesmen of South Carolina belongs the invention, and upon the citizens of that State will unfortunately fall the evils of reducing it to practice....

The right to secede is deduced from the nature of the Constitution, which, they say, is a compact between sovereign States who have preserved their whole sovereignty and therefore are subject to no superior; that because they made the compact they can break it when in their opinion it has been departed from by the other States. Fallacious as this course of reasoning is, it enlists State pride and finds advocates in the honest prejudices of those who have not studied the nature of our Government sufficiently to see the radical error on which it rests.

The people of the United States formed the Constitution, acting through the State legislatures in making the compact, to meet and discuss its provisions, and acting in separate conventions when they ratified those provisions; but the terms used in its construction show it to be a Government in which the people of all the States, collectively, are represented. We are one people in the choice of President and Vice-President. Here the States have no other agency to direct the mode in which the votes shall be given. The candidates having the majority of all the votes are chosen. The electors of a majority of States may have given their votes for one candidate, and yet another may be chosen. The people, then, and not the States, are represented in the executive branch.

In the House of Representatives there is this difference, that the people of one State do not, as in the case of President and Vice-President, all vote for the same officers. The people of all the States do not vote for all the members, each State electing only its own representatives. But this creates no material distinction. When chosen, they are all representatives of the United States, not representatives of the particular State from which they come. They are paid by the United States, not by the State; nor are they accountable to it for any act done in the performance of their legislative functions; and however

they may in practice, as it is their duty to do, consult and prefer the interests of their particular constituents when they come in conflict with any other partial or local interest, to promote the general good.

The Constitution of the United States, then, forms a government, not a league; and whether it be formed by compact between the States or in any other manner, its character is the same. It is a Government in which all the people are represented, which operates directly on the people individually, not upon the States; they retained all the power they did not grant. But each State, having expressly parted with so many powers as to constitute, jointly with other States, a single nation, can not, from that period, possess any right to secede, because such secession does not break a league, but destroys the unity of a nation; and any injury to that unity is not only a breach which would result from the contravention of a compact, but it is an offense against the whole Union. To say that any State may at pleasure secede from the Union is to say that the United States are not a nation, because it would be a solecism to contend that any part of a nation might dissolve its connection with the other parts, to their injury or ruin, without committing any offense. Secession, like any other revolutionary act, may be morally justified by the extremity of oppression; but to call it a constitutional right is confounding the meaning of terms, and can only be done through gross error to deceive those who are willing to assert a right, but would pause before they made a revolution or incur the penalties consequent on a failure.

Because the Union was formed by a compact, it is said the parties to that compact may, when they feel themselves aggrieved, depart from it; but it is precisely because it is a compact that they can not. A compact is an agreement or binding obligation. It may by its terms have a sanction or penalty for its breach, or it may not. If it contains no sanction, it may be broken with no other consequence than moral guilt; if it have a sanction, then the breach incurs the designated or implied penalty....

Fellow citizens of my native State, let me not only admonish you, as the First Magistrate of our common country, not to incur the penalty of its laws, but use the influence that a father would over his children whom he saw rushing to certain ruin. In that paternal language, with that paternal feeling, let me tell you, my countrymen, that you are deluded by men who are either deceived themselves or wish to deceive you. Mark under what pretenses you have been led on to the brink of insurrection and treason on which you stand…. Let those among your leaders who once approved and advocated the principle of protective duties answer the question; and let them choose whether they will be considered as incapable then of perceiving or as imposing upon your confidence and endeavoring to mislead you now. In either case they are unsafe guides in the perilous path they urge you to tread. Ponder well on this circumstance, and you will know how to appreciate the exaggerated language they address to you. They are not champions of liberty, emulating the fame of our Revolutionary fathers, nor are you an oppressed people, contending, as they repeat to you, against worse than colonial vassalage. You are free members of a flourishing and happy Union. There is no settled design to oppress you. You have indeed felt the unequal operation of laws which may have been unwisely, not unconstitutionally, passed; but that inequality must necessarily be removed. At the very moment when you were madly urged on to the unfortunate course you have begun a change in public opinion had commenced. The nearly approaching payments of the public debt and the consequent necessity of a diminution of duties had already produced a considerable reduction, and that, too, on some articles of general consumption in your State….

I adjure you, as you honor their memory, as you love the cause of freedom, to which they dedicated their lives, as you prize the peace of your country, the lives of its best citizens, and your own fair fame, to retrace your steps. Snatch from the archives of your State the disorganizing edict of its convention; bid its members to reassemble and promulgate the decided expressions of your will to remain in the path which alone can conduct you to safety, prosperity, and honor. Tell them that compared to disunion all other evils are light, because that brings with it an accumulation of all. Declare that you will never take the field unless the star-spangled banner of your country shall float over you; that you will not be stigmatized when dead, and dishonored and scorned while you live, as the authors of the first attack on the Constitution of your country. Its destroyers you can not be.

❧ "Sending many a redskin to his long home"

KIT CARSON

Christopher "Kit" Carson was born on the Kentucky frontier in 1809 and lived his life as a scout, trapper, Indian fighter and adventurer in the West. He helped lead several expeditions by explorer John C. Fremont who mapped overland trails to California and Oregon. In his autobiography Carson recalled some of his experiences to a public eager to read about the adventure and romance of the West.

In January, 1833, a party of men who had been out hunting returned about dark. Their horses were very poor, having been fed during the winter on cottonwood bark, and they turned them out to gather such nourishment as they could find. That night a party of about fifty Crow Indians came to our camp and stole nine of the horses that were loose. In the morning we discovered sign of the Indians and twelve of us took the trail and traveled about forty miles. It was getting late. Our animals were fatigued for the snow was deep, and the passing of many herds of buffaloes during the day caused us a great deal of difficulty in keeping the trail. At length we saw a grove of timber at a distance of two or three miles. Taking into consideration the condition of our animals, we concluded to make for it and camp for the night. On our arrival, however, we saw fires about four miles ahead of us. We tied our animals to trees, and as soon as it became dark, took a circuitous route for the Indian camp.

We planned to come upon the Indians from the direction in which they were traveling. It took us some time to get close enough to the camp to discover their strength, as we had to crawl, and use all the means that we were aware of to elude detection. After maneuvering in this direction for some time, we came within about one hundred yards of their camp. The Indians were in two forts of about equal strength. They were dancing and singing, and passing the night jovially in honor of their robbery of the whites. We spied our horses, which were tied near the entrance of one of the forts. Let come what would, we were bound to get them. We remained concealed in the brush, suffering severely from the cold, until the Indians laid down to sleep.

When we thought they were all asleep, six of

us crawled towards our animals, the rest remaining where they were as a reserve for us to fall back on in case we did not meet with success. We hid behind logs and crawled silently towards the fort, the snow being of great service to us for when crawling we were not liable to make any noise. We finally reached the horses, cut the ropes, and by throwing snow balls at them drove them to where our reserve was stationed. We then held a council, taking the views of each in regard to what had best be done. Some were in favor of retiring; having recovered their property and received no damage, they were willing to return to camp. Not so with those that had lost no animals. They wanted satisfaction for the trouble and hardships they had gone through while in pursuit of the thieves. Myself and two others were the only ones that had not lost horses and we were determined to have satisfaction, let the consequences be ever so fatal. The peace party could not get a convert to their side. Seeing us so determined to fight (there is always a brotherly affection existing among trappers and the side of danger is always their choice), it was not long before all agreed to join us in our perilous enterprise.

We started the horses that had been retaken to the place where we had tied our other animals, with three of our men acting as an escort. We then marched directly for the fort from which we had taken our horses. When we were within a few paces of it, a dog discovered us and began to bark. The Indians were alarmed and commenced to get up, when we opened a deadly fire, each ball taking its victim. We killed nearly every Indian in the fort. The few that remained were wounded and made their escape to the other fort, whose inmates commenced firing on us, but without any effect, since we kept concealed behind trees, firing only when we were sure of our object. It was now near day, and the Indians could see our force, which was so weak they concluded to charge on us. We received them calmly, and when they got very close fired on them, killing five, and the balance returned to their fort. After some deliberation among themselves, they finally made another attempt, which met with greater success. We had to retreat, but there was much timber in the vicinity, and we had but little difficulty in making our camp, where, being reinforced by the three men with the horses, we awaited the approach of the enemy. Since they did not attack us, we started for our main camp and arrived there in the evening. During our pursuit of the lost animals we suffered considerably, but in the success of recovering our horses and sending many a redskin to his long home, our sufferings were soon forgotten. We remained in our camp without any further molestation until spring, when we started for Laramie River on another trapping expedition.

"We are menaced by our old enemies, avarice and ambition"

WILLIAM LEGGETT

As the assistant editor of the *New York Evening Post,* the radical politician-poet William Leggett provided one of the most vitriolic voices against the concentration of wealth in the 1830s. This 1834 editorial expresses simmering resentments against special privilege that helped fuel Jackson's rise to power.

The rich perceive, acknowledge, and act upon a common interest, and why not the poor? Yet the moment the latter are called upon to combine for the preservation of their rights, forsooth the community is in danger. Property is no longer secure and life in jeopardy. This cant has descended to us from those times when the poor and laboring classes had no stake in the community and no rights except such as they could acquire by force. But the times have changed though the cant remains the same. The scrip nobility of this Republic have adopted towards the free people of this Republic the same language which the feudal barons and the despot who contested with them the power of oppressing the people used towards their serfs and villains, as they were opprobriously called.

These would-be lordlings of the Paper Dynasty cannot or will not perceive that there is some difference in the situation and feelings of the people of the United States and those of the despotic governments of Europe. They forget that at this moment our people—we mean emphatically the class which labors with its own hands—is in possession of a greater portion of the property and intelligence of this country, ay, ten times over, than all the creatures of the "paper credit system" put together. This property is indeed more widely and equally distributed among the people than among the phantoms of the paper system, and so much the better. And as to their intelligence, let any man talk with them, and if he does not learn something it is his own fault. They are as well acquainted with the rights of person and property and have as just a regard for them as the most illustrious lordling of the scrip nobility. And why should they not? Who and what are the great majority of the wealthy people of this city, we may say of this country? Are they not—we say it not in disparagement, but in high commendation—are they not men who began the world comparatively poor with ordinary education and ordinary means? And what should make them so much wiser than their neighbors? Is it because they live in better style, ride in carriages, and have more money or at least more credit than their poorer neighbors? Does a man become wiser, stronger, or more virtuous and patriotic because he has a fine house over his head? Does he love his country the better because he has a French cook and a box at the opera? Or does he grow more learned, logical, and profound by intense study of the daybook, ledger, bills of exchange, bank promises, and notes of hand?

Of all the countries on the face of the earth or that ever existed on the face of the earth, this is the one where the claims of wealth and aristocracy are the most unfounded, absurd, and ridiculous. With no claim to hereditary distinctions, with no exclusive rights except what they derive from monopolies, and no power of perpetuating their estates in their posterity, the assumption of aristocratic airs and claims is supremely ridiculous. Tomorrow they themselves may be beggars for aught they know, or at all events their children may become so. Their posterity in the second generation will have to begin the world again and work for a living as did their forefathers. And yet the moment a man becomes rich among us, he sets up for wisdom; he despises the poor and ignorant; he sets up for patriotism; he is your only man who has a stake in the community and therefore the only one who ought to have a voice in the state. What folly is this? And how contemptible his presumption? He is not a whit wiser, better, or more patriotic than when he commenced the world, a wagon driver. Nay, not half so patriotic, for he would see his country disgraced a thousand times rather than see one fall of the stocks, unless perhaps he had been speculating on such a contingency. To him a victory is only of consequence as it raises, and a defeat only to be lamented as it depresses a loan. His soul is Wrapped up in a certificate of scrip or a bank note. Witness the conduct of these pure patriots during the late War, when they, at least a large proportion of them, not only withheld all their support from the Government but used all their influence to prevent others from giving their assistance. Yet these are the people who alone have a stake in the community and, of course, exclusively monopolize patriotism.

But let us ask what and where is the danger of a combination of the laboring classes in vindication of their political principles or in defense of their menaced rights? Have they not the right to act in concert when their opponents act in concert? Nay, is it not their bounden duty to combine against the only enemy they have to fear as yet in this free country: monopoly and a great paper system that grinds them to the dust? Truly, this is strange republican doctrine, and this is a strange republican country, where men cannot unite in one common effort, in one common cause, without rousing the cry of danger to the rights of person and property. Is not this a government of the people, founded on the rights of the people, and instituted for the express object of guarding them against the encroachments and usurpations of power? And if they are not permitted the possession of common interest, the exercise of a common feeling, if they cannot combine to resist by constitutional means these encroachments, to what purpose were they declared free to exercise the right of suffrage in the choice of rulers and the making of laws?

And what, we ask, is the power against which the people not only of this country but of almost all Europe are called upon to array themselves, and the encroachment on their rights they are summoned to resist? Is it not emphatically the power of monopoly and the encroachments of corporate privileges of every kind which the cupidity of the rich engenders to the injury of the poor?

It was to guard against the encroachments of power, the insatiate ambition of wealth, that this government was instituted by the people themselves. But the objects which call for the peculiar jealousy and watchfulness of the people are not now what they once were. The cautions of the early writers in favor of the liberties of mankind have in some measure become obsolete and inapplicable. We are menaced by our old enemies, avarice and ambition, under a new name and form. The tyrant is changed from a steel-clad feudal baron or a minor despot, at the head of thousands of ruffian followers, to a mighty civil gentleman who comes mincing and bowing to the people with a quill behind his ear, at the head of countless millions of magnificent promises. He promises to make everybody rich; he promises to pave cities with gold; and he promises to pay. In short he is made up of promises.

He will do wonders such as never were seen or heard of, provided the people will only allow him to make his promises equal to silver and gold and human labor, and grant him the exclusive benefits of all the great blessings he intends to confer on them. He is the sly, selfish, grasping and insatiable tyrant the people are now to guard against. A concentrated money power; a usurper in the disguise of a benefactor; an agent exercising privileges which his principal never possessed; an impostor who, while he affects to wear chains, is placed above those who are free; a chartered libertine that pretends to be manacled only that he may the more safely pick our pockets and lord it over our rights. This is the enemy we are now to encounter and overcome before we can expect to enjoy the substantial realities of freedom.

✏️ "The dangers from Popery"

SAMUEL F. B. MORSE

A wave of Irish and German immigrants started to arrive in the United States in the 1830s. Many longstanding citizens reacted in horror. Nativism swept parts of New England. Complaints arose that the new residents drank too much, drove wages down and incited crime. A strain of intolerance emerged especially against Catholic immigrants. Natives such as Samuel Morse (who would invent the telegraph in 1844) believed the Catholic religion was at odds with democratic principles and would undermine the country. Although Morse's 1835 article against "Popery" did not advocate violence against Catholics, riots and fights did break out as a result of its publication.

I deem it a duty to warn the Christian community against the temptation to which they were exposed, in guarding against the political dangers arising from Popery could invite or force them, it might keep a jubilee, for its triumph would be sure. The propensity to resist by unlawful means the encroachments of an enemy, because that enemy uses such means against us, belongs to human nature. We are very apt to think, in the irritation of being attacked, that we may lawfully hurl back the darts of a foe, whatever may be their character; that we may "fight the Devil with fire," instead of the milder, yet more effective weapon of "the Lord rebuke thee." The same spirit of Christianity which forbids us to return railing for railing, and persecution for persecution, forbids the use of unlawful or even doubtful means of defence, merely because an enemy uses them to attack us. If Popery, (as is unblushingly the case,) organizes itself at our elections, it interferes politically and sells itself to this or that political demagogue or party, it should be remembered that this is notoriously the true character of Popery. It is its nature. It cannot act otherwise. Intrigue is its appropriate business. But all this foreign to Christianity. Christianity must not enter the political arena with Popery, nor be mailed in Popish armor. The weapons and stratagems of Popery suit not with the simplicity and frankness of Christianity....

But whilst deprecating a union of religious sects to act politically against Popery, I must not be misunderstood as recommending no political opposition to Popery by the American community. I have endeavored to rouse Protestants to a renewed and more vigorous use of their religious weapons in their moral war with Popery, but I am not unmindful of another duty, the political duty, which the double character of Popery makes it necessary to urge upon American citizens, with equal force, the imperious duty of defending the distinctive principles of our civil government. It must be sufficiently manifest to every republican citizen that the civil polity of Popery is in direct opposition to all which he deems sacred in government. He must perceive that Popery cannot from its very nature tolerate any of those civil rights which are the peculiar boast of Americans. Should Popery increase but for a little time longer in this country with the alarming rapidity with which, as authentic statistics testify, it is advancing at the present time, (and it must not be forgotten that despotism in Europe, in its desperate struggles for existence, is lending its powerful aid to the enterprise) we may even in this generation learn by sad experience what common sagacity and ordinary research might now teach, in time to arrest the evil, that Popery cannot tolerate our form of government in any of its essential principles.

Popery does not acknowledge the right of the people to govern; but claims for itself the supreme right to govern all people and all rulers by divine right.

It does not tolerate the Liberty of the Press; it takes advantage indeed of our liberty of the press to use its own press against our liberty; but it proclaims in the thunders of the Vatican, and with a voice which it pronounces infallible and unchangeable, that it is a liberty "never sufficiently to be execrated and detested."

It does not tolerate liberty of conscience nor liberty of opinion. The one is denounced by the Sovereign Pontiff as "a most pestilential error," and the other, "a pest of all others most to be dreaded in a state."

It is not responsible to the people in its financial matters. It taxes at will, and is accountable to none but itself.

Now these are political tenets held by Papists in close union with their religious belief, yet these are not religious but civil tenets; they belong to despotic government. Conscience cannot be pleaded against our dealing politically with them. They are separable from religious belief; and if Papists will separate them, and repudiate these noxious principles, and teach and act accordingly, the political duty of exposing and opposing Papists, on the ground of the enmity of their political tenets to our republican government, will cease. But can they do it? If they can, it behoves them to do it without delay. If they cannot, or will not, let them not complain of religious persecution, or of religious intolerance, if this republican people, when it shall wake to a sense of the danger that threatens its blood-bought institutions, shall rally to their defence with some show of indignation. Let them not whine about religious oppression, if the democracy turns its searching eye upon this secret treason to the state, and shall in future scrutinize with something of suspicion, the professions of those foreign friends, who are so ready to rush to a fraternal embrace. Let them not raise the cry of religious proscription, if American republicans shall stamp an indelible brand upon the liveried slaves of a foreign despot,… who now sheltered behind the shield of our religious liberty, dream of security, while sapping the foundations of our civil government…. America may for a time, sleep soundly, as innocence is wont to sleep, unsuspicious of hostile attack; but if any foreign power, jealous of the increasing strength of the embryo giant, sends its serpents to lurk within his cradle, let such presumption be assured that the waking energies of the infant are not to be despised, that once having grasped his foes, he will neither be tempted from his hold by admiration of their painted and gilded covering, nor by fear of the fatal embrace of their treacherous folds.

❧ "The Spirit of God breathes through the combined intelligence of the people"

GEORGE BANCROFT

The first major American historian and author of *History of the United States,* George Bancroft provided the Jacksonian democracy movement with intellectual force. In this 1835 address at Williams College, Bancroft expressed his faith in the ultimate wisdom of public opinion versus the knowledge of individuals, no matter how expert they may be.

The best government rests on the people and not on the few, on persons and not on property, on the free development of public opinion and not on authority; because the munificent Author of our being has conferred the gifts of mind upon every member of the human race without distinction of outward circumstances. Whatever of other possessions may be engrossed, mind asserts its own independence. Lands, estates, the produce of mines, the prolific abundance of the seas, may be usurped by a privileged class. Avarice, assuming the form of ambitious power, may grasp realm after realm, subdue continents, compass the earth in its schemes of aggrandizement, and sigh after other worlds; but mind eludes the power of appropriation; it exists only in its own individuality; it is a property which cannot be confiscated and cannot be torn away; it laughs at chains; it bursts from imprisonment; it defies monopoly. A government of equal rights must, therefore, rest upon mind; not wealth, not brute force, the sum of the moral intelligence of the community should rule the State. Prescription can no more assume to be a valid plea for political injustice; society studies to eradicate established abuses, and to bring social institutions and laws into harmony with moral right; not dismayed by the natural and necessary imperfections of all human effort, and not giving way to despair, because every hope does not at once ripen into fruit.

The public happiness is the true object of legislation, and can be secured only by the masses of mankind themselves awakening to the knowledge and the care of their own interests. Our free institutions have reversed the false and ignoble distinctions between men; and refusing to gratify the pride of caste, have acknowledged the common mind to be the true material for a commonwealth. Every thing has hitherto been done for the happy few. It is not possible to endow an aristocracy with greater benefits than they have already enjoyed; there is no room to hope that individuals will be more highly gifted or more fully developed than the greatest sages of past times. The world can advance only through the culture of the moral and intellectual powers of the people. To accomplish this end by means of the people themselves is the highest purpose of government. If it be the duty of the individual to strive after a perfection like the perfection of God, how much more ought a nation to be the image of Deity. The common mind is the true Parian marble, fit to be wrought into likeness to a God. The duty of America is to secure the culture and the happiness of the masses by their reliance on themselves.

The absence of the prejudices of the old world leaves us here the opportunity of consulting independent truth; and man is left to apply the instinct of freedom to every social relation and public interest. We have approached so near to nature, that we can hear her gentlest whispers; we have made Humanity our lawgiver and our oracle; and, therefore, the nation receives, vivifies and applies principles, which in Europe the wisest accept with distrust. Freedom of mind and of conscience, freedom of the seas, freedom of industry, equality of fran-

chises, each great truth is firmly grasped, comprehended and enforced; for the multitude is neither rash nor fickle. In truth, it is less fickle than those who profess to be its guides. Its natural dialectics surpass the logic of the schools. Political action has never been so consistent and so unwavering, as when it results from a feeling or a principle, diffused through society. The people is firm and tranquil in its movements, and necessarily acts with moderation, because it becomes but slowly impregnated with new ideas; and effects no changes, except in harmony with the knowledge which it has acquired. Besides, where it is permanently possessed of power, there exists neither the occasion nor the desire for frequent change. It is not the parent of tumult; sedition is bred in the lap of luxury, and its chosen emissaries are the beggared spendthrift and the impoverished libertine. The government by the people is in very truth the strongest government in the world. Discarding the implements of terror, it dares to rule by moral force, and has its citadel in the heart.

Such is the political system which rests on reason, reflection, and the free expression of deliberate choice. There may be those who scoff at the suggestion, that the decision of the whole is to be preferred to the judgment of the enlightened few. They say in their hearts that the masses are ignorant; that farmers know nothing of legislation; that mechanics should not quit their workshops to join in forming public opinion. But true political science does indeed venerate the masses. It maintains, not as has been perversely asserted, that "the people can make right," but that the people can DISCERN right. Individuals are but shadows, too often engrossed by the pursuit of shadows; the race is immortal: individuals are of limited sagacity; the common mind is infinite in its experience: individuals are languid and blind; the many are ever wakeful: individuals are corrupt; the race has been redeemed: individuals are time-serving; the masses are fearless: individuals may be false, the masses are ingenuous and sincere: individuals claim the divine sanction of truth for the deceitful conceptions of their own fancies; the Spirit of God breathes through the combined intelligence of the people. Truth is not to be ascertained by the impulses of an individual; it emerges from the contradictions of personal opinions; it raises itself in majestic serenity above the strifes of parties and the conflict of sects; it acknowledges neither the solitary mind, nor the separate faction as its oracle; but owns as its only faithful interpreter the dictates of pure reason itself, proclaimed by the general voice of mankind. The decrees of the universal conscience are the nearest approach to the presence of God in the soul of man.

Thus the opinion which we respect is, indeed, not the opinion of one or of a few, but the sagacity of the many. It is hard for the pride of cultivated philosophy to put its ear to the ground, and listen reverently to the voice of lowly humanity; yet the people collectively are wiser than the most gifted individual, for all his wisdom constitutes but a part of theirs. When the great sculptor of Greece was endeavoring to fashion the perfect model of beauty, he did not passively imitate the form of the loveliest woman of his age; but he gleaned the several lineaments of his faultless work from the many. And so it is, that a perfect judgment is the result of comparison, when error eliminates error, and truth is established by concurring witnesses. The organ of truth is the invisible decision of the unbiased world; she pleads before no tribunal but public opinion; she owns no safe interpreter but the common mind; she knows no court of appeals but the soul of humanity. It is when the multitude give counsel, that right purposes find safety; theirs is the fixedness that cannot be shaken; theirs is the understanding which exceeds in wisdom; theirs is the heart, of which the largeness is as the sand on the sea-shore.

It is not by vast armies, by immense natural resources, by accumulations of treasure, that the greatest results in modern civilization have been accomplished. The traces of the career of conquest pass away, hardly leaving a scar on the national intelligence. The famous battle grounds of victory are, most of them, comparatively indifferent to the human race; barren fields of blood, the scourges of their times, but affecting the social condition as little as the raging of a pestilence. Not one benevolent nor one ameliorating principle in the Roman state, was a voluntary concession of the aristocracy; each useful element was borrowed from the Democracies of Greece, or was a reluctant concession to the demands of the people. The same is true in modern political life. It is the confession of an enemy to Democracy, that "ALL THE GREAT AND NOBLE INSTITUTIONS OF THE WORLD HAVE COME FROM POPULAR EFFORTS."

🌿 "The power of the people are disseminated"

ALEXIS DE TOCQUEVILLE

Like many curious Europeans in the 19th century, Alexis de Tocqueville visited the United States and wrote about his experiences. He published his book *Democracy in America* in 1835, offering an especially insightful analysis of the American psyche. Tocqueville—a politician himself—was impressed by the remarkable success the United States enjoyed in making democracy work. Two of the underpinnings of that strength, he observed, were freedom of the press and the respect for the law that prevailed.

Liberty of the Press

The influence of the liberty of the press does not affect political opinions alone, but extends to all the opinions of men, and modifies customs as well as laws… I confess that I do not entertain the firm and complete attachment to the liberty of the press which is wont to be excited by things that are supremely good in their very nature. I approve of it from a consideration more of the evils it prevents, than of the advantages it insures. If any one could point out an intermediate and yet a tenable position between the complete independence and the entire servitude of opinion, I should, perhaps, be inclined to adopt it; but the difficulty is, to discover this intermediate position. Intending to correct the licentiousness of the press, and to restore the use of orderly language, you first try the offender by a jury; but if the jury acquits him, the opinion which was that of a single individual becomes the opinion of the whole country. Too much and too little has therefore been done; go farther, then. You bring the delinquent before permanent magistrates; but even here, the cause must be heard before it can be decided; and the very principles which no book would have ventured to avow are blazoned forth in the pleadings, and what was obscurely hinted at in a single composition is thus repeated in a multitude of other publications. The language is only the expression, and (if I may so speak) the body of the thought, but it is not the thought itself. Tribunals may condemn the body, but the sense, the spirit, of the work is too subtle for their authority. Too much has still been done to recede, too little to attain your end; you must go still farther. Establish a censorship of the press. But the tongue of the public speaker will still make itself heard, and your purpose is not yet accomplished; you have only increased the mischief. Thought is not, like physical strength, dependent upon the number of its agents; nor can authors be counted like the troops which compose an army. On the contrary, the authority of a principle is often increased by the small number of men by whom it is expressed. The words of one strong-minded man, addressed to the passions of a listening assembly, have more power than the vociferations of a thousand orators; and if it be allowed to speak freely in any one public place, the consequence is the same as if free speaking was allowed in every village. The liberty of speech must therefore be destroyed, as well as the liberty of the press. And now you have succeeded, everybody is reduced to silence. But your object was to repress the abuses of liberty, and you are brought to the feet of a despot. You have been led from the extreme of independence to the extreme of servitude, without finding a single tenable position on the way at which you could stop....

The small influence of the American journals is attributable to several reasons, amongst which are the following.

The liberty of writing, like all other liberty, is most formidable when it is a novelty; for a people who have never been accustomed to hear state affairs discussed before them, place implicit confidence in the first tribune who presents himself. The Anglo-Americans have enjoyed this liberty ever since the foundation of the Colonies; moreover, the press cannot create human passions, however skillfully it may kindle them where they exist. In America, political life is active, varied, even agitated, but is rarely affected by those deep passions which are excited only when material interests are impaired: and in the United States, these interests are prosperous. A glance at a French and an American newspaper is sufficient to show the difference which exists in this respect between the two nations. In France, the space allotted to commercial advertisements is very limited, and the news-intelligence is not considerable; but the essential part of the journal is the discussion of the politics of the day. In America, three quarters of the enormous sheet are filled with advertisements, and the remainder is frequently occupied by political intelligence or trivial anecdotes; it is only from time to time, that one finds a corner devoted to passionate discussions, like those which the journalists of France every day give to their readers.

It has been demonstrated by observation, and discovered by the sure instinct even of the pettiest despots, that the influence of a power is increased in proportion as its direction is centralized. In France, the press combines a two-fold centralization; almost all its power is centered in the same spot, and, so to speak, in the same hands; for its organs are far from numerous. The influence of a public press thus constituted, upon a sceptical nation, must be almost unbounded. It is an enemy with whom a government may sign an occasional truce, but which it is difficult to resist for any length of time.

Neither of these kinds of centralization exists in America. The United States have no metropolis; the intelligence and the power of the people are disseminated through all the parts of this vast country, and instead of radiating from a common point, they cross each other in every direction; the Americans have nowhere established any central direction of opinion, any more than of the conduct of affairs. The difference arises from local circumstances, and not from human power; but it is owing to the laws of the Union that there are no licenses to be granted to printers, no securities demanded from editors, as in France, and no stamp duty, as in France and England. The consequence is, that nothing is easier than to set up a newspaper, as a small number of subscribers suffices to defray the expenses.

Hence the number of periodical and semi-periodical publications in the United States is almost incredibly large. The most enlightened Americans attribute the little influence of the press to this excessive dissemination of its power; and it is an axiom of political science in that country, that the only way to neutralize the effect of the public journals is to multiply their number. I cannot see how a truth which is so self-evident should not already have been more generally admitted in Europe. I can see why the persons who hope to bring about revolutions by means of the press should be desirous of confining it to a few powerful organs; but it is inconceivable that the official partisans of the existing state of things, and the natural supporters of the laws, should attempt to diminish the influence of the press by concentrating its power. The governments of Europe seem to treat the press with the courtesy which the knights of old showed to their opponents; having found from their own experience that centralization is a powerful weapon, they have furnished their enemies with it, in order doubtless to have more glory for overcoming them.

In America, there is scarcely a hamlet which has not its newspaper. It may readily be imagined, that neither discipline nor unity of action can be established among so many combatants; and each one consequently fights under his own standard. All the political journals of the United States are, indeed, arrayed on the side of the administration or against it; but they attack and defend it in a thousand different ways. They cannot form those great currents of opinion which sweep away the strongest dikes. This division of influence of the press produces other consequences scarcely less remarkable. The facility with which a newspaper can be established produces a multitude of them; but as the competition prevents any considerable profit, persons of much capacity are rarely led to engage in these undertakings. Such is the number of the public prints, that, even if they were a source of wealth, writers of ability could not be found to direct them all. The journalists of the United States are generally in a very humble position, with a scanty education and a vulgar turn of mind. The will of the majority is the most general of laws, and it established certain habits to which every one must then conform; the aggregate of these common habits is what is called the class-spirit of each profession; thus there is the class-spirit of the bar, of the court, etc. The class-spirit of the French journalists consists in a violent, but frequently eloquent and lofty, manner of discussing the great interest of the state: and the exceptions to this mode of writing are only occasional. The characteristics of the American journalist consist in an open and coarse appeal to the passions of his readers; he abandons principles to assail the characters of individuals, to track them into private life, and disclose all their weaknesses and vices....

But, although the press is limited to these resources, its influence in America is immense. It causes political life to circulate through all the parts of that vast territory. Its eye is constantly open to detect the secret springs of political designs, and to summon the leaders of all parties in turn to the bar of public opinion. It rallies the interests of the community round certain principles, and draws up the creed of every party; for it affords a means of intercourse between those who hear and address each other, without ever coming into immediate contact. When many organs of the press adopt the same line of conduct, their influence in the long run becomes irresistible; and public opinion, perpetually assailed from the same side, eventually yields to the attack. In the United States, each separate journal exercises but little authority; but the power of the periodical press is second only to that of the people.

Respect for the Law

It is not always feasible to consult the whole people, either directly or indirectly, in the formation of the law; but it cannot be denied that, when this is possible, the authority of the law is much augmented. This popular origin, which impairs the excellence and the wisdom of legislation, contributes much to increase its power. There is an amazing strength in the expression of the will of a whole people; and when it declares itself, even the imagination of those who would wish to contest it is overawed. The truth of this fact is well known by parties; and they consequently strive to make out a majority whenever they can. If they have not the greater number of votes on their side, they assert that the true majority abstained from voting; and if they are foiled even there, they have recourse to those who had no right to vote.

In the United States, except slaves, servants, and paupers supported by the townships, there is no class of persons who do not exercise the elective franchise, and who do not indirectly contribute to make the laws. Those who wish to attack the laws must consequently either change the opinion of the nation, or trample upon its decision.

A second reason, which is still more direct and weighty, may be adduced: in the United States, every one is personally interested in enforcing the obedience of the whole community to the law; for as the minority may shortly rally the majority to its principles, it is interested in professing that respect for the decrees of the legislator which it may soon have occasion to claim for its own. However irksome an enactment may be, the citizen of the United States complies with it, not only because it is the work of the majority, but because it is his own, and he regards it as a contract to which he is himself a party.

In the United States, then, that numerous and turbulent multitude does not exist, who, regarding the law as their natural enemy, look upon it with fear and distrust. It is impossible, on the contrary, not to perceive that all classes display the utmost reliance upon the legislation of their country, and are attached to it by a kind of parental affection.

I am wrong, however, in saying all classes; for as, in America, the European scale of authority is inverted, the wealthy are there placed in a position analogous to that of the poor in the Old World, and it is the opulent classes who frequently look upon the law with suspicion. I have already observed that the advantage of democracy is not, as has been sometimes asserted, that it protects those of the majority. In the United States, where the poor rule, the rich have always something to fear from the abuse of their power. This natural anxiety of the rich may produce a secret dissatisfaction; but society is not disturbed by it, for the same reason, which withholds the confidence of the rich from the legislative authority, makes them obey its mandates: their wealth, which prevents them from making the law, prevents them from withstanding it. Amongst civilized nations, only those who have nothing to lose ever revolt; and if the laws of a democracy are not always worthy of respect, they are always respected; for those who usually infringe the laws cannot fail to obey those which they have themselves made, and by which they are benefited, whilst the citizens who might be interested in the infraction of them are induced, by their character and station, to submit to the decisions of the legislature, whatever they may be. Besides, the people in America obey the law, not only because it is their work, but because, first, it is a self-imposed evil, and secondly, it is an evil of transient duration.

🍂 Compulsory school attendance

MASSACHUSETTS LEGISLATURE

While on the forefront of the American industrial revolution, Massachusetts also held a leading place in education reform. The press for child labor was taking children out of the classroom and onto the factory floor. Alarmed by this dangerous trend, the Massachusetts Legislature in 1836 passed the first legislation in the United States making education compulsory.

Be it enacted by the Senate and House of Representatives, in General Court assembled and by the authority of the same, as follows:

Section 1. From and after the first day of April, in the year eighteen hundred and thirty seven, no child under the age of fifteen years shall be employed to labor in any manufacturing establishment, unless such child shall have attended some public or private day school, where instruction is given by a teacher qualified ... at least three months of the twelve months next preceding any and every year, in which such child shall be so employed.

Section 2. The owner, agent or superintendent of any manufacturing establishment contrary to the provisions of this act, shall forfeit the sum of fifty dollars for each offence, to be recovered by indictment, to the use of common schools in the towns respectively where said establishments may be situated.

🍂 California beachcombers

RICHARD HENRY DANA

Richard Henry Dana came from a distinguished Boston family. As a young Harvard man he enlisted on the brig *Pilgrim* in 1834 for a two-year voyage around the Cape Horn to the California coast. He recorded the hardships of the sailor's life and the decidedly casual Californian lifestyle. Upon returning to Boston, he published his journal as the book *Two Years Before the Mast*. At once bemused and critical of the relaxed ways of the Mexicans and Anglos who lived on the West Coast, Dana here describes some of the "beachcombers" he encountered.

There was but one man in the only house here, and

him I shall always remember as a good specimen of a California ranger. He had been a tailor in Philadelphia, and, getting intemperate and in debt, joined a trapping party, and went to the Columbia river, and thence down to Monterey, where he spent everything, left his party, and came to the Pueblo de los Angeles to work at his trade. Here he went dead to leeward among the pulperias, gambling rooms, etc., and came down to San Pedro to be moral by being out of temptation. He had been in the house several weeks, working hard at his trade, upon orders which he had brought with him, and talked much of his resolution, and opened his heart to us about his past life. After we had been here some time, he started off one morning, in fine spirits, well dressed, to carry the clothes which he had been making to the Pueblo, and saying that he would bring back his money and some fresh orders the next day. The next day came, and a week passed, and nearly a fortnight, when one day, going ashore, we saw a tall man, who looked like our friend the tailor, getting out of the back of an Indian's cart, which had just come down from the Pueblo. He stood for the house, but we bore up after him; when, finding that we were overhauling him, he hove to and spoke us. Such a sight! Barefooted, with an old pair of trousers tied round his waist by a piece of green hide, a soiled cotton shirt, and a torn Indian hat; "cleaned out" to the last real, and completely "used up." He confessed the whole matter; acknowledged that he was on his back; and now he had a prospect of a fit of the horrors for a week, and of being worse than useless for months. This is a specimen of the life of half the Americans and the English who are adrift along the coasts of the Pacific and its islands—commonly called "beachcombers." One of the same stamp was Russell, who was master of the hide house at San Diego while I was there, but had been afterward dismissed for his misconduct. He spent his own money, and nearly all the stores among the half-bloods upon the beach, and went up to the presidio, where he lived the life of a desperate "loafer," until some rascally deed him off "between two days," with men on horseback, dogs, and Indians in full cry after him, among the hills. One night he burst into our room at the hide house, breathless, pale as a ghost, covered with mud, and torn by thorns and briers, nearly naked, and begged for a crust of bread, saying he had neither eaten nor

slept for three days. Here was the great Mr. Russell, who a month before was "Don Tomas," capitan de la playa, maestro de la casa, &c., &c. begging food and shelter of Kanakas and sailors. He stayed with us till he had given himself up, and was dragged off to the calabozo.

Another, and a more amusing, specimen was one whom we saw at San Francisco. He had been a lad on board the ship *California*, in one of her first voyages, and ran away and commenced ranchero, gambling, stealing horses, &c. He worked along up to San Francisco, and was living on a rancho near there while we were in port. One morning, when we went ashore in the boat, we found him at the landing place, dressed in California style—a wide hat, faded velveteen trousers, and a blanket thrown over his shoulders—and wishing to go off in the boat, saying he was going to *pasear* with our captain a little. We had many doubts of the reception he would meet with; but he seemed to think himself company for anyone. We took him aboard, landed him at the gangway, and went about our work, keeping an eye upon the quarterdeck, where the captain was walking. The lad went up to him with complete assurance, and, raising his hat, wished him a good afternoon. Captain Thompson turned round, looked at him from head to foot, and, saying coolly, "Hallo! Who the hell are you?" kept on his walk. This was a rebuff not to be mistaken, and the joke passed about among the crew by winks and signs at different parts of the ship. Finding himself disappointed at headquarters, he edged along forward to the mate, who was overseeing some work upon the forecastle, and tried to begin a yarn; but it would not do. The mate had seen the reception he had met with aft, and would have no cast-off company. The second mate was aloft, and the third mate and myself were painting the quarter boat, but the joke had got before him, and he found everybody busy and silent. Looking over the rail a few moments afterward, we saw him at the galley door talking with the cook. This was indeed a comedown, from the highest seat in the synagogue to a seat in the galley with the black cook. At night, too, when supper was called, he stood in the waist for some time, hoping to be asked down with the officers, but they went below, one after another, and left him. His next chance was with the carpenter and sailmaker, and he lounged round the after hatchway until the last had gone down. We had now had fun enough out of him, and, taking pity on him, offered him a pot of tea, and a cut at the kid, with the rest, in the forecastle. He was hungry, and it was growing dark, and he began to see that there was no use in playing the caballero any longer, and came down into the forecastle, put into the "grub" in sailor's style, threw off all his airs, and enjoyed the joke as much as anyone; for a man must take a joke among sailors. He gave us an account of his adventures in the country, roguery and all, and was very entertaining. He was a smart, unprincipled fellow, was in many of the rascally doings of the country, and gave us a great deal of interesting information as to the ways of the world we were in.

CHAPTER FOUR

1837–1860

America in Transition

"Check this spirit of monopoly"

ANDREW JACKSON

Jackson's farewell address in 1837 was marked by his warning to the people about the dangers of his old enemy, concentrated wealth. Despite slaying the national bank, Jackson noted that the mass of working people would remain in danger of losing their wealth and influence over the direction of the government if they were not wary of moneyed interests. "You will, in the end, find that the most important powers of Government have been given or bartered away, and the control over your dearest interest ... passed into the hands of these corporations," Jackson predicted.

It is one of the serious evils of our present system of banking that it enables one class of society, and that by no means a numerous one, by its control over the currency to act injuriously upon the interests of all the others and to exercise more than its just proportion of influence in political affairs. The agricultural, the mechanical, and the laboring classes have little or no share in the direction of the great moneyed corporations; and from their habits and the nature of their pursuits, they are incapable of forming extensive combinations to act together with united force. Such concert of action may sometimes be produced in a single city or in a small district of country by means of personal communications with each other; but they have no regular or active correspondence with those who are engaged in similar pursuits in distant places; they have but little patronage to give to the press and exercise but a small share of influence over it; they have no crowd of dependents above them who hope to grow rich without labor by their countenance and favor and who are, therefore, always ready to exercise their wishes. The planter, the farmer, the mechanic, and the laborer all know that their success depends upon their own industry and economy and that they must not expect to become suddenly rich by the fruits of their toil. Yet these classes of society form the great body of the people of the United States; they are the bone and sinew of the country; men who love liberty and desire nothing but equal rights and equal laws and who, moreover, hold the great mass of our national wealth, although it is distributed in moderate amounts among the millions of freemen who possess it. But, with overwhelming numbers and wealth on their side, they are in constant danger of losing their fair influence in the Government and with difficulty maintain their just rights against the incessant efforts daily made to encroach upon them. The mischief springs from the power which the moneyed interest derives from a paper currency which they are able to control; from the multitude of corporations with exclusive privileges which they have succeeded in obtaining in the different States and which are employed altogether for their benefit; and unless you become more watchful in your States and check this spirit of monopoly and thirst for exclusive privileges, you will, in the end, find that the most important powers of Government have been given or bartered away, and the control over your dearest interests has passed into the hands of these corporations.

The paper money system and its natural associates—monopoly and exclusive privileges—have already struck their roots deep in the soil; and it will require all your efforts to check its further growth and to eradicate the evil. The men who profit by the abuses and desire to perpetuate them will continue to besiege the halls of legislation in the General Government as well as in the States and will seek, by every artifice, to mislead and deceive the public servants. It is to yourselves that you must look for safety and the means of guarding and perpetuating your free institutions. In your hands is rightfully placed the sovereignty of the country and to you every one placed in authority is ultimately responsible. It is always in your power to see that the wishes of the people are carried into faithful execution, and their will, when once made known, must sooner or later be obeyed. And while the people remain, as I trust they ever will, uncorrupted and incorruptible and continue watchful and jealous of their rights, the Government is safe, and the cause of freedom will continue to triumph over all its enemies.

"Pure, unmixed, personal idolatry"

JOHN CALHOUN

During Jackson's second term as president, the Senate formally criticized the president's decision to veto a new charter for the national bank and subsequent decision to allocate its money to state banks. Stopping short of an impeachment that would not have succeeded against the popular president, the Senate instead passed a resolution condemning Jackson's action as unconstitutional.

In January 1837, Jackson's allies sought to expunge the resolution from the Senate's record. John C. Calhoun, who had stepped down as Jackson's vice president to become a South Carolina senator and bitter opponent of Jackson's, fought the resolution. He declared the censure constitutional and the pending decision to withdraw the censure as an exercise in "personal idoltary."

The gentleman from Virginia [Mr. Rives] says that the argument in favor of this expunging resolution has not been answered. Sir, there are some questions so plain that they cannot be argued. Nothing can make them more plain; and this is one. No one not blinded by party zeal can possibly be insensible that the measure proposed is a violation of the Constitution. The Constitution requires the Senate to keep a journal; this resolution goes to expunge the journal. If you may expunge a part, you may expunge the whole; and if it is expunged, how is it kept? The Constitution says the journal shall be kept; this resolution says it shall be destroyed. It does the very thing which the Constitution declares shall not be done. That is the argument, the whole argument. There is none other. Talk of precedents? and precedents drawn from a foreign country? They don't apply. No, sir. This is to be done, not in consequence of argument, but in spite of argument. I understand the case. I know perfectly well the gentlemen have no liberty to vote otherwise. They are coerced by an exterior power. They try, indeed, to comfort their conscience by saying that it is the will of the people, and the voice of the people. It is no such thing. We all know how these legislative returns have been obtained. It is by dictation from the White House. The president himself, with that vast mass of patronage which he wields, and the thousand expectations he is able to hold up, has obtained these votes of the state legislatures; and this, forsooth, is said to be the voice of the people. The voice of the people! Sir, can we forget the scene which was exhibited in this chamber when that expunging resolution was first introduced here? Have we forgotten the universal giving way of conscience, so that the senator from Missouri was left alone? I see before me senators who could not swallow that resolution; and has its nature changed

since then? Is it any more constitutional now than it was then? Not at all. But executive power has interposed. Talk to me of the voice of the people! No, sir. It is the combination of patronage and power to coerce this body into a gross and palpable violation of the Constitution. Some individuals, I perceive, think to escape through the particular form in which this act is to be perpetrated. They tell us that the resolution on your records is not to be expunged, but is only to be endorsed "Expunged." Really, sir, I do not know how to argue against such contemptible sophistry. The occasion is too solemn for an argument of this sort. You are going to violate the Constitution, and you get rid of the infamy by a falsehood. You yourselves say that the resolution is expunged by your order. Yet you say it is not expunged. You put your act in express words. You record it, and then turn round and deny it.

But what is the motive? What is the pretext for this enormity? Why, gentlemen tell us the Senate has two distinct consciences—a legislative conscience and a judicial conscience. As a legislative body we have decided that the president has violated the Constitution. But gentlemen tell us that this is an impeachable offense; and, as we may be called to try it in our judicial capacity, we have no right to express the opinion. I need not show how inconsistent such a position is with the eternal, imprescriptible fight of freedom of speech, and how utterly inconsistent it is with precedents drawn from the history of our British ancestors, where the same liberty of speech has for centuries been enjoyed. There is a shorter and more direct argument in reply. Gentlemen who take that position cannot, according to their own showing, vote for this resolution; for if it is unconstitutional for us to record a resolution of condemnation, because we may afterwards be called to try the case in a judicial capacity, then it is equally unconstitutional for us to record a resolution of acquittal. If it is unconstitutional for the Senate to declare before a trial that the president has violated the Constitution, it is equally unconstitutional to declare before a trial that he has not violated the Constitution. The same principle is involved in both. Yet, in the very face of this principle, gentlemen are here going to condemn their own act.

But why do I waste my breath? I know it is all utterly vain. The day is gone; night approaches, and night is suitable to the dark deed we meditate. There is a sort of destiny in this thing. The act must be performed; and it is an act which will tell on the political history of this country forever. Other preceding violations of the Constitution (and they have been many and great) filled my bosom with indignation, but this fills it only with grief. Others were done in the heat of partisanship. Power was, as it were, compelled to support itself by seizing upon new instruments of influence and patronage; and there were ambitious and able men to direct the process. Such was the removal of the deposits, which the president seized upon by a new and unprecedented act of arbitrary power—an act which gave him ample means of rewarding friends and punishing enemies. Something may, perhaps, be pardoned to him in this matter, on the old apology of tyrants—the plea of necessity. But here there can be no such apology. Here no necessity can so much as be pretended. This act originates in pure, unmixed, personal idolatry. It is the melancholy evidence of a broken spirit, ready to bow at the feet of power. The former act was such as one as might have been perpetrated in the days of Pompey or Caesar; but an act like this could never have been consummated by a Roman Senate until the times of Caligula and Nero.

"Victory or Death"

WILLIAM BARRET TRAVIS

The first Anglo settlers in Texas arrived in the 1820s and rapidly grew to outnumber Mexicans two to one. The brief "Fredonia Rebellion" of 1826-27 highlighted tensions between the two cultures. In 1829 Mexico banned slavery and imposed new taxes, triggering resistance in Texas that culminated on March 2, 1836, with the Texas declaration of independence.

Fighting between Americans and Texans had already broken out and a Mexican army had surrounded a contingent of Texan soldiers at the Alamo, including Davy Crockett, Jim Bowie and the commander William B. Travis. Shortly before the Mexicans assaulted the doomed fort, Travis wrote a message seeking help from other Texan forces, ending it with the famous defiant words "Victory or death." At great cost to themselves, the Mexicans captured the Alamo on March 6 and killed all 187 of its defenders in a bloody battle.

One month later at the Battle of San Jacinto, an outnumbered Texan army led by Sam Houston defeated the Mexican army to the battle cry, "Remember the Alamo!"

Lieutenant-Colonel-Commandant of the Alamo
To the People of Texas & all Americans in the world—

Fellow Citizens & Compatriots: I am besieged, by a thousand or more of the Mexicans under Santa Anna—I have sustained a continual Bombardment & cannonade for 24 hours & have not lost a man—The enemy has demanded a surrender at discretion, otherwise the garrison are to be put to the sword, if the fort is taken—I have answered the demand with a cannon shot, & our flag still waves proudly from the walls—I shall never surrender or retreat. Then, I call on you in the name of Liberty, of patriotism & everything dear to the American character, to come to our aid, with all dispatch—The enemy is receiving reinforcements daily & will no doubt increase to three or four thousand in four or five days. If this call is neglected, I am determined to sustain myself as long as possible & die like a soldier who never forgets what is due to his own honor & that of his country—
VICTORY OR DEATH

The Trail of Tears

A NATIVE OF MAINE

In the 1830s, President Jackson instituted an "Indian removal policy" in which friendly Native American tribes in the Southeast such as the Cherokee and Creek were forcibly relocated to what is today Oklahoma, Kansas and Nebraska. Having fought as allies with Jackson, adapted to the white system of government and established themselves anew as farmers, the Cherokees strongly resisted the policy, which was designed to hand over their farms to white settlers.

The Cherokees lost a legal challenge and in 1838 an estimated 16,000 went on a forced march from their traditional homeland to the relatively barren western territory. More than 4,000 died en route on "The Trail of Tears." A Maine newspaper correspondent witnessed the march as the Cherokees passed through Kentucky in 1838.

On Tuesday evening we fell in with a detachment of the poor Cherokee Indians…. That poor despised people are now on their long and tedious march to their place of destination beyond the Mississippi River. In the first detachment which we met, were about eleven hundred Indians—sixty wagons—six hundred horses, and perhaps forty pairs of oxen. We found them in the forest camped for the night by the road side, comfortable—if comfortable they might be in a December night, and under a severe fall of rain accompanied with heavy wind. With their canvass for a shield from the inclemency of the weather, and the cold wet ground for a resting place, after the fatigue of the day, they spent the night with probably as little of the reality as the appearance of comfort. We learned from the officers and overseers of the detachment in the morning, that many of the aged Indians were suffering extremely from the fatigue of the journey, and the ill health consequent upon it. Several were then quite ill, and one aged man we were informed was then in the last struggles of death. There were about ten officers and overseers in each detachment whose business it was to provide supplies for the journey, and attend to the general wants of the company. The cost of the journey is paid by the American Government as one of the conditions of the pretended treaty which many of the Indians still call fraudulent.

The officers informed us that the Indians were very unwilling to go—so much so that some two hundred had escaped, in collecting them together, and secreted themselves in the mountains in Georgia and the eastern part of Tennessee, and those who were on the way were so unwilling to pursue their journey, that it was some days quite late in the evening before they could get them under way—and even then they went reluctantly. I know it is said that "only a few were unwilling to go"—"the most go willingly and think the remove on the whole, an advantage to the nation." The testimony of the officers and observation have both tended to confirm the belief, however, in my mind that the great majority of the nation feel that they are wronged—grievously wronged, and nothing but arbitrary power compels them to remove…

The last detachment which we passed on the 7th, embraced rising two thousand Indians with horses and mules in proportion. The forward part of the train we found just pitching their tents for the night, and notwithstanding some thirty or forty wagons were already stationed, we found the road literally filled with the procession for about three miles in length. The sick and feeble were carried in wagons—about as comfortable for travelling as a New England ox cart with a covering over it—a great many ride on horseback and mul-

titudes go on foot—even aged females, apparently, nearly ready to drop into the grave—were travelling with heavy burdens attached to the back—on the sometimes frozen ground, and sometimes muddy streets, with no covering for the feet except what nature had given them. We were some hours making our way through the crowd, which brought us in close contact with the wagons and the multitude, so much that we felt fortunate to find ourselves freed from the crowd without leaving any part of our carriage. We learned from the inhabitants on the road where the Indians passed that they buried fourteen to fifteen at every stopping place—and they make a journey of ten miles per day only on an average…. One aged Indian, who was commander of the friendly Creeks and Seminoles in a very important engagement in company with General Jackson, was accosted on arriving in a little village in Kentucky by an aged man residing there, and who was one of Jackson's men in the engagement referred to, and asked if he (the Indian) recollected him? The aged Chieftain looked him in the face and recognised him, and with a down-cast look and heavy sigh, referring to the engagement, he said, "Ah! My life and the lives of my people were then at stake for you and your country. I then thought Jackson my best friend. But, ah! Jackson no serve me right. Your country no do me justice now."

"I have wept in the land of my birth over slavery"

ANGELINA GRIMKÉ

With an angry mob outside pelting stones at the Philadelphia building that held the National Anti-Slavery Convention in 1838, Angelina Grimké gave a stirring address condemning slavery. A Quaker born in South Carolina, she and her sister Sarah grew up amongst slaves and as adults condemned the institution.

Angelina first gained recognition when William Lloyd Garrison published a letter of hers in 1835 in *The Liberator.* One year later the publication of her pamphlet *An Appeal to the Christian Women of the South* helped spur the abolitionist movement in the North. But in her native South Carolina, the pamphlet was publicly burned.

A few days after the following address was delivered May 16, 1838, the building was destroyed by fire. A year later, Grimké published the abolitionist book *American Slavery as It Is; Testimony of a Thousand Witnesses*. The Grimké sisters also championed women's rights, an issue which divided the abolitionists.

Do you ask, "What has the North to do with slavery?" Hear it, hear it! Those voices without tell us that the spirit of slavery is here and has been roused to wrath by our conventions; for surely liberty would not foam and tear herself with rage, because her friends are multiplied daily, and meetings are held in quick succession to set forth her virtues and extend her peaceful kingdom. This opposition shows that slavery has done its deadliest work in the hearts of our citizens. Do you ask, then, "What has the North to do?" I answer, cast out first the spirit of slavery from your own hearts, and then lend your aid to convert the South. Each one present has a work to do, be his or her situation what it may, however limited their means or insignificant their supposed influence. The great men of this country will not do this work; the church will never do it. A desire to please the world, to keep the favor of all parties and of all conditions, makes them dumb on this and every other unpopular subject.

As a Southerner, I feel that it is my duty to stand up here tonight and bear testimony against slavery. I have seen it! I have seen it! I know it has horrors that can never be described. I was brought up under its wing. I witnessed for many years its demoralizing influences and its destructiveness to human happiness. I have never seen a happy slave. I have seen him dance in his chains, it is true, but he was not happy. There is a wide difference between happiness and mirth. Man cannot enjoy happiness while his manhood is destroyed. Slaves, however, may be, and sometimes are mirthful. When hope is extinguished, they say, "Let us eat and drink, for tomorrow we die."

What is a mob? What would the breaking of every window be? What would the leveling of this hall be? Any evidence that we are wrong, or that slavery is a good and a wholesome institution? What if the mob should now burst upon us, break up our meeting, and commit violence on our persons? Would that be anything compared with what the slaves endure? No, no; and we do not remember them, "as bound with them," if we shrink in the time of peril, or feel unwilling to sacrifice ourselves, if need be, for their sake. I thank the Lord that

there is yet life enough left to feel the truth, even though it rages at it; that conscience is not so completely seared as to be unmoved by the truth of the living God.

How wonderfully constituted is the human mind! How it resists, as long as it can, all efforts to reclaim it from error! I feel that all this disturbance is but an evidence that our efforts are the best that could have been adopted, or else the friends of slavery would not care for what we say and do. The South knows what we do. I am thankful that they are reached by our efforts. Many times have I wept in the land of my birth over the system of slavery. I know of none who sympathized in my feelings; I was unaware that any efforts were made to deliver the oppressed; no voice in the wilderness was heard calling on the people to repent and do works meet for repentance, and my heart sickened within me. Oh, how should I have rejoiced to know that such efforts as these were being made. I only wonder that I had such feelings. But in the midst of temptation I was preserved, and my sympathy grew warmer, and my hatred of slavery more inveterate, until at last I have exiled myself from my native land, because I could no longer endure to hear the wailing of the slave.

I fled to the land of Penn; for here, thought I, sympathy for the slave will surely be found. But I found it not. The people were kind and hospitable, but the slave had no place in their thoughts. I therefore shut up my grief in my own heart. I remembered that I was a Carolinian, from a state which framed this iniquity by law. Every Southern breeze wafted to me the discordant tones of weeping and wailing, shrieks and groans, mingled with prayers and blasphemous curses. My heart sank within me to the abominations in the midst of which I had been born and educated. What will it avail, cried I, in bitterness of spirit, to expose to the gaze of strangers the horrors and pollutions of slavery, when there is no ear to hear nor heart to feel and pray for the slave? But how different do I feel now! Animated with hope, nay, with an assurance of the triumph of liberty and good will to man, I will lift up my voice like a trumpet, and show this people what they can do to influence the Southern mind and overthrow slavery.

We often hear the questions asked: "What shall we do?" Here is an opportunity. Every man and every woman present may do something by showing that we fear not a mob, and in the midst of revilings and threatenings, pleading the cause of those who are ready to perish. Let me urge everyone to buy the books written on the subject; read them and lend them to your neighbors. Give your money no longer for things which pander to pride and lust, but aid in scattering "the living coals of truth upon the naked heart of the nation," in circulating appeals to the sympathies of Christians in behalf of the outraged slave.

But it is said by some, our "books and papers do not speak the truth"; why, then, do they not contradict what we say? They cannot. Moreover, the South has entreated, nay, commanded us, to be silent, and what greater evidence of the truth of our publications could be desired?

Women of Philadelphia! Allow me as a Southern woman, with much attachment to the land of my birth, to entreat you to come up to this work. Especially, let me urge you to petition. Men may settle this and other questions at the ballot-box, but you have no such right. It is only through petitions that you can reach the legislature. It is, therefore, peculiarly your duty to petition. Do you say, "It does no good!" The South already turns pale at the number sent. They have read the reports of the proceedings of Congress and they have seen that among other petitions were very many from the women of the North on the subject of slavery. Men who hold the rod over slaves rule in the councils of the nation; and they deny our right to petition and remonstrate against the abuses of our sex and our kind. We have these rights, however, from our God. Only let us exercise them, and, though often turned away unanswered, let us remember the influence of importunity upon the unjust judge and act accordingly. The fact that the South looks jealously upon our measures shows that they are effectual. There is, therefore, no cause for doubting or despair.

It was remarked in England that women did much to abolish slavery in her colonies. Nor are they now idle. Numerous petitions from them have recently been presented to the queen to abolish apprenticeship, with its cruelties, nearly equal to those of the system whose place it supplies. One petition, two miles and a quarter long, has been presented. And do you think these labors will be in vain? Let the history of the past answer. When the women of these states send up to Congress such a petition our legislators will arise, as did those of

England, and say: "When all the maids and matrons of the land are knocking at our doors we must legislate." Let the zeal and love, the faith and works of our English sisters quicken ours; that while the slaves continue to suffer, and when they shout for deliverance, we may feel the satisfaction of "having done what we could."

⚜ "Guilty of excusable homicide"

PHILIP HONE

The western frontier was a tough place. In 1838, Philip Hone of New York recorded in his diary the events of a knife fight that took place in the Arkansas House of Representatives between the Speaker of the House and a fellow legislator.

Some time last winter a personal dispute occurred, during the session of the House of Representatives of the State of Arkansas, between a Mr. Wilson, the Speaker then presiding, and Major Anthony, a member, in the course of which the former came down from his chair, drew a large knife (a weapon which it appears these modern barbarians carry about their persons), attacked his adversary and killed him on the spot. Anthony endeavoured to defend himself (he had also his knife); but the movement of the honourable Speaker was so sudden as to render his efforts ineffectual, and I suppose it was "out of order" for other members to interfere in the parliamentary discipline of their presiding officer.

Wilson has been tried for this flagrant outrage. There is a full account of the trial in the newspapers, taken from the Arkansas "Gazette." From the testimony it does not appear that any violent provocation was offered by the deceased, and the facts above-states were substantially proved, notwithstanding which the verdict of the jury was as follows: "Guilty of excusable homicide, and not guilty in any manner or form as charged in the indictment;" and the prisoner was discharged from custody. Further accounts state that immediately after this mockery of justice, the jurors, with the sheriffs and witnesses, had a grand drinking frolic at the expense of the defendant.

"And looks the world in the face"

HENRY WADSWORTH LONGFELLOW

Henry Wadsworth Longfellow was one of the first great American poets. Immensely popular, he helped the young nation forge a cultural identity distinct from Europe by using American subject matters. He published several poems in 1839, including "The Village Blacksmith" and "Psalm of Life" celebrating the values of a hard work. Longfellow also wrote the narrative poems "Evangeline" in 1847, "The Song of Hiawatha" in 1855, and "Paul Revere's Ride" in 1863.

"The Village Blacksmith"

Under a spreading chestnut tree
The village smithy stands;
The smith, a mighty man is he,
With large sinewy hands;
And the muscles of his brawny arms
Are strong as iron bands.

His hair is crisp, and black, and long,
His face is like the tan;
His brow is wet with honest sweat,
He earns whate'er he can;
And looks the whole world in the face,
For he owes not any man.

Week in, week out, from morn till night,
You can hear his bellows blow;
You can hear him swing his heavy sledge,
With measured beat and slow;
Like a sexton ringing the village bell,
When the evening sun is low.

And children coming home from school
Look in at the open door;
They love to see the flaming forge,
And hear the bellows roar;
And catch the burning sparks that fly
Like chaff from a threshing floor.

He goes on Sunday to the church,
And sits among his boys;
He hears the parson pray and preach,
He hears his daughter's voice;
Singing in the village choir,
And it makes his heart rejoice.

It sounds to him like her mother's voice,
Singing in Paradise!
He needs must think of her once more,
How in the grave she lies;

And with his hard, rough hand he wipes
A tear out of his eyes.

Toiling—rejoicing—sorrowing
Onward through life he goes;
Each morning sees some task begin,
Each evening sees it close;
Something attempted, something done,
Has earned a night's repose.

Thanks, thanks to thee, my worthy friend,
For the lesson thou has taught!
Thus at the flaming forge of life
Our fortunes must be wrought;
Thus on its sounding anvil shaped
Each burning deed and thought!

"Psalm of Life"

Tell me not, in mournful numbers,
    Life is but an empty dream!
For the soul is dead that slumbers,
    And things are not what they seem.

Life is real! Life is earnest!
    And the grave is not its goal;
Dust thou art, to dust returnest,
    Was not spoken of the soul.

Not enjoyment, and not sorrow,
    Is our destined end or way;
But to act, that each to-morrow
    Find us farther than to-day.

Art is long, and Time is fleeting,
    And our hearts, though stout and brave,
Still, like muffled drums, are beating
    Funeral marches to the grave.

In the world's broad field of battle,
    In the bivouac of Life,
Be not like dumb, driven cattle!
    Be a hero in the strife!

Trust no Future, howe'er pleasant!
    Let the dead Past bury its dead!
Act,—act in the living Present!
    Heart within, and God o'erhead!

Lives of great men all remind us
    We can make our lives sublime,
And, departing leave behind us
    Footprints on the sands of time;

Footprints, that perhaps another,
    Sailing o'er life's solemn main,
A forlorn and shipwrecked brother
    Seeing, shall take heart again.

Let us, then, be up and doing,
    With a heart for any fate;

Still achieving, still pursuing,
    Learn to labor and to wait.

❧ "A man is born to be a reformer"

RALPH WALDO EMERSON

Ralph Waldo Emerson served an inspiration to reformers and was the leader of the Transcendental movement of the 1830s-40s in New England. A mediocre student at Harvard and unsuccessful in his first ministry, Emerson soared to prominence in 1837 with his famous address on "The American Scholar," daring scholars to chart their own intellectual course. Emerson's sermons, lectures, essays and poems helped make him a towering figure in American literature and one of the leading influences of his time. This essay, "Man the Reformer," was written in 1841.

In the history of the world the doctrine of Reform had never such scope as at the present hour. Lutherans, Herrnhuters, Jesuits, Monks, Quakers, Knox, Wesley, Swedenborg, Bentham, in their accusations of society, all respected something,—church or state, literature or history, domestic usages, the market town, the dinner table, coined money. But now all these and all things else hear the trumpet, and must rush to judgment, Christianity, the laws, commerce, schools, the farm, the laboratory; and not a kingdom, town, statute, rite, calling, man, or woman, but is threatened by the new spirit.

What if some of the objections whereby our institutions are assailed are extreme and speculative, and the reformers tend to idealism? That only shows the extravagance of the abuses which have driven the mind into the opposite extreme. It is when your facts and persons grow unreal and fantastic by too much falsehood that the scholar flies for refuge to the world of ideas, and aims to recruit and replenish nature from that source. Let ideas establish their legitimate sway again in society, let life be fair and poetic, and the scholars will gladly be lovers, citizens, and philanthropists.

It will afford no security from the new ideas that the old nations, the laws of centuries, the property and institutions of a hundred cities, are built on other foundations. The demon of reform has a secret door into the heart of every lawmaker, of every inhabitant of every city. The fact that a

new thought and hope have dawned in your breast should apprize you that in the same hour a new light broke in upon a thousand private hearts. That secret which you would fain keep,—as soon as you go abroad, lo! there is one standing on the doorstep to tell you the same. There is not the most bronzed and sharpened money-catcher who does not, to your consternation almost, quail and shake the moment he hears a question prompted by the new ideas. We thought he had some semblance of ground to stand upon, that such as he at least would die hard; but he trembles and flees. Then the scholar says, "Cities and coaches shall never impose on me again; for behold every solitary dream of mine is rushing to fulfilment. That fancy I had, and hesitated to utter because you would laugh,—the broker, the attorney, the market-man are saying the same thing. Had I waited a day longer to speak, I had been too late. Behold, State Street thinks, and Wall Street doubts, and begins to prophesy!"

It cannot be wondered at that this general inquest into abuses should arise in the bosom of society, when one considers the practical impediments that stand in the way of virtuous young men. The young man, on entering life, finds the way to lucrative employments blocked with abuses. The ways of trade are grown selfish to the borders of theft, and supple to the borders (if not beyond the borders) of fraud. The employments of commerce are not intrinsically unfit for a man, or less genial to his faculties; but these are now in their general course so vitiated by derelictions and abuses at which all connive that it requires more vigor and resources than can be expected of every young man to right himself in them; he is lost in them; he cannot move hand or foot in them. Has he genius and virtue? the less does he find them fit for him to grow in, and if he would thrive in them, he must sacrifice all the brilliant dreams of boyhood and youth as dreams; he must forget the prayers of his childhood and must take on him the harness of routine and obsequiousness. If not so minded, nothing is left him but to begin the world anew, as he does who puts the spade into the ground for food. We are all implicated of course in this charge; it is only necessary to ask a few questions as to the progress of the articles of commerce from the fields where they grew, to our houses, to become aware that we eat and drink and wear perjury and fraud in a hundred commodities....

The idea which now begins to agitate society has a wider scope than our daily employments, our households, and the institutions of property. We are to revise the whole of our social structure, the State, the school, religion, marriage, trade, science, and explore their foundations in our own nature; we are to see that the world not only fitted the former men, but fits us, and to clear ourselves of every usage which has not its roots in our own mind. What is a man born for but to be a Reformer, a Remaker of what man has made; a renouncer of lies; a restorer of truth and good, imitating that great Nature which embosoms us all, and which sleeps no moment on an old past, but every hour repairs herself, yielding us every morning a new day, and with every pulsation a new life? Let him renounce everything which is not true to him, and put all his practices back on their first thoughts, and do nothing for which he has not the whole world for his reason. If there are inconveniences and what is called ruin in the way, because we have so enervated and maimed ourselves, yet it would be like dying of perfumes to sink in the effort to re-attach the deeds of every day to the holy and mysterious recesses of life.

The power which is at once spring and regulator in all efforts of reform is the conviction that there is an infinite worthiness in man, which will appear at the call of worth, and that all particular reforms are the removing of some impediment. Is it not the highest duty that man should be honored in us? I ought not to allow any man because he has broad lands to feel that he is rich in my presence. I ought to make him feel that I can do without his riches, that I cannot be bought,—neither by comfort, neither by pride,—and though I be utterly penniless, and receiving bread from him, that he is the poor man beside me. And if, at the same time, a woman or a child discovers a sentiment of piety, or a juster way of thinking than mine, I ought to confess it by my respect and obedience, though it go to alter my whole way of life....

Let our affection flow out to our fellows; it would operate in a day the greatest of all revolutions. It is better to work on institutions by the sun than by the wind. The State must consider the poor man, and all voices must speak for him. Every child that is born must have a just chance for his bread. Let the amelioration in our laws of property proceed from the concession of the rich, not from the grasping of the poor. Let us begin by habitual imparting. Let us understand that the equitable rule is that no one should take more than his share, let him be ever so rich. Let me feel that I am to be a lover. I am to see to it that the world is the better for me, and to find my reward in the act. Love would put a new face on this weary old world in which we dwell as pagans and enemies too long, and it would warm the heart to see how fast the vain diplomacy of statesmen, the impotence of armies, and navies, and lines of defence, would be superseded by this unarmed child. Love will creep where it cannot go, will accomplish that by imperceptible methods,—being its own lever, fulcrum, and power,—which force could never achieve. Have you not seen in the woods, in a late autumn morning, a poor fungus of mushroom,—a plant without any solidity, nay, that seemed nothing but a soft mush or jelly,—by its constant, total, and inconceivably gentle pushing, manage to break its way up through the frosty ground, and actually to lift a hard crust on its head? It is the symbol of the power of kindness. The virtue of this principle in human society in application to great interests is absolute and forgotten. Once or twice in history it has been tried in illustrious instances, with signal success. This great, overgrown, dead Christendom of ours still keeps alive at least the name of a lover of mankind. But one day all men will be lovers; and every calamity will be dissolved in the universal Sunshine.

"We cannot perceive, that it is criminal for men to agree together to exercise their rights"

LEMARD SHAW

Up until *Commonwealth v. Hunt* courts had deemed trade union activities as illegal conspiracies. But in 1840 the Bootmakers' Society in Boston appealed a municipal case in which it was found guilty for compelling an employer to fire a shoemaker who refused to join the trade union. The Supreme Judicial Court overthrew the conviction, thus removing the stigma of criminality from union activities. Justice Lemard Shaw wrote the unanimous 1842 opinion stating that a combination of workers could work in concert to achieve goals through legal activities. Although most courts continued to look unfavorably on unions, Shaw's decision made it possible for unions to organize, grow and work for higher wages and better working conditions.

This was an indictment against the defendants (seven in number), for a conspiracy. The first count alleged that the defendants, together with divers other persons unknown to the grand jurors, "on the first Monday of September 1840, at Boston, being workmen and journeymen in the art and manual occupation of boot-makers, unlawfully, perniciously and deceitfully designing and intending to continue, keep up, form, and unite themselves into an unlawful club, society and combination...did unlawfully assemble and meet together, and...did then and there unjustly and corruptly...agree together, that none of them would work for any master or person whatsoever, in the said art, mystery or occupation, who should employ any workman or journeyman, or other person, in the said art, who was not a member of said club, society or combination, after notice given him to discharge such workman from the employ of such master; to the great damage and oppression, not only of their said masters employing them in said art and occupation, but also of divers other workmen and journeymen in the said art, mystery and occupation; to the evil example of all others in like case offending, and against the peace and dignity of the Commonwealth."

The second count charged that the defendants, and others unknown, at the time and place mentioned in the first count, "did unlawfully assemble, meet, conspire, confederate and agree together, not to work for any master or person who should employ any workman not being a member of a club, society or combination, called the Boston Journeymen Bootmakers' Society in Boston, in Massachusetts, or should break any of their by-laws, unless such workman should pay to said club and society such sum as should be agreed upon as a penalty for the breach of such unlawful rules, orders and by-laws; and by means of said conspiracy, they did compel one Isaac B. Wait, a master cordwainer in said Boston, to turn out of his employ one Jeremiah Home, a journeyman bootmaker, because said Horne would not pay a sum of money to said society for an alleged penalty of some, of said unjust rules, orders and by-laws."...

The defendants were found guilty, at the October term, 1840, of the municipal court, and thereupon several exceptions were alleged by them to the ruling of the judge at the trial. The only exception, which was considered in this court, was this: "The defendants' counsel contended that the indictment did not set forth any agreement to do a criminal act, or to do any lawful act by criminal means; and that the agreements, therein set forth, did not constitute a conspiracy indictable by any law of this Commonwealth; and they moved the court so to instruct the jury: But the judge refused so to do, and instructed the jury that the indictment against the defendants did, in his opinion, describe a confederacy among the defendants to do an unlawful act, and to effect the same by unlawful means: That the society, organized and associated for the purpose described in the indictment, was an unlawful conspiracy, against the laws of this Commonwealth ....

...We have no doubt, that by the operation of the constitution of this Commonwealth, the general rules of the common law, making conspiracy an indictable offence, are in force here, and that this is included in the description of laws which had, before the adoption of the constitution, been used and approved in the Province, Colony, or State of Massachusetts Bay, and usually practised in the courts of law .... Still it is proper in this connexion to remark, that although the common law in regard to conspiracy in this Commonwealth is in force, yet it will not necessarily follow that every indictment at common law for this offence is a precedent for a similar indictment in this State. The general rule of the common law is, that it is a criminal and indictable offence, for two or more to confederate and Combine together, by concerted means, to do that which is unlawful or criminal, to the injury of the public, or portions or classes of the community, or even to the rights of an individual. This rule of law may be equally in force as a rule of the common law, in England and in this Commonwealth; and yet it must depend upon the local laws of each country to determine, whether the purpose to be accomplished by the combination, or the concerted means of accomplishing it, be unlawful or criminal in the respective countries. All those laws of the parent country, whether rules of the common law, or early English statutes, which were made for the purpose of regulating the wages of laborers, the settlement of paupers, and making it penal for anyone

to use a trade or handicraft to which he had not
served a full apprenticeship—not being adapted to
the circumstances of our colonial condition—were
not adopted, used or approved, and therefore do
not come within the description of the laws adopted and confirmed by the provision of the constitution already cited....

Stripped then of these introductory recitals
and alleged injurious consequences, and of the
qualifying epithets attached to the facts, the aver-
ment is this; that the defendants and others formed
themselves into a society, and agreed not to work
for any person who should employ any journeyman
or other person, not a member of such society, after
notice given him to discharge such workman. The
manifest intent of the association is, to induce all
those engaged in the same occupation to become
members of it. Such a purpose is not unlawful. It
would give them a power which might be exerted
for useful and honorable purposes, or for dangerous
and pernicious ones. If the latter were the real and
actual object, and susceptible of proof, it should
have been specially charged. Such an association
might be used to afford each other assistance in
times of poverty, sickness and distress; or to raise
their intellectual, moral and social condition; or to
make improvement in their art; or for other proper
purposes. Or the association might be designed for
purposes of oppression and injustice....

Nor can we perceive that the objects of this
association, whatever they may have been, were to
be attained by criminal means. The means which
they proposed to employ, as averred in this count,
and which, as we are now to presume, were established by the proof, were, that they would not work
for a person, who, after due notice, should employ a
journeyman not a member of their society.
Supposing the object of the association to be laudable and lawful, or at least not unlawful, are these
means criminal? The case supposes that these persons are not bound by contract, but free to work for
whom they please, or not to work, if they so prefer.
In this state of things, we cannot perceive, that it is
criminal for men to agree together to exercise their
own acknowledged rights, in such a manner as best
to subserve their own interests. One way to test
this is, to consider the effect of such an agreement,
where the object of the association is acknowledged
on all hands to be a laudable one. Suppose a class
of workmen, impressed with the manifold evils on

intemperance, should agree with each other not to
work in a shop in which ardent spirit was furnished, or not to work in a shop with any one who
used it, or not to for an employer, who should, after
notice, employ a journeyman who habitually used
it. The consequences might be the same. A workman, who should still persist in the use of ardent
spirit, would find it more difficult to get employment; a master employing such an one might at
times, experience inconvenience in his work in losing the services of a skillful but intemperate workman. Still it seems to us, that as the object would
be lawful, and the means not unlawful, such an
agreement could not be pronounced a criminal
conspiracy....

We think, therefore, that associations may be
entered into, the object of which is to adopt measures that may have a tendency to impoverish
another, that is, to diminish his gains and profits,
and Yet so far from being criminal or unlawful, the
object may be highly meritorious and public spirited. The legality of such an association will therefore depend upon the means to be used for its
accomplishment....

❧ "Individual accumulation will be seen in its naked selfishness"

ELIZABETH PEABODY

Throughout the United States a series of Utopian communities were established with the goal of trying to create a perfect society removed from the tawdry and corrupt influences
of an increasingly industrialized society. Some, such as the
Shakers, were inspired by religion. Others, such as the
Nashoba community for emancipated slaves and Robert
Owens' socialist New Harmony community, were founded on
political ideals. Brook Farm in West Roxbury, Massachusetts,
was founded in 1841 with the goal of creating an equal society where self-interest gave way to community goals. Brook
Farm prospered until 1846 when fire destroyed the farm.
Elizabeth Peabody, who was involved in the planning of
Brook Farm but was not a member, wrote about the commu-
nity in 1843.

In order to live a religious and moral life worthy
the name, they feel it is necessary to come out in
some degree from the world, and to form themselves into a community of property, so far as to

exclude competition and the ordinary rules of trade; while they reserve sufficient private property, or the means of obtaining it, for all purposes of independence, and isolation at will. They have bought a farm, in order to make agriculture the basis of their life, it being the most direct and simple in relation to nature. A true life, although it aims beyond the highest star, is redolent of the healthy earth. The perfume of clover lingers about it. The lowing of cattle is the natural bass to the melody of human voices....

The plan of the Community, as an economy, is in brief this: for all who have property to take stock, and receive a fixed interest thereon: then to keep house or board in commons, as they shall severally desire, at the cost of provisions purchased at wholesale, or raised on the farm; and for all to labor in community, and be paid at a certain rate an hour, choosing their own number of hours, and their own kind of work. With the results of this labor and their interest, they are to pay their board, and also purchase whatever else they require at cost, at the warehouses of the Community, which are to be filled by the Community as such. To perfect this economy, in the course of time they must have all trades and all modes of business carried on among themselves, from the lowest mechanical trade, which contributes to the health and comfort of life, to the finest art, which adorns it with food or drapery for the mind.

All labor, whether bodily or intellectual, is to be paid at the same rate of wages; on the principle that as the labor becomes merely bodily, it is a greater sacrifice to the individual laborer to give his time to it; because time is desirable for the cultivation of the intellectual, in exact proportion to ignorance. Besides, intellectual labor involves in itself higher pleasures, and is more its own reward, than bodily labor.

After becoming members of this Community, none will be engaged merely in bodily labor. The hours of labor for the Association will be limited by a general law, and can be curtailed at the will of the individual still more; and means will be given to all for intellectual improvement and for social intercourse, calculated to refine and expand. The hours redeemed from labor by community, will not be re-applied to the acquisition of wealth, but to the production of intellectual goods. This Community aims to be rich, not in the metallic representative of wealth, but in the wealth itself, which money should represent; namely, LEISURE TO LIVE IN ALL THE FACULTIES OF THE SOUL. As a Community, it will traffic with the world at large, in the products of agricultural labor; and it will sell education to as many young persons as can be domesticated in the families, and enter into the common life with their own children. In the end it hopes to be enabled to provide, not only all the necessaries, but all the elegances desirable for bodily and for spiritual health: books, apparatus, collections for science, works of art, means of beautiful amusement. These things are to be common to all; and thus that object, which alone gilds and refines the passion for individual accumulation, will no longer exist for desire, and whenever the sordid passion appears, it will be seen in its naked selfishness. In its ultimate success, the Community will realize all the ends which selfishness seeks, but involved in spiritual blessings, which only greatness of soul can aspire after.

And the requisitions on the individuals, it is believed, will make this the order forever. The spiritual good will always be the condition of the temporal. Every one must labor for the Community in a reasonable degree, or not taste its benefits.... Whoever is willing to receive from his fellow men that for which he gives no equivalent, will stay away from its precincts forever. But whoever shall surrender himself to its principles, shall find that its yoke is easy and its burden light. Everything can be said of it, in a degree, which Christ said of his kingdom, and therefore it is believed that in some measure it does embody his idea. For its gate of entrance is strait and narrow. It is literally a pearl hidden in a field. Those only who are willing to lose their life for its sake shall find it. Its voice is that which sent the young man sorrowing away: "Go sell all thy goods and give to the poor, and then come and follow me." "Seek first the kingdom of Heaven and its righteousness, and all other things shall be added to you."...

There may be some persons at a distance, who will ask, To what degree has this Community gone into operation? We can not answer this with precision, but we have a right to say that it has purchased the farm which some of its members cultivated for a year with success, by way of trying their love and skill for agricultural labor; that in the only house they are as yet rich enough to own, is collected a large family, including several boarding scholars, and that all work and study together. They seem to be glad to know of all who desire to join them in the spirit, that at any moment, when they are able to enlarge their habitations, they may call together those that belong to them.

❧ "I beg, I implore, I demand pity"

DOROTHEA DIX

Dorothea Dix was one of the great champion reformers of her day, successfully raising the consciousness of the nation to the plight of the mentally ill. In January 1843 Dix presented a petition to the Massachusetts Legislature detailing the cruel treatment that the insane suffered in jails and calling for the separation of the mentally ill from the criminal. Her work led to the creation of state-supported institutions for the mentally ill in Massachusetts and several other states.

In 1854, after eight years of lobbying by Dix, Congress passed an act allocating 12.2 million acres of public land among the states to support institutions for the insane and the deaf. President Pierce vetoed the bill saying that federal aid would bring to an end state and local "fountains of charity." During the Civil War Dix imposed demanding standards as the superintendent of women nurses on the Union side. This is from her 1843 petition to the Massachusetts Legislature.

Gentlemen,—I respectfully ask to present this Memorial, believing that the cause, which actuates to and sanctions so unusual a movement, presents no equivocal claim to public consideration and sympathy. Surrendering to calm and deep convictions of duty my habitual views of what is womanly and becoming, I proceed briefly to explain what has conducted me before you unsolicited and unsustained, trusting, while I do so, that the memorialist will be speedily forgotten in the memorial
....

I come to present the strong claims of suffering humanity. I come to place before the Legislature of Massachusetts the condition of the miserable, the desolate, the outcast. I come as the advocate of helpless, forgotten, insane, and idiotic men and women; of beings sunk to a condition from which the most unconcerned would start with real horror; of beings wretched in our prisons, and more wretched in our almshouses. And I cannot suppose it needful to employ earnest persuasion, or stubborn argument, in order to arrest and fix attention upon a subject only the more strongly pressing in its claims because it is revolting and disgusting in its details.

I must confine myself to few examples, but am ready to furnish other and more complete details, if required. If my pictures are displeasing, coarse, and severe, my subjects, it must be recollected, offer no tranquil, refined, or composing features. The condition of human beings, reduced to the extremest states of degradation and misery, cannot be exhibited in softened language, or adorn a polished page.

I proceed, gentlemen, briefly to call your attention to the present state of insane persons confined within this Commonwealth, in cages, closets, cellars, stalls, pens! Chained, naked, beaten with rods, and lashed into obedience.

As I state cold, severe facts, I feel obliged to refer to persons, and definitely to indicate localities. But it is upon my subject, not upon localities or individuals, I desire to fix attention; and I would speak as kindly as possible of all wardens, keepers, and other responsible officers, believing that most of these have erred not through hardness of heart and wilful cruelty so much as want of skill and knowledge, and want of consideration. Familiarity with suffering, it is said, blunts the sensibilities, and where neglect once finds a footing other injuries are multiplied. This is not all, for it may justly and strongly be added that, from the deficiency of adequate means to meet the wants of these cases, it has been an absolute impossibility to do justice in this matter. Prisons are not constructed in view of being converted into county hospitals, and almshouses are not founded as receptacles for the insane. And yet, in the face of justice and common sense, wardens are by law compelled to receive, and the masters of almshouses not to refuse, insane and idiotic subjects in all stages of mental disease and privation.

It is the Commonwealth, not its integral parts, that is accountable for most of the abuses which have lately and do still exist. I repeat it, it is defective legislation which perpetuates and multiplies these abuses. In illustration of my subject, I offer the following extracts from my Notebook and Journal:

SPRINGFIELD. In the jail, one lunatic woman, furiously mad, a State pauper, improperly situated, both in regard to the prisoners, the keepers, and herself. It is a case of extreme self-forgetfulness and oblivion to all the decencies of life, to describe which would be to repeat only the grossest scenes. She is much worse since leaving Worcester. In the almshouse of the same town is a woman apparently only needing judicious care, and some well chosen employment, to make it unnecessary to confine her in solitude, in a dreary unfurnished room. Her appeals for employment and companionship are most touching, but the mistress replied "she had no time to attend to her."…

CONCORD. A woman from the hospital in a cage in the almshouse. In the jail several, decently cared for in general, but not properly placed in a prison. Violent, noisy, unmanageable most of the time.

LINCOLN. A woman in a cage. Medford. One idiotic subject chained, and one in a close stall for seventeen years. Pepperell. One often doubly chained, hand and foot; another violent; several peaceable now. Brookfield. One man caged, comfortable. Granville. One often closely confined; now losing the use of his limbs from want of exercise. Charlemont. One man caged. Savoy. One man caged. Lenox. Two in the jail, against whose unfit condition there the jailer protests.

DEDHAM. The insane disadvantageously placed in the jail. In the almshouse, two females in stalls, situated in the main building; lie in wooden bunks filled with straw; always shut up. One of these subjects is supposed curable. The overseers of the poor have declined giving her a trial at the hospital, as I was informed, on account of expense.

FRANKLIN. One man chained; decent. Taunton. One woman caged. Plymouth. One man stall-caged; from Worcester Hospital. Scituate. One man and one woman stall-caged. West Bridgewater. Three idiots. Never removed from one room. Barnstable. Four females in pens and stalls. Two chained certainly. I think all. Jail, one idiot. Wellfleet. Three insane. One man and one woman chained, the latter in a bad condition. Brewster. One woman violently mad, solitary. Could not see her, the master and mistress being absent, and the paupers in charge having strict orders to admit no one. Rochester. Seven insane; at present none caged. Milford. Two insane, not now caged. Cohasset. One idiot, one insane; most miserable condition. Plympton. One insane, three idiots; condition wretched.

Besides the above, I have seen many who, part of the year, are chained or caged. The use of cages all but universal. Hardly a town but can refer to some not distant period of using them; chains are less common; negligences frequent; wilful abuse less frequent than sufferings proceeding from ignorance, or want of consideration. I encountered during the last three months many poor creatures wandering reckless and unprotected through the country. Innumerable accounts have been sent me of persons who had roved away unwatched and unsearched after; and I have heard that responsible persons, controlling the almshouses, have not thought themselves culpable in sending away from their shelter, to cast upon the chances of remote relief, insane men and women. These, left on the highways, unfriended and incompetent to control or direct their own movements, sometimes have found refuge in the hospital, and others have not been traced. But I cannot particularize. In traversing the State, I have found hundreds of insane persons in every variety of circumstance and condition, many whose situation could not and need not be improved; a less number, but that very large, whose lives are the saddest pictures of human suffering and degradation. I give a few illustrations; but description fades before reality.

DANVERS. November. Visited the almshouse. A large building, much out of repair. Understand a new one is in contemplation. Here are from fifty-six to sixty inmates, one idiotic, three insane; one of the latter in close confinement at all times.

Long before reaching the house, wild shouts, snatches of rude songs, imprecations and obscene language, fell upon the ear, proceeding from the occupant of a low building, rather remote from the principal building to which my course was directed. Found the mistress, and was conducted to the place which was called "the home" of the forlorn maniac, a young woman, exhibiting a condition of neglect and misery blotting out the faintest idea of comfort, and outraging every sentiment of decency. She had been, I learnt, a respectable person, industrious and worthy. Disappointments and trials shook her mind, and, finally, laid prostrate reason and self-control. She became a maniac for life. She had been at Worcester Hospital for a considerable time, and had been returned as "incurable." The mistress told me she understood that, "while there, she was comfortable and decent." Alas, what a change was here exhibited! She had passed from one degree of violence to another, in swift progress. There she stood, clinging to or beating upon the bars of her caged apartment, the contracted size of which afforded space only for increasing accumulations of filth, a loud spectacle. There she stood with naked arms and dishevelled hair, the unwashed frame invested with fragments of unclean garments, the air so extremely offensive, though ventilation was afforded on all sides save one, that it was not possible to remain beyond a few moments without retreating for recovery to the outward air. Irritation of body, produced by utter filth and exposure, incited her to the horrid process of tearing off her skin by inches. Her face, neck, and person were thus disfigured to hideousness. She held up a fragment just rent off. To my exclamation of horror, the mistress replied: "Oh, we can't help it. Half the skin is off sometimes. We can do nothing with her; and it makes no difference what she eats, for she consumes her own filth as readily as the food which is brought her."…

Men of Massachusetts, I beg, I implore, I demand pity and protection for these of my suffering, outraged sex. Fathers, husbands, brothers, I would supplicate you for this boon; but what do I say? I dishonor you, divest you at once of Christianity and humanity, does this appeal imply distrust. If it comes burdened with a doubt of your righteousness in this legislation, then blot it out; while I declare confidence in your honor, not less than your humanity. Here you will put away the cold, calculating spirit of selfishness and self-seeking; lay off the armor of local strife and political opposition; here and now, for once, forgetful of the earthly and perishable, come up to these halls and consecrate them with one heart and one mind to works of righteousness and just judgment. Become the benefactors of your race, the just guardians of the solemn rights you hold in trust. Raise up the fallen, succor the desolate, restore the outcast, defend the helpless, and for your eternal and great reward receive the benediction, "Well done, good and faithful servants, become rulers over many things!"…

Gentlemen, I commit to you this sacred cause. Your action upon this subject will affect the present and future condition of hundreds and of thousands.

"The annexation of Texas to the United States"

SAM HOUSTON

After defeating Mexican forces in the battlefield, Texas declared itself an independent republic in 1836. Military hero Sam Houston became its first president, and would later serve as its last from 1841 to 1844. United States President Andrew Jackson formally recognized the Republic of Texas on his last day in office in 1837. Texas then petitioned for annexation to the United States, but opposition from antislavery forces stalled the effort.

Texas carried forward as an independent but in 1842 Mexico invaded the Lone Star republic to regain its lost territory. The Texans repulsed the invasion, but renewed their efforts to join the United States. In 1844, Houston wrote this letter to Jackson to enlist his support in the effort. Finally, in 1845 Texas was annexed by the United States, becoming the 28th state and the 15th slave state. When the Civil War broke out 15 years later, Houston was one of the few prominent leaders from the deep South to urge against secession.

Venerated Friend,

Your several favors of the last month have reached me safely and with expedition. I have given all the attention to their contents which your views as well as the subject matter itself demanded. You are fully aware that every circumstance in which you feel a deep interest, or whatever concerns you individually, awakens in me emotions of the liveliest regard.

It is natural to suppose that the subject of the annexation of Texas to the U. States has commanded the most profound deliberation of which I am capable. Heretofore, the demeanor of the U. States towards us, has been such as to discourage any hope which the friends of the measure might entertain. Our situation, also, has been peculiar and difficult. I have found myself surrounded with internal difficulties as well as external dangers. It was my duty, as Executive, to have an eye to every emergency which might possibly arise. My situation might have excused, or even justified, a compromittal on my part, with the hope of securing for my country a respite from existing calamities. I am happy to assure you, however, that I have incurred no committal prejudicial to her interest or my own honor. I am free to take any action which her future welfare may require, and be perfectly vindicated from any imputation of bad faith towards any nation or individual....

I am determined upon immediate annexation to the United States. It is not the result of feeling; nor do I believe that the measure would be as advantageous to Texas, if she had permanent peace, as it is indispensably necessary to the United States. Texas with peace could exist without the U. States; but the U. States cannot, without great hazard to the security of their institutions, exist without Texas. The U. States are one of the rival powers of the earth, and from their importance as well as the peculiarity of their institutions and the extent of their commercial relations, they must expect at no distant day, wars, the object of which will be to prevent their continuance, if possible, as a nation.

Situated as Texas is in point of locality, with peace she has nothing to apprehend for years to come. Other nations would not dread her rivalry, but rather court her friendship for commercial advantage. Her people would have nothing to divert them from their agricultural pursuits. Her advancement in the arts of peace and commerce would be inevitable. With a government requiring trifling expenditure, and a tariff much lower than that of the United States, she would invite the commerce of all nations to her ports (as is already to some extent the case); and while she thus increased the demand for her productions she would drive the manufactures of the United States from her markets, from the fact that American manufacturers could not so well compete with those of Europe. In this way, the immense trade of the Northern Mexican States as well as Texas would fall into the hands of European merchants and pass through our ports and territory. In a few years the loss to the American manufacturer would not be a small amount. But, on the other hand, by annexation, these advantages would be secured to the American merchant to the exclusion of the European; for we should then be but one government.

The exchange of commodities between Texas and Europe, would give rise to a feeling of reciprocal benefit; and there would be nothing in all this to excite national cupidity or jealousy towards her. Thus situated, Texas might remain at peace for a half century: nor is it probably that she would then have war, unless it were with Mexico. Her resources having accumulated for this period, she would have

sufficient means and ample capacity to subjugate Mexico whenever she might choose so to do. The efficiency and hardy character of her population would, also, enable wise leaders to render subservient the means of Mexico to her own subjugation—This is an imperfect glance at some of the advantages which Texas might hope for as a separate power.

By immediate annexation we relieve ourselves of the solicitude which we have felt as to our situation: yet that would be no guaranty for immediate peace. Mexico might take annexation as cause of war, and inflict annoyances upon us. It might be some time before the proper aid from the U. States would be available for our defence against incursion. Such an incursion would seriously interrupt our citizens in their peaceful avocations....

There is a sameness or unity in our institutions and national interests in Texas which does not exist in the U. States. All our population is agricultural and we have no sectional institution or diversified interests. It is different in the U.S. Their legislation is embarrassed by these interests. The farming, manufacturing, maritime and mercantile interests all claim the peculiar consideration of the national Congress. Texas, independent, would be free from the agitations arising from this condition of things. The interests of the north and the south, in the U. States render it almost two distinct nations. The question of slavery cannot on this subject be arrayed against another. By annexation we should subject ourselves to the hazard of our tranquility and peace on this subject, which, as a separate power, would not exist. The debt of Texas is a mere "drop in the bucket." Our public domain comprises at least one hundred and fifty millions of acres of arable land, with every delightful variety of climate and every natural advantage which a country of the same extent could possibly enjoy....

I wish to reside in a land where all will be subordinate to law, and where none dare defy its mandates. I have arrived at that period of life, when I earnestly desire retirement and an assurance that whatever I possess will be secured to me by just laws wisely administered. This privilege I would deem a rich requital for whatever I may have performed useful in life....

A special minister, together with our resident Charge, has been appointed, with full powers, and despatched to consummate the work of annexation.

But that you may be the more perfectly informed of everything interesting connected with the subject, I have directed my Private Secretary and confidential friend, W. D. Miller, Esq., to convey my personal salutations and embraces to you, with authority to communicate everything upon every subject....

Now, my venerated friend, will you perceive that Texas is presented to the United States... but if, in the confident hope of the union, she should be rejected, her mortification would be indescribable. She has been sought by the United States, and this is the third time she has consented. Were she now to be spurned, it would forever terminate expectation on her part; and it would then not only be left for the United States to expect that she would seek some other friend, but all Christendom would justify her in a course dictated by necessity and sanctioned by wisdom. However adverse this might be to the wishes or the interests of the United States, in her present situation she could not ponder long. The course adopted by the U. States, if it stop short of annexation, will displease France, irritate England and exasperate Mexico. An effort to postpone it to a more convenient season may be tried in the U. States, to subserve party purposes and make a President; Let them beware! I take it that it is of too great magnitude for any impediment to be interposed to its execution.

That you may live to see your hopes in relation to it crowned with complete success, I sincerely desire. In the event that it speedily takes place, I hope it will afford me an opportunity of visiting you again at the Hermitage. It is the ardent desire of Mrs. Houston to see the day when you can lay your hand on our little boy's head and bestow upon him your benediction. Be assured, General, I should rejoice if circumstances should afford an opportunity for an event so desirable to us.

Be pleased to make the united salutations of Ms. Houston and myself to your family. We unite our prayers for your happiness, and join in the expression of our affectionate regard for you.

Truly your friend,
Sam Houston

❧ Expanding westward

JAMES K. POLK

Texas's petition for annexation was accepted by a receptive United States, eager to push its borders westward. President James K. Polk embraced the nation's expansionist ambitions. In his March 4, 1845, inaugural address, Polk not only declared his strong support for accepting Texas into the Union, but also claimed the United States' right to territories beyond the Rocky Mountains. Within two years, Polk had acquired Texas, taken a huge swath of land in the Southwest from Mexico by force and signed an agreement dividing the Oregon Territory with Great Britain at the 49th parallel.

The Republic of Texas has made known her desire to come into our Union, to form a part of our confederacy and enjoy with us the blessings of liberty secured and guaranteed by our Constitution. Texas was once part of our country—was unwisely ceded away to a foreign power—is not independent, and possesses an undoubted right to dispose of a part or the whole of her territory and to merge her sovereignty as a separate and independent state in ours. I congratulate my country that by an act of the late Congress of the United States the assent of this government has been given to the reunion, and it only remains for the two countries to agree upon the terms to consummate an object so important to both.

I regard the question of annexation as belonging exclusively to the United States and Texas. They are independent powers competent to contract, and foreign nations have no right to interfere with them or to take exceptions to their reunion. Foreign powers do not seem to appreciate the true character of our government. Our Union is a confederation of independent states, whose policy is peace with each other and all the world. To enlarge its limits is to extend the dominions of peace over additional territories and increasing millions. The world has nothing to fear from military ambitions in our government....

Foreign powers should therefore look on the annexation of Texas to the United States not as the conquest of a nation seeking to extend her dominions by arms and violence, but as the peaceful acquisition of a territory once her own, by adding another member to our confederation, with the consent of that member, thereby diminishing the chances of war and opening to them new and ever-increasing markets for their products.

To Texas the reunion is important, because the strong protecting arm of our government would be extended over her, and the vast resources of her fertile soil and genial climate would be speedily developed....

Is there one among our citizens who would not prefer perpetual peace with Texas to occasional wars, which so often occur between bordering nations? Is there one who would not prefer free intercourse with her to high duties on all our products and manufactures which enter her ports or cross her frontiers? Is there one who would not prefer an unrestricted communication with her citizens to the frontier obstructions which must occur if she remains out of the Union? Whatever is good or evil in the local institutions of Texas will remain her own whether annexed to the United States or not. None of the present states will be responsible for them any more than they are for the local institutions of each other. They have confederated together for certain specified objects. Upon the same principle that they would refuse to form a perpetual union with Texas because of her local institutions our forefathers would have been prevented from forming our present Union.... I shall on the broad principle which formed the basis and produced the adoption of our Constitution, and not in any narrow spirit of sectional policy, endeavor by all constitutional, honorable, and appropriate means to consummate the expressed will of the people and government of the United States by the reannexation of Texas to our Union at the earliest practicable period.

Nor will it become in a less degree my duty to assert and maintain by all constitutional means the right of the United States to that portion of our territory which lies beyond the Rocky Mountains. Our title to the country of the Oregon is "clear and unquestionable," and already are our people preparing to perfect that title by occupying it with their wives and children. But eighty years ago our population was confined on the west by the ridge of the Alleghanies. Within that period—within the lifetime, I might say, of some of my hearers—our people, increasing to many millions, have filled the eastern valleys of the Mississippi, adventurously ascended the Missouri to its headspring, and are already engaged in establishing the blessings of self-government in valleys of which the rivers flow to the Pacific. The world beholds the peaceful triumphs of the industry of our emigrants. To us belongs the duty of protecting them adequately wherever they may be upon our soil. The jurisdiction of our laws and the benefits of our republican institutions should be extended over them in the distant regions which they have selected for their homes.

A Christian Defense of Slavery

THE REVEREND RICHARD FULLER

By the 1840s the South had become increasingly defensive of slavery. Many seethed at the accusations and incriminations of the abolitionist movement. In response, the slave-owning South issued increasingly strident defenses of slavery. Some of the most effective defenders were clergymen. The Reverend Richard Fuller of South Carolina wrote this Christian defense of slavery in 1845 citing Biblical passages to bolster the South's God-given right to own slaves. Slavery split several national churches during the antebellum period. Just as Southern ministers objected to their Northern colleagues abolitionist views, many Northern ministers could not abide the Southern Christian community's defense of slavery.

The issue now before us regards the essential moral character of slavery; and on such a question I am strongly disposed to pass by all ethical and metaphysical dissertation, and appeal at once to the only standard of right and wrong which can prove decisive. For my own part, I am heartily sick and weary of the controversies and debates waged and waging on every side, in which each party is contending, not for truth, but victory, and which have effected just nothing, for the want of some arbiter recognised by all, and whose decree shall be final and infallible. Now such an umpire we have. Whatever importance others may attach to the deductions of human reasoning, and thus impiously array against the Scriptures those "oppositions of science falsely so called," which the Apostle terms "profane and vain babblings," you and I have long since put on our shields one motto—"Let God be true and every man a liar."...

Now, in order to clear away rubbish, and arrive at once at the point, let me remind you that it is simply the essential character of slavery which we are discussing; and that slavery is a term whose meaning can be easily and accurately defined. Slavery is bondage. It is (to give Paley's idea in other language) the condition of one to whose service another has a fight, without the consent or contract of the servant….

Is it necessarily a crime in the sight of God to control or curtail the natural personal liberty of a human being? A question admitting no debate at all.

It will not be disputed that government is the ordinance of God. But government is restraint; the very idea of government includes an abridgment of that personal freedom which a savage has in the forest, and a modification of it into political freedom, or civil rights and privileges.

Is it, then, necessarily a crime for a government to discriminate between those whom it controls, in the distribution of civil privileges and political liberty? It would surely be preposterous to affirm this. Every government has necessarily a fight to pass laws indispensable to its existence; and it has a right, also, to establish those regulations which shall best promote the good of the whole population. Whether any particular enactments be necessary, and whether they do secure the greatest good, are points as to which error may be committed, but as to which each government is the judge; and if it acts uprightly, with all the lights possessed, there is no crime. We boast of our liberties, and are forever quoting the words of the Declaration of Independence; yet in this country it has been deemed most for the good of the whole, that one half of the citizens (and I believe by far the noblest, purest, and best half) should be disenfranchised of a great many civil rights. This is true, also, of all citizens until they reach an age wholly conventional, viz. twenty-one. Is this a sin? Will it be urged that all are born free and equal, and that it is wicked to violate the indefeasible rights of women and minors? The day is coming, I venture to predict, when our regenerators will utter such frantic arguments; for they drive on, unrecking and unheeding alike the plainest dictates of reason and experience, and the stern lessons of the French Revolution, and the warning voice which spoke in such fearful accents amid the havoc and butchery and desolation of St. Domingo. But no good citizen considers the inequalities existing in these States criminal ….

As soon as slavery is mentioned at the North, there is conjured up, in the minds of many persons, I know not what confused, revolting combination, and heart-rending spectacle, of chains, and whips, and cruelty, and crime, and wretchedness. But, I repeat it, even at the peril of tediousness, that necessarily and essentially—(and in a multitude of instances, practically and actually)—slavery is nothing more than the condition of one who is deprived of political power, and does service,—without his contract and consent, it is true, but yet it may be, cheerfully and happily, and for a compensation reasonable and certain, paid in modes of return best for the slave himself. With what is strictly physical liberty, the master interferes no more, in such cases, than you do with a hired servant. The work assigned is confessedly very light—scarcely one half of that performed by a white laborer with you. When that is performed, the slaves (to use an expression common with them) are "their own masters." And if you ever allow us the pleasure of seeing you at the South, you will find slaves tilling land for themselves; working as mechanics for themselves, and selling various articles of merchandise for themselves; and when you inquire of them some explanation, they will speak of their rights, and their property, with as clear a sense of what is due to them, and as much confidence, as they could if free; and tell you (to use another of their phrases) that they do all this "in their own time."…

Having described the condition of a slave, I ought now to advert to the obligations of the master; but I have not space, nor is it requisite. Let me only say, (and with the most solemn earnestness, for God forbid I should ever utter a word which may perpetuate cruelty and sin,) that the right of the master not only does not give him any such license of wholesale oppression and wrong as you suppose, but really places him under the deepest corresponding obligations to promote the interest, temporal and eternal, of his slaves. And though we have all been "verily guilty concerning our brethren" who are dependent on us, yet I trust the South is becoming every day more alive to its responsibility. Already much has been effected; and, as a class, I believe our slaves to be now better compensated, and, in moral, intellectual, and religious condition, superior to most operatives in Europe. From parliamentary reports, it appears that in Ireland three millions and a half of people live in mud hovels, having one room, and without chimney or window. In England and Wales there are three millions of people without any pastoral provision. In London itself the statistics of misery and vice are appalling. On one occasion, said a speaker in Exeter Hall, four families occupied one small room, each hiring a corner; and in one of these corners there was a corpse lately dead, and four men using it as a table to play cards upon. And if this be so in Great Britain, need I speak of Spain and Russia, or attest what I myself have seen of ignorance and superstition and degradation in Italy? We are far, however, from having acquitted ourselves of our duty; and I do not wish to palliate, much less defend by recrimination, the unfaithfulness of the South to the sacred trust imposed upon us....

The natural descendants of Abraham were holders of slaves, and God took them into special relation to himself. "He made known his ways unto Moses, his acts unto the children of Israel;" and he instituted regulations for their government, into which he expressly incorporated a permission to buy and hold slaves. These institutes not only recognise slavery as lawful, but contain very minute directions. It is not necessary for me to argue this point, as it is conceded by you. Slaves were held by the priests. "A sojourner of a priest, or an hired servant, shall not eat of the holy thing. But if the priest buy any soul with his money, he shall eat of it, and he that is born in his house, they shall eat of it." (Lev. xxii. 10, 11.) They might be bought of the Canaanites around, or of strangers living among the Hebrews. "Both thy bondmen, and thy bondmaids, which thou shalt have, shall be of the heathen that are round about you; of them shall ye buy bondmen and bondmaids. Moreover, of the children of the strangers that do sojourn among you, of them shall ye buy, and of their families that are with you, which they begat in your land; and they shall be your possession." (Lev. xxv.) They were regarded as property, and were called "money," "possession:" "If a man smite his servant or his maid, with a rod, and he die under his hand; he shall be surely punished. Notwithstanding, if he continue a day or two, he shall not be punished: for he is his money." (Exod. xxi. 20, 21.) They might be sold. This is implied in the term "money;" but it is plainly taken for granted: "Thou shalt not make

merchandise of her, because thou hast humbled her." (Deut. xxi. 14.) See also Exod. xxi. 7, 8. "And if a man sell his daughter to be a maid-servant, she shall not go out as the menservants do. If she please not her master, who hath betrothed her to himself, then shall he let her be redeemed: to sell her to a strange nation he shall have no power, seeing he hath dealt deceitfully with her." The slavery thus expressly sanctioned was hereditary and perpetual: "Ye shall take them as an inheritance for your children after you, to inherit them for a possession. They shall be your bondmen forever." (Lev. xxv.) Lastly, Hebrews, if bought, were to be treated, not as slaves, but as hired servants, and to go free at the year of jubilee. "If thy brother that dwelleth by thee be waxen poor, and be sold unto thee, thou shalt not compel him to serve as a bondservant; but as an hired servant and as a sojourner shall he be with thee, and shall serve thee unto the year of jubilee: and then shall he depart from thee, both he and his children with him, and shall return unto his own family, and unto the possession of his father shall he return." (Lev. xxv. 29.) If during the Hebrew's time of service he married a slave, and had children, the wife and children were not set at liberty with him. If he consented, he might become a slave for life: "If thou buy a Hebrew servant, six years shall he serve: and in the seventh he shall go out free for nothing. If he came in by himself, he shall go out by himself: if he were married, then his wife shall go out with him. If his master have given him a wife, and she have borne him sons or daughters, the wife and her children shall be her master's, and he shall go out by himself. And if the servant shall plainly say, I love my master, my wife, and my children; I will not go out free: Then his master shall bring him unto the judges: he shall also bring him to the door, or unto the door-post; and his master shall bore his ear through with an awl; and he shall serve him forever." (Exod. xxi. 2-6.)

Such are some parts of the Mosaic institution. Let me add, also, that the decalogue twice recognises slavery, and forbids one Israelite to covet the man-servant or maid-servant of another. And, now, how does all this appear if your assumption be for a moment tenable, that slavery is as great a crime as can be committed? Suppose these regulations had thus sanctioned piracy, or idolatry, would they ever have commanded the faith of the world as divine? How conclusive is this that slavery is not among crimes in the estimation of mankind, and according to the immutable and eternal principles of morality!...

The New Testament is not silent as to slavery; it recognises the relation, and commands slaves to obey their masters; and what I now affirm is this, that, when we consider the previous permission by the Old Testament, such commands to slaves are not only a *suppressio veri,*
but a *suggestio falsi*—not only a suppression of the truth, but a suggestion of what is false—if slavery be a sin of appalling magnitude. Let it be borne in mind that the previous sanction had been both by God's conduct and express precept, and demanded, therefore, a countervailing revelation of no equivocal sort. Yet, not only is no condemnation uttered, but slaves are addressed as such, and required to obey...

You affirm ... that although the apostles did not condemn slavery by express precept, they did so by the inculcation of truths that must abolish slavery. As to which allegation, occupying the ground I now do, it would be quite enough for me to reply, that no matter what truths the apostles taught, if they received slaveholders into the churches, and pronounced them "faithful and beloved," they put to silence the charge that slaveholding is always and everywhere a sin.

If you had said that the gospel, wherever received, at once eradicated the Roman system of slavery, and made the relation "a very different thing;" and if you had added, that everywhere the gospel requires of a master the moral and intellectual improvement of his slaves; I at least should have had no controversy with you. Then, too, while Christians at the South are enjoined to perform their solemn duty, the good and the wise through the Union might consult in the spirit of a prospective and far-seeing philanthropy, as to the designs of God for the African race. But the proposition defended by you has no connection with all this. Slavery is averred by you to be always, and every moment, a sin of appalling magnitude....

Slavery may be a sin; and may be rendered so by the manner in which the present master obtained his power, or by the abuse of that power, or by the means employed to perpetuate that power. But supposing there is no sin (as there is manifestly none) in being the heir or legatee of this power, then the use of it may be most virtuous; as

in the bequests mentioned in my third letter; and in all cases where slaves are unprepared for liberty, and the master's authority is exercised for their truest benefit, temporal and eternal.

🍂 *"Cotton and negroes are the constant theme"*

J. H. INGRAM

With the minor exceptions of 1809, 1815 and the Civil War years, cotton was the number one export of the United States from 1807 until 1890. Eli Whitney's invention of the cotton gin in 1793 made cotton a profitable cash crop of far-reaching implications. By eliminating the time consuming task of processing raw cotton, Whitney initiated the rapid expansion of the textile industry and entrenched the slave system.

Farming cotton was a labor-intensive, brutal undertaking that required rich soil and cheap, unskilled labor. The Mississippi Valley's virgin soil and abundant slaves provided the ingredients to build cotton plantations and personal fortunes. The Deep South turned to cotton with a vengeance in the early nineteenth century, creating a foundation from which to build the regional economy and provide Northern textile manufacturers with their raw materials.

J. H. Ingram was born and raised in New England but moved to Natchez, Mississippi, in 1830 when he was 21 years old. Ingram had a great affection for the South and its ways. In his 1835 book *The South-West* he explained the inextricable relationship between the economy, slaves, and "King Cotton." This combination helped fuel Southerners' drive to defend slavery and emboldened them to believe they were in a position to back up their threats of secession.

There are many causes, both moral and physical, which concur to render the inhabitants of the south dissimilar to those of the north. Some of these may be traced to climate, more to education and local relations, and yet more to that peculiar state of things which necessarily prevails in a planting country and all newly organized states. The difference is clearly distinguishable through all its grades and ramifications, and so strongly marked as to stamp the southern character with traits sufficiently distinctive to be dignified with the term national.

A plantation well stocked with hands, is the *ne plus ultra* of every man's ambition who resides at the south. Young men who come to this country, "to make money," soon catch the mania, and nothing less than a broad plantation, waving with the snow white cotton bolls, can fill their mental vision, as they anticipate by a few years in their dreams of the future, the result of their plans and labours. Hence, the great number of planters and the few professional men of long or eminent standing in their several professions. In such a state of things no men grow old or gray in their profession if at all successful. As soon as the young lawyer acquires sufficient to purchase a few hundred acres of the rich alluvial lands, and a few slaves, he quits his profession at once, though perhaps just rising into eminence, and turns cotton planter. The bar at Natchez is composed, with but few exceptions, entirely of young men. Ten years hence, probably not four out of five of these, if living, will remain in their profession. To the prevalence of this custom of retiring so early from the bar, and not to want of talent, is to be attributed its deficiency of distinguished names. There is much talent now concentrated at this bar, and throughout the state. But its possessors are young men; and this mania for planting will soon deprive the state of any benefit from it in a professional point of view. As the lawyers are young, the judges cannot of course be much stricken in years. The northerner, naturally associates with the locks of snow, a suit of title of Judge, a venerable, dignified personage, with sober black, and powdered queue, shoe-buckles, and black silk stockings. Judge my surprise at hearing at the public table a few days since, a young gentleman, apparently not more than four or five and twenty, addressed as "judge!" I at first thought it applied as a mere "soubriquet," till subsequently assured that he was really on the bench....

Cotton and negroes are the constant theme—the ever harped upon, never worn out subject of conversation among all classes. But a small portion of the broad rich lands of this thriving state is yet appropriated. Not till every acre is purchased and cultivated—not till Mississippi becomes one vast cotton field, will this mania, which has entered into the very marrow, bone and sinew of a Mississippian's system, pass away. And not then, till the lands become exhausted and wholly unfit for farther cultivation. The rich loam which forms the upland soil of this state is of a very slight depth—and after a few years is worn away by constant culture and the action of the winds and rain. The fields are then "thrown out" as useless. Every ploughfurrow becomes the bed of a rivulet after heavy rains—these uniting are increased into torrents, before which the impal-

pable soil dissolves like ice under a summer's sun. By degrees, acre after acre, of what was a few years previous beautifully undulating ground, waving with the dark green, snow-crested cotton, presents a wild scene of frightful precipices, and yawning chasms, which are increased in depth and destructively enlarged after every rain. There are many thousand acres within twenty miles of the city of Natchez, being the earliest cultivated portions of the country, which are now lying in this condition, presenting an appearance of wild desolation, and not unfrequently, of sublimity....

To sell cotton in order to buy negroes—to make more cotton to buy more negroes, "ad infinitum," is the aim and direct tendency of all the operations of the thorough-going cotton planter; his whole soul is wrapped up in the pursuit. It is, apparently, the principle by which he "lives, moves, and has his being." There are some who "work" three and four hundred negroes, though the average number is from thirty to one hundred. "This is all very fine," you say, "but the slaves!—there's the rub." True; but without slaves there could be no planters, for whites will not and cannot work cotton plantations, beneath a broiling southern sun.— Without planters there could be no cotton; without cotton no wealth. Without them Mississippi would be a wilderness, and revert to the aboriginal possessors. Annihilate them tomorrow, and this state and every southern state might be bought for a song. I am not advocating this system; but destroy it—and the southern states become at once comparative ciphers in the Union. Northerners, particularly Yankees, are at first a little compunctious on the subject of holding slaves. They soon, however, illustrate the truth contained in the following lines, but slightly changed from their original application. With half-averted eyes they at first view slavery as

"—A monster of such horrid mien,
That to be hated needs but to be seen:
But seen too oft, familiar with her face,
They soon endure—and in the end embrace."

Many of the planters are northerners. When they have conquered their prejudices, they become thorough, driving planters, generally giving themselves up to the pursuit more devotedly than the regular-bred planter. Their treatment of their slaves is also far more rigid. Northerners are entirely unaccustomed to their habits, which are perfectly understood and appreciated by southerners, who have been familiar with Africans from childhood; whom they have had for their nurses, play-fellows, and "bearers," and between whom and themselves a reciprocal and very natural attachment exists, which, on the gentleman's part, involuntarily extends to the whole dingy race, exhibited in a kindly feeling and condescending familiarity, for which he receives gratitude in return. On the part of the slave, this attachment is manifested by an affection and faithfulness which only cease with life. Of this state of feeling, which a southern life and education can only give, the northerner knows nothing. Inexperience leads him to hold the reins of government over his novel subjects with an unsparing severity, which the native ruler of these domestic colonies finds wholly unnecessary. The slave always prefers a southern master, because he knows that he will be understood by him. His kindly feelings toward, and sympathies with slaves, as such, are as honourable to his heart as gratifying to the subjects of them. He treats with suitable allowance those peculiarities of their race, which the unpractised northerner will construe into idleness, obstinacy, laziness, revenge, or hatred. There is another cause for their difference of treatment to their slaves. The southerner, habituated to their presence, never fears them, and laughs at the idea. It is the reverse with the northerner: he fears them, and hopes to intimidate them by severity.

❧ Baseball's Original Rules

ALEXANDER CARTWRIGHT

Alexander Cartwright is credited with inventing the basic rules of baseball and laying out the first baseball diamond with four bases 90 feet apart in Hoboken, New Jersey, in 1845. The first known organized game was played between the New York Knickerbockers—a team made up primarily of businessmen—and the New York Nine, consisting of a team of manual laborers and clerks. With Cartwright as umpire, the game lasted four innings. The New York Nine won 23-1.

Baseball's popularity boomed during the Civil War as soldiers not engaged on the front lines played it to pass the time. The sport soon became the national pastime. Many people have seen it as embracing the American ideal of equality, whereby success is determined by individual merit in the context of a group enterprise. By the turn of the century baseball was the favorite spectator sport in the United States and would remain so throughout the 20th century.

1st. Members must strictly observe the time agreed upon for exercise, and be punctual in their attendance.

2nd. When assembled for exercise, the President, or in his absence, the Vice-President, shall appoint an Umpire, who shall keep the game in a book provided for that purpose, and note all violations of the By-Laws and Rules during the time of exercise.

3rd. The presiding officer shall designate two members as Captains, who shall retire and make the match to be played, observing at the same time that the players opposite to each other should be as nearly equal as possible, the choice of sides to be then tossed for, and the first in hand to be decided in like manner.

4th. The bases shall be from "home" to second base, forty-two paces; from first to third base, forty-two paces, equidistant.

5th. No stump match shall be played on a regular day of exercise.

6th. If there should not be a sufficient number of members of the Club present at the time agreed upon to commence exercise, gentlemen not members may be chosen in to make up the match, which shall not be broken up to take in members that may afterwards appear; but in all cases, members shall have the preference, when present, at the making or a match.

7th. If members appear after the game is commenced, they may be chosen in if mutually agreed upon.

8th. The game to consist of twenty-one counts, or aces; but at the conclusion an equal number of hands must be played.

9th. The ball must be pitched, not thrown, for the bat.

10th. A ball knocked out of the field, or outside the range of the first or third base, is foul.

11th. Three balls being struck at and missed and the last one caught, is a hand out; if not caught is considered fair, and the striker bound to run.

12th. If a ball be struck, or tipped, and caught, either flying or on the first bound, it is a hand out.

13th. A player running the bases shall be out, if the ball is in the hands of an adversary on the base, or the runner is touched with it before he makes his base; it being understood, however, that in no instance is a ball to be thrown at him.

14th. A player running who shall prevent an

adversary from catching or getting the ball before making his base, is a hand out.

15th. Three hands out, all out.

16th. Players must take their strike in regular turn.

17th. All disputes and differences relative to the game, to be decided by the Umpire, from which there is no appeal.

18th. No ace or base can be made on a foul strike.

19th. A runner cannot be put out in making one base, when a balk is made by the pitcher.

20th. But one base allowed when a ball bounds out of the field when struck.

🌿 "We are destined to be a great manufacturing people"

HENRY A. MILES

In 1846 Henry A. Miles wrote the book *Lowell, As It Was, and It Is* describing the rapid growth of Lowell, Massachusetts, the pre-eminent manufacturing town in the Northeast. On the leading edge of the American Industrial Revolution, the story of Lowell was repeated hundreds of times across the country over the next century as towns grew into small manufacturing cities.

Using the Merrimack River to power its mills, its access to Boston (made easy by the construction of a railroad), cotton from the South, credit from local banks and labor from the surrounding countryside and immigrant ships, Lowell went from being a typical country village to a booming textile manufacturing city in less than 20 years. Clearly proud of his hometown's accomplishments, Miles describes the process in glowing terms.

While emphasizing the benefits of progress, Miles hints at some of the problems associated with rapid industrialization. On the one hand, the city is growing, adding public buildings and extraordinary advances in commerce. Miles assigns the credit to the vision of the manufacturing companies and their able superintendents who oversee both the work and personal lives of their employees. But Miles also acknowledges that the rapid growth has caused some problems, a need to build a facility for juvenile delinquents and hints at a profound imbalance in the wealth distribution between the owners and the laborers.

The ten years that succeeded the incorporation of Lowell as a town [in 1826] were marked by as great revolutions in the business concerns of the country,

as could be found in any ten years that might be named. There was the great depression of 1827 and 1828, when so many manufacturing companies in New England became bankrupt, and the universal gloom prevailed. This was followed by the great rage for speculation which reigned in 1831 and the few following years. The fortunes of the young town were affected like those of all other places. A cloud rested upon her prospects in the former period, and when the bubble of the latter period burst, many were ruined who had here purchased lands at enormously extravagant prices. Yet through all this the growth of Lowell was in the main steadily onward. She was extending the plan, and laying broad and deep foundations of a great community. New streets were opened, houses and stores were put up, churches were erected, canals were dug, manufacturing operations were extended, and within the ten years named above, the population of the town was multiplied six fold. The increase was without parallel in any place in any country. This prosperity was the result of the sagacity, enterprize, and energy of the capitalists and manufacturers, by whom the fortunes of the place were guided.

A few of the leading events of these years will be here briefly noticed. The Lowell Bank—the first in the town—was incorporated March 11, 1828, with a capital of one hundred thousand dollars. That same year two new manufacturing companies were incorporated—the Appleton and Lowell—both of which immediately proceeded to the erection of mills. An Institution for Savings was incorporated, and went into operation in 1829. A vast increase of the business of Lowell was planned in 1830, by the construction of the Western, of Suffolk, Canal. This was dug in 1831 and 1832, at an expense of seventy thousand dollars. Instead of using the whole fall of thirty-two feet once, it was proposed to divide it into two falls of sixteen feet each; and thus power was obtained for three new corporations. The Suffolk, Tremont, and Lawrence Companies were all incorporated in the winter and spring of 1831, and forthwith commenced the erection of mills and boarding houses. That same year the Railroad Bank was incorporated and went into operation with a capital of eight hundred thousand dollars. Simultaneously with these movements a new company, incorporated June 5, 1830, by the name of the Middlesex Manufacturing Company, purchased the water privilege before owned by

Thomas Hurd, and proceeded to put up a large brick mill for the manufacture of wool. A bleaching company, with a capital of fifty thousand dollars, was incorporated in 1832. Still another canal was dug in 1835, at an expense of thirty-five thousand dollars, to carry water to the mills of the Boott Company, incorporated March 27th of that year, and which proceeded to put up five large factories and eight blocks of boarding houses.

Nor was it merely in this extension of her manufacturing operations that Lowell began at once to assume the importance of a great town. Other buildings were erected, such as usually belonged to such a town. A spacious hall for town purposes, with committee rooms and stores underneath, was completed in 1830, at an expense of thirty thousand dollars. Churches for the Baptist, Orthodox, Universalist, and Unitarian denominations were erected; the latter, a substantial brick building, with a chaste and beautiful interior, dedicated December 25, 1832, and costing twenty-eight thousand dollars. A large hotel—the Merrimack House—was built the same year. This House belongs to the first class of similar establishments, and cost thirty thousand dollars. Another public hall, with reading and library rooms, was built in 1835, for the use of the Middlesex Mechanics' Association, on land given by the Locks and Canal Company, and at a cost of twenty thousand dollars; nearly the whole of which was paid by contributions from the different manufacturing companies. About this time also two large Grammar School Houses were erected, at an expense to the town of twenty-one thousand dollars. A large Alms-house and Poor Farm were provided for the town, a little over a mile distant from its centre, the cost of which was eighteen thousand five hundred dollars…. The opening of the Railroad, July 4, 1835, which connects Boston with Lowell, brought the thriving town within an hour's ride of the metropolis.

These are some of the progressive steps of the rapid and unexampled advancement of this place. A simple statement of the population of the town, at different periods within ten years here alluded to, will still further illustrate its growth. Population of Lowell in 1826, two thousand five hundred inhabitants. In 1828, three thousand five hundred thirty-two. In 1830, six thousand four hundred seventy-seven. In 1832, ten thousand two hundred

forty-four. In 1833, twelve thousand three hundred sixty-three. In 1836, seventeen thousand six hundred thirty-three. Lowell was incorporated as a city March 30, 1836….

The City of Lowell

During the nine years that Lowell has been a city, it has undergone great changes, though not so many nor so striking as during its history as a town. The attention of the new municipal government was at once directed towards improving the general condition of the city, by constructing sidewalks, lighting the streets, the preservation of the public health, the erection of new edifices for the use of the public schools, and the establishment of sewers, which are permanent and costly structures, effectually draining the most densely settled parts of the city. It was not till 1844 that the experiment was made of paving a public street. The success of the plan has lead to an extension of paving this year.

In 1837 a large Market-house was completed. The building is of brick, one hundred and fifty feet long, and forty-five feet wide, three stories high, and contains twenty-two stalls for meat, vegetables, and fish. In the second and third stories are the court-rooms for the county courts, and police court of the city, with offices and jury-rooms. The cost of this building, with the land, was forty-six thousand, one hundred and five dollars. The first court was held in it in April 1837.

Since the incorporation of Lowell as a city, two new companies have erected extensive works. The Massachusetts Manufacturing Company was chartered in 1839, and has built four large mills now in successful operation, together with several blocks of boarding-houses. The Prescott Company was incorporated in 1843, and have erected a mammoth mill on the banks of the Concord river. It has not yet received its machinery. An extensive foundry was built in 1840 by the Locks and Canal Company, at a cost of thirty thousand dollars. Here about seventy men are constantly employed, making the castings which are used in the machine-shops and factories of the city. Among the other improvements which have been made within: new churches; the purchase and establishment, in 1839, of a hospital; the building of a jail, in 1839, on the modern plan of separate cells; the consecration in 1840, of a beautiful Cemetery…; and the purchase, this year, by the city, of two large commons, one of twenty acres, the other of nine, which are to be forever kept open for walks, parades, and other uses. To these should be added the establishment, this year, of a City Library; and the fact that the first steps have been taken to provide immediately for a house of reformation for juvenile offenders.

A mention of these improvements reminds us what after all has been the best change within the last few years—a change in the feelings of the citizens of Lowell. They have begun to cultivate home attachments to the place. They have manifested a disposition to make this their residence for life. They have felt prompted, therefore, to efforts to improve and adorn the place, to establish the conveniences and comforts which a large city demands, and to leave no practicable means untried which promise to elevate the tone and character of society. The existence of the disposition referred to is attested by the kind of improvements above indicated, and by the fact that a large number of residences, and some of them commodious and costly dwellings, have recently been erected....

Lowell in 1845

Lowell has at present a population of nearly thirty thousand souls. About one third of this whole number are operatives, either in the mills, or connected with the mechanical employments ... viz. six thousand three hundred and twenty females, and two thousand nine hundred and fifteen males. There are thirty-three mills beside the print works, and about five hundred and fifty houses belonging to the corporations. The capital stock here invested in manufacturing and mechanical enterprises is twelve millions of dollars. There are made in Lowell, every week, one million four hundred and fifty-nine thousand one yards of cloth amounting to seventy-five million eight hundred and sixty-eight thousand yards per year. This is nearly enough to belt the globe twice round. Sixty-one thousand one hundred bales of cotton are worked up every year. Of printed calico there are made annually fourteen millions of yards. The annual consumption in the Lowell manufactories is, of coal, twelve thousand five hundred tons; of wood, three thousand two hundred and seventy cords; of oil, sixty-seven thousand eight hundred and forty-two gallons; of charcoal, six hundred thousand bushels; of starch, eight hundred thousand pounds. Over one million and a

half dollars are paid out every year for labor, and that sum has been received as the profits one year in this immense business. At no time have the business prospects of the city been more encouraging than they are now....

A Lowell Corporation

Lowell has been highly commended by some, as a model community, for its good order, industry, spirit of intelligence, and general freedom from vice. It has been strongly condemned, by others, as a hotbed of corruption, tainting and polluting the whole land. We all, in New England, have an interest in knowing what are the exact facts of the case. We are destined to be a great manufacturing people. The influences that go forth from Lowell, will go forth from many other manufacturing villages and cities. If these influences are pernicious, we have a great calamity impending over us. Rather than endure it, we should prefer to have every factory destroyed; the character of our sons and daughters being of infinitely more importance than any considerations "wherewithal they shall be clothed. If, on the other hand, a system has been introduced, carefully provided with checks and safeguards, and strong moral and conservative influences, it is our duty to see that this system be faithfully carried out, so as to prevent the disastrous results which have developed themselves in the manufacturing towns of other countries....

As preparing the way to a more intelligent view of the case, a brief description may be here given of a Lowell Corporation.

On the banks of the river, or of a canal, stands a row of mills, numbering, on different corporations, from two to five. A few rods from these, are long blocks of brick boarding-houses, containing a sufficient number of tenements to accommodate the most of the operatives employed by the Corporation. Between the boarding-houses and the mills is a line of a one story brick building, containing the counting room, superintendent's room, clerk's and store rooms. The mill yard is surrounded by enclosures, that the only access is through the counting room, in full view of those whose business it is to see that no improper persons intrude themselves upon the premises.

Thus the superintendent, from his room, has the whole of the Corporation under his eye. On the one side are the boarding-houses, all of which are under his care, and are rented only to known and approved tenants; on the other side are the mills, in each room of which he has stationed some carefully selected overseer, who is held responsible for the work, good order, and proper management of his room. Within the yard, also, are repair shops, each department of which, whether of iron, leather, or wood, has its head overseer. There is a superintendent of the yard, who, with a number of men under his care, has charge of all the out-door work of the establishment. There is a head watchman, having oversight of the night watch, who are required to pass through every room in the mills a prescribed number of times every night.

This, then, is the little world over which the superintendent presides. Assisted by his clerk, who keeps the necessary records, by the paymaster, who, receiving his funds from the treasurer of the Corporation, disburses their wages to the operatives, and not forgetting even the "runner," as he is called, who does the errands of the office, the superintendent's mind regulates all; his character inspires all; his plans, matured and decided by the directors of the company, who visit him every week, control all. He presides over one of the most perfect systems of subdivided and yet well-defined responsibility. Of course everything depends upon the kind of man who fills such a post as this. No pecuniary considerations have ever stood who could be found. To their remarkable and universally acknowledged success in this respect, to their selection of individuals highly distinguished both for their general force of character, and for their integrity, conscientiousness, and magnanimity, is Lowell chiefly indebted, both for the profitableness of her operations, and the character which she has sustained.

❧ "A real picture of factory life"

LOWELL WOMAN'S PROTEST

For those who worked in the factories themselves, Lowell's success yielded few benefits. Factory life was monotonous, the hours long and the work dehumanizing. Female workers, in particular, earned low wages. The average female worker in the 1830s made $3.25 for a 70-plus-hour work-week. Because room and board expenses were withdrawn from the salary, the take-home pay was two dollars per week. This anonymous 1845 description of a female factory worker's experience reflected the frustrations of laborers stuck in a system they were powerless to change.

For the purpose of illustration, let us go with that light-hearted, joyous young girl who is about for the first time to leave the home of her childhood, that home around which clusters so many beautiful and holy associations, pleasant memories, and quiet joys; to leave, too, a mother's cheerful smile, a father's care and protection; and wend her way toward this far famed "city of spindles," this promised land of the imagination, in whose praise she has doubtless heard so much.

Let us trace her progress during her first year's residence, and see whether she indeed realizes those golden prospects which have been held out to her. Follow her now as she enters that large gloomy looking building—she is in search of employment, and has been told that she might here obtain an eligible situation. She is sadly wearied with her journey, and withal somewhat annoyed by the noise, confusion, and strange faces all around her. So, after a brief conversation with the overseer, she concludes to accept the first situation which he offers; and reserving to herself a sufficient portion of time in which to obtain the necessary rest after her unwonted exertions, and the gratification of a stranger's curiosity regarding the place in which she is now to make her future home, she retires to her boarding house, to arrange matters as much to her mind as may be.

The intervening time passes rapidly away, and she soon finds herself once more within the confines of that close noisy apartment, and is forthwith installed in her new situation—first, however, premising that she has been sent to the Counting-room, and receives therefrom a Regulation paper, containing the rules by which she must be governed while in their employ; and lo! Here is the beginning of mischief; for in addition to the tyrannous and oppressive rules which meet her astonished eyes, she finds herself compelled to remain for the space of twelve months in the very place she then occupies, however reasonable and just cause of complaint might be hers, or however strong the wish for dismission; thus, in fact, constituting herself a slave, a very slave to the caprices of him for whom she labors. Several incidents coming to the knowledge of the writer, might be somewhat interesting in this connection, as tending to show the prejudicial influence exerted upon the interest of the operative by this unjust requisition. The first is of a lady who has been engaged as an operative for a number of years, and recently entered a weaving room on the Massachusetts Corporation: the overseers having assured her previous to her entrance, that she should realize the sum of $2.25 per week, exclusive of board; which she finding it impossible to do, appealed to the Counting-room for a line enabling her to engage elsewhere but it was peremptorily refused....

But to return to our toiling Maiden, the next beautiful feature which she discovers in this glorious system is, the long number of hours which she is obliged to spend in the above named close, unwholesome apartment. It is not enough, that like the poor peasant of Ireland, or the Russian serf who labors from sun to sun, but during one half of the year, she must still continue to toil on, long after Nature's lamp has ceased to lend its aid—nor will even this suffice to satisfy the grasping avarice of her hasty meals, which is in winter simply one half hour at noon—in the spring she is allowed the same at morn, and during the summer is added 15 minutes to the half hour at noon. Then too, when she is at last released from her wearisome day's toil, still may she not depart in peace. No! Her footsteps must be dogged to see that they do not stray beyond the corporation limits, and she must, whether she will or no, be subjected to manifold inconveniences of a large crowded boarding-house, where too, the price paid for her accommodation is so utterly insignificant, that it will not ensure to her the common comforts of life; she is obliged to sleep in a small comfortless, half ventilated apartment containing some half a dozen occupants each; but no matter, she is an operative—it is all well enough for her; there is no "abuse" about it; no, indeed, so think our employers—but do we think so? Time will show....

Reader will you pronounce this a mere fancy sketch, written for the sake of effect? It is not so. It is a real picture of "Factory life"; nor is it one half so bad as might truthfully and justly have been drawn. But it has been asked, and doubtless will be asked again, why, if these evils are so aggravating, have they been so long and so peacefully borne? Ah! And why have they? It is a question well worthy of our consideration, and we would call upon every operative in our city, aye, throughout the length and breadth of the land, to awake from the lethargy which has fallen upon them, and assert and maintain their rights. We call upon you for action—united and immediate action. But, says one, let us wait till we are stronger. In the language of one of old, we ask, when shall we be stronger? Will it be the next week or the next year? Will it be when we are reduced to the service conditions of the poor operatives of England? For verily we shall be and that right soon, if matters be suffered to remain as they are. Says another, how shall we act? We are but one amongst a thousand, what shall we do that our influence may be felt in this vast multitude? We answer there is in this city an Association called the Female Labor Reform Association, having for its professed object, the amelioration of the condition of the operative. Enrolled upon its records are the names of five hundred members—come then, and add thereto five hundred or rather five thousand more, and in the strength or our united influence we will soon show these drivelling cotton lords, this mushroom aristocracy of New England, who arrogantly aspire to lord it over God's heritage, that our rights cannot be trampled upon with impunity; that we will no longer submit to that arbitrary power which has for the last ten years been so abundantly exercised over us....

❧ *Manifest Destiny*

JOHN L. O'SULLIVAN

As the editor of the Democratic Party's *United States Magazine and Democratic Review* John L. Sullivan first coined the term "manifest destiny" to justify United States expansion into the western territories. Although he was specifically discussing the annexation of Texas in an 1845 article on the United States' inherent right to occupy and "overspread the continent," the term quickly encompassed all the country's expansionary goals and was adopted by all political parties as "an American right." By the end of the century, the manifest destiny doctrine was also applied to American ambitions in Latin America, Cuba, Hawaii and the Philippines.

Texas is now ours. Already, before these words are written, her Convention has undoubtedly ratified the acceptance, by her Congress, of our proffered invitation into the Union; and made the requisite changes in her already republican form of constitution to adapt it to its future federal relations. Her star and her stripe may already be said to have taken their place in the glorious blazon of our common nationality; and the sweep of our eagle's wing already includes within its circuit the wide extent of her fair and fertile land....

Why, were other reasoning wanting, in favor of now elevating this question of the reception of Texas into the Union, out of the lower region of our past party dissensions, up to its proper level of a high and broad nationality, it surely is to be found, found abundantly, in the manner in which other nations have undertaken to intrude themselves into it, between us and the proper parties to the case, in a spirit of hostile interference against us, for the avowed object of thwarting our policy and hampering our power, limiting our greatness and checking the fulfilment of our manifest destiny to overspread the continent allotted by Providence for the free development of our yearly multiplying millions. This we have seen done by England, our old rival and enemy; and by France, strangely coupled with her against us, under the influence of the Anglicism strongly tinging the policy of her present prime minister, Guizot. The zealous activity with which this effort to defeat us was pushed by the representatives of those governments, together with the character of intrigue accompanying it, fully constituted that case of foreign interference, which Mr. Clay himself declared should, and would unite us all in maintaining the common cause of our country against the foreigner and the foe....

It is wholly untrue, and unjust to ourselves, the pretence that the Annexation has been a measure of spoliation, unrightful and unrighteous—of military conquest under forms of peace and law—of territorial aggrandizement at the expense of justice, and justice due by a double sanctity to the weak.... The independence of Texas was complete and absolute. It was an independence, not only in fact, but of right. No obligation of duty towards Mexico tended in the least degree to restrain our right to effect the desired recovery of the fair province once our own—whatever motives of policy might have prompted a more deferential consideration of her feelings and her pride, as involved in the question. If Texas became peopled with an American population, it was by no contrivance of our government, but on the express invitation of that of Mexico herself; accompanied with such guaranties of State independence, and the maintenance of a federal system analogous to our own, as constituted a compact fully justifying the strongest measures of redress on the part of those afterwards deceived in this guaranty, and sought to be enslaved under the yoke imposed by its violation. She was released, rightfully and absolutely released, from all Mexican allegiance, or duty of cohesion to the Mexican political body, by the acts and fault of Mexico herself, and Mexico alone. There never was a clearer case. It was not revolution; it was resistance to revolution: and resistance under such circumstances as left independence the necessary resulting state, caused by the abandonment of those with whom her former federal association had existed. What then can be more preposterous than all this clamor by Mexico and the Mexican interest, against Annexation, as a violation of any rights of hers, any duties of ours?...

Nor is there any just foundation for the charge that Annexation is a great pro-slavery measure— calculated to increase and perpetuate that institution. Slavery had nothing to do with it. Opinions were and are greatly divided, both at the North and South, as to the influence to be exerted by it on Slavery and the Slave States. That it will tend to facilitate and hasten the disappearance of Slavery from all the northern tier of the present Slave States, cannot surely admit of serious question. The greater value in Texas of the slave labor now employed in those States, must soon produce the effect of draining off that labor southwardly, by the same unvarying law that bids water descend the slope that invites it. Every new Slave State in Texas will make at least one Free State from among those in which that institution now exists—to say nothing of those portions of Texas on which slavery cannot spring and grow—to say nothing of the far more rapid growth of new States in the free West and North-west, as these fine regions are overspread by the emigration fast flowing over them from Europe, as well as from the Northern and Eastern States of the Union as it exists. On the other hand, it is undeniably much gained for the cause of the eventual voluntary abolition of slavery; that it should have been thus drained off towards the only outlet which appeared to furnish much probability of the ultimate disappearance of the negro race from our borders. The Spanish-Indian

American populations of Mexico, Central America and South America, afford the only receptacle capable of absorbing that race whenever we shall be prepared to slough it off—to emancipate it from slavery, and (simultaneously necessary) to remove it from the midst of our own. Themselves already of mixed and confused blood, and free from the "prejudices" which among us so insuperably forbid the social amalgamation which can alone elevate the Negro race out of a virtually servile degradation, even though legally free, the regions occupied by those populations must strongly attract the black race in that direction; and as soon as the destined hour of emancipation shall arrive, will relieve the question of one of its worst difficulties, if not absolutely the greatest....

California will, probably, next fall away from the loose adhesion which, in such a country as Mexico, holds a remote province in a slight equivocal kind of dependence on the metropolis. Imbecile and distracted, Mexico never can exert any real governmental authority over such a country. The impotence of the one and the distance of the other, must make the relation one of virtual independence; unless, by stunting the province of all natural growth, and forbidding that immigration which can alone develop its capabilities and fulfil the purposes of its creation, tyranny may retain a military dominion, which is no government in the legitimate sense of the term. In the case of California this is now impossible. The Anglo-Saxon foot is already on its borders. Already the advance guard of the irresistible army of Anglo-Saxon emigration has begun to pour down upon it, armed with the plough and the rifle, and marking its trail with schools and colleges, courts and representative halls, mills and meeting-houses. A population will soon be in actual occupation of California, over which it will be idle for Mexico to dream of dominion. They will necessarily become independent. All this without agency of our government, without responsibility of our people in the natural flow of events, the spontaneous working of principles, and the adaptation of the tendencies and wants of the human race to the elemental circumstances in the midst of which they find themselves placed. And they will have a right to independence—to self-government—to the possession of the homes conquered from the wilderness by their own labors and dangers, sufferings and sacrifices—a better and a truer right than the artificial

title of sovereignty in Mexico, a thousand miles distant, inheriting from Spain a title good only against those who have none better. Their right to independence will be the natural right of self-government belonging to any community strong enough to maintain it—distinct in position, origin and character, and free from any mutual obligations of membership of a common political body, binding it to others by the duty of loyalty and compact of public faith....

❧ The Oregon Treaty

JAMES K. POLK

The United States and Great Britain resolved 50 years of disputes over the boundary of the Oregon Territory with the signing of the Oregon Treaty in 1846. Previously, the two countries had agreed in 1818 to hold the territory from the 42nd and the 54th parallel jointly. The Oregon Treaty, signed on June 15, 1846, set the boundary at the 49th parallel. The securing of Oregon helped spur emigration to the territory by American settlers.

Article I. From the point on the forty-ninth parallel of north latitude, where the boundary laid down in existing treaties and conventions between the United States and Great Britain terminates, the line of boundary between the territories of the United States and those of her Britannic Majesty shall be continued westward along the said forty-ninth parallel of north latitude to the middle of the channel which separates the continent from Vancouver's Island, and thence southerly through the middle of the said channel, and of Fuca's Straits, to the Pacific ocean: Provided, however, That the navigation of the whole of the said channel and straits, south of the forty-ninth parallel of north latitude, remain free and open to both parties.

Article II. From the point at which the forty-ninth parallel of north latitude shall be found to intersect the great northern branch of the Columbia River, the navigation of the said branch shall be free and open to the Hudson's bay company, and to all British subjects trading with the same, to the point where the said branch meets the main stream of the Columbia, and thence down the said main stream to the ocean, with free access into and through the said river or rivers, it being understood that all the usual portages along the line thus described shall, in like manner, be free and open. In navigating the said river or rivers, British subjects, with their goods and produce, shall be treated on the same footing as citizens of the United States; it being, however, always understood that nothing in this article shall be construed as preventing, or intended to prevent, the government of the United States from making any regulations respecting the navigation of the said river or rivers not inconsistent with the present treaty.

Article III. In the future appropriation of the territory south of the forty-ninth parallel of north latitude, as provided in the first article of this treaty, the possessory rights of the Hudson's Bay Company, and of all British subjects who may be already in the occupation of land or other property lawfully acquired within the said territory, shall be respected.

Article IV. The farms, lands, and other property of every description, belonging to the Puget's Sound Agricultural Company, on the north side of the Columbia River, shall be confirmed to the said company. In case, however, the situation of those farms and lands should be considered by the United States to be of public and political importance, and the United States government should signify a desire to obtain possession of the whole, or of any part thereof, the property so required shall be transferred to the said government, at a proper valuation, to be agreed upon between the parties.

❧ On Our Way to Rio Grande

GEORGE WASHINGTON DIXON

Because Mexico never recognized Texan independence, the United States' annexation of Texas was technically considered an act of war by Mexicans. Polk, whose expansionist goals were well known, sent General Zachary Taylor to Texas and in 1846 ordered him to go to the Rio Grande. This triggered a border dispute with Mexican troops as Mexico claimed the Nueces River further north was the Texan border.

Mexican troops attacked a scouting group of American soldiers. Polk used the skirmish to claim that Mexico had invaded the United States and asked Congress to declare war, which it did. American troops quickly won victories in California and embarked on three campaigns to seize what is today the American Southwest and captured Mexico City

with a force commanded by General Winfield Scott.

American soldiers won a series of victories. The war was very popular at home. A spate of books, newspaper stories, poems and songs celebrated the American war, the first to take place outside of its own borders. George Washington Dixon was a popular black-face minstrel who contributed his part to the pro-war popular culture with the 1846 song "On Our Way to Rio Grande."

The Mexicans are on our soil
In war they wish us to embroil
They've tried their best and worst to vex us
By murdering our brave men in Texas
We're on our way to Rio Grande
On our way to Rio Grande
On our way to Rio Grande
And with arms they'll find us handy

We are the boys who fear no noise
We'll leave behind us all our joys
To punish them half savage scamps
Who've slain our brethren in their camps
The God of War, the mighty Mars
Has smiled upon our stripes and stars
And in spite of any ugly rumors
We'll vanquish all the Montezumas
We're on our way to Matamoros
On our way to Matamoros
On our way to Matamoros
And we'll conquer all before us!

❧ "Peace Between the United States of America and the Mexican Republic"

TREATY OF GUADELUPE HIDALGO

Defying an order from Polk to be recalled to Washington D.C., United States delegate N. P. Trist signed the Treaty of Guadelupe Hidalgo on February 2, 1848, ending the Mexican War. The treaty called for Mexico handing over more than 500,000 square miles of territory to the United States for $15 million. The transaction included California, Nevada, Utah, and parts of Wyoming, Colorado, New Mexico and Arizona. The United States pledged it would assume any debts owed to its citizens by the Mexican government and promised to respect the cultural and property rights of Mexicans living in the territory. Many years later, this promise helped prompt the development of bilingual education programs in schools with Hispanic populations.

Although the transaction represented the second largest territorial acquisition by the United States in its continental expansion, Polk and others were dissatisfied with the treaty. Polk wanted significantly more territory in what is today northwestern Mexico. He contemplated not presenting the pact to the Senate for approval, but eventually gave his public endorsement of the treaty. The Senate ratified it May 30, 1848.

Article I. there shall be firm and universal peace between the United States of America and the Mexican Republic and between their respective countries, territories, cities, towns, and people, without exception of place or persons....

Article V. the boundary line between the two Republics shall commence in the gulf of Mexico, three leagues from land, opposite the mouth of the Rio Grande, otherwise called Rio Bravo del Norte, or opposite the mouth of its deepest branch, if it should have more than one branch emptying directly into the sea; from thence up the middle of that river, following the deepest channel, where it has more than one, to the point where it strikes the southern boundary of New Mexico; thence, westwardly, along the whole southern boundary of New Mexico (which runs north of the town called Paso) to its western termination; thence, northward, along the western line of New Mexico, until it intersects the first branch of the River Gila; (or if it should not intersect any branch of that river, then to the point on the said line nearest to such branch, and thence in a direct line to the same;) thence down the middle of the said branch, and thence in a direct line to the same;) thence down the middle of the said branch and of the said river, until it empties into the Rio Colorado; thence across the Rio Colorado, following the division line between Upper and Lower California, to the Pacific ocean....

Article VII. The River Gila, and the part of the Rio Bravo del Norte lying below the southern boundary of New Mexico, being, agreeably to the fifth article, divided in the middle between the two republics, the navigation of the Gila and of the Bravo below said boundary shall be free and common to the vessels and citizens of both countries; and neither shall, without the consent of the other, construct any work that may impede or interrupt, in whole or in part, the exercise of this right; not even for the purpose of favoring new methods of navigation....

Article VIII. Mexicans now established in territories previously belonging to Mexico, and which remain for the future within the limits of the United States, as defined by the present treaty, shall be free to continue where they now reside, or to remove at any time to the Mexican republic, retaining the property which they possess in the said territories, or disposing thereof, and removing the proceeds wherever they please, without being subjected, on this account, to any contribution, tax, or charge whatever....

Article XII. In consideration of the extension acquired by the boundaries of the United States, as defined in the fifth article of the present treaty, the Government of the United States engages to pay to that of the Mexican Republic the sum of fifteen million dollars....

Article XIII. The United States engage, moreover, to assume and pay to the claimants all the amounts now due them, and those hereafter to become due, by reason of the claims already liquidated and decided against the Mexican Republic, under the conventions between the two republics severally concluded on the eleventh day of April, eighteen hundred and thirty-nine, and on the thirtieth day of January, eighteen hundred and forty-three, so that the Mexican Republic shall be absolutely exempt, for the future from all expense whatever on account of the said claims.

Article XIV. The United States do furthermore discharge the Mexican Republic from all claims of citizens of the United States not heretofore decided against the Mexican Government, which may have arisen previously to the date of the signature of this treaty; which discharge shall be final and perpetual, whither the said claims be rejected or be allowed by the board of commissioners provided for in the following article, and whatever shall be the total amount of those allowed....

Article XV. The United States, exonerating Mexico from all demands on account of the claims of their citizens mentioned in the preceding article, and considering them entirely and forever cancelled, whatever their amount may be, undertake to make satisfaction for the same, to an amount not exceeding three and one quarter million dollars....

Article XXI. If unhappily any disagreement should hereafter arise between the governments of the two republics, whether with respect to the interpretation of any stipulation in this treaty, or with respect to any other particular concerning the political or commercial relations of the two nations, the said governments, in the name of those nations, do promise to each other that they will endeavor, in the most sincere and earnest manner, to settle the differences so arising, and to preserve the state of peace and friendship in which the two countries are now placing themselves; using, for this end, mutual representations and pacific negotiations. And if, by these means, they should not be enabled to come to an agreement, a resort shall not, on this account, be had to reprisals, aggression, or hostility of any kind, by the one republic against the other, until the Government of that which deems itself aggrieved shall have maturely considered, in the spirit of peace and good neighborship, whether it would not be better that such difference should be settled by the arbitration of commissioners appointed on each side, or by that of a friendly nation. And should such course be proposed by either party, it shall be acceded to by the other, unless deemed by it altogether incompatible with the nature of the difference, or circumstances of the case.

🍃 *Civil Disobedience*

HENRY DAVID THOREAU

Like many abolitionists who opposed the Mexican War, Henry David Thoreau believed the conflict was designed to expand slavery westward. As an act of protest to the war, Thoreau refused to pay his poll tax and spent a night in jail before a relative paid the tax on Thoreau's behalf—much to his annoyance. He explained his action in his speech to his fellow townsmen in Concord, Massachusetts. Three years later Thoreau's lecture was published as "On the Duty of Civil Disobedience."

Widely ignored or scorned in its day, Thoreau's essay on the duties of an individual to act upon his conscience has had a worldwide influence, impacting the writings of Leo Tolstoy, Gandhi's revolutionary movement and the American civil rights movement of the 1950s and 1960s.

I heartily accept the motto, "That government is best which governs least"; and I should like to see it acted up to more rapidly and systematically. Carried out, it finally amounts to this, which I also believe, "That government is best which governs not at all"; and when men are prepared for it, that will be the kind of government which they will have. Government is at best but an expedient; but most

governments are usually, and all governments are sometimes, inexpedient. The objections which have been brought against a standing army, and they are many and weighty, and deserve to prevail, may also at last be brought against a standing government. The standing army is only an arm of the standing government. The government itself, which is only the mode which the people have chosen to execute their will, is equally liable to be abused and perverted before the people can act through it. Witness the present Mexican war, the work of comparatively a few individuals using the standing government as their tool; for, in the outset, the people would not have consented to this measure.

This American government, what is it but a tradition, though a recent one, endeavoring to transmit itself unimpaired to posterity, but each instant losing some of its integrity? It has not the vitality and force of a single living man; for a single man can bend it to his will. It is a sort of wooden gun to the people themselves. But it is not the less necessary for this; for the people must have some complicated machinery or other, and hear its din, to satisfy that idea of government which they have. Governments show thus how successfully men can be imposed on, even impose on themselves, for their own advantage. It is excellent, we must all allow. Yet this government never of itself furthered any enterprise, but by the alacrity with which it got out of its way. It does not keep the country free. It does not settle the West. It does not educate. The character inherent in the American people has done all that has been accomplished; and it would have done somewhat more, if the government had not sometimes got in its way. For government is an expedient by which men would fain succeed in letting one another alone; and, as has been said, when it is most expedient, the governed are most let alone by it. Trade and commerce, if they were not made of India-rubber, would never manage to bounce over the obstacles which legislators are continually putting in their way; and, if one were to judge these men wholly by the effects of their actions and not partly by their intentions, they would deserve to be classed and punished with those mischievous persons who put obstructions on railroads.

But, to speak practically and as a citizen, unlike those who call themselves no-government men, I ask for, not at once no government, but at once a better government. Let every man make known what kind of government would command respect, and that will be one step toward obtaining it.

After all, the practical reason why, when the power is once in the hands of the people, a majority are permitted, and for a long period continue, to rule, is not because they are most likely to be in the right, nor because this seems fairest to the minority, but because they are physically the strongest. But a government in which the majority rule in all cases cannot be based on justice, even as far as men understand it. Can there not be a government in which majorities do not virtually decide right and wrong, but conscience?—in which majorities decide only those questions to which the role of expediency is applicable? Must the citizen ever for a moment, or in the least degree, resign his conscience to the legislator? Why has every man a conscience, then? I think that we should be men first, and subjects afterward. It is not desirable to cultivate a respect for the law, so much as for the right. The only obligation which I have the right to assume, is to do at any time what I think right. It is truly enough said, that a corporation has no conscience; but a corporation of conscientious men is a corporation with a conscience. Law never made men a whit more just; and, by means of their respect for it, even the well-disposed are daily made the agents of injustice. A common and natural result of an undue respect for law is, that you may see a file of soldiers, colonel, captain, corporal, privates, powder-monkeys, and all, marching in admirable order over hill and dale to the wars, against their wills, ay, against their common sense and consciences, which makes it very steep marching indeed, and produces a palpitation of the heart. They have no doubt that it is a damnable business in which they are concerned; they are all peaceably inclined. Now, what are they? Men at all? or small movable forts and magazines, at the service of some unscrupulous man in power? Visit the Navy Yard, and behold a marine, such a man as an American government can make, or such as it can make a man with its black arts, a mere shadow and reminiscence of humanity, a man laid out alive and standing, and already, as one may say, buried under arms with funeral accompaniments, though it may be,—

"Not a drum was heard, not a funeral note,
As his corse to the rampart we hurried;

Not a soldier discharged his farewell shot
O'er the grave where our hero we buried."

The mass of men serve the state thus, not as men mainly, but as machines, with their bodies. They are the standing army, and the militia, jailers, constables, posse comitatus, &c. In most cases there is no free exercise whatever of the judgment or of the moral sense; but they put themselves on a level with wood and earth and stones; and wooden men can perhaps be manufactured that will serve the purpose as well. Such command no more respect than men of straw or a lump of dirt. They have the same sort of worth only as horses and dogs. Yet such as these even are commonly esteemed good citizens. Others,—as most legislators, politicians, lawyers, ministers, and officeholders,—serve the state chiefly with their heads; and, as they rarely make any moral distinctions, they are as likely to serve the Devil, without intending it, as God. A very few, as heroes, patriots, martyrs, reformers in the great sense, and men, serve the state with their consciences also, and so necessarily resist it for the most part; and they are commonly treated as enemies by it. A wise man will only be useful as a man, and will not submit to be "clay," and "stop a hole to keep the wind away," but leave that office to his dust at least:—

"I am too high-born to be propertied,
To be a secondary at control,
Or useful serving-man and instrument
To any sovereign state throughout the world."

He who gives himself entirely to his fellow-men appears to them useless and selfish; but he who gives himself partially to them is pronounced a benefactor and philanthropist.

How does it become a man to behave toward this American government to-day? I answer, that he cannot without disgrace be associated with it. I cannot for an instant recognize that political organization as my government which is the slave's government also.

All men recognize the right of revolution; that is, the right to refuse allegiance to, and to resist, the government, when its tyranny or its inefficiency are great and unendurable. But almost all say that such is not the case now. But such was the case, they think, in the Revolution of '75. If one were to tell me that this was a bad government because it taxed certain foreign commodities brought to its ports, it is most probable that I should not make an ado about it, for I can do without them. All machines have their friction; and possibly this does enough good to counterbalance the evil. At any rate, it is a great evil to make a stir about it. But when the friction comes to have its machine, and oppression and robbery are organized, I say, let us not have such a machine any longer. In other words, when a sixth of the population of a nation which has undertaken to be the refuge of liberty are slaves, and a whole country is unjustly overran and conquered by a foreign army, and subjected to military law, I think that it is not too soon for honest men to rebel and revolutionize. What makes this duty the more urgent is the fact, that the country so overrun is not our own, but ours is the invading army.

Paley, a common authority with many on moral questions, in his chapter on the "Duty of Submission to Civil Government," resolves all civil obligation into expediency; and he proceeds to say, "that so long as the interest of the whole society requires it, that is, so long as the established government cannot be resisted or changed without public inconveniency, it is the will of God that the established government be obeyed, and no longer…This principle being admitted, the justice of every particular case of resistance is reduced to a computation of the quantity of the danger and grievance on the one side, and of the probability and expense of redressing it on the other." Of this, he says, every man shall judge for himself. But Paley appears never to have contemplated those cases to which the rule of expediency does not apply, in which a people, as well as an individual, must do justice, cost what it may. If I have unjustly wrested a plank from a drowning man, I must restore it to him though I drown myself. This, according to Paley, would be inconvenient. But he that would save his life, in such a case, shall lose it. This people must cease to hold slaves, and to make war on Mexico, though it cost them their existence as a people….

I meet this American government, or its representative, the State government, directly, and face to face, once a year and no more—in the person of its tax-gatherer; this is the only mode in which a man situated as I am necessarily meets it; and it then says distinctly, Recognize me; and the simplest, the most effectual, and, in the present posture of affairs, the indispensablest mode of treating with it on this head, of expressing your little satisfaction with and love for it, is to deny it then. My civil neighbor, the tax-gatherer, is the very man I have to deal with, for it is, after all, with men and not with parchment that I quarrel, and he has voluntarily chosen to be an agent of the government. How shall he ever know well what he is and does as an officer of the government, or as a man, until he is obliged to consider whether he shall treat me, his neighbor, for whom he has respect, as a neighbor and well-disposed man, or as a maniac and disturber of the peace, and see if he can get over this obstruction to his neighborliness without a ruder and more impetuous thought or speech corresponding with his action. I know this well, that if one thousand, if one hundred, if ten men whom I could name, if ten honest men only, nay, if one HONEST man, in this State of Massachusetts, ceasing to hold slaves, were actually to withdraw from this copartnership, and be locked up in the county jail therefor, it would be the abolition of slavery in America. For it matters not how small the beginning may seem to be: what is once well done is done forever. But we love better to talk about it: that we say is our mission. Reform keeps many scores of newspapers in its service, but not one man. If my esteemed neighbor, the State's ambassador, who will devote his days to the settlement of the question of human rights in the Council Chamber, instead of being threatened with the prisons of Carolina, were to sit down the prisoner of Massachusetts, that State which is so anxious to foist the sin of slavery upon her sister,—though at present she can discover only an act of inhospitality to be the ground of a quarrel with her,—the Legislature would not wholly waive the subject the following winter.

Under a government which imprisons any unjustly, the true place for a just man is also a prison. The proper place to-day, the only place which Massachusetts has provided for her freer and less desponding spirits, is in her prisons, to be put out and locked out of the State by her own act, as they have already put themselves out by their principles. It is there that the fugitive slave, and the Mexican prisoner on parole, and the Indian come to plead the wrongs of his race, should find them; on that separate, but more free and honorable ground, where the State places those who are not with her, but against her, the only house in a slave State in which a free man can abide with honor. If any think that their influence would be lost there, and their voices no longer afflict the ear of the State, that they would not be as an enemy within its walls, they do not know by how much truth is stronger than error, nor how much more eloquently and effectively he can combat injustice who has experienced a little in his own person. Cast your whole vote, not a strip of paper merely, but your whole influence. A minority is powerless while it conforms to the majority; it is not even a minority then; but it is irresistible when it clogs by its whole weight. If the alternative is to keep all just men in prison, or give up war and slavery, the State will not hesitate which to choose. If a thousand men were not to pay their tax-bills this year, that would not be a violent and bloody measure, as it would be to pay them, and enable the State to commit violence and shed innocent blood. This is, in fact, the definition of a peaceable revolution, if any such is possible. If the tax-gatherer, or any other public officer, asks me, as one has done, "But what shall I do?" my answer is, "If you really wish to do anything, resign your office." When the subject has refused allegiance, and the officer has resigned his office, then the revolution is accomplished. But even suppose blood should flow. Is there not a sort of blood shed when the conscience is wounded? Through this wound a man's real manhood and immortality flow out, and he bleeds to an everlasting death. I see this blood flowing now....

The authority of government, even such as I am willing to submit to,—for I will cheerfully obey those who know and can do better than I, and in many things even those who neither know nor can do so well,—is still an impure one: to be strictly just, it must have the sanction and consent of the governed. It can have no pure fight over my person and property but what I concede to it. The progress from an absolute to a limited monarchy, from a limited monarchy to a democracy, is a progress toward a true respect for the individual. Even the Chinese philosopher was wise enough to regard the individual as the basis of the empire. Is a democracy, such as we know it, the last improvement possible in government? Is it not possible to take a step further towards recognizing and organizing the rights of man? There will never be a really free and enlightened State, until the State comes to recognize the individual as a higher and independent power, from which all its own power and authority are derived,

and treats him accordingly. I please myself with imagining a State at last which can afford to be just to all men, and to treat the individual with respect as a neighbor; which even would not think it inconsistent with its own repose, if a few were to live aloof from it, not meddling with it, nor embraced by it, who fulfilled all the duties of neighbors and fellowmen. A State which bore this kind of fruit, and suffered it to drop off as fast as it ripened, would prepare the way for a still more perfect and glorious State, which also I have imagined, but not yet anywhere seen.

"My master was my father"

FREDERICK DOUGLASS

Born as a slave in Maryland, Frederick Bailey escaped in 1838 to Massachusetts where he changed his name to Frederick Douglass. A powerful orator, Douglass emerged as the leading African-American abolitionist of the pre-Civil War era. He became an agent of the Massachusetts Anti-Slavery Society and raised enough money from speaking engagements to purchase his freedom.

In 1847, Douglass founded and co-edited the abolitionist paper *North Star*. During the Civil War he played a leading role in recruiting African-American soldiers for the Union cause.

The following excerpt from his 1845 autobiography, *Narrative of the Life of Frederick Douglass, Written by Himself*, describes his childhood. The book helped raise awareness in the North of the miserable conditions slaves lived under in the South.

I was born in Tuckahoe, near Hillsborough, and about twelve miles from Easton, in Talbot county, Maryland. I have no accurate knowledge of my age, never having seen any authentic record containing it. By far the larger part of the slaves know as little of their age as horses know of theirs, and it is the wish of most masters within my knowledge to keep their slaves thus ignorant. I do not remember to have ever met a slave who could tell of his birthday. They seldom come nearer to it than planting-time, harvest-time, cherry-time, spring-time, or fall-time. A want of information concerning my own was a source of unhappiness to me even during childhood. The white children could tell their ages. I could not tell why I ought to be deprived of the same privilege. I was not allowed to make any inquiries of my master concerning it. He deemed all such inquiries on the part of a slave improper and impertinent, and evidence of a restless spirit. The nearest estimate I can give makes me now between twenty-seven and twenty-eight years of age. I come to this, from hearing my master say, some time during 1835, I was about seventeen years old.

My mother was named Harriet Bailey. She was the daughter of Isaac and Betsey Bailey, both colored, and quite dark. My mother was of a darker complexion than either my grandmother or grandfather.

My father was a white man. He was admitted to be such by all I ever heard speak of my parentage. The opinion was also whispered that my master was my father; but of the correctness of this opinion, I know nothing; the means of knowing was withheld from me. My mother and I were separated when I was but an infant—before I knew her as my mother. It is a common custom, in the part of Maryland from which I ran away, to part children from their mothers at a very early age. Frequently, before the child has reached its twelfth month, its mother is taken from it, and hired out on some farm a considerable distance off, and the child is placed under the care of an old woman, too old for field labor. For what this separation is done, I do not know, unless it be to hinder the development of the child's affection toward its mother, and to blunt and destroy the natural affection of the mother for the child. This is the inevitable result.

I never saw my mother, to know her as such, more than four or five times in my life; and each of these times was very short in duration, and at night. She was hired by a Mr. Stewart, who lived about twelve miles from my home. She made her journeys to see me in the night, travelling the whole distance on foot, after the performance of her day's work. She was a field hand, and a whipping is the penalty of not being in the field at sunrise, unless a slave has special permission from his or her master to the contrary—a permission which they seldom get, and one that gives to him that gives it the proud name of being a kind master. I do not recollect of ever seeing my mother by the light of day. She was with me in the night. She would lie down with me and get me to sleep, but long before I waked she was gone. Very little communication ever took place between us. Death soon ended what little we could have while she lived, and with it her hardships and suffering. She died when I was about seven years old, on one of my master's farms, near Lee's Mills. I was not allowed to be present during her illness, at her death, or burial. She was gone long before I knew any thing about it. Never having enjoyed, to any considerable extent, her soothing presence, her tender and watchful care, I received the tidings of her death with much the same emotions I should have probably felt at the death of a stranger.

Called thus suddenly away, she left me without the slightest intimation of who my father was. The whisper that my master was my father, may or may not be true; and, true or false, it is of but little consequence to my purpose whilst the fact remains, in all its glaring odiousness, that slaveholders have ordained, and by law established, that the children of slave women shall in all cases follow the condition of their mothers; and this is done too obviously to administer to their own lusts, and make a gratification of their wicked desires profitable as well as pleasurable; for by this cunning arrangement, the slaveholder, in cases not a few, sustains to his slaves the double relation of master and father.

I know of such cases; and it is worthy of remark that such slaves invariably suffer greater hardships, and have more to contend with, than others. They are, in the first place, a constant offence to their mistress. She is ever disposed to find fault with them; they can seldom do any thing to please her; she is never better pleased than when she sees them under the lash, especially when she suspects her husband of showing to his mulatto children favors which he withholds from his black slaves. The master is frequently compelled to sell this class of his slaves, out of deference to the feelings of his white wife; and, cruel as the deed may strike any one to be, for a man to sell his own children to human flesh-mongers, it is often the dictate of humanity for him to do so; for, unless he does this, he must not only whip them himself, but must stand by and see one white son tie up his brother, of but few shades darker complexion than himself, and ply the gory lash to his naked back; and if he lisp one word of disapproval, it is set down to his parental partiality, and only makes a bad matter worse, both for himself and the slave whom he would protect and defend.

"*Let me make you a present of this little nigger*"

WILLIAM WELLS BROWN

William Wells Brown was a former slave who recounted his experiences as an assistant to a slavetrader in his 1847 book *Narrative of the Life of William Brown.* He became a prominent abolitionist and was one of the first people to write about the history of African-Americans in the United States. Accounts such as this helped enflame anti-slavery sentiments in the North.

He soon commenced purchasing to make up the third gang. We took steamboat, and went to Jefferson City, a town on the Missouri river. Here we landed, and took stage for the interior of the State. He bought a number of slaves as he passed the different farms and villages. After getting twenty-two or twenty-three men and women, we arrived at St. Charles, a village on the banks of the Missouri. Here he purchased a woman who had a child in her arms, appearing to be four or five weeks old.

We had been travelling by land for some days, and were in hopes to have found a boat at this place for St. Louis, but were disappointed. As no boat was expected for some days, we started for St. Louis by land. Mr. Walker had purchased two horses. He rode one, and I the other. The slaves were chained together, and we took up our line of march, Mr. Walker taking the lead, and I bringing up the rear. Though the distance was not more than twenty miles, we did not reach it the first day. The road was worse than any that I have ever travelled.

Soon after we left St. Charles, the young child grew very cross, and kept up a noise during the greater part of the day. Mr. Walker complained of its crying several times, and told the mother to stop the child's d—d noise, or he would. The women tried to keep the child from crying, but could not. We put up at night with an acquaintance of Mr. Walker, and in the morning, just as we were about to start, the child again commenced crying. Walter stepped to her, and told her to give the child to him. The mother trembling obeyed. He took the child by one arm, as you would a cat by the leg, walked into the house, and said to the lady.

"Madam, I will make you a present of this little nigger; it keeps such a noise that I can't bear it."

"Thank you, sir," said the lady.

The mother, as soon as she saw that her child was to be left, ran up to Mr. Walker, and falling upon her knees begged him to let her have her child; she clung around his legs, and cried, "Oh, my child! O, do, do, do. I will stop its crying, if you will only let me have it again." When I saw this woman crying for her child so piteously, a shudder,—a feeling akin to horror shot through my frame.

Mr. Walker commanded her to return into the ranks with the other slaves. Women who had children were not chained, but those who had none were. As soon as her child was disposed of, she was chained in the gang.

The Trials of Girlhood

HARRIET JACOBS

Rape was a constant threat for many slaves. They had little recourse to resist predatory white men. Harriet Jacobs wrote about her unsuccessful attempts to fend off the approaches of her owner, a respected doctor, before escaping to the North. She recalled her experiences in her 1861 narrative *The Trials of Girlhood,* noting that slavery made women even more vulnerable than men to the demands of their masters.

During the first years of my service in Dr. Flint's family, I was accustomed to share some indulgences with the children of my mistress. Though this seemed to me no more than right, I was grateful for it, and tried to merit the kindness by the faithful discharge of my duties. But I now entered on my fifteenth year—a sad epoch in the life of a slave girl. My master began to whisper foul words in my ear. Young as I was, I could not remain ignorant of their import. I tried to treat them with indifference or contempt. The master's age, my extreme youth, and the fear that his conduct would be reported to my grandmother, made him bear this treatment for many months. He was a crafty man, and resorted to many means to accomplish his purposes. Sometimes he had stormy, terrific ways, that made his victims tremble; sometimes he assumed a gentleness that he thought must surely subdue. Of the two, I preferred his stormy moods, although they left me trembling. He tried his utmost to corrupt the pure principles my grandmother had instilled. He peopled my young mind with unclean images, such as only a vile monster could think of. I turned from him with disgust and hatred. But he was my master. I was compelled to live under the same roof with him— where I saw a man forty years my senior daily violating the most sacred commandments of nature. He told me I was his property; that I must be subject to his will in all things. My soul revolted against the mean tyranny. But where could I turn for protection? No matter whether the slave girl be as black as ebony or as fair as her mistress. In either case, there is no shadow of law to protect her from insult, from violence, or even from death; all these are inflicted by fiends who bear the shape of men. The mistress, who ought to protect the helpless victim, has no other feelings towards her but those of jealousy and rage. The degradation, the wrongs, the vices, that grow out of slavery, are more than I can describe. They are greater than you would willingly believe. Surely, if you credited one half the truths that are told you concerning the helpless millions suffering in this cruel bondage, you at the north would not help to tighten the yoke. You surely would refuse to do for the master, on your own soil, the mean and cruel work which trained bloodhounds and the lowest class of whites do for him at the south.

Every where the years bring to all enough of sin and sorrow; but in slavery the very dawn of life is darkened by these shadows. Even the little child, who is accustomed to wait on her mistress and her children, will learn, before she is twelve years old, why it is that her mistress hates such and such a one among the slaves. Perhaps the child's own mother is among those hated ones. She listens to violent outbreaks of jealous passion, and cannot help understanding what is the cause. She will become prematurely knowing in evil things. Soon she will learn to tremble when she hears her master's footfall. She will be compelled to realize that she is no longer a child. If God has bestowed beauty upon her, it will prove her greatest curse. That which commands admiration in the white woman only hastens the degradation of the female slave. I know that some are too much brutalized by slavery to feel the humiliation of their position; but many slaves feel it most acutely, and shrink from the memory of it. I cannot tell how much I suffered in the presence of these wrongs, nor how I am still pained by the retrospect. My master met me at every turn, reminding me that I belonged to him, and swearing by heaven and earth that he would compel me to submit to him. If I went out for a breath of fresh air, after a day of unwearied toil, his footsteps dogged me. If I knelt by my mother's grave, his dark shadow fell on me even there. The light heart which nature had given me became heavy with sad forebodings. The other slaves in my master's house noticed the change. Many of them pitied me; but none dared to ask the cause. They had no need to inquire. They knew too well the guilty practices under that roof; and they were aware that to speak of them was an offence that never went unpunished.

I longed for some one to confide in. I would have given the world to have laid my head on my grandmother's faithful bosom, and told her all my troubles. But Dr. Flint swore he would kill me, if I was not as silent as the grave. Then, although my grandmother was all in all to me, I feared her as well as loved her. I had been accustomed to look up to her with a respect bordering upon awe. I was very young, and felt shamefaced about telling her such impure things, especially as I knew her to be very strict on such subjects. Moreover, she was a woman of a high spirit. She was usually very quiet in her demeanor; but if her indignation was once roused, it was not very easily quelled. I had been told that she once chased a white gentleman with a loaded pistol, because he insulted one of her daughters. I dreaded the consequences of a violent outbreak; and both pride and fear kept me silent. But though I did not confide in my grandmother, and even evaded her vigilant watchfulness and inquiry, her presence in the neighborhood was some protection to me. Though she had been a slave, Dr. Flint was afraid of her. He dreaded her scorching rebukes. Moreover, she was known and patronized by many people; and he did not wish to have his villany made public. It was lucky for me that I did not live on a distant plantation, but in a town not so large that the inhabitants were ignorant of each other's affairs. Bad as are the laws and customs in a slaveholding community, the doctor, as a professional man, deemed it prudent to keep up some outward show of decency.

O, what days and nights of fear and sorrow that man caused me! Reader, it is not to awaken sympathy for myself that I am telling you truthfully what I suffered in slavery. I do it to kindle a flame of compassion in your hearts for my sisters who are still in bondage, suffering as I once suffered.

I once saw two beautiful children playing together. One was a fair white child; the other was her slave, and also her sister. When I saw them embracing each other, and heard their joyous laughter, I turned sadly away from the lovely sight. I foresaw the inevitable blight that would fall on the little slave's heart. I knew how soon her laughter would be changed to sighs. The fair child grew up to be a still fairer woman. From childhood to womanhood her pathway was blooming with flowers, and overarched by a sunny sky. Scarcely one day of her life had been clouded when the sun rose on her happy bridal morning.

How had those years dealt with her slave sister, the little playmate of her childhood? She, also, was very beautiful; but the flowers and sunshine of love were not for her. She drank the cup of sin, and shame, and misery, whereof her persecuted race are compelled to drink.

In view of these things, why are ye silent, ye free men and women of the north? Why do your tongues falter in maintenance of the right? Would that I had more ability! But my heart is so full, and my pen is so weak! There are noble men and women who plead for us, striving to help those who cannot help themselves. God bless them! God give them strength and courage to go on! God bless those, every where, who are laboring to advance the cause of humanity!

❧ "Halleluiah! Halleluiah!"

FREDERIKA BREMER

White Southerners were generally eager to have their slaves converted to Christianity as a way to preserve white dominance and often out of a genuine concern for their souls. African-American slaves abandoned their traditional African religions to embrace the redemptive qualities of Christianity. It was a way to find solace in their bonded state. Many black churches were formed throughout the South and were often lead by charismatic African-American preachers. Fredrika Bremer of Sweden attended a black church in New Orleans in 1849 and later wrote about the startling spiritual experience in her travel book *The Homes of the New World.*

I must now tell you about a real African tornado which Anne W. and I witnessed last Sunday after-noon. It was in the African Church, for even here, in this gay, light-hearted city of New Orleans, has Christianity commenced its work of renovated life; and they have Sunday-schools for negro children, where they receive instruction about the Savior; and the negro slaves are able to serve God in their own church.

We came too late to hear the sermon in this African Church, whither we had betaken ourselves. But at the close of the service, a so-called class-meeting was held. I do not know whether I have already said that the Methodists form, within their community, certain divisions or classes, which elect their own leaders or exhorters. These exhorters go round at the class-meeting to such of the members of their class as they deem to stand in need of consolation or encouragement, talk to them, aloud or in an under voice, receive their confessions, impart advice to them, and so on. I had seen such a class-meeting at Washington, and knew, therefore, what was the kind of scene which we might expect. But my expectations were quite exceeded here. Here we were nearer the tropical sun than at Washington.

The exhorters went round, and began to converse here and there with the people who sat on the benches. Scarcely, however, had they talked for a minute before the person addressed came into a state of exaltation, and began to speak and to perorate more loudly and more vehemently than the exhorter himself, and so to overpower him. There was one exhorter in particular, whose black, good-natured countenance was illumined by so great a degree of the inward light, by so much good-humor and joy, that it was a pleasure to see him, and to hear him too; for, although his phrases were pretty much the same, and the same over again, yet they were words full of Christian pith and marrow, and they were uttered with so much cordiality, that they could not do other than go straight to the heart with enlivening power. Sometimes his ideas seemed to come to an end, and he stood, as it were, seeking for a moment; but then he would begin again with what he had just now said, and his words always brought with them the same warmth and faithfulness, and he looked like a life-infusing sunbeam. And it was only as the messenger of the joy in Christ that he preached:

"Hold fast by Christ! He is the Lord! He is the mighty One! He will help! He will do every thing well! Trust in him, my sister, my brother. Call upon him. Yes. Yes. Hold fast by Christ! He is the Lord!" &c., &c.

By degrees the noise increased in the church, and became a storm of voices and cries. The words were heard, "Yes, come Lord Jesus! Come, oh come, oh glory!" and they who thus cried aloud began to leap—leaped aloft with a motion as of a cork flying out of a bottle, while they waved their arms and their handkerchiefs in the air, as if they were endeavoring to bring something down, and all the while crying aloud, "Come, oh come!" And as they leaped, they twisted their bodies round in a sort of cork-screw fashion, and were evidently in a state of convulsion; sometimes they fell down and rolled in the aisle, amid loud, lamenting cries and groans. I saw our tropical exhorter, the man with the sun-bright countenance, talking to a young negro with a crooked nose and eyes that squinted, and he too very soon began to talk and to preach, as he sprung high into the air, leaping up and down with incredible elasticity. Whichever way we looked in the church, we saw somebody leaping up and fanning the air; the whole church seemed transformed into a regular Bedlam, and the noise and the tumult was horrible. Still, however, the exhorters made their rounds with beaming countenances, as if they were in their right element, and as if every thing were going on as it ought to do. Presently we saw our hearty exhorter address a few words to a tall, handsome mulatto woman, who sat before us, and while he was preaching to her she began to preach to him; both talked for some time with evident enchantment, till she also got into motion, and sprang aloft with such vehemence, that three other women took hold of her by the skirts, as if to hold her still on the earth. Two of these laughed quietly, while they continued to hold her down, and she to leap up and throw her arms around. At length she fell and rolled about amid convulsive groans. After that she rose up and began to walk about, up and down the church, with outspread arms, ejaculating every now and then, "Halleluiah!" Her appearance was now calm, earnest, and really beautiful. Amid all the wild tumult of crying and leaping, on the right hand and the left, she continued to walk up and down the church, in all directions, with outspread arms, eyes cast upward, exclaiming, in a low voice, "Halleluiah! Halleluiah!" At length she sank down upon her knees on the platform by the altar, and there she became still.

After the crying and the leaping had continued for a good quarter of an hour longer, several negroes raised the mulatto woman, who was lying prostrate by the altar. She was now quite rigid. They bore her to a bench in front of us, and laid her down upon it.

"What has happened to her?" inquired Anne W. from a young negro girl whom she knew.

"Converted!" said she laconically, and joined those who were softly rubbing the pulses of the converted.

I laid my hand upon her brow. It was quite cold, so also were her hands.

When, by degrees, she had recovered consciousness, her glance was still fixed, but it seemed to me that it was directed rather inwardly than outwardly; she talked to herself in a low voice, and such a beautiful, blissful expression was portrayed in her countenance, that I would willingly experience that which she then experienced, saw, or perceived. It was no ordinary, no earthly scene. Her countenance was as it were transfigured. As soon as, after deep sighs, she had returned to her usual state, her appearance became usual also. But her demeanor was changed; she wept much, but calmly and silently.

The tornado gradually subsided in the church; shrieking and leaping, admonishing and preaching, all became hushed; and now people shook hands with each other, talked, laughed, congratulated one another so heartily, so cheerfully, with such cordial warmth and good-will, that it was a pleasure to behold. Of the whole raging, exciting scene there remained merely a feeling of satisfaction and pleasure, as if they had been together at some joyful feast.

I confess, however, to having been thoroughly amused by the frolic. Not so Anne W., who regarded that disorderly, wild worship with a feeling of astonishment, almost of indignation; and when our warm-hearted exhorter came up to us, and, turning especially to her, apologized for not having observed us before, that it was with no intention to neglect us, and so on, I saw her lovely coral-red upper lip curl with a bitter scorn as she replied, "I can not see in what respect you have neglected us." The man looked as if he would have been glad, with all his heart, to have preached to us, and, for my own part, I would gladly have listened to his Christian exhortation, given with its

African ardor. We shook hands, however, in the name of our common Lord and Master.

, And in spite of all the irrationality and the want of good taste which may be felt in such scenes, I am certain that there is in them, although as yet in a chaotic state, the element of true African worship. Give only intelligence, order, system to this outbreak of the warm emotions, longings, and presentiments of life, and then that which now appears hideous will become beautiful, that which is discordant will become harmonious. The children of Africa may yet give us a form of divine worship in which invocation, supplication, and songs of praise may respond to the inner life of the fervent soul!

How many there are, even in our cold North, who in their youthful years have felt an Africa of religious life, and who might have produced glorious flowers and fruits if it only could have existed—if it had not been smothered by the snow and the gray coldness of conventionality—had not been imprisoned in the stone church of custom.

I have visited some other churches in New Orleans, a Unitarian, an Episcopalian, and a Catholic Church, the last with the name dear to me, that of St. Theresa. But the heavenly spirit of St. Theresa was not there. An Irishman jabbered an unintelligible jargon, and in not one of these houses of God could I observe or obtain that which I sought for—edification. There was, at all events, life and ardor in the church of the negro assembly.

❧ "All men and women are created equal"

SENECA FALLS DECLARATION

In 1848 five women in Seneca Falls, New York, took it upon themselves to call for a convention for a declaration of women's rights modeled on the American Declaration of Independence. Initiated by Elizabeth Cady Stanton and Lucretia Mott, these five women prepared a draft declaration of sentiments and resolutions and invited men and women to participate in the event. The proposal included a resolution inserted by Stanton asserting a woman's right to vote. After a two-day convention, 68 women and 32 men signed the declaration.

The declaration prompted a largely negative reaction from the national press, particularly the call for women suffrage, which was controversial even among men who con-

sidered themselves to be progressive reformers. Nevertheless, the declaration prompted a series of annual conventions on women's rights and has come to be considered the starting point of the feminist movement in the United States. The right for women to vote became the movement's galvanizing issue over the next 70 years as women believed that they could not impact the legal, economic and social inequalities until they had political influence. Only one of the declaration's signers, Charlotte Woodward Pierce, lived long enough to vote in the 1920 election, the first time women were allowed to participate in a national election.

1. Declaration of Sentiments

When, in the course of human events, it becomes necessary for one portion of the family of man to assume among the people of the earth a position different from that which they have hitherto occupied, but one to which the laws of nature and of nature's God entitle them, a decent respect to the opinions of mankind requires that they should declare the causes that impel them to such a course.

We hold these truths to be self-evident: that all men and women are created equal; that they are endowed by their Creator with certain inalienable rights; that among these are life, liberty, and the pursuit of happiness; that to secure these rights governments are instituted, deriving their just powers from the consent of the governed. Whenever any form of government becomes destructive of these ends, it is the right of those who suffer from it to refuse allegiance to it, and to insist upon the institution of a new government, laying its foundation on such principles, and organizing its powers in such form, as to them shall seem most likely to effect their safety and happiness. Prudence, indeed, will dictate that governments long established should not be changed for light and transient causes; and accordingly all experience hath shown that mankind are more disposed to suffer while evils are sufferable, than to right themselves by abolishing the forms to which they were accustomed. But when a long train of abuses and usurpations, pursuing invariably the same object, evinces a design to reduce them under absolute despotism, it is their duty to throw off such government, and to provide new guards for their future security. Such has been the patient sufferance of the women under this government, and such is now the necessity which constrains them to demand the equal station to which they are entitled.

The history of mankind is a history of repeated injuries and usurpations on the part of man toward woman, having in direct object the establishment of an absolute tyranny over her. To prove this, let facts be submitted to a candid world.

He has never permitted her to exercise her inalienable right to the elective franchise.

He has compelled her to submit to laws, in the formation of which she had no voice.

He has withheld from her rights which are given to the most ignorant and degraded men—both natives and foreigners.

Having deprived her of this first right of a citizen, the elective franchise, thereby leaving her without representation in the halls of legislation, he has oppressed her on all sides.

He has made her, if married, in the eye of the law, civilly dead.

He has taken from her all right in property, even to the wages she earns.

He has made her, morally, an irresponsible being, as she can commit many crimes with impunity, provided they be done in the presence of her husband. In the covenant of marriage, she is compelled to promise obedience to her husband, he becoming, to all intents and purposes, her master—the law giving him power to deprive her of her liberty, and to administer chastisement.

He has so framed the laws of divorce, as to what shall be the proper causes, and in case of separation, to whom the guardianship of the children shall be given, as to be wholly regardless of the happiness of women—the law, in all cases, going upon a false supposition of the supremacy of man, and giving all power into his hands.

After depriving her of all rights as a married woman, if single, and the owner of property, he has taxed her to support a government which recognizes her only when her property can be made profitable to it.

He has monopolized nearly all the profitable employments, and from those she is permitted to follow, she receives but a scanty remuneration. He closes against her all the avenues to wealth and distinction which he considers most honorable to himself. As a teacher of theology, medicine, or law, she is not known.

He has denied her the facilities for obtaining a thorough education, all colleges being closed against her.

He allows her in Church, as well as State, but a subordinate position, claiming Apostolic authority for her exclusion from the ministry, and, with some exceptions, from any public participation in the affairs of the Church.

He has created a false public sentiment by giving to the world a different code of morals for men and women, by which moral delinquencies which exclude women from society, are not only tolerated, but deemed of little account in man.

He has usurped the prerogative of Jehovah himself, claiming it as his right to assign for her a sphere of action, when that belongs to her conscience and to her God.

He has endeavored, in every way that he could, to destroy her confidence in her own powers, to lessen her self-respect and to make her willing to lead a dependent and abject life.

Now, in view of this entire disenfranchisement of one-half the people of this country, their social and religious degradation—in view of the unjust laws above mentioned, and because women do feel themselves aggrieved, oppressed, and fraudulently deprived of their most sacred rights, we insist that they have immediate admission to all the rights and privileges which belong to them as citizens of the United States.

In entering upon the great work before us, we anticipate no small amount of misconception, misrepresentation, and ridicule; but we shall use every instrumentality within our power to effect our object. We shall employ agents, circulate tracts, petition the State and National legislatures, and endeavor to enlist the pulpit and the press in our behalf. We hope this Convention will be followed by a series of Conventions embracing every part of the country.

2. Resolutions

Whereas, The great precept of nature is conceded to be, that "man shall pursue his own true and substantial happiness." Blackstone in his Commentaries remarks, that this law of Nature being coeval with mankind, and dictated by God himself, is of course superior in obligation to any other. It is binding over all the globe, in all countries and at all times; no human laws are of any validity if contrary to this, and such of them as are valid, derive all their force, and all their validity, and all their authority, mediately and immediately, from this original; therefore,

Resolved, That all laws which prevent woman from occupying such a station in society as her conscience shall dictate, or which place her in a position inferior to that of man, are contrary to the great precept of nature, and therefore of no force or authority.

Resolved, That woman is man's equal—was intended to be so by the Creator, and the highest good of the race demands that she should be recognized as such.

Resolved, That the women of this country ought to be enlightened in regard to the laws under which they live, that they may no longer publish their degradation by declaring themselves satisfied with their present position, nor their ignorance, by asserting that they have all the rights they want.

Resolved, That inasmuch as man, while claiming for himself intellectual superiority, does accord to woman moral superiority, it is pre-eminently his duty to encourage her to speak and teach, as she has an opportunity, in all religious assemblies.

Resolved, That the same amount of virtue, delicacy, and refinement of behavior that is required of woman in the social state, should also be required of man, and the same transgressions should be visited with equal severity on both man and woman.

Resolved, That the objection of indelicacy and impropriety, which is so often brought against woman when she addresses a public audience, comes with a very ill-grace from those who encourage, by their attendance, her appearance on the stage, in the concert, or in feats of the circus.

Resolved, That woman has too long rested satisfied in the circumscribed limits which corrupt customs and a perverted application of the Scriptures have marked out for her, and that it is time she should move in the enlarged sphere which her great Creator has assigned her.

Resolved, That it is the duty of the women of this country to secure to themselves their sacred right to the elective franchise.

Resolved, That the equality of human rights results necessarily from the fact of the identity of the race in capabilities and responsibilities.

Resolved, That the speedy success of our cause depends upon the zealous and untiring efforts of both men and women, for the overthrow of the monopoly of the pulpit, and for the securing to women an equal participation with men in the various trades, professions, and commerce.

Resolved, therefore, That, being invested by the creator with the same capabilities, and the same consciousness of responsibility for their exercise, it is demonstrably the right and duty of woman, equally with man, to promote every righteous cause by every righteous means; and especially in regard to the great subjects of morals and religion, it is self-evidently her right to participate with her brother in teaching them, both in private and in public, by writing and by speaking, by any instrumentalities proper to be used, and in any assemblies proper to be held; and this being a self-evident truth growing out of the divinely implanted principles of human nature, any custom or authority adverse to it, whether modern or wearing the hoary sanction of antiquity, is to be regarded as a self-evident falsehood, and at war with mankind.

❧ "And ain't I a woman?"

SOJOURNER TRUTH

Sojourner Truth was born into slavery in New York State, but was given her freedom when New York emancipated slaves in 1827. She was originally named Isabella but changed it to Sojourner Truth in 1843 when she became an evangelist preaching her religious and abolitionist ideas. When the fledgling women's movement started in 1848, she became one of the few African-American participants. Nevertheless, her impact was significant. Using plain, frank language she presented a compelling case for women's rights. This speech was given at the 1851 Ohio Women's Rights Convention in Akron.

Well, children, where there is so much racket there must be something out of kilter. I think that 'twixt the Negroes of the South and the women of the North, all talking about rights, the white men will be in a fix pretty soon. But what's all this here talking about?

That man over there says that women need to be helped into carriages, and lifted over ditches, and to have the best place everywhere. Nobody ever helps me into carriages, or over mud puddles, or gives me any best place! And ain't I a woman? Look at me! Look at my arm. I have plowed and planted, and gathered into barns, and no man could head me! And ain't I a woman? I could work as much and eat as much as a man—when I could get it—and bear the lash as well! And ain't I a woman? I have borne thirteen children, and seen them most all sold off to slavery, and when I cried out with my mother's grief, none but Jesus heard me! And ain't I a woman?

Then they talk about this thing in the head; what's this they call it? [Someone tells her, "intellect."] That's it, honey. What's that got to do with women's rights or Negro's rights? If my cup won't hold but a pint, and yours holds a quart, wouldn't you be mean not to let me have my little half-measure full?

Then that little man in black there, he says women can't have as much rights as men, 'cause Christ wasn't a woman! Where did your Christ come from? Where did your Christ come from? From God and a woman!! Man had nothing to do with him.

If the first woman God ever made was strong enough to turn the world upside down all alone, these women together ought to be able to turn it back, and get it right side up again! And now they is asking to do it, the men better let them.

Obliged to you for hearing me, and now old Sojourner ain't got nothing more to say.

❧ "Sexual love is not naturally restricted to pairs"

JOHN NOYES

The most successful and notorious of the utopian communities during the age of reform was the Oneida Community in upstate New York, which encouraged very progressive sexual relations between men and women. Radical social reformer John Noyes moved the community from Putney, Vermont, to Oneida in 1848 because of local objections to the community's "complex marriage" system. Noyes sought to reshape relations between men and women. He developed a complex communal marriage system that shocked outsiders. Nevertheless, the community prospered as a commercial and agricultural enterprise for many years before disbanding in 1881. Noyes wrote this description of the marriage system in 1870.

CHAPTER II. Showing that Marriage is not an institution of the Kingdom of Heaven, and must give place to Communism.
PROPOSITION 5. In the Kingdom of

Heaven, the institution of marriage, which assigns the exclusive possession of one woman to one man, does not exist. Matt. 22: 23—30.

6. In the Kingdom of Heaven the intimate union of life and interest, which in the world is limited to pairs, extends through the whole body of believers; i.e. complex marriage takes the place of simple. John 17:21...

8. Admitting that the Community principle of the day of Pentecost, in its actual operation at that time, extended only to material goods, yet we affirm that there is no intrinsic difference between property in persons and property in things; and that the same spirit which abolished exclusiveness in regard to money, would abolish, if circumstances allowed full scope to it, exclusiveness in regard to women and children. Paul expressly places property in women and property in goods in the same category, and speaks of them together, as ready to be abolished by the advent of the Kingdom of Heaven. "The time," says he, "is short; it remaineth that they that have wives be as though they had none; and they that buy as though they possessed not; for the fashion of this world passeth away." I Cor. 7: 29-31.

9. The abolishment of appropriation is involved in the very nature of a true relation to Christ in the gospel. This we prove thus: The possessive feeling which expresses itself by the possessive pronoun mine, is the same in essence when it relate to persons, as when it relates to money or any other property. Amativeness and acquisitiveness are only different channels of one stream. They converge as we trace them to their source....

10. The abolishment of exclusiveness is involved in the love-relation required between all believers by the express injunction of Christ and the apostles, and by the whole tenor of the New Testament. "The new commandment is, that we love one another," and that, not by pairs, as in the world, but en masse. We are required to love one another fervently. The fashion of the world forbids a man and woman who are otherwise appropriated, to love one another fervently. But if they obey Christ they must do this; and whoever would allow them to do this, and yet would forbid them (on any other ground than that of present expediency), to express their unity, would "strain at a gnat and swallow a camel"; for unity of hearts is as much more important than any external expression of it,

as a camel is larger than a gnat....

13. The law of marriage is the same in kind with the Jewish law concerning meats and drinks and holy days, of which Paul said that they were "contrary to us, and were taken out of the way, being nailed to the cross." Col. 2: 14. The plea in favor of the worldly, social system, that it is not arbitrary, but founded in nature, will not bear investigation. All experience testifies (the theory of the novels to the contrary notwithstanding), that sexual love is not naturally restricted to pairs. Second marriages are contrary to the one-love theory, and yet are often the happiest marriages. Men and women find universally (however the fact may be conceded), that their susceptibility to love is not burnt out by one honey-moon, or satisfied by one lover. On the contrary, the secret history of the human heart will bear out the assertion that it is capable of loving any number of times and any number of persons, and that the more it loves the more it can love. This is the law of nature, thrust out of sight and condemned by common consent, and yet secretly known to all.

14. The law of marriage "worketh wrath." 1. It provokes to secret adultery, actual or of the heart. 2. It ties together unmatched natures. 3. It sunders matched natures. 4. It gives to sexual appetite only a scanty and monotonous allowance, and so produces the natural vices of poverty, contraction of taste and stinginess or jealousy. It makes no provision for the sexual appetite at the very time when that appetite is the strongest. By the custom of the world, marriage, in the average of cases, takes place at about the age of twenty-four; whereas puberty commences at the age of fourteen. For ten years, therefore, and that in the very flush of life, the sexual appetite is starved. This law of society bears hardest on females, because they have less opportunity of choosing their time of marriage than men. This discrepancy between the marriage system and nature, is one of the principal sources of the peculiar diseases of women, of prostitution, masturbation, and licentiousness in general.

❧ *"An act to limit hours"*

PENNSYLVANIA LEGISLATURE

Starting in the 1830s, state legislatures began to respond to a public outcry against manufacturers for the abuse of children in factories and the lengthy hours all employees were forced to work. Legislation prohibiting child labor and setting restrictions on hours did not come in earnest until the late 1840s. This 1848 Pennsylvania legislation prohibited the use of children under 12 in textile factories and set a ten-hour-a-day limit on all textile factory workers. Like much of the similar legislation passed at the time, no proof of age requirements were imposed and no enforcement provisions were included. As a result, the law was frequently ignored.

The labor performed during a period of ten hours, on any secular day, of all cotton, woolen, silk, paper, bagging and flax factories, shall be considered a legal day's labor; and that hereafter, no minor or adult engaged in any such factories, shall be holden or required to work more than ten hours on any secular day, or sixty hours in any secular week, and that after the fourth day of July, of the present year, no man shall be admitted as a worker, under the age of twelve years, in any cotton, woolen, silk or flax factory, within this commonwealth; that any owner of or employer in any such factories aforesaid, shall employ any such minor, he shall be adjudged to pay a penalty of fifty dollars one-half thereof to the party so employed, and the other half to the commonwealth, to be recovered in like manner as fines of like amount are now recoverable by law: Provided, That nothing contained in any act shall be constructed to prevent minors, above the age of fourteen years, from being employed more than ten hours in any day, if the same be done by special contract with their parents or guardians.

❧ *"Education is the great equalizer of the condition of men"*

HORACE MANN

As president of the Massachusetts Senate, Horace Mann oversaw the approval of the state's 1837 act improving the quality of education and creating a Board of Education. He subsequently resigned his seat to serve as secretary of the Board of Education and began to implement a personal campaign to elevate the condition of public schools in Massachusetts. Every year Mann delivered an annual report to the Board of Education. In 1848 he delivered his twelfth and last report, outlining the critical need for publicly funded universal education for the economic, medical and intellectual well-being of the state and the nation. He equated the need for an educated population to a robust economy and a functioning democratic government. Mann, who was subjected to abusive and ignorant teachers as a child, played a major role in abolishing corporal punishment in schools, emphasizing the importance of early education and breaking schools down into classes.

...A cardinal object which the government of Massachusetts, and all the influential men in the State, should propose to themselves, is the physical well-being of all the people, —the sufficiency, comfort, competence, of every individual in regard to food, raiment, and shelter. And these necessaries and conveniences of life should be obtained by each individual for himself, or by each family for themselves, rather than accepted from the hand of charity or extorted by poor-laws. It is not averred that this most desirable result can, in all instances, be obtained; but it is, nevertheless, the end to be aimed at. True statesmanship and true political economy, not less than true philanthropy, present this perfect theory as the goal, to be more and more closely approximated by our imperfect practice. The desire to achieve such a result cannot be regarded as an unreasonable ambition; for, though all mankind were well fed, well clothed, and well housed, they might still be half civilized.

According to the European theory, men are divided into classes, some to toil and earn, others to seize and enjoy. According to the Massachusetts theory, all are to have an equal chance for earning, and equal security in the enjoyment of what they earn. The latter tends to equality of condition; the former, to the grossest inequalities. Tried by any Christian standard of morals, or even by any of the better sort of heathen standards, can any one hesitate, for a moment, in declaring which of the two will produce the greater amount of human welfare, and which, therefore, is the more conformable to the divine will? The European theory is blind to what constitutes the highest glory as well as the highest duty of a State....

Our ambition as a State should trace itself to a different origin, and propose to itself a different object. Its flame should be lighted at the skies. Its radiance and its warmth should reach the darkest and the coldest of abodes of men. It should seek the solution of such problems as these: To what extent can competence displace pauperism? How nearly can we free ourselves from the low-minded and the vicious, not by their expatriation, but by their elevation? To what extent can the resources and powers of Nature be converted into human welfare, the peaceful arts of life be advanced, and the vast treasures of human talent and genius be developed? How much of suffering, in all its forms, can be relieved? Or, what is better than relief, how much can be prevented? Cannot the classes of crimes be lessened, and the number of criminals in each class be diminished?...

Now two or three things will doubtless be admitted to be true, beyond all controversy, in regard to Massachusetts. By its industrial condition, and its business operations, it is exposed, far beyond any other State in the Union, to the fatal extremes of overgrown wealth and desperate poverty. Its population is far more dense than that of any other State. It is four or five times more dense than the average of all the other States taken together; and density of population has always been one of the proximate causes of social inequality. According to population and territorial extent there is far more capital in Massachusetts—capital which is movable, and instantaneously available—than in any other State in the Union; and probably both these qualifications respecting population and territory could be omitted without endangering the truth of the assertion....

Now surely nothing but universal education can counterwork this tendency to the domination of capital and the servility of labor. If one class possesses all the wealth and the education, while the residue of society is ignorant and poor, it matters not by what name the relation between them may be called: the latter, in fact and in truth, will be the servile dependents and subjects of the former. But, if education be equally diffused, it will draw property after it by the strongest of all attractions; for such a thing never did happen, and never can happen, as that an intelligent and practical body of men should be permanently poor. Property and labor in different classes are essentially antagonistic; but property and labor in the same class are essentially fraternal. The people of Massachusetts have, in some degree, appreciated the truth that the unexampled prosperity of the State—its comfort, its competence, its general intelligence and virtue—is attributable to the education, more or less perfect, which all its people have received; but are they sensible of a fact equally important,—namely, that it is to this same education that two-thirds of the people are indebted for not being to-day the vassals of as severe a tyranny, in the form of capital, as the lower classes of Europe are bound to in any form of brute force?

Education then, beyond all other devices of human origin, is a great equalizer of the conditions of men,—the balance wheel of the social machinery. I do not here mean that it so elevates the moral nature as to make men disdain and abhor the oppression of their fellow men. This idea pertains to another of its attributes. But I mean that it gives each man the independence and the means by which he can resist the selfishness of other men. It does better than to disarm the poor of their hostility toward the rich: it prevents being poor. Agrarianism is the revenge of poverty against wealth. The wanton destruction of the property of others—the burning of hay-ricks, and corn-ricks, the demolition of machinery because it supersedes hand-labor, the sprinkling of vitriol on rich dresses—is only agrarianism run mad. Education prevents both the revenge and the madness. On the other hand, a fellow-feeling for one's class or caste is the common instinct of hearts not wholly sunk in selfish regard for a person or for a family. The spread of education, by enlarging the cultivated class or caste, will open a wider area over which the social feelings will expand; and, if this education should be universal and complete, it would do more than all things else to obliterate factitious distinctions in society....

For the creation of wealth, then, for the existence of a wealthy people and a wealthy nation, intelligence is the grand condition. The number of improvers will increase as the intellectual constituency, if I may so call it, increases. In former times, and in most parts of the world even at the present day, not one man in a million has ever had such a development of mind as made it possible for him to become a contributor to art or science.... Let this development proceed, and contributions ... of inestimable value, will be sure to follow. That political economy, therefore, which busies itself about capital and labor, supply and demand, inter-

ests and rents, favorable and unfavorable balances of trade, but leaves out of account the elements of a wide-spread mental development, is naught but stupendous folly. The greatest of all the arts in political economy is to change a consumer into a producer; and the next greatest is to increase the producing power,—and this to be directly obtained by increasing his intelligence. For mere delving, an ignorant man is but little better than a swine, whom he so much resembles in his appetites, and surpasses in his power of mischief....

The Compromise of 1850

HENRY CLAY

The acquisition of western territories widened the schism between the South and North. Fearing they would lose their political power to resist the increasing calls for the abolition of slavery, the slave-holding states wanted to make sure that new states admitted to the Union permitted slaves. But in 1848 the Oregon Territory banned slavery and in 1849 California adopted a constitution prohibiting slavery. It appeared as if the political balance would tip in favor of the free states at a time when abolitionist calls for the banning of slavery were gaining increasing popular support in the North.

Southerners threatened to secede from the Union. At the beginning of 1850 the country was on the verge of falling apart. On January 29, Kentucky senator Henry Clay introduced a series of resolutions laying forth the framework for a compromise agreement to keep the Union intact. His plan called for California being admitted as a free state, adopting a stricter fugitive slave law, the prohibition of slavery in Washington D.C., postponing the decision of slavery in Utah and New Mexico, defining Texas' border, and the federal assumption of the $10 million Texan debt.

Clay, who became known as "The Great Compromiser," gave a two-day address to Congress on February 5 and 6 imploring the country to avoid dissolving into regional confederacies. He envisioned a bitter, protracted and bloody war between the states if they could not agree to stay united. He vigorously supported the preservation of the union at all costs, including going to war to preserve it.

If the Union is to be dissolved for any existing causes, it will be dissolved because slavery is interdicted or not allowed to be introduced into the ceded territories; because slavery is threatened to be abolished in the District of Columbia, and because fugitive slaves are not returned, as in my opinion they ought to be, and restored to their masters. These, I believe, will be the causes, if there be any causes, which can lead to the direful event to which I have referred.

Well, now, let us suppose that the Union has been dissolved. What remedy does it furnish for the grievances complained of in its united condition? Will you be able to push slavery into the ceded territories? How are you to do it, supposing the North—all the states north of the Potomac, and which are opposed to it—are in possession of the navy and army of the United States? Can you expect, if there is a dissolution of the Union that you can carry slavery into California and New Mexico? You cannot dream of such a purpose. If it were abolished in the District of Columbia, and the Union were dissolved, would the dissolution of the Union restore slavery in the District of Columbia? Are you safer in the recovery of your fugitive slaves, in a state of dissolution or of severance of the Union, than you are in the Union itself? Why, what is the state of the fact in the Union? You lose some slaves. You recover some others. Let me advert to a fact which I ought to have introduced before, because it is highly creditable to the courts and juries of the free states. In every case, so far as my information extends, where an appeal has been made to the courts of justice for the recovery of fugitives, or for the recovery of penalties inflicted upon persons who have assisted in decoying slaves from their masters and aiding them in escaping from their masters—as far as I am informed, the courts have asserted the rights of the owner, and the juries have promptly returned adequate verdicts in favor of the owner. Well, this is some remedy. What would you have if the Union were dissevered? Why, sir, then the severed parts would be independent of each other—foreign countries! Slaves taken from the one into the other would be then like slaves now escaping from the United States into Canada. There would be no right of extradition; no right to demand your slaves; no right to appeal to the courts of justice to demand your slaves which escape, or the penalties for decoying them. Where one slave escapes now, by running away from his owner, hundreds and thousands would escape if the Union were severed in parts—I care not where nor how you run the line, if independent sovereignties were established....

But, I must take the occasion to say that, in my opinion, there is no right on the part of one or more of the states to secede from the Union. War and the dissolution of the Union are identical and inseparable. There can be no dissolution of the Union, except by consent or by war. No one can expect, in the existing state of things, that that consent would be given, and war is the only alternative by which a dissolution could be accomplished. And, Mr. President, if consent were given—if possibly we were to separate by mutual agreement and by a given line, in less than sixty days after such an agreement had been executed, war would break out between the free and slaveholding portions of this Union—between the two independent portions into which it would be erected in virtue of the act of separation....

But how are you going to separate them? In my humble opinion, Mr. President, we should begin at least with three confederacies—the Confederacy of the North, the Confederacy of the Atlantic Southern States (the slaveholding states), and the Confederacy of the Valley of the Mississippi. My life upon it, sir, that vast population that has already concentrated, and will concentrate, upon the headwaters and tributaries of the Mississippi, will never consent that the mouth of that river shall be held subject to the power of any foreign state whatever. Such, I believe, would be the consequences of dissolution of the Union. But other confederacies would spring up, from time to time, as dissatisfaction and discontent were disseminated over the country. There would be the Confederacy of the Lakes—perhaps the Confederacy of New England and of the Middle States....

Mr. President, I am directly opposed to any purpose of secession, of separation. I am for staying within the Union and defying any portion of this Union to expel or drive me out of the Union. I am for staying within the Union and fighting for my rights—if necessary, with the sword—within the bounds and under the safeguard of the Union. I am for vindicating these rights, but not by being driven out of the Union rashly and unceremoniously by any portion of this confederacy. Here I am within it, and here I mean to stand and die; as far as my individual purposes or wished can go—within it to protect myself and to defy all power upon earth to expel me or drive me from the situation in which I am placed. Will there not be more safety in fighting within the Union than without it?...

I said that I thought that there was no right on

the part of one or more of the states to secede from this Union. I think that the Constitution of the thirteen states was made, not merely for the generation which then existed, but for posterity, undefined, unlimited, permanent, and perpetual—for this posterity, and for every subsequent state which might come into the union, binding themselves by that indissoluble bond. It is to remain for that posterity now and forever. Like another of the great relations of private life, it was a marriage that no human authority can dissolve or divorce the parties from; and, if I may be allowed to refer to this same example in private life, let us say what man and wife say to each other: "We have mutual faults; nothing in the form of human beings can be perfect. Let us then be kind to each other, forbearing, conceding; let us live in happiness and peace."

Mr. President, I have said what I solemnly believe—that the dissolution of the Union and war are identical and inseparable; that they are convertible terms.

Such a war, too, as that would be, following the dissolution of the Union!... And what would be its termination? Standing armies and navies, to an extent draining the revenues of each portion of the disseevered empire, would be created; exterminating wars would follow—not a war of two nor three years, but of interminable duration—an exterminating war would follow, until some Philip or Alexander, some Caesar or Napoleon would rise to cut the Gordian knot, and solve the problem of the capacity of man for self-government, and crush the liberties of both the disseevered portions of this Union. Can you doubt it? Look at history—consult the pages of all history, ancient or modern; look at human nature—look at the character of the contest in which you would be engaged in the supposition of a war following the dissolution of the Union such as I have suggested—and I ask you if it is possible for you to doubt that the final but perhaps distant termination of the while will be some despot treading down the liberties of the people?—that the final result will be the extinction of this last and glorious light, which is leading all mankind, who are gazing upon it, to cherish hope and anxious expectation that the liberty which prevails here will sooner or later be advanced throughout the civilized world? Can you, Mr. President, lightly contemplate the consequence? Can you yield yourself to a torrent of passion, amidst dangers which I

have depicted in colors far short of what would be the reality, if the event should ever happen? I conjure gentlemen—whether from the South or the North, by all they hold dear in this world—by all their love of liberty—by all their veneration for their ancestors—by all their regard for posterity—by all their gratitude to him who has bestowed upon them such unnumbered blessings—by all the duties which they owe to mankind, and all the duties they owe to themselves—by all these considerations I implore them to pause—solemnly to pause—at the edge of the precipice before the fearful and disastrous leap is taken in the yawning abyss below, which will inevitably lead to certain an irretrievable destruction.

And, finally, Mr. President, I implore, as the best blessing which heaven can bestow upon me on earth, that if the direful and sad event of the dissolution of the Union shall happen, I may not survive to behold the sad and heart-rending spectacle.

✿ "[The South] has little left to surrender"

JOHN C. CALHOUN

Clay's proposal, which was in part crafted by Illinois Senator Stephen A. Douglas, prompted one of the great Congressional debates in American history. Senators wrestled with how to keep the Union intact without compromising their regional interests. South Carolina Senator John C. Calhoun had represented Southern state and pro-slavery interests throughout his career. A month before his own death, he gave his final deliberation against Northern aggressions. Too sick to deliver the speech himself, James A. Mason read the speech to Congress as the enfeebled Calhoun sat and watched.

Calhoun defended the Southern right to slavery and laid the issue of secession on the steps of the North. Compromise would not solve the essential dispute, he said, unless the North relented to the South's need to be allowed to keep slavery as a lawful institution in perpetuity.

I have, Senators, believed from the first that the agitation of the subject of slavery would, if not prevented by some timely and effective measure, end in disunion. I have, on all proper occasions, endeavored to call the attention of both the two great parties which divide the country to adopt some measure to prevent so great a disaster, but without success. The agitation has been permitted to proceed, with almost no attempt to resist it, until it has reached a period when it can no longer be disguised or denied, that the Union is in danger. You have thus had forced upon you the greatest and the gravest question that can ever come under your consideration: how can the Union be preserved?...

Indeed, as events are now moving, it will not require the South to secede, to dissolve the Union. Agitation will of itself effect it, of which past history furnishes abundant proof...

It is a great mistake to suppose that disunion can be effected by a single blow. The cords which bind these states together in one common Union are far too numerous and powerful for that. Disunion must be the work of time. It is only through a long process, and successively, that the cords can be snapped, until the whole fabric falls asunder. Already the agitation of the slavery question has snapped some of the most important, and has greatly weakened all the others, as I shall proceed to show.

The cords which bind the states together are not only many, but various in character. Among them, some are spiritual or ecclesiastical; some political; others social. Others pertain to the benefit conferred by the Union, and others to the feelings of duty and obligation.

The strongest of those of a spiritual and ecclesiastical nature consisted in the unity of the great religious denominations, all of which originally embraced the Union. All these denominations, with the exception perhaps of the Catholics, were organized very much upon the principle of our political institutions. Beginning with smaller meetings, corresponding with the political divisions of the country, their organization terminated in one great central assemblage, corresponding very much with the character of Congress. At these meetings the principal clergymen and lay members of the respective denominations from all parts of the Union, met to transact business relating to their common concerns. It was not confined to what appertained to the doctrines and discipline of the respective denominations, but extended to plans for disseminating the Bible, establishing missionaries, distributing tracts, and of establishing presses for the publication of tracts, newspapers, and periodicals, with a view of diffusing religious information and for the support of the doctrines and creeds of the denominations.

All this combined contributed greatly to strengthen the bonds of the Union. The ties which held each denomination together formed a strong cord to hold the whole Union together. But, powerful as they were, they have not been able to resist the explosive effect of slavery agitation. There is but one way by which [the Union] can with any certainty be saved, and that is a full and final settlement, on the principle of justice, of all the questions at issue between the two sections. The South asks for justice, simple justice, and less she ought not to take. She has no compromise to offer, but the Constitution; and no concession or surrender to make. She has already surrendered so much that she has little left to surrender. Such a settlement would go to the root of the evil, and remove all cause of discontent, and satisfy the South that she could remain honorably and safely in the Union; and thereby restore the harmony and fraternal feelings between the sections, which existed anterior to the Missouri agitation. Nothing else can, with any certainty, finally and forever settle the questions at issue, terminate agitation, and save the Union.

But can this be done? Yes, easily; not by the weaker parry, for it can of itself do nothing—not even protect itself—but by the stronger. The North has only to will it, to do justice and perform her duty, in order to accomplish it: to do justice by conceding to the South an equal right in the acquired territory, and to do her duty by causing the stipulations relative to fugitive slaves to be faithfully fulfilled: to cease the agitation of the slave question, and to provide for the insertion of a provision in the Constitution, by an amendment, which will restore to the South in substance the power she possessed of protecting herself, before the equilibrium between the sections was destroyed by the action of this government. There will be no difficulty in devising such a provision. One that will protect the South, and which, at the same time, will improve and strengthen the government, instead of impairing or weakening it.

But will the North agree to do this? It is for her to answer the question. But I will say, she cannot refuse, if she has half the love of the Union which she professes to have, or without justly exposing herself to the charge that her love of power and aggrandizement is far greater than her love of the Union. At all events, the responsibility of saving the Union is on the North and not the South. The South cannot save it by any act of hers, and the North may save it without any sacrifice whatever, unless to do justice and to perform her duties under the Constitution be regarded by her as a sacrifice.

It is time, Senators, that there should be an open and manly avowal on all sides, as to what is intended to be done. If the question is not now settled, it is uncertain whether it ever can hereafter be; and we, as the representatives of the states of this Union, regarded as governments, should come to a distinct understanding as to our respective views, in order to ascertain whether the great questions at issue between the two sections can be settled or not. If you, who represent the stronger portion, cannot agree to settle them on the broad principles of justice and duty, say so; and let the states we both represent agree to separate and part in peace. If you are unwilling we should part in peace, tell us so; and we shall know what to do, when you reduce the question to submission or resistance. If you remain silent, you then compel us to infer what you intend. In that case, California will become the test question. If you admit her, under all the difficulties that oppose her admission, you compel us to infer that you intend to exclude us from the whole of the acquired territories, with the intention of destroying irretrievably the equilibrium between the two sections. We would be blind not to perceive in that case that your real objects are power and aggrandizement, and infatuated not to act accordingly…

I have now, Senators, done my duty in expressing my opinions fully, freely, and candidly, on this solemn occasion. In doing so, I have been governed by the motives which have governed me in all the stages of the agitation of the slavery question since its commencement; and exerted myself to arrest it, with the intention of saving the Union, if it could be done; and, if it cannot, to save the section where it has pleased Providence to cast my lot, and which I sincerely believe has justice and the Constitution on its side. Having faithfully done my duty to the best of my ability, both to the Union and my section, throughout the whole of this agitation, I shall have the consolation, let what will come, that I am free from all responsibility.

"Let us not be pigmies in a case that calls for men"

DANIEL WEBSTER

The great orator Massachusetts Senator Daniel Webster threw his behind support Clay's compromise and thereby helped preserved the Union. Webster's stance stunned his supporters. He not only endorsed a tougher fugitive slave law, but also condemned abolitionists who he accused of enflaming Southern passions. As Webster said in his March 7, 1850, speech in the Senate, the most important issue was the preservation of the Union. Several months later, Congress passed Clay's compromise in a series of five acts. Within two years, both Webster and Clay died.

Mr. President, in the excited times in which we live, there is found to exist a state of crimination and recrimination between the North and South. There are lists of grievances produced by each; and those grievances, real or supposed, alienate the minds of one portion of the country from the other, exasperate the feelings, and subdue the sense of fraternal attention, patriotic love, and mutual regard. I shall bestow a little attention, sir, upon these various grievances existing on the one side and on the other. I begin with complaints of the South. I will not answer, further than I have, the general statements of the honorable senator from South Carolina, that the North has prospered at the expense of the South in consequence of the manner of administering the government, in the collecting of its revenues, and so forth. These are disputed topics, and I have no inclination to enter into them. But I will allude to other complaints of the South, and especially to one which has in my opinion just foundation; and that is, that there has been found at the North, among individuals and among legislators, a disinclination to perform fully their constitutional duties in regard to the return of persons bound to service who have escaped into the free states. In that respect, the South, in my judgment, is right, and the North is wrong.

Every member of every Northern legislature is bound by oath, like every other officer in the country, to support the Constitution of the United States; and the article of the Constitution which says to these states they shall deliver up fugitives from service is as binding in honor and conscience as any other article. No man fulfills his duty in any legislature who sets himself to find excuses, evasions, escapes from this constitutional obligation. I have always thought that the Constitution addressed itself to the legislatures of the states or to the states themselves. It says that these persons escaping into another state, and coming therefore within the jurisdiction of that state, shall be delivered up, it seems to me the import of the clause is that the state itself, in obedience to the Constitution, shall cause him to be delivered up. That is my judgment. I have always entertained that opinion, and I entertain it now. But when the subject, some years ago, was before the Supreme Court of the United States, the majority of the judges held that the power to cause fugitives from service to be delivered up was a power to be exercised under the authority of this government. I do not know, on the whole, that it may not have been a fortunate decision. My habit is to respect the result of judicial deliberations and the solemnity of judicial decisions.

As it now stands, the business of seeing that these fugitives are delivered up resides in the power of Congress and the national judicature, and my friend at the head of the Judiciary Committee has a bill on the subject now before the Senate, which, with some amendments to it, I propose to support, with all its provisions, to the fullest extent. And I desire to call the attention of all sober-minded men at the North, of all conscientious men, of all men who are not carried away by some fanatical idea or some false impression, to their constitutional obligations. I put it to all the sober and sound minds at the North as a question of morals and a question of conscience. What right have they, in their legislative capacity or any other capacity, to endeavor to get round this Constitution, or to embarrass the free exercise of the rights secured by the Constitution to the persons whose slaves escape from them? None at all; none at all....

Then, sir, there are the abolition societies, of which I am unwilling to speak, but in regard to which I have very clear notions and opinions. I do not think them useful. I think their operations for the last twenty years have produced nothing good or valuable. At the same time, I believe thousands of their members to be honest and good men, perfectly well-meaning men. They have excited feelings; they think they must do something for the cause of liber-

ty; and, in their sphere of action, they do not see what else they can do than to contribute to an abolition press, or an abolition society, or to pay an abolition lecturer. I do not mean to impute gross motives even to the leaders of these societies, but I am not blind to the consequences of their proceedings. I cannot but see what mischiefs their interference with the South has produced. And is it not plain to every man? Let any gentleman who entertains doubts on this point recur to the debates in the Virginia House of Delegates in 1832, and he will see with what freedom a proposition made by Mr. Jefferson Randolph for the gradual abolition of slavery was discussed in that body. Every one spoke of slavery as he thought, very ignominious and disparaging names and epithets were applied to it. The debates in the House of Delegates on that occasion, I believe, were all published. They were ready by every colored man who could read, and to those who could not read, those debates were read by others. At that time Virginia was not unwilling or afraid to discuss this question, and to let that part of her population know as much of the discussion as they could learn. That was in 1832. As has been said by the honorable member from South Carolina, these abolition societies commenced their course of action in 1835. It is said, I do not know how true it may be, that they send incendiary publications into the slave states; at any rate, they attempted to arouse, and did arouse, a very strong feeling; in other words, they created great agitation in the North against Southern slavery. Well, what was the result? The bonds of the slaves were bound more firmly than before, their rivets were more strongly fastened. Public opinion, which in Virginia had begun to be exhibited against slavery, and was opening out for the discussion of the question, drew back and shut itself up in its castle....

Mr. President, I should much prefer to have heard from every member on this floor declarations of opinion that this Union could never be dissolved, than the declaration of opinions by any body, that, in any case, under the pressure of any circumstances, such a dissolution was possible. I hear with distress and anguish the word "secession," especially when it falls from the lips of those who are patriotic, and known to the country, and known all over the world, for their political services. Secession! Peaceable secession! Sir, your eyes and mine are never destined to see that miracle.

The dismemberment of this vast country without convulsion! The breaking up of the fountains of the great deep without ruffling the surface! Who is foolish, I beg everybody's pardon, as to expect to see any such thing? Sir, he who sees these states, now revolving in harmony around a common center, and expects to see them quit their places and fly off without convulsion, may look the next hour to see the heavenly bodies rush from their spheres and jostle against each other in the realms of space, without causing the wreck of the universe. There can be no such thing as a peaceable secession. Peaceable secession is an utter impossibility. Is the great Constitution under which we live, covering this whole country, is it to be thawed and melted away by secession, as the snows on the mountain melt under the influence of a vernal sun, disappear almost unobserved, and run off? No, sir! No, sir!...

Peaceable secession! Peaceable secession! The concurrent agreement of all the members of this great republic to separate! A voluntary separation, with alimony on one side and on the other. Why, what would be the result? Where is the line to be drawn? What states are to secede? What is to remain American? What am I to be? An American no longer? Am I to become a sectional man, a local man, a separatist, with no country in common with the gentlemen who sit around me here, or who fill the other house of Congress? Heaven forbid! Where is the flag of the republic to remain? Where is the eagle still to tower? Or is he to cower, and shrink, and fall to the ground?...

What is to become of the army? What is to become of the navy? What is to become of the public lands? How is each of the thirty states to defend itself? I know, although the idea has not been state distinctly, there is to be, or it is supposed possible that there will be, a Southern Confederacy. I do not mean to say that it is true, but I have heard it suggested elsewhere, that the idea has been entertained, that, after the dissolution of this Union, a Southern Confederacy might be formed. I am sorry, sir, that it has ever been thought of, talked of, or dreamed of, in the wildest flights of human imagination. But the idea, so far as it exists, must be of a separation, assigning the slave states to one side and the free states to the other. Sir, I may express myself too strongly perhaps, but there are impossibilities in the natural as well as in the physical world, and I hold the idea of a separation of these

states, those that are free to form one government, and those that are slave-holding to form another, as such an impossibility. We could not separate the states by any such line, if we were to draw it. We could not sit down here today and draw a line of separation that would satisfy any five men in the country. There are natural causes that would keep and tie us together, and there are social and domestic relations which we could not break if we would, and which we should not if we could....

And now, Mr. President, instead of speaking of the possibility or the utility of secession, instead of dwelling in those caverns of darkness, instead of groping with those ideas so full of all that is horrid and horrible, let us come out into the light of day; let us enjoy the fresh air of liberty and union; let us cherish those hopes which belong to us; let us devote ourselves to those great objects that are fit for our consideration and our action; let us raise our conceptions to the magnitude and the importance of the duties that devolve upon us; let our comprehension be as broad as the country for which we act, our aspirations as high as its certain destiny; let us not be pigmies in a case that calls for men. Never did there devolve on any generation of men higher trusts than now devolve upon us, for the preservation of this Constitution and the harmony and peace of all who are destined to live under it. Let us make our generation one of the strongest and brightest links in the golden chain which is destined, I fondly believe, to grapple the people of all the states to this Constitution for ages to come.

❧ "It was a new world to them"

NEW YORK DAILY TIMES

Immigration soared in the early 1850s to as many as 400,000 people a year. All told, 2.3 million Europeans moved to the United States in the 1850s—or almost 20 times the number of immigrants in the 1820s. The new waves of the migration directly impacted the urbanization and industrialization of the Northeast. Expanding industries such as textile, construction and iron absorbed the inflows. Nevertheless, the cities could not handle the flood of unskilled workers. Many immigrant families struggled in crammed slums. Boston, New York and other cities complained of the burden on their charitable causes and the increasing crime rates. This article in the New York *Daily Times* was written in 1853 describing the scene that greeted immigrants as they disembarked.

If you would see, for a moment, one of the streams in the great current which is always pouring through New-York, go down a Summer afternoon to the North River wharves. A German emigrant ship has just made fast. The long wharf is crowded full of trucks and carts, and drays, waiting for the passengers. As you approach the end you come upon a noisy crowd of strange faces and stranger costumes. Moustached peasants in Tyrolese hats are arguing in unintelligible English with truck-drivers; runners from the German hotels are pulling the confused women hither and thither; peasant girls with bare heads, and the rich-flushed, nut brown faces you never see here, are carrying huge bundles to the heaps of baggage; children in doublets and hose, and queer little caps, are mounted on the trunks, or swung off amid the laughter of the crowd with ropes from the ship's sides. Some are just welcoming an old face, so dear in the strange land, some are letting down the huge trunks, some swearing in very genuine low Dutch, at the endless noise and distractions. They bear the plain marks of the Old World. Healthy, stout frames, and low, degraded faces with many stamps of inferiority; dependence, servitude on them; little graces of costume too—a colored headdress or a fringed coat—which never could have originated here; and now and then a sweet face, with the rich bloom and the dancing blue eye, that seem to reflect the very glow and beauty of the vine hills of the Rhine.

It is a new world to them—oppression, bitter poverty behind—here, hope, freedom, and a chance to work, and food to the laboring man. They may have the vaguest ideas of it all—still, to the dullest some thoughts come of the New Free World.

Every one in the great City, who can make a living from the freshly arrived immigrant, is here. Runners, sharpers, peddlers, agents of boarding-houses, of forwarding-offices, and worst of all, of the houses where many a simple emigrant girl, far from friends and home, comes to a sad end. Very many of these, who are now arriving, will start to-morrow at once for the far West. Some will hang about the German boarding-houses in Greenwich-street, each day losing their money, their children getting out of control, until they at last seek a refuge in Ward's island, or settle down in the Eleventh Ward, to add to the great mass of foreign poverty and misery there gathered. From there, you shall see their children sallying out these summer mornings, as soon as light, to do the petty work of the City, rag-picking, bone-gathering, selling chips, peddling by the thousands, radishes, strawberries and fruit through every street.

❧ "We have our Five Points"

GEORGE TEMPLETON STRONG

George Templeton Strong observed in his diary in 1851 the social problems that were emerging in New York City's immigrant neighborhoods.

Yet we have our Five Points, our emigrant quarters, our swarms of seamstresses to whom their utmost toil in monotonous daily drudgery gives only bare subsistence, a life barren of hope and of enjoyment; our hordes of dock thieves, and of children who live in the streets and by them. No one can walk the length of Broadway without meeting some hideous troop of ragged girls, from twelve years old down, brutalized already almost beyond redemption by premature vice, clad in filthy refuse of the rag-picker's collections, obscene of speech, the stamp of childhood gone from their faces, hurrying along with harsh laughter and foulness on their lips that some of them have learned by rote, yet too young to understand it; with thief written in their cunning eyes and whore on their depraved faces, though so unnatural, foul, and repulsive in every look and gesture, that that last profession seems utterly beyond their aspirations. On a rainy day such crews may be seen by dozens. They haunt every other crossing and skulk away together, when the sun comes out and the mud is dry again. And such a group I think the most revolting object that the social diseases of a great city can produce. A gang of blackguard boys is lovely by the side of it.

The Rich Men of Massachusetts

A. FORBES AND J.W. GREENE

With capitalism in full blossom by the mid 1850s, Americans developed a fascination with wealth. In 1851, A. Forbes and J.W. Greene published a book, *The Rich Men of Massachusetts,* chronicling the histories and status of the wealthiest men in Massachusetts. The authors wrote that the aim of the book was "to furnish encouragement to the young, from the contemplation of success resulting from a suitable combination of those sterling qualities, Perserverance, Energy, Carefulness, Economy, Integrity."

Brewster, Osmyn $100,000

Of the firm of Crocker & Brewster. A printer; learned his trade in the place where he now keeps, and where, men and boys, he and his partner have been for more than forty years. At first they were apprentices to, then partners with, and subsequently successors of Samuel T. Armstrong. In this establishment fortunes have been made in the sale of religious books, it being the only place in Boston, for many years, denominated a "religious book store." Mr. Brewster has ever been a close applicant to business, and has earned the respect of his fellow-citizens, who have often honored him with their confidence.

Humphrey, Benjamin $750,000

Began poor. Formerly merchant. Born in Weymouth; an only son. At the age of fourteen came to Boston, and obtained a situation with Abraham Wild, a merchant engaged in extensive business. At twenty, with the consent of his master, he commenced business in Fore, now Ann Street, and by close attention, laid the foundation of his present prosperity.

Coffin, Jared $300,000

Began his career as a cooper on board a Nantucket Whaler; finally became master and owner of a ship, and acquired large wealth by his enterprise and fact for saving. He is a rough sort of a stick, as might be expected, and things none the less of his dignity because it is back by a fat purse.

Douglass, Robert $100,000

Began poor. Confectioner. At the age of sixteen he was left fatherless, with eight brothers and sisters and a mother. He supported them all; brought up all the children and provided for them, and still provides for his mother. The ordinary terms expressive of efficiency, and benevolence, are altogether too tame to be applied to Robert Douglass. The world has few instances of such "great men."

Allen, Phineas $60,000

Began poor. Entered as an apprentice at the printer's trade in Southampton, but ran away before his time was up. Came to Pittsfield, and started a Democratic paper (the "Pittsfield Sun") by which he made his money. A man of extremely regular business habits. Always about his business; a correct, go-ahead man, but no speculator. He has been a member of both branches of the Legislature.

"The precocious depravity of San Francisco"

WILLIAM KELLY

The discovery of gold in California triggered one of the great gold mining rushes in American history. Tens of thousands of prospectors flocked to California in search of instant fortunes. San Francisco, which served as the main supply station for gold miners, boomed into a thriving city. The population exploded from 1,000 to 35,000 in two years. William Kelly described in 1851 the runaways prices, lust for profit and bawdy conditions that marked Western boomtowns through the 19th century. San Francisco withstood the test of time and remained a prosperous city, serving as California's largest and most important city for many years.

There are numerous houses of worship in the city, but none of them externally distinguishable as such save the Roman Catholic chapel—a new frame building of capacious dimensions—erected on an eminence, which makes it quite a feature of the city. It is to be regretted, however, that their influence is exceedingly circumscribed, if any inference can be deduced from the limited attendance; for while their congregations are so lamentably thin, the dens of iniquity, the gaming-houses, are crammed to suffocation; the sacrilegious din of their crashing banks rending the solemn stillness of the Sabbath, penetrating to the shrine of worship even during the hour of prayer—the rampant bleatings of the golden calf drowning the mild tones of Christian piety.

The world's progress furnishes no parallel for the precocious depravity of San Francisco. The virgin soil of a new settlement did not use to be a garden for vice and evil. There it was the kindly philanthropist looked to find the ruddy virtues blooming in a kindred clay in an uncontaminated atmosphere, fading and sickening only in the tedious revolution of time, as moral culture degenerated into voluptuous lethargy, accumulated wealth morbidly craving the incentives of luxury, and enervating enjoyments supplanting the healthy exercise of enterprise, when, with drooping heads and shrivelled stems, they shrank into decay, choked by the rank weeds of artificial society. But in Francisco a new and anomalous phase has arisen; the infant phenomenon exhibiting the tokens of senility in its cradle, with the gangrene of vicious indulgence staining its soft cheek before it is well emancipated from its swaddling-clothes—which predicate for it the proudest position amongst all the cities within the vast bay of oceans between the Capes of Horn and Good Hope.

In Francisco nothing is natural—everything is forced; it is a hotbed where all pursuits are stimulated by the fierce fire of one predominant lust. Trade or business is not embarked in there to be the honourable occupation of a lifetime; professions are not solely followed to secure a permanent practice and social elevation; men engage in both the one and the other to build up fortunes in a hurry with whatever materials they can grasp, to win a large stake by any means and then withdraw, confounding the tactics of the gambler with the zealous integrity of the merchant, until conscience is left without a corner to hide in, and even common decency is obliged to pick her steps through the mire....

Lot property, in and about Francisco, is, and will continue for some time, to be valuable and in demand, from the unceasing stream of emigration, both by sea and land, one-fourth of whom either stay in or return to the city; and as there are no such things as empty houses or untenanted stores, those who come with an intention of starting business have no alternative but to purchase a lot and erect a tenement; so that, I repeat, lot property contiguous to the city is for the present an improving investment; but I wish to emphasize contiguous, because surveys and allotments have been made out to ridiculously remote points, that cannot possibly come into occupation if ever, for a number of years; for you will meet, as you travel towards the city, miles from its turmoil, posts surmounted with boards, that wayfarers approach to learn the distance, but them headed with the names of streets, and notifications "that the adjoining lots are for sale"—causing the bewildered stranger to strain his optics in search of the outlines of a town, impressed, as he proceeds with amazement, and vague notions of earthquakes and such like vagaries of nature.

But I cannot refrain from expressing my opinion—the question of title apart—that the present extravagant value of property in Francisco cannot continue to be long sustained, because commerce and business, which are its life and soul, are on an unsound and fictitious basis, that must be revolutionised to become stable and permanent. The standard of property is relatively regulated by the profits of trade, and as those profits become necessarily depressed as the vast appliances of steam open fresh facilities for intercourse and transit, its value must subside in like ratio. No sane man could put faith in the continuance of a system having to bear up against the feverish pulse of a money-market beating at an average of eight per cent per month, against rents five hundred per cent above those of New York or London, against wages and salaries equally exorbitant, with an exhausting domestic expenditure, despite of the most self-denying economy, and without the guarantee of insurance to cover the ruinous risks of the place from fire.

Besides, regarding it in another light, how is it possible that a city claiming to contain 50,000 inhabitants, can be supported in its present career by so scant a population as that California is said to contain, which, according to an average of the very best estimates, does not exceed 200,000, cities, diggings, ranches, and all; an amount, too, that is gradually on the decrease, as the placer diggings—which alone can be worked by individual energy and labour—are giving evidences of exhaustion;

results that will steadily progress until the mining operations of the country are concentrated in a few large associated companies, constrainedly employing machinery instead of manual labor in stamping and grinding the quartz, amalgamations, etc., to the consequent diminution of the population, who have not the attraction of agricultural resources to induce them to settle in the country; for it is a notorious fact, borne out by experience, that not one out of every hundred emigrants either start with the intention of permanent settlement, or see reason to change their minds after a season's residence in the country.

There is a constantly shifting population, the one coming with the determination of working hard, and saving rapidly for home enjoyment, the other returning with the fruits of their labor and economy. At first the flood was stronger, but latterly the ebb tide is the more impetuous, carrying along with each receding wave a portion of the sandy foundation on which this marvellous city has been built.

San Francisco, to be upheld in its present overweening pretensions, would require a thriving population of at least a couple of million at its back.

❧ "A spectacle unequaled in past history"

ANDREWS REPORT

By the early 1850s the industrial North and Midwest had enjoyed extraordinary growth, particularly in small cities. The construction of the Erie Canal and other smaller canals had opened the interior of the United States to trade. The subsequent boom in railroads starting in the late 1830s also perpetuated that growth.

Internal improvements became a mantra of American business interests, as this 1853 report to Congress by Israel D. Andrews reflects. The unprecedented growth led to tremendous optimism about the country's future.

[The Illinois and Michigan canal] was opened in May, 1848, and the first section of the Chicago and Galena railroad in March, 1849.... In 1840 the population of Chicago was 4,479, and the valuation of property not far from $250,000; while in 1851 the population was about 36,000, and the assessed valuation of real and personal property was

$8,562,717. In 1847 the population, according to the city census, was 16,859; in 1848 it was 20,023; in 1849, 23,047; and in 1850, according to the United States census, 29,963; having increased twice more rapidly than before, since the completion of the canal. The population of Chicago at this time—August, 1852—is nearly, if not quite, 40,000.

In regard to this train of argument, and to this view of the effect of internal improvements on the growth of the West, and on the commercial condition of that portion of the country, it will be well to follow up the same train of examination in relation to the growth of certain points to the east of the great lakes, such as Buffalo, New York, Oswego, Boston and other cities directly affected by the same commerce through the internal channels of communication in New York and Massachusetts....

Between the years 1800 and 1850 the population of New York doubled itself once in every 15 years; Philadelphia, in 18; Boston, in 18; Albany, in 16; Cincinnati, in 7; St. Louis, in 9; Buffalo, in 8; and Detroit, in 8....

... [F]rom 1840 to 1850—a period of ten years, during which nearly the whole western population had become exporters by means of the Ohio, New York, and Philadelphia canals, and the various lines of railway—the effect of these influences and New York, has been truly astonishing; but the same influence, reacted and reflected from the East upon the western cities is yet more wonderful....

It appears that every new improvement is bound by inevitable laws to pay its tribute to some great channel of internal commerce. The existence of such a channel has indirectly created the necessity for the improvement; and the same law which called it into existence as necessarily requires it, by a reactionary impulse, to indemnify its creator.

Before the present century shall have passed away, the United State will undoubtedly present to the world a spectacle unequalled in past history. More than fifty millions of republican freeman, all equal citizens of a confederacy of independent States, united by congenial sympathies and hopes; by a devotion to the principles of political and religious freedom, and of self-government; bound together by a common language and harmonious laws, and by a sacred compact of union, will also be firmly cemented with one another by indissoluble bonds of mutual dependence and common interests. The remote sections of the confederacy will be made near neighbors by means of canals. Railroads will chain all the several parts each to each; the whole people from the pacific to the North Atlantic ocean, from the great lakes to the Gulf of Mexico, cultivating the arts of peace and science, and incited by a genuine rivalry for the accomplishment of the real mission of the American people.

McGuffey's Eclectic First Reader

WILLIAM H. MCGUFFEY

William McGuffey was a college professor who, starting in the 1830s, wrote the *McGuffey Readers*, a series of textbooks designed to promote moral improvement and patriotism. An estimated 122 million copies of his texts were sold, influencing generations of elementary students. This excerpt, entitled "Poor Old Man," was from *McGuffey's Eclectic First Reader* published in 1853.

Jane, there is a poor old man at the door.
He asks for something to eat. We will give him
      some bread and cheese.
He is cold. Will you give him some clothes too?
I will give him a suit of old clothes, which will be
      new to him.
Poor man! I wish he had a warm house to live in,
      and kind friends to live with him; then he
      would not have to beg from door to door.
We should be kind to the poor. We may be as poor
      as this old man, and need as much as he.
Shall I give him some cents to buy a pair of shoes?
No; you may give him a pair of shoes.
It is hard for the poor to have to beg from house to
      house.
Poor boys and girls some-times have to sleep out of
      doors all night. When it snows, they are very
      cold, and when it rains, they get quite wet.
Who is it that gives us food to eat, and clothes to
      make us warm?
It is God, my child; he makes the sun to shine, and
      sends the rain upon the earth, that we may
      have food.
God makes the wool grow upon the little lambs,
      that we may have clothes to keep us warm.

The Kansas Emigrants

JOHN GREENLEAF WHITTIER

In 1854, Congress passed the Kansas-Nebraska Act repealing the Missouri Compromise and establishing that the issue of slavery in the territories of Kansas and Nebraska would be determined according to the principles of popular sovereignty. The residents themselves would decide whether to allow slavery. Anti- and pro-slavery settlers flocked to Kansas to advocate and vote for their respective causes. Popular northern poet John Greenleaf Whittier praised the abolitionist settlers who moved to Kansas in support of freedom in his poem "The Kansas Emigrants." For the next four years intermittent battles were fought between the two sides in a bitter conflict marked by retaliatory massacres. In 1858 Kansas entered the Union as a free state.

We cross the prairie as of old
the pilgrims crossed the sea,
to make the West, as they the East,
The homestead of the free!
We go to rear a wall of men
On Freedom's southern line,
and plant beside the cotton-tree
the rugged Northern pine!
We're flowing from our native hills
As our free rivers flow:
The blessing of our Mother-land
Is on us as we go.
We go to plant her common schools
On distant prairie swells,
and give the Sabbaths of the wild
The music of her bells.
Upbearing, like the Ark of old,
The Bible in our van,
We go to test the truth of God
Against the fraud of man.
No pause, nor rest, save where the streams
that feed the Kansas run,
Save where our Pilgrim gonfalon
Shall flout the setting sun!
We'll tread the prairie as of old
Our fathers sailed the sea,
and make the West, as they the East,
The homestead of the free!

❧ "We may be brothers after all"

CHIEF SEATTLE

Chief Seattle led the Duwamish and Suquamish tribes in the Pacific Northwest in mid-1800s. Westward settlement of the Oregon Territories placed pressure on the tribes. The United States offered a treaty to Seattle for his tribes to settle in land reservations. Agreeing to the offer, the chief responded with this speech in 1854, recorded many years later by Dr. Henry Smith.

There was a time when our people covered the land as the waves of a wind-ruffled sea covers its shell-paved floor, but that time long since passed away with the greatness of tribes that are now but a mournful memory. I will not dwell on, nor mourn over, our untimely decay, nor reproach my pale-faced brothers with hastening it as we too may have been somewhat to blame.

When our young men grow angry at some real or imagined wrong and disfigure their faces with black paint, their hearts, also, are disfigured and turn black, and then their cruelty is relentless and knows no bounds, and our old men are not able to restrain them.

But let us hope that hostilities between the red man and his pale-faced brothers may never return. We would have everything to lose and nothing to gain.

True it is that revenge, with our young braves, is considered gain, even at the cost of their own lives, but old men who stay at home in times of war, and old women who have sons to lose, know better.

Our good father at Washington—for I presume he is now our father as well as yours, since King George has moved his boundaries further north—our great and good father, I say, sends us word that if we do as he desires he will protect us. His brave armies will be to us a bristling wall of strength, and his great ships of war will fill our harbors so that our ancient enemies far to the northward, the Simsians and Hydas, will no longer frighten our women and old men. Then he will be our father, and we will be his children.

But can this ever be? Your God is not our God! Your God loves your people and hates mine. He folds his strong protecting arms lovingly about the pale face and leads him by the hand as a father leads his infant son; but He has forsaken His red children—if they really are his. Our God, the Great Spirit, seems also to have forsaken us. Your God makes your people wax strong every day. Soon they will fill all the land. Our people are ebbing away like a rapidly receding tide that will never return. The white man's cannot love our people or He would protect them.... We are two distinct races with separate origins and separate destinies. There is little in common between us.

To us the ashes of our ancestors are sacred and their resting place is hallowed ground. You wander far from the graves of your ancestors and seemingly without regret. Your religion was written upon tables of stone by the iron finger of your God so that you could not forget. The red man could never comprehend nor remember it. Our religion is the traditions of our ancestors—the dreams of our old men, given them in solemn hours of night by the Great Spirit, and the visions of our sachems—and is written in the hearts of our people.

Your dead cease to love you and the land of their nativity as soon as they pass the portals of the tomb and wander away beyond the stars. They are soon forgotten and never return. Our dead never forget the beautiful world that gave them being. They still love its verdant valleys, its murmuring rivers, its magnificent mountains, sequestered vales and verdant lined lakes and bays, and ever yearn in tender, fond affection over the lonely hearted living, and often return from the Happy Hunting Ground to visit, guide, console, and comfort them.

Day and night cannot dwell together. The red man has ever fled the approach of the white man, as the morning mist flees before the morning sun.

However, your proposition seems fair and I think that my people will accept it and will retire to the reservation you offer them. Then we will dwell apart in peace, for the words of the Great White Chief seem to be the words of nature speaking to my people out of dense darkness.

It matters little where we pass the remnant of our days. They will not be many. The Indians' night promises to be dark. Not a single star of hope hovers above his horizon. Sad-voiced winds moan in the distance. Grim fate seems to be on the red man's trail, and wherever he goes he will hear the approaching footsteps of his fell destroyer and prepare stolidly to meet his doom, as does the wounded doe that hears the approaching footsteps of the hunter....

But why should I mourn at the untimely fate of my people? Tribe follows tribe, and nation follows nation, like the waves of the sea. It is the order of nature, and regret is useless. Your time of decay may be distant, but it will surely come, for even the white man whose God walked and talked with him as friend with friend, cannot be exempt from the common destiny. We may be brothers after all. We will see.

We will ponder your proposition and when we decide we will let you know. But should we accept it, I here and now make this condition—that we will not be denied the privilege without molestation of visiting at any time the tombs of our ancestors, friends and children. Every part of this soil is sacred in the estimation of my people. Every hillside, every valley, every plain and grove has been hallowed by some sad or happy event in days long vanished....

And when the last red man shall have perished, and the memory of my tribe shall have become a myth among the white men, these shores will swarm with the invisible dead of my tribe, and when your children's children think themselves alone in the field, the store, the shop, upon the highway, or in the silence of the pathless woods, they will not be alone. In all the earth there is no place dedicated to solitude. At night when the streets of your cities and villages are silent and you think them deserted, they will throng with the returning hosts that once filled them and still love this beautiful land. The white man will never be alone.

Let him be just and deal kindly with my people, for the dead are not powerless. Dead, did I say? There is no death, only a change of worlds.

❧ Massachusetts Personal Liberty Act

MASSACHUSETTS LEGISLATURE

Five years after Massachusetts Senator Daniel Webster salvaged the Missouri Compromise by throwing his support behind the Fugitive Slave Act of 1850, the Massachusetts Legislature made it almost impossible to enforce the act within the state. The Massachusetts Personal Liberty Act, passed in the wake of the outcry of the arrest and return of a fugitive slave. It gave several rights to runaway slaves and raised the standard of proof for owners of slaves to an extraordinarily high level. The legislation made it illegal for state officers to enforce the Fugitive Slave Act, stripped lawyers who represented slave-owning claimants of their commission, forbade the local militia to enforce the Fugitive Slave Act and prohibited the use of state jails and buildings for detaining fugitive slaves.

Passed over the governor's veto, the legislation infuriated the South, confirming the region's suspicions that the North could not be relied on to return runaway slaves and was bent on ending slavery.

Section 2. The meaning of the one hundred and eleventh chapter of the Revised Statutes is hereby declared to be, that every person imprisoned or restrained of his liberty is entitled, as of right and of course, to the writ of *habeus corpus*, except in the second section of that chapter....

Section 6. If any claimant shall appear to demand the custody or possession of the person for whose benefit such writ is sued out, such claimant shall state in writing the facts on which he relies, with precision and certainty; and neither the claimant of the alleged fugitive, nor any person interested in his alleged obligation to service or labor, nor the alleged fugitive, shall be permitted to testify at the trial of the issue; and no confessions, admissions or declarations of the alleged fugitive against himself shall be given in evidence. Upon every question of fact involved in the issue, the burden of proof shall be on the claimant, and the facts alleged and necessary to be established must be proved by the testimony of at least two credible witnesses, or other legal evidence equivalent thereto, and by the rules of evidence known and secured by the common law; and no ex parte deposition or affidavit shall be received in proof in behalf of the claimant, and no presumption shall arise in favor of the claimant from any proof that the alleged fugitive or any of his ancestors had actually been held as a slave, without proof that such holding was legal.

Section 7. If any person shall removed from the limits of the Commonwealth, or shall assist in removing therefrom, or shall come into the Commonwealth with the intention of removing or of assisting in the removing therefrom, or shall procure or assist in procuring to be so removed, any person being in the peace thereof who is not "held to service or labor" by the "party" making "claim," or who has not "escaped" from the "party" making 'claim," within the meaning of those words in the constitution of the United States, on the pretence that such person is so held or has so escaped, or that his "service or labor" is so "due," or with the intent to subject him to such "service or labor," he shall be punished by a fine of not less than one thousand, nor more than five thousand dollars, and by imprisonment in the State Prison not less than one, nor more than five years....

Section 9. No person, while holding any office of honor, trust, or emolument, under the laws of this Commonwealth, shall, in any capacity, issue any warrant or other process, or grant any certificate, under or by virtue of [the Federal Fugitive Slave Acts of 1793 and 1850] ... or shall in any capacity, serve any such warrant or other process.

Section 10. Any person who shall grant any certificate under or by virtue of the acts of congress, mentioned in the preceding section, shall be deemed to have resigned any commission from the Commonwealth which he may possess, his office shall be deemed vacant, and he shall be forever thereafter ineligible to any office or trust, honor or emolument under the laws of this Commonwealth.

Section 11. Any person who shall act as counsel or attorney for any claimant of any alleged fugitive from service or labor, under or by virtue of the acts of congress mentioned in the ninth section of this act, shall be deemed to have resigned any commission from the Commonwealth that he may possess, and he shall be thereafter incapacitated from appearing as counsel or attorney in the courts of this Commonwealth....

Section 14. Any person holding any judicial office under the constitution or laws of this Commonwealth, who shall continue, for ten days after passage of this act, to hold the office of United States commissioner, or any office ... which qualifies him to issue any warrant or other process ... under the [Fugitive Slave Acts] shall be deemed to have violated good behavior, to have given reason for the loss of public confidence, and furnished sufficient ground either for impeachment or for removal by address.

Section 15. Any sheriff, deputy sheriff, jailer, coroner, constable, or other officer of this Commonwealth, or the police of any city or town, or any district, county, city or town officer, or any officer or other member of the volunteer militia of this Commonwealth, who shall hereafter arrest ... any person for the reason that he is claimed or adjudged to be a fugitive from service or labor, shall be punished by fine ... and by imprisonment....

Section 16. The volunteer militia of the Commonwealth shall not act in any manner in the seizure .... of any person for the reason that he is claimed or adjudged to be a fugitive from service or labor....

Section 19. No jail, prison, or other place of confinement belonging to, or used by, either the Commonwealth of Massachusetts or any county therein, shall be used for the detention or imprisonment of any person accused or convicted of any offence created by [the fugitive Slave Acts] ... or accused or convicted of obstructing or resisting any process, warrant, or order issued under either of said acts, or of rescuing, or attempting to rescue any person arrested or detained under any of the provisions of either of the said acts....

🌿 Walden

HENRY DAVID THOREAU

Reacting against the onslaught of industrial progress, Henry David Thoreau withdrew from society to live alone at Walden Pond outside of Concord, although he did interact occasionally with friends and neighbors. Thoreau described the experience in his 1854 book *Walden,* a widely influential book that explored self-reliance, the joys of living a simple life in harmony with nature and man's place in nature. *Walden* and other writings by Thoreau helped provide the intellectual foundation for the environmental movement.

I do not propose to write an ode to dejection, but to brag as lustily as chanticleer in the morning, standing on his roost, if only to wake my neighbors up.

When I wrote the following pages, or rather the bulk of them, I lived alone, in the woods, a mile from any neighbor, in a house which I had built myself, on the shore of a Walden pond, in Concord, Massachusetts, and earned my living by the labor of my hands only. I lived there two years and two months. At present I am a sojourner in civilized life again....

I would fain say something, not so much concerning the Chinese and Sandwich Islanders as you who read these pages, who are said to live in New

England; something about your condition or circumstance in this world, in this town, what it is, whether it is necessary that it be as bad as it is, whether it cannot be improved as well as not. I have traveled a good deal in Concord; and every where, in shops, and offices, and fields, the inhabitants have appeared to me to be doing penance in a thousand remarkable ways. What I have heard of Bramins sitting exposed to four fires and looking in the face of the sun; or hanging suspended, with their heads downward, over flames; or looking at the heavens over their shoulders "until it becomes impossible for them to resume their natural position, while from the twist of the neck nothing but liquids can pass into the stomach;" or dwelling, chained for life, at the foot of a tree; or measuring with their bodies, like caterpillars, the breadth of vast empires; or standing on one leg on the tops of pillars,—even these forms of conscious penance are hardly more incredible and astonishing than the scenes which I daily witness. The twelve labors of Hercules were trifling in comparison with those which my neighbors have undertaken; for they were only twelve, and had an end; but I could never see that these men slew or captured any monster or finished any labor. They have no friend Iolas to burn with a hot iron the root of the hydra's head, but as soon as one head is crushed, two spring up.

I see young men, my townsmen, whose misfortune it is to have inherited farms, houses, barns, cattle, and farming tools; for these are more easily acquired than got rid of. Better if they had been born in the open pasture and suckled by a wolf, that they might have seen with clearer eyes what field they were called to labor in. Who made them serfs of the soil? Why should they eat their sixty acres, when man is condemned to eat only his peck of dirt? Why should they begin digging their graves as soon as they are born? They have got to live a man's life, pushing all these things before them, and get on as well as they can. How many a poor immortal soul have I met well nigh crushed and smothered under its load, creeping down the road of life, pushing before it a barn seventy-five feet by forty, its Augean stables never cleansed, and one hundred acres of land, tillage, mowing, pasture, and wood-lot! The portionless, who struggle with no such unnecessary inherited encumbrances, find it labor enough to subdue and cultivate a few cubic

feet of flesh.

But men labor under a mistake. The better part of the man is soon ploughed into the soil for compost. By a seeming fate, commonly called necessity, they are employed, as it says in an old book, laying up treasures which moth and rust will corrupt and thieves break through and steal. It is a fool's life, as they will find when they get to the end of it, if not before. It is said that Deucelion and Pyrrha created men by throwing stones over their heads behind them:—

Inde genus durum sumus, experiesque laborum,
Et documenta damus qua simus origine nati.

Or, as Raleigh rhymes it in his sonorous way,—

"From thence our kind hard-hearted is, enduring pain and care,
Approving that our bodies of a stony nature are."

So much for a blind obedience to a blundering oracle, throwing the stones over their heads behind them, and not seeing where they fell.

Most men, even in this comparatively free country, through mere ignorance and mistake, are so occupied with the factitious cares and superfluously coarse labors of life that its finer fruits cannot be plucked by them. Their fingers, from excessive toil, are too clumsy and tremble too much for that. Actually, the laboring man has not leisure for a true integrity day by day; he cannot afford to sustain the manliest relations to man; his labor would be depreciated in the market. He has no time to be any thing but a machine. How can he remember well his ignorance—which his growth requires—who has so often used his knowledge? We should feed and clothe him gratuitously sometimes, and recruit him with our cordials, before we judge him. The finest qualities of our nature, like the bloom on fruits, can be preserved only by the most delicate handling. Yet we do not treat ourselves nor one another thus tenderly.

Some of you, we all know, are poor, find it hard to live, are sometimes, as it were, gasping for breath. I have no doubt that some of you who read this book are unable to pay for all the dinners which you have actually eaten, or for the coats and shoes which are fast wearing or are already worn out, and have come to this page to spend borrowed or stolen time, robbing your creditors of an hour. It is very evident what mean and sneaking lives many of you live, for my sight has been whetted by experience;

always on the limits, trying to get into business and trying to get out of debt, a very ancient slough, called by the Latins aes alienum, another's brass, for some of their coins were made of brass; still living, and dying, and buried by this other's brass; always promising to pay, promising to pay, tomorrow, and dying today, insolvent; seeking to curry favor, to get custom, by how many modes, only not state-prison offenses; lying, flattering, voting, contracting yourselves into a nutshell of civility, or dilating into an atmosphere of thin and vaporous generosity, that you may persuade your neighbor to let you make his shoes, or his hat, or his coat, or his carriage, or import his groceries for him; making yourselves sick, that you may lay up something against a sick day, something to be tucked away in an old chest, or in a stocking behind the plastering, or, more safely, in the brick bank; no matter how much or how little.

I sometimes wonder that we can be so frivolous, I may almost say, as to attend to the gross but somewhat foreign form of servitude called Negro Slavery, there are so many keen and subtle masters that enslave both north and south. It is hard to have a southern overseer; it is worse to have a northern one; but worst of all when you are the slave-driver of yourself. Talk of a divinity of man! Look at the teamster on the highway, wending to market by day or night; does any divinity stir within him? His highest duty is to fodder and water his horses! What is his destiny compared with the shipping interests? Does not he drive for Squire Make-a-stir? How godlike, how immortal, is he? See how he cowers and sneaks, how vaguely all the day he fears, not being immortal nor divine, but the slave and prisoner of his own deeds. Public opinion is a weak tyrant compared with our own private opinion. What a man thinks of himself, that it is which determines, or rather indicates, his fate. Self-emancipation even in the West Indian provinces of the fancy and imagination,—what Wilberforce is there to bring that about? Think, also, of the ladies of the land weaving toilet cushions against the last day, not to betray too green an interest in their fates! As if you could kill time without injuring eternity.

The mass of men lead lives of quiet desperation. What is called resignation is confirmed desperation. From the desperate city you go into the desperate country, and have to console yourself with the bravery of minks and muskrats. A stereotyped but unconscious despair is concealed even under what are called the games and amusements of mankind. There is no play in them, for this comes after work. But it is a characteristic of wisdom not to do desperate things.

When we consider what, to use the words of the catechism, is the chief end of man, and what are the true necessaries and means of life, it appears as if men had deliberately chosen the common mode of living because they preferred it to any other. Yet they honestly think there is no choice left. But alert and healthy natures remember that the sun rose clear. It is never too late to give up our prejudices. No way of thinking or doing, however ancient, can be trusted without proof. What everybody echoes or in silence passes by as true today may turn out to be falsehood tomorrow, mere smoke of opinion, which some had trusted for a cloud that would sprinkle fertilizing rain on their fields. What old people say you cannot do, you try and find that you can. Old deeds for old people, and new deeds for new. Old people did not know enough once, perchance, to fetch fresh fuel to keep the fire a-going; new people put a little dry wood under a pot, and are whirled round the globe with the speed of birds, in a way to kill old people, as the phrase is. Age is no better, hardly so well, qualified for an instructor as youth, for it has not profited so much as it has lost. One may almost doubt if the wisest man has learned anything of absolute value by living. Practically, the old have no very important advice to give the young, their own experience has been so partial, and their lives have been such miserable failures, for private reasons, as they must believe; and it may be that they have some faith left which belies that experience, and they are only less young than they were. I have lived some thirty years on this planet, and I have yet to hear the first syllable of valuable or even earnest advice from my seniors. They have told me nothing, and probably cannot tell me anything to the purpose. Here is life, an experiment to a great extent untried by me; but it does not avail me that they have tried it. If I have any experience which I think valuable, I am sure that this my Mentors said nothing about.

One farmer says to me, "You cannot live on vegetable food solely, for it furnishes nothing to make bones with;" and so he religiously devotes a part of his day to supplying his system with the raw material of bones; walking all the while he talks behind his oxen, which, with vegetable-made bones, jerk him and his lumbering plow along in spite of every obstacle. Some things are really necessaries of life in some circles, the most helpless and diseased, which in others are luxuries merely, and in others still are entirely unknown.

The whole ground of human life seems to some to have been gone over by their predecessors, both the heights and valleys, and all things to have been cared for. According to Evelyn, "the wise Solomon prescribed ordinances for the very distance of trees; and the Roman praetors have decided how often you may go into your neighbor's land to gather acorns which fall on it without trespass, and what share belongs to that neighbor." Hippocrates has even left directions how we should cut our nails; that is, even with the ends of the fingers neither shorter nor longer. Undoubtedly the very tedium and ennui which presume to have exhausted the variety and the joys of life are as old as Adam. But man's capacities have never been measured; nor are we to judge of what he can do by any precedents, so little has been tried. Whatever have been thy failures hitherto, "be not afflicted, my child, for who shall assign to thee what thou hast left undone?"

We might try our lives by a thousand simple tests; as, for instance, that the same sun that ripens my beans illumines at once a system of earths like ours. If I had remembered this it would have prevented some mistakes. This was not the light in which I hoed them. The stars are the apexes of what wonderful triangles! What distant and different beings in the various mansions of the universe are contemplating the same one at the same moment! Nature and human life are as various as our several constitutions. Who shall say what prospect life offers to another? Could a greater miracle take place than for us to look through each other's eyes for an instant? We should live in all the ages of the world in an hour; nay, in all the worlds of all the ages. History, Poetry, Mythology!—I know of no reading of another's experience so startling and informing as this would be.

The greater part of what my neighbors call good I believe in my soul to be bad, and if I repent of anything, it is very likely to be my good behavior. What demon possessed me that I behaved so well? You may say the wisest thing you can, old man,—you who have lived seventy years, not without honor of a kind,—I hear an irresistible voice which invites me away from all that. One generation abandons the enterprises of another like stranded vessels.

I think that we may safely trust a good deal more than we do. We may waive just so much care of ourselves as we honestly bestow elsewhere. Nature is as well adapted to our weakness as to our strength. The incessant anxiety and strain of some is a well-nigh incurable form of disease. We are made to exaggerate the importance of what work we do; and yet how much is not done by us! or, what if we had been taken sick? How vigilant we are! Determined not to live by faith if we can avoid it; all day long on the alert, at night we unwillingly say our prayers and commit ourselves to uncertainties. So thoroughly and sincerely are we compelled to live, reverencing our life, and denying the possibility of change. This is the only way, we say; but there are as many ways as there can be drawn radii from one center. All change is a miracle to contemplate; but it is a miracle which is taking place every instant. Confucius said, "To know that we know what we know, and that we do not know what we do not know, that is true knowledge." When one man has reduced a fact of the imagination to be a fact of his understanding, I foresee that all men will at length establish their lives on that basis.

❧ "Americans must rule America"

AMERICAN PARTY 1856 PLATFORM

A new political party emerged in the 1850s in reaction against the surge of Irish and German immigrants in the previous decade. The American, or "Know-Nothing," Party was formed in upstate New York and in the 1854 mid-term congressional elections made a strong showing in several states. Concerned about the growing influence of immigrants in government, their allegedly corrupting influence on society and the job competition foreigners offered, the American Party attempted to tighten qualifications for citizenship and limit opportunities and influence of foreign-born residents.

In 1856 the American Party nominated former President Millard Fillmore (who had assumed the office after Zachary Taylor's death in 1850) as their presidential candidate and issued a national political platform. Fillmore garnered 22 percent of the vote. Divided over the slavery issue, however, the party split and faded from national politics.

2. The perpetuation of the Federal Union and Constitution, as the palladium of our civil and religious liberties, and the only sure bulwarks of American Independence.

3. Americans must rule America; and to this end native-born citizens should be selected for all State, Federal and municipal offices of government employment, in preference to all others. Nevertheless,

4. Persons born of American parents residing temporarily abroad, should be entitled to all the rights of native-born citizens.

5. No person should be selected for political station (whether of native or foreign birth), who recognizes any allegiance or obligation of any description to any foreign prince, potentate or power, or who refuses to recognize the Federal and State Constitutions (each within its sphere) as paramount to all other laws, as rules of political action.

6. The unqualified recognition and maintenance of the reserved rights of the several States, and the cultivation of harmony and fraternal good will between the citizens of the several States, and to this end, non-interference by Congress with questions appertaining solely to the individual States, and non-intervention by each State with the affairs of any other State.

7. The recognition of the right of native-born and naturalized citizens of the United States, permanently residing in any territory thereof, to frame their constitution and laws, and to regulate their domestic and social affairs in their own mode, subject only to the provisions of the Federal Constitution, with the privilege of admission into the Union whenever they have the requisite population for one Representative in Congress: Provided, always, that none but those who are citizens of the United States, under the Constitution and laws thereof, and who have a fixed residence in any such Territory, ought to participate in the formation of the Constitution, or in the enactment of laws for said Territory or State.

8. An enforcement of the principles that no State or Territory ought to admit others than citizens to the right of suffrage, or of holding political offices of the United States.

9. A change in the laws of naturalization, making a continued residence of twenty-one years, of all not heretofore provided for, an indispensable

requisite for citizenship hereafter, and excluding all paupers, and persons convicted of crime, from landing upon our shores; but no interference with the vested rights of foreigners.

10. Opposition to any union between church and State; no interference with religious faith or worship, and no test oaths for office....

🍂 On the Oregon Trail

HELEN CARPENTER

In 1842 Elijah White led the first wagon train on a cross-country journey to establish a settlement on Oregon's Pacific Coast. Two years later, John C. Frémont and Kit Carson blazed the Oregon and California trails, establishing a pathway for thousands of pioneers to follow in settling the West during the next 20 years. The journey was arduous and perilous, fraught with danger from weather, hostile Native American tribes and an inhospitable climate. Many people died from starvation and disease or were killed. This 1857 record of pioneer Helen Carpenter's trip on the Oregon Trail offers a glimpse into the courage and perseverance that the pioneers drew on to realize their goal of settling a new territory.

Although there is not much to cook, the difficulty and inconvenience in doing it amounts to a great deal—so by the time one has squatted around the fire and cooked bread and bacon, and made several dozen trips to and from the wagon—washed the dishes...and gotten things ready for an early breakfast, some of the others already have their night caps on—at any rate it is time to go to bed. In respect to women's work, the days are all very much the same—except when we stop...then there is washing to be done and light bread to make and all kinds of odd jobs. Some women have very little help about the camp, being obliged to get the wood and water...make camp fires, unpack at night and pack up in the morning—and if they are Missourians they have the milking to do if they are fortunate enough to have cows. I am lucky in having a Yankee for a husband, so am well waited on...
.

When the sun was just peeping over the top of the mountain, there was suddenly heard a shot and a blood curdling yell, and immediately the Indians we saw yesterday were seen riding at full speed directly toward the horses...father put his gun to his shoulder as though to shoot....The Indians kept…circling…and halooing…bullets came whizzing through the camp. None can know the horror of it, who have not been similarly situated…[the Indians] did not come directly toward us, but all the time in a circular way, from one side of the road to the other, each time they passed, getting a little nearer, and occasionally firing a shot….Father and Reel could stand it no longer, they must let those Indians see how far their Sharps rifles would carry. Without aiming to hit them, they made the earth fly….

It is now 18 days since we have seen a train…[we] found the body of a nude woman on the bank of the slough….A piece of hair rope was around her neck….From appearances it was thought she had been tortured by being drawn back and forth through the slough, by this rope around her neck. The body was given the best burial that was possible, under the circumstances….

A Handbook for Overland Expeditions

RANDOLPH MARCY

A captain in the army, Randolph Marcy wrote *The Prairie Traveler, A Handbook for Overland Expeditions* in 1859 to assist the thousands of settlers who were traversing the country to settle the West. As this excerpt shows, the seemingly simple and fundamental task of providing, storing and preparing food for overland treks was a complicated, tedious and, at times, perilous task.

Supplies for a march should be put up in the most secure, compact, and portable shape.

Bacon should be packed in strong sacks of a hundred pounds to each; or, in very hot climates, put in boxes and surrounded with bran, which in a great measure prevents the fat from melting away.

Flour should be packed in stout double canvas sacks well sewed, a hundred pounds in each sack.

Butter may be preserved by boiling it thoroughly, and skimming off the scum as it rises to the top until it is quite clear like oil. It is then placed in tin canisters and soldered up. This mode of preserving butter has been adopted in the hot climate of southern Texas, and it is found to keep sweet for a great length of time, and its flavor is but little impaired by the process.

Sugar may be well secured in India-rubber or gutta-percha sacks, or so placed in the wagon as not to risk getting wet.

Desiccated or dried vegetables are almost equal to the fresh, and are put up in such a compact and portable form as easily to be transported over the plains. They have been extensively used in the Crimean war, and by our own army in Utah, and have been very generally approved. They are prepared by cutting the fresh vegetables into thin slices and subjecting them to a very powerful press, which removes the juice and leaves a solid cake, which after having been thoroughly dried in an oven, becomes almost as hard as a rock. A small piece of this, about half the size of a man's hand, when boiled, swells up so as to fill a vegetable dish, and is sufficient for four men. It is believed that the antiscorbutic properties of vegetables are not impaired by desiccation, and they will keep for years if not exposed to dampness. Canned vegetables are very good for campaigning, but are not so portable as when put up in the other form….

When the deer are lying down in the smooth prairie, unless the grass is tall, it is difficult to get near them, as they are generally looking around, and become alarmed at the least noise.

The Indians are in the habit of using a small instrument which imitates the bleat of the young fawn, with which they lure the doe within range of their rifles. The young fawn gives out no scent upon its track until it is sufficiently grown to make good running, and instinct teaches the mother that this wise provision of nature to preserve the helpless little quadruped from the ravages of wolves, panthers, and other carnivorous beasts, will be defeated if she remains with it, as her tracks can not be concealed. She therefore hides her fawn in the grass, where it is almost impossible to see it, even when very near it, goes off to some neighboring thicket within call, and makes her bed alone. The Indian pot-hunter, who is but little scrupulous as to the means he employs in accomplishing his ends, sounds the bleat along near the places where he thinks the game is lying, and the unsuspicious doe, who imagines that her offspring is in distress, rushes with headlong impetuosity toward the sound, and often goes within a few yards of the hunter to receive her death-wound….

I once undertook to experiment with the instrument myself, and made my first essay in attempting to call up an antelope which I discovered in the distance. I succeeded admirably in luring the way victim within shooting range, had raised upon my knees, and was just in the act of pulling trigger, when a rustling in the grass to my left drew my attention in that direction, where, much to my surprise, I beheld a huge panther within about twenty yards, bounding with gigantic strides directly toward me. I turned my rifle, and in an instant, much to my relief and gratification, its contents were lodged in the heart of the beast.

❧ Dred Scott v. Sandford: "The right of property in a slave is distinctly and expressly affirmed in the Constitution"

SUPREME COURT JUSTICE ROGER B. TANEY

Dred Scott was a slave in Missouri, a slave state, who in 1834 was taken by his master to Illinois, a free state. He then went to the Wisconsin Territory, where the Missouri Compromise of 1820 prohibited slavery, before returning to Missouri. In 1846, Scott filed a lawsuit, *Dred Scott v. Sandford,* seeking his freedom on the grounds that his living in Illinois and Wisconsin freed him from bondage. The case made it to the Supreme Court. In 1857 the court ruled seven to two against Scott.

The court's decision held that African-Americans are not citizens but rather property, that the federal government has no authority to prohibit slavery in the territories (thus overturning Congress's Missouri Compromise), and that living in a free state does not provide grounds for obtaining freedom. The decision sparked enormous protest in the North where abolitionists vehemently rejected the decision and widespread fears emerged that slavery would be legalized throughout the country. Supreme Court Justice Roger B. Taney's written decision below thus helped heighten tensions between North and South even further and led to the passing of the 13th and 14th amendments after the Civil War.

There are two leading questions presented by the record:

1. Had the Circuit Court of the United States jurisdiction to hear and determine the case between these parties? And,

2. If it had jurisdiction, is the judgment it has given erroneous or not?

The plaintiff in error, who was also the plaintiff in the court below, was, with his wife and children, held as slaves by the defendant, in the State of Missouri, and he brought this action in the Circuit Court of the United States for that district, to assert the title of himself and his family to freedom.

The declaration is...that he and the defendant are citizens of different States; that is, that he is a citizen of Missouri, and the defendant a citizen of New York.

The defendant pleaded in abatement to the jurisdiction of the court, that the plaintiff was not a citizen of the State of Missouri, as alleged in his declaration, being a negro of African descent whose ancestors were of pure African blood, and who were brought into this country and sold as slaves.

To this plea the plaintiff demurred, and the defendant joined in demurrer....

The question is simply this: Can a negro, whose ancestors were imported into this country, and sold as slaves, become a member of the political community formed and brought into existence by the Constitution of the United States, and as such become entitled to all the rights, and privileges, and immunities, guarantied by that instrument to the citizen? One of which rights is the privilege of suing in a court of the United States in the cases specified in the Constitution.

It will be observed, that the plea applies to that class of persons only whose ancestors were negroes of the African race, and imported into this country, and sold and held as slaves. The only matter in issue before the court, therefore, is, whether the descendants of such slaves, when they shall be emancipated, or who are born of parents who had become free before their birth, are citizens of a State, in the sense in which the word citizen is used in the Constitution of the United States. And this being the only matter in dispute on the pleadings, the court must be understood as speaking in this opinion of that class only, that is of persons who are the descendants of Africans who were imported into this country and sold as slaves....

We proceed to examine the case as presented by the pleadings. The words "people of the United States" and "citizens" are synonymous terms, and mean the same thing. They both describe the political body who, according to our republican institutions, form the sovereignty, and who hold the power and conduct the government through their representatives. They are what we familiarly call the "sovereign people," and every citizen is one of this people, and a constituent member of this sovereignty. The question before us is, whether the class of persons described in the plea in abatement compose a portion of this people, and are constituent members of this sovereignty? We think they are not, and that they are not included, and were not intended to be included, under the word "citizens" in the Constitution, and can, therefore, claim none of the rights and privileges which that instrument provides for and secures to citizens of the United States. On the contrary, they were at that time considered as a subordinate and inferior class of beings, who had been subjugated by the dominant race, and whether emancipated or not, yet remained subject to their authority, and had no rights or privileges but such as those who held the power and the government might choose to grant them....

In discussing this question, we must not confound the rights of citizenship which a state may confer within its own limits, and the rights of citizenship as a member of the Union. It does not by any means follow, because he has all the rights and privileges of a citizen of a State, that he must be a citizen of the United States. He may have all of the rights and privileges of the citizen of a State, and yet not be entitled to the rights and privileges of a citizen in any other State. For, previous to the adoption of the Constitution of the United States, every State had the undoubted right to confer on whomsoever it pleased the character of a citizen, and to endow him with all its rights. But this character, of course, was confined to the boundaries of the State, and gave him no rights or privileges in other States beyond those secured to him by the laws of nations and the comity of States. Nor have the several States surrendered the power of conferring these rights and privileges by adopting the Constitution of the United States. Each State may still confer them upon an alien, or any one it thinks proper, or upon any class or description of persons; yet he would not be a citizen in the sense in which that word is used in the Constitution of the United States, nor entitled to sue as such in one of its courts, nor to the privileges and immunities of a citizen in the other States. The

rights which he would acquire would be restricted to the State which gave them....

It is very clear, therefore, that no State can, by any Act or law of its own, passed since the adoption of the Constitution, introduce a new member into the political community created by the Constitution of the United States. It cannot make him a member of this community by making him a member of its own. And for the same reason it cannot introduce any person, or description of persons, who were not intended to be embraced in this new political family, which the Constitution brought into existence, but were intended to be excluded from it.

The question then arises, whether the provisions of the Constitution, in relation to the personal rights and privileges to which the citizen of a State should be entitled, embraced the negro African race, at that time in this country, or who might afterwards be imported, who had then or should afterwards be made free in any State; and to put it in the power of a single State to make him a citizen of the United States, and endow him with the full rights of citizenship in every other State without their consent. Does the Constitution of the United States act upon him whenever he shall be made free under the laws of a State, and raised there to the rank of a citizen, and immediately clothe him with all the privileges of a citizen in every other State, and in its own courts?

The court think the affirmative of these propositions cannot be maintained. And if it cannot, the plaintiff in error could not be a citizen of the State of Missouri, within the meaning of the Constitution of the United States, and, consequently, was not entitled to sue in its courts.

It is true, every person, and every class and description of persons, who were at the time of the adoption of the Constitution recognized as citizens in the several States, became also citizens of this new political body; but none other; it was formed by them, and for them and their posterity, but for no one else. And the personal rights and privileges guarantied to citizens of this new sovereignty were intended to embrace those only who were then members of the several state communities, or who should afterwards, by birthright or otherwise, become members, according to the provisions of the Constitution and the principles on which it was founded....

In the opinion of the court, the legislation and histories of the times, and the language used in the Declaration of Independence, show, that neither the class of persons who had been imported as slaves, nor their descendants, whether they had become free or not, were then acknowledged as a part of the people, nor intended to be included in the general words used in that memorable instrument....

There are two clauses in the Constitution which point directly and specifically to the negro race as a separate class of persons, and show clearly that they were not regarded as a portion of the people or citizens of the Government then formed.

One of these clauses reserves to each of the thirteen States the right to import slaves until the year 1808, if he thinks it proper. And the importation which it thus sanctions was unquestionably of persons of the race of which we are speaking, as the traffic in slaves in the United States had always been confined to them. And by the other provision the States pledge themselves to each other to maintain the right of property of the master, by delivering up to him any slave who may have escaped from his service, and be found within their respective territories.... And these two provisions show, conclusively, that neither the description of persons therein referred to, nor their descendants, were embraced in any of the other provisions of the Constitution: for certainly these two clauses were not intended to confer on them or their posterity the blessings of liberty, or any of the personal rights so carefully provided for the citizen....

Indeed, when we look to the condition of this race in the several States at the time, it is impossible to believe that these rights and privileges were intended to be extended to them....

Undoubtedly, a person may be a citizen, that is, a member of the community who form the sovereignty, although he exercises no share of the political power, and is incapacitated from holding particular offices....

So, too, a person may be entitled to vote by the law of the State, who is not a citizen even of the State itself. And in some of the States of the Union foreigners not naturalized are allowed to vote. And the State may give the right to free negroes and mulattoes, but that does not make them citizens of the State, and still less of the United States. And the provision in the Constitution giving privileges and immunities in other States, does not apply to them.

Neither does it apply to a person who, being the citizen of a State, migrates to another State. For then he becomes subject to the laws of the State in which he lives, and he is no longer a citizen of the State from which he removed. And the State in which he resides may then, unquestionably, determine his status or condition, and place him among the class of persons who are not recognized as citizens, but belong to an inferior and subject race; and may deny him the privileges and immunities enjoyed by its citizens....

But if he ranks as a citizen of the State to which he belongs, within the meaning of the Constitution of the United States, then, whenever he goes into another State, the Constitution clothes him, as to the rights of person, with all the privileges and immunities which belong to citizens of the State. And if persons of the African race are citizens of a state, and of the United States, they would be entitled to all of these privileges and immunities in every State, and the State could not restrict them; for they would hold these privileges and immunities, under the paramount authority of the Federal Government, and its courts would be bound to maintain and enforce them, the Constitution and laws of the State to the contrary notwithstanding....

And upon a full and careful consideration of the subject, the court is of opinion that, upon the facts stated in the plea in abatement, Dred Scott was not a citizen of Missouri within the meaning of the Constitution of the United States, and not entitled as such to sue in its courts; and, consequently, that the Circuit Court had no jurisdiction of the case, and that the judgment on the plea in abatement is erroneous....

We proceed, therefore, to inquire whether the facts relied on by the plaintiff entitled him to his freedom....

In considering this part of the controversy, two questions arise: 1st. Was he, together with his family, free in Missouri by reason of the stay in the territory of the United States herein before mentioned? And 2d, If they were not, is Scott himself free by reason of his removal to Rock Island, in the State of Illinois, as stated in the above admissions?

The Act of Congress, upon which the plaintiff relies, declares that slavery and involuntary servitude, except as a punishment for crime, shall be forever prohibited in all that part of the territory ceded by France, under the name of Louisiana, which lies north of thirty-six degrees thirty minutes north latitude, and not included within the limits of Missouri. And the difficulty which meets us at the threshold of this part of the inquiry is, whether Congress was authorized to pass this law under any of the powers granted to it by the Constitution; for if the authority is not given by that instrument, it is the duty of this court to declare it void and inoperative, and incapable of conferring freedom upon any one who is held as a slave under the laws of any one of the States.

The counsel for the plaintiff has laid much stress upon that article in the Constitution which confers on Congress the power "to dispose of and make all needful rules and regulations respecting the territory or other property belonging to the United States;" but, in the judgment of the court, that provision has no bearing on the present controversy, and the power there given, whatever it may be, is confined, and was intended to be confined, to the territory which at that time belonged to, or was claimed by, the United States, and was within their boundaries as settled by the treaty with Great Britain, and can have no influence upon a territory afterwards acquired from a foreign Government. It was a special provision for a known and particular territory, and to meet a present emergency, and nothing more....

If this clause is construed to extend to territory acquired by the present Government from a foreign nation, outside of the limits of any charter from the British Government to a colony, it would be difficult to say, why it was deemed necessary to give the Government the power to sell any vacant lands belonging to the sovereignty which might be found within it; and if this was necessary, why the grant of this power should precede the power to legislate over it and establish a Government there; and still more difficult to say, why it was deemed necessary so specially and particularly to grant the power to make needful rules and regulations in relation to any personal or movable property it might acquire there. For the words, other property necessarily, by every known rule of interpretation, must mean property of a different description from territory or land. And the difficulty would perhaps be insurmountable in endeavoring to account for

the last member of the sentence, which provides that "nothing in this Constitution shall be so construed as to prejudice any claims of the United States or any particular State," or to say how any particular State could have claims in or to a territory ceded by a foreign Government, or to account for associating this provision with the preceding provisions of the clause, with which it would appear to have no connection....

The rights of private property have been guarded with equal care. Thus the rights of property are united with the rights of person, and placed on the same ground by the Fifth Amendment to the Constitution.... An Act of Congress which deprives a person of the United States of his liberty or property merely because he came himself or brought his property into a particular Territory of the United States, and who had committed no offense against the laws, could hardly be dignified with the name of due process of law....

If the Constitution recognizes the right of property of the master in a slave, and makes no distinction between that description of property and other property owned by a citizen, no tribunal, acting under the authority of the United States, whether it be legislative, executive, or judicial, has a right to draw such a distinction, or deny to it the benefit of the provisions and guarantees which have been provided for the protection of private property against the encroachments of the Government.

Now... the right of property in a slave is distinctly and expressly affirmed in the Constitution. The right to traffic in it, like an ordinary article of merchandise and property, was guaranteed to the citizens of the United States, in every State that might desire it, for twenty years. And the Government in express terms is pledged to protect it in all future time, if the slave escapes from his owner.... And no word can be found in the Constitution which gives Congress a greater power over slave property, or which entitles property of that kind to less protection than property of any other description. The only power conferred is the power coupled with the duty of guarding and protecting the owner in his rights.

Upon these considerations, it is the opinion of the court that the Act of Congress which prohibited a citizen from holding and owning property of this kind in the territory of the United States north of the line therein mentioned, is not warranted by the Constitution, and is therefore void; and that neither Dred Scott himself, nor any of his family, were made free by being carried into this territory; even if they had been carried there by the owner, with the intention of becoming a permanent resident....

Upon the whole, therefore, it is the judgment of this court, that it appears by the record before us that the plaintiff in error is not a citizen of Missouri, in the sense in which that word is used in the Constitution; and that the Circuit Court of the United States, for that reason, had no jurisdiction in the case, and could give no judgment in it.

Its judgment for the defendant must, consequently, be reversed, and a mandate issued directing the suit to be dismissed for want of jurisdiction.

❧ A plea for Southern cities

HILTON R. HELPER

In stark contrast to the North which was building railroads and factories at a rapid clip, the South's manufacturing efforts were relatively meek. Relying instead on its cash crops such as cotton, the South was largely agricultural. Only one in ten Southerners lived in cities compared to one in three in the North.

Hilton R. Helper identified this disparity in his 1857 book *The Impending Crisis of the South: How to Meet It,* calling for the South to redirect its economic and social system away from a slave-based agricultural economy and to embrace the industrial revolution. Helper's plea, however, was largely ignored and came too late. When the Civil War broke out in 1861 the South's economy, with a fraction of the railroads and manufacturing capacity, was ill-equipped to withstand a sustained conflict with the larger, wealthier and more industrialized North.

Our theme is a city—a great Southern importing, exporting, and manufacturing city, to be located at some point or port on the coast of the Carolinas, Georgia, or Virginia, where we can carry on active commerce, buy, sell, fabricate, receive the profits which accrue from the exchange of our own commodities, open facilities for direct communication with foreign countries, and establish all those collateral sources of wealth, utility, and adornment, which are the usual concomitants of a metropolis,

and which add so very materially to the interest and importance of a nation. Without a city of this kind, the South can never develop her commercial resources nor attain to that eminent position to which those vast resources would otherwise exalt her. According to calculations based upon reasonable estimates, it is owing to the lack of a great commercial city in the South, that we are now annually drained of more than One Hundred and Twenty Millions of Dollars! We should, however, take into consideration the negative loss as well as the positive. Especially should we think of the influx of emigrants, of the visits of strangers and cosmopolites, of the patronage to hotels and public halls, of the profits of travel and transportation, of the emoluments of foreign and domestic trade, and of numerous other advantages which have their origin exclusively in wealthy, enterprising, and densely populated cities.

Nothing is more evident than the fact, that our people have never entertained a proper opinion of the importance of home cities. Blindly, and greatly to our own injury, we have contributed hundreds of millions of dollars towards the erection of mammoth cities at the North, while our own magnificent bays and harbors have been most shamefully disregarded and neglected. Now, instead of carrying all our money to New York, Philadelphia, Boston, and Cininnati, suppose we had kept it on the south side of Mason and Dixon's line—as we would have done, had it not been for slavery—and had disbursed it in the upbuilding of Norfolk, Beaufort, Charleston, or Savannah, how much richer, better, greater, would have been our population. How many hundred thousand natives of the South would now be thriving at home, instead of adding to the wealth and political power of the Union. How much greater would be the number and length of our railroads, canals, turnpikes, and telegraphs. How much greater would be the extent and diversity of our manufactures. How much greater would be the grandeur, and how much larger would be the number of our churches, theatres, schools, colleges, lyceums, banks, hotels, stores, and private dwellings. How many more clippers and steamships would we have sailing on the ocean, how vastly more reputable would we be abroad, how infinitely more respectable, progressive, and happy, would we be at home.

That we may learn something of the importance of cities in general, let us look for a moment at the great capitals of the world. What would England be without London? What would France be without Paris? What would Turkey be without Constantinople? Or to come nearer home, what would Maryland be without Baltimore? What would Louisiana be without New Orleans? What would South Carolina be without Charleston? Do we ever think of these countries or States without thinking of their cities also? If we want to learn the news of the country, do we not go to the city, or to the city papers? Every metropolis may be regarded as the nucleus or epitome of the country in which it is situated; and the more prominent features and characteristics of a country, particularly of the people of a country, are almost always to be seen within the limits of its capital city. Almost invariably do we find the bulk of floating funds, the best talent, and the most vigorous energies of a nation concentrated in its chief cities; and does not this concentration of wealth, energy, and talent, conduce, in an extraordinary degree, to the growth and prosperity of the nation? Unquestionably. Wealth develops wealth, energy develops energy, talent develops talent. What, then, must be the condition of those countries which do not possess the means or faculties of centralizing their material forces, their energies, and their talents? Are they not destined to occupy an inferior rank among the nations of the earth? Let the South answer.

❧ "A house divided by itself cannot stand"

ABRAHAM LINCOLN

Abraham Lincoln gave his famous speech declaring that "a house divided by itself cannot stand" at the close of the 1858 Illinois Republican convention in which he was nominated to oppose Stephen Douglas in the coming election for U.S. senator. Lincoln sharply criticized Douglas for the prominent role he had played in the perceived gains that the slave states had achieved since the Compromise in 1850, particularly the Kansas-Nebraska Act, which Douglas had crafted. This speech and his speeches in the Lincoln-Douglas debates helped propel him on to the national stage. Although he narrowly lost the election for senator, two years later Lincoln defeated Douglas in the presidential election.

Mr. President and Gentlemen of the Convention.

If we could first know where we are, and whither we are tending, we could then better judge what to do, and how to do it.

We are now far into the fifth year, since a policy was initiated, with the avowed object, and confident promise, of putting an end to slavery agitation.

Under the operation of that policy, that agitation has not only not ceased, but has constantly augmented.

In my opinion, it will not cease, until a crisis shall have been reached, and passed.

"A house divided against itself cannot stand."

I believe this government cannot endure, permanently half slave and half free.

I do not expect the Union to be dissolved—I do not expect the house to fall—but I do expect it will cease to be divided. It will become all one thing, or all the other.

Either the opponents of slavery, will arrest the further spread of it, and place it where the public mind shall rest in the belief that it is in course of ultimate extinction; or its advocates will push it forward, till it shall become alike lawful in all the States, old as well as new—North as well as South. Have we no tendency to the latter condition?

Let anyone who doubts, carefully contemplate that now almost complete legal combination—piece of machinery so to speak—compounded of the Nebraska doctrine, and the Dred Scott decision. Let him consider not only what work the machinery is adapted to do, and how well adapted; but also, let him study the history of its construction, and trace, if he can, or rather fail, if he can, to trace the evidences of design, and concert of action, among its chief bosses, from the beginning.

The new year of 1854 found slavery excluded from more than half the States by State Constitutions, and from most of the national territory by Congressional prohibition.

Four days later, commenced the struggle, which ended in repealing that Congressional prohibition.

This opened all the national territory to slavery; and was the first point gained.

But, so far, Congress only, had acted; and an indorsement by the people, real or apparent, was indispensable, to save the point already gained, and give chance for more.

This necessity had not been overlooked; but

had been provided for, as well as might be, in the notable argument of "squatter sovereignty," otherwise called "sacred right of self government," which latter phrase, though expressive of the only rightful basis of any government, was so perverted in this attempted use of it as to amount to just this: That if any one man, choose to enslave another, no third man shall be allowed to object.

That argument was incorporated into the Nebraska bill itself, in the language which follows: "It being the true intent and meaning of this act not to legislate slavery into any Territory or state, nor to exclude it therefrom; but to leave the people thereof perfectly free to form and regulate their domestic institutions in their own way, subject only to the Constitution of the United States."

Then opened the roar of loose declamation in favor of "Squatter Sovereignty," and "Sacred right of self government."

"But," said opposition members, "let us be more specific—let us amend the bill so as to expressly declare that the people of the territory may exclude slavery." "Not we," said the friends of the measure; and down they voted the amendment.

While the Nebraska bill was passing through congress, a law case, involving the question of a negroe's freedom, by reason of his owner having voluntarily taken him first into a free state and then a territory covered by the congressional prohibition, and held him as a slave, for a long time in each, was passing through the U.S. Circuit Court for the District of Missouri; and both Nebraska bill and law suit were brought to a decision in the same month of May, 1854. The negroe's name was "Dred Scott," which name now designates the decision finally made in the case.

Before the then next Presidential election, the law case came to, and was argued in the Supreme Court of the United States; but the decision of it was deferred until after the election. Still, before the election, Senator Trumbull, on the floor of the Senate, requests the leading advocate of the Nebraska bill to state his opinion whether the people of a territory can constitutionally exclude slavery from their limits; and the latter answers, "That is a question for the Supreme Court."

The election came. Mr. Buchanan was elected, and the indorsement, such as it was, secured. That was the second point gained. The indorsement, however, fell short of a clear popular majority by nearly four hundred thousand votes, and so, perhaps, was not overwhelmingly reliable and satisfactory.

The outgoing President, in his last annual message, as impressively as possible echoed back upon the people the weight and authority of the indorsement.

The Supreme Court met again; did not announce their decision, but ordered a re-argument.

The Presidential inauguration came, and still no decision of the court; but the incoming President, in his inaugural address, fervently exhorted the people to abide by the forthcoming decision, whatever it might be.

Then, in a few days, came the decision.

The reputed author of the Nebraska bill finds an early occasion to make a speech at this capitol indorsing the Dred Scott Decision, and vehemently denouncing all opposition to it.

The new President, too, seizes the early occasion of the Silliman letter to indorse and strongly construe that decision, and to express his astonishment that any different view had ever been entertained.

At length a squabble springs up between the President and the author of the Nebraska bill, on the mere question of fact, whether the Lecompton constitution was or was not, in any just sense, made by the people of Kansas; and in that squabble the latter declares that all he wants is a fair vote for the people, and that he cares not whether slavery be voted down or voted up. I do not understand his declaration that he cares not whether slavery be voted down or voted up, to be intended by him other than as an apt definition of the policy he would impress upon the public mind—the principle for which he declares he has suffered much, and is ready to suffer to the end.

And well may he cling to that principle. If he has any parental feeling, well may he cling to it. That principle, is the only shred left of his original Nebraska doctrine. Under the Dred Scott decision, "squatter sovereignty" squatted out of existence, tumbled down like temporary scaffolding—like the mould at the foundry served through one blast and fell back into loose sand—helped to carry an election, and then was kicked to the winds. His late joint struggle with the Republicans, against the Lecompton Constitution, involves nothing of the original Nebraska doctrine. That struggle was made on a point, the right of a people to make their own constitution, upon which he and the Republicans have never differed.

The several points of the Dred Scott decision, in connection with Senator Douglas' "care not" policy, constitute the piece of machinery, in its present state of advancement. This was the third point gained.

The working points of that machinery are:

First, that no negro slave, imported as such from Africa, and no descendant of such slave can ever be a citizen of any State, in the sense of that term as used in the Constitution of the United States.

This point is made in order to deprive the negro, in every possible event, of the benefit of this provision of the United States Constitution, which declares that—

"The citizens of each State shall be entitled to all privileges and immunities of citizens in the several States."

Secondly, that "subject to the Constitution of the United States," neither Congress nor a Territorial Legislature can exclude slavery from any United States territory.

This point is made in order that individual men may fill up the territories with slaves, without danger of losing them as property, and thus to enhance the chances of permanency to the institution through all the future.

Thirdly, that whether the holding of a negro in actual slavery in a free State, makes him free, as against the holder, the United States courts will not decide, but will leave to be decided by the courts of any slave State the negro may be forced into by the master.

This point is made, not to be pressed immediately; but, if acquiesced in for awhile, and apparently indorsed by the people at an election, then to sustain the logical conclusion that what Dred Scott's master might lawfully do with Dred Scott, in the free State of Illinois, every other master may lawfully do with any other one, or one thousand slaves, in Illinois, or in any other free State.

Auxiliary to all this, and working hand in hand with it, the Nebraska doctrine, or what is left of it, is to educate and mould public opinion, at least Northern public opinion, to not care whether slavery is voted down or voted up.

This shows exactly where we now are; and partially also, whither we are tending.

It will throw additional light on the latter, to go back, and run the mind over the string of historical facts already stated. Several things will now appear less dark and mysterious than they did when they were transpiring. The people were to be left "perfectly free" "subject only to the Constitution." What the Constitution had to do with it, outsiders could not then see. Plainly enough now, it was an exactly fitted niche, for the Dred Scott decision to afterwards come in, and declare the perfect freedom of the people, to be just no freedom at all.

Why was the amendment, expressly declaring the right of the people to exclude slavery, voted down? Plainly enough now, the adoption of it, would have spoiled the niche for the Dred Scott decision.

Why was the court decision held up? Why, even a Senator's individual opinion withheld, till after the Presidential election? Plainly enough now, the speaking out then would have damaged the "perfectly free" argument upon which the election was to be carried.

Why the outgoing President's felicitation on the indorsement? Why the delay of a reargument? Why the incoming President's advance exhortation in favor of the decision?

These things look like the cautious patting and petting of a spirited horse, preparatory to mounting him, when it is dreaded that he may give the rider a fall. And why the hasty after indorsements of the decision by the President and others?

We can not absolutely know that all these exact adaptations are the result of preconcert. But when we see a lot of framed timbers, different portions of which we know have been gotten out at different times and places and by different workmen—Stephen, Franklin, Roger and James, for instance—and when we see these timbers joined together, and see they exactly make the frame of a house or a mill, all the tenons and mortices exactly fitting, and all the lengths and proportions of the different pieces exactly adapted to their respective places, and not a piece too many or too few—not omitting even scaffolding—or, if a single piece be lacking, we can see the place in the frame exactly fitted and prepared to yet bring such piece in—in such a case, we find it impossible to not believe that Stephen and Franklin and Roger and James all understood one another from the beginning, and all worked upon a common plan or draft drawn up before the first lick was struck.

It should not be overlooked that, by the Nebraska bill, the people of a State as well as Territory, were to be left "perfectly free" "subject only to the Constitution."

Why mention a State? They were legislating for territories, and not for or about States. Certainly the people of a State are and ought to be subject to the Constitution of the United States; but why is mention of this lugged into this merely territorial law? Why are the people of a territory and the people of a state therein lumped together, and their relation to the Constitution therein treated as being precisely the same?

While the opinion of the Court, by Chief Justice Taney, in the Dred Scott case, and the separate opinions of all the concurring Judges, expressly declare that the Constitution of the United States neither permits Congress nor a Territorial legislature to exclude slavery from any United States territory, they all omit to declare whether or not the same Constitution permits a state, or the people of a State, to exclude it.

Possibly, this was a mere omission; but who can be quite sure, if McLean or Curtis had sought to get into the opinion a declaration of unlimited power in the people of a state to exclude slavery from their limits, just as Chase and Macy sought to get such declaration, in behalf of the people of a territory, into the Nebraska bill—I ask, who can be quite sure that it would not have been voted down, in the one case, as it had been in the other.

The nearest approach to the point of declaring the power of a State over slavery is made by Judge Nelson. He approaches it more than once, using the precise idea, and almost the language too, of the Nebraska act. On one occasion his exact language is, "except in cases where the power is restrained by the Constitution of the United States, the law of the State is supreme over the subject of slavery within its jurisdiction."

In what cases the power of the states is so restrained by the U.S. Constitution, is left an open question, precisely the same question, as to the restraint on the power of the territories was left open in the Nebraska act. Put that and that together, and we have another nice little niche, which we may, ere long, see filled with another Supreme

Court decision, declaring that the Constitution of the United States does not permit a state to exclude slavery from its limits.

And this may especially be expected if the doctrine of "care not whether slavery be voted down or voted up," shall gain upon the public mind sufficiently to give promise that such a decision can be maintained when made.

Such a decision is all that slavery now lacks of being alike lawful in all the States.

Welcome or unwelcome, such decision is probably coming, and will soon be upon us, unless the power of the present political dynasty shall be met and overthrown.

We shall lie down pleasantly dreaming that the people of Missouri are on the verge of making their State free; and we shall awake to the reality instead, that the Supreme Court has made Illinois a slave State.

To meet and overthrow the power of that dynasty is the work now before all those who would prevent that consummation.

That is what we have to do.

But how can we best do it?

There are those who denounce us openly to their own friends, and yet whisper us softly, that Senator Douglas is the aptest instrument there is, with which to effect that object. They do not tell us, nor has he told us, that he wishes any such object to be effected. They wish us to infer all, from the facts, that he now has a little quarrel with the present head of the dynasty; and that he has regularly voted with us, on a single point, upon which, he and we, have never differed.

They remind us that he is a very great man, and that the largest of us are very small ones. Let this be granted. But "a living dog is better than a dead lion." Judge Douglas, if not a dead lion for this work, is at least a caged and toothless one. How can he oppose the advances of slavery? He doesn't care anything about it. His avowed mission is impressing the "public heart" to care nothing about it.

A leading Douglas Democratic newspaper thinks Douglas' superior talent will be needed to resist the revival of the African slave trade.

Does Douglas believe an effort to revive that trade is approaching? He has not said so. Does he really think so? But if it is, how can he resist it? For years he has labored to prove it a sacred right of

white men to take negro slaves into the new territories. Can he possibly show that it is less a sacred
right to buy them where they can be bought cheapest? And, unquestionably they can be bought
cheaper in Africa than in Virginia.

He has done all in his power to reduce the
whole question of slavery to one of a mere right of
property; and as such, how can he oppose the foreign slave trade—how can he refuse that trade in
that "property" shall be "perfectly free"—unless he
does it as a protection to the home production?
And as the home producers will probably not ask
the protection, he will be wholly without a ground
of opposition.

Senator Douglas holds, we know, that a man
may rightfully be wiser to-day than he was yesterday—that he may rightfully change when he finds
himself wrong.

But, can we for that reason, run ahead, and
infer that he will make any particular change, of
which he, himself, has given no intimation? Can
we safely base our action upon any such vague
inference?

Now, as ever, I wish to not misrepresent Judge
Douglas' position, question his motives, or do ought
that can be personally offensive to him.

Whenever, if ever, he and we can come
together on principle so that our great cause may
have assistance from his great ability, I hope to
have interposed no adventitious obstacle.

But clearly, he is not now with us—he
does not pretend to be—he does not promise
to ever be.

Our cause, then, must be intrusted to, and conducted by its own undoubted friends—those whose
hands are free, whose hearts are in the work—who
do care for the result.

Two years ago the Republicans of the nation
mustered over thirteen hundred thousand strong.

We did this under the single impulse of resistance to a common danger, with every external circumstance against us.

Of strange, discordant, and even, hostile elements, we gathered from the four winds, and armed
and fought the battle through, under the constant
hot fire of a disciplined, proud, and pampered
enemy.

Did we brave all then, to falter now?—now—
when that same enemy is wavering, dissevered and
belligerent?

The result is not doubtful. We shall not fail—if
we stand firm, we shall not fail.

Wise councils may accelerate or mistakes delay
it, but, sooner or later the victory is sure to come.

"This government can exist"

STEPHEN DOUGLAS

Douglas and Lincoln engaged in seven debates in the 1858
Illinois campaign. Employing humor, logic, popular appeal,
legal stances and rhetoric, the two men articulated their
positions on slavery. In the last debate held October 15 in
Alton, Illinois, Douglas accuses Lincoln for misleading listen-
ers with the statement that he would not abolish slavery in
slave states.

By prohibiting slavery in the federal territories, Douglas
says, Lincoln would tip the political balance in Congress
against the slave states and then abolish slavery from the
United States altogether. In contrast to Lincoln's position that
the country could not remain "half slave and half free,"
Douglas believed the country could endure, so long as the
federal government did not interfere in a state or territory's
right to allow slaves or not.

Mr. Lincoln has concluded his remarks by saying
that there is not such an abolitionist as I am in all
America. If he could make the abolitionists of
Illinois believe that, he would not have much show
for the Senate. Let him make the abolitionists
believe the truth of that statement, and his political back is broken....

Mr. Lincoln tries to avoid the main issue by
attacking the truth of my proposition that our
fathers made this government divided into free and
slave states, recognizing the right of each to decide
all its local questions for itself. Did they not thus
make it? It is true that they did not establish slavery in any of the states, or abolish it in any of
them, but finding thirteen states, twelve of which
were slave and one free, they agreed to form a government uniting them together as they stood divided into free and slave states and to guarantee forever to each state the right to do as it pleased on the
slavery question? Having thus made the government, and conferred this right upon each state forever, I assert that this government can exist as they
made it, divided into free and slave states, if any
one state chooses to retain slavery. He says that he

looks forward to a time when slavery shall be abolished everywhere. I look forward to a time when each state shall be allowed to do as it pleases. If it chooses to keep slavery forever, it is not my business, but its own; if it chooses to abolish slavery, it is its own business—not mine. I care more for the great principle of self-government, the right of the people to rule, than I do for all the Negroes in Christendom. I would not endanger the perpetuity of this Union, I would not blot out the great inalienable rights of the white men, for all the Negroes that ever existed. Hence, I say, let us maintain this government on the principles that our fathers made it, recognizing the right of each state to keep slavery as long as its people determine, or to abolish it when they please. But Mr. Lincoln says that when our fathers made this government they did not look forward to the state of things now existing, and therefore he thinks the doctrine was wrong; and he quotes Brooks, of South Carolina, to prove that our fathers then thought that probably slavery would be abolished by each state acting for itself before this time. Suppose they did; suppose they did not foresee what has occurred, does that change the principles of our government? They did not probably foresee the telegraph that transmits intelligence by lightning, nor did they foresee the railroads that now form the bonds of union between the different states, or the thousand mechanical inventions that have elevated mankind. But do these things change the principles of the government? Our fathers, I say, made this government on the principle of the right of each state to do as it pleases in its own domestic affairs, subject to the Constitution, and allowed the people of each to apply to every new change of circumstances such remedy as they may see fit to improve their condition. This right they have for all time to come.

Mr. Lincoln went on to tell you that he does not at all desire to interfere with slavery in the states where it exists, nor does his party. I expected him to say that down here. Let me ask him, then, how he expects to put slavery in the course of ultimate extinction everywhere, if he does not intend to interfere with it in the states where it exists? He says that he will prohibit it in all territories, and the inference is, then, that unless they make free states out of them he will keep them out of the Union; for, mark you, he did not say whether or not he would

vote to admit Kansas with slavery or not, as her people might apply; he did not say whether or not he was in favor of bringing the territories now in existence into the Union on the principle of Clay's Compromise Measures on the slavery question. I told you that he would not. His idea is that he will prohibit slavery in all the territories and thus force them all to become free states, surrounding the slave states with a cordon of free states, and hemming them in, keeping the slaves confined to their present limits whilst they go on multiplying, until the soil on which they live will no longer feed them, and he will thus be able to put slavery in a course of ultimate extinction by starvation.

He will extinguish slavery in the Southern states as the French general exterminated the Algerines when he smoked them out. He is going to extinguish slavery by surrounding the slave states, hemming in the slaves, and starving them out of existence, as you smoke a fox out of his hole. He intends to do that in the name of humanity and Christianity, in order that we may get rid of the terrible crime and sin entailed upon our fathers of holding slaves. Mr. Lincoln makes out that line of policy and appeals to the moral sense of justice and to the Christian feeling of the community to sustain him. He says that any man who holds to the contrary doctrine is in the position of the king who claimed to govern by divine right. Let us examine for a moment and see what principle it was that overthrew the divine right of George III to govern us. Did not these colonies rebel because the British Parliament had no right to pass laws concerning our property and domestic and private institutions without our consent? We demanded that the British government should not pass such laws unless they gave us representation in the body passing them, and this the British government insisting on doing, we went to war, on the principle that the Home government should not control and govern distant colonies without giving them a representation. Now, Mr. Lincoln proposes to govern the territories without giving them a representation and calls on Congress to pass laws controlling their property and domestic concerns without their consent and against their will. Thus, he asserts for his party the identical principle asserted by George III and the Tories of the Revolution.

I ask you to look into these things and then tell me whether the democracy or the abolitionists are right. I hold that the people of a territory, like those of a state (I use the language of Mr. Buchanan in his letter of acceptance), have the right to decide for themselves whether slavery shall or shall not exist within their limits. The point upon which Chief Justice Taney expresses his opinion is simply this: that slaves, being property, stand on an equal footing with other property, and consequently that the owner has the same right to carry that property into a territory that he has any other, subject to the same conditions. Suppose that one of your merchants was to take fifty or one hundred thousand dollars' worth of liquors to Kansas. He has a right to go there, under that decision, but when he gets there he finds the Maine liquor law in force, and what can he do with his property after he gets it there? He cannot sell it; he cannot use it; it is subject to the local law, and that law is against him; and the best thing he can do with it is to bring it back into Missouri or Illinois and sell it. If you take Negroes to Kansas, as Colonel Jeff Davis said in his Bangor speech, from which I have quoted today, you must take them there subject to the local law. If the people want the institution of slavery, they will protect and encourage it; but if they do not want it they will withhold that protection, and the absence of local legislation protecting slavery excludes it as completely as a positive prohibition. You slaveholders of Missouri might as well understand what you know practically, that you cannot carry slavery where the people do not want it. All you have a right to ask is that the people shall do as they please; if they want slavery, let them have it; if they do not want it, allow them to refuse to encourage it.

My friends, if, as I have said before, we will only live up to this great fundamental principle, there will be peace between the North and the South. Mr. Lincoln admits that under the Constitution, on all domestic questions, except slavery, we ought not to interfere with the people of each state. What right have we to interfere with the people of each state? What right have we to interfere with slavery any more than we have to interfere with any other question? He says that this slavery question is now the bone of contention. Why? Simply because agitators have combined in all the free states to make war upon it? Suppose the agitators in the states should combine in one-half of the Union to make war upon the railroad system of the other half. They would thus be driven to the same

sectional strife. Suppose one section makes war upon any other particular institution of the opposite section, and the same strife is produced. The only remedy and safety is that we shall stand by the Constitution as our fathers made it, obey the laws as they are passed, while they stand the proper test, and sustain the decisions of the Supreme Court and the constituted authorities.

❧ *"To rouse the South"*

EDMUND RUFFIN

Edmund Ruffin first gained notoriety in 1837 when he founded the *Farmers' Registrar,* a publication advocating for advanced agricultural practices. Among other things, he promoted the application of marl, deeper plowing and animal husbandry. By the 1850s, however, his strident calls for secession made him one of the leading "fire-eaters" of the South.

In 1858, as Lincoln and Douglas debated slavery and most national leaders struggled to keep the country together, Ruffin and his compatriots longed for a final rift to break the South's ties with the North. Ruffin's diary reflects his frustrations at the lack of leadership from Southern politicians to lead a secession movement. He correctly anticipated that the 1860 election might serve as a catalyst for disunion if the Democratic Party collapsed from the schism between Northern and Southern interests.

Aug. 4. Immediately after breakfast proceeded on my way, & in 12 miles more, reached Linden, in Westmoreland, the residence of Willoughby Newton. Found him awaiting my arrival. We were soon engaged in earnest discussion on the great Southern question, & in regard to our respective recent actions therein—his disunion address, on July 4th, before the Va. Military Institute, & my published scheme of association of "United Southerners." For his part, he has been strongly assailed in the newspapers—& I have, for my share, only escaped with less denunciation because of the greater obscurity of myself & my scheme. Newton & I have exchanged several long letters on these particular points, & the whole general subject. But much was left untouched for our expected personal meeting & free conversation. We agree entirely as to the necessity for, & the advantages of a separation & independent confederacy of the slave-holding states. Also we agree that nearly all the leading & prominent men of the south, even when agreeing with us in general opinion, are rendered timid, & silent, & unwilling to make any public avowal of disunion sentiments, because they are fearful they are on the much weaker side, & that such avowals would destroy all their political hopes, & favor, from the majority. The aspirants to the presidency, of whom nearly every very prominent southern politician is one, are bribed by their entirely vain hopes, either to openly & actively go into the service of our enemies, to buy northern votes, (as Douglas, Wise, & Jeff Davis have done,) or otherwise, like Hunter & others to remain silent & inactive, for fear of offending the North, in cases where justice to the South requires their active defence. While it is, to my view, a vain hope that any southern man can ever be again elected President of the present United States, yet scores of political leaders, & their thousands of the most active & influential several partizans, are, either actively or passively, working to further the supremacy of the North & the submission of the South, as the means of attaining their own selfish & base objects. So now, & it will increase with the nearer approach of the presidential election in 1860, every man who hopes to gain anything from the continuance of the Union, will be loud & active in shouting for its integrity & permanence. The many & zealous recent defenders of the Union, & denouncers of its enemies, have been stimulated by the fear that…upholding the southern party will operate to overthrow the national democratic party, by driving off the smaller northern wing of that party. If the success of this party is to be best effected by injuring (& still more if by destroying) the supporters of southern rights, then I shall more anxiously wish for the speedy overthrow of the national democratic party, & its being beaten by the "Black Republican" or abolition party, in the next presidential election. This is wanting to unite southern men under the banner of the south, disentangled from all northern alliances. Newton has convinced me, (& I readily yield to his better judgment,) that in this view of prospects, it will be bad policy for me to endeavor to establish associations of "United Southerners," or in any such manner to separate & identify our true & boldest men. For, under present circumstances, not one in 100 of those who think with us, will dare to avow their opinions, & to commit themselves by such open action. And the very few who would so move, would be by our opposers counted as being all of the disunionists—& we would be powerless, & sink in our apparent weakness. I admit fully the force of these views, & I will desist from any further effort for the present time—

hoping that the events of 1860 will change circumstances, so that the dishonest & the timid southern men may then be as strongly bribed by their selfish views to stand up for the South, as now to stoop & truckle to the North.—Walked out with Newton, to see from the nearest edge of the high table land, the magnificent view thence of the broad lowgrounds, of the Potomac, with the head water of that river, & of Mechadack creek, seen in various detached places, as if of islands filling the larger surface of an extensive lake. Conversation on various subjects, but mostly of southern politics, to bed-time.

Aug. 16. After breakfast, Mr. Newton took me in his light carriage to drive over some of the neighboring country, so as to see fair samples of the peculiar lands of this long & narrow peninsula between the lower Potomac & Rappahannock, known as the Northern Neck. It is a beautiful & valuable agricultural region, with many advantages, & especially in regard to the contiguity of deep navigable waters on one or the other side…. Afternoon, several gentlemen came in & among them Jos. Mayo jr. of this neighborhood, but now assistant editor, in Petersburg, of the South-Side Democrat.—The last number of "The South" contained another editorial… more contemptuous & offensive in manner than the preceding. [James L.] Orr & Keitt of S.C. have both lately delivered what are called "conservative" speeches, in public meetings, & Jefferson Davis, a candidate for the Presidency, in a speech delivered at the North, has vied with Wise in fishing for northern votes, by lauding the Union. Hammond's late speech is reported to be in the same "conservative" tone—though in his letter to me he denied the correctness of all the newspaper reports. All these demonstrations, together with Pryor's strange change of attitude, seem to indicate a concerted purpose, & arranged plan, to sustain the "national democratic party," by courting & submitting to the northern & small portion of it, by silencing & postponing, if not sacrificing the just claims of the south. If the northern members of the democratic party should not be retained, there will be no possible chance to elect the next president—& still less that he will be a southern man. It is to effect the latter impossible object, & each one favoring his own selfish ends, that all our southern aspirants have become such good union men. And all their respective partisans & followers obey the commands of their leaders, & follow their course. Scarcely a dozen men in Va. (& not one of them aspirants to political station,) who will now even speak openly, much less act, in defence of the south to the extent that was avowed very generally a year or two ago. Under these circumstances, there is no use in attempting to collect auxiliaries, or to make any arrangement for action. Nearly all, even of those who think with me, are either under this corrupt influence, for themselves or their leaders, or otherwise intimidated by the prevailing outcry, so that all fear to act to sustain the South. All that these few of us can do, will be, from time to time, to continue to proclaim resistance through the newspapers, & to show that all have not submitted. There have been sundry attacks in the newspapers on Newton's disunion Address on the 4th of July. He will use them merely as an excuse to defend his views, & set them forth at length & elaborately, in another publication. I hope this argument in support of the political necessity, and also the many & great prospective benefits to the South, of seceding from the Northern States, will attract notice, & have good effects in future time, even though now no voice shall be raised in concurrence or approval. When the issue of the next presidential election shall be known, in 1860, & all southern candidates defeated & their hopes shown to be baseless, & their aspirations desperate, they may come to their senses, & to their former southern support. Still better if this "national" democratic party shall then be defeated & ruptured, & an abolitionist elected. Then perhaps the South may act for its defence & only salvation. If not, then submission to northern oppression will be the fixed course of the South, & its fate sealed....

Aug. 28. I do not believe that anything can be done at present to rouse the South. All the prominent politicians are either aspirants to the presidency, or seeking other high offices, & know they can only reach their objects by support of northern votes. Hence they desire especially to conciliate the north, & particularly now, for the nomination of a candidate for the presidency in 1860. All the newspapers are in the service of one or other of these aspirants, & obey their bidding. The great mass merely follow the directions given by their leaders through the newspapers— and as the cue is now to laud the union, it is vain to say anything against it. Nothing can be done

until after the nomination & election of 1860. Then these southern leaders, blinded now by their ambition, will all be disappointed, & may understand the truth that no southern man can be made president, or as a candidate, receive the support of the northern democrats. To obtain their support, everything must be yielded to their wishes, prejudices, & interests—& by so doing, the South may rule, as it is called. This disappointment, or some new outrage, or the entire separation (as I hope may occur) between the Southern & Northern democrats, may dispose the South again to resist. At present everything that can be said to that purpose, is addressed to deaf ears. I will trouble myself no more about it, until a suitable time shall come.

❧ "Mingle my blood with the blood of my children"

JOHN BROWN

A fervid abolitionist, John Brown led a small band of followers to capture the federal armory at Harper's Ferry, Virginia, on October 16, 1859. He hoped to spark a slave rebellion and use the weapons seized in the arsenal. However, federal troops commanded by Colonel Robert E. Lee surrounded the building and captured Brown after a brief battle. Seven of Brown's followers—including two of his sons—were killed as were ten federal soldiers.

Brown (who had previously killed five men in Kansas for the cause of abolitionism) was tried for treason and conspiring with slaves to commit murder, convicted and hanged. During his trail he delivered the following speech. Abolitionists hailed Brown as a hero and a martyr to their cause. But Brown's rebellion, the reaction from the North and the fact that his venture was financed by prominent New Englanders and New Yorkers enraged the South.

I have, may it please the court, a few words to say. In the first place, I deny everything but what I have all along admitted—of a design on my part to free slaves. I intended certainly to have made a clean thing of that matter, as I did last winter, when I went into Missouri and there took slaves without the snapping of a gun on either side, moving them through the country, and finally leaving them in Canada. I designed to have done the same thing again, on a larger scale. That was all I intended. I never did intend murder, or treason, or the destruction of property, or to excite or incite slaves to rebellion, or to make insurrection.

I have another objection, and that is that it is unjust that I should suffer such a penalty. Had I interfered in the manner which I admit, and which I admit has been fairly proved (for I admire the truthfulness and candor of the greater portion of the witnesses who have testified in this case)—had I so interfered in behalf of the rich, the powerful, the intelligent, the so-called great, or in behalf of any of their friends, either father, mother, brother, sister, wife, or children, or any of that class, and suffered and sacrificed what I have in this interference, it would have been all right. Every man in this court would have deemed it an act worthy of reward rather than punishment.

This court acknowledges, too, as I suppose, the validity of the law of God. I see a book kissed, which I suppose to be the Bible, or at least the New Testament, which teaches me that all things whatsoever I would that men should do to me, I should do even so to them. It teaches me, further, to remember them that are in bonds, as bound with them. I endeavored to act up to that instruction. I say, I am yet too young to understand that God is any respecter of persons. I believe that to have interfered as I have done, as I have always freely admitted I have done, in behalf of His despised poor, was no wrong, but right. Now if it is deemed necessary that I should forfeit my life for the furtherance of the ends of justice, and mingle my blood further with the blood of my children and with the blood of millions in this slave country whose rights are disregarded by wicked, cruel, and unjust enactments—I say, let it be done.

Let me say one word further.

I feel entirely satisfied with the treatment I have received on my trial. Considering all the circumstances, it has been more generous than I expected. But I feel no consciousness of guilt. I have stated from the first what was my intention and what was not. I never had any design against liberty of any person, nor any disposition to commit treason, or excite slaves to rebel, or make any general insurrection. I never encouraged any man to do so but always discouraged any idea of that kind.

Let me say, also, a word in regard to the statements made by some of those who were connected with me. I hear it has been stated by some of them that I induced them to join me. But the contrary is true. I do not this to injure them, but as regretting their weakness. No one but joined me of his own accord, and the greater part at their own expense. A number of them I never saw, and never had a word of conversation with, till the day they came to me, and that was for the purpose I have stated.

Now I have done.

"We denounce those threats of Disunion"

REPUBLICAN PARTY PLATFORM

The Republican Party's 1860 political platform called for the preservation of the Union, reaffirmed states' rights and sought the abolition of slavery in federal territories. It thus articulated the goal of allowing existing states to retain slavery if they chose. But the restrictions on expanding slavery enraged the South which simply did not believe the North would not eventually prohibit slavery altogether. Many Southern states refused to even place the Republican presidential candidate, Abraham Lincoln, on the election ballots. When Lincoln won the election against a divided Democratic Party, secessionists cited the Republican platform as a reason to leave the Union. The platform also included provisions to encourage westward expansion and industrial development. These positions would later be enacted by the Republic administration and Congress during the Civil War.

Resolved, That we, the delegated representatives of the Republican electors of the United States, in convention assembled, in discharge of the duty we owe to our constituents and our country, united in the following declarations:

1. That the history of the nation, during the last four years, has fully established the propriety and necessity of the organization and perpetuation of the Republican party, and that the causes which called it into existence are permanent in their nature, and now, more than ever before, demand its peaceful and constitutional triumph.

2. That the maintenance of the principles promulgated in the Declaration of Independence and embodied in the Federal Constitution, "That all men are created equal; that they are endowed by their

Creator with certain inalienable rights; that among these are life, liberty and the pursuit of happiness; that, to secure these rights, governments are instituted among men, deriving their just powers from the consent of the governed," is essential to the preservation of our Republican institutions; and that the Federal Constitution, the Rights of the States, must and shall be preserved.

3. That to the Union of the States this nation owes its unprecedented increase in population, its surprising development of material resources, its rapid augmentation of wealth, its happiness at home and its honor abroad; and we hold in abhorrence all schemes of Disunion, come from whatever source they may; And we congratulate the country that no Republican member of Congress has uttered or countenanced the threats of Disunion so often made by Democratic members, without rebuke and with applause from their political associates; and we denounce those threats of Disunion, in case of a popular overthrow of their ascendency, as denying the vital principles of a free government, and as an avowal of contemplated treason, which it is the imperative duty of an indignant People sternly to rebuke and forever silence.

4. That the maintenance inviolate of the rights of the States, and especially the right of each State to order and control its own domestic institutions according to its own judgment exclusively, is essential to the that balance of powers on which the perfection and endurance of our political fabric depends; and we denounce the lawless invasion by armed force of the soil of any State or Territory, no matter under what pretext, as among the gravest crimes....

7. That the new dogma that the Constitution, of its own force, carries Slavery into any or all of the Territories of the United States, is a dangerous political heresy, at variance with the explicit provisions of that instrument itself, with contemporaneous exposition, and with legislative and judicial precedent; is revolutionary in its tendency, and subversive of the peace and harmony of the country.

8. That the normal condition of all the territory of the United States is that of freedom; That as our Republican fathers, when they had abolished slavery in all our national territory, ordained that "no persons should be deprived of life, liberty, or

property, without due process of law," it becomes our duty, by legislation, whenever such legislation is necessary, to maintain this provision of the Constitution against all attempts to violate it; and we deny the authority of Congress, of a territorial legislature, or of any individuals, to give legal existence to Slavery in any Territory of the United States.

9. That we brand the recent re-opening of the African slave-trade, under the cover of our national flag, aided by perversions of judicial power, as a crime against humanity and a burning shame to our country and age; and we call upon Congress to take prompt and efficient measures for the total and final suppression of that execrable traffic....

10. That in the recent vetoes, by their Federal Governors, of the acts of the legislatures of Kansas and Nebraska, prohibiting Slavery in those Territories, we find a practical illustration of the boasted Democratic principle of Non-Intervention and Popular Sovereignty embodied in the Kansas-Nebraska bill, and demonstration of the deception and fraud involved therein.

11. That Kansas should, of right, be immediately admitted as a State under the Constitution recently formed and adopted by her people, and accepted by the House of Representatives.

12. That, while providing revenue for the support of the General Government by duties upon imports, sound policy requires such an adjustment of these imposts as to encourage the development of the industrial interests of the whole country; and we commend that policy of national exchanges which secures to the working men liberal wages, to agriculture remunerating prices, to mechanics and manufacturers an adequate reward for their skill, labor and enterprise, and to the nation commercial prosperity and independence.

13. That we protest against any sale or alienation to others of the Public Lands held by actual settlers, and against any view of the Homestead policy which regards the settlers as paupers or supplicants for public bounty; and we demand the passage by Congress of the complete and satisfactory Homestead measure which has already passed the house....

16. That a Railroad to the Pacific Ocean is imperatively demanded by the interests of the

whole country; that the Federal government ought to render immediate and efficient aid in its construction; and that, as preliminary thereto, a daily overland Mail should be promptly established....

CHAPTER FIVE

1861–1865

Civil War and a New Birth of Freedom

"The die is cast"

MARY CHESNUT

The election of the hated Republican Abraham Lincoln as president in November 1860 sent the South into a fury of rebellion. Mary Chesnut was a leading member of the South Carolina aristocracy. She, like those around her, was delighted by the prospect of secession. Anticipating an eventful and exciting future, Chesnut decided to keep a journal.

Charleston, South Carolina
November 8, 1860

Yesterday on the train, just before we reached Fernandina, a woman called out: "That settles the hash." Tanny touched me on the shoulder and said: "Lincoln's elected." "How do you know?" "The man over there has a telegram."

The excitement was very great. Everybody was talking at the same time. One, a little more moved than the others, stood up and said despondently: "The die is cast: no more vain regrets, sad forebodings are useless: the stake is life or death." "Did you ever!" was the prevailing exclamation, and someone cried out: "Now that the black radical Republicans have the power I suppose they will Brown us all." No doubt of it.

I have always kept a journal after a fashion of my own, with dates and a line of poetry or prose, mere quotations, which I understood and no else, and I have kept letters and extracts from the papers. From today forward I will tell my story in my own way. I now wish I had a chronicle of the two delightful and eventful years that have just passed. Those delights have fled and one's breath is taken away to think what events have since crowded in. Like the woman's record in her journal, we have had "earthquakes, as usual"...daily shocks.

At Fernandina I saw young men running up a Palmetto flag, and shouting a little prematurely, "South Carolina has seceded!" I was overjoyed to find Florida so sympathetic, but Tanny told me the young men were Gadsdens, Porchers, and Gourdins, names as inevitably South Carolinian as Moses and Lazrarus are Jewish.

From my window I can hear a grand and mighty flow of eloquence. Bartow and a delegation from Savannah are having a supper given to them in the dining room below. The noise of the speaking and cheering is pretty hard on a hard traveler. Suddenly I found myself listening with pleasure.

Voice, tenor, temper, sentiment, language all were perfect.

"Separate and equal among the nations"

SOUTH CAROLINA DECLARATION OF CAUSES OF SECESSION

Six weeks later, South Carolina formally triggered a series of secessions. A convention of delegates formally severed South Carolina's ties with the federal government. Fearing that a Lincoln presidency would bring about the end of slavery—upon which the region's economy was built—the southernmost states opted to form a new nation, the Confederate States of America. South Carolina's declaration was soon echoed in Mississippi, Florida, Alabama, Georgia, Louisiana, and Texas.

December 24, 1860

The people of the State of South Carolina in Convention assembled, on the 2d day of April, A.D. 1852, declared that the frequent violations of the Constitution of the United States by the Federal Government, and its encroachments upon the reserved rights of the States, fully justified this State in their withdrawal from the Federal Union; but in deference to the opinions and wishes of the other Slaveholding States, she forbore at that time to exercise this right. Since that time these encroachments have continued to increase, and further forbearance ceases to be a virtue.

And now the State of South Carolina having resumed her separate and equal place among nations, deems it due to herself, to the remaining United States of America, and to the nations of the world, that she should declare the immediate causes which have led to this act.

In 1787, Deputies were appointed by the States to revise the articles of Confederation; and on 17th September, 1787, these Deputies recommended, for the adoption of the States, the Articles of Union, known as the Constitution of the United States.

Thus was established by compact between the States, a Government with defined objects and powers, limited to the express words of the grant.... We hold that the Government thus established is subject to the two great principles asserted in the

Declaration of Independence; and we hold further, that the mode of its formation subjects it to a third fundamental principle, namely the law of compact. We maintain that in every compact between two or more parties, the obligation is mutual; that the failure of one of the contracting parties to perform a material part of the agreement, entirely releases the obligation of the other; and that, where no arbiter is provided, each party is remitted to his own judgement to determine the fact of failure, with all its consequences.

In the present case, that fact is established with certainty. We assert that fourteen of the States have deliberately refused for years to fulfill their constitutional obligations and we refer to their own statutes for the proof.

The Constitution of the United States, in its fourth Article, provides as follows:

"No person held to service or labor in one State under the laws thereof, escaping into another, shall, in consequence of any law or regulation therein, be discharged from such service or labor, but shall be delivered up, on claim of the party to whom such service or labor may be due."

This stipulation was so material to the compact that without it that compact would not have been made. The greater number of the contracting parties held slaves, and they had previously evinced their estimate of the value of such a stipulation by making it a condition in the Ordinance for the government of the territory ceded by Virginia, which obligations, and the laws of the General Government, have ceased to effect the objects of the Constitution. The States of Maine, New Hampshire, Vermont, Massachusetts, Connecticut, Rhode Island, New York, Pennsylvania, Illinois, Indiana, Michigan, Wisconsin and Iowa, have enacted laws which either nullify the acts of Congress, or render useless any attempt to execute them. In many of these States the fugitive is discharged from the service of labor claimed, and in none of them has the State Government complied with the stipulation made in the Constitution. The State of New Jersey, at an early day, passed a law in conformity with her constitutional obligation; but the current of Anti-Slavery feeling has led her more recently to enact laws which render inoperative the remedies provided by her own laws and the laws of Congress. In the State of New York even the right of transit for a slave has been denied by her tribunals; and the States of Ohio and Iowa have refused to surrender to justice fugitives

charged with murder, and with inciting servile insurrection in the State of Virginia. Thus the constitutional compact has been deliberately broken and disregarded by the non-slaveholding States; and the consequence follows that South Carolina is released from her obligation....

We affirm that these ends for which the Government was instituted have been defeated, and the Government itself has been destructive of them by the action of the non-slaveholding States. Those States have assumed the right of deciding upon the property of our domestic institutions; and have denied the rights of property established in fifteen of the States and recognized by the Constitution; they have denounced as sinful the institution of Slavery; they have permitted the open establishment among them of societies, whose avowed object is to disturb the peace of and eloin the property of the citizens of other States. They have encouraged and assisted thousands of our slaves to leave their homes; and those who remain, have been incited by emissaries, books, and pictures, to servile insurrection.

For twenty-five years this agitation has been steadily increasing, until it has now secured to its aid the power of the common Government. Observing the forms of the Constitution, a sectional party has found within that article establishing the Executive Department, the means of subverting the Constitution itself. A geographical line has been drawn across the Union, and all the States north of that line have united in the election of a man to the high office of President of the United States whose opinions and purposes are hostile to Slavery. He is to be intrusted with the administration of the administration of the common Government, because he has declared that "Government cannot endure permanently half slave, half free," and that the public mind must rest in the belief that Slavery is in the course of ultimate extinction.

This sectional combination for the subversion of the Constitution has been aided, in some of the States, by elevating to citizenship persons who, by the supreme law of the land, are incapable of becoming citizens; and their votes have been used to inaugurate a new policy, hostile to the South, and destructive to its peace and safety.

On the 4th of March next this party will take possession of the Government. It has announced that the South shall be excluded from the common territory, that the Judicial tribunal shall be made sectional, and that a war must be waged against Slavery until it shall cease throughout the Unites States.

The guarantees of the Constitution will then no longer exist; the equal rights of the States will be lost. The slaveholding States will no longer have the power of self-government, or self-protection, and the Federal Government will have become their enemy.

Sectional interest and animosity will deepen the irritation; and all hope of remedy is rendered vain, by the fact that the public opinion at the North has invested a great political error with the sanctions of a more erroneous religious belief.

We, therefore, the people of South Carolina, by our delegates in Convention assembled, appealing to the Supreme Judge of the world for the rectitude of our intentions, have solemnly declared that the union heretofore existing between this State and the other States of North America is dissolved, and that the State of South Carolina has resumed her position among the nations of the world, as a separate and independent state, with full power to levy war, conclude peace, contract alliances, establish commerce, and to do all other acts and things which independent States may of right do.

❧ "Negro slavery shall be recognized and protected"

CONSTITUTION OF THE CONFEDERATE STATES OF AMERICA

The fledgling Confederacy hastily prepared a new Constitution for its breakaway government in the winter of 1861. Ratified days after Lincoln's inauguration, the Confederate Constitution relied heavily on the United States Constitution of 1787, with some critical modifications reflecting Southerners' misgivings of the political structure they had abandoned. The basic structure of government remained the same with a bicameral legislature, president, and judicial system all performing approximately the same duties as the U. S. government. Guarantees of individual liberties (except for slaves) were retained as constitutional rights. The ban on importing slaves was also kept. Whole sections of the U.S. Constitution pertaining to basic operations of the government were simply lifted for the Confederate version.

But major changes were made. As the preamble states,

the source of the national government's authority would lie with the states. States became responsible for financing the central government, thus weakening the national government's ability to act. Congress was assigned the constitutional duty to protect the institution of slavery within the Confederacy and its territories. Slaves were to be considered by the legal system as property. The president was given the right to make line-item vetoes and control of budgetary appropriations.

Paradoxically, the desire to bolster states' rights—which led to secession—hindered the Confederacy's ability to wage war as states were often at odds with each other and the central government. Whereas Lincoln consolidated and strengthened central authority (for which he was sharply criticized) to wage war, Confederate President Jefferson Davis did not have the same political levers.

We the people of the Confederate States, each state acting in its sovereign and independent character, in order to from a permanent government, establish justice, insure domestic tranquillity, and secure the blessings of liberty to ourselves and our posterity—invoking the favor and guidance of Almighty God—do ordain and establish this Constitution for the Confederate States of America.

Article I. Section 1. All legislative powers herein delegated shall be vested in Congress of the Confederate States, which shall consist of a Senate and House of Representatives.

Section 2. (1) The House of Representatives shall be…chosen every second year by the people of the several States; and the electors of each State shall be citizens of the Confederate States, and have the qualifications requisite for electors of the most numerous branches of the State Legislature; but no person of foreign birth, not a citizen of the Confederate States, shall be allowed to vote for any officer, civil, or political, State or Federal….

(2) Representatives and direct taxes shall be apportioned among the several States which may be included among the several States which may be included within this Confederacy, according to their respective numbers, which shall be determined by adding to the whole number of free persons, including those bound to service for a term of years, and excluding Indians not taxed, three-fifths of all slaves. The actual enumeration shall be made within three years after the first meeting of the Congress of the Confederate States, and within every subsequent term of ten years, in such manner as they shall by law direct. The number of Representatives shall not exceed one for every fifty

thousand, but each State shall have at least one Representative; and until such enumeration shall be made the State of South Carolina shall be entitled to choose six; the State of Georgia ten; the State of Alabama nine; the State of Florida two; the State of Mississippi seven; the State of Louisiana six; and the State of Texas six....

Section 9. (1) The importation of negroes of the African race, from any foreign country, other than the slaveholding States or Territories of the United States of America, is hereby forbidden; and Congress is required to pass such laws as shall effectually prevent the same.

(2) Congress shall have the power to prohibit the introduction of slaves from any State not a member of, or Territory not belonging to, this Confederacy....

Article IV. Section 2. (1) The citizens of each State shall be entitled to all the privileges and immunities of citizens of the several States, and shall have the right of transit and sojourn in any State of this Confederacy, with their slaves and other property; and the right of property in said slaves shall not be thereby impaired....

(3) No slave or other person held to service or labor in any State or Territory of the Confederate States, under the laws thereof, escaping or [un]lawfully carried into another, shall, in consequence of any law or regulation therein, be discharged from such service or labor; but shall be delivered up on claim of the party to whom such slaves belongs, or to whom such service or labor may be due....

Section 3. (3) The Confederate States may acquire new territory; and Congress shall have power to legislate and provide governments for the inhabitants of all territory belonging to the Confederate States, lying without the limits of the several States, and may permit them, at such times, and in such manner as it may be law provide, to form States to be admitted into the Confederacy. In all such territory, the institution of negro slavery, as it now exists in the Confederate States, shall be recognized and protected by Congress and by the territorial government; and the inhabitants of the several Confederate States and Territories shall have the right to take to such territory any slaves lawfully held by them in any of the States or Territories of the Confederate States....

Article V. Section 1. (1) Upon the demand of any three States, legally assembled in their several Conventions, the Congress shall summon a Convention of all the States, to take into consideration such amendments to the Constitution as the said States shall concur in suggesting at the time when the said demand is made; and should any of the proposed amendments to the Constitution be agreed on by the said Convention—voting by States—and the same be ratified by the Legislatures of two-thirds thereof—as the one or the other mode of ratification may be proposed by the general convention—they shall thenceforward form a part of this Constitution. But no State shall, without its consent, be deprived of its equal representation in the Senate....

Article VII. 1. The ratification of the conventions of five States shall be sufficient for the establishment of this Constitution between the States so ratifying the same.

2. When five States shall have ratified this Constitution in the manner before specified, the Congress, under the provisional Constitution, shall prescribe the time for holding the election of president and Vice-President, and for the meeting of the electoral college, and for counting the votes and inaugurating the President. They shall also prescribe the time for holding the first election of members of Congress under this Constitution, and the time for assembling the same. Until the assembling of such Congress, the Congress under the provisional Constitution shall continue to exercise the legislative powers granted them; not extending beyond the time limited by the Constitution of the Provisional Government.

Adopted unanimously by the Congress of the Confederate States of South Carolina, Georgia, Florida, Alabama, Mississippi, Louisiana, and Texas, sitting in convention at the capitol, in the city of Montgomery, Alabama, on the Eleventh day of March, in the year Eighteen Hundred and Sixty-One.

❧ "We must not be enemies"

ABRAHAM LINCOLN'S FIRST INAUGURAL ADDRESS

When Abraham Lincoln took his oath of office, he faced a perilous situation. Not only had seven states seceded, several others were actively considering whether to join them. Lincoln's address represented a cross between a plea to the South to stay in the Union and a lengthy, legal explanation of why he would not recognize the nation's dissolution. Lincoln did not want to initiate military action against the South for fear of pushing other states out of the Union. He sought to find a middle ground.

March 4, 1861

Fellow citizens of the United States, in compliance with a custom as old as the Government itself, I appear before you to address you briefly, and to take in your presence the oath prescribed by the Constitution of the United States to be taken by the President "before he enters on the execution of his office."

Apprehension seems to exist among the people of the southern states that by the accession of a Republican administration of their property and their peace and personal security are to be endangered. There has never been any reasonable cause for such apprehension. Indeed, the most ample evidence to the contrary has all the while existed and been open to their inspection. It is found in nearly all the published speeches of him who now addresses you. I do but quote from one of these speeches when I declare that "I have no purpose, directly or indirectly, to interfere with the institution of slavery in the States where it exists. I believe I have no lawful right to do so, and I have no inclination to do so."

I now reiterate these sentiments; and in doing so, I only press upon the public attention the most conclusive evidence of which the case is susceptible, that the property, peace and security of no section are to be in any wise endangered by the now incoming administration. I add, too, that all the protection which, consistently with the Constitution and the laws, can be given, will be cheerfully given to all the States when lawfully demanded, for whatever cause—as cheerfully to one section as to another.

I take the official oath today with no mental reservations, and with no purpose to construe the Constitution or laws by any hypercritical rules. And, while I do not choose now to specify particular acts of Congress as proper to be enforced, I do suggest that it will be much safer for all, both in officials and private situations, to conform to and abide by all those acts which stand unrepealed, than to violate any of them, trusting to find impunity in having them held to be unconstitutional.

A disruption of the Federal Union, heretofore only menaced, is now formidably attempted.

I hold that, in contemplation of universal law and of the Constitution, the Union of these States is perpetual. Perpetuity is implied, if not expressed, in the fundamental law of all national governments. It is safe to assert that no government proper ever had a provision in its organic law for its own termination. Continue to execute all the express provisions for our national Constitution, and the Union will endure forever—it being impossible to destroy it except by some action not provided for in the instrument itself.

Again, if the United States be not a government proper, but an association of States in the nature of contract merely, can it as a contract be peacefully unmade by less than all the parties who made it? One party to a contract may violate it—break it, so to speak; but does it not require all to lawfully rescind it?

Descending from these general principles, we find the proposition that in legal contemplation the Union is perpetual confirmed by the history of the Union itself. The Union is much older than the Constitution. It was formed, in fact, by the Articles of Association in 1774. It was matured and continued by the Declaration of Independence in 1776. It was further matured, and the faith of all the then thirteen States expressly plighted and engaged that it should be perpetual, by the Articles of Confederation in 1778. And, finally, in 1787 one of the declared objects for ordaining and establishing the Constitution was "to form a more perfect Union."

But if the destruction of the Union by one or by a part only of the States be lawfully possible, the Union is less perfect than before the Constitution, having lost the vital element of perpetuity.

It follows from these views that no State upon its own mere motion can lawfully get out of the Union; that resolves and ordinances to that effect are legally void; and that acts of violence, within any State or States, against the authority of the United States, are insurrectionary or revolutionary, according to circumstances.

I therefore consider that, in view of the Constitution and the laws, the Union is unbroken; and to the extent of my ability I shall take care, as the Constitution itself expressly enjoins upon me, that the laws of the Union be faithfully executed in all the States. Doing this I deem to be only a simple duty on my part; and I shall perform it so far as practicable, unless my rightful masters, the American people, shall withhold the requisite means, or in some authoritative manner direct the contrary. I trust this will not be regarded as a menace, but only as the declared purpose of the Union that it will constitutionally defend and maintain itself.

In doing this there needs to be no bloodshed or violence; and there shall be none, unless it be forced upon the national authority. The power confided to me will be used to hold, occupy, and possess the property and places belonging to the government, and to collect the duties and imposts; but beyond what may be necessary for these objects, there will be no invasion, no using of force against or among the people anywhere. Where hostility to the United States, in any interior locality, shall be so great and universal as to prevent competent resident citizens from holding the Federal offices, there will be no attempt to force obnoxious strangers among the people for that object. While the strict legal right may exist in the government to enforce the exercise of these offices, the attempt to do so would be so irritating, and so nearly impracticable withal, that I deem it better to forego for the time the uses of such offices.

The mails, unless repelled, will continue to be furnished in all parts of the Union. So far as possible, the people everywhere shall have that sense of perfect security which is most favorable to calm thought and reflection. The course here indicated will be followed unless current events and experience shall show a modification or change to be proper, and in every case and exigency my best discretion will be exercised according to circumstances actually existing, and with a view and a hope of a peaceful solution of the national troubles and the restoration of fraternal sympathies and affections.

That there are persons in one section or another who seek to destroy the Union at all events, and are glad of any pretext to do it, I will neither affirm nor deny; but if there be such, I need address no word to them. To those, however, who really love the Union may I not speak?

Before entering upon so grave a matter as the destruction of our national fabric, with all its benefits, its memories, and its hopes, would it not be

wise to ascertain precisely why we do it? Will you hazard so desperate a step while there is any possibility that any portion of the ills you fly from have no real existence? Will you, while the certain ills you fly to are greater than all the real ones you fly from—will you risk the commission of so fearful a mistake?

All profess to be content in the Union if all constitutional rights can be maintained. Is it true, then, that any right, plainly written in the Constitution, has been denied? I think not. Happily the human mind is so constituted that no party can reach to the audacity of doing this. Think, if you can, of a single instance in which a plainly written provision of the Constitution has ever been denied. If by mere force of numbers a majority should deprive a minority of any clearly written constitutional right, it might, in a moral point of view, justify revolution—certainly would if such a right were a vital one. But such is not our case. All the vital rights of minorities and of individuals are so plainly assured to them by affirmations and negations, guaranties, and prohibitions, in the Constitution, that controversies never arise concerning them. But no organic law can ever be framed with a provision specifically applicable to every question which may occur in practical administration. No foresight can anticipate, nor any document of reasonable length contain, express provisions for all possible questions. Shall fugitives from labor be surrendered by national or by State authority? The Constitution does not expressly say. May Congress prohibit slavery in the Territories? The Constitution does not expressly say. Must Congress protect slavery in the territories? The Constitution does not expressly say.

From questions of this class spring all our constitutional controversies, and we divide upon them into majorities and minorities. If the minority will not acquiesce, the majority must, or the government must cease. There is no other alternative; for continuing the government is acquiescence on one side or the other.

If a minority in such case will secede rather than acquiesce, they make a precedent which in turn will divide and ruin them; for a minority of their own will secede from them whenever a majority refuses to be controlled by such minority. For instance, why may not any portion of a new confederacy a year or two hence arbitrarily secede from it? All who cherish disunion sentiments are now being educated to the exact temper of doing this.

Is there such a perfect identity of interest among the States to compose a new Union as to produce harmony only, and prevent renewed secession?

Plainly, the central idea of secession is the essence of anarchy. A majority held in restraint by the constitutional checks and limitations, and always changing easily with deliberate changes of popular opinions and sentiments, is the only true sovereign of a free people. Whoever rejects it does, of necessity, fly to anarchy or to despotism. Unanimity is impossible; the rule of a minority, as a permanent arrangement, is wholly inadmissible; so that, rejecting the majority principle, anarchy or despotism in some form is all that is left.

I do not forget the position assumed by some, that constitutional questions are to be decided by the Supreme Court, nor do I deny that such decisions must be binding, in any case, upon the parties to a suit, as to the object of that suit, while they are also entitled to a very high respect and consideration in all parallel cases by all other department of the government. And, while it is obviously possible that such decision may be erroneous in any given case, still the evil effect following it, being limited to that particular case, with the chance that it may be overruled and never become a precedent for other cases, can better be borne than could the evils of a different practice. At the same time, the candid citizen must confess that if the policy of the government, upon vital questions affecting the whole people, is to be irrevocably fixed by decisions of the Supreme Court, the instant they are made, in ordinary litigation between parties in personal actions, the people will have ceased to be their own rulers, having to that extent practically resigned the government into the hands of that eminent tribunal. Nor is there in this view any assault upon the court or the judges. It is a duty from which they may not shrink to decide cases properly brought before them, and it is no fault of theirs if others seek to turn their decisions to political purposes.

One section of our country believes slavery is right, and ought to be extended, while the other believes it is wrong, and ought not to be extended. This is the only substantial dispute. The fugitive slave clause of the Constitution and the law for the suppression of the foreign slave trade are each as well enforced, perhaps as any law can ever be in a community where the moral sense of the people imperfectly supports the law itself. The great body of the people abide by the dry legal obligation in both cases, and a few break over in each. This, I think, cannot be perfectly cured; and it would be worse in both cases after the separation of the sections than before. The foreign slave trade, now imperfectly suppressed, would be ultimately revived, without restriction, in one section, while fugitive slaves, now only partially surrendered, would not be surrendered at all by the other.

Physically speaking, we cannot separate. We cannot remove our respective sections from each other, nor build an impassable wall between them. A husband and wife may be divorced and go out of the presence and beyond the reach of each other; but the different parts of our country cannot do this. They cannot but remain face to face, and intercourse, either amicable or hostile, must continue between them. Is it possible, then, to make that intercourse more advantageous or more satisfactory after separation than before? Can aliens make treaties easier than friends can make laws? Can treaties be more faithfully enforced between aliens than laws can among friends? Suppose you go to war, you cannot fight always and when, after much loss on both sides, and no gain on either, you cease fighting, the identical old questions as to terms of intercourse are again upon you.

This country, with its institutions belongs to the people who inhabit it. Whenever they shall grow weary of the existing government, they can exercise their constitutional right to dismember or overthrow it. I cannot be ignorant of the fact that many worthy and patriotic citizens are desirous of having the national Constitution amended. While I make no recommendation of amendments, I fully recognize the rightful authority of the people over the whole subject, to be exercised in either of the modes prescribed in the instrument itself, and I should, under existing circumstances, favor rather than oppose a fair opportunity being afforded the people to act upon it. I will venture to add that to me the convention mode seems preferable, in that it allows amendments to originate with the people themselves, instead of only permitting them to take or reject propositions originated by others not especially chosen for the purpose, and which might not be precisely such as they would wish to either accept or refuse. I understand a proposed amendment to the Constitution—which amendment, however, I have not seen—has passed Congress, to the effect that the Federal Government shall never interfere with the domestic institutions of the States, including that of persons held to service. To avoid misconstruction of what I have said, I depart from my purpose not to speak of particular amendments so far as to say that, holding such a provision to now be implied constitutional law, I have no objection to its being made express and irrevocable.

Why should there not be a patient confidence in the ultimate justice of the people? Is there any better or equal hope in the world? In our present differences is either party without faith of being in the right? If the Almighty Ruler of nations, with his eternal truth and justice, be on your side of the North, or on yours of the South, that truth and that justice will surely prevail by the judgment of this great tribunal of the American people.

By the frame of the government under which we live, this same people have wisely given their public servants but little power for mischief; and have, with equal wisdom, provided for the return of that little to their own hands at very short intervals. While the people retain their virtue and vigilance, no administration, by any extreme of wickedness or folly, can very seriously injure the government in the short space of four years.

My countrymen, one and all, think calmly and well upon this whole subject. Nothing valuable can be lost by taking time. If there be an object to hurry any of you in hot haste to a step which you would never take deliberately, that object will be frustrated by it. Such of you as are now dissatisfied still have the old Constitution unimpaired, and, on the sensitive point, the laws of your own framing under it; while the new administration will have no immediate power, if it would, to change either. If it were admitted that you who are dissatisfied hold the right side in the dispute, there still is no single good reason for precipitate action. Intelligence, patriotism, Christianity, and a firm reliance on Him who has never yet forsaken this favored land, are still competent to adjust in the best way all our present difficult[y]

In your [ha]y dissatisfied fellow-countrymen, and not [in m]ine, is the momentous issue of civil war. The government will not assail you. You can have no conflict without being yourselves the aggressors. You have no oath registered in heaven to destroy the government, while I shall have the most solemn one to "preserve, protect, and defend" it.

I am loath to close. We are not enemies, but friends. We must not be enemies. Though passion may have strained, it must not break, our bonds of affection. The mystic chords of memory, stretching from every battlefield and patriot grave to every living heart and hearthstone all over this broad land, will yet swell the chorus of the Union when again touched, as surely they will be, by the better angels of our nature.

🍂 The Cornerstone Speech

ALEXANDER STEPHENS

Despite Lincoln's plea, the South pushed forward with its decision to form a new government and constitution. Alexander Stephens was one of the more articulate and influential southern leaders prior to secession. The Georgia politician actually opposed secession after Lincoln's election, but once the decision was made, joined his state. When the Montgomery Convention formed the new Confederate government, it named Stephens as vice president. Although Stephens proved to be a less-than-successful vice president, his views reflected the prevailing sentiment behind the formation of the Confederate States of America. The dispute over slavery caused the "revolution," Stephens said in this Savannah, Georgia speech, and the supremacy of whites over blacks was the fundamental cornerstone of the new nation.

March 21, 1861

The new Constitution has put at rest forever all the agitating questions relating to our peculiar institutions—African slavery as it exists among us—the proper status of the negro in our form of civilization. This was the immediate cause of the late rupture and present revolution. Jefferson, in his forecast, had anticipated this, as the "rock upon which the old Union would split." He was right. What was the conjecture with him, is now realized fact. But whether he fully comprehended the great truth upon which that rock stood and stands, may be doubted. The prevailing ideas entertained by him and most of the leading statesmen at the time of the formation of the old Constitution were, that the enslavement of the African was in violation of the laws of nature; that it was wrong in principle, socially, morally and politically. It was an evil they knew not well how to deal with; but the general opinion of the men of that day was that, somehow or other, in the order of Providence, the institution would be evanescent and pass away. This idea, though not incorporated in the Constitution, was the prevailing idea at the time. The Constitution, it is true, secured every essential guarantee to the institution while it should last, and hence no argument can be justly used against the constitutional guarantees thus secured, because of the common sentiment of the day. Those ideas, however, were fundamentally wrong. They vested upon the assumption of the equality of races. This was an error. It was a sandy foundation, and the idea of a Government built upon it—when the "storm came and the wind blew, it fell."

Our new Government is founded upon exactly the opposite ideas; its foundations are laid, its cornerstone rests, upon the great truth that the negro is not equal to the white man; that slavery, subordination to the superior race, is his natural and moral condition. This, our new Government, is the first, in the history of the world, based upon this great physical, philosophical, and moral truth.

As I have stated, the truth of this principle may be slow in development, as all truths are, and ever have been, in the various branches of science. It was so with the principles announced by Galileo—it was so with Adam Smith and the principles of political economy. It was so with Harvey, and his theory of the circulation of the blood. It is stated that not a single one of the medical profession, living at the time of the announcement of the truths made by him, admitted them. Now, they are universally acknowledged. May we not therefore look with confidence to the ultimate universal acknowledgement of the truths upon which our system rests? It is the first government ever instituted upon principles in strict conformity to nature, and the ordination of Providence, in furnishing the materials of human society. Many Governments have been founded upon the principles of certain classes; but the classes thus enslaved, were of the same race, and in violation of the laws of nature. Our system commits no such violation of nature's laws. The negro by nature, or by the curse against Canaan, is fitted for that condition which he occupies in our system. The architect, in the construction of buildings, lays the foundation with proper material—the granite—then comes the brick or the marble. The substratum of our society is made of the material fitted by nature for it, and by experience we know that it is the best, not only for the superior but for the inferior race, that it should be so. It is, indeed, in conformity with the Creator. It is not for us to inquire into the wisdom of His ordinances or to question them. For His own purposes He has made one race to differ from another, as He has made "one star to differ from another in glory."

The great objects of humanity are best attained, when conformed to his laws and degrees, in the formation of Governments as well as in all things else. Our Confederacy is founded upon principles in strict conformity with these laws. The stone which was rejected by the first builders "is become the chief stone of the corner" in our new edifice.

❧ "The Confederate States can no longer delay"

FORT SUMTER BOMBING

One month after Lincoln's inauguration, all eyes turned to Fort Sumter in Charleston Harbor. A federal garrison commanded by Major Robert Anderson was stationed in the island-fort awaiting supplies. Although Lincoln said he would not force federal policies on the South, he wanted to maintain a presence and he sent a ship to provision Fort Sumter. The Confederacy, however, wanted to expel the federal soldiers from the new nation. The government asked General Beauregard, commander of the Confederate forces, to seek the evacuation of Fort Sumter. Anderson refused. Early on the morning of April 12, Confederate forces bombarded the garrison. Thirty-four hours later, Anderson surrendered. Three of the exchanges in the correspondence follow.

Headquarters, Provisional Army, C.S.A.
Charleston, S.C., April 11, 1861
Sir:

The Government of the Confederate States has hitherto forborne from any hostile demonstration against Fort Sumter, in the hope that the Government of the United States, with a view to the amicable adjustment of all questions between the two Governments, and to avert the calamities of war, would voluntarily evacuate it. There was reason at one time to believe that such would be the course pursued by the Government of the United States; and under that impression my government has refrained from making any demand for the surrender of the fort.

But the Confederate States can no longer delay assuming actual possession of a fortification commanding the entrance of one of their harbors, and necessary to its defence and security.

I am ordered by the Government of the Confederate States to demand the evacuation of Fort Sumter. My Aids, Colonel Chesnut and Captain Lee, are authorized to make such demand of you. All proper facilities will be afforded for the removal of yourself and command, together with company, arms, and property, and all private property, to any post in the United States which you may elect. The flag which you have upheld so long and with so much fortitude, under the most trying circumstances, may be saluted by you on taking it down.

Colonel Chesnut and Captain Lee will, for a reasonable time, await your answer.

I am sir, very respectfully,
Your obedient servant,
G.T. Beauregard
Brigadier-General Commanding.

Headquarters, Fort Sumter, S.C.
April 11th, 1861
General:

I have the honor to acknowledge the receipt of your communication demanding the evacuation of this fort; and to say in reply thereto that it is a demand with which I regret that my sense of honor and of my obligations to my Government prevent my compliance.

Thanking you for the fair, manly, and courteous terms proposed, and for the high compliment paid me,

I am, General, very respectfully,
Your obedient servant,
Robert Anderson,
Major U.S. Army, Commanding

Fort Sumter, S.C.
April 12, 1861, 3:20 a.m.
Sir:

By authority of Brigadier-General Beauregard, commanding the Provisional Forces of the Confederate States, we have the honor to notify you that he will open the fire of his batteries on Fort Sumter in one hour from this time.

We have the honor to be, very respectfully,
Your obedient servants,

James Chesnut, jr.
Aide-de-Camp.
Stephen D. Lee,
Captain S.C. Army and Aide-de-Camp.

"I have endeavored to do what I thought right"

ROBERT E. LEE

Lincoln responded to the bombing by declaring the South in a state of rebellion and calling for volunteers to serve in the military. Refusing to accede in the suppression of their sister states, North Carolina, Virginia, Tennessee and Arkansas joined the Confederacy. As states voted to secede from or stay with the United States, thousands of young men were faced with the dilemma of what to do. The stakes for Robert E. Lee were enormous—both for him personally and the nation. An enormously successful soldier in the Mexican War, he was a leading candidate to take command of the Union Army. But Lee hailed from Virginia. As his letter to his sister, Anne Marshall, shows, Lee's loyalties were deeply divided between his devotion to his state and to his country. The second letter is to his commander, General Winfield Scott, who had recommended Lee to take over command of the Union forces.

Arlington, Virgina, April 20, 1861
My dear Sister: I am grieved at my inability to see you. I have been waiting for a 'more convenient season,' which has brought to many before me deep and lasting regret. Now we are in a state of war which will yield to nothing. The whole South is in a state of revolution, into which Virginia, after a long struggle, has been drawn; and though I recognize no necessity for this state of things, and would have foreborne and pleaded to the end for redress of grievances, real or supposed, yet in my own person I had to meet the question whether I should take part against my native State.

With all my devotion to the Union and the feeling of loyalty and duty of an American citizen, I have not been able to make up by mind to raise my hand against my relatives, my children, my home. I have therefore resigned my commission in the Army, and save in defense of my native State, with the sincere hope that my poor services may never be needed, I hope I may never be called on to draw my sword. I know you will blame me; but you must think as kindly of me as you can, and believe that I have endeavoured to do what I thought right.

To show you the feeling and struggle it has cost me, I send you a copy of my letter of resignation. I have no time for more. May God guard and protect you and yours, and shower upon you everlasting blessings, is the prayer of your devoted brother.

R. E. Lee

Arlington, Virginia, April 20, 1861

General: Since my interview with you on the 18th inst. I have felt that I ought no longer to retain my commission in the Army. I therefore tender my resignation, which I request you will recommend for acceptance. It would have been presented at once but for the struggle it has cost me to separate myself from a service to which I have devoted the best years of my life, and all the ability I possessed.

During the whole of that time—more than a quarter of a century—I have experienced nothing but kindness from my superiors and most cordial friendship from my comrades. To no one, General, have I been as much indebted as to yourself for uniform kindness and consideration, and it has always been my ardent desire to merit your approbation. I shall carry to the grave the most grateful recollections of your kind consideration, and your name and fame shall always be dear to me.

Save in the defense of my native State, I never desire again to draw my sword.

Be pleased to accept my most earnest wishes for the continuance of your happiness and prosperity, and believe, most truly yours,

R. E. Lee

❧ "I will not dwell upon the awful scene"

PHILIP POWERS

With war declared, armies for both the North and South prepared for a quick victory. But when the first major conflict was fought at the First Battle of Bull Run, the euphoria evaporated. Both sides would have to brace for a long and decidedly unromantic war. This letter from Philip Powers, a sergeant major with the 1st Virginia Cavalry, reflected the dismay of battle, even for the victors.

Camp at Fairfax Courthouse
July 23, 1861
My Dearest Wife:

Several Clark men, among them Knelles, were in our camp for a short time this evening but I was so busy I had not time even to drop you a line, and fearing lest the same thing may occur again, I write tonight, though excessively fatigued.

Yesterday we had a drenching rain all day and most of last night, and being without tents we could not escape the rain and mud. We broke our camp however about midnight and marched to this place accompanied by two regiments of infantry and one battery of artillery. I was glad to leave, for as I wrote you we were near by a hospital of the enemy where [there were] over three hundred of their wounded, dead and dying. Many of them necessarily left out in all the inclemency of weathers to die. To pass by it was enough to soften and sicken the hardest heart. I will not dwell upon the awful scene.

The battle was nothing to this after piece. The excitement of the contest, the cheering of the soldiers, the triumph of victory and the whole field of many of its terrors—nothing could lessen the horrors of the field by moonlight. Enough—I cannot, I will not describe it. May God, in his infinite mercy, avert a second such calamity. Our march after we got beyond the scenes of the fight was rather cheering than otherwise. For twelve miles the road was literally strewn with every description of baggage, wagons, ambulances, barrels of sugar, crackers, ground coffee and thousands of axes, spades, shovels, picks, arms by the thousands, clothing of every description, cooking utensils—in fact, everything—and all left behind to expedite their flight, which was never stopped until they reached Washington.

Our troops have been busily engaged in appropriating everything they might possibly need, from a pin cushion to the finest army tent. In this place we found in several houses clothing enough to fill every room in our house. Their army was splendidly equipped with every possible convenience and comfort. But I cannot account for their utter confusion and panic. Their own papers give our regiment the credit for turning the tide of victory on our side. The papers if you can see them will give you all the particulars.

I do not know what our next move will be but suppose it will be upon Alexandria. All I desire is to drive them from our soil and secure peace—I would not shed another drop.

I cannot write now. Farewell! I pray that my

wife and little children may be protected and comforted at all times.

Ever Yours,
P. H. Powers

❧ *"This imbecile,*
pro-slavery government
does try me so"

LYDIA MARIA CHILD

Lydia Maria Child was one of America's best-selling authors
and a rabid abolitionist. The author of *Hobomok* (1824), *The
Frugal Housewife* (1829) and *Letters from New York* (1843-45),
Child later turned her pen to push for the abolition of slavery.
Her position was so harsh that she outraged her readers and
was banned from certain circles in her native New England.
Nonetheless, she would not relent and represented an extreme
Northern position that pressed upon Lincoln to free slaves. In
1865, she published *The Freedmen's Book,* a series of biogra-
phies of black historical figures as well as writings by leading
abolitionists and blacks. This excerpt comes from a letter written to a friend, Lucy Searle.

October 11, 1861

I did not mean to talk so much about public affairs;
but this imbecile, pro-slavery government does try
me so, that it seems as if I must shoot somebody.
Willis is out again with a florid description of Mrs.
Lincoln's autumn bonnet, called "The Princess."
"Rose-colored velvet, with guipine medallions,
trimmed with black thread lace, put on full, and
this again trimmed on the edge with a deeper fringe
of minute black marabout and ostrich feathers. &x
&c…"

So this is what the people are taxed for! To
deck out this vulgar doll with foreign flippery! And
oppressed millions must groan on, lest her "noble
native State" should take offence, if Government
made use of the beneficent power God has so
miraculously placed in its hands. To see these
things, and have no power to change them, to see
the glorious opportunity so near, yet slipping away,
leaving the nation to sink deeper and deeper into
the abyss of degradation—this is really the torment
of Tantalus.

❧ *"The tide is against us"*

JEFFERSON DAVIS

Jefferson Davis was appointed the President of the Confederacy
on February 18, 1861, during the constitutional convention in
Alabama. One year later, after a permanent constitution had
been formed, Davis was officially elected by a popular vote. His
second inaugural address on February 22, 1862, sought a devoted call to arms that would bring on a Southern victory, despite
some early setbacks in the year-old war.

Fellow Citizens: On this the birthday of the man
most identified with the establishment of American
independence, and beneath the monument erected
to commemorate his heroic virtues and those of his
compatriots, we have assembled to usher into existence the permanent government of the
Confederate States. Through this instrumentality,
under the favor of Divine Providence, we hope to
perpetuate the principles of our Revolutionary
fathers. The day, the memory, and the purpose
seem fitly associated.

It is with mingled feelings of humility and
pride that I appear to take, in the presence of the
people and before high heaven, the oath prescribed
as a qualification for the exalted station to which
the unanimous voice of the people has called me.
Deeply sensible of all that is implied by this manifestation of the people's confidence, I am yet more
profoundly impressed by the vast responsibility of
the office and humbly feel my own unworthiness.

When a long course of class legislation,
directed not to the general warfare but to the
aggrandizement of the Northern section of the
Union, culminated in a warfare on the domestic
institutions of the Southern states—when the
dogmas of a sectional party, substitutes for the
provisions of the constitutional compact, threatened to destroy the sovereign rights of the
states—six of those states, withdrawing from the
Union, confederated together to exercise the right
and perform the duty of instituting a government
which would better secure the liberties for the
preservation of which that Union was established.

Whatever of hope some may have entertained
that a returning sense of justice would remove the
danger with which our rights were threatened, and
render it possible to preserve the Union of the
Constitution, must have been dispelled by the
malignity and barbarity of the Northern states in
the prosecution of the existing war. The confidence

of the most hopeful among us must have been destroyed by the disregard they have recently exhibited for all the time-honored bulwarks of civil and religious liberty.

Bastilles filled with prisoners, arrested without civil processor indictment duly found; the writ of habeas corpus suspended by executive mandate; a state legislature controlled by the imprisonment of members whose avowed principles suggested to the federal executive that there might be another added to the list of seceded states; elections held under threats of a military power; civil officers, peaceful citizens, and gentlewomen incarcerated for opinion's sake—proclaimed the incapacity of our late associates to administer a government as free, liberal, and humane as that established for our common use.

For proof of the sincerity of our purpose to maintain our ancient institutions, we may point to the Constitution of the Confederacy and the laws enacted under it, as well as to the fact that through all the necessities of an unequal struggle there has been no act on our part to impair personal liberty or the freedom of speech, of thought, or of the press. The courts have been open, the judicial functions fully executed, and every right of the peaceful citizen maintained as securely as if a war of invasion had not disturbed the land.

The people of the states now confederates became convinced the government of the United States had fallen into the hands of a sectional majority, who would pervert that most sacred of all trusts to the destruction of the rights which it was pledged to protect. They believed that to remain longer in the Union would subject them to a continuance of a disparaging discrimination, submission to which would be inconsistent with their welfare and intolerable to a proud people. They therefore determined to sever its bonds and establish a new confederacy for themselves.

The first year in our history has been the most eventful in the annals of this continent. A new government has been established, and its machinery put in operation over an area exceeding seven hundred thousand square miles. The great principles upon which we have been willing to hazard everything that is dear to man have made conquests for us which could never have been achieved by the sword. Our Confederacy has grown from six to thirteen states; and Maryland, already united to

us by hallowed memories and material interests, will, I believe, when able to speak with unstifled voice, connect her destiny with the South.

Our people have rallied with unexampled unanimity to the support of the great principles of constitutional government, with firm resolve to perpetuate by arms the right which they could not peacefully secure. A million of men, it is estimated, are now standing in hostile array and waging war along a frontier of thousands of miles. Battles have been fought, sieges have been conducted, and although the contest is not ended, and the tide for the moment is against us, the final result in our favor is not doubtful.

This great strife has awakened in the people the highest emotions and qualities of the human soul. It is cultivating feelings of patriotism, virtue, and courage. Instances of self-sacrifice contending are rife throughout the land. Never has a people evinced a more determined spirit than that now animating men, women, and children in every part of our country. Upon the first call, the men fly to arms; and wives and mothers send their husbands and sons to battle without a murmur of regret.

It is a satisfaction that we have maintained the war by our unaided exertions. We have neither asked nor received assistance from any quarter. Yet the interest involved is not wholly our own. The world at large is concerned in opening our markets to its commerce. When the independence of the Confederate States is recognized by the nations of the earth, and we are free to follow our interests and inclinations by cultivating foreign trade, the Southern states will offer to manufacturing nations the most favorable markets which ever invited their commerce. Cotton, sugar, tobacco, provisions, timber, and naval stores will furnish attractive exchanges.

The tyranny of an unbridled majority, the most odious and least responsible form of despotism, has denied us both the rights and the remedy. Therefore we are in arms to renew such sacrifices as our fathers made to the holy cause of constitutional liberty. At the darkest hour of our struggle the provisional gives place to the permanent government. After a series of successes and victories, which covered our arms with glory, we have recently met with serious disasters. But in the heart of a people resolved to be free, these disasters tend but to stimulate to increased resistance.

To show ourselves worthy of the inheritance

bequeathed to us by the patriots of the Revolution, we must emulate that heroic devotion which made reverse to them but the crucible in which their patriotism was refined.

With confidence in the wisdom and virtue of those who will share with me the responsibility and aid me in the conduct of public affairs; securely relying on the patriotism and courage of the people, of which the present war has furnished so many examples, I deeply feel the weight of the responsibilities I now, with unaffected diffidence, am about to assume; and fully realizing the inequality of human power to guide and to sustain, my hope is reverently fixed on Him whose favor is ever vouchsafed to the cause which is just. With humble gratitude and adoration, acknowledge the Providence which has so visibly protected God! I trustingly commit myself, and prayerfully invoke Thy blessing on my country and its cause.

❧ *"The South only asked to be let alone"*

CONFEDERATE TEXTBOOK

Despite the demands of war, the South produced new textbooks for their children. This excerpt from *Geographical Reader of the Dixie Children* written in 1863 offers a Confederate version of the causes of the Civil War. Other texts incorporated the themes of the war. Math texts posed questions such as "If one Southerner can whip three Yankees, how many Southerners does it take to whip fifteen Yankees?"

The United States

1. This was once the most prosperous country in the world. Nearly a hundred years ago it belonged to England, but the English made such hard laws that the people said they would not obey them. After a long, bloody war of seven years, they gained their independence; and for many years were prosperous and happy.

2. In the mean time both English and American ships went to Africa and brought away many of those poor heathen negroes, and sold them for slaves. Some people said it was wrong and asked the King of England to stop it. He replied that "he knew it was wrong; but that slave trade brought much money into his treasury, and it should continue." But both countries afterwards did pass laws

to stop this trade. In a few years, the Northern States finding their climate too cold for the negro to be profitable, sold them to the people living farther South. Then the Northern States passed laws to forbid any person owning slaves in their borders.

3. Then the northern people began to preach, to lecture, and to write about the sin of slavery. The money for which they sold their slaves, was not partly spent trying to persuade Southern States to sent their slaves back to Africa. And when the territories were settled they were not willing for any of them to become slaveholding. This would soon have made the North much stronger than the South; and many of the men said they would vote for a law to free all the negroes in the country. The Southern men tried to show them how unfair this would be, but they still kept on.

4. In the year 1860 the Abolitionists become strong enough to elect one of their own men for president. Abraham Lincoln was a weak man, and the South believed he would deprive them of their rights. So the Southern States seceded, and elected Jefferson Davis for their President. This so enraged President Lincoln that he declared war, and has exhausted nearly all the strength of the nation, in vain attempt to whip the South back into the Union. Thousands of lives have been lost, and the earth has been drenched with blood; but still Abraham is unable to conquer the "Rebels" as he calls the south. The South only asked to be let alone, and divide the public property equally. It would have been wise in the North to have said to her Southern sisters, "If you are not content to dwell with us longer, depart in peace. We will divide the inheritance with you, and may you be a great nation."

5. This country possesses many ships, has fine cities and towns, many railroads, steamboats, canals, manufacturers, etc. the people are ingenious, and enterprising, and are noted for their tact in "driving a bargain." They are refined, and intelligent on all subjects but that of negro slavery, on this they are mad.

6. The large lakes, the long rivers, the tall mountains, with the beautiful farms and pretty towns and villages, make this a very interesting country to travelers.

ꙮ Civil War legislation

CONGRESS

When southern congressmen and senators left the U.S. Congress, the main obstacle to the Republican agenda of economic growth evaporated. Several key legislative acts were passed that would set the stage for the country's industrial explosion and western expansion for the rest of the 19th century. The Homestead Act, the Pacific Railway Act and the Morrill Act would all pave the way for one of the most dynamic eras of growth in the nation's history.

Homestead Act, May 20, 1862

Be it enacted, That any person who is the head of a family, or who has arrived at the age of twenty-one years, and is a citizen of the United States, or who shall have filed his intention to become such, as required by the naturalization laws of the United States, and who has never borne arms against the United States Government or given aid and comfort to its enemies, shall, from and after the first of January, 1863, be entitled to enter one quarter-section or a less quantity of unappropriated public lands, upon which said person may have filed a pre-emption claim, or which may, at the time the application is made, be subject to pre-emption at one dollar and twenty-five cents, or less, per acre; or eighty acres or less of such unappropriated lands, at two dollars and fifty cents per acre, to be located in a body, in conformity to the legal subdivisions of the public lands, and after the same shall have been surveyed: Provided, That any person owning or residing on land may, under the provisions of this act, enter other land lying contiguous to his or her said land, which shall not, with the land so already owned and occupied exceed in the aggregate one hundred and sixty acres.

Sec. 2. That the person applying for the benefit of this act shall, upon application to the register of the land office in which he or she is about to make such entry, make affidavit before the said register or receiver that he or she is the head of a family, or is twenty-one or more years of age, or shall have performed service in the Army or Navy of the United States, and that he has never borne arms against the Government of the United States or given aid and comfort to its enemies, and that such application is made for his or her exclusive use and benefit, and that said entry is made for the purpose of actual settlement and cultivation, and not,

either directly or indirectly, for the use or benefit of any other person or persons whomsoever, and upon filing the said affidavit with the register or receiver, and on payment of ten dollars, he or she shall thereupon be permitted to enter the quantity of land specified: Provided, however, that no certificate shall be given or patent issued therefor until the expiration of five years from the date of such entry—or if he be dead, his widow, or in case of her death, his heirs or devisee; or in case of a widow making such entry, her heirs or devisee, in case of her death—shall prove by two credible witnesses that he, she, or they have resided upon or cultivated the same for the term of five years immediately succeeding the time of filing the affidavit aforesaid, and shall make affidavit that no part of said land has been alienated, and that he has borne true allegiance to the Government of the United States; then in such cases he, she, or they, if at that time a citizen of the United States, shall be entitled to a patent, as in other cases provided for by law: And provided, further, That in case of the death of both father and mother, leaving an infant child or children under twenty-one years of age, the right and fee shall inure to the benefit of said infant child or children; and the executor, administrator, or guardian may, at any time within two years after the death of the surviving parent, and in accordance with the laws of the State in which such children for the time being have their domicile, sell said land for the benefit of said infants, but for no other purpose; and the purchaser shall acquire the absolute title by the purchase, and be entitled to a patent from the United States, on payment of the office fees and sum of money herein specified.

ꙮ *"Aid in the construction of a Railroad and Telegraph line...to the Pacific Ocean"*

PACIFIC RAILWAY ACT, JULY 1, 1862

An act to aid in the Construction of a Railroad and Telegraph Line from the Missouri River to the Pacific Ocean

Be it enacted, That Walter S. Burgess together with five commissioners to be appointed by the Secretary of the Interior…and hereby created and erected into body corporate by the name of "The Union Pacific Railroad Company"…; and said corporation is hereby authorized and empowered to lay out, locate, construct, furnish, maintain and enjoy a continuous railroad and telegraph…from a point on the one hundredth meridian of longitude west from Greenwich, between the south margin of the wall of the Republican River and the north margin of the valley of the Platte River, to the western boundary of Nevada Territory, upon the route and terms hereinafter provided….

Sec. 2. That the right of way through the public lands be granted to said company for the construction of said railroad and telegraph line; and the right is hereby given to said company to take from the public lands adjacent to the line of said road, earth, stone, timber, and other materials for the construction thereof; said right of way is granted to said railroad to the extent of two hundred feet in width on each side of said railroad when it may pass over the public lands, including all necessary grounds for stations, buildings, workshops, and depots, machine shops, switches, side tracks, turn tables, and water stations. The United States shall extinguish as rapidly as may be the Indian titles to all lands falling under the operation of this act….

Sec. 3. That there be granted to the said company, for the purpose of aiding in the construction of said railroad and telegraph line, and to secure the safe and speedy transportation of mails, troops, munitions of war and public stores thereon, every alternative section of public land, designated by odd numbers, to the amount of five alternate sections per mile on each side of said railroad, on the line thereof, and within the limits of ten miles on each side of said road…Provided that all mineral lands shall be excepted from the operation of this act; but where the same shall contain timber, the timber thereon is granted to said company….

Sec. 5. That for the purposes herein mentioned the Secretary of Treasury shall…in accordance with the provisions of this act, issue to said company bonds of the United States of one thousand dollars each, payable in thirty years after date, paying six per centum per annum interest…to the amount of sixteen of said bonds per mile for each section of forty miles; and to secure the repayment to the United States…of the amount of said bonds…the issue of said bonds…shall ipso facto constitute a first mortgage on the whole line of the railroad and telegraph….

Sec. 9. That the Leavenworth, Pawnee and Western Railroad Company of Kansas are hereby authorized to construct a railroad and telegraph line…upon the same terms and conditions in all respects as are provied [for the construction of the Union Pacific Railroad]…. The Central Pacific Railroad Company of California are hereby authorized to construct a railroad and telegraph line from the Pacific coast to the eastern boundaries of California, upon the same terms and conditions in all respects [as provided for the Union Pacific Railroad].

Sec. 10.…The Central Pacific Railroad Company of California after completing its road across said State, is authorized to continue the construction of said railroad and telegraph through the Territories of the United States to the Missouri River upon the terms and conditions provided in this act in relation to the Union Pacific Railroad Company, until said roads shall meet and connect….

Sec. 11. That for three hundred miles of said road most mountainous and difficult of construction, to wit: one hundred and fifty miles westerly from the eastern base of the Rocky Mountains, and one hundreds and fifty miles eastwardly from the western base of the Sierra Nevada mountains…the bonds to be issued to aid in the construction thereof shall be treble the number per mile hereinbefore provided; and between the sections last named of one hundred and fifty miles each, the bonds to be issued to aid in the construction thereof shall be double the number per mile first mentioned.

"Provide colleges for the benefit of agriculture and the mechanic arts"

MORRILL ACT, JULY 2, 1862

An Act donating Public Lands to the several States and Territories which may provide Colleges for the Benefit of Agriculture and the Mechanic Arts.

Be it enacted by the Senate and House of

Representatives of the United States of America in Congress assembled, That there be granted to the several States, for the purposed hereinafter mentioned, an amount of public land, to be apportioned to each State a quantity equal to thirty thousand acres for each senator and representative in Congress to which the States are respectively entitled by the apportionment under the census of 1860; Provided, That no mineral lands shall be selected or purchased under the provisions of this act.

Sec. 2. And be it further enacted, That the land aforesaid, after being surveyed, shall be apportioned to the several States in sections or subdivisions of sections, not less than one quarter of a section; and whenever there are public lands in a State subject to sale at private entry at one dollar and twenty-five cents per acre, the quantity to which said State shall be entitled shall be selected from such lands within the limits of such State, and the Secretary of the Interior is hereby directed to issue to each of the States in which there is not the quantity of public lands subject to sale at private entry at one dollar and twenty-five cents per acre; to which said State may be entitled under the provisions of this act, land scrip to the amount in acres for the deficiency of its distributive share: said scrip to be sold by said States and the proceeds thereof applied to the uses and purposed prescribed in this act, and for other use or purpose whatsoever....

Sec. 4. And be it further enacted, That all moneys derived from the sale of the lands aforesaid by the States to which the lands are apportioned, and from the sale of land scrip hereinbefore provided for, shall be invested in stocks of the United States, or of the States, or some other safe stocks, yielding not less than five per centum upon the par value of said stocks; and that the moneys so invested shall constitute a perpetual fund, the capital of which shall remain forever undiminished, (except so far as may be provided in section fifth of this act,) and the interest of which shall be inviolably appropriated, by each State which may take and claim the benefit of this act, to the endowment, support, and maintenance of at least one college where the leading object shall be, without excluding other scientific and classical studies, and including military tactics, to teach such branches of learning as are related to agriculture and mechanic arts, in such manner as the legislatures of the State may respectively prescribe,

in order to promote the liberal and practical education of the industrial classes in the several pursuits and professions in life.

Sec. 5. No State while in a condition of rebellion or insurrection against the government of the United States shall be entitled to the benefit of this Act.

❧ "If we are regarded as an evil here"

THE REVEREND HENRY M. TURNER

In April 1862, Lincoln signed a new law freeing slaves in Washington, D. C. The law designated $100,000 "to aid in the colonization and settlement" of freed African Americans to "Hayti, Liberia, or any such country beyond the limits of the United States." No clear plan had emerged over what to do with emancipated slaves. Lincoln and the vast majority of whites did not view African Americans as equals and were at a loss over what role freed slaves would play in society.

Many African Americans were keenly aware of this problem. Several schemes emerged to create new colonies abroad. Hundreds emigrated to Haiti after the war broke out. In April 1862, forty of the leading African American citizens in Washington D.C. wrote the following petition to Congress seeking financial assistance to colonize land in Central America.

To the Honorable Senate and House of Representatives of the United States of America, in Congress assembled:

The undersigned, for themselves, their relatives, and friends, whom they represent; desire, by this memorial, most respectfully to show to the Congress and people of this great country—of which, too, they are natives, but humbly born—that they appreciate, to the fullest extent, the humane actions which are now inaugurated to give freedom to their so long oppressed colored race; but they believe that this freedom will result in injuriously, unless there shall be opened to the colored people a region, to which they may immigrate—a country which is suited to their organization, and in which they may seek and secure, by their own industry, that mental and physical development which will allow them an honorable position in the families of God's great world.

That there is ignorance in the mass of the colored race, is not to be denied: this is caused by the peculiar condition in which they have been raised—without the advantages of general education so wisely and freely accorded to the white citizens. But there are those amongst them who have secured the blessings of knowledge, and who are capable of informing their brethren of what is for their ultimate good, as the leaders of the Pilgrim Fathers informed those who with them to plant civil and religious liberty upon this continent.

To these we are indebted for the knowledge that Liberia is too distant from the land of our birth, and that however kindly and wisely the original plans of colonization may have been laid for that country, neither those plans, nor that region, are suited to our present condition, and that it will be impossible for us ever to move there in sufficient numbers to secure for us the full liberties of the human race, the elements of which we have learned here.

From there, too, we have learned the deep degradation and wretchedness in which our relatives were sunk, who were induced by heartless speculators to immigrate to Hayti. Slavery, if it must be borne, is more endurable under a race we have long been taught to look up to and regard as superior, than under one originated in Africa, degraded by abject slavery under Spanish and French greed, and still further brutalized by unrestrained and licentious liberty, such as exists with those who hold the power to control the poor immigrant in Hayti, or either of the Afro-West India Islands.

Of our own will, we cannot go either to Liberia or these islands. We have, in the United States, been taught to venerate virtue, to strive to attain it, and we can, with humble price, point to as wide spread examples of the benefit of these teachings, as can any similar number of men, with no greater advantages than ourselves. Therefore we wish to shun those countries where the opposite of virtue rules, where vice reigns supreme, where our very blood would be required if we opposed its indulgence.

Though colored, and debarred from rights of citizenship, our hearts none the less, cling to the land of our birth. We do not wish to be driven beyond the Ocean, where old hands of kindness cannot reach us, where we cannot hear from those with whom we have grown up, with all the fond remembrances of childhood.

We now number as many souls as won the freedom of your sires from British rule. We may not now be as capable to govern ourselves as they were, but we will, with your aid, be as zealous, and with God's blessing, we will be as successful.

There is a land—part of this your own continent—to which we wish to go. It is that portion generally called Central America. There are land there without inhabitants, yet bearing spontaneously all that is suited to our race.

Aid us to get there—protect us for a short while, and we will prove ourselves worthy and grateful. The labor, which, in servitude, has raised cotton, sugar, and tobacco, will do the same, not in the blood of bondage, but in the free spirit of liberty, and with the exultant knowledge, that it is to be part of your commerce, and to be given in exchange for the productions of our old native land.

If we are regarded as an evil here, (and we may become so by our competing with your white labor while here for the necessities of existence), send us where, instead of being an evil, we may be made a blessing, by increasing the value of that white labor, while at the same time we offer it greater comforts in reducing the costs in producing, by our own labor, those articles in abundance which all require for health and sustenance.

Do not, we beseech you, recognize and build up foreign nations of the black race, who have no sympathy or thought or language with that race which has grown up with you, and who only seek by such recognition, shaped as it is, by European diplomacy, to sow discord and trouble with us here, that you and ourselves may be involved in a common ruin.

Send us—our prayer is, send us—to that country we have indicated, that we may not be wholly excluded from you, that we may aid in bringing to you that great commerce of the Pacific, which will still further increase the wealth and power of your country: and your petitioners will ever pray.

☙ "The Prayer of Twenty Millions"

GREELEY'S APPEAL TO LINCOLN

In the summer of 1862 Confederate armies soundly repulsed Union attacks in the Peninsular Campaign and at the Second Battle of Bull Run. Cries of discontent were rising in the North and it appeared as if England and France might assist the Confederate States of America. While some Northerners wanted to abandon the war altogether, others such as the influential New York *Tribune* editor Horace Greeley pushed to broaden the war aims to include the abolition of slavery. Greeley wrote a column expressing that view in the form of a letter to Lincoln. Lincoln responded that his goal was to preserve the union above all else.

August 19, 1862

Dear Sir:

We complain that the Union cause has suffered, and is now suffering immensely, from mistaken deference to rebel Slavery. Had you, sir, in your Inaugural Address, unmistakably given notice that, in case the rebellion already commenced, were persisted in, and your efforts to preserve the Union and enforce the laws should be resisted by armed force, you would recognize no loyal person as rightfully held in Slavery by a traitor, we believe the rebellion would therein have received a staggering if not fatal blow....

On the face of this wide earth, Mr. President, there is not one disinterested, determined, intelligent champion of the Union cause who does not feel that all attempts to put down the rebellion and at the same time uphold its inciting cause are preposterous and futile—that the rebellion, if crushed out tomorrow, would be renewed within a year if Slavery were left in full vigor—and that every hour of deference to Slavery is an hour of added and deepened peril to the Union. I appeal to the testimony of your ambassadors in Europe. It is freely at your service, not at mine. Ask them to tell you candidly whether the seeming subserviency of your policy to the slaveholding, slavery-upholding interest, is not the perplexity, the despair of statesmen of all parties, and be admonished by the general answer!

I close as I began with the statement that what an immense majority of the loyal millions of your countrymen require of you is a frank, declared, unqualified, ungrudging execution of the laws of the land, more especially of the Confiscation Act. That act gives freedom to the slaves of rebels coming within our lines, or whom those lines may at any time inclose—we ask you to render it due obedience by publicly requiring all your subordinates to recognize and obey it. The rebels are everywhere using the late anti-Negro riots in the North, as they have long used your officers' treatment of Negroes in the South, to convince the slaves that they have nothing to hope from a Union success—that we mean in that case to sell them into a bitter bondage to defray the cost of the war. Let them impress this as a truth on the great mass of their ignorant and credulous bondmen, and the Union will never be restored—never. We cannot conquer ten millions of people united in solid phalanx against us, powerfully aided by Northern sympathizers and European allies. We must have scouts, guides, spies, cooks, teamsters, diggers and choppers from the blacks of the South, whether we allow them to fight for us or not, or we shall be baffled and repelled. As one of the millions who would gladly have avoided this struggle at any sacrifice but that of principle and honor, but who now feel that the triumph of the Union is indispensable not only to the existence of our country but to the well-being of mankind, I entreat you to render a hearty and unequivocal obedience to that law of the land.

Yours,

Horace Greeley

LINCOLN'S RESPONSE

August 22, 1862

Hon. Horace Greeley:

Dear Sir: I have just read yours of the nineteenth, addressed to myself through the New York Tribune. If there be in it statements or assumptions of fact which I may know to be erroneous, I do not know and here argue against them. If there be in it any inferences which I may believe to be falsely drawn, I do not now and here argue against them. If there be perceptible in it an impatient and dictatorial tone, I waive it in deference to an old friend, whose heart I have always supposed to be right.

As to the policy I "seem to be pursuing," as you say, I have not meant to leave anyone in doubt.

I would save the Union. I would save it the shortest way under the Constitution. The sooner the National authority can be restored, the nearer the Union will be "the Union as it was." If there be those who would not save the Union unless they could at the same time save Slavery, I do not agree with them. If there be those who would not save the Union unless they could at the same time destroy Slavery, I do not agree with them. My paramount object in this struggle is to save the Union, and is not either to save or destroy Slavery. If I could save the Union without freeing any slave, I would do it; and if I could save it by freeing all the slaves, I would do it; and if I could do it by freeing some and leaving others alone, I would also do that. What I do about Slavery and the colored race, I do because I believe it helps to save this Union; and what I forbear, I forbear because I do not believe it would help to save the Union. I shall do less whenever I shall believe what I am doing hurts the cause, and I shall do more whenever I shall believe doing more will help the cause. I shall try to correct errors when shown to be errors; and I shall adopt new views so fast as they shall appear to be true views. I have here stated my purpose according to my view of official duty, and I intend no modification of my oft-expressed personal wish that all men, everywhere, could be free.

Yours,
Lincoln

🍂 *Emancipation Proclamation*

ABRAHAM LINCOLN

In September, 1862, Union forces fought Lee's invading army at Antietam, Maryland, to a stalemate, compelling Lee to withdraw back to Virginia. The battle, the bloodiest single day of the war, gave Lincoln the opportunity to announce the Emancipation Proclamation freeing slaves in the rebellious states. Ever mindful of the impact of abolishing slavery in the slave states that remained loyal to the Union, Lincoln fulfilled his promise to Greeley that he might free some slaves and leave others alone if it would help preserve the Union. The declaration effectively removed the possibility of England and France, which had both abolished slavery decades earlier, supporting the pro-slavery Confederacy.

Whereas, on the 22nd day of September, in the year of our Lord 1862, a proclamation was issued by the President of the United States, containing, among other things, the following, to wit:

That on the 1st day of January, in the year of our Lord 1863, all persons held as slaves within any state or designated part of a state, the people whereof shall then be in rebellion against the United States, shall be then, thenceforward, and forever free; and the executive government of the United States, including the military and naval authority thereof, will recognize and maintain the freedom of such persons and will do no act or acts to repress such person, or any of them, in any efforts they may make for their actual freedom.

Then the executive will, on the 1st day of January aforesaid, by proclamation, designate the states and parts of states, if any, in which the people thereof, respectively, shall then be in rebellion against the United States; and the fact that any state or the people thereof shall on that day be in good faith represented in the Congress of the United States by members chosen thereto at elections wherein a majority of the qualified voters of such states shall have participated shall, in the absence of strong countervailing testimony, be deemed conclusive evidence that such state and the people thereof are not then in rebellion against the United States.

Now, therefore, I, Abraham Lincoln, President of the United States, by virtue of the power in me vested as commander in chief of the Army and Navy of the United States, in time of actual armed rebellion against the authority and government of the United States, and as a fit and necessary war measure for suppressing said rebellion, do, on this 1st day of January, in the year of our Lord 1863, and in accordance with my purpose so to do, publicly proclaimed for the full period of 100 days from the day first above mentioned, order and designate as the states and parts of states wherein the people thereof, respectively, are this day in rebellion against the United States to following, to wit:

Arkansas, Texas, Louisiana (except the parishes of St. Bernard, Plaquemines, Jefferson, St. John, St. Charles, St. James, Ascension, Assumption, Terrebonne, Lafourche, St. Mary, St. Martin, and Orleans, including the city of New Orleans), Mississippi, Alabama, Florida, Georgia, South Carolina, North Carolina, and Virginia (except the forty-eight counties designated as West Virginia, and also the counties of Berkeley, Accomac, Northampton, Elizabeth City, York, Princess Anne, and Norfolk, including the cities of Norfolk and Portsmouth), and which excepted parts are for the present left precisely as if this proclamation were not issued.

And, by virtue of the power and for the purpose aforesaid, I do order and declare that all persons held as slaves within said designated states and parts of state are, and henceforward shall be, free; and that the executive government of the United States, including the military and naval authorities thereof, will recognize and maintain the freedom of said persons.

And I hereby enjoin upon the people so declared to be free to abstain from all violence, unless in necessary self-defense; and I recommend that, in all cases when allowed, they labor faithfully for reasonable wages.

And I further declare and make known that such persons of suitable condition will be received into the armed service of the United States to garrison forts, positions, stations, and other places, and to man vessels of all sorts in said service.

And upon this act, sincerely believed to be an act of justice, warranted by the Constitution upon military necessity, I invoke the considerate judgment of mankind and the gracious favor of Almighty God.

❧ "To the working-men of Manchester"

ABRAHAM LINCOLN

At the outbreak of the Civil War the British government's sympathies lay with the Confederacy. A weak and divided United States served England's interests. The British had strong trade ties with the South, which supplied cotton for its textile mills, as opposed to the North, which competed with British manufacturers. In addition, the prospect of a breakaway former colony falling apart was not viewed as a bad thing by British leadership bent on building a global empire. Although the British government did not formerly ally itself with the Confederate government, it allowed the Confederacy to buy supplies, use its ports, and seek financing from England.

When Lincoln issued the Emancipation Proclamation freeing slaves, the British establishment condemned the action. *The Times* declared it "a very sad document." But for several decades the British had led Europe's abolitionist movement. With Lincoln's action, the Civil War became about slavery, changing the international implications of British support for the Confederacy.

On December 31, 1862, the citizens of Manchester,

England—many of whom had lost work because of the Northern blockade on Southern cotton—wrote a stirring letter of support to Lincoln assuring him of their support.

"We rejoice in your greatness as an outgrowth of England, whose blood and language you share, whose orderly and legal freedom you have applied to new circumstances, over a region immeasurably greater than our own," the address stated. "The vast progress you have made in the short space of twenty months fills us with hope that every stain on your freedom will shortly be removed, and that the erasure of that foul blot upon civilization and Christianity—chattel slavery—during your Presidency will cause the name of Abraham Lincoln to be honored and revered by posterity…. Our interests, moreover, our identified with yours. We are truly one people, though locally separate. And if you have any ill-wishers here, be assured they are chiefly those who oppose liberty at home, and that they will be powerless to stir up quarrels between us, from the very day in which your country becomes, undeniably and without exception, the home of the free. Accept our high admiration of your firmness in upholding the proclamation of freedom."

Lincoln replied with the following letter.

To the Working-Men of Manchester:
I have the honor to acknowledge the receipt of the address and resolutions which you sent me on the eve of the new year. When I came, on the 4th of March, 1861, through a free and constitutional election to preside in the government of the United States, the country was found at the verge of civil war. Whatever might have been the cause, or whosoever the fault, one duty, paramount to all others, was before me, namely, to maintain and preserve at once the Constitution and the integrity of the Federal Republic. A conscientious purpose to perform this duty is the key to all the measures of administration which have been and to all which will hereafter be pursued. Under our frame of government and my official oath, I could not depart from this purpose if I would. It is not always in the power of government to enlarge or restrict the scope of moral results which follow the policies that they may deem it necessary for the public safety from time to time to adopt.

I have understood well that the duty of self-preservation rests solely with the American people;

but I have at the same time been aware that favor or disfavor of foreign nations might have a material influence in enlarging or prolonging the struggle with disloyal men in which the country is engaged. A fair examination of history has served to authorize a belief that the past actions and influences of the United States were generally regarded as having been beneficial toward mankind. I have, therefore, reckoned upon the forbearance of nations. Circumstances—to some of which you kindly allude—induce me especially to expect that if justice and good faith should be practised by the United States, they would encounter no hostile influence on the part of Great Britain. It is now a pleasant duty to acknowledge the demonstration you have given of your desire that a spirit of amity and peace toward this country may prevail in the councils of your Queen, who is respected and esteemed in your own country only more than she is by the kindred nation which has its home on this side of the Atlantic.

I know and deeply deplore the sufferings which the working-men of Manchester, and in all Europe, are called to endure in this crisis. It has been often and studiously represented that the attempt to overthrow this government, which was built upon the foundation of human rights, and to substitute for it one which should rest exclusively on the basis of human slavery, was likely to obtain the favor of Europe. Through the action of our disloyal citizens, the working-men of Europe have been subjected to severe trials, for the purpose of forcing their sanction to that attempt. Under the circumstances, I cannot but regard your decisive utterances upon the question as an instance of sublime Christian heroism which has not been surpassed in any age or in any country. It is indeed an energetic and reinspiring assurance of the inherent power of truth and of the ultimate and universal triumph of justice, humanity, and freedom. I do not doubt that the sentiments you have expressed will be sustained by your great nation; and, on the other hand, I have no hesitation in assuring you that they will excite admiration, esteem and the most reciprocal feelings of friendship among the American people, I hail this interchange of sentiment, therefore, as an augury that whatever misfortune may befall your country or my own, the peace and friendship which now exist between the two nations will be, as it shall be my desire to make them, perpetual.

❧ Gettysburg Diary

ELISHA HUNT RHODES

Flushed with a series of victories in the spring of 1863, General Robert E. Lee made a bold gamble to move the war into the Northern states. A victory there, he reasoned, might push waning Northern support for the war over the brink and compel the Union to end the war. Quite by accident, Lee's army found itself at Gettysburg, Pennsylvania, fighting the Army of the Potomac under the command of General George Meade. The three-day battle became the turning point of the war. Elisha Hunt Rhodes of the 2nd Rhode Island Volunteers recorded his role in the events several days after the battle ended.

Middletown, Md., July 8, 1863

The great battle of the war has been fought and thanks to God the Army of the Potomac has been victorious at last. But how can I describe the exciting events of the past few days? On the night of July 1st we were in camp near Manchester, Md. Rumors of fighting in Pennsylvania have been heard all the days, but the distance was so great to the battlefield that we knew little about it. The men were tired and hungry and lay down to rest early in the evening. At nine o'clock orders came for us to move and we in great haste packed up and started on the road towards Pennsylvania. General Hooker has been relieved and Gen. George G. Meade of Penn. assigned to the command of the Army of the Potomac. What does it all mean? Well, it is none of our affairs and we obey orders and march out into the road. We struggle on through the night, the men almost dead for lack of sleep and falling over their own shadows. But still we go on in the warm summer night. Little is said by any one, for we were too weary to talk, only now and then an officer sharply orders the men to close up. Sometimes the column would halt for a moment as obstructions were met in the advance, and then we would run to catch up. Daylight brought no halt and what little hard bread we had was taken from the haversacks and eaten as we marched on. On the morning of July 2nd we heard the firing in front and then we understood the reason for such great haste. I was taken sick upon the road and fell helpless to the ground. The Surgeon, Dr. Carr, gave me a remedy and a pass for admittance to an ambulance. I lay upon the road side until several Regiments had passed when I began to revive. I immediately hurried on and soon came up with my Co. "B." The boys received me well, and went on without further trouble. The firing in our front grew loud and more distinct and soon we met the poor wounded fellows being carried to the rear. At a place called Littlestown we saw large numbers of our wounded men, and all kinds of carriages were being used to take them to the hospitals. At about 2 o'clock pm we reached the Battlefield of Gettysburg, Penn. having made a march of thirty-four miles without a halt. The men threw themselves upon the ground exhausted, but were soon ordered forward. We followed the road blocked with troops and trains until 4 pm when the field of battle with the long lines of struggling weary soldiers burst upon us. With loud cheers the old Sixth Corps took up the double quick and were soon in line of battle near the left of the main line held by the 5th Corps. The 5th Corps were in reserve, but we took their place, moved forward and took part in the fight. Our Division was finally sent to the front and relieved Gen. Sykes' Division of Regulars. Picket firing was kept up until long after dark, when we were relieved and returned a short distance. The men threw themselves upon the ground, and oblivious to the dead and dying around us we slept the sleep of the weary.

July 3rd 1863. This morning the troops were under arms before light and ready for the great battle that we knew must be fought. The firing began, and our Brigade was hurried to the right of the line to reinforce it. While not in the front line yet we were constantly exposed to the fire of the Rebel Artillery, while bullets fell around us. We moved from point to point, wherever danger to be imminent until noon when we were ordered to report to the line held by Gen. Birney. Our Brigade marched down the road until we reached the house used by General Meade as Headquarters. The road ran between hedges of rocks while the fields were strewn with boulders. To our left was a hill on which we had many Batteries posted. Just as we reached Gen. Meade's Headquarters, a shell burst over our heads, and it was immediately followed by showers of iron. More than two hundred guns were belching forth their thunder, and most of the shells that came over the hill struck in the road on which our Brigade was moving. Solid shot would strike the large rocks and split them as if exploded by gunpowder. The flying iron and pieces of stone struck men down in every direction. It is said that

this fire continued for about two hours, but I have no idea of the time. We could not see the enemy, and we could only cover ourselves the best we could behind the rocks and trees. About 30 men of our Brigade were killed or wounded by this fire. Soon the Rebel yell was heard, and we have found since that the Rebel General Pickett made a charge with his Division and was repulsed after reaching some of our batteries. Our lines of Infantry in front of us rose up and poured in a terrible fire. As we were only a few yards in rear of our lines we saw all the fight. The firing gradually died away, and but for an occasional shot all was still. But what a scene it was. Oh the dead and the dying on this bloody field. The 2nd R.I. lost only one man killed and five wounded. One of the latter belonged to my Co. "B." Again night came upon us and again we slept amid the dead and the dying.

July 4th, 1863. Was ever the Nation's Birthday celebrated in such a way before. This morning the 2nd R.I. was sent out to the front and found that during the night General Lee and his Rebel Army had fallen back. It was impossible to march across the field without stepping upon dead or wounded men, while horses and broken Artillery lay on every side. We advanced to a sunken road (Emmitsburg Road) where we deployed as skirmishers and lay down behind a bank of earth. Berdan's Sharpshooters joined us, and we passed the day in firing upon any Rebels that showed themselves. At 12 AM National Salute was shotted guns was fired from several of our Batteries, and the shells passed over our heads toward the Rebel lines. At night we were relieved and went to the rear for a little rest and sleep.

July 5th, 1863. Glorious news! We have won the victory, thank God, and the Rebel Army is fleeing to Virginia. We have news that Vicksburg has fallen. We have thousands of prisoners, and they seem to be stupified with the news. This morning our Corps (the 6th) started in pursuit of Lee's Army. We have had rain and the roads are bad, so we move slow. Every house we see is a hospital, and the road is covered with the arms and equipments thrown away by the Rebels.

❧ "Attacked by an armed mob"

U.S. ARMY RECORD

By 1863, the Civil War was not a popular war in the North. Discontent with the way it was being waged, high casualties, and general weariness sapped enthusiasm for preserving the Union. Led by the Democratic "Copperheads," an anti-war movement emerged. Many northerners did not want to risk their lives for the sake of the Union, much less to free slaves.

To keep the war effort going, however, more men were needed to fill the army's ranks. On March 3, 1863, Congress passed a law authorizing conscription and clamping down on objections to the measure. Exemptions were made for men who were the sole support of women and children. Men could also avoid service by finding a substitute or paying a $300 fee to the government. Objection to the war was not a grounds for exemption.

Tensions rose and draft riots broke out in several cities. In July 1863, riots erupted throughout New York City against the draft. African Americans and army stations were targeted by rioters. Eventually, Union troops fresh from the Battle of Gettysburg were sent to restore order. In the end more than 1,000 people were killed or wounded. The following report from a Union officer described the riot.

About six o'clock P.M., General Dodge and Colonel Mott informed General Brown, that the troops at Grammercy Park had marched down Twenty-second Street, and been attacked by an armed mob; that they had been driven back, leaving their dead in the street. The general ordered me to take my company, and a portion of the Twentieth and Twenty-eighth New York volunteer batteries, about eighty men, armed as infantry, commanded by Lieutenant B. F. Ryer. Lieutenant Ryer had with him Lieutenant Robert F. Joyce and Lieutenant F. M. Chase, Twenty-eight battery. My whole company amounted to one hundred and sixty men.

With this force I marched to the Grammercy Hotel. At a short distance from the hotel, I saw some of the rioters fire from a house on some of Colonel Mott's command. I immediately sent Lieutenant Joyce with a few men to search the house. The search was fruitless, the men having escaped to the rear. I then told the women in the house that the artillery would open on the house, if any more shots were fired from it. We then marched down Twenty-second Street, between Second and third Avenues, found the body of a sergeant of Davis' Cavalry, who had been killed two hours before. I ordered a livery-stable keeper to put his horses to a carriage, and accompany me, for the purpose of carrying the dead and wounded. He replied that the mob would kill him if he did, and that he dare not do it. He was informed that he would be protected if he went, but if he refused he would be instantly shot. The horses were speedily harnessed, and the body put into the carriage. The mob at this time commenced firing on us from the houses. We at once commended searching the houses, while my skirmishers drove the rioters back from every window and from the roofs. The houses were searched from cellar to the roof. The mob made a desperate fight, and evidently seemed to think they could whip us. Every house that was used to conceal these rioters was cleared. A large number was killed, and several prisoners taken. We then marched to Second Avenue, where we found the mob in great force and concealed in houses. They fired on us from the house-tops, and from windows, and also from cross streets. We soon cleared the streets, and then commenced searching the houses. We searched thirteen houses, killed those within that resisted, and took the remainder prisoners. Some of them fought like incarnate fiends, and would not surrender. All such were shot on the spot. The soldiers captured a large number of revolvers of large size, which I allowed them to keep. The mob at this place were well armed; nearly every one had some kind of fire-arms, and had one blunderbuss which they fired on us.

If they had been cool and steady, they might have done us great harm. As it was, they fired wildly, running to a window and firing, and then retreating back out of danger.

When my soldiers once got into a house they made short work of it. The fight lasted about forty minutes and was more severe than all the rest in which my company was engaged. There were none of my men killed. Sergeant Cadro, of company F, Twelfth Infantry (my own) was slightly wounded in the hand; private Krouse was also slightly wounded.

The mob being entirely dispersed, we returned to head-quarters.

❧ Charleston

HENRY TIMROD

Henry Timrod was the unofficial poet laureate of the Confederacy. His poems celebrated the virtues of the cause.

Here he praises Charleston, which started the Civil War, in an 1863 poem shortly after it repulsed a Northern siege.

Calm as that second summer which precedes
The first fall of the snow,
In the broad sunlight of heroic deeds,
The city bides the foe.
As yet, behind their ramparts, stern and proud,
Her bolted thunders sleep—
Dark Sumter, like a battlemented cloud,
Looms o'er the solemn deep.

No Calpe frowns from lofty cliff to scaur
To guard the holy strand;
But Moultrie holds in leash her dogs of war
Above the level sand.

And down the dunes a thousand guns lie couched,
Unseen, beside the flood—
Like tigers in some Orient jungle crouched,
That wait and watch for blood.

Meanwhile, through streets still echoing with trade,
Walk grave and thoughtful men,
Whose hands may one day wield the patriot's blade
As lightly as the pen.
And maidens, with such eyes as would grow dim
Over a bleeding hound,
Seem each one to have caught the strength of him
Whose sword she sadly bound.

Thus girt without and garrisoned at home,
Day patient following day,
Old Charleston looks from roof and spire and
    dome,
Across her tranquil bay.

Ships, through a hundred foes, from Saxon lands
And spicy Indian ports,
Bring Saxon steel and iron to her hands,
And summer to her courts.
But still, along yon dim Atlantic line,
The only hostile smoke
Creeps like a harmless mist above the brine,
From some frail floating oak.

Shall the spring dawn, and she, still clad in smiles,
And with an unscathed brow,
Rest in the strong arms of her palm-crowned isles,
As fair and free as now?

We know not; in the temple of the Fates
God has inscribed her doom:
And, all untroubled in her faith, she waits
The triumph or the tomb.

❧ *"Are we Soldiers, or are we Labourers?"*

CORPORAL JAMES HENRY GOODING

CAPTAIN JAMES W. GRACE

In 1862, the United States War Department authorized the recruitment of blacks for military duty. Although recruits were promised they would receive the same pay (thirteen dollars per month) as white soldiers, Congress had only authorized paying black laborers ten dollars a month. The Union Army was only willing to pay black soldiers the lesser amount. Soldiers of the all-black 54th Massachusetts Regiment refused to accept a laborer's wage.

The regiment took part in the doomed attack on Fort Wagner outside of Charleston, South Carolina, in July 1863. The regiment suffered casualties of almost 50 percent, including the death of their commander, Colonel Robert Gould Shaw. Shaw and the other dead soldiers were buried in a mass grave outside the fortress. Despite the defeat, the bravery of the black regiment dispelled widespread skepticism about black soldiers' capacity to fight. The decision to let blacks serve in the army and their bravery in battle played a major role in the ultimate Union victory: the abolition of slavery and the granting of equal rights.

Corporal James Henry Gooding of New Bedford, Massachusetts, served with the regiment. A free black man prior to the war, he wrote a column for his hometown newspaper, The *New Bedford Mercury,* throughout his time of service. After the Battle of Fort Wagner, he wrote a letter to Abraham Lincoln asking that he and his fellow black soldiers receive equal pay.

Camp of the 54th Massachusetts colored regt., Morris Island.
Dept. Of the South. Sept. 28th, 1863.
Your Excellency, Abraham Lincoln:

Your Excellency will pardon the presumption of an humble individual like myself, in addressing you, but the earnest Solicitation of my comrades in Arms beside the genuine interest felt by myself in the matter is my excuse, for placing before the Executive head of the Nation our Common Grievance.

On the 6th day of the last Month, the

Paymaster of the department informed us, that if we would decide to receive the sum of $10 per month, he would come and pay us that sum, but that, on the sitting of Congress, the Regt., would, in his opinion, be allowed the other three. He did not give us any guarantee that this would be, as he hoped; certainly he had no authority for making any such guarantee, and we cannot suppose him acting in any way interested.

Now the main question is, Are we Soldiers, or are we Labourers? We are fully armed and equipped, have done all the various Duties pertaining to a Soldier's life, have conducted ourselves to the complete satisfaction of General Officers, who were, if any[thing], prejudiced against us, but who now accord us all the encouragement and honour due us; have shared the perils and Labour of Reducing the first stronghold that flaunted a Traitor Flag; and more, Mr. President. Today the Anglo-Saxon Mother, Wife, or Sister are not alone in tears for departed Sons, Husbands and Brothers. The patient, trusting Descendants of Africa's Clime have dyed the ground with blood, in defense of the Union, and Democracy. Men, too, your Excellency, who know in a measure the cruelties of the Iron heel of oppression, which in years gone by, the very Power their blood is now being spilled to maintain, ever ground them to the dust.

But When the war trumpet sounded o'er the land, when men knew not the Friend from the Traitor, the Black man laid his life at the Altar of the Nation—and he was refused. When the arms of the Union were beaten, in the first year of the War, and the Executive called more food for its ravaging maw, again the black man begged the privilege of aiding his country in her need, to be again refused.

And now he is in the War, and how has he conducted himself? Let their dusky forms rise up, out the mires of James Island, and give the answer. Let the rich mould around Wagner's parapets be upturned, and there will be found an Eloquent answer. Obedient and patient and Solid as a wall as are they. All we lack is a paler hue and a better acquaintance with the Alphabet.

Now your Excellency, we have done a Soldier's Duty. Why Can't we have a Solider's pay? You caution the Rebel Chieftain, that the United States knows no distinction in her Soldiers. She insists on having all her Soldiers of whatever creed or Color, to be treated according to the usages of War. Now

if the United States exacts uniformity of treatment of her Soldiers from the Insurgents, would it not be well and consistent to set the example herself by paying all her Soldiers alike?

We of this Regt. were not enlisted under any "contraband" act. But we do not wish to be understood as rating our Service of more Value to the Government than the service of the ex-slave. Their Service is undoubtedly worth much to the Nation, but Congress made express provision touching their case, as slaves freed by military necessity, and assuming the Government to be their temporary Guardian. Not so with us. Freemen by birth and consequently having the advantage of thinking and acting for ourselves so far as the laws would allow us, we do not consider ourselves fit subject for the Contraband act.

We appeal to you, Sir, as the Executive of the Nation, to have us justly Dealt with. The Regt. do pray that they be assured their service will be fairly appreciated by paying them as American Soldiers, not as menial hirelings. Black men, you may well know, are poor; three dollars per month for a year will supply their needy Wives and little ones with fuel. If you, as Chief magistrate of the Nation, will assure us of our whole pay, we are content. Our Patriotism, our enthusiasm will have a new impetus, to exert our energy more and more to aid our Country. Not that our hearts ever flagged in Devotion, spite the evident apathy displayed in our behalf, but We feel as though our Country spurned us, now that we are sworn to serve her. Please give this a moment's attention.

James Henry Gooding

Five months later, Gooding was killed in action at the Battle of Olustee Station in Florida. Captain James W. Grace, wrote a letter to the *New Bedford Mercury* informing Gooding's editors of his death, as well as the resolution on pay for black soldiers.

Jacksonville, Fla., Feb. 25, 1864

Messrs. Editors:

I am pained to inform you that Corporal James H. Gooding was killed in battle on the 20th inst. at Olustee Station. He was one of the Color Corporals and was with the colors at the time. So great was the rout of our troops that we left nearly all our dead and wounded on the field. The fight lasted four hours. We were badly beaten that night, and the next day we kept falling back, until we reached Jacksonville. The fifty-fourth did honor to themselves and our city. All concede that no regiment fought like it.

James H. Buchanan, of New Bedford, was killed; and Sergeant Wharton A. Williams, also of our city, was wounded in the hand. Many others of Co. C were wounded, but none of them from our city.

The regiment is pleased to learn that the bill to pay them $13 per month passed.

The total loss of the regiment, I am unable to give you at this time. All we want now is more troops; with them we would go forward again and drive the rebels from the State.

Your friend
James W. Grace
Fifty-Fourth Regiment

The Gettysburg Address

ABRAHAM LINCOLN

Four months after the climactic Battle of Gettysburg, a great memorial service was given. Abraham Lincoln gave a brief speech commemorating the dead and the underlying principles of the nation. Brief and eloquent, it is arguably the most important speech in American history.

Fourscore and seven years ago our fathers brought forth on this continent a new nation, conceived in Liberty, and dedicated to the proposition that all men are created equal.

Now we are engaged in a great civil war, testing whether that nation or any nation so conceived and so dedicated, can long endure. We are met on a great battlefield of that war. We have come to dedicate a portion of that field, as a final resting place for those who here gave their lives that that nation might live. It is altogether fitting and proper that we should do this.

But, in a larger sense, we can not dedicate—we can not consecrate—we can not hallow—this ground. The brave men, living and dead, who struggled here, have consecrated it, far above our poor power to add or detract. The world will little note nor long remember what we say here, but it can never forget what they did here. It is for us the living, rather, to be dedicated here to the unfinished work which they who fought here have

thus far so nobly advanced. It is rather for us to be here dedicated to the great task remaining before us—that from these honored dead we take increased devotion to that cause for which they gave the last full measure of devotion—that we here highly resolve that these dead shall not have died in vain—that this nation, under God, shall have a new birth of freedom—and that government of the people, by the people, for the people, shall not perish from the earth.

"Let us live to make men free"

CIVIL WAR SONGS

Between the horrors of battle, soldiers withstood the tedium of camp life. In part to fill the time and also to draw inspiration for their respective causes, hundreds of songs were written during the Civil War. Two musical staples of the Civil War have withstood the test of time.

Battle Hymn of the Republic
Julia Ward Howe

Mine eyes have seen the glory of the coming of the
    Lord;
He is trampling out the vintage where the grapes of
    wrath are stored;
He hath loosed the fateful lightning of His terrible
    swift sword:
His truth is marching on.

I have seen Him in the watch-fires of a hundred
    circling camps;
They have builded Him an altar in the evening
    dews and damps;
I can read His righteous sentence by the dim and
    flaring lamps:
His day is marching on.

I have read a fiery gospel writ in burnished rows of
    steel:
"As ye deal with my condemners, so with you my
    grace shall deal;
Let the Hero, born of woman, crush the serpent
    with his heel,
Since God is marching on."
He has sounded forth the trumpet that shall never
    call retreat;

He is sifting out the hearts of men before His judg-
ment-seat;
Oh, be swift, my soul, to answer Him! Be jubilant,
my feet!
Our God is marching on.

In the beauty of the lilies Christ was born across
the sea,
With a glory in his bosom that transfigures you and
me:
As he died to make men holy, let us live to make
men free,
While God is marching on.

Dixie

I wish I was in the land of cotton, old times there
are not forgotten,
Look away, look away, look away, Dixie land.
In Dixie land where I was born in, early on a frosty
mornin',
Look away, look away, look away, Dixie land.

Then I wish I was in Dixie, hooray! Hooray!
In Dixie land I'll take my stand to live and die in
Dixie,
Away, away, away down South in Dixie,
Away, away, away down South in Dixie.

Old Missus marry Weill de Weaber, Will-yum was a
gay deceaber,
Look away, look away, look away, Dixie land.
But when he put his arm around her, smiled as
fierce as a forty pounder,
Look away, look away, look away, Dixie land.

Old Missus acted the foolish part, and died for a
man that broke her heart,
Look away, look away, look away, Dixie land.
So here's a health to the next old Missues or the
gals that long to kiss us,
Look away, look away, look away, Dixie land.

Dars buckwheat cakes an' ingen batter, makes you
fat or a little fatter,
Look away, look away, look away, Dixie land.
Den hoe it down and scratch your grabble, to
Dixie's land I'm bound to travel,
Look away, look away, look away, Dixie land.

❧ "The real war will never get into the books"

WALT WHITMAN

Walt Whitman served the Union cause in Northern hospitals in Washington, D.C., working as an aid. He frequently went up to the front and had many friends and relatives in the military. Throughout the war he kept a diary, wrote letters and poems and published articles recording his observations of the men who actually fought the war. His perspective mixed the good, bad and tragic into an all-too-human picture of the war and its toil.

A Glimpse of War's Hell-Scenes

In one of the late movements of our troops in the valley (near Upperville, I think), a strong force of Moseby's guerrillas attacked a train of wounded and the guard of cavalry convoying them. The ambulances contained about sixty wounded, quite a number of them officers of rank. The Rebels were in strength, and the capture of the train and its partial guard after a short snap was effectually accomplished. No sooner had our men surrendered, the Rebels instantly commenced robbing the train and murdering their prisoners, even the wounded. Here is the scene or a sample of it—ten minutes after.

Among the wounded officers in the ambulances were one, a lieutenant of the regulars, and another, of higher rank. These two were dragged out on the ground on their backs and were now surrounded by the guerrillas, a demoniac crowd, each member of which was stabbing them in different parts of their bodies. One of the officers had his feet pinned firmly to the ground by bayonets stuck through them and thrust into the ground. These two officers, as afterwards found on examination, had received twenty such thrusts, some of them through the mouth, face, etc. The wounded had all been dragged (to give a better chance for plunder) out of their wagons; some had been effectually dispatched, and their bodies were lying there lifeless and bloody. Others, not yet dead but horribly mutilated, were moaning or groaning. Of our men who surrendered, most had been thus maimed or slaughtered.

At this instant, a force of our cavalry, who had been following the train at some interval, charged suddenly upon the Secesh captors, who proceeded at once to make the best escape they could. Most of them got away, but we gobbled two officers and seventeen men in the very acts just described. The sight was one which admitted of little discussion, as may be imagined. The seventeen captured men and two officers were put under guard for the night, but it was decided there and then that they should die.

The next morning the two officers were taken in town—separate places—put in the centre of the street and shot. The seventeen men were taken on to an open ground a little to one side. They were placed in a hollow square, half encompassed by two of our cavalry regiments, one of which regiments had three days before found the bloody corpses of three of their men hamstrung and hung up by the heels to limbs of trees by Mosby's guerrillas; and the other had not long before had twelve men, after surrendering, shot and then hung by the neck to limbs of trees, and jeering inscriptions pinned to the breast of one of the corpses, who had been a sergeant.

Those three, and those twelve, had been found, I say by these environing regiments. Now, with revolvers, they formed the grim cordon of the seventeen prisoners. The latter were placed in the midst of the hollow square, unfastened, and the ironical remark made to them that they were now to be given "a chance for themselves." A few ran for it. But what use? From every side the deadly pills came. In a few minutes the seventeen corpses strewed the hollow square.

I was curious to know whether some of the Union soldiers, some few (some one or two at least of the youngsters), did not abstain from shooting on the helpless men. Not one. There was no exultation, very little said—almost nothing—yet every man there contributed his shot.

Multiply the above by scores, aye hundreds; verify it in all the forms that different circumstances, individuals, places could afford; light it with every lurid passion—the wolf's, the lion's lapping thirst for blood; the passionate, boiling volcanoes of human revenge for comrades, brothers slain; with the light of burning farms and heaps of smutting, smouldering black embers—and in the human heart everywhere, black, worse embers—and you have an inkling of the war.

Two Brothers, One North, One South
May 28–29

I stayed tonight a long time by the bedside of a new patient, a young Baltimorean aged about nineteen years. W.S.P. (2nd Maryland, Southern), very feeble, right leg amputated, can't sleep hardly at all; has taken a great deal of morphine, which, as usual, is costing more than it comes to. Evidently very intelligent and well bred, very affectionate, held on to my hand and put it to his face, not willing to let me leave.

As I was lingering, soothing him in his pain, he says to me suddenly: "I hardly think you know who I am; I don't wish to impose on you—I am a Rebel soldier." I said I did not know that, but it made no difference. Visited him daily for about two weeks after that, while he lived (death had marked him and he was quite alone). I loved him much, always kissed him and he did me.

In an adjoining ward I found his brother, an officer of rank, a Union soldier, a brave and religious man, Colonel Clifton K. Prentiss, 6th Maryland Infantry, 6th Corps, wounded in one of the engagments at Petersburg, April 2; lingered, suffered much, died in Brooklyn, August 20, '65. It was in the same battle both were hit. One was a strong Unionist, the other Secesh; both fought on their respective sides, both badly wounded, and both brought together here after a separation of four years. Each died for his cause.

Death of a Hero

I wonder if I could ever convey to another—to you, for instance, reader dear—the tender and terrible realities of such cases, (many, many happened,) as the one I am now going to mention. Stewart C. Glover, company E, 5th Wisconsin—was wounded May 5, in one of those fierce tussles of the Wilderness—died May 21—aged about 20. He was a small and beardless young man—a splendid soldier—in fact almost an ideal American, of his age. He had served nearly three years, and would have been entitled to his discharge in a few days. He was in Hancock's corps.

The fighting had about ceased for the day, when the general commanding the brigade rode by and call'd for volunteers to bring in the wounded. Glover responded among the first—went out gayly—but while in the act of bearing in a wounded sergeant to our lines, was shot in the knee by a rebel sharpshooter; consequence, amputation and death. He had resided with his father, John Glover, an aged and feeble man, in Batavia, Genesee county, N.Y., but was at school in Wisconsin, after the war broke out, and there enlisted—soon took to soldier-life, liked it, was very manly, was beloved by officers and comrades. He kept a little diary, like so many of the soldiers. On the day of his death he wrote the following in it, to-day the doctor says I must die—all is over with me—ah, so young to die. On another blank leaf he pencilled to his brother, dear brother Thomas, I have been brave but wicked—pray for me.

Come Up From The Fields Father

Come up from the fields father, here's a letter from
 our Pete,
And come to the front door mother, here's a letter
 from thy dear son.
Lo, 'tis autumn,
Lo, where the trees, deeper green, yellower and red-
 der,
Cool and sweeten Ohio's villages with leaves flut-
 tering in the moderate wind,
Where apples ripe in the orchards hang and grapes
 on the trellis'd vines,
(Smell you the smell of the grapes on the vines?
Smell you the buckwheat where the bees were late-
 ly buzzing?)

Above all, lo, the sky so calm, so transparent after
 the rain, and with wondrous clouds,
Below too, all calm, all vital and beautiful, and the
 farm prospers well.
Down in the fields all prospers well,
But now from the fields come father, come at the
 daughter's call,
And come to the entry mother, to the front door
 come right away.

Fast as she can she hurries, something ominous, her
 steps trembling,
She does not tarry to smooth her hair nor adjust
 her cap.
Open the envelope quickly,
O this is not our son's writing, yet his name is
 sign'd,
O a strange hand writes for our dear son, O strick-
 en mother's soul!
All swims before her eyes, flashes with black, she
 catches the main words only,
Sentences broken, *gunshot wound in the breast, cavalry skirmish, taken to hospital,*

At present low, but will soon be better.

Ah now the single figure to me,
Amid all teeming and wealthy Ohio with all its
 cities and farms,
Sickly white in the face and dull in the head, very
 faint,
By the jamb of a door leans.

Grieve not so, dear mother, (the just-grown daughter
 speaks through her sobs,
The little sisters huddle around speechless and dismay'd,)
*See, dearest mother, the letter says Pete will soon be
 better.*

Alas, poor boy, he will never be better, (nor may-be
 needs to be better, that brave and simple soul,)
While they stand at home at the door, he is dead
 already,
The only son is dead.

But the mother needs to be better,
She with thin form presently drest in black,
By day her meals untouch'd, then at night fitfully
 sleeping, often waking,
In the midnight waking, weeping, longing with one
 deep longing,
O that she might withdraw unnoticed, silent from
 life escape and withdraw,
To follow, to seek, to be with her dear dead son.

"I see the President almost every day"
August 12, 1863

I see the President almost every day, as I happen to live where he passes to and from his lodgings out of town. He never sleeps at the White House during the hot season, but has quarters at a health location some three miles north of the city—the Soldiers' Home—a United States military establishment.

 I saw him this morning about 8:30 coming in to business, riding on Vermont Avenue, near L Street. He always has a company of twenty-five or thirty cavalry, with sabres drawn and held upright over their shoulders. They say the guard was against his personal wish, but he let counselors have their way.

 The party makes no great show in uniform or horses. Mr. Lincoln on the saddle generally rides a good-sized, easygoing, gray horse; is dressed in plain black, somewhat rusty and dusty; wears a stiff black hat; and looks about as ordinary in attire, etc. as the commonest man. A lieutenant with yellow straps rides at his left; and following behind, two by two, come the cavalry men in their yellow-striped jackets. They are generally going at a slow trot, as that is the pace set them by the one they wait upon. The sabres and accoutrements clank, and the entirely ornamental cortege as it trots toward Lafayette Square arouses no sensation; only some curious stranger stops and gazes.

I see very plainly Abraham Lincoln's dark brown face, with deep-cut lines, the eyes always, to me with a deep latent sadness in the expression. We have got so that we exchange bows, and very cordial ones.

Sometimes the President goes and comes in an open barouche. The cavalry always accompany him, with drawn sabres. Often I notice, as he goes out evenings and sometimes in the morning when he returns early, he turns off and halts at the large and handsome residence of the Secretary of War on K Street and holds conference there. If in his barouche, I can see from my window he does not alight, but sits in his vehicle, and Mr. Stanton comes out to attend him. Sometimes one of his sons, a boy of ten or twelve, accompanies him, riding at his right on a pony.

Earlier in the summer I occasionally saw the President in the face fully, as they were moving slowly; and his look, though abstracted, happened to be directed steadily in my eye. He bowed and smiled, but far beneath the smile I noticed well the expression I have alluded to. None of the artists or pictures have caught the deep though subtle and indirect expression of this man's face. There is something else there. One of the great portrait painters of two or three centuries ago is needed.

"The real war will never get in the books"

And so good-bye to the war. I know not how it may have been or may be to others—to me the main interest I found (and still, on recollection, find) in the rank and file of the armies, both sides, and in those specimens amid the hospitals and even the dead on the field. To me, the points illustrating the latent personal character and eligibilities of these States in the two or three millions of American young and middle-aged men, North and South,

embodied in those armies—and especially the one third or one fourth of their number stricken by wounds or disease at some time in the course of the contest—were of more significance even than the political interests involved. (As so much of a race depends on how it faces death, and how it stands personal anguish and sickness; as, in the glints of emotions under emergencies, and the indirect traits and asides in Plutarch, we get far profounder clues to the antique world than all its more formal history.)

Future years will never know the seething hell and the black infernal background of countless minors scenes and interiors (not the official surface courteousness of the generals, not the few great battles) of the Secession War; and it is best they should not. The real war will never get in the books.

🌿 Doings in Nevada

MARK TWAIN

When the Civil War broke out, Samuel Clemens joined a Confederate unit in Missouri. He did not enjoy military life, however, and soon departed for more interesting prospects out West. Clemens, who soon took on the pen name Mark Twain, was not alone. Wanting no part in the Civil War, thousands of young men headed west to start farms and prospect mines. Removed from the war, but not unaware of its implications, settlers (who were mainly sympathetic to the Northern cause) continued to seek new opportunities. Twain took on a career as a newspaper correspondent and started to build his reputation as a keen observer with a biting wit. Here, he describes some of the considerations that all frontier territories confronted in forming self-governing bodies.

Carson City, Nevada Territory
January 4, 1864

Editor T. T.: The concentrated wisdom of Nevada Territory (known unto and respected by the nations of the earth as "Washoe") assembled in convention at Carson recently, and framed a constitution. It was an excellent piece of work in some respects, but it had one or two unfortunate defects which debarred it from assuming to be an immaculate conception. The chief of these was a clause authorizing the taxing of the mines. The people will not stand that. There are some 30,000 gold and silver mining incorporations here, or mines, or claims, or which you please, or all, if it suits you better. Very little of the kind of property thus represented is improved yet, or "developed" as we call it; it will take two or three years to get it in a developed and paying condition, and will require an enormous outlay of capital to accomplish such a result. And until it does begin to pay dividends, the people will not consent that it shall be burdened and hindered by taxation. Therefore, I am satisfied they will refuse to ratify our new constitution on the 19th inst.

It had an amusing feature in it, also. That was the Great Seal of the State. It had snow-capped mountains in it; and tunnels and shafts, and pickaxes and quartz-mills, and pack-trains, and mule-teams. These things were good; what there were of them. And it had railroads in it, and telegraphs, and stars, and suspension-bridges, and other romantic fictions foreign to sand and sage-brush. But the richest of it was the motto. It took them thirty days to decide whether it should be "Volens et Potens" (which they said meant "Able and Willing"), or "The Union Must and Shall be preserved." Either would have been presumptuous, and surpassingly absurd just at present. Because we are not able and willing, thus far, to do a great deal more than locate wild-cat mining-claims and reluctantly sell them to confiding strangers at a ruinous sacrifice—of conscience. And if it were left to us to preserve the Union, in case the balance of the country failed in the attempt, I seriously believe we couldn't do it. Possibly, we might make it mighty warm for the Confederacy if it came prowling around here, but ultimately we would have to forsake our high trust, and quit preserving the Union. I am confident of it. And I have thought the matter over a good deal, off and on, as we say in Paris. We have an animal here whose surname is the "jackass rabbit". It is three feet long, has legs liking a counting-house stool, ears of monstrous length, and no tail to speak of. It is swifter than a greyhound, and as meek and harmless as an infant. I might mention, also, that it is as handsome as most infants; however, it would be foreign to the subject, and I do not know that a remark of that kind would be popular in all circles. Let it pass, then—I will say nothing about it, though it would be a greater comfort to me to do it, if people would consider the source and overlook it. Well, somebody proposed a substitute for that pictorial Great Seal, a figure of a jackass-rabbit reposing in the shade of his native sage-brush, with the motto "Volens enough, but not some d—d Potens". Possibly that had something to do with the rejection of one of the proposed mottoes by the Convention.

🐝 "Oh, if it could all end, and this terrible turmoil cease"

CAPTAIN PHILIP POWERS

In the spring of 1864, General Ulysses S. Grant made an all-out push against the Confederate Army. General William T. Sherman launched his drive on Atlanta; General Nathaniel Banks moved to take Mobile, Alabama, from New Orleans and Grant himself led his Army of the Potomac to attack Lee's Army of Northern Virginia.

Grant's plan was to apply the weight of Northern resources and manpower on the comparatively weak South from all sides. The Civil War was becoming a war of attrition, and as this letter from Confederate Captain Powers shows, it was starting to wear on Southern forces. He wrote the letter three days after the Battle of Yellow Tavern where the dashing Southern hero General J.E.B. Stuart was killed. Powers was serving with the Quartermaster Department, Cavalry Corps, Confederate Army of Northern Virginia.

Spotsylvania, Va.
May 15, 1864
My Dear Wife:

The Sabbath morn opens upon us sadly this morning, and with a heart depressed with a deep and bitter grief I long to commune with some heart which can sympathize with me. We heard yesterday of the death of our noble leader, Genl. Stuart and the news has thrown a gloom upon us all. Since the death of the lamented Jackson, no event, no disaster, has so affected me. Jackson was a great loss to his country and to the cause. Genl. Stuart is a great loss to his country. But to us, who have been intimately associated with him—and to me in particular—his loss is irreparable, for in him, I have lost my best friend in the army.

I cannot realize that he is gone, that I am to see his gallant figure, nor hear his cheering voice, no more. "God's will be done," a great man has fallen, and his faults are now swallowed up and forgotten in the recollection of his eminent virtues—his glorious valor and patriotism. May God in his mercy comfort his poor widow. My heart sorrows for her, as for one very near to me.

The two armies here still confront each other in line of battle, though there has been no serious engagement since Thursday, when Genl. Johnson's Division was repulsed and himself and many of his men captured. The position and some of the artillery was recovered but not the prisoners, though in the same day we repulsed every other attack.

It has been raining for three days, and you can hardly imagine how uncomfortable we are lying in the mud and wet every day. Fortunately, my neuralgia attack has worn itself out and affects me but very slightly, though I am worn out and wearied in mind with continued anxiety. Oh, if it could all end, and this terrible turmoil cease.

For nearly two weeks our men have been in line of battle, exposed to all the inclemency of the weather, fac[ing] the insufferable heat and now the drenching rains—and yet they stand and fight. The wounded and the maimed and the dying lie around on the cold wet ground. No dear ones to minister to their wants—and the last breath is caught by the passing breeze and no listening ear of affection ever hears the sound. How long will a merciful God permit this war? And will the wail of the woe that rises from bloody battlefields never cease?

Love to the children and kisses for the babes. God be with you, my good wife.

Ever Yours,
P.H. Powers

🍃 The Union Assault at Cold Harbor

ULYSSES S. GRANT

General Grant continued to press against the Rebel forces, engaging them in almost constant conflict for the next three weeks as he pushed south. The Union campaign culminated in an early-morning assault on Confederate defenses at Cold Harbor on June 3. Almost 10,000 Union soldiers fell in the doomed assault. In the *Personal Memoirs of U.S. Grant* written twenty years after the event, Grant acknowledged that the attack was a mistake. The battle proved the futility of frontal assaults against embedded defenders, a lesson Lee had learned at Gettysburg with Pickett's Charge.

Two weeks later, the two exhausted armies faced each other at Petersburg and dug in for what would become a ten-month stalemate. The Petersburg campaign marked the first time trench warfare was waged. Neither side could break the defensive lines of their enemies. It proved to be a precursor of the Western Front in World War I.

The corps commanders were to select the points in their respective fronts where they would make their assaults. The move was to commence at half-past four in the morning. Hancock sent Barlow and Gibbon forward at the appointed hour, with Birney as a reserve. Barlow pushed forward with great vigor, under a heavy fire of both artillery and musketry, through thickets and swamps. Notwithstanding all the resistance of the enemy and the natural obstructions to overcome, he carried a position occupied by the enemy outside their main line where the road makes a deep cut through a bank affording as good a shelter for troops as if it had been made for that purpose. Three pieces of artillery had been captured here, and several hundred prisoners. The guns were immediately turned against the men who had just been using them. No assistance came to him, he (Barlow) intrenched under fire and continued to hold his place. Gibbon was not so fortunate in his front. He found the ground over which he had to pass cut up with deep ravines, and a morass difficult to cross. But his men struggled on until some of them got up to the very parapet covering the enemy. Gibbon gained ground much nearer the enemy than that which he left, and here intrenched and held fast.

Wright's corps moving in two lines captured the outer rifle-pits in their front, but accomplished nothing more. Smith's corps also gained the outer rifle-pits in its front. The ground over which this corps (18th) had to move was the most exposed of any over which charges were made. An open plain intervened between the contending forces at this point, which was exposed both to a direct and a cross fire. Smith, however, finding a ravine running towards his front, sufficiently deep to protect him in it from cross fire, and somewhat from a direct fire, put Martindale's division in it, and with Brooks supporting him on the left and Devens on the right succeeded in gaining the outer—and probably—picket rifle pits. Warren and Burnside also advanced and gained ground—which brought the whole army on one line.

This assault cost us heavily and probably without benefit to compensate: but the enemy was not cheered by the occurrence sufficiently to induce him to take the offensive. In fact, nowhere after the battle of Wilderness did Lee show any disposition to leave his defences far behind him.

Fighting was substantially over by half-past seven in the morning....

I have always regretted that the last assault at Cold Harbor was ever made. I might say the same thing of the assault of the 22nd of May, 1863 at Vicksburg. At Cold Harbor no advantage whatever was gained to compensate for the heavy loss we sustained. Indeed, the advantages other than those of relative losses, were on the Confederate side. Before that, the Army of Northern Virginia seemed to have acquired a wholesome regard for the courage, endurance, and soldierly qualities generally of the Army of the Potomac. They no longer wanted to fight them "one Confederate to five Yanks." Indeed, they seemed to have given up any idea of gaining any advantage of their antagonist in the open field. They had come to much prefer breastworks in their front to the Army of the Potomac. This charge seemed to revive their hopes temporarily; but it was of short duration. The effect upon the Army of the Potomac was the reverse. When we reached the James River, however, all the effects of the battle of Cold Harbor seemed to have disappeared.

❧ "Life on the Sea Islands"

CHARLOTTE FORTEN

A young black Massachusetts school teacher, Charlotte Forten sailed to the occupied South Carolina islands in 1862 to help educate recently freed slaves. She came from a distinguished Philadelphia family and was bent on helping to make a difference on behalf of former slaves. In 1864 she wrote an article for *Atlantic Monthly* magazine about her experiences in South Carolina. She wanted to show that emancipated slaves were able to improve their lot. That spirit would influence much of the Northern sentiment behind the post-Civil War Reconstruction policies.

May/June 1864

It was on the afternoon of a warm, murky day late in October that our steamer, the United States, touched the landing at Hilton Head. A motley assemblage had collected on the wharf, officers, soldiers, and "contrabands" of every size and hue: black was, however, the prevailing color. The first view of Hilton Head is desolate enough, a long low, sandy point, stretching out into the sea, with no visible dwellings upon it, except the rows of small white-roofed houses which have lately been built for the freed people.

From Hilton Head to Beaufort the same long, low line of sandy coast, bordered by trees; formida-

ble gunboats in the distance, and the gray ruins of an old fort, said to have been built by the Huguenots more than two hundreds years ago.... A large building which was once the Public Library is now a shelter for freed people from Fernandia. Did the Rebels know it, they would doubtless upturn their aristocratic noses, and exclaim in disgust, "To what base uses," etc. We confess that it was highly satisfactory to us to see how the tables are turned, now that the "whirlgig of time has brought about its revenge."...There were indications that already Northern improvements had reached this Southern town. Among them was a wharf, a convenience that one wonders how the Southerners could so long existed without. The more we know of their mode of life, the more we are inclined to marvel at its utter shiftlessness.

Little colored children of every hue were playing about the streets, looking as merry and happy as children ought to look, now that the evil shadow of Slavery no longer hangs over them. Some of the officers we met did not impress us favorably. They talked flippantly, and sneeringly at the negroes, whom they found we had come down to teach, using an epithet more offensive than gentlemanly....

The next morning L. and I were awakened by the cheerful voices of men and women, children and chickens, in the yard below. We ran to the window, and looked out. Women in bright-colored handkerchiefs, some carrying pails on their heads, were crossing the yard, busy with their morning work; children were playing and tumbling around them. On every face there was a look of serenity and cheerfulness. My heart gave a great throb of happiness as I looked at them and thought, "They are free! So long down-trodden, so long crushed to the earth, but now in their old homes, forever free!" And I thanked God that I had lived to see this day.

The first day of school was rather trying. Most of my children were very small, and consequently restless. Some were too young to learn the alphabet. These little ones were brought to school because the older children—in whose care their parents leave them while at work—could not come without them. We were therefore willing to have them come, although they seemed to have discovered the secret of perpetual motion, and tried one's patience sadly. But after some days of positive, though not severe treatment, order was brought out of chaos, and I found but little difficulty in managing and quieting the tiniest and most restless spirits. I never before saw children so eager to learn, although I had had several years' experience in New England schools. Coming to school is a constant delight and recreation to them. They come here as other children go to play. The older ones, during the summer, work in the fields from early morning until eleven or twelve o'clock, and then come into school, after their hard toil in the hot sun, as bright and as anxious to learn as ever.

Of course, there are some stupid ones, but these are the minority. The majority learn with wonderful rapidity. Many of the grown people are desirous of learning to read. It is wonderful how a people who have been so long crushed to the earth, so imbruted as these have been, and they are said to be among the most degraded negroes of the South, can have so great a desire for knowledge, and such a capability for attaining it. One cannot believe that the haughty Anglo-Saxon race, after centuries of such an experience as these people have had, would they themselves use every means in their power to crush and degrade them, denying them every right and privilege, closing against them every avenue of elevation and improvement. Were they, under such circumstances, intellectual and refined, they would certainly be vastly superior to any other race that ever existed....

❧ Letter to Mrs. Bixby

ABRAHAM LINCOLN

On November 21, 1864, after the bloody campaigns in Virginia and Georgia, Abraham Lincoln wrote a letter to Lydia Bixby, the mother of five sons who were killed in battle fighting on the Union side. Lincoln wrote the letter shortly after winning re-election as president and at a time when it was becoming increasingly clear that the North would triumph in its cause of union and freedom for slaves.

Dear Madam:

I have been shown in the files of the War Department a statement of the Adjutant general of Massachusetts that you are the mother of five sons who have died gloriously on the field of battle. I feel how weak and fruitless must be any words of mine which should attempt to beguile you from the grief of a loss so overwhelming, but I cannot refrain from tendering to you the consolation that may be found in the thanks of the Republic that they died to save. I pray that the heavenly Father may assuage the anguish of your bereavement, and leave you only the cherished memory of the loved and lost, and the solemn pride that must be yours to have laid so costly a sacrifice upon the altar of freedom.

❧ Massacre of the Cheyenne Indians

JOHN SMITH

While most of the country was embroiled in the midst of the Civil War, out West tensions between settlers and Indians continued unabated. Prospectors in the Pike's Peak gold rush compelled the United States to purchase land from Indians and set aside territory in barren southeastern Colorado for the Cheyenne and Arapaho tribes. Some of the Indians rebelled against the transaction and attacked settlements. The southern Cheyenne, however, stuck to the conditions of the peace treaty and sought protection from United States troops. In fact, Cheyenne chief Black Kettle had met with military leaders, including Colonel J. M. Chivington, and was assured his tribe would be protected.

Colorado militia, however, were bent on revenge. Unable or unwilling to distinguish between peaceful and warrior tribes, Chivington, a Methodist preacher, ordered his troops to swoop down on Black Kettle's unsuspecting Cheyenne camp at Sand River Creek at dawn on a November morning in 1864. The soldiers massacred an estimated 450 men, women and children, ignoring a white flag of surrender and a large American flag in front of Black Kettle's tent. Abraham Lincoln had given Black Kettle the flag. Local newspapers celebrated the massacre as a great victory and hailed Chivington and his soldiers as heroes.

But as word of the massacre filtered east, more sympathetic sensibilities were outraged. After the Civil War ended, Congress launched an investigation into the massacre, including this interview with Indian agent John S. Smith.

Testimony of John S. Smith before the Joint Committee on the Conduct of the War
QUESTION. Were the women and children slaughtered indiscriminately, or only so far as they were with the warriors?

JOHN SMITH. Indiscriminately.

QUESTION. Were there any acts of barbarity perpetrated there that came under your own observation?

SMITH. Yes, sir; I saw the bodies of those lying

there cut all to pieces, worse mutilated than any I ever saw before; the women cut all to pieces.

QUESTION. How cut?

SMITH. With knives; scalped; their brains knocked out; children two or three months old; all ages lying there, from sucking infants up to warriors. They were terribly mutilated, lying there in the water and sand; most of them in the bed of the creek, dead and dying, making many struggles. They were so badly mutilated and covered with sand and water that it was very hard for me to tell one from another.

QUESTION. Did you see it done?

SMITH. Yes sir; I saw them fall.

QUESTION. Fall when they were killed?

SMITH. Yes, sir.

QUESTION. Did you see them when they were mutilated?

SMITH. Yes, sir.

QUESTION. By whom were they mutilated?

SMITH. By the United States troops.

QUESTION. Do you know whether or not it was done by the direction or consent of any of the officers?

SMITH. I do not. I hardly think it was.

QUESTION. Were there any other barbarities and atrocities committed there other than those you have mentioned, that you saw?

SMITH. Yes, sir; I had a half-breed son there, who gave himself up. He started at the time the Indians fled; being a half-breed he had but little hope of being spared, and seeing them fire at me, he ran away with the Indians for the distance of about a mile. During the fight up there he walked back to my camp and went into the lodge. It was surrounded by soldiers at the time. He came in quietly and sat down; he remained there that day, that night, and the next day in the afternoon; about four o'clock in the evening, as I was sitting inside the camp, a soldier came up outside of the lodge and called me by name. I got up and went out; he took me by the arm and walked towards Colonel Chivington's camp, which was about 60 yards from my camp. Said he, "I am sorry to tell you, but they are going to kill your son Jack." I knew the feeling towards the whole camp of Indians, and that there was no use to make any resistance. I said, "I can't help it." I then walked on towards where Colonel Chivington was standing by his camp-fire; when I had got within a few feet of him I heard a gun fired, and saw a crowd run to my lodge, and they told me Jack was dead.

QUESTION. What action did Colonel Chivington take in regard to that matter?

SMITH. Major Anthony, who was present, told Colonel Chivington that he had heard some remarks made, indicating that they were desirous of killing Jack; and that [Colonel Chivington] had it in his power to save him, and that by saving him he might make him a very useful man, as he was well acquainted with all the Cheyenne and Arapahoe country, and he could be used as a guide or interpreter. Colonel Chivington replied to Major Anthony, as the Major himself told me, that he had no orders to receive and no advice to give.

"Oh, what a horrible thing war is"

ELIZA FRANCES ANDREWS

By early 1865 the Civil War was in its death throes. Suffering from the effects of the naval blockade, famine, and four years of wars, Southerners found luxury in the simplest of items, as this entry from Eliza Frances's journal reflects. The young Georgia woman's entry also discusses the toll of the war on Union prisoners at Andersonville, who in the previous summer died at a rate of one every 11 minutes. At the beginning of the war, prisoners were routinely exchanged. Often, released prisoners re-enlisted as soldiers.

But in 1864 prisoner exchanges ceased. The Confederate Army refused to acknowledge African-American soldiers as being anything but runaway slaves. Captured African-American Union soldiers were massacred on the spot or sold into slavery. Grant ordered an end to the prisoner exchange until the South formally agreed to recognize "no distinction whatever in the exchange between white and colored prisoners." This policy coincided with Grant's desire to deprive the South of manpower to replenish its dwindling army.

Already inadequate for the job, prisoner of war camps became death traps. Disease, freezing temperatures and non-existent sanitary measures led to thousands of deaths in Union camps. But the North at least had the resources to feed its prisoners—not so in the South, where prisoners suffered terrible deprivations.

Worst of all was Andersonville. As many as 33,000 prisoners were crammed into the twenty-six-acre camp, making it the fifth largest city in the Confederacy. Each inmate's daily ration was a teaspoon of salt, three tablespoons of beans, and half a pint of cornmeal. The prison commandant refused to provide shelter or clothing. Seeking shade from the sweltering mid-day sun, prisoners dug tunnels that attracted vermin. Of the 50,000 Union soldiers who entered Andersonville,

10,000 died. In all, more than 50,000 soldiers died in Union and Confederate prison camps during the war.

January 25, 1865. While going our rounds in the morning we found a very important person in Peter Louis, a paroled Yankee prisoner, in the employ of Captain Bonham. The captain keeps him out of the stockade, feeds and clothes him, and in return reaps the benefit of his skill. Peter is a French Yankee, a shoemaker by trade, and makes as beautiful shoes as I ever saw imported from France. My heart quite softened toward him when I saw his handiwork, and little Mrs. Sims was so overcome that she gave him a huge slice of her Confederate fruitcake. I talked French with him, which pleased him greatly, and Mett and I engaged him to make us each a pair of shoes. I will feel like a lady once more, with good shoes on my feet. I expect the poor Yank is glad to get away from Anderson on any terms. Although matters have improved somewhat with the cool weather, the tales that are told of the condition of things there last summer are appalling. Mrs. Brisbane heard all about it from Father Hamilton, a Roman Catholic priest from Macon, who has been working like a good Samaritan in those dens of filth and misery. It is a shame to us Protestants that we have let a Roman Catholic get so far ahead of us in this work of charity and mercy. Mrs. Brisbane says Father Hamilton told her that during the summer the wretched prisoners burrowed in the ground like moles to protect themselves from the sun. It was not safe to give them material to build shanties as they might use it for clubs to overcome the guard. These underground huts, he said, were alive with vermin and stank like charnel houses. Many of the prisoners were stark naked, having not so much as a shirt to their backs. He told a pitiful story of a Pole who had no garment but a shirt, and to make it cover him better, he put his legs into the sleeves and tied the tail around his neck. The others guyed him so on his appearance and the poor wretch was so disheartened by suffering that one day he deliberately stepped over the dead line and stood there till the guard was forced to shoot him. But what I can't understand is that a Pole of all people in the world, should come over here and try to take away our liberty when his own country is in the hands of oppressors. One would think that the Poles, of all nations in the world, ought to sympathize with a people fighting for their liberties. Father Hamilton said that at one time the prisoners died at the rate of a hundred and fifty a day, and he saw some of them die on the ground without a rag to lie on or a garment to cover them. Dysentery was the most fatal disease, and as they lay on the ground in their own excrements, the smell was so horrible that the good father says he was often obliged to rush from their presence to get a breath of pure air. It is dreadful. My heart aches for the poor wretches, Yankees though they are, and I am afraid God will suffer some terrible retribution to fall upon us for letting such things happen. If the Yankees ever should come to southwest Georgia and go to Anderson and see the graves there, God have mercy on the land! And yet what can we do? The Yankees themselves are really more to blame than we, for they won't exchange prisoners, and our poor, hard-pressed Confederacy had not the means to provide for them when our own soldiers are starving in the field. Oh, what a horrible thing war is when stripped of all its pomp and circumstance!

"With malice toward none"

ABRAHAM LINCOLN'S SECOND INAUGURAL ADDRESS

With the re-election of Abraham Lincoln in 1864, a string of military victories in the field and crumbling Confederate resolve, there was a widespread expectation in the North that the Union would prevail. When Abraham Lincoln made his Second Inaugural Address March 4, 1865, he was starting to lay the groundwork for the hard work of reconciliation. Invoking biblical terms, Lincoln remained intent on finishing the war that had divided the country and forging a new nation, bound together in peace.

Fellow Countrymen:
At this second appearing to take the oath of the presidential office, there is less occasion for an extended address than there was at the first. Then a statement, somewhat in detail, of a course to be pursued, seemed fitting and proper. Now, at the expiration of four years, during which public declarations have been constantly called forth on every point and phase of the great contest which still absorbs the attention, and engrosses the energies of the nation, little that is

new could be presented. The progress of our arms, upon which all else chiefly depends, is as well known to the public as to myself; and it is, I trust, reasonably satisfactory and encouraging to all. With high hope for the future, no prediction in regard to it is ventured.

On the occasion corresponding to this four years ago, all thoughts were anxiously directed to an impending civil war. All dreaded it—all sought to avert it. While the inaugural address was being delivered from this place, devoted altogether to saving the Union without war, insurgent agents were in the city seeking to destroy it without war— seeking to dissolve the Union, and divide effects, by negotiation. Both parties deprecated war; but one of them would make war rather than let the nation survive; and the other would accept war rather than let it perish. And the war came.

One-eighth of the whole population were colored slaves, not distributed generally over the Union, but localized in the Southern part of it. These slaves constituted a peculiar and powerful interest. All knew that this interest was, somehow, the cause of the war. To strengthen, perpetuate, and extend this interest was the object for which the insurgents would rend the Union, even by war; while the government claimed no right to do more than to restrict the territorial enlargement of it. Neither party expected for the war the magnitude, or the duration, which it has already attained. Neither anticipated that the cause of the conflict might cease with, or even before, the conflict itself should cease. Each looked for an easier triumph, and a result less fundamental and astounding. Both read the same Bible, and pray to the same God; and each invokes His aid against the other. It may seem strange that any men should dare to ask a just God's assistance in wringing their bread from the sweat of other men's faces; but let us judge not that we be not judged. The prayers of both could not be answered; that of neither has been answered fully. The Almighty has His own purposes. "Woe unto the world because of offenses! For it must needs be that offences come; but woe to that man by whom the offense cometh!" If we shall suppose that American Slavery is one of those offenses which, in the providence of God, must needs come, but which, having continued through His appointed time, He now wills to remove, and that He gives to both North and South, this terrible war, as the woe due to those by whom the offense came, shall we discern therein any departure from those divine attributes which the believers in a Living God always ascribe to Him? Fondly do we hope— fervently do we pray—that this mighty scourge of war may speedily pass away. Yet, if God wills that it continue, until all the wealth plied by the bondman's two hundred and fifty years of unrequited toil shall be sunk, and until every drop of blood drawn with the lash, shall be paid by another drawn with the sword, as was said three thousand years ago, so still it must be said, "the judgments of the Lord, are true and righteous altogether."

With malice toward none; with charity for all; with firmness in the right, as God gives us to see the right, let us strive on to finish the work we are in; to bind up the nation's wounds; to care for him who shall have borne the battle, and for his widow, and his orphan—to do all which may achieve and cherish a just, and a lasting peace, among ourselves, and with all nations.

🍂 "We did not want to exult over their downfall"

ULYSSES S. GRANT

In early April 1865, Grant at last broke the siege at Petersburg. Lee's army dashed westward attempting to escape. But Grant's armies surrounded Lee at Appomatox. Hoping to end the bloodshed, Grant offered to discuss terms of surrender on April 7. After holding out hope for an escape route for two days, Lee responded that he would meet with Grant to negotiate a surrender. Grant, who was known as "Unconditional Surrender Grant," realized that the loss of Lee's army would end the conflict. As his memoirs reflect, Grant heeded Lincoln's embracing attitude toward the defeated South. Grant was respectful of Lee and his soldiers, offering to let the former rebels keep their horses and mules. Grant also ordered his quartermaster to deliver 25,000 rations to the starving Southern troops.

When I had left camp that morning I had not expected so soon the result that was then taking place, and consequently was in rough garb. I was without a sword, as I usually was when on horseback on the field, and wore a soldier's blouse for a coat, with the shoulder straps of my rank to indicate to the army who I was. When I went into the house I found General Lee. We greeted each other, and after shaking hands took our seats. I had my staff with me, a good portion of whom were in the room during the whole of the interview.

What General Lee's feelings were I do not know. As he was a man of much dignity, with an impassable face, it was impossible to say whether he felt inwardly glad that the end had finally come, or felt sad over the result, and was too manly to show it. Whatever his feelings, they were entirely concealed from my observation; but my own feelings, which had been quite jubilant on the receipt of his letter, were sad and depressed. I felt like anything rather than rejoicing at the downfall of a foe who had fought so long and valiantly, and had suffered so much for a cause, though that cause was, I believe, one of the worst for which a people ever fought, and one for which there was the least excuse. I do not question, however, the sincerity of the great mass of those who were opposed to us.

General Lee was dressed in a full uniform which was entirely new, and was wearing a sword of considerable value, very likely the sword which had been presented by the State of Virginia; at all events it was an entirely different sword from the one that would ordinarily be worn in the field. In my rough traveling suit, the uniform of a private with the straps of a lieutenant-general, I must have contrasted very strangely with a man so handsomely dressed, six feet high and of faultless form. But this was not a matter that I thought of until afterwards. We soon fell into a conversation about old army times. He remarked that he remembered me very well in the old army; and I told him that as a matter of course I remembered him perfectly, but from the difference in our rank and years (there being about sixteen years' difference in our ages), I had thought it very likely that I had not attracted his attention sufficiently to be remembered by him after such a long interval. Our conversation grew so pleasant that I almost forgot the object of our meeting. After the conversation had run on this style for some time, General Lee called my attention to the object of our meeting, and said that he had asked for this interview for the purpose of getting from me the terms I proposed to give his army. I said that I meant merely that his army should lay down their arms, not to take them up again during the continuance of the war unless duly and properly exchanged. He said that he had understood my letter....

I then said to him that I thought this would be about the last battle of the war—I sincerely hoped so; and I said further I took it that most of the men in the ranks were small farmers. The whole country had been so raided by the two armies that it was doubtful whether they would be able to put in a crop to carry themselves and their families through the next winter without the aid of the horses they were then riding. The United States did not want them and I would, therefore, instruct the officers I left behind to receive the paroles of his troops to let every man of the Confederate army who claimed to own a horse or mule take the animal to his home. Lee remarked again that this would have a happy effect....

When news of the surrender first reached our lines our men commenced firing a salute of a hundred guns in honor of the victory. I at once sent word, however, to have it stopped. The confederates were now our prisoners, and we did not want to exult over their downfall.

❧ Farewell to his Army

ROBERT E. LEE

Having surrendered his forces to Grant the day before, Lee wrote a final farewell message to his soldiers.

Headquarters, Army of Northern Virginia
April 10, 1865

After four years of arduous service marked by unsurpassed courage and fortitude, the Army of Northern Virginia has been compelled to yield to overwhelming numbers and resources.

I need not tell the survivors of so many hard-fought battles who have remained steadfast to the last that I have consented to this result from no distrust of them; but feeling that valor and devotion could accomplish nothing that would compensate for the loss that must have attended the continuance of the contest, I determined to avoid the useless sacrifice of those whose past services have endeared them to their countrymen. By the terms of the agreement, officers and men can return to their homes and remain until exchanged.

You may take with you the satisfaction that proceeds from the consciousness of duty faithfully performed, and I earnestly pray that a merciful God will extend to you His blessing and protection. With an increasing admiration of your constancy, and a grateful remembrance of your kind and generous consideration of myself, I bid you an affectionate farewell.

R. E. Lee,
General

❧ "I am lost in amazement that the struggle could have been so prolonged"

JUDAH BENJAMIN

After the Civil War was over, Judah Benjamin wrote to a Confederate colleague, Charles Marshall, reflecting on the deficiencies of the Confederate States of America that contributed to their defeat. Benjamin had variously served as Attorney General, Secretary of War and Secretary of State. The fledgling nation, the letter makes clear, was plagued by internal strife and massive logistical deficiencies. Ironically, the issue of state's rights, which precipitated the conflict, proved to also sap the strength of the Confederate war effort.

As soon as war became certain, every possible effort was made by the President and his advisers to induce Congress to raise an army enlisted "for the war." The fatal effects of enlistments for short terms, shown by the history of the War of Independence against England, were invoked as furnishings a lesson for our guidance. It was all in vain. The people as we were informed by the members would not volunteer for the war, but they would rise in mass as volunteers for twelve months. We did not wish them to rise in mass nor in great numbers for any such short term, for the reason that we could not arm them, and their term of service would expire before we could equip them. I speak from memory as to numbers, but only a moderate force was raised (all that we could provide with arms) for twelve months service, and thus a provisional army was formed, but the fatal effect of the short term of service, combined with the painful deficiency of supplies, were felt long before

the end of the year. While the Northern States after the Battle of Manassas were vigorously engaged in preparing for an overwhelming descent upon Virginia, our own army was falling to pieces.

The representatives of the people could not be persuaded to pass measures unpalatable to the people; and the unthinking multitude upon whose voluntary enlistments Congress forced us to depend were unable to foresee or appreciate the dangers of the policy against which we protested. It was only the imminent danger of being left without any army by the return home in mass of the first levy of twelve-month volunteers that drove Congress into passing a law for enlistments for the war, and in order to induce the soldiers under arms to re-enlist we were driven to the fatal expedient of granting them not only bounties but furloughs to return from Virginia to their homes in the far South, and if our actual condition had been at all suspected by the enemy they might have marched through Virginia with but the faintest show of resistance.

As to supplies of munitions I will give a single instance of the straits to which we were reduced. I was Secretary of War ad interim for a few months, during which Roanoke Island, commanded by General Wise, fell into the hands of the enemy. The report of that General shows that the capture was due in great measure to the persistent disregard by the Secretary of War of his urgent demands for munitions and supplies. Congress appointed a committee to investigate the conduct of the Secretary. I consulted the President whether it was best for the country that I should submit to unmerited censure or reveal to a Congressional Committee our poverty and my utter inability to supply the requisitions of General Wise, and thus run the risk that the fact should become known to some of the spies of the enemy of whose activity we were well assured. It was thought best for the public service that I should suffer the blame in silence and a report of censure on me was accordingly made by the Committee of Congress.

The dearth even of powder was so great during the descent of the enemy on Roanoke, General Wise having sent me a despatch that he was in instant need of ammunition, I ordered by telegraph General Huger at Norfolk to send an immediate supply; this was done but accompanied by a despatch from General Huger protesting against this exhausting of his small store, and saying that it was insufficient to defend Norfolk for a day.

General Lee was therefore ordered to send a part of his very scanty supply to Norfolk, General Lee being in his turn aided by a small cargo of powder which had just run into one of the inlets on the coast of Florida.

Another source of trouble, disorganization and inefficiency was the incurable jealousy in many states of the General Government. Each State has its own mode of appointing officers, generally by election. Until disaster forced Congress to pass the Conscription law, all that we could do was to get laws passed calling for certain quotas of troops from the states, and in order to prevent attempts made to prevent attempts made to create officers of higher rank than the Confederate officers, who would thus have been placed under the orders of raw militia generals, we resorted to the expedient of refusing to receive any higher organisation than a regiment. But the troops being State troops officered by the State officers, the army was constantly scandalized by electioneering to replace regimental officers, and Confederate Commanders were without means of enforcing discipline and efficiency except through the cumbrous and most objectionable expedient of Courts Martial. Another fatal defect was that we had no power to consolidate regiments, battalions, and companies. If a company was reduced to five men or a regiment to fifty, we had no power to remedy this. The message of the President of the 12th of August, 1862, showed the fatal effects of our military system, and a perusal of that message will shed a flood of light on the actual position of things and the helplessness to which the Executive was reduced by the legislation of Congress, and the restrictions imposed on his power to act efficiently for military success by the jealousy of Congress and the States. When I look back on it all, I am lost in amazement that the struggle could have been so prolonged, and one of the main, if not the main strength and encouragement to the Executive was the genius, ability, constancy, fidelity, and firmness of General Lee.

❧ "They are everywhere, these Yankees"

MARY CHESNUT

Lee's surrender effectively ended the war. The South was destroyed. What had started for the white population with such hope and celebration ended in despondency and poverty. When South Carolina first declared secession, Mary Chesnut could not sleep because of the celebrations going on downstairs. At the conclusion of the war, Chesnut's home served as a bivouac for weary, defeated soldiers.

April 19th (1865)—Just now, when Mr. Clay dashed upstairs, pale as a sheet, saying, "General Lee has capitulated," I saw it reflected in Mary Darby's face before I heard him speak. Staggered to the table, sat down, and wept aloud. Mr. Clay's eyes were not dry. Quite beside herself Mary shrieked, "Now we belong to negroes and Yankees!" Buck said, "I do not believe it."

How different from ours of them is their estimate of us. How contradictory is their attitude toward us. To keep the despised and iniquitous South within their borders as part of their country, they are willing to enlist millions of men at home and abroad, and to spend billions, and we know they do not love fighting, per se, nor spending money. They are perfectly willing to have three killed for our one. We hear they have all grown rich, through "shoddy," whatever that is. Genuine Yankees can make a fortune trading jackknives.

"Somehow it is borne in on me that we will have to pay the piper," was remarked today. "No; blood can not be squeezed from a turnip. You can not pour anything out of an empty cup. We have no money even for taxes or to be confiscated."

While the Preston girls are here, my dining-room is given up to them, and we camp on the landing, with our one table and six chairs. Beds are made on the dining-room floor. Otherwise there is no furniture, except buckets of water and bath-tubs in their impoverished chamber. Night and day this landing and these steps are crowded with the elite of the Confederacy, going and coming, and when night comes, or rather, bedtime, more beds are made on the floor of the landing-place for the war-worn soldiers to rest upon. The whole house is a bivouac. As Pickens said of South Carolina in 1861, we are "an armed camp."

My husband is rarely at home. I sleep with the girls, and my room is given up to soldiers. General Lee's few, but undismayed, his remnant of an army, or the part from the South and West, sad and crest-fallen, pass through Chester. Many discomfited heroes find their way up these stairs. They say Johnston will not be caught as Lee was. Sherman in the hill country of Georgia, what will he do but retreat in the plains of North Carolina with Grant, Sherman, and Thomas all to the fore?

We are to stay here. Running is useless now; so we mean to bide a Yankee raid, which they say is imminent. Why fly? They are everywhere, these Yankees, like red ants, like the locusts and frogs which were the plagues of Egypt.

The assassination of Mr. Lincoln

EDWIN BATES

Just five days after Lee surrendered, on April 14, 1865, exactly four years to the day after Fort Sumter was captured to begin the war, John Wilkes Booth shot Abraham Lincoln at Ford's Theatre. The nation was stunned as questions about an uncertain future arose. Lincoln's successor, Andrew Johnson, would continue a policy of reconstructing the South, much to the dismay of Congress.

As for Booth, his escape from the theater left him with a broken leg and a death warrant on his head. Twelve days later he and a fellow conspirator were tracked to barn in Virginia, where, following a shoot-out, Booth and his partner were killed. Four others involved in the assassination plot were hanged, three were sentenced to life in prison and an eighth, the man who held Booth's horse while he shot the president, was sentenced to six years in jail. Four years later, Johnson would pardon those in jail.

The following letter was written by Edwin Bates to his parents shortly after he witnessed the assassination as a member of the audience in the theater.

I went to the theatre last night & saw him for the first time—& soon after an event did occur—not happy as I had predicted in my letter, but one the most horrible & atrocious that that as ever been recorded in the annals of history—the assassination of Mr. Lincoln. I was accompanied by Mr. Sawyer the gentleman that wrote you about me last fall & was seated in the orchestra chairs next to the stage & nearly underneath the box occupied by Mr. Lincoln & friends.

I first heard the report of a pistol & immediately after a man jumped from Mr. Lincolns box a distance of 10 or 15 feet upon the stage right before & not more than 10 feet from me. He fell partly upon his side but instantly rose & with a long dagger in hand rushed rapidly across the stage & disappeared before any in the vast house full of people could realise what had occurred. He was a fine looking man dressed in a full suit of black & it was my impression at the first instant that some body had fired a pistol at him & he had jumped down upon the stage for safety or had been knocked down. I rec this impression from the fact that a pistol had been fired & he had no pistol in his hand but his dagger I saw & before he had got half way across the stage I comprehended that the man was an assassin & that some deadly attack had been made upon Mr. Lincoln. The audience generally seemed about the same time to comprehend the whole matter & began to cry catch him, kill him, but before any could get upon the stage he had disappeared from view behind the scenes. It was in the midst of a play, "Our American Cousin" in which the "yankee" is represented to be a Vermonter hailing from Brattleboro & is on a visit to England to see his English relatives, the piece is amusing & it was between two of the acts of this play while a few actors were just coming on the stage that it occurred. The actors seemed no more to comprehend the matter than the audience or they might perhaps have stopped the man as he ran right past them if they had not been intimidated by his dagger. As it was he rushed out at the rear of the theatre mounted a horse & disappeared & disappeared & has not yet been caught although recognised by a dozen different people in the theatre. His name is John Wilkes Booth an actor & who has frequently played in this theatre & conversant with the different places of egress from it. He had not until last night ever succeeded in attaining any reputation in his profession as an actor but now he has acquired a reputation in tragedy which will render him famous & infamous in history in all time. In the box with Mr. Lincoln was Mrs. Lincoln & also another gentleman & lady. This gentleman I hear was also stabbed by the man. Those who got first to Mr. Lincoln were those seated in the part of the house I was, who jumped upon the stage & by the assistance of each other & climbing up the posts they could get up to near the box & the lady I mentioned as being in the party & apparently 25 or 30 years of age assisted them in, there was immediately a call for water & stimulants from those who first reached the box & the whole of the vast audience was under the wildest excitement & indignation when it became known that Mr. Lincoln was mortally wounded. They were all soon requested to leave the theatre but before all had done so Mr. Lincoln was carried out insensible to a house opposite in which condition he remained until he expired this morning. I forgot to mention that as the man rose as he partially fell upon his knees as he touched the stage he raised the dagger & as he ran across the stage uttered the words "Sic semper tyrannis." As Mr. S & myself walked slowly to the hotel we agreed that the probability was that the man when found would be discovered to be some insane person, that the lowest depths of human depravity even in a rebel of the worst type would not permit to commit such a horrible deed in so bold a manner before thousands of people & where there could be so little chance of escape. But soon after we got to the hotel news came that Mr. Seward & all his household had been assassinated, that it was a grand conspiracy, that the other members of the Cabinet were safe but that suspicious persons had been seen about the residence of Mr. Stanton & Co., also that Gen Grant who left on the evening train for Philadelphia had been shot in the cars. This morning this contradicted & to day the General has returned here. It appears from letters found in Booths room that this murder had been premeditated for some time & it was the intention to have it come off at the inaugural on 4th March but opportunity did not offer, that all the Cabinet & other leading men were to be included is now supposed, that Gen Grant was to be included last night was very probable—as it was reported in the papers of yesterday morning that he would accompany the President to the theatre in the evening.

Booth is a native of Baltimore, & before it was known with any certainty that it was him I heard a gentleman state (who knew him well, he said), that

he could not be the man—for he had long known him & had never known him to be a secessionist that he has taken no part in the rebellion—had been out West, "acting" for last two years or two & latter had been in the petrolium business. It is certain that two & probably more are in the plot, that it was got up in Baltimore, some think also it was known to the Confederate authorities at Richmond. Even if they had succeeded in accomplishing all they desired & destroyed all—President Cabinet & Generals—what good could result to the southern cause at this stage of the war? Once such a blow might have staggered the north but now that time is past.

The excitement here is terrific, the street-corners & hotels are crowded with people swearing deep & deadly vengance to all rebels & the whole south—& so it will be over the north & what the results will be none can tell. Mr. Lincoln was certainly a "Saul among the people" & the early peace & prosperity that I had hoped under his hand would soon return to the country I am afraid now is far distant. His conciliatory policy I am satisfied although distasteful to the radicals & perhaps a majority of the people was surest & quickest road to peace. The rebel armies dispersed soon peace & prosperity would have been restored to the South. That policy may now be changed. Mr. Johnson who is now President is more vindictive. I heard him say in a speech last week that the leaders in the rebellion he would hang as high as Haman.

No event except those of the family history has ever filled me with such profound sadness as this. I have no heart to prosecute further the business upon which I came here & which I had reason to hope I would soon successfully accomplish. I think now I shall leave here in a day or two & return South on the next steamer. I hope for the sake of the Union men of the South & the south generally that it will be found when the assassins are caught & examined that no part of this plot was concocted at the South or was known to Southern leaders.

CHAPTER SIX

1865–1892

Reconstruction and Redefinition

🐦 "Prominent citizens became piesellers"

MYRTA LOCKETT AVARY

At the conclusion of the Civil War much of the South was in a state of ruin and confusion. Cities were destroyed, towns sacked, fields laid fallow and the economy in shambles. Thousands of people died of starvation. For millions, the main goal in the immediate months after the war was survival. Myrta Lockett Avary recalled how even the wealthiest and most prestigious Southerners had become destitute.

We did anything and everything we could to make a living. Prominent citizens became piesellers. Colonel Cary, of General Magruder's staff, came home to find his family desperately poor, as were all respectable folks. He was a brave soldier, an able officer—before the war, principal of a male academy at Hampton. Now he did not know to what he could turn his hand for the support of himself and family. He walked around his place, came in, and said to his wife: "My dear, I have taken stock of our assets. You pride yourself on your apple pies. We have an apple tree and a cow. I will gather the apples and milk the cow, and you will make the pies, and I will go around and sell them."

Armed with pies, he met his aforetime antagonists at Camp Grant and conquered them quite. The pies were delicious; the seller was a soldier, an officer of distinction, in hard luck; and the men at Camp Grant were soldiers too. There was sharp demand and good prices; only the elite—officers of rank—could afford to indulge in these confections. Well it was that Yankee mothers had cultivated in their sons an appetite for pies. One Savannah lady made thirty dollars selling pies to Sherman's soldiers; in Georgia's aristocratic "city by the sea" highbred dames stood at basement windows selling cakes and pies to whoever would buy.

Colonel Cary had thrifty rivals throughout Dixie. A once-rich Planter near Columbia made a living by selling flowers; a Charleston aristocrat peddled tea by the pound and molasses by the quart to his former slaves. General Stephen Elliott sold fish and oysters which he caught with his own hands. His friend, Captain Stoney, did likewise. Gentlemen of position and formerly of wealth did not pause to consider whether they would be discredited by pursuing occupations quite as humble.

Men of high attainments, without capital, without any basis upon which to make a new start in life except "grit," did whatever they could find to do and made merry over it.

For months after the surrender, Confederates were passing through the country to their homes, and hospitality was free to every ragged and footsore soldier; the poor best the larder of every mansion afforded was at the command of the grayjacket. How diffidently proud men would ask for bread, their empty pockets shaming them! When any man turned them off with cold words, it was not well for his neighbors to know; for so he was like to have no more respectable guests. The soldiers were good company, bringing news from far and wide. Most were cheerful, glad they were going home, undaunted by long tramps ahead. The soldier was used to hard marches. Now that his course was set toward where loved ones watched for his coming, life had its rosy outlook that turned to gray for some who reached the spot where home had stood to find only a bank of ashes. Reports of country through which they came were often summed up: "White folks in the fields, Negroes flocking to towns. Freedmen's Bureau offices everywhere thronged with blacks."

A man who belonged to the crippled squad, not one of whom had a full complement of arms and legs, told this story: As four of them were limping along near Lexington, they noticed a gray-headed white man in rough, mud-stained clothes turning furrows with a plow and behind him a white girl dropping corn. Taking him for a hired man, they hallooed: "Hello, there!" The man raised his head. "Say," they called, "can you tell us where we can get something to eat?" He waved them towards a house where a lady who was on the porch asked them to have a seat and wait while she had food cooked.

They had an idea that she prepared with her own hands the dinner to which they presently sat down, of hot hoecakes, buttermilk, and a little meat so smothered in lettuce leaves that it looked a great deal. When they had cleared up the table, she said: "I am having more bread cooked if you can wait a few minutes. I am sorry we have not more meat and milk. I know this has been a very light repast for hungry men, but we have entertained others this morning, and we have not much left. We hate to send our soldiers hungry from the door; they ought to have the best of everything when they have fought so long and bravely and suffered so much." The way she spoke made them proud of the arms and legs they didn't have.

Now that hunger was somewhat appeased, they began to note surroundings. The dwelling was that of a military man, and a man of piety and culture. A lad running in addressed the lady as Mrs. Pendleton and said something about "where General Pendleton is plowing."

They stumbled to their crutches! and in blushing confusion humble apologies, all the instincts of the soldier shocked at the liberties they had taken with an officer of such high grade and at the ease of manner with which they had sat at his table to be served by his wife. They knew their host for William Nelson Pendleton, late brigadier general, C.S.A., chief of artillery of the Army of Northern Virginia, a fighting preacher. She smiled when they blundered out the excuse that they had mistaken him for a day laborer.

"The mistake has been made before," she said. "Indeed, the General is a day laborer in his own field, and it does not mortify him in the least now that all our people have to work. He is thankful his strength is sufficient, and for the help that the schoolboys and his daughters give him." She put bread into their haversacks and sent them on their way rejoicing. The day laborer and his plow were close to the roadside, and as they passed, they drew themselves up in line and brought all the hands they had to their ragged caps in salute.

Doctor Robert G. Stephens, of Atlanta, tells me of a Confederate soldier who, returning armless to his Georgia home, made his wife hitch him to a plow which she drove; and they made a crop. A Northern missionary said in 1867, to a Philadelphia audience, that he had seen in North Carolina a white mother hitch herself to a plow which her eleven-year-old son drove, while another child dropped into the furrows seeds Northern charity had given.

❧ "Neither slavery nor involuntary servitude shall exist"

THIRTEEN AMENDMENT

In January 1865 Congress passed legislation for the Thirteenth Amendment to the Constitution banning slavery from the United States. Northern states quickly approved the amendment, but to secure ratification by three-quarters of the states, at least some Southern states needed to approve it. Ratification by legislatures in former Confederate states became a condition for restoring relations with the Union. The amendment received final ratification on December 6, 1865, ensuring the freedom of more than 4 million African-American slaves from bondage.

Section 1. Neither slavery nor involuntary servitude, except as a punishment for crime whereof the party shall have been duly convicted, shall exist within the United States, or any place subject to their jurisdiction.

Section 2. Congress shall have the power to enforce this article by appropriate legislation.

❧ The Blue and the Gray

FRANCIS MILES FINCH

With 500,000 men killed in the Civil War, the country struggled for a national reconciliation. Francis Miles Finch's poem "The Blue and the Gray" appeared in *The Atlantic Monthly* in 1867. A New York judge, he commemorated the deaths of soldiers from both the North and the South. The poem became a staple at Memorial Day services (which was designated to honor the Civil War dead from both sides) and was later printed in *McGuffey's Reader,* making it even more widely known.

By the flow of the inland river,
Whence the fleets of iron have fled,
Where the blades of the grave grass quiver,
Asleep are the ranks of the dead;—
Under the one, the Blue;
Under the other, the Gray.

These in the robings of glory,
Those in the gloom of defeat,
All with the battle blood gory,
In the dusk of eternity meet;—
Under the sod and the dew,
Waiting the judgment day;—
Under the laurel, the Blue;
Under the willow, the Gray.

From the silence of sorrowful hours
The desolate mourners go,

Lovingly laden with flowers
Alike for the friend and the foe,—
Under the sod and the dew,
Waiting the judgment day;—
Under the roses, the Blue;
Under the lillies, the Gray.

So with an equal splendor
The morning sun rays fall,
With a touch, impartially tender,
On the blossoms blooming for all;—
Under the sod and the dew,
Waiting the judgment day;—
'Broidered with gold, the Blue;
Mellowed with gold, the Gray.

So, when the summer calleth,
On forest and field of grain
With an equal murmur falleth
The cooling drip of the rain;—
Under the sod and the dew,
Waiting the judgment day;—
Wet with the rain, the Blue;
Wet with the rain, the Gray.

Sadly, but not with upbraiding,
The generous deed was done;
In the storm of the years that are fading,
No braver battle was won;—
Under the sod and the dew,
Waiting the judgment day;—
Under the blossoms, the Blue;
Under the garlands, the Gray.

No more shall the war cry sever,
Or the winding rivers be red;
They banish our anger forever
When they laurel the graves of our dead!
Under the sod and the dew,
Waiting the judgment day;—
Love and tears for the Blue,
Tears and love for the Gray.

"Rebel States shall be divided into military districts"

FIRST RECONSTRUCTION ACT

Vice President Andrew Johnson ascended to the presidency after Lincoln's assassination. He continued Lincoln's relatively lenient reconstruction policy of creating provisional state governments. With the victory of the Radical Republican Party in the 1866 election, however, Congress imposed a more extreme reconstruction policy calling for military control over the former Confederate states. In order to be readmitted into the Union, state conventions were required, in which delegates were elected by universal male suffrage, with the exception of anyone who had participated in the Confederate war effort. As a result, state conventions consisted almost entirely of freed slaves and newly arrived citizens from the North, derisively known as "carpetbaggers." Johnson vetoed the act saying it was unconstitutional. Congress overrode the veto.

Whereas no legal State governments or adequate protection for life or property now exists in the rebel States of Virginia, North Carolina, South Carolina, Georgia, Mississippi, Alabama, Louisiana, Florida, Texas, and Arkansas; and whereas it is necessary that peace and good order should be enforced in said States until loyal and republican State governments can be legally established: therefore,

Be it enacted by the Senate and House of Representatives of the United States of America in Congress assembled, That said rebel States shall be divided into military districts and made subject to the military authority of the United States as in hereinafter prescribed, and for that purpose Virginia shall constitute the first district; North Carolina and South Carolina the second district; Georgia, Alabama, and Florida the third district; Mississippi and Arkansas the fourth district; and Louisiana and Texas the fifth district.

Section 2. And be it further enacted, That it shall be the duty of the President to assign to the command of each of said districts an officer of the army, not below the rank of brigadier-general, and to detail a sufficient military force to enable such officer to perform his duties and enforce his authority within the district to which he is assigned.

Section 3. And be it further enacted, That it shall be the duty of each officer assigned as aforesaid, to protect all persons in their rights of person and property, to suppress insurrection, disorder, and violence, and to punish, or cause to be punished, all disturbers of the public peace and criminals; and to this end he may allow local civil tribunals to take jurisdiction of and to try offenders, or, when in his judgment it may be necessary for the trial of offenders, he shall have power to organize military commissions or tribunals for that purpose, and all interference under color of State authority with the exercise of military authority under this act, shall be null and void.

Section 4. And be it further enacted, That all persons put under military arrest by virtue of this act shall be tried without unnecessary delay, and no cruel or unusual punishment shall be inflicted, and no sentence of any military commission or tribunal hereby authorized, affecting the life or liberty of any person, shall be executed until it is approved by the officer in command of the district, and the laws and regulations for the government of the army shall not be affected by this act, except in so far as they conflict with its provisions: Provided, That no sentence of death under the provisions of this act shall be carried into effect without the approval of the President.

Section 5. That when the people of any one of said rebel States shall have formed a constitution of government in conformity with the Constitution of the United States in all respects, framed by a convention of delegates elected by the male citizens of said State twenty-one years old and upward, of whatever race, color, or previous condition, who have been resident in said State for one year previous to the day of such election, except such as may be disenfranchised for participation in the rebellion or for felony at common law, and when such constitution shall provide that the elective franchise shall be enjoyed by all such persons as have the qualifications herein states for electors of delegates, and when such constitution shall be ratified by a majority of the persons voting on the question of ratification who are qualified as electors for delegates, and when such constitution shall have been submitted to Congress for examination and approval, and Congress shall have approved the same, and when said State, by a vote of its legislature elected under said constitution, shall have adopted the amendment to the Constitution of the United States said State shall be declared entitled

to representation in Congress, and senators and representatives shall be admitted therefrom on their taking the oath prescribed by law, and then and thereafter the preceding sections of this act shall be inoperative in said States: Provided, That no person excluded from the privilege of holding office by said proposed amendment to the Constitution of the United States, shall be eligible to election as a member of the convention to frame a constitution for any of said rebel States, nor shall any such person vote for members of such convention.

"Seward's Folly"

THE PURCHASE OF ALASKA

Secretary of State William Seward pursued an aggressive expansionary policy after the Civil War, applying military pressure against French intervention in Mexico and negotiating a treaty of friendship and commerce with China. In 1867, Seward arranged for the United States to buy the Virgin Islands from Denmark for $7.5 million and Alaska from Russia for $7.2 million. The Senate rejected the purchase of the Virgin Islands but approved the Alaskan treaty, prompting howls of protest that the United States was taken in the deal.

The transaction was derided as "Seward's Folly" and "Seward's Ice Box." Russia—which had acquired the remote region primarily for its abundant fur trade—was eager to sell the territory when it appeared as if the British might take it. Despite domestic scorn for the transaction, the purchase of the Alaskan Territory at two cents an acre proved to be an extraordinary boon to the United States when gold was discovered near the end of the century. Alaska became a state in 1959. Seward's birthday is now a state holiday.

The United States of America and his Majesty the Emperor of all the Russias, being desirous of strengthening, if possible, the good understanding which exists between them, have, for that purpose, appointed as their plenipotentaries: the President of the United States, William H. Seward, Secretary of State; and his Majesty the Emperor of all the Russias, the privy counsellor Edward de Stoeckl, his envoy extraordinary and minister plenipotentiary to the United States.

And the said plenipotentiaries, having exchanged their full powers, which were found to be in due form, have agreed upon and signed the following articles:—

Article I—His Majesty the Emperor of all the

Russias agrees to cede to the United States, by this convention, immediately upon the exchange of the ratifications thereof, all the territory and dominion now possessed by his said Majesty on the continent of America and in the adjacent islands, the same being contained within the geographical limits herein set forth, to wit: the eastern limit is the line of demarcation between the Russian and the British possessions in North America, as established by the convention between Russia and Great Britain, of February 28-16, 1825, and described in Articles III. and IV. of said convention, in the following terms:—

Commencing from the southernmost point of the island called Prince of Wales Island, which point lies in the parallel of 54 degrees 40 minutes north latitude, and between the 131st and 133d degree of west longitude (meridian of Greenwich), the said line shall ascend to the north along the channel called Portland Channel, as far as the point of the continent where it strikes the 56th degree of north latitude; from this last-mentioned point the line of demarcation shall follow the summit of the mountains situated parallel to the coast as far as the point of intersection of the 141st degree of west longitude (of the same meridian); and finally, from the said point of intersection, the said meridian line of the 141st degree, in its prolongation as far as the Frozen Ocean.

Article III. The inhabitants of the ceded territory, according to their choice, reserving their natural allegiance, may return to Russia within three years; but, if they should prefer to remain in the ceded territory, they, with the exception of uncivilized native tribes, shall be admitted to the enjoyment of all the rights, advantages, and immunities of citizens of the United States, and shall be maintained and protected in the free enjoyment of their liberty, property, and religion. The uncivilized tribes will be subject to such laws and regulations as the United States may from time to time adopt in regard to aboriginal tribes of that country....

IV. With reference to the line of demarcation laid down in the preceding article, it is understood—

1st. That the island called Prince of Wales Island shall belong wholly to Russia (now by this cession to the United States).

2d. That whenever the summit of the mountains which extend in a direction parallel to the coast from the 56th degree of north latitude to the point of intersection of the 141st degree of west longitude shall prove to be at the distance of more than ten marine leagues from the ocean, the limit between the British possessions and the line of coast which is to belong to Russia as above mentioned (that is to say, the limit to the possessions ceded by this convention) shall be formed by a line parallel to the winding of the coast, and which shall never exceed the distance of ten marine leagues therefrom.

The western limit within which the territories and dominion conveyed are contained passes through a point in Behring's Straits on the parallel of 65 degrees 30 minutes north latitude, at its intersection by the meridian which passes midway between the islands of Krusenstern, or Ignalook, and the island of Ratmanoff, or Noonarbook, and proceeds due north, without limitation, into the same Frozen Ocean. The same western limit, beginning at the same initial point, proceeds thence in a course nearly southwest, through Behring's Straits and Behring's Sea, so as to pass midway between the northwest point of the island of St. Lawrence and the southeast point of Cape Choukotski, to the meridian of 72 west longitude; thence, from the intersection of that meridian, in a southwesterly direction, so as to pass midway between the island of Attou and the Copper Island of the Kormandorski couplet or group in the North Pacific Ocean, to the meridian of 193 degrees west longitude, so as to include in the territory conveyed the whole of the Aleutian Islands east of that meridian.

Article II. In the cession of territory and dominion made by the preceding article are included the right of property in all public lots and squares, vacant lands, and all public buildings, fortifications, barracks, and other edifices which are not private individual property. It is, however, understood and agreed that the churches which have been built in the ceded territory by the Russian government shall remain the property of such members of the Greek Oriental Church resident in the territory as may choose to worship therein. Any government archives, papers, and documents relative to the territory and dominion aforesaid, which may be now existing there, will be left in the possession of the agent of the United States; but an authenticated copy of such of them as may be required will be at all times given by the

United States to the Russian government, or to such Russian officers or subjects as they may apply for.

Article V. Immediately after the exchange of the ratifications of this convention, any fortifications or military posts which may be in the ceded territory shall be delivered to the agent of the United States, and any Russian troops which may be in the territory shall be withdrawn as soon as may be reasonably and conveniently practicable.

Article VI. In consideration of the cession aforesaid the United States agrees to pay at the treasury in Washington, within ten months after the exchange of the ratifications of this convention, to the diplomatic representative or other agent of his Majesty the Emperor of all the Russias, duly authorized to receive the same, seven million two hundred thousand dollars in gold....

🍃 Ragged Dick

HORATIO ALGER

In 1867 Horatio Alger published the first in his enormously popular series of rags-to-riches stories. An 1860 graduate of the Harvard Divinity School, Alger's stories described how young boys could improve their lot through hard work, honesty, and thriftiness. The stories embodied and perpetuated the popular notion that in America a person rose or fell in society according to his or her merit. The following excerpts are from the first story, "Ragged Dick," which was initially published as a magazine series in *Student and Schoolmate* and later put into book format in 1868.

There was another way in which Dick sometimes lost money. There was a noted gambling-house on Baxter Street, which in the evening was sometimes crowded with these juvenile gamesters, who staked their hard earnings, generally losing of course, and refreshing themselves from time to time with a vile mixture of liquor at two cents a glass. Sometimes Dick strayed in here, and played with the rest.

I have mentioned Dick's faults and defects, because I want it understood, to begin with, that I don't consider him a model boy. But there were some good points about him nevertheless. He was above doing anything mean or dishonorable. He would not steal, or cheat, or impose upon younger boys, but was frank and straight-forward, manly and self-reliant. His nature was a noble one, and had

saved him from all mean faults. I hope my young readers will like him as I do, without being blind to his faults. Perhaps, although he was only a boot-black, they may find something in him to imitate.

• • •

"That's a pretty good story," said Dick, "but I don't believe all the cats in New York will ever make me mayor."

"No probably not, but you may rise in some other way. A good many distinguished men have once been poor boys. There's hope for you, Dick, if you'll try."

"Nobody ever talked to me so before," said Dick. "They just called me Ragged Dick, and told me I'd grow up to be a vagabond (boys who are better educated need not be surprised at Dick's blunders) and come to the gallows."

"Telling you so won't make it turn out so, Dick. If you'll try to be somebody, and grow up into a respectable member of society, you will. You may not become rich—it isn't everybody that becomes rich, you know—but you can obtain a good position, and be respected."

"I'll try," said Dick, earnestly, "I needn't have been Ragged Dick so long if I hadn't spent my money in goin' to the theatre, and treatin' boys to oyster-stews, and bettin' money on cards and such like."

• • •

"I believe he is a good boy," said Mr. Whitney. "I hope, my lad, you will prosper and rise in the world. You know in this free country poverty in early life is no bar to a man's advancement. I haven't risen very high myself," he added, with a smile, "but have met with moderate success in life; yet there was a time when I was as poor as you."

"Were you sir?" asked Dick, eagerly.

"Yes, my boy, I have known the time when I have been obliged to go without my dinner because I didn't have enough money to pay for it."

"How did you get up in the world?" asked Dick, anxiously.

"I entered a printing-office as an apprentice, and worked for some years. Then my eyes gave out and I was obliged to give that up. Not knowing what else to do, I went into the country, and worked on a farm. After a while I was lucky enough to invent a machine, which has brought me in a great deal of money. But there was one thing I got while I was in the printing-office which I value more than money."

"What was that, sir?"

"A taste for reading and study…"

• • •

Our hero took his bank-book, and gazed on the entry "Five Dollars" with a new sense of importance. He had been accustomed to joke about Erie shares; but now, for the first time, he felt himself a capitalist; on a small scale, to be sure, but still it was no small thing for Dick to have five dollars which he could call his own. He firmly determined that he would lay by every cent he could spare from his earnings towards the fund he hoped to accumulate.

But Dick was too sensible not to know that there was something more than money needed to win a respectable position in the world. He felt that he was very ignorant. Of reading and writing he only knew the rudiments, and that, with a slight acquaintance with arithmetic, was all he did know of books. Dick knew he must study hard, and he dreaded it. He looked upon learning as attended with greater difficulties than it really possesses. But Dick had good pluck. He meant to learn, nevertheless, and resolved to buy a book with his first spare earnings.

When Dick went home at night he locked up his bankbook in one of the drawers of the bureau. It was wonderful how much more independent he felt whenever he reflected upon the contents of that drawer, and with what an important air of joint ownership he regarded the bank building in which his small savings were deposited.

• • •

Dick left the counting-room, hardly knowing whether he stood on his head or his heels, so over-joyed was he at the sudden change in his fortunes. Ten dollars a week was to him a fortune, and three times as much as he had expected to obtain at first. Indeed he would have been glad, only the day before, to get a place at three dollars a week. He reflected that with the stock of clothes which he had now on hand, he could save up at least half of it, and even then live better than he had been accustomed to do; so that his little fund in the savings bank, instead of being diminished, would be steadily increasing. Then he was to be advanced if he deserved it. It was indeed a bright prospect for a boy, who, only a year before, could neither read nor write, and depended for a night's lodging upon the chance hospitality of an alleyway or old wagon. Dick's great ambition to "grow up 'spectable" seemed likely to be accomplished after all.

"The end of the white man's government"

NEW ORLEANS TRIBUNE

The New Orleans *Tribune* was the first daily newspaper published by African-Americans. In the wake of the end of the Civil War it served as a voice for freed slaves. The November 22, 1867, editorial below shows that despite resentments of how the federal military had implemented Reconstruction policies, renewed federal initiatives to enfranchise and empower African-Americans offered hope that freed slaves—who represented more than 35 percent of the total population in the South—might gain political power.

After three years' hesitation and delay the National Government concluded at last to take the right step for reconstruction. Every way was first tried except the sound and logical one. The first attempt at reconstruction was through military power. Provisional officers, taken from the army, were appointed as governors and mayors; provost marshals and freedmen's bureau agents were intrusted with the supervision of affairs in the country parishes. They understood very little of the political situation. Governor Shepley discarded the propositions of the Free State Committee. Provost marshals showed the rebels more courtesy and granted them more favors than they did to poor but devoted Union men. Agents of the Freedmen's Bureau might have been designated as planters' agents. They took more trouble to procure hands for the owners of large plantations than to protect the freed people and defend their rights. We still recollect Gen. Banks' order on "small-pox passes," by which, under the absurd plea of preventing the spreading of small-pox, the colored people were placed under a law of exception as far as their movements were concerned. They were not allowed to change plantations, they could not leave a place and hunt for work—which is the natural right of all free laborers—unless they first obtained a pass from their former employer, who, of course, refused to give them any. The hypocritical "small-pox passes" remain on Gen. Banks' record, as one of the most flagrant failures to understand and to establish freedom.

The pro-slavery spirit inspired the act of the military administration. The military was not the power to understand civil liberty; generals used to arbitrary command, felt better disposed in favor of the common laborers. They were, moreover, unwilling to take the responsibility of any important change. And after Butler—who was an exception to the rule—had left us, they did, perhaps unconsciously, as much as they could for the slave power, and as little as they could for the cause of liberty and the rights of man.

At last, however, the military government relinquished its hold. The Convention of 1864 assembled, and under the Constitution they framed, a civil government having its legislative, its executive, and judicial officers, was inaugurated. The attempt was made under the inspiration of the military, and could be, of course, but a continuance of the same errors already made. A very small number of the people of a small number of parishes was called upon to vote. The representatives of the old Union minority of white men met at the City Hall, and ignoring the change of the times, believing themselves the legitimate successors of King Cotton, they made an oligarchical Constitution, nearly as bad, for it was as partial as that of 1852. They forgot through pride and presumption, that they had no power by themselves to uphold the white union oligarchy thus created. The fact is that the very day when military rule came to an end, and the qualified voters—the white voters—under the Constitution of 1864 went to the polls, the Union oligarchs were put aside and rebel officers reinstated in their stead. It did not take great power of intellect to foresee the result. The *Union* and subsequently the *Tribune* warned our white friends, at the time, of the evident fate in store for them. Still they kept up their illusions; for could they listen to a black organ? The dullest among them believed himself smarter than any colored man in the land; and down they went, having consummated their own ruin. Gov. Wells vindicated our forebodings. He promptly turned them out of office; and then they could see whether the black organ

had seen things correctly or not. From that day they began to call again at our office; they said they were ready to retrieve their faults, and to proclaim universal suffrage. But the golden opportunity had passed away, they had been blind at the opportune time; they had played in their enemies hands. And rebels showed at the Mechanics' Institute how they intended to treat them.

This was the end of the Union white man's government. Since the eventful day of the 30th of July, 1866, we have lived under the grasp of the rebel oligarchy, restored to power. But congress has finally given us the means of relief. After governments of minorities, we are at last enabled to organize a government of the people. Let us hope that the Convention of 1867 will have more foresight, a sounder judgment and more liberalism than had the Convention of 1864. They have to work in the interest of the whole people and secure the rights of all classes of citizens, of whatever race or color, unless they want to see the fabric they will attempt to build up crumble to piece, and partake of the fate of the government erected in 1864.

🍂 "The masculine element"

ELIZABETH CADY STANTON

As one of the principal authors of the Seneca Falls Declaration of Rights, Elizabeth Cady Stanton held a long-standing reputation as an advocate for women's rights when she spoke before the 1868 Woman Suffrage Convention in Washington, D.C. The convention took place at a time when recent constitutional amendments were either secured or being considered to free slaves, guarantee equal rights among all citizens and enfranchise African-Americans with the right to vote. Woman suffragists, who had worked on behalf of abolitionists, hoped that the reform movement would embrace their call for the right to vote. Many were bitterly disappointed when that did not happen. Rather than emphasizing the finer qualities of women, Stanton's address in support of an amendment giving women the right to vote was a withering attack on "the masculine element."

I urge a sixteenth amendment, because "manhood suffrage," or a man's government, is civil, religious, and social disorganization. The male element is a destructive force, stern, selfish, aggrandizing, loving war, violence, conquest, acquisition, breeding in the material and moral world alike discord, disorder, disease, and death. See what a record of blood and cruelty the pages of history reveal! Through what slavery, slaughter, and sacrifice, through what inquisitions and imprisonments, pains and persecutions, black codes and gloomy creeds, the soul of humanity has struggled for the centuries, while mercy has veiled her face and all hearts have been dead alike to love and hope!

The male element has held high carnival thus far; it has fairly run riot from the beginning, overpowering the feminine element everywhere, crushing out all the diviner qualities in human nature, until we know but little of true manhood and womanhood, of the latter comparatively nothing, for it has scarce been recognized as a power until within the last century. Society is but the reflection of man himself, untempered by woman's thought; the hard iron rule we feel alike in the church, the state, and the home. No one need wonder at the disorganization, at the fragmentary condition of everything, when we remember that man, who represents but half a complete being, with but half an idea on every subject, has undertaken the absolute control of all sublunary matters.

People object to the demands of those whom they choose to call the strong-minded, because they say "the right of suffrage will make the women masculine." That is just the difficulty in which we are involved today. Though disenfranchised, we have few women in the best sense; we have simply so many reflections, varieties, and dilutions of the masculine gender. The strong, natural characteristics of womanhood are repressed and ignored in dependence, for so long as man feeds woman she will try to please the giver and adapt herself to his condition. To keep a foothold in society, woman must be as near like man as possible, reflect his ideas, opinions, virtues, motives, prejudices, and vices. She must respect his statutes, though they strip her of every inalienable right, and conflict with that higher law written by the finger of God on her own soul.

She must look at everything from its dollar-and-cent point of view, or she is a mere romancer. She must accept things as they are and make the best of them. To mourn over the miseries of others, the poverty of the poor, their hardships in jails, prisons, asylums, the horrors of war, cruelty, and brutality in every form, all this would be mere sen-

timentalizing. To protest against the intrigue, bribery, and corruption of public life, to desire that her sons might follow some business that did not involve lying, cheating, and a hard, grinding selfishness, would be arrant nonsense.

In this way man has been molding woman to his ideas by direct and positive influences, while she, if not a negation, has used indirect means to control him, and in most cases developed the very characteristics both in him and herself that needed repression. And now man himself stands appalled at the results of his own excesses, and mourns in bitterness that falsehood, selfishness, and violence are the law of life. The need of this hour is not territory, gold mines, railroads, or specie payments but a new evangel of womanhood, to exalt purity, virtue, morality, true religion, to lift man up into the higher realms of thought and action.

We ask woman's enfranchisement, as the first step toward the recognition of that essential element in government that can only secure the health, strength, and prosperity of the nation. Whatever is done to lift woman to her true position will help to usher in a new day of peace and perfection for the race.

In speaking of the masculine element, I do not wish to be understood to say that all men are hard, selfish, and brutal, for many of the most beautiful spirits the world has known have been clothed with manhood; but I refer to those characteristics, though often marked in woman, that distinguish what is called the stronger sex. For example, the love of acquisition and conquest, the very pioneers of civilization, when expended on the earth, the sea, the elements, the riches and forces of nature, are powers of destruction when used to subjugate one man to another or to sacrifice nations to ambition.

Here that great conservator of woman's love, if permitted to assert itself, as it naturally would in freedom against oppression, violence, and war, would hold all these destructive forces in check, for woman knows the cost of life better than man does, and not with her consent would one drop of blood ever be shed, one life sacrificed in vain.

With violence and disturbance in the natural world, we see a constant effort to maintain an equilibrium of forces. Nature, like a loving mother, is ever trying to keep land and sea, mountain and valley, each in its place, to hush the angry winds and waves, balance the extremes of heat and cold, of rain and drought, that peace, harmony, and beauty may reign supreme. There is a striking analogy between matter and mind, and the present disorganization of society warns us that in the dethronement of woman we have let loose the elements of violence and ruin that she only has the power to curb. If the civilization of the age calls for an extension of the suffrage, surely a government of the most virtuous educated men and women would better represent the whole and protect the interests of all than could the representation of either sex alone.

❧ *"Multitudes bitterly opposed the schools"*

CONGRESSIONAL REPORT ON THE FREEDMEN'S BUREAU

Congress created the Bureau of Refugees, Freedmen and Abandoned Lands in March 1865 to help alleviate conditions for the 4 million African-Americans who had escaped from slavery, been granted freedom, or were about to be freed at the conclusion of the Civil War. Almost all of the slaves were illiterate. Having gained their freedom, many lost their means for survival. They did not have property, training or experience in the free market.

The Freedmen's Bureau went about the task of establishing schools to teach freed slaves how to read and write and provide them with a basic education. The bureau also provided food, set up courts to protect emancipated slaves' civil rights and founded savings banks. From 1865 to 1972 the bureau spent more than $6 million on education, $15 million on food and gave more than 500,000 people medical assistance. But as this 1868 Congressional Report on the Freedmen's Bureau makes clear, the agency made significant accomplishments in the face of a hostile political environment. The report's conclusion that military enforcement would be necessary to perpetuate the agency's programs proved correct. When Reconstruction ended and the military was withdrawn, white hostility pushed back many of the bureau's gains.

When our armies entered the South two facts became apparent: first, a surprising thirst for knowledge among the negroes; second, a large volunteer force of teachers for their instruction.

Without delay schools were successfully established and the earliest efforts to impart knowledge found the freedmen ready for its reception. Teachers of character and culture were ready from the first. To some extent the army had carried its own instructors. Negro servants of officers studied at the campfires of fellow servants. Chaplains of colored troops became instructors. In the campaigns of 1864 and 1865 the Christian Commission employed 50 teachers in colored camps and regiments.

At the close of the war it is believed that 20,000 colored soldiers could read intelligently, and a much larger number were learning their first lessons.

Really wonderful results had been accomplished through the disinterested efforts of benevolent associations working in connection with the government. But arrangements were soon made to give, on a larger scale, systematic and impartial aid to all of them. This consisted in turning over for school use temporary government buildings no longer needed for military purposes, and buildings seized from disloyal owners; also transportation for teachers, books, and school furniture, with quarters and rations for teachers and superintendants when on duty.

Schools were taken in charge by the Bureau, and in some States carried on wholly (in connection with local efforts) by use of the "refugees and freemen's fund." Teachers came under the general direction of the assistant commissioners, and protection through the department commanders was given to all engaged in the work.

Superintendants of schools for each State were appointed July 12, 1865, whose duty it was "to work as much as possible in connection with State officers who may have had school matters in charge, and to take cognizance of all that was being done to educate refugees and freedmen, secure protection to schools and teachers, promote method and efficiency, and to correspond with the benevolent agencies which were supplying his field."

The total number of pupils January 1, 1866, in all the colored schools, as near as could be ascertained, was 90,589; teachers, 1,314; schools, 740.

Whenever our troops broke through the lines of the enemy, schools followed. At Hampton, Beaufort, North Carolina, Roanoke Island, and New Orleans, they were soon in operation. A very efficient system was instituted for Louisiana in the early part of 1864, by Major General Banks, then in command of that State. It was supported by a military tax upon the whole population. Schools were opened in Savannah, Georgia, on the entrance of General Sherman, in December, 1864, and 500 pupils were at once enrolled. Ten intelligent colored persons were the first teachers, and nearly $81,000 were immediately contributed by the negroes for their support. This work was organized by the Secretary of the American Tract Society, Boston. Two of the largest of these schools were in "Bryan's slave mart," where platforms occupied a few days before with bondmen for sale became crowded with children learning to read.

At the end of the school year, July 1, 1866, it was found that while complete organization had not been reached, the schools in nearly all the States were steadily gaining in numbers, attainment, and general influence.

The official reports of superintendants gave 975 schools, 1,405 teachers, and 90,778 pupils. But these figures were not a true exhibit of the actual increase. They did not include many schools which failed to report. It was estimated that in all the different methods of teaching there had been, during the preceding six months, 150,000 freedmen and their children earnestly and successfully occupied in study.

Some change of sentiment had, at this time, been observed among the better classes of the South; those of higher intelligence acknowledging that education must become universal. Still, multitudes bitterly opposed the schools. Teachers were proscribed and ill-treated; school-houses were burned; many schools could not be opened, and others, after a brief struggle, had to be closed. Nevertheless, the country began to feel the moral power of this movement. Commendations came from foreign lands, and the universal demand of good men was that the work should go on.

As showing the desire for education among the freedmen, we give the following facts: When the collection of the general tax for colored schools was suspended in Louisiana by military order, the consternation of the colored population was intense. Petitions began to pour in. I saw one from the plantations across the river, at least thirty feet in length, representing ten thousand negroes. It was affecting to examine it, and note the names and marks [X] of such a long list of parents, ignorant themselves, but begging that their children might

be educated, promising that from beneath their present burdens, and out of their extreme poverty, they would pay for it.

In September, 1865, J. W. Alvord, the present general superintendant, was appointed "Inspector of Schools." He traveled through nearly all the States lately in insurrection, and made the first general report to the Bureau on the subject of education, January 1, 1866.

Extracts from this report give the condition of the freedmen throughout the whole South. He says, "The desire of the freedmen for knowledge has not been overstated. This comes from several causes.

"1. The natural thirst for knowledge common to all men.

"2. They have seen power and influence among white people always coupled with learning; it is the sign of that elevation to which they now aspire.

"3. Its mysteries, hitherto hidden from them in written literature, excite to the special study of books.

"4. Their freedom has given wonderful stimulus to all effort, indicating a vitality which augurs well for their whole future condition and character.

"5. But, especially, the practical business of life now upon their hands shows their immediate need of education.

"This they all feel and acknowledge; hence their unusual welcome of and attendance upon schools is confined to no one class or age. Those advanced in life throw up their hands at first in despair, but a little encouragement places even these as pupils at the alphabet.

"Such as are in middle life, the laboring classes, gladly avail themselves of evening and Sabbath-schools. They may be often seen during the intervals of toil, when off duty as servants, on steamboats, along the railroads, and when unemployed in the streets in the city, or on plantations, with some fragment of a spelling-book in their hands, earnestly at study.

"Regiments of colored soldiers have nearly all made improvement in learning. In some of them, where but few knew their letters at first, nearly every man can now read, and many of them write. In other regiments one-half or two-thirds can do this.

"Even in hospitals I discovered very commendable efforts at such elementary instruction.

"But the great movement is among children of the usual school age. Their parents, if at all intelligent, encourage them to study. Your officers add their influence, and it is a fact, not always true of children, that among those recently from bondage, the school-house, however rough and uncomfortable, is of all places the most attractive. A very common punishment for misdemeanor is the threat of being kept at home for a day. The threat, in most cases, is sufficient."

The report goes on to say, "Much opposition has been encountered from those who do not believe in the elevation of the negro. A multitude of facts might be given. It is the testimony of all superintendants that if military power should be withdrawn, our schools would cease to exist.

"This opposition is sometimes ludicrous as well as inhuman. A member of the legislature, in session while I was at New Orleans, was passing one of the schools with me, having at the time its recess, the grounds about the building being filled with children. He stopped and looked intently, then earnestly inquired 'Is this a school?' 'Yes,' I replied. 'What! of niggers?' 'These are colored children, evidently,' I answered. 'Well! Well!' said he, and raising his hands, 'I have seen many an absurdity in my lifetime, but this is the climax of absurdities!' I am sure he did not speak from effect, but as he felt. He left me abruptly, and turned the next corner to take his seat with legislators similarly prejudiced."

The act of July 16, 1866, enlarged the powers of the Bureau in regard to education. It sanctioned co-operation with private benevolent associations, and with agents and teachers accredited by them. It directed the Commissioner to "hire or provide, by lease, buildings for purposes of education whenever teachers and means of instruction, without cost to the government, should be provided." And, also, that he should "furnish such protection as might be required for the safe conduct of such schools."

The schools, on the passage of this act, assumed in all respects a more enlarged and permanent character. Schools in the cities and larger towns began to be graded. Normal or high schools were planned, and a few came into existence. The earliest of these were at Norfolk, Charleston, New Orleans and Nashville.

Industrial schools for girls, in which sewing, knitting, straw-braiding, etc., were taught, were encouraged. School buildings, by rent or construction, were largely provided, and new stimulus was given to every department.

The freedmen, in view of new civil rights, and what the Bureau had undertaken for them, had gained an advanced standing, with increasing self-respect and confidence that a vastly improved condition was within their reach.

Up to this time it had been questioned, whether colored children could advance rapidly into the higher branches, but it was found that 23,727 pupils were in writing, 12,970 in geography, 31,692 in arithmetic, and 1,573 in higher branches; and that out of 1,430 teachers of the day and night schools, 458 were colored persons.

The January report stated that "the actual results reached since these schools commenced, both in numbers and in advancement, were surprising." At the end of the school year, July 1, 1867, it could be said, "We look back with astonishment at the amount accomplished. Such progress as is seen under auspices admitted to be unfavorable; the permanency of the schools, scarcely one failing when once commenced; the rapid increase of general intelligence among the whole colored population, are matters of constant remark by every observer. Thus far this educational effort, considered as a whole, has been eminently successful. The country and the world are surprised to behold a depressed race, so lately and so long in bondage, springing to their feet and entering the lists in hopeful competition with every rival."

Reports from all the States show that there are 1,839 day and night schools, 2,087 teachers, and 111,442 pupils. By adding industrial schools, and those "within the knowledge of the superintendant," the number will be 2,207 schools, 2,442 teachers, and 130,735 pupils.

Sabbath-schools also show much larger numbers during the past year, the figures being 1,126 schools and 80,647 pupils; and if we add those "not regularly reported," the whole number of Sabbath-schools will be 1,468, with 105,786 pupils; totals, schools of all kinds, as reported, 3,695; pupils, 238,342. Of these schools 1,086 are sustained wholly or in part by the freedmen, and 391 of the buildings in which these schools are held are owned by themselves; 699 of the teachers in the day and night schools are colored and 1,388 white; 28,068 colored pupils have paid tuition, the average amount per month being $12,720.96, or a fraction over 45 cents per scholar. Only 8,743 pupils were free before the war.

As showing the progress of the Schools, it will be observed that 42,879 pupils are now in writing, 23,957 in geography, 40,454 in arithmetic, and 4,661 in higher branches. Twenty-one normal or high schools are in operation, with 1,821 pupils, the schools having doubled in number during the last year with three times the number of pupils. Of these schools not many are far advanced, but they are intended to be what their name implies.

There are now 35 industrial schools, giving instruction to 2,124 pupils in the various kinds of female labor, not including 4,185 in the day schools, who are taught needle-work. The average daily attendance in all the above schools has been nearly 75 per cent of the enrollment.

There are now connected with these schools 44 children's temperance societies, called the "Vanguard of Freedom," having, in the aggregate, 3,000 members. These societies are constantly increasing, and doing much to train children in correct moral habits.

Education in thrift and economy is effected through the influence of the "Freedmen's Savings and Trust Company," chartered by Congress, and placed under the protection of this Bureau. Twenty branches of this institution, located in as many of the central cities and larger towns of the Southern States, are now in operation. Six of these banks have, at this time (January 1,1868), on deposit an average of over $50,000 each, the whole amount now due depositors at all the branches being $585,770.17. Four times this amount has been deposited and drawn out for use in important purchases, homesteads etc. Both the business and the influence of the banks are rapidly increasing. Multitudes of these people never before had the first idea of saving for future use. Their former industry was only a hard, profitless task, but under the instructions of the cashiers the value of money is learned, and they are stimulated to earn it.

❧ "A full pardon"

ANDREW JOHNSON

On December 25, 1868, Andrew Johnson issued an amnesty proclamation pardoning everyone who participated in the Confederate war effort and restoring their full rights as citizens. The amnesty was similar to Lincoln's 1863 Proclamation of Amnesty and Reconstruction. The restoration of citizenship rights went contrary to Congress's reconstruction program. Armed with the ability to vote, Southerners used their restored political authority against the state governments established by the federal governments.

[W]hereas, the authority of the Federal Government having been re-established in all the States and Territories within the jurisdiction of the United States,…and that a universal amnesty and pardon for participation in said rebellion extended to all who have borne any part therein will tend to secure permanent peace, order, and prosperity throughout the land, and to renew and fully restore confidence and fraternal feeling among the whole people, and their respect for and attachment to the National Government, designed by its patriotic founders for the general good:

Now, therefore, be it known that I, Andrew Johnson,…hereby proclaim and declare unconditionally, and without reservation, to all and to every person who directly or indirectly participated in the late resurrection or rebellion, a full pardon and amnesty for the offence of treason against the United States, or of adhering to their enemies during the late civil war, with restoration of all rights, privileges, and immunities under the constitution and the laws which have been made in pursuance thereof.

In testimony whereof, I have signed these presents with my hand, and have caused the seal of the United States to be hereunto affixed.

❧ "Guilty or not guilty as charged in this article of impeachment?"

GEORGE JULIAN

Andrew Johnson found himself at odds with the Republican Congress almost from the moment he succeeded Lincoln. When the radical wing of the Republican Party won several seats in the election of 1866 tensions between Johnson and Congress reached a fevered pitch. A flurry of presidential vetoes and override votes marked the increasingly strained relations between Johnson and Congress. These included the Civil Rights Act of 1865 giving former slaves the right to citizenship, two Reconstruction acts designed to impose Congressional control on the South and the Tenure of Office Act of 1867 in which Congress required the President to gain permission from the Senate before dismissing Cabinet officers.

In the summer of 1867 Johnson dismissed Secretary of War Edwin Stanton while Congress was in recess. Republicans accused Johnson of violating the Tenure of Office Act. On February 24, 1868, the House of Representatives resolved to impeach Johnson. Two weeks later the impeachment was presented to the Senate. On May 16, 1868, the Senate voted 35-19 to impeach Johnson, one vote shy of the required two-thirds majority for conviction. Congressman George Julian recalled the impeachment trial in his memoir *Political Recollections* and regretted his role in the impeachment.

On the 24th of February, 1868, the House, by a vote of one hundred and twenty-six to forty-seven, declared in favor of impeachment. The crowds in the galleries, in the lobbies, and on the floor were unprecedented and the excitement at high tide. The fifty-seven who had voted for impeachment in December were now happy. They felt at last that the country was safe. The whole land seemed to be electrified, as they believed it would have been at any previous time if the House had had the nerve to go forward, and they rejoiced that the madness of Johnson had at last compelled Congress to face the great duty. A committee of seven was appointed by the Speaker to prepare articles of impeachment, of whom Thaddeus Stevens was chairman. He was now rapidly failing in strength and every morning had to be carried upstairs to his seat in the House, but his humor never failed him, and on one of these occasions he said to the young men who had him in charge, "I wonder, boys, who will carry me when you are dead and gone." He was very thin, pale, and haggard. His eye was bright, but his face was "scarred by the crooked autograph of pain." He was a constant sufferer, and during the sessions of the committee kept himself stimulated by sipping a little wine or brandy; but he was its ruling spirit and greatly speeded its work by the clearness of his perceptions and the strength of his will. His mental force seemed to defy the power of disease. The articles of impeachment were ready for submission in a few days and adopted by the House on the second of March by a majority of considerably more than two-thirds, when the case was transferred to the Senate.

The popular feeling against the President was now rapidly nearing its climax and becoming a sort of frenzy. Andrew Johnson was no longer merely a "wrongheaded and obstinate man" but a "genius in depravity," whose hoarded malignity and passion were unfathomable. He was not simply "an irresolute mule," as General Schenck had styled him, but was devil-bent upon the ruin of his country; and his trial connected itself with all the memories of the war, and involved the nation in a new and final struggle for its life. Even so sober and unimaginative a man as Mr. Boutwell, one of the managers of the impeachment in the Senate, lost his wits and completely surrendered himself to the passions of the hour.

No extravagance of speech or explosion of wrath was deemed out of order during this strange dispensation in our politics.

The trial proceeded with unabated interest, and on the afternoon of the eleventh of May the excitement reached its highest point. Reports came from the Senate, then in secret session, that Grimes, Fessenden, and Henderson were certainly for acquittal, and that other senators were to follow them. An indescribable gloom now prevailed among the friends of impeachment, which increased during the afternoon and at night when the Senate was again in session. At the adjournment there was some hope of conviction, but it was generally considered very doubtful. On meeting my old antislavery friend, Doctor Brisbane, he told me he felt as if he were sitting up with a sick friend who was expected to die. His face was the picture of despair. To such men it seemed that all the trials of the war were merged in this grand issue and that it involved the existence of free government on this continent.

The final vote was postponed till the sixteenth, owing to Senator Howard's illness, and on the morning of that day the friends of impeachment felt more confident. The vote was first taken on the eleventh article. The galleries were packed, and an indescribable anxiety was written on every face. Some of the members of the House near me grew pale and sick under the burden of suspense. Such stillness prevailed that the breathing in the galleries could be heard at the announcement of each senator's vote. This was quite noticeable when any of the doubtful senators voted, the people holding their breath as the words "guilty" or "not guilty" were pronounced and then giving it simultaneous vent. Every heart throbbed more anxiously as the name of Senator Fowler was reached and the Chief Justice propounded to him the prescribed question: "How say you, is the respondent, Andrew Johnson, President of the United States, guilty or not guilty of a high misdemeanor, as charged in this article of impeachment?" The senator, in evident excitement, inadvertently answered "guilty," and thus lent a momentary relief to the friends of impeachment; but this was immediately dissipated by correcting his vote on the statement of the Chief Justice that he did not understand the Senator's response to the question. Nearly all hope of conviction fled when Senator Ross of Kansas voted "not guilty," and a long breathing of disappointment and despair followed the like vote of Van Winkle, which settled the case in favor of the President.

It is impossible now to realize how perfectly overmastering was the excitement of these days. The exercise of calm judgment was simply out of the question. As I have already stated, passion ruled the hour and constantly strengthened the tendency to one-sidedness and exaggeration. The attempt to impeach the President was undoubtedly inspired mainly by patriotic motives, but the spirit of intolerance among Republicans toward those who differed with them in opinion set all moderation and common sense at defiance. Patriotism and party animosity were so inextricably mingled and confounded that the real merits of the controversy could only be seen after the heat and turmoil of the strife had passed away. Time has made this manifest. Andrew Johnson was not the devil incarnate he was then painted, nor did he monopolize entirely the wrongheadedness of the times. No one will now dispute that the popular estimate of his character did him very great injustice. It is equally certain that great injustice was done to Trumbull, Fessenden, Grimes, and other senators who voted to acquit the President and gave proof of their honesty and independence by facing the wrath and scorn of the party with which they had so long been identified. The idea of making the question of impeachment a matter of party discipline was utterly indefensible and preposterous.

"Equal protection of the laws"

FOURTEENTH AMENDMENT

Recalling Supreme Court Chief Justice Roger B. Taney's ruling in the Dred Scott decision that African-Americans—whether free or enslaved—could be considered as citizens, the post-Civil War Republican Congress initiated the Fourteenth Amendment defining citizenship and guaranteeing the equal protection of laws. The immediate effect of the amendment was thus to secure the civil rights of the freedmen. The long-term impact of the equal protection clause, however, embraced a wider range of constituencies (such as women and corporations) and had much broader implications on a spectrum of legal issues.

The second, third, and fourth sections of the Fourteenth Amendment were specifically directed at reshaping the South and punishing those who had assisted the Confederate war effort. The second section gives Southern states the choice of either accepting African-American voters or losing seats in the House of Representatives, thus all but compelling them to enfranchise former slaves. The third section wiped out the South's former political leadership by banning former Confederate leaders from taking public office without swearing an oath in support of the Constitution. Finally, the fourth section disavowed Confederate war debt, validated the United States war debt and disallowed all claims for loss of property, including slaves.

Section 1. All persons born or naturalized in the United States, and subject to the jurisdiction thereof, are citizens of the United States and of the State wherein they reside. No state shall make or enforce any law which shall abridge the privileges or immunities of citizens of the United States; nor shall any State deprive any person of life, liberty, or property, without due process of law; nor deny to any person within its jurisdiction the equal protection of the laws.

Section 2. Representatives shall be apportioned among the several States according to their respective numbers, counting the whole number of persons in each State, excluding Indians not taxed. But when the right to vote at any election for the choice of electors for President and Vice-President of the United States, Representatives in Congress, the Executive and Judicial officers of a State, or the members of the Legislature thereof, is denied to any of the male inhabitants of such State, being twenty-one years of age, and citizens of the United States, or in any way abridged, except for participation in rebellion, or other crime, the basis of representation therein shall be reduced in the proportion which the number of such male citizens shall bear to the whole number of male citizens twenty-one years of age in such State.

Section 3. No person shall be a Senator or Representative in Congress, or elector of President and Vice-President, or hold any office, civil or military, under the United States, or under any State, who, having previously taken an oath, as a member of Congress, or as an officer of the United States, or as a member of any State, to support the Constitution of the United States, shall have engaged in insurrection or rebellion against the same; or given aid or comfort to the enemies thereof. But Congress may by a vote of two-thirds of each House, remove such disability.

Section 4. The validity of the public debt of the United States, authorized by law, including debts incurred for payment of pensions and bounties for services in suppressing insurrection or rebellion, shall not be questioned. But neither the United States nor any State shall assume or pay any debt or obligation incurred in aid of insurrection or rebellion against the United States, or any claim for the loss or emancipation of any slave; but all such debts, obligations, and claims shall be held illegal and void.

Section 5. The congress shall have the power to enforce, by appropriate legislation, the provisions of this article.

❧ "I do solemnly swear"

OATH OF OFFICE

The authors of the Constitution explicitly rejected the notion of federal employees and officers—with the exception of the President—submitting to an oath of loyalty. "A good government did not need them," said James Wilson, "and a bad government ought not to be supported." Instead, the framers of the Constitution enacted a simple one-sentence statement swearing to support the Constitution. The outbreak of the Civil War in 1861, however, complicated matters as the federal government became quite concerned about disloyal government officers. In 1862 Congress enacted the "iron-clad test oath," a lengthy statement swearing to past, present and future loyalty to the government that required all officers, employees and even contractors to pledge. When the war ended it became obvious that the oath had to be changed if any former Confederate officers or soldiers were going to serve in the federal government. On July 11, 1868, Congress created a new oath of office that has remained in place to

this day. The issue of the oath of office remained a dormant one until the Cold War in the 1940s. Concerns about Communist influence in the government during the post-World War II "Red Scare" re-ignited the issue of the oath of office. Ironically, the re-emergence of the issue also rekindled objections to the oath on the basis of it being a violation of a citizen's right to free speech.

I do solemnly swear (or affirm) that I will support and defend the Constitution of the United States against all enemies, foreign and domestic; that I take this obligation freely, without any mental reservation or purpose of evasion, and that I will well and truthfully discharge the duties of the office on which I am about to enter. So help me God.

❧ "The right to vote shall not be denied on account of race"

FIFTEENTH AMENDMENT

In early 1869 the Republican Congress initiated the Fifteenth Amendment enfranchising African-American men. Many former Confederate states had already given former slaves the right to vote in their new state constitutions, but radical Republicans were concerned that when the Reconstruction period ended the new state governments would retract that right. The immediate effect of the amendment was to enfranchise African-Americans in the North. Nevertheless, Republican fears were well founded as Southern Democrats imposed a series of obstacles for African-American voters in the late 1800s, including the poll tax, highly restrictive registration laws, literacy and property qualifications and a variety of other loopholes. In many parts of the Deep South African-Americans were effectively barred from voting until the Civil Rights movements in the 1960s.

Section 1. The right of citizens of the United States to vote shall not be denied or abridged by the United States or by any State on account of race, color, or previous condition of servitude.

Section 2. The Congress shall have power to enforce this article by appropriate legislation.

"Wild Bill, then as now the most famous scout on the Plains"

GEORGE CUSTER

The West of the late 1800s was a wild, often lawless place. Legendary figures rose and fell based on their gun-shooting skills. One of the most celebrated gunfighters was James "Wild Bill" Hickok, reputed to be the fastest shot in the West. Along with Wyatt Earp, he was considered to be among the frontier's greatest "peace officers." Born in 1837 in Illinois, he moved to Kansas when he was 18 and became a stage driver. His exploits started on July 12, 1861, when the McCanles Gang attacked him at Rock Creek Station, Nebraska. Hickok killed McCanles and two others in the gunfight. He then served as a sharpshooter, scout and spy for the Union Army in the Civil War, was a scout for the U. S. Army during the Indian wars after the Civil War and a U.S. marshal at Hays City and Abilene, Kansas, in the 1870s. Hickok scouted for General George Custer after the Civil War. He was murdered in 1876 at Deadwood in the Dakota Territory. Custer wrote about Hickok in his book *My Life on the Plains.*

In addition to the regularly organized companies of soldiers which made up the pursuing column, I had with me a detachment of white scouts or Plainsmen, and one of friendly Indians, the latter belonging to the tribe of Delawares, once so famous in Indian wars. Of the Indians one only could speak English; he acted as interpreter for the party. Among the white scouts were numbered some of the most noted of their class. The most prominent man among them was "Wild Bill," whose highly varied career was made the subject of an illustrated sketch in one of the popular monthly periodicals a few years ago. "Wild Bill" was a strange character, just the one which a novelist might gloat over. He was a Plainsman in every sense of the word, yet unlike any other of his class. In person he was about six feet one in height, straight as the straightest of the warriors whose implacable foe he was; broad shoulders, well-formed chest and limbs, and a face strikingly handsome; a sharp, clear, blue eye, which stared you straight in the face when in conversation; a finely-shaped nose, inclined to be aquiline; a well-turned mouth, with lips only partially concealed by a handsome moustache. His hair and complexion were those of the perfect blond. The former was worn in uncut ringlets falling carelessly over his powerfully formed shoulders. Add to this figure a costume blending the immaculate neatness of the dandy with the extravagant taste and style of the frontiersman, and you have Wild Bill, then as now the most famous scout on the Plains. Whether on foot or on horseback, he was one of the most perfect types of physical manhood I ever saw. Of his courage there could be no question; it had been brought to the test on too many occasions to admit of a doubt. His skill in the use of the rifle and pistol was unerring; while his deportment was exactly the opposite of what might be expected from a man of his surroundings. It was entirely free from all bluster or bravado. He seldom spoke of himself unless requested to do so. His conversation, strange to say, never bordered either on the vulgar or blasphemous. His influence among the frontiersmen was unbounded, his word was law; and many are the personal quarrels and disturbances which he has checked among his comrades by his simple announcement that "this has gone far enough," if need be followed by the ominous warning that when persisted in or renewed the quarreller "must settle it with me." "Wild Bill" is anything but a quarrelsome man; yet no one but himself can enumerate the many conflicts in which he has been engaged, and which have almost invariably resulted in the death of his adversary. I have a personal knowledge of at least half a dozen men whom he has at various times killed, one of these being at the time a member of my command. Others have been severely wounded, yet he always escapes unhurt.

On the Plains every man openly carries his belt with its invariable appendages, knife and revolver, often two of the latter. Wild Bill always carried two handsome ivory-handled revolvers of the large size; he was never seen without them. Where this is the common custom, brawls or personal difficulties are seldom if ever settled by blows. The quarrel is not from a word to a blow, but from a word to the revolver, and he who can draw and fire first is the best man. No civil law reaches him; none is applied for. In fact there is no law recognized beyond the frontier but that of "might makes right." Should death result from the quarrel, as it usually does, no coroner's jury is impanelled to learn the cause of death, and the survivor is not arrested. But instead of these old-fashioned proceedings, a meeting of citizens takes place, the survivor is requested to be present when the circumstances of the homicide are inquired into, and the unfailing verdict of "justifiable," "self-defence," etc., is pronounced, and the law stands vindicated. That justice is often deprived to a victim there is not a doubt. Yet in all of the many affairs of this kind in which "Wild Bill" has performed a part, and which have come to my knowledge, there is not a single instance in which the verdict of twelve fair-minded men would not be pronounced in his favor. That the even tenor of his way continues to be disturbed by little events of this description may be inferred from an item which has been floating lately through the columns of the press, and which states that "the funeral of 'Jim Bludso,' who was killed the other day by 'Wild Bill,' took place to-day." It then adds: "The funeral expenses were borne by 'Wild Bill.'" What could be more thoughtful than this? Not only to send a fellow mortal out of the world, but to pay the expenses of the transit.

❧ "A Buffalo-killing match"

BUFFALO BILL CODY

The introduction of the horse to America by European explorers and settlers allowed some Native American tribes to venture out into the Great Plains where 50 million or more buffaloes roamed. Tribes used the buffalo hides, meat, dung and organs for clothing, food, shelter, fuel and a variety of other purposes. Starting with Lewis and Clark, white explorers and settlers hunted buffalo as well, but were often indiscriminate in their practices. Although buffalo meat and hides were utilized by white settlers and railroad work crews, buffalo hunting also became a sport. After the Civil War the military encouraged wholesale buffalo hunting to deprive Native American tribes of their food source. "Until the buffalo is destroyed," General Philip Sheridan wrote, "it is the only way to bring lasting peace and allow civilization to advance." By 1875 there were less than 1 million buffaloes, and in 1895 there were fewer than 1,000.

William Cody—better known as Buffalo Bill—earned a reputation as the greatest buffalo hunter of the West. He claimed to have killed 4,280 buffaloes in 17 months. Buffalo Bill's adventures also included being a Pony Express rider, prospector, horse wrangler and army scout. In 1883, Buffalo Bill started his famous Wild West Show featuring cowboys and Native Americans who engaged in mock battles. The show toured the United States and Europe. Buffalo Bill wrote about his experiences on the frontier, including this description of a competitive buffalo hunt to determine who was the greatest buffalo hunter in the West.

Shortly after the adventures mentioned in the preceding chapter, I had my celebrated buffalo hunt with Billy Comstock, a noted scout, guide and interpreter, who was then chief of scouts at Fort Wallace, Kansas. Comstock had the reputation, for a long time, of being a most successful buffalo hunter, and the officers in particular, who had seen him kill buffaloes, were very desirous of backing him in a match against me. It was accordingly arranged that I should shoot him a buffalo-killing match, and the preliminaries were easily and satisfactorily agreed upon. We were to hunt one day of eight hours, beginning at eight o'clock in the morning, and closing at four o'clock in the afternoon. The wager was five hundred dollars a side, and the man who should kill the greater number of buffaloes from on horseback was to be declared the winner.

The hunt took place about twenty miles east of Sheridan, and as it had been pretty well advertised and noised abroad, a large crowd witnessed the interesting and exciting scene. An excursion party, mostly from St. Louis, consisting of about a hundred gentlemen and ladies, came out on a special train to view the sport, and among the number was my wife, with little baby Arta, who had come to remain with me for a while.

The buffaloes were quite plenty, and it was agreed that we should go into the same herd at the same time and "make a run," as we called it, each one killing as many as possible. A referee was to follow each of us on horseback when we entered the herd, and count the buffaloes killed by each man. The St. Louis excursionists, as well as the other spectators, rode out to the vicinity of the hunting grounds in wagons and on horseback, keeping well out of sight of the buffaloes, so as not to frighten them, until the time came for us to dash into the herd; when they were to come up as near as they pleased and witness the chase.

We were fortunate in the first run in getting good ground. Comstock was mounted on one of his favorite horses, while I rode old Brigham. I felt confident that I had the advantage of Comstock in two things—first, I had the best buffalo horse that ever made a track; and second, I was using what was known at that time as the needle-gun, a breech-loading Springfield rifle—calibre 50,—it was my favorite old "Lucretia," which has already been introduced to the notice of the reader; while

Comstock was armed with a Henry rifle, and although he could fire a few shots quicker than I could, yet I was pretty certain that it did not carry powder and lead enough to do execution equal to my calibre 50.

At last the time came to begin the match. Comstock and I dashed into a herd, followed by the referees. The buffaloes separated; Comstock took the left bunch and I the right. My great forte in killing buffaloes from horseback was to get them circling by riding my horse at the head of the herd, shooting the leaders, thus crowding their followers to the left, till they would finally circle round and round.

On this morning the buffaloes were very accommodating, and I soon had them running in a beautiful circle, when I dropped them thick and fast, until I had killed thirty-eight; which finished my run.

Comstock began shooting at the rear of the herd, which he was chasing, and they kept straight on. He succeeded, however, in killing twenty-three, but they were scattered over a distance of three miles, while mine lay close together. I had "nursed" my buffaloes, as a billiard-player does the balls when he makes a big run.

After the result of the first run had been duly announced, our St. Louis excursion friends—who had approached to the place where we had stopped—set out a lot of champagne, which they had brought with them, and which proved a good drink on a Kansas prairie, and a buffalo hunter was a good man to get away with it.

While taking a short rest, we suddenly spied another herd of buffaloes coming toward us. It was only a small drove, and we at once prepared to give the animals a lively reception. They proved to be a herd of cows and calves—which, by the way, are quicker in their movements than the bulls. We charged in among them, and I concluded my run with a score of eighteen, while Comstock killed fourteen. The score now stood fifty-six to thirty-seven, in my favor.

Again the excursion party approached, and once more the champagne was tapped. After we had eaten a lunch which was spread for us, we resumed the hunt. Striking out for a distance of three miles, we came up close to another herd. As I was so far ahead of my competitor in the number killed, I thought I could afford to give an extra

exhibition of my skill. I had told the ladies that I would, on the next run, ride my horse without saddle or bridle. This had raised the excitement to fever heat among the excursionists, and I remember one fair lady who endeavored to prevail upon me not to attempt it.

"That's nothing at all," said I; "I have done it many a time, and old Brigham knows as well as I what I am doing, and sometimes a great deal better."

So, leaving my saddle and bridle with the wagons, we rode to the windward of the buffaloes, as usual, and when within a few hundred yards of them we dashed into the herd. I soon had thirteen laid out on the ground, the last one of which I had driven down close to the wagons, where the ladies were. It frightened some of the tender creatures to see the buffalo coming at full speed directly toward them; but when he had got within fifty yards of one of the wagons, I shot him dead in his tracks. This made my sixty-ninth buffalo, and finished my third and last run, Comstock having killed forty-six.

As it was now late in the afternoon, Comstock and his backers gave up the idea that he could beat me, and thereupon the referees declared me the winner of the match, as well as the champion buffalo-hunter of the plains.

"Atlantic and Pacific were joined together"

GRENVILLE M. DODGE

On March 10, 1869, railroad officials, political leaders and work gangs converged at Promontory Point, Utah, to drive in the last spike of the Pacific Railroad, the first of five transcontinental railroads built in the 19th century. The driving of the spike linked the Union Pacific line built from east to west with the Central Pacific, which had commenced construction in California.

General Grenville M. Dodge had served as Sherman's engineer in the Atlanta Campaign and near the end of the war was made chief engineer of the Union Pacific. Dodge's efficient and hard-working ways helped propel construction three years ahead of the government's timeline. Work crews carved a railbed through the Rocky Mountains, often in the face of attacks from Native American tribes. As many as 10,000 laborers worked on each line at any given time. The ceremony marked a high point in the golden age of railroading in the United States.

From 1865 to 1914 the nation's railway network grew almost eight-fold from 35,000 to 254,000 miles. The federal government gave railroads more than 100 million acres and $64 million in loans and tax breaks to finance the expansion, which also helped generate enormous profits for many of the railroad companies. The advent of a rail system led to the introduction of four standard time zones in the country to permit for a national schedule system. Railroads paved the way for the uniting of the country as a single economic entity, tying the Atlantic to the Pacific, farmers to manufacturers and producers to consumers.

On the morning of May 10, 1869, Hon. Leland Stanford, Governor of California and President of the Central Pacific, accompanied by Messrs. Huntington, Hopkins, Crocker and trainloads of California's distinguished citizens, arrived from the west. During the forenoon Vice President T. C. Durant and Directors John R. Duff and Sidney Dillon and Consulting Engineer Silas A. Seymour of the Union Pacific, with other prominent men, including a delegation of Mormons from Salt Lake City, came in on a train from the east. The National Government was represented by a detachment of "regulars" from Fort Douglass, Utah, accompanied by a band, and 600 others, including Chinese, Mexicans, Indians, half-breeds, negroes and laborers, suggesting an air of cosmopolitanism, all gathered around the open space where the tracks were to be joined. The Chinese laid the rails from the west end, and the Irish laborers laid them from the east end, until they met and joined.

Telegraphic wires were so connected that each blow of the descending sledge could be reported instantly to all parts of the United States. Corresponding blows were struck on the bell of the City Hall in San Francisco, and with the last blow of the sledge a cannon was fired at Fort Point. General Stafford presented a spike of gold, silver and iron as the offering of the Territory of Arizona. Governor Tuttle of Nevada presented a spike of silver from his state. The connecting tie was of California laurel, and California presented the last spike of gold in behalf of that state. A silver sledge had also been presented for the occasion. A prayer was offered. Governor Stanford of California made a few appropriate remarks on behalf of the Central Pacific and the chief engineer responded for the Union Pacific.

Then the telegraphic inquiry from the Omaha office, from which the circuit was to be started, was answered: "To everybody: Keep quiet. When the last spike is driven at Promontory Point we will say 'Done.' Don't break the circuit, but watch for the signals of the blows of the hammer. The spike will soon be driven. The signal will be three dots for the commencement of the blows."

The magnet tapped one two three then paused "Done." The spike was given its first blow by President Stanford and Vice President Durant followed. Neither hit the spike the first time, but hit the rail, and were greeted by the lusty cheers of the onlookers, accompanied by the screams of the locomotives and the music of the military band. Many other spikes were driven on the last rail by some of the distinguished persons present, but it was seldom that they first hit the spike. The original spike, after being tapped by the officials of the companies, was driven home by the chief engineers of the two roads. Then the two trains were run together, the two locomotives touching at the point of junction, and the engineers of the two locomotives each broke a bottle of champagne on the other's engine. Then it was declared that the connection was made and the Atlantic and Pacific were joined together never to be parted.

"Gonna be a steel-drivin' man"

THE BALLAD OF JOHN HENRY

John Henry was an African-American steel driver who in the early 1870s helped excavate the Big Bend Tunnel, the longest tunnel in the country stretching a mile and a quarter under wild terrain in West Virginia. The Chesapeake and Ohio Railroad, like all rail companies at the time, had updated and standardized their equipment to make the laborious task of building a railway more efficient. Among the many innovations was a steam drill designed to replace the work of tunneling with hand drillers or "steel drivers." Using large hammers, steel drivers slammed pieces of steel into rock to place dynamite for blasting. It was dangerous, back-breaking work. The work crews—typically made up of gangs of former slaves—often sang ballads while working to relieve the tedium of their task.

John Henry engaged in a contest with the steam drill and won, but subsequently died. Although some claim the tale is a myth, scholars believe there was a John Henry and the contest really did happen. There has been some discrepancy in the details of the event, such as whether he died on the spot, exhausted from the contest or shortly afterwards in a dynamite explosion. Nevertheless, the event was celebrated as a folk song by rail workers. The ballad did not come to national attention until the 20th century when it started to appear in folk song anthologies. The rhythmic song celebrates a convergence of trends—the emergence of African-American free labor, the railroad construction boom and the triumph of the spirit of man over machine. This helped contribute to the song's popularity and made it one of the most important folk songs in American tradition.

John Henry was a little baby boy
You could hold him in the palm of your hand.
He gave a long and lonesome cry,
 "Gonna be a steel-drivin' man, Lawd, Lawd,
Gonna be a steel-drivin' man."
They took John Henry to the tunnel,
Put him in the lead to drive,
The rock was so tall, John Henry so small,
That he laid down his hammer and cried, "Lawd,
    Lawd,"
Laid down his hammer and he cried.
John Henry started on the right hand,
The steam drill started on the left,
 "Fo' I'd let that stream drill beat me down,
I'd hammer my fool self to death, Lawd, Lawd,
Hammer my fool self to death."
John Henry told his captain,
 "A man ain't nothin' but a man,
Fo' I let your steam drill beat me down
I'll die with this hammer in my hand, Lawd, Lawd,
Die with this hammer in my hand."
Now the captain told John Henry,
 "I believe my tunnel's sinkin' in."
 "Stand back, Captain, and doncha be afraid,
That's nothin' but my hammer catchin' wind,
    Lawd, Lawd,
That's nothin' but my hammer catchin' wind."
John Henry told his cap'n,
"Look yonder, boy, what do I see?
Your drill's done broke and your hole's done choke,
And you can't drive steel like me, Lawd, Lawd,
You can't drive steel like me."
John Henry hammerin' in the mountain,
Till the handle of his hammer caught on fire,
He drove so hard till he broke his po' heart,
Then he laid down his hammer and he died, Lawd,
    Lawd,
He laid down his hammer and he died.
They took John Henry to the tunnel,
And they buried him in the sand,
An' every locomotive come rollin' by
Say, "There lies a steel-drivin' man, Lawd, Lawd,
There lies a steel-drivin' man."

The Public Park Movement

FREDERICK LAW OLMSTED

The rapid, unchecked growth of cities in the 1800s alarmed the public. Crowded, dirty and crime-ridden, cities were built by private developers. Profit—not public good—was the primary motivation in city planning. Increasingly, reformers called for public input in their planning and development. Frederick Law Olmsted led the movement for devising new ways to build cities.

Olmsted was a landscape architect who in 1857 was selected, along with Calvert Vaux, to design Central Park in New York City. Fighting real estate developers and city politicians to accomplish the goal, their design for Central Park as a pastoral, rambling sanctuary became a model city park.

Olmsted and others argued that plantings, appropriate planning and the construction of parks would improve the moral and physical health of city residents, as he explained in this 1870 address. Olmsted's work had a direct impact on the way cities looked (he designed major parks in Boston, Chicago, Montreal and more than a dozen other communities) and led to the City Beautiful Movement at the end of the century. The imprint of his work can be found in almost every city in the United States today.

It is hardly a matter of speculation, I am disposed to think, but almost of demonstration, that the larger a town becomes simply because of its advantages for commercial purposes, the greater will be the convenience available to those who live in and near it for cooperation, as well with reference to the accumulation of wealth in the higher forms—as in seats of learning, of science, and of art—as with reference to merely domestic economy and the emancipation of both men and women from petty, confining, and narrowing cares.

It also appears to be nearly certain, then, that towns which of late have been increasingly rapidly on account of their commercial advantages are likely to be still more attractive to population in the future; that there will in consequence soon be larger towns than any the world has yet known, and that the further progress of civilization is to depend mainly upon the influences by which men's minds and characters will be affected while living in large towns.

Now, knowing that the average length of the life of mankind in towns has been much less than in the country, and that the average amount of disease and misery and of vice and crime has been much greater in towns, this would be a very dark prospect for civilization, if it were not that modern Science has beyond all question determined many of the causes of the special evils by which men are afflicted in towns, and placed means in our hands for guarding against them. It has shown, for example, that under ordinary circumstances, in the interior parts of large and closely built towns, a given quantity of air contains considerably less of the elements which we require to receive through the lungs than the air of the country or even of the outer and more open parts of a town, and that instead of them it carries into the lungs highly corrupt and irritating matters, the action of which tends strongly to vitiate all our sources of vigor—how strongly may perhaps be indicated in the shortest way by the statement that even metallic plates and statues corrode and wear away under the atmospheric influences which prevail in the midst of large towns, more rapidly than in the country....

It has happened several times within the last century, when old artificial obstructions to the spreading out of a city have been removed, and especially when there has been a demolition of and rebuilding on a new ground plan so some part which had previously been noted for the frequency of certain crimes, the prevalence of certain diseases, and the shortness of life among its inhabitants, that a marked improvement in all these respects has followed, and has been maintained not alone in the dark parts, but in the city as a whole.... Strange to say, however, here in the New World, where great towns by the hundred are springing into existence, no care at all is taken to avoid bad plans. The most brutal Pagans to whom we have sent our missionaries have never shown greater indifference to the suffering of others than is exhibited in the plans of some of our most promising cities, for which men now living in them are responsible....

It is evident that if we go on in this way, the progress of civilized mankind in health, virtue, and happiness will be seriously endangered.

It is practically certain that the Boston of to-day is the mere nucleus of the Boston that is to be. It is practically certain that it is to extend over many miles of country now thoroughly rural in character, in parts of which farmers are now laying out roads with a view to shortening the teaming distance between their wood-lots and a railway station, being governed in their courses by old property lines, which were first run simply with reference to the equitable division of heritages, and in other parts of which, perhaps, some wild speculators are having streets staked off from plans which they have formed with a rule and pencil in a broker's office, with a view chiefly of impressions they would make when seen by other speculators on a lithographed map. And by this manner of planning, unless views of duty or interest prevail that are not yet common, if Boston continues to grow at its present rate even for but a few generations longer, and then simply holds its own until it shall be as old as the Boston in Lincolnshire now is, more men, women, and children are to be seriously affected in health and morals than are now living on this Continent....

Let us proceed, then, to the question of means, and with a seriousness in some degree befitting a question, upon our dealing with which we know the misery or happiness of many millions of our fellow-beings will depend.

We will for the present set before our minds the two sources of wear and corruption which we have seen to be remediable and therefore preventible. We may admit that commerce requires that in some parts of a town there shall be an arrangement of buildings, and a character of streets and of traffic in them which will establish conditions of corruption and of irritation, physical and mental. But commerce does not require the same conditions to be maintained in all parts of a town.

Air is disinfected by sunlight and foliage. Foliage also acts mechanically to purify the air by screening it. Opportunity and inducement to escape at frequent intervals from the confined and vitiated air of the commercial quarter, and to supply the lungs with air screened and purified by trees, and recently acted upon by sunlight, together with opportunity and inducement to escape from conditions requiring vigilance, wariness, and activity toward other men—if these could be supplied economically, our problem would be solved....

Would trees for seclusion and shade and beauty, be out of place, for instance by the side of certain of our streets? It will, perhaps, appear to you that it is hardly necessary to ask such a question, as throughout the United States trees are commonly planted at the sides of streets. Unfortunately they are seldom so planted as to have fairly settled the question of the desirableness of systematically maintaining trees under these circumstances. In the first place, the streets are planned, wherever they are, essentially alike. Trees are planted in the space assigned for sidewalks, where at first, while they are saplings, and the vicinity is rural or suburban, they are not much in the way, but where, as they grow larger, and the vicinity becomes urban, they take up more and more space, while space is more and more required for passage. That is not all. Thousands and tens of thousands are planted every year in a manner and under conditions as nearly certain as possible either to kill them outright, or to so lessen their vitality as to prevent their natural and beautiful development, and to cause premature decrepitude. Often, too, as their lower limbs are found inconvenient, no space having been provided for trees in laying out the street, they are deformed by butcherly amputations. If by rare good fortune they are suffered to become beautiful, they still stand subject to be condemned to death at any time, as obstructions in the highway.

What I would ask is, whether we might not with economy make special provision in some of our streets—in a twentieth or a fiftieth part, if you please, of all—for trees to remain as a permanent furniture of the city? I mean, to make a place for them in which they would have room to grow naturally and gracefully. Even if the distance between the houses should have to be made half as much again as it is required in our commercial streets, could not the space be afforded? Out of town space is not costly when measures to secure it are taken early. The assessments for benefits where such streets were provided for, would, in nearly all cases, defray the cost of the land required. The strips of ground reserved for the trees, six, twelve, twenty feet wide, would cost nothing for paving or flagging.

The change both of scene and air which would be obtained by people engaged for the most part in the necessarily confined interior commercial parts of the town, on passing into a street of this character after the trees had became stately and graceful, would be worth a good deal. If such streets were made still broader in some parts, with spacious malls, the advantage would be increased. If each of them were given the proper capacity, and laid out with laterals and connections in suitable directions to serve as a convenient trunkline of communications between two large districts of the town or the business center and the suburbs, a very great number of people might thus be placed every day under influences counteracting those with which we desire to contend….

I have next to see what opportunities are wanted to induce people to engage in what I have termed neighborly receptive recreations, under conditions which shall be highly counteractive to the prevailing bias to degeneration and demoralization in large towns. To make clearer what I mean, I need an illustration which I find in a familiar domestic gathering, where the prattle of the children mingles with the easy conversation of the more sedate, the bodily requirements satisfied with good cheer, fresh air, agreeable light, moderate temperature, snug shelter, and furniture and decorations adapted to please the eye, without calling for profound admiration on the one hand, or tending to the fatigue or disgust on the other. The circumstances are all favorable to a pleasurable wakefulness of the mind without stimulating exertion; and the close relation of family life, the association of children, of mothers, of lovers, of those who give play to faculties such as may be dormant in business or on the promenade; while at the same time the cares of providing in detail for all the wants of the family, guidance, instruction, reproof, are, as matters of conscious exertion, as far as possible laid aside.

There is an instinctive inclination to this social, neighborly, unexertive form of recreation among all of us. In one way or another it is sure to be constantly operating upon those millions on millions of men and women who are to pass their lives within a few miles of where we now stand. To what extent it shall operate so as to develop health and virtue, will, on many occasions, be simply a question of opportunity and inducement. And this question is one for the determination of which for a thousand years we here to-day are largely responsible….

If the great city to arise here is to be laid out little by little, and chiefly to suit the views of landowners, acting only individually, and thinking only of how what they do is to effect the value in the next week or the next year of the few lots that each may hold at the time, the opportunities of so obeying this inclination as at the same time to give the lungs a bath of pure sunny air, to give the mind a suggestion of rest from the devouring eagerness and intellectual strife of town life, will always be few to any, to many will amount to nothing.

But is it possible to make public provision for recreation of this class, essentially domestic and secluded as it is?

It is a question which can, of course, be conclusively answered only from experience. And from experience in some slight degree I shall answer it. There is one large American town, in which it may happen that a man of any class shall say to his wife, when he is going out in the morning: "My dear, when the children come home from school, put some bread and butter and salad in a basket, and go to the spring under the chestnut-tree where we found the Johnsons last week. I will join you there as soon as I can get away from the office. We will walk to the dairy-man's cottage and get some tea, and some fresh milk for the children, and take our supper by the brook-side;" and this shall be no joke, but the most refreshing earnest.

❧ "Descriptions of the Ku Klux Klans"

FRANKFORT, KENTUCKY, CONGRESSIONAL PETITION

Responding against the enfranchisement of African-Americans, Southern whites formed several secret organizations during the Reconstruction Era to undermine federal policies and intimidate African-Americans. The most notorious and largest group was the Ku Klux Klan founded in 1866 in Pulaski, Tennessee. These organizations murdered, whipped and terrorized African-Americans who attempted to exercise their newfound rights as citizens.

The letter below presented by African-American residents in Frankfort, Kentucky, was one of several formal complaints brought to Congress alerting the federal government to the extent of terrorism that was being inflicted on them. This particular letter cites 64 specific incidents in which more than 50 African-Americans were murdered by the Ku Klux Klan or mobs. Congress responded to the rising violence by making violent abuse of civil and political rights a federal crime and directing the military to crack down on Klan activities. Hundreds of people were arrested, leading to a decline in terrorism.

The end of Reconstruction in 1877, however, prompted a resurgence in lynchings. One hundred or more African-Americans were lynched every year for the last 20 years of the 19th century. Violence against African-Americans was typically used as a way to intimidate them from attempting to elevate their suppressed status in society.

To the Senate and house of Representatives in Congress assembled: We the Colored Citizens of Frankfort and vicinity to this day memorialize your honorable bodies upon the condition of affairs now existing in this the state of Kentucky.

We would respectfully state that life, liberty and property are unprotected among the colored races of this state. Organized Bands of desperate and lawless men mainly composed of soldiers of the late Rebel armies, Armed disciplined and disguised and bound by Oath and secret obligations, have by force terror and violence subverted all civil society among Colored people, thus utterly rendering insecure the safety of persons and property overthrowing all those rights which are the primary basis and objects of the government which are expressly guaranteed to us by the Constitution of the United States as amended; We believe you are not familiar with the description of the Ku Klux Klans riding nightly over the country going from County to County and in the County towns spreading terror wherever they go, by robbing whipping ravishing and killing our people without provocation, compelling Colored people to brake the ice and bathe in the Chilly waters of the Kentucky River.

The Legislature has adjourned; they refused to enact any laws to suppress Ku Klux disorder. We regard them as now being licensed to continue their dark and bloody deeds under cover of the dark night. They refuse to allow us to testify in the state Courts where a white man is concerned. We find their deeds are perpetrated only upon Colored men and white Republicans. We also find that for our services to the Government and our race we have become the special object of hatred and persecution at the hands of the Democratic party. Our people are driven from their homes in great numbers having no redress only the U.S. Courts which is in many cases unable to reach them. We would state that we have been law abiding citizens, pay our tax and in many parts of the state our people have been driven from the poles, refused the right to vote. Many have been slaughtered while attempting to vote, we ask how long is this state of things to last.

We appeal to you as law abiding citizens to enact some laws that will protect us. And that will enable us to exercise the rights of citizens. We see that the senator from this state denies there being organized Bands of desperaders in the state for information we lay before you a number of violent acts occurred during his Administration. Although he [Governor

John. W.] Stevenson says half Dozen instances of violence did occur these are not more than one half the acts that have occured. The Democratic party has here a political organization composed only of Democrats not a single Republican can join them where many of these acts have been committed it has been proven that they were the men, done with Armies from the State Arsenal. We pray you will take steps to remedy these evils.

Done by a Committee of Grievances appointed at a meeting of all the Colored Citizens of Frankfort & vicinity.

Mar. 25, 1871
Henry Marrs, Teacher colored school
Henry Lynn, Livery stable keeper
N. N. Trumbo, Grocer
Samuel Damsey
B. Smith
B. T. Crampton, Barber

1. A mob visited Harrodsburg in Mercer County to take from jail a man named Robertson, Nov. 14, 1867.
2. Smith attacked and whipped by regulation in Zelun County Nov. 1867.
3. Colored school house burned by incendiaries in Breckinridge Dec. 24, 1867.
4. A Negro Jim Macklin taken from jail in Frankfort and hung by mob January 28, 1868.
5. Sam Davis hung by mob in Harrodsburg May 28, 1868.
6. Wm. Pierce hung by a mob in Christian July 12, 1868.
7. Geo. Roger hung by a mob in Bradsfordville Martin County July 11, 1868.
8. Colored school Exhibition at Midway attacked by a mob July 31, 1868.
9. Seven person ordered to leave their homes at Standford, Ky. Aug. 7, 1868.
10. Silas Woodford age sixty badly beaten by disguised mob. Mary Smith Curtis and Margaret Mosby also badly beaten, near Keene Jessemine County Aug. 1868.
11. Cabe Fields shot—and killed by disguised men near Keene Jessamine County Aug. 3, 1868.
12. James Gaines expelled from Anderson by Ku Klux Aug. 1868.
13. James Parker killed by Ku Klux Pulaski, Aug. 1868.
14. Noah Blankenship whipped by a mob in Pulaski County Aug. 1868.
15. Negroes attacked robbed and driven from Summerville in Green County Aug. 21, 1868.
16. William Gibson and John Gibson hung by a mob in Washington County Aug. 1868.
17. F. H. Montford hung by a mob near Cogers landing in Jessamine County Aug. 28, 1868.
18. Wm. Glassgow killed by a mob in Warren Country Sep. 5, 1868.
19. Negro hung by a mob Sep. 1868.
20. Two Negros beaten by Ku Klux in Anderson county Sept. 11, 1868.
21. Mob attacked house of Oliver Stone in Fayette county Sept. 11, 1868.
22. Mob attacked Cumins house in Pulaski County. Cumins, his daughter and a man named adams killed in the attack Sept. 18, 1868.
23. U. S. Marshall Meriwether attacked captured and beatened with death in Larue County by mob Sept. 1868.
24. Richardson house attacked in Conishville by mob and Crasban killed Sept. 28 1868.
25. Mob attacks Negro cabin at hanging forks in Lincoln County. John Mosteran killed & Cash & Coffey killed Sept. 1869.
26. Terry Laws & James Ryan hung by mob at Nicholasville oct. 26, 1868.
27. Attack on Negro cabin in Spencer County—a woman outraged Dec. 1868.
28. Two negroes shot by Ku Klux at Sulphur Springs in Union County Dec. 1868.
29. Negro shot at Morganfield Union Country, Dec. 1868.
30. Mob visited Edwin Burris house in Mercer County, January, 1869.
31. William Parker whipped by Ku Klux in Lincoln County Jan. 20, 1869.
32. Mob attacked and fired into house of Jesse Davises in Lincoln County Jan. 20, 1868.
33. Spears taken from his room at Harrodsburg by disguise men Jan. 19, 1869.
34. Albert Bradford killed by disguise men in Scott County, Jan. 20, 1869.
35. Ku Klux whipped boy at Standford March 12, 1869.
36. Mob attacked Frank Bournes house in Jessamine County. Roberts killed March 1869.
37. Geo Bratcher hung by mob on sugar creek in Garrard County March 30, 1869.

38. John Penny hung by a mob at Nevada Mercer County May 29, 1869.

39. Ku Klux whipped Lucien Green in Lincoln County June 1869.

40. Miller whipped by Ku Klux in Madison Country July 2d, 1869.

41. Chas Henderson shot and his wife killed by mob on silver creek Madison County July 1869.

42. Mob decoy from Harrodsburg and hangs Geo Bolling July 17, 1869.

43. Disguise band visited home of I. C. Vanarsdall and T. J. Vanarsdall in Mercer County July 18, 1869.

44. Mob attack Ronsey's house in Casey County three men and one woman killed July 1869.

45. James Crowders hung by mob near Lebanon Merion County Aug. 9, 1869

46. Mob tar and feather a citizen of Cynthiana in Harrison County Aug. 1869.

47. Mob whipped and bruised a Negro in Davis County Sept. 1869.

48. Ku Klux burn colored meeting-house in Carrol County Sept. 1869.

49. Ku Klux whipped a negro at John Carmins's farm in Fayette County Sept. 1869.

50. Wiley Gevens killed by Ku Klux at Dixon Webster County Oct. 1869.

51. Geo. Rose killed by Ku Klux near Kirkville in Madison County Oct. 18, 1869.

52. Ku Klux ordered Wallace Sinkhorn to leave his home near Parkville Boyle County Oct. 1869.

53. Man named Shepherd shot by mob near Parksville Oct. 1869.

54. Regulator killed Geo Tanehly in Lincoln County Nov. 2d. 1869.

55. Ku Klux attacked Frank Searcy house in madison County one man shot Nov. 1869.

56. Searcy hung by mob madison County at Richmond Nov. 4th, 1869.

57. Ku Klux killed Robt. Mershon daughter shot Nov. 1869.

58. Mob whipped Pope Hall and Willett in Washington County Nov. 1869.

59. Regulators whipped Cooper in Pulaski County Nov. 1869.

60. Ku Klux ruffians outraged negroes in Hickman County Nov. 20, 1869.

61. Mob take two Negroes from jail Richmond Madison County one hung one whipped Dec. 12, 1869.

62. Two Negroes killed by mob while in civil custody near Mayfield Graves County Dec. 1869.

63. Allen Cooper killed by Ku Klux in Adair County Dec. 24th, 1869.

64. Negroes whipped while on Scott's farm in Franklin County Dec. 1869.

❧ "No Indian nation shall be recognized as an independent nation"

U. S. CONGRESS

In 1871 Congress inserted a clause in an appropriations bill wiping out the government's obligation to treat Native American tribes as sovereign nations. The effect of this was to give the government the ability to negate promises made in past treaties with Native American nations. This helped clear the way for the Congress to interfere in the internal affairs of Native American tribes and to impose federal laws, regulations and programs on them without their consultation and often against their will.

Be it enacted by the Senate and House of Representatives of the United States of America in Congress assembled, that the following sums be, and they are hereby, appropriated, out of any money in the treasury not otherwise appropriated, for the purpose of paying the current and contingent expenses of the Indian department, and fulfilling treaty stipulations with the various Indian tribes....

For insurance and transportation of goods for the Yankons, one thousand five hundred dollars: Provided, That hereafter no Indian nation or tribe within the territory of the United States shall be acknowledged or recognized as an independent nation, tribe, or power with whom the United States may contract by treaty: Provided further, That nothing herein contained shall be construed to invalidate or impair the obligation of any treaty heretofore lawfully made and ratified with any such Indian nation or tribe....

"All of my sex are doomed to political subjection"

SUSAN B. ANTHONY

Susan B. Anthony and Elizabeth Cady Stanton founded the national Woman Suffrage Association in 1869 to advocate for the women's right to vote. The daughter of Massachusetts Quakers, Anthony challenged state law in Rochester, New York, when she voted in the 1872 presidential election. She was arrested and in June 1873 went to trial.

Shortly before the trial, Anthony delivered a speech outlining her case. Citing the Declaration of Independence, U.S. Constitution and the Fourteenth Amendment, she forcefully argued for the women's right to vote. Anthony lost the case. After the reading of the verdict, Anthony bitterly complained of the handling of her trial in a fiery exchange with the judge who imposed a one-hundred-dollar fine. Anthony refused to pay. Judge Hunt, in turn, declined to put Anthony in jail, thus preventing her from appealing the case to the Supreme Court.

JUDGE HUNT: The prisoner will stand up. Has the prisoner anything to say why sentence shall not be pronounced?

ANTHONY: Yes, your honor, I have many things to say; for in your ordered verdict of guilty, you have trampled underfoot, every vital principle of our government. My natural rights, my civil rights, my political rights, are all alike ignored. Robbed of the fundamental privilege of citizenship, I am degraded from the status of a citizen to that of a subject; and not only myself individually, but all of my sex, are, by your honor's verdict, doomed to political subjection under this so-called republican government.

HUNT: The Court can not listen to a rehearsal of arguments the prisoner's counsel has already consumed three hours in presenting.

ANTHONY: May it please your honor, I am not arguing the question, but simply stating the reasons why sentence can not, in justice, be pronounced against me. Your denial of my citizen's rights to vote is the denial of my right of consent as one of the governed, the denial of my right of representation as one of the taxed, the denial of my right to a trial by a jury of my peers as an offender against the law, therefore, the denial of my sacred rights to life, liberty, property, and—

HUNT: The Court can not allow the prisoner to

go on.

ANTHONY: Of all my prosecutors,...not one is my peer, but each and all are my political sovereigns; and had your honor submitted my case to the jury, as was clearly your duty, even then I should have had cause of protest, for not one those men was my peer; but, native or foreign, white or black, rich or poor, educated or ignorant, awake or asleep, sober or drunk, each and every man of them was political superior; hence, in no sense, my peer.... [J]ury, judge, counsel, must all be of the superior class.

HUNT: The Court must insist—the prisoner has been tried according to the established forms of law.

ANTHONY: Yes, your honor, but by forms of law all made by men, interpreted by men, administered by men, in favor of men, and against women; and hence, your honor's ordered verdict of guilty, against a United States citizen for the exercise of "that citizen's right to vote," simply because that citizen was a woman and not a man. But, yesterday, the same man-made forms of law declared it a crime punishable with $1,000 fine and six months' imprisonment, for you, or me, or any of us, to give a cup of cold water, a crust of bread, or a night's shelter to a panting fugitive as he was tracking his way to Canada. And every man or woman in whose veins coursed a drop of human sympathy violated that wicked law, reckless of consequences, and was justified in so doing. As then the slaves who got their freedom [had to] take it over, or under, or through the unjust forms of law, precisely so now must women, to get their right to a voice in this Government, take it; and I have taken mine, and mean to take it at every possible opportunity.

HUNT: The Court orders the prisoner to sit down. It will not allow another word.

ANTHONY: When I was brought before your honor for trial, I hoped for a broad and liberal interpretation of the Constitution and its recent amendments, that should declare all United States citizens under its protecting aegis—that should declare equality of rights the national guarantee to all persons born or naturalized in the United States. But failing to get this justice—failing, even, to get a jury not of my peers—I ask not leniency at your hands—but rather the full rigors of the law.

HUNT: The court must insist— The prisoner will stand up. The sentence of the Court is that you pay a fine of one hundred dollars and the costs of the prosecution.

ANTHONY: May it please your honor, I shall never pay a dollar of your unjust penalty. All the stock in trade I possess is a $10,000 debt, incurred by publishing my paper—The Revolution—four years ago, the sole object of which was to educate all women to do precisely as I have done, rebel against your man-made, unjust, unconstitutional forms of law, that tax, fine, imprison, and hang women, while they deny them the right of representation in the Government; and I shall work on with might and main to pay every dollar of that honest debt, but not a penny shall go to this unjust claim. And I shall earnestly and persistently continue to urge all women to the practical recognition of the old revolutionary maxim, that "Resistance to tyranny is obedience to God."

HUNT: Madam, the Court will not order you committed until the fine is paid.

❧ "Oh, give me a home, where the buffalo roam"

HOME ON THE RANGE

Authorship of "Home on the Range" has never been resolved and no copyrights were ever given for the popular ballad. Written in the 1870s, the song reflected the romance of the Great American West.

Oh, give me a home,
Where the buffalo roam,
Where the deer and the antelope play;
Where seldom is heard a discouraging word,
And the skies are not cloudy all day.

Home, home on the range,
Where the deer and the antelope play;
Where seldom is heard a discouraging word,
And the skies are not cloudy all day.

How often at night when the heavens are bright
With the lights of the glittering stars,
Have I stood there amazed and asked as I gazed
If their glory exceed that of ours.

Oh, give me a land where the bright

diamond sand
Flows leisurely down the stream;
Where the graceful white swan goes gliding along
Like a maid in a heavenly dream.

Where the air is so pure, the zephyrs so free,
The breezes so balmy and light,
That I would not exchange my home on the range,
For all the cities so bright.

❧ "Very few become Americanized"

ANTI-CHINESE TESTIMONY

Responding to a need for cheap labor in California and difficult economic conditions in China, more than 150,000 Chinese immigrated to California from 1850 to 1880. Thousands of Chinese were employed in work gangs to build the transcontinental railroads. Possessing an alien culture, a completely different religion and a willingness to work long hours at low pay, Chinese immigrants presented a threat. Further, many Chinese went to the United States simply to make money and return to their homeland enriched. In the 1870s a wave of anti-Chinese sentiment swept the West, prompting violent attacks against Chinese.

Congress held hearings on Chinese immigration in 1876. The testimony below was given by a nativist minister who strongly objected to Chinese "heathenism" and believed the Chinese represented a significant threat to the United States. In 1882 Congress passed the Chinese Exclusion Act, prohibiting Chinese immigration for ten years. This was followed by the United States-China Treaty of 1894 barring the exchange of immigrants between the two countries, with some exceptions, for another ten years.

Slavery gave the master power to destroy all the distinctive heathenism which the African brought with him, and he did destroy it. But coolieism gives the employer no such power, and he does not do it. Slavery changed the whole early acquired character of the African, leaving almost or quite nothing of his idolatrous religion, language, customs, habits, morals, tastes, and prejudices, educating him and elevating him up to a whole new character, as an American Christian citizen, in the use of the American language, with American feelings, views, and aspirations.

Coolieism, with very slight exceptions, leaves the Chinese just what they were in their native land, with all their idolatry, immorality, vice, and heathen customs, habits, dress, tastes, prejudices, and most unacquirable language a large, distinct class of people, adverse to all that is American. Slavery rendered impossible any clanship or race combination among Africans in conflict with our interests or our Government; but coolieism gives the Chinese full opportunity to unite all their energies in any schemes they may devise in their supposed interests, to enforce and perpetuate their numerical influence, their heathen worship, their idolatrous customs, their temple ceremonies, their degrading habits, immoralities, vices, dress, prostitution, language, and every feature of abomination so common in their own country.

Already they have a perfect government among themselves distinct from our own, with their laws, their secret courts of trial, and their police, executive, and other officers, the object of which is to perpetuate their race peculiarities, their clanship interests, and their religion, with terrible sanctions of law, even the death penalty, to enforce their regulations.

They are managing a perfect and increasingly efficient "imperium in imperio," to enforce obedience to their requirements, however adverse to American interests or government. They now number full 150,000 in our country, of whom about 130,000 are in California, being nearly one-sixth of our whole population. Others in large numbers are coming, amounting (when unchecked by intimidation) to 25,000 a year. Very few of these ever change in character, to become Americanized. Only about 500 in the last twenty-five years have renounced their native heathenism to profess Christianity. Thus do they remain and rapidly increase in our country, a vast united class, distinct from us in all important characteristics, tastes, habits and language, exerting an influence adverse to our interests, soon, if unrestrained, to number 5,000,000 or even 10,000,000.

✖ "The success of the Standard Oil Company"

JOHN D. ROCKEFELLER

Oil was discovered in Titusville, Pennsylvania, in 1859, sparking a spectacular boom in western Pennsylvania that transformed American industry. John D. Rockefeller was one of thousands that participated in the oil frenzy. He quickly identified the refining and transportation of oil as the most lucrative entry into the oil explosion. In the late 1860s and 1870s Rockefeller moved aggressively—many would say ruthlessly—to consolidate the oil industry under his control. Rockefeller founded Standard Oil Trust in 1882—the nation's first megacorporation—which eventually controlled more than 80 percent of the country's oil production. Rockefeller's vision, relentless faith in oil, ceaseless drive and cut-throat tactics made him the richest man in United States history. This is Rockefeller's description of the founding of Standard Oil and its success as told in the book *Random Reminiscences of Man and Events.*

The story of the early history of the oil trade is too well known to bear repeating in detail. The cleansing of crude petroleum was a simple and easy process, and at first the profits were very large. Naturally, all sorts of people went into it; the butcher, the baker, and the candlestick maker began to refine oil, and it was only a short time before more of the finished product was put on the market than could possibly be consumed. The price went down and down until the trade was threatened with ruin. It seemed absolutely necessary to extend the market for oil by exporting to foreign countries, which required a long and most difficult development, and also to greatly improve the processes of refining so that oil could be made and sold cheaply, yet with a profit, and to use as by-products all of the materials which in the less efficient plants were lost or thrown away.

These were the problems which confronted us almost at the outset, and this great depression led to consultations with our neighbors and friends in the business in the effort to bring some order out of what was rapidly becoming a state of chaos. To accomplish all these tasks of enlarging the market and improving the methods of manufacture in a large way was beyond the power or ability of any concern as then constituted. It could only be done, we reasoned, by increasing our capital and availing ourselves of the best talent and experience.

It was with this idea that we proceeded to buy the largest and best refining concerns and centralize the administration of them with a view to securing greater economy and efficiency. The business grew faster than we anticipated.

This enterprise, conducted by men of application and ability working hard together, soon built up unusual facilities in manufacture, in transportation, in finance, and in extending markets. We had our troubles and setbacks; we suffered from some severe fires; and the supply of crude oil was most uncertain. Our plans were constantly changed by changed conditions. We developed great facilities in an oil center, erected storage tanks, and connected pipe lines; then the oil failed and our work was thrown away. At best it was a speculative trade, and I wonder that we managed to pull through so often, but we were gradually learning how to conduct a most difficult business....

I ascribe the success of the Standard Oil Company to its consistent policy of making the volume of its business large through the merit and cheapness of its products. It has spared no expense in utilizing the best and most efficient method of manufacture. It has sought for the best superintendents and workmen and paid the best wages. It has not hesitated to sacrifice old machinery and old plants for new and better ones. It has placed its manufactories at the points where they could supply markets at the least expense. It has not only sought markets for its principal products but for all possible by-products, sparing no expense in introducing them to the public in every nook and corner of the world. It has not hesitated to invest millions of dollars in methods for cheapening the gathering and distribution of oils by pipe lines, special cars, tank-steamers, and tank-wagons. It has erected tank stations at railroad centers in every part of the country to cheapen the storage and delivery of oil. It has had faith in American oil and has brought together vast sums of money for the purpose of making it what it is and for holding its market against the competition of Russia and all the countries which are producers of oil and competitors against American products.

❧ "All the soldiers were now killed"

TWO MOON DESCRIBES CUSTER'S LAST STAND

After the Civil War the United States renewed its westward expansion resulting in a series of conflicts with Native Americans. More than 200 battles were fought between 1869 and 1874. Throughout the entire 19th century an estimated 5,000 Native Americans and 7,000 soldiers were killed in battle (although most Native American deaths in this era resulted from starvation and disease.) President Ulysses Grant developed a policy in which Native Americans would live on reservations under the care of agents. This helped put a temporary end to the wars.

In 1875, however, the government permitted gold-prospectors to swarm into the Black Hills, prompting an all-out war with the Sioux and other tribes. On June 26, 1876, General George Custer—a Civil War hero and renowned Indian fighter—attacked a huge gathering of Sioux, Cheyenne and other tribes at Little Big Horn. Hopelessly outnumbered, Custer and 265 men were surrounded and wiped out in the battle, while two other smaller contingents attached to Custer's unit managed to escape. News of the defeat reached the East just as most Americans were about to celebrate the centennial of the Declaration of Independence. The Battle of Little Big Horn prompted cries of retribution and the military stomped down hard on Native American resistance. Most of the tribes involved in the battle surrendered to the United States the following year. This account of the Battle of Little Big Horn by Cheyenne Chief Two Moon was reported by Hamlin Garland and published in the September 1898 *McClure's Magazine*.

As we topped the low, pine-clad ridge and looked into the hot, dry valley, Wolf Voice, my Cheyenne interpreter, pointed at a little log cabin, toward the green line of alders wherein the Rosebud ran, and said: "His house—Two Moon."

As we drew near we came to a puzzling fork in the road. The left branch skirted a corner of a wire fence, the right turned into a field. We started to the left, but the waving of a blanket in the hands of a man at the cabin door directed us to the right. As we drew nearer we perceived Two Moon spreading blankets in the scant shade of his log cabin. Some young Cheyennes were grinding a sickle. A couple of children were playing about the little log stables. The barn-yard and buildings were like those of a white settler on the new and arid sod. It was all barren and unlovely—the home of poverty.

As we dismounted at the door Two Moon came out to meet us with hand outstretched. "How?" he said, with the heartiest, long-drawn note of welcome. He motioned us to be seated on the blankets which he had spread for us upon seeing our approach. Nothing could exceed the dignity and sincerity of his greeting.

As we took seats he brought out tobacco and a pipe. He was a tall old man, of a fine, clear brown complexion, big-chested, erect, and martial of bearing. His smiling face was broadly benignant, and his manners were courteous and manly.

While he cut his tobacco Wolf Voice interpreted my wishes to him. I said, "Two Moon, I have come to hear your story of the Custer battle, for they tell me you were a chief there. After you tell me the story, I want to take some photographs of you. I want you to signal with a blanket as the great chiefs used to do in fight."

Wolf Voice made this known to him, delivering also a message from the agents, and at every pause Two Moon uttered deep-voiced notes of comprehension. "Ai," "A-ah," "Hoh,"—these sounds are commonly called "grunts," but they were low, long-drawn expulsions of breath, very expressive.

Then a long silence intervened. The old man mused. It required time to go from the silence of the hot valley, the shadow of his little cabin, and the wire fence of his pasture, back to the days of his youth. When he began to speak, it was with great deliberation. His face became each moment graver and his eyes more introspective.

"Two Moon does not like to talk about the days of fighting; but since you are to make a book, and the agent says you are a friend to Grinnell, I will tell you about it—the truth. It is now a long time ago, and my words do not come quickly.

"That spring I was camped on Powder River with fifty lodges of my people—Cheyennes. The place is near what is now Fort McKenney. One morning soldiers charged my camp. They were in command of Three Fingers [Colonel McKenzie]. We were surprised and scattered, leaving our ponies. The soldiers ran all our horses off. That night the soldiers slept, leaving the horses on one side; so we crept up and stole them back again, and then we went away.

"We traveled far, and one day we met a big camp of Sioux at Charcoal Butte. We camped with the Sioux, and had a good time, plenty grass, plenty game, good water. Crazy Horse was head chief of the camp. Sitting Bull was camped a little ways below, on the Little Missouri River.

"Crazy Horse said to me, 'I'm glad you are come. We are going to fight the white man again.'

"The camp was already full of wounded men, women, and children.

"I said to Crazy Horse, 'All right. I am ready to fight. I have fought already. My people have been killed, my horses stolen; I am satisfied to fight.'"

Here the old man paused a moment, and his face took on a lofty and somber expression.

"I believed at that time the Great Spirits had made Sioux, put them there,"—he drew a circle to the right—"and white men and Cheyennes here,"—indicating two places to the left—"expecting them to fight. The Great Spirits I thought liked to see the fight; it was to them all the same like playing. So I thought then about fighting." As he said this, he made me feel for one moment the power of a sardonic god whose drama was the wars of men.

"About May, when the grass was tall and the horses strong, we broke camp and started across the country to the mouth of the Tongue River. Then Sitting Bull and Crazy Horse and all went up the Rosebud. There we had a big fight with General Crook, and whipped him. Many soldiers were killed—few Indians. It was a great fight, much smoke and dust.

"From there we all went over the divide, and camped in the valley of Little Horn. Everybody thought, 'Now we are out of the white man's country. He can live there, we will live here.' After a few days, one morning when I was in camp north of Sitting Bull, a Sioux messenger rode up and said, 'Let everybody paint up, cook, and get ready for a big dance.'

"Cheyennes then went to work to cook, cut up tobacco, and get ready. We all thought to dance all day. We were very glad to think we were far away from the white man.

"I went to water my horses at the creek, and washed them off with cool water, then took a swim myself. I came back to the camp afoot. When I got near my lodge, I looked up the Little Horn towards Sitting Bull's camp. I saw a great dust rising. It looked like a whirlwind. Soon Sioux horseman came rushing into camp shouting: 'Soldiers come! Plenty white soldiers.'

"I ran into my lodge, and said to my brother-in-law, 'Get your horses; the white man is coming. Everybody run for horses.'

"Outside, far up the valley, I heard a battle cry, Hay-ay, hay-ay! I heard shooting, too, this way [clapping his hands very fast]. I couldn't see any Indians. Everybody was getting horses and saddles. After I had caught my horse, a Sioux warrior came again and said, 'Many soldiers are coming.'

"Then he said to the women, 'Get out of the way, we are going to have hard fight.' "I said, 'All right, I am ready.'

"I got on my horse, and rode out into my

camp. I called out to the people all running about: 'I am Two Moon, your chief. Don't run away. Stay here and fight. You must stay and fight the white soldiers. I shall stay even if I am to be killed.'

"I rode swiftly toward Sitting Bull's camp. There I saw the white soldiers fighting in a line [Reno's men]. Indians covered the flat. They began to drive the soldiers all mixed up—Sioux, then soldiers, then more Sioux, and all shooting. The air was full of smoke and dust. I saw the soldiers fall back and drop into the river-bed like buffalo fleeing. They had no time to look for a crossing. The Sioux chased them up the hill, where they met more soldiers in wagons, and then messengers came saying more soldiers were going to kill the women, and the Sioux turned back. Chief Gall was there fighting, Crazy Horse also.

"I then rode toward my camp, and stopped squaws from carrying off lodges. While I was sitting on my horse I saw flags come up over the hill to the east like that [he raised his finger-tips]. Then the soldiers rose all at once, all on horses, like this [he put his fingers behind each other to indicate that Custer appeared marching in columns of fours]. They formed into three bunches [squadrons] with a little ways between. Then a bugle sounded, and they all got off horses, and some soldiers led the horses back over the hill.

"Then the Sioux rode up the ridge on all sides, riding very fast. The Cheyennes went up the left way. Then the shooting was quick, quick. Pop— pop—pop very fast. Some of the soldiers were down on their knees, some standing. Officers all in front. The smoke was like a great cloud, and everywhere the Sioux went the dust rose like smoke. We circled all round him—swirling like water round a stone. We shoot, we ride fast, we shoot again. Soldiers drop, and horses fall on them. Soldiers in line drop, but one man rides up and down the line—all the time shouting. He rode a sorrel horse with white face and white fore-legs. I don't know who he was. He was a brave man.

"Indians keep swirling round and round, and the soldiers killed only a few. Many soldiers fell. At last all horses killed but five. Once in a while some man would break out and run toward the river, but he would fall. At last about a hundred men and five horsemen stood on the hill all bunched together. All along the bugler kept blowing his commands. He was very brave too. Then a chief was killed. I hear it was Long Hair [Custer], I don't

know; and then five horsemen and the bunch of men, may be so forty, started toward the river. The man on the sorrel horse led them, shouting all the time. He wore a buckskin shirt, and had long black hair and mustache. He fought hard with a big knife. His men were all covered with white dust. I couldn't tell whether they were officers or not. One man all alone ran far down toward the river, then round up over the hill. I thought he was going to escape, but a Sioux fired and hit him in the head. He was the last man. He wore braid on his arms [sergeant].

"All the soldiers were now killed, and the bodies were stripped. After that no one could tell which were officers. The bodies were left where they fell. We had no dance that night. We were sorrowful.

"Next day four Sioux chiefs and two Cheyennes and I, Two Moon, went upon the battlefield to count the dead. One man carried a little bundle of sticks. When we came to dead men, we took a little stick and gave it to another man, so we counted the dead. There were 388. There were thirty-nine Sioux and seven Cheyennes killed, and about a hundred wounded.

"Some white soldiers were cut with knives, to make sure they were dead; and the war women had mangled some. Most of them were left just where they fell. We came to the man with big mustache; he lay down the hills toward the river. The Indians did not take his buckskin shirt. The Sioux said, 'That is a big chief. That is Long Hair.' I don't know. I had never seen him. The man on the white-faced horse was the bravest man.

"That day as the sun was getting low our young men came up the Little Horn riding hard. Many white soldiers were coming in a big boat, and when we looked we could see the smoke rising. I called my people together, and we hurried up the Little Horn, into Rotten Grass Valley. We camped there three days, and then rode swiftly back over our old trail to the east. Sitting Bull went back into the Rosebud and down the Yellowstone, and away to the north. I did not see him again."

೪ Invention of the telephone

ALEXANDER GRAHAM BELL

A Scottish immigrant, Alexander Graham Bell founded a training school for teachers of the deaf in Boston, Massachusetts in 1872. He later invented a telegraph multiplexing system, which in turn led to his interest in transmitting sounds. In March 1876, Bell successfully transmitted words to his assistant, Thomas Watson. The invention of the telephone signaled the ascension of the United States as an advanced industrial power and completely transformed the communications industry.

Bell soon patented the telephone, later founded Bell Telephone Company and in 1915 placed the first transcontinental telephone call from New York to San Francisco. The following is Bell's journal entry the first day he spoke with Watson over the telephone.

I then shouted into M [the mouth piece] the following sentence: "Mr. Watson—Come here—I want to see you." To my delight he came and declared that he had heard and understood what I said. I asked him to repeat the words. He answered "You said—'Mr. Watson—Come here—I want to see you.'" We then changed places and I listened at S [the receiver] while Mr. Watson read a few passages from a book into the mouth piece M. It was certainly the case that articulate sounds proceeded from S. The effect was loud but indistinct and muffled. If I had read beforehand the passage given by Mr. Watson I should have recognized every word. As it was I could not make out the sense—but an occasional word here and there was quite distinct. I made out "to" and "out" and "further"; and finally the sentence "Mr. Bell do you understand what I say? Do—you—un—der—stand—what—I—say" came quite clearly intelligibly.

೪ "Certain combination of men against law exist"

ULYSSES S. GRANT

The federal government's Reconstruction policies were under severe strains in the 1870s. Corruption in President Ulysses Grant's administration had infected the federal agencies charged with overseeing Reconstruction. Southern whites bitterly resented the elevation of political rights to African-Americans and northern "carpetbaggers." A reign of intimidation by organizations such as the Ku Klux Klan helped southern white Democrats reclaim their political clout. By 1876, only three states were still under Republican control—Florida, Louisiana and South Carolina. Democratic resistance against the Republican administrations was rising. In South Carolina, former Confederate General Wade Hampton led an informal militia known as the "Red Shirts" who increasingly engaged in violent resistance to Republican policies. Several armed conflicts prompted Republican South Carolina Governor Daniel H. Chamberlain to request Grant authorize the use of federal troops. Grant agreed to the request and declared martial law over South Carolina.

Whereas it has been satisfactorily shown to me that insurrection and domestic violence exist in several counties of the State of South Carolina, and that certain combinations of men against law exist in many counties of said State known as "rifle clubs," who ride up and down by day and night in arms, murdering some peaceable citizens and intimidating others, which combinations, though forbidden by the laws of the State, can not be controlled or suppressed by the ordinary course of justice; and

Whereas it is provided in the Constitution of the United States that the United States shall protect every State in this Union, on application of the legislature, or of the executive (when the legislature can not be convened), against domestic violence; and

Whereas by laws in pursuance of the above it is provided (in the laws of the United States) that in all cases of insurrection in any State or of obstruction to the laws thereof it shall be lawful for the President of the United States, on application of the legislature of such State, or of the executive (when the legislature can not be convened), to call forth the militia of any other State or States, or to employ such part of the land and naval forces as shall be judged necessary, for the purpose of suppressing such insurrection or causing the laws to be duly executed; and

Whereas the legislature of said State is not now in session and can not be convened in time to meet the present emergency, and the executive of said State, under section 4 of Article IV of the Constitution of the United States and the laws passed in pursuance thereof, has therefore made due application to me in the premises for such part of the military force of the United States as may be necessary and adequate to protect said State and the citizens thereof against domestic violence and to enforce the due execution of the laws; and

Whereas it is required that whenever it may be necessary, in the judgment of the President, to use the military force for the purpose of aforesaid, he shall forthwith, by proclamation, command such insurgents to disperse and retire peaceably to their respective homes within a limited time:

Now, therefore, I, Ulysses S. Grant, President of the United States, do hereby make proclamation and command all persons engaged in said unlawful and insurrectionary proceedings to disperse and retire peaceably to their respective abodes within three days from this date, and hereafter abandon said combinations and submit themselves to the laws and constituted authorities of said State.

And I invoke the aid and cooperation of all good citizens thereof to uphold the laws and preserve the public peace.

"Mistakes have been made"

ULYSSES S. GRANT

President Grant's administration was wracked by corruption scandals at almost all levels. The most notorious case of corruption involved a dummy corporation called Crédit Mobilier to hold diverted public funds dedicated for the construction of the Union Pacific Railroad. The money was siphoned off for top Republican officials. When the scheme was revealed in 1872-73 Grant's vice president, Schuyler Colfax, and several congressmen were implicated. Grant was never directly involved in any of the scandals that plagued his administration. Nevertheless, at the conclusion of his eight-year tenure as president, Grant offered an apology for his administration's conduct when he delivered his eighth annual message to Congress in 1876.

To the Senate and House of Representatives:

In submitting my eighth and last annual message to Congress it seems proper that I should refer to and in some degree recapitulate the events and official acts of the past eight years.

It was my fortune, or misfortune, to be called to the office of Chief Executive without any previous political training. From the age of 17 I had never even witnessed the excitement attending a Presidential campaign but twice antecedent to my own candidacy, and at but one of them was eligible as a voter.

Under such circumstances it is but reasonable to suppose that errors of judgment must have occurred. Even had they not, differences of opinion between the Executive, bound by an oath to the strict performance of his duties, and writers and debaters must have arisen. It is not necessarily evidence of blunder on the part of the Executive because there are these differences of views. Mistakes have been made, as all can see and I admit, but it seems to me oftener in the selections made of the assistants appointed to aid in carrying out the various duties of administering the Government—in nearly every case selected without a personal acquaintance with the appointee, but upon recommendations of their representatives chosen directly by the people. It is impossible, where so many trusts are to be allotted, that the right parties should be chosen in every instance. History shows that no Administration from the time of Washington to the present has been free from these mistakes. But I leave comparisons to history, claiming only that I have acted in every instance from a conscientious desire to do what was right, constitutional, within the law, and for the very best interests of the whole people. Failures have been errors of judgment, not of intent....

"The uneducated negro was too weak"

DANIEL CHAMBERLAIN

Controversy and fraud marked the 1876 presidential election between the Republican Rutherford B. Hayes and Democratic Samuel J. Tilden. A special commission was formed to resolve 20 disputed electoral votes. On a strictly partisan 8-7 vote, the commission assigned all the disputed votes to Hayes, meaning he would win the electoral vote 185-184. Infuriated Democrats threatened to contest the election but instead struck a deal with Hayes and the Republicans. In exchange for removing troops from the South, naming a Southerner to the cabinet and allocating federal aid to the South, the Southern Democrats agreed to support the commission's finding. As a result, Democrats regained state political control throughout the region. Former South Carolina Governor Daniel Chamberlain wrote about the fall of the Republican Party in South Carolina to William Lloyd Garrison in June 1877.

Dear Mr. Garrison....

Your prophecy is fulfilled, and I am not only overthrown, but as a consequence I am now a citizen of New York. It seems to me a remarkable experience indeed, though I hope I do not egotistically exaggerate it, for I am sure it will soon be forgotten by most men in the press and hurry of new events. Why I write this line now and send it to Boston when I know you are in Europe, is because I feel like putting on record my main reflections on my experiences of the last three years....

First, then, my defeat was inevitable under the circumstances of time and place which surrounded me. I mean here exactly that the uneducated negro was too weak, no matter what his numbers, to cope with the whites.

We had lost too, the sympathy of the North, in some large measure, though we never deserved it so certainly as in 1876 in South Carolina.

The Presidential contest also endangered us and doubtless defeated us. The hope of electing Tilden incited our opponents, and the greed of office led the defeated Republicans under Hayes to sell us out. There was just as distinct a bargain to do this at Washington as ever existed which was not signed and sealed on paper. And the South is not to be blamed for it, if anybody is; but rather those leaders, like Evarts, who could never see their Constitutional obligations towards the South until the offices were slipping away from their party.

So the end came, but not as you expected....

"A general reestablishment of order"

RUTHERFORD B. HAYES

When President Rutherford B. Hayes delivered his first annual message to Congress in December 1877 all of the conditions in the political agreement between the Republicans and the Democrats had been accomplished. The Reconstruction Era ended and a century-long dominance of segregationist Democratic state governments in the South had been initiated. Hayes—who was a decorated Civil War veteran and a Radical Republican who had voted for Johnson's impeachment—emphasized the need for North and South to continue the reconciliation of differences. Hayes praised the progress that had been made in the South in reestablishing its economy, political stability and judicial system.

To complete and make permanent the pacification of the country continues to be, and until it is fully accomplished must remain, the most important of all our national interests. The earnest purpose of good citizens generally to unite their efforts in this endeavor is evident. It found decided expression in the resolutions announced in 1876 by the national conventions of the leading political parties of the country. There was a widespread apprehension that the momentous results in our progress as a nation marked by the recent amendments to the Constitution were in imminent jeopardy; that the good understanding which prompted their adoption, in the interest of a loyal devotion to the general welfare, might prove a barren truce, and that the two sections of the country, once engaged in civil strife, might be again almost as widely severed and disunited as they were when arrayed in arms against each other.

The course to be pursued, which, in my judgment, seemed wisest in the presence of this emergency, was plainly indicated in my inaugural address. It pointed to the time, which all our people desire to see, when a genuine love of our whole country and of all that concerns its true welfare shall supplant the destructive forces of the mutual animosity of races and of sectional hostility. Opinions have differed widely as to the measures best calculated to secure this great end. This was to be expected. The measures adopted by the Administration have been subjected to severe and varied criticism. Any course whatever which might have been entered upon would certainly have encountered distrust and opposition. These measures were, in my judgment, such as were most in harmony with the Constitution and with the genius of our people, and best adapted, under all the circumstances, to attain the end in view. Beneficent results, already apparent, prove that these endeavors are not to be regarded as a mere experiment, and should sustain and encourage us in our efforts. Already, in the brief period which has elapsed, the immediate effectiveness, no less than the justice, of the course pursued is demonstrated, and I have an abiding faith that time will furnish its ample vindication in the minds of the great majority of my fellow-citizens. The discontinuance of the use of the Army for the purpose of upholding local governments in two States of the Union was no less a constitutional duty and requirement, under the circumstances existing at the time, than it was a much-needed measure for the restoration of local self-government and the promotion of national harmony. The withdrawal of the troops from such employment was effected deliberately, and with solicitous care for the peace and good order of society and the protection of the property and persons and every right of all classes of citizens.

The results that have followed are indeed significant and encouraging. All apprehension of danger from remitting those States to local self-government is dispelled, and a most salutary change in the minds of the people has begun and is in progress in every part of that section of the country once the theater of unhappy civil strife, substituting for suspicion, distrust, and aversion, concord, friendship, and patriotic attachment to the Union. No unprejudiced mind will deny that the terrible and often fatal collisions which for several years have been of frequent occurrence and have agitated and alarmed the public mind have almost entirely ceased, and that a spirit of mutual forbearance and hearty national interest has succeeded. There has been a general reestablishment of order and of the orderly administration of justice. Instances of remaining lawlessness have become of rare occurrence; political turmoil and turbulence have disappeared; useful industries have been resumed; public credit in the Southern States has been greatly strengthened, and the encouraging benefits of a revival of commerce between the sections of the country lately embroiled in civil war are fully enjoyed. Such are some of the results already attained, upon which the country is to be congratulated. They are of such importance that we may with confidence patiently await the desired consummation that will surely come with the natural progress of events....

❧ "We had only our ignorance"

ANONYMOUS AFRICAN-AMERICAN

With the end of Reconstruction in the South, protections and opportunities provided to freed slaves evaporated. Southern white Democratic state governments passed laws sharply restricting the newfound rights of African-Americans, segregating blacks from white society. Plantation owners found new ways to bind their former slaves as miserably paid workers through sharecropping and other arrangements. For all practical purposes, many African-Americans found themselves in virtually the same position they had occupied before their emancipation. This personal story of one former Georgia slave published in *Independent* magazine illustrates the chicanery, corruption and brute force that characterized race relations in the post-Reconstruction South.

I am a Negro and was born some time during the war in Elbert County, Ga., and I reckon by this time I must be a little over forty years old. My mother was not married when I was born, and I never knew who my father was or anything about him. Shortly after the war my mother died, and I was left to the care of my uncle. All this happened before I was eight years old, and so I can't remember very much about it. When I was about ten years old my uncle hired me out to Captain.... I was told that the Captain wanted me for his house-boy, and that later on he was going to train me to be his coachman. To be a coachman in those days was considered a post of honor, and young as I was, I was glad of the chance.

But I had not been at the Captain's a month before I was put to work on the farm, with some twenty or thirty other Negroes men, women and children. From the beginning the boys had the same tasks as the men and women. There was no difference. We all worked hard during the week, and would frolic on Saturday nights and often on Sundays. And everybody was happy. The men got $3 a week and the women $2. I don't know what the children got. Every week my uncle collected my money for me, but it was very little of it that I ever saw. My uncle fed and clothed me, gave me a place to sleep, and allowed me ten or fifteen cents a week for "spending change," as he called it.

I must have been seventeen or eighteen years old before I got tired of that arrangement, and felt that I was man enough to be working for myself and handling my own wages.... Unknown to my uncle or the Captain I went off to a neighboring plantation and hired myself out to another man. The new landlord agreed to give me forty cents a day and furnish me one meal. I thought that I was doing fine. Bright and early one Monday morning I started for work, still not letting the others know anything about it. But they found it out before sundown. The Captain came over to the new place and brought some kind of officer of the law. The officer pulled out a long piece of paper from his pocket and read it to my new employer. When this was done I heard my new boss say:

"I beg your pardon, Captain. I didn't know this nigger was bound out to you, or I wouldn't have hired him."

"He certainly is bound out to me," said the Captain. "He belongs to me until he is twenty-one, and I'm going to make him know his place."

So I was carried back to the Captain's. That night he made me strip off my clothing down to my waist, had me tied to a tree in his backyard, ordered his foreman to give me thirty lashes with a buggy whip across my bare back, and stood by until it was done. After that experience the Captain made me stay on his place night and day, but my uncle still continued to "draw" my money.

I was a man nearly grown before I knew how to count from one to one hundred. I was a man nearly grown before I ever saw a colored school teacher. I never went to school a day in my life. To-day I can't write my own name, though I can read a little. I was a man nearly grown before I ever rode on a railroad train, and then I went on an excursion from Elberton to Athens. What was true of me was true of hundreds of other Negroes around me—'way off there in the country, fifteen or twenty miles from the nearest town.

When I reached twenty-one the Captain told me I was a free man, but he urged me to stay with him. He said he would treat me right, and pay me as much as anybody else would. The Captain's son and I were about the same age, and the Captain said that, as he had owned my mother and uncle during slavery, and as his son didn't want me to leave them (since I had been with them so long), he wanted me to stay with the old family. And I stayed. I signed a contract—that is, I made my mark for one year. The captain was to give me $3.50 a week, and furnish me a little house on the plantation—a one-room log cabin similar to those used by his other laborers.

During that year I married Mandy. For several years Mandy had been the house-servant for the Captain, his wife, his son and his three daughters, and they all seemed to think a good deal of her. As an evidence of their regard they gave us furniture, which cost about $25, and we set up housekeeping in one of the Captain's two-room shanties. I thought I was the biggest man in Georgia. Mandy still kept her place in the "Big House" after our marriage. We did so well for the first year that I

renewed my contract for the second year, and the third, fourth and fifth year I did the same tiring.

Before the end of the fifth year the Captain had died, and his son, who had married some two or three years before, took charge of the plantation. Also, for two or three years, this son had been serving at Atlanta in some big office to which he had been elected. I think it was in the Legislature or something of that sort anyhow, all the people called him Senator. At the end of the fifth year the Senator suggested that I sign up a contract for ten years; then, he said, we wouldn't have to fix up papers every year. I asked my wife about it; she consented; and so I made a ten-year contract.

Not long afterward the Senator had a long, low shanty built on his place. A great big chimney, with a wide, open fireplace, was built at one end of it, and on each side of the house, running lengthwise, there was a row of flames or stalls just large enough to hold a single mattress.... They looked for all the world like stalls for horses.... Nobody seemed to know what the Senator was fixing for.

All doubts were put aside one bright day in April when about forty able-bodied Negroes, bound in iron chains, and some of them handcuffed, were brought out to the Senator's farm in three big wagons. They were quartered in the long, low shanty, and it was afterward called the stockade. This was the beginning of the Senator's convict camp. These men were prisoners who had been leased by the Senator from the State of Georgia at about $200 each per year, the State agreeing to pay for guards and physicians, for necessary inspection, for inquests, all rewards for escaped convicts, the cost of litigation and all other incidental camp expenses. When I saw these men in shackles, and the guards with their guns, I was scared nearly to death. I felt like running away, but I didn't know where to go. And if there had been any place to go to, I would have had to leave my wife and child behind.

We free laborers held a meeting. We all wanted to quit. We sent a man to tell the Senator about it. Word came back that we were all under contract for ten years and that the Senator would hold us to the letter of the contract, or put us in chains and lock us up—the same as the other prisoners. It was made plain to us by some white people we talked to that in the contracts we had signed we had all agreed to be locked up in a stockade at night or at any other time that our employer saw fit; further, we learned that we could not lawfully break our contract for any reason and go and hire ourselves to somebody else without the consent of our employer; and, more than that, if we got mad and ran away, we could be run down by bloodhounds, arrested without process of law, and be returned to our employers, who, according to the contract, might beat us brutally or administer any other kind of punishment that he thought proper.

In other words, we had sold ourselves into slavery—and what could we do about it? The white folks had all the courts, all the guns, all the hounds, all the railroads, all the telegraph wires, all the newspapers, all the money, and nearly all the land, and we had only our ignorance, our poverty and our empty hands. We decided that the best thing to do was to shut our mouths, say nothing, and go back to work. And most of us worked side by side with those convicts during the remainder of the ten years.

But this first batch of convicts was only the beginning. Within six months another stockade was built, and twenty or thirty other convicts were brought to the plantation, among them six or eight women! The Senator had bought an additional thousand acres of land, and to his already large cotton plantation he added two great big saw-mills and went into the lumber business. Within two years the Senator had in all nearly 200 Negroes working on his plantation about half of them free laborers, so called, and about half of them convicts. The only difference between the free laborers and the others was that the free laborers could come and go as they pleased, at night that is, they were not locked up at night, and were not, as a general thing, whipped for slight offenses.

The troubles of the free laborers began at the close of the ten-year period. To a man, they all wanted to quit when the time was up. To a man, they all refused to sign new contracts—even for one year, not to say anything of ten years. And just when we thought that our bondage was at an end we found that it had really just begun. Two or three years before, or about a year and a half after the Senator had started his camp, he had established a large store, which was called the commissary. All of us free laborers were compelled to buy our supplies—food, clothing, etc. from the store. We never used any money in our dealings at the commissary, only tickets or orders, and we had a general settle-

ment once each year, in October. In this store we were charged all sorts of high prices for goods, because every year we would come out in debt to our employer. If not that, we seldom had more than $5 or $10 coming to us and that for a whole year's work. Well, at the close of the tenth year, when we kicked and meant to leave the Senator, he said to some of us with a smile (and I never will forget that smile—I can see it now):

"Boys, I'm sorry you're going to leave me. I hope you will do well in your new places—so well that you will be able to pay me the little balances which most of you owe me."

Word was sent out for all of us to meet him at the commissary at 2 o'clock. There he told us that, after we had signed what he called a written acknowledgment of our debts, we might go and look for new places. The store-keeper took us one by one and read to us statements of our accounts. According to the books there was no man of us who owed the Senator less than $100; some of us were put down for as much as $200. I owed $165, according to the bookkeeper. These debts were not accumulated during one year, but ran back for three and four years, so we were told in spite of the fact that we understood that we had had a full settlement at the end of each year. But no one of us would have dared to dispute a white man's word— o, no; not in those days. Besides, we fellows didn't care anything about the amounts we were after getting away; and we had been told that we might go, if we signed the acknowledgments. We would have signed anything, just to get away. So we stepped up, we did, and made our marks.

That same night we were rounded up by a constable and ten or twelve white men, who aided him, and we were locked up, every one of us, in the Senator's stockades. The next morning it was explained to us by the two guards appointed to watch us that, in the papers we had signed the day before, we had not only made acknowledgment of our indebtedness, but that we had also agreed to work for the Senator until the debts were paid by hard labor. And from that day forward we were treated just like convicts. Really we had made ourselves lifetime slaves, or peons, as the laws called us. But, call it slavery, peonage, or what not, the truth is we lived in a hell on earth what time we spent in the Senator's peon camp.

I lived in that camp, as a peon, for nearly three

years. My wife fared better than I did, as did the wives of some of the other Negroes, because the white men about the camp used these unfortunate creatures as their mistresses. When I was first put in the stockade, my wife was still kept for a while in the "Big House," but my little boy, who was only nine years old, was given away to a Negro family across the river in South Carolina, and I never saw or heard of him after that. When I left the camp, my wife had had two children by some one of the white bosses, and she was living in fairly good shape in a little house off to herself.

But the poor Negro women who were not in the class with my wife fared about as bad as the helpless Negro men. Most of the time the women who were peons or convicts were compelled to wear men's clothes. Sometimes, when I have seen them dressed like men, and plowing or hoeing or hauling logs or working at the blacksmith's trade, just the same as men, my heart would bleed and my blood would boil, but I was powerless to raise a hand. It would have meant death on the spot to have said a word. Of the first six women brought to the camp, two of them gave birth to children after they had been there more than twelve months and the babies had white men for their fathers!

The stockades in which we slept were, I believe, the filthiest places in the world. They were cesspools of nastiness. During the three years that I was there I am willing to swear that a mattress was never moved after it had been brought there, except to turn it over once or twice a month. No sheets were used, only dark-colored blankets. Most of the men slept every night in the clothing that they had worked in all day. Some of the worst characters were made to sleep in chains. The doors were locked and barred each night, and tallow candles were the only lights allowed. Really the stockades were but little more than cow sheds, horse stables or hog pens....

But I didn't tell you how I got out. I didn't get out—they put me out. When I had served as a peon for nearly three years—and you remember that they claimed that I owed them only $165—when I had served for nearly three years, one of the bosses came to me and said that my time was up. He happened to be the one who was said to be living with my wife. He gave me a new suit of overalls, which cost about seventy-five cents, took me in a buggy and carried me across the Broad River

into South Carolina, set me down and told me to "git." I didn't have a cent of money, and I wasn't feeling well, but somehow I managed to get a move on me. I begged my way to Columbia. In two or three days I ran across a man looking for laborers to carry to Birmingham, and I joined his gang. I have been here in Birmingham district since they released me, and I reckon I'll die either in a coal mine or an iron furnace. It don't make much difference which. Either is better than a Georgia peon camp. And a Georgia peon camp is hell itself.

"I will fight no more forever"

CHIEF JOSEPH

The Nez Percé tribe—who 70 years earlier had rescued the Lewis and Clark expedition—refused in 1877 to resettle on a reservation. Chief Joseph led his tribe on an extraordinary 1,500-mile escape through Wyoming, Idaho and Montana from the U.S. army. Outnumbered and outgunned, Chief Joseph successfully employed guerilla tactics to avoid capture for many months. But with the arrival of winter in 1878 and his tribe starving, Chief Joseph finally announced his decision to surrender to the U.S. military.

Tell General Howard I know his heart. What he told me before, I have it in my heart. I am tired of fighting. Our chiefs are killed; Looking-Glass is dead, Ta-Hool-Hool-Shute is dead. The old men are all dead. It is the young men who say yes or no. He who led on the young men is dead. It is cold, and we have no blankets; the little children are freezing to death. My people, some of them, have run away to the hills, and have no blankets, no food. No one knows where they are—perhaps freezing to death. I want to have time to look for my children, and see how many of them I can find. Maybe I shall find them among the dead. Hear me, my chiefs! I am tired; my heart is sick and sad. From where the sun now stands I will fight no more forever.

❧ "The Silent General"

WALT WHITMAN

Walt Whitman was one of the great observers of 19th century America and American democracy. On September 28, 1879, he wrote a diary entry about Ulysses S. Grant, who was now an ordinary citizen.

So General Grant, after circumambiating the world, has arrived home again—landed in San Francisco yesterday, from the ship City of Tokio from Japan. What a man he is! what a history! what an illustration—his life—of the capacities of that American individuality common to us all. Cynical critics are wondering "what the people can see in Grant" to make such a hubbub about. They aver (and it is no doubt true) that he has hardly the average of our day's literary and scholastic culture, and absolutely no pronounc'd genius or conventional eminence of any sort. Correct: but proves how an average western farmer, mechanic, boatman, carried by tides of circumstances, perhaps caprices, into a position of incredible military or civic responsibilities, (history has presented none more trying, no born monarch's, no more shining for attack or envy,) may steer his way fitly and steadily through them all, carrying the country and himself with credit year after year—command over a million armed men—fight more than fifty pitch'd battles—rule for eight years a land larger than all the kingdoms of Europe combined—and then, retiring, quietly (with a cigar in his mouth) make the promenade of the whole world, through its courts and coteries, and kings and czars and mikados, and splendidest glitters and etiquettes, as phlegmatically as he ever walk'd the portico of a Missouri hotel after dinner. I say all this is what people like—and I am sure I like it. Seems to me it transcends Plutarch. How those old Greeks, indeed, would have seized on him! A mere plain man—no art, no poetry—only practical sense, ability to do, or try his best to do, what devolv'd upon him. A common trader, money-maker, tanner, farmer of Illinois—general for the republic, in its terrific struggle within itself, in the war of attempted secession—President following (a task of peace, more difficult than the war itself)—nothing heroic, as the authorities put it—and yet the greatest hero. The gods, the destinies, seem to have concentrated upon him president, and I suppose it's just one of the risks he takes.

❧ Pioneers! O Pioneers!

WALT WHITMAN

Having first achieved national literary fame in 1855 with the publication of *Leaves of Grass,* Walt Whitman continued to write poetry, often about contemporary American themes. He wrote "Pioneers! O Pioneers!" to commemorate the courage and fortitude of the settlers of the American West.

Come my tan-faced children,
Follow well in order, get your weapons ready,
Have you your pistols? have you your sharp-edged
    axes?
Pioneers! O Pioneers!
For we cannot tarry here,
We must march my darlings, we must bear the
    brunt of danger,
We the youthful sinewy races, all the rest on us
    depend,
Pioneers! O Pioneers!
O you youths, Western youths,
So impatient, full of action, full of manly pride and
    friendship,
Plain I see you Western youths, see you tramping
    with the foremost,
Pioneers! O Pioneers!
Have the elder races halted?
Do they droop and end their lesson, wearied over
    there beyond the seas?
We take up the task eternal, and the burden and
    the lesson,
Pioneers! O pioneers!
All the past we leave behind,
We debouch upon a newer mightier world, varied
    world,
Fresh and strong the world we seize, world of labor
    and the march,
Pioneers! O pioneers!
We detachments steady throwing,
Down the edges, through the passes, up the moun-
    tains steep,
Conquering, holding, daring, venturing as we go
    the unknown ways,
Pioneers! O pioneers!
We primeval forests felling,
We the rivers stemming, vexing we and piercing
    deep the mines within,
We the surface broad surveying, we the virgin soil
    upheaving,
Pioneers! O pioneers!

Colorado men are we,
From the peaks gigantic, from the great sierras and
the high plateaus,
From the mine and from the gully, from the hunt-
ing trail we come,
Pioneers! O pioneers!
From Nebraska, from Arkansas,
Central inland race are we, from Missouri, with the
continental blood intervein'd,
All the hands of comrades clasping, all the
Southern, all the Northern,
Pioneers! O pioneers!
O resistless restless race!
O beloved race in all! O my breast aches with ten-
der love for all!
O I mourn and yet exult, I am rapt with love
for all,
Pioneers! O pioneers!
Raise the mighty mother mistress,
Waving high the delicate mistress, over all the star-
ry mistress, (bend your heads all,)
Raise the fang'd and warlike mistress, stern, impas-
sive, weapon'd mistress,
Pioneers! O pioneers!
See my children, resolute children,
By those swarms upon our rear we must never yield
or falter,
Ages back in ghostly millions frowning there
behind us urging,
Pioneers! O pioneers!
On and on the compact ranks,
With accessions ever waiting, with the places of
the dead quickly fill'd,
Through the battle, through defeat, moving yet and
never stopping,
Pioneers! O pioneers!
O to die advancing on!
Are there some of us to droop and die? has the
hour come?
Then upon the march we fittest die, soon and sure
the gap is fill'd,
Pioneers! O pioneers!
All the pulses of the world,
Falling in they beat for us, with the Western move-
ment beat,
Holding single or together, steady moving to the
front, all for us,
Pioneers! O pioneers!
Life's involv'd and varied pageants,

All the forms and shows, all the workmen at their
work,
All the seamen and the landsmen, all the
masters with their slaves,
Pioneers! O pioneers!
All the hapless silent lovers,
All the prisoners in the prisons, all the righteous
and the wicked,
All the joyous, all the sorrowing, all the living, all
the dying,
Pioneers! O pioneers!
I too with my soul and body,
We, a curious trio, picking, wandering our
way,
Through these shores amid the shadows, with the
apparitions pressing,
Pioneers! O pioneers!
Lo, the darting bowling orb!
Lo, the brother orbs around, all the clustering suns
and planets,
All the dazzling days, all the mystic nights with
dreams,
Pioneers! O pioneers!
These are of us, they are with us,
All for primal needed work, while the followers
there in embryo wait behind,
We today's procession heading, we the route for
travel clearing,
Pioneers! O pioneers!
O you daughters of the West!
O you young and elder daughters! O you mothers
and you wives!
Never must you be divided, in our ranks you move
united,
Pioneers! O pioneers!
Minstrels latent on the prairies!
(Shrouded bards of other lands, you may rest, you
have done your work,)
Soon I hear you coming warbling, soon you rise
and tramp amid us,
Pioneers! O pioneers!
Not for delectations sweet,
Not the cushion and the slipper, not the peaceful
and the studious,
Not the riches safe and palling, not for us the tame
enjoyment,
Pioneers! O pioneers!
Do the feasters gluttonous feast?
Do the corpulent sleepers sleep? have they lock'd

and bolted doors?
Still be ours the diet hard, and the blanket on the
    ground,
Pioneers! O pioneers!
Has the night descended?
Was the road of late so toilsome? did we stop dis-
    couraged nodding on our way?
Yet a passing hour I yield you in your tracks to
    pause oblivious,
Pioneers! O pioneers!
Till with sound of trumpet,
Far, far off the daybreak calls—hark! how loud and
    clear I hear it wind,
Swift! to the head of the army!—swift! spring to
    your places,
Pioneers! O pioneers!

A Century of Dishonor

HELEN HUNT JACKSON

Born in Massachusetts, Helen Hunt Jackson moved to
Colorado in 1872. She soon became interested in the plight
of Native Americans on the Great Plains. Shocked at what
she discovered, Jackson wrote a scathing indictment of the
government's treatment of Native Americans. She published
A Century of Dishonor at her own expense in 1881 and distributed a copy to every member of Congress.

The following excerpt describes the experience of the
Northern Cheyenne who were forced on to a reservation designated for another tribe against their will. Almost half the
tribe died from disease. A large group who fled from the
reservation to return to their northern homeland were later
captured and badly mistreated in prison. A second prison-
break ended in their massacre.

A Century of Dishonor helped prick the nation's consciousness about the government's abusive treatment of
Native Americans. The book, however, came at the tail end
of the subjugation of Native Americans that dated back more
than 250 years. The Plains Indians were the last tribes to
succumb to the nation's expansionary policies in the continental United States.

The winter of 1877 and summer of 1878 were terrible
seasons for the Cheyennes. Their fall hunt had
proved unsuccessful. Indians from other reservations
had hunted the ground over before them, and driven
the buffalo off; and the Cheyennes made their way
home again in straggling parties, destitute and hungry. Their agent reports that the result of this hunt
has clearly proved that "in the future the Indian must

rely on tilling the ground as the principal means of
support; and if this conviction can be firmly established, the greatest obstacle to advancement in agriculture will be overcome. With the buffalo gone, and
their pony herds being constantly decimated by the
inroads of horse-thieves, they must soon adopt, in all
its varieties, the way of the white man."

The ration allowed to these Indians is reported
as being "reduced and insufficient," and the small
sums they have been able to earn by selling buffalo
hides are said to have been "of material assistance" to
them in "supplementing" this ration. But in this year
there have been sold only $657 worth of skins by the
Cheyennes and Arapahoes together. In 1876 they
sold $17,600 worth. Here is a falling off enough to
cause very great suffering in a little community of five
thousand people. But this was only the beginning of
their troubles. The summer proved one of unusual
heat. Extreme heat, chills and fever, and "a reduced
and insufficient ration," all combined, resulted in an
amount of sickness heart-rending to read of. "It is no
exaggerated estimate," says the agent, "to place the
number of sick people on the reservation at two
thousand. Many deaths occurred which might have
been obviated had there been a proper supply of anti-
malarial remedies at hand. Hundreds applying for
treatment have been refused medicine."

The Northern Cheyennes grew more and more
restless and unhappy. "In council and elsewhere
they profess an intense desire to be sent North,
where they say they will settle down as the others
have done," says the report; adding, with an
obtuseness which is inexplicable, that "no difference has been made in the treatment of the
Indians," but that the "compliance of these
Northern Cheyennes has been of an entirely different nature from that of the other Indians," and that
it may be "necessary in the future to compel what
so far we have been unable to effect by kindness
and appeal to their better natures."

If it is "an appeal to men's better natures" to
remove them by force from a healthful Northern
climate, which they love and thrive in, to a malarial Southern one, where they are struck down by
chills and fever—refuse them medicine which can
combat chills and fever, and finally starve them—
there indeed, might be said to have been most
forcible appeals made to the "better natures" of
these Northern Cheyennes. What might have been

predicted followed.

Early in the autumn, after this terrible summer, a band of some three hundred of these Northern Cheyennes took the desperate step of running off and attempting to make their way back to Dakota. They were pursued, fought desperately, but were finally overpowered, and surrendered. They surrendered, however, only on the condition that they should be taken to Dakota. They were unanimous in declaring that they would rather die than go back to the Indian Territory. This was nothing more, in fact, than saying that they would rather die by bullets than of chills and fever and starvation.

These Indians were taken to Fort Robinson, Nebraska. Here they were confined as prisoners of war, and held subject to the orders of the Department of the Interior. The department was informed of the Indians' determination never to be taken back alive to Indian Territory. The army officers in charge reiterated these statements, and implored the department to permit them to remain at the North; but it was of no avail. Orders came—explicit, repeated, finally stern—insisting on the return of these Indians to their agency. The commanding officer at Fort Robinson has been censured severely for the course he pursued in his effort to carry out those orders. It is difficult to see what else he could have done, except to have resigned his post. He could not take three hundred Indians by sheer brute force and carry them hundreds of miles, especially when they were so desperate that they had broken up the iron stoves in their quarters, and wrought and twisted them into weapons with which to resist. He thought perhaps he could starve them into submission. He stopped the issue of food; he also stopped the issue of fuel to them. It was midwinter; the mercury froze in that month at Fort Robinson. At the end of two days he asked the Indians to let their women and children come out that he might feed them. Not a woman would come out. On the night of the fourth day—or, according to some accounts, the sixth—these starving, freezing Indians broke prison, overpowered the guards, and fled, carrying their women and children with them. They held the pursuing troops at bay for several days; finally made a last stand in a deep ravine, and were shot down—men, women, and children together. Out of the whole band there were left alive some fifty women and children and seven men, who, having been confined in another part of the fort, had not had the good fortune to share in this outbreak and meet their death in the ravine. These, with their wives and children, were sent to Fort Leavenworth to be put in prison; the men to be tried for murders committed in their skirmishes in Kansas on their way to the north. Red Cloud, a Sioux chief, came to Fort Robinson immediately after this massacre and entreated to be allowed to take the Cheyenne widows and orphans into his tribe to be cared for. The Government, therefore, kindly permitted twenty-two Cheyenne widows and thirty-two Cheyenne children—many of them orphans—to be received into the band of the Ogallalla Sioux.

An attempt was made by the Commissioner of Indian Affairs, in his Report for 1879, to show by tables and figures that these Indians were not starving at the time of their flight from Indian Territory. The attempt only redounded to his own disgrace; it being proved, by the testimony given by a former clerk of the Indian Bureau before the Senate committee appointed to investigate the case of the Northern Cheyennes, that the commissioner had been guilty of absolute dishonesty in his estimates, and that the quantity of beef actually issued to the Cheyenne Agency was hundreds of pounds less than he had reported it, and that the Indians were actually, as they had claimed, "starving."

The testimony given before this committee by some of the Cheyenne prisoners themselves is heart-rending. One must have a callous heart who can read it unmoved.

When asked by Senator [John T.] Morgan [of Alabama], "Did you ever really suffer from hunger?" one of the chiefs replied. "We were always hungry; we never had enough. When they that were sick once in awhile felt as though they could eat something, we had nothing to give them."

"Did you not go out on the plains sometimes and hunt buffalo, with the consent of the agent?"

"We went out on a buffalo-hunt, and nearly starved while out; we could not find any buffalo hardly; we could hardly get back with our ponies; we had to kill a good many of our ponies to eat, to save ourselves from starving." "How many children got sick and died?"

"Between the fall of 1877 and 1878 we lost fifty children. A great many of our finest young men died, as well as many women."

"Old Crow," a chief who served faithfully as Indian scout and ally under General [George] Crook for years, said: "I did not feel like doing anything for awhile, because I had no heart. I did not want to be in this country. I was all the time wanting to get back to the better country where I was born, and where my children are buried, and where my mother and sister yet live. So I have laid in my lodge most of the time with nothing to think about but that, and the affair up north at Fort Robinson, and my relatives and friends who were killed there. But now I feel as though, if I had a wagon and a horse or two, and some land, I would try to work. If I had something, so that I could do something, I might not think so much about these other things. As it is now, I feel as though I would just as soon be asleep with the rest."

The wife of one of the chiefs confined at Fort Leavenworth testified before the committee as follows: "The main thing I complained of was that we didn't get enough to eat; my children nearly starved to death; then sickness came, and there was nothing good for them to eat; for a long time the most they had to eat was corn-meal and salt. Three or four children died every day for awhile, and that frightened us."

When asked if there were anything she would like to say to the committee, the poor woman replied: "I wish you would do what you can to get my husband released. I am very poor here, and do not know what is to become of me. If he were released he would come down here, and we would live together quietly, and do no harm to anybody, and make no trouble. But I should never get over my desire to get back north; I should always want to get back where my children were born, and died, and were buried. That country is better than this in every respect. There is plenty of good, cool water there—pure water—while here the water is not good. It is not hot there, nor so sickly. Are you going where my husband is? Can you tell when he is likely to be released?"...

It is stated also that there was not sufficient clothing to furnish each Indian with a warm suit of clothing, "as promised by the treaty," and that, "by reference to official correspondence, the fact is established that the Cheyennes and Arapahoes are judged as having no legal rights to any lands, having forfeited their treaty reservation by a failure to settle thereon," and their "present reservation not having been, as yet, confirmed by Congress. Inasmuch as the Indians fully understood, and were assured that this reservation was given to them in lieu of their treaty reservation, and have commenced farming in the belief that there was no uncertainty about the matter it is but common justice that definite action be had at an early day, securing to them what is their right."

It would seem that there could be found nowhere in the melancholy record of the experiences of our Indians a more glaring instance of confused multiplication of injustices than this. The Cheyennes were pursued and slain for venturing to leave this very reservation, which, it appears, is not their reservation at all, and they have no legal right to it. Are there any words to fitly characterize such treatment as this from a great, powerful, rich nation, to a handful of helpless people?

❧ "Wanted: Jesse James"

MISSOURI GOVERNOR THOMAS T. CRITTENDEN

Missouri witnessed perhaps the most vicious fighting of the Civil War. The state was bitterly divided and erupted into a series of guerrilla campaigns, murderous raids and wholesale killings. C. W. Quantrell led one of the most notorious guerrilla forces for the Confederacy. Jesse James joined Quantrell as a 15-year-old and when the war ended was shot and badly wounded after he surrendered. Embittered and trained to kill, James embarked on one of the most notorious criminal careers in United States history. Along with his brother Frank, the James gang murdered, robbed and plundered their way through the West for 15 years. In 1881, Missouri Governor Thomas T. Crittenden finally issued a reward of $10,000 for the capture—dead or alive—of the two James brothers. Gang members Robert and Charles Ford shot and killed Jesse James at his St. Joseph, Missouri, home on April 3, 1882.

Proclamation of the Governor of Missouri
Rewards for the arrest of express and train robbers

State of Missouri Executive Department

WHEREAS, It has been made known to me, as the Governor of the State of Missouri, that certain parties, whose names are to me unknown, have confederated and banded themselves together for the purpose of committing robberies within this State; and

WHEREAS, Said parties did, on or about the Eighth day of October, 1879, stop a train near Glendale, in the County of Jackson, in said State, and, with force and violence, take, steal and carry away the money and other express matter being carried thereon; and

WHEREAS, On the fifteenth day of July, 1881, said parties and their confederates did stop a train upon the line of the Chicago, Rock Island and Pacific Railroad, near Winston, in the County of Daviess, in said State, and, with force and violence, take, steal, and carry away the money and other express matter being carried thereon; and, in perpetration of the robbery last aforesaid, the parties engaged therein did kill and murder one WILLIAM WESTFALL, the conductor of the train together with one JOHN McCuLLOCH, who was at the time in the employ of said company, then on said train; and WHEREAS, Frank James and Jesse W. James stand indicted in the Circuit Court of said Daviess County, for the murder of John W. Sheets, and the parties engaged in the robberies and murders aforesaid have fled from justice and have absconded and secreted themselves:

Now, THEREFORE, in consideration of the premises and in lieu of all other rewards heretofore offered, for the arrest or conviction of the parties aforesaid, or either of them, by any person or corporation, I, THOMAS T. CRITTENDEN, Governor of the State of Missouri, do hereby offer a reward of five thousand dollars ($5,000.00) for the arrest and conviction of each person participating in either of the robberies or murders aforesaid, excepting the said FRANK JAMES and JESSE W. JAMES; and for the arrest and delivery of said

FRANK JAMES and JESSE W. JAMES,

and each or either of them, to the sheriff of said Daviess County, I hereby offer a reward of five thousand dollars ($5,000.00) and for the conviction of either of the parties last aforesaid of participation in either of the murders or robberies above mentioned, I hereby offer a further reward of five thousand dollars ($5,000.00).

IN TESTIMONY WHEREOF, I have hereunto set my hand and caused to be affixed the GREAT SEAL of the State of Missouri. Done at the City of Jefferson on this 28th day of July, A. D. 1881.

THOMAS T. CRITTENDEN

By the Governor:

MICHAL K. McGRATH, Sec'y of State.

❧ "I was christened Calamity Jane"

CALAMITY JANE

Martha Cannary, or Calamity Jane as she became known, was one of the great characters of the Wild West. A scout for General Custer, mistress to Wild Bill Hickok and a gunslinger, Calamity Jane seemed to play a role in many of the western frontier's most famous stories. She was born in 1852, emigrated from Missouri with her family to Wyoming as a girl, and grew up to be the extraordinary Calamity Jane. By the 1890s, however, Calamity Jane was a washed-up drunk. Like Buffalo Bill, she turned to entertaining to make a livelihood. To help promote her career she wrote a brief autobiography. Although some scholars believe the account is more fiction than fact, the story has become part of the mythology of the West.

Her life story also reflects the kind of rough, self-reliant lifestyle that women in the West were compelled to live. Not surprisingly, women in the West were the first to be given the right to vote. In 1869, Wyoming Territory became the first political entity in the United States to allow women to vote and hold office.

My maiden name was Martha Cannary, was born in Princeton, Missouri, May 1st, 1852. Father and mother natives of Ohio. Had two brothers and three sisters, I being the oldest of the children. As a child I always had a fondness for adventure and out-door exercise and especial fondness for horses which I began to ride at an early age and continued to do so until I became an expert rider, being able to ride the most vicious and stubborn of horses, in fact the greater portion of my life in early times was spent in this manner.

In 1865 we emigrated from our homes in Missouri by the overland route to Virginia City, Montana, taking five months to make the journey. While on the way the greater portion of my time was spent in hunting along with the men and hunters of the party, in fact I was at all times with the men when there was excitement and adventures to be had. By the time we reached Virginia City I was considered a remarkable good shot and a fearless rider for a girl of my age. I remember many occurrences on the journey from Missouri to Montana. Many times in crossing the mountains the conditions of the trail were so bad that we frequently had to lower the wagons over ledges by hand with ropes, for they were so rough and rugged that horses were of no use. We also had many exciting times fording streams, for many of the streams in our way were noted for quicksand and boggy places, where, unless we were very careful, we would have lost horses and all. Then we had many dangers to encounter in the way of streams swelling on account of heavy rains. On occasions of that kind the men would usually select the best places to cross the streams, myself on more than one occasion have mounted my pony and swam across the stream several times merely to amuse myself and have had many narrow escapes from having both myself and pony washed away to certain death, but as the pioneers of those days had plenty of courage we overcome all obstacles, and reached Virginia City in safety.

Mother died at Black Foot, Montana, 1866, where we buried her. I left Montana in spring of 1866, for Utah, arriving at Salt Lake city during the summer. Remained in Utah until 1867, where my father died, then went to Fort Bridger, Wyoming Territory, where we arrived May 1, 1868. Remained around Fort Bridger during 1868, then went to Piedmont, Wyoming, with U. P. Railway. Joined General Custer as a scout at Fort Russell, Wyoming, in 1870, and started for Arizona for the Indian campaign. Up to this time I had always worn the costume of my sex. When I joined Custer I donned the uniform of a soldier. It was a bit awkward at first but I soon got to be perfectly at home in men's clothes.

Was in Arizona up to the winter of 1871 and during that time I had a great many adventures with the Indians, for as a scout I had a great many dangerous missions to perform and while I was in many close places always succeeded in getting away safely, for by this time I was considered the most reckless and daring rider and one of the best shots in the western country.

After that campaign I returned to Fort Sanders, Wyoming, remained there until spring of 1872, when we were ordered out to the Muscle Shell or Nursey Pursey [Nez Perce] Indian outbreak. In that war Generals Custer, Miles, Terry and Cook were all engaged. This campaign lasted until fall of 1873.

It was during this campaign that I was christened Calamity Jane. It was on Goose Creek, Wyoming, where the town of Sheridan is now located, Captain Egan was in command of the post. We were ordered out to quell an uprising of the Indians, and were out for several days, had numerous skirmishes during which six of the soldiers were killed and several severely wounded. When on

returning to the post we were ambushed about a mile and a half from our destination. When fired upon Captain Egan was shot. I was riding in advance and on hearing the firing turned in my saddle and saw the captain reeling in his saddle as though about to fall. I turned my horse and galloped back with all haste to his side and got there in time to catch him as he was falling. I lifted him onto my horse in front of me and succeeded in getting him safely to the fort. Captain Egan, on recovering, laughingly said: "I name you Calamity Jane, the heroine of the plains." I have borne that name up to the present time. We were afterwards ordered to Fort Custer, where Custer City now stands, where we arrived in the spring of 1874; remained around Fort Custer all summer and were ordered to Fort Russell in fall of 1874, where we remained until spring of 1875; was then ordered to the Black Hills to protect miners, as that country was controlled by the Sioux Indians and the government had to send the soldiers to protect the lives of the miners and settlers in that section. Remained there until fall of 1875, and wintered at Fort Laramie. In spring of 1876, we were ordered north with General Cook to join Generals Miles, Terry and Custer at Big Horn river. During this march I swam the Platte river at Fort Fetterman as I was the bearer of important dispatches. I had a ninety mile ride to make, being wet and cold, I contracted a severe illness and was sent back in Gen. Crook's ambulance to Fort Fetterman where I laid in the hospital for fourteen days. When able to ride I started for Fort Laramie where I met Wm. Hickock, better known as Wild Bill, and we started for Deadwood, where we arrived about June.

During the month of June I acted as a pony express rider carrying the U. S. mail between Deadwood and Custer, a distance of fifty miles, over one of the roughest trails in the Black Hills country. As many of the riders before me had been held up and robbed of their packages, mail and money that they carried, for that was the only means of getting mail and money between these points. It was considered the most dangerous route in the Hills, but as my reputation as a rider and quick shot was well known, I was molested very little, for the toll gatherers looked on me as being a good fellow, and they knew that I never missed my mark. I made the round trip every two days which was considered pretty good riding in that country. Remained around Deadwood during the summer visiting all the camps within an area of 100 miles. My friend, Wild Bill, remained in Deadwood during the summer with the exception of occasional visits to the camps. On the 2d of August, while setting at a gambling table in the Bell Union saloon, in Deadwood, he was shot in the back of the head by the notorious Jack McCall, a desperado. I was in Deadwood at the time and on hearing of the killing made my way at once to the scene of the shooting and found that my friend had been killed by McCall. I at once started to look for the assassin and found him at Shurdy's butcher shop and grabbed a meat cleaver and made him throw up his hands; through the excitement on hearing of Bill's death, having left my weapons on the post of my bed. He was then taken to a log cabin and locked up, well secured as every one thought, but he got away and was afterwards caught at Fagan's ranch on Horse creek, on the old Cheyenne road, and was then taken to Yankton, Dakota, where he was tried, sentenced and hung.

I remained around Deadwood locating claims, going from camp to camp until the spring of 1877, when one morning I saddled my horse and rode towards Crook city. I had gone about 12 miles from Deadwood, at the mouth of Whitewood creek, when I met the overland mail running from Cheyenne to Deadwood. The horses on a run, about two hundred yards from the station; upon looking closely I saw they were pursued by Indians. The horses ran to the barn as was their custom. As the horses stopped I rode along the side of the coach and found the driver, John Slaughter, lying face downwards in the boot of the stage, he having been shot by the Indians. When the stage got to the station the Indians hid in the bushes. I immediately removed all baggage from the coach except the mail. I then took the driver's seat and with all haste drove to Deadwood, carrying the six passengers and the dead driver.

I left Deadwood in the fall of 1877 and went to Bear Butte Creek with the 7th Cavalry. During the fall and winter we built Fort Meade and the town of Sturgis. In 1878 I left the command and went to Rapid city and put in the year prospecting.

In 1879 I went to Fort Pierre and drove trains from Rapid city to Fort Pierce for Frank Witcher, then drove teams from Fort Pierce to Sturgis for Fred Evans. This teaming was done with oxen as they were better fitted for the work than horses, owing to the rough nature of the country.

In 1881 I went to Wyoming and returned in 1882 to Miles City and took up a ranch on the Yellowstone, raising stock and cattle, also kept a way-side inn, where the weary traveler could be accommodated with food, drink, or trouble, if he looked for it. Left the ranch in 1883, went to California, going through the states and territories, reached Ogden the latter part of 1883, and San Francisco in 1884. Left San Francisco in the summer of 1884 for Texas, stopping at Fort Yuma, Arizona, the hottest spot in the United States. Stopping at all points of interest until I reached El Paso in the fall. When in El Paso I met Mr. Clinton Burk, a native of Texas, who I married in August, 1885. As I thought I had traveled through life long enough alone and thought it was about time to take a partner for the rest of my days. We remained in Texas leading a quiet home life until 1889. On October 29th, 1887, I became the mother of a girl baby, the very image of its father, at least that is what he said, but who has the temper of its mother.

When we left Texas we went to Boulder, Colo., where we kept a hotel until 1893, after which we travelled through Wyoming, Montana, Idaho, Washington, Oregon, then back to Montana, then to Dakota, arriving in Deadwood October 9th, 1895, after an absence of seventeen years.

My arrival in Deadwood after an absence of so many years created quite an excitement among my many friends of the past, to such an extent that a vast number of the citizens who had come to Deadwood during my absence who had heard so much of Calamity Jane and her many adventures in former years were anxious to see me. Among the many whom I met were several gentlemen from eastern cities, who advised me to allow myself to be placed before the public in such a manner as to give the people of the eastern cities an opportunity of seeing the Woman Scout who was made so famous through her daring career in the west and Black Hills countries.

An agent of Kohl & Middleton, the celebrated museum men, came to Deadwood, through the solicitation of the gentlemen whom I had met there and arrangements were made to place me before the public in this manner. My first engagement began at the Palace museum, Minneapolis, January 20th, 1896, under Kohl & Middleton's management.

Hoping that this little history of my life may interest all readers, I remain as in the older days.

Yours,

Mrs. M. Burk, better known as Calamity Jane.

🌿 "The red hand of murder"

JAMES BLAINE

James Garfield was elected president in 1880, the compromise Republican choice after a bitter political feud. He was selected on the 36th ballot of the Republican convention with the support of Maine Senator James Blaine who had been a leading candidate himself. Garfield, an Ohio congressman, had been a war hero with a reputation for courage.

Upon taking office, Garfield attempted to check government corruption. But on July 2 a disappointed office-seeker assassinated Garfield in the Washington railroad station. Garfield died of the gunshot wound September 19. Vice President Chester Arthur succeeded Garfield. Arthur, who had garnered a small personal fortune running the New York Custom House, initially did nothing to check the spoils system that Garfield had fought. Public outrage, however, prompted him to initiate several reforms.

Blaine, who had served as Garfield's secretary of state, delivered this eulogy of the felled president five months after the president's death.

For the second time in this generation the great departments of the government of the United States are assembled in the Hall of Representatives, to do honor to the memory of a murdered president. Lincoln fell at the close of a mighty struggle, in which the passions of men had been deeply stirred. The tragical termination of his great life added but another to the lengthened succession of horrors which had marked so many lintels with the blood of the firstborn. Garfield was slain in a day of peace, when brother had been reconciled to brother, and when anger and hate had been banished from the land....

Great in life, he was surpassingly great in death. For no cause in the very frenzy of wantonness and wickedness, by the red hand of murder, he was thrust from the full tide of this world's interest, from its hopes, its aspirations, its victories, into the visible presence of death—and he did not quail.

Not alone for one short moment in which, stunned and dazed, he could give up life, hardly aware of its relinquishment, but through days of deadly languor, through weeks of agony, that was not less agony because silently borne, with clear sight and calm courage he looked into his open grave. What blight and ruin met his anguished eyes, whose lips may tell—what brilliant, broken plans, what baffled, high ambitions, what sundering of strong, warm, manhood's friendship, what bitter rending of sweet household ties! Behind him a proud, expectant nation, a great host of sustaining friends, a cherished and happy mother, wearing the full, rich honors of her early toil and tears; the wife of his youth, whose whole life lay in his; the little boys not yet emerged from childhood's day of frolic; the fair young daughter; the sturdy sons just springing into closest companionship, claiming every day and every day rewarding a father's love and care; and in his heart the eager, rejoicing power to meet all demands. And his soul was not shaken.

His countrymen were thrilled with instant, profound, and universal sympathy. Masterful in his mortal weakness, he became the center of a nation's love, enshrined in the prayers of a world. But all the love and all the sympathy could not share with him his suffering. He trod the winepress alone. With unfaltering front he faced death. With unfailing tenderness he took leave of life. Above the demoniac hiss of the assassin's bullet he heard the voice of God. With simple resignation he bowed to the divine decree.

As the end drew near, his early craving for the sea returned. The stately mansion of power had been to him the wearisome hospital of pain, and he begged to be taken from his prison walls, from its oppressive, stifling air, from its homelessness and its hopelessness. Gently, silently, the love of a great people bore the pale sufferer to the longed-for healing of the sea, to live or to die, as God should will, within sight of the heaving billows, within sound of its manifold voices.

With a wan, fevered face, tenderly lifted to the cooling breeze, he looked out wistfully upon the ocean's changing wonders; on its far sails; on its restless waves, rolling shoreward to break and die beneath the noonday sun; on the red clouds of evening, arching low to the horizon; on the serene and shining pathway of the star. Let us think that his dying eyes read a mystic meaning which only the rapt and parting soul may know. Let us believe that in the silence of the receding world he heard the great waves breaking on a further shore and felt already upon his wasted brow the breath of the eternal morning.

✣ *The New Colossus*

EMMA LAZARUS

The French Republic gave the United States in 1876 a massive sculpture—the Statue of Liberty by Frédéric Auguste Bartholdi—to celebrate the two nations' friendship. For the next decade the Pedestal Fund Committee raised money for the construction of a pedestal to hold the statue. In 1883 the committee organized an art exhibition for the struggling project. Emma Lazarus, a Jewish scholar submitted a portfolio of work including "The New Colossus." Lazarus wrote the poem as a sympathetic gesture to the thousands of desperate Jews who were arriving in New York City as refugees from the anti-Jewish pogroms in Russia. Lazarus, who won a $1,500 award for her entry, died four years later, and the poem faded into obscurity. But in 1903 Georgina Schuyler, an elderly New York society women, secured permission to place the poem on a bronze tablet on the second floor of the Statue of Liberty. Neither the poem nor the event attracted public attention for another 30 years.

Immigration at the time Lazarus wrote the poem and Schuyler displayed it to the public was hardly an issue that most people celebrated. In fact, the bias at the time was against immigration. New immigrants were widely perceived as bringing alien religions and immoral behavior to American shores with the affect of driving wages down and increasing the crime rate. By the 1930s, however, after a series of tight restrictions on immigration had been imposed, the perception of immigrants from the public—who were mostly immigrants or descendents of immigrants themselves—had become quite favorable. The journalist Louis Adamic initiated a crusade to popularize Lazarus's poem. His efforts found a willing public that eagerly embraced the poem as part of the American spirit of redemption. In 1945 the bronze tablet was moved from the second floor to the main entrance. The poem has become enshrined as an integral part of American nationalism.

Not like the brazen giant of Greek fame,
With conquering limbs astride from land to land;
Here at our sea-washed, sunset gates shall stand
A mighty woman with a torch, whose flame
Is the imprisoned lightning, and her name
Mother of Exiles. From her beacon-hand
Glows world-wide welcome; her mild eyes
    command
The air-bridged harbor that twin cities frame.

"Keep, ancient lands, your storied pomp!" cries she
With silent lips. "Give me your tired, your poor,

Your huddled masses yearning to breathe free,
The wretched refuse of your teeming shore.
Send these, the homeless, the tempest-tost to me,
I lift my lamp beside the golden door!"

✣ *"The people of both races will have equal accommodation"*

J. A. SCOTT

The demise of Reconstruction in the South was quickly replaced with a new policy of segregation. White state governments throughout the South imposed laws that separated public facilities and accommodations for white and African-American citizens. Facilities for whites were almost universally better than those for African-Americans. In 1883 J. A. Scott, an African-American attorney from Birmingham, Alabama, testified to the United States Senate about the unequal accommodations available on trains.

There has been a universal discrimination here in Alabama, and, indeed, all over the South, in the treatment of the colored people as to cars they are permitted to ride in. The white people have always labored under the impression that whenever a colored man attempted to go into a ladies' car, he did it simply because it was a car for white people. Now if the white people looked at it as we look at it, taking a common-sense view of it, they would see that that idea is erroneous and false. We go into those cars simply because there are better accommodations there, and because we secure better protection in the ladies' car, for the general sentiment of the white men certainly protects their ladies. But in the cars allotted to the colored people a white man comes in and smokes cigars, chews tobacco, and curses and swears, and all that kind of thing, and the conductors on the various roads don't exercise their powers for the protection of the colored passengers. We made these complaints to the railroad commission, and the president of the commission told us that it was a matter within their jurisdiction, and that they would take cognizance of it, and would see that those complaints were looked into, and those evils remedied. We asked simply for equal accommodation and protection with the white people in riding on the railroads, and the 22d day of this month was set for a final hearing, and the superintendent of railroads was summoned to be there at the final hearing of the matter, and we have the assurance of the gentlemen of the commission that the subject will be acted upon promptly, and that the vexed question—for this is one of the most vexed questions that we have to deal with in the South—will be settled. We expect, therefore, that so far as Alabama is concerned, the people of both races will have equal accommodation. Our people do not care whether they are put in the front of the train or in the middle or at the tail end, so long as they have proper accommodation and proper protection.

❧ "Giving the Negro fair play"

FREDERICK DOUGLASS

A powerful voice for emancipation before and during the Civil War, Frederick Douglass remained an articulate and forceful spokesman for African-American rights for more than 40 years afterwards. He was a staunch supporter of the Republican party and was named as marshal of the District of Columbia in 1877, the district's recorder of the deeds in 1881 and as minister to Haiti in 1889. Nevertheless, Douglass was frequently shunned in Republican social circles and at ceremonial services.

Douglass championed equal opportunity for all citizens, saying that African-American citizens had a right to "voting at the same ballot-box, using the same cartridge-box, going to the same schools, attending the same churches, travelling in the same street cars, in the same railroad cars, on the same steam-boats, proud of the same country, fighting the same war and enjoying the same peace and all its advantages." Douglass delivered his message to the American Missionary Association in 1884. Frustrated by the lack of progress in achieving his goal of equal opportunity, Douglass was said to have advised a college student in 1895 shortly before he died that the best way to advance the cause was "Agitate! Agitate! Agitate!"

In answer to the question as to what shall be done with the Negro, I have sometimes replied, "Do nothing with him, give him fair play and let him alone." But in reporting me, it has been found convenient and agreeable to place the emphasis of my speech on one part of my sentence. They willingly accepted my idea of letting the Negro alone, but not so my idea of giving the Negro fair play. It has always been easier for some of the American people to imitate the priest and the Levite, rather than the

example of the good Samaritan; to let the Negro alone rather than to give him fair play. Even here in New England—the most enlightened and benevolent section of our country—the Negro has been excluded from nearly all profitable employments. I speak from experience. I came here from the South fifty-six years ago, with a good trade in my hands, and might have commanded by my trade three dollars a day, but my white brethren, while praying for their daily bread, were not willing that I should obtain mine by the same means open to them. I was compelled to work for one dollar a day, when others working at my trade were receiving three dollars a day.

But to return. When we consider the long years of slavery, the years of enforced ignorance, the years of injustice, of cruel strifes and degradation to which the Negro was doomed, the duty of the nation is not, and cannot be, performed by simply letting him alone.

If Northern benevolence could send a missionary to a very dark corner of the South, if it could place a church on every hilltop in the South, a schoolhouse in every valley, and support a preacher in the one, and a teacher in the other, for fifty years to come, they could not then even compensate the poor freedmen for the long years of wrong and suffering he has been compelled to endure. The people of the North should remember that slavery and the degradation of the Negro were inflicted by the power of the nation, that the North was a consenting party to the wrong, and that a common sin can only be atoned and condoned by a common repentance.

Under the whole heavens, there never was a people emancipated under conditions more unfavorable to mental, moral and physical improvement than were the slaves of our Southern States. They were emancipated not by the moral judgment of the nation as a whole; they were emancipated not as a blessing for themselves, but as a punishment to their master; not to strengthen the emancipated but to weaken the rebels, and, naturally enough, taking the emancipation in this sense, the old master class have resented it and have resolved to make his freedom a curse rather than a blessing to the Negro. In many instances they have been quite successful in accomplishing this purpose. Then the manner of emancipation was against the Negro. He was turned loose to the open sky without a foot of earth on which to stand; without a single farming implement; he was turned loose to the elements, to hunger, to destitution; without money, without friends; and to endure the pitiless storm of the old master's wrath. The old master had in his possession the land and the power to crush the Negro, and the Negro in return had no power of defense. The difference between his past condition and his present condition is that in the past the old master class could say to him, "You shall work for me or I will whip you to death;" in the present condition he can say to him, "You shall work for me or I will starve you to death." And today the Negro is in this latter condition....

With all the discouraging circumstances that now surround what is improperly called the Negro problem, I do not despair of a better day. It is sometimes said that the condition of the colored man today is worse than it was in the time of slavery. To me this is simply extravagance. We now have the organic law of the land on our side. We have thousands of teachers, and hundreds of thousands of pupils attending schools; we can now count our friends by the million. In many of the States we have elective franchise; in some of them we have colored office-holders. It is no small advantage that we are citizens of this Republic by special amendment of the Constitution. The very resistance that we now meet on Southern railroads, steamboats and hotels is evidence of our progress. It is not the Negro in his degradation that is objected to, but the Negro educated, cultivated and refined. The Negro who fails to respect himself, who makes no provision for himself or his family, and is content to live the life of a vagabond, meets no resistance. He is just where he is desired by his enemies. Perhaps you will say that this proves that education, wealth and refinement will do nothing for the Negro; but the answer to this is, "that the hair of the dog will cure the bite" eventually. All people suddenly springing from a lowly condition have to pass through a period of probation. At first they are denounced as "upstarts," but the "upstarts" of one generation are the elite of the next.

The history of the great Anglo-Saxon race should encourage the Negro to hope on and hope ever, and work on and work ever. They were once the slaves of Normans; they were despised and insulted. They were looked upon as the coarser clay than the haughty Norman. Their language was despised and repudiated, but where today is the haughty Norman? What people and what language now rock the world by their power?

My hope for the Negro is largely based upon his enduring qualities. No persecutions, no proscriptions, no hardships are able to extinguish him. He neither dies out, nor goes out. He is here to stay, and while here he will partake of the blessings of your education, your progress, your civilization, and your Christian religion. His appeal to you today is for an equal chance in the race of life, and dark and stormy as the present appears, his appeal will not go unanswered.

The Adventures of Huckleberry Finn

MARK TWAIN

Mark Twain emerged in the late 1800s as the foremost writer and humorist in the United States. A brilliant satirist, Twain—whose real name was Samuel Clemens—wrote in 1884 *The Adventures of Huckleberry Finn,* one of the great novels in American history. Twain's story centered around Huckleberry Finn and the runaway slave Jim as they took a raft down the Mississippi River in the antebellum South. Using the vernacular language of the Mississippi, Twain's classic served as a metaphor of the American predicament. In the following excerpt, Huck and Jim rescue two men who claimed to be the Duke of Bridgewater and the long-lost Dauphin of France.

One morning about day-break, I found a canoe and crossed over a chute to the main shore—it was only two hundred yards—and paddled about a mile up a crick amongst the cypress woods, to see if I couldn't get some berries. Just as I was passing a place where a kind of a cow-path crossed the crick, here comes a couple of men tearing up the path as tight as they could foot it. I thought I was a goner, for whenever anybody was after anybody I judged it was me—or maybe Jim. I was about to dig out from there in a hurry, but they was pretty close to me then, and sung out and begged me to save their lives—said they hadn't been doing nothing, and was being chased for it—said there was men and dogs acoming. They wanted to jump right in, but I says—

"Don't you do it. I don't hear the dogs and horses yet; you've got time to crowd through the brush and get up the crick a little ways; then you take to the water and wade down to me and get in—that'll throw the dogs off the scent."

They done it, and soon as they were aboard I lit out for our tow-head, and in about five or ten minutes we heard the dogs and the men a way off, shouting. We heard them come along towards the crick, but couldn't see them; they seemed to stop and fool around a while; then, as we got further and further away all the time, we couldn't hardly hear them at all; by the time we had left a mile of woods behind us and struck the river, everything was quiet, and we paddled over to the tow-head and hid in the cotton-woods and was safe.

One of these fellows was about seventy, or upwards, and had a bald head and very gray whiskers. He had an old battered-up slouch hat on, and greasy blue woolen shirt, and ragged old blue jeans britches stuffed into his boot tops, and home-knit galluses—no, he only had one. He had an old long-tailed blue jeans coat with slick brass buttons, flung over his arm, and both of them had big fat ratty-looking carpet-bags.

The other fellow was about thirty and dressed about as ornery. After breakfast we all laid off and talked, and the first thing that come out was that these chaps didn't know one another.

"What got you into trouble?" says the baldhead to t'other chap.

"Well, I'd been selling an article to take the tartar off the teeth—and it does take it off, too, and generly the enamel along with it—but I staid about one night longer than I ought to, and was just in the act of sliding out when I ran across you on the trail this side of town, and you told me they were coming, and begged me to help you to get off. So I told you I was expecting trouble myself and would scatter out with you. That's the whole yarn-what's yourn?"

"Well, I'd ben a-runnin' a little temperance revival thar, 'bout a week, and was the pet of the women-folks, big and little for I was making' it might warm for the rummies. I tell you, and takin' as much as five or six dollars a night—ten cents a head, children and niggers free—and business a growin' all the time; when somehow or another a little report got around, last night, that I had a way of puttin' my time with a private jug, on the sly. A nigger rousted me out this mornin', and told me the people was getherin' on the quiet,

with their dogs and horses, and they'd be along pretty soon and give me 'bout half an hour's start, and then run me down, if they could; and if they got me they'd tar and feather me and ride me on a rail, sure. I didn't wait for no breakfast—I warn't hungry."

"Old man," says the young one, "I reckon we might double-team it together; what do you think?"

"I ain't undisposed. What's your line—mainly?"

"Jour printer, by trade, do a little in patent medicines; theatre-actor—tragedy, you know; take a turn at mesmerism and phrenology when there's a chance; teach singing-geography school for a change; sling a lecture, sometimes—oh, I do lots of things—most anything that comes handy, so it ain't work. What's your lay?"

"I've done considerable in the doctoring way in my time. Laying' on o' hands is my best holt—for cancer, and paralysis, and sich things; and I k'n tell a fortune pretty good, when I've got somebody along to find out the facts for me. Preachin's my line, too; and workin' camp-meetin's; and mission-aryin around."

Nobody never said anything for a while; then the young man hove a sigh and says—

"Alas!"

"What're you alassin' about?" says the bald-head.

"To think I should have lived to be leading such a life, and be degraded down into such company." And he begun to wipe the corner of his eye with a rag.

"Dern your skin, ain't the company good enough for you?" says the baldhead, pretty pert and uppish.

"Yes, it is good enough for me; it's as good as I deserve; for who fetched me so low, when I was so high? I did myself. I don't blame you, gentlemen—far from it; I don't blame anybody. I deserve it all. Let the cold world do its worst; one thing I know—there's a grave somewhere for me. The world may go on just as its always done, and take everything from me—loved ones, property, everything—but it can't take that. Some day I'll lie down in it and forget it all, and my broken heart will be at rest." He went on a-wiping.

"Drot your pore broken heart," says the bald-head; "what are you heaving your pore broken heart at us f'r? We hain't done nothing."

"No, I know you haven't. I ain't blaming you, gentlemen. I brought myself down—yes, I did it myself. It's right I should suffer—perfectly right—I don't make any moan."

"Brought you down from what? Whar was you brought down from?"

"Ah, you would not believe me; the world never believes—let it pass—'tis no matter. The secret of my birth—"

"The secret of your birth? Do you mean to say—"

"Gentlemen," says the young man, very solemn, "I will reveal it to you, for I feel I may have confidence in you. By rights I am a duke!"

Jim's eyes bugged out when hear that; and I reckon mine did, too. Then the baldhead says: "No! You can't mean it?"

"Yes. My great-grandfather, eldest son of the Duke of Bridgewater, fled to this country about the end of the last century, to breathe the pure air of freedom; married here, and died, leaving a son, his own father dying about the same time. The second son of the late duke seized the titles and estates—the infant real duke was ignored. I am the lineal descendant of that infant—I am the rightful Duke of Bridgewater; and here am I, forlorn, torn from my high estate, hunted of men, despised by the cold world, ragged, worn, heart-broken, and degraded to the companionship of felons on a raft!"

Jim pitied him ever so much, and so did I. We tried to comfort him, but he said it warn't much use, he couldn't be much comforted; said if we was a mind to acknowledge him, that would do him more good than most anything else; so we said we would, if he would tell us how. He said we ought to bow, when we spoke to him, and say, "Your Grace," or "My Lord," or "Your Lordship"—and he wouldn't mind if we called him plain "Bridgewater," which he said was a title, anyway, and not a name; and one of us ought to wait on him at dinner, and do any little thing for him he wanted done.

Well, that was all easy, so we done it. All through dinner Jim stood around and waited and waited on him, and says, "Will yo' Grace have some o' dis, or some o' dat?" and so on, and a body could see it was mighty pleasing to him.

But the old man got pretty silent, by-and-by— didn't have much to say, and didn't look pretty comfortable over all that petting that was going on around that duke. He seemed to have something on his mind. So, along in the afternoon, he says:

"Looky here, Bilgewater," he says, "I'm nation sorry for you, but you ain't the only person that's had troubles like that."

"No?"

"No, you ain't. You ain't the only person that's ben snaked down wrongfully out'n a high place."

"Alas!"

"No, you ain't the only person that's had a secret of his birth." And by jing, he begins to cry.

"Hold! What do you mean?"

"Bilgewater, kin I trust you?" says the old man, still sort of sobbing.

"To the bitter death!" He took the old man by the hand and squeezed it, and says, "The secret of your being: speak!"

"Bilgewater, I am the late Dauphin!"

You bet you Jim and me started, this time. Then the duke says:

"You are what?"

"Yes, my friend, it is too true—your eyes is lookin' at this very moment on the pore disappeared Dauphin, Looy the Seventeen, son of Looy the Sixteen and Marry Antonette."

"You! At your age! No! You mean you're the late Charlemagne; you must be six or seven hundred years old, at the very least."

"Trouble has done it, Bilgewater, trouble has done it; trouble has brung these gray hairs and this premature balditude. Yes, gentlemen, you see before you, in blue jeans and misery, the wanderin', exiled, trampled-on and sufferin' rightful King of France."

Well, he cried and took on so, that me and Jim didn't know hardly what to do, we was so sorry—and so glad and proud we'd got him with us, too. So we set in, like we done before with the duke, and tried to comfort him. But he said it warn't no use, nothing but to be dead and done with it all could do him any good; though he said it often made him feel easier and better for a while if people treated him according to his rights, and got down on one knee to speak to him, and always called him "Your Majesty", and waited on him first at meals, and didn't set down in his presence till he asked them. So Jim and me set to majestying him, and doing this and that and t'other for him, and standing up till he told us we might set down. This done him heaps of good, and so he got cheerful and comfortable. But the duke kind of soured on him, and didn't look a bit satisfied with the way things was going; still, the king acted real friendly towards him, and said the duke's great-grandfather and all the Dukes of Bilgewater was a good deal thought of by his father and was allowed to come to the palace considerable; but the duke staid huffy a good while, till by-and-by the king says:

"Like as not we got to be together a blamed long time, on this h-yer raft, Bilgewater, and so what's the use o' your bein' sour? It'll only make things oncomfortable. It ain't my fault I warn't born a duke, it ain't your fault you warn't born a king—so what's the use to worry? Make the best o'things the way you find 'em, says I—that's my motto. This ain't no bad thing that we've struck here—plenty grub and an easy life—come, give us your hand, Duke, and less all be friends."

The duke done it, and Jim and me was pretty glad to see it. It took away all the uncomfortableness, and we felt might good over it, because it would a been a miserable business to have any unfriendliness on the raft; for what you want, above all things, on a raft, is for everybody to be satisfied, and feel right and kind towards the others.

It didn't take me long to make up my mind that these liars warn't no kings nor dukes, all, but just low-down humbugs and frauds. But I never said nothing, never let on; kept it to myself; it's the best way; then you don't have no quarrels, and don't get into no trouble. If they wanted us to call them kings and dukes, I hadn't no objections, 'long as it would keep peace in the family; and it wan't no use to tell Jim, so I didn't tell him. If I never learnt nothing else out of pap, I learnt that the best way to get along with his kind of people is to let them have their own way.

❧ "The New South"

HENRY W. GRADY

In 1886 Henry W. Grady, editor of the *Atlanta Constitution*, was invited to New York City to speak to the New England Society that included some of the wealthiest and most influential men in the country. Grady's topic was "The New South"—a new phrase that applied to the post-Civil War southern economy and culture. In a speech greeted by frequent and prolonged applause, Grady addressed the common bonds of North and South, praising Abraham Lincoln as a great American but at the same time honoring the soldiers of the Confederacy. He called for a reconciliation, pledging that the South had set bitterness aside and adapted its economy to move forward without slavery. Grady invited the North to embrace the South in its efforts to continue to rebuild its economy and heal the rift of the Civil War.

The impact of Grady's speech was immediate. In a single address he helped forge a new positive identity for the South to build upon in creating a new, stronger regional economy. Grady did not invent the term, but his definition of "The New South" placed a renewed emphasis on the potential of the region, as opposed to its forlorn past. The speech also assured northern capitalists that the South had entered a new era of stability. A new wave of capital investments flowed to the South, helping to spur its manufacturing capacity. Although the speech was criticized by some southerners as being too conciliatory and some northerners as being insincere, Grady helped define how the North and South would mend their difference in the pursuit of forging a single, unified nation.

There was a South of slavery and secession—that South is dead. There is a South of union and freedom—that South, thank God, is living and breathing growing every hour....

[T]he Cavalier as well as the Puritan was on the Continent in its early days, and that he was "up and able to be about." I have read your books carefully and I find no mention of that fact, which seems to me an important one for preserving a sort of historical equilibrium if for nothing else.

Let me remind you that the Virginia Cavalier first challenged France on this continent that Cavalier John Smith gave New England its very name, and was so pleased with the job that while Miles Standish was cutting off men's ears for courting a girl without her parents' consent, and forbade men to kiss their wives on Sunday, the Cavalier was courting everything in sight, and that the Almighty had vouchsafed great increase to the Cavalier colonies, the huts in the wilderness being as full as the nests in the woods.

But having incorporated the Cavalier as a fact in your charming little books I shall let him work out his own salvation, as he has always done with engaging gallantry, and we will hold no controversy as to his merits. Why should we? Neither Puritan nor Cavalier long survived as such. The virtues and traditions of both happily still live for the inspiration of their sons and the saving of the old fashion. Both Puritan and Cavalier were lost in the storm of the first Revolution; and the American citizen, supplanting both and stronger than either, took possession of the Republic bought by their common blood and fashioned to wisdom, and charged himself with teaching men government and establishing the voice of the people as the voice of God.

My friends, Dr. Talinage has told you that the typical American has yet to come. Let me tell you that he has already come. Great types like valuable plants are slow to flower and fruit. But from the union of these colonist Puritans and Cavaliers, from the straightening of their purposes and the crossing of their blood, slow perfecting through a century, came he who stands as the first typical American, the first who comprehended within himself all the strength and gentleness, all the majesty and grace of this republic—Abraham Lincoln. He was the sum of Puritan and Cavalier, for in his ardent nature were fused the virtues of both, and in the depths of his great soul the faults of both were lost. He was greater than Puritan, greater than Cavalier, in that he was American, and that in his homely form were first gathered the vast and thrilling forces of his ideal government, charging it with such tremendous meaning and so elevating it above human suffering that martyrdom, though infamously aimed, came as a fitting crown to a life consecrated from the cradle to human liberty. Let us, each cherishing the traditions and honoring his fathers, build with reverent hands to the type of this simple but sublime life, in which all types are honored; and in Our common glory as Americans there will be plenty and to spare for your forefathers and for mine.

In speaking to the toast with which you have honored me, I accept the term, "The New South," as in no sense disparaging to the old. Dear to me, sir, is the home of my childhood and the traditions of my people. I would not, if I could, dim the glory they won in peace and war, or by word or deed take aught from the splendor and grace of their civilization—never equalled and, perhaps, never to be equalled in its chivalric strength and grace. There is a New South, not through protest against the old, but because of new conditions, new adjustments and, if you please new ideas and aspirations. It is to this that I address myself....

Think of [the defeated Confederate soldier] as ragged, half-starved, heavy hearted, enfeebled by want and wounds; having fought to exhaustion, he surrenders his gun, wrings the hands of his comrades in silence, and lifting his tear-stained and pal-

lid face for the last time to the graves that dot the old Virginia hills, pulls his gray cap over his brow and begins the slow and painful journey. What does he find—let me ask you, who went to your homes eager to find in the welcome you had justly earned, lull payment for four years' sacrifice—what does he find when, having followed the battlestained cross against overwhelming odds, dreading death not half so much as surrender, he reaches the home he left so prosperous and beautiful? He finds his house in ruins, his farm devastated, his slaves free, his stock killed, his barns empty, his trade destroyed, his money worthless; his social system, feudal in its magnificence, swept away; his people without law or legal status, his comrades slain, and the burdens of others heavy on his shoulders. Crushed by defeat, his very traditions are gone: without money, credit, employment, material or training; and beside all this, confronted with the gravest problem that ever met human intelligence the establishing of a status for the vast body of his liberated slaves.

What does he do—this hero in gray with a heart of gold? Does he sit down in sullenness and despair? Not for a day. Surely God, who had stripped him of his prosperity, inspired him in his adversity. As ruin was never before so overwhelming, never was restoration swifter. The soldier stepped from the trenches into the furrow, horses that had charged Federal guns marched before the plow, and fields that ran red with human blood in April were green with the harvest in June; women reared in luxury cut up their dresses and made breeches for their husbands, and, with a patience and heroism that fit women always as a garment, gave their hands to work. There was little bitterness in all this. Cheerfulness and frankness prevailed. "Bill Arp" struck the keynote when he said: "Well, I killed as many of them as they did of me, and now I am going to work."...

But in all this what have we accomplished? What is the sum of our work? We have found out that in the general summary the free negro counts more than he did as a slave, We have planted the schoolhouse on the hilltop and made it free to white and black. We have sowed towns and cities in the place of theories and put business above politics. We have challenged your spinners in Massachusetts and your ironmakers in Pennsylvania. We have learned that the $400,000,000 annually received from our cotton crop will make us rich, when the supplies that make it are home-raised. We have reduced the commercial rate of interest from 24 to 6 per cent., and are floating 4 per cent. bonds. We have learned that one northern immigrant is worth fifty foreigners, and have smoothed the path to southward, wiped out the place where Mason and Dixon's line used to be, and hung our latchstring to you and yours. We have reached the point that marks perfect harmony in every household, when the husband confesses that the pies which his wife cooks are as good as those his mother used to bake; and we admit that the sun shines as brightly and the moon as softly as it did "before the war." We have established thrift in city and country. We have fallen in love with work. We have restored comfort to homes from which culture and elegance never departed. We have let economy take root and spread among us as rank as the crab grass which sprung from Sherman's cavalry camps, until we are ready to lay odds on the Georgia Yankee, as he manufactures relics of the battlefield in a one-story shanty and squeezes pure olive oil out of his cotton seed, against any Down-easter that ever swapped wooden nutmegs for flannel sausages in the valleys of Vermont. Above all, we know that we have achieved in these "piping times of peace" a fuller independence for the South than that which our fathers sought to win in the forum by their eloquence or compel on the field by their swords.

It is a rare privilege, sir, to have had part, however humble, in this work. Never was nobler duty confided to human hands than the uplifting and upbuilding of the prostrate and bleeding South, misguided, perhaps, but beautiful in her suffering, and honest, brave and generous always. In the record of her social, industrial, and political illustration we wait with confidence the verdict of the world....

[W]hen Lee surrendered, I say, and Johnston quit, the South became, and has since been, loyal to this union. We fought hard enough to know that we were whipped, and in perfect frankness accepted as final the arbitrament of the sword to which we had appealed. The South found her jewel in the toad's head of defeat. The shackles that had held her in narrow limitations fell forever when the shackles of the negro slave were broken. Under the old regime the negroes were slaves to the South, the South was a slave to the system. The old plantation, with its simple police regulation and its feu-

dal habit, was the only type possible under slavery. Thus was gathered in the hands of a splendid and chivalric oligarchy the substance that should have been diffused among the people, as the rich blood, under certain artificial conditions, is gathered at the heart, filling that with affluent rapture, but leaving the body chill and colorless.

The old South rested everything on slavery and agriculture, unconscious that these could neither give nor maintain healthy growth. The new South presents a perfect Democracy, the oligarchs leading in the popular movement a social system compact and closely knitted, less splendid on the surface but stronger at the core—a hundred farms for every plantation, fifty homes for every palace, and a diversified industry that meets the complex needs of this complex age.

The new South is enamored of her new work. Her soul is stirred with the breath of a new life. The light of a grander day is falling fair on her face. She is thrilling with the consciousness of growing power and prosperity. As she stands upright, full-statured and equal among the people of the earth, breathing the keen air and looking out upon the expanding horizon, she understands that her emancipation came because in the inscrutable wisdom of God her honest purpose was crossed and her brave armies were beaten.

This is said in no spirit of time-serving or apology. The South has nothing for which to apologize. She believes that the late struggle between the States was war and was not rebellion, revolution, and not conspiracy, and that her convictions were as honest as yours. I should be unjust to the dauntless spirit of the South and to my own convictions if I did not make this plain in this presence. The South has nothing to take back. In my native town of Athens is a monument that crowns its central hill a plain, white shaft. Deep cut into its shining side is a name dear to me above the names of men, that of a brave and simple man who died in brave and simple faith. Not for all the glories of New England—from Plymouth Rock all the way would I exchange the heritage he left me in his soldier's death. To the foot of that shaft I shall send my children's children to reverence him who ennobled their name with his heroic blood. But, sir, speaking from the shadow of that memory, which I honor as I do nothing else on earth, I say that the cause in which he suffered and for which he gave his life was adjudged by higher and fuller wisdom than his or mine, and I am glad that the omniscient God held the balance of battle in His Almighty hand, and that human slavery was swept forever from American soil—the American Union saved from the wreck of war.

This message, Mr. President, comes to you from consecrated ground. Every foot of the soil about the city in which I live is as sacred as a bat-tle-ground of the republic. Every hill that invests it is hallowed to you by the blood of your broth-ers, who died for your victory, and doubly hal-lowed to us by the blow of those who died hope-less, but undaunted, in defeat sacred soil to all of us, rich with memories that make us purer and stronger and better, silent but staunch witnesses in its red desolation of the matchless valor of American hearts and the deathless glory of American arms—speaking an eloquent witness in its white peace and prosperity to the indissoluble union of American States and the imperishable brotherhood of the American people.

Now, what answer has New England to this message? Will she permit the prejudice of war to remain in the hearts of the conquerors, when it has died in the hearts of the conquered? Will she transmit this prejudice to the next generation, that in their hearts, which never felt the generous ardor of conflict, it may perpetuate itself? Will she with-hold, save in strained courtesy, the hand which straight from his soldier's heart Grant offered to Lee at Appomattox? Will she make the vision of a restored and happy people, which gathered above the couch of your dying captain, filling his heart with grace, touching his lips with praise and glori-fying his path to the grave; will she make this vision on which the last sigh of his expiring soul breathed a benediction, a cheat and a delusion? If she does, the South, never abject in asking for comradeship, must accept with dignity its refusal; but if she does not; if she accepts in frankness and sincerity this message of good-will and friendship, then will the prophecy of Webster, delivered in this very Society forty years ago amid tremendous applause, be verified in its fullest and final sense, when he said: "Standing hand to hand and clasp-ing hands, we should remain united as we have been for sixty years, citizens of the same country, members of the same government, united, all unit-ed now and united forever. There have been diffi-culties, contentions, and controversies, but I tell you that in my judgment

Those opposed eyes,
Which like the meteors of a troubled heaven,
All of one nature, of one substance bred,
Did lately meet in th'intestine shock,
Shall now, in mutual well beseeming ranks,
March all one way."

"To arms, we call you, to arms!"

AUGUST SPIES

Labor unrest marked much of the 1880s. In 1886 workers at the McCormick Harvesting Machine Company in Chicago went on strike. During the protest police fired into a crowd killing several workers. The next day anarchists organized a protest rally at Haymarket Square. The circular below was written by a man named August Spies calling for workers to take part in the demonstration. During the protest a bomb exploded, triggering an exchange of gunfire. Seven police-men and four workers were killed in the exchange. Eight anarchists were tried and convicted of conspiracy. Four were executed (including Spies), one committed suicide and three were imprisoned. The violence of the Haymarket Square protest triggered widespread concern about the tactics of labor organizations, helped incite anti-immigration sentiment and led to the passage of the Merritt Conspiracy Act designed to stifle radical labor activities.

REVENGE! WORKINGMEN! TO ARMS!

Your masters sent out their bloodhounds—the police—they killed six of your brothers at McCormick's this afternoon. They killed the poor wretches, because they, like you, had courage to disobey the supreme will of your bosses. They killed them because they dared ask for the shortening of the hours of toil. They killed them to show you "free American citizens" that you must be sacrificed and contented with whatever your bosses conde-scend to allow you, or you will get killed!

You have for years endured the most abject humiliations; you have for years suffered immeasur-able iniquities; you have worked yourselves to death; you have endured the pangs of want and hunger; your children you have sacrificed to the factory lords—in short, you have been miserable and obedient slaves all these years. Why? To satisfy the insatiable greed and fill the coffers of your lazy thieving masters! When you ask him now to lessen your burden, he sends his bloodhounds out to shoot you, to kill you!

If you are men, if you are the sons of your grand-sires, who have their blood to free you, then you will rise in your might, Hercules, and destroy the hideous monster that seeks to destroy you.

To arms, we call you, to arms!
YOUR BROTHERS

❧ *"The dives of New York are hot-beds of its crime"*

GEORGE W. WALLING

Anti-city literature was very popular in the United States in the late 1800s. Writers revealed the sins of the cities to an audience that was at once fascinated and repulsed by the cities' seamier side of life. George W. Walling's *Recollections of a New York Chief of Police,* written in 1887, was typical of this type of writing. Passages such as the one below describing the "Haymarket" outraged moralists who increasingly called for a crackdown on immoral behavior and a prohibition of alcohol.

The dives of New York are hot-beds of its crime. Under the brilliant glare of gas-jets and the seductive strains of music vice germinates, grows, buds and yields its bitter fruit. Every stage of crime is reflected in a true picture of these holes of viciousness. The "dance of death" begins with the Haymarket, grows feeble in "Billy McGlory's," or the "Black-and-Tan," and ends in the river or the potter's field. A pure girl who visits the Haymarket, if such a one ever does visit it, attracted by the gay scenes and the fascination of the waltz, may feel sure of her own power to keep from going lower in the scale of sensuality; but as surely as a displaced stone goes tumbling down a hillside, she rushes onward to the black fate which awaits her, and virtue, youth, beauty, health and soul are lost in the downward course to ruin. A terrible fate it is, yet many are they who reach it yearly.

New York is well provided with what is commonly known as dives, although fortunately, under the awakening moral sense of the community some

of the more notorious dens of iniquity are being closed. There are enough left, however, to amuse and corrupt the crowds which nightly flock to them. For the uninitiated let it be said that by dives is meant, in general, the dance-halls in various parts of the town, where abandoned women congregate to try their charms on easily tempted men. These dance-halls are all more or less alike. They vary only in the classes of people patronizing them. I will not say they vary in the degree of vice carried on, for I believe there is as much wickedness in the Cremorne and Haymarket and Tom Gould's, as in the low resort down town. They all have music and dancing and female attaches and gaudily decorated halls, and liquors. One of these attractions would be worthless without the others. All taken together make a combination which many men find it hard to resist.

The men who own and run such places are *sui generis*—of their own kind. From the enormous amount of their ill-gotten gains they are able to own expensive houses and live in extravagant style. Beneath their smiling features there is the consciousness, no, perhaps not consciousness, but at least the remembrance of almost every sort of crime. Conscience is a foreign word to men of this foul business. Honest and generous are they sometimes called? Well, yes, when it pays. They are tyrants of the worst sort. The women who frequent their resorts are not their accomplices in iniquity, but their tools. They use them as travelling showmen do a trained bear—prod them when they refuse to dance or when they become useless, treat them as we do faded flowers—throw them into the gutter to die.

In order that the full significance of the evil influence which surrounds these places may be appreciated, I have thought it best to describe in detail each of the better known dives. Some may seem almost too well known to need description, but it strikes me they cannot be made too familiar.

First, there is the Haymarket, situated on Sixth Avenue, just below Thirtieth Street. On the outside it is not a particularly ornate building; in fact, by daylight the structure is rather repulsive, but then the Haymarket is only an ordinary building in the daytime. At night it shines with the brilliancy of a Broadway theater and becomes animate with the licentious life of the avenue. The easily swinging doors which open from the sidewlk creak half the night with the entrance or exit of depraved women and their masculine escorts. Let the reader who has never visited this illuminated den go with me in imagination, and see the wicked character of the place, pictured as well as I am able to paint it. At the entrance one reads by the pale electric light the only indication of the purposes to which the building is put— "Haymarket, Grand Soiree Dansante." We push the swinging doors and pay our entrance fee of twenty-five cents for males, nothing for females, to a man behind a narrow window. We push another swinging door and then pause to become accustomed to the gay glare and the whirl of human figures. We are in a long and broad room, whose center is a polished dancing floor. At the extreme end is a sort of a stage with a brilliantly painted curtain, and the chairs of the musicians. The latter are playing their instruments at full blast, and to the entrancing strains of a waltz a dozen or more young men and women are moving in a slow measure over the floor. Along on either side of the wall is a row of seats, and here we sit for a few moments and look about us. We hear the clink of glasses and look up to discover that the dancing-hall is not all of the Haymarket. There is a gallery above us and it seems to be the popular part of the place. It is crowded with men and women, drinking and smoking and filling the room and ribald laughter and blasphemous words. The galleries extend around three sides of the room; and so well filled are they with the Haymarket's patrons and patronesses that it is with difficulty that the waiters, who carry, everything, from lemonade to whiskey, are able to work their way through the throngs, without smashing glasses and tipping over tables.

The galleries are arranged with tables and chairs, and on the northern side connected by passage-ways with the gallery, is the bar. There are tables in the bar-room also, and they are well filled with glasses, and surrounded by abandoned women and the men whom they have "roped" in. It does not take us long to discover that the attraction of the Haymarket is not so much in its dance floor as in its gallery. It is here the that the habitues of the place congregate, and mingle vile jokes with beer and whiskey and tobacco smoke. There are all sorts of women here. Some are extremely young and pretty; others are fat and homely and awkward. Some are demure, others coarse and loud-mouthed. Some have painted their faces to hide the ravages which vice has been making in their features. Some are dressed with taste; others are arrayed in brilliant colors and cheap tawdry fabrics. Some even are bashful and modest appearing, hesitating to approach the men who patronize the place. Others are brazen in their conduct. They address without compunction those with whom they wish to talk—even fling their arms around them and breathe lascivious thoughts into their ears.

The females who visit the Haymarket range in age from seventeen to thirty-five years, and most of them are not more than twenty-five. They are most of them inmates of disreputable houses, and congregate in this dance-hall like harpies, to seize upon and devour the weak. The owners of the Haymarket allow them free admission to and from the building, and pile up their riches by squeezing the prey of these prostitutes. The amount of liquor that is sold here is enormous. Of course fancy prices are put on every drink, and the girls who frequent the place are supposed to call for the most expensive liquors, and drink as much as they are able.

As I hinted in the previous part of this chapter, I consider the Haymarket as bad in its influence as some of the down-town resorts. The language and conversation which one hears here are something terrible in their way. I remember once when I was obliged to be in the place in an official capacity, I noticed a young girl there whose face was peculiarly sweet and winning. She had an air of refinement about her that at once distinguished her from her companions. She looked bright and seemed to talk with vivacity. I was struck by the girl's face, and made up my mind that she must have been persuaded to visit the resort by companions who were older in years and depravity. My curiosity to confirm my good opinion of her was great, I admit, and I had not long to wait before my curiosity was satisfied in a most shocking manner. The girl saw me standing alone and came where I was. She introduced the conversation with some flippant remark, and after a word or two in reply from me, she launched into such a tirade of oaths and foul speech as fairly took my breath away. I was almost struck dumb. The shock to my impressions was impossible to overcome. I have seen many hardened human beings in the course of my life, but the depravity of none of them ever surprised me as did the foul words which came from what I supposed were pure lips.

So the demoralizing effect of the Haymarket is not in the actual crime committed there, as is the case in the Bleeker Street dives for instance, but in the temptations which are held out so seductively to young men by the devils in female forms who make their homes there.

❧ The Dawes Act

CONGRESS

The Dawes Act of 1887 represented an attempt by Congress to absorb Native Americans into the United States' culture and economy. The act—named after Massachusetts Senator Henry L. Dawes—granted as much as 160 acres to Native American families for agricultural purposes. Participants in the program, which was also known as the Indian Homestead Act, were granted United States citizenship and permission to sell the property after 25 years. Although well meaning, the Dawes Act failed. Native American tribes were based on communal lifestyles. The culture was not conducive to private ownership and a capitalist economy. The policies of the Dawes Act were overturned by the Indian Reorganization Act of 1934.

Be it enacted &c. That in all cases where any tribe or band of Indians has been, or shall hereafter be, located upon any reservation created for their use, either by treaty stipulation or by virtue of an act of Congress or executive order setting apart the same for their use, the President of the United States be, and he hereby is, authorized, whenever in his opinion any reservation or any part thereof of such Indians is advantageous for agriculture and grazing purposes to cause said reservation, or any part thereof, to be surveyed, or resurveyed if necessary, and to allot the lands in said reservation in severalty to any Indian located thereon in quantities as follows:

To each head of a family, one-quarter of a section;

To each single person over eighteen years of age, one-eighth of a section; and,

To each other single person under eighteen years now living, or who may be born prior to the date of the order of the President directing an allotment of the lands embraced in any reservation, one-sixteenth of a section....

Section 2. That all allotments set apart under the provisions of this act shall be selected by the Indians, heads of families selecting for their minor children, and the agents shall select for each orphan child, and in such manner as to embrace the improvements of the Indians making the selection....

Provided, That if any one entitled to an allotment shall fail to make a selection within four years after the President shall direct that allotments may be made on a particular reservation, the Secretary of the Interior may direct the agent of such tribe or band, if such there be, and if there be no agent, then a special agent appointed for that purpose, to make a selection for such Indian, which selection shall be allotted as in cases where selections are made by the Indians, and patents shall issue in like manner....

Section 4. That where any Indian not residing upon a reservation, or for whose tribe no reservation has been provided by treaty, act of Congress or executive order, shall make settlement upon any surveyed or unsurveyed lands of the United States not otherwise appropriated, he or she shall be entitled, upon application to the local land office for the district in which the lands are located, to have the same allotted to him or her, and to his or her children, in quantities and manner as provided in this act for Indians residing upon reservations; and when such settlement is made upon unsurveyed lands, the grant to such Indians shall be adjusted upon the survey of the lands so as to conform thereto; and patents shall be issued to them for such lands in the manner and with the restrictions as herein provided....

Section 5.... And provided further, That at any time after lands have been allotted to all the Indians of any tribe as herein provided, or sooner if in the opinion of the President it shall be for the best interests of said tribe, it shall be lawful for the Secretary of the Interior to negotiate with such Indian tribe for the purchase and release by said tribe in conformity with the treaty or statute under which such reservation is held, of such portions of its reservation not allotted as such tribe shall, from time to time, consent to sell....

Section 6.... And every Indian born within the territorial limits of the United States to whom allotments shall have been made under the provisions of this act, or under any law or treaty, and every Indian born within the territorial limits of the United States who has voluntarily taken up, within said limits, his residence separate and apart from any tribe of Indians therein, and has adopted the habits of civilized life, is hereby declared to be a citizen of the United States, and is entitled to all the rights, privileges, and immunities of such citizens, whether said Indian has been or not, by birth or otherwise, a member of any tribe of Indians within the territorial limits of the United States without in any manner impairing or otherwise affecting the right of any such Indian to tribal or other property....

❧ "My ambition is to build a great Industrial Works"

THOMAS EDISON

Born in 1847, Thomas Alva Edison transformed American industry and technology. Starting his career manufacturing telegraph equipment, Edison's innovative mind applied to the business of invention. He founded the nation's fist research laboratory for the purpose of making inventions in 1876 at Menlo Park, New Jersey. Combining advanced equipment, learned scientists and clever machinists, the Edison Laboratory cranked out an incredible 400 inventions over the next ten years, including the first phonograph (the first recording was "Mary had a little lamb"), the incandescent electric lamp, the electrically powered locomotive and the two-electrode vacuum bulb. In 1887 Edison built a new laboratory in West Orange, New Jersey, ten times larger with many more scientists and engineers on staff. The letter below describes the new laboratory to J. Hood Wright, one of many financial backers who helped transform Edison's inventions into manufactured products. By the end of his life in 1931, Edison had more than 1,000 patents credited to him.

Prior to Edison the typical inventor was a solitary innovator who tinkered in an attic or work shed trying to devise new machines that might save labor. Inventors such as Eli Whitney, Benjamin Franklin and John Deere helped create new machines and tools for a country marked by a shortage of labor and abundance of natural resources. They were individuals who devised new inventions on pure ingenuity and circumstance. Edison created an invention factory, he hired people for the specific purposes of making inventions and applied significant financial resources to the endeavor. Henry Ford described Edison's research facilities as the birthplace of modern American technology. After Edison the purview of invention left the work shed and entered the corporate research laboratory. Bell Systems,

Eastman Kodak, General Electric and other major companies created their own research centers devoted to research and development.

My laboratory will soon be completed. The dimensions are one building 250 ft long 50 ft wide & 3 stories [high] 4 other bldgs. 25 x 100 ft one story high all of brick. I will have the best equipped and largest laboratory extant, and the facilities incomparably superior to any other for rapid and cheap development of an invention, & working it up into Commercial shape with models, patterns & special machinery. In fact there is no similar institution in Existence. We do our own castings forgings. Can build anything from a ladys watch to a Locomotive.

The Machine shop is sufficiently large to employ 50 men & 30 men can be worked in other parts of the works. Inventions that formerly took months & cost a large sum can now be done 2 or 3 days with very small expense, as I shall carry a stock of almost every conceivable material of every size and with the latest machinery a man will produce 10 times as much as in a laboratory which has but little material, not of a size, delays of days waiting for castings and machinery not universal or modern....

You are aware from your long acquaintance with me that I do not fly any financial Kites, or speculate, and that the works which I control are well managed. In the early days of the shops it was necessary that I should largely manage them, first because the art had to be created. Second, because I could get no men who were competent in such a new business. But as soon as it was possible I put other persons in charge. I am perfectly well aware of the fact that my place is in the laboratory; but I think you will admit that I know how a shop should be managed & also know how to select men to manage them.

With this prelude I will come to business.

My ambition is to build up a great Industrial Works in the Orange Valley starting in a small way & gradually working up. The Laboratory supplying the perfected inventions, models, patterns & fitting up necessary special machinery in the factory for each invention.

My plan contemplates to working of only that class of inventions which requires by small investments.... Such a work in time could be running on 30 or 40 special things of so diversified nature that the average profit could scarcely be [varied] by competitors. Now Mr. Wright, do you think this is practicable. If so can you help me along with it.

❧ The Lady's Guide to Perfect Gentility

EMILY THORNWELL

The urbanization of America and the rapid rise of a wealthy elite changed expectations of how people should conduct themselves. In 1887 Emily Thornwell wrote *The Lady's Guide to Perfect Gentility* to help define how women were supposed to conduct themselves.

Gait and carriage—A lady ought to adopt a modest and measured gait; too great hurry injures the grace which ought to characterize her. She should not turn her head on one side and on the other, especially in large towns or cities, where this bad habit seems to be an invitation to the impertinent. A lady should not present herself alone in a library, or a museum, unless she goes there to study, or work as an artist.

Gentlemen's attendance—After twilight, a young lady would not be conducting herself in a becoming manner, by walking alone; and if she passes the evening with any one, she ought, beforehand, to provide some one to come for her at a stated hour; but if this is not practicable, she should politely ask of the person whom she is visiting, to permit a servant to accompany her. But, however much this may be considered proper, and consequently an obligation, a married lady, well educated, will disregard it if circumstances prevent her being able, without trouble, to find a conductor.

Raising the dress—When tripping over the pavement, a lady should gracefully raise her dress a little above her ankle. With the right hand, she should hold together the folds of her gown, and draw them towards the right side. To raise the dress on both sides, and with both hands, is vulgar. This ungraceful practice can only be tolerated for a moment, when the mud is very deep.

Receiving visitors—When we see persons enter, whether announced or not, we rise immediately, advance towards them, request them to sit down, avoiding however the old form of, "Take the trouble to be seated." If it is a young man, we offer him an arm-chair, or a stuffed one; if an elderly man, we insist upon his accepting the arm-chair; if a lady, we beg her to be seated upon the ottoman....

In winter, the most honorable places are those at the corner of the fireplace; in proportion as they place you in front of the fire, your seat is considered inferior in rank. Moreover, when it happens to be a respectable married lady, and one to whom we wish to do honor, we take her by the hand and conduct her to the corner of the fireplace. If this place is occupied by a young lady, she should rise and offer her seat to the married lady, taking for herself a chair in the middle of the circle.

Propriety of movement and general demeanor in company—To look steadily at any one, especially if you are a lady and are speaking to a gentleman; to turn the head frequently on one side and the other during conversation...to cross your legs...to admire yourself with complacency in a glass...to fold carefully your shawl, instead of throwing it with graceful negligence upon a table...to laugh immoderately...to place your hand upon the person with whom you are conversing; to take him by the buttons, the collar of his cloak, the cuffs, the waist, etc.... to roll the eyes or raise them in affectation...to play continually with your chain or fan...to beat time with the feet and hands...to shake with your feet the chair of your neighbor; to rub your face or your hands; wink your eyes; shrug up your shoulders; stamp with your feet, &c.;—all these bad habits...are in the highest degree displeasing.

❧ "A typical day's work"

ILLINOIS FARMER'S WIFE

Most women in the United States had more pressing concerns than how to navigate city sidewalks in a lady-like fashion. Until the twentieth century, most Americans worked on farms. Husbands and wives labored long hours doing demanding work, as this anonymous Illinois farmer's wife attested.

No man can run a farm without some one to help him, and in this case I have always been called upon and expected to help to do anything that a man would be expected to do; I began this when we were first married, when there were few household duties and no reasonable excuse for refusing to help.

I was reared on a farm, was healthy and strong, was ambitious, and the work was not disagreeable, and having no children for the first six years of married life, the habit of going whenever asked to became firmly fixed, and he had no thought of hiring a man to help him, since I could no anything for which he needed help.

I was always religiously inclined; brought up to attend Sunday school, not in a haphazard way, but to attend every Sunday all the year round, and when I was twelve years old I was appointed teacher to a Sunday school class, a position I proudly held until I was married at eighteen years of age.

I was an apt student at school and before I was eighteen I had earned a teacher's certificate of the second grade and would gladly have remained in school a few more years, but I had, unwittingly, agreed to marry the man who is now my husband, and though I begged to be released, his will was so much stronger that I was unable to free myself without wounding a loving heart, and could not find it in my nature to do so....

My work is so varied that it would be difficult, indeed, to describe a typical day's work.

Any bright morning in the latter part of May I am out of bed at four o'clock; next, after I have dressed and combed my hair, I start a fire in the kitchen stove, and while the stove is getting hot I go to the flower garden and gather a choice, half-blown rose and a spray of bride's wreath, and arrange them in my hair, and sweep the floors and then cook breakfast.

While the other members of the family are eating breakfast I strain away the morning's milk (for my husband milks the cows while I get breakfast), and fill my husband's dinner-pail, for he will go to work on our other farm for the day.

By this time it is half-past five o'clock, my husband is gone to his work, and the stock loudly pleading to be turned out into the pastures. The younger cattle, a half-dozen steers, are left in the pasture at night, and I now drive the two cows a half-quarter mile and turn them in with the others, come back, and then there's a horse in the barn that belongs in a field where there is no water, which I take to a spring quite a distance from the barn; bring it back and turn it into a field with the sheep, a dozen in number, which are housed at night.

The young calves are then turned out into the warm sunshine, and the stock hogs, which are kept in a pen, are clamoring for feed, and I carry a pailful of swill to them, and hasten to the house and turn out the chickens and put out feed and water for them, and it is, perhaps, 6.30 a.m.

I have not eaten breakfast yet, but that can wait; I make the beds next and straighten things up in the living room, for I dislike to have the early morning caller find my house topsy-turvy. When this is done I go to the kitchen, which also serves as a dining room, and uncover the table, and take a mouthful of food occasionally as I pass to and fro at my work until my appetite is appeased.

By the time the work is done in the kitchen it is about 7.15 a.m., and the cool morning hours have flown, and no hoeing done in the garden yet, and the children's toilet has to be attended to and churning has to be done.

Finally the children are washed and the churning done, and it is eight o'clock, and the sun getting hot, but no matter, weeds die quickly when cut down in the heat of the day, and I use the hoe to a good advantage until the dinner hour, which is 11.30 a.m. We come in, and I comb my hair, and put fresh flowers in it, and eat a cold dinner, put out feed and water for the chickens; set a hen, perhaps, sweep the floors again; sit down and rest, and read a few moments, and it is nearly one o'clock, and I sweep the door yard while I am waiting for the clock to strike the hour.

I make and sow a flower bed, dig around some shrubbery, and go back to the garden to hoe until time to do the chores at night, but ere long some hogs come up to the back gate, through the wheat field, and when I go to see what is wrong I find that the cows have torn the fence down, and they, too, are in the wheat field.

With much difficulty I get them back into their own domain and repair the fence. I hoe in the garden till four o'clock; then I go into the house and get supper, and prepare something for the dinner pail tomorrow; when supper is all ready it is set aside, and I pull a few hundred plants of tomato, sweet potato or cabbage for transplanting, get them in a cool, moist place where they will not wilt, and I then go after the horse, water him, and put him in the barn; call the sheep and house them, and go after the cows and milk them, feed the hogs, put down hay for the horses, and put oats and corn in their troughs, and set those plants and come in and fasten up the chickens, and it is dark. By this time it is 8 o'clock p.m.; my husband has come home, and we are eating supper; when we are through eating I make the beds ready, and the children and their father go to bed, and I wash the dishes and get things in shape to get breakfast quickly next morning.

It is now about 9 o'clock p.m., and after a short prayer I retire for the night.

As a matter of course, there's hardly two days together which require the same routine, yet every day is as fully occupied in some way or other as this one, with varying tasks as the seasons change....

I have never had a vacation, but if I should be allowed one I should certainly be pleased to spend it in an art gallery.

"Plain surroundings, like plain living, might be conducive to high thinking"

INDIA HARRIS SIMMONS

Having settled the West, homesteaders went about the business of creating permanent communities. One of the central community institutions was school. But with few resources, settlers had to do with what they could scrounge together. In 1888, India Harris Simmons traveled to Kearny County, Kansas to meet her homesteading parents and teach in a one-room school made of a converted Prairie mud house. In this journal entry, she describes the school.

School opened in October of 1888 with nineteen pupils. Not wishing to postpone the opening of school until a suitable building could be secured, the patrons decided to use a dugout which had served as a dwelling for a pre-empter, who had 'proved up' and gone.

The outlook, or speaking more exactly, the inlook, was not reassuring. The floor and walls were just plain dirt, not even adobe plaster, and the one window and the cellar type of doorway gave scant illumination. Plain benches without backs ran around three sides of the room. There were no blackboards or other school equipment. Decorating

it, or improving it in any substantial way would take at least a little money which could not be spared by the district until more land was 'proved up' and made taxable.

So, clean 'gunny bags,' a kind of coarse burlap bag, were ripped apart and fastened against the walls to keep the dirt away from the clothing. Use had somewhat packed and hardened the floor, which they cleared of loose dirt, and then laid down old rugs and pieces of carpet, on which the children's feet could rest. They cleaned the tiny four-paned window, at each side of which they hung a bright piece of cheap drapery, being careful not to obscure any of the precious light.

A small wooden box, with a clean paper on top, held the water jug and the common drinking cup. A taller box, with a shelf inside and a pretty stand cover on it, served as the teacher's desk, and her chair was one of the home-made kind with a broad board nailed on slantingly for a back, quite common in the dugout homes. A little Topsy stove, on which the bachelor claim holder had baked his morning flap-jacks, was the final piece of furniture.

When the little group had been called in, and nineteen happy expectant faces greeted her from the row of benches, the young teacher had a sense of misgiving as to her ability to change that crude little dirt-walled room into a hall of learning.... But breathing a prayer that plain surroundings, like plain living, might be conducive to high thinking, she began the opening exercises which dedicated the lowly dwelling to its new high use.

The nondescript supply of books which each pupil had brought from whatever state was 'back home' to him was placed on the bench by his side. Slates, which had to take the place of both blackboard and tablets, were of all sizes and descriptions, from Jimmy's tiny one with the red felt covered frame and pencil tied to it with a string, to Mary's big double one with the wide home-made frames fastened together with strong hinges and cut deep with initials and hearts. She had found it packed away among grandfather's books, which he had used away back in Ohio. There were histories from Illinois, spellers and writing books from Iowa, readers from St. Louis city schools, and even some old blue-backed spellers, with their five-syllabled puzzlers.

From this motley array the teacher made the assignments and arranged the classifications, depending entirely upon her own judgment. The pupils had been without school privileges long enough to be glad to have an opportunity to study, and their rapid progress showed they came, for the most part, from intelligent families. True, there was not a suspension globe for explaining mathematical geography, but an apple and a ball did very well. There was no case of the latest wall maps on rollers, but the large ones in the books answered the purpose when care was taken to hold them correctly.

Society as I Have Found It

WARD MCALLISTER

The rapid industrialization of the United States created a tremendous concentration of wealth into the hands of a relatively small elite class. In 1900 one ten-thousandth of 1 percent of the population held more than 20 percent of the nation's wealth. The average wealth of a family in the top 1 percent was $264,000 versus $150 for the average wealth for a family in the bottom 50 percent. The boom in wealth fostered a new society founded on conspicuous spending. The wealthy did not just spend money, they wanted to be seen spending money. Elaborate mansions were built in New York City and Newport, Rhode Island. Travel, art and gala parties became distinguishing characteristics in the lifestyles of the rich and famous. Mark Twain dubbed the era "The Gilded Age" for its social ostentation, worship of wealth and venal politics. Ward McAllister rose to prominence within this privileged society and wrote an autobiographical book, *Society as I Have Found It,* in 1890 describing the frivolous lifestyles of the super rich.

We here reach a period when New York society turned over a new leaf. Up to this time for one to be worth a million of dollars was to be rated as a man of fortune, but now bygones must be bygones. New York's ideas as to values, when fortune was named, leaped boldly up to ten millions, fifty millions, one hundred millions; and the necessities and luxuries followed suit. One was no longer content with a dinner of a dozen or more, to be served by a couple of servants. Fashion demanded that you be received in the hall of the house in which you were to dine by from five to six servants, who, with the butler, were to serve the repast—the butler, on such occasions, to do alone the headwork, and under him he had these men in livery to serve the dinner,

he to guide and direct them. Soft strains of music were introduced between the courses, and in some houses gold replaced silver in the way of plate; and everything that skill and art could suggest was added to make the dinners not a vulgar display but a gastronomic effort evidencing the possession by the host of both money and taste.

The butler, from getting a salary of forty dollars a month, received then from sixty to seventy-five dollars a month. The second man jumped up from twenty to thirty-five and forty dollars, and the extra men, at the dinner of a dozen people or more, would cost twenty-four dollars. Then the orchids, being the most costly of all flowers, were introduced in profusion. The canvasback that we could buy at two dollars and a half a pair went up to eight dollars a pair; the terrapin were four dollars apiece. Our forefathers would have been staggered at the cost of the hospitality of these days....

The six quadrilles were really the event of the ball, consisting of the hobbyhorse quadrille, the men who danced in it being dressed in "pink" and the ladies wearing red hunting coats and white satin skirts, all of the period of Louis XIV. In the Mother Goose quadrille were Jack and Jill, Little Red Riding Hood, Bo-Peep, Goody Two-Shoes, Mary, Mary, Quite Contrary, and My Pretty Maid. The opera bouffe quadrille was most successful, but of all of them, the star quadrille, containing the youth and beauty of the city, was the most brilliant. The ladies in it were arrayed as twin stars in four different colors, yellow, blue, mauve, and white. Above the forehead of each lady, in her hair, was worn an electric light, giving a fairy and elflike appearance to each of them. The Dresden quadrille, in which the ladies wore white satin with powdered hair and the gentlemen white satin knee breeches and powdered wigs, with the Dresden mark, crossed swords, on each of them, was effective. The hostess appeared as a Venetian princess, with a superb jeweled peacock in her hair. The host was the Duke de Guise for that evening. The host's eldest brother wore a costume of Louis XVI. His wife appeared as the electric light in white satin trimmed with diamonds, and her head one blaze of diamonds. The most remarkable costume and one spoken of to this day was that of a cat, the dress being of cats' tails and white cats' heads, and a bell with "Puss" on it in large letters. A distinguished beauty dressed as a phoenix, adorned with diamonds and rubies, was superb, and with the Capuchin monk, with hood and sandals, inimitable. But to name the most striking would be to name all.

The great social revolution that had occurred in New York this winter, like most revolutionary waves, reached Newport. Our distinguished New York journalist then made Newport his summer home, buying the fine granite house that for years had been first known as the Middleton mansion, afterward the Sidney Brooks residence, and filling it with distinguished Europeans. His activity and energy gave new life to the place.

One fine summer morning one of his guests, an officer in the English army, a bright spirit and admirable horseman, riding on his polo pony up to the Newport Reading Room, where all the fossils of the place, the nobs and the swells, daily gossiped, he was challenged to ride the pony into the hall of this revered old club, and being bantered to do it, he actually did ride the pony across the narrow piazza and into the hall of the club itself. This was enough to set Newport agog. What sacrilege! an Englishman to ride in upon us, not respecting the sanctity of the place. It aroused the old patriots, who were members of that institution, with the spirit of '76; and a summary note was sent to the great-journalist, withdrawing the invitation the club had previously given his guest. The latter in turn felt aggrieved and retaliated with this result: building for Newport a superb casino, embracing a club, a ballroom, and a restaurant, opposite his own residence. All this evidencing that agitation of any kind is as beneficial in social circles as to the atmosphere we breathe.

Then our journalist conceived and gave a handsome domino ball, all the ladies in domino, much after the pattern of the one previously given by the Duchess de Dino and in many respects resembling it, having a huge tent spread behind the house, and all the rooms on the first floor converted into a series of charming supper rooms, each table decorated most elaborately with beautiful flowers—as handsome a ball as one could give. I took the wife of the attorney general to it in domino, who, after her life in Washington, was amazed at the beauty of the scene. The grounds, which were very handsome, were all, even the plants themselves, illuminated with electric lights -- that is, streams of electric light were cunningly thrown

under the plants, giving an illumination *a giorno* and producing the most beautiful effect.

At this ball there appeared a blue domino that set all the men wild. Coming to the ball in her own carriage (her servants she felt she could not trust not to betray her) she dashed into the merry throng, and gliding from one to the other, whispered airy nothings into men's ears. But they contained enough to excite the most intense curiosity as to who she was. She was the belle of the evening; she became bold and daring at times, attacking men about the inmost secrets of their hearts, so as to alarm them; and when she had worked them all up to a fever heat, she came to me to take her to the door that she might make good her escape. A dozen men barricaded the way, but with the rapidity of a deer she dashed through them, reached the sidewalk, and her footman literally threw her into the carriage. Her coachman, well drilled, dashed off at a furious rate, and to this day no one has ever found out who the fair creature was.

🌿 Looking Backward

EDWARD BELLAMY

Edward Bellamy wrote the utopian novel *Looking Backward* in 1888 envisioning a future society based on economic equality. In the book the main character falls asleep and wakes up in the year 2000 in the United States. Society has rid itself of classes, education is universal and crime has disappeared. Bellamy's vision of an ideal socialist future had an enormous influence by both highlighting what was wrong with contemporary society and presenting a goal for which to aspire.

"If I were to give you in one sentence, a key to what may seem the mysteries of our civilization as compared with that of your age, I should say that it is the fact that the solidarity of the race and the brotherhood of man, which to you were but fine phrases, are, to our thinking and feeling, ties as real and as vital as physical fraternity.

"But even setting that consideration aside, I do not see why it so surprises you that those who cannot work are conceded the full right to live on the produce of those who can. Even in your day, the duty of military service for the protection of the nation, to which our industrial service corresponds, while obligatory on those able to discharge it, did not operate to deprive of the privileges of citizenship those who were unable. They stayed at home, and were protected by those who fought, and nobody questioned their right to be, or thought less of them. So, now, the requirement of industrial service from those able to render it does not operate to deprive of the privileges of citizenship, which now implies the citizen's maintenance, him who cannot work. The worker is not a citizen because he works, but works because he is a citizen. As you recognize the duty of the strong to fight for the weak, we now that fighting is gone by, recognize his duty to work for him.

"A solution which leaves an unaccounted-for residuum is no solution at all; and our solution of the problem of human society would have been none at all had it left the lame, the sick, and the blind outside with the beasts, to fare as they might. Better far have left the strong and well unprovided for than these burdened ones, toward whom every heart must yearn, and for whom ease of mind and body should be provided, if for no others. Therefore it is, as I told you this morning, that the title of every man, woman, and child to the means of existence rests on no basis less plain, broad, and simple than the fact that they are fellows of one race— members of one human family. The only coin current is the image of God, and that is good for all we have.

"I think there is no feature of the civilization of your epoch so repugnant to modern ideas as the neglect with which you treated your dependent classes. Even if you had no pity, no feeling of brotherhood, how was it that you did not see that you were robbing the incapable class of their plain right in leaving them unprovided for?"

"However earnestly a man may long for leisure for purposes of study or meditation," I remarked, "he cannot get out of the harness, if I understand you rightly, except in these two ways you have mentioned. He must either by literary, artistic, or inventive productiveness indemnify the nation for the loss of his services, or must get a sufficient number of other people to contribute to such an indemnity."

"It is most certain," replied Dr. Leete, "that no able-bodied man nowadays can evade his share of work and live on the toil of others, whether he

calls himself by the fine name of student or confesses to being simply lazy. At the same time our system is elastic enough to give free play to every instinct of human nature which does not aim at dominating others or living on the fruit of others' labor. There is not only the remission by indemnification but the remission by abnegation. Any man in his thirty-third year, his term of service being then half done, can obtain an honorable discharge from the army, provided he accepts for the rest of his life one half the rate of maintenance other citizens receive. It is quite possible to live on this amount, though one must forego the luxuries and elegancies of life, with some, perhaps, of its comforts."

❧ Forty Years of Hull House

JANE ADDAMS

Jane Addams was the preeminent social worker of her time. In 1889 she and Ellen Gates Starr founded Hull House in the slums of Chicago. The idea of settlement houses originated in London, England. Trained professionals "settled" in impoverished neighborhoods to help relieve poverty. It was replicated in major American cities starting in the late 1880s. Hull House quickly became a lively community center, fulfilling a wide range of needs for impoverished working families.

Addams and Starr confronted a wide spectrum of problems. Municipal corruption often worsened situations rather than improved them. Single working mothers were often compelled to lock their children in dangerous tenement apartments while they were away. In one case, the social workers discovered a child whose spine was curved as the result of being tied to a table every day for three years while his mother was away working. Every problem required a different solution involving determination, initiative and work. The following excerpt from Addam's book *Forty Years of Hull House* describes battling city officials and corrupt workers to remove garbage from the streets.

During their tenure at Hull House, Addams and Starr established a day nursery, theater, working girls' home, labor museum, boys' club, reading parties, English-language classes and several other programs designed to rectify problems, stimulate community activity, and match problems with solutions. Hull House and other settlement houses were on the forefront of the social reform movement that marked the turn of the century. Employing grassroots involvement, they played a major role in advocating for improvements in child labor laws and housing conditions. The women who served in the settlement houses became leading academics, political leaders and virtually created the profession of social work.

Addams was a founder of the Women's Peace Party in 1915, the Women's International League for Peace and Freedom in 1919 and the American Civil Liberties Union in 1929. She won the Nobel Prize in 1931, the first American woman to achieve the honor.

One of the striking features of our neighborhood twenty years ago, and one to which we never became reconciled, was the presence of huge wooden garbage boxes fastened to the street pavement in which the undisturbed refuse accumulated day by day. The system of garbage collecting was inadequate throughout the city but it became the greatest menace in a ward such as ours, where the normal amount of waste was much increased by the decayed fruit and vegetables discarded by the Italian and Greek fruit peddlers, and by the residuum left over from the piles of filthy rags which were fished out of the city dumps and brought to the homes of the rag pickers for further sorting and washing.

The children of our neighborhood twenty years ago played their games in and around these huge garbage boxes. They were the first objects that the toddling child learned to climb; their bulk afforded a barricade and their contents provided missiles in all the battles of the older boys, and finally they became the seats upon which absorbed lovers held enchanted converse....

During our first three years on Halsted Street, we had established a small incinerator at Hull-House and we had many times reported the untoward conditions of the ward to the city hall. We had also arranged many talks for the immigrants, pointing out that although a woman may sweep her own doorway in her native village and allow the refuse to innocently decay in the open air and sunshine, in a crowded city quarter, if the garbage is not properly collected and destroyed, a tenement-house mother may see her children sicken and die, and that the immigrants must therefore not only keep their own houses clean, but must also help the authorities to keep the city clean.

Possibly our efforts slightly modified the worst conditions, but they still remained intolerable, and the fourth summer...we began a systematic investigation of the city system of garbage collection, both as to its efficiency in other wards and its possible connection with the death rate in the various wards of the city.

The Hull-House Woman's Club had been organized the year before by the resident kindergartner who had first inaugurated a mothers' meeting. The members came together, however, in quite a new way that summer when we discussed with them the high death rate so persistent in our ward. After several meetings devoted to the subject, despite the fact that the death rate rose highest in the congested foreign colonies and not in the streets in which most of the Irish American club women lived, twelve of their number undertook in connection with the residents, to carefully investigate the condition of the alleys. During August and September the substantiated reports of violations of the law sent in from Hull-House to the health department were one thousand and thirty-seven. For the club woman who had finished a long day's work of washing or ironing followed by the cooking of a hot supper, it would have been much easier to sit on her doorstep during a summer evening than to go up and down ill-kept alleys and get into trouble with her neighbors over the condition of their garbage boxes. It required both civic enterprise and moral conviction to be willing to do this three evenings a week during the hottest and most uncomfortable months of the year. Nevertheless, a certain number of women persisted, as did the residents, and three city inspectors in succession were transferred from the ward because of unsatisfactory services. Still the death rate remained high and the condition seemed little improved throughout the next winter. In sheer desperation, the following spring when the city contracts were awarded for the removal of garbage, with the backing of two well-known business men, put in a bid for the garbage removal of the nineteenth ward. My paper was thrown out on a technicality but the incident induced the mayor to appoint me the garbage inspector of the ward.

The salary was a thousand dollars a year, and the loss of that political "plum" made a great stir among the politicians. The position was no sinecure whether regarded from the point of view of getting up at six in the morning to see that the men were early at work; or of following the loaded wagons, uneasily dropping their contents at intervals, to their dreary destination at the dump; or of insisting that the contractor must increase the number of his wagons from nine to thirteen and from thirteen to seventeen, although he assured me that he lost money on every one and that the former inspector had let him off with seven; or of taking careless landlords into court because they would not provide the proper garbage receptacles; or of arresting the tenant who tried to make the garbage wagons carry away the contents of his stable.

With the two or three residents who nobly stood by, we set up six of those doleful incinerators which are supposed to burn garbage with the fuel collected in the alley itself. The one factory in town which could utilize old tin cans was a window weight factory, and we deluged that with ten times as many tin cans as it could use—much less would pay for. We made desperate attempts to have the dead animals removed by the contractor who was paid most liberally by the city for that purpose but who, we slowly discovered, always made the police ambulances do the work, delivering the carcasses upon freight cars for shipment to a soap factory in Indiana where they were sold for a good price although the contractor himself was the largest stockholder in the concern.

✤ "The true Gospel concerning Wealth"

ANDREW CARNEGIE

Andrew Carnegie's rise to prosperity was a Horatio Alger story come to life. He arrived in Allegheny City, Pennsylvania, as a young Scottish immigrant in 1848. He started to work as a child, saved money, showed enterprise and elevated his position within a steel mill by dint of hard work and skill. By 1873 he had his own company and started to consolidate the Pittsburgh steel industry into the Carnegie Steel Company. He turned Pittsburgh into a major industrial steel center. His companies were known for their hard-driving tactics. In 1892 Carnegie ordered a small army of Pinkerton detectives to break a strike at his steel plant in Homestead, Pennsylvania. Seven strikers were killed in the conflict. In 1901 Carnegie sold his company in a merger with J. P. Morgan who created U. S. Steel. When he retired, the former penniless immigrant had $250 million, making him one of the wealthiest men in the country.

Carnegie wrote the article "Wealth" in 1889 for the *North American Review* as an explanation of how the rich accumulated their fortunes and an exploration how they should spend their "surplus wealth." Carnegie was a personal friend of Herbert Spencer who had applied Darwin's survival-of-the-fittest theory of evolution to the marketplace. Like most industrialists at the time, Carnegie subscribed to Spencer's theory that the accumulation of large sums of money for individuals was justified as being part of the natural order and good for society at large. One of the great philanthropists in American history, Carnegie also believed that the wealthy needed to return the vast majority of their money to society. Carnegie suggested that the wealthy donate their money to enterprises that would provide opportunities for the poor to elevate themselves. Carnegie gave away more than $350 million in his lifetime to more than 2,800 libraries and philanthropies. Critics, however, charged Carnegie as a miserly hypocrite who deprived his workers of living wages for the sake of advancing his own philanthropic goals.

The problem of our age is the proper administration of wealth, so that the ties of brotherhood may still bind together the rich and poor in harmonious relationship. The conditions of human life have not only been changed, but revolutionized, within the past few hundred years. In former days there was little difference between the dwelling, dress, food, and environment of the chief and those of his retainers. The Indians are today where civilized man then was. When visiting the Sioux, I was led to the wigwam of the chief. It was just like the others in external appearance, and even within the difference was trifling between it and those of the poorest of his braves. The contrast between the palace of the millionaire and the cottage of the laborer with us today measures the change which has come with civilization.

This change, however, is not to be deplored, but welcomed as highly beneficial. It is well, nay, essential for the progress of the race, that the houses of some should be homes for all that is highest and best in literature and the arts, and for all the refinements of civilization, rather than that none should be so. Much better this great irregularity than universal squalor. Without wealth there can be no Maecenas. The "good old times" were not good old times. Neither master nor servant was as well situated then as today. A relapse to old conditions would be disastrous to both—not the least so to him who serves—and would sweep away civilization with it. But whether the change be for good or ill, it is upon us, beyond our power to alter, and therefore to be accepted and made the best of. It is a waste of time to criticise the inevitable.

It is easy to see how the change has come. One illustration will serve for almost every phase of the cause. In the manufacture of products we have the whole story. It applies to all combinations of human industry, as stimulated and enlarged by the inventions of this scientific age. Formerly articles were manufactured at the domestic hearth or in small shops which formed part of the household. The master and his apprentices worked side by side, the latter living with the master, and therefore subject to the same conditions. When these apprentices rose to be masters, there was little or no change in their mode of life, and they, in turn, educated in the same routine succeeding apprentices. There was, substantially, social equality, and even political equality, for those engaged in industrial pursuits had then little or no political voice in the State.

But the inevitable result of such a mode of manufacture was crude articles at high prices. Today the world obtains commodities of excellent quality at prices which even the generation preceding this would have deemed incredible. In the commercial world similar causes have produced similar results, and the race is benefited thereby. The poor enjoy what the rich could not before afford. What were the luxuries have become the necessaries of life. The laborer has now more comforts than the farmer had a few generations ago. The farmer has more luxuries than the landlord had, and is more richly clad and better housed. The landlord has books and pictures rarer, and appointments more artistic, than the King could then obtain.

The price we pay for this salutary change is, no doubt, great. We assemble thousands of operatives in the factory, in the mine, and in the counting-house, of whom the employer can know little or nothing, and to whom the employer is little better than a myth. All intercourse between them is at an end. Rigid Castes are formed, and, as usual, mutual ignorance breeds mutual distrust. Each Caste is without sympathy for the other, and ready to credit anything disparaging in regard to it. Under the law of competition, the employer of thousands is forced into the strictest economies, among which the rates paid to labor figure prominently, and often there is friction between the employer and the employed, between capital and labor, between rich and poor. Human society loses homogeneity.

The price which society pays for the law of competition, like the price it pays for cheap comforts and luxuries, is also great; but the advantages of this law are also greater still, for it is to this law that we owe our wonderful material development, which brings improved conditions in its train. But, whether the law be benign or not, we must say of it, as we say of the change in the conditions of men

to which we have referred: It is here; we cannot evade it; no substitutes for it have been found; and while the law may be sometimes hard for the individual, it is best for the race, because it insures the survival of the fittest in every department. We accept and welcome, therefore, as conditions to which we must accommodate ourselves, great inequality of environment, the concentration of business, industrial and commercial, in the hands of a few, and the law of competition between these, as being not only beneficial, but essential for the future progress of the race. Having accepted these, it follows that there must be great scope for the exercise of special ability in the merchant and in the manufacturer who has to conduct affairs upon a great scale. That this talent for organization and management is rare among men is proved by the fact that it invariably secures for its possessor enormous rewards, no matter where or under what laws or conditions. The experienced in affairs always rate the man whose services can be obtained as a partner as not only the first consideration, but such as to render the question of his capital scarcely worth considering, for such men soon create capital; while, without the special talent required, capital soon takes wings. Such men become interested in firms or corporations using millions; and estimating only simple interest to be made upon the capital invested, it is inevitable that their income must exceed their expenditures, and that they must accumulate wealth. Nor is there any middle ground which such men can occupy, because the great manufacturing or commercial concern which does not earn at least interest upon its capital soon becomes bankrupt. It must either go forward or fall behind: to stand still is impossible. It is a condition essential for its successful operation that it should be thus far profitable, and even that, in addition to interest on capital, it should make profit. It is a law, as certain as any of the others named, that men possessed of this peculiar talent for affairs, under the free play of economic forces, must, of necessity, soon be in receipt of more revenue than can be judiciously expended upon themselves; and this law is as beneficial for the race as the others.

Objections to the foundations upon which society is based are not in order, because the condition of the race is better with these than it has been with any others which have been tried. Of the effect of any new substitutes proposed we cannot be sure. The Socialist or Anarchist who seeks to overturn present conditions is to be regarded as attacking the foundation upon which civilization itself rests, for civilization took its start from the day that the capable, industrious workman said to his incompetent and lazy fellow, "If thou dost not sow, thou shalt not reap," and thus ended primitive Communism by separating the drones from the bees. One who studies this subject will soon be brought face to face with the conclusion that upon the sacredness of property civilization itself depends—the right of the laborer to his hundred dollars in the savings bank, and equally the legal right of the millionaire to his millions. To those who propose to substitute Communism for this intense Individualism the answer, therefore, is: The race has tried that. All progress from that barbarous day to the present time has resulted from its displacement. Not evil, but good, has come to the race from the accumulation of wealth by those who have the ability and energy that produce it. But even if we admit for a moment that it might be better for the race to discard its present foundation, Individualism,—that it is a nobler ideal that man should labor, not for himself alone, but in and for a brotherhood of his fellows, and share with them all in common, realizing Swedenborg's idea of Heaven, where, as he says, the angels derive their happiness, not from the laboring for self, but for each other,—even admit all this, and a sufficient answer is, This is not evolution, but revolution. It necessitates the changing of human nature itself a work of eons, even if it were good to change it, which we cannot know. It is not practicable in our day or in our age. Even if desirable theoretically, it belongs to another and long-succeeding sociological stratum. Our duty is with what is practicable now; with the next step possible in our day and generation. It is criminal to waste our energies in endeavoring to uproot, when all we can profitably or possibly accomplish is to bend the universal tree of humanity a little in the direction most favorable to the production of good fruit under existing circumstances. We might as well urge the destruction of the highest existing type of man because he failed to reach our ideal as to favor the destruction of Individualism, Private Property, the Law of Accumulation of Wealth, the Law of Competition; for these are the highest results of human experience, the soil in which society so far has produced the best fruit. Unequally or unjustly, as these laws sometimes operate, and imperfect as they appear to the Idealist, they are, nevertheless, like the highest type of man: the best and most valuable of all that humanity has yet accomplished.

We start, then, with a condition of affairs under which the best interests of the race are promoted, but which inevitably gives wealth to the few. Thus far, accepting conditions as they exist, the situation can be surveyed and pronounced good. The question then arises,—and, if the foregoing be correct, it is the only question with which we have to deal,—What is the proper mode of administering wealth after the laws upon which civilization is founded have thrown it into the hands of the few? And it is of this great question that I believe I offer the true solution. It will be understood that fortunes are here spoken of, not moderate sums saved by many years of effort, the returns from which are required for the comfortable maintenance and education of families. This is not wealth, but only competence, which it should be the aim of all to acquire.

There are but three modes in which surplus wealth can be disposed of. It can be left to the families of the decedent; or it can be bequeathed for public purposes; or, finally, it can be administered during their lives by its possessors. Under the first and second modes most of the wealth of the world that has reached the few has hitherto been applied. Let us in turn consider each of these modes. The first is the most injudicious. In monarchical countries, the estates and the greatest portion of the wealth are left to the first son, that the vanity of the parent may be gratified by the thought that his name and title are to descend to succeeding generations unimpaired. The condition of this class in Europe today teaches the futility of such hopes or ambitions. The successors have become impoverished through their follies or from the fall in the value of land. Even in Great Britain the strict law of entail has been found inadequate to maintain the status of an hereditary class. Its soil is rapidly passing into the hands of the stranger. Under republican institutions the division of property among the children is much fairer, but the question which forces itself upon thoughtful men in all lands is: Why should men leave great fortunes to their children? If this is done from affection, is it not misguided affection? Observation teaches that, generally speaking, it is not well for the children that they should be so burdened. Neither is it well for the state. Beyond providing for the wife and daughters moderate sources of income, and very moderate allowances indeed, if any, for the sons, men may well hesitate, for it is no longer questionable that great sums bequeathed oftener work more for the injury than for the good of the recipients. Wise men will soon conclude that, for the best interests of the members of their families and of the state, such bequests are an improper use of their means....

As to the second mode, that of leaving wealth at death for public uses, it may be said that this is only a means for the disposal of wealth, provided a man is content to wait until he is dead before it becomes of much good in the world. Knowledge of the results of legacies bequeathed is not calculated to inspire the brightest hopes of much posthumous good being accomplished. The cases are not few in which the real object sought by the testator is not attained, nor are they few in which his real wishes are thwarted. In many cases the bequests are so used as to become only monuments of his folly....

There remains, then, only one mode of using great fortunes; but in this we have the true antidote for the temporary unequal distribution of wealth, the reconciliation of the rich and the poor—a reign of harmony another ideal, differing, indeed, from that of the Communist in requiring only the further evolution of existing conditions, not the total overthrow of our civilization. It is founded upon the present most intense individualism, and the race is prepared to put it in practice by degrees whenever it pleases. Under its sway we shall have an ideal state, in which the surplus wealth of the few will become, in the best sense, the property of the many, because administered for the common good, and this wealth, passing through the hands of the few, can be made a much more potent force for the elevation of our race than if it had been distributed in small sums to the people themselves. Even the poorest can be made to see this, and to agree that great sums gathered by some of their fellow-citizens and spent for public purposes, from which the masses reap the principal benefit, are more valuable to them than if scattered among them through the course of many years in trifling amounts.

If we consider what results flow from the Cooper Institute, for instance, to the best portion of the race in New York not possessed of means, and compare these with those which would have arisen for the good of the masses from an equal sum distributed by Mr. Cooper in his lifetime in the form of wages, which is the highest form of distribution, being for work done and not for charity, we can form some estimate of the possibilities for the improvement of the race which lie embedded in the present law of the accumulation of wealth. Much of this sum, if distributed in small quantities among the people, would have been wasted in the indulgence of appetite, some of it in excess, and it may be doubted whether even the part put to the best use, that of adding to the comforts of the home, would have yielded results for the race, as a race, at all comparable to those which are flowing and are to flow from the Cooper Institute from generation to generation. Let the advocate of violent or radical change ponder well this thought.

We might even go so far as to take another instance, that of Mr. Tilden's bequest of five millions of dollars for a free library in the city of New York, but in referring to this one cannot help saying involuntarily, How much better if Mr. Tilden had devoted the last years of his own life to the proper administration of this immense sum; in which case neither legal contest nor any other cause of delay could have interfered with his aims. But let us assume that Mr. Tilden's millions finally become the means of giving to this city a noble public library, where the treasures of the world contained in books will be open to all forever, without money and without price. Considering the good of that part of the race which congregates in and around Manhattan Island, would its permanent benefit have been better promoted had these millions been allowed to circulate in small sums through the hands of the masses? Even the most strenuous advocate of Communism must entertain a doubt upon this subject. Most of those who think will probably entertain no doubt whatever.

Poor and restricted are our opportunities in this life; narrow our horizon; our best work most imperfect; but rich men should be thankful for one inestimable boon. They have it in their power during their lives to busy themselves in organizing benefactions from which the masses of their fellows will derive lasting advantage, and thus dignify their own lives. The highest life is probably to be reached, not by such imitation of the life of Christ as Count Tolstoi gives us, but, while animated by Christ's spirit, by recognizing the changed conditions of this age, and adopting modes of expressing this spirit suitable to the changed conditions under which we live; still laboring for the good of our fellows, which was the essence of his life and teaching, but laboring in a different manner.

This, then, is held to be the duty of the man of Wealth: First, to set an example of modest, unostentatious living, shunning display or extravagance; to provide moderately for the legitimate wants of those dependent upon him; and after doing so to consider all surplus revenues which come to him simply as trust funds, which he is called upon to administer, and strictly bound as a matter of duty to administer in the manner which, in his judgment, is best calculated to produce the most beneficial results for the community—the man of wealth thus becoming the mere agent and trustee for his poorer brethren, bringing to their service his superior wisdom, experience, and ability to administer, doing for them better than they would or could do for themselves....

The best uses to which surplus wealth can be put have already been indicated. Those who would administer wisely must, indeed, be wise, for one of the serious obstacles to the improvement of our race is indiscriminate charity. It were better for mankind that the millions of the rich was thrown into the sea than so spent as to encourage the slothful, the drunken, the unworthy. Of every thousand dollars spent in so called charity today, it is probable that $950 is unwisely spent; so spent, indeed, as to produce the very evils which it proposes to mitigate or cure. A well known writer of philosophic books admitted the other day that he had given a quarter of a dollar to a man who approached him as he was coming to visit the house of his friend. He knew nothing of the habits of this beggar; knew not the use that would be made of this money, although he had every reason to suspect that it would be spent improperly. This man professed to be a disciple of Herbert Spencer; yet the quarter-dollar given that night will probably work more injury than all the money which its thoughtless donor will ever be able to give in true charity will do good. He only gratified his own feelings, saved himself from annoyance, and this was probably one of the most selfish and very worst actions of his life, for in all respects he is most worthy.

In bestowing charity, the main consideration should be to help those who will help themselves; to provide part of the means by which those who desire to improve may do so; to give those who desire to rise the aids by which they may rise; to assist, but rarely or never to do all. Neither the individual nor the race is improved by alms-giving. Those worthy of assistance, except in rare cases, seldom require assistance. The really valuable men of the race never do, except in cases of accident or sudden change. Every one has, of course, cases of individuals brought to his own knowledge where temporally assistance can do genuine good, and these he will not overlook. But the amount which can be wisely given by the individual for individuals is necessarily limited by his lack of knowledge of the circumstances connected with each. He is the only true reformer who is as careful and as anxious not to aid the unworthy as he is to aid the worthy, and, perhaps, even more so, for in alms-giving more injury is probably done by rewarding vice than by relieving virtue.

The rich man is thus almost restricted to following the examples of Peter Cooper, Enoch Pratt of Baltimore, Mr. Pratt of Brooklyn, Senator Stanford, and others, who know that the best means of benefiting the community is to place within its reach the ladders upon which the aspiring can rise parks, and means of recreation, by which men are helped in body and mind; works of art, certain to give pleasure and improve the public taste, and public institutions of various kinds, which will improve the general condition of the people; in this manner returning their surplus wealth to the mass of their fellows in the forms best calculated to do them lasting good.

Thus is the problem of Rich and Poor to be solved. The laws of accumulation will be left free; the laws of distribution free. Individualism will continue, but the millionaire will be but a trustee for the poor; intrusted for a season with a great part of the increased wealth of the community, but administering it for the community far better than it could or would have done for itself. The best minds will thus have reached a stage in the development of the race in which it is clearly seen that there is no mode of disposing of surplus wealth creditable to thoughtful and earnest men into whose hands it flows save by using it year by year for the general good. This day already dawns. But a little while, and although, without incurring the pity of their fellows, men may die sharers in great business enterprises from which their capital cannot be or has not been withdrawn, and is left chiefly at death for public uses, yet the man who dies leaving behind him millions of available wealth, which was his to administer during life, will pass away "unwept, unhonored, and unsung," no matter to what uses he leaves the dross which he cannot take with him. Of such as these the public verdict will then be: "The man who dies thus rich dies disgraced."

Such, in my opinion, is the true Gospel concerning Wealth, obedience to which is destined some day to solve the problem of the rich and the Poor, and to bring "Peace on earth, among men Good-Will."

❧ How the Other Half Lives

JACOB A. RIIS

As a police reporter for the *New York Tribune,* Jacob A. Riis saw first-hand the abject conditions of New York City's Lower East Side. In 1890 the Danish-American reporter-turned-reformer published *How the Other Half Lives* documenting the overcrowded, dangerous and destitute conditions that marked immigrant city life. Riis used photographs to illustrate his explanations of urban slum life. Images of filthy tenement houses, barefoot boys dressed in rags sleeping on the street and dangerous alleyways with hoodlums poised menacingly alarmed the public. Photographs showed the problems in ways that words never could. As a result, Riis brought impetus to a tenement reform movement in the city and a national effort aimed at improving urban conditions. For the first time, photography was used as a tool in promoting social reform.

The street Arab is as much of an institution in New York as Newspaper Row, to which he gravitates naturally, following his Bohemian instinct. Crowded out of the tenements to shift for himself, and quite ready to do it, he meets the host of adventurous runaways from every State in the Union and from across the sea, whom New York attracts with a queer fascination, as it attracts older emigrants from all parts of the world. A census of the population in the Newsboys' Lodging-house on

any night will show such an odd mixture of small humanity as could hardly be got together in any other spot. It is a mistake to think that they are helpless little creatures, to be pitied and cried over because they are alone in the world. The unmerciful "guying" the good man would receive, who went to them with such a programme, would soon convince him that that sort of pity was wasted, and would very likely give him the idea that they were a set of hardened little scoundrels, quite beyond the reach of missionary effort.

But that would only be his second mistake. The Street Arab has all the faults and all the virtues of the lawless life he leads. Vagabond that he is, acknowledging no authority and owing no allegiance to anybody or anything, with his grimy fist raised against society whenever it tries to coerce him, he is as bright and sharp as the weasel, which, among all the predatory beasts, he most resembles. His sturdy independence, love of freedom and absolute self-reliance, together with his rude sense of justice that enables him to govern his little community, not always in accordance with municipal law or city ordinances, but often a good deal closer to the saving line of "doing to others as one would be done by"—these are strong handles by which those who know how can catch the boy and make him useful. Successful bankers, clergymen, and lawyers all over the country, statesmen in some instances of national repute, bear evidence in their lives to the potency of such missionary efforts. There is scarcely a learned profession, or branch of honorable business, that has not in the last twenty years borrowed some of its brightest light from the poverty and gloom of New York's streets.

Anyone, whom business or curiosity has taken through Park Row or across Printing House Square in the midnight hour, when the air is filled with the roar of great presses spinning with printers' ink on endless rolls of white paper the history of the world in twenty-four hours that have just passed away, has seen little groups of these boys hanging about the newspaper offices; in winter, when snow is on the streets, fighting for warm spots around the grated vent-holes that let out the heat and steam from the underground rooms with their noise and clatter, and in summer playing craps and 7-11 on the curb for their hard-earned pennies, with all the absorbing concern of hardened gamblers. This is their beat. Here the agent for the Society for the

Prevention of Cruelty to Children finds those he thinks too young for "business," but does not always capture them. Like rabbits in their burrows, the little ragamuffins sleep with at least one eye open, and every sense alert to the approach of danger: of their enemy, the policeman, whose chief business in life is to move them on, and of the agent bent on robbing them of their cherished freedom. At the first warning shot they scatter and are off. To pursue them would be like chasing the fleet-footed mountain goat in his rocky fastnesses.

❧ "Luck is not chance"

EMILY DICKINSON

Emily Dickinson lived a quiet, largely secluded life in Amherst, Massachusetts, from 1830 to 1886. Although she wrote more than 1,700 poems, few were published during her lifetime. In 1890, several of the poems were gathered together and published for the first time as a book. Dickinson's poetry has since become considered one of the great achievements of American literature—a single woman's musing about the great themes of life explored in simple, direct language.

Luck is not chance—
It's Toil—
Fortune's expensive smile
Is earned—.

I took one Draught of Life—
I'll tell you what I paid—
Precisely an existence—
The market price, they said.
They weighed me, Dust by Dust—
They balanced Film with Film,
Then handed me my Being's worth—
A single Dram of Heaven!

That such have died enable us
The tranquiller to die;
That such have lived, certificate
For immortality.

❧ "The labor movement is a fixed fact"

SAMUEL GOMPERS

A cigar maker, Samuel Gompers helped found the American Federation of Labor in 1886 and served as its president for almost 40 years. The AFL rapidly grew to become the most powerful single union in the United States at the turn of the century, boasting more than 1.7 million members in 1904. Gompers solidified the union's strength by focusing attention on the core membership issues of wages and hours of work, and rejecting radical efforts for comprehensive labor reform. Gompers delivered this address on May 1, 1890, in Louisville, Kentucky.

My friends, we have met here today to celebrate the idea that has prompted thousands of working-people of Louisville and New Albany to parade the streets of [your city]; that prompts the toilers of Chicago to turn out by their fifty or hundred thousand men; that prompts the vast army of wage-workers in New York to demonstrate their enthusiasm and appreciation of the importance of this idea; that prompts the toilers of England, Ireland, Germany, France, Italy, Spain, and Austria to defy the manifestos of the autocrats of the world and say that on May the first, 1890, the wage-workers of the world will lay down their tools in sympathy with the wage-workers of America, to establish a principle of limitations of hours of labor to eight hours for sleep, eight hours for work, and eight hours for what we will.

It has been charged time and again that were we to have more hours of leisure we would merely devote it to debauchery, to the cultivation of vicious habits—in other words, that we would get drunk. I desire to say this in answer to that charge: As a rule, there are two classes in society who get drunk. One is the class who has no work to do, because it can't get any, and gets drunk on its face. I maintain that that class in our social life that exhibits the greatest degree of sobriety is that class who are able, by a fair number of hours of day's work to earn fair wages—not overworked. The man who works twelve, fourteen, and sixteen hours a day requires some artificial stimulation to restore the life ground out of him in the drudgery of the day....

We ought to be able to discuss this question on a higher ground, and I am pleased to say that the movement in which we are engaged will stimulate us to it. They tell us that the eight-hour movement can not be enforced, for the reason that it must check industrial and commercial progress. I say that the history of this country, in its industrial and commercial relations, shows the reverse. I say that is the plane on which this question ought to be discussed—that is the social question. As long as they make this question an economic one, I am willing to discuss it with them. I would retrace every step I have taken to advance this movement did it mean industrial and commercial stagnation. But it does not mean that. It means greater prosperity; it means a greater degree of progress for the whole people; it means more advancement and intelligence, and a nobler race of people....

They say they can't afford it. Is that true? Let us see for one moment. If a reduction in the hours of labor causes industrial and commercial ruination, it would naturally follow increased hours of labor would increase the prosperity, commercial and industrial. If that were true, England and America ought to be at the tail end, and China at the head of civilization.

Is it not a fact that we find laborers in England and the United States, where the hours are eight, nine and ten hours a day—do we not find that employers and laborers are more successful? Don't we find them selling articles cheaper? We do not need to trust the modern moralist to tell us those things. In all industries where the hours of labor are long, there you will find the least development of the power of invention. Where the hours of labor are long, men are cheap, and where men are cheap there is no necessity for invention. How can you expect a man to work ten or twelve or fourteen hours at his calling and then devote any time to the invention of a machine or discovery of a new principle or force? If he be so fortunate as to be able to read a paper he will fall asleep before he has read through the second or third line.

Why, when you reduce the hours of labor, say an hour a day, just think what it means. Suppose men who work ten hours a day had the time lessened to nine, or men who work nine hours a day have it reduced to eight hours; what does it mean. It means millions of golden hours and opportunities for thought. Some men might say you will go to sleep. Well, some men might sleep sixteen hours a day; the ordinary man might try that, but he would soon find he could not do it long. He would have to do something. He would probably go to the theater one night, to a concert another night, but could not do that every night. He would probably become interested in some study and the hours that have been taken from manual labor are devoted to mental labor, and the mental labor of one hour will produce for him more wealth than the physical labor of a dozen hours.

I maintain that this is a true proposition—that men under the short-hour system not only have opportunity to improve themselves, but to make a greater degree of prosperity for their employers. Why, my friends, how is it in China, how is it in Spain, how is it in India and Russia, how is it in Italy? Cast your eye throughout the universe and observe the industry that forces nature to yield up its fruits to man's necessities, and you will find that where the hours of labor are the shortest the progress of invention in machinery and the prosperity of the people are the greatest. It is the greatest impediment to progress to hire men cheaply. Wherever men are cheap, there you find the least degree of progress. It has only been under the great influence of our great republic, where our people have exhibited their great senses, that we can move forward, upward and onward, and are watched with interest in our movements of progress and reform....

The man who works the long hours has no necessities except the barest to keep body and soul together, so he can work. He goes to sleep and dreams of work; he rises in the morning to go to work; he takes his frugal lunch to work; he comes home again to throw himself down on a miserable apology for a bed so that he can get that little rest that he may be able to go to work again. He is nothing but a veritable machine. He lives to work instead of working to live.

My friends, the only thing the working people need besides the necessities of life, is time. Time. Time with which our lives begin; time with which our lives close; time to cultivate the better nature within us; time to brighten our homes. Time, which brings us from the lowest condition up to the highest civilization; time, so that we can raise men to a higher plane.

My friends, you will find that it has been ascertained that there is more than a million brothers and sisters—able-bodied men and women—on the streets, and on the highways and byways of our country willing to work but cannot find it. You know that it is the theory of our government that we can work or cease to work at will. It is only a theory. You know that it is only a theory and not a fact. It is true that we can cease to work when we want to, but I deny that we can work when we will, so long as there are a million idle men and women tramping the streets of our cities, searching for work. The theory that we can work or cease to work when we will is a delusion and a snare. It is a lie.

What we want to consider is, first, to make our employment more secure, and, secondly, to make wages more permanent, and, thirdly, to give these poor people a chance to work. The laborer has been regarded as a mere producing machine…but the back of labor is the soul of man and honesty of purpose and aspiration. Now you can not, as the political economists and college professors [do], say that labor is a commodity to be bought and sold. I say we are American citizens with the heritage of all the great men who have stood before us; men who have sacrificed all in the cause except honor. Our enemies would like to see this movement thrust into Hades, they would like to see it in a warmer climate, but I say to you that this labor movement has come to stay. Like Banquo's ghost, it will not stay down. I say the labor movement is a fixed fact. It has grown out of the necessities of the people, and, although some may desire to see it fail, still the labor movement will be found to have a strong lodgment in the hearts of the people, and we will go on until success has been achieved.

We want eight hours and nothing less. We have been accused of being selfish, and it has been said that we will want more; that last year we got an advance of ten cents and now we want more. We do want more. You will find that a man generally wants more. Go and ask a tramp what he wants, and if he doesn't want a drink, he wants a good, square meal. You ask a workingman, who is getting two dollars a day, and he will say that he wants ten cents more. Ask a man who gets five dollars a day and he will want fifty cents more. The man who receives five thousand dollars a year wants six thousand dollars a year, and the man who owns eight or nine hundred thousand dollars will want a hundred thousand dollars more to make it a million, while the man who has his millions will want everything he can lay his hands on and then raise his voice against the poor devil who wants ten cents more a day. We live in the later part of the nineteenth century. In the age of electricity and steam that has produced wealth a hundred fold, we insist that it has been brought about by the intelligence and energy of the workingmen, and while we find that is now easier to produce it is harder to live. We do want more, and when it becomes more, we shall still want more. And we shall never cease to demand more until we have received the results of our labor.

❧ Sherman Antitrust Act

U. S. CONGRESS

By 1890 there was widespread popular discontent with the rise of business "trusts" that controlled entire industrial sectors. Both Republican and Democratic political parties in 1888 included anti-monopoly plans in their platforms. To check the power of business monopolies, Congress passed the Sherman Antitrust Act of 1890. Although the legislation was a landmark in that it represented the first time the government attempted to impose controls on monopolistic practices, the act was very ambiguous and vague. It proved to be very difficult to enforce its provisions against businesses. Ironically, the act was successfully used to prevent labor unions from taking collective action. In 1892, a Connecticut manufacturer claimed that a nationwide boycott organized by a hatters' union was a form of restraint of trade prohibited by the Sherman Antitrust Act. The Supreme Court agreed. When the Clayton Act was passed in 1914 to strengthen the antitrust act, the new legislation specifically exempted labor unions.

Be it enacted by the Senate and House of Representatives of the United States of America in Congress assembled,

Section 1. Every contract, combination in the form of trust or otherwise, or conspiracy, in restraint of trade or commerce among the several States, or with foreign nations, is hereby declared to be illegal. Every person who shall make any such contract or engage in any such combination or conspiracy, shall be deemed guilty of a misdemeanor, and, on conviction thereof, shall be punished by fine not exceeding five thousand dollars, or by imprisonment not exceeding one year, or by both said punishments, in the discretion of the court.

Section 2. Every person who shall monopolize, or attempt to monopolize, or combine or conspire with any other person or persons, to monopolize any part of the trade or commerce among the several States, or with foreign nations, shall be deemed guilty of a misdemeanor, and, on conviction thereof, shall be punished by fine not exceeding one year, or by both said punishments, in the discretion of the court.

Section 3. Every contract, combination in form or otherwise, or conspiracy, in restraint of trade or commerce in any Territory of the United States or of the District of Columbia, or in restraint of trade or commerce between any such Territory and another, or between any such Territory or Territories and any State or States or the District of Columbia, or with foreign nations, or between the District of Columbia and any State or States or foreign nations, is hereby deemed illegal. Every person who shall make any such contract or engage in any such combination or conspiracy, shall be deemed guilty of a misdemeanor, and, on conviction thereof, shall be punished by fine not exceeding five thousand dollars, or by imprisonment not exceeding one year, or by both said punishments, in the discretion of the court.

Section 4. The several circuit courts of the United States are hereby invested with jurisdiction to prevent and restrain violations of this act.… Such proceedings may be by way of petition setting forth the case and praying that such violation shall be enjoined or otherwise prohibited.…

Section 7. Any person who shall be injured in his business or property by any other person or corporation by reason of anything forbidden or declared to be unlawful by this act, may sue therefor…and shall recover three fold the damages by him sustained, and the costs of suit, including a reasonable attorney's fee.

❧ "It was one long grave of butchered women and children and babies"

BLACK ELK RECALLS WOUNDED KNEE

Imprisoned, decimated by disease and trapped on unwanted Indian reservations, Native Americans from the Great Plains turned to a new mysticism for spiritual relief. A religious ceremony known as the Ghost Dance became very popular. The ceremony was based on the belief that a great prophet would arrive and make the whites vanish. Concerned that the Ghost Dance would prompt resistance, government authorities sought to ban the ceremony. Soldiers came to arrest Lakota Sioux Chief Sitting Bull on December 15, 1890, because of fears that he would endorse the Ghost Dance. A fight broke out, however, and Sitting Bull was killed.

Afraid of further military retribution, Sitting Bull's tribe, the Minicounjous, fled. The army tracked the tribe down on December 28 and took them to Wounded Knee Creek at the Pine Ridge Sioux Reservation. The next morning, as the troops were disarming the tribe, shots broke out and a massacre ensued. As many as 300 men, women and children were killed. Survivors totaled four men and forty-seven women and children. The incident marked the last armed conflict between Native Americans and the United States. Black Elk recalled the battle many years later.

That evening before it happened, I went in to Pine Ridge and heard these things, and while I was there, soldiers started for where the Big Foots were. These made about five hundred soldiers that were there next morning. When I saw them starting I felt that something terrible was going to happen. That night I could hardly sleep at all. I walked around most of the night.

In the morning I went out after my horses, and while I was out I heard shooting off toward the east, and I knew from the sound that it must be wagon-guns going off. The sounds went right through my body, and I felt that something terrible would happen.

When I reached camp with the horses, a man rode up to me and said: "Hey-hey-hey! The people that are coming are fired on! I know it!"

I saddled up my buckskin and put on my sacred shirt. It was one I had made to be worn by no one but myself. It had a spotted eagle outstretched on the back of it, and the daybreak star was on the left shoulder, because when facing south that shoulder is toward the east. Across the breast, from the left shoulder to the right hip, was the flaming rainbow, and there was another rainbow around the neck, like a necklace, with a star at the bottom. At each shoulder, elbow, and wrist was an eagle feather; and over the whole shirt were red streaks of lightning. You will see that this was from my great vision, and you will know how it protected me that day.

I painted my face all red, and in my hair I put one eagle feather for the One Above. It did not take me long to get ready, for I could still hear the shooting over there.

I started out alone on the old road that ran across the hills to Wounded Knee. I had no gun. I carried only the sacred bow of the west that I had seen in my great vision. I had gone only a little way when a band of young men came galloping after me. The first two who came up were Loves War and Iron Wasichu. I asked what they were going to do, and they said they were just going to see where the shooting was. Then others were coming up, and some older men.

We rode fast, and there were about twenty of us now. The shooting was getting louder. A horseback from over there came galloping very fast toward us, and he said: "Hey-hey-hey! They have murdered them!" Then he whipped his horse and rode away faster toward Pine Ridge.

In a little while we had come to the top of the ridge where, looking to the east, you can see for the first time the monument and the burying ground on the little hill where the church is. That is where the terrible thing started. Just south of the burying ground on the little hill a deep dry gulch runs about east and west, very crooked, and it rises westward to nearly the top of the ridge where we were. It had no name, but the Wasichus sometimes call it Battle Creek now. We stopped on the ridge not far from the head of the dry gulch. Wagon-guns were still going off over there on the little hill, and they were going off again where they hit along the gulch. There was much shooting down yonder, and there were many cries, and we could see cavalrymen scattered over the hills ahead of us. Cavalrymen were riding along the gulch and shooting into it, where the women and children were running away and trying to hide in the gullies and the stunted pines.

A little way ahead of us, just below the head of the dry gulch, there were some women and chil-dren who were huddled under a clay bank, and some cavalrymen were there pointing guns at them.

We stopped back behind the ridge, and I said to the others: "Take courage. These are our relatives. We will try to get them back." Then we all sang a song which went like this:

A thunder being nation I am, I have said.
A thunder being nation I am, I have said.
You shall live. You shall live.
You shall live. You shall live.

Then I rode over the ridge and the others after me, and we were crying: "Take courage! It is time to fight!" The soldiers who were guarding our relatives shot at us and then ran away fast, and some more cavalrymen on the other side of the gulch did too. We got our relatives and sent them across the ridge to the northwest where they would be safe.

I had no gun, and when we were charging, I just held the sacred bow out in front of me with my right hand. The bullets did not hit us at all.

We found a little baby lying all alone near the head of the gulch. I could not pick her up just then, but I got her later and some of my people adopted her. I just wrapped her up tighter in a shawl that was around her and left her there. It was a safe place, and I had other work to do.

The soldiers had run eastward over the hills where there were some more soldiers, and they were off their horses and lying down. I told the others to stay back, and I charged upon them holding the sacred bow out toward them with my right hand. They all shot at me, and I could hear bullets all around me, but I ran my horse right close to them, and then swung around. Some soldiers across the gulch began shooting at me too, but I got back to the others and was not hurt at all.

By now many other Lakotas, who had heard the shooting, were coming up from Pine Ridge, and we all charged on the soldiers. They ran eastward toward where the trouble began. We followed down along the dry gulch, and what we saw was terrible. Dead and wounded women and children and little babies were scattered all along there where they had been trying to run away. The soldiers had followed along the gulch, as they ran, and murdered them in there. Sometimes they were in heaps because they had huddled together, and some were scattered all along. Sometimes bunches of them had been killed and torn to pieces where the wagon-guns hit them. I saw a little baby trying to suck its mother, but she was bloody and dead.

There were two little boys at one place in this gulch. They had guns and they had been killing soldiers all by themselves. We could see the soldiers they had killed. The boys were all alone there, and they were not hurt. These were very brave little boys.

When we drove the soldiers back, they dug themselves in, and we were not enough people to drive them out from there. In the evening they marched off up Wounded Knee Creek, and then we saw all that they had done there.

Men and women and children were heaped and scattered all over the flat at the bottom of the little hill where the soldiers had their wagon-guns, and westward up the dry gulch all the way to the high ridge, the dead women and children and babies were scattered.

When I saw this I wished that I had died too, but I was not sorry for the women and children. It was better for them to be happy in the other world, and I wanted to be there too. But before I went there I wanted to have revenge. I thought there might be a day, and we should have revenge.

After the soldiers marched away, I heard from my friend, Dog Chief, how the trouble started, and he was right there by Yellow Bird when it happened. This is the way it was:

In the morning the soldiers began to take all the guns away from the Big Foots, who were camped in the flat below the little hill where the monument and burying ground are now. The people had stacked most of their guns, and even their knives, by the tepee where Big Foot was lying sick. Soldiers were on the little hill and all around, and there were soldiers across the dry gulch to the south and over east along Wounded Knee Creek too. The people were nearly surrounded, and the wagon guns were pointing at them.

Some had not yet given up their guns, and so the soldiers were searching all the tepees, throwing things around and poking into everything. There was a man called Yellow Bird, and he and another man were standing in front of the tepee where Big Foot was lying sick. They had white sheets around and over them, with eyeholes to look through, and they had guns under these. An officer came to search them. He took the other man's gun, and then started to take Yellow Bird's. But Yellow Bird would not let go. He wrestled with the officer, and while they were wrestling, the gun went off and killed the officer. Wasichus and some others have said he meant to do this, but Dog Chief was standing right there, and he told me it was not so. As soon as the gun went off, Dog Chief told me, an officer shot and killed Big Foot who was lying sick inside the tepee.

Then suddenly nobody knew what was happening, except that the soldiers were all shooting and the wagon-guns began going off right in among the people.

Many were shot down right there. The women and children ran into the gulch and up west, dropping all the time, for the soldiers shot them as they ran. There were only about a hundred warriors and there were nearly five hundred soldiers. The warriors rushed to where they had piled their guns and knives. They fought soldiers with only their hands until they got their guns.

Dog Chief saw Yellow Bird run into a tepee with his gun, and from there he killed soldiers until the tepee caught fire. Then he died full of bullets.

It was a good winter day when all this happened. The sun was shining. But after the soldiers marched away from their dirty work, a heavy snow began to fall. The wind came up in the night. There was a big blizzard, and it grew very cold. The snow drifted deep in the crooked gulch, and it was one long grave of butchered women and children and babies, who had never done any harm and were only trying to run away.

CHAPTER SEVEN

1892–1918

Progressive Era

🌿 "The interests of rural and civic labor are the same; their enemies are identical"

THE POPULIST PARTY PLATFORM

Plunging grain prices devastated farmers during the 1880s and 1890s. Saddled with mortgages, farmers struggled to meet loan payments as their incomes fell. Many banks foreclosed on farms. Farmers resented the high costs of hauling their goods to markets by rail. Facing a desperate situation, farmers united with the labor movement to form the Populist Party demanding a wide range of reform aimed at curtailing the nation's money interests.

In 1892 the energized fledgling party met in Omaha, Nebraska, to nominate former Iowa Congressman Robert Weaver as its presidential candidate and to forge a party platform. They called for the nationalization of railroads, a national monetary system regulated by the federal government, a graduated income tax, labor reform, an eight-hour day, a single-term limit for the presidency, the direct election of senators, immigration restrictions and several other reforms. Weaver garnered more than 1 million votes and 22 electoral votes from Colorado, Idaho, Kansas and Nevada. Several seats from western states were also won by Populist candidates.

The party collapsed in 1896 when the Democrats nominated Populist William Jennings Bryant for president, undermining the fledgling party's support. Nevertheless, many of the Populist Party's proposals were enacted by the government over the next 20 years during the Progressive Era.

Assembled upon the 116th anniversary of the Declaration of Independence, the People's Party of America, in their fist national convention, invoking upon their action the blessing of Almighty God, put forth in the name and on behalf of the people of this country, the following preamble and declaration of principles:

Preamble

The conditions which surround us best justify our co-operation; we meet in the midst of a nation brought to the verge of moral, political, and material ruin. Corruption dominates the ballot box, the legislatures, the Congress, and touches even the ermine of the bench. The people are demoralized; most of the states have been compelled to isolate the voters at the polling places to prevent universal intimidation and bribery. The newspapers are large-

ly subsidized or muzzled, public opinion silenced, business prostrated, homes covered with mortgages, labor impoverished, and the land concentrating in the hands of capitalists. The urban workmen are denied the right to organize for self-protection, imported pauperized labor beats down their wages, a hireling standing army, unrecognized by our laws, is established to shoot them down, and they are rapidly degenerating into European conditions. The fruits of the toil of millions are boldly stolen to build up colossal fortunes for a few, unprecedented in the history of mankind; and the possessors of those, in turn, despise the Republic and endanger liberty. From the same prolific womb of governmental injustice we breed the two great classes— tramps and millionaires.

The national power to create money is appropriated to enrich bondholders; a vast public debt payable in legal tender currency has been funded into gold-bearing bonds, thereby adding millions to the burdens of the people.

Silver, which has been accepted as coin since the dawn of history, has been demonetized to add to the purchasing power of gold by decreasing the value of all forms of property as well as human labor, and the supply of currency is purposely abridged to fatten usurers, bankrupt enterprise, and enslave industry. A vast conspiracy against mankind has been organized on two continents, and it is rapidly taking possession of the world. If not met and overthrown at once, it forebodes terrible social convulsions, the destruction of civilization, or the establishment of an absolute despotism.

We have witnessed for more than a quarter of a century the struggles of the two great political parties for power and plunder, while grievous wrongs have been inflicted upon the suffering people. We charge that the controlling influences dominating both these parties have permitted the existing dreadful conditions to develop without serious effort to prevent or restrain them. Neither do they now promise us any substantial reform. They have agreed together to ignore, in the coming campaign, every issue but one. They propose to drown the outcries of a plunderer people with the uproar of a sham battle over the tariff, so that capitalists, corporations, national banks, rings, trusts, watered stock, the demonetization of silver, and the oppressions of the usurers may all be lost sight of. They propose to sacrifice our homes, lives, and children on the altar of mammon; to destroy the multitude in order to secure corruption funds from the millionaires....

We seek to restore the government of the Republic to the hands of "the plain people," with which class it originated. We assert our purposes to be identical with the purposes of the national Constitution; to form a more perfect union and establish justice, insure domestic tranquility, provide for the common defense, promote the general welfare, and secure the blessings of liberty for ourselves and our posterity.

We declare that this Republic can only endure as a free government while built upon the love of the people for each other and for the nation; that it cannot be pinned together by bayonets; that the Civil War is over, and that every passion and resentment which grew out of it must die with it, and that we must be in fact, as we are in name, one united brotherhood of free men.

Our country finds itself confronted by conditions for which there is no precedent in the history of the world; our annual agricultural productions amount to billions of dollars in value, which must, within a few weeks or months, be exchanged for billions of dollars' worth of commodities consumed in their production; the existing currency supply is wholly inadequate to make this exchange; the results are falling prices, the formation of combines and rings, the impoverishment of the producing class. We pledge ourselves that if given power we will labor to correct these evils by wise and reasonable legislation, in accordance with the terms of our platform.

We believe that the power of government—in other words, of the people—should be expanded (as in the case of the postal service) as rapidly and as far as the good sense of an intelligent people and the teachings of experience shall justify, to the end that oppression, injustice, and poverty shall eventually cease in the land....

[W]e ask all men to first help us to determine whether we are to have a republic to administer before we differ as to the conditions upon which it is to be administered, believing that the forces of reform this day organized will never cease to move forward until every wrong is righted and equal rights and equal privileges securely established for all the men and women of this country.

We declare, therefore:

First: That the union of the labor forces of the United States this day consummated shall be permanent and perpetual....

Second: Wealth belongs to him who creates it, and every dollar taken from industry without an equivalent is robbery. "If any will not work, neither shall he eat." The interests of rural and civic labor are the same; their enemies are identical.

Third: We believe that the time has come when the railroad corporations will either own the people or the people must own the railroads, and should the government enter upon the work of owning and managing all railroads, we should favor an amendment to the Constitution by which all persons engaged in the government service shall be placed under a civil service regulation of the most rigid character, so as to prevent the increase of the power of the national administration by the use of such additional government employees.

Finance: We demand a national currency, safe, sound, and flexible, issued by the general government only, a full legal tender for all debts, public and private, and that without the use of banking corporations, a just, equitable, and efficient means of distribution direct to the people....

Transportation: Transportation being a means of exchange and a public necessity, the government should own and operate the railroads in the interest of the people. The telegraph and telephone, like the post-office system, being a necessity for the transmission of news, should be owned and operated by the government in the interest of the people.

Land: The land, including all the natural sources of wealth, is the heritage of the people, and should not be monopolized for speculative purposes, and alien ownership of land should be prohibited. All land now held by railroads and other corporations in excess of their actual needs, and all lands now owned by aliens should be reclaimed by the government and held for actual settlers only....

1. Resolved, That we demand a free ballot and a fair count in all elections, and pledge ourselves to secure it...[for] every legal voter without federal intervention, through the adoption by the states of the unperverted Australian, or secret ballot, system.

2. Resolved, That the revenue derived from a graduated income tax should be applied to the reduction of the burden of taxation now levied upon the domestic industries of this country.

3. Resolved, That we pledge our support to fair and liberal pensions to ex-Union soldiers and sailors.

4. Resolved, That we condemn the fallacy of protecting American labor under the present system, which opens our ports to the pauper and criminal classes of the world and crowds out our wage earners; and we denounce the present ineffective laws against contract labor, and demand the further restriction of undesirable emigration.

5. Resolved, That we cordially sympathize with the efforts of organized workingmen to shorten the hours of labor, and demand a rigid enforcement of the existing eight-hour law on government work, and ask that a penalty clause be added to the said law.

6. Resolved, That we regard the maintenance of a large standing army of mercenaries, known as the Pinkerton system, as a menace to our liberties, and we demand its abolition; and we condemn the recent invasion of the territory of Wyoming by the hired assassins of plutocracy, assisted by federal officers.

7. Resolved, That we commend to the favorable consideration of the people and the reform press the legislative system known as the initiative and referendum.

8. Resolved, That we favor a constitutional provision limiting the office of President and Vice-President to one term, and providing for the election of Senators of the United States by a direct vote of the people.

9. Resolved, That we oppose any subsidy or national aid to any private corporation for any purpose.

10. Resolved, That this convention sympathizes with the Knights of Labor and their righteous contest with the tyrannical combine of clothing manufacturers of Rochester, and declare it to be the duty of all who hate tyranny and oppression to refuse to purchase the goods made by the said manufacturers, or to patronize any merchants who sell such goods.

❧ "The frontier has gone"

FREDERICK JACKSON TURNER

On July 12, 1893, historian Frederick Jackson Turner read his essay "The Significance of the Frontier in American History" to the American Historical Association in Chicago, instantly changing the way Americans viewed their own history. Before the young Wisconsin man delivered his address, American history was viewed as an extension of Europe. Turner opened an entirely new interpretation, saying that the source of American innovation and democracy was derived from the western frontier. Having grown up on the frontier in Wisconsin and studied European history, Turner argued that the West shaped the character of the United States, helping to forge a national image of individual self-reliance and a democratic society.

Turner's thesis—which coincided with the end of the Western frontier on the continental United States—was widely accepted at the time but has since been marked by controversy. Critics have objected to Turner's insensitivity to Native Americans and for placing too much of an emphasis on the benefits of individualism. Nevertheless, the concept of finding new frontiers stayed in the forefront of the American conscience throughout the 20th century, whether it meant physically finding new frontiers through imperialistic adventures at the turn of the century or achieving new idealized states of equality or opportunity.

In a recent bulletin of the superintendent of the census for 1890 appear these significant words: "Up to and including 1880 the country had a frontier of settlement, but at present the unsettled area has been so broken into by isolated bodies of settlement that there can hardly be said to be a frontier line. In the discussion of its extent, its westward movement, etc., it cannot, therefore, any longer have a place in the census reports." This brief official statement marks the closing of a great historic movement. Up to our own day American history has been in a large degree the history of the colonization of the Great West. The existence of an area of free land, its continuous recession, and the advance of American settlement westward explain American development.

Behind institutions, behind constitutional forms and modifications, lie the vital forces that call these organs into life and shape them to meet changing conditions. The peculiarity of American institutions is the fact that they have been compelled to adapt themselves to the changes of an expanding people—to the changes involved in crossing a continent, in winning a wilderness, and in developing at each area of this progress, out of the primitive economic and political conditions of the frontier, the complexity of city life. Said Calhoun in 1817, "We are great, and rapidly—I was about to say fearfully—growing!" So saying, he touched on the distinguishing feature of American life. All peoples show development: the germ theory of politics has been sufficiently emphasized. In the case of most nations, however, the development has occurred in a limited area; and if the nation has expanded, it has met other growing peoples whom it has conquered. But in the case of the United States we have a different phenomenon. Limiting our attention to the Atlantic coast, we have the familiar phenomenon of the evolution of institutions in a limited area, such as the rise of representative government; the differentiation of simple colonial governments into complex organs; the progress from primitive industrial society, without division of labor, up to manufacturing civilization. But we have in addition to this a recurrence of the process of evolution in each Western area reached in the process of expansion. Thus American development has exhibited not merely advance along a single line but a return to primitive conditions on a continually advancing frontier line, and a new development for that area. American social development has been continually beginning over again on the frontier. This perennial rebirth, this fluidity of American life, this expansion westward with its new opportunities, its continuous touch with the simplicity of primitive society, furnish the forces dominating American character. The true point of view in the history of this nation is not the Atlantic coast, it is the Great West. Even the slavery struggle, which is made so exclusive an object of attention by writers like Professor von Hoist, occupies its important place in American history because of its relation to westward expansion.

In this advance the frontier is the outer edge of the wave—the meeting point between savagery and civilization. Much has been written about the frontier from the point of view of border warfare and the chase, but as a field for the serious study of the economist and the historian it has been neglected.

What is the frontier? It is not the European frontier—a fortified boundary line running through dense populations. The most significant thing about it is that it lies at the hither edge of free land. In the census reports it is treated as the margin of that settlement which has a density of two or more people to the square mile. The term is an elastic one, and for our purpose does not need sharp definition. We shall consider the whole frontier belt, including the Indian country and the outer margin of the "settled area" of the census

reports. This paper will make no attempt to treat the subject exhaustively; its aim is simply to call attention to the frontier as a fertile field for investigation, and to suggest some of the problems which arise in connection with it.

In the settlement of America we have to observe how European life entered the continent, and how America modified and developed that life, and reacted on Europe. Our early history is the study of European germs developing in an American environment. Too exclusive attention has been paid by institutional students to the Germanic origins, too little to the American factors. The frontier is the line of most rapid and effective Americanization. The wilderness masters the colonist. It finds him a European in dress, industries, tools, modes of travel, and thought. It takes him from the railroad car and puts him in the birch canoe. It strips off the garments of civilization, and arrays him in the hunting shirt and the moccasin. It puts him in the log cabin of the Cherokee and the Iroquois, and runs an Indian palisade around him. Before long he has gone to planting Indian corn and plowing with a sharp stick; he shouts the war cry and takes the scalp in orthodox Indian fashion. In short, at the frontier the environment is at first too strong for the man. He must accept the conditions which it furnishes, or perish, and so he fits himself into the Indian clearings and follows the Indian trails. Little by little he transforms the wilderness, but the outcome is not the old Europe, not simply the development of Germanic germs, any more than the first phenomenon was a case of reversion to the Germanic mark. The fact is that here is a new product that is American. At first the frontier was the Atlantic coast. It was the frontier of Europe in a very real sense. Moving westward, the frontier became more and more American. As successive terminal moraines result from successive glaciations, so each frontier leaves its traces behind it, and when it becomes a settled area the region still partakes of the frontier characteristics. Thus the advance of the frontier has meant a steady movement away from the influence of Europe, a steady growth of independence on American lines. And to study this advance, the men who grew up under these conditions, and the political, economic, and social results of it, is to study the really American part of our history....

Growth of Democracy

[T]he most important effect of the frontier has been in the promotion of democracy here and in Europe. As has been pointed out, the frontier is productive of individualism. Complex society is precipitated by the wilderness into a kind of primitive organization based on the family. The tendency is anti-social. It produces antipathy to control, and particularly to any direct control. The tax-gatherer is viewed as a representative of oppression. Professor Osgood, in an able article, has pointed out that the frontier conditions prevalent in the colonies are important factors in the explanation of the American Revolution, where individual liberty was sometimes confused with absence of all effective government. The same conditions aid in explaining the difficulty of instituting a strong government in the period of the confederacy. The frontier individualism has from the beginning promoted democracy.

The frontier states that came into the Union in the first quarter of a century of its existence came in with democratic suffrage provisions, and had reactive effects of the highest importance upon the older states whose peoples were being attracted there. It was western New York that forced an extension of suffrage in the constitutional convention of that state in 1821; and it was western Virginia that compelled the tidewater region to put a more liberal suffrage provision in the constitution framed in 1830, and to give to the frontier region a more nearly proportionate representation with the tidewater aristocracy. The rise of democracy as an effective force in the nation came in with Western preponderance under Jackson and William Henry Harrison, and it meant the triumph of the frontier—with all of its good and with all of its evil elements.

An interesting illustration of the tone of frontier democracy in 1830 comes from the debates in the Virginia convention already referred to. A representative from western Virginia declared: "But, sir, it is not the increase of population in the West which this gentleman ought to fear. It is the energy which the mountain breeze and western habits impart to those emigrants. They are regenerated, politically I mean, sir. They soon become working politicians; and the difference, sir, between a talking and a working politician is immense. The Old Dominion has long been celebrated for producing great orators; the ablest metaphysicians in policy; men that can split hairs in all abstruse questions of political economy. But at home, or when they return from congress, they have negroes to fan them asleep. But a Pennsylvania, a New York, an Ohio, or a western Virginia statesman, though far inferior in logic, metaphysics and rhetoric to an old Virginia statesman, has this advantage, that when he returns home he takes off his coat and takes hold of the plough. This gives him bone and muscle, sir, and preserves his republican principles pure and uncontaminated."

So long as free land exists, the opportunity for a competency exists, and economic power secures political power. But democracy born of free land, strong in selfishness and individualism, intolerant of administrative experience and education, and pressing individual liberty beyond its proper bounds, has its dangers as well as its benefits. Individualism in America has allowed a laxity in regard to governmental affairs which has rendered possible the spoils system, and all the manifest evils that follow from the lack of a highly developed civic spirit. In this connection may be noted also the influence of frontier conditions in permitting lax business honor, inflated paper currency, and wildcat banking. The colonial and Revolutionary frontier was the region whence emanated many of the worst forms of an evil currency. The West in the War of 1812 repeated the phenomenon on the frontier of that day, while the speculation and wildcat banking of the period of the crisis of 1837 occurred on the new frontier belt of the next tier of states. Thus each one of the periods of lax financial integrity coincides with periods when a new set of frontier communities had arisen, and coincides in area with these successive frontiers, for the most part. The recent Populist agitation is a case in point. Many a state that now declines any connection with the tenets of the Populists itself adhered to such ideas in an earlier stage of the development of the state. A primitive society can hardly be expected to show the intelligent appreciation of the complexity of business interests in a developed society. The continual recurrence of these areas of paper-money agitation is another evidence that the frontier can be isolated and studied as a factor in American history of the highest importance....

Intellectual Traits

From the conditions of frontier life came intellectual traits of profound importance. The works of travelers along each frontier from colonial days onward describe for each certain traits, and these traits have, while softening down, still persisted as survivals in the place of their origin, even when a higher social organization succeeded. The result is that to the frontier the American intellect owes its striking characteristics. That coarseness and strength combined with acuteness and inquisitiveness, that practical, inventive turn of mind, quick to find expedients, that masterful grasp of material things, lacking in the artistic but powerful to effect great ends, that restless, nervous energy, that dominant individualism, working for good and for evil, and withal that buoyancy and exuberance which comes with freedom, these are traits of the frontier, or traits called out elsewhere because of the existence of the frontier. Since the days when the fleet of Columbus sailed into the waters of the New World, America has been another name for opportunity, and the people of the United States have taken their tone from the incessant expansion which has not only been open but has even been forced upon them. He would be a rash prophet who should assert that the expansive character of American life has now entirely ceased. Movement has been its dominant fact, and, unless this training has no effect upon a people, the American intellect will continually demand a wider field for its exercise. But never again will such gifts of free land offer themselves. For a moment at the frontier the bonds of custom are broken, and unrestraint is triumphant. There is no tabula rasa. The stubborn American environment is there with its imperious summons to accept its conditions; the inherited ways of doing things are also there; and yet, in spite of environment, and in spite of custom, each frontier did indeed furnish a new field of opportunity, a gate of escape from the bondage of the past; and freshness, and confidence, and scorn of older society, impatience of its restraints and its ideas, and indifference to its lessons, have accompanied the frontier. What the Mediterranean Sea was to the Greeks, breaking the bond of custom, offering new experiences, calling out new institutions and activities, that, and more, the ever retreating frontier has been to the United States directly, and to the nations of Europe more remotely. And now, four centuries from the discovery of America, at the end of a hundred years of life under the Constitution, the frontier has gone, and with its going has closed the first period of American history.

✌ "My sister…forgot, and talked, and just that minute her finger was off"

HELEN CAMPBELL

Hundreds of thousands of children helped provide the labor to fuel the industrial boom of late 19th and early 20th century. Helen Campbell, a New York City missionary, was one of several people to help raise public awareness of the horrendous conditions many small children labored under. Her book *Darkness and Daylight, or Lights and Shadows of New York Life* described what she witnessed in the slums of New York during the 1890s.

Unions such as the Knights of Labor advocated for legislation prohibiting child labor. The Progressive movement of the early 1900s made child labor reform a central plank in its political platform. Several states passed legislation banning child labor. In 1916 Congress passed a child labor law that in 1918 the Supreme Court deemed unconstitutional for interfering in local labor conditions. In 1924 Congress passed a constitutional amendment banning child labor but the proposal fell short of the required state support. It was not until the Fair Labor Standards Act of 1938 that the federal government effectively banned the employment of children 16 and under in manufacturing and mining.

In one night-school eighty of them [girls] registered as "nurses." Being interpreted, this means that they take care of the baby at home while the mother goes out to "day's work." It is astonishing to see the real motherliness of the little things, who lug about the baby with devotion; and if they feed it on strange diet they are but following in the footsteps of the mothers, who regard the baby at six months old as the sharer of whatever the family bill of fare has to offer. The small German child is early to take his portion of lager;…the Irish children have tea or coffee and even a sup of the "craytur…."

I have seen a six-year-old girl scrubbing the floor of the one room in which lived a widowed mother and three children.

"She's a widdy washerwoman," said the dot, a creature with big blue eyes and a thin eager little face. "Yes, ma'am, she's a widdy washerwoman, an' I keep house. That's the baby there, an' he's good all the time, savin' whin his teeth is too big for him. It's teeth that's hard on babies, but I mind him good an' he thinks more o' me than he does of mother. See how beautiful he sucks at the pork."

The small housekeeper pointed with pride to the bed, where the tiny baby lay, a strip of fat pork in his mouth.

"He's weakly like, an' mother gives him the pork to set him up. An' he takes his sup o' tay beautiful too. Whin the summer comes we'll get to have him go to the Children's Home at Bath, maybe, or down to Coney Island or somewhere. I might be a 'Fresh Air' child meself, but I have to keep house you know, an' so mother can't let me go."

This is one phase of child-labor, and the most natural and innocent one, though it is a heavy burden to lay on small shoulders, and premature age and debility are its inevitable results. Far truer is this of the long hours in shop or manufactory. A child of eight—one of a dozen in a shop on Walker Street—stripped feathers, and had for a year earned three dollars a week. In this case the father was dead and the mother sick, and the little thing went home to do such cooking as she could. Like many a worker, she had already learned to take strong tea and to believe that it gave her strength. She was dwarfed in growth from confinement in the air of the workshop, from lack of proper food and no play, and thousands of these little feather-strippers are in like case.

In another workshop in the same neighborhood, children of from eight to ten, and one much younger, cut the feathers from cock-tails. The hours were from eight to six, and so for ten hours daily they bent over the work, which included cutting from the stem, steaming, curling, and packing.

Eight thousand children make envelopes at three and a half cents a thousand. They gum, separate, and sort. The hours are the same, but the rooms are generally lighter and better ventilated than the feather workers' surroundings. Many more burnish china, for, strange as it may seem, the most delicate ware is entrusted to children of ten or twelve. The burnishing instrument is held close against the breast, and this is a fruitful source of sickness, since the constant pressure brings with it various stomach and other troubles, dyspepsia being the chief.

Paper collars employ a host. The youngest bend over them, for even a child of five can do this. One child of twelve counts and boxes twenty thousand a day, and one who pastes the lining on the Buttonholes does five thousand a day. Over ten thousand children make paper boxes. Even in the making of gold-leaf a good many are employed, though chiefly young girls of fifteen and upwards. It is one of the most exhausting of the trades, as no air can be admitted, and the atmosphere is stifling.

Feathers, flowers, and tobacco employ the greatest number. A child of six can strip tobacco or cut feathers. In one great firm, employing over a thousand men, women, and children, a woman of eighty and her grandchild of four sit side by side and strip the leaves.... With the exception of match-making and one or two other industries there is hardly a trade so deadly in its effects. There are many operations which children are competent to carry on, and the phases of work done at home in the tenement-houses often employ the entire family....

In a report of the State Bureau of Labor it is stated that in one room less than twelve by fourteen feet, whose duplicate can be found at many points, a family of seven worked. Three of these, all girls, were under ten years of age. Tobacco lay in piles on the floor and under the long table at one end where cigars were rolled. Two of the children sat on the floor, stripping the leaves, and another sat on a small stool. A girl of twenty sat near them, and all had sores on lips, cheeks, and hands. Some four thousand women are engaged in this industry, and an equal number of unregistered young children share it with them. As in sewing, a number of women often club together and use one room, and in such cases their babies crawl about in the filth on the wet floors, playing with the damp tobacco and breathing the poison with which the room is saturated.

Skin diseases of many sorts develop in the children who work in this way, and for the women and girls nervous and hysterical complaints are common, the direct result of poisoning by nicotine....

Twine-factories are clean and well-ventilated, but they are often as disastrous in their effects. The twisting-room is filled with long spindles, innocent-looking enough, but taking a finger along with the flax as silently and suddenly as the thread forms....

One [child] explained how it happened in her case:

"You see you mustn't talk or look off a minute. They just march right along. My sister was like me. She forgot and talked, and just that minute her finger was off, and she didn't even cry till she picked it up. My little finger always did stick out, and I was trying to twist fast like the girl next to me, and somehow it caught in the flax. I tried to jerk away, but it wasn't any use. It was off just the same as hers, and it took a great while before I could come back. I'm sort of afraid of them, for any minute your whole hand might go and you'd hardly know till it was done."

In a small room on Hester Street a woman at work on overalls for the making of which she received one dollar a dozen said:—

"I couldn't do as well if it wasn't for Jinny and Mame there. Mame has learned to sew on buttons first-rate, and Jinny is doing almost as well. I'm alone to-day, but most days three of us sew together here, and Jinny keeps right along. We'll do better yet when Mame gets a bit older."

As she spoke the door opened and a woman with an enormous bundle of overalls entered and sat down on the nearest chair with a gasp.

"Them stairs is killin'," she said. "It's lucky I've not to climb 'em often."

Something crept forward as the bundle slid to the floor, and busied itself with the string that bound it.

"Here you, Jinny," said the woman, "don't you be foolin'. What do you want anyhow?"

Then something shook back a mat of thick hair and rose to its feet, a tiny child who in size seemed scarcely three, but whose countenance indicated the experience of three hundred.

"It's the string I want," the small voice said. "Me and Mame was goin' to play with it."

"There's small time for play," said the mother; "there'll be two pair more in a minute or two, an' you are to see how Mame does one an' do it good, too, or I'll find out why not."

Mame had come forward and stood holding to the one thin garment which but partly covered Jinny's little bones. She, too, looked out from a wild thatch of black hair, and with the same expression of deep experience, the pallid, hungry little faces lighting suddenly as some cheap cakes were produced. Both of them sat down on the floor and ate their portion silently.

"Mame's seven, and Jinny's goin' on six," said the mother, "but Jinny's the smartest. She could sew on buttons when she wasn't much over four. I had five, but the Lord took 'em all but these two. I couldn't get on if it wasn't for Marme."

Mame looked up, but said no word, and, as I

left the room, settled herself with her back against the wall, Jinny at her side, laying the coveted string near at hand for use if any minute for play arrived.

"I pledge allegiance"

FRANCIS BELLAMY

The pledge of allegiance was first introduced in the magazine *The Youth's Companion* in 1892 to help mark the 400th anniversary of the landing of Christopher Columbus in America. Schools adapted the pledge almost immediately. The pledge had two revisions. In 1924 "my Flag" was replaced with "the flag of the United States of America," and in 1954 Congress added "under God." Congress also determined in 1954 that the appropriate way to deliver the pledge was to stand upright with no headgear on and to have the right hand over the heart.

I pledge allegiance to my Flag and to the Republic for which it stands; one nation, indivisible, with liberty and justice for all.

America the Beautiful

KATHERINE LEE BATES

Katherine Lee Bates, an English professor at Wellesley College, wrote "America the Beautiful" in 1893, but it was not published until two years later.

O beautiful for spacious skies,
For amber waves of grain,
For purple mountain majesties
Above the fruited plan!
America! America!
God shed His grace on thee,
And crown thy good with brotherhood
From sea to shining sea!

O beautiful for pilgrim feet,
Whose stern, impassioned stress
A thoroughfare for freedom beat
Across the wilderness!
America! America!
God mend thine every flaw,
Confirm thy soul in self-control,
Thy liberty in law!

O beautiful for heroes proved
In liberating strife,
Who more than self their country loved,
And mercy more than life!
America! America!
May God thy gold refine,
Till all success be nobleness
And every gain divine!

O beautiful for patriot dream
That sees beyond the years
Thine alabaster cities gleam
Undimmed by human tears!
America! America!
God shed His grace on thee,
And crown thy good with brotherhood
From sea to shining sea!

"To Eugene v. Debs and the American Railway Union"

GROVER CLEVELAND

The United States went into a prolonged depression in 1893 creating widespread unemployment and bank failures. Speculation and overextended industrial production came to a dramatic end, forcing companies to scale back their work force and investments. Workers seethed with resentment as they suffered pay cuts and job losses. A wave of strikes swept the country in 1894, the most violent and dramatic of which was the Pullman strike organized by American Railway Union leader Eugene V. Debs.

The strike shut down railroad transportation from Chicago to the West Coast. President Grover Cleveland intervened on the side of the railroad companies. He sent 2,000 troops to run the trains and issued an injunction, citing the Sherman Antitrust Act, restraining Debs and the union from any activities designed to hamper the operation of trains. Debs ignored the order and was arrested. Federal troops fired on striking workers, killing 13 and wounding 50. This prompted workers in 26 states to join the strike resulting in yet more violence.

The President of the United States of America to Eugene V. Debs…and the American Railway Union. And all other persons combining and conspiring with them, and to all other persons whomsoever:

You are hereby restrained, commanded, and enjoined absolutely to desist and refrain from in any way or manner interfering with, hindering, obstructing, or stopping any of the business of any of the following-named railroads: [twenty-three railroad companies listed] as common carriers of passengers and freight between or among any States of the United States, and from in any way interfering with, hindering, obstructing, or stopping any mail trains, express trains, whether freight or passenger, engaged in interstate commerce, or carrying passengers or freight between or among the States;…and from compelling or inducing, or attempting to compel or induce, threats, intimidation, persuasion, force, or violence, any of the employees of any of said railroads to refuse or fail to perform any of their duties as employees of any of said railroads in connection with the interstate business or commerce of such railroads, or the transportation of passengers or property between or among the States;…and from doing any act whatever in furtherance of any conspiracy or combination to restrain either of said railroad companies in the free and unhindered control and handling of interstate commerce over the lines of said railroads, and of transportation of persons and freight between and among the States; and from ordering, directing, aiding, assisting, or abetting, in any manner whatever, any person or persons to commit any or either of the acts aforesaid.

And Eugene V. Debs and all other persons are hereby enjoined and restrained from sending out any letters, messages, or communications directing, inciting, encouraging, or instructing any person whatsoever to interfere with the business or affairs, directly or indirectly, of any of the railway companies hereinabove named, or from persuading any of the employees of said railway companies while in the employment of their respective companies to fail or refuse to perform the duties of their employment….

✥ "Give employment to any idle man applying for work"

JACOB S. COXEY

Economic hardship sparked a nationwide demand for federal intervention. More than a dozen "armies" of unemployed workers coalesced and marched on Washington in 1894. As many as 10,000 people took part in the marches. The most famous of these was led by "General" Jacob S. Coxey, a quarry owner and Populist from Massillon, Ohio. Wearing a sombrero and silver-dollar buttons on his coat, Coxey demanded that the government issue bonds to hire the unemployed for a nationwide road-construction project. Federal officials refused to meet with Coxey. Instead, they had him arrested for walking on the grass and then ordered police to break up his "army" with clubs. Widely derided as a crank at the time, Coxey's call for public infrastructure spending to help stimulate business and employment has since become a standard fiscal tool to keep a balanced economy. Coxey's proposed bills are excerpted below.

Non-Interest Bearing Bond Bill

Be it enacted…That whenever any State, Territory, County, township, municipality, or incorporated town or village deems it necessary to make any public improvements, they shall deposit with the Secretary of the Treasury of the United States a non-interest bearing twenty-five year bond, not to exceed one-half of the assessed valuation of the property in said State, Territory, County, township, municipality or incorporated town or village, and said bond to be retired at the rate of four per centum per annum.

Section 2. That whenever the foregoing section of this Act has been complied with it shall be mandatory upon the Secretary of the Treasury of the United States to have…printed Treasury notes in the denomination of one, two, five, and ten dollars each, which shall be full legal tender for all debts, public and private to the face value of said bond, and deliver to said State…ninety-nine per centum of said notes, and retain one per centum for expense of engraving and printing same.

Section 3. That after the passage of this Act it shall be compulsory upon every incorporated town or village, municipality, township, County, State or Territory, to give employment to any idle man applying for work, and that the rate be not less than one dollar and fifty cents per day for common

labor and three dollars and fifty cents per day for teams and labor, and that eight hours per day shall constitute a day's labor under this act.

Coxey's Roads Bill

Section 1. Be it enacted…That the Secretary of the Treasury of the United States is hereby authorized and instructed to have engraved and printed…five hundred millions of dollars of treasury notes, as legal tender for all debts, public and private, said notes to be in denominations of one, two, five and ten dollars, and to be placed in a fund to be known as the "general county road fund system of the United States," and to be expended solely for the said purpose.

Section 2…. That it shall be the duty of the Secretary of War to take charge of the construction of the general County Road System in the United States, and said construction to commence as soon as…said fund is available…when it shall be the duty of the Secretary of War to inaugurate the work and expend the sum of twenty millions of dollars per month, pro rata with the number of miles of roads in each state and territory in the United States.

Section 3…. That all labor other than that of the Secretary of War…shall be paid by the day, and that the rate be not less than one dollar and fifty cents per day for common labor, and three dollars and fifty cents per day for teams and labor, and that eight hours shall constitute a day's labor under the provisions of this bill.

✥ "Influence of Machinery on Labor"

CARROLL D. WRIGHT

President Chester B. Arthur named Carroll D. Wright as the nation's first Labor Commissioner in 1884 and directed him to write a report on the cause of industrial depressions. The report delivered in 1886 concluded that technological progress was reaching its maturity and that new markets might be difficult to find.

Almost a decade later, in 1895, Wright wrote *Industrial Evolution of the United States* with a very different conclusion: industrial development was creating its own new markets. Instead of industrial progress coming at the expense of labor, statistical evidence showed that workers were a beneficiary of labor-saving inventions. Although the argument was based on primitive calculations and evidence, the report represented one of the first economic explanations of this counter-intuitive phenomena.

Chapter XXVVII: The Influence of Machinery on Labor

In the manufacture of agricultural implements new machinery has, in the opinion of some of the best manufacturers of such implements, displaced fully fifty per cent of the muscular labor formerly employed, as, for instance, hammers and dies have done away with the most particular labor on a plow. In one of the most extensive establishments engaged in the manufacture of agricultural implements in one of the Western States it is found that 600 men, with the use of machinery, are now doing the work that would require 2,145 men, without the aid of machinery, to perform; that is to say, there has been in this particular establishment a loss of labor to 1,545, the proportion of loss being 3.57 to 1.

In the manufacture of small arms, where one man, by manual labor, was formerly able to "turn" and "fit" one stock for a musket in one day of ten hours, three men now, by a division of labor and the use of power machinery, will turn out and fit from 125 to 150 stocks in ten hours. By this statement it is seen that one man individually turns out and fits the equivalent of forty-two to fifty in ten hours, as against one stock in the same length of time under former conditions. In this particular calling, then, there is a displacement of forty-four to forty-nine men in one operation.

Looking at a cruder industry, that of brickmaking, improved devices have displaced ten per cent of labor, while in making fire-brick forty per cent of the labor formerly employed is now dispensed with, and yet in many brickmaking concerns no displacement whatsoever has taken place.

The manufacture of boots and shoes offers some very wonderful facts in this connection. In one large and long-established manufactory in one of the Eastern States the proprietors testify that it would require five hundred persons, working by hand processes and in the old way in the shops by the roadside, to make as many women's boots and shoes as one hundred persons now make with the aid of machinery and by congregated labor, a contraction of eighty per cent in this particular case. In another division of the same industry the number of men required to produce a given quantity of

boots and shoes has been reduced one half, while, in still another locality, and on another quality of boots, being entirely for women's wear, where formerly a first-class workman could turn out six pairs in one week, he will not turn out eighteen pairs. A well-known firm in the West engaged in the manufacture of boots and shoes finds that it would take one hundred and twenty persons, working by hand, to produce the amount of work done in its factory by sixty employees, and that the handwork would not compare in workmanship and appearance by fifty per cent. By the use of Goodyear's sewing machine for turned shoes one man will sew two hundred and fifty pairs in one day. It would require eight men, working by hand, to sew the same number in the same time. By the use of a heel-shaver or trimmer one man will trim three hundred pairs of shoes in one day, while formerly three men would have been required to do the same work; and with the McKay machine one operator will handle three hundred pairs of shoes in one day, while without the machine he could handle but five pairs in the same time. So, in nailing on heels, one man, with the aid of machinery, can heel three hundred pairs of shoes per day, while five men would have to work all day to accomplish this by hand. A large Philadelphia house which makes boys' and children's shoes entirely, has learned that the introduction of new machinery within the past thirty years has displaced employees in proportion of six to one, and that the cost of the product has been reduced one half....

In another line labor has been displaced to such an extent that only one-third the number of operatives formerly required is now in employment. In the days of the single-spindle hand-wheel, one spinner, working fifty-six hours continuously, could spin five hanks of number thirty-two twist. At the present time, with one pair of self-acting mule-spinning machines, having 2,124 spindles, one spinner, with the assistance of two small boys, can produce 55,098 hanks of number thirty-two twist in the same time. It is quite generally agreed that there has been a displacement, taking all processes of cotton manufacture into consideration, in the proportion of three to one. The average number of spindles per operative in the cotton-mills of this country in 1831 was 25.2; it is now over 64.82, an increase of nearly 157 per cent; and along with this increase of the number of spindles per operative there has been an increase of product per operative of over 145 per cent, so far as spinning alone is concerned. In weaving in the olden time, in this country, a fair adult hand-loom weaver wove from forty-two to forty-eight yards of common shirting per week. Now a weaver, tending six power-looms in a cotton factory, will produce 1,500 yards and over in a single week; and now a recent invention will enable a waver to double this product....

And so illustrations might be accumulated in very many directions—in the manufacture of furniture, in the glass industry, in leather-making, in sawing lumber, in the manufacture of machines and machinery, in the production of metals and metallic goods of all kinds, or of wooden-ware, in the manufacture of musical instruments, in mining, in the oil industry, in the manufacture of musical instruments, in mining, in the oil industry, in the manufacture of paper, in pottery, in the production of railroad supplies, in the manufacture of rubber boots, of saws, of silk goods, of soap, of tobacco, of trunks, in building vessels, in making wine, and in the production of woolen goods.

It is impossible to arrive at an accurate statement as to the number of persons it would require under the old system to produce the goods made by the present industrial system with the aid of invention and power machinery. Any computation would be a rough estimate. In some branches of work such a rough estimate would indicate that each employee at the present represents, on an average, fifty employees under the old system. In many other branches the estimate would involve the employment of one now where three were employed. Looking at this question without any desire to be mathematically accurate, it is fair to say, perhaps, that it would require from fifty to one hundred million persons in this country, working under the old system, to produce the goods made and do the work performed by the workers of to-day with the aid of machinery. This computation may, of course, be very wide of the truth, but any computation is equally startling, and when it is considered that in spinning alone 1,100 threads are easily spun now at one time where one was spun under the old system, no estimate can be successfully disputed.

All these facts and illustrations simply show that there has been, economically speaking, a great displacement of labor by the use of inventions; power machinery has come in as a magical assistant to the power of muscle and mind, and it is this side of the question that usually causes alarm. Enlightenment has taught the wage-receiver some of the advantages of the introduction of inventions as his assistants, but he is not yet fully instructed as to their influence in all directions. He does see the displacement; he does see the difficulty of turning his hand to other employment or of finding employment in the same direction. These are tangible influences which present themselves squarely in the face of the man involved, and to him no philosophical, economic, or ethical answer is sufficient. It is therefore impossible to treat of the influence of inventions, so far as the displacement of labor is concerned, as one of the leading influences, on the individual basis. We must take labor abstractly. So, having shown the powerful influence of the use of ingenious devices in the displacement or contraction of labor, as such, it is proper to show how such devices have influenced the expansion of labor or created employments and opportunities for employment which did not exist before their inception and application. A separate chapter is given to this part of the subject.

Chapter XXVIII: The Influence of Machinery on Labor Expansion

As incredible as the facts given in the preceding chapter appear to one who has not studied them, the ability to crystallize in individual cases and show the fairly exact displacement of labor exists. An examination of the opposite influence of inventions, that of the expansion or creation of employments not before existing, reveals a more encouraging state or condition of things, but one in which the statistician can make but very little headway. The influences under the expansion of labor have various ramifications. The people at large, and especially those who work for wages, have experienced these influences in several directions, and contemporaneous with the introduction and use of inventions, the chief economic influence being in the direction of expansion, the other influences being more thoroughly ethical, and these should be considered under that broad title. The statistical method helps in some respects in studying the expansive power of inventions, and especially in the direction of great staples used as raw material in manufacturing processes and in the increase of the number of people employed relative to the number of the population. If there has been a great increase in the consumption per capita of great staples for manufacturing purposes, there must have been a corresponding expansion of labor necessary for the production of goods in like directions.

Taking up some of the leading staples, the facts show that the per capita consumption of cotton in this country in 1930 was 5.9 pounds; in 1880, 13.91 pounds; while in 1890 the per capita consumption had increased to nearly 19 pounds. These figures are for cotton consumed in our own country, and clearly and positively indicate that the labor necessary for such consumption has been kept up to the standard, if not beyond the standard, of the olden time—that is, as to the number of people employed.

In iron the increase has been as great proportionately. In 1870 the per capita consumption of iron in the United States was 105.64 pounds, in 1880 it had risen to 204.99, and in 1890 to 283.38. While processes in manufacturing iron have been improved, and labor displaced to a certain extent by such processes, this great increase in the consumption of iron is a most encouraging fact, and proves that there has been an offset to the displacement.

The consumption of steel shows like results. In 1880 it was 46 pounds per capita, and in 1890, 144 pounds. The application of iron and steel in all directions, in the building trades as well as in the mechanical arts, in great engineering undertakings, and in a multitude of directions, only indicates that labor must be actively employed, or such extensions could not take place. But a more conclusive offset to the displacement of labor, considered abstractly, is shown by the statistics of persons engaged in all occupations. From 1860 to 1890, a period of thirty years, and the most prolific period in this country of inventions, and therefore of the most intensified influence in all directions of their introduction, the population increased 99.16 per cent, while during the same period the number of persons employed in all occupations—manufacturing, agriculture. Domestic service, everything—increased 176.07 per cent. In the twenty years, 1870 to 1890, the population increased 62.41 per cent, while the number of persons in all occupations increased 81.80 per cent. An analysis of these statements shows that the increase of the number of those engaged in manufacturing, mechanical, and mining industries, those in which the influence of inventions is most keenly felt, for the period from 1860 to 1890 was 172.27 per cent, as against 99.16 per cent increase in the total population. If statistics

could be as forcibly applied to show the new occupations brought into existence by invention, it is believed that the result would be still more emphatic.

If we could examine scientifically the number of created occupations, the claim that inventions have displaced labor on the whole would be conclusively and emphatically refuted. Taking some of the great industries that now exist, and which did not exist prior to the inventions which made them, we must acknowledge the power of the answer. In telegraphy thousands and thousands of people employed where no one has ever been displaced. The construction of the lines, the manufacture of the instruments, the operation of the lines—all these divisions and subdivisions of great industry have brought thousands of intelligent men and women into remunerative employment where no one had ever been employed before. The telephone has only added to this accumulation and expansion, and the whole field of electricity, in providing for the employment of many skilled workers, has not trenched upon the privileges of the past. Electroplating, a modern device, has not only added wonderfully to the employed list by its direct influence, but indirectly by the introduction of a class of goods which can be secured by all persons. Silverware is no longer the luxury of the rich. Through the invention of electroplating, excellent ware, with most artistic design, can be found in almost every habitation in America. The application of electroplating to nickel furnished and subsidiary industry to that of electroplating generally, and nickelplating had not been known half a dozen years before more than thirty thousand people were employed in the industry, where no one had ever been employed prior to the invention....

It is certainly true—and the statement is simply cumulative evidence of the truth of the view that expansion of labor through inventions has been equal or superior to any displacement that has taken place—that in those countries given to the development and use of machinery there is found the greatest proportion of employed persons, and that in those countries where machinery has been developed to little or no purpose poverty reigns, ignorance is the prevailing condition, and civilization consequently far in the rear.

The expansion of values as the result of the influence of machinery has been quite marvelous as in any other direction, for educated labor, supplemented by machinery, has developed small quantities of inexpensive material into products of great value. This truth is illustrated by taking cotton and iron ore as the starting-point. A pound of cotton, costing at the time this calculation was made but 13 cents, has been developed into muslin which sold in the market for 80 cents, and into chintz which sold for $4. Seventy-five cents' worth of common iron ore has been developed into $5 worth of bar-iron, or into $10 worth of horse-shoes, or into $180 worth of table knives, or into $6,800 worth of fine needles, or into $29,480 worth of shirt buttons, or $200,000 worth of watch-springs, or $400,000 worth of hair-springs, and the same quantity of common iron ore can be made into $2,500,000 worth of pallet arbors.

The illustrations given, both of the expansion of labor and the expansion of values, are sufficiently suggestive of a line of study which, carried in any direction, will show that machinery is the friend and not the enemy of man, especially when man is considered as a part of society and not as an individual.

❧ Atlanta Exposition Address

BOOKER T. WASHINGTON

Born into slavery in 1856, Booker T. Washington was one of the most accomplished African-Americans of the post-Civil War era. Working his way through school as a janitor, he attended Wayland Seminary in Washington, D.C., to become a school instructor. In 1881 he organized Alabama's Tuskegee Institute to train African-Americans in trades and professions. He was the principal there until 1915. He wrote several books, such as *Up from Slavery* in 1901, advocating the importance of education and hard work.

In 1895, Washington spoke to a racially mixed audience at the Cotton States' Exposition delivering a famous address on the importance of African-Americans to be contrite and to submit to segregation. Social and political equality would have to be earned through self-reliance and economic advancement, he said. Although whites applauded Washington's speech, it received a mixed response from African-Americans. Washington's African-American contemporary W. E. B. DuBois dubbed the speech as the "Atlanta Compromise."

Mr. President and Gentlemen of the Board of Directors and Citizens: One-third of the population of the South is of the Negro race. No enterprise seeking the material, civil, or moral welfare of this section can disregard this element of our population and reach the highest success. I but convey to you, Mr. President and directors, the sentiment of the masses of my race when I say that in no way have the value and manhood of the American Negro been more fittingly and generously recognized than by the managers of this magnificent exposition at every stage of its progress. It is a recognition that will do more to cement the friendship of the two races than any occurrence since the dawn of our freedom.

Not only this, but the opportunity here afforded will awaken among us a new era of industrial progress. Ignorant and inexperienced, it is not strange that in the first years of our new life we began at the top instead of the bottom; that a seat in Congress or the state legislature was more sought than real estate or industrial skill; that the political convention or stump speaking had more attractions than starting a dairy farm or truck garden.

A ship lost at sea for many days suddenly sighted a friendly vessel. From the mast of the unfortunate vessel was seen a signal, "Water, water; we die of thirst!" The answer from the friendly vessel at once came back, "Cast down your bucket where you are." And a third and fourth signal for water was answered, "Cast down your bucket where you are." The captain of the distressed vessel, at last heeding the injunction, cast down his bucket, and it came up full of fresh sparkling water from the mouth of the Amazon River. To those of my race who depend on bettering their condition in a foreign land or who underestimate the importance of cultivating friendly relations with the Southern white man, who is their next-door neighbor, I would say: "Cast down your bucket where you are"—cast it down in making friends in every manly way of the people of all races by whom we are surrounded.

Cast it down in agriculture, mechanics, in commerce, in domestic service, and in the professions. And in this connection it is well to bear in mind that whatever other sins the South may be called to bear, when it comes to business, pure and simple, it is in the South that the Negro is given a man's chance in the commercial world, and in nothing is this exposition more eloquent than in emphasizing this chance. Our greatest danger is that in the great leap from slavery to freedom we may overlook the fact that the masses of us are to live by the productions of our hands, and fail to keep in mind that we shall prosper in proportion as we learn to dignify and glorify common labor and put brains and skill into the common occupations of life; we shall prosper in proportion as we learn to draw the line between the superficial and the substantial, the ornamental gew-gaws of life and the useful. No race can prosper till it learns that there is as much dignity in tilling a field as in writing a poem. It is at the bottom of life we must begin, and not at the top. Nor should we permit our grievances to overshadow our opportunities.

To those of the white race who look to the incoming of those of foreign birth and strange tongue and habits for the prosperity of the South, were I permitted I would repeat what I say to my own race, "Cast down your bucket where you are." Cast it down among the eight millions of Negroes whose habits you know, whose fidelity and love you have tested in days when to have proved treacherous meant the ruin of your firesides. Cast down your bucket among these people who have, without strikes and labor wars, tilled your fields, cleared your forests, built your railroads and cities, and brought forth treasures from the bowels of the earth, and helped make possible this magnificent representation of the progress of the South. Casting down your bucket among my people, helping and encouraging them as you are doing on these grounds, and to education of head, hand, and heart, you will find that they will buy your surplus land, make blossom the waste places in your fields, and run your factories. While doing this, you can be sure in the future, as in the past, that you and your families will be surrounded by the most patient, faithful, law-abiding, and unresentful people that the world has seen. As we have proved our loyalty to you in the past, in nursing your children, watching by the sick-beds of your mothers and fathers, and often following them with tear-dimmed eyes to their graves, so in the future, in our humble way, we shall stand by you with a devotion that no foreigner can approach, ready to lay down our lives, if need be, in defense of yours, interlacing our industrial, commercial, civil and religious life with yours in a way that shall make the interests of both races one. In all things that are purely social we can be as separate as the fingers, yet one as the hand in all things essential to mutual progress.

There is no defense or security for any of us except in the highest intelligence and development of all. If anywhere there are efforts tending to curtail the fullest growth of the Negro, let these efforts be turned into stimulating, encouraging, and making him the most useful and intelligent citizen. Effort or means so invested will pay a thousand percent interest. These efforts will be twice blessed— "blessing him that gives and him that takes."

There is no escape through the law of man or God from the inevitable:

The laws of changeless justice bind
Oppressor with oppressed;
And close as sin and suffering joined
We march to fate abreast.

Nearly sixteen million of hands will aid you in pulling the load upward; or they will pull against you the load downward. We shall constitute one-third and more of the ignorance and crime of the South, or one-third its intelligence and progress; we shall contribute one-third to the business and industrial prosperity of the South, or we shall prove a veritable body of death, stagnating, depressing, retarding every effort to advance the body politic.

Gentlemen of the exposition, as we present to you our humble effort at an exhibition of our progress, you must not expect overmuch. Starting thirty years ago with ownership here and there in a few quilts and pumpkins and chickens (gathered from miscellaneous sources), remember the path that has led from these to the inventions and production of agricultural implements, buggies, steam engines, newspapers, books, statuary, carving, paintings, the management of drugstores and banks, has not been trodden without contact with thorns and thistles. While we take pride in what we exhibit as a result of our independent efforts, we do not for a moment forget that our part in this exhibition would fall far short of your expectations but for the constant help that has come to our educational life, not only from the Southern states, but especially from Northern philanthropists, who have made their gifts a constant stream of blessing and encouragement.

The wisest among my race understand that the agitation of questions of social equality is the extremest folly, and that progress in the enjoyment of all the privileges that will come to us must be the result of severe and constant struggle rather than of artificial forcing. No race that has anything to contribute to the markets of the world is long in any degree ostracized. It is important and right that all privileges of the law be ours, but it is vastly more important that we be prepared for the exercises of these privileges. The opportunity to earn a dollar in a factory just now is worth infinitely more than the opportunity to spend a dollar in an opera house.

In conclusion, may I repeat that nothing in thirty years has given us more hope and encouragement, and drawn us so near to you of the white race, as this opportunity offered by the exposition; and here bending, as it were, over the altar that represents the results of the struggles of your race and mine, both starting practically empty-handed three decades ago, I pledge that in your effort to work out the great and intricate problems which God has laid at the doors of the South, you shall have at all times the patient, sympathetic help of my race; only let this be constantly in mind, that, while from representations in these buildings of the produce of field, of forest, of mine, of factory, letters, and art, much good will come, yet far above and beyond material benefits will be that higher good, that, let us pray God, will come, in a blotting out of sectional differences and racial animosities and suspicions, in a determination to administer absolute justice, in a willing, obedience among all classes to the mandates of law. This, this, coupled with our material prosperity, will bring into our beloved South a new heaven and a new earth.

✤❧ *Plessy v. Ferguson: "Separate but equal"*

SUPREME COURT JUSTICE
HENRY BILLINGS BROWN,
SUPREME COURT JUSTICE
JOHN HARLAN MARSHALL

By the 1890s the South had enacted a series of "Jim Crow" laws that required separate facilities for black and white citizens. Homer Plessy was one-eighth African-American. While sitting in the white section of a railway car in Lousiana he was ordered to move to the black section of the train. He refused and was arrested for violating a Louisiana law requiring separate railroad cars for blacks and whites. Judge John H. Ferguson found him guilty. Plessy appealed the verdict claiming that the law violated the Fourteenth Amendment.

By a seven to two vote, the Supreme Court upheld the decision, stating that if railroad cars offer equal accommodations, then segregation is not discriminatory. The decision affirmed the "separate but equal" doctrine that provided the legal justification for the "Jim Crow" laws. The doctrine was not struck down until *Brown v. Board of Education of Topeka* in 1954. Below are excerpts from the majority opinion and the dissent by Supreme Court Justice John Marshall Harlan.

Justice Henry Billings Browns's Majority Opinion

This case turns upon the constitutionality of an act of the general assembly of the state of Louisiana, passed in 1890, providing for separate railway carriages for the white and colored races....

The constitutionality of this act is attacked upon the ground that it conflicts both with the 13th Amendment of the Constitution, abolishing slavery, and the 14th Amendment, which prohibits certain restrictive legislation on the part of the states.

That it does not conflict with the 13th Amendment, which abolished slavery and involuntary servitude, except as a punishment for crime, is too clear for argument....

The object of the [14th] amendment was undoubtedly to enforce the absolute equality of the two races before the law, but in the nature of things it could not have been intended to abolish distinctions based upon color, or to enforce social, as distinguished from political, equality, or a commingling of the two races upon terms unsatisfactory to either. Laws permitting, and even requiring their separation in places where they are liable to be brought into contact do not necessarily imply the inferiority of either race to the other, and have been generally, if not universally, recognized as within the competency of the state legislatures in the exercise of their police power. The most common instance of this is connected with the establishment of separate schools for white and colored children, which have been held to be a valid exercise of the legislative power even by courts of states where the political rights of the colored race have been longest and most earnestly enforced....

It is claimed by the plaintiff in error that, in any mixed community, the reputation of belonging to the dominant race, in this instance the white race, is property, in the same sense that a right of action, or of inheritance, is property. Conceding this to be so, for the purposes of this case, we are unable to see how this statute deprives him of, or in any way affects his right to, such property. If he be a white man and assigned to a colored coach, he may have his action for damages against the company for being deprived of his so-called property. Upon the other hand, if he be a colored man and be so assigned, he has been deprived of no property, since he is not lawfully entitled to the reputation of being a white man….

So far, then, as a conflict with the 14th Amendment is concerned, the case reduces itself to the question whether the statute of Louisiana is a reasonable regulation, and with respect to this there must necessarily be a large discretion on the part of the legislature. In determining the question of reasonableness it is at liberty to act with reference to the established usages, customs, and traditions of the people, and with a view to the promotion of their comfort, and the preservation of the public peace and good order. Gauged by this standard, we cannot say that a law which authorizes or even requires the separation of the two races in public conveyances is unreasonable or more obnoxious to the 14th Amendment than the acts of Congress requiring separate schools for colored children in the District of Columbia, the constitutionality of which does not seem to have been questioned, or the corresponding acts of state legislatures.

We consider the underlying fallacy of the plaintiff's argument to consist in the assumption that the enforced separation of the two races stamps the colored race with a badge of inferiority. If this be so, it is not by reason of anything found in the act, but solely because the colored race chooses to put that construction upon it. The argument necessarily assumes that if, as has been more than once the case, and is not unlikely to be so again, the colored race should become the dominant power in the state legislature, and should enact a law in precisely similar terms, it would thereby relegate the white race to an inferior position. We imagine that the white race, at least, would not acquiesce in this assumption. The argument also assumes that social prejudice may be overcome by legislation, and that equal rights cannot be secured to the Negro except by an enforced commingling of the two races. We cannot accept this proposition. If the two races are to meet on terms of social equality, it must be the result of natural affinities, a mutual appreciation of each other's merits and a voluntary consent of individuals….

Legislation is powerless to eradicate racial instincts or to abolish distinctions based upon physical differences, and the attempt to do so can only result in accentuating the difficulties of the present situation. If the civil and political right of both races be equal, one cannot be inferior to the other civilly or politically. If one race be inferior to the other socially, the Constitution of the United States cannot put them upon the same plane.

Justice John Marshall Harlan's dissent

The white race deems itself to be the dominant race in this country. And so it is, in prestige, in achievements, in education, in wealth, and in power. So, I doubt not, it will continue to be for all time, if it remains true to its great heritage and holds fast to the principles of constitutional liberty. But in view of the Constitution and in the eye of the law, there is in this country no superior, dominant, ruling class of citizens. There is no caste here. Our Constitution is color-blind, and neither knows nor tolerates classes among citizens. In respect to civil rights, all citizens are equal before the law. The humblest is the peer of the most powerful. The law regards man as man, and takes no account of his surroundings or of his color when his civil rights as guaranteed by the supreme law of the land are involved. It is, therefore, to be regretted that this high tribunal, the final expositor of the fundamental law of the land, has reached the conclusion that it is competent for a State to regulate the enjoyment by citizens of their civil rights solely upon the basis of race.

The destinies of the two races, in this country, are indissolubly linked together, and the interests of both require that the common government of all shall not permit the seeds of race hate to be planted under the sanction of law. What can more certainly arouse race hate, what more certainly create and perpetuate a feeling of distrust between these races, than state enactments, which, in fact, proceed on the ground that colored citizens are so inferior and degraded that they cannot be allowed to sit in public coaches occupied by white citizens? That, as all will admit, is the real meaning of such legislation as was enacted in Louisiana.

The arbitrary separation of citizens, on the basis of race, while they are on a public highway, is a badge of servitude wholly inconsistent with the civil freedom and the equality before the law established by the Constitution. It cannot be justified upon any legal grounds.

If evils will result from the commingling of the two races upon public highways established for the benefit of all, they will be infinitely less than those that will surely come from state legislation regulating the enjoyment of civil rights upon the basis of race. We boast of the freedom enjoyed by our people above all other peoples. But it is difficult to reconcile that boast with a state of the law which, practically, puts the brand of servitude and degradation upon a large class of our fellow-citizens, our equals before the law. The thin disguise of "equal" accommodations for passengers in railroad coaches will not mislead any one, nor atone for the wrong this day done.

🌿 *"The Cross of Gold"*

WILLIAM JENNINGS BRYAN

Burdened by high debts and low commodity prices, farmers and debtors across the country wanted the federal government to loosen monetary policy by going off the strict gold standard. Silver coinage would help spur inflation which would make it easier for debtors to pay back their loans. Banks vigorously opposed the silver platform.

William Jennings Bryan of Nebraska became the leading spokesman for the free-silver issue and in 1896 at the Democratic convention delivered his famous "Cross of Gold" speech. The address catapulted Bryan on to the national arena. He became the Democratic candidate for president. Bryan used the cross of gold analogy in more than four hundred speeches in the campaign, but to no avail as he lost the election to William McKinley. Bryan ran again for president in 1900 and 1908, losing both times. He later served as Secretary of State for Woodrow Wilson.

Never before in the history of this country has there been witnessed such a contest as that through which we have just passed. Never before in the history of American politics has a great issue been fought out as this issue has been, by the voters of a great party. On the fourth of March, 1895, a few Democrats, most them members of Congress, issued an address to the Democrats of the nation, asserting that the money question was the paramount issue of the hour; declaring that a majority of the Democratic party had the right to control the action of the party on this paramount issue; and concluding with the request that the believers in the free coinage of silver in the Democratic party should organize, take charge of, and control the policy of the Democratic party. Three months later, at Memphis, an organization was perfected, and the silver Democrats went forth openly and coura-

geously proclaiming their belief and declaring that, if successful, they would crystallize into a platform the declaration which they had made. Then began the conflict. With a zeal approaching the zeal which inspired the Crusaders who followed Peter the Hermit, our silver Democrats went forth from victory unto victory until they are now assembled, not to discuss, not to debate, but to enter up the judgment already rendered by the plain people of this country. In this contest brother has been arrayed against brother, father against son. The warmest ties of love, acquaintance and association have been disregarded; old leaders have been cast aside when they have refused to give expression to the sentiments of those whom they would lead, and new leaders have sprung up to give direction to this cause of truth. Thus has the contest been waged, and we have assembled here under as binding and solemn instructions as were ever imposed upon representatives of the people....

They tell us that this platform was made to catch votes. We reply to them that changing conditions make new issues, that the principles on which Democracy rests are as everlasting as the hills, but that they must be applied to new conditions make new issues, that the principles on which Democracy rests are as everlasting as the hills, but that they must be applied to new conditions as they arise. Conditions have arisen, and we are here to meet those conditions. They tell us that the income tax ought not be brought in here; that it is a new idea. They criticize us for our criticism of the Supreme Court of the United States. My friends, we have not criticized; we have simply called attention to what you already know. If you want criticisms, read the dissenting opinions of the court. There you will find criticisms. They say that we passed an unconstitutional law; we deny it. The income tax law was not unconstitutional when it was passed; it was not unconstitutional when it went before the Supreme Court for the first time; it did not become unconstitutional until one of the judges changed his mind, and we cannot be expected to know when a judge will change his mind. The income tax is just. It simply intends to put the burdens of government upon the backs of the people. I am in favor of an income tax. When I find a man who is not willing to bear his share of the burdens of the government which protects him, I find a man who is unworthy to enjoy the blessings of a government like ours....

We say in our platform that we believe that the right to coin and issue money is a function of government. We believe it. We believe that it is a part of sovereignty and can no more with safety be delegated to private individuals the power to make penal statutes or levy taxes. Mr. Jefferson, who was once regarded as good Democratic authority, seems to have differed in opinion from the gentleman who has addressed us on the part of the minority. Those who are opposed to this proposition tell us that the issue of paper money is a function of the bank, and that the government ought to go out of the banking business. I stand with Jefferson rather than with them and tell them, as he did, that the issue of money is a function of government and that banks ought to go out of the governing business....

We go forth confident that we shall win. Why? Because upon the paramount issue of this campaign there is not a spot of ground upon which the enemy will dare to challenge battle. If they tell us that the gold standard is a good thing, we shall point to their platform and tell them that their platform pledges the party to get rid of the gold standard and substitute bimetalism. If the gold standard is a good thing, why try to get rid of it? I call your attention to the fact that some of the very people who are in this convention today and who tell us that we ought to declare in favor of international bimetalism—thereby declaring that the gold standard is wrong and that the principle of bimetalism is better—these very people four months ago were open and avowed advocates of the gold standard, and were then telling us that we could not legislate two metals together, even with the aid of all the world. If the gold standard is a good thing, we ought to declare in favor of its retention and not in favor of abandoning it; and if the gold standard is a bad thing, why should we wait until other nations are willing to help us let go?

Here is the line of battle, and we care not upon which issue they force the fight; we are prepared to meet them on either issue or on both. If they tell us that the gold standard is the standard of civilization, we reply to them that this, the most enlightened of all the nations of the earth, has never declared for a gold standard and that both the great parties this year are declaring against it. If the gold standard is the standard of civilization,

why, my friends, should we not have it?...

Mr. Carlisle said in 1878 that this was a struggle between "the idle holders of idle capital" and "the struggling masses, who produce the wealth and pay the taxes of the country"; and, my friends, the question we are to decide is: Upon which side will the Democratic party fight? Upon the side of the "the idle holders of idle capital" or upon the side of "the struggling masses"? That is the question which the party must answer first, and then it must be answered by each individual hereafter. The sympathies of the Democratic party as shown by the platform, are on the side of the struggling masses who have ever been the foundation of the Democratic party. There are two ideas of government. There are those believe that, if you will only legislate to make the well-to-do prosperous, their prosperity will leak through on those below. The Democratic idea, however, [is] that if you legislate to make the masses prosperous, their prosperity will find its way up through every class which rests upon them....

My friends, we declare that this nation is able to legislate for its own people on every question, without waiting for the aid or consent of any other nation on earth; and upon that issue we expect to carry every state in the Union. I shall not slander the inhabitants of the fair state of Massachusetts nor the inhabitants of New York by saying that, when they are confronted with the proposition, they will declare that this nation is not able to attend its own business. It is the issue of 1776 over again. Our ancestors, when but three million in number, had the courage to declare their political independence of every other nation; shall we, their descendents, when we have grown to seventy millions, declare that we are less independent than our forefathers? No, my friends, that will never be the verdict of our people. Therefore we care not upon what lines the battle is fought. If they say bimetalism is good, but that we cannot have it until the other nations help us, we reply that, instead of having a gold standard because England has, we will restore bimetalism and then let England have bimetalism because the United States has it. If they dare to come out in the open field and defend the gold standard as a good thing, we will fight them to the uttermost. Having behind us the producing masses of this nation and the world, supported by the commercial interests, the laboring interests and the toilers everywhere, we will answer their demand for a gold standard by saying to them: You shall not press down upon the brow of labor this crown of thorns; you shall not crucify mankind upon a cross of gold.

❧ "The Tall Office Building"

LOUIS SULLIVAN

Improvements in technology and urbanization allowed for the construction of new, taller buildings in American cities after the Civil War. The first "skyscrapers" were built in New York City, but architects could not devise a satisfactory style to fit the new, elongated buildings. In some cases, they appeared to be houses stacked on top of each other and in others, almost ludicrously designed big homes. The Great Chicago Fire of 1871 created an opportunity for architects to confront the issue. Out of the decimated city center, a massive new reconstruction effort took place. Initial buildings looked cumbersome and awkward. But in the 1880s and 1890s a new style of architecture emerged out of Chicago that set the standard for "skyscrapers." Louis Sullivan played a defining role in the development of this modern sensibility. With his partner Dankmar Adler, he designed The Auditorium (1886) and The Garrick Theater (1891-92) in Chicago, as well as the Wainwright building (1890-91) in St. Louis. Rather than seeking to imitate past architectural styles, Sullivan sought to reflect the qualities—height, splendor, utility—of the new modern buildings. "Form follows function," he famously declared. Sullivan's edict helped spawn an entire school of architects in the 20th century, particularly in the design of industrial buildings. This excerpt comes from an article Sullivan wrote, "The Tall Office Building," for *Lippincott's Magazine* in 1896.

The architects of this land and generation are now brought face to face with something new under the sun—namely, that evolution and integration of social conditions, that special grouping of them, that results in a demand for the erection of tall office buildings.

It is not my purpose to discuss the social conditions; I accept them as the fact, and say at once that the design of the tall office building must be recognized and confronted at the outset as a problem to be solved—a vital problem, pressing for a true solution.

Let us state the conditions in the plainest manner. Briefly, they are these: offices are necessary for the transaction of business; the invention and perfection of the high-speed elevators make vertical travel, that was once tedious and painful, now easy and comfortable; development of steel manufacture

has shown the way to safe, rigid, economical constructions rising to a great height; continued growth of population in the great cities, consequent congestion of centers and rise in value of ground, stimulate an increase in number of stories; these successfully piled one upon another, react on ground values—and so on, by action and reaction, interaction and inter-reaction. Thus has come about that form of lofty construction called the "modern office building." It has come in answer to a call, for in it a new grouping of social conditions has found a habitation and a name.

Up to this point all in evidence is materialistic, an exhibition of force, of resolution, of brains in the keen sense of the word. It is the joint product of the speculator, the engineer, the builder.

Problem: How shall we impart to this sterile pile, this crude, harsh, brutal agglomeration, this stark, staring exclamation of eternal strife, the graciousness of those higher forms of sensibility and culture that rest on the lower and fiercer passions? How shall we proclaim from the dizzy height of this strange, weird, modern housetop the peaceful evangel of sentiment, of beauty, the cult of a higher life?

This is the problem; and we must seek the solution of it in a process analogous to its own evolution—indeed, a continuation of it—namely, by proceeding step by step from general to special aspects, from coarser to finer considerations....

All things in nature have a shape, that is to say, a form, an outward semblance, that tells us what they are, that distinguishes them from ourselves and from each other.

Unfailingly in nature these shapes express the inner life, the native quality, of the animal, tree, bird, fish, that they present to us; they are so characteristic, so recognizable, that we say, simply, it is "natural" it should be so. Yet the moment we peer beneath this surface of things, the moment we look through the tranquil reflection of ourselves and the clouds above us, down into the clear, fluent, unfathomable depth of nature, how startling is the silence of it, how amazing the flow of life, how absorbing the mystery. Unceasingly the essence of things is taking shape in the matter of things, and this unspeakable process we call birth and growth. Awhile the spirit and the matter fade away together, and it is this that we call decadence, death. These two happenings seem jointed and interdependent, blended into one like a bubble and its iridescence, and they seem borne along upon a slowly moving air. This air is wonderful past all understanding.

Yet to the steadfast eye of one standing upon the shore of things, looking chiefly and most lovingly upon that side on which the sun shines and that we feel joyously to be life, the heart is ever gladdened by the beauty, the exquisite spontaneity, with which life seeks and takes on its forms in an accord perfectly responsive to its needs. It seems ever as though the life and the form were absolutely one and inseparable, so adequate is the sense of fulfillment.

Whether it be the sweeping eagle in his flight or the open apple-blossom, the toiling work-horse, the blithe swan, the branching oak, the winding stream at its base, the drifting clouds, over all the coursing sun, form ever follows function, and this is the law. Where function does not change form does not change. The granite rocks, the ever-brooding hills, remain for ages; the lightning lives, comes into shape, and dies in a twinkling.

It is the pervading law of all things organic, and inorganic, of all things physical and metaphysical, of all things human and all things superhuman, of all true manifestations of the head, of the heart, of the Soul, that the life is recognizable in its expression, that form ever follows function. This is the law.

Shall we, then, daily violate this law in our art? Are we so decadent, so imbecile, so utterly weak of eyesight, that we cannot perceive this truth so simple, so very simple? Is it indeed a truth so transparent that we see through it but do not see it? Is it really then, a very marvelous thing, or is it rather so commonplace, so everyday, so near a thing to us, that we cannot perceive that the shape, form, outward expression, design or whatever we may choose, of the tall office building should in the very nature of things follow the functions of the building, and that where the function does not change, the form is not to change?

Does this not readily, clearly, and conclusively show that the lower one or two stories will take on a special character suited to the special needs, that the tiers of typical offices, having the same unchanging function, shall continue in the same unchanging form, and that as to the attic, specific and conclusive as it is in its very nature, its function shall equally be so in force, in significance, in continuity, in conclusiveness of outward expres-

sion? From this results, naturally, spontaneously, unwittingly, a three-part division, not from any theory, symbol, or fancied logic.

And thus the design of the tall office building takes its place with all other architectural types made when architecture, as has happened once in many years, was a living art. Witness the Greek temple, the Gothic cathedral, the medieval fortress.

And thus when native instinct and sensibility shall govern the exercise of our beloved art; when the known law, the respected law, shall be that form ever follows function; when architects shall cease struggling and prattling handcuffed and vainglorious in the asylum of a foreign school; when it is truly felt, cheerfully accepted, that this law opens up the airy sunshine of green fields, and gives to us a freedom that the very beauty and sumptuousness of the out-working of the law itself as exhibited in nature will deter any sane, any sensitive man from changing into license, when it becomes evident that we are merely speaking a foreign language with a noticeable American accent, whereas each and every architect in the land might, under the benign influence of this law, express in the simplest, most modest, most natural way that which it is in him to say; that he might really and would surely develop his own characteristic individuality, and that the architectural art with him would certainly become a living form of speech, a natural form of utterance, giving surcease to him and adding treasures small and great to the growing art of his land; when we know, and feel that Nature is our friend, not our implacable enemy—that an afternoon in the country, an hour by the sea, a full open view of one single day, through dawn, high noon, and twilight, will suggest to us so much that is rhythmical, deep, and eternal in the vast art of architecture, something so deep, so true, that all the narrow formalities, hard-and-fast rules, and strangling bonds of the schools cannot stifle it in us then it may be proclaimed that we are on the high-road to a natural and satisfying art, an architecture that will soon become a fine art in the true, the best sense of the word, an art that will live because it will be of the people, for the people, and by the people.

🍂 "Overwhelming victory"

WILLIAM McKINLEY

On February 15, 1898, an explosion killed 266 United States sailors on the *Maine* while the warship was anchored in Havana, Cuba. Investigations many years later showed that the disaster was triggered by a fire in the ship's coal bunker. Nevertheless, the accident came at a time when expansionary fever ran high in the United States. Many newspapers and politicians actively encouraged anti-Spanish resentment for the treatment of Cuban revolutionaries. When the *Maine* blew up in the Spanish harbor, newspapers, politicians and the public demanded retribution against Spain.

On April 11, 1898, President William McKinley asked Congress for a declaration of war, even though the day before Spain had agreed to United States demands in Cuba. On April 25, war was formally declared. Starting in the 1880s, naval officers such as Alfred Thayer Mahan and Commodore George Dewey strongly advocated a naval buildup as the key to the United States securing national greatness. By the time the Spanish-American War arrived, the United States boasted a heavily armed, modern navy.

Less than two weeks after declaring war McKinley directed Dewey to employ the navy in an attack on the Spanish navy in the Philippines, which was part of Spain's empire. In a matter of hours, Dewey sunk nine out of ten Spanish warships, killing 381 men. The United States lost no ships and no fatalities. McKinley detailed Dewey's exploits to Congress on May 9, 1898.

On the 24th of April I directed the Secretary of the Navy to telegraph orders to Commodore George Dewey, of the United States Navy, commanding the Asiatic Squadron, then lying in the port of Hong Kong, to proceed forthwith to the Philippine Islands, there to commence operations and engage the assembled Spanish fleet.

Promptly obeying that order, the United States squadron, consisting of the flagships *Olympia*, *Baltimore*, *Raleigh*, *Boston*, *Concord*, and *Petrel*, with the revenue cutter *McCulloch* as an auxiliary dispatch boat, entered the harbor of Manila at daybreak on the 1st of May and immediately engaged the entire Spanish fleet of eleven ships; which were under the protection of the fire of the land forts. After a stubborn fight, in which the enemy suffered great loss, these vessels were destroyed or completely disabled and the water battery at Cavite silenced. Of our brave officers and men not one was lost and only eight injured, and those slightly. All of our ships escaped any serious damage.

By the 4th of May, Commodore Dewey had taken possession of the naval station at Cavite, destroying the fortifications there and at the entrance of the bay and paroling their garrisons. The waters of the bay are under his complete control. He has established hospitals within the American lines where 250 of the Spanish sick and wounded are assisted and protected.

The magnitude of this victory can hardly be measured by the ordinary standard of naval warfare. Outweighing any material advantage is the moral effect of this initial success. At this unsurpassed achievement the great heart of our nation throbs, not with boasting or with greed of conquest, but with deep gratitude that this triumph has come in a just cause and that by the grace of God an effective step has thus been taken toward the attainment of the wished-for peace. To those whose skill, courage, and devotion have won the fight, to the gallant commander and the brave officers and men who aided him, our country owes an incalculable debt.

Feeling as our people feel, and speaking in their name, I at once sent a message to Commodore Dewey thanking him and his officers and men for their splendid achievement and overwhelming victory and informing him that I had appointed him an acting rear-admiral.

I now recommend that, following our national precedents and expressing the fervent gratitude of every patriotic heart, the thanks of Congress be given Acting Rear-Admiral George Dewey, of the United States Navy, for highly distinguished conduct in conflict with the enemy, and to the officers and men under his command for their gallantry in the destruction of the enemy's fleet and the capture of the enemy's fortifications in the bay of Manila.

🍂 "To the charge!"

STEPHEN BONSAL

A United States expeditionary force of 18,000 soldiers landed a few miles from Santiago, Cuba, on June 22, 1898, to wrest the island from a 200,000-man Spanish army. Despite being poorly armed and badly provisioned, the army laid siege on Santiago. On July 1, "The Rough Riders" charged up San Juan Hill by foot to take an entrenched Spanish position overlooking San Juan. The successful frontal assault made Colonel Theodore Roosevelt—who was the only person to make the charge on a horse—a national hero and catapulted him to the vice presidency. Stephen Bonsal, who took part in the attack, wrote about the experience in his book *The Fight for Santiago*.

When the line was nearly formed and the last of his men were coming up, General Hawkins, accompanied by Schroeder, the gallant bugler, stepped forward into the open field and, standing by the wire fence, surveyed the slopes which he had never seen plainly before, up which he was now to send his handful of men upon their desperate errand. While engaged in this he noticed half a dozen of his men crouching for cover in the thicket nearby. Suddenly one of the men got up and walked away from the group in the cover, though the other men tried to detain him. Hawkins heard the brave fellow say: "No, I'll be blanked if I do; I won't lie down when a general and a better man is standing!" And so he stood up, with his rifle before him, with muscles taut and neck, outstretched, only awaiting the order for the rush which was momentarily expected. When Hawkins turned around, he saw that the others were following this man's example. Walking over to where they stood, he said: "Our duties are different here, my men. I must see all I can, and you must be seen as little as possible. Lie down!" And then he resumed his survey of the Spanish positions.

The word was given, and Schroeder put it to the shrill clarion music, and the men of the two little, decimated regiments rushed across the field of guinea grass in a race which lay between victory and death, and, as any military man would have said, with the odds decidedly in favor of death. General Hawkins stood out in the open field, a shining mark indeed, urging the men up on the heights as fast as they emerged from the forest, with their eyes blinking as they came out into the sunlight. Not that they required much urging—they went up the heights to avenge the cruel losses they had met in their advance and because they knew the capture of the blockhouse offered the only hope of turning the adverse tide of battle. When they reached the foothills of the heights, they secured some protection and a better footing and crept up the heights in little bunches, availing themselves of what shelter the inequalities of the ground offered, while Hawkins by his presence and his voice spurred them on to attempt the impossible. Now the three regiments of the Third Brigade (Wikoff's) emerged from the forest, swarmed up the heights some distance to the left of the blockhouse, and overlapping the

Spanish line and flanking the Spanish trenches as they did, contributed to the fire of the men of the Sixth and Sixteenth in making the blockhouse untenable.

The Spanish blockhouses, wreathed in the gorgeous red flowers of the flame-tree, rose straight before our advancing columns. Now and again a gleam of the sunlight upon a rifle and the high-crowned guano hat of a Spanish soldier fascinate your gaze. You listen as in a dream to the quick, insistent tone of the orders, for the Spaniards are firing in volleys and not at will; and again you rub your eyes and smile incredulously, for the sun is shining peacefully on the heights, and there is not a speck of smoke anywhere to be seen to tell you from whence the firing comes. And yet, as the little clumps of blue coats that dot the fields and the roadside reveal to you only too truly, this is the stern reality of war. From every trench and blockhouse—you can only guess where they all are in a general way—the volleys are delivered as though by some quick-firing automaton. You hear the mechanical click of the rifle and often the very words of command. As the First Brigade (Hawkins') starts up the hill to the left of the fort, you see that the Spaniards who have been holding the blue house on Kettles Hill to the right with such stubborn resistance are wavering. Then they hurry out of the trenches and run swiftly away down the hill to the right of the little lagoon, and the yellow flag of the Cavalry Division rises over the hill and bursts upon our gaze like a harvest moon; and then appear, like satellites in its wake, the innumerable troop guidons of red and white and yellow. The Spaniards have lost their advanced position, and we have gained one.

The cavalry do not rest long, and some forward spirits rush down the hill and are pretty well mixed up with the infantry brigades before that final charge is delivered which leaves the bullet-swept heights in our possession. Far from relaxing, the fire from the Spanish trenches, which our artillery has utterly failed to keep down, redoubles in vigor. The Spaniards fully recognize that the critical moment has come, and from their vantage they pour a leaden stream down into the valley, where our second line is coming up to the charge. Perhaps, over and above the rattle of the musketry, they also hear and understand the bugle call of the white-haired brigadier as he passes with the bugler along the line, feeling the heartbeat of his men, as it were, and collecting them for the charge he is soon to lead. It is certainly magnificent, it is certainly not war, and had it failed, it would have been called quixotic. These two thin, depleted brigades, the First and Third, are absolutely unsupported by artillery save the Gatling guns, while from the Spanish right they are swept by the shrapnel fire of the heavy batteries. This fire in itself is destructive and upon men of less sturdy fiber could not have failed to exert a depressing effect.

And now, right in front, as if the small-arms fire with all its automatic regularity were not enough, you see the bushes shattered and whole lines of the guinea grass lose their tassels as though falling under the mighty sweep of a scythe in the grasp of some strong, invisible hand. You do not need to hear the turning of the cog-wheel crank faster and ever faster to recognize that the Spaniards are pouring upon our men a steady stream of missiles from their machine guns. Then, over the roar of musketry and the booming of the great guns and the quick moans of those who fall, you hear a sharp note of the bugle, and every man steps out, putting into word and into action the trumpet note which spells in martial music the words, "To the charge!"

From right to left one little band rushes fifty yards, crouches, and fires; the platoon on the left passes them, crouches, and fires. And so they go, platoon after platoon. You have no eyes for the writhing masses of blue which mark their progress, particularly by the wire fences where the advance is slow; you only follow that line which rises and falls with the mechanical regularity of a piston rod. In a moment they are under the hill and with a short, breathless cheer commence to swarm up the slope. The fire of the Spaniards almost ceases, then begins again, wild, irregular, and dies away in a desultory pitter-patter. The Spaniards sullenly retire, while the five infantry regiments swarm over the crest of the hill and take possession of the blockhouse and the trenches which the Spaniards fought for with such obstinacy and relinquished with such reluctance. The red and yellow flag disappears, and soon the blue flag of the infantrymen and the Stars and Stripes of us all float over the blockhouse. On the right the six regiments of the cavalry division sweep around the right of the lagoon, all except some of the Third Cavalry who come around the left and have fought almost shoulder to shoulder with the doughboys. The cavalry climb the heights before them in open skirmish order under the hacienda a quarter of a mile to the right of the fort; the Spaniards give way all along the line; and we hold the heights of San Juan. But you cannot please everybody. The fire-eating major of the Second Infantry, Major S—, of the first regiment of the reserve brigade, crouching behind a little foothill five hundred yards away, heaves a mighty sigh as he swings his men out into the open and leads them around to the left. "We were to go in, boys, the moment they wavered; but they didn't waver worth a cent. And so you've all missed being in the greatest charge that our army has ever made."

"Cession is accepted, ratified, and confirmed"

ANNEXATION OF HAWAII

Americans began settling Hawaii in the mid-1800s because its land was fertile for sugar and fruit production. In 1893 the United States proclaimed the kingdom as a protectorate after Queen Liliuokalani took the throne. Sugar magnates feared she would impose her authority on their plantations. In addition, naval strategist Alfred Thayer Mahan strongly advocated for the United States to acquire Hawaii as a naval base to protect the West Coast and serve as a station for American expansion in the Pacific Ocean. At the time, President Benjamin Harrison proposed the islands be annexed by the United States. His successor, Grover Cleveland, however, was an isolationist and withdrew an annexation treaty from the Senate. Hawaii became an independent republic.

Five years later, McKinley proposed the islands be annexed. The Spanish-American War broke out while the treaty was being considered. Hawaii served as a military base for the United States' war effort. On July 7, 1898, Congress annexed the islands by a joint resolution.

Whereas the Government of the Republic of Hawaii having, in due form, signified its consent, in the manner provided by its constitution, to cede absolutely and without reserve to the United States of America all rights of sovereignty of whatsoever kind in and over the Hawaiian Islands and their dependencies, and also to cede and transfer to the United States the absolute fee and ownership of all public, Government, or Crown lands, public buildings or edifices, ports, harbors, military equipment, and all other public property of every kind and description belonging to the Government of the Hawaiian Islands, together with every right and appurtenance thereunto appertaining: Therefore,

Resolved, That said cession is accepted, ratified, and confirmed, and that the said Hawaiian Islands and their dependencies be, and they are hereby, annexed as a part of the territory of the United States and are subject to the sovereign dominion thereof, and that all singular the property and rights hereinbefore mentioned are vested in the United States of America.

The existing laws of the United States relative to public lands shall not apply to such lands in the Hawaiian Islands; but the Congress of the United States shall enact special laws for their management and disposition: Provided, That all revenue from or proceeds of the same, except as regards such part thereof as may be used or occupied for the civil, military, or naval purposes of the United States, or may be assigned for the use of the local government, shall be used solely for the benefit of the inhabitants of the Hawaiian Islands for educational and other public purposes.

Until Congress shall provide for the government of such islands all the civil, judicial, and military powers exercised by the officers of the existing government in said islands shall be vested in such person or persons and shall be exercised in such manner as the President of the United States shall direct; and the president shall have power to remove said officers and fill the vacancies so occasioned.

The existing treaties of the Hawaiian Islands with foreign nations shall forthwith cease and determine, being replaced by such treaties as may exist, or as may be hereafter concluded, between the United States and such foreign nations. The municipal legislation of the Hawaiian Islands, not enacted for the fulfillment of the treaties so extinguished, and not inconsistent with this joint resolution nor contrary to the Constitution of the United States, shall remain in force until the Congress of the United States shall otherwise determine.

Until legislation shall be enacted extending the United States customs laws and regulations to the Hawaiian Islands with the United States and other countries shall remain unchanged.

The public debt of the Republic of Hawaii, lawfully existing at the date of the passage of this joint resolution, including the amounts due to depositors in the Hawaiian Postal Savings Bank, is hereby assumed by the Government of the United States; but the liability of the United States in this regard shall in no case exceed four million dollars. So long, however, as the existing Government and the present commercial relations of the Hawaiian Islands are continued as hereinbefore provided said Government shall continue to pay the interest on said debt.

There shall be no further immigration of Chinese into the Hawaiian Islands, except upon such conditions as are now or may hereafter be allowed by the laws of the United States; and no Chinese, by reason of anything herein contained, shall be allowed to enter the United States from the Hawaiian Islands.

The President shall appoint five commissioners, at least two of whom shall be residents of the Hawaiian Islands, who shall, as soon as reasonably practicable, recommend to Congress such legislation concerning the Hawaiian Islands as they shall deem necessary or proper…

"Spain relinquishes all claim of sovereignty over and title to Cuba"

TREATY OF PARIS

The Spanish-American War was a one-sided, brief affair. The Cuban invasion lasted ten weeks and all of the Spanish forces in the Philippines had surrendered by the middle of August. On August 12, 1898, an armistice went into effect. The Treaty of Paris concluding the war was signed on December 10, 1898.

By the terms of the treaty, Spain granted independence to Cuba and ceded Puerto Rico and Guam to the United States. The United States bought the Philippines for $20 million. The acquisitions helped slake a national thirst for foreign expansion. But holding the new territories proved more difficult than acquiring them. Insurgents in the Philippines rebelled at United States rule. An estimated 100,000 people were killed when the United States crushed the rebellion.

Whereas, a Treaty of Peace between the United States of America and Her Majesty the Queen

Regent of Spain, in the name of her August Son, Don Alfonso XIII, was concluded and signed by their respective plenipotentiaries at Paris on the tenth day of December, 1898, the original of which Convention being in the English and Spanish languages, is word for word as follows:…

Article I. Spain relinquishes all claim of sovereignty over and title to Cuba.

And as the island is, upon its evacuation by Spain, to be occupied by the United States, the United States will, so long as such occupation shall last, assume and discharge the obligations that may under international law result from the fact of its occupation, for the protection of life and property.

Article II. Spain cedes to the United States the island of Porto Rico and other islands now under Spanish sovereignty in the West Indies, and the island of Guam in the Marianas or Ladrones.

Article III. Spain cedes to the United States the archipelago known as the Philippine Islands, and comprehending the islands lying within the following line:…

The United States will pay to Spain the sum of twenty million dollars ($20,000,000) within three months after the exchange of the ratifications of the present treaty.

Article IV. The United States will, for the term of ten years from the date of the exchange of the ratifications of the present treaty, admit Spanish ships and merchandise to the ports of the Philippine Islands on the same terms as ships and merchandise of the United States.

Article V. The United States will, upon the signature of the present treaty, send back to Spain, at its own cost, the Spanish soldiers taken as prisoners of war on the capture of Manila by the American forces. The arms of the soldiers in question shall be restored to them.…

Article XVI. It is understood that any obligations assumed in this treaty by the United States with respect to Cuba are limited to the time of its occupancy thereof but it will upon the termination of such occupancy, advise any Government established in the island to assume the same obligations.…

"The Strenuous Life"

THEODORE ROOSEVELT

Theodore Roosevelt emerged out of the Spanish-American War as a new national hero and spokesman for United States expansion. Indomitable, energetic, robust and accomplished, Roosevelt's spirit matched the country's. The United States entered the new century eager to flex its newfound strength as a united, economically powerful nation. Roosevelt delivered his famous address on "The Strenuous Life" on April 10, 1899, to the Hamilton Club in Chicago. The next year he was elected as vice president in McKinley's second term.

I wish to preach, not the doctrine of ignoble ease, but the doctrine of the strenuous life, the life of toil and effort, of labor and strife; to preach that highest form of success which comes, not to the man who desires mere easy peace, but to the man who does not shrink from danger, from hardship, or from bitter toil, and who out of these wins the splendid ultimate triumph.

A life of slothful ease, a life of that peace which springs merely from lack either of desire or of power to strive after great things, is as little worthy of a nation as of an individual. I ask only that what every self-respecting American demands from himself and from his sons shall be demanded of the American nation as a whole.… A mere life of ease is not in the end a very satisfactory life, and, above all, it is a life which ultimately unfits those who follow it for serious work in the world.…

As it is with the individual, so it is with the nation. It is a base untruth to say that happy is the nation that has no history. Thrice happy is the nation that has a glorious history. Far better it is to dare mighty things, to win glorious triumphs, even though checkered by failure, than to take rank with those poor spirits who neither enjoy much nor suffer much, because they live in the gray twilight that knows not victory nor defeat. If in 1861 the men who loved the Union had believed that peace was the end of all things, and war and strife the worst of all things, and had acted up to their belief, we would have saved hundreds of thousands of lives, we would have saved hundreds of millions of dollars. Moreover, besides saving all the blood and treasure we then lavished, we would have prevented the heartbreak of many women, the dissolution of many homes, and we would have spared the country those months of gloom and shame when it seemed as if our armies marched only to defeat. We could have avoided all this suffering simply by shrinking from strife. And if we had thus avoided it, we would have shown that we were weaklings, and that we were unfit to stand among the great nations of the earth. Thank God for the iron in the blood of our fathers, the men who upheld the wisdom of Lincoln, and bore sword or rifle in the armies of Grant! Let us, the children of the men who proved themselves equal to the mighty days, let us, the children of the men who carried the great Civil War to a triumphant conclusion, praise the God of our fathers that the ignoble counsels of peace were rejected; that the suffering and loss, the blackness of sorrow and despair, were unflinchingly faced, and the years of strife endured; for in the end the slave was freed, the Union restored, and the mighty American republic placed once more as a helmeted queen among nations.

We of this generation do not have to face a task such as that our fathers faced, but we have our tasks, and woe to us if we fail to perform them! We cannot, if we would, play the part of China, and be content to rot by inches in ignoble ease within our borders, taking no interest in what goes on beyond them, sunk in a scrambling commercialism; heedless of the higher life, the life of aspiration, of toil and risk, busying ourselves only with the wants of our bodies for the day, until suddenly we should find, beyond a shadow of question, what China has already found, that in this world the nation that has trained itself to a career of unwarlike and isolated ease is bound, in the end, to go down before other nations which have not lost the manly and adventurous qualities. If we are to be a really great people, we must strive in good faith to play a great part in the road. We cannot avoid meeting great issues. All that we can determine for ourselves is whether we shall meet them well or ill. In 1898 we could not help being brought face to face with the problem of war with Spain. All we could decide was whether we should shrink like cowards from the contest, or enter into it as beseemed a brave and high-spirited people; and, once in, whether failure or success should crown our banners. So it is now. We cannot avoid the responsibilities that confront us in Hawaii, Cuba, Porto Rico, and the Philippines. All we can decide is whether we shall meet them in a way that will redound to the national credit, or whether we shall make of our

dealings with these new problems a dark and shameful page in our history. To refuse to deal with them at all merely amounts to dealing with them badly. We have a given problem to solve. If we undertake the solution, there is, of course, always danger that we may not solve it aright; but to refuse to undertake the solution simply renders it certain that we cannot possibly solve it aright.

We cannot sit huddled within our own borders and avow ourselves merely an assemblage of well-to-do hucksters who care nothing for what happens beyond. Such a policy would defeat even its own end; for as the nations grow to have ever wider and wider interests, and are brought into closer and closer contact, if we are to hold our own in the struggle for naval and commercial supremacy, we must build up our power without our own borders. We must build the isthmian canal, and we must grasp the points of vantage which will enable us to have our say in deciding the destiny of the oceans of the East and the West.

So much for the commercial side. From the standpoint of international honor the argument is even stronger. The guns that thundered off Manila and Santiago left us echoes of glory, but they also left us a legacy of duty. If we drove out a medieval tyranny only to make room for savage anarchy, we had better not have begun the task at all. It is worse than idle to say that we have no duty to perform, and can leave to their fates the islands we have conquered. Such a course would be the course of infamy. It would be followed at once by utter chaos in the wretched islands themselves. Some stronger manlier power would have to step in and do the work, and we would have shown ourselves weaklings, unable to carry to successful completion the labors that great and high-spirited nations are eager to undertake.

The work must be done; we cannot escape our responsibility and if we are worth our salt, we shall be glad of the chance to do the work, glad of the chance to show ourselves equal to one of the great tasks set modern civilization. But let us not deceive ourselves as to the importance of the task. Let us not be misled by vainglory into underestimating the strain it will put on our powers. Above all, let us, as we value our own self-respect, face the responsibilities with proper seriousness, courage, and high resolve. We must demand the higher order of integrity and ability in our public men who are to grapple with these new problems. We must hold to a rigid accountability those public servants who show unfaithfulness to the interests of the nation or inability to rise to the high level of the new demands upon our strength and our resources.

Now, apply all this to our public men of today. Our army has never been built up as it should be built up. I shall not discuss with an audience like this the puerile suggestion that a nation of seventy millions of freemen is in danger of losing its liberties from the existence of an army of one hundred thousand men, three-fourths of whom will be employed in certain foreign islands, in certain coast fortresses, and on Indian reservations. No man of good sense and stout heart can take such a proposition seriously. If we are such weaklings as the proposition implies, then we are unworthy of freedom in any event. To no body of men in the United States is the country so much indebted as to the splendid officers and enlisted men of the regular army and navy. There is no body from which the country has less to fear, and none of which it should be prouder, none which it should be more anxious to upbuild.

Our army needs complete reorganization—not merely enlarging—and the reorganization can only come as the result of legislation. A proper general staff should be established, and the positions of ord-nance, commissary, and quartermaster officers should be filled by detail from the line. Above all, the army must be given the chance to exercise in large bodies. Never again should we see, as we saw in the Spanish war, major-generals in command of divisions who had never before commanded three companies together in the field. Yet, incredible to relate, Congress has shown a queer inability to learn some of the lessons of the war. There were large bodies of men in both branches who opposed the declaration of war, who opposed the ratification of peace, who opposed the upbuilding of the army, and who even opposed the purchase of armor at a reasonable price for the battle-ships and cruisers, thereby putting an absolute stop to the building of any new fighting-ships for the navy. If, during the years to come, any disaster should befall our arms, afloat or ashore, and thereby any shame come to the United States, remember that the blame will lie upon the men whose names appear upon the roll-calls of Congress on the wrong side of these great questions. On them will lie the burden of any loss of our soldiers and sailors, of any dishonor to the flag; and upon you and the people of this country will lie the blame if you do

not repudiate, in no unmistakable way, what these men have done. The blame will not rest upon the untrained commander of untried troops, upon the civil officers of a department the organization of which has been left utterly inadequate, or upon the admiral with an insufficient number of ships; but upon the public men who have so lamentably failed in forethought as to refuse to remedy these evils long in advance, and upon the nation that stands behind those public men.

In the West Indies and the Philippines alike we are confronted by most difficult problems. It is cow-ardly to shrink from solving them in the proper way; for solved they must be, if not by us, then by some stronger and more manful race. If we are too weak, too selfish, or too foolish to solve them, some bolder and abler people must undertake the solution. Personally, I am far too firm a believer in the great-ness of my country and the power of my countrymen to admit for one moment that we shall ever be driven to the ignoble alternative.

The problems are different for the different islands. Porto Rico is not large enough to stand alone. We must govern it wisely and well, primarily in the interest of its own people. Cuba, is, in my judgment, entitled ultimately to settle for itself whether it shall be an independent state or an inte-gral portion of the mightiest of republics. But until order and stable liberty are secured, we must remain in the island to insure them, and infinite tact, judgment, moderation, and courage must be shown by our military and civil representatives in keeping the island pacified, in relentlessly stamping out brigandage, in protecting all alike, and yet in showing proper recognition to the men who have fought for Cuban liberty. The Philippines offer a yet graver problem. Their population includes half-caste and native Christians, warlike Moslems, and wild pagans. Many of their people are utterly unfit for self-government, and show no signs of becom-ing fit. Others may in time become fit but at pre-sent can only take part in self-government under a wise supervision, at once firm and beneficent. We have driven Spanish tyranny from the islands. If we now let it be replaced by savage anarchy, our work has been for harm and not for good. I have scant patience with those who fear to undertake the task of governing the Philippines, and who openly avow that they do fear to undertake it, or that they shrink from it because of the expense and trouble;

but I have even scanter patience with those who make a pretense of humanitarianism to hide and cover their timidity, and who cant about "liberty" and the "consent of the governed," in order to excuse themselves for their unwillingness to play the part of men. Their doctrines, if carried out, would make it incumbent upon us to leave the Apaches of Arizona to work out their own salvation, and to decline to interfere in a single Indian reservation. Their doctrines condemn your forefathers and mine for ever having settled in these United States.

England's rule in India and Egypt has been of great benefit to England, for it has trained up generations of men accustomed to look at the larger and loftier side of public life. It has been of even greater benefit to India and Egypt. And finally, and most of all, it has advanced the cause of civilization. So, if we do our duty aright in the Philippines, we will add to that national renown which is the highest and finest part of national life, will greatly benefit the people of the Philippine Islands, and, above all, we will play our part well in the great work of uplifting mankind. But to do this work, keep ever in mind that we must show in a very high degree the qualities of courage, of honesty, and of good judgment. Resistance must be stamped out. The first and all-important work to be done is to establish the supremacy of our flag. We must put down armed resistance before we can accomplish anything else, and there should be no parleying, no faltering, in dealing with our foe. As for those in our own country who encourage the foe, we can afford contemptuously to disregard them; but it must be remembered that their utterances are not saved from being treasonable merely by the fact that they are despicable.

When once we have put down armed resistance, when once our rule is acknowledged, then an even more difficult task will begin, for then we must see to it that the islands are administered with absolute honesty and with good judgment. If we let the public service of the islands be turned into the prey of the spoils politician, we shall have begun to tread the path which Spain trod to her own destruction. We must send out there only good and able men, chosen for their fitness, and not because of their partisan service, and these men must not only administer impartial justice to the natives and serve their own government with honesty and

fidelity, but must show the utmost tact and firmness, remembering that, with such people as those with whom we are to deal, weakness is the greatest of crimes, and that next to weakness comes lack of consideration for their principles and prejudices.

I preach to you, then, my countrymen, that our country calls not for the life of ease but for the life of strenuous endeavor. The twentieth century looms before us big with the fate of many nations. If we stand idly by, if we seek merely swollen, slothful ease and ignoble peace, if we shrink from the hard contests where men must win at hazard of their lives and at the risk of all they hold dear, then the bolder and stronger peoples will pass us by, and will win for themselves the domination of the world. Let us therefore boldly face the life of strife, resolute to do our duty well and manfully; resolute to uphold righteousness by deed and by word; resolute to be both honest and brave, to serve high ideals, yet to use practical methods. Above all, let us shrink from no strife, moral or physical, within or without the nation, provided we are certain that the strife is justified, for it is only through strife, through hard and dangerous endeavor, that we shall ultimately win the goal of true national greatness.

❧ Open Door Policy

WILLIAM W. ROCKHILL

At the dawn of the new century, the United States wanted to increase the commercial benefits of Chinese trade without accepting the burden of running a foreign colony. A weak Chinese government had allowed several European countries to develop "spheres of influence" along its heavily populated coast. The United States wanted part of the action.

American diplomat William W. Rockhill wrote a memorandum to Secretary of State John Hay in 1899 recommending the United States pursue an "open door" trade policy with China in which it developed its own sphere of influence through negotiations with China and other European powers. One year later 2,500 United States troops helped intervene in China to suppress the Boxer Rebellion, an anti-foreign uprising. For the next 50 years the United States remained tightly involved in Chinese domestic affairs, helping to spur Japanese tensions prior to World War II.

We find today in China that the policy of the "Open Door," the untrammeled exercise of the rights insured to Treaty Powers by the Treaty of Tientsin, and other treaties copied on it or under the most favored nation clause, is claimed by the mercantile classes of the United States and other powers as essential to the healthy extension of trade in China. We see, on the other hand, that the political interests and the geographical relations of Great Britain, Russia, and France to China have forced those countries to divide up China proper into areas or spheres of interest (or influence) in which they enjoy special rights and privileges, the ultimate scope of which is not yet determined, and that at the same time Great Britain, in its desire not to sacrifice entirely its mercantile interests, is also endeavoring to preserve some of the undoubted benefits of the "open door" policy, but "spheres of influence" are an accomplished fact, this cannot be too much insisted upon....

Such being the condition of things, and in view of the probability of complications soon arising between the interested powers in China, whereby it will become difficult, if not impossible, for the United States to retain the rights guaranteed them by treaties with China, what should be our immediate policy? To this question there can, it seems, be but one answer, we should at once initiate negotiations to obtain from those powers who have acquired zones of interest in China formal assurances that (1.) they will in no way interfere within their so-called spheres of interest with any treaty port or with vested rights in it of any nature; (2.) that all ports they may open in their respective spheres shall apply to all merchandise landed or shipped, no matter to what nationality belonging, and that the dues and duties provided for by the treaty shall be collected by the Chinese Government; and (3.) that they will levy no higher harbor dues on vessels of other nationalities frequenting their ports in such spheres than shall be levied on their national vessels, and that they will also levy no higher railroad charges on merchandise belongings to or destined for subjects of other powers transported through their spheres than shall be levied on similar merchandise belonging to its own nationality.

In other words, we should insist on absolute equality of treatment in the various zones, for equality of opportunity with the citizens of the favored powers we cannot hope to have, in view of the well known method now in vogue for securing privileges and concessions, though we should continually, by every proper means, seek to gain this also.

Such understandings with the various powers, and it is confidently believed that they could be

reached at present, would secure an open market throughout China for our trade on terms of equality with all other foreigners, and would further remove dangerous sources of irritation and possible conflict between the contending powers, greatly tending to re-establish confidence, and prepare the way for concerted action by the Powers to bring about the reforms in Chinese administration and the strengthening of the Imperial Government, recognized on all sides as essential to the maintenance of peace.

"The nation should assume power of regulation over all corporations"

THEODORE ROOSEVELT

On September 6, 1901, deranged anarchist Leon Czolgosz shot President McKinley twice at close range in Buffalo, New York. McKinley died eight days later. Theodore Roosevelt—described by industrialist Mark Hanna as that "damned cowboy"—became president. Roosevelt wasted little time in letting the nation know his concerns about what he called big business. In his first annual message to Congress on December 3, 1901, Roosevelt promised to apply the resources of the national government to restrain monopolies and trusts. The energetic Roosevelt initiated 44 lawsuits against trusts during his presidency and advocated for reforms such as the Food and Drug Act.

To the Senate and House of Representatives:
There is a widespread conviction in the minds of the American people that the great corporations known as trusts are in certain of their features and tendencies hurtful to the general welfare. This…is based upon sincere conviction that combination and concentration should be, not prohibited, but supervised and within reasonable limits controlled; and in my judgment this conviction is right.

It is no limitation upon property rights or freedom of contract to require that when men receive from government the privilege of doing business under corporate form, which frees them from individual responsibility, and enables them to call into their enterprises the capital of the public, they shall do so upon absolutely truthful representations as to the value of the property in which the capital is to be invested. Corporations engaged in interstate commerce should be regulated if they are found to exercise a license working to the public injury. It should be as much the aim of those who seek for social betterment to rid the business world of crimes of cunning as to rid the entire body politic of crimes of violence. Great corporations exist only because they are created and safeguarded by our institutions; and it is therefore our right and our duty to see that they work in harmony with these institutions.

The first essential in determining how to deal with the great industrial combinations is knowledge of the facts—publicity. In the interest of the public, the government should have the right to inspect and examine the workings of the great corporations engaged in interstate business. Publicity is the only sure remedy which we can now invoke. What further remedies are needed in the way of governmental regulation, or taxation, can only be determined after publicity has been obtained, by process of law, and in the course of administration. The first requisite is knowledge, full and complete—knowledge which may be made public to the world....

· The large corporations, commonly called trusts, though organized in one State, always do business in many States, often doing very little business in the State where they are incorporated. There is utter lack of uniformity in the State laws about them; and as no State has any exclusive interest in or power over their acts, it has in practice proved impossible to get adequate regulation through State action. Therefore, in the interest of the whole people, the nation should, without interfering with the power of the States in the matter itself, also assume power of supervision and regulation over all corporations doing an interstate business. This is especially true where the corporation derives a portion of its wealth from the existence of some monopolistic element or tendency in its business. There would be no hardship in such supervision; banks are subject to it, and in their case it is now accepted as a simple matter of course. Indeed, it is now probable that supervision of corporations by the National Government need not go so far as is now the case with the supervision exercised over them by so conservative a State as Massachusetts, in order to produce excellent results.

When the Constitution was adopted, at the end of the eighteenth century, no human wisdom could foretell the sweeping changes, alike in industrial and political conditions, which were to take place by the beginning of the twentieth century. At that time it was accepted as a matter of course that the several States were the proper authorities to regulate, so far as was then necessary, the comparatively insignificant and strictly localized corporate bodies of the day. The conditions are now wholly different and wholly different action is called for. I believe that a law can be framed which will enable the National Government to exercise control along the lines above indicated; profiting by the experience gained through the passage and administration of the Interstate Commerce Act. If, however, the judgment of the Congress is that it lacks the constitutional power to pass such an act, then a constitutional amendment should be submitted to confer the power.

❧ "As Regards Patriotism"

MARK TWAIN

The United States victory in the Spanish-American War and Roosevelt's "big stick" expansionary policy marked the high point in American imperial ambitions. But not everyone in the United States favored expansion. Observing that America had once been a colony itself, many questioned the need, morality and wisdom of the United States becoming a colonial power, particularly in the Philippines. Satirist Mark Twain opposed the country's imperial ambitions and in 1901 wrote a satirical essay "As Regards Patriotism" questioning American motives.

It is agreed, in this country, that if a man can arrange his religion so that it perfectly satisfies his conscience, it is not incumbent upon him to care whether the arrangement is satisfactory to anyone else or not.

In Austria and some other countries this is not the case. There the State arranges a man's religion for him, he has no voice in it himself.

Patriotism is merely a religion—love of country, worship of country, devotion to the country's flag and honor and welfare.

In absolute monarchies it is furnished from the Throne, cut and dried, to the subject; in England and America it is furnished, cut and dried, to the citizen by the politician and the newspaper.

The newspaper-and-politician-manufactured Patriot often gags in private over his dose; but he takes it, and keeps it on his stomach the best he can. Blessed are the meek.

Sometimes, in the beginning of an insane and shabby political upheaval, he is strongly moved to revolt, but he doesn't do it—he knows better. He knows that his maker would find it out—the maker of his Patriotism, the windy and incoherent six-dollar sub-editor of his village newspaper—and would bray out in print and call him a Traitor. And how dreadful that would be. It makes him tuck his tail between his legs and shiver. We all know—the reader knows it quite well—that two or three years ago nine-tenths of the human tails in England and America performed just that act. Which is to say, nine-tenths of the Patriots in England and America turned Traitor to keep from being called Traitor. Isn't it true? You know it to be true. Isn't it curious?

Yet it was not a thing to be very seriously ashamed of. A man can seldom—very, very seldom—fight a winning fight against his training; the odds are too heavy. For many a year—perhaps always—the training of the two nations had been dead against independence in political thought, persistently inhospitable toward Patriotism manufactured on a man's own premises, Patriotism reasoned out in the man's own head and fire-assayed and tested and proved in his own conscience. The resulting Patriotism was a shop-worn product procured at second hand. The Patriot did not know just how or when or where he got his opinions, neither did he care, so long as he was with what seemed the majority—which was the main thing, the safe thing, the comfortable thing. Does the reader believe he knows three men who have actual reasons for their pattern of Patriotism—and can furnish them? Let him not examine, unless he wants to be disappointed. He will be likely to find that his men got their Patriotism at the public trough, and had no hand in their preparation themselves.

Training does wonderful things. It moved the people of this country to oppose the Mexican war; then moved them to fall in with what they supposed was the opinion of the majority—majority-Patriotism is the customary Patriotism—and go down there and fight. Before the Civil War it made the North indifferent to slavery and friendly to the slave interest; in that interest it made Massachusetts hostile to the American flag, and she would not allow it to be hoisted on her State House—in her eyes it was the flag of a faction. Then by and by,

training swung Massachusetts the other way, and she went raging South to fight under that very flag and against their foretime protected-interest of hers.

Training made us nobly anxious to free Cuba; training made us give her a noble promise; training has enabled us to take it back. Long training made us revolt at the idea of wantonly taking any weak nation's country and liberties away from it, a short training has made us glad to do it, and proud of having done it. Training made us loathe Weyler's cruel concentration camps, training has persuaded us to prefer them to any other device for winning the love of our "wards."

There is nothing that training cannot do. Nothing is above its reach or below it. It can turn bad morals to good, good morals to bad; it can destroy prinicples, it can re-create them; it can debase angels to men and lift men to angelships. And it can do any one of these miracles in a year—even in six months.

Then men can be trained to manufacture their own Patriotism. They can be trained to labor it out in their own heads and hearts, and in the privacy and independence of their own premises. It can train them to stop taking it by command, as the Austrian takes his religion.

"If you strike that dog again, I'll kill you"

JACK LONDON

Gold was discovered in Alaska at the turn of the century, triggering one of the last great gold rushes in United States history. Alaska's population doubled to nearly 70,000. Between $17 million and $49 million of gold boullion was excavated annually from Alaska until 1916, often by lone miners who struck it rich. The risks and dangers of Alaska, however, were great. The weather was harsh and the landscape bleak. Mining proved difficult and laying railroads was even more so. By 1911 only one major railway had been built.

In 1903 Jack London—who had gone to Alaska to mine for gold—published *Call of the Wild,* his first best-selling novel. The story, told from the view of the dog "Buck," showed the hardships miners encountered in their quest for instant fortunes. The following excerpt reflects how ill-prepared some of the fortune-seekers were to face the Alaskan frontier. London's gritty, man-against-nature style was very popular and became part of a new genre of American literature.

Three days passed, by which time Buck and his mates

found how really tired and weak they were. Then, on the morning of the fourth day, two men from the States came along and bought them, harness and all, for a song. The men addressed each other as Hal and Charles. Charles was a middle-aged, lightish-colored man, with weak and watery eyes and a mustache that twisted fiercely and vigorously up, giving the lie to the limply drooping lip it concealed. Hal was a youngster of nineteen or twenty, with a big Colt's revolver and a hunting knife strapped about him on a belt that fairly bristled with cartridges. This belt was the most salient thing about him. It advertised his callowness–a callowness sheer and unutterable. Both men were manifestly out of place, and why such as they should adventure North is part of the mystery of things that passes understanding.

Buck heard the chaffering, saw the money pass between the man and the Government agent, and knew that the Scotch half-breed and the mail-train drivers were passing out of his life on the heels of Perrault and François and the others who had gone before. When driven with his mates to the new owners' camp, Buck saw a slipshod and slovenly affair, tent halfstretched, dishes unwashed, everything in disorder; also, he saw a woman. Mercedes the men called her. She was Charles's wife and Hal's sister–a nice family party.

Buck watched them apprehensively as they proceeded to take down the tent and load the sled. There was a great deal of effort about their manner, but no businesslike method. The tent was rolled into an awkward bundle three times as large as it should have been. The tin dishes were packed away unwashed. Mercedes continually fluttered in the way of her men and kept up an unbroken chattering of remonstrance and advice. When they put a clothes sack on the front of the sled, she suggested it should go on the back; and when they had put it on the back, and covered it over with a couple of other bundles, she discovered overlooked articles which could abide nowhere else but in that very sack, and they unloaded again.

Three men from a neighboring tent came out and looked on, grinning and winking at one another.

"You've got a right smart load as it is," said one of them; "and it's not me should tell you your business, but I wouldn't tote that tent along if I was you."

"Undreamed of!" cried Mercedes, throwing up her hands in dainty dismay. "However in the world could I manage without a tent?"

"It's springtime, and you won't get any more cold weather," the man replied.

She shook her head decidedly, and Charles and Hal put the last odds and ends on top the mountainous load.

"Think it'll ride?" one of the men asked.

"Why shouldn't it?" Charles demanded rather shortly

"Oh, that's all right, that's all right," the man hastened meekly to say. "I was just a-wonderin' that is all. It seemed a mite top heavy."

Charles turned his back and drew the lashings down as well as he could, which was not in the least well.

"An' of course the dogs can hike along all day with that contraption behind them," affirmed a second of the men.

"Certainly," said Hal, with freezing politeness, taking hold of the gee pole with one hand and swinging his whip from the other. "Mush!" he shouted. "Mush on there!"

The dogs sprang against the breastbands, strained hard for a few moments, then relaxed. They were unable to move the sled.

"The lazy brutes, I'll show them," he cried, preparing to lash out at them with the whip.

But Mercedes interfered, crying, "Oh, Hal, you mustn't," as she caught hold of the whip and wrenched it from him. "The poor dears! Now you must promise you won't be harsh with them for the rest of the trip, or I won't go a step."

"Precious lot you know about dogs," her brother sneered; "and I wish you'd leave me alone. They're lazy, I tell you, and you've got to whip them to get anything out of them. That's their way. You ask anyone. Ask one of those men."

Mercedes looked at them imploringly, untold repugnance at sight of pain written in her pretty face.

"They're weak as water, if you want to know," came the reply from one of the men. "Plumb tuckered out, that's what's the matter. They need a rest."

"Rest be blanked," said Hal, with his beardless lips; and Mercedes said, "Oh!" in pain and sorrow at the oath.

But she was a clannish creature, and rushed at

once to the defense of her brother. "Never mind that man," she said pointedly. "You're driving our dogs, and you do what you think best with them."

Again Hal's whip fell upon the dogs. They threw themselves against the breastbands, dug their feet into the packed snow, got down low to it, and put forth all their strength. The sled held as though it were an anchor. After two efforts, they stood still, panting. The whip was whistling savagely, when once more Mercedes interfered. She dropped on her knees before Buck, with tears in her eyes, and put her arms around his neck.

"You poor, poor dears," she cried sympathetically, "why don't you pull hard?–then you wouldn't be whipped." Buck did not like her, but he was feeling too miserable to resist her, taking it as part of the day's miserable work.

One of the onlookers, who had been clenching his teeth to suppress hot speech, now spoke up:

"It's not that I care a whoop what becomes of you, but for the dogs' sakes I just want to tell you, you can help them a mighty lot by breaking out that sled. The runners are froze fast. Throw your weight against the gee pole, right and left, and break it out."

A third time the attempt was made, but this time, following the advice, Hal broke out the runners which had been frozen to the snow. The overloaded and unwieldy sled forged ahead, Buck and his mates struggling frantically under the rain of blows. A hundred yards ahead the path turned and sloped steeply into the main street. It would have required an experienced man to keep the top-heavy sled upright, and Hal was not such a man. As they swung on the turn the sled went over, spilling half its load through the loose lashings. The dogs never stopped. The lightened sled bounded on its side behind them. They were angry because of the ill treatment they had received and the unjust load. Buck was raging. He broke into a run, the team following his lead. Hal cried "Whoa! whoa!" but they gave no heed. He tripped and was pulled off his feet. The capsized sled ground over him, and the dogs dashed up the street, adding to the gaiety of Skagway as they scattered the remainder of the outfit along its chief thoroughfare.

Kindhearted citizens caught the dogs and gathered up the scattered belongings. Also, they gave advice. Half the load and twice the dogs, if they ever expected to reach Dawson, was what was said. Hal and his sister and brother-in-law listened unwillingly, pitched tent, and overhauled the outfit. Canned goods were turned out that made men laugh, for canned goods on the Long Trail are a thing to dream about. "Blankets for a hotel," quoth one of the men who laughed and helped. "Half as many is too much; get rid of them. Throw away that tent, and all those dishes—who's going to wash them, anyway? Good Lord, do you think you're traveling on a Pullman?"

And so it went, the inexorable elimination of the superfluous. Mercedes cried when her clothes bags were dumped on the ground and article after article was thrown out. She cried in general, and she cried in particular over each discarded thing. She clasped hands about knees, rocking back and forth broken heartedly. She averred she would not go an inch, not for a dozen Charleses. She appealed to everybody and to everything, finally wiping her eyes and proceeding to cast out even articles of apparel that were imperative necessaries. And in her zeal, when she had finished with her own, she attacked the belongings of her men and went through them like a tornado.

This accomplished, the outfit, though cut in half, was still a formidable bulk. Charles and Hal went out in the evening and bought six Outside dogs. These, added to the six of the original team, and Teek and Koona, the huskies obtained at the Rink Rapids on the record trip, brought the team up to fourteen. But the Outside dogs, though practically broken in since their landing, did not amount to much. Three were short-haired pointers, one was a Newfoundland, and the other two were mongrels of indeterminate breed. They did not seem to know anything, these newcomers. Buck and his comrades looked upon them with disgust, and though he speedily taught them their places and what not to do, he could not teach them what to do. They did not take kindly to trace and trail. With the exception of the two mongrels, they were bewildered and spirit-broken by the strange, savage environment in which they found themselves and by the ill treatment they had received. The two mongrels were without spirit at all; bones were the only things breakable about them.

With the newcomers hopeless and forlorn, and the old team worn out by twenty-five hundred miles of continuous trail, the outlook was anything but bright. The two men, however, were quite cheerful. And they were proud, too. They were doing the thing in style, with fourteen dogs. They had seen other sleds depart over the Pass for Dawson, or come in from Dawson, but never had they seen a sled with so many as fourteen dogs. In the nature of Arctic travel there was a reason why fourteen dogs should not drag one sled, and that was that one sled could not carry the food for fourteen dogs. But Charles and Hal did not know this. They had worked the trip out with a pencil, so much to a dog, so many dogs, so many days, Q.E.D. Mercedes looked over their shoulders and nodded comprehensively, it was all so very simple.

Late next morning Buck led the long team up the street. There was nothing lively about it, no snap or go in him and his fellows. They were starting dead weary. Four times he had covered the distance between Salt Water and Dawson, and the knowledge that, jaded and tired, he was facing the same trail once more, made him bitter. His heart was not in the work, nor was the heart of any dog. The Outsides were timid and frightened, the Insides without confidence in their masters.

Buck felt vaguely that there was no depending upon these two men and the woman. They did not know how to do anything, and as the days went by it became apparent that they could not learn. They were slack in all things, without order or discipline. It took them half the night to pitch a slovenly camp, and half the morning to break that camp and get the sled loaded in fashion so slovenly that for the rest of the day they were occupied in stopping and rearranging the load. Some days they did not make ten miles. On other days they were unable to get started at all. And on no day did they succeed in making more than half the distance used by the men as a basis in their dog-food computation.

By this time all the amenities and gentlenesses of the Southland had fallen away from the three people. Shorn of its glamour and romance, Arctic travel became to them a reality too harsh for their manhood and womanhood. Mercedes ceased weeping over the dogs, being too occupied with weeping over herself and with quarreling with her husband and brother. To quarrel was the one thing they were never too weary to do. Their irritability arose out of their misery, increased with it, doubled upon it, outdistanced it. The wonderful patience of the trail which comes to men who toil hard and suffer sore, and remain sweet of speech and kindly, did not come to these two men and the woman. They had

no inkling of such a patience. They were stiff and in pain; their muscles ached, their bones ached, their very hearts ached; and because of this they became sharp of speech, and hard words were first on their lips in the morning and last at night.

It was beautiful spring weather, but neither dogs nor humans were aware of it. Each day the sun rose earlier and set later. It was dawn by three in the morning, and twilight lingered till nine at night. The whole long day was a blaze of sunshine. The ghostly winter silence had given way to the great spring murmur of awakening life. This murmur arose from all the land, fraught with the joy of living. It came from the things that lived and moved again, things which had been as dead and which had not moved during the long months of frost. The sap was rising in the pines. The willows and aspens were bursting out in young buds. Shrubs and vines were putting on fresh garbs of green. Crickets sang in the nights, and in the days all manner of creeping, crawling things rustled forth into the sun. Partridges and woodpeckers were booming and knocking in the forest. Squirrels were chattering, birds singing, and overhead honked the wild fowl driving up from the south in cunning wedges that split the air.

From every hill slope came the trickle of running water, the music of unseen fountains. All things were thawing, bending, snapping. The Yukon was straining to break loose the ice that bound it down. It ate away from beneath; the sun ate from above. Air holes formed, fissures sprang and spread apart, while thin sections of ice fell through bodily river. And amid all this bursting, rending, throbbing of the soft-sighing breezes, like wayfarers to death, staggered the two men, the woman, and the huskies.

With the dogs falling, Mercedes weeping and riding, Hal swearing innocuously, and Charles's eyes wistfully watering, they staggered into John Thornton's camp at the mouth of White River. When they halted, the dogs dropped down as though they had all been struck dead. Mercedes dried her eyes and looked at John Thornton. Charles sat down on a log to rest. He sat down very slowly and painstakingly what of his great stiffness. Hal did the talking. John Thornton was whittling the last touches on an ax handle he had made from a stick of birch. He whittled and listened, gave monosyllabic replies, and, when it was asked, terse advice. He knew the breed, and he gave his advice in the certainty that it would not be followed.

"They told us up above that the bottom was dropping out of the trail and that the best thing for us to do was to lay over," Hal said in response to Thornton's warning to take no more chances on the rotten ice. "They told us we couldn't make White River, and here we are." This last with a sneering ring of triumph in it.

"And they told you true," John Thornton answered. "The bottom's likely to drop out at any moment. Only fools, with the blind luck of fools, could have made it. I tell you straight, I wouldn't risk my carcass on that ice for all the gold in Alaska."

"That's because you're not a fool, I suppose," said Hal. "All the same, we'll go on to Dawson." He uncoiled his whip. "Get up there, Buck! Hi! Get up there! Mush on!"

Thornton went on whittling. It was idle, he knew, to get between a fool and his folly; while two or three fools more or less would not alter the scheme of things.

But the team did not get up at the command. It had long since passed into the stage where blows were required to rouse it. The whip flashed out, here and there, on its merciless errands. John Thornton compressed his lips. Sol-leks was the first to crawl to his feet. Teek followed. Joe came next, yelping with pain. Pike made painful efforts. Twice he fell over, when half up, and on the third attempt managed to rise. Buck made no effort. He lay quietly where he had fallen. The lash bit into him again and again, but he neither whined nor struggled. Several times Thornton started, as though to speak, but changed his mind. A moisture came into his eyes, and, as the whipping continued, he arose and walked irresolutely up and down.

This was the first time Buck had failed, in itself a sufficient reason to drive Hal into a rage. He exchanged the whip for the customary club. Buck refused to move under the rain of heavier blows which now fell upon him. Like his mates, he was barely able to get up, but, unlike them, he had made up his mind not to get up. He had a vague feeling of impending doom. This had been strong upon him when he pulled in to the bank, and it had not departed from him. With the thin and rotten ice he had felt under his feet all day, it seemed that he sensed disaster close at hand, out there ahead on the ice where his master was trying to drive him. He refused to stir. So greatly had he suffered, and so far gone was he, that the blows did not hurt much. And as they continued to fall upon him, the spark of life within flickered and went down. It was nearly out. He felt strangely numb. As though from a great distance, he was aware that he was being beaten. The last sensations of pain left him. He no longer felt anything, though very faintly he could hear the impact of the club upon his body. But it was no longer his body, it seemed so far away.

And then, suddenly, without warning, uttering a cry that was inarticulate and more like the cry of an animal, John Thornton sprang upon the man who wielded the club. Hal was hurled backward, as though struck by a falling tree. Mercedes screamed. Charles looked on wistfully, wiped his watery eyes, but did not get up because of his stiffness.

John Thornton stood over Buck, struggling to control himself, too convulsed with rage to speak.

"If you strike that dog again, I'll kill you," he at last, managed to say in a choking voice.

"It's my dog," Hal replied, wiping the blood from his mouth as he came back. "Get out of my way, or I'll fix you. I'm going to Dawson."

Thornton stood between him and Buck, and evinced no intention of getting out of the way. Hal drew his long hunting knife. Mercedes screamed, cried, laughed, and manifested the chaotic abandonment of hysteria. Thornton rapped Hal's knuckles with the ax handle, knocking the knife to the ground. He rapped his knuckles again as he tried to pick it up. Then he stooped, picked it up himself, and with two strokes cut Buck's traces.

Hal had no fight left in him. Besides, his hands were full with his sister, or his arms, rather; while Buck was too near dead to be of further use in hauling the sled. A few minutes later they pulled out from the bank and down the river. Buck heard them go and raised his head to see. Pike was leading, Sol-leks was at the wheel, and between were Joe and Teek. They were limping and staggering. Mercedes was riding the loaded sled. Hal guided at the gee pole, and Charles stumbled along in the rear.

As Buck watched them, Thornton knelt beside him and with rough, kindly hands searched for broken bones. By the time his search had disclosed nothing more than many bruises and a state of terrible starvation, the sled was a quarter of a mile away. Dog and man watched it crawling along over the ice. Suddenly, they saw its back end drop down, as into a rut, and the gee pole, with Hal clinging to it, jerk into the air. Mercedes's scream came to their ears. They saw Charles turn and make one step to run back, and then a whole section of ice give way and dogs and humans disappear. A yawning hole was all that was to be seen. The bottom had dropped out of the trail.

John Thornton and Buck looked at each other.

"You poor devil," said John Thornton, and Buck licked his hand.

❧ "The Oil War of 1872"

IDA M. TARBULL

In 1903 *McClure's Magazine* published a series of articles by investigative journalist Ida M. Tarbull detailing the ruthless business tactics used by John D. Rockefeller to gain a monopoly in the oil business. Shattering the popular image that hard work and perseverance were the keys to Rockefeller's success, Tarbull showed how Rockefeller employed chicanery and back-room deals with railroad companies to squash the competition.

More than any other single writer, Tarbull—whose father had been forced out of the oil business by Rockefeller—aroused public anger at the trusts that held a tight grip on American industry. Her articles generated a public outcry for action against Rockefeller's Standard Oil Trust, in particular, and business trusts in general. In 1911, Standard Oil was ordered to dismantle into several smaller companies.

Tarbull was one of several "muckraking" journalists of the time who exposed public corruption, abusive practices by industry leaders and the squalid conditions of the poor and working classes.

It was inevitable that under the pressure of their indignation and resentment some person or persons should be fixed upon as responsible, and should be hated accordingly. Before the lifting of the embargo this responsibility had been fixed. It was the Standard Oil Company of Cleveland, so the Oil Regions decided, which was at the bottom of the business, and the "Mephistopheles of the Cleveland Company," as they put it, was John D. Rockefeller. Even the *Cleveland Herald* acknowledged this popular judgment. "Whether justly or unjustly," the editor wrote, "Cleveland has the odium of having originated the scheme." This opinion gained ground as the days passed. The activity of the president of the Standard in New York, in trying to save

the contracts with the railroads, and his constant appearance with Mr. Watson, and the fact brought out by the Congressional investigation that a larger block of the South Improvement Company's stock was owned in the Standard than in any other firm, strengthened the belief. But what did more than anything else to fix the conviction was what they had learned of the career of the Standard Oil Company in Cleveland. Before the oil war the company had been known simply as one of several successful firms in that city. It drove close bargains, but it paid promptly, and was considered a desirable customer. Now the Oil Regions learned for the first time of the sudden and phenomenal expansion of the company. Where there had been at the beginning of 1872 twenty-six refining firms in Cleveland, there were but six left. In three months before and during the oil war the Standard had absorbed twenty plants. It was generally charged by the Cleveland refiners that Mr. Rockefeller had used the South Improvement scheme to persuade or compel his rivals to sell to him. "Why," cried the oil men, "the Standard Oil Company has done already in Cleveland what the South Improvement Company set out to do for the whole country, and it has done it by the same means."

By the time the blockade was raised, another unhappy conviction was fixed on the Oil Regions–the Standard Oil Company meant to carry out the plans of the exploded South Improvement Company. The promoters of the scheme were partly responsible for the report. Under the smart of their defeat they talked rather more freely than their policy of silence justified, and their remarks were quoted widely. Mr. Rockefeller was reported in the "Derrick" to have said to a prominent oil man of Oil City that the South Improvement Company could work under the charter of the Standard Oil Company, and to have predicted that in less than two months the gentleman would be glad to join him. The newspapers made much of the following similar story reported by a New York correspondent:

A prominent Cleveland member of what was the South Improvement Company had said within two days, "The business now will be done by the Standard Oil Company. We have a rate of freight by water from Cleveland to New York at 70 cents. No man in the trade shall make a dollar this year. We propose so manipulating the market as to run the price of crude on the Creek as low as two and a half. We mean to show the world that the South Improvement Company was organized for business and means business in spite of opposition. The same thing has been said in substance by the leading Philadelphia member."

"The trade here regards the Standard Oil Company as simply taking the place of the South Improvement Company and as being ready at any moment to make the same attempt to control the trade as its progenitors did," said the *New York Bulletin* about the middle of April. And the *Cleveland Herald* discussed the situation under the heading, "South Improvement Company alias Standard Oil Company." The effect of these reports in the Oil Regions was most disastrous. Their open war became a kind of guerrilla opposition. Those who sold oil to the Standard were ostracized, and its president was openly scorned.

Mr. Rockefeller Begins All Over Again

If Mr. Rockefeller had been an ordinary man the outburst of popular contempt and suspicion which suddenly poured on his head would have thwarted and crushed him. But he was no ordinary man. He had the powerful imagination to see what might be done with the oil business if it could be centered in his hands—the intelligence to analyze the problem into its elements and to find the key to control. He had the essential element to all great achievement, a steadfastness to a purpose once conceived which nothing can crush. The Oil Regions might rage, call him a conspirator and those who sold him oil traitors; the railroads might withdraw their contracts and the legislature annul his charter; undisturbed and unresting he kept at his great purpose. Even if his nature had not been such as to forbid him to abandon an enterprise in which he saw promise of vast profits, even if he had not had a mind which, stopped by a wall, burrows under or creeps around, he would nevertheless have been forced to desperate efforts to save his business. He had increased his refining capacity in Cleveland to 10,000 barrels on the strength of the South Improvement Company contracts. These contracts were annulled, and in their place was one signed by officials of all the oil-shipping roads refusing rebates to everybody. His geographical position was such that it cost him under these new contracts 50 cents more to get oil from the wells to New York than it

did his rivals on the Creek. What could he do?

Mr. Rockefeller Gets A Rebate

He got a rebate. In spite of the binding nature of the contracts signed in New York on March 25th by representatives of all the railroads, before the middle of April the Standard Oil Company was shipping oil eastward from Cleveland for $1.25–this by the sworn testimony of Mr. H.M. Flagler before a commission of the Ohio State Legislature, in March, 1879. How much less a rate than $1.25 Mr. Rockefeller had before the end of April the writer does not know. Of course the rate was secret, and he probably understood now, as he had not two months before, how essential it was that he keep it secret. His task was more difficult now, for he had an enemy active, clamorous, contemptuous, whose suspicions had reached that acute point where they could believe nothing but evil of him–the producers and independents of the Oil Regions. It was utterly impossible that he should ever silence this enemy, for their points of view were diametrically opposed.

They believed in independent effort–every man for himself and fair play for all. They wanted competition, loved open fight. They considered that all business should be done openly–that the railways were bound as public carriers to give equal rates–that any combination which favored one firm or one locality at the expense of another was unjust and illegal.

Mr. Rockefeller's Opinions And Character

Mr. Rockefeller's point of view was different. He believed that the "good of all" was in a combination which would control the business as the South Improvement Company proposed to control it. Such a combination would end at once all the abuses the business suffered. As rebates and special rates were essential to this control, he favored them. Of course Mr. Rockefeller knew that the railroad was a public carrier, and that its charter forbade discrimination. But he knew that the railroads did not pretend to obey the laws governing them, that they regularly granted special rates and rebates to those who had large amounts of freight. That is, you could bargain with the railroads as you could with a man carrying on a strictly private business depending in no way on a public franchise. Moreover, Mr. Rockefeller knew that if he did not get rebates somebody else would; that they were for the wariest, the shrewdest, the most persistent. If somebody was to get rebates, why not he? This point of view was no uncommon one. Many men held it and felt a sort of scorn, as practical men always do for theorists, when it was contended that the shipper was as wrong in taking rates as the railroads in granting them.

Thus, on one hand there was an exaggerated sense of personal independence, on the other a firm belief in combination; on one hand a determination to root out the vicious system of rebates practised by the railway, on the other a determination to keep it alive and profit by it. Those theories which the body of oil men held as vital and fundamental Mr. Rockefeller and his associates either did not comprehend or were deaf to. This lack of comprehension by many men of what seems to other men to be the most obvious principles of justice is not rare. Many men who are widely known as good, share it. Mr. Rockefeller was "good." There was no more faithful Baptist in Cleveland than he. Every enterprise of that church he had supported liberally from his youth. He gave to its poor. He visited its sick. He wept with its suffering. Moreover, he gave unostentatiously to many outside charities of whose worthiness he was satisfied. He was simple and frugal in his habits. He never went to the theater, never drank wine. He was a devoted husband, and he gave much time to the training of his children, seeking to develop in them his own habits of economy and of charity. Yet he was willing to strain every nerve to obtain for himself special and illegal privileges from the railroads which were bound to ruin every man in the oil business not sharing them with him. Religious emotion and sentiments of charity, propriety and self-denial seem to have taken the place in him of notions of justice and regard for the rights of others.

Unhampered, then, by any ethical consideration, undismayed by the clamor of the Oil Regions, believing firmly as ever that relief for the disorders in the oil business lay in combining and controlling the entire refining interest, this man of vast patience and foresight took up his work. The day after the newspapers of the Oil Regions printed the report of the Congressional Committee on Commerce denouncing the South Improvement Company as "one of the most gigantic and dangerous conspiracies ever attempted," and declaring

that if it had not been checked in time it "would have resulted in the absorption and arbitrary control of trade in all the great interests of the country," Mr. Rockefeller and several other members of the South Improvement Company appeared in the Oil Regions. They had come, they explained, to present a new plan of cooperation, and to show the oil men that it was to their interest to go into it. Whether they would be able to obtain by persuasion what they had failed to obtain by assault was now an interesting uncertainty.

❧ "The United States guarantees and will maintain the independence of Panama"

PANAMA CANAL TREATY

Eager to avoid the lengthy and dangerous voyage around South America, the United States and European countries sought ways to build a canal through Central America for many years. In 1850, the United States and Great Britain signed a treaty pledging to build a canal in cooperation with each other. In 1891, France started to construct an aqueduct in Nicaragua, but construction floundered due to disease and inadequate machinery.

In 1902, a United States commission selected a narrow portion of Panama as the best place to build a canal. Colombia rejected an offer to purchase the land. President Roosevelt turned to gunboat diplomacy. With United States support and an American gunboat off shore to back them up, Panama rebels declared independence on November 6, 1903. Two weeks later, the United States and Panama signed the Hay-Buneau-Varilla Treaty with virtually the identical terms offered to Colombia granting the United States land and permission to build the Panama Canal.

Work commenced on the 40 mile project in 1906. It took eight years, $300 million and more than five thousand lives to complete the Panama Canal—the largest construction project in world history up to that time. Colombia did not recognize Panama until 1925.

Article I. The United States guarantees and will maintain the independence of the Republic of Panama.

Article II. The Republic of Panama grants to the United States in perpetuity the use, occupation and control of a zone of land and land under water for the construction, maintenance, operation, sanitation and protection of said Canal of the width of ten miles extending to the distance of five miles on each side of the center line of the route of the canal to be constructed; the said zone beginning in the Caribbean Sea, three marine miles from mean low water mark, and extending to and across the Isthmus of Panama into the Pacific Ocean to a distance of three marine miles from mean low water mark, with the proviso that the cities of Panama and Colon and the harbors adjacent to said cities, which are included within the boundaries of the zone above described, shall not be included within this grant. The Republic of Panama further grants to the United States in perpetuity the use, occupation and control of any other lands and waters outside of the zone above described which may be necessary and convenient for the construction, maintenance, operation, sanitation and protection of the said Canal or of any auxiliary Canals or other works necessary and convenient for the construction, maintenance, operation, sanitation and protection of the said enterprise.

The Republic of Panama further grants in like manner to the United States in perpetuity all islands within the limits of the zone above described and in addition thereto the group of small islands in the Bay of Panama, named Perico, Naos, Culebra and Flamenco....

Article V. The Republic of Panama grants to the United States in perpetuity a monopoly for the construction, maintenance and operation of any system of communication by means of canal or railroad across its territory between the Caribbean Sea and the Pacific Ocean....

Article VIII. The Republic of Panama grants to the United States all rights which it now has or hereafter may acquire to the property of the New Panama Canal Company and the Panama Railroad Company as a result of the transfer of sovereignty from the Republic of Colombia to the Republic of Panama over the Isthmus of Panama and authorizes the New Panama Canal Company to sell and transfer to the United States its rights, privileges, properties and concessions as well as the Panama Railroad and all the shares or part of the shares of that company.

Article IX. The United States agrees that the ports at either entrance of the Canal and the waters thereof and the Republic of Panama agrees that the towns of Panama and Colon shall be free for all time so that there shall not be imposed or collected custom house tolls, tonnage, anchorage, lighthouse, wharf, pilot or quarantine dues or any other charges or taxes of any kind upon any vessel using or passing through the Canal or belonging to or employed by the United States, directly or indirectly, in connection with the construction, maintenance, operation, sanitation and protection of the main Canal, or auxiliary works, or upon the cargo, officers, crew or passengers of any such vessels, except such tolls and charges as may be imposed by the United States for the use of the Canal and other works, and except tolls and charges imposed by the Republic of Panama upon merchandise destined to be introduced for the consumption of the rest of the Republic of Panama, and upon vessels touching at the ports of Colon and Panama and which do not cross the Canal.

The Government of the Republic of Panama shall have the right to establish in such ports and in the towns of Panama and Colon such houses and guards as it may deem necessary to collect duties on importations destined to other portions of Panama and to prevent contraband trade. The United States shall have the right to make use of the towns and harbors of Panama and Colon as places of anchorage, and for making repairs, for loading, unloading, depositing or trans-shipping cargoes either in transit or destined for the service of the canal and for other works pertaining to the canal.

Article X. The Republic of Panama agrees that there shall not be imposed any taxes, national, municipal, departmental or of any other class upon the Canal, the railways and auxiliary works, tugs and other vessels employed in the service of the canal, storehouse, workshops, offices, quarters for laborers, factories of all kinds, warehouses, wharves, machinery and other works, property, and effects appertaining to the Canal or railroad and auxiliary works, or their officers or employees, situated within the cities of Panama and Colon, and that there shall not be imposed contributions or charges of a personal character of any kind upon officers, employees, laborers and other individuals in the service of the Canal and railroad and auxiliary works....

Article XIV. As the price or compensation for the rights, powers and privileges granted in this convention by the Republic of Panama to the United States, the Government of the United

States agrees to pay to the Republic of Panama the sum of ten million dollars ($10,000,000) in gold coin of the United States on the exchange of the ratification of this convention and also an annual payment during the life of this convention of two hundred and fifty thousand dollars ($250,000) in like gold coin, beginning nine years after the date aforesaid.

The provisions of this article shall be in addition to all other benefits assured to the Republic of Panama under this convention.

But no delay or difference of opinion under this article or any other provisions of this treaty shall affect or interrupt the full operation and effect of this convention in all other respects....

Article XVIII. The Canal, when constructed, and the entrances thereto shall be neutral in perpetuity, and shall be opened upon the terms provided for by Section 1 of Article III of, and in conformity with all the stipulations of, the treaty entered into by the Governments of the United States and Great Britain on November 18, 1901.

Article XXIII. If it should become necessary at any time to employ armed forces for the safety or protection of the Canal, or of the ships that make use of the same, or the railways and auxiliary works, the United States shall have the right, at all times and in its discretion, to use its police and its land and naval forces or to establish fortifications for these purposes.

Article XXIV. No change either in the Government or in the laws and treaties of the Republic of Panama shall, without the consent of the United States, affect any right of the United States under the present convention, or under any treaty stipulation between the two countries that now exists or may hereafter exist touching the subject matter of this convention.

If the Republic of Panama shall hereafter enter as a constituent into any other Government or into any union or confederation of States, so as to merge her sovereignty or independence in such Government, union or confederation, the rights of the United States under this convention shall not be in any respect lessened or impaired.

Article XXV. For better performance of the engagements of this convention and to the end of the efficient protection of the Canal and the preservation of its neutrality, the Government of the Republic of Panama will sell or lease to the United States lands adequate and necessary for naval or coaling stations on the Pacific coast and on the western Caribbean coast of the Republic at certain points to be agreed upon with the President of the United States....

"It was my dream to come [to the United States]"

JESÚS GARCIA

Between 1900 and 1920 more than 500,000 Mexicans, mostly young men, migrated to Texas, New Mexico, Arizona and California looking for work. Several factors led to the northward migration. Many fled the violent revolution that was taking place in Mexico. Economic opportunities were limited and violence was ever present. In the United States Southwest, however, the Reclamation Act of 1902 helped lead to the irrigation of desert land into agricultural fields. Restrictions on Asian immigration increased the need for other sources of cheap farm labor. Railroads also sought Mexican workers. In 1910, nearly 2,000 Mexicans a month were taking jobs on railroad construction crews.

Mexican-American relations, however, deteriorated. Cultures clashed, Mexicans were discriminated against and lynchings began to occur. Border conflicts with Mexican soldiers and revolutionaries also heightened tensions for Mexican immigrants. Jesús Garcia came to America at the turn of the century in an attempt to find better work, better living conditions and better wages. He described his experience in 1931 to sociologist Manuel Gamio for his collection of oral histories, *The Mexican Immigrant: His Life Story*.

Since I was very small I had the idea of going out to know the world, to go about a lot in every direction. As I heard a lot about the United States, it was my dream to come here....I was in school where my father was a teacher but when the revolution came and months went by without their paying him and there was a lot of trouble, my father resigned. He then started a store but I went on in a school where an uncle of mine was a professor. This uncle, however, didn't take much interest in my learning so I quit school and studied at home and helped my father in the store....

When I was about twenty I decided to leave home and come here. I waited one day until my father went out and then I took money out of the strong box, gold coins especially. I took out enough to take me to San Antonio and took the train for

Nuevo Laredo. I crossed the border there. I had no trouble, although it was the first time I had come. I paid my $8, passed my examination, then changed my Mexican coins for American money and went to San Antonio, Texas.

When I arrived there, I looked for work but couldn't find any so that I went to [a labor contractor]. They said I was to go and work on the tracks. I didn't know what that was but I contracted to work because my money was giving out. I only had three dollars left. I gave one to the contractor, and he then took me with a lot of Mexicans to a railroad camp.

I worked all day, but as I wasn't used to such a heavy kind of work I thought of leaving. I could hardly finish out working that first day. I thought I was going to die because the work was so hard. At night I asked the boys slyly where Dallas, Texas, was or some other large city and they told me down the tracks and said that if I wanted to go I should catch a freight train and go as a tramp. But I didn't let them suspect anything but told them I was only fooling. I also asked them how one could get there on foot and they said by following the tracks but that one should be careful and cross the bridges in a hurry so that a train wouldn't overtake one. In that part of Texas there are many bridges. On the next day, without their noticing it, I left on foot, and went down the tracks. I left at about seven in the morning and reached the outskirts of Dallas at about six in the evening. It was already getting dark and I only had a dollar with me as I hadn't even gotten my day's pay.

On reaching the outskirts of Dallas, I saw a man who seemed to me to be a Negro and at the same time a Mexican and I thought of speaking to him. As I didn't know English I said to myself, if he is a Negro he isn't going to pay any attention to me. Finally I spoke to him in Spanish and it turned out that he was Mexican, although to tell the truth he looked like a Negro. I told him how I had come and he said that I could spend the night there in his house. He gave me something to eat and a mattress on which to sleep.

On the next day the same man took me to the house of an old man who rented rooms. The old man received me very kindly into his home and gave me a room. When I told him that I didn't have either money or a job he said that I shouldn't worry. I could pay him when I had some. I was

there about a month without working and the man and his wife, both of them quite old, took as good care of me as though I was paying them. They gave me food, my room, and even cleaned my clothes. They had some children now grown up.

Finally I managed to get work laying pipes and I was working for two weeks earning $2.50 a day. Then they laid me off because they said that I wasn't strong enough for hard work…. Then a Mexican advised me to look for work in the hotels and restaurants because that fitted me, but I couldn't find that, because it is necessary to speak English for those jobs. Then I got a job with an electric company….They wanted me to go down into a well with a pick and make it deeper. I think that it was 20 meters deep and I also had to wheel stones. This work was so hard that I could hardly finish the day, for at about four o'clock in the afternoon the foreman wanted me to lift a rock so big that I couldn't even move it much less lift it. He then said that if I couldn't do that it was better that I quit so that I asked for my time, and they gave me $2.50.

I kept on looking for work and in about three days I found one in a restaurant as "vegetable man" (peeling vegetables). I stayed there about two months and on account of a Mexican who went to tell the manager that I couldn't do that work they fired me. Then I went to another restaurant and hotel and there they gave me a job as dish-washer. I was then learning a little English. When they needed a new "vegetable man," I told the foreman that I could do the work and he gave it to me with an increase in pay. I think that they paid me $45 a month and my food. That boss was an American but very good and he told me that he was going to teach me how to do everything so that when anyone was missing I could take their place. He taught me to be a cook and to do all the work of the kitchen, bake, etc. He even increased my pay until I was getting $75 a month and my food.

By that time I stopped living at the house of the old man of whom I have told you. That was because I don't like to live at the edges of the town. In the outskirts there are no police nor authorities and one can be assaulted and even killed and no one will notice it. But I have remained very thankful to that old man and I told him that I would always be his friend and would go to visit him. I paid the old man there $4 a month but then I found a good friend with whom I took in the downtown district a room for which we paid between the two of us $15 a month, $7.50 each. I worked ten hours a day and he did also. My pal was Mexican and we cared for each other more than brothers. When one didn't have money the other did and we helped each other in everything....Once I told my friend that we should go to Mexico but he said not, because he was in love with a girl who was his sweetheart.

I then told the boss to give me my time. The boss asked me why I wanted to go and if I wanted permission to go he would let me go for two weeks or a month. I then told him that I was going to Mexico to see my people. He answered that if I was going I should know that I always had my job there anytime that I should come back.

I then went to Aguascalientes taking a lot of clothes with me and a little money. I went to my home and my parents were very happy. But I found everything different, very dull, and very changed. I no longer wished to stay there but to return to Dallas. Then without my people knowing it I left again leaving all of my clothes for I only brought what I had on and a little money. I came to Ciudad Juarez and from there I went to El Paso without any trouble. There I sent a telegram to my boss in Dallas. He answered saying that my job was ready for me there.

I was all ready to go to Dallas when some friends told me that Los Angeles was very pretty, that one could earn a lot of money there and a lot of things, so that I took the train to Los Angeles. But as I came on the train I got sick and I decided to stay in Phoenix for I was afraid of getting sicker. As soon as I was well I began to look for work. Earlier I didn't mind being without work for weeks but now I did.

I soon found work at a sanatorium of the city, there in the outskirts. They paid me $65 a month and my board and room but I worked more than 10 hours for as soon as a patient came I had to give him water and food and had a lot of trouble. Once a patient got hard-boiled because I was late with the food. It wasn't my fault for the cook was late. I told him so and he said, "Shut up, Mexican." I then called him "a son of a viche" and he said that he was going to ask to have me fired. I told him all right and then went to the doctor and asked him to give me my time. Then I told him what had happened and he

told me not to answer the patients, not to pay any attention to them for they were like children or crazy people and said that the reason why we Mexicans don't get ahead is because we can't get used to staying in one place. I told him to give me my time and that was all, for I wasn't used to have anyone shout at me. He gave me my time but he told me that when I wanted to come back he would give me work.

Then I got a job as a "vegetable-man" but when the boss saw that I knew how to cook and everything he raised my pay to $75 and put me as a cook together with the other cooks who are Americans or Greeks. I am the only Mexican there is in this hotel. The only thing is that here we don't have a day off as there is little business. They have a few cooks and they can't substitute very easily. Only once in a while when I ask for rest do they give it to me and put a boy in my place....

"The machine started off with its ups and downs"

ORVILLE WRIGHT

On a windy December 17, 1903, bicycle mechanics Orville and Wilbur Wright made the first successful sustained manned flight in a gasoline-powered aircraft on the beach at Kitty Hawk, North Carolina. The Wright brothers made four attempts with the longest one covering 852 feet during 59 seconds. This account comes from Orville's diary.

When we got up a wind of between 20 and 25 miles was blowing from the north. We got the machine out early and put out the signal for the men at the station.... After running the engine and propellers a few minutes to get them in working order, I got on the machine at 10:35 for the first trial....On slipping the rope the machine started off increasing in speed to probably 7 or 8 miles. The machine lifted from the truck just as it was entering on the fourth rail. Mr. Daniels took a picture just as it left the tracks. I found the control of the front rudder quite difficult on account of its being balanced too near the center and thus had a tendency to turn itself when started so that the rudder was turned too far on one side and then too far on the other. As a result the machine would rise suddenly to about 10 ft. and then as suddenly, on turning the rudder, dart for the ground. A sudden dart went out about 100 feet from the end of the tracks ended the flight. Time about 12 seconds (not known exactly as watch was not promptly stopped). The lever for throwing off the engine was broken, and the skid under the rudder cracked. After repairs, at 20 min. after 11 o'clock Will made the second trial. The course was about like mine, up and down but a little longer over the ground though about the same in time. Dist. not measured but about 175 ft. Wind speed not quite so strong. With the aid of the station men present, we picked the machine up and carried it back to the starting ways. At about 20 minutes till 12 o'clock I made the third trial. When out about the same distance as Will's, I met with a strong gust from the left which raised the left wing and sidled the machine off to the right in a lively manner. I immediately turned the rudder to bring the machine down and then worked the end control….At just 12 o'clock Will started on the fourth and last trip.

The machine started off with its ups and downs as it had before, but by the time he had gone over three or four hundred feet he had it under much better control, and was traveling on a fairly even course. It proceeded in this manner till it reached a small hummock out about 800 feet from the starting ways, when it began its pitching again and suddenly darted into the ground. The front rudder frame was badly broken up, but the main frame suffered none at all. The distance over the ground was 852 feet in 59 seconds. The engine turns was 1071, but this included several seconds while on the starting ways and probably about a half second after landing. The jar of landing had set the watch on machine back so that we have no exact record for the 1071 turns. Will took a picture of my third flight just before the gust struck the machine. The machine left the ways successfully at every trial, and the tail was never caught by the truck as we had feared.

After removing the front rudder, we carried the machine back to camp. We set the machine down a few feet west of the building, and while standing about discussing the last flight, a sudden gust of wind struck the machine and started to turn it over. All rushed to stop it. Will who was near one end ran to the front, but too late to do any good. Mr. Daniels and myself seized spars [uprights] at the rear, but to no purpose. The machine gradually turned over on

us. Mr. Daniels, having had no experience in handling a machine of this kind, hung on to it from the inside, and as a result was knocked down and turned over and over with it as it went. His escape was miraculous, as he was in with the engine and chains. The engine legs were all broken off, the chain guides badly bent, a number of uprights, and nearly all the rear ends of the ribs were broken.

"I seen my opportunities and I took 'em"

GEORGE WASHINGTON PLUNKITT

George Washington Plunkitt was a plain-spoken ward boss in New York City's notorious Tammany Hall political machine. In a series of interviews with *New York Evening Post* reporter William L. Riordon, Plunkitt explained how city politics worked. Contemptuous of political reformers, the Irish-American politician made his own distinction between "honest graft and dishonest graft" in city politics and explained the advantages of using party machines to run city governments.

Riordon published the interviews in 1905 as a series of articles and in the book *Plunkitt of Tammany Hall.* Plunkitt's assessment illustrated how politics and business overlapped in the operations of a city, and also the inherent problems of reformers efforts to purify city politics. The interviews offer an insight into the way city politics operated throughout the country, reflecting the ingrained problems they created. Many of the reform efforts to eradicate corrupt practices took on social-religious undertones as most political machines were operated by Catholic immigrants while the reformers were usually Protestants.

Everybody is talkin' these days about Tammany men growin' rich on graft, but nobody thinks of drawin' the distinction between honest graft and dishonest graft. There's all the difference in the world between the two. Yes, many of our men have grown in politics. I have myself. I've made a big fortune out of the game, and I'm getting richer every day, but I've not gone in for dishonest graft—blackmailin' gamblers, saloon-keepers, disorderly people, etc.—and neither has any of the men who made big fortunes in politics.

There's an honest graft, and I'm an example of how it works. I might sum up the whole thing by sayin': "I seen my opportunities and I took 'em."

Just let me explain by examples. My party's in power in the city and it's goin' to undertake a lot of public improvements. Well, I'm tipped off, say, that they're going to lay out a new park at a certain place.

I see my opportunity and I take it. I go that place and I buy up all the land I can get in the neighborhood. Then the board of this or that makes its plan public, and there is a rush to get my land, which nobody cared particular before.

Ain't it perfectly honest to charge a good price and make a profit on my investment and foresight? Of course it is. Well, that's honest graft.

Or, supposin' it's a new bridge they're goin' to build. I get tipped off and I buy as much property as I can that has to be taken for approaches. I sell at my own price later on and drop some more money in the bank.

Wouldn't you? It's just like lookin' ahead in Wall Street or in the coffee market. It's honest graft, and I'm lookin' for it every day in the year. I will tell you frankly that I've got a good lot of it, too.

I'll tell you of one case. They were goin' to fix up a big park, no matter where. I got on to it, and went lookin' about for land in that neighborhood.

I could get nothin' at a bargain but a big piece of swamp, but I took it fast enough and held on to it. What turned out was just what I counted on. They couldn't make the park complete without Plunkitt's swamp, and they had to pay a good price for it. Anything dishonest in that?

Up in the watershed I made some money, too. I bought up several bits of land there some years ago and made a pretty good guess that they would be bought up for water purposes later by the city.

Somehow, I always guessed about right, and shouldn' I enjoy the profit of my foresight? It was rather amusin' when the condemnation commissioners came along and found piece after piece of the land in the name of George Plunkitt of the Fifteenth Assembly District, New York City. They wondered how I knew just what to buy. The answer is—I seen my opportunity and I took it. I haven't confined myself to land; anything that pays is in my line.

For instance, the city is repavin' a street and has several hundred thousand old granite blocks to sell. I am on hand to buy, and I know just what they are worth.

How? Never mind that. I had a sort of monop-oly of this business for a while, but once a newspaper tried to do me. It got some outside men to come over from Brooklyn and New Jersey to bid against me.

Was I done? Not much. I went to each of the men and said: "How many of these 250,000 stones do you want?" One said 20,000, and another wanted 15,000, and another wanted 10,000. I said: "All right, let me bid for the lot, and I'll give each of you all you want for nothin'."

They agreed, of course. Then the auctioneer yelled: "How much am I bid for these 250,000 fine pavin' stones?"

"Two dollars and fifty cents," says I.

"Two dollars and fifty cents!" screamed the auctioneer. "Oh, that's a joke. Give me a real bid."

He found the bid was real enough. My rivals stood silent. I got the lot for $2.50 and gave them their share. That's how the attempt to do Plunkitt ended, and that's how all such attempts end.

I've told you how I got rich by honest graft. Now, let me tell you that most politicians who are accused of robbin' the city get rich the same way.

They didn't steal a dollar from the city treasury. They just seen their opportunities and took them. That is why, when a reform administration comes in and spend a half million dollars a tryin' to find the public robberies they talked about in the campaign, they don't find them.

The books are always right. The money in the city treasury is all right. Everything is all right. All they can show is that the Tammany heads of departments looked after their friends, within the law, and gave them what opportunities they could to make honest graft. Now, let me tell you that's never goin' to hurt Tammany with the people. Every good man looks after his friends, and any man who doesn't isn't likely to be popular. If I have a good thing to hand out in private life, I give it to a friend. Why shouldn't I do the same in public life?

Another kind of honest graft. Tammany has raised a good many salaries. There was an awful howl by the reformers, but don't you know that Tammany gains ten votes for every one it lost by salary raisin'?

The Wall Street banker thinks it shameful to raise a department clerk's salary from $1,500 to $1,800 a year, but every man who draws a salary himself says: "That's all right. I wish it was me."

And he feels very much like votin' the Tammany ticket on election day, just out of sympathy.

Tammany was beat in 1901 because the people were deceived into believin' that it worked dishonest graft. They didn't draw a distinction between dishonest and honest graft, but they saw that some Tammany men grew rich, and supposed they had been robbin' the city treasury or levyin' blackmail on disorderly houses or workin' in with the gamblers and lawbreakers.

As a matter of policy, if nothing else, why should the Tammany leaders go into such dirty business when there is so much honest graft lyin' around when they are in power? Did you ever consider that?

Now, in conclusion, I want to say that I don't own a dishonest dollar. If my worst enemy was given the job of writin' my epitaph when I'm gone, he couldn't do more than write:

"George W. Plunkitt. He Seen His Opportunities, and He Took 'Em."

Reformers Only Mornin' Glories

College professors and philosophers who go up in a balloon to think are always discussin' the question: "Why Reform Administrations Never Succeed Themselves!" The reason is plain to anybody who has learned the a, b, c, of politics.

I can't tell just how many of these movements I've seen started in New York during my forty years in politics, but I can tell you how many have lasted more than a few years—one. There have been reform committees of fifty, of sixty, of seventy, of one hundred and all sorts of numbers that started out to do up the regular political organizations. They were mornin' glories—looked lovely in the mornin' and withered up in a short time, while the regular machines went on flourishin' forever, like fine old oaks. Say, that's the first poetry I ever worked off. Ain't it great?

Just look back a few years. You remember the People's Municipal League that nominated Frank Scott for mayor in 1890? Do you remember the reformers that got up that league? Have you ever heard of them since? I haven't. Scott himself survived because he had always been a first-rate politician, but you'd have to look in the newspaper almanacs of 1891 to find out who made up the People's Municipal League. Oh, yes! I remember one name: Ollie Teal; dear, pretty Ollie and his big dog. They're about all that's left of the League.

Now take the reform movement of 1894. A lot of good politicians joined in that—the Republicans, the State Democrats, the Stecklerites and the O'Brienites, and they gave us a lickin', but the real reform part of the affair, the Committee of Seventy that started the thing goin' what's become of those reformers? What's become of Charles Stewart Smith? Where's Bangs? Do you ever hear of Cornell, the iron man, in politics now? Could a search party find R. W. G. Welling? Have you seen the name of Fulton McMahon or McMahon Fulton—I ain't sure which—in the papers lately? Or Preble Tucker? Or—but it's no use to go through the list of the reformers who said they sounded in the death knell of Tammany in 1894. They're gone for good, and Tammany's pretty well, thank you. They did the talkin' and posin', and the politicians in the movement got all the plums. It's always the case.

The citizens' Union has lasted a little bit longer than the reform crowd that went before them, but that's because they learned a thing or two from us. They learned how to put up a pretty good bluff—and bluff counts a lot in politics. With only a few thousand members, they had the nerve to run the whole Fusion movement, make the Republicans and other organizations come to their headquarters to select a ticket and dictate what every candidate must do or not do. I love nerve, and I've had a sort of respect for the Citizens' Union lately, but the Union can't last. Its people haven't been trained to politics, and whenever Tammany calls their bluff they lay right down. You'll never hear of the Union again after a year or two.

And, by the way, what's become of the good government clubs, the political nurseries of a few years ago? Do you ever hear of Good Government Club D and P and Q and Z any more? What's become of the infants who were to grow up and show us how to govern the city? I know what's become of the nursery that was started in my district. You can find pretty much the whole outfit over in my headquarters, Washington Hall.

The fact is that a reformer can't last in politics. He can make a show for a while, but he always comes down like a rocket. Politics is as much a regular business as the grocery or dry-goods or the drug business. You've got to be trained up to it or you're sure to fall. Suppose a man who knew nothing about the grocery trade suddenly went into business and tried to conduct it according to his own ideas. Wouldn't he make a mess of it? He might make a splurge for a while, as long as his money lasted, but his store would soon be empty. It's just the same with a reformer. He hasn't been brought up in the difficult business of politics and he makes a mess of it every time.

I've been studyin' the political game for forty-five years, and I don't know it all yet. I'm learnin' somethin' all the time. How, then, can you expect what they call "business men" to turn into politics all at once a make a success of it? It is just as if I went to Columbia University and started to teach Greek. They usually last about as long in politics as I would last at Columbia.

You can't begin too early in politics if you want to succeed at the game. I began several years before I could vote, and so did every successful leader in Tammany Hall. When I was twelve years old I made myself useful around the district headquarters and did work at the polls on election day. Later on, I hustled about gettin' out voters who had jags on or who were too lazy to come to the polls. There's a hundred ways that boys can help, and they get an experience that's the first real step in statesmanship. Show me a boy that hustles for the organization on election day, and I'll show you a comin' statesman.

That's the a, b, c of politics. It ain't easy work to get up to y and z. You have to give nearly all your time and attention to it. Of course, you may have some business or occupation on the side, but the great business of your life must be politics if you want to succeed in it. A few years ago Tammany tried to mix politics and business in equal quantities by havin' two leaders for each district, a politician and a business man. They wouldn't mix. They were like oil and water. The politician looked after the politics of his district; the businessman looked after his grocery store or his milk route, and whenever he appeared at an executive meeting, it was only to make trouble. The whole scheme turned out to be a farce and was abandoned mighty quick.

Do you understand now, why it is that a reformer goes down and out in the first or second round, while a politician answers to the gong every time? It is because the one has gone into the fight without trainin', while the other trains all the time and knows every fine point of the game.

❧ The Jungle

UPTON SINCLAIR

Upton Sinclair's novel *The Jungle* was published in 1906 as a harsh critique of modern industry's brutal impact on individuals. The muckraking book's greatest impact, however, came from Sinclair's description of a meat-packing factory. The exposé prompted federal investigations into the food industry and resulted in the Pure Food and Drug Act of 1906 creating national standards and federal inspectors to enforce them. To Sinclair's disappointment, however, no action was taken to ease working conditions for the meat packers themselves. An excerpt of the book follows.

There was another interesting set of statistics that a person might have gathered in Packingtown—those of the various afflictions of the workers. When Jurgis had first inspected the packing plants with Szedvilas, he had marveled while he listened to the tale of all the things that were made out of the carcasses of animals and of all the lesser industries that were maintained there; now he found that each one of these lesser industries was a separate little inferno, in its way as horrible as the killing-beds, the source and fountain of them all. The workers in each of them had their own peculiar diseases. And the wandering visitor might be skeptical about all the swindles, but he could not be skeptical about these, for the worker bore the evidence of them about on his own person—generally he had only to hold out his hand.

There were the men in the pickle rooms, for instance, where old Antanas had gotten his death; scarce a one of these had not some spot of horror on his person. Let a man so much as scrape his finger pushing a truck in the pickle rooms, and he might have a sore that would put him out of the world; all the joints in his fingers might be eaten by the acid, one by one. Of the butchers and floormen, the beef boners and trimmers, and all those who used knives, you could scarcely find a person who had the use of his thumb; time and time again the base of it had been slashed, till it was a mere lump of flesh against which the man pressed the knife to hold it. The hands of these men would be criss-crossed with cuts, until you could no longer pretend to count them or to trace them. They would have no nails—they had worn them off pulling hides; their knuckles were swollen so that their fingers spread out like a fan. There were men who worked in the cooking rooms, in the midst of steam and sickening odors, by artificial light; in these rooms the germs of tuberculosis might live for two years, but the supply was renewed every hour. There were the beef luggers, who carried two-hundred-pound quarters into the refrigerator cars, a fearful kind of work, that began at four o'clock in the morning, and that wore out the most powerful man in a few years. There were those who worked in the chilling rooms, and whose special disease was rheumatism; the time limit that a man could work in the chilling rooms was said to be five years. There were the wool pluckers, whose hands went to pieces even sooner than the hands of the pickle men; for the pelts of the sheep had to be painted with acid to loosen the wool, and then the pluckers had to pull out this wool with their bare hands, till the acid had eaten their fingers off. There were those who made the tins for the canned meat, and their hands, too, were a maze of cuts, and each cut represented a chance for blood poisoning. Some worked at the stamping machines, and it was very seldom that one could work long there at the pace that was set, and not give out and forget himself, and have a part of his hand chopped off. There were the "hoisters," as they were called, whose task it was to press the lever which lifted the dead cattle off the floor. They ran along upon a rafter, peering down through the damp and the steam, and as old Durham's architects had not built the killing room for the convenience of the hoisters, at every few feet they would have to stoop under a beam, say four feet above the one they ran on, which got them into the habit of stooping, so that in a few years they would be walking like chimpanzees. Worst of any, however, were the fertilizer men, and those who served in the cooking rooms. These people could not be shown to the visitor—for the odor of a fertilizer man would scare any ordinary visitor at a hundred yards, and as for the other men, who worked in tank rooms full of steam and in some of which there were open vats near the level of the floor, their peculiar trouble was that they fell into the vats; and when they were fished out, there was never enough of them left to be worth exhibiting—sometimes they would be overlooked for days, till all but the bones of them had gone out to the world as Durham's Pure Leaf Lard!

🍂 "A beginning in forest preservation"

THEODORE ROOSEVELT

Teddy Roosevelt was an avid outdoorsman who placed nature conservation on the forefront of national policy. During his tenure, Roosevelt set aside almost 150 million acres of timber land and 85 million acres of mineral lands in Alaska, created 51 wild bird refuges, doubled the number of national parks from five to ten and enacted National Monument protection for 16 sites, including redwood forests in California, Mount Olympus in Washington and the Grand Canyon. Land conservation was in many ways Roosevelt's greatest legacy.

In his 1907 message to Congress Roosevelt explained the importance of preserving the natural environment and their relationship to the economy. Western land barons and business interests, however, objected to Roosevelt's conservation policies. When William Taft succeeded Roosevelt as president he fired chief forester Gifford Pinchot, who had been instrumental in Roosevelt's conservation programs. Taft's decision to rollback the national conservation program was one of the reasons Roosevelt decided in 1912 to form a third political party and run for president against Taft.

Optimism is a good characteristic, but if carried to an excess it becomes foolishness. We are prone to speak of the resources of this country as inexhaustible; this is not so. The mineral wealth of the country, the coal, iron, oil, gas, and the like, does not reproduce itself, and therefore is certain to be exhausted ultimately; and wastefulness in dealing with it today means that our descendants will feel the exhaustion a generation or two before they otherwise would. But there are certain other forms of waste which could be entirely stopped—the waste of soil by washing, for instance, which is among the most dangerous of all wastes now in progress in the United States, is easily preventable, so that this present enormous loss of fertility is entirely unnecessary. The preservation or replacement of the forests is one of the most important means of preventing this loss. We have made a beginning in forest preservation, but...so rapid has been the rate of exhaustion of timber in the United States in the past, and so rapidly is the remainder being exhausted, that the country is unquestionably on the verge of a timber famine which will be felt in every household in the land....The present annual consumption of lumber is certainly three times as great as the annual growth; and if the consumption and growth continue unchanged, practically all our lumber will be exhausted in another generation, while long before the limit to complete exhaustion is reached the growing scarcity will make itself felt in many blighting ways upon our national welfare. About twenty per cent of our forested territory is now reserved in national forests; but these do not include the most valuable timberlands, and in any event the proportion is too small to expect that the reserves can accomplish more than a mitigation of the trouble which is ahead for the nation…. We should acquire in the Appalachian and White Mountain regions all the forest-lands that it is possible to acquire for the use of the nation. These lands, because they form a national asset, are as emphatically national as the rivers which they feed, and which flow through so many States before they reach the ocean….

Take Me Out To The Ballgame

ALBERT VON TILZER AND JACK NORWORTH

Written in 1908, "Take Me Out To The Ballgame" has become as much a part of Americana as the ballgame itself, routinely sung during the "seventh-inning stretch" of most professional baseball games. Von Tilzer—who had never even been to a game when he wrote the music for the piece—was one of the most popular songwriters of the era. Norworth played vaudeville and wrote "Shine On, Harvest Moon" the same year.

Katie Casey was baseball mad,
Had the fever and had it bad;
Just to root for the home town crew, ev'ry sou,
    Katie blew
On a Saturday, her young beau
Called to see if she'd like to go,
To see a show but Miss Kate said, "No,
I'll tell you what you can do":

Take me out to the ball game,
Take me out with the crowd
Buy me some peanuts and crackerjack,
I don't care if I never get back,

Let me root, root, root for the home team,
If they don't win it's a shame

For it's one, two, three strikes you're out,
At the old ball game.

Katie Casey saw all the games,
Knew the players by their first names,
Told the umpire he was wrong, all along, good and
    strong
When the score was just two to two,
Katie Casey knew just what to do,
Just to cheer up the boys she knew,
She made the gang sing this song:

Take me out to the ball game,
Take me out with the crowd
Buy me some peanuts and crackerjack,
I don't care if I never get back,

Let me root, root, root for the home team,
If they don't win it's a shame
For it's one, two, three strikes you're out,
At the old ball game.

"Pittsburgh cannot afford to have over 500 workingmen killed every year"

PAUL KELLOGG

As a national center for steel manufacturing, Pittsburgh stood on the forefront of the American industrial revolution—for good and bad. Nonexistent planning, poor regulations and inadequate enforcement created squalid living conditions and dangerous work environments. The population grew faster than accommodations could be built. Pittsburgh had the world's highest death rate from typhoid. At the turn of the century a series of social surveys were conducted to explore the economic and social problems of America's cities. Paul Kellogg led one such survey called the Pittsburgh Survey, in 1908.

…[T]he housing problem is not a city problem alone. It is repeated in each of the mill towns. I could cite instances in Braddock, Duquesne, McKeesport, Sharpsburg, where old buildings are filthy and over-crowded and where new buildings are put up in violation of every canon of scientific housing—back-to-back houses such as were condemned in England 75 years ago as breeding places of disease. Homestead, for instance, has no ordinance against overcrowding, no ordinance requiring adequate water supply, or forbidding privy vaults in congested neighborhoods. The foreigners live in the Second Ward between the river and the railroads. In twenty-two courts studied in this district, only three houses had running water inside the house. One hundred ten people were found using one yard pump. Fifty-one out of 239 families lived in one room. Twenty-six of the two room apartments are used by eight or more people; one two room apartment sheltered 13; two, 12; two, 11. A crude reflection of the effect of these conditions is indicated by the death rate in this second ward. Of every three children born there one dies before it reaches two years of age, as against one in every six in the rest of Homestead, where detached, and livable dwellings prevail.

The Gamble of Health

This comparison of health conditions in a small town is true in a large, cruel way of Pittsburgh itself. In cooperation with the Typhoid Fever Commission we have analyzed by wards the death certificates of people dying in Pittsburgh for the past five years. We have grouped these wards into districts, the living conditions of which are more or less of a kind. Let me compare the mortality figures of wards nine and ten and twelve—a group of river wards in the old city, near the mills, peopled for the most part with a wage-earning population of small income—compare these wards with ward twenty-two, a new residential district in the East End. What are the chances of life of the men, women and children living in the one and in the other? The chance of a man's dying of bronchitis in the river wards is two and a half as against one in the East End, it is four of his dying from pneumonia as against one in the East End, five of his dying of typhoid as against one in the East End, six of his dying a violent death as against one in the East End. These are rough proportions merely, but they are of terrific significance. Our American boast that everybody has an equal chance falls flat before them. The dice are loaded in Pittsburgh when it comes to a man's health; his health is the workingman's best asset; and the health and vigor of its working population are in the long run the vital and irreplaceable resource of an industrial center.

This brings us to a point where we can define more concretely the plain civic responsibility of democracy in an industrial district. That responsibility is to contrive and to operate the social machinery of the community, and to make living conditions in the district, such as will attract and hold for the industries on which the prosperity of the district must depend, a strong and vigorous labor force. Here lies the responsibility of the community to the individual manufacturer—and the responsibility of the community to its own future—that the efficiency of its workers shall not be mortgaged before they go to work in the morning.

The Human Waste of Industrial Accidents

This carries a counter responsibility. In the interests of the community as a whole, in the interests of all the industries as against the interests of any single one, the public cannot afford to have such a working force impaired or wasted by unsanitary or health taxing conditions during the working hours. What I mean will perhaps be clearest by illustrating in the case of industrial accidents. Pittsburgh cannot afford to have over 500 workingmen killed every year in the course of employment, or the unknown number of men who are seriously injured. During the past year, the Pittsburgh Survey has made an intensive inquiry into the facts surrounding the deaths of the entire roster of men killed in industry during twelve months, and of the accident cases treated in the hospitals of the district during three months—not with the idea of raising anew the question of responsibility for particular accidents, but to see if there are any indications as to whether these accidents could be prevented and whether the burden of them falls where in justice it should. The work has been done by a staff of five people, including a lawyer, an engineer and interpreters, and we have had the cooperation of claim agents, superintendents, foremen, trade union officials and others. We found that of the 526 men killed in the year studied in Allegheny County, the accidents fell on Americans as well as foreigners; 224 were native born. The ranks of steel workers and train men suffer most—the pick of the workmen in the district. There were 195 steel workers killed, 125 railroad men, 71 mine workers, and 135 in other occupations. It was found that it was the young men of the district who go down in the course of industry. Eighty-two were under 20 years of age, 221 in between 20 and 30. Over half the men killed were earning less than $15 a week, a fact which raises the question if the law is fair in assuming, as it does in Pennsylvania, that wages cover risk. Fifty-one percent of the men killed were married with families to support; an additional 30 percent were single men, partly, or wholely, supporting a family. It was shown that the greatest losses are not due to the spectacular accidents, but to everyday causes. In the steel industry for instance, 42 deaths were due to the operation of electric cranes, 31 to the operation of broad and narrow gauge railroads in the mills and yards, and 24 to falls from a height or into pits, vats, etc. Pittsburgh has stamped out smallpox; its physicians are fighting tuberculosis; the municipality is checking typhoid. Cannot engineers, foremen, employers and workmen come together in a campaign to reduce accidents? Considerable has already been done in this direction by progressive employers. The problem is that of bringing up the whole district to progressive standards.

On the other hand we have put these industrial accident cases to that same test of human measurement which we found of such significance in gauging the losses due to typhoid fever. This steady march of injury and death means an enormous economic loss. Is the burden of this loss justly distributed? What takes the place of the wages of these bread-winners? What resources of their own have these families to fall back on? What share of the loss is shouldered by the employer? What share falls in the long run upon the community itself, in the care of the sick and dependent? Is the Pennsylvania law fair that exempts the employer from paying anything to the family of a killed alien if that family lives in a foreign country? Are the risks which the law assumes that the workman assumes when he hires out for wages, fair risks under modern conditions of production? Is it in the long run, to the interest of the employer to leave to the haphazard, embittered gamble of damage suits, this question of meeting in a fair way the human loss which with even the best processes and the greatest care is involved in the production of utilities? I am not in a position here to put forward the economic facts brought out by our inquiries; but I can say that on every hand, among employers and claim agents and workmen, there is profound dissatisfaction and an increasing open-mindedness toward some such sane and equitable system or workingmen's compensation as those in operation in Germany and in England.

"The ship ride to America was miserable"

JAKE KREIDER

In 1910, 15 percent of the population was foreign born and the proportion was rising. Immigrants were a despised class of people. Woodrow Wilson described them in a 1902 book as being of the "lowest class" and coming from the "sordid and hapless elements." A majority of the immigrants came through Ellis Island in New York Harbor. Jake Kreider, who was born in Austria, made the trans-Atlantic passage in 1911.

The ship ride to America was miserable. This was a German ship, and I spoke German so I got along, but I remember there were some Russian kids there, and they didn't like the Russians at all.

I used to do the shopping on the ship. Passengers would give me money and I would buy whatever they wanted from the canteen on the ship. Oranges, lemons, whatever they had. And then they would tip me. Tip me like crazy. Because they were nauseated. They were throwing up. They thought they were going to die. Money didn't mean a thing to them. I used to say, "Don't give me so much money." "Ah, what good is the money? I'm gonna die anyhow." They were so seasick they thought they were going to die.

I was so frightened, so disgusted. The people were all feeling lousy, scratching. They were dirty. They didn't get no attention. It was terrible. At least we had a shower in our room, we could shower, keep clean. When we got off the boat, got to Ellis Island, people were sitting on the benches scratching from the lice. They were loaded with lice. Ellis Island looked like a great barn with benches. We all sat on benches. Driven in there like a bunch of cattle.

It was about noon when we arrived. We were examined by the eye doctor, the medical doctor. And we all passed. But the ship was two days early, my father was supposed to meet us and there was no way of contacting him. "You'll have to lay on a bench and go to sleep," one of the officers said. I said, "That's not possible. This place is lousy. I can't take this. Why do we have to stay here? Why can't we go to my father?"

"Well," he said, "someone has to meet you. There has to be a certain amount of financial responsibility."

"What are you worrying about finances? We have plenty of money!"

"What do you mean, you have plenty of money?"

"Yeah, we have plenty of money. My mother's got it in her money belt."

They took my mother with a nurse into a room. My mother undressed, and she took out the money belt, and they opened it up. The officer took one look at it. He said, "Oh, my God, I haven't seen so much money in years!"

"You don't have to stay," he said. "You've got the money. You can take the ferry to New York."

So we packed up and left. We got to New York, but we had to get to Newark, New Jersey. So I tried to find someone who could speak German or Jewish or Polish. And what surprised me was seeing so many black people. In our country the only black people we knew were the Gypsies. And I was under the impression that's who they were, Gypsies. It didn't make sense to me to see so many black people.

Finally we found someone, got the directions. We took a trolley car to the Hudson tubes and Newark. And then another trolley to Springfield Avenue. We were a block and a half away from my father's house when we got out. A four-room house across the street from a livery stable where he worked. He was sitting on the front porch steps. And I recognized him, and I was delighted. But there was no affection from him. No real affection. Nothing. As though he saw us yesterday.

"I will do my best"

BOY SCOUTS AND GIRL SCOUTS

The Boy Scouts were founded in 1910 and the Girl Scouts two years later. It was a time when the country was seeking a renewed sense of national identity. The oaths and laws to which the young members pledged their allegiance to have come to serve as a model of the ideal American ethic. Since the founding of the organizations, more than 90 million people have been in the Boys Scouts and 40 million in the Girl Scouts.

Boy Scout Oath
On my honor I will do my best
To do my duty to God and my country
And to obey the Scout Law;
To help other people at all times;
To keep myself physically strong,
Mentally awake, and morally straight.

The Boy Scout Law
A Scout is Trustworthy
A Scout is Loyal
A Scout is Helpful
A Scout is Friendly
A Scout is Courteous
A Scout is Kind
A Scout is Obedient
A Scout is Cheerful
A Scout is Thrifty
A Scout is Brave
A Scout is Clean
A Scout is Reverent

Girl Scout Oath
On my honor, I will try:
To serve God and my country,
To help people at all times,
And to live by the Girl Scout Law.

The Girl Scout Law
I will do my best:
To be honest
To be fair
To help where I am needed
To be cheerful
To be friendly and considerate
To be a sister to every Girl Scout
To respect authority
To use resources wisely
To protect and improve the world around me
To show respect for myself and others through my
   words and actions.

Results of Equal Suffrage in California

NATIONAL WOMAN SUFFRAGE ASSOCIATION

When California adopted woman suffrage it became the sixth and by far the largest state to do so. The National Woman Suffrage Association, in an attempt to win favor in other states, decided to take a more aggressive stance on the issue of suffrage. This bulletin was published in an effort to show how California could serve as a model for why women should be granted the vote. Contrary to the critics' expectations, the association stated, giving women the right to vote did not have dire consequences.

Women Do Not Neglect Their Homes. Political activity and service are carried on by women whose children are grown, by women without children or by unmarried women, just as club activities are carried on.

Suffrage Has Proved to Be Another Bond of Common Interest between husband and wife. They do not always agree in opinion, but discussion has added to their information and has not broken up any homes.

Women Seldom Seek Political Office. No woman ran for the legislature is the first two state elections after their enfranchisement and few have been elected to any but minor positions. Many have been appointed to political positions. Women show a desire to fit themselves for office before seeking it.

Women Do Not Pay a Poll Tax. The Poll Tax is not a voting tax but a school and military tax imposed upon men only, citizens and aliens alike.

Women Are Registered in Their Homes. The regular biennial registration is largely made by house-to-house visits of Deputy County Clerks. There is no trouble or inconvenience about registering.

Women Attend Political Meetings, Often Taking Their Children with them.

Women Conduct Schools of Voting and Teach Men as well as women how to vote correctly.

Polling Places Have Been Made Entirely Desirable. Schools, churches, libraries, club houses and tents are now used extensively. The use of livery stables, barns, barber shops and similar places has been stopped. No man would question the desirability of having his wife go to the polls.

Women Frequently Serve as Election Judges. They are interested, conscientious and reliable. Several of the county clerks have stated that they prefer to have women as judges.

As a Rule Women Do Not Vote Unless They Understand a Question. Men frequently vote "No" on all propositions they do not understand, but women refrain from voting.

Women Vote More Rapidly and With Fewer Mistakes than men. This is generally commented upon by elected officials. It is due to the fact that women study the sample ballots and know exactly how they are going to vote.

A Petition to Appeal the Suffrage Amendment Was Stopped as soon as the first few elections demonstrated the sensible way that women would vote.

Those Who Were Anti-Suffragists Register and Vote as faithfully as the Suffragists. Most of them honestly believed that women were not ready for the responsibility of the ballot, but since they have a duty to perform they have accepted their share.

❧ "The Titanic went under"

JAMES B. MCGOUGH

In April 1912 the "unsinkable" *Titanic* set off on its maiden voyage, carrying more than 2,220 passengers from the docks of Southampton, England. While the ocean liner sped toward New York City in an attempt to break a trans-Atlantic speed record, it struck an iceberg south of the Grand Banks of Newfoundland minutes before midnight on April 14. The *Titanic* sank in less than three hours. Having removed half the life boats to make room on the ship's decks, there were not enough boats to hold all the passengers. With many life boats only partially filled, 1,553 died in the tragedy, including some of the most prominent and wealthiest men and women in society. As the ship was going down, the ship's crew gave priority to placing first-class passengers in the rescue boats and often dispatched boats before they were filled, meaning hundreds of people not in first class would never have a chance to escape the sinking ship. James B. McGough of Philadelphia survived and sent a message to his mother upon arriving in New York City.

I am here, safe, the collision which caused the loss of the Titanic, occurred about 11:40 o'clock. I had an outer state room on the side toward the iceberg against which the ship crashed. Flynn who occupied the room with me, had just gone to bed. Calderhead was in bed in a state room adjoining.

When the crash came, I ran to the porthole. I saw the ice pressed close against the side of the ship. Chunks of it were ground off, and they fell into the window. I happened to glance at my watch, and it showed me exactly the hour.

I knew that something was seriously wrong, and hastily got into my clothes. I took time, also, to get my watch and money. Flynn, in the meantime, had run over to Calderhead's stateroom and had awakened him. When I had dressed I ran outside.

I saw the iceberg. The boat deck stood about ninety feet out of the water and the berg towered above us for at least fifty feet. I judge the berg stood between 140 and 150 feet out of the water.

Many of the women on board, I am sure, did not leave their staterooms at once. They stayed there, at least for a time. I believe that many of them did not awaken to their danger until near the last.

One statement I want to correct, the lights did not go out, at least not while I was on board. When I ran to the deck I heard Captain Smith order that the air chambers be examined. An effort was made to work the doors closing the compartments, but to no avail. When the ship ran upon the iceberg, the sharp pointed berg cut through both thicknesses of the bottom and left it in such a position that it filled rapidly.

I remember that it was a beautiful night. There was no wind and the sea was calm. But for this it is certain that when the boats were launched most all of us would have perished in the ice-covered sea. At first the captain ordered the hatches over the steerage fastened down. This was to prevent the hysterical passengers in that part of the ship rushing to the deck and increasing the panic. Before we left, however, those passengers were released.

Two sailors were put into each of the boats. When the boats were lowered the women hung back. They feared to go down the long, steep ladder to the water. Seeing them hesitate, I cried: "Someone has to be first," and started down the ladder.

I had hardly started before I regretted I had not waited on deck. But I feel if I had not led the way the women would not have started and the death list would have been much larger. Flynn and Calderhead led the way into other boats.

It was only a short time before the boat was filled. We had fifty-five in our boat, nearly all of them women. We had entered the craft so hastily that we did not take time to get a light.

For a time we bobbed about on the ocean. Then we started to row slowly away. I shall never forget the screams that flowed over the ocean toward us from the sinking ship. At the end there was a mad rush and scramble.

It was fearfully hard on the women. Few of them were completely dressed. Some wore only their night gowns, with some light wrapper or

kimono over them. The air was pitilessly cold.

There were so few men in the boat the women had to row. This was good for some of them, as it kept their blood in circulation, but even then it was the most severe experience for them imaginable. Some of them were half-crazed with grief or terror. Several became ill from the exposure.

I saw Mr. Widener just before I left, and afterward, while we were rowing away from the vessel I had a good glimpse of him. He appeared as calm and collected as though he were taking a walk on Broad St. When the rush for the boats began he and his son Harry, stood back.

At the end sailors had to tear Mrs. Widener from him, and she went down the ladder, calling to him pitifully. The ship went down at 2:20 o'clock exactly. The front end went down gradually. We saw no men shot, but just before the finish we heard several shots.

I was told that Captain Smith or one of the officers shot himself on the bridge just before the *Titanic* went under. I heard also that several men had been killed as they made a final rush for the boats, trying to cut off the women and children.

While we were floating around the sailors set off some red fire, which illuminated the ocean for miles around. This was a signal of distress. Unfortunately there was no one near enough to answer in time.

John B. Thayer, Jr., was saved after he had gone down with the ship. Just as the vessel took the plunge he leaped over the side. He struck out for a life raft and reached it. There he clung for several hours until, half-frozen, he was taken into one of the boats which was a trifle less crowded than the others.

For six hours we bobbed around in the ocean. We rowed over to a boat that was provided with a light, and tied the two small crafts together. Finally daylight came, and the sun rose in a clear sky. There we were, a little fleet, alone in the limitless ocean, with the ice cakes tossing about on all sides.

It was after 8 o'clock in the morning when we saw the masts of a steamship coming up over the horizon. It was the most blessed sight our eyes ever saw. It meant an end to the physical suffering, a relief to the strain under which we had been laboring. Many broke down when they saw it.

The ship, of course, was the *Carpathia*. While it was hurrying toward us the crew and passengers had made the most generous preparations for us. When they took us on board they had blankets, clothing, food and warm liquids all ready. Their physicians were ready to care for the sick. The passengers gave up their warm beds to us.

During the time we were in the water we bumped frequently into the bodies that floated about us. A great many of the men jumped into the water before the boat sank, and they were ther bodies that we struck.

❧ "The experiment of an assembly line"

HENRY FORD

Henry Ford built his first gasoline-powered car in 1896. Seven years later he founded the Henry Ford Motor Company. His first great success was the Model T, built in 1908. In four years he introduced the assembly line to build cars with speed and precision unlike ever before. Each worker was assigned specific, narrow tasks in the construction process and only worked eight hours a day for five dollars, a handsome wage at the time. The cost of a Model T was $750. Ford thus transformed the manufacturing process and was able to mass produce cars at a rate of more than 9,000 a day, simultaneously making automobiles more affordable to the middle class in the United States.

A Ford car contains about five thousand parts—that is counting screws, nuts, and all. Some of the parts are fairly bulky and others are almost the size of watch parts. In our first assembling we simply started to put a car together at a spot on the floor and workmen brought to it the parts as they were needed in exactly the same way that one builds a house. When we started to make parts it was natural to create a single department of the factory to make that part, but usually one workman performed all of the operations necessary on a small part. The rapid press of production made it necessary to devise plans of production that would avoid having the workers falling over one another....

The first step forward in assembly came when we began taking the work to the men instead of the men to the work. We now have two general principles in all operations—that a man shall never have to take more than one step, if possibly it can be avoided, and that no man need ever stoop over.

The principles of assembly are these:

(1)Place the tools and the men in the sequence of the operation so that each component part shall travel the least possible distance while in the process of finishing.

(2)Use work slides or some other form of carrier so that when a workman completes his operation, he drops the part always in the same place—which place must always be the most convenient place to his hand—and if possible have gravity carry the part to the next workman for his operation.

(3)Use sliding assembling lines by which the parts to be assembled are delivered at convenient distances.

The net result of the application of these principles is the reduction of the necessity for thought on the part of the worker and the reduction of his movements to a minimum. He does as nearly as possible only one thing with only one movement....

Along about April 1, 1913, we first tried the experiment of an assembly line. We tried it on assembling the fly-wheel magneto. We try everything in a little way first—we will rip out anything once we discover a better way, but we have to know absolutely that the new way is going to be better than the old before we do anything drastic.

I believe that this was the first moving line ever installed. The idea came in a general way from the overhead trolley that the Chicago packers use in dressing beef. We had previously assembled the fly-wheel magneto in the usual method. With one workman doing a complete job he could turn out from thirty-five to forty pieces in a nine-hour day, or about twenty minutes to an assembly. What he did alone was then spread into twenty-nine operations; that cut down the assembly time to thirteen minutes, ten seconds. Then we raised the height of the line eight inches—this was in 1914—and cut the time to seven minutes. Further experimenting with the speed that the work should move at we cut the time down to five minutes. In short, the result is this: by the aid of scientific study one man is now able to do somewhat more than four did only a comparatively few years ago. That line established the efficiency of the method and we now use it everywhere. The assembling of the motor, formerly done by one man, is now divided into eighty-four operations—those men do the work that three times their number formerly did.

"The power to lay and collect taxes on income"

THE SIXTEENTH AMENDMENT

The early 20th century was marked by an enormous schism between the wealthy and the poor. Resentment against the wealthy ran high. The Populist Party in 1892 had called for a progressive income tax in their initial political platform. The proposal gained momentum, especially during Roosevelt's presidency when he aggressively expanded federal government programs. In 1909, Congress passed the Sixteenth Amendment giving itself the authority to tax incomes. The state ratified the measure in 1913. Although initial income tax rates were very modest, the tax rate gradually increased and has become the most important source of revenue for the federal government.

The Congress shall have power to lay and collect taxes on incomes, from whatever source derived, without apportionment among the several States, and without regard to any census or enumeration.

"Senators elected by the people"

THE SEVENTEENTH AMENDMENT

The original Constitution called for state legislatures to elect U.S. senators as a way to balance the impact of popular opinion in the crafting of legislation by the directly elected House of Representatives. By the early 1900s, however, sentiment had swung strongly against this indirect form of election because of the rampant corruption in the government. The direct election of senators became a central goal of the Progressive movement. In 1909 Congress approved the proposal. It was ratified four years later by the states making senators more directly accountable to the voters.

The Senate of the United States shall be composed of two Senators from each State, elected by the people thereof, for six years; and each Senator shall have one vote. The electors in each State shall have the qualifications requisite for electors of the most numerous branch of the State legislatures.

When vacancies happen in the representation of any State in the Senate, the executive authority of such State shall issue writs of election to fill such vacancies: *Provided,* That the legislature of any

State may empower the executive thereof to make temporary appointments until the people fill the vacancies by election as the legislature may direct.

This amendment shall not be so construed as to affect the election or term of any Senator chosen before it becomes valid as part of the Constitution.

"The establishment of Federal reserve banks"

THE FEDERAL RESERVE ACT

By 1913 there was widespread demand for federal banking reforms. Southern and western farmers objected to the concentration of wealth into the hands of eastern private bankers and accused J.P. Morgan and others of controlling a "Money Trust." Conservative bankers were concerned that crises such as the financial panic of 1907 would continue so long as the currency remained inflexible and credit inelastic.

President Woodrow Wilson found common ground between these two constituencies by forming the Federal Reserve Bank. Based on the structure of the Bank of England and the old Second United States Bank, the Federal Reserve Act created an efficient banking system. The Federal Reserve Board and its twelve regional banks eased and tightened credit according to financial conditions, oversaw the regulation of private banks, and took responsibility for maintaining the strength of the dollar. The act was widely hailed by both constituencies for restoring financial stability.

An Act to provide for the establishment of Federal reserve banks, to furnish an elastic currency, to afford means of rediscounting commercial paper, to establish a more effective supervision of banking in the United States, and for other purposes....

Federal Reserve Board

Section 10. A Federal Reserve Board is hereby created which shall consist of seven members, including the Secretary of the Treasury and the Comptroller of the Currency, who shall be members ex officio, and five members appointed by the President of the United States, by and with the advice and consent of the Senate. In selecting five appointive members of the Federal Reserve Board, not more than one of whom shall be selected from any one Federal reserve district, the President shall have due regard to a fair representation of the different commercial, industrial and geographical divisions of the country....

The members of said board, the Secretary of

the Treasury, the Assistant Secretaries of the Treasury, and the Comptroller of the Currency shall be ineligible during the time that they are in office and for two years thereafter to hold any office, position, or employment in any member bank. Of the five members thus appointed by the President at least two shall be persons experienced in banking or finance. One shall be designated by the President to serve for two, one for four, one for six, one for eight, and one for ten years, and thereafter each member so appointed shall serve for a term of ten years unless sooner removed for cause by the President. Of the five persons thus appointed, one shall be designated by the President as governor and one as vice governor of the Federal Reserve Board. The governor of the Federal Reserve Board, subject to its supervision, shall be the active executive officer....

Section 11. The Federal Reserve Board shall be authorized and empowered:

(a) To examine at its discretion the accounts, books and affairs of each Federal reserve bank and of each member bank and to require such statements and reports as it may deem necessary. The said board shall publish once each week a statement showing the condition of each Federal reserve bank and a consolidated statement for all Federal reserve banks....

(b) To permit, or, on the affirmative vote of at least five members of the Reserve Board to require reserve banks to rediscount the discounted paper of other Federal reserve banks at rates of interest to be fixed by the Federal Reserve Board.

(c) To suspend for a period not exceeding thirty days, and from time to time to renew such suspension for periods not exceeding fifteen days, any reserve requirement specified in this Act: *Provided,* That it shall establish graduated tax upon the amounts by which the reserve requirements of this Act may be permitted to fall below the level hereinafter specified: *And provided further,* That when the gold reserve held against Federal reserve notes falls below forty per centum, the Federal Reserve Board shall establish a graduated tax of not more than one per centum per annum upon such deficiency until the reserves fall to thirty-two and one-half per centum, and when said reserve falls below thirty-two and one-half per centum, a tax at the rate increasingly of not less than one and one-half per centum per annum upon each two and on-half per centum or fraction

thereof that such reserve falls below thirty-two and one-half per centum. The tax shall be paid by the reserve bank, but the reserve bank shall add an amount equal to said tax to the rates of interest and discount fixed by the Federal Reserve Board.

(d) To supervise and regulate through the bureau under the charge of the Comptroller of the Currency the issue and retirement of Federal reserve notes, and to prescribe rules and regulations under which such notes may be delivered by the Comptroller to the Federal reserve agents applying therefor.

(e) To add to the number of cities classified as reserve and central reserve cities under existing law in which national banking associations are subject to the reserve requirements set forth in section twenty of this Act; or to reclassify existing reserve and central reserve cities or to terminate their designation as such....

Powers of Federal Reserve Banks

Section 13. Any Federal reserve bank may receive from any of its member banks, and from the United States, deposits of current funds in lawful money, national-bank notes, Federal reserve notes, or checks and drafts upon solvent member banks, payable upon presentation; or, solely for exchange purposes, may receive from other Federal reserve banks deposits of current funds in lawful money, national-bank notes, or checks and drafts upon solvent member or other Federal reserve banks, payable upon presentation.

Upon the indorsement of any of its member banks, with a waiver of demand, notice and protest by such bank, any Federal reserve bank may discount notes, drafts, and bills of exchange arising out of actual commercial transactions; that is, notes, drafts, and bills of exchange issued or drawn for agricultural, industrial, or commercial purposes, or the proceeds of which have been used, or are to be used, for such purposes, the Federal Reserve Board to have the right to determine or define the character of the paper thus eligible for discount, within the meaning of this Act. Nothing in this Act contained shall be construed to prohibit such notes, drafts, and bills of exchange secured by staple agricultural products, or other goods, wares, or merchandise from being eligible for such discount; but such definition shall not include notes, drafts, or bills covering merely investments or issued or drawn for the purpose of carrying or trading in stocks, bonds, or other investment securities, except bonds and notes of the Government of the United States. Notes, drafts, and bills admitted to discount under the terms of this paragraph have a maturity at the time of discount of not more than ninety days: *Provided,* That notes, drafts, and bills drawn or issued for agricultural purposes or based on live stock and having a maturity not exceeding six months may be discounted in an amount to be limited to a percentage of the capital of the Federal reserve bank to be ascertained fixed by the Federal Reserve Board.

Any Federal reserve bank may discount acceptances are based on the importation or exportation of goods and which have a maturity at time of discount of not more than three months, and indorsed by at least one member bank. The amount of acceptances so discounted shall at no time exceed one-half the paid-up capital stock and surplus of the bank for which the rediscounts are made....

Any member bank may accept drafts or bills of exchange drawn upon it and growing out of transactions involving the importation or exportation of goods having not more than six months sight to run; but no bank shall accept such bills to an amount equal at any time in the aggregate to more than one-half its paid-up capital stock and surplus....

Open-Market Operations

Section 14. Any Federal reserve bank may, under rules and regulations prescribed by the Federal Reserve Board, purchase and sell in the open market, at home or abroad, either from or to domestic or foreign banks, firms, corporations, or individuals, cable transfers and bankers' acceptances and bills of exchange of the kinds and maturities by this Act made eligible for rediscount, with or without indorsement of a member bank.

Every Federal reserve bank shall have power:

(a)To deal in gold coin and boullion at home or abroad, to make loans thereon, exchange Federal reserve notes for gold, gold coin, or gold certificates, and to contract for loans of gold coin or bullion, giving therefor, when necessary, acceptable security, including the hypothecation of United States bonds or other securities which Federal reserve banks are authorized to hold.

(b) To buy and sell, at home or abroad, bonds and notes of the United States, and bills, notes, revenue bonds, and warrants with a maturity from date of purchase of not exceeding six months, issued in anticipation of the collection of taxes or in anticipation of the receipt of assured revenues by any State, county, district, political subdivision, or municipality in the continental United States, including irrigation, drainage and reclamation districts, such purchases to be made in accordance with rules and regulations prescribed by the Federal Reserve Board;

(c) To purchase from member banks and to sell, with or without its indorsement, bills of exchange arising out of commercial transactions, as hereinbefore defined;

(d) To establish from time to time, subject to review and determination of the Federal Reserve Board, rates of discount to be charged by the Federal reserve bank for each class of paper, which shall be fixed with a view of accommodating commerce and business;

(e) To establish accounts with other Federal reserve banks for exchange purposes and, with the consent of the Federal Reserve Board, to open and maintain banking accounts in foreign countries, appoint correspondents, and establish agencies in such countries wheresoever it may deem best for the purpose of purchasing, selling, and collecting bills of exchange, and to buy and sell with or without its indorsement, through such correspondents or agencies, bills of exchange arising out of actual commercial transactions which have not more than ninety days to run and which bear the signature of two or more responsible parties.

Section 15. The moneys held in the general fund of the Treasury, except the five per centum fund for the redemption of outstanding national-bank notes and the funds provided in this Act for the redemption of Federal reserve notes may, upon the direction of the Secretary of the Treasury be deposited in Federal reserve banks, which banks, when required by the Secretary of the Treasury, shall act as fiscal agents of the United States; and the revenues of the Government or any part thereof may be deposited in such banks, and disbursements may be made by checks against such deposits.

No Public funds of the Philippine Islands, or of the postal savings, or any Government funds, shall be deposited in the continental United States in any bank not belonging to the system established by this Act: *Provided, however,* That nothing in this Act shall be construed to deny the right of the Secretary of the Treasury to use member banks as depositories.

Note Issues

Section 16. Federal reserve notes, to be issued at the discretion of the Federal Reserve Board for the purpose of making advances to Federal reserve banks through the Federal reserve agents as hereinafter set forth and for no other purpose, are hereby authorized. The said notes shall be obligations of the United States and shall be receivable by all national and member banks and Federal reserve banks and for all taxes, customs, and other public dues. They shall be redeemed in gold on demand at the Treasury Department of the United States, in the city of Washington District of Columbia, or in gold or lawful money at any Federal reserve bank.

Any Federal reserve bank may make application to the local Federal reserve agent for such amount of the Federal reserve notes hereinbefore provided for as it may require. Such application shall be accompanied with a tender to the local Federal reserve agent of collateral in amount equal to the sum of the Federal reserve notes thus applied for and issued pursuant to such application. The collateral security thus offered shall be notes and bills, accepted for rediscount under the provisions of section thirteen of this Act, and the Federal reserve agent shall each day notify the Federal Reserve Board of all issues and withdrawals of Federal Reserve notes to and by the Federal reserve bank to which he is accredited. The said Federal Reserve Board may at any time call upon a Federal reserve bank for additional security to protect the Federal reserve notes issued to it.

Every Federal reserve bank shall maintain reserves in gold or lawful money of not less than thirty-five per centum against its deposits and reserves in gold of not less than forty per centum against its Federal reserve notes in actual circulation, and not offset by gold or lawful money deposited with the Federal reserve agent....Notes presented for redemption at the Treasury of the United States shall be paid out of the redemption fund and returned to the Federal reserve banks through which they were originally issued, and thereupon such Federal reserve bank shall, upon demand of the Secretary of the Treasury,

reimburse such redemption fund in lawful money or, if such Federal reserve notes have been redeemed by the Treasurer in gold or gold certificates, then such funds shall be reimbursed to the extent deemed necessary by the Secretary of the Treasury in gold or gold certificates...Federal reserve notes received by the Treasury, otherwise than for redemption, may be exchanged for gold out of the redemption fund hereinafter provided and returned to the reserve bank through which they were originally issued, or they may be returned to such bank for the Credit of the United States. Federal reserve notes unfit for circulation shall be returned by the Federal reserve agents to the Comptroller of the Currency for cancellation and destruction.

The Federal Reserve Board shall require each Federal reserve bank to maintain on deposit in the Treasury of the United States a sum in gold sufficient in the judgment of the Secretary of the Treasury for the redemption of the Federal reserve notes issued to such bank, but in no event less than five per centum; but such deposit of gold Shall be counted and included as part of the forty per centum reserve hereinbefore required....

"It shall be unlawful... to create a monopoly in any line of commerce"

CLAYTON ANTI-TRUST ACT

On October 15, 1914 Congress passed the Clayton Anti-Trust Act to strengthen the Sherman Anti-Trust Act. The legislation, sponsored by President Wilson and supported by labor unions, prohibited the use of the anti-trust laws on labor organizations and provided specificity on what monopolistic practices were illegal. Coupled with another act creating the Federal Trade Commission, the new legislation provided the federal government with the regulatory authority to regulate unfair business practices.

....Sec. 2. That it shall be unlawful for any person engaged in commerce, in the course of such commerce, either directly or indirectly to discriminate in price between different purchasers of commodities which commodities are sold for use, consumption, or resale within the United States or any...other place under the jurisdiction of the United States, where the effect of such discrimination may be to substantially lessen competition or tend to create a monopoly in any line of commerce....

Sec. 3. That it shall be unlawful for any person engaged in commerce, to lease or make a sale of goods,...or other commodities,...for use, consumption or resale within the United States or...other place under the jurisdiction of the United States, or fix a price charged therefor, or discount from, or rebate upon, such price, on the condition,...that the lessee or purchaser thereof shall not use or deal in the goods,...or other commodities of a competitor or competitors of the lessor or seller, where the effect of such lease, sale, or contract for sale or such condition, agreement, or understanding may be to substantially lessen competition or tend to create a monopoly in any line of commerce...

Sec. 6. That the labor of a human being is not a commodity or article of commerce. Nothing contained in the anti-trust laws shall be construed to forbid the existence and operation of labor, agricultural, or horticultural organizations, instituted for the purposes of mutual help, and not having capital stock or conduced for profit, or to forbid or restrain individual members of such organizations from lawfully carrying out the legitimate objects thereof; nor shall such organizations, or the members thereof, be held or construed to be illegal combinations or conspiracies in restraint of trade, under the anti-trust laws.

Sec. 7. That no corporation engaged in commerce shall acquire, directly or indirectly, the whole or any part of the stock or other share capital of another corporation engaged also in commerce, where the effect of such acquisition may be to substantially lessen competition between the corporations whose stock is so acquired and the corporation making the acquisition, or to restrain such commerce in any section or community, or tend to create a monopoly of any line of commerce...

This section shall not apply to corporations purchasing such stock solely for investment and not using the same by voting or otherwise to bring about, or in attempting to bring about, the substantial lessening of competition...

Sec. 8. That from and after two years from the date of the approval of this act no person shall at the same time be a director or other officer or employee of more than one bank, banking associa-

tion or trust company, organized or operating under the laws of the United States, either of which has deposits, capital, surplus, and undivided profits aggregating more than $5,000,000; and no private banker or person who is a director in any bank or trust company, organized and operating under the laws of a State, having deposits, capital, surplus, and undivided profits aggregating more than $5,000,000, shall be eligible to be a director in any bank or banking association organized or operating under thc laws of the United States...

That from and after two years from the date of the approval of this Act no person at the same time shall be a director in any two or more corporations, any one of which has capital, surplus, and undivided profits aggregating more than $1,000,000, engaged in whole or in part in commerce, other than banks, banking associations, trust companies and common carriers subject to the Act to regulate commerce, approved February 4th, 1887, if such corporations are or shall have been theretofore, by virtue of their business and location of operation, competitors, so that the elimination of competition by agreement between them would constitute a violation of any of the provisions of any of the anti-trust laws...

Sec. 10. That after two years from the approval of this Act no common carrier engaged in commerce shall have any dealings in securities, supplies, or other articles of commerce...to the amount of more than $50,000, in the aggregate, in any one year, with another corporation, firm, partnership or association when the said common carrier shall have upon its board of directors or as its president, manager, or as its purchasing or selling officer, or agent in the particular transaction, any person who is at the same time a director, manager, or purchasing or selling officer of, or who has any substantial interest in, such other corporation, firm, partnership, or association, unless and except such purchases shall be made from, or such dealings shall be with, the bidder whose bid is the most favorable to such common carrier, to be ascertained by competitive bidding under regulations to be prescribed by rule or otherwise by the Interstate Commerce Commission...

Sec. 20. That no restraining order or injunction shall be granted by any court of the United States, or a judge or the judges thereof, in any case between an employer and employees or between employers and employees, or between employees, or between persons employed and persons seeking employment, involving, or growing out of, a dispute concerning terms or conditions of employment, unless necessary to prevent irreparable injury to property, or to a property right, of the party making the application, for which injury there is no adequate remedy at law, and such property or property right must be described with a particularity in the application, which must be in writing and sworn to by the applicant or by his agent or attorney.

And no such restraining order or injunction shall prohibit any person or persons, whether singly or in concert, from terminating any relation of employment, or from ceasing to perform any work or labor, or from recommending, advising, or persuading others by peaceful means so to do; or from attending at any place where any such person or persons may lawfully be, for the purpose of peacefully obtaining or communicating information, or from peacefully persuading any person to work or to abstain from working; or from ceasing to patronize or to employ any party to such dispute, or from recommending, advising, or persuading others by peaceful and lawful means so to do; or from paying or giving to, or withholding from, any person engaged in such dispute, any strike benefits or other moneys or things of value; or from peaceably assembling in a lawful manner, and for lawful purposes; or from doing any act or thing which might lawfully be done in the absence of such dispute by any party thereto; nor shall any of the acts specified in this paragraph be considered or held to be violations of any law of the United States.

❧ *"There is a class struggle in society"*

WILLIAM "BIG BILL" HAYWOOD

William "Big Bill" Haywood was one of the more radical labor leaders of the early 1900s. Having lost his eye in a mining accident when he was nine years old, Haywood served as the leader of the Western Federation of Miners and was a founder of the Industrial Workers of the World. The IWW (known as the "Wobblies") organized some of the most destitute workers in the country—Western miners, itinerant farmers, immigrant textile workers and others that the larger American Federation of Labor ignored. Militant and confrontational in its approach, the IWW employed strikes to

obtain recognition of industrial unions.

While imprisoned on a charge of assassinating the governor of Idaho, Haywood ran as a candidate for the murdered governor's seat. He lost the election but was acquitted of the murder charge. In 1915, Haywood testified before the Industrial Relations Commission to describe working conditions and defend union practices.

CHAIRMAN WALSH: Are you familiar with the formation of the Western Federation of Miners?

HAYWOOD: Yes; being a miner, of course I kept acquainted with what the miners were doing and remember when that Federation of Miners was organized, and have since become acquainted with all of the circumstances that brought about the Federation of Miners.

WALSH: Will you please describe the conditions that led to the formation of the Western Federation of Miners?

HAYWOOD: It was organized as the result of a strike that occurred in the Coeur d'Alene.... In 1902 and 1903 came the strike that is so well known as the Cripple Creek strike, and that strike was in the nature of a sympathetic strike. The men who were working in the mills in Colorado City, although entitled to the benefits of the 8-hour law which had been passed in Colorado at that time, were working 12 hours a day [on average:] 11 hours on the day shift and 13 hours on the night shift.

This condition prevails in the smelting plants of Colorado at the present time, and in some of the milling plants. They went out on strike in September, I think, 1902.

WALSH: Was the attention of the authorities called to the condition—that is, that the law was being violated with reference to the hours of labor?

HAYWOOD: Oh, yes, indeed.

WALSH: Was the law inoperative, or why didn't they prosecute the officials?

HAYWOOD: The smelter officials, or mine owners, do you mean?

WALSH: Yes.

HAYWOOD: Did you ever hear of a mine owner or of a manufacturer being prosecuted for violation of a law? Well, they were not, anyway. The courts don't work that way.

They were striking as they struck ten years before, for the enforcement of a state law. The laws at that time were inoperative at Cripple Creek. The militia ran the district. They threw the officers out of office. Sheriff Robinson, I remember, had a rope thrown at his feet and was told to resign or they would hang him....Habeas corpus was denied. I recall Judge Seed's court, where he had three men brought in that were being held by the militia. While his court was in session it was surrounded by soldiers who had their gatling guns and rifles trained on the door. He ordered those three prisoners released, and the soldiers went after them and they were taken back to trial. That strike was not won.... The authorities of the city took up the side of the employment sharks, and between 500 and 600 men and women, members of the organization, were thrown into prison..... [E]verywhere, I might say, that I have seen courts in action; they took the side of the capitalists.... [T]here is a class struggle in society, with workers on one side of that struggle and the capitalists on the other; that the workers have nothing but their labor power and the capitalists have the control of and the influence of all branches of government—legislative, executive, and judicial; that they have on their side of the question all of the forces of law; they can hire detectives, they can have the police force for the asking or the militia, or the Regular Army.

There are workers who have come to the conclusion that there is only one way to win this battle. We don't agree at all with the statement that you heard reiterated here day after day–that there is an identity of interests between capital and labor. We say to you frankly that there can be no identity of interests between labor, who produces all by their own labor power and their brains, and such men as John D. Rockefeller, Morgan, and their stockholders, who neither by brain or muscle or by any other effort contribute to the productivity of the industries that they own.

COMMISSIONER WEINSTOCK: Well then, summing up, we find that I.W.W.'ism teaches the following:...

HAYWOOD: Read me that over again.

WEINSTOCK: "(a) that the workers are to use any and all tactics that will get the results sought with the least possible expenditure of time and energy."

HAYWOOD: Yes; I believe in the worker using any kind of tactics that will get results....

WEINSTOCK: "(b) The question of right or wrong is not to be considered."

HAYWOOD: What is right and wrong? What I think is right in my mind or what you think is right

in your mind?

WEINSTOCK: "(c) The avenging sword is to be unsheathed, with all hearts resolved on victory or death."

HAYWOOD: What that means is a general strike.

WEINSTOCK: "(d) The workman is to help himself when the proper time comes."

HAYWOOD: When the proper time comes, when he needs it let him go and get it.

WEINSTOCK: "(e) No agreement with an employer of labor is to be considered by the worker as sacred or inviolable."

HAYWOOD: ...You can let that about contract and agreement stand.

WEINSTOCK: "(f) The worker is to produce inferior goods and kill time"–we will cut that out, that which relates to the production of inferior goods and killing time; that is out of the subject.

HAYWOOD: Yes.

WEINSTOCK: "(g) The worker is to look forward to the day when he will confiscate the factories and drive out the owners."

HAYWOOD: I would drive them in instead of out.

WEINSTOCK: And the last is, "(i) Strikers are to disobey and treat with contempt all judicial injunctions."

HAYWOOD: Well, I have been plastered up with injunctions until I do not need a suit of clothes, and I have treated them with contempt.

WEINSTOCK: And you advocate that?

HAYWOOD: I do not believe in that kind of law at all. I think that is a usurpation on the part of the courts of a function that was never vested in the courts by the Constitution.

WEINSTOCK: ...As I understand it, I.W.W.'ism is socialism, with this difference—

HAYWOOD: With its working clothes on.

WEINSTOCK: As an I.W.W., are you a believer in free speech?

HAYWOOD: Yes, sir.

WEINSTOCK: Are you a believer in free press?

HAYWOOD: Yes, sir.

WEINSTOCK: Now, if your idea prevails and you went to bed tonight under the capitalistic system and woke up tomorrow morning under your system, the machinery of production and distribution would belong to all the people.

HAYWOOD: Under our system it would be under the management of the working class.

WEINSTOCK: ...[W]ill you briefly outline to us, Haywood, how would you govern and direct the affairs under your proposed system of 100,000,000 of people, as we are in this country today?

HAYWOOD: Well, how are the affairs of the hundred million people conducted at the present time? The workers have no interest, have no voice in anything except the shops. Many of the workers are children. They certainly have no interest and no voice in the franchise. They are employed in the shops, and of course my idea is that children who work should have a voice in the way they work—in the hours they work, in the wages that they should receive—that is, children who labor. The same is true of women. The political state, the Government, says that women are not entitled to vote—that is, except in the 10 free States of the West; but they are industrial units; they are productive units....My idea is that they should have a voice in the control or disposition of their labor power, and the only place where they can express themselves to the fullest as citizens of industry, if you will, as to the purpose of their work and the conditions under which they will labor. Now, you recognize that in conjunction with women and children.

The black men of the South are on the same footing. They are all citizens of this country, but they have no voice in its government. Millions of black men are disenfranchised, who if organized would have a voice in saying how they should work and how the conditions of labor should be regulated. But unorganized they are as helpless and in the same condition of slavery as they were before the [Civil W]ar. This is not only true of women and children and black men, but it extends to the foreigner who comes to this country and is certainly a useful member of society. Most of them at once go into industries, but for five years they are not citizens. They plod along at their work and have no voice in the control or use of their labor power. And as you have learned through this commission there are corporations who direct the manner in which these foreigners shall vote. Certainly you have heard something of that in connection with the Rockefeller interests in the Southern part of Colorado. You know that the elections there were never carried on straight, and these foreigners were directed as to how their ballot should be placed.

They are not the only ones who are disenfranchised, but there is also the workingman who is born in this country, who is shifted about from place to place by industrial depressions; their homes are broken up and they are compelled to go from one city to another, and each State requires a certain period of residence before a man has the right to vote. Some States say he must be a resident 1 year, others say 2 years; he must live for a certain length of time in the county; he must live for 30 days or such a matter in the precinct before he has any voice in the conduct of government. Now, if a man was not a subject of a State or Nation, but a citizen of industry, moving from place to place, belonging to his union, wherever he went he would step in the union hall, show his card, register, and he at once has a voice in the conduct of the affairs pertaining to his welfare. That is the form of society I want to see, where the men who do the work, and who are the only people who are worth while—understand me, Mr. Weinstock, I think that the workingman, even doing the meanest kind of work, is a more important member of society than any judge on the Supreme Bench and other useless members of society. I am speaking for the working class, and I am a partisan to the workers....

COMMISSIONER HARRIMAN: Haywood, I understand that you do not believe in war. Now, if you don't believe in war, why do you believe in violence in labor disputes? One is war between nations, and the other is war between—

HAYWOOD: You say I believe in violence?

HARRIMAN: I thought you did.

HAYWOOD: Probably I do; but I don't want it to be taken for granted without giving me an opportunity to explain what violence means. I think you will agree that there is nothing more violent that you can do to the capitalist than to drain his pocketbook. In that sort of violence I believe, and we are trying to make it impossible for the growth of more capitalists and to make useful citizens out of the existing capitalists.

🐝 *"In Porto Rico no blood will be shed"*

LUIS MUÑOZ RIVERA

While World War I raged in Europe, the United States expanded its holdings in the Caribbean. President Wilson purchased the Virgin Islands from Denmark for $25 million. The nation also sought to clarify its relationship with Puerto Rico. Although Congress wanted to grant citizenship to Puerto Ricans, many Puerto Ricans opposed the proposal. They wanted their island to become an independent nation. If that could not be accomplished, they sought statehood.

On May 5, 1916, Luis Muñoz Rivera, the Puerto Rican commissioner in Washington, spoke to the US House of Representatives in a final attempt to prevent the passing of the Jones Act, an act which would grant citizenship and nothing more. The bill passed in the House two weeks after this speech. Wilson signed it into law on February 20, 1917.

On the 18th day of October, 1898, when the flag of this great Republic was unfurled over the fortresses of San Juan, if anyone had said to my countrymen that the United States, the land of liberty, was going to deny their right to form a government of the people, by the people, and for the people of Porto Rico, my countrymen would have refused to believe such a prophecy, considering it sheer madness. The Porto Ricans were living at that time under a regime of ample self-government, discussed and voted by the Spanish Cortes, on the basis of the parliamentary system in use among all the nations of Europe. Spain sent to the islands a governor, whose power, strictly limited by law, made him the equivalent of those constitutional sovereigns who reign but do not govern. The members of the cabinet, without whose signature no executive order was valid, were natives of the island; the representatives in the senate and in the house were natives of the island; and the administration in its entirety was in the hands of natives of the island. The Spanish Cortes, it is true, retained the power to make statutory laws for Porto Rico, but in the Cortes were 16 Porto Rican representatives and 3 Porto Rican senators having voice and vote. And all the insular laws were made by the insular parliament.

Two years later, in 1900, after a long period of military rule, the Congress of the United States approved the Foraker Act. Under this act all of the 11 members of the executive council were appointed by the President of the United States; 6 of them were the heads of departments; 5 exercised legislative functions only. And this executive council, or in practice, the bureaucratic majority of the council, was, and is in reality, with the governor, the supreme arbiter of the island and of its interests. It represents the most absolute contradiction of republican principles.

For 16 years we have endured this system of government, protesting and struggling against it, with energy and without result. We did not lose hope, because if one national party, the Republican, was forcibly enforcing this system upon us, the other national party, the Democratic, was encouraging us by its declarations in the platforms of Kansas City, St. Louis, and Denver. Porto Rico waited, election after election, for the Democratic Party to triumph at the polls and fulfill its promises. At last the Democratic Party did triumph. It is here. It has a controlling majority at this end of the Capitol and at the other end; it is in possession of the White House. On the Democratic Party rests the sole and undivided responsibility for the progress of events at this juncture. It can, by a legislative act, keep alive the hopes of the people of Porto Rico or it can deal these hopes their death blow.

The Republican Party decreed independence for Cuba and thereby covered itself with glory; the Democratic Party is bound by the principles written into its platforms and by the recorded speeches of its leaders to decree liberty for Porto Rico. The legislation you are about to enact will prove whether the platforms of the Democratic Party are more than useless paper, whether the words of its leaders are more than soap bubbles, dissolved by the breath of triumph. Here is the dilemma with its two unescapable horns: You must proceed in accordance with the fundamental principles of your party or you must be untrue to them. The monarchies of the Old World, envious of American success and the republics of the New World, anxious to see clearly the direction in which the American initiative is tending, are watching and studying the Democratic administration. Something more is at stake than the fate of Porto Rico—poor, isolated, and defenseless as she is—the prestige and the good name of the United States are at stake. England learned the hard lessons of Saratoga and Yorktown in the eighteenth century. And in the nineteenth century she established self-government, complete, sincere, and honorable, in Canada, Australia, and New Zealand. Then in the twentieth century, immediately after the Anglo-Boer War, she established self-government, complete, sincere, and honorable, for the Orange Free State and the Transvaal, her enemies of the day before. She turned over the reins of power to insurgents who were still wearing uniforms stained with British blood.

In Porto Rico no blood will be shed. Such a thing is impossible in an island of 3,600 square miles. Its narrow confines never permitted and never will permit armed resistance. For this very reason Porto Rico is a field of experiment unique on the globe. And if Spain, the reactionary monarchy, gave Porto Rico the home rule which she was enjoying in 1898, what should the United States, the progressive Republic, grant her? This is the mute question which Europe and America are writing today in the solitudes of the Atlantic and on the waters of the Panama Canal. The reply is the bill which is now under discussion. This bill can not meet the earnest aspirations of my country. It is not a measure of self-government ample enough to solve definitely our political problem or to match your national reputation, established by a successful championship for liberty and justice throughout the world since the very beginning of your national life. But, meager and conservative as the bill appears when we look at its provision from our own point of view, we sincerely recognize its noble purposes and willingly accept it as a step in the right direction and as a reform paving the way for others more acceptable and satisfactory which shall come a little later, provided that my countrymen will be able to demonstrate their capacity, the capacity they possess, to govern themselves. In regard to such capacity, it is my duty, no doubt, a pleasant duty, to assure Congress that the Porto Ricans will endeavor to prove their intelligence, their patriotism, and their full preparation to enjoy and to exercise a democratic regime.

Our behavior during the past is a sufficient guaranty for our behavior in the future. Never a revolution there, in spite of our Latin blood: never an attempt to commercialize our political influence; never an attack against the majesty of law. The ever-reigning peace was not at any time disturbed by the illiterate masses, which bear their suffering with such stoic fortitude and only seek comfort in their bitter servitude, confiding in the supreme protection of God.

There is no reason which justifies American statesmen in denying self-government to my country and erasing from their programs the principles of popular sovereignty. Is illiteracy the reason? Because if in Porto Rico 60 per cent of the electorate can not read, in the United States in the early days of the

Republic 80 per cent of the population were unable to read; and even today there are 20 Republics and twenty monarchies which acknowledge a higher percentage of illiteracy than Porto Rico. It is not the coexistence of two races on the island, because here in North America more than 10 States show a higher proportion of Negro population than Porto Rico, and the District of Columbia has precisely the same proportion, 67 white to 33 per cent colored. It is not our small territorial extent, because two States have a smaller area than Porto Rico. It is not a question of population, for by the last census there were 18 States with a smaller population than Porto Rico. Nor is it a matter of real and personal property, for the taxable property in New Mexico is only one-third that of Porto Rico. There is a reason and only one reason—the same sad reason of war and conquest which let loose over the South after the fall of Richmond thousands and thousands of office seekers, hungry for power and authority, and determined to report to their superiors that the rebels of the South were unprepared for self-government. We are the southerners of the twentieth century.

The House of Representatives has never been influenced by this class of motives. The House of Representatives has very high motives, and, if they are studied thoroughly, very grave reasons for redeeming my country from bureaucratic greed and confiding to it at once the responsibility for its own destinies and the power to fix and determine them. They are reasons of an international character which affect the policy of the United States in the rest of America. Porto Rico, the only one of the former colonies of Spain in this hemisphere which does not fly its own flag or figure in the family of nations, is being closely observed with assiduous vigilance by the Republics of the Caribbean Sea and the Gulf of Mexico. Cuba, Santo Domingo, Venezuela, Colombia, Costa Rica, Honduras, Nicaragua, Salvador, Guatemala maintain with us a constant interchange of ideas and never lose sight of the experiment in the colonial government which is being carried on in Porto Rico. If they see that the Porto Ricans are living happily, that they are not treated with disdain, that their aspirations are being fulfilled, that their character is being respected, that they are not being subjected to an imperialistic tutelage, and that the right to govern their own country is not being usurped, these nations will recognize the superiority of American methods and will feel the influence of the American Government. This will smooth the way to the moral hegemony which you are called by your greatness, by your wealth, by your traditions, and your institutions to exercise in the New World. On the other hand, if these communities, Latin like Porto Rico, speaking the same language as Porto Rico, branches of the same ancestral trunk that produced Porto Rico, bound to Porto Rico by so many roots striking deep in a common past, if these communities observe that your insular experiment is a failure and that you have not been able to keep the affections of a people who awaited from you their redemption and their happiness, they will be convinced that they must look, not to Washington but to London, Paris, or Berlin when they seek markets for their products, sympathy for their misfortunes, and guarantees for their liberty.

What do you gain along with the discontent of my countrymen? You as Members of Congress? Nothing. And the Nation loses a part of its prestige, difficulties are created in the path of its policies, its democratic ideals are violated, and it must abdicate its position as leader in every progressive movement on the planet. Therefore if you undertake a reform, do it sincerely. A policy of subterfuge and shadows might be expected in the Italy of the Medicis, in the France of the Valois, in the England of the Stuarts, or the Spain of the Bourbons, but it is hard to explain in the United States of Cleveland, McKinley, Roosevelt, and Wilson.

I come now to treat a problem which is really not a problem for Porto Rico, as my constituents look at it, because it has been solved already in the Foraker Act. The Foraker Act recognizes the Porto Rican citizenship of the inhabitants of Porto Rice. We are satisfied with this citizenship and desire to prolong and maintain it—our natural citizenship, founded not on the conventionalism of law but on the fact that we were born on an island and love that island above all else, and would not exchange our country for any other country, though it were one as great and as free as the United States. If Porto Rico were to disappear in a geological catastrophe and there survived a thousand or ten thousand or a hundred thousand Porto Ricans, and they were given the choice of all the citizenships of the world, they would choose without a moment's hesitation that of the United States. But so long as Porto Rico exists on the surface of the ocean, poor

and small as she is, and even if she were poorer and smaller, Porto Ricans will always choose Porto Rican citizenship. And the Congress of the United States will have performed an indefensible act if it tries to destroy so legitimate a sentiment and to annul through a law of its own making a law of the oldest and wisest legislators of all time—a law of nature.

It is true that my countrymen have asked many times, unanimously, for American citizenship. They asked for it when through the promise of General Miles on his disembarkation in Ponce, and when through the promises of the Democratic Party when it adopted the Kansas City platform—they believed it not only possible but probable, not only probable but certain, that American citizenship was the door by which to enter, not after a period of 100 years nor of 10, but immediately into the fellowship of the American people as a State of the Union. Today they no longer believe it. From this floor the most eminent statesmen have made it clear to them that they must not believe it. And my countrymen, who, precisely the same as yours, have their dignity and self-respect to maintain, refuse to accept a citizenship of an inferior order, a citizenship of the second class, which does not permit them to dispose of their own resources nor to live their own lives nor to send to this Capitol their proportional representation. To obtain benefits of such magnitude they were disposed to sacrifice their sentiments of filial love for the motherland. These advantages have vanished, and the people of Porto Rico have decided to continue to be Porto Ricans; to be so each day with increasing enthusiasm; to retain their own name, claiming for it the same consideration, the same respect, which they accord to the names of other countries, above all to the name of the United States. Give us statehood and your glorious citizenship will be welcome to us and to our children. If you deny us statehood, we decline your citizenship, frankly, proudly, as befits a people who can be deprived of their civil liberties but who, although deprived of their civil liberties, will preserve their conception of honor, which none can take from them, because they bear it in their souls, a moral heritage from their forefathers.

We have a profound consideration for your national ideas; you must treat our local ideas with a similar consideration. As the representative of Porto Rico, I propose that you convoke the people of the island to express themselves in full plebiscite on the question of citizenship and that you permit the people of Porto Rico to decide by their votes whether they wish the citizenship of the United States or whether they prefer their own natural citizenship. It would be strange if, having refused it so long as the majority of people asked for it, you should decide to impose it by force now that the majority of the people decline it.

You, citizens of a free fatherland, with its own laws, its own institutions, and its own flag, can appreciate the unhappiness of the small and solitary people that must await its laws from your authority, that lacks institutions created by their will, and who does not feel the pride of having the colors of a national emblem to cover the homes of its families and the tombs of its ancestors.

Give us now the field of experiment which we ask of you, that we may show that it is easy for us to constitute a stable republican government with all possible guarantees for all possible interests. And afterwards, when you acquire the certainty that you can, found in Porto Rico a republic like that founded in Cuba and Panama, like the one you will found at some future day in the Philippines, give us our independence and you will stand before humanity as the greatest of the great; that which neither Greece nor Rome nor England ever were, a great creator of new nationalities and a great liberator of oppressed peoples.

❧ "Rights due political prisoners"

SUFFRAGIST PRISONERS

In the 1916 national election Jeannette Rufkin was elected in Montana to serve in the United States House of Representatives, making her the first woman to hold a national elected office. Women were also encouraged by the re-election of Wilson who had expressed support for their cause. But after the election Wilson did not press the issue.

Infuriated by inaction, woman suffragists stepped up their activities and became increasingly militant. Women picketed the White House in 1917 and later engaged in more drastic tactics such as hunger strikes, public burnings of Wilson's speeches on democracy and burning Wilson in effigy.

Many were imprisoned for the their demonstrations. In jail they lobbied for different treatment than common criminals. In 1917, eleven women petitioned to be treated as political prisoners. Authorities refused their request, placed them in solitary confinement and took away several privileges. In response, women engaged in hunger strikes.

Wilson did not lobby Congress to pass the National Suffrage Amendment until September 1918. He subsequently worked to ensure they would be able to participate in the 1920 election.

To The Commissioners Of The District of Columbia:

As political prisoners, we, the undersigned, refuse to work while in prison. We have taken this stand as a matter of principle after careful consideration, and from it we shall not recede.

This action is a necessary protest against an unjust sentence. In reminding President Wilson of his pre-election promises toward woman suffrage we were exercising the right of peaceful petition, guaranteed by the Constitution…

Conscious, therefore, of having acted in accordance with the highest standards of citizenship, we ask the Commissioners of the District to grant us the rights due political prisoners. We ask that we no longer be segregated and confined under locks and bars in small groups, but permitted to see each other, and that Miss Lucy Burns, who is in full sympathy with this letter, be released from solitary confinement in another building and given back to us.

We ask exemption from prison work, that our legal right to consult counsel be recognized, to have food sent to us from outside, to supply ourselves with writing material for as much correspondence as we may need, to receive books, letters, newspapers, our relatives and friends.

Our united demand for political treatment has been delayed, because on entering the workhouse we found conditions so very bad that before we could ask that the suffragists be treated as political prisoners, it was necessary to make a stand for the ordinary rights of human beings for all the inmates. Although this has not been accomplished we now wish to bring the important question of the status of political prisoners to the attention of the commissioners, who, we are informed, have full authority to make what regulations they please for the District prison and workhouse.

The Commissioners are requested to send us a written reply so that we may be sure this protest has reached them.

"There is nothing here for the colored man"

AFRICAN-AMERICAN JOB SEEKER

Between 1914 and 1920, more than 500,000 African-Americans moved from the South to northern cities to work in factories. Northern industrialists advertised in the South seeking workers and promising better lives and more money. Known as the "Great Migration," the demographic shift helped reshape northern cities and spurred the development of African-American art, music and literature. The migration, however, also triggered a new wave of racism in the North, spawning race riots and the rebirth of the Ku Klux Klan. The following letter was written by an African-American from Mobile, Alabama, responding to an advertisement for a job in the North.

April 26, 1917

Dear Sir Bro.: I take great pane in droping you a few lines hopeing that this will find you enjoying the best of health as it leave me at this time present. Dear sir I seen in the Defender where you was helping us a long in securing a posission an I can do cement work an stone work. I written to a firm in Birmingham an they sent me a blank stateing $2.00 would get me a ticket an pay 10 per ct of my salary for the 1st month and $24.92c would be paid after I reach Detroit and went to work where they sent me to work. I had to stay there until I pay them the sum of $24.92c so I want to leave Mobile for there. If there nothing there for me to make a support for my self and family. My wife is seamstress. We want to get away the 15 or 20 of May so please give this matter your earnest consideration an let me hear from you by return mail as my bro. in law want to get away to. He is a carpenter by trade. So please help us as we are in need of your help as we wanted to go to Detroit but if you says no we go where ever you sends us until we can get to Detroit. We expect to do whatever you says. There is nothing here for the colored man but a hard time wich these southern crackers gives us. We has not had any work to do in 4 wks. and every thing is high to the colored man so please let me hear from you by return mail. Please do this for your brother.

"We propose an alliance...with Mexico"

THE ZIMMERMAN NOTE

When Woodrow Wilson ran for re-election in 1916 he pledged to keep the United States out of the war. Isolationist sentiment ran deep in the United States. Further, at the outset of the war it was unclear which side the United States would take. Many German- and Irish-Americans opposed intervening on the side of the allies. In 1916 United States troops had engaged in several border conflicts with Mexico after the United States had attempted to influence domestic politics. Although the two countries had reached a peace agreement, tensions remained.

By early 1917, however, the United States found it increasingly difficult to maintain its neutral stance. There were strong financial ties between the British and American financial communities. In addition, Germany had used submarines to sink merchant vessels. Although it had suspended the sinking of neutral vessels, Germany was poised to restore the policy. Confident that Germany was on the verge of knocking Russia out of the war, German Foreign Minister Arthur Zimmerman sent a telegram proposing that Mexico and Japan ally themselves with Germany if the United States entered the war when Germany lifted its ban on unrestricted submarine warfare.

The British intercepted the telegram and forwarded it to the United States. Six weeks later Wilson released its contents to the public, swinging American sentiment strongly to the Allied cause and alerting the nation that the war was not a strictly European affair.

Berlin, January 19, 1917

On the first of February we intend to begin submarine warfare unrestricted. In spite of this it is our intention to keep neutral the United States of America.

If this attempt is not successful we propose an alliance on the following basis with Mexico: That we shall make war together and together make peace. We shall give general financial support, and it is understood that Mexico is to reconquer the lost territory in New Mexico, Texas, and Arizona. The details are left for your settlement.

You are instructed to inform the President of Mexico of the above in the greatest confidence as soon as it is certain there will be an outbreak of war with the United States, and we suggest that the President of Mexico on his own initiative should communicate with Japan suggesting adherence at once to this plan; at the same time offer to mediate between Germany and Japan.

Please call to the attention of the President of Mexico that the employment of ruthless submarine warfare now promises to compel England to make peace in a few months.

🌺 "Neutrality, it now appears, is impracticable"

WILSON'S DECLARATION OF WAR AGAINST GERMANY

With the resumption of submarine attacks on neutral ships in the Atlantic Ocean, President Wilson decided to seek a declaration of war from Congress. When Wilson made the request on April 2, 1917, 209 Americans had died in the attacks, 28 of them on American ships, since the start of World War I in 1914. The most spectacular sinking had been of the British ship *Lusitania* on May 7, 1915, killing 128 Americans. Germany claimed (correctly as it turned out) that the ocean liner was carrying ammunition bound for Great Britain. Nevertheless, Americans were outraged at the German aggression. Two days after Wilson's speech, Congress declared war on Germany.

I have called the Congress into extraordinary session because there are serious, very serious, choices of policy to be made, and made immediately, which it was neither right nor constitutionally permissible that I should assume the responsibility of making.

On the third of February last I officially laid before you the extraordinary announcement of the Imperial German Government that on and after the first day of February it was its purpose to put aside all restraints of law or of humanity and use its submarines to sink every vessel that sought to approach either the ports of Great Britain and Ireland or the western coasts of Europe or any of the ports controlled by the enemies of Germany within the Mediterranean. That had seemed to be the object of the German submarine warfare earlier in the war, but since April of last year the Imperial Government had somewhat restrained the commanders of its undersea craft in conformity with its promise then given to us that passenger boats should not be sunk and that due warning would be given to all other vessels which its submarines might seek to destroy, when no resistance was offered or escape attempted, and care taken that their crews were given at least a fair chance to save their lives in their open boats. The precautions taken were meager and haphazard enough, as was proved in distressing instance after instance in the progress of the cruel and unmanly business, but a certain degree of restraint was observed. The new policy has swept every restriction aside. Vessels of every kind, whatever their flag, their character, their cargo, their destination, their errand, have been ruthlessly sent to the bottom without warning and without thought of help or mercy for those on board, the vessels of friendly neutrals along with those of belligerents. Even hospital ships and ships carrying relief to the sorely bereaved and stricken people of Belgium, though the latter were provided with safe conduct through the proscribed areas by the German Government itself and were distinguished by unmistakable marks of identity, have been sunk with the same reckless lack of compassion or of principle.

I was for a little while unable to believe that such things would in fact be done by any government that had hitherto subscribed to the humane practices of civilized nations. International law had its origin in the attempt to set up some law which would be respected and observed upon the seas, where no nation had right of dominion and where lay the free highways of the world....This minimum of right the German Government has swept aside under the plea of retaliation and necessity and because it had no weapons which it could use at sea except these which it is impossible to employ as it is employing them without throwing to the winds all scruples of humanity or of respect for the understandings that were supposed to underlie the intercourse of the world. I am not now thinking of the loss of property involved, immense and serious as that is, but only of the wanton and wholesale destruction of the lives of non-combatants, men, women, and children, engaged in pursuits which have always, even in the darkest periods of modern history, been deemed innocent and legitimate. Property can be paid for; the lives of peaceful and innocent people cannot be. The present German submarine warfare against commerce is a warfare against mankind.

It is a war against all nations. American ships have been sunk, American lives taken in ways which it has stirred us very deeply to learn of, but the ships and people of other neutral and friendly nations have been sunk and overwhelmed in the waters in the same way. There has been no discrimination. The challenge is to all mankind. Each nation must decide for itself how it will meet it. The choice we make for ourselves must be made with a moderation of counsel and a temperateness of judgment befitting our character and our motives as a nation. We must put excited feeling away. Our motive will not be revenge or the victorious assertion of the physical might of the nation, but only the vindication of right, of human right, of which we are only a single champion.

When I addressed the Congress on the twenty-sixth of February last I thought that it would suffice to assert our neutral rights with arms, our right to use the seas against unlawful interference, our right to keep our people safe against unlawful violence. But armed neutrality, it now appears, is impracticable. Because submarines are in effect outlaws when used as the German submarines have been used against merchant shipping, it is impossible to defend ships against their attacks as the law of nations has assumed that merchantmen would defend themselves against privateers or cruisers, visible craft giving chase upon the open sea. It is common prudence in such circumstances, grim necessity indeed, to endeavor to destroy them before they have shown their own intention. They must be dealt with upon sight, if dealt with at all. The German Government denies the right of neutrals to use arms at all within the areas of the sea which it has proscribed even in the defense of rights which no modern publicist has ever before questioned their right to defend. The intimation is conveyed that the armed guards which we have placed on our merchant ships will be treated as beyond the pale of law and subject to be dealt with as pirates would be. Armed neutrality is ineffectual enough at best; in such circumstances and in the face of such pretensions it is worse than ineffectual: it is likely only to produce what it was meant to prevent; it is practically certain to draw us into the war without either the rights or the effectiveness of belligerents. There is one choice we cannot make, we are incapable of making: we will not choose the path of submission and suffer the most sacred rights of our Nation and our people to be ignored or violated. The wrongs against which we now array ourselves are no common wrongs; they cut to the very roots of human life.

With a profound sense of the solemn and even tragical character of the step I am taking and of the grave responsibilities which it involves, but in unhesitating obedience to what I deem my constitutional duty, I advise that the Congress declare the recent course of the Imperial German Government to be in fact nothing less than war against the government and people of the United States; that it formally accept the status of belligerent which has thus been thrust upon it; and that it take immediate steps not only to put the country in a more thorough state of defense but also to exert all its power and employ all its resources to bring the Government of the German Empire to terms and end the war.

What this will involve is clear. It will involve the utmost practicable cooperation in counsel and action with the governments now at war with Germany, and, as incident to that, the extension to those governments of the most liberal financial credits, in order that our resources may so far as possible be added to theirs. It will involve the organization and mobilization of all the material resources of the country to supply the materials of war and serve the incidental needs of the Nation in the most abundant and yet the most economical and efficient way possible. It will involve the immediate full equipment of the navy in all respects but particularly in supplying it with the best means of dealing with the enemy's submarines. It will involve the immediate addition to the armed forces of the United States already provided for by law in case of war at least five hundred thousand men, who should, in my opinion, be chosen upon the principle of universal liability to service, and also the authorization of subsequent additional increments of equal force so soon as they may be needed and can be handled in training. It will involve also, of course, the granting of adequate credits to the Government, sustained, I hope, so far as they can equitably be sustained by the present generation, by well conceived taxation....

While we do these things, these deeply momentous things, let us be very clear, and make very clear to all the world what our motives and our objects are. My own thought has not been driven from its habitual and normal course by the unhappy events of the last two months, and I do not believe that the thought of the Nation has been altered or clouded by them. I have exactly the same things in mind now that I had in mind when I addressed the Senate on the twenty-second of January last; the same that I had in mind when I addressed the Congress on the third of February and on the twenty-sixth of February. Our object now, as then, is to vindicate the principles of peace and justice in the life of the world as against selfish and autocratic power and to set up amongst the really free and self-governed peoples of the world such a concert of purpose and of action as will henceforth insure the observance of those principles. Neutrality is no longer feasible or desirable where the peace of the world is involved and the freedom of its peoples, and the menace to that peace and freedom lies in the existence of autocratic governments backed by organized force which is controlled wholly by their will, not by the will of their people. We have seen the last of neutrality in such circumstances. We are at the beginning of an age in which it will be insisted that the same standards of conduct and of responsibility for wrong done shall be observed among nations and their governments that are observed among the individual citizens of civilized states.

We have no quarrel with the German people. We have no feeling towards them but one of sympathy and friendship. It was not upon their impulse that their government acted in entering this war. It was not with their previous knowledge or approval. It was a war determined upon as wars used to be determined upon in the old, unhappy days when peoples were nowhere consulted by their rulers and wars were provoked and waged in the interest of dynasties or of little groups of ambitious men who were accustomed to use their fellow men as pawns and tools....

We are accepting this challenge of hostile purpose because we know that in such a Government, following such methods, we can never have a friend; and that in the presence of its organized power, always lying in wait to accomplish we know not what purpose, there can be no assured security for the democratic Governments of the world. We are now about to accept gauge of battle with this natural foe to liberty and shall, if necessary, spend the whole force of the nation to check and nullify its pretensions and its power. We are glad, now that we see the facts with no veil of false pretense about them, to fight thus for the ultimate peace of the world and for the liberation of its peoples, the German peoples included: for the rights of nations great and small and the privilege of men everywhere to choose their way of life and of obedience.

The world must be made safe for democracy. Its peace must be planted upon the tested foundations of political liberty. We have no selfish ends to serve. We desire no conquest, no dominion. We seek no indemnities for ourselves, no material compensation for the sacrifices we shall freely make. We are but one of the champions of the rights of mankind. We shall be satisfied when those rights have been made as secure as the faith and the freedom of nations can make them.

Just because we fight without rancor and without selfish object, seeking nothing for ourselves but what we shall wish to share with all free peoples, we shall, I feel confident, conduct our operations as belligerents without passion and ourselves observe with proud punctilio the principles of right and of fair play we profess to be fighting for.

I have said nothing of the Governments allied with the Imperial Government of Germany because they have not made war upon us or challenged us to defend our right and our honor. The Austro-Hungarian Government has, indeed, avowed its unqualified indorsement and acceptance of the reckless and lawless submarine warfare adopted now without disguise by the Imperial German Government, and it has therefore not been possible for this Government to receive Count Tarnowski, the Ambassador recently accredited to this Government by the Imperial and Royal Government of Austria-Hungary; but that Government has not actually engaged in warfare against citizens of the United States on the seas, and I take the liberty, for the present at least, of postponing a discussion of our relations with the authorities at Vienna. We enter this war only where we are clearly forced into it because there are no other means of defending our rights.

It will be all the easier for us to conduct ourselves as belligerents in a high spirit of right and fairness because we act without animus, not in enmity towards a people or with the desire to bring any injury or disadvantage upon them, but only in armed opposition to an irresponsible government which has thrown aside all considerations of humanity and of right and is running amuck. We are, let me say again, the sincere friends of the German people, and shall desire nothing so much as the early reestablishment of intimate relations of mutual advantage between us—however hard it may be for them, for the time being, to believe that this is spoken from our hearts. We have borne with their present Government through all these bitter months because of that friendship—exercising a patience and forbearance which would otherwise have been impossible. We shall, happily, still have an opportunity to prove that friendship in our daily attitude and actions towards the millions of men and women of German birth and native sympathy who live amongst us and share our life, and we shall be proud to prove it towards all who are in fact loyal to their neighbors and to the Government in the hour of test. They are, most of them, as true and loyal Americans as if they had never known any other fealty or allegiance. They will be prompt to stand with us in rebuking and restraining the few who may be of a different mind and purpose. If there should be disloyalty, it will be dealt with with a firm hand of stern repression; but, if it lifts its head at all, it will lift it only here and there and without countenance except from a lawless and malignant few.

It is a distressing and oppressive duty, Gentlemen of the Congress, which I have performed in thus addressing you. There are, it may be, many months of fiery trial and sacrifice ahead of us. It is a fearful thing to lead this great peaceful people into war, into the most terrible and disastrous of all wars, civilization itself seeming to be in the balance. But the right is more precious than peace, and we shall fight for the things which we have always carried nearest our hearts—for democracy, for the right of those who submit to authority to have a voice in their own Governments, for the rights and liberties of small nations, for a universal dominion of right by such a concert of free peoples as shall bring peace and safety to all nations and make the world itself at last free. To such a task we can dedicate our lives and our fortunes, everything that we are and everything that we have, with the pride of those who know that the day has come when America is privileged to spend her blood and her might for the principles that gave her birth and happiness and the peace which she has treasured. God helping her, she can do no other.

❧ "Over There"

GEORGE M. COHAN

Broadway song-and-dance man George M. Cohan wrote the patriotic war song "Over There" in late 1917. The nation almost immediately adopted it as the theme song of World War I. Cohan, who had also written "You're a Grand Old Flag," "Yankee Doodle Dandy" and "Give My Regards to Broadway," was awarded the Congressional Medal of Honor for composing "Over There."

Johnnie get your gun, get your gun, get your gun,
Take it on the run, on the run, on the run;
Hear them calling you and me;
Ev'ry son of liberty.
Hurry right away, no delay, go today,
Make your daddy glad, to have had such a lad,
Tell your sweetheart not to pine,
To be proud her boy's in line.

Over there, over there,
Send the word, send the word over there,
That the Yanks are coming,
The Yanks are coming,
The drums rum-tumming ev'ry where—

So prepare, say a pray'r,
Send the word, send the word to beware,
We'll be over, we're coming over,
And we won't come back till it's over, over there.

Johnnie get your gun, get your gun, get your gun,
Johnnie show the Hun, you're a son-of-a-gun,
Hoist the flag and let her fly,
Like true heroes, do or die.
Pack your little kit, show your grit, do your bit,
Soldiers to the ranks from the towns and the tanks,
Make your mother proud of you,
And to liberty be true.

❧ "We kept the Germans from getting into Paris"

WILLIAM BROWN

When the United States entered World War I on the side of England, France and Russia, Europe had already been engaged in a bloody, stalemated conflict for three years. United States "doughboys" under General "Black Jack" Pershing began to arrive in France in the summer of 1917 to fight in the trenches of the Western Front. By the time the war was over on November 11, 1918, 1.4 million American soldiers saw active combat in Europe and 116,516 were killed in action or died of wounds. William Brown of the 9th Infantry kept a journal of his front-line experiences before being wounded in battle.

Our trenches here were only three feet deep—so we needed the entanglements, for, in case of an enemy attack, our rifles could do a deadly amount of work before the Huns got through the wire.

The troops stationed back of the front line, usually in a small wood, formed details and cut stakes for us and brought them and the wire down to us, two miles ahead, after it grew dark.

Then a platoon was detailed from the front line trenches to string the wire. Odd, but the coils of wire used to make me homesick for the ranch. I'd strung so much of it there, for such a different purpose.

Anyway, we left the trenches at ten and worked until two in the morning. A machine gun and gunners were always sent out ahead of us, in case of an attack, so we felt just as safe as if we were on our own doorstep and even grew so bold that we talked out loud. Soldiers have a queer way of getting used to most anything, and we are all fatalists after a fashion.

We usually went out about sixty yards in front of our first line and if we worked fast and it wasn't too muddy, we could string seventy-five yards of entanglements in a night. The French and German strung their wire criss-cross, about the height of the knee, to tangle up advancing soldiers, but the Yanks used a different system. We drove a middle stake, leaving about four feet above the ground. The tall men of the platoon had to drive these. We used a wooden mallet covered with a gunnysack to drown the sound of the blows. Then, on each side of the row of tall stakes, we drove a row of shorter ones and then we strung the wire. Sometimes we had gloves—usually we didn't—and we had to be careful or we either got tangled in our own wire or got our hands badly torn.

A wire was first strung along the tall stakes. No staples were used, the wire was just wound around them. Then wires were strung criss-cross from these stakes to the short ones on either side and lastly, along tile two rows of short ones. Twisting it around the stakes was usually where we tore our hands and swore at the Germans. We blamed everything on

them, you know, from the mud, up to delayed letters from our sweethearts.

Sometimes a lieutenant, sometimes a sergeant, was boss of the platoon. We worked until the first streaks of morning light shot across the sky.

Before an attack at dawn our engineers crept out and cut the German wire entanglements. Sometimes the tanks would break them down for us, but they couldn't clear the wire away and I have often had my leggings cut to ribbons.

All our trench digging was done at night also. In front of our first line another trench was always dug to be used for day and night work by observers, machine gunners and snipers. When we were through digging, we always camouflaged the thrownout dirt with hay for this reason: It is very hard for the aerial observer in an aeroplane to distinguish the changes such as trenches, shellholes, etc., made in the night. So aerial photographs are taken and these are very carefully compared and the changes there seen noted. Thus we tried to camouflage our digging so as to show no change in the German air photographers' work.

When a Hun aeroplane would come over our lines, we usually stood very still. That made it hard for the aviator to see us. But there was one plane that used to come over our lines every morning and take photographs. We watched him quietly for about five mornings, then we got tired"of this "bird"—so we decided to shoot at him the next morning if he came. By George, he was right there on the dot. When he was about two hundred feet above us, we all let go at him. We thought he had a charmed life, for our shots never fazed him. Next morning, we let him have it again, but he sat up there absolutely unconcerned and took his blamed pictures, so we were ordered to bring an anti-aircraft gun up and place it on the front line. The next morning, when he came back that gun made quick work of him. He was brought down in our lines and placed on the "croaking sheet."

The construction of the aeroplane was new to us. The body was made of steel, oval-shaped—no wonder our rifle bullets just glanced off when we hit it. But the bullets from "anti" didn't—bad luck to the aviator.

An observation balloon didn't last very long at the front either. They were used principally to direct artillery fire on the ammunition and food stuffs trains or autos going up to the German lines.

The aviators would finish these balloons up in a hurry. They would soar up in the clouds, dive down over the balloon and drop a fire bomb which would set it afire. All we would see was a large burst of flame. Then the signal man in the balloon would jump out—the parachute attached to his back would open up and he would land safely in our lines ready to go up in another balloon and spy on "Fritzy."

The signal men of the army had very dangerous work to do, and were under shell-fire most of the time, laying lines of communication as fast as the doughboys advanced, and they had to work fast to keep up with us. They laid lines of communication to the artillery also, in order to direct the barrage fire. Without a barrage in front of us, an advance would have been almost certain death. Not that we feared death, but we didn't want to waste any good men.

Practically all the "day fighting" was done by means of these communication lines run to the artillery by the signal men and their hazardous work kept them on the jump. They slept when and where they could and worked with shells flying all the time, and their lines had to be strung on something even tho the trees and fences were almost obliterated.

I remember once when a soldier had been killed and almost buried by a high explosive shell. Only his arm still stuck up out of the earth.

A signal man came by with his wire and not finding anything else, wound it around the upright hand and from there to the stump of a tree that had been blown to pieces by artillery fire.

Another signal man came by with a touch of sentiment in him and took time to scribble something on a piece of wood and stick it up beside the upright arm. It was "Still doing his bit." It showed the spirit of our boys—game to the end.

The signal work at night consisted of sending up rockets and lighted parachutes. They spoke a language all their own that "Fritzy" couldn't understand. A code wouldn't have done him any good for sometimes the rockets meant one thing and sometimes another.

The rockets or flares were used principally to locate enemy patrols and to watch for any advance the enemy might try to make. The lighted parachutes were used to signal the artillery, in ease they were falling short, as was sometimes the ease.

If I found wire-stringing interesting, I certainly found night patrol work exciting. We always went out at ten o'clock at night and what was left of us came back at two in the morning, just before dawn.

There were always eight or twelve of us with a sergeant in command. We blackened our faces like "nigger" comedians, put gunny sacks over our well-worn shiny helmets, crawled through our barbed wire and began our hunt in the dark, in "No Man's Land" for a German patrol. We carried both rifles and hand grenades.

Now, there are nearly always forty men in a German patrol—about ten with rifles and the rest with hand grenades, which we called "potato mashers" from their shapes. These mashers are dangerous contrivances and being near one when it explodes means "lights out" for you—so we sure had to keep our eyes open, or rather ears open, when we were out on night patrol.

What we wanted principally was prisoners for information. So when we met a German patrol, in a bunch, we used our grenades; if we met them singly, we used our rifles. The men in the trenches, of course, knew we were having a skirmish, but they always let us fight it out alone. If any of our men were hurt—other men were sent out from our trenches to bring them in.

If we brought in any German prisoners, we used to scare the life out of them and say!—the poor fools would come through with all kinds of information and it was generally the truth. Talk about cowards—they were so dead scared of being shot that they couldn't get their information out fast enough and they all ran true to form, with few exceptions. Sometimes, we've had them sneak out of their trenches and walk straight over to ours, give themselves up, and tell everything they knew about their military situation.

Out at night, we had to exercise all the skill and strategy that we knew, for sometimes German patrols would pull off some new stunt that we weren't wise to. Usually the whole patrol worked together, sending one or two men out to meet our patrol—if we ran across each other—while the others would conceal themselves nearby, ready to slice us up.

Fritz thought we'd be fools enough to go at him in a bunch, but we didn't. We'd send one or two men out to flank them while the rest would get ready to do up the rest of their bunch.

I remember a skirmish one night on the Paris road. It ran between our trenches—a broad beautiful road, that had been bordered by two rows of beautiful trees, now torn and shattered and uprooted by shell-fire.

We bumped into one of "Jerry's" patrols, threw our grenades into it and used our rifles with telling effect for we could hear the wounded Germans a-hollering.

It got pretty hot for us, too, for they threw their beastly "potato mashers." Three of our men were wounded and the rest of us scattered and hunted for shell-holes until we could find our way back to our trenches—crawl back, you know, through the mud. When we finally got back, another patrol was sent out to look for the wounded Huns, but they had been gathered up by their own men and carried back to the trenches. A few nights later, one of our patrols brought us in some prisoners who gave us information that helped us later when we attacked Vaux.

Rainy nights made the work harder, for the boys had to crawl through the mud and slime until they were wet through and caked with mud and sometimes when we jumped into a shell hole for safety we would land in three or four feet of water. But the work paid, for the information we dug out of our prisoners, helped a lot in planning our attacks.

When we were in the front line trenches our rations and "chuck" came up to us at 10:00 P. M. and 2:00 A. M.—just four hours apart and that had to do us for the whole next day—so we always ate the "chow" at night and saved our rations for the daytime. You see, if the "chow detail," as we called the doughboys who brought our food up to us, came up in the daytime, sure as fate, Fritz would spot them and shells would come from all directions—Fritz would do anything to keep us from getting something to eat.

For thirty-nine days we held that line under continuous shell-fire and kept the Germans from getting into Paris. This wasn't what the Yanks came over for tho'—they wanted action and they soon got it. Holding the line wasn't sufficient, however, for it soon became imperative to push the enemy back in order to capture his strong positions and observation posts.

🍂 Wilson's Address to Congress January 8, 1918

THE FOURTEEN POINTS

Woodrow Wilson had sought a negotiated peace in Europe since its outbreak in 1914. With the United States now in the war, he hoped to conclude "the war to end all wars" with a lasting peace settlement. On January 8, 1918, Wilson presented Congress with the Fourteen Points, a program for a lasting and just post-war settlement. Wilson hoped the plan would begin a new era of international diplomacy based on freedom, self-determination and the establishment of a League of Nations to maintain international peace.

At the Paris Peace Conference following World War I, many of the points were dropped or modified. The European Allies, particularly France, sought a harsher peace than Wilson. Nevertheless, the idea of the League of Nations was retained. Ironically, the stiffest opposition to the League came from the United States when the peace treaty was presented to the Senate in 1919.

Gentlemen of the Congress:

...It will be our wish and purpose that the processes of peace, when they are begun, shall be absolutely open and that they shall involve and permit henceforth no secret understandings of any kind. The day of conquest and aggrandizement is gone by; so is also the day of secret covenants entered into in the interest of particular governments and likely at some unlooked-for moment to upset the peace of the world. It is this happy fact, now clear to the view of every public man whose thoughts do not still linger in an age that is dead and gone, which makes it possible for every nation whose purposes are consistent with justice and the peace of the world to avow now or at any other time the objects it has in view.

We entered this war because violations of right had occurred which touched us to the quick and made the life of our own people impossible unless they were corrected and the world secured once for all against their recurrence. What we demand in this war, therefore, is nothing peculiar to ourselves. It is that the world be made fit and safe to live in; and particularly that it be made safe for every peace-loving nation which, like our own, wishes to live its own life, determine its own institutions, be assured of justice and fair dealing by the other peoples of the world as against force and selfish aggression. All the peoples of the world are in effect partners in this interest, and for our own part we see very clearly that unless justice be done to others it will not be done to us. The program of the world's peace, therefore, is our program; and that program, the only possible program, as we see it, is this:

I. Open covenants of peace, openly arrived at, after which there shall be no private international understandings of any kind but diplomacy shall proceed always frankly and in the public view.

II. Absolute freedom of navigation upon the seas, outside territorial waters, alike in peace and in war, except as the seas may be closed in whole or in part by international action for the enforcement of international covenants.

III. The removal, so far as possible, of all economic barriers and the establishment of an equality of trade conditions among all the nations consenting to the peace and associating themselves for its maintenance.

IV. Adequate guarantees given and taken that national armaments will be reduced to the lowest point consistent with domestic safety.

V. A free, open-minded, and absolutely impartial adjustment of all colonial claims, based upon a strict observance of the principle that in determining all such questions of sovereignty the interests of the populations concerned must have equal weight with the equitable claims of the government whose title is to be determined.

VI. The evacuation of all Russian territory and such a settlement of all questions affecting Russia as will secure the best and freest cooperation of the other nations of the world in obtaining for her an unhampered and unembarrassed opportunity for the independent determination of her own political development and national policy and assure her of a sincere welcome into the society of free nations under institutions of her own choosing; and, more than a welcome, assistance also of every kind that she may need and may herself desire. The treatment accorded Russia by her sister nations in the months to come will be the acid test of their good will, of their comprehension of her needs as distinguished from their own interests, and of their intelligent and unselfish sympathy.

VII. Belgium, the whole world will agree, must be evacuated and restored, without any attempt to limit the sovereignty which she enjoys in common with all other free nations. No other single act will serve as this will serve to restore confidence among the nations in the laws which they have themselves set and determined for the government of their relations with one another. Without this healing act the whole structure and validity of international law is forever impaired.

VIII. All French territory should be freed and the invaded portions restored, and the wrong done to France by Prussia in 1871 in the matter of Alsace-Lorraine, which has unsettled the peace of the world for nearly fifty years, should be righted, in order that peace may once more be made secure in the interest of all.

IX. A readjustment of the frontiers of Italy should be effected along clearly recognizable lines of nationality.

X. The peoples of Austria-Hungary, whose place among the nations we wish to see safeguarded and assured, should be accorded the freest opportunity of autonomous development.

XI. Rumania, Serbia, and Montenegro should be evacuated; occupied territories restored; Serbia accorded free and secure access to the sea; and the relations of the several Balkan states to one another determined by friendly counsel along historically established lines of allegiance and nationality; and international guarantees of the political and economic independence and territorial integrity of the several Balkan states should be entered into.

XII. The Turkish portions of the present Ottoman Empire should be assured a secure sovereignty, but the other nationalities which are now under Turkish rule should be assured an undoubted security of life and an absolutely unmolested opportunity of autonomous development, and the Dardanelles should be permanently opened as a free passage to the ships and commerce of all nations under international guarantees.

XIII. An independent Polish state should be erected which should include the territories inhabited by indisputably Polish populations, which should be assured a free and secure access to the sea, and whose political and economic independence and territorial integrity should be guaranteed by international covenant.

XIV. A general association of nations must be formed under specific covenants for the purpose of affording mutual guarantees of political independence and territorial integrity to great and small states alike.

In regard to these essential rectifications of wrong

and assertions of right we feel ourselves to be intimate partners of all the governments and peoples associated together against the Imperialists. We cannot be separated in interest or divided in purpose. We stand together until the end.

For such arrangements and covenants we are willing to fight and to continue to fight until they are achieved; but only because we wish the right to prevail and desire a just and stable peace such as can be secured only by removing the chief provocations to war, which this program does not remove. We have no jealousy of German greatness, and there is nothing in this program that impairs it. We grudge her no achievement or distinction of learning or of pacific enterprise such as have made her record very bright and very enviable. We do not wish to injure her or to block in any way her legitimate influence or power. We do not wish to fight her either with arms or with hostile arrangements of trade if she is willing to associate herself with us and the other peace-loving nations of the world in covenants of justice and law and fair dealing. We wish her only to accept a place of equality among the peoples of the world—the new world in which we now live—instead of a place of mastery.

🌿 "While there is a lower class, I am in it"

EUGENE DEBS

A five-time Socialist presidential candidate, Eugene Debs was vehemently opposed to United States involvement in World War I. He was arrested in 1918 and charged with violating the Espionage Act. On September 14, 1918, after being convicted, Debs addressed the court articulating his opposition to the war. Unmoved by Debs's eloquence, the judge sentenced Debs to ten years of prison. Debs ran as the Socialist nominee for president in 1920, garnering 915,000 from a federal penitentiary. President Warren Harding pardoned Debs in 1921.

Years ago I recognized my kinship with all living beings, and I made up my mind that I was not one bit better than the meanest on earth. I said then, and I say now, that while there is a lower class, I am in it; while there is a criminal element, I am of it; and while there is a soul in prison, I am not free.

I listened to all that was said in this court in support and justification of this prosecution, but my mind remains unchanged. I look upon the Espionage Law as a despotic enactment in flagrant conflict with democratic principles and with the spirit of free institutions....

Your Honor, I have stated in this court that I am opposed to the social system in which we live, that I believe in a fundamental change—but if possible by peaceable and orderly means....

Standing here this morning, I recall my boyhood. At fourteen I went to work in a railroad shop; at sixteen I was firing a freight engine on a railroad. I remember all the hardships and privations of that earlier day, and from that time until now my heart has been with the working class. I could have been in Congress long ago. I have preferred to go to prison....

In this country—the most favored beneath the bending skies—we have vast areas of the richest and most fertile soil, material resources in inexhaustible abundance, the most marvelous productive machinery on earth, and millions of eager workers ready to apply their labor to that machinery to produce in abundance for every man, woman, and child—and if there are still vast numbers of our people who are the victims of poverty and whose lives are an unceasing struggle all the way from youth to old age, until at last death comes to their rescue and still their aching hearts and lulls these hapless victims to dreamless sleep, it is not the fault of the Almighty: it cannot be charged to nature, but it is due entirely to the outgrown social system in which we live, that ought to be abolished not only in the interest of the toiling masses but in the higher interest of all humanity....

I believe, Your Honor, in common with all socialists, that this nation ought to own and control its own industries. I believe, as all socialists do, that all things that are jointly needed and used ought to be jointly owned—that industry, the basis of our social life, instead of being the private property of the few and operated for their enrichment, ought to be the common property of all, democratically administered in the interest of all....

I am opposing a social order in which it is possible for one man who does absolutely nothing that is useful to amass a fortune of hundreds of millions of dollars, while millions of men and women who work all the days of their lives secure barely enough for a wretched existence.

This order of things cannot always endure...we shall have the universal commonwealth—the harmonious cooperation of every nation with every other nation on earth....

I can see the dawn of the better day for humanity. The people are awakening. In due time they will and must come to their own....

I am now prepared to receive your sentence.

1919–1941

Boom, Bust and the New Deal

✿ "I must think of the United States first"

HENRY CABOT LODGE

Determined to avoid repeating the mistakes that led to World War I, President Wilson threw his support behind the creation of the League of Nations—an entity which would monitor and control overly aggressive countries. When the war ended he went to Versailles to urge the Allies to create this new international organization for peace. Disgusted with war, most of the world leaders agreed.

But, in the United States, sentiment had swung away from international involvement of any kind. The country had prospered without getting itself involved in European affairs for more than a century and many people saw no need to change direction. For many, American involvement in World War I had been too costly; more than 110,000 men were killed in the war.

Senator Henry Cabot Lodge helped lead the fight in the Senate against American participation in the League of Nations. Despite a determined effort by Wilson to convince the general public otherwise, Lodge prevailed. As a result, the League of Nations went forward without one of its fiercest advocates and without the largest economic power in the world. The League ultimately failed to fulfill its mission, but the lessons learned in its demise helped forge a stronger international agency—after World War II—in the form of the United Nations.

I object in the strongest possible way to having the United States agree, directly or indirectly, to be controlled by a league which may at any time, and perfectly lawfully and in accordance with the terms of the covenant, be drawn in to deal with internal conflicts in other countries, no matter what those conflicts may be. We should never permit the United States to be involved in any internal conflict in another country, except by the will of her people expressed through the Congress which represents them.

Those of us, Mr. President, who are either wholly opposed to the League or who are trying to preserve the independence and the safety of the United States by changing the terms of the League, and who are endeavoring to make the League, if we are to be a member of it, less certain to promote war instead of peace have been reproached with selfishness in our outlook and with a desire to keep our country in a state of isolation. So far as the question of isolation goes, it is impossible to isolate the United States. I well remember the time, twenty years ago, when eminent senators and other distinguished gentlemen who were opposing the

Philippines and shrieking about imperialism sneered at the statement made by some of us, that the United States had become a world power. I think no one now would question that the Spanish war marked the entrance of the United States into world affairs to a degree which had never obtained before. It was both inevitable and an irrevocable step, and our entrance into the war with Germany certainly showed once and for all that the United States was not unmindful of its world responsibilities.

We may set aside all this empty talk about isolation. Nobody expects to isolate the United States or to make it a hermit nation, which is a sheer absurdity. But there is a wide difference between taking a suitable part and bearing a due responsibility in world affairs and plunging the United States into every controversy and conflict on the face of the globe. By meddling in all the differences which may arise among any portion or fragment of humankind, we simply fritter away our influence and injure ourselves to no good purpose. We shall be of far more value to the world and its peace by occupying, so far as possible, the situation which we have occupied for the last twenty years and by adhering to the policy of Washington and Hamilton, of Jefferson and Monroe, under which we have risen to our present greatness and prosperity.

It has been reiterated here on this floor, and reiterated to the point of weariness, that in every treaty there is some sacrifice of sovereignty. That is not a universal truth by any means, but it is true of some treaties and it is a platitude which does not require reiteration. The question and the only question before us here is how much of our sovereignty we are justified in sacrificing. In what I have already said about other nations putting us into war, I have covered one point of sovereignty which ought never to be yielded—the power to send American soldiers and sailors everywhere, which ought never to be taken from the American people or impaired in the slightest degree. Let us beware how we palter with our independence....

Contrast the United States with any country on the face of the earth today, and ask yourself whether the situation of the United States is not the best to be found. I will go as far as anyone in world service, but the first step to world service is the maintenance of the United States. You may call me selfish if you will, conservative or reactionary, or use any other harsh adjective you see fit to apply, but an American I was born, an American I have remained all my life. I can never be anything else but an American, and I must think of the United States first, and when I think of the United States first in an arrangement like this I am thinking of what is best for the world, for if the United States fails, the best hopes of mankind will fail with it. I have never had but one allegiance—I cannot divide it now. I have loved but one flag, and I cannot share that devotion and give affection to the mongrel banner invented for a league. Internationalism, illustrated by the Bolsheviks and by the men to whom all countries are alike provided they can make money out of them, is to me repulsive. National I must remain, and in that way, I like all other Americans, can render the amplest service to the world. The United States is the world's best hope, but if you fetter her in the interests and quarrels of other nations, if you tangle her in the intrigues of Europe, you will destroy her power for good and endanger her very existence. Leave her to march freely through the centuries to come as in the years that have gone. Strong, generous, and confident, she has nobly served mankind. Beware how you trifle with your marvelous inheritance, this great land of ordered liberty, for if we stumble and fall, freedom and civilization everywhere will go down in ruin.

We are told we shall "break the heart of the world" if we do not take this League just as it stands. I fear that the hearts of the vast majority of mankind would beat on strongly and steadily and without any quickening if the League were to perish altogether. If it should be effectively and beneficiently changed, the people who would lie awake in sorrow for a single night could be easily gathered in one not very large room, but those who would draw a long breath of relief would reach to millions.

We hear much of visions, and I trust we shall continue to have visions and dream dreams of a fairer future for the race. But visions are one thing and visionaries are another, and the mechanical appliances of the rhetorician designed to give a picture of a present which does not exist and of a future which no man can predict are as unreal and short-lived as the steam or canvas clouds, the angels suspended on wires, and the artificial lights of the stage. They pass with the moment of effect and are shabby and tawdry in the daylight. Let us at least be real. Washington's entire honesty of mind and his fearless look into the face of all facts are qualities which can never go out of fashion and which we should all do well to imitate....

No doubt many excellent and patriotic people see a coming fulfillment of noble ideals in the words "league for peace." We all respect and share these aspirations and desires, but some of us see no hope, but rather defeat, for them in this murky covenant. For we, too, have our ideals, even if we differ from those who have tried to establish a monopoly of idealism, giving service to all her people and to the world. Our ideal of the future is that she should continue to render that service of her own free will. She has great problems of her own to solve, very grim and perilous problems, and a right solution, if we can attain to it, would largely benefit mankind. We would have our country strong to resist a peril from the West, as she has flung back the German menace from the East. We would not have our politics distracted and embittered by the dissensions of other lands. We would not have our country's vigor exhausted, or her moral force abated, by everlasting meddling and muddling in every quarrel, great and small, which afflicts the world. Our ideal is to make her ever stronger and better and finer, because in that way alone, as we believe, can she be of the greatest service to the world's peace and to the welfare of mankind.

❧ *"The working class and the employing class have nothing in common"*

PREAMBLE OF THE INDUSTRIAL WORKERS OF THE WORLD

The Industrial Workers of the World, one of the most radical left-wing unions in the nation, was founded in 1905. The union mainly represented laborers from the farms, mines and lumber camps of the West. Echoing the socialist and communist sentiments of European radicals, the organization met in Chicago shortly after World War I to call for the overthrow of the existing wage system and an overthrow of capitalism.

The working class and the employing class have nothing in common. There can be no peace so long as hunger and want are found among millions of working people and the few, who make up the employing class, have all the good things of life.

Between these two classes a struggle must go on until the workers of the world organize as a class, take possession of the earth and the machinery of production and abolish the wage system.

We find that centering of the management of industries into fewer and fewer hands makes the trade unions unable to cope with the ever growing power of the employing class. The trade unions foster a state of affairs which allows one set of workers to be pitted against another set of workers in the same industry, thereby helping defeat one another in wage wars. Moreover the trade unions aid the employing class to mislead the workers into the belief that the working class have interests in common with their employers.

These conditions can be changed and the interest of the working class upheld only by an organization formed in such a way that all its members in any one industry, or in all industries if necessary, cease work whenever a strike or lockout is on in any department thereof, thus making an injury to one an injury to all.

Instead of the conservative motto, "A fair day's wage for a fair day's work," we must inscribe on our banner the revolutionary watchword, "Abolition of the wage system." It is the historic mission of the working class to do away with capitalism. The arm of production must be organized not only for the everyday struggle with capitalists, but also to carry on production when capitalism shall have been overthrown. By organizing industrially we are forming the structure of the new society within the shell of the old.

❧ "Any person who displays a red flag… is guilty of a felony"

CALIFORNIA RED FLAG LAW

Mass paranoia swept the country after World War I. The communist overthrow of Czarist Russia and the resulting civil war, combined with a wave of socialist-communist unrest in parts of Europe and a growing restlessness among American workers, whipped up a fearful mania in the United States known as The Red Scare.

The government cracked down hard on suspected socialists, communists and other radicals, who were often subsequently imprisoned or exiled. In many cases, the victims were immigrants and labor leaders. One outgrowth of The Red Scare was the legal prohibition of the use of red flags or other symbols of opposition to government. Thirty-three states passed anti-red flag laws between 1917 and 1921. The Supreme Court declared the California Red Flag Law unconstitutional in 1931.

California Penal Code Section 403a

An act to add a new section to the Penal Code…prohibiting the use of a red flag in aid of anarchistic or seditious activities. (Approved, April 30, 1919, in effect, July 22, 1919)

The people of the State of California do enact as follows:…

403a. Any person who displays a red flag, banner or badge or any flag, badge, banner, or device of any color or form whatever in any public place or in any meeting place or public assembly, or from or on any house, building or window as a sign, symbol or emblem of opposition to organized government or as an invitation or stimulus to anarchistic action or as an aid to propaganda that is of a seditious character is guilty of a felony.

❧ Abrams v. United States: "The best test of the truth is the power of the thought"

SUPREME COURT JUSTICE OLIVER WENDELL HOLMES, JR.

Despite the hysteria of the Red Scare, not everyone in government buckled to the urgency to squash diversity of opinion. Justice Oliver Wendell Holmes, Jr., resisted the pressures of the Red Scare, as evidenced in his dissenting opinion in the 1918 case Abrams v. United States.

Russia was in the midst of civil war—the Bolsheviks had seized power and were fighting off the counter-revolutionary "White Army" in a desperate struggle. Fearful of the spread of communism, the Allied forces sent expeditionary forces to assist the White Army. A 7,000-man contingent of U.S. soldiers occupied Vladivostok on the Russian Pacific Coast.

This action prompted a wave of protest within the United States from communist sympathizers, including five self-described anarchist or socialist Russian immigrants who published and distributed a leaflet in New York City protesting the Allied efforts and sharply criticizing the American government. They were arrested and convicted for violating the Espionage Act of 1917 by attempting to incite rebellion. The case went into appeals, eventually landing in the Supreme Court. The majority of the court affirmed the decision, but Holmes dissented.

Persecution for the expression of opinions seems to me perfectly logical. If you have no doubts of your premises or your power and want a certain result with all your heart you naturally express your wishes in law and sweep away all opposition. To allow opposition by speech seems to indicate that you think speech impotent, as when a man says that he has squared the circle, or that you do not care wholeheartedly for the result, or that you doubt either your power or your premises. But when men have realized that time has upset many fighting faiths, they may come to believe even more than they believe the very foundations of their own conduct that the ultimate good desired is better reached by free trade in ideas—that the best test of truth is the power of the thought to itself accepted in the competition of the market, and that truth is the only ground upon which their wishes safely can be carried out. That at any rate is the theory of our Constitution. It is an experiment, as all life is an experiment. Every year, if not every day, we have to wager our salvation upon some prophecy based upon imperfect knowledge. While that experiment is part of our system I think that we should be eternally vigilant against attempts to check the expression of opinions that we loathe and believe to be fraught with death, unless they so imminently threaten immediate interference with the lawful and pressing purposes of the law that an immediate check is required to save the country.

Schenck v. United States: "A clear and present danger"

SUPREME COURT JUSTICE OLIVER WENDELL HOLMES, JR.

While Holmes expressed a tolerant sentiment in *Abrams v. United States,* he made a distinction between the exercise of

free speech and legitimate threats to the American government. *Schenck v. United States* pitted a draft resister against the government. Schenk claimed that his First Amendment right to free speech was denied when he was arrested for distributing anti-war materials to soldiers. Lower federal courts convicted Schenck, the Supreme Court upheld the decision. Holmes, a Civil War veteran, wrote the majority opinion in which he enunciates the "clear and present danger" doctrine.

This indictment charges a conspiracy to violate the Espionage Act of June 15, 1917, by causing and attempting to cause insubordination…in the military and naval forces of the United States, and to obstruct the recruiting and enlistment service of the United States, when the United States was at war with the German Empire, to wit, that the defendant wilfully conspired to have printed and circulated to men who had been called and accepted for military service…a document set forth and alleged to be calculated to cause such insubordination and obstruction. The count alleges overt acts in pursuance of the conspiracy, ending in the distribution of the document set forth…. They set up the First Amendment to the Constitution forbidding Congress to make any law abridging the freedom of speech, or of the press….

The document in question upon its first printed side recited the first section of the Thirteenth Amendment, said that the idea embodied in it was violated by the conscription act and that a conscript is little better than a convict. In impassioned language it intimated that conscription was despotism in its worst form and a monstrous wrong against humanity in the interest of Wall Street's chosen few. It said, "Do not submit to intimidation," but in form at least confined itself to peaceful measures such as a petition for the repeal of the act. The other and later printed side of the sheet was headed "Assert Your Rights." It stated reasons for alleging that anyone violated the Constitution when he refused to recognize "your right to assert your opposition to the draft," and went on, "If you do not assert and support your rights, you are helping to deny or disparage rights which it is the solemn duty of all citizens and residents of the United States to retain." It described the arguments on the other side as coming from cunning politicians and a mercenary capitalist press, and even silent consent to the conscription law as helping to support an infamous conspiracy. It denied the power to send our citizens away to foreign shores to shoot up the people of other lands, and added that words could not express the condemnations such cold-blooded ruthlessness deserves, &c., &c., winding up, "You must do your share to maintain, support and uphold the rights of the people of this country." Of course the document would not have been sent unless it had been intended to have some effect, and we do not see what effect it could be expected to have upon persons subject to the draft except to influence them to obstruct the carrying of it out. The defendants do not deny that the jury might find against them on this point.

But it is said, suppose that that was the tendency of this circular, it is protected by the First Amendment of the Constitution.... We admit that in many places and in ordinary times the defendants in saying all that was said in the circular would have been within their constitutional rights. But the character of every act depends upon the circumstances in which it is done. The most stringent protection of free speech would not protect a man in falsely shouting fire in a theater and causing a panic. It does not even protect a man from injunction against uttering words that may have all the effect of force. The question in every case is whether the words used are in such circumstances and are of such a nature as to create a clear and present danger that they will bring about the substantive evils that Congress has a right to prevent. It is a question of proximity and degree. When a nation is at war many things that might be said in time of peace are such a hindrance to its effort that their utterance will not be endured so long as men fight and that no Court could regard them as protected by any constitutional right. It seems to be admitted that if an actual obstruction of the recruiting service were proved, liability for words that produced that effect might be enforced. The statute of 1917 punishes conspiracies to obstruct as well as actual obstruction. If the act, (speaking, or circulating a paper) its tendency and the intent with which it is done are the same, we perceive no ground for saying that success alone warrants making the act a crime.

"No person shall possess any intoxicating liquor"

THE VOLSTEAD ACT

The National Prohibition Act, or Volstead Act, was approved by Congress in 1919 to enforce the 18th Amendment banning the recreational drinking of alcohol in the United States. Prohibition was a product of a revived religious movement of the late nineteenth and early twentieth century championed by evangelical preacher Billy Sunday.

Prohibition was perhaps the single greatest failure in American social and legislative history. Not only was the ban widely ignored, it forced the manufacturing, transportation and sale of alcohol underground. Though it was illegal, bootlegging was extremely profitable. Gangsters rapidly took over the liquor business, prompting violent gang wars. Chicago became the nation's crime capital and its leading mobster, Al Capone, catapulted to international fame.

In 1933, the 21st Amendment repealed Prohibition.

Be it Enacted....That the short title of this Act shall be the "National Prohibition Act."

Prohibition of Intoxicating Beverages

Section 3. No person shall on or after the date when the eighteenth amendment to the Constitution of the United States goes into effect, manufacture, sell, barter, transport, import, export, deliver, furnish or possess any intoxicating liquor except as authorized in this Act, and all the provisions of this Act shall be liberally construed to the end that the use of intoxicating liquor as a beverage may be prevented.

Liquor for nonbeverage purposes and wine for sacramental purposes may be manufactured, purchased, sold, bartered, transported, imported, exported, delivered, furnished and possessed, but only as herein provided and the commissioner may, upon application, issue permits therefor: Provided, That nothing in this Act shall prohibit the purchase and sale of warehouse receipts covering distilled spirits on deposit in Government bonded warehouses, and no special tax liability shall attach to the business of purchasing and selling such warehouse receipts....

Section 6. No one shall manufacture, sell, purchase, transport, or prescribe any liquor without first obtaining a permit from the commissioner so to do, except that a person may, without a permit, purchase and use liquor for medicinal purposes when prescribed by a physician as herein provided, and except that any person who in the opinion of the commissioner is conducting a bona fide hospital or sanatorium engaged in the treatment of persons suffering from alcoholism, may, under such rules, regulations, and conditions as the commissioner shall prescribe, purchase and use, in accordance with the methods in use in such institutions, liquor, to be administered to the patients of such institution under the direction of a duly qualified physician employed by such institution.

All permits to manufacture, prescribe, sell, or transport, liquor, may be issued for one year, and shall expire on the 31st day of December next succeeding the issuance thereof:

Permits to purchase liquor shall specify the quantity and kind to be purchased and the purpose for which it is to be used. No permit shall be issued to any person who within one year prior to the application therefore or issuance thereof shall have violated the terms of any permit issued under this Title or any law of the United States or of any State regulating traffic in liquor. No permit shall be issued to anyone to sell liquor at retail, unless the sale is to be made through a pharmacist designated in the permit and duly licensed under the laws of his State to compound and dispense medicine prescribed by a duly licensed physician. No one shall be given a permit to prescribe liquor unless he is a physician duly licensed to practice medicine and actively engaged in the practice of such profession.

Nothing in this title shall be held to apply to the manufacture, sale, transportation, importation, possession, or distribution of wine for sacramental purposes, or like religious rites, except section 6 (saves the same requires a permit to purchase) see section 10 hereof, and the provisions of this Act prescribing penalties for the violation of either of said sections. No person to whom a permit may be issued to manufacture, transport, import, or sell wines for sacramental purposes or like religious rites shall sell, barter, exchange, or furnish any such to any person not a rabbi, minister of the gospel, priest, or an officer duly authorized for the purpose by any church or congregation, not to any such except upon an application duly subscribed by him, which application, authenticated as regulations may prescribe, shall be filed and preserved by the seller. The head of any conference of diocese or other ecclesiastical jurisdiction may designate any rabbi, minister, or priest to supervise the manufacture of wine to be used for the purposes and rites in this section mentioned, and the person so designated may, in the discretion of the commissioner, be granted a permit to supervise such manufacture.

Section 7. No one but a physician holding a permit [may] prescribe liquor. And no physician shall prescribe liquor unless after careful physical examination of the person for whose use such prescription is sought, or if such examination is found impracticable, then upon the best information obtainable, he in good faith believes that the use of such liquor as a medicine by such person is necessary and will afford relief to him from some known ailment. Not more than a pint of spirituous liquor to be taken internally shall be prescribed for use by the same person within any period of ten days and no prescription shall be filled more than once. Any pharmacist filling a prescription shall at the time indorse upon it over his own signature the word "canceled," together with the date when the liquor was delivered, and then make the same a part of the record that he is required to keep as herein provided....

Section 18. It shall be unlawful to advertise, manufacture, sell, or possess for sale any utensil, contrivance, machine, preparation, compound, tablet, substance, formula direction, recipe advertised, designated, or intended for use in the unlawful manufacture of intoxicating liquor....

Section 21. Any room, house, building, boat, vehicle, structure, or place where intoxicating liquor is manufactured, sold, kept or bartered in violation of this title, and all intoxicating liquor and property kept and used in maintaining the same, is hereby declared to be a common nuisance, and any person who maintains such a common nuisance shall be guilty of a misdemeanor and upon conviction thereof shall be fined not more than $1,000 or be imprisoned for not more than one year, or both....

Section 25. It shall be unlawful to have or possess any liquor or property designed for the manufacture of liquor intended for use in violating this title or which has been so used, and no property rights shall exist in any such liquor or property.

No search warrant shall issue to search any private dwelling occupied as such unless it is being used for the unlawful sale of intoxicating liquor, or unless it is in part used for some business purposes such as a store, shop, saloon, restaurant, hotel, or boarding house....

Section 29. Any person who manufactures or sells liquor in violation of this title shall for a first offense be fined not more than $1,000, or imprisoned not exceeding six months, and for a second or subsequent offense shall be fined not less than $200 not more than $2,000 and be imprisoned not less than one month nor more than five years.

Any person violating the provisions of any permit, or who makes any false record, report, or affidavit required by this title, or violates any of the provisions of this title, for which offense a special penalty is not prescribed, shall be fined for a first offense not more than $500; for a second offense not less than $100 nor more than $1,000, or be imprisoned not more than ninety days; for any subsequent offense he shall be fined not less than $500 and be imprisoned not less than three months nor more than two years....

Section 33. After February 1, 1920, the possession of liquors by any person not legally permitted under this title to possess liquor shall be prima facie evidence that such liquor is kept for the purpose of being sold, bartered, exchanged, given away, furnished, or otherwise disposed of in violation of the Provisions of this title but it shall not be unlawful to possess liquors in one's private dwelling while the same is occupied and used by him as his dwelling only and such liquor need not be reported, provided such liquors are for use only for the personal consumption of the owner thereof and his family residing in such dwelling and of his bona fide guests when entertained by him therein; and the burden of proof shall be upon the possessor in any action concerning the same to prove that such liquor was lawfully acquired, possessed, and used.

❧ The Hallmarks of American

H. L. MENCKEN

At the beginning of the 20th century, *Baltimore Sun* columnist H.L. Mencken was one of the leading newspapermen in the country. Pushing the boundaries of English to its creative limits, he brought life to his writings with a blunt, distinctive style. In 1919, Mencken preached what he practiced when he wrote *The American Language,* a vibrant description of the English language in America. He explored the origins of American words and used American English as a metaphor for the American experience.

The American Language was written at a time when the United States was discovering its own identity. A nation of immigrants, the country strove for a commonality that joined the diverse backgrounds and interests of a multicultural society. Language was a common denominator for all Americans. Its vibrancy and fluidity reflected the changing, dynamic character of the people who spoke it. Mencken eventually wrote several editions of the book. This excerpt comes from the fourth edition.

The characters chiefly noted of American English are, first, its general uniformity throughout the country; second, its impatient disregard for grammatical, syntactical and phonological rule and precedent; and, third, its large capacity (distinctly greater than that of the English of present-day England) for taking in new words and phrases from outside sources, and for manufacturing them of its own material.

The first of these characters has struck every observer, native and foreign. In place of the discordant dialects of nearly all the other major countries, including England, we have a general *Volkssprache* for the whole nation, conditioned on minor differences in pronunciation and vocabulary and by the linguistic struggles of various groups of newcomers. No other country can show such linguistic solidarity, not even Canada, for there a large minority of the population resists speaking English altogether. The Little Russian of the Ukraine is unintelligible to the citizen of Moscow; the northern Italian can scarcely follow a conversation in Sicilian; the Low German from Hamburg is a foreigner in Munich; the Breton flounders in Gascony. Even in the United Kingdom there are wide differences. There are some regional peculiarities in American English,...but all Americans use pretty much the same words in the same way.

Of the intrinsic differences that separate American from English, the chief have their roots in the disparity between the environment and traditions of two peoples since the 17th century. The English have lived under a relatively stable social order, and it has impressed upon their souls their characteristic respect for precedent. The Americans felt no such restraint and acquired no such habit of conformity. They plunged to the other extreme, for life in their country put a high value upon the qualities of curiosity and daring, and so they acquired that character of restlessness, that disdain for the dead hand, which still broadly marks them. The American is not, of course, lacking in a capacity for discipline; he submits to leadership readily, and even to tyranny. But, curiously, it is not the leadership that is old and decorous that commonly fetches him, but the leadership that is new and extravagant. He will resist dictation out of the past, but he will follow a new messiah with almost Russian willingness, and into the wildest vagaries of economics, religion, morals and speech. A new fallacy in politics spreads faster in the United States than anywhere else on earth, and so does a new revelation of God, or a new shibboleth, or metaphor, or piece of slang. The American likes to make his language as he goes along. A novelty loses nothing by the fact that it is a novelty, particularly if it meets the national fancy for the terse, the vivid, and, above all, the bold and imaginative. The characteristic American habit of reducing complex concepts to the starkest abbreviations was already noticeable in colonial times, and such typical Americanisms as O.K., N.G. and P.D.Q. have been traced back to the early days of the Republic. In so modest an operation as that which has evolved bunk and buncombe there is evidence of a phenomenon which the philologian recognizes as belonging to the most lusty stages of speech.

But more important than the sheer inventions, if only because more numerous, are the extensions of the vocabulary by the devices of rhetoric. The American, from the beginning, has been the most ardent of recorded rhetoricians. His politics bristles with pungent epithets; his whole history has been bedizened with tall talk; his fundamental institutions rest far more upon brilliant phases than upon logical ideas. He exercises continually an incomparable capacity for projecting hidden and often fantastic relationships into his speech. Such a term as rubberneck is almost a complete treatise on American psychology; it has precisely the boldness and contempt for ordered forms that are so characteristically American. The same qualities are in roughhouse, has-been, lame duck and a thousand other such racy substantives, and in all the great stock of native verbs and adjectives. There is, indeed, but a shadowy boundary in these new coinages between the various parts of speech. Corral, borrowed from Spanish, immediately becomes a verb and the father of an adjective. Bust, carved out of burst, erects itself into a noun. Bum, coming by way of an earlier bummer from the German, becomes a noun, adjective, verb and adverb. Verbs are fashioned out of substantives:

to engineer, to stump, to hog, to style. Others are made by torturing nouns with harsh affixes, as to burglarize and to itemize, or by groping for the root, as to resurrect and to jell. Yet others are changed from intransitive to transitive: a sleeping car sleeps thirty passengers.

All these processes are to be observed in the history of the English of England; at the time of its sturdiest growth they flourished. More than one observer noted the likeness between the situation of American English today and that of British English at the end of the Sixteenth Century. The Englishmen of that time had not yet come under the yoke of grammarians and lexicographers, and were free to mold their language to the throng of new ideas that marked an era of adventure and expansion. Their situation closely resembled that of the American pioneers who swarmed into the West following the War of 1812, and they met linguistic needs with the same boldness. By a happy accident they had a group of men who could bring to the business of word-making a degree of ingenuity and taste far beyond the common; above all, they had the aid of a really first-rate genius, Shakespeare. The result was a renovation of old ways of speech and a proliferation of new and useful terms that has had no parallel, to sate, save on this side of the Atlantic. Standard English in the Eighteenth Century, succumbed to pedants whose ignorance of language process was only equaled by their impudent assumption of authority: Swift, Horace Walpole, Thomas Gray of the oft-misquoted "Elegy" and, above all, Samuel Johnson. No eminent lexicographer was ever more ignorant of speechways than he was. In his Dictionary of 1755 he thundered idiotically against many words that are now universally recognized as sound English, e.g., to wabble, to bamboozle and touchy. To wabble he described as "low, barbarous," and to bamboozle and touchy as "low," and at other times he denounced to swap, to coax, to budge, fib, banter, fop, fun, stingy, swimmingly, row (in the sense of disturbance), chaperon and to derange. Under the influence of Johnson and his Nineteenth Century apes, the Standard Southern dialect of English has been arrested in its growth and burdened with irrational affectations. Its tendency is to combat all that expansive gusto which made for its pliancy and resilience in the days of Shakespeare. In place of the old loose-footedness there is a preciosity which, in one direction, takes the form of clumsy artificialities in the spoken language, and in another shows itself in the even clumsier Johnsonese of so much current English writing—the jargon denounced by Sir Arthur Quiller-Couch in his Cambridge lectures.

American has so far escaped such suffocating formalism. Of course, we have our occasional practitioners of the authentic English jargon. "Once upon a time," says Jacques Barzun, of Columbia University, "American speech was really known for its racy colloquial creations—barnstorm, boom, boost, bulldoze, pan out, splurge and so on. Now it is the flaccid polysyllable that expresses the country's mind. Pioneer has yielded to pedant, and one begins to wonder whether the German word-order had better not be adopted to complete the system." What fevers Barzun, of course, is the artificial pseudo-English that school ma'ams, whether in panties or pantaloons, try to foist upon their victims, and the even worse jargon that Dogberrys in and out of office use for their revelations to the multitude. But in the main our faults lie precisely the opposite direction. That is to say, we incline toward a directness of statement which, at its greatest, lacks restraint and urbanity altogether, and toward a hospitality which often admits novelties for the mere sake of their novelty, and is quite uncritical of the difference between a genuine improvement in succinctness and clarity, and mere extravagant raciness.

This revolt against conventional bounds and restraints is most noticeable, of course, on the lower levels of American speech. But even in the upper regions there are rebels aplenty, some of such authority that it is impossible to dismiss them. A glance through the speeches of Woodrow Wilson, a conscientious purist and Anglomaniac, reveals in a few moments half a dozen locutions that an Englishman in like position would certainly hesitate to use, among them we must get a move on, to gumshoe, and that is going some. John Dewey, the country's most respectable metaphysician, unhesitatingly used dope for opium. In recent years certain English magnificoes have shown signs of going the same route, but whenever they yield they are accused, and rightly, of succumbing to American influence.

Let American confront a novel problem alongside English, and immediately its superior imaginativeness and resourcefulness become obvious. Movie is better than cinema. Billboard is better than hoarding. Officeholder is more honest, more picturesque, more thoroughly Anglo-Saxon than public servant. Turn to the terminology of railroading (itself, by the way, an Americanism): its creation fell upon the two peoples equally, but they tackled the job independently. The English, seeking a figure to describe the wedge-shaped fender in front of the locomotive, called a plough; the American gave it the pungent name of cowcatcher. So with the casting which guides the wheels from one rail to another. The English called it a crossing-plate; the Americans, more responsive to the suggestion in its shape, called it a frog. One pictures the common materials being dumped into a pot, exotic flavorings added, and the bubblings assiduously and expectantly skimmed. "When we Americans are through with the English language," says Mr. Dooley, "it will look as if it had been run over by a musical comedy."

All this boldness of conceit, of course, makes for vulgarity. It flowers in such barbaric inventions as tasty, goof and semi-occasional. But vulgarity, after all, means no more than yielding to natural impulses in the face of conventional inhibitions— the heart of all healthy language-making. The history of English, like the history of American and of every other living tongue, is a history of vulgarisms that, by their accurate meeting of real needs, have forced their way into sound usage, and even into the lifeless catalogues of the grammarians. In our own case the greater conservatism of the English restrains our native tendency to go too far, but the process itself is as inexorable in its workings as the precession of the equinoxes, and if we yield to it more eagerly than the English, it is only a proof, perhaps, that the future of what was once the Anglo-Saxon tongue lies on this side of the water.

❧ Meyer v. Nebraska: "The knowledge of German cannot reasonably be regarded as harmful"

SUPREME COURT JUSTICE
JAMES C. MACREYNOLDS

The United States' entry into World War I sparked a wave of anti-German sentiment. Americans not only became anti-Germany, they lashed out at German immigrants and German culture within the United States. The prejudice manifested itself in many ways, ranging from public condemnation of the use of innocuous words such as *frankfurter* and *sauerkraut* to serious violence.

In 1919—a year after the war ended—German prejudice lingered as Nebraska passed an "emergency measure" making it a criminal offense to teach any language other than English to students who had not completed the eighth grade. *Meyer v. Nebraska* tested the constitutionality of the law. A Nebraska court convicted Meyer of teaching German to a ten-year-old boy. In 1923, the Supreme Court reversed the decision, setting a limit on the government's authority to foster patriotism, even in wartime.

The Supreme Court of the State affirmed the judgment of conviction. It declared the offense charged and established was "the direct and intentional teaching of the German language as a distinct subject to a child who had not passed the eighth grade," in the parochial school maintained by Zion Evangelical Lutheran Congregation, a collection of biblical stories being used therefore. And it held that the statute forbidding this did not conflict with the Fourteenth Amendment, but was a valid exercise of the police power. The following excerpts from the opinion sufficiently indicate the reasons advanced to support the conclusion.

"The salutary purpose of the statute is clear. The legislature had seen the baneful effects of permitting foreigners, who had taken residence in this country, to rear and educate their children in the language of their native land. The result of that condition was found to be inimical to our own safety. To allow the children of foreigners, who had emigrated here, to be taught from early childhood the language of the country of their parents was to rear them with that language as their mother tongue. It was to educate them so that they must always think in that language, and, as a consequence, naturally inculcate in them the ideas and sentiments foreign to the best interests of this country. The statute, therefore, was intended not only to require that the education of all children be conducted in the English language and until it had become a part of them, they should not in the schools be taught any other language. The obvious purpose of this statute was that the English language should be and become the mother tongue of all children reared in this state."

The problem for our determination is whether the statute as construed and applied unreasonably infringes the liberty guaranteed to the plaintiff in error by the Fourteenth Amendment. "No State shall...deprive any person of life, liberty, or property, without due process of law."

The American people have always regarded education and acquisition of knowledge as matters of supreme importance which should be diligently promoted....

Practically, education of the young is only possible in schools conducted by especially qualified persons who devote themselves thereto. The calling always has been regarded as useful and honorable, essential, indeed, to the public welfare. Mere knowledge of the German language cannot reasonably be regarded as harmful. Heretofore it has been commonly looked upon as helpful and desirable. Plaintiff in error taught this language in school as part of his occupation. His right thus to teach and the right of parents to engage him so to instruct their children, we think, are within the liberty of the Amendment.

It is said the purpose of the legislation was to promote civil development by inhibiting training and education of the immature in foreign tongues and ideals before they could learn English and acquire American ideals; and "that the English language should be and become the mother tongue of all children reared in this State." It is also affirmed that the foreign born population is very large, that certain communities commonly use foreign words, follow foreign leaders, move in a foreign atmosphere, and that the children are thereby hindered from becoming citizens of the most useful type and the public safety is impaired.

That the State may do much, go very far, indeed, in order to improve the quality of its citizens, physically, mentally and morally, is clear; but the individual has certain fundamental rights which must be respected. The protection of the Constitution extends to all, to those who speak other languages as well to those born with English on the tongue. Perhaps it would be highly advantageous if all had ready understanding of our ordinary speech, but this cannot be coerced by methods which conflict with the Constitution—a desirable end cannot be promoted by prohibited means.

...In order to submerge the individual and develop ideal citizens, Sparta assembled the males at seven into barracks and intrusted their subsequent education and training to official guardians. Although such measures have been deliberately approved by men of genius, their ideas touching the relation between individual and State were wholly different from those upon which our institutions rest; and it hardly will be affirmed that any legislature could impose such restrictions upon the people of a State without doing violence to both letter and spirit of the Constitution.

The desire of the legislature to foster a homogenous people with American ideals prepared readily to understand current discussions of civil matters is easy to appreciate. Unfortunate experiences during the late war and aversion toward every characteristic of truculent adversaries were certainly enough to quicken that aspiration. But the means adopted, we think, exceed the limitations on the power of the State and conflict with rights assured to plaintiff in error. The interference is plain enough and no adequate reason therefore in time of peace and domestic tranquility has been shown.

The power of the State to compel attendance at some school and to make reasonable regulations for all schools, including a requirement that they shall give instructions to English, is not questioned…. No emergency has risen which renders knowledge by a child of some language other than English so clearly harmful as to justify its inhibition with the consequent infringement of rights long freely enjoyed. We are constrained to conclude that the statute as applied is arbitrary and without reasonable relation to any end within the competency of the State.

Reversed.

❦ *Suffrage prevails*

19TH AMENDMENT

On August 18, 1920, the 19th Amendment—giving women the right to vote—was ratified, ending more than seventy years of political pressure by suffragists. Ironically, the amendment came three years after the first woman, Jeannette Rankin, had been elected to the House of Representatives, and eight years after Julia Clifford Lathrop was named director of the Children's Bureau, representing the first time a woman headed a federal agency.

Also in 1920, The League of Women Voters was organized to educate women about politics and promote the status and rights of women. Three years later, the first version of a women's equal rights amendment was submitted to Congress.

The right of citizens of the United States to vote shall not be denied or abridged by the United States or by any State on account of sex.

Congress shall have power to enforce this article by appropriate legislation.

❦ *"Woman must not accept; she must challenge"*

MARGARET SANGER

As a public health nurse, Margaret Sanger witnessed first hand the deaths of women who attempted self-induced abortions and the hardships of impoverished women saddled with unwanted pregnancies. She called for birth control, a term she coined, and opened the country's first birth control clinic, founded the Birth Control League (now Planned Parenthood) in 1921, and was a forceful advocate for the development of a birth control pill. In 1920, she wrote about the subject in her book, *Women and the New Race*.

The problem of birth control has arisen directly from the effort of the feminine spirit to free itself from bondage. Woman herself has wrought that bondage through her reproductive powers and while enslaving herself has enslaved the world. The physical suffering to be relieved is chiefly woman's. Hers, too, is the love life that dies first under the blight of too-prolific breeding. Within her is wrapped up the future of the race—it is hers to make or mar. All of these considerations point unmistakably to one fact—it is woman's duty as well as her privilege to lay hold of the means of freedom. Whatever men may do, she cannot escape the responsibility. For ages she has been deprived of the opportunity to meet this obligation. She is now emerging from her helplessness. Even as no one can share the suffering of the overburdened mother, so no one can do this work for her. Others may help, but she and she alone can free herself.

The basic freedom of the world is woman's freedom. A free race cannot be born of slave mothers. A woman enchained cannot choose but give a measure of that bondage to her sons and daughters. No woman can call herself free who does not own and control her body. No woman can call herself free until she can choose consciously whether she will or will not be a mother.

It does not greatly alter the case that some women call themselves free because they earn their own livings, while others profess freedom because they defy the conventions of sex relationships. She who earns her own living gains a sort of freedom that is not to be undervalued, but in quantity it is of little account beside the untrammeled choice of mating or not mating, of being a mother or not being a mother. She gains food and clothing and shelter, at least, without submitting to the charity of her companion, but the earning of her own living does not give her the development of her inner sex urge, far deeper and more powerful in its outworkings than any of these externals. In order to have that development, she must still meet and solve the problem of motherhood.

With the so-called "free" woman, who chooses a mate in defiance of convention, freedom is largely a question of character and audacity. If she does attain an unrestricted choice of a mate, she is still in a position to be enslaved through her reproductive powers. Indeed, the pressure of law and custom upon the woman not legally married is likely to make her more of a slave than the woman fortunate enough to marry the man of her choice.

Look at it from any standpoint you will, suggest any solution you will, conventional or unconventional, sanctioned by law or in defiance of law, woman is in the same position, fundamentally, until she is able to determine for herself whether she will be a mother and to fix the number of her offspring. This unavoidable situation is alone enough to make birth control, first of all, a woman's problem. On the very face of the matter, voluntary motherhood is chiefly the concern of the woman.

It is persistently urged, however, that since sex expression is the act of two, the responsibility of controlling the results should not be placed upon woman alone. Is it fair, it is asked, to give her, instead of the man, the task of protecting herself when she is, perhaps, less rugged in physique than her mate, and has, at all events, the normal, periodic inconveniences of her sex?

We must examine this phase of her problem in two lights—that of the ideal, and of the conditions working toward the ideal. In an ideal society, no doubt, birth control would become the concern of the man as well as the woman. The hard, inescapable fact which we encounter today is that man has not only refused any such responsibility, but has individually and collectively sought to prevent woman from obtaining knowledge by which she could assume this responsibility for herself. She is still in the position of a dependent today because her mate has refused to consider her as an individual apart from his needs. She is still bound because she has in the past left the solution of the problem to him. Having left it to him, she finds that instead of rights, she has only such privileges as she has gained by petitioning, coaxing and cozening. Having left it to him, she is exploited, driven and enslaved to his desires.

While it is true that he suffers many evils as the consequence of that situation, she suffers vastly more. While it is true that he should be awakened to the cause of these evils, we know that they come home to her with crushing force every day. It is she who has the long burden of carrying, bearing and rearing the unwanted children. It is her heart that the sight of the deformed, subnormal, the undernourished, the overworked child smites first and oftenest and hardest. It is her love life that dies first in the fear of undesired pregnancy. It is her opportunity for self-expression that perished first and most hopelessly because of it.

Conditions, rather than theories, facts, rather than dreams, govern the problem. They place it squarely upon the shoulders of woman. She has learned that whatever the moral responsibility of the man in this direction may be, he does not discharge it. She has learned that, lovable and considerate as the individual husband may be, she has nothing to expect from men in the mass, when they make laws and decree customs. She knows that regardless of what ought to be, the brutal, unavoidable fact is that she will never receive her freedom until she takes it for herself.

Having learned this much, she has yet something more to learn. Women are too much inclined to follow in the footsteps of men, to try to think as men think, to try to solve the general problems of life as men solve them. If after attaining their freedom, women accept conditions in the spheres of government, industry, art, morals and religion as they find them, they will be but taking a leaf out of man's book. The woman is not needed to do man's work. She is not needed to think man's thoughts. She need not fear that the masculine mind, almost universally dominant, will fail to take care of its own. Her mission is not to enhance the masculine spirit, but to express the feminine; hers is not to preserve a man-made world, but to create a human world by the infusion of the feminine element into all of its activities.

Woman must not accept; she must challenge. She must not be awed by that which has been built up around her; she must reverence that within her which struggles for expression. Her eyes must be less upon what is and more clearly upon what should be. She must listen only with a frankly questioning attitude to the dogmatized opinions of man-made society. When she chooses her new, free course of action, it must be in the light of her own opinion—of her own intuition. Only so she can give play to the feminine spirit. Only thus can she free her mate from the bondage which he wrought for himself when he wrought hers. Only thus can she restore to him that of which he robbed himself in restricting her. Only thus can she remake the world.

✑ The Revolution in Manners and Morals

FREDERICK LEWIS ALLEN

Written in 1931, Frederick Lewis Allen's book *Only Yesterday* looked back at the Roaring 1920s knowing how they would end. The stock market crash of 1929—and resulting Great Depression—would lay the good times to rest. Nevertheless, many of the great themes of the era would come back when prosperity returned.

Near the top of this list was the luxury of discovering and acting out youthful rebellion. It reads like a watered-down version of parental complaints two and three generations later. The 1920s were marked by the ongoing clash between those who wanted to stretch the limits of moral behavior and those who wanted to tighten them. This was especially the case of women, who having recently been enfranchised to vote could exercise their independence in other ways. Allen described the phenomenon in his book, attributing it to the impacts of World War I, the suffragette movement, Sigmund Freud's writings, prohibition, and the rise of automobiles, movies and advertising.

A first-class revolt against the accepted American order was certainly taking place during those early years of the Post-war decade, but it was one with which Nikolai Lenin had nothing whatever to do. The shock troops of the rebellion were not alien agitators, but the sons and daughters of well-to-do American families, who knew little about Bolshevism and cared distinctly less, and their defiance was expressed not in obscure radical publications or in soap-box speeches, but right across the family breakfast table into the horrified ears of conservative fathers and mothers. Men and women were still shivering at the Red Menace when they awoke to the no less alarming Problem of the Younger Generation, and realized that if the Constitution were not in danger, the moral code of the country certainly was.

This code, as it currently concerned young people, might have been roughly summarized as follows: Women were the guardians of morality; they were made of finer stuff than men and were expected to act accordingly. Young girls must look forward in innocence (tempered perhaps with a modicum of physiological instruction) to a romantic love match which would lead them to the altar and to living-happily-ever-after; and until the "right man" came along they must allow no male to kiss them. It was expected that some would succumb to the temptations of sex, but only with a special class of outlawed women; girls of respectable families were supposed to have no such temptations. Boys and girls were permitted large freedom to work and play together, with decreasing and well-nigh nominal chaperonage, but only because the code worked so well on the whole that a sort of honor system was supplanting supervision by their elders; it was taken for granted that if they had been well brought up they would never take advantage of this freedom. And although the attitude toward smoking and drinking by girls differed widely in different strata of society and different parts of the country, majority of opinion held that it was morally wrong for them to smoke and could hardly imagine them showing the effects of alcohol.

The war had not long been over when cries of alarm from parents, teachers, and moral preceptors began to rend the air. For the boys and girls just growing out of adolescence were making mince-meat of this code.

The dresses that the girls—and for that matter most of the older women—were wearing seemed alarming enough. In July, 1920, a fashion-writer reported in the *New York Times* that "the American woman…has lifted her skirts far beyond any modest limitation," which was another way of saying that the hem was now all of nine inches above the ground. It was freely predicted that skirts would come down again in the winter of 1920-21, but instead they climbed a few scandalous inches farther. The flappers wore thin dresses, short-sleeved and occasionally (in the evening) sleeveless; some of the wilder young things rolled their stockings below their knees, revealing to the shocked eyes of virtue a fleeting glance of shin-bones and knee-cap; and many of them were visibly using cosmetics. "The intoxication of rouge," earnestly explained Dorothy Speare in *Dancers in the Dark*, "is an insidious vintage known to more girls than mere man can ever believe." Useless for frantic parents to insist that no lady did such things; the answer was that the daughters of ladies were doing it, and even retouching their masterpieces in public. Some of them, furthermore, were abandoning their corsets. "The men won't dance with you if you wear a corset," they were quoted as saying.

The current mode in dancing created still more consternation. Not the romantic violin but the barbaric saxophone now dominated the orchestra, and to its passionate crooning and wailing the fox-trotters moved in what the editor of the Hobart College *Herald* disgustedly called a "syncopated embrace." No longer did even an inch of space separate them; they danced as if glued together, body to body, cheek to cheek. Cried the *Catholic Telegraph* of Cincinnati in righteous indignation, "The music is sensuous, the embracing of partners—the female only half-dressed—is absolutely indecent; and the motions—they are such as may not be described, with any respect for propriety, in a family newspaper. Suffice it to say that there are certain houses appropriate for such dances; but those houses have been closed by law."

Supposedly "nice" girls were smoking cigarettes—openly and defiantly, if often rather awkwardly and self-consciously. They were drinking—somewhat less openly but often all too efficaciously. There were stories of daughters of the most exemplary parents getting drunk— "blotto," as their companions cheerfully put it—on the contents of the hip-flasks of the new prohibition regime, and going out joyriding with men at four in the morning. And worst of all, even at well-regulated dances they were said to retire where the eye of the most sharp-sighted chaperon could not follow, and in darkened rooms or in parked cars to engage in the unspeakable practice of petting and necking.

It was not until F. Scott Fitzgerald, who had hardly graduated from Princeton and ought to know what his generation was doing, brought out *This Side of Paradise* in April, 1920, that fathers and mothers realized fully what was afoot and how long it had been going on. Apparently the "petting party" had been current as early as 1916, and was now widely established as an indoor sport. "None of the Victorian mothers—and most of the mothers were Victorian—had any idea how casually their daughters were accustomed to be kissed," wrote Mr. Fitzgerald. "…Amory saw girls doing things that even in his memory would have been impossibe: eating three-o'clock, after-dance suppers in impossible cafes, talking of every side of life with an air half of earnestness, half of mockery, yet with a furtive excitement that Amory considered stood for a real moral let-down. But he never realized how widespread it was until he saw the cities between New York and Chicago as one vast juvenile intrigue." The book caused a shudder to run down the national spine; did not Mr. Fitzgerald represent one of his well-nurtured heroines as brazenly confessing, "I've kissed dozens of men. I suppose I'll kiss dozens more;" and another heroine as saying to a young man (to a young man!), "Oh, just one person in fifty has any glimmer of what sex is, I'm hipped on Freud and all that, but it's rotten that every bit of real life in the world is ninety-nine percent passion and one little soupcon of jealousy?"

It was incredible. It was abominable. What did it all mean? Was every decent standard being thrown over? Mothers read the scarlet words and wondered if they themselves "had any idea how often their daughters were accustomed to be kissed."…But no, this must be an exaggerated account of the misconduct of some especially depraved group. Nice girls couldn't behave like that and talk openly about passion. But in due course other books appeared to substantiate the findings of Mr. Fitzgerald: *Dancers in the Dark*, *The Plastic Age*, *Flaming Youth*. Magazine articles and newspapers reiterated the scandal. To be sure, there were plenty of communities where nice girls did not, in actual face "behave like that"; and even in the more sophisticated urban centers there were plenty of girls who did not. Nevertheless, there was enough fire beneath the smoke of these sensational revelations to make the Problem of the Younger Generation a topic of anxious discussion from coast to coast.

The forces of morality rallied to the attack. Dr. Francis E. Clark, founder and president of the Christian Endeavor Society, declared that the modern "indecent dance" was "an offense against womanly purity, the very fountainhead of our family and civil life." The new style of dancing was denounced in religious journals as "impure, polluting, corrupting, debasing, destroying spirituality, increasing carnality," and the mothers and sisters and church members of the land were called upon to admonish and instruct and raise the spiritual tone of these dreadful young people. President Murphy of the University of Florida cried out with true Southern warmth, "The low-cut gowns, the rolled hose and short skirts are born of the Devil and his angels, and are carrying the present and future generations to chaos and destruction." A group of Episcopal church-women in New York, speaking with the authority of wealth and social position (for they included Mrs. J. Pierpont Morgan, Mrs. Borden Harriman, Mrs. Henry Phipps, Mrs. James Roosevelt, and Mrs. E. H. Harriman), proposed an organization to discourage fashions involving an "excess of nudity" and "improper ways of dancing." The Y. W. C. A. conducted a national campaign against immodest dress among high-school girls, supplying newspapers with printed materials carrying headlines such as "Working Girls Responsive to Modesty Appeal" and "High Heels Losing Ground Even in France." In Philadelphia a Dress Reform Committee of prominent citizens sent a questionnaire to over a thousand clergymen to ask them what would be their idea of a proper dress, and although the gentlemen of the cloth showed a distressing variety of opinion, the committee proceeded to design a "moral gown" which was endorsed by ministers of fifteen denominations. The distinguishing characteristics of this moral gown were that it was very loose-fitting, that the sleeves reached just below the elbows, and that the hem came within seven and a half inches of the floor.

Not content with example and reproof, legislators in several states introduced bills to reform feminine dress once and for all. The New York American reported in 1921 that a bill was pending in Utah providing fine and imprisonment for those who wore on the streets "skirts higher than three inches above the ankle." A bill was laid before the Virginia legislature which would forbid any woman from wearing shirtwaists or evening gowns which displayed "more than three inches of her throat." In Ohio the proposed limit of decolletage was two inches; the bill introduced in the Ohio legislature aimed also to prevent the sale of any "garment which unduly displays or accentuates the lines of the female figure," and to prohibit any "female over fourteen years of age" from wearing "a skirt which does not reach to that part of the foot known as the instep."

Meanwhile innumerable families were torn with dissension over cigarettes and gin and all-night automobile rides. Fathers and mothers lay awake asking themselves whether their children were not utterly lost; sons and daughters evaded questions, lied miserably and unhappily, or flared up to reply rudely that at least they were not dirty-minded hypocrites, that they saw no harm in what they were doing and proposed to go right on doing it. From those liberal clergymen and teachers who prided themselves on keeping step with all that was new came a chorus of reassurance: these young people were at least franker and more honest than their elders had been; having experimented for themselves, would they not soon find out which standards were outworn and which represented the accumulated moral wisdom of the race? Hearing such hopeful words, many good people took heart again. Perhaps this flare-up of youthful passion was a flash in the pan, after all. Perhaps in another year or two the boys and girls would come to their senses and everything would be all right again.

They were wrong, however. For the revolt of the younger generations was only the beginning of a revolution in manners and morals that was already beginning to affect men and women of every age in every part of the country.

❧ "To keep eternally ablaze the sacred fire of a fervent devotion to a pure Americanism"

KU KLUX KLAN DECLARATION

The revival of the Ku Klux Klan in the 1920s spoke to the rising racism, xenophobia and anti-Catholicism that marked the era. The dubious organization had been founded in the Reconstruction South to resist the Northern occupation, including efforts to elevate the status of blacks in society.

In 1922, white Protestant men revived the Klan to maintain, among other things, the supremacy of whites and "pure Americanism." Dressed in white sheets, the KKK terrorized blacks, immigrants and Catholics—not just in the South. They commonly lynched blacks with the tacit approval of police.

The rise of the KKK represented one of the more virulent strains of intolerance that has plagued the nation's history. As this 1922 proclamation makes clear, however, KKK members saw their role in a very different, very noble light.

We solemnly declare to all mankind: that the Knights of the Ku Klux Klan, incorporated, is the original Ku Klux Klan organized in the year 1866, and active during the Reconstruction period of American history; and by and under its corporate name is revived, remodeled and expanded into a ritualistic, fraternal, patriotic society of national scope, duly incorporated (under the laws of the State of Georgia) in the years of 1915 and 1916, and dedicated to the same principles and spiritual purposes as more particularly set forth in Article II, of the Constitution and Laws of the society.

We do further declare to the world: that our original Prescript used as the governing law of the Ku Klux Klan, during the period of its former activities, and all official titles, mannerisms, usages and things therein prescribed have not been abandoned by us; but on the contrary, all of these, together with designs of paraphernalia, regalia, flags, banners, emblems, symbols, or other insignia and things prescribed or previously used by or under the authority of the Ku Klux Klan are the property of the Ku Klux Klan under and by virtue of its corporate name of Knights of Ku Klux Klan, and are held sacred by us as a precious heritage, which we shall jealously preserve, forever maintain and valiantly protect from profanation.

The Imperial Proclamation

To the lovers of law, order, peace and justice of all nations, people, tribes and tongues of the whole earth, Greetings:

I, and the citizens of the Invisible Empire, through me, make declaration to you:

We, the members of this order, desiring to promote patriotism toward our civil government; honorable peace among men and nations; protection for and happiness in the homes of our people; manhood, brotherhood, and love among ourselves, and

liberty, justice and fraternity among all mankind; believing we can best accomplish these noble purposes through a mystic, social, patriotic, benevolent association, having a perfected lodge system, with an exalted ritualistic form of work and an effective form of government, not for selfish profit, but for the mutual betterment, benefit and protection of our oath-bound associates, and their loved ones; do physically, socially, morally and vocationally:

Proclaim to the World

That we are dedicated to the sublime duty of providing generous aid, tender sympathy and fraternal assistance amid fortune and misfortune in the effulgent light of life and amid the sable shadows of death, and to the exalted privilege of demonstrating the practical utility of the great (yet most neglected) doctrine of the Fatherhood of God and the brotherhood of man as a vital force in the lives and affairs of men.

We invite all men who can qualify to become citizens of the Invisible Empire to approach the portal of our beneficent domain, join us in our noble work of extending its boundaries, and in disseminating the gospel of "Klancraft," thereby encouraging, conserving, protecting and making vital the fraternal relationship in the practice of an honorable clannishness; to share with us the glory of performing the sacred duty of protecting womanhood; to maintain forever the God-given supremacy of the White race; to commemorate the holy and chivalric achievements of our fathers; to safeguard the sacred rights, privileges and institutions of our civil government; to bless mankind and to keep eternally ablaze the sacred fire of a fervent devotion to a pure Americanism.

The Invisible Empire is founded on sterling character, and immutable principles based upon sacred sentiment and cemented by noble purposes. It is promoted by a sincere, unselfish devotion of the souls of men, and is governed by their consecrated intelligence. It is the soul of chivalry, virtue's impenetrable shield and the devout impulse of an unconquered race.

Done in the aulic of His Majesty, the Emperor of the Invisible Empire, Knights of the Ku Klux Klan, in the Imperial Palace, in the Imperial City of Atlanta, Commonwealth of Georgia, United States of America.

This the 29th day of November, Anno Domini, Nineteen Hundred and Twenty-two,

Anno Klan LVI.
William Joseph Simmons
Imperial Wizard

❧ *"He had seen four of his six brothers die by violence, three of them killed by white men"*

MALCOLM X

Born in the 1920s, Malcolm X suffered the sting of the Ku Klux Klan's tactics as a child. His father, a minister who preached the word of African nationalist Marcus Garvey, was the frequent target of the KKK and other white supremacist groups. His grandfather was a white man who had raped Malcolm X's black grandmother. Four of Malcolm X's uncles, in addition to his father, would be killed by white men.

Malcolm X recalled this violence-ridden childhood in his 1965 autobiography. In describing the environment in which he and other blacks lived—and were powerless to do anything about for many years—he helped to highlight the courage of blacks who later fought against racism in the 1950s and explain the resentment of blacks in the 1960s.

When my mother was pregnant with me, she told me later, a party of hooded Ku Klux Klan riders galloped up to our home in Omaha, Nebraska, one night. Surrounding the house, brandishing their shotguns and rifles, they shouted for my father to come out. My mother went to the front door and opened it. Standing where they could see her pregnant condition, she told them that she was alone with her three small children, and that my father was away, preaching, in Milwaukee. The Klansmen shouted threats and warnings at her that we had better get out of town because "the good Christian white people" were not going to stand for my father's "spreading trouble" among the "good" Negroes of Omaha with the "back to Africa" preachings of Marcus Garvey.

My father, the Reverend Earl Little, was a Baptist minister, a dedicated organizer for Marcus Aurelius Garvey's U.N.I.A. (Universal Negro Improvement Association). With the help of such disciples as my father, Garvey, from his headquarters in New York City's Harlem, was raising the banner of black-race purity and exhorting the Negro masses to return to their ancestral African homeland—a cause which had made Garvey the most controversial black man on earth.

Still shouting threats, the Klansmen finally spurred their horses and galloped around the house, shattering every window pane with their gun butts. Then they rode off into the night, their torches flaring, as suddenly as they had come.

My father was enraged when he returned. He decided to wait until I was born—which would be soon—and then the family would move. I am not sure why he made this decision, for he was not a frightened Negro, as most then were, and many still are today. My father was a big, six-foot-four, very black man. He had only one eye. How he had lost the other one I have never known. He was from Reynolds, Georgia, where he had left school after the third, or maybe fourth grade. He believed, as did Marcus Garvey, that freedom, independence and self-respect could never be achieved by the Negro in America, and that therefore the Negro should leave America to the white man and return to his African land of origin. Among the reasons my father had decided to risk and dedicate his life to help disseminate this philosophy among his people was that he had seen four of his six brothers die by violence, three of them killed by white men, including one by lynching. What my father could not know then was that of the remaining three, including himself, only one, my Uncle Jim, would die in bed, of natural causes. Northern white police were later to shoot my Uncle Oscar. And my father was finally himself to die by the white man's hands.

It has always been my belief that I, too, will die by violence. I have done all that I can to be prepared.

I was my father's seventh child. He had three children by a previous marriage—Ella, Earl, and Mary, who lived in Boston. He had met and married my mother in Philadelphia, where their first child, my oldest full brother, Wilfred, was born. They moved from Philadelphia to Omaha, where Hilda and Philbert were born.

I was next in line. My mother was twenty-eight when I was born on May 19, 1925, in an Omaha hospital. Then we moved to Milwaukee, where Reginald was born. From infancy, he had some kind of hernia condition which was to handicap him physically for the rest of his life.

Louise Little, my mother, who was born in

Grenada, in the British West Indies, looked like a white woman. Her father was white. She had straight black hair, and her accent did not sound like a Negro's. Of this white father of hers, I know nothing except her shame about it. I remember hearing her say she was glad that she had never seen him. It was, of course, because of him that I got my reddish-brown "mariny" color of skin, and my hair of the same color. I was the lightest child in our family. (Out in the world later on, in Boston and New York, I was among the millions of Negroes who were insane enough to feel that it was some kind of status symbol to be light-complexioned—that one was actually fortunate to be born thus. But, still later, I learned to hate every drop of that white rapist's blood that is in me.)

Our family stayed only briefly in Milwaukee, for my father wanted to find a place where he could raise our own food and perhaps build a business. The teachings of Marcus Garvey stressed becoming independent of the white man. We went next, for some reason, to Lansing, Michigan. My father bought a house and soon, as had been his pattern, he was doing free-lance Christian preaching in local Negro Baptist churches, and during the week he was roaming about spreading word of Marcus Garvey.

He had begun to lay away savings for the store he had always wanted to own when, as always, some stupid local Uncle Tom Negroes began to funnel stories about his revolutionary beliefs to the local white people. This time, the get-out-of-town threats came from a local hate society called The Black Legion. They wore black robes instead of white. Soon, nearly everywhere my father went, Black Legionnaires were reviling him as an "uppity nigger" for wanting to own a store, for living outside the Lansing Negro district, for spreading unrest and dissension among "the good niggers."

As in Omaha, my mother was pregnant again, this time with my youngest sister. Shortly after Yvonne was born came the nightmare night in 1929, my earliest vivid memory. I remember being suddenly snatched awake into a frightening confusion of pistol shots and shouting and smoke and flames. My father had shouted and shot at the two white men who had set the fire and were running away. Our home was burning down around us. We were lunging and bumping and tumbling all over each other trying to escape. My mother, with the baby in her arms,

just made it into the yard before the house crashed in, showering sparks. I remember we were outside in the night in our underwear, crying and yelling our heads off. The white police and firemen came and stood around watching as the house burned to the ground.

❧ The Immigration Act of 1924

CONGRESS

Soured by the United States' experience in World War I and alarmed by the number of southern European immigrants who were arriving in the United States, Congress passed the Immigration Act of 1921. This historic piece of legislation set a limit on the number of foreigners allowed into the country, imposed country quotas and placed a cap of three percent of immigrants in relation to the number of nationals in the country, based on the 1910 census.

Three years later, however, Congress decided that they had not been restrictive enough in their impositions. From their nativist perspective, too many immigrants from places other than northern and western Europe were piling into the country. The Immigration Act of 1924 remedied this. The number of immigrants permitted by nationality was reduced to two percent and the base date was changed to 1890, when there were significantly fewer southern Europeans in the United States.

The "Immigration Act of 1924" which supplants the so-called quota limit act of May 19, 1921, the latter having expired by limitation at the close of the fiscal year just ended, makes several very important changes not only in our immigration policy but also in the administrative machinery of the Immigration Service. Some of the more important changes in these respects will be briefly referred to.

It will be remembered that the quota limit act of May, 1921, provided that the number of aliens of any nationality admissible to the United States in any fiscal year should be limited to 3 percent of the number of persons of such nationality who were resident in the United States according to the census of 1910, it being also provided that no more than 20 percent of any annual quota could be admitted in any one month. Under the act of 1924 the number of each nationality who may be admitted annually is limited to 2 percent of the population of such nationality resident in the United States according to the census of 1890, and not more than 10 percent of any annual quota may be admitted in any month except in cases where such quota is less than 300 for the entire year.

Under the act of May, 1921, the quota area was limited to Europe, the Near East, Africa, and Australasia. The countries of North and South America, with adjacent islands, and countries immigration from which was otherwise regulated, such as China, Japan, and countries within the Asiatic barred zone, were not within the scope of the quota law. Under the new act, however, immigration from the entire world, with the exception of the Dominion of Canada, Newfoundland, the Republic of Mexico, the Republic of Cuba, the Republic of Haiti, the Dominican Republic, the Canal Zone, the independent countries of Central and South America, is subject to quota limitations. The various quotas established under the new law are shown in the following proclamation of the President, issued on the last day of the present fiscal year:

By The President of The United States Of America

A Proclamation

Whereas, it is provided in the act of Congress approved May 26, 1924, entitled "An act to limit the immigration of aliens into the United States, and for other purposes" that —

"The annual quota of any nationality shall be two per centum of the number of foreign-born individuals of such nationality resident in continental United States as determined by the United States census of 1890, but the minimum quota of any nationality shall be 100 (Sec. 11(a)).

"The Secretary of State, the Secretary of Commerce, and the Secretary of Labor, jointly, shall, as soon as feasible after the enactment of this act, prepare a statement showing the number of individuals of the various nationalities resident in continental United States as determined by the United States census of 1890, which statement shall be, the population basis for the purposes of subdivision (a) of section 11 (Sec. 12(b)).

"Such officials shall, jointly, report annually to the President the quota of each nationality under subdivisions (a) of section 11, together with the statements, estimates, and revisions provided for in this section. The President shall proclaim and make known the quotas so reported." (Sec. 12 (e)).

Now, therefore, I Calvin Coolidge, President of the United States of America acting under and by virtue of the power in me vested by the aforesaid act of Congress, do hereby proclaim and make known that on and after July 1, 1924, and throughout the fiscal year 1924-1925, the quota of each nationality provided in said Act shall be as follows:

Country or area of birth	Quota 1924-1925
Afghanistan	100
Albania	100
Andorra	100
Arabian peninsula (1, 2)	100
Australia, including Papua, Tasmania, and all islands Appertaining to Australia (3, 4)	121
Austria	785
Belgium (5)	512
Bhutan	100
Bulgaria	100
Cameroon (proposed British mandate)	100
Cameroon (French mandate)	100
China	100
Czechoslovakia	3,073
Danzig, Free City of	228
Denmark (5, 6)	2,789
Egypt	100
Estonia	124
Ethiopia (Abyssinia)	100
Finland	70
France (1, 5, 6)	3,954
Germany	51,227
Great Britain and Northern Ireland (1, 3, 5, 6)	34,007
Greece	100
Hungary	473
Iceland	100
India (3)	100
Iraq (Mesopotamia)	100
Irish Free State (3)	28,567
Italy, including Rhodes, Dodekanesia and Castellorizzo (5)	3,845
Japan	100
Latvia	142
Liberia	100
Lichtenstein	100
Lithuania	344
Luxemburg	100

Monaco	100
Morocco (French and Spanish Zones and Tangier)	100
Muscat (Oman)	100
Nauru (proposed British mandate) (4)	100
Nepal	100
Netherlands (1, 5, 6)	648
New Zealand (including appertaining islands) (3, 4)	100
Norway (5)	6,453
New Guinea, and other Pacific Islands under proposed Australian mandate (4)	100
Palestine (with Trans-Jordan, proposed British mandate)	100
Persia (1)	100
Poland	5,982
Portugal (1, 5)	503
Ruanda and Urundi (Belgium mandate)	100
Rumania	603
Russia, European and Asiatic (1)	2,248
Samoa, Western (4) (proposed mandate of New Zealand)	100
San Marino	100
Siam	100
South Africa, Union of (3)	100
South West Africa (proposed mandate of Union of South Africa)	100
Spain (5)	131
Sweden	9,561
Switzerland	1,081
Syria and Lebanon (French mandate)	100
Tanganyika (proposed British mandate)	100
Togoland (proposed British mandate)	100
Togoland (French mandate)	100
Turkey	100
Yap and other Pacific islands (under Japanese mandate) (4)	100
Yugoslavia	671

(a) Persons born in the portions of Persia, Russia or the Arabian peninsula situation within the barred zone, and who are admissible under the immigration laws of the United States as quota immigrants, will be charged to the quotas of these countries; and (b) persons born in the colonies, dependencies, or protectorates, or portions thereof, within the barred zone, or France, Great Britain, the Netherlands, or Portugal, who are admissible under the immigration laws of the United States as quota immigrants, will be charged to the quota of the country to which such colony of dependency belongs or by which it is administered as a protectorate.

The quota-area denominated "Arabian peninsula" consists of all territory except Muscat and Aden, situated in the portion of that peninsula and adjacent islands, to the southeast of Iraq, of Palestine with Trans-Jordan and of Egypt.

Quota immigrants born in the British self-governing dominions or in the Empire of India, will be charged to the appropriate quota rather than to that of Great Britain and Northern Island. There are no quota restrictions for Canada and Newfoundland.

Quota immigrants eligible to citizenship in the United States, born in a colony, dependency, or protectorate of any country to which a quota applies will be charged to the quota of that country.

In contract with the law of 1921, the Immigration Act of 1924 provides that persons born in the colonies or dependencies of European countries situated in Central American, South America, or the islands adjacent to the American continents (except Newfoundland and islands pertaining to Newfoundland, Labrador and Canada), will be charged to the quota of the country to which such colony or dependency belongs.

General Note—The immigration quotas assigned to the various countries and quota-area should not be regarded as having any political significance whatever, or as involving recognition of new governments, or of new boundaries, or of transfers of territory except as the United States Government has already made such recognition in a formal and official manner .

Calvin Coolidge

❧ *"The highest possible moral and artisitc standards"*

THE HAYS FORMULA

As president of the Motion Picture Producers and Distributors of America, Will H. Hays imposed a code of guidelines on

Hollywood movies from 1924 to 1945. The Hays Code (or Hays Formula) was created in response to some of the more racy movies being produced in the 1920s and the resulting criticism. The former chairman of the Republican National Committee, Hays wanted to preserve the moral integrity of the film industry.

Although several movies in the late 1920s exceeded the bounds of the code, by the early 1930s Hays' guidelines became more or less institutionalized and stayed in place for thirty years. Hays, however, did allow some exceptions. David O. Selznick, for example, sought and received special permission for Rhett Butler to use the word "damn" in *Gone With the Wind*.

Whereas, the member of the Motion Picture Producers and Distributors of America, Inc., in their continuing effort "to establish and maintain the highest possible moral and artistic standards of motion picture production" are engaged in a special effort to prevent the prevalent type of book and play from becoming the prevalent type of picture; to exercise every possible care that only books or plays which are of the right type are used for screen presentation; to avoid the picturization of books or plays which can be produced after such chances as to leave the producer subject to a charge of deception; to avoid using titles which are indicative of a kind of picture which should not be produced, or by their suggestiveness seek to obtain attendance by deception, a thing equally reprehensible; and to prevent misleading, salacious or dishonest advertising:

Now, therefore, be it resolved by the board of directors of the Motion Picture Producers and Distributors of America, Inc., That said Association does hereby reaffirm its determination to carry out its purposes above set out; and does hereby repledge the best efforts of the members of the Association to that end; and does hereby further declare that they will not produce or promote the production, exhibit or promote the exhibition, or aid in any way whatsoever in the production, distribution or exhibition by the members of this Association or by companies subsidiary to said members or by any other person, firm or corporation producing, distributing or exhibiting pictures, of any picture or pictures by whomsoever produced, distributed or exhibited, which because of the unfit character of title, story, exploitation or picture itself, do not meet the requirements of this preamble and resolution or hinder the ful-

fillment of the purposes of the Association set out herein.

Resolved, That those things which are included in the following list shall not appear in pictures produced by the members of the Association, irrespective of the manner in which they are treated:

Pointed profanity—by either title or lip—this includes the words "God," "Lord," "Jesus," "Christ" (unless they be used reverently in connection with proper religious ceremonies), "hell," "damn," "Gawd," and every other profane and vulgar expression however it may be spelled;

Any licentious or suggestive nudity—in fact or in silhouette; and any lecherous or licentious notice thereof by other characters in the picture;

The illegal traffic in drugs;

Any inference of sex perversion;

White slavery;

Miscegenation (sex relationships between the white and black races);

Sex hygiene and veneral diseases;

Scenes of actual childbirth—in fact or in silhouette;

Children's sex organs;

Ridicule of the clergy;

Willful offense to any nation, race or creed.

And be it further Resolved, That special care be exercised in the manner in which the following subjects are treated, to the end that vulgarity and suggestiveness may be eliminated and that good taste may be emphasized:

The use of flags;

International relations (avoiding picturization in an unfavorable light another country's religion, history, institutions, prominent people, and citizenry);

Arson;

The use of firearms;

Theft, robbery, safe-cracking, and dynamiting of trains, mines, buildings, etc. (having in mind the effect which a too-detailed description of these may have upon the moron);

Brutality and possible gruesomeness;

Technique of committing murder by whatever method;

Methods of smuggling;

Third-degree methods;

Actual hangings or electrocutions as legal punishment for crime;

Sympathy for criminals;

Attitude toward public characters and institutions;

Sedition;

Apparent cruelty to children and animals;

Branding of people or animals;

The sale of women, or of a woman selling her virtue;

Rape or attempted rape;

First-night scenes;

Man and woman in bed together;

Deliberate seduction of girls;

The institution of marriage;

Surgical operations;

The use of drugs;

Titles or scenes having to do with the law enforcement or law-enforcing officers;

Excessive lustful kissing, particularly when one character or the other is a "heavy."

❧ *Teapot Dome*

JOINT RESOLUTION OF CONGRESS RESPECTING PROSECUTION FOR CANCELLATION OF OIL, FEBRUARY 8, 1924

President Warren Harding's administration was repeatedly marred by scandal—the most damaging of which was Teapot Dome. Publicly owned oil fields were fraudulently leased to private interests, stirring a public outcry against government corruption.

Secretary of the Navy Albert Bacon Fall secretly leased the Teapot Dome reserve in Wyoming to Harry F. Sinclair and the Elk Hill reserve in California to E. L. Doheny. When the arrangement was discovered, Congress annulled the lease and called for an investigation. Fall, who had accepted hundreds of thousands of dollars and a herd of cattle for the deal, was imprisoned for ten months on bribery charges. Harding died just before the public learned the facts of the scandal.

A joint resolution directing the President to institute and prosecute suits to cancel certain leases of oil lands and incidental contracts, and for other purposes.

Whereas it appears from evidence taken by the Committee on Public Lands and Surveys of the United States Senate that certain lease of naval reserve No. 3, in the State of Wyoming, bearing date April 7, 1922, made in form by the Government of the United States, through Albert B. Fall, Secretary of the Interior, and Edwin Denby, Secretary of the Navy, as lessor, to the Mammoth Oil Co., as lessee, and that certain contract between the Government of the United States and the Pan American Petroleum & Transport Co., dated April 25, 1922, signed by Edward C. Finney, Acting Secretary of the Interior, and Edwin Denby, Secretary of the Navy, relating among other things to the construction of oil tanks at Pearl Harbor, Territory of Hawaii, and that certain lease of naval reserve No. 1, in the State of California, bearing date December 11, 1922, made in form by the Government of the United States through Albert B. Fall, Secretary of the Interior, and Edwin Denby, Secretary of the Navy, as lessor, to the Pan American Petroleum Co., as lessee, were executed under circumstances indicating fraud and corruption; and

Whereas the said leases and contract were entered into without authority on the part of the officers purporting to act in the execution of the same for the United States and in violation of the laws of Congress; and

Whereas such leases and contract were made in defiance of the settled policy of the Government adhered to through three successive administrations, to maintain in the ground a great reserve supply of oil adequate to the needs of the Navy in any emergency threatening the national security: Therefore be it.

Resolved, etc., That the said leases and contract are against the public interest and that the lands embraced therein should be recovered and held for the purpose to which they were dedicated; and

Resolved further, That the President of the United States be, and he hereby is, authorized and directed immediately to cause suit to be instituted and prosecuted for the annulment and cancellation of the said leases and contract and all contracts incidental or supplemental thereto, to enjoin further extraction of oil from the said reserves under said leases or from the territory covered by the same, to secure any further appropriate incidental relief, and to prosecute such other actions or proceedings, civil and criminal, as may be warranted by the facts in relation to the making of the said leases and contract.

And that President is further authorized and directed to appoint, by and with the advice and consent of the Senate, special counsel who shall have charge and control of the prosecution of such litigation, anything in the statutes touching the powers of the attorney General of the Department of Justice to the contrary notwithstanding.

Among the Believers

H. L. MENCKEN

John T. Scopes was a Tennessee schoolteacher who was charged with teaching the theory of evolution and brought to court for the transgression. Prosecuted by William Jennings Bryan and defended by Clarence Darrow, the 1925 case in rural Dayton, Tennessee, became a national event. Religious belief went head to head with progressive intellectualism in this landmark case.

H.L. Mencken was the leading commentator of the 1920s. His *Baltimore Sun* columns lampooned American morals. In an era when Prohibition forbade liquor and alcoholism was on the rise, Mencken's biting satires on American hypocrisy struck a responsive chord.

The Scopes Trial was fertile fodder for Mencken's sharp pen. He traveled to Tennessee to cover the trial, where he reported not just on the trial itself, but on the heavily religious South that rejected modern science. Scopes was found guilty and sentenced to pay a $100 fine—a debt that was promptly covered by the *Baltimore Sun.*

It was hot weather when they tried the infidel Scopes at Dayton, Tenn., but I went down there very willingly, for I was eager to see something of evangelical Christianity as a going concern. In the big cities of the Republic, despite the endless efforts of consecrated men, it is laid up with a wasting disease. The very Sunday-school superintendents, taking jazz from the stealthy radio, shake their fire-proof legs; their pupils, moving into adolescence, no longer respond to the proliferating hormones by enlisting for missionary service in Africa, but resort to necking instead. Even in Dayton, I found, though the mob was up to do execution upon Scopes, there was a strong smell of antinominalism. The nine churches of the village were half empty on Sunday, and weeds choked their yards. Only two or three of the resident pastors managed to sustain themselves by their ghost-

ly science; the rest had to take orders for mail-order pantaloons or work in the adjacent strawberry fields; one, I heard, was a barber. On the courthouse green a score of sweating theologians debated the darker passages of Holy Writ day and night, but I soon found that they were all volunteers, and that the local faithful, while interested in their exegesis as an intellectual exercise, did not permit it to impede the indigenous debaucheries. Exactly twelve minutes after I reached the village I was taken in tow by a Christian man and introduced to the favorite tipple of the Cumberland Range: half corn liquor and half Coca-Cola. It seemed a dreadful dose to me, but I found that the Dayton illuminati got it down with gusto, rubbing their tummies and rolling their eyes. I include among them the chief local proponents of the Mosaic cosmogony. They were all hot for Genesis, but their faces were far too florid to belong to teetotalers, and when a pretty girl came tripping down the main street, which was very often, they reached for the places where their neckties should have been with all the amorous enterprise of movie actors. It seemed somehow strange.

An amiable newspaper woman of Chattanooga, familiar with those uplands, presently enlightened me. Dayton, she explained, was simply a great capital like any other. That is to say, it was to Rhea County what Atlanta was to Georgia or Paris to France. That is to say, it was predominantly Epicurean and sinful. A country girl from some remote valley of the county, coming into town for her semi-annual bottle of Lydia Pinkham's Vegetable Compound, shivered on approaching Robinson's drug-store quite as a country girl from upstate New York might shiver on approaching the Metropolitan Opera House. In every village lout she saw a potential white-slaver. The hard sidewalks hurt her feet. Temptations of the flesh bristled to all sides of her, luring her to Hell. This newspaper woman told me of a session with just such a visitor, holden a few days before. The latter waited outside one of the town hot-dog and Coca-Cola shops while her husband negotiated with a hardware merchant across the street. The newspaper woman, idling along and observing that the stranger was badly used by the heat, invited her to step into the shop for a glass of Coca-Cola. The invitation brought forth only a gurgle of terror. Coca-Cola, it quickly appeared, was prohibited by the country lady's pastor, as a levantine and Hell-sent narcotic. He also prohibited coffee and tea—and pies! He had his doubts about white bread and boughten meat. The newspaper woman, interested, inquired about ice-cream. It was, she found, not specifically prohibited, but going into a Coca-Cola shop to get it would be clearly sinful. So she offered to get a saucer of it, and bring it out to the sidewalk. The visitor vacillated—and came near being lost. But God saved her in the nick of time. When the newspaper woman emerged from the place she was in full flight up the street. Later on her husband, mounted on a mule, overtook her four miles out the mountain pike. This newspaper woman, whose kindness covered city infidels as well as Alpine Christians, offered to take me back in the hills to a place where the old-time religion was genuinely on tap. The Scopes jury, she explained, was composed mainly of its customers, with a few Dayton sophisticates added to leaven the mass. It would thus be instructive to climb the heights and observe the former at their ceremonies.... But foreigners, it appeared, would have to approach the sacred grove cautiously, for the upland worshipers were very shy, and at the first sight of a strange face they would adjourn their orgy and slink into the forest.

Slowly and cautiously we crossed what seemed to be a pasture, and then we stealthily edged further and further. The light now grew larger and we could begin to make out what was going on. We went ahead on all fours, like snakes in the grass.

From the great limb of a mighty oak hung a couple of crude torches of the sort that car inspectors thrust under Pullman cars when a train pulls in at night. In the guttering glare was the preacher, and for a while we could see no one else. He was an immensely tall and thin mountaineer in blue jeans, his collarless shirt open at the neck and his hair a tousled mop. As he preached he paced up and down under the smoking flambeaux, and at each turn he thrust his arms into the air and yelled "Glory to God!" We crept nearer in the shadow of the cornfield, and began to hear more of his discourse. He was preaching on the Day of Judgment. The high kings of the earth, he roared, would all fall down and die; only the sanctified would stand up to receive the Lord God of Hosts. One of these kings he mentioned by name, the king of what he called Greece-y. The king of Greece-y, he said, was doomed to Hell.

The preacher stopped at last, and there arose out of the darkness a woman with her hair pulled back into a light tight knot. She began so quietly that we couldn't hear what she said, but soon her voice rose resonantly and we could follow her. She was denouncing the reading of books. Some wandering book agent, it appeared, had come to her cabin and tried to sell her a specimen of his wares. She refused to touch it. Why, indeed, read a book? If what was in it true, then everything in it was already in the Bible. If it was false, then reading it would imperil the soul. This syllogism from the Caliph Omar complete, she sat down.

Finally, we got tired of the show and returned to Dayton. It was nearly eleven o'clock—an immensely late hour for those latitudes—but the whole town was still gathered in the courthouse yard, listening to the disputes of theologians. The Scopes trial had brought them in from all directions. There was a friar wearing a sandwich sign announcing that he was the Bible champion of the world. There was a Seventh Day Adventist arguing that Clarence Darrow was the beast with seven heads and ten horns described in Revelation XIII, and that the end of the world was at hand. There was an evangelist made up like Andy Gump, with the news that atheists in Cincinnati were preparing to descend upon Dayton and burn the town. There was an ancient who maintained that no Catholic could be a Christian. There was the eloquent Dr. T. T. Martin, of Blue Mountain, Miss., come to town with a truck-load of torches and hymn-books to put Darwin in his place. There was a singing brother bellowing apocalyptic hymns. There was William Jennings Bryan, followed everywhere by a gaping crowd. Dayton was having a roaring time. It was better than the circus. But the note of devotion was simply not there; the Daytonians, after listening a while, would slip away to Robinson's drugstore to regale themselves with Coca-Cola, or to the lobby of the Aqua Hotel, where the learned Raulston sat in state, judicially picking his teeth. The real religion was not present. It began at the bridge over the town creek, where the road makes off for the hills.

Mother to Son

LANGSTON HUGHES

The 1920s saw the rise of a new, sophisticated black culture centered in New York City. The Harlem Renaissance brought forth a diverse array of talented black musicians, writers and artists with a distinctive style marked by the toils of their lives and the sense of freedom that comes from having little to lose. Most famously, jazz grew out of the black culture and by the 1920s had been accepted by much of white culture.

Langston Hughes was a talented member of the Harlem Renaissance and a leading spokesman. "Jazz to me is one of the inherent expressions of Negro life in America: the eternal tom-tom beating in the Negro soul," Hughes wrote, "the tom-tom of revolt against the weariness of the white world, a world of subway trains, and work, work, work; the tom-tom of joy and laughter, and pain swallowed in a smile.... To my mind, it is the duty of the younger Negro artist...to change the force of his art from that old whispering 'I want to be white,' hidden in the aspirations of his people, to 'Why should I want to be white? I am Negro—and beautiful.'"

The culture of the Harlem Renaissance served as a source of identity for an emerging black culture. The following poems, "Mother to Son" and "Litany" by Hughes are examples of his own contribution to American culture.

Mother to Son

Well, son, I'll tell you:
Life for me ain't been no crystal stair.
It's had tacks in it,
And splinters,
And boards torn up,
And places with no carpet on the floor—
Bare.
But all the time
I'se been a-climbin' on,
And reachin' landin's,
And turnin' corners,
And sometimes goin' in the dark
Where there ain't been no light.
So boy, don't you turn back.
Don't you set down on the steps
Cause you finds it kiner hard.
Don't you fall no—
For I'se still goin', honey,
I's still combin',
And life for me ain't been no crystal stair.

Litany

Gather up

In the arms of your pity
The sick, the depraved,
The desperate, the tired,
All the scum
Of our weary city
Gather up
In the arms of your pity.
Gather up
In the arms of your love—
Those who expect
No love from above.

"American investments and business interests will be very seriously affected"

COOLIDGE EXPLAINS AMERICAN INTERVENTION IN NICARAGUA

While the United States was working hard to avoid entanglements in Europe, it did not keep its distance from foreign affairs in Latin America. The events of the late 1920s would serve as a prelude to less direct American intervention in Nicaragua sixty years later.

In 1927, revolution threatened the U.S.-backed Nicaraguan government. Claiming that this represented a threat to American business interests and possible access to the Panama Canal, President Calvin Coolidge sent 5,000 troops to restore order. Coolidge delivered the following message to Congress justifying military intervention in Nicaragua.

The troops contained the fighting on behalf of the reactionary Nicaraguan government and land interests. A truce was imposed and a special election held the following year. Ironically, one of the rebel generals won the election. U.S. troops did not withdraw from the Central Americal country until 1933.

It is well known that in 1912 the United States intervened in Nicaragua with a large force and put down a revolution, and that from that time to 1925 a legation guard of American marines was, with the consent of the Nicaraguan Government, kept in Managua to protect American lives and property. In 1923 representatives of the five Central American countries, namely, Costa Rica, Guatemala, Honduras, Nicaragua, and Salvador, at the invitation of the United States, met in Washington and entered into a series of treaties. These treaties dealt with limitation of armament, a Central American tribunal for arbitration and the general subject of peace and amity. The treaty last referred to specifically provides in Article II that the Governments of the contracting parties will not recognize any other government which may come into power in any of the five Republics through a coup d'etat, or revolution, and disqualifies the leaders of such coup d'etat, or revolution, from assuming the presidency or vice presidency

The United States was not a party to this treaty, but it was made in Washington under the auspices of the Secretary of State, and this Government has felt a moral obligation to apply its principles in order to encourage the Central American States in their efforts to prevent revolution and disorder

The Nicaraguan constitution provides in article 106 that in the absence of the President and Vice President the Congress shall designate one of its members to complete the unexpired term of President.

The action of Congress in designating Señor Diaz was perfectly legal and in accordance with the constitution. Therefore the United States Government on November 17 extended recognition to Señor Diaz. Immediately following the inauguration of President Diaz and frequently since that date he has appealed to the United States for support, has informed this Government of the aid which Mexico is giving to the revolutionists, and has stated that he is unable solely because of the aid given by Mexico to the revolutionists to protect the lives and property of American citizens and other foreigners. When negotiations leading up to the Corinto conferences began, I immediately placed an embargo on the shipment of arms and ammunition to Nicaragua

At the end of November, after spending some time in Mexico City, Doctor Sacasa went back to Nicaragua, landing at Puerto Cabezas, near Bragmans Bluff. He immediately placed himself at the head of the insurrection and declared himself President of Nicaragua. He has never been recognized by any of the Central American Republics nor by any other government, with the exception of Mexico, which recognized him immediately. As arms and munitions in large quantities were reach-

ing the revolutionists, I deemed it unfair to prevent the recognized government from purchasing arms abroad, and accordingly, the Secretary of State has notified the Diaz Government that licenses would be issued for the export of arms and munitions purchased in this country. It would be thoroughly inconsistent for this country not to support the government recognized by it while the revolutionists were receiving arms and munitions from abroad.

For many years numerous Americans have been living in Nicaragua, developing its industries and carrying on business. At the present time there are large investments in lumbering, mining, coffee growing, banana culture, shipping, and also in general mercantile and other collateral business.

In addition to these industries now in existence, the Government of Nicaragua, by a treaty entered into on the 5th day of August, 1914, granted in perpetuity to the United States the exclusive proprietary rights necessary and convenient for the construction, operation, and maintenance of an oceanic canal.

There is no question that if the revolution continues American investments and business interests in Nicaragua will be very seriously affected, if not destroyed.

Manifestly the relation of this Government to the Nicaraguan situation and its policy in the existing emergency, are determined by the facts which I have described. The proprietary rights of the United States in the Nicaraguan canal route, with the necessary implications growing out of it affecting the Panama Canal, together with the obligations flowing from the investments of all classes of our citizens in Nicaragua, place us in a position of peculiar responsibility. I am sure it is not the desire of the United States to intervene in the internal affairs of Nicaragua or of any other Central American Republic. Nevertheless it must be said that we have a very definite and special interest in the maintenance of order and good government in Nicaragua at the present time, and that the stability, prosperity, and independence of all Central American countries can never be a matter of indifference to us. The United States can not, therefore, fail to view with deep concern any serious threat to stability and constitutional government in Nicaragua tending toward anarchy and jeopardizing American interests, especially if such state of affairs is contributed to or brought about by outside influences or by any foreign power. It has always been and remains the policy of the United States in such circumstances to take the steps that may be necessary for the preservation and protection of the lives, the property, and the interests of its citizens and of this Government itself. In this respect I propose to follow the path of my predecessors.

Consequently, I have deemed it my duty to use the powers committed to me to insure the adequate protection of all American interests in Nicaragua, whether they be endangered by internal strife or by outside interference in the affairs of that Republic.

❧ "I have suffered because I am a radical"

BARTOLOMEO VANZETTI'S LAST STATEMENT IN COURT

In 1921, Italian immigrants Nicola Sacco and Bartolomeo Vanzetti were convicted in Braintree, Massachusetts of a murder during a shoe-factory robbery and sentenced to death. Outraged by the preponderance of evidence about the two men's radical politics and the lack of evidence about the incident itself, a groundswell of opposition to the sentence emerged. The case attracted national attention.

The governor appointed a special commission which sharply criticized the presiding judge's conduct, but sustained the findings. The execution was carried out on August 23, 1927, although many people believed the two were innocent. Vanzetti's last statement in court was made on April 9, 1927.

Yes. What I say is that I am innocent, not only of the Braintree crime but also of the Bridgewater crime. That I am not only innocent of these two crimes, but in all my life I have never stolen and I have never killed and I have never spilled blood. That is what I want to say. And it is not all. Not only am I innocent of these two crimes, not only in all my life I have never stole, never killed, never spilled blood, but I have struggled all my life, since I began to reason, to eliminate crime from the earth.

Everybody that knows these two arms knows very well that I did not need to go in between the street and kill a man to take the money. I can live with my two arms and live well. But besides that, I can live even without work with my arms for other people. I have had plenty of chance to live independently and to live what the world conceives to be a higher life than not to gain our bread with the sweat of our brow.

Well, I want to reach a little point farther, and it is this—that not only have I not been trying to steal in Bridgewater, not only have I not been in Braintree to steal and kill and have never steal or kill or spilt blood in all my life, not only have I struggled hard against crimes, but I have refused myself the commodity or glory of life, the pride of life of a good position because in my consideration it is not right to exploit man.

Now, I should say that I am not only innocent of all these things, not only have I never committed a real crime in my life—though some sins, but not crimes—not only have I struggled all my life to eliminate crimes that the official law and the official moral condemns, but also the crime that the official moral and the official law sanctions and sanctifies, exploitation and the oppression of the man by the man, and if there is a reason why I am here as a guilty man, if there is a reason why you in a few minutes can doom me, it is this reason and none else.

I beg your pardon. There is the more good man I ever cast my eyes upon since I lived, a man that will last and will grow always more near and more dear to the people, as far as into the heart of the people, so long as admiration for goodness and for sacrifice will last. I mean Eugene Debs. He know, and not only he but every man of understanding in the world, not only in this country but also in the other countries, men that we have provided a certain amount of a record of the times, they all stick with us, the flower of mankind of Europe, the better writers, the greatest thinkers, of Europe, have pleaded in our favor. The scientists, the greatest scientists, the greatest statesmen of Europe, have pleaded in our favor. The people of foreign nations have pleaded in our favor.

Is it possible that only a few on the jury, only two or three men, who would condemn their mother for worldly honor and for earthly fortune; is it possible that they are right against what the world, the whole world has say it is wrong and that I know that it is wrong? If there is one that I should know it, if it is right or if it is wrong, it is I and this man. You see it is seven years that we are in jail. What we have suffered during those years no human tongue can say, and yet you see me before you, not trembling, you see me looking you in your eyes straight, not blushing, not changing color, not ashamed or in fear.

We have proved that there could not have been another Judge on the face of the earth more prejudiced and more cruel than you have been against us. We have proved that. Still they refuse the new trial. We know, and you know in your heart, that you have been against us from the very beginning, before you see us. Before you see us you already know that we were radicals, that we were underdogs, that we were the enemy of the institution that you can believe in good faith in their goodness—I don't want to condemn that—and that it was easy on the time of the first trial to get a verdict of guiltiness.

We know that you have spoke yourself and have spoke your hostility against us, and your despisement against us with friends of yours on the train, at the University Club of Boston, and the Gold Club of Worcester, Massachusetts. I am sure that if the people who know all what you say against us would have the civil courage to take the stand, maybe your Honor—I am sorry to say this because you are an old man, and I have an old father—but maybe you would be beside us in good justice at this time.

When you sentenced me at the Plymouth trial you say, to the best part of my memory, of my good faith, that crimes were in accordance with my principle—something of that sort—and you take off one charge, if I remember it exactly, from the jury. The jury was so violent against me that they found me guilty of both charges, because there were only two.

We were tried during a time that has now passed into history. I mean by that, a time when there was hysteria of resentment and hate against the people of our principles, against the foreigner, against slackers, and it seems to me—rather, I am positive, that both you and Mr. Katzmann has done all what it were in your power in order to work out, in order to agitate still more the passion of the juror, the prejudice of the juror, against us.

Well, I have already say that I now only am not guilty of these crimes, but I never commit a crime in my life—I have never steal and I have never kill and I have never spilt blood, and I have fought against the crime, and I have fought and I have sacrificed myself even to eliminate the crimes that the law and the church legitimate and sanctify.

That is what I say: I would not wish to a dog or to a snake, to the most low and misfortunate creature on the earth—I would not wish to any of them what I have had to suffer for things that I am not guilty of. But my conviction is that I have suffered for things that I am guilty of. I am suffering because I am a radical and indeed I am a radical; I have suffered because I was an Italian, and indeed I am an Italian; I have suffered more for my family and for my beloved than for myself; but I am so convinced to be right that if you could execute me two times, I would live again to do what I have done already. I have finished. Thank you.

❧ "Which way to Ireland?"

CHARLES LINDBERGH

Charles Lindbergh was arguably the world's first media hero. Handsome, articulate, and dashing, Lindbergh was a pilot with a hunger for adventure. Airplanes represented the possibilities of technology and Lindbergh embodied its promise.

Before his famous flight, however, Lindbergh, the son of a congressman, was relatively unknown to the world. He was simply one of several people who hoped to make a solo flight across the Atlantic. On May 19, 1927, when the weather report turned favorable, Lindbergh took off from New York City in his single-engine airplane, The Spirit of St. Louis, to realize his dream. When he landed in Paris 33 hours and 3,600 miles later, Lindbergh was a world hero.

On the morning of May nineteenth, a light rain was falling and sky was overcast. Weather reports from land stations and ships along the great circle were unfavorable and there was apparently no prospect of taking off for Paris for several days at least. But at about six o'clock I received a special report from the New York Weather Bureau. A high pressure area was over the entire North Atlantic and the low pressure area over Nova Scotia and Newfoundland was receding. It was apparent that the prospects of the fog clearing up were as good as I might expect for some time to come. The North Atlantic should be clear with only local storms on the coast of Europe. The moon had just passed full and the percentage of days with fog over Newfoundland and the Grand Banks was increasing so that there seemed to be no advantage in waiting longer.

We went to Curtiss Field as quickly as possible and made arrangements for the barograph to be sealed and installed, and for the plane to be serviced and checked.

We decided partially to fill the fuel tanks in the hangar before towing the ship on a truck to Roosevelt Field which adjoins Curtiss on the east, where the servicing would be completed.

I left the responsibility for conditioning the plane in the hands of the men on the field while I went into the hotel for about two and one-half hours of rest; but at the hotel there were several more details which had to be completed and I was unable to get any sleep that night.

I returned to the field before daybreak on the morning of the twentieth. A light rain was falling which continued until almost dawn; consequently we did not move the ship to Roosevelt Field until much later than we had planned, and the take off was delayed from daybreak until nearly eight o'clock.

At dawn the shower had passed, although the sky was overcast, and occasionally there would be some slight precipitation. The tail of the plane was lashed to a truck and escorted by a number of motorcycle police. The slow trip from Curtiss to Roosevelt was begun.

The ship was placed at the extreme west end of the field heading along the east and west runway and the final fueling commenced.

About 7:40 am the motor was started and at 7:52 I took off on the flight for Paris.

The field was a little soft due to the rain during the night and the heavily loaded plane gathered speed very slowly. After passing the halfway mark, however, it was apparent that I would be able to clear the obstruction at the end. I passed over a tractor by about fifteen feet and a telephone line by about twenty, with a fair reserve of flying speed. I believe that the ship would have taken off from a hard field with at least five hundred pounds more weight.

I turned slightly to the right to avoid some high trees on a hill directly ahead, but by the time I had gone a few hundred yards I had sufficient alti-

tude to clear all obstructions and throttled the engine down to 1750 rpm I took up a compass course at once and soon reached Long Island Sound where the Curtiss Oriole with its photographer, which had been escorting me, turned back.

The haze soon cleared and from Cape Cod and Nova Scotia I passed within view of numerous fishing vessels.

The northern part of Nova Scotia contained a number of storm areas and several times I flew through cloudbursts.

As I neared the northern coast, snow appeared in patches on the ground and far to the eastward the coastline was covered with fog.

For many miles between Nova Scotia and Newfoundland the ocean was covered with caked ice, but as I approached the coast the ice disappeared entirely and I saw several ships in this area.

I had taken up a course for St. John's, which is south of the great circle from New York to Paris, so that there would be no question of the fact that I had passed Newfoundland in case I was forced down in the North Atlantic.

I passed over numerous icebergs after leaving St. John's, but saw no ships except the coast.

Darkness set in about 8:15 and a thin, low fog formed over the sea through which the white bergs showed up with surprising clearness. This fog became thicker and increased in height until within two hours I was just skimming the top of storm clouds at about ten thousand feet. Even at this altitude there was a thick haze through which only the stars directly overhead could be seen.

There was no moon and it was very dark. The tops of some of the storm clouds were several thousand feet above me and at one time, when I attempted to fly through one of the larger clouds, sleet started to collect on the plane and I was forced to turn around and get back into clear air immediately and then fly around any clouds which I could not get over.

The moon appeared on the horizon after about two hours of darkness; then the flying was much less complicated.

Dawn came at about 1 am, New York time, and the temperature had risen until there was practically no remaining danger of sleet.

Shortly after sunrise the clouds became more broken, although some of them were far above me and it was often necessary to fly through them, navigating by instruments only.

As the sun became higher, holes appeared in the fog. Through one the open water was visible, and I dropped down until less than a hundred feet above the waves. There was a strong wind blowing from the northwest and the ocean was covered with white caps.

After a few miles of fairly clear weather the ceiling lowered to zero and for nearly two hours I flew entirely blind through the fog at an altitude of about 1,500 feet. Then the fog raised and the water was visible again.

On several more occasions it was necessary to fly by instrument for short periods; then the fog broke up into patches. These patches took on forms of everyday description. Numerous shorelines appeared with trees perfectly outlined against the horizon. In fact, the mirages were so natural that, had I not been in mid-Atlantic and known that no land existed along my route, I would have taken them to be actual islands.

As the fog cleared I dropped down closer to the water, sometimes flying within ten feet of the waves and seldom higher than two hundred.

There is a cushion of air close to the ground or water through which a plane flies with less effort than when at a higher altitude, and for hours at a time I took advantage of this factor.

Also, it was less difficult to determine the wind drift near the water. During the entire flight the wind was strong enough to produce white caps on the waves. When one of these formed, the foam would be blown off, showing the wind direction and approximate velocity. This foam remained on the water long enough for me to obtain a general idea of my drift.

During the day I saw a number of porpoises and a few birds but no ships, although I understand that two different boats reported me passing over.

The first indication of my approach to the European Coast was a small fishing boat which I first noticed a few miles ahead and slightly to the south of my course. There were several of these fishing boats grouped within a few miles of each other.

I flew over the first boat without seeing any signs of life. As I circled over the second, however, a man's face appeared, looking out of the cabin window.

I have carried on short conversations with peo-ple on the ground by flying low with throttled engine, and shouting a question, and receiving the answer by some signal. When I saw this fisherman I decided to try to get him to point towards land. I had no sooner made the decision than the futility of the effort became apparent. In all likelihood he could not speak English, and even if he could he would undoubtedly be too astounded to answer. However, I circled again and closing the throttle as the plane passed within a few feet of the boat I shouted, "Which way to Ireland?" Of course the attempt was useless, and I continued on my course.

Less than an hour later a rugged and semi-mountainous coastline appeared to the northeast. I was flying less than two hundred feet from the water when I sighted it. The shore was fairly dis-tinct and not over ten or fifteen miles away. A light haze coupled with numerous storm areas had pre-vented my seeing it from a long distance.

The coastline came down from the north and curved towards the east. I had very little doubt that it was the southwestern end of Ireland, but in order to make sure I changed my course towards the nearest point of land.

I located Cape Valencia and Dingle Bay, then resumed by compass course towards Paris.

After leaving Ireland I passed a number of steamers and was seldom out of sight of a ship.

In a little over two hours the coast of England appeared. My course passed over southern England and a little south of Plymouth; then across the English Channel, striking France over Cherbourg.

I was flying at about fifteen-hundred-foot alti-tude over England and as I crossed the Channel and passed over Cherbourg, France, I had probably seen more of that part of Europe than many native Europeans. The visibility was good and the country could be seen for miles around.

The sun went down shortly after passing Cherbourg and soon the beacons along the Paris-London airway became visible.

I first saw the lights of Paris a little before 10 pm, or 5 pm, New York time, and a few minutes later I was circling the Eiffel Tower at an altitude of about four thousand feet.

The lights of Le Bourget were plainly visible, but appeared to be very close to Paris. I had under-stood that the field was farther from the city, so continued out to northeast into the country for four or five miles to make sure that there was not another field farther out which might be Le Bourget. Then I returned and spiralled down closer to the lights. Presently I could make out long lines of hangars, and the roads appeared to be jammed with cars.

I flew low over the field once, then circled around into the wind and landed.

❧ Future of Women in the Air

AMELIA EARHART

Like fellow pilot Charles Lindbergh, Amelia Earhart captured the nation's imagination. She was the first woman to fly across the Atlantic Ocean in an aircraft in 1928. Four years later, she became the first woman to fly solo to Europe, leaving from Newfoundland and landing in Wales in a 15-hour flight. In 1935 she was the first person to fly two different solo flights, one from Hawaii to the United States mainland and the other from Mexico City to New York.

Earhart's daring flights both helped make the world seem a smaller place and set a new standard of accomplishment for women. In this February 1931 address, she explained some of the potential for airplanes. Earhart disappeared in the Pacific during a round-the-world flight attempt in 1937.

Obviously, research regarding technological unemployment is as vital today as further refinement or production of labor saving and comfort giving devices. Among all the marvels of modern invention, that with which I am most concerned is of course air transportation.

Flying is perhaps the most dramatic of recent scientific attainments. In the brief span of thirty-odd years, the world has seen an inventor's dream, first materialized by the Wright brothers at Kitty Hawk, become an everyday actuality.

Perhaps I am prejudiced, but to me it seems that no other phase of modern progress can try to maintain such a brimming measure of romance and beauty coupled with utility as does aviation. Within itself this industry embraces many of those scientific accomplishments which yesterday seemed fantastic in possibility.

The pilot winging his way above the earth at 200 mph talks by radio telephone to ground stations or to other planes in the air. In thick weather he is guided by radio beams, and receives detailed reports of conditions ahead beamed through special instruments and new methods of meteorological calculations.

He sits behind engines, reliability of which, measured by yardsticks of the past is all but unbelievable. I myself, still fly a Wasp motor which has carried me over the North Atlantic, part of the Pacific, to and from Mexico City and many times across this continent.

Aviation, this young modern giant, exemplifies the possible relationship of women and the creations of science. Although women as yet, have not taken full advantage of its use and benefits, air travel is as available to them as to men.

❧ "You ain't heard nothing yet"

HOLLYWOOD ENGINEER GEORGE GROVES

In 1927, the Hollywood movie studio Warner Brothers changed everything with the film *The Jazz Singer*. In the movie, vaudeville actor Al Jolson famously turns to the cameras and proclaims "Mama, you ain't heard nothin' yet," ending the era of silent movies, and ushering in the new age of "talkies."

Audiences loved it. They no longer had to be read the narrative in awkward passages and the music ceased to come from a piano player or musical band playing in the theater itself. But talkies threw Hollywood upside down. Movie stars with high voices and foreign accents suddenly found themselves out of work and theatrical performers who might have shunned Hollywood were in high demand for their dramatic talents.

Engineer George Groves—who worked at Bell Labs, the company that developed the sound system—recalled his role in the invention of talking movies in an oral history project done by the American Film Institute. He later worked directly for Warner Brothers.

Warner Brothers were given credit for inventing sound for motion pictures, and they did to the extent that they were the first to make a commercially acceptable sound system and equip theaters and, in conjunction with the Western Electric Company, be able to distribute product all over the country with sound.

Now, it so happened during [1925-27], that a great invention was being developed in the Bell

Labs, and that was the change from acoustic recording of phonograph records, where you just played into a horn, and had a stylus driven by acoustical power, to electrical recording.... They had invented, along with electrical recording of phonograph records, a means of synchronizing a record, as it played, with a motion picture....

And they staged a demonstration of their system, to Sam Warner. He was tremendously impressed, and convinced his brothers that they should go ahead and do something about it. Simultaneously with the development of the Bell Labs, there were other developments going on.... However, all of these different systems were deficient in fidelity and lack of power to fill an auditorium when they played the product.

So in the Bell laboratories, they developed amplifiers and loudspeakers to fill an auditorium. And, in course of time, Warner Brothers took over the development and exploitation of the system, under contract with Western Electric Company, and did experimental work in the Vitagraph Studios in Brooklyn. It was there that I think the first experimental job that I know of, that happened when I was there—I was transferred over to Warner Brothers with the equipment when this deal went through—was to record Lee Duncan, the owner of Rin Tin Tin, directing his dog from the sidelines. It was a pretty crude demonstration, but nevertheless it worked, and you could hear him talk....

When Warner Brothers became convinced that the thing was a practical device, and decided to put a big program on, and show it, they took over the Manhattan Opera House on 35th Street in New York, and converted it into a studio.

The seats were all taken out, the stage was extended over the whole auditorium, we moved in bags and baggage. The boxes were made into recording rooms. Dressing rooms were used as machine rooms and repair shops. And the only convenient place where a mixer could sit was in the Masonic Shrine room on the sixth floor of the building, in front of the building. So all the microphone lines from the stage were run up through the grille where the ventilating air normally came out, and the mixer panel fastened onto that grille. That's where I sat, and spent a lot of my time, recording the first Vitaphone programs. Anytime there was a change of set-up or a slight case of trou-

ble, I had to go down six flights in an elevator, then up the stage, get back up, and go back upstairs. And I did a lot of running. I kept in good condition.

At that time, the speed of commercial records was 78 revolutions per minute, rpm. In order to accommodate ten minutes of playing time, which was the running time of a thousand feet of film at 90 feet a minute, they had to reduce the speed of the turntable to 33 1/3. Otherwise it would have been an enormous thing to run a half an hour. So the whole system was designed to run on a turntable that ran at 33 1/3, which, interestingly enough, has remained the standard speed for LPs to this day....

We finally put on the Vitaphone program in New York, on August 6, 1926. Of course it was a great success. And along with that, we had some rather ambitious short subjects with Metropolitan Opera stars....

We stayed there in New York until April 1927 when Warner Brothers decided to move the whole crew and installation to Hollywood. There we made a few short subjects, but the main object of the changeover was the decision to put talking sequences, or singing sequences, rather, in addition to the score, in *The Jazz Singer*. As I remember, *The Jazz Singer* had been shot as a silent picture.

One thing that has impressed me during the passing of time is that nobody thought at that time of putting talking sequences in. Everything we did, somebody was singing, either an opera or a vaudeville act of some kind. The only talking thing that ever happened, in the early days, was a speech by Will Hays, which was made for the opening of Vitaphone.... That was a talking thing, but somehow or other it never seemed to dawn on anybody that they should talk in motion pictures.

When we recorded *The Jazz Singer,* at one moment in the picture Al Jolson sat down to play the piano and sing a song for his mother, after he had been on the stage as a singer, much to the annoyance of his father, who was a cantor in the church and wanted his son to follow in his footsteps. Jolson sat down at the piano, and before he sang, he said something to the effect of "Mama, you ain't heard nothin' yet." This speech has been quoted as being very prophetic, and quoted many, many times. And it seemed to take everybody by surprise. "By golly! He talked." After that, it was decided to put talking sequences in pictures.

🐦 "Matters of public concern should be freely expressed"

AMERICAN CIVIL LIBERTIES UNION CREED

The American Civil Liberties Union was formed in 1921 as a successor to the National Civil Liberties Bureau. Some of the leading liberals in the country created the organization to secure the rights of free speech and oppose the suppression of opinion. Among the leaders of the ACLU were Norman Thomas, who ran for president as a Socialist several times, and Jane Addams, a social reformer who would win the Nobel Peace Prize in 1931 for her work.

A Statement Defining the Position of the American Civil Liberties Union on the Issues of the United States Today

(Adopted by the National Committee)
We stand on the general principle that all thought on matters of public concern should be freely expressed without interference. Orderly social progress is promoted by unrestricted freedom of opinion. The punishment of mere opinion, without overt acts, is never in the interest of orderly progress. Suppression of opinion makes for violence and bloodshed.

The principle of freedom of speech, press and assemblage, embodied in our constitutional law, must be reasserted in its application to American conditions today. That application must deal with various methods now used to repress new ideas and democratic movements. The following paragraphs cover the most significant of the tactics of repression in the United States today.

1. Free Speech. There should be no control whatever in advance over what any person may say. The right to meet and to speak freely without permit should be unquestioned.

There should be no prosecutions for the mere expression of opinion on matters of public concern, however radical, however violent. The expression of all opinions, however radical, should be tolerated. The fullest freedom of speech should be encouraged by setting aside special places in streets or parks and in the use of public buildings, free of charge, for public meetings of any sort.

2. Free Press. There should be no censorship over the mails by the post-office or any other agency at any time or in any way. Privacy of communication should be inviolate. Printed matter should never be subject to a political censorship. The granting or revoking of second class mailing privileges should have nothing whatever to do with a paper's opinions and policies.

If libelous, fraudulent, or other illegal matter is being circulated, it should be seized by proper warrant through the prosecuting authorities, not by the post-office department. The business of the post-office department is to carry the mails, not to investigate crime or to act as censors.

There should be no control over the distribution of literature at meetings or hand to hand in public or in private places. No system of licenses for distribution should be tolerated.

3. Freedom of Assemblage. Meetings in public places, parades and processions should be freely permitted, the only reasonable regulation being the advance notification to the police of the time and place. No discretion should be given the police to prohibit parades or precessions, but merely to alter routes in accordance with the imperative demands of traffic in crowded cities. There should be no laws or regulations prohibiting the display of red flags or other political emblems.

The right of assemblage is involved in the right to picket in time of strike. Peaceful picketing, therefore, should not be prohibited, regulated by injunction, by order of court or by police edict. It is the business of the police in places where picketing is conducted merely to keep traffic free and to handle specific violations of law against persons upon complaint.

4. The Right to Strike. The right of workers to organize in organizations of their own choosing, and to strike, should never be infringed by law.

Compulsory arbitration is to be condemned not only because it destroys the workers' right to strike, but because it lays emphasis on one set of obligations alone, those of workers to society.

5. Law Enforcement. The practice of deputizing privately paid police as general police officers should be opposed. So should the attempts of private company employees to police the streets or property other than that of the company.

The efforts of private associations to take into their own hands the enforcement of law should be opposed at every point. Public officials, employees of private corporations, and leaders of mobs, who interfere with the exercise of the constitutionally established rights of free speech and free assembly, should be vigorously proceeded against.

The sending of troops into areas of industrial conflict to maintain law and order almost inevitably results in the government taking sides in an industrial conflict in behalf of the employer. The presence of troops, whether or not martial law is declared, very rarely affects the employer adversely, but it usually results in the complete denial of civil rights to the workers.

6. *Search and Seizure*. It is the custom of certain federal, state and city officials, particularly in cases involving civil liberty, to make arrests without warrant, to enter upon private property, and to seize papers and literature without legal process. Such practices should be contested. Officials so violating constitutional guarantees should be proceeded against.

7. *The Right to a Fair Trial*. Every person charged with an offense should have the fullest opportunity for a fair trial, for securing counsel and bail in a reasonable sum. In the case of a poor person, special aid should be organized to secure a fair trial, and when necessary, an appeal. The legal profession should be alert to defend cases involving civil liberty. The resolutions of various associations of lawyers against taking cases of radicals are wholly against the traditions of American liberty.

8. *Immigration, Deportation, and Passports*. No person should be refused admission to the United States on the ground of holding objectionable opinions. The present restrictions against radicals of various beliefs is wholly opposed to our tradition of political asylum.

No alien should be deported merely for the expression of opinion or for membership in a radical or revolutionary organization. This is as un-American a practice as the prosecution of citizens for expression of opinion.

The attempt to revoke naturalization papers in order to declare a citizen an alien subject to deportation is a perversion of a law which was intended to cover only cases of fraud.

Citizenship papers should not be refused to any alien because of the expression of radical views, or

activities in the cause of labor.

The granting of passports to or from the United States should not be dependent merely upon the opinions of citizens or membership in radical or labor organizations.

9. *Liberty in Education*. The attempts to maintain a uniform orthodox opinion among teachers should be opposed. The attempts of educational authorities to inject into public school and college instruction propaganda in the interest of any particular theory of society to the exclusion of others should be opposed.

10. *Race Equality*. Every attempt to discriminate between races in the application of all principles of civil liberty here set forth should be opposed.

How to get Civil Liberty:

We realize that these standards of civil liberty cannot be attained as abstract principles or as constitutional guarantees. Economic or political power is necessary to assert and maintain all "rights." In the midst of any conflict they are not granted by the side holding the economic and political power, except as they may be forced by the strength of the opposition. However, the mere public assertion of the principle of freedom of opinion in the words or deeds of individuals, or weak minorities, helps win it recognition, and in the long run makes for tolerance and against resort to violence.

Today the organized movements of labor and of the farmers are waging the chief fight for civil liberty throughout the United States as part of their effort for increased control of industry. Publicity, demonstrations, political activities and legal aid are organized nationally and locally. Only by such an aggressive policy of insistence can rights be secured and maintained. The union of organized labor, the farmers, radical and liberal movements is the most effective means to this.

It is these forces which the American Civil Liberties Union serves in their efforts for civil liberty. The practical work of free speech demonstrations, publicity and legal defense is done primarily in the struggles of the organized labor and farmers movements.

❧ "Something distinctly different from our former experience is taking place"

THE NEW DISCOVERY OF AMERICA

At the end of 1929 Americans could not help but look back upon the decade with swelled pride. Unbridled prosperity had made the United States the envy of the world. Summing up the reasons for the country's commercial success, a group of scholars under Harvard Professor Edwin F. Gay prepared the *Report of the Committee on Recent Economic Changes in the United States.* Gay prophesied that the boom-and-bust economic cycles that had plagued the country's history were most likely at an end. He was premature in this statement. By the end of the year, the country was barelling head-first into its worst depression of the century.

During the last six or seven years, books, reports and articles, in many languages, describing, explaining or criticizing the economic and social situation in the United States have appeared in unparalleled quantity. This has been heralded as the New Discovery of America.

Despite such divergence of opinion among these contemporaneous observers as to causes and conditions, there is marked unanimity as to the fact which is chiefly responsible for this extraordinary interest. They agree that of late there has been an "immense advance in America." Our visitors are "impressed, everywhere and every day, by the evidences of an ebullient prosperity and a confidence in the future."...

It is needless to enlarge on the numerous clashes in the testimony of the foreign observers. It is more to point to indicate that, despite their varying origins and predilections, there is a considerable degree of concurrence, although with differing emphasis, regarding certain main factors in the recent economic and social experience of this country. These factors may here be briefly summarized.

1. The natural resources of the United States are unrivaled, especially those which are fundamental to modern large-scale industrialism....

2. In this vast expanse of territory, historically so recently opened to European migration and settlement, labor is relatively scarce and wages are relatively high...there is in the United States a markedly higher standard of living, and this profoundly influences the American outlook.

3. In consequence of the juxtaposition of rich resources and an inadequate labor supply, there has resulted a progressive development of labor-supplementing machine equipment, in agriculture, transportation and industry, and also a remarkable utilization of power....

4. Many observers hold that of even greater importance than the technical progress is the great domestic market.... the resulting "mass consumption" makes mass production possible and profitable....

5. The problem of correlating abundant resources, expensive labor, and unsurpassed machine equipment, to serve the greatest of markets, has put a high premium on management and organizing capacity....

6. In order to obtain the effective utilization of the worker's effort and to lower costs, American management has begun more systematically to improve industrial relations....

7. A related factor in American economic efficiency is the open mindedness of American management....

8. Emphasis is unanimously laid upon the dominant national trait of optimistic energy, as an underlying element in these various phenomena of American economic activity. The individual in America is mobile.... He sometimes appears docile, but it is because he is tolerant of social inconveniences which his experience tells him are only incidental and temporary....

But it will serve our present purpose to point out that most of the eight significant features of the existing economic conditions in the United States upon which we have found our foreign visitors in substantial agreement are also characteristic of former major periods of prosperity in our history. The fundamental conditions of our existence on this continent have thus far remained substantially unchanged, and the responses have therefore been similar, not so much in external form as in their essential character. Even the successive maladjustments of economic growth show, behind their external dissimilarities, an underlying likeness. With superabundant natural resources, for example, we

have always been open to the charge of wastefulness, and this is easily explicable, but with insufficient man power it seems, at first thought, curious
that we are now and have ever been wasteful of
human life....

Another serious maladjustment has been constantly observable in the extreme to which we have
carried the swings of prosperity and business depression, the fierce bursts of speculative activity and
the sharp reactions. Again, our environment and
its needs may help to explain this feverish pulse-
beat; yet here also another slogan, "stability," may
be symptomatic of coming fundamental change. It
is, furthermore, highly characteristic of all our periods of expansion that the rapidity and vigor of
growth of some elements is so great as seriously to
unbalance the whole organism....

The shifting of psychological attitude, here
indicated, seems to suggest that something distinctly different from our former experience is taking
place. The chief characteristics of the present economic phase, agreed upon by our numerous visitors
from abroad, are, it is true, evolved logically from
what has preceded.... But there seems now to be
differences of degree which approach differences in
kind. In this sense we may say that the unprecedented utilization of power and its wide dispersion
by automobile and tractor, in which this country
leads the way, is a new addition of enormous potentiality to our resources. With the general increase
of wealth, the growth in the number of millionaires
has been accompanied by a remarkable rise in the
real wages of industrial workers, and wide diffusions
of investments. The profession of management is
clearly emerging, and there is visible an increasing
professional spirit in business, which springs from
and entails recognized social responsibilities. The
"self-policing" of business, with its code of ethics,
has been assisted by the recent development of
trade-associations and the increasing influence of
research and professional education. The strength
and stability of the our financial structure, both
governmental and commercial, is of modern
growth. The great corporate development of business enterprise...has gone on to new heights. It
may be creating, as some think, a new type of social
organization, but in any case the open-mindedness
of the public, and of the state which is its instrument, toward this growing power of business corporations appears to be novel in American history.

Here are the beginnings of new answers to the
old problem. But more than this. Some of the basic
elements of the problem are evidently in process of
change. The resources of the country, still enormous, are no longer regarded as limitless; the labor
of the world is no longer invited freely to exploit
them. The capital flow has turned outward; private
and public interests and responsibilities have a new
world-wide scope. These changes must have far-
reaching consequences and entail further and more
perplexing adjustments.

❧ *"True liberalism seeks all legitimate freedom"*

HERBERT HOOVER SPEAKS ON RUGGED INDIVIDUALISM

As an international businessman and prominent government
official, Herbert Hoover had first-hand experience on the relative efficiencies of private enterprise and governmental oversight. While recognizing the need for governmental authority
in certain situations, he was a forceful advocate of individual
initiative. In 1922, he wrote *American Individualism: The
Challenge of Liberty* in which he explored the tenuous balance of economic liberties.

Near the end of his 1928 campaign for President against
New York Governor Al Smith, Hoover revisited the issue in an
hour-long speech to Republican supporters in New York City.
Although the tedium of his lengthy speech drove more than
5,000 people in Madison Square Audience out of the auditorium, Hoover's address articulated the Republican philosophy
of rugged individualism. It both justified his Republican predecessor's laissez-faire policies of the 1920s and foreshadowed Hoover's vigorous opposition to governmental intervention to reverse the impact of the Great Depression.

This campaign now draws near a close. The platform of the two parties defining principles and
offering solutions of various national problems have
been presented and are being earnestly considered
by our people.

In my acceptance speech I endeavored to outline the spirit and ideals by which I would be guided in carrying that platform into administration.
Tonight I will not deal with the multitude of issues
which have been already well canvassed. I intend
rather to discuss some of those more fundamental
principles and ideals upon which I believe the gov-

ernment of the United States should be conducted.

After the war, when the Republican Party assumed administration of the country, we were faced with the problem of determination of the very nature of our national life. During one hundred and fifty years we have builded up a form of self-government and a social system which is peculiarly our own. It differs essentially from all others in the world. It is the American system. It is just as definite and positive a political and social system as has ever been developed on earth. It is founded upon a particular conception of self-government in which decentralized local responsibility is the very base. Further than this, it is founded upon the conception that only through ordered liberty, freedom, and equal opportunity to the individual will his initiative and enterprise spur on the march of progress. And in our insistence upon equality of opportunity has our system advanced beyond all the world.

During the war we necessarily turned to the government to solve every difficult economic problem. The government having absorbed every energy of our people for war, there was no other solution. For the preservation of the state the Federal Government became a centralized despotism which undertook unprecedented responsibilities, assumed autocratic powers, and took over the business of citizens. To a large degree we regimented our whole people temporarily into a socialistic state. However justified in time of war if continued in peace-time it would destroy not only our American system but with it our progress and freedom as well.

When the war closed, the most vital of all issues both in our own country and throughout the world was whether governments should continue their wartime ownership and operations of many instrumentalities of production and distribution. We were challenged with a peace-time choice between the American system of rugged individualism and a European philosophy of diametrically opposed doctrines—doctrines of paternalism and state socialism. The acceptance of these ideas would have meant the destruction of self-government through centralization of government. It would have meant the undermining of the individual initiative and enterprise through which our people have grown to unparalleled greatness.

The Republican Party from the beginning resolutely turned its face away from these ideas and these war practices.

When the Republican Party came into full power it went at once resolutely back to our fundamental conception of the state and the rights and responsibilities of the individual. Thereby it restored confidence and hope in the American people, it freed and stimulated enterprise, it restored the government to its position as an umpire instead of a player in the economic game. For these reasons the American people have gone forward in progress while the rest of the world has halted, and some countries have even gone backwards. If anyone will study the causes of retarded recuperation in Europe, he will find much of it due to stifling of private initiative on one hand, and overloading of the government with business on the other.

There has been revived in this campaign, however, a series of proposals which, if adopted, would be a long step toward the abandonment of our American system and a surrender to the destructive operation of governmental conduct of commercial business. Because the country is faced with difficulty and doubt over certain national problems—that is prohibition, farm relief, and electrical power—our opponents propose that we must thrust government a long way into the businesses which give rise to these problems. In effect, they abandon the tenets of their own party and turn to state socialism as a solution for the difficulties presented by all three. It is proposed that we shall change from prohibition to the state purchase and sale of liquor. If their agricultural relief program means anything, it means that the government shall directly or indirectly buy and sell and fix prices of agricultural products. And we are to go into the hydroelectric power business. In other words, we are confronted with a huge program of government in business.

There is, therefore, submitted to the American people a question of fundamental principle. That is: shall we depart from the principles of our American political and economic system, upon which we have advanced beyond all the rest of the world, in order to adopt methods based on principles destructive of its very foundations? And I wish to emphasize the seriousness of these proposals. I wish to make my position clear; for this goes to the very roots of American life and progress.

I should like to state to you the effect that this projection of government in business would have upon our system of self-government and our economic system. That effect would reach to the daily life of every man and woman. It would impair the very basis of liberty and freedom not only for those left outside the fold of expanded bureaucracy but for those embraced within it.

Let us first see the effect upon self-government. When the Federal Government undertakes to go into commercial business it must at once set up the organization and administration of that business, and it immediately finds itself in a labyrinth, every alley of which leads to the destruction of self-government.

Commercial business requires a concentration of responsibility. Self-government requires decentralization and many checks and balances to safeguard liberty. Our government to succeed in business would need to become in effect a despotism. There at once begins the destruction of self-government.

It is a false liberalism that interprets itself into the government operation of commercial business. Every step of bureaucratizing of the business of our country poisons the very roots of liberalism—that is, political equality, free speech, free assembly, free press, and equality of opportunity. It is the road not to more liberty, but to less liberty. Liberalism should be found not striving to spread bureaucracy but striving to set bounds to it. True liberalism seeks all legitimate freedom first in the confident belief that without such freedom the pursuit of all other blessings and benefits is vain. That belief is the foundation of all American progress, political as well as economic.

Liberalism is a force truly of the spirit, a force proceeding from the deep realization that economic freedom cannot be sacrificed if political freedom is to be preserved. Even if governmental conduct of business could give us more efficiency instead of less efficiency, the fundamental objection to it would remain unaltered and unabated. It would destroy political equality. It would increase rather than decrease abuse and corruption. It would stifle initiative and invention. It would undermine the development of leadership. It would cramp and cripple the mental and spiritual energies of our people. It would extinguish equality and opportunity. It would dry up the spirit of liberty and progress. For these reasons primarily it must be resisted. For a hundred and fifty years liberalism has found its true spirit in the American system, not in the European systems.

I do not wish to be misunderstood in this statement. I am defining a general policy. It does not mean that our government is to part with one iota of its national resources without complete protection to the public interest. I have already stated that where the government is engaged in public works for purposes of flood control, of navigation, or irrigation, of scientific research or national defense, or in pioneering a new art, it will at times necessarily produce power or commodities as a by-product. But they must be a by-product of the major purpose, not the major purpose itself.

Nor do I wish to be misinterpreted as believing that the United States is free-for-all and devil-take-the-hindmost. The very essence of equality of opportunity and of American individualism is that there shall be not domination by any group or combination in this republic, whether it be business or political. On the contrary, it demands economic justice as well as political and social justice. It is no system of laissez faire.

I feel deeply on this subject because during the war I had some practical experience with governmental operation and control. I have witnessed not only at home but abroad the many failures of government in business. I have seen its tyrannies, its injustices, its destruction of self-government, its undermining of the very instincts which carry our people forward to progress. I have witnessed the lack of advance, the lowered standards of living, the depressed spirits of people working under such a system. My objection is based not upon theory or upon a failure to recognize wrong or abuse, but I know the adoption of such methods would strike at the very roots of American life and would destroy the very basis of American progress.

Our people have the right to know whether we can continue to solve our great problems without abandonment of our American system. I know we can.

And what have been the results of the American system? Our country has become the land of opportunity to those born without inheritance, not merely because of the wealth of its resources and industry but because of this freedom of initiative and enterprise. Russia has natural resources equal to ours. Her people are equally industrious, but she has not had the blessings of one hundred and fifty years of our form of government and our social system.

By adherence to the principles of decentralized

self-government, ordered liberty, equal opportunity, and freedom to the individual, our American experiment in human welfare has yielded a degree of well-being unparalleled in all the world. It has come nearer to the abolition of poverty, to the abolition of fear of want, than humanity has ever reached before. Progress of the past seven years is the proof of it. This along furnishes the answer to our opponents, who ask us to introduce destructive elements into the system by which this has been accomplished.

I have endeavored to present to you that the greatness of America has grown out of a political and social system and a method of control of economic forces distinctly its own—our American system—which has carried this great experiment in human welfare farther than ever before in all history. We are nearer today to the ideal of the abolition of poverty and fear from the lives of men and women than ever before in any land. And I again repeat that the departure from our American system by injecting principles destructive to it which our opponents propose, will jeopardize the very liberty and freedom of our people, and will destroy equality of opportunity not only to ourselves but to our children.

❧❧ "Demoralization was unprecedented"

THE WALL STREET JOURNAL REPORTS OCTOBER, 1929 STOCK MARKET CRASH

All through the 1920s, the stock market enjoyed an extraordinary boom. The Dow Jones Industrial Average soared from a low of 63.9 in the doldrums of 1921 to 381.17 in the autumn of 1929. In October, the market crashed, dropping almost 50 percent in a week.

Panicked bankers scurried to rally the market. They enjoyed a short-lived success, as this October 25, 1929, *Wall Street Journal* article conveys. Within two weeks, the market had regained more than half of its losses reaching a post-crash high of 294.07 points. But the good times did not last. The market renewed its descent and did not reach a bottom until the summer of 1932 when the Dow Jones Industrial Average scraped its floor at 41.22 points. Speculators, investment banks, brokerage houses, major corporations and

others were wiped out completely.

The market crash proved to be a precursor to the Great Depression, although some economists insist it did not cause the decline in the real economy. Nevertheless, within the next three years, the national income dropped by almost 50 percent, unemployment reached 25 percent, and more than 5,500 banks were suspended.

Bankers Halt Stock Debacle

Strong banking support thrown behind the stock market shortly after noon on Thursday stopped the tremendous wave of liquidation which had brought about in the first two hours of trading probably the most demoralized condition in stock market history.

With stocks breaking wide open, the tape two hours late and sellers finding bids only at wide concessions, leading bank executives gathered at the office of J. P. Morgan & Co. This conference was followed by a checking of the decline, and then by a substantial rally which was sustained to the closing gong.

In such matters, of course, no official admission is ever made as to the amount of support thrown behind the market. But that it was of unusual size can hardly be doubted, in view of the manner in which the general list recovered from the debacle of the early trading, and the size of the institutions represented.

The heads of four large banks, representing in excess of six billion dollars of resources, met in the conference at the Morgan office. The banks, whose executive heads were present were the Chase National, National City, Bankers Trust and Guaranty Trust. Soon thereafter, supporting bids appeared in leading stocks; when the scale buying orders had checked the break they were followed by bidding for stocks. The Street's estimate was that the banking support of as much as a billion dollars had been put behind the market for leading equities in American industry.

The rally which ensued brought many stocks out of the slough of despond, for it meant real bids were present where before only dozens of "air pockets" existed. Many stocks rallied 25 to 50 points from previous breaks which had marked prices down 50 to 150 points in two hours of trading. Steel common alone rallied more than 12 points to close at a small gain for the day. Another constructive development was the statement by Col. J. W. Prentiss of Hornblower & Weeks, that his firm regarded the break as having gone too far and that a real rally should ensue. The firm is following this up with a nationwide advising in its opinion "present conditions are favorable for advantageous in standard American securities."

Late in the day representatives of 30 leading Stock Exchange houses, representing leading wire and commission houses, held a meeting called by Colonel Prentiss. The sense of this gathering was that the situation warranted a more hopeful view regarding the immediate outlook for prices. Brokerage opinion, therefore, should take on an optimistic tone. In this regard, Hornblower & Weeks' market letter for today says: "commencing with today's trading the markets should start laying the foundation for the constructive advance which we believe will characterize 1930. We believe yesterday's wide-open collapse will prove as excessive on the down side as the mid-summer speculation did on the up side."

In such a violent wave of liquidation, particular emphasis was made in many banking quarters on the manner in which brokerage houses had maintained their strong position in face of the unusual speculative fever which had preceded the collapse in prices. The spokesman for the meeting of large bankers said that their canvass of the situation showed no house to be in trouble. This condition, in view, of the widespread drop in prices, was regarded as a remarkable demonstration of stability.

The view expressed by the spokesman for the gathering of bankers was that the break was a technical one and not based on anything fundamentally wrong; that the market had run into a situation where there were urgent and heavy offerings of stocks in the face of a decided absence of bids; this brought about the terrific breaks in prices, with stocks for a time going for almost any price offered.

Charles E. Mitchell, one of the conferees at the meeting in the Morgan offices, reiterated his statement of a few days previously that he regarded the market break as purely technical and saw nothing to worry about in the general situation.

The volume of trading of 12,894,600 shares on the Stock Exchange broke all previous records, being some 50 percent larger than the previous record on March 26 last. With trading on the Curb Exchange in excess of 6,000,000 shares the two exchanges handled 20,000,000 shares for the day. The Stock Exchange tape did not finish recording prices until 7:08 pm, compared with the previous

late record of 5:14 pm, on March 26, last.

Demoralization in the early trading was unprecedented. Not only was it hard to sell stocks, for they were 10 to 30 points below the quotations appearing, but it was equally difficult for those desiring to buy. They were almost wholly in the dark as to what they would have to pay for their stocks.

The principal selling appeared to come from large operators who had suffered heavy beatings in the major decline in their pet issues over the past few weeks. At the opening there were no less than 42 separate issues in which the first sale exceeded 5,000 shares and ran as high as 20,000 in some cases. Prices were generally lower, but the avalanche of selling did not hit the market until close to 11 o'clock. Then it came from all points of the compass as impaired margin accounts were thrown overboard. It was undoubtedly the most drastic cleaning out of a long position the Street has ever witnessed in such a short period of time.

✣ Brother, Can You Spare a Dime?

E. Y. HARBURG

The Great Depression stunned the nation. Hard-working men and women who a few years earlier appeared to be part of building a great nation found themselves out of work, starving, and at a complete loss of what to do. The confidence of the 1920s had evaporated into a time of self-doubt, and for some humiliation. The "American Dream" had been replaced by the agony of Depression.

Yip Harburg's "Brother, Can You Spare a Dime?" written in 1932 with music by Jay Gorney captured the pathos that gripped the nation.

They used to tell me I was building a dream,
And so followed the mob
When there was earth to plough or guns to
    bear
I was always there on the job
They used to tell me I was building a dream
With peace and glory ahead
Why should I be standing in line just waiting for
    bread?

Once I built a railroad, made it run,
Made it race against time.
Once I built a railroad,
Now it's done
Brother, can you spare a dime?

Once I built a tower to the sun.
Brick and rivet and lime,
Once I built a tower,
Now it's done,
Brother, can you spare a dime?

Once in khaki suits
Gee, we looked swell
Full of that Yankee-Doodle-de-dum.
Half a million boots went sloggin' thru Hell,
I was the kid with the drum.
Say don't you remember,
they call me Al
It was Al all the time
Say, don't you remember
I'm your Pal!
Buddy, can you spare a dime?

🌿 *Pretty Boy Floyd*

WOODY GUTHRIE

Hard times provoked defiance. Folk singer Woody Guthrie's song "Pretty Boy Floyd" glorified the gangsters that stole from the rich and (sometimes) gave to the poor. From the perspective of destitute farmers whose land was taken by the banks for failing to pay the mortgage, the distinction between robbers and bankers was not always clear. Several robbers gained notoriety during the 1930s, including Bonnie and Clyde, Pretty Boy Floyd and John Dilinger.

If you'll gather round me children,
A story I will tell
About Pretty Boy Floyd, the outlaw,
Oklahoma knew him well.
It was in the town of Shawnee,
It was Saturday afternoon,
His wife beside him in the wagon
As into town they rode.
There a deputy Sheriff approached him,
In a manner rather rude,
Using vulgar words of language,
And his wife she overheard.

Pretty Boy grabbed a log chain,
And the deputy grabbed a gun,
And in the fight that followed
He laid that deputy down.
He took to the trees and timbers,
And he lived a life of shame,
Every crime in Oklahoma
Was added to his name.
Yes, he took to the trees and timbers,
On that Canadian River's shore,
And Pretty Boy found a welcome
At many a farmer's door.
There's many a starvin' farmer,
The same old story told,
How this outlaw paid their mortgage,
And saved their little home.
Others tell you 'bout a stranger,
That come to beg a meal,
And underneath his napkin
Left a thousand dollar bill.
It was in Oklahoma City
It was on Christmas Day,
There came a whole car load of groceries,
With a letter that did say:
 "You say that I'm an outlaw,
You say that I'm a thief,
Here's a Christmas dinner
For the families on relief."
Now as through this world I ramble,
I see lots of funny men,
Some will rob you with a six-gun,
And some with a fountain pen.
But as through this life you travel,
As through your life you roam,
You won't never see an outlaw,
Drive a family from their home.

🌿 *"Fathers had killed themselves, so the family could have the insurance"*

RECALLING THE DEPRESSION

Forty years after the Depression struck, Studs Terkel interviewed a wide spectrum of men and women who lived through it. He recorded their recollections in the book *Hard Times: An Oral History of the Great Depression.* Anecdotes from two of the interviewees, Kitty McCulloch and Pauline Kael, reflect some of the anguish, humor and tensions caused by the desperate economic times.

Kitty McCulloch

There were many beggars, who would come to your back door, and they would say they were hungry. I wouldn't give them money because I didn't have it. But I did take them in and put them in my kitchen and give them something to eat.

This one man came in—it was right before Christmas. My husband had a very nice suit, tailored. It was a black suit with a fine white pinstripe in it. He put it to one side. I thought he didn't like the suit. I said to this man, "You're clothes are all ragged. I think I have a nice suit for you." So I gave him this suit.

The following Sunday my husband was to go to a wake. He said, "Where's my good suit?" And I said, "Well, Daddy, you never wore it. I—well, it's gone." He said. "Where's it gone to?" I said, "I gave it to a man who had such shabby clothes. Anyway, you got three other suits and he didn't have any. So I gave it to him." He said, "You're the limit, Mother."

One elderly man that had white whiskers and all, he came to my back door. He was pretty much of a philosopher. He was just charming. A man probably in his sixties. And he did look like St. Nicholas, I'll tell you that. I gave him a good, warm meal. He said, "Bring me a pencil and paper and I'll draw you a picture." So he sketched. And was really good. He was an artist.

(Laughing) A man came to my door, and I could smell liquor a little. He said, "You don't suppose you could have a couple of shirts you could give me, old shirts of your husband's?" I said, "Oh, I'm so very sorry, my husband hasn't anything but old shirts, really. That's all he has right now and he wears those." He said. "Lady, if I get some extra ones, I'll come back and give them to you." I said, "Go on, mind your own business."

And another one, I smelled liquor on his breath, too. He wanted to know if he could have a few pennies. I said, "Are you hungry?" He said, "I haven't any food. I'd like some money to buy some food." I said, "I'll make you a nice sandwich." So I made him a sandwich with mayonnaise and chicken and lettuce, a double sandwich, put it in wax paper. He gave me a dirty look and started down the alley. I watched him when he got, oh, two or three doors down, he threw it down the street.

Pauline Kael

When I attended Berkeley in 1936, so many of the kids had actually lost their fathers. They had wandered off in disgrace because they couldn't support their families. Other fathers had killed themselves, so the family could have the insurance. Families had totally broken down. Each father took it as his personal failure. These middle-class men apparently had no social sense of what was going on, so they killed themselves.

It was still the Depression. There were kids who didn't have a place to sleep, huddling under bridges on the campus. I had a scholarship, but there were times when I didn't have food. The meals were often three candy bars. We lived communally and I remember feeding other kids by cooking up more spaghetti than I can ever consider again.

There was an embarrassment at college where a lot of the kids were well-heeled. I still have a resentment against the fraternity boys and the sorority girls with their cashmere sweaters and the pearls. Even now, when I lecture at colleges, I have this feeling about those terribly overdressed kids. It wasn't a hatred because I wanted these things, but because they didn't understand what was going on.

I was a reader for seven courses a semester, and I made $50 a month. I think I was the only girl on the labor board at Berkeley. We were trying to get the minimum wage on campus raised to forty cents an hour. These well-dressed kids couldn't understand our interest. There was a real division between the poor who were trying to improve things on the campus and the rich kids who didn't give a damn.

Berkeley was a cauldron in the late Thirties. You no sooner enrolled than you got an invitation from the Trotskyites and the Stalinists. Both were wooing you. I enrolled at sixteen, so it was a little overpowering at the time. I remember joining the Teachers Assistants Union. We had our own version of Mario Savio. He's now a lawyer specialized in bankruptcies. We did elect a liberal as president of the student body. It was a miracle in those days.

The fraternity boys often acted as strikebreakers in San Francisco—the athletes and the engineering students. And the poor boys were trying to get their 40 cents an hour. The college administration could always count on the frat boys to put down any student movement.

🍂 The Bonus Army

HERBERT HOOVER

Soldiers who fought for their country in World War I were given noticeably modest assistance when the hostilities ended. Each veteran was given sixty dollars as special pay for their contribution to the war effort. Frustrated by their negligible compensation, veterans demanded more and in 1924 Congress and President Calvin Coolidge approved an "adjusted compensation" bill to bridge the difference between what veterans would have received as civilians versus their actual military pay. Each veteran was given a bonus certificate that could be redeemed for five hundred dollars in 1945.

But in 1932, with work almost impossible to come by and their families destitute, thousands of veterans determined that they could not wait until 1945. A "bonus expeditionary force" or "bonus army" of up to 25,000 former veterans marched on Washington, D.C., and camped out in the nation's capital demanding that the government immediately honor the certificates. Congress voted against the measures in June, but authorized funds for transportation costs of the encamped veterans back to their homes. More than half left the city, but others remained, refusing to comply with local police demands to leave.

Suspecting a communist plot to overthrow the government, President Hoover ordered that federal troops under Chief of Staff Douglas MacArthur remove the protesting veterans on July 28. Armed with tanks, tear gas, machine guns, and fixed bayonets, Majors Dwight D. Eisenhower and George S. Patton (both World War I veterans themselves) led American soldiers in a dawn attack on the encampment. Two veterans and two policemen were killed in the assault. (In 1936, Congress overrode President Franklin D. Roosevelt's veto to authorize the immediate redemption of the bonus certificates.)

The attack represented a low point in the Great Depression, staining Hoover's reputation as a humanitarian. Hoover, however, remained resolute in his hostility toward the veterans and the agitators that he believed created the problem. The following passages are Hoover's comments in a press conference after the assault, as well as a letter he wrote to Washington, D.C., Police Commissioner Luther Reichelderfer urging him to crack down on the remnants of the bonus army.

A challenge to the authority of the United States Government has been met, swiftly and firmly.

After months of patient indulgence, the Government met overt lawlessness as it always must be met if the cherished processes of self-government are to be preserved. We cannot tolerate the abuse of Constitutional rights by those who would destroy all government, no matter who they may be. Government cannot be coerced by mob rule.

The Department of Justice is pressing its investigation into the violence which forced the call for Army detachments, and it is my sincere hope that those agitators who inspired yesterday's attack upon the Federal authority may be brought speedily to trial in the civil courts. There can be no safe harbor in the United States of America for violence.

Order and civil tranquility are the first requisites in the great task of economic reconstruction to which our whole people now are devoting their heroic and noble energies. The national effort must not be retarded in even the slightest degree by organized lawlessness. The first obligation of my office is to uphold and defend the Constitution and the authority of the law. This I propose always to do.

My Dear Mr. Commissioner:

In response to your information that the police of the District were overwhelmed by an organized attack by several thousand men, and were unable to maintain law and order, I complied with your request for aid from the Army to the police. It is a matter of satisfaction that, after the arrival of this assistance, the mobs which were defying the municipal government were dissolved without the firing of a shot or the loss of a life.

I wish to call attention of the District Commissioners to the fact that martial law has not been declared: that responsibility for order still rests upon your commission and the police. The civil government of Washington must function uninterrupted. The Commissioners, through their own powers, should now deal with this question decisively.

It is the duty of the authorities of the District to at once find the instigators of this attack on the police and bring them to justice. It is obvious that, after the departure of the majority of the veterans, subversive influences obtained control of the men remaining in the District, a large part of whom were not veterans, secured repudiation of their elected leaders and inaugurated and organized this attack.

They were undoubtedly led to believe that the civil authorities could be intimidated with impunity because of attempts to conciliate by lax enforcement of city ordinances and laws in many directions. I shall expect the police to strictly enforce every ordinance of the District in every part of the city. I wish every violator of the law to be instantly arrested and prosecuted under due process of law.

I have requested the law enforcement agencies of the Federal Government to cooperate with the District authorities to this end.

There is no group, no matter what its origins, that can be allowed either to violate the laws of this city or to intimidate the Government.

Yours faithfully,
Herbert Hoover

❧ *"The only thing we have to fear is fear itself"*

FRANKLIN D. ROOSEVELT'S FIRST INAUGURAL ADDRESS

When Franklin D. Roosevelt swore the oath of presidency in March 1933, the country was in the depths of the Depression. One-quarter of American farmers had lost their farms. Steel mills were operating at one-fifth their capacity. More than 5,000 banks were insolvent. The county was weary and eager to embrace a new leader with new vision.

Roosevelt did not disappoint. With his opening words, Roosevelt firmly assumed his leadership role, bringing a decisive shift in policy and outlook. Instead of rejecting governmental innovation based on Hoover's discredited faith in rugged individualism, Roosevelt sought action to reverse course. The government was going to do something to help its citizens. The vigor, humanity, and courage that marked his inaugural speech set the tone for the "New Deal" that Roosevelt promised.

This is a day of national consecration, and I am certain that my fellow-Americans expect that on my induction into the Presidency I will address them with a candor and a decision which the present situation of our nation impels.

This is pre-eminently the time to speak the truth, the whole truth, frankly and boldly. Nor need we shrink from honestly facing conditions in our country today. This great nation will endure as it has endured, will revive and will prosper.

So first of all let me assert my firm belief that the only thing we have to fear is fear itself—namely, unreasoning, unjustified terror which paralyzes needed efforts to convert retreat into advance.

In every dark hour of our national life a leadership of frankness and vigor has met with that understanding and support of the people themselves which is essential to victory. I am convinced that you will again give that support to leadership in these critical days.

In such a spirit on my part and on yours we face our common difficulties. They concern, thank God, only material things. Values have shrunken to fantastic levels; taxes have risen; our ability to pay has fallen, government of all kinds is faced by serious curtailment of income; the means of exchange are frozen in the currents of trade; the withered leaves of industrial enterprise lie on every side; farmers find no markets for their produce; the savings of many years in thousands of families are gone.

More important, a host of unemployed citizens face the grim problem of existence, and an equally great number toil with little return. Only a foolish optimist can deny the dark realities of the moment.

Yet our distress comes from no failure of substance. We are stricken by no plague of locusts. Compared with the perils which our forefathers conquered because they believed and were not afraid, we have still much to be thankful for. Nature still offers her bounty and human efforts have multiplied it. Plenty is at our doorstep, but a generous use of it languishes in the very sight of the supply.

Primarily, this is because the rulers of the exchange of mankind's goods have failed through their own stubbornness and their own incompetence, have admitted their failure and abdicated. Practices of the unscrupulous money changers stand indicted in the court of public opinion, rejected by the hearts and minds of men.

True, they have tried, but their efforts have been cast in the pattern of an outworn tradition. Faced by failure of credit, they have proposed only the lending of more money.

Stripped of the lure of profit by which to induce our people to follow their false leadership, they have resorted to exhortations, pleading tearfully for restored confidence. They know only the rules of a generation of self-seekers.

They have no vision, and when there is no vision the people perish.

The money changers have fled from their high seats in the temple of our civilization. We may now restore that temple to the ancient truths.

The measure of the restoration lies in the extent to which we apply social values more noble than mere monetary profit.

Happiness lies not in the mere possession of money; it lies in the joy of achievement, in the thrill of creative effort.

The joy and moral stimulation of work no longer must be forgotten in the mad chase of evanescent profits. These dark days will be worth all they cost us if they teach us that our true destiny is not to be ministered unto but to minister to ourselves and to our fellow-men.

Recognition of the falsity of material wealth as the standard of success goes hand in hand with the abandonment of the false belief that public office and high political position are to be valued only by the standards of pride of place and personal profit; and there must be an end to a conduct in banking and in business which too often has given to a sacred trust the likeness of callous and selfish wrongdoing.

Small wonder that confidence languishes, for it thrives only on honesty, on honor, on the sacredness of obligations, on faithful protection, on unselfish performance. Without them it cannot live.

Restoration calls, however, not for changes in ethics alone. This nation asks for action, and action now.

Our greatest primary task is to put people to work. This is no unsolvable problem if we face it wisely and courageously.

It can be accomplished in part by direct recruiting by the government itself, treating the task as we would treat the emergency of a war, but at the same time, through this employment, accomplishing greatly needed projects to stimulate and reorganize the use of our natural resources.

Hand in hand with this, we must frankly recognize the overbalance of population in our industrial centers and, by engaging on a national scale in the redistribution, endeavor to provide a better use of the land for those best fitted for the land.

The task can be helped by definite efforts to raise the values of agricultural products and with this the power to purchase the output of our cities.

It can be helped by preventing realistically the tragedy of the growing loss, through foreclosure, of our small homes and our farms.

It can be helped by insistence that the Federal, State and local governments act forthwith on the demand that their cost be drastically reduced.

It can be helped by the unifying of relief activities which today are often scattered, uneconomical and unequal. It can be helped by national planning for and supervision of all forms of transportation and of communications and other utilities which have a definitely public character.

There are many ways in which it can be helped, but it can never be helped merely by talking about it. We must act, and act quickly.

Finally, in our progress toward a resumption of work we require two safeguards against a return of the evils of the old order; there must be a strict supervision of all banking and credits and investments; there must be an end to speculation with other people's money, and there must be provision for an adequate but sound currency.

These are the lines of attack. I shall presently urge upon a new Congress in special session detailed measures for their fulfillment, and I shall seek the immediate assistance of the several States.

Through this program of action we address ourselves to putting our own national house in order and making income balance outgo....

If I read the temper of our people correctly, we now realize as we have never before, our interdependence on each other; that we cannot merely take, but we must give as well; that if we are to go forward we must move as a trained and loyal army willing to sacrifice for the good of a common discipline, because, without such discipline, no progress is made, no leadership becomes effective.

"People will turn out all right if you give them a proper chance"

JOHN DOS PASSOS

In 1933, as part of Roosevelt's first "One Hundred Days" initiative, Congress passed the American Agricultural Act, offering assistance to farmers. American farmers had been devastated. Even before the stock market crash, farmers were struggling to survive. Low prices, deteriorating soil conditions and the collapse of banks to finance them put millions of farmers in desperate straits.

The AAA and later the Soil Conservation and Domestic Allotment Act offered badly needed assistance. The Farm Security Administration was created to lend money to farmers at low rates to reinvest in their farms. Close to a million rehabilitation loans were made to help struggling farmers get back on their feet.

Acclaimed American writer John Dos Passos accompanied a Farm Security Administration agent in the southeast to get a first-hand look at the results of the new farming policy. This excerpt, describing some of what he found, comes from his 1943 book *State of the Nation*.

The relocation agent was driving me out past the steaming gray buildings of the chemical factories, over the hill that gave us, as the road looped, a backward view of the whole busy little northern Alabama industrial town with its trainyards and warehouses and the great pile of the steel mill and the long corrugated iron sheds of the pipe works lying in the bowl-shaped valley under a ceiling of soft-coal smoke. We passed a few tourist cabins turned into permanent residences and a last row of temporary shacks for chemical industry workers and turned onto a country road through a bleak shallow valley between scrubby pine woods. Counting all the war dislocations in together, the agent was telling me six hundred and ninety-nine families had had to move off farms in this county alone. Of these Farm Security Administration had helped five hundred and twenty-three. So far as he knew those figures were about average for the dislocated areas in the Southeast.

Of the families Farm Security had helped, thirty-four had been set up in dairying (he had hoped to raise that figure to ninety-six before long), twenty-seven in the chicken business, fifteen in beef cattle and the rest were raising cotton, as they were

accustomed to. Seemed a drop in the bucket, didn't it? But you had to begin slowly in a thing like this. If the experiment worked, it would be easy enough to multiply the number of farms.

The agent was a ruddy-faced young man immensely absorbed in what he was doing. He stopped the car on the side of the road and pointed proudly to a one-story house on a little knoll of red clay barely fuzzed with new green grass. "This is the first of our dairy farms. These places are already making cash money every two weeks selling milk to the army camp through the cooling plant. Let's take a look."

Across the road beyond the new barbed wire fence oats were sprouting in even rows in the red land. "That'll be our permanent pasture."

The house was clean and new with screened windows and a screened porch. The milking shed with its concrete floor was clean and new. The small cows, by a Jersey bull out of local scrub stock, looked clean and new. Only the farmer and his wife, a lanky weather-beaten pair, the man in overalls, the woman in Mother Hubbard and poke bonnet, had the old-time back-country look. Their clothes were clean though patched like crazy quilts, they were keeping the place clean all right, but they still looked ill at ease as if they hadn't settled down yet to feel this was really their home. The man kept talking about his water pump in a worried way, kept saying he was afraid it was going to break down. His wife was complaining about the faucet in the sink in the milking shed.

"It's not his pump that's worrying him," the agent said, grinning as he drove off. "It's the loan he had to make to buy the cows. He's accustomed to making a crop loan of a couple of hundred dollars and twelve hundred seems a terrible lot. When I tell him that he's selling a hundred dollars worth of milk every two weeks the figures just don't sink in. He's doing fine but he can't believe it…. Of course the high price of feed isn't doing us any good. About half of what we make on the milk goes into feed. Even so we are making out. The project's making out and the dairymen are making out."

In another county there were colored people living in the small, new low white houses. At the place where we stopped the mother and father had gone to town because it was Saturday afternoon. We looked at the young chicks and the hogs and the neat hills of earth the man's sweet potatoes were stored in. "This feller's going to be all right," the agent said. "There's one across the railroad tracks that isn't turning out so good, spends all his time working off his farm."

A little barefooted black girl in a clean pink dress had been following us around timidly. "How much preserving did your mother do last year?" the agent asked. "Let's see them…oh yes, canning is part of the program. Every client has a pressure kettle and is shown how to use it."

The little girl was too scared to open her mouth but she ran on the tips of her toes to the kitchen door and opened it and beckoned us in. The kitchen looked as if it had just been scrubbed that morning. With a look of reverence as if she were showing off some sacred magical object in a niche the little girl pulled open the door of the closet opposite the back door. From floor to ceiling clear shining jars of corn and beans and tomatoes and okra packed every carefully scrubbed shelf. They looked like the bright-colored vegetables you see wining prizes at country fairs.

"They look all right," said the agent. He couldn't help puffing out his chest, you could see, as he showed them off. "That means they've been eating something more than white meat and sweet potatoes this winter. That's a balanced diet."

As we drove back down the scrawny back road where Negro families lived in identically the same demountable white houses that were put up in other regions for the whites I couldn't help thinking that maybe in the electric brooders for chicks, in the electric pumps and the preserving kettles and the boilers for sterilizing the pails in the dairies and the vegetable patches and the clean hog pens there was the germ of a new way of life for the countryside.

"Is this sort of thing going to catch on?" I asked.

"Is Congress going to let us go ahead with it?" the agent asked me back….

The office of Farm Security was over an implement store on the other side of the courthouse. When I walked in the door a six-foot lantern-jawed backwoodsman in stained overalls with a quid of tobacco as big as an apple in his cheek stood leaning over the desk counting out ten-dollar bills while the administrator made out a receipt.

"Well, that jest about clars me up," he said as he slapped down the last greenback on the pile on the desk. He lifted the window a little with a long leathery flipper and spat delicately out into the yellow branches of a willow tree just feathered with early green.

"Feel better?" asked the administrator.

"Right smart…Good-day, gentlemen…I'll be goin'," said the man gravely and stalked out of the office.

"To go by the speeches in Congress I've just seen something that never happens, a Farm Security client paying off his loan."

"A very high percentage pay off their loans," said the administrator sharply; "higher all the time."

He was a quiet, studious-looking man with a long, closely cropped head. He wore a leather jacket and boots. He sat there at his desk for some time without speaking. Then he said suddenly, "I'll tell you a funny thing," and threw himself back in his chair and stared up at the peeling ceiling above his head. "You know when we started up this relocation work we picked our clients very carefully, made all sorts of investigations of their character and background to see if they'd be a good risk or not. Now we just take them as they come. Statistically the random clients work out as well or better than the hand-picked clients."

"What do you figure that means?"

"You tell me what it means."

While I sat there trying to figure out an answer he straightened himself up at his desk and picked up a pencil in a businesslike way as if he were going to start writing with it. "What it means to me is that the great majority of people will turn out all right if you give them a proper chance…I said the proper chance." He paused again and smiled. "Maybe that was the sort of thing the men who founded this country figured on." He jumped to his feet in a hurry as if he were afraid he'd said too much. "Suppose you and me go across the street and get us some dinner before they run out of everything," he said in a voice suddenly warm and good-natured.

"To encourage national industrial recovery"

THE NATIONAL RECOVERY ACT

June 16, 1933

The National Recovery Act was one of the most dramatic pieces of legislation in American history. Part of the One Hundred Days program by Roosevelt and the 73rd Congress, this legislation asserted federal control over American industry. It was designed to jump-start the economy through a combination of sweeping measures.

New control mechanisms were put in place through government codes, the government virtually seized control of the oil pipeline system and major public works projects were established to hire tens of thousands of unemployed. General Hugh Johnson was named chief administrator of the program—which became a centerpiece for the New Deal. The NRA, however, floundered. It was plagued by administrative problems and in 1935 the Supreme Court struck down the act's industrial codes.

An Act to encourage national industrial recovery, to foster fair competition, and to provide for the construction of certain useful public works, and for other purposes.

Title I—Industrial Recovery
Declaration of Police
Section 1. A national emergency productive of widespread unemployment and disorganization of industry, which burdens interstate and foreign commerce, affects the public welfare, and undermines the standards of living of the American people, is hereby declared to exist. It is hereby declared to be the policy of Congress to remove obstructions to the free flow of interstate and foreign commerce which tend to diminish the amount thereof; and to provide for the general welfare by promoting the organization of industry for the purpose of cooperative action among trade groups, to induce and maintain united action of labor and management under adequate governmental sanctions and supervision, to eliminate unfair competitive practices, to promote the fullest possible utilization of the present productive capacity of industries, to avoid undue restriction of production (except as may be temporarily required), to increase the consumption of industrial and agricultural products by increasing purchasing power, to reduce and relieve unemployment, to improve standards to labor, and otherwise to rehabilitate industry and to conserve national resources.

Administrative Agencies
Section 2.(c) This title shall cease to be in effect and any agencies established hereunder shall cease to exist at the expiration of two years after the date of enactment of this Act, or sooner if the President shall by proclamation or the Congress shall by joint resolution declare that the emergency recognized by Section 1 has ended.

Codes of Fair Competition
Section 3. (a) Upon the application to the President by one or more trade or industrial associations or groups, the President may approve a code or codes or fair competition for the trade of industry or subdivision thereof, represented by the applicant or applicants, if the President finds (1) that such associations or groups impose no inequitable restrictions on admission to membership therein and are truly representative of such trades or industries or subdivisions thereof, and (2) that such code or codes are not designed to promote monopolies or to eliminate or oppress small enterprises and will not operate to discriminate against them, and will tend to effectuate the policy of this title Provided, That such code or codes shall not permit monopolies or monopolistic practices.

Provided further, That where such code or codes affect the services and welfare of persons engaged in other steps of the economic process, nothing in this section shall deprive such persons of the right to be heard prior to approval by the President of such code or codes. The President may, as a condition of his approval of any such code, impose such conditions (including requirements for the making of reports and the keeping of accounts) for the protection of consumers, competitors, employees, and others, and in furtherance of the public interest, and may provide such exceptions to and exemptions from the provisions of such code, as the President in his discretion deems necessary to effectuate the policy herein declared.

After the President shall have approved any such code, the provisions of such code shall be the standards of fair competition for such trade or industry or subdivision thereof. Any violation of such standards in any transaction in or affecting interstate or foreign commerce shall be deemed an unfair method of competition in commerce within the meaning of the Federal Trade Commission Act, as amended; but nothing in this title shall be construed to impair the powers of the Federal Trade Commission under such Act, as amended.

Upon his own motion, or if complaint is made to the President that abuses inimical to the public interest and contrary to the policy herein declared are prevalent in any trade or industry or subdivision thereof, and if no code of fair competition therefor has theretofore been approved by the President, the President, after such public notice and hearing as he shall specify, may prescribe and approve a code of fair competition for such trade or industry or subdivision thereof, which shall have the same effect as a code of fair competition approved by the President under subsection (a) of this section.

Agreements and Licenses
Section 4. (a) The President is authorized to enter into agreements with, and to approve voluntary agreements between and among, persons engaged in a trade or industry, labor organizations, and trade or industrial organizations, associations, or groups, relating to any trade or industry, if in his judgment such agreements will aid in effectuating the policy of this title with respect to transactions in or affecting interstate or foreign commerce, and will be consistent with the requirements of clause (2) of subsection (a) of section 3 for a code of fair competition.

Whenever the President shall find that destructive wage or price cutting or other activities contrary to the policy of this title are being practiced in any trade or industry or any subdivision thereof, and after such public notice and hearing as he shall specify, shall find it essential to license business enterprises in order to make effective a code of fair competition or an agreement under this title or otherwise to effectuate the policy of this title, and shall publicly so announce, no person shall, after a date fixed in such announcement, engage in or carry on any business, in or affecting interstate or foreign commerce, specified in such announcement, unless he shall have first obtained a license issued pursuant to such regulations as the President shall prescribe. The President may suspend or revoke any such license, after due notice and opportunity for hearing, for violations of the terms or conditions thereof. Any order of the President suspending or revoking any such license shall be final if in accordance with law.

Oil Regulation
Section 9. (a) The President is further authorized to initiate before the Interstate Commerce Commission proceedings necessary to prescribe regulations to control the operations of oil pipe lines and to fix reasonable, compensatory rates for the transportation of petroleum and its products by pipe lines, and the Interstate Commerce Commission shall grant preference to the hearings and determination of such cases.

The President is authorized to institute proceedings to divorce from any holding company any pipe-line company controlled by such holding company which pipe-line company by unfair practices or by exorbitant rates in the transportation of petroleum or its products tends to create a monopoly.

The President is authorized to prohibit the transportation in interstate and foreign commerce of petroleum and the products thereof produced or withdrawn from storage in excess of the amount permitted to be produced or withdrawn from storage by any State law or valid regulation or order prescribed thereunder, by any board, commission, officer, or other duly authorized agency of a State.

Title II—Public Works and Construction Projects
Federal Emergency Administration of Public Works
Section 201. (a) To effectuate the purposes of this title, the President is hereby authorized to create a Federal Emergency Administration of Public Works, all the powers of which shall be exercised by a Federal Emergency Administrator of Public Works.

Section 202. The Administrator, under the direction of the President, shall prepare a comprehensive program of public works, which shall include among other things the following: (a) Construction, repair, and improvement of public highways and park ways, public buildings, and any publicly owned instrumentalities and facilities; (b) conservation and development of natural resources, including control, utilization, and purification of waters, prevention of soil or coastal erosion, development of water power, transmission of electrical energy, and construction of river and harbor improvements and flood control and also the construction of any river or drainage improvement required to perform or satisfy any obligation incurred by the United States through a treaty with a foreign Government heretofore ratified and to restore or develop for the use of any State or its citizens water taken from or denied to them by performance on the part of the United States of treaty obligations heretofore assumed: Provided, that no river or harbor improvements shall be carried out unless they shall have heretofore or hereafter been adopted by the Congress or are recommended by the Chief of Engineers of the United States Army; (c) any projects of the character heretofore constructed or carried on either directly by public authority or with public aid to serve the interests of the general public; (d) construction, reconstruction, alteration, or repair under public regulation or control of low-cost housing and slum-clearance projects; (e) any project (other than those included in the foregoing classes) of any character heretofore eligible for loans under subsection (a) of section 201 of the Emergency Relief and Construction Act of 1932, as amended, and paragraph (3) of such subsection (a) shall for such purposes be held to include loans for the construction or completion of hospitals the operation of which is partly financed from public funds, and of reservoirs and pumping plants and for the construction of dry docks; and if in the opinion of the President it seems desirable, the construction of naval vessels within the terms and/or limits established by the London Naval Treaty of 1930 and of aircraft required therefor and construction of heavier-than-air aircraft and technical construction for the Army Air Corps and such Army housing projects as the President may approve, and provision of original equipment for the mechanization or motorization of such Army tactical units as he may designate: Provided, however, That in the event of an international agreement for the further limitation of armament, to which the United States is signatory, the President is hereby authorized and empowered to suspend, in whole or in part, any such naval or military construction or mechanization and motorization of Army units.

Section 203. (a) With a view to increasing employment quickly (while reasonably securing any loans made by the United States) the President is authorized and empowered, through the Administrator or through such other agencies as he may designate or create, (1) to construct, finance, or aid in the construction or financing of any public-works project included in the program prepared pursuant to section 202; (2) upon such terms as the President shall prescribe, to make grants to States, municipalities, or other public bodies for the construction, repair, or improvement or any such project, but no such grant shall be in excess of 30 per centum of the cost of the labor and materials employed upon such project; (3) to acquire by purchase, or by exercise of the power of eminent domain, any real or personal property in connection with the construction of any such project, and to sell any security acquired or any property so constructed or acquired or to lease any such property with or without the privilege or purchase: Provided, That all moneys received from any such sale or lease or the repayment of any loan shall be used to retire obligations issued pursuant to section 209 of this Act, in addition to any other moneys required to be used for such purpose; (4) to aid in the financing of such railroad maintenance and equipment as may be approved by the Interstate Commerce Commission as desirable for the improvement of transportation facilities; Provided, That in deciding to extend any aid or grant hereunder to any State, county, or municipality the President may consider whether action is in process or in good faith assured therein reasonably designed to bring the ordinary current expenditures thereof within the prudently estimated revenues thereof.

The President, in his discretion, and under such terms as he may prescribe, may extend any of the benefits of this title to any State, county, or municipality notwithstanding any constitutional or legal restriction or limitation on the right or power of such State, county, or municipality to borrow money or incur indebtedness.

Section 4 (a) For the purpose of providing for emergency construction of public highways and related projects, the President is authorized to make grants to the highway departments of the several States in an amount not less than $400,000,000 to be expended by such departments in accordance with the provisions of the Federal Highway Act, approved November 9, 1921, as amended and supplemented...

Section 205 (a) Not less than $50,000,000 of

the amount made available by this Act shall be allotted for (A) national forest highways, (B) national forest roads, trails, bridges, and related projects, (C) national park roads and trails in national parks owned or authorized, (D) roads on Indian reservations, and (E) roads through public lands, to be expended in the same manner as provided in paragraph (2) of section 301 of the Emergency Relief and Construction Act of 1932, in the case of appropriations allocated for such purposes, respectively, in such section 301, to remain available until expended.

❧ *"My nation, behold it in kindness!"*

BLACK ELK SPEAKS

Black Elk was an Oglala Lakota Indian holy man who, working with author John G. Neihardt, wrote an autobigraphical history called *Black Elk Speaks* in 1932. The official government policy at the time was to try to strip Native Americans of their culture and Americanize them. Black Elk, however, sought to preserve the culture of his people and told stories of Native American ceremonies and games, such as the following excerpt from his book.

Although *Black Elk Speaks* did not have a significant impact in the 1930s, when it was republished in 1961, it helped stimulate a renewed interest in Native American literature and stimulate the Native American's resolve to preserve their identity.

Twenty days passed, and it was time to perform the dog vision with heyokas. But before I tell you how we did it, I will say something about heyokas and the heyoka ceremony, which seems to be foolish, but is not so.

Only those who have had visions of the thunder beings of the west can act as heyokas. They have sacred power and they share some of this with the people, but they do it through funny actions. When a vision comes from the thunder beings of the west, it comes with terror like a thunder storm; but when the storm of vision has passed, the world is greener and happier; for wherever the truth of vision comes upon the world, it is like rain. The world, you see, is happier after the terror of the storm.

But in the heyoka ceremony, everything is

backwards, and it is planned that the people shall be made to feel jolly and happy first, so that it may be easier for the power to come to them. You have noticed that the truth comes into this world with two faces. One is sad, and the other laughs; but it is the same face, laughing or weeping. When people are already in despair, maybe the laughing face is better for them; and when they feel good and are too sure of being safe, maybe the weeping face is better for them to see. And so I think that is what the heyoka ceremony is for.

There was a man by the name of Wachpanne (Poor) who took charge of this ceremony for me because he had acted as a heyoka many times and knew all about it. First he told all the poor to gather in a circle on the flat near Pine Ridge, and in the center, near a sacred teepee that was set there, he placed a pot of water which was made to boil by dropping hot stones from a fire into it. First, he had to make an offering of sweet grass to the west. He sat beside the fire with some sweet grass in his hand, and said: "To the Great Spirit's day, to that day grown old and wise, I will make an offering." Then, as he sprinkled the grass upon the fire and the sweet smoke arose, he sang:

> This I burn as an offering.
> Behold it!
> A sacred praise I am making.
> A sacred praise I am making.
> My nation, behold it in kindness!
> The day of the sun has been my strength.
> The path of the moon shall be my robe.
> A sacred praise I am making.
> A sacred praise I am making.

Then the dog had to be killed quickly and without making any scar, as lightning kills, for it is the power of the lightning that the heyokas have.

Over the smoke of the sweet grass a rawhide rope was held to make it sacred. Then two heyokas tied a slip noose in the rope and put this over the neck of the dog. Three times they pulled the rope gently, one at each end of the rope, and the fourth time they jerked it hard, breaking the neck. Then Wachpanne singed the dog and washed it well, and after he cut away everything but the head, the spine and the tail. Now walking six steps away from the pot, one for each of the Powers, he turned to the west, offering the head and spine to the thunder beings, then to the north, the east and the south, then to the Spirit above and to the Mother Earth.

After this, standing where he was, six steps away, he faced the pot and said: "In a sacred manner I thus boil this dog." Three times he swung it, and the fourth time he threw it so that it fell head first into the boiling water. Then he took the heart of the dog and did with it what he had done with the head and the spine.

During all this time, thirty heyokas, one for each day of a moon, were doing foolish tricks among the people to make them feel jolly. They were all dressed and painted in such funny ways that everybody who saw them had to laugh. One Side and I were fellow clowns. We had our bodies painted all over and streaked with black lightning. The right sides of our heads were shaved, and the hair on the left side was left hanging long. This looked very funny, but it had a meaning; for when we looked toward where you are always facing (the south) the bare sides of our heads were toward the west, which showed that we were humble before the thunder beings who had given us power. Each of us carried a very long bow, so long that nobody could use it, and it was very crooked too. The arrows that were carried were very long and very crooked, so that it looked crazy to have them. We were riding sorrels with streaks of black lightning all over them, for we were to represent the two men of my dog vision.

Wachpanne now went into the sacred teepee, where he sang about the heyokas:

These are sacred,
These are sacred,
They have said,
They have said.
These are sacred,
They have said.

Twelve times he sang this, once for each of the moons.

Afterward, while the pot was boiling, One Side and I, sitting on our painted sorrels, faced the west and sang:

In a sacred manner they have sent voices.
Half the universe has sent voices.
In a sacred manner they have sent voices to you.

Even while we were singing thus, the heyokas were doing foolish things and making laughter. For instance, two heyokas with crooked bows and arrows painted in a funny way, would come to a lit-

tle shallow puddle of water. They would act as though they thought it was a wide, deep river that they had to cross; so, making motions, but saying nothing, they would decide to see how deep the river was. Taking their long crooked arrows, they would thrust these into the water, not downwards, but flat-wise just under the surface. This would make the whole arrow wet. Standing the arrows up beside them, they would show that the water was far over their heads in depth, so they would get ready to swim. One would then plunge into the shallow puddle head first, getting his face in the mud and fighting the water wildly as though he were drowning. Then the other would plunge in to save his comrade, and there would be more fun antics in the water to make the people laugh.

After One Side and I had sung to the west, we faced the pot, where the heart and the head of the dog had been boiling. With sharp pointed arrows, we charged on horseback upon the pot and past it. I had to catch the head upon my arrow and One Side had to catch the heart, for we were representing the two men I had seen in the vision. After we had done this, the heyokas all chased us, trying to get a piece of the meat, and the people rushed to the pot, trying to get a piece of the sacred flesh. Ever so little of it would be good for them, for the power of the west was in it now. It was like giving them medicine to make them happier and stronger.

When the ceremony was over, everybody felt a great deal better, for it had been a day of fun. They were better able now to see the greenness of the world, the wideness of the sacred day, the colors of the earth, and to set these in their minds.

The Six Grandfathers have placed in this world many things, all of which should be happy. Every little thing is sent for something, and in that thing there should be happiness and the power to make happy. Like the grasses showing tender faces to each other, thus we should do, for this was the wish of the Grandfathers of the World.

"The Economics of Man-made Weather"

WILLIS H. CARRIER

Out of the economic wreckage of the Great Depression, several innovations were emerging that would help change the daily of lives of future Americans. One was the air conditioner.

A young engineer—just graduated from Cornell University in 1902—Willis H. Carrier devised a new machine for a Brooklyn printer that reduced humidity in the production area, allowing color to be applied properly to paper. Previously, the pages would expand and shrink as the humidity rose and fell. Carrier's innovation was the precursor to the modern air conditioner.

Carrier continued to improve the device and applied it to a wide range of industrial purposes. Enabling people and companies to "make their own weather," chocolate factories could operate in the summer, bakeries did not have to be stifling hot, munitions factories could control the heat, and railroads could provide comfort for their passengers. "Every day a good day," Carrier proclaimed in 1919 when he promoted air-conditioned theaters.

By 1933, air conditioners were used widely in industry, but had barely been introduced into homes. Carrier envisioned the day when air conditioners would improve the daily lives of Americans in their homes. He described that vision in this article, "The Economics of Man-made Weather" in *Scientific American.* Carrier was right. Air conditioners became big business starting in the 1950s and have become a standard appliance in homes across the country. In addition to providing comfort, air conditioners literally made the South a cool place to work. They helped lead to the revival of the South as a business center.

Less than a century ago farm laborers who toiled from dawn to dusk at 75 cents per day rioted and destroyed the first mowing machines. Poorly paid spinners and weavers wrecked some of the first spinning jennies and power looms in England.

At this time we again hear the cry of those who would place upon the "machine age" the responsibility for unemployment and economic instability.

The mobility of labor and the flexibility of industry as well as the stability of credit, to avert recurrence of these conditions, is a problem yet to be solved. The immediate situation imposes a crying need for new industries which will contribute wealth and employment in a degree comparable to that produced by the automobile, the radio, and the household refrigerator. In the anxiety to identify such a bright spot, some economists have pointed to the field of air conditioning. Although I do not feel that this new industry or any other single industry can be called upon to produce an immediate and miraculous recovery, it is my own opinion that air conditioning will contribute substantially, in numerous direct and indirect ways, to business improvement and to the maintenance of the tempo of our advancement.

Climate has always exerted a dominant influence upon the destinies and advancement of the races. Ages ago we learned to heat the air and thus make it possible to inhabit, throughout cold seasons, sections of the earth which otherwise would have been forbidding. But temperature is only one phase in our new command of the conditions of the air which surrounds us. We have also learned to clean the air, to free it from dust and objectionable foreign matter.

We have learned to establish and control any desired condition of humidity—which is just as important to our comfort and health as the temperature of the air. In summer, we can by dehumidification relieve the muggy oppression of humid days; in winter, we can add moisture to the air to alleviate that parching, arid condition common to the artificially heated, but un-humidified home or office….

While textile mills at one time could be successful only in regions having a naturally moist climate, great mills are operating today in the cotton fields near the source of supply because air conditions best suited to each manufacturing process are maintained within the mills by modern air conditioning equipment.

Air conditioning is applied to a great variety of industrial processes and, therefore, there is necessary a wide diversity in the character and method of its application. In some installations the primary purpose is to produce a humid climate with only a reasonable degree of temperature reduction which, though of practical advantage, is merely incidental. In many other cases, a rigid control of temperature with a lowering of the relative humidity is required.

This last-mentioned type of air conditioning has a much larger field as it applies to all processes that are affected by temperature as well as humidity. This is true in the manufacture of confectionery, in modern bakeries, in the manufacture of cigars and cigarettes, and in lithographing. It is used in the automatic packaging and wrapping of goods and in the drying of certain products at low temperatures, such as photographic films, chewing gum, and summer sausage. It is used successfully in many processes of the manufacture of ceramics from terra cotta to tiles and dishes. The Simonds Saw and Tool Company, Fitchburg, Massachusetts, have applied it as a necessary adjunct to their windowless factory where saws are to be manufactured under artificial light and artificial ventilation, maintaining ideal conditions regardless of external conditions.

More than 200 industries have already found air conditioning an indispensable servant, freeing the progressive manufacturer from daily weather uncertainties, improving the quality of his product, and contributing to the health and efficiency of his workers....

There is another field of air conditioning which creates a new demand, a new market, and has the possibilities of much more than making up for the economies of labor resulting from the application of air conditioning to industry. I refer to air conditioning for human comfort. This is a new and most fascinating field, and it is this field which, to my mind, has the greatest potentialities for making air conditioning a great industry.

Although the basic principles and practice of air conditioning have been well known for more than 20 years, it is only within the last eight years that its vast importance in increasing human comfort and efficiency has begun to receive public acceptance.

As a pioneer in this particular field, as well as in the general field of air conditioning, I am naturally enthusiastic concerning its future prospects. Any economic predictions that I may make might well be prejudiced, but I find that I have plenty of excellent company. Others who view the possibilities of the industry from the outside often outdo me in their enthusiasm concerning future possibilities in this field....

What are the returns in air conditioning? The first installation of air conditioning in a theater in New York City in 1924 paid for the entire installation the first summer that it was operated. It increased the summer attendance fully 50 percent and the average yearly attendance from 12 to 15 percent while the cost of air conditioning varies from 5 to 10 percent.

In the department store, air conditioning pays its way. The lower floor and basement where nearly one half the sales are made are usually air conditioned. The cost of owning and operating an air conditioning system is less than one-half of 1 percent of the total sales for the year. Since it is the summer sales that are chiefly increased, it requires less than a 2 percent increase for a three months period. Judging from the results of air conditioning at Macy's, as an illustration, the increase in purchasers, and presumably the increase in sales, during this period is several times this amount.

I am confident in predicting that within a few years the office building that is not air conditioned in summer as well as in winter will be wholly obsolete....

Air conditioning applied to human comfort not only contributes to human welfare but creates a new and rapidly increasing demand usefully aiding and taking up the slack of unemployment in technological advance in this and other fields. It may be the key to the successful exploitation of the wealth of the tropics. As an industry, it is yet in its infancy, and of its possibilities the surface only has been scratched. Upon the development of industries such as this our future industrial and social progress and well-being depend.

Woolworth's $250,000,000 Trick

FORTUNE MAGAZINE

F.H. Woolworth changed retailing in America. To introduce the "five-and-ten-cent" store, Woolworth revolutionized the way retail stores were organized. In the 1870s Woolworth left farming to work in Chicago as a salesman, a task he was not suited to do. In one of his first jobs, he was demoted for his lack of selling ability—but Woolworth had a knack for displays. Instead of trying to convince customers to buy products with his words, he set up displays that allowed the products to sell themselves.

In 1879, he opened his first F.H. Woolworth store in Utica, New York, employing techniques which he perfected over the next several years. Red storefronts, gold letters, alluring (but inexpensive) merchandise prominently displayed in glass windows, shining jewelry, "sold" signs, all became part of the standard Woolworth storefront. Clever displays cut down on the cost of sales people, allowing him to just use salesclerks to wrap packages and process the sales.

To keep prices down, Woolworth had to keep costs down. As he built his chain of retail stores, he constantly sought economies of scale and at the same time developed new management techniques to ensure quality control. By the early 1930s, Woolworth himself was out of the business, but his system had survived and prospered, so much so that a new Woolworth in town presented a threat to surrounding smaller, local merchants. Woolworth was a national institution with tremendous buying power and a corporate structure that others copied. The store became a precursor for the national retail outlets that dominate contemporary America.

This 1933 *Fortune* magazine article describes some of those techniques and the flavor of the Woolworth company.

Keenoflex razor blades, 4 for 10 cents...a 12 x 16 print of Rheims Cathedral, 20 cents...Othello Selected Dates, 1/2 lb., 10 cents...Hi-flier Big boy Tailless Dancing Kite...President Roosevelt, 8 x 12...Rubber Snap Gun, harmless, but amusing...La Vierge Folle perfume...Venetian Night incense...globes, 20 cents, it's a small world...Triple Heder ice-cream cone, three dippers...pants pockets, you get the pockets and sew them on to the pants....

Because F.W. Woolworth Co. commenced the year 1933 with 1,932 stores in the U.S., Canada, and Cuba and 563 stores in the rest of the world (mostly the British Isles), F.W. Woolworth Co. is a big chain. Because F.W. Woolworth has bought as much as $200,000,000 of merchandise in a year's time, it has a big buying power. Because all the Woolworth stores have red fronts with gold letters and wide corridors and plenty of electric lights, the company is said to have "standardized its units." And because of these several becauses there has arisen the legend that Woolworth can be explained by a reference to big buying power, standardized stores, and organization in the sense that somebody down in the Woolworth Building pushes a button and 1,932 stores take the green gumdrops out of Window No. 3 and put pink ribbons in their place. This is a totally erroneous conception.

Mr. Ernest Munroe Swingle lives in Red Bank, New Jersey. Mr. Swingle is a large man—six-feet high, 200-pounds heavy. He stands very straight and with his round, smooth face, his close-cut, smoothly brushed hair, and his brown, twinkling eyes, he looks younger than his forty-two years. Yet a certain amplitude of chin and belt indicates that Mr. Swingle has reached the age of maturity and is engaged in perhaps not a sedentary (Mr. Swingle doesn't sit much) but at least an indoor occupation.

Commuting from Red Bank to Manhattan, via the Hudson River tube, Mr. Swingle emerges at Herald Square, halts at the northwest corner of Thirty-fifth and Broadway. His next-door neighbor (across Thirty-fifth Street) is R.H. Macy. Across the street is a Rogers Peet shop. And over beyond the Square, where William Earl Dodge (Phelps Dodge Copper) sits in grimy bronze under the "L" structure, the tall straight tower of the Empire State Building fills the eye and the skyline. Industrially, the neighborhood is mostly cloaks and suits. But from a retail standpoint the corner is excellent. Besides Macy and Rogers Peet (and Mr. Swingle), there is nearby a Loft's, a Child's, a Liggett's, Saks 34th St., and Gimbel's. A good place for a store, a good place for Mr. Swingle.

For Mr. Swingle is a storekeeper. He is not precisely a merchant, inasmuch as the F.W. Woolworth Co. supplies his capital, pays his bills, and collects such of the profits as are not allotted to Mr. Swingle who works on a percentage of the net. But he is very much more than a clerk.

He is the boss of about 300 people whom he can hire and fire at will. In addition to the main floor and the basement Woolworth visited by his customers, he has an upstairs Woolworth where he keeps an inventory of 20,000 items with a value close to $175,000. When items need reordering it is Mr. Swingle who reorders them. And he buys directly from the manufacturer and not from a Woolworth warehouse. (Woolworth has 1,932 stores, three U.S. warehouses.) Figures on individual stores are not matters for publication, but it is conservative to estimate that Mr. Swingle's sales run in the neighborhood of $2,000,000 a year. And Mr. Swingle would be distinctly shocked if his operating profit did not safely exceed 10 to 12 per cent of his gross. Neighbor Percy Straus is a world-famed merchant and in 1932 Macy's made about $3,000,000. Storekeeper Swingle is just a Woolworth manager, but at between a fifth and quarter of a million dollars his earnings can hardly be considered negligible. If Mr. Swingle so desired he could move down to the Woolworth Building and become an Executive. But Mr. Swingle has no interest in moving. He is a storekeeper....

All Woolworth merchandise is divided into twenty-eight departments, for which there are twenty-four buyers (some of the smaller departments being lumped together). The buyer spends his working hours in the Woolworth Building—and busy hours they are. To him come a dozen, two dozen, three dozen manufacturers a day. Often selling Woolworth is their life objective, for Woolworth may take 50 percent, 75 per cent, even 100 percent of their output. They pour out of the elevators on the twenty-fourth floor of the Woolworth Building. They wait, restless and nervous, in the reception hall. They proceed, eventually, into the presence of the buyer.

And they meet a man who is much more than a purchasing agent. True, there is plenty of price dickering. Broadly speaking, Woolworth gets for six and one-half cents what it sells for ten cents, and around the half a cent wages many a battle. But price is not the only—it is often not the significant—topic, nor the most exciting. Here is a good five-cent article—but how about making the package date from 1933 instead of 1892? Here is a round gadget which would be better as a square gadget; how about squaring the circle while staying in the price field? Or here is something which, desirable in every way, simply cannot be made to sell for ten cents regardless of Woolworth volume. Then how about making it in a cheaper material or omitting something or in some manner cutting the pattern to fit the cloth? Suggestions vary from improving the method of displaying safety pins to establishing a complete new line of Woolworth cosmetics (Embassy line) sold in jars and bottles of a slickness and smartness hitherto unheard of in the five-, ten-, and twenty-cent world. Woolworth is not a manufacturer but neither is it a catchall for what the manufacturer brings it. First Woolworth buying lesson: never let well enough alone.

Notice that the manufacturers do not sell to the Woolworth stores: they sell to the Woolworth buyers. And the buyers are a highly centralized group headed by Charles Wurtz Deyo, Vice President in charge of Merchandising. Heavy-set, square-jawed, slow-spoken, Mr. Deyo firmly grasps the responsibility for spending upwards of 160,000,000 Woolworth dollars a year. Then what becomes of the 1,900 independent Mr. Swingles? How can the buyers buy for Woolworth while the Swingles buy for the stores?

The answer is the Approved List of Woolworth Manufacturers. It is a catalogue. It is the net result of thousands of manufacturers and the twenty-four Woolworth buyers. The result, too, of infinite trial-and-error, of months, even of years of labor. From this catalogue, the 1,900 Mr. Swingles choose....

We have called Woolworth decentralized. It is. But it is not chaotic. What we have been describ-ing is the Woolworth system functioning as it ought to function. When the system develops an ache in Store No. 765 or a pain in Item No. 3,492, in come the doctors. And with them comes the element of control.

Immediate control is exerted by the District Managers. There are thirteen District Managers, each heading one of the districts into which Woolworth has divided the U.S. (and Canada). The Manhattan district has 145 stores, the Chicago district 184 stores, the San Francisco district 164 stores, and so on. Under the District Manager are merchandising men and superintendents. The merchandising men scout competitive stores, ponder the ever-present problem of merchandise improvement, act as a clearing house for new ideas and new items. The superintendents might better be called inspectors. There is, roughly, one superintendent for each twenty stores. They travel from store to store in visits of inspection, as the gas company meter-reader travels from house to house. Furthermore, the store manager sends the district office a daily report of sales. In this way, Woolworth keeps the finger on the pulse.

Store troubles develop most frequently because a competitor has arrived to cut into sales and profits. This is unfortunate, but not a great deal can be done about it. The other trouble is poor handling of the stock. The store manager may have got himself loaded up with slow-moving items and caught short of the best sellers. Under the previous regime there was a tendency to solve the problem by firing the store manager, but the present method is to correct the cause rather than to pass the buck. Sometimes the home office will recapitalize the store and advance the manager funds with which to buy fast-moving merchandise and write off the old stock. Eventually it may be necessary to off with the store manager's head, but even then there is a careful investigation to find out who trained the store manager and where he came from and how he got the job.

Ultimate Woolworth control resides in the Woolworth building. It centers about a peculiarly Woolworthian entity known as "Diamond W." The Diamond W is the operating profit of all the stores. It is composed of 1,932 Diamond W's in the form of the operating profit for each store. The Home Office Mind pictures what each Diamond W should be, what the big Diamond W should amount to. The store manager's mind pictures the memory of how brightly his jewel shone in the previous year. Not always does the home office demand that each store's Diamond should each year contain more carats. Allowances are made for local conditions, for the general state of trade. But each store manager has an ideal to realize, an objective to attain. And everybody is interested in attaining it. For not only is the store manager paid out of the profits of his store. Profit-sharing also are the superintendents, the merchandising men, the district manager. A loss in any store is a loss to everyone's income.

Which brings us to a definition of quality which sets Woolworth apart from every other U.S. corporation. At Woolworth, everybody has gone through the mill. The Chairman ran a Woolworth store when there were only two Woolworth stores. The President opened boxes in the ninth Woolworth. Nobody comes in from the outside and starts halfway up the ladder, or quarter way up, or even on the second rung. They all begin at the beginning.

A young man walks into a Woolworth store and gets a job. It may be a year or more before he penetrates into the store that the customer sees. He is down in the basement (or up in the attic) learning how to take the head off a barrel and how to check an invoice. He is called, officially, a "learner" (and there are 1,800 learners now studying Woolworth's primary lessons). After he has learned inventory by heart, he is graduated to the stores itself. He beholds the customers, the counters, the salesgirls, the Outside World. He helps the managers with windows and counters and buying and reporting. One fine day he gets his own store—a Class-Four store with a volume of less than $50,000 a year. Then—according to his stature—come larger stores, until he reaches Class One (more than $500,000 a year). If he shows more interest in merchandise than in selling merchandise, he may deviate from the stores to the districts; may aim at becoming a district manager, and eventually be graduated into the home-office executive staff. But no matter how high a Woolworthian he may become, he will never forget the store training received in his formative years.

In Aldous Huxley's *Brave New World* children were bred in bottles and brought up in hatcheries to be either Alphas (the upper class) or betas (the middle class) or Gammas, Deltas, and Epsilons (the progressively inferior classes). Object: to produce a civilization in which each man's task fitted each man's capacity. In Woolworth the selection does not begin with this conception and the design is not so clearly visualized. But a process of natural selection produces the same result. A Beta-minus finds himself going no farther than a $100,000-a-year store, but a $100,000-a-year store is precisely suited to his capacity. A Beta-plus lands in a big-town store with a million-dollar volume, and having reached his limit neither receives nor desires more, while the Alphas ultimately climb up to the twenty-fourth floor of the Woolworth Building and grope with the executive problems to which their intellects are fitted. Meanwhile, Alphas, Betas, and Gammas (if Gammas survive) have all become Woolworthians. It is not the red fronts and the gold letters that give Woolworth stores their inherent unity. It is the psychological standardization of the store managers, plus the fact that even the topmost executives are simply store managers who are so superior that they have the capacity to do even more than manage stores.

❧ "Successful analysis requires a rational atmosphere"

BENJAMIN GRAHAM AND DAVID DODD

Out of the rubble of the 1929-30 stock market crash came *Security Analysis* by Benjamin Graham and David Dodd, published in 1934. *Security Analysis* became the most influential book written on investing, providing the fundamental structure for analyzing financial securities for the next 60 years in its thorough 600 pages.

Graham and Dodd's approach, which later became known as "value investing," placed a heavy emphasis on the proven abilities of the company being assessed and a sober examination of its prospects. The most famous practitioner of this approach became Warren Buffett, a student of Graham's in the 1940s, whose successful investment of a few thousand dollars eventually made him one of the two richest men in America by the 1990s.

In the last three decades the prestige of security analysis in Wall Street has experienced both a brilliant rise and an ignominious fall—a history related but by no means parallel to the course of stock prices. The advance of security analysis proceeded uninterruptedly until about 1927, covering a long period in which increasing attention was paid on all sides to financial reports and statistical data. But the "new era" commencing in 1927 involved at bottom the abandonment of the analytical approach; and while emphasis was still seemingly placed on facts and figures, these were manipulated by a sort of pseudo-analysis to support the delusions of the period. The market collapse in October 1929 was no surprise to such analysts as had kept their heads, but the extent of the business collapse which later developed, with its devastating effects on established earning power, again threw their calculations out of gear. Hence the ultimate result was that serious analysis suffered a double discrediting: the first—prior to the crash—due to the persistence of imaginary values, and the second—after the crash—due to the disappearance of real values….

The extreme fluctuations and vicissitudes of that period are not likely to be duplicated soon again. Successful analysis, like successful investment, requires a fairly rational atmosphere to work in and at least some stability of values to work with.

Three Functions of Analysis

1. Descriptive Function

The functions of security analysis may be described under three headings: descriptive, selective, and critical. In its more obvious form, descriptive analysis consists of marshalling the important facts relating to an issue and presenting them in a coherent, readily intelligible manner. This function is adequately performed for the entire range of marketable corporate securities by the various manuals…. A more penetrating type of description seeks to reveal the strong and weak points in the position of an issue, compare its exhibit with that of others of similar character, and appraise the factors which are likely to influence its future performance. Analysis of this kind is applicable to almost every corporate issue, and it may be regarded as an adjunct not only to investment but also to intelligent speculation in that it provides an organized factual basis for the application of judgment for purposes of investment or speculation.

2. The Selective Function of Security Analysis

In its selective function, security analysis goes further and expresses specific judgments of its own. It seeks to determine whether a given issue should be bought, sold, retained, or exchanged for some other. What types of securities or situations lend themselves best to this more positive activity of the analyst, and to what handicaps or limitations is it subject? It may be well to start with a group of examples of analytical judgments, which could later serve as a basis for a more general inquiry.

Examples of Analytical Judgments. In 1928 the public was offered a large issue of a 6% noncumulative preferred stock of St. Louis-San Francisco Railway Company priced at 100. The record showed that in no year had earnings been equivalent to as much as 1&! times the fixed charges and preferred dividends combined. The application of well-established standards of selection to the facts in this case would have led to the rejection of the issue as insufficiently protected.

A contrasting example: In June 1932 it was possible to purchase 5% bonds of Owens-Illinois Glass Company, due 1939, at 70 yielding 11% to maturity. The company's earnings were many times interest requirements—not only on the average but even at the time of the severe depression. The bond issue was amply covered by current assets alone, and it was followed by common and preferred stock with a very large aggregate market value, taking their lowest quotations. Here, analysis would have led to the recommendation of this issue as a strongly entrenched and attractively priced investment.

Let us take an example from the field of common stocks. In 1922, prior to the boom in aviation securities, Wright Aeronautical Corporation stock was selling on the New York Stock Exchange at only $8, although it was paying a $1 dividend, had for some time been earning over $2 a share, and showed more than $8 per share in cash assets in the treasury. In this case analysis would readily have established that the intrinsic value of the issue was substantially above the market price.

Again, consider the same issue in 1928 when it

had advanced to $280 per share. It was then earning at the rate of $8 per share, as against $3.77 in 1927. The dividend rate was $2; the net-asset value was less than $50 per share. A study of this picture must have shown conclusively that the market price represented for the most part the capitalization of entirely conjectural future prospects—in other words, that the intrinsic value was far less than the market quotation….

Intrinsic Value vs. Price. From the foregoing examples it will be seen that the work of the securities analyst is not without concrete results of considerable practical value, and that it is applicable to a wide variety of situations. In all of these instances he appears to be concerned with the intrinsic value of the security and more particularly with the discovery of discrepancies between the intrinsic value and the market price. We must recognize, however, that intrinsic value is an elusive concept. In general terms it is understood to be that value which is justified by the facts, e.g., the assets, earnings, dividends, definite prospects, as distinct, let us say, from market quotations established by artificial manipulation or distorted by psychological excesses. But it is a great mistake to imagine that intrinsic value is as definite and as determinable as is the market price. Some time ago intrinsic value (in the case of a common stock) was thought to be about the same thing as "book value," i.e., it was equal to the net assets of the business, fairly priced. This view of intrinsic value was quite definite, but it proved almost worthless as a practical matter because neither the average earnings nor the average market price evinced any tendency to be governed by the book value.

Intrinsic Value and "Earning Power." Hence this idea was superseded by a newer view, viz., that the intrinsic value of a business was determined by its earning power. But the phrase "earning power" must imply a fairly confident expectation of certain future results. It is not sufficient to know what the past earnings have averaged, or even that they disclose a definite line of growth or decline. There must be plausible grounds for believing that this average or this trend is a dependable guide to the future. Experience has shown only too forcibly that in many instances this is far from true. This means that the concept of "earning power," expressed as a definite figure, and the derived concept of intrinsic value, as something equally definite and ascertain-

able, cannot be safely accepted as a general premise of security analysis….

The Critical Function of Security Analysis
The principles of investment finance and the methods of corporation finance fall necessarily within the province of security analysis. Analytical judgments are reached by applying standards to facts. The analyst is concerned, therefore, with the soundness and practicability of the standards of selection. He is also interested to see that securities, especially bonds and preferred stocks, be issued with adequate protective provisions, and—more important still—that proper methods of enforcement of these covenants be part of accepted financial practice.

It is a matter of great moment to the analyst that the facts be fairly presented, and this means that he must concern himself with all corporate policies affecting the security owner, for the value of the issue which he analyzes may be largely dependent upon the acts of the management. In this category are included questions of capitalization set-up, for dividend and expansion policies, of managerial compensation, and even of continuing or liquidating an unprofitable business.

On these matters of varied import, security analysis may be competent to express critical judgments, looking to the avoidance of mistakes, to the correction of abuses, and to the better protection of those owning bonds or stocks.

✒ *"To protect the national banking system"*

THE SECURITIES EXCHANGE ACT OF 1934

Five years after the stock market crash, President Roosevelt signed The Securities Exchange Act, which imposed strict new rules on the market designed to ensure that the deceptive, misleading, and speculative practices that many believed contributed to the crash would not reoccur. Among the most important reforms were the creation of the Securities and Exchange Commission, new reporting requirements by all publicly held companies, and new mechanisms for the exchange of securities. In addition, specific market practices were prohibited and the Federal Reserve Board was given control over margin requirements on brokers' loans.

Roosevelt named Joseph Kennedy, a notorious stock manipulator in the 1920s, as the first chairman of the exchange, reasoning that Kennedy was best equipped to identify inappropriate stock practices. He was right—Kennedy did an excellent job, and the market steadily reflected the wisdom of the restructuring.

....Section 2. For the reasons hereinafter enumerated transactions in securities as commonly conducted...are affected with a national public interest which makes it necessary to provide for regulation and control of such transactions...to require appropriate reports and to make such regulation and control reasonably complete and effective in order to protect interstate commerce, the national credit...to protect and make more effective the national banking system and Federal Reserve system, and to insure the maintenance of fair and honest markets in such transactions:

(1) Such transactions (a) are carried on in large volume by the public generally and in large part originate outside the States in which the exchanges and over-the-counter markets are located and/or are affected by means of the mails and instrumentalities of interstate commerce; (b) constitute an important part of the current of interstate commerce; (c) involve in large part the securities of issuers engaged in interstate commerce; (d) involve the use of credit, directly affect the financing of trade, industry, and transportation in interstate commerce, and directly affect and influence the volume of interstate commerce, and affect the national credit.

(2) The prices established and offered in such transactions are generally disseminated and quoted throughout the United States and foreign countries and constitute a basis for determining and establishing the prices at which securities are bought and sold, the amount of certain taxes owing to the United States and to the several States by owners, buyers, and sellers of securities, and the value of collateral for bank loans.

(3) Frequently the prices of securities on such exchanges and markets are susceptible to manipulation and control, and the dissemination of such prices gives rise to excessive speculation, resulting in sudden and unreasonable fluctuations in the prices of securities which (a) cause alternately unreasonable expansion and unreasonable contraction of the volume of credit available for trade, transportation, and industry in interstate commerce, (b) hinder the proper appraisal of the value of securities and thus prevent a fair calculation of taxes owing to the United States and to the several States by owners, buyers, and sellers of securities, and (c) prevent the fair valuation of collateral for bank loans and/or obstruct the effective operation of the national banking system and Federal Reserve System.

(4) National emergencies, which produce widespread unemployment and the dislocation of trade, transportation, and industry, and which burden interstate commerce and adversely affect the general welfare, are precipitated, intensified, and prolonged by manipulation and sudden and unreasonable fluctuations of security prices and by excessive speculation on such exchanges and markets, and to meet such emergencies the Federal Government is put to such great expense as to burden the national credit....

Securities and Exchange Commission
Section 4. (a) There is hereby established a Securities and Exchange Commission (hereinafter referred to as the "Commission") to be composed of five commissioners to be appointed by the President by and with the advice and consent of the Senate. Not more than three of such commissioners shall be members of the same political party, and in making appointments members of different political parties shall be appointed alternately as nearly as may be practicable. No commissioners shall engage in any other business, vocation, or employment than that of serving as commissioner, nor shall any commissioner participate, directly or indirectly, in any stock-market operations or transactions of a character subject to regulation by the Commission pursuant to this title....

Transaction of Unregistered Exchanges
Section 5. It shall be unlawful for any broker, dealer, or exchange, directly or indirectly, to make use of the mails or any means of instrumentality of interstate commerce for the purpose of using any facility of an exchange within or subject to the jurisdiction of the United States to effect any transaction in a security, or to report any such transaction, unless such exchange (1) is registered as a national securities exchange under section 6 of this

title, or (2) is exempted from such registration upon application by the exchange because, in the opinion of the Commission, by reason of the limited volume of transaction effected on such exchange, it is not practicable and not necessary or appropriate in the public interest or for the protection of investors to require such registration.

Registration of National Securities Exchanges

Section 6. (a) Any exchange may be registered with the Commission as a national securities exchange under the terms and conditions hereinafter provided in this section, by filing a registration statement in such form as the Commission may prescribe....

Registration Requirements for Securities

Section 12. (a) It shall be unlawful for any member, broker, or dealer to effect any transaction in any security (other than an exempted security) on a national securities exchange unless a registration is effective as to such security for such exchange in accordance with the provisions of this title and the rules and regulations thereunder.

A security may be registered on a national securities exchange by the issuer filing an application with the exchange (and filing with the commission such duplicate originals thereof as the Commission may require), which application shall contain—

(1) Such information, in such detail, as to the issuer and any person directly or indirectly controlling or controlled by, or under direct or indirect common control with, the issuer, and any guarantor of the security as to principal or interest or both, as the Commission may by rules and regulations require, as necessary or appropriate in the public interest or for the protection of investors, in respect of the following:

(A) The organization, financial structure and nature of the business;

(B)The terms, positions, rights, and privileges of the different classes of securities outstanding;

(C) The terms on which their securities are to be, and during the preceding three years have been, offered to the public or otherwise;

(D) The directors, officers, and underwriters, and each security holder or record holding more than 10 per centum of any class of any equity security of the issuer (other than an exempted security),

their renumeration and their interests in the securities of, and their material contracts with, the issuer and any person directly or indirectly controlling or controlled by, or under direct or indirect common control with, the issuer;

(E) Renumeration to others than directors and officers exceeding $20,000 per annum;

(F) Bonus and profit-sharing arrangements;

(G) Management and service contracts;

(H) Options existing or to be created in respect of their securities:

(I) Balance sheets for not more than the three preceding fiscal years, certified if required by the rules and regulations of the Commission by independent public accountants;

(J) Profit and loss statements for not more than the three preceding fiscal years, certified if required by the rules and regulations of the Commission by independent public accountants; and

(K) Any further financial statements which the Commission may deem necessary or appropriate for the protection of investors....

Periodical and Other Reports

Section 13. (a) Every issuer of a security registered on a national securities exchange shall file the information, documents, and reports below specified with the exchange (and shall file with the Commission such duplicate originals thereof as the Commission may require), in accordance with such rules and regulations as the Commission may prescribe as necessary or appropriate for the proper protection of investors and to insure fair dealing in the security—

Such information and documents as the Commission may require to keep reasonably current the information and documents filed pursuant to section 12.

Such annual reports certified if required by the rules and regulations of the Commission by independent public accountant, and such quarterly reports, as the Commission may prescribe....

❧ The Grapes of Wrath

JOHN STEINBECK

Among the worst hit in the Depression were the farmers of the Great Plains. Dust storms, the lowest wheat prices in 300 years, and the stifled economy brought desperation to the Midwest. With no options at home and the promise of opportunity in California, thousands of farmers took their families west in search of jobs and new lives.

John Steinbeck wrote about the Dust Bowl and the "Okie" migration to California in his extraordinary book *The Grapes of Wrath.* The novel about the Joads explored the trials of the journey, the struggles and disappointments they found in California and the strain it placed on a formerly proud family, torn apart by the forces of a national tragedy.

Once California belonged to Mexico and its land to Mexicans; and a horde of tattered feverish Americans poured in. And such was their hunger for land that they took the land—stole Sutter's land, Guerrero's land, took the grants and broke them up and growled and quarreled over them, those frantic hungry men; and they guarded with guns the land they had stolen. They put up houses and barns, they turned the earth and planted crops. And these things were possession, and possession was ownership.

The Mexicans were weak and fled. They could not resist, because they wanted nothing in the world as frantically as the Americans wanted land.

Then, with time, the squatters were no longer squatters, but owners; and their children grew up and had children on the land. And the hunger was gone from them, the feral hunger, the gnawing, tearing hunger for land, for water and earth and the good sky over it, for the green thrusting grass, for the swelling roots. They had these things so completely that they did not know about them any more. They had no more the stomach-tearing lust for a rich acre and a shining blade to plow it, for seed and a windmill beating its wings in the air. They arose in the dark no more to hear the sleepy birds' first chittering, and the morning wind around the house while they waited for the first light to go out to the dear acres. These things were lost, and crops were reckoned in dollars, and land was valued by the principal plus interest, and crops were bought and sold before they were planted. Then crop failure, drought, and flood were no longer lit-tle deaths within life, but simple losses of money. And all their love was thinned with money, and all their fierceness dribbled away in interest until they were no longer farmers at all, but little shopkeepers of crops, little manufacturers who must sell before they can make. Then those farmers who were not good shopkeepers lost their land to the good shop-keepers. No matter how clever, how loving a man might be with earth and growing things, he could not survive if he was not a good shopkeeper. And as time went on, the business men had the farms, and the farms grew larger, but there were fewer of them....

And then the dispossessed were drawn west— from Kansas, Oklahoma, Texas, New Mexico; from Nevada and Arkansas families, tribes, dusted out, tractored out. Carloads, caravans, homeless and hungry; twenty thousand and fifty thousand and a hundred thousand and two hundred thousand. They streamed over the mountains, hungry and restless—restless as ants, scurrying to find work to do—to lift, to push, to pull, to pick, to cut—any-thing, any burden to bear, for food. The kids are hungry. We got no place to live. Like ants scurrying for work, for food, and most of all for land.

We ain't foreign. Seven generations back Americans, and beyond that Irish, Scotch, English, German. One of our folks was in the Revolution, an' they was lots of our folks in the Civil War— both sides. Americans.

They were hungry and they were fierce. And they had hoped to find a home, and they found only hatred. Okies—the owners hated them because the owners knew they were soft and the Okies strong, that they were fed and the Okies hungry; and perhaps the owners had heard from their grandfathers how easy it is to steal land from a soft man if you are fierce and hungry and armed. The owners hated them because they had no money to spend. There is no shorter path to a storekeeper's contempt, and all his admirations are exactly opposite. The town men, little bankers, hated Okies because there was nothing to gain from them. They had nothing. And the laboring people hated Okies because a hungry man must work, and if he must work, if he has to work, the wage payer automatically gives him less for his work; and then no one can get more.

And the dispossessed, the migrants, flowed into California, two hundred and fifty thousand,

and three hundred thousand. Behind them new tractors were going on the land and the tenants were being forced off. And the new waves were on the way, new waves of the dispossessed and the homeless, hardened, intent, and dangerous.

And while the Californians wanted many things, accumulation, social success, amusement, luxury, and a curious banking security, the new barbarians wanted only two things—land and food; and to them the two were one. And whereas the wants of the Californians were nebulous and undefined, the wants of the Okies were beside the roads, lying there to be seen and coveted: the good fields with water to be dug for, the good green fields, earth to crumble experimentally in the hand, grass to smell, oaten stalks to chew until the sharp sweetness was in the throat. A man might look at a fallow field and know, and see in his mind that his own bending back and his own straining arms would bring the cabbages into the light, and the golden eating corn, the turnips and carrots.

And a homeless, hungry man, driving the roads with his wife beside him and his thin children in the back seat, could look at the fallow fields which might produce food but not profit, and that man could know how a fallow field is a sin and the unused land a crime against the thin children. And such a man drove along the roads and knew temptation at every field, and knew the lust to take these fields and make them grow strength for his children and a little comfort for his wife. The temptation was before him always. The fields goaded him, and the company ditches with good water flowing were a goad to him.

And in the south he saw the golden oranges hanging on the trees, the little golden oranges on the dark green trees; and guards with shotguns patrolling the lines so a man might not pick an orange for a thin child, oranges to be dumped if the price was low.

He drove his old car into a town. He scoured the farms for work. Where can we sleep tonight?

Well, there's Hooverville on the edge of the river. There a whole raft of Okies there.

He drove his old car to Hooverville. He never asked again, for there was a Hooverville on the edge of every town.

The rag town lay close to water; and the houses were tents, and the weed-thatched enclosures, paper houses, a great junk pile. The man drove his family in and became a citizen of Hooverville—always they were called Hooverville. The man put up his own tent as near to water as he could get; or if he had no tent, he went to the city dump and brought back cartons and built a house of corrugated paper. And when the rains came the house melted and washed away. He settled in Hooverville and he scoured the countryside for work, and the little money he had went for gasoline to look for work. In the evening the men gathered and talked together. Squatting on their hams they talked of the land they had seen.

"Every Man a King"

HUEY LONG

Huey Long terrified and enthralled the country. Despite the breadth of reforms introduced by Roosevelt's New Deal legislation, it did not pull the country out of the Depression. Millions of unemployed still cluttered the city streets and entire farming communities were wiped out. Long spoke to the discontented, taking advantage of their simmering resentment.

Elected as governor of Louisiana in 1928, Long ruled his state with an iron fist, but he also brought schools and hope to the poverty-stricken. He was elected to the senate in 1930 and quickly made a name for himself on the national stage. Railing against the rich and the deficiencies of government policy, Long called for a radical redistribution of wealth. He promised every family food, a house and four-hour workdays. It was an appealing offer coming from the flamboyant and charismatic Long. So much so that Roosevelt feared Long more than he did the Republicans in the 1936 election.

Long, however, was assassinated in 1935. Nevertheless, his proclamation "Every Man a King" had struck a chord and reflected the radical solutions that were being tossed about during the difficult years of the Great Depression. This radio speech was delivered from Washington, D.C., in January 1935.

I contend, my friends, that we have no difficult problem to solve in America, and that is the view of nearly everyone with whom I have discussed the matter here in Washington and elsewhere throughout the United States—that we have no very difficult problem to solve.

It is not the difficulty of the problem which we have; it is the fact that the rich people of this country—and by rich people I mean the super-rich—will not allow us to solve the problems, or rather the one little problem that is afflicting this country, because in order to cure all of our woes it is necessary to scale down the big fortunes, that we may scatter the wealth to be shared by all of the people....

I believe that was the judgment and the view and the law of the Lord, that we would have to distribute wealth every so often, in order that there could not be people starving to death in a land of plenty, as there is in America today.

We have in America today more wealth, more goods, more food, more clothing, more houses than we have ever had. We have everything in abundance here.

We have the farm problem, my friends, because we have too much cotton, because we have too much wheat, and have too much corn, and too much potatoes.

We have a home-loan problem, because we have too many houses, and yet nobody can buy them and live in them.

We have trouble, my friends, in the country, because we have too much money owing, the greatest indebtedness that has ever been given to civilization, where it has been shown that we are incapable of distributing the actual things that are here, because the people have not money enough to supply themselves with them, and because the greed of a few men is such that they think it is necessary that they own everything, and their pleasure consists in the starvation of the masses, and in their possessing things they cannot use, and their children cannot use, but who bask in the splendor of sunlight and wealth, casting darkness and despair and impressing it on everyone else.

"So, therefore," said the Lord in effect, "if you see these things that now have occurred and exist in this and other countries, there must be·a constant scattering of wealth in any country if this country is to survive."

Now, my friends, if you were off on an island where there were a hundred lunches, you could not let one man eat up the hundred lunches, or take the hundred lunches and not let anybody else eat any of them. If you did, there would not be anything else for the balance of the people to consume.

So, we have in America today, my friends, a condition by which about ten men dominate the means of activity in at least 85 percent of the activities that you own. They either own directly every-

thing or they have got some kind of mortgage on it, with a very small percentage to be expected. They own the banks, they own the steel mills, they own the railroads, they own the bonds, they own the mortgages, they own the stores, and they have chained the country from one end to the other until there is not any kind of business that a small, independent man could go into today and make a living, and there is not any kind of business that an independent man can go into and make any money to buy an automobile with; and they have finally and gradually and steadily eliminated everybody from the fields in which there is a living to be made, and still they have got little enough sense to think they ought to be able to get more business out of it anyway.

If you reduce a man to the point where he is starving to death and bleeding and dying, how do you expect that man to get hold of any money to spend with you? It is not possible.

Then, ladies and gentlemen, how do you expect people to live, when the wherewith cannot be had by the people?

Now, we have organized a society, and we call it Share Our Wealth Society, a society with the motto "Every Man a King."

Every man a king, so there would be no such thing as a man and woman who did not have the necessities of life, who would not be dependent upon the whims and caprices and ipse dixit of the financial barons for a living. What do we propose by this society? We propose to limit the wealth of big men in the country. There is an average of $15,000 in wealth to every family in America. That is right here today.

We do not propose to divide it up equally. We do not propose a division of wealth, but we propose to limit poverty that we will allow to be inflicted upon any man's family. We will not say we are going to try to guarantee any equality, or 415,000 to a family. No; but we do say that one-third of the average is low enough for any one family to hold, that there should be a guarantee of a family wealth of around $5,000; enough for a home, an automobile, a radio, and the ordinary conveniences, and the opportunity to educate their children; a fair share of the income of this land thereafter to that family so there will be no such thing as merely the select to have those things, and so there will be no such thing as a family living in poverty and distress.

We have to limit fortunes. Our present plan is that we will allow no one man to own more than $50 million. We think that with that limit we will be able to carry out the balance of the program. It may be necessary that we limit it to less than $50 million. It may be necessary, in working out of the plans that no man's fortune would be more than $10 million or $15 million. But be that as it may, it will still be more than any one man, or any one man and his children and their children, will be able to spend in their lifetimes; and it is not necessary or reasonable to have wealth piled up beyond that point where we cannot prevent poverty among the masses.

Another thing we propose is old-age pension of thirty dollars a month for everyone that is sixty years old. Now, we do not give this pension to a man making $1,000 a year, and we do not give it to him if he has $10,000 in property, but outside of that we do.

We will limit hours of work. There is not any necessity of having overproduction. I think all you have got to do, ladies and gentlemen, is just limit the hours of work to such an extent as people will work only so long as it is necessary to produce enough for all of the people to have what they need. Why, ladies and gentlemen, let us say that all of these labor-saving devices reduce hours down to where you do not have to work but four hours a day; that is enough for these people, and then praise be the name of the Lord, if it gets that good. Let it be good and not a curse, and then we will have five hours a day and five days a week, or even less than that, and we might give a man a whole month off during a year, or give him two months; and we might do what other countries have seen fit to do, and what I did in Louisiana, by having schools by which adults could go back and learn the things that have been discovered since they went to school.

We will not have any trouble taking care of the agricultural situation. All you have to do is balance your production with your consumption. You simply have to abandon a particular crop that you have too much of, and all you have to do is store the surplus for the next year, and the government will take over.

Those are the things we propose to do. "Every Man a King." Every man to when there is something to eat; all to wear something when there is

something to wear. That makes us all a sovereign.

And we ought to take care of the veterans of the wars in this program. That is a small matter. Suppose it does cost a billion dollars a year—that means that the money will be scattered throughout this country. We ought to pay them a bonus. We can do it....

Now, my friends, we have got to hit the root with the ax. Centralized power in the hands of a few, with centralized credit in the hands of a few, is the trouble.

Get together in your community tonight or tomorrow and organize one of our Share Our Wealth Societies. If you do not understand it, write me and let me send you the platform; let me give you the proof of it.

This is Huey P. Long talking, United States senator, Washington, D.C. Write me and let me send you the data on this proposition. Enroll with us. Let us make known to the people what we are going to do. I will send you a button, if I have got enough of them left. We have got a little button that some of our friends designed, with our message around the rim of the button, and in the center "Every Man a King."...

Now that I have but a minute left, I want to say that I suppose my family is listening in on the radio on New Orleans, and I will say to my wife and three children that I am entirely well and hope to be home before many more days, and I hope they have listened to my speech tonight, and I wish them and all of their neighbors and friends everything good that may be had.

I thank you, my friends, for your kind attention, and I hope you will enroll with us, take care of your own work of this government, and share or help in our Share Our Wealth Societies.

❧ "To diminish the causes of labor disputes"

THE NATIONAL LABOR RELATIONS ACT

July 5, 1935

When the Supreme Court invalidated the National Recovery Act, Congress passed the National Labor Relations Act enabling the government with the ability to intervene in the increasingly violent labor disputes that were erupting all over the nation. It was also known as the Wagner Act in recognition of its chief sponsor, New York Senator Robert F. Wagner.

The act recognized labor's right to organize and to bargain collectively. The establishment of the independent National Labor Relations Board created a mechanism to investigate labor complaints, safeguard the right to collective bargaining, impose cease-and-desist orders and arbitrate labor disputes. Although effective, both labor and ownership sharply criticized many of the Board's decisions, claiming it was biased to the other side.

The Act to diminish the causes of labor disputes burdening or obstructing interstate and foreign commerce, to create a National Labor Relations Board, and for other purposes.

Be it enacted,

Findings and Policy

Section 1. The denial by employers of the right of employees to organize and the refusal by employers to accept the procedure of collective bargaining lead to strikes and other forms of industrial strife or unrest, which have the intent or the necessary effect or burdening or obstructing commerce by (a) impairing the efficiency, safety, or operation of the instrumentalities of commerce; (b) occurring in the current of commerce; (c) materially affecting, restraining, or controlling the flow of raw materials or manufactured or processed goods from or into the channels of commerce, or the prices of such materials or goods in commerce; or (d) causing diminution of employment and wages in such volume as substantially to impair or disrupt the market for goods flowing from or into the channels of commerce.

The inequality of bargaining power between employees who do not possess full freedom of association or actual liberty of contract, and employers who are organized in the corporate or other forms of ownership association substantially burdens and affects the flow of commerce, and tends to aggravate recurrent business depressions, by depressing wage rates and the purchasing power of wage earners in industry and by preventing the stabilization of competitive wage rates and working conditions within and between industries.

Experience has proved that protection by law of the right of employees to organize and bargain collectively safeguards commerce from injury, impairment, or interruption, and promotes the flow of commerce by removing certain recognized sources of industrial strife and unrest, by encouraging practices fundamental to the friendly adjustment of industrial disputes arising out of differences as to wages, hours, or other working conditions, and by restoring equality of bargaining power between employers and employees.

It is hereby declared to be the policy of the United States to eliminate the causes of certain substantial obstructions to the free flow of commerce and to mitigate and eliminate these obstructions when they have occurred by encouraging the practice and procedure of collective bargaining and by protecting the exercise by workers of full freedom of association, self-organization, and designation of representatives of their own choosing, for the purpose of negotiating the terms and conditions of their employment or other mutual aid or protection.

National Labor Relations Board

Section 3. (a) There is hereby created a board, to be known as the "National Labor Relations Board," which shall be composed of three members, who shall be appointed by the President, by and with the advice and consent of the Senate. One of the original members shall be appointed for a term of one year, one for a term of three years, and one for a term of five years, but their successors shall be appointed for terms of five years each, except that any individual chosen to fill a vacancy shall be appointed only for the unexpired term of the member whom he shall succeed. The President shall designate one member to serve as chairman of the Board. Any member of the Board may be removed by the President, upon notice and hearing, for neglect of duly or malfeasance in office, but for no other cause

Section 4. (a) Each member of the Board shall receive a salary of $10,000 a year, shall be eligible for reappointment, and shall not engage in any other business, vocation or employment.

Section 5. (a) The Board may establish or utilize such regional, local, or other agencies, and utilize such voluntary and uncompensated services, as may from time to time be needed

Section 6. (a) The Board shall have authority from time to time to make, amend, and rescind such rules and regulations as may be necessary to carry out the provisions of this Act. Such rules and regulations shall be effective upon publication in the manner which the Board shall prescribe.

Rights of Employees
Section 7. Employees shall have the right of self-organization, to form, join, or assist labor organizations, to bargain collectively through representatives of their own choosing, and to engage in concerted activities, for the purpose of collective bargaining or other mutual aid or protection.

Section 8. It shall be an unfair labor practice for an employer to interfere with, restrain, or coerce employees in the exercise of the rights guaranteed in section 7.

To dominate or interfere with the formation or administration of any labor organization or contribute financial or other support to it: Provided, That subject to rules and regulations made and published by the Board pursuant to section 6 (a), an employer shall not be prohibited from permitting employees to confer with him during working hours without loss of time or pay.

By discrimination in regard to hire or tenure of employment or any term or condition of employment to encourage or discourage membership in any labor organization: Provided, That nothing in this Act, or in the National Industrial Recovery Act (U.S.C. Supp. VII, Title 15, secs. 701-712), as amended from time to time, or in any code or agreement approved or prescribed thereunder, or in any other statute of the United States, shall preclude an employer from making an agreement with a labor organization (not established, maintained, or assisted by any action defined in this Act as an unfair labor practice) to require as a condition of employment membership therein, if such labor organization is the representative of the employees as provided in section 9 (a), in the appropriate collective bargaining unit covered by such agreement when made.

To discharge or otherwise discriminate against an employee because he has filed charges or given testimony under this Act.

To refuse to bargain collectively with the representatives of his employees, subject to the provisions of Section 9 (a).

Representatives and Elections
Section 9. (a) Representatives designated or selected for the purposes of collective bargaining by the majority of the employees in a unit appropriate for such purposes, shall be the exclusive representatives of all the employees in such unit for the purposes of collective bargaining in respect to rates of pay, wages, hours of employment, or other conditions of employment: Provided, That any individual employee or a group of employees shall have the right at any time to present grievances to their employer.

The Board shall decide in each case whether, in order to insure to employees the full benefit of their right to self-organization and to collective bargaining, and otherwise to effectuate the policies of this Act, the unit appropriate for the purposes of collective bargaining shall be the employer unit, craft unit, plant unit, or subdivision thereof.

Whenever a question affecting commerce arises concerning the representation of employees, the Board may investigate such controversy and certify to the parties, in writing, the name or names of the representatives that have been designated or selected. In any such investigation, the Board shall provide for an appropriate hearing upon due notice, either in conjunction with a proceeding under section 10 or otherwise, and may take a secret ballot of employees, or utilize any other suitable method to ascertain such representatives.

Whenever an order of the Board made pursuant to section 10 (c) is based in whole or in part upon facts certified following an investigation pursuant to subsection (c) of this section, and there is a petition for the enforcement or review of such order, such certification and the record of such investigation shall be included in the transcript of the entire record required to be filed under subsections 10 (e) or 10 (f), and thereupon the decree of the court enforcing modifying or setting aside in whole or in part the order of the Board shall be made and entered upon the pleadings, testimony, and proceedings set forth in such transcript.

Prevention of Unfair Labor Practices
Section 10. (a) The Board is empowered, as hereinafter provided, to prevent any person from engaging in any unfair labor practice (listed in section 8) affecting commerce. This power shall be exclusive, and shall not be affected by any other means of adjustment or prevention that has been or may be established by agreement, code, law, or otherwise.

Whenever it is charged that any person has engaged in or is engaging in any such unfair labor practice, the Board, or any agent or agency designated by the Board for such purposes, shall have power to issue and cause to be served upon such person a complaint stating the charges in that respect, and containing a notice of hearing before the Board or a member thereof, or before a designated agent or agency, at a place therein fixed, not less than five days after the serving of said complaint. Any such complaint may be amended by the member, agent or agency conducting the hearing or the Board in its discretion at any time prior to the issuance of an order based thereon. The person so complained of shall have the right to file an answer to the original or amended complaint and to appear in person or otherwise and give testimony at the place and time fixed in the complaint. At the discretion of the member, agent or agency conducting the hearing or the Board, any other person may be allowed to intervene in the said proceeding and to present testimony. In any such proceeding the rules of evidence prevailing in courts of law or equity shall not be controlling.

The testimony taken by such member, agent or agency or the Board shall be reduced to writing and filed with the Board. Thereafter, in its discretion, the Board upon notice may take further testimony or hear argument. If upon all the testimony taken the Board shall be of the opinion that any person named in the complaint has engaged in or is engaging in any such unfair labor practice, then the Board shall state its finding of fact and shall issue and cause to be served on such person an order requiring such person to cease and desist from such unfair labor practice, and to take such affirmative action, including reinstatement of employees with or without back pay, as will effectuate the policies of this Act. Such order may further require such person to make reports from time to time showing the extent to which it has complied with the order. If upon all the testimony taken the Board shall be of the opinion that no person named in the complaint has engaged in or is engaging in any such unfair labor practice, then the Board shall state its findings of fact and shall issue an order dismissing the said complaint.

The Board shall have power to petition any circuit court of appeals of the United States, or if all the circuit courts of appeals to which application may be made are in vacation, any district court of the United States, within any circuit or district, respectively, wherein the unfair labor practice in question occurred or wherein such person resides or transacts business, for the enforcement of such order and for appropriate temporary relief or restraining order, and shall certify and file in the court a transcript of the entire record in the proceeding, including the pleadings and testimony upon which such order was entered and the findings and order of the Board. Upon such filing, the court shall cause notice thereof to be served upon such person, and thereupon shall have jurisdiction of the proceeding and of the question determined therein, and shall have power to grant such temporary relief or restraining order as it deems just and proper, and to make and enter upon the pleadings, testimony, and proceedings set forth in such transcript a decree enforcing, modifying and enforcing a so modified, or setting aside in whole or in part the order of the Board. No objection that has not been urged before the Board, its member, agent or agency, shall be considered by the court, unless the failure or neglect to urge such objection shall be excused because of extraordinary circumstances. The findings of the Board as to the facts, if supported by evidence, shall be conclusive

The Board may modify its finding as to the facts, or make new findings, by reason of additional evidence so taken and filed, and it shall file such modified or new findings, which, if supported by evidence, shall be conclusive, and shall file its recommendations, if any, for the modification or setting aside of its original order. The jurisdiction of the court shall be exclusive and its judgment and decree shall be final, except that the same shall be subject to review by the appropriate circuit court of appeals if application was made to the district court as hereinabove provided, and by the Supreme Court of the United States upon writ of certiorari or certification

Any person aggrieved by a final order of the Board granting or denying in whole or in part the relief sought may obtain a review of such order in any circuit court of appeals of the United States in the circuit wherein the unfair labor practice in question was alleged to have been engaged in or wherein such person resides or transacts business.

The commencement of proceedings under subsection (e) or (f) of this section shall not, unless specifically ordered by the court, operate as a stay of the Board's order.

Petitions filed under this Act shall be heard expeditiously, and if possible within ten days after they have been docketed.

❧ "A law that will take care of human needs"

THE SOCIAL SECURITY ACT OF 1935

Dramatically improving the prospects for the elderly in the United States, the Social Security Act of 1935 represented the first time that the federal government took responsibility for the protection of the elderly from poverty. Although individual states had introduced social security legislation starting in 1929, it had never been done a national basis.

The law, considered dangerously radical by many people at the time, established a federal pension for retirees, to be funded with a payroll tax. The act also provided funds to assist children, the blind and the unemployed, to institute vocational training programs and provide family health programs. It has since become a central bulwark of the government. Prior to Social Security, the elderly routinely faced the prospect of poverty upon retirement—that fear has dissipated. The following are remarks made by Roosevelt upon signing the Social Security Act and passages of the legislation itself.

Roosevelt on The Social Security Act

Today a hope of many years standing is in large part fulfilled. The civilization of the past hundred years, with its startling industrial changes, has tended more and more to make life insecure. Young people have come to wonder what would be their lot when they came to old age. The man with a job has wondered how long the job would last.

This Social Security measure gives at least some protection to thirty million of our citizens who will reap direct benefits through unemployment compensation, through old-age pensions, and through increased services for the protection of children and the prevention of ill-health.

We can never ensure 100 percent of the population against 100 percent of the hazards and vicissitudes of life, but we have tried to frame a law which will give some measure of protection to the average citizen and to his family against the loss of a job and against poverty-ridden old age.

This law, too, represents a cornerstone in a structure which is being built but is by no means complete—a structure intended to lessen the force of possible future depressions, to act as a protection to future administrations of the government against the necessity of going deeply into debt to furnish relief to the needy—a law to flatten out the peaks and valleys of deflation and of inflation—in other words, a law that will take care of human needs and at the same time provide for the United States an economic structure of vastly greater soundness.

The Social Security Act

August 14, 1935

An Act to provide for the general welfare by establishing a system of Federal old-age benefits, and by enabling the several States to make more adequate provision for aged persons, blind persons, dependent and crippled children, maternal and child welfare, public health, and the administration of their unemployment compensation laws; to establish a Social Security Board; to raise revenue; and for other purposes.

Be it enacted by the Senate and House of Representatives of the United States of America in Congress assembled,

Title I. Grants to States for Old Age Assistance

Appropriation
Section 1. For the purpose of enabling each State to furnish financial assistance, as far as practicable under the conditions in such State, to aged needy individuals, there is hereby authorized to be appropriated for the fiscal year ending June 30, 1936, the sum of $4,750,000 and there is hereby authorized to be appropriated for each fiscal year thereafter a sum sufficient to carry out the purposes of this title. The sums made available under this section shall be used for making payments to States which have submitted, and had approved by the Social Security Board established by Title VII, State plans for old-age assistance.

State Old-Age Assistance Plans
Section 2. (a) A State plan for old-age assistance must (1) provide that it shall be in effect in all political subdivisions of the State, and, if administered by them, be mandatory upon them; (2) pro-

vide for financial participation by the State; (3) either provide for the establishment or designation of a single State agency to administer the plan, or provide for the establishment or designation of a single State agency to supervise the administration of the plan; (4) provide for granting to any individual, whose claim for old-age assistance is denied, an opportunity for a fair hearing before such State agency; (5) provide such methods of administration (other than those relating to selection, tenure of office, and compensation of personnel) as are found by the Board to be necessary for the efficient operation of the plan; (6) provide that the State agency will make such reports in such form and containing such information, as the Board may from time to time require, and comply with such provisions as the Board may from time to time find necessary to assure the correctness and verification of such reports; and (7) provide that, if the State or any of its political subdivisions collects from the estate of any recipient of old-age assistance any amount with respect to old-age assistance furnished him under the plan, one-half of the net amount so collected shall be promptly paid to the United States. Any payment so made shall be deposited in the Treasury to the credit of the appropriation for the purposes of this title.

The Board shall approve any plan which fulfills the conditions specified in subsection (a), except that it shall not approve any plan which imposes, as a condition of eligibility for old-age assistance under the plan.

An age requirement of more than sixty-five years, except that the plan may impose, effective until January 1, 1940, an age requirement of as much as seventy years; or

Any residence requirement which excludes any resident of the State who has resided therein five years during the nine years immediately preceding the application for old-age assistance and has resided therein continuously for one year immediately preceding the application; or

Any citizenship requirement which excludes any citizen of the United States.

Payment to States
Section 3. (a) From the sums appropriated therefor, the Secretary of the Treasury shall pay to each State which has an approved plan for old-age assistance, for each quarter, beginning with the quarter

commencing July 1, 1935, (1) an amount, which shall be used exclusively as old-age assistance, equal to one-half of the total of the sums expended during such quarter as old-age assistance under the State plan with respect to each individual who at the time of such expenditure is sixty-five years of age or older and is not an inmate of a public institution, not counting so much of such expenditure with respect to any individual for any month as exceeds $30, and (2) 5 per centum of such amount, which shall be used for paying the costs of administering the State plan or for old-age assistance, or both, and for no other purpose....

Old-Age Benefit Payments
Section 202. (a) Every qualified individual shall be entitled to receive, with respect to the period beginning on the date he attains the age of sixty-five, or on January 1, 1942, whichever is the later, and ending on the date of his death, an old-age benefit (payable as nearly as practicable in equal monthly installments) as follows:

If the total wages determined by the Board to have been paid to him, with respect to employment after December 31, 1936, and before he attained the age of sixty-five, were not more than $3,000, the old-age benefit shall be at a monthly rate of one-half of 1 per centum of such total wages;

If such total wages were more than $3,000, the old-age benefit shall be at a monthly rate equal to the sum of the following:

One-half of 1 per centum of $3,000; plus

One-twelfth of 1 per centum of the amount by which such total wages exceeded $3,000 and did not exceed $45,000; plus;

One-twenty-fourth of 1 per centum of the amount by which such total wages exceeded $45,000.

In no case shall the monthly rate computed under subsection (a) exceed $85

Payments Upon Death
Section 203. (a) If any individual dies before attaining the age of sixty-five, there shall be paid to his estate an amount equal to 3 1/2 per centum of the total wages determined by the Board to have been paid to him, with respect to employment after December 31, 1936...

Title III. Grants to States for Unemployment

Compensation Administration
Appropriation
Section 301. For the purpose of assisting the States in the administration of their unemployment compensation laws, there is hereby authorized to be appropriated, for the fiscal year ending June 30, 1936, the sum of $4,000,000, and for each fiscal year thereafter the sum of 49,000,000, to be used as hereinafter provided.

Title IV. Grants to States for Aid to Dependent Children
Appropriation
Section 401. For the purpose of enabling each State to furnish financial assistance, as far as practicable under the conditions in such State, to needy dependent children, there is hereby authorized to be appropriated for the fiscal year ending June 30, 1936, the sum of $24,750,000, and there is hereby authorized to be appropriated for each fiscal year thereafter a sum sufficient to carry out the purposes of this title. The sums made available under this section shall be used for making payments to States which have submitted, and had approved by the Board, State plans for aid to dependent children.

Payment to States
Section 403. (a) From the sums appropriated therefor, the Secretary of the Treasury shall pay to each State which has an approved plan for aid to dependent children, for each quarter, beginning with the quarter commencing July 1, 1935, an amount, which shall be used exclusively for carrying out the State plan, equal to one-third of the total of the sums expended during such quarter under such plan, not counting so much of such expenditure with respect to any dependent child for any month as exceeds $18, or if there is more than one dependent child in the same home, as exceeds $18 for any month with respect to one such dependent child and $12 for such month with respect to each of the other dependent children.

Definition.
Section 406. When used in this title, the term "dependent child" means a child under the age of sixteen who has been deprived of parental support or care by reason of death, continued absence from the home, or physical or mental incapacity of a parent, and who is living with his father, mother, grandfather, grandmother, brother, sister, stepfather, stepmother, stepbrother, stepsister, uncle, or aunt, in a place of residence maintained by one or more of such relatives as his or their own home.

Title V. Grants to State for Maternal and Child Welfare
Part 1. Maternal and Child Health Services
Appropriation
Section 501. For the purpose of enabling each State to extend and improve, as far as practicable under the conditions in such State, services for promoting the health of mothers and children, especially in rural areas and in areas suffering from severe economic distress, there is hereby authorized to be appropriated for each fiscal year, beginning with the fiscal year ending June 30, 1936, the sum of $3,800,000. The sums made available under this section shall be used for making payments to States which have submitted, and had approved by the Chief of the Children's Bureau, State plans for such services.

Allotments to States
Section 502. (a) Out of the sums appropriated pursuant to section 501 for each fiscal year the Secretary of Labor shall allot to each State $20,000, and such part of $1,800,000 as he finds that the number of live births in such State bore to the total number of live births in the United States, in the latest calendar year for which the Bureau of the Census has available statistics.

Out of the sums appropriated pursuant to section 501 for each fiscal year the Secretary of Labor shall allot to the States $980,000 (in addition to the allotments made under subsection (a), according to the financial need for each State for assistance in carrying out its State plan, as determined by him after taking into consideration the number of live births in such State.

Approval of State Plans
Section 503. (a) A State plan for maternal and child-health services must (1) provide for financial participation by the State; (2) provide for the administration of the plan by the State health agency or the supervision of the administration of the plan by the State health agency; (3) provide such methods of administration (other than those relating to selection, tenure of office, and compen-

sation of personnel) as are necessary for the efficient operation of the plan; (4) provide that the State health agency will make such reports, in such form and containing such information, as the Secretary of Labor may from time to time require, and comply with such provisions as he may from time to time find necessary to assure the correctness and verification of such reports; (5) provide for the extension and improvement of local maternal and child-health services administered by local child-health units; (6) provide for cooperation with medical, nursing, and welfare groups and organizations; and (7) provide for the development of demonstration services in needy areas and among groups in special need.

Part 2. Services for Crippled Children
Appropriation
Section 511. For the purpose of enabling each State to extend and improve (especially in rural areas and in areas suffering from severe economic distress), as far as practicable under the conditions in such State, services for locating crippled children, and for providing medical, surgical, corrective, and other services and care, and facilities for diagnosis, hospitalization, and aftercare, for children who are crippled or who are suffering from conditions which lead to crippling, there is hereby authorized to be appropriated for each fiscal year, beginning with the fiscal year ending June 30, 1936, the sum of $2,850,000. The sums made available under this section shall be used for making payments to States which have submitted, and had approved by the Chief of the Children's Bureau, State plans for such services.

Part 3 - Child-Welfare Services
Section 521. (a) For the purpose of enabling the United States, through the Children's Bureau, to cooperate with State public-welfare agencies in establishing, extending, and strengthening, especially in predominately rural areas, public-welfare services (hereinafter in this section referred to as "child-welfare services") for the protection and care of homeless, dependent, and neglected children, and children in danger of becoming delinquent, there is hereby authorized to be appropriated for each fiscal year, beginning with the fiscal year ending June 30, 1936, the sum of $1,500,000. Such amount shall be allotted by the Secretary of Labor

for use by cooperating State public-welfare agencies on the basis of plans developed jointly by the State agency and the Children's Bureau, to each State $10,000 and the remainder to each State on the basis of such plans, not to exceed such part of the remainder as the rural population of such State bears to the total rural population of the United States. The amount so allotted shall be expended for payment of part of the cost of district, county or other local child-welfare services in areas predominantly rural, and for developing State services for the encouragement and assistance of adequate methods of community child-welfare organization in areas predominantly rural and other areas of special need.

Part 4. Vocational Rehabilitation
Section 531. (a) In order to enable the United States to cooperate with the States and Hawaii in extending the strengthening their programs of vocational rehabilitation of the physically disabled, and to continue to carry out the provisions and purposes of the Act entitled "An Act to provide for the promotion of vocational rehabilitation of persons disabled in industry or otherwise and their return to civil employment," approved June 2, 1920, there is hereby authorized to be appropriated for the fiscal years ending June 30, 1936, and June 30, 1937, the sum of $841,000 for each such fiscal year in addition to the amount of the existing authorization, and for each fiscal year thereafter the sum of $1,938,000.

Title VI. Public Health Work
Appropriation
Section 601. For the purpose of assisting States, counties, health districts, and other political subdivisions of the States in establishing and maintaining adequate public-health services, including the training of personnel for State and local health work, there is hereby authorized to be appropriated for each fiscal year, beginning with the fiscal year ending June 30, 1936, the sum of $8,000,000 to be used as hereinafter provided...

Investigations
Section 603. (a) There is hereby authorized to be appropriated for each fiscal year, beginning with the fiscal year ending June 30, 1936, the sum of $2,000,000 for expenditure by the Public Health

Service for investigation of disease and problems of sanitation....

Title VIII. Taxes with Respect to Employment
Income Tax on Employees
Section 801. In addition to other taxes, there shall be levied, collected, and paid upon the income of every individual a tax equal to the following percentages of the wages (as defined in section 811) received by him after December 31, 1936, with respect to employment (as defined in section 811) after such date:

With respect to employment during the calendar years 1937, 1938, and 1939, the rate shall be 1 per centum.

With respect to employment during the calendar years 1940, 1941, and 1942, the rate shall be 1 1/2 per centum.

With respect to employment during the calendar years 1943, 1944, and 1945, the rate shall be 2 per centum.

With respect to employment during the calendar years 1946, 1947, and 1948, the rate shall be 2 1/2 per centum.

With respect to employment after December 31, 1948, the rate shall be 3 per centum.
Deduction of Tax from Wages
Section 802. (a) The tax imposed by section 801 shall be collected by the employer of the taxpayer, by deducting the amount of the tax from wages as and when paid....

Excise Tax on Employees
Section 804. In addition to other taxes, every employer shall pay an excise tax with respect to having individuals in his employ, equal to the following percentages of wages (as defined in section 811) paid by him after December 31, 1936, with respect to employment (as defined in Section 811) after such date:

With respect to employment during the calendar years 1937, 1938, and 1939, the rate shall be 1 per centum.

With respect to employment during the calendar years 1940, 1941, and 1942, the rate shall be 1 1/2 per centum.

With respect to employment during the calendar years 1943, 1944 and 1945, the rate shall be 2 per centum.

With respect to employment during the calen-

dar years 1946, 1947 and 1948, the rate shall be 2 1/2 per centum.

With respect to employment after December 31, 1948, the rate shall be 3 per centum.

Title X. Grants to States or Aid to the Blind
Appropriation
Section 1001. For the purpose of enabling each State to furnish financial assistance, as far as practicable under the conditions in such State, to needy individuals who are blind, there is hereby authorized to be appropriated for the fiscal year ending June 30, 1936, the sum of $3,000,000, and there is hereby authorized to be appropriated for each fiscal year thereafter a sum sufficient to carry out the purposes of this title. The sums made available under this section shall be used for making payments to States which have submitted, and had approved by the Social Security Board, State plans for aid to the blind.

❧ *Commonplace*

NORMAN ROCKWELL

From the earliest settlers, Americans sought to find an identity for themselves that was distinct from Europe. A nation of immigrants, Americans found it difficult to break their cultural ties. By the early twentieth century, however, that sense of cultural self-identity was finally starting to blossom in an American Renaissance. Instead of turning to Europe for inspiration, Americans were looking to their own history and their own lives to adopt new cultural icons for themselves. The construction of the Lincoln Memorial, the rise of jazz and authors such as Sinclair Lewis who focused on uniquely American sources, were all creating a distinctly American culture. The famed illustrator Norman Rockwell was part of this phenomenon. His humorous paintings for the *Saturday Evening Post*—which reached almost one in ten homes in this pre-television era—were popular and influential in creating a cohesive identity for Americans. In this 1936 column he talks about his approach to art.

When I was younger I went to France to paint. Like many young artists, I thought I needed stimulation—something outside of myself and my environment—to make my work more interesting and important. But after seven months in France I realized that exotic and unusual things had not changed me. Indeed, I could not work as well in France as I could at home among the ordinary, familiar things.

I know that all I need in my work is at hand. Whether I make the best use of it depends entirely upon my ability to see, to feel, and to understand. The commonplaces of America are to me the richest subjects in art. Boys batting flies on vacant lots; little girls playing jacks on the front steps; old men plodding home at twilight, umbrellas in hand—all of these things arouse feeling in me.

Commonplaces never become tiresome. It is we who become tired when we cease to be curious and appreciative. We may fly from our ordinary surroundings to escape commonplace, but we go along. After a moment's excitement with a new scene, it becomes commonplace again. And we find that it is not a new scene which we needed, but a new viewpoint.

Right now I am engaged in the most delightful task of illustrating an edition of Mark Twain's *Tom Sawyer*—recording the trivial events in the lives of two ordinary American boys. While literary men of fifty years ago were imitating European novelists and poets, Mark Twain was immortalizing the prosaic environment of Hannibal, Missouri. His books have been published in many languages. They have enabled the rest of the world to understand and appreciate us. And they have enabled us to better understand ourselves and so improve.

When I go to farms or little towns, I am always surprised at the discontent I find. The farm family so often looks with envious eyes upon the town, the town upon the cities and the cities upon New York. And New York, too often, has looked across the sea toward Europe. And all of us who turn our eyes away from what we have are missing life.

But I am not being pessimistic. America is becoming more and more aware of itself—its own beauty, its political freedom, its traditions—its commonplaces. Artists, writers, and scientists are reporting and investigating life around them. They are discovering the things we have seen all our lives, and overlooked.

I am not urging placid acceptance of things as they are. I am suggesting that we take stock of what we have around us, explore it with appreciative understanding—and criticism. That is the beginning of change and growth—of a greater America.

🌿 *"I might have had a bad break, but I have an awful lot to live for"*

LOU GEHRIG

Lou Gehrig was the iron man of baseball. He played first base for the New York Yankees in every game for more than fifteen years as one of the country's premier hitters. All told, he played 2,130 consecutive games, a mark of endurance that would last for almost sixty years. He finally pulled himself out of the lineup in 1939, having been weakened by a fatal neurological disease that would later be named after him.

On May 2, 1939, the Yankees honored Gehrig, whose work ethic, professionalism and simple honesty came to represent the best of American values. This was his farewell statement to the fans.

Fans, for the past two weeks you have been reading about a bad break I got. Yet today I consider myself the luckiest man on the face of the earth.

I have been in ballparks for seventeen years and I have never received anything but kindness and encouragement from you fans. Look at these grand men. Which of you wouldn't consider it the highlight of his career just to associate with them for even one day? Sure, I'm lucky. Who wouldn't have considered it an honor to have known Jacob Ruppert? Also, the builder of baseball's greatest empire, Ed Barrow? To have spent six years with that wonderful little fellow Miller Huggins?

Then to have spent the next nine years with that outstanding leader, that smart student of psychology, the best manager in baseball today, Joe McCarthy? Sure, I'm lucky. When the New York Giants, a team you would give your right arm to beat and vice versa, sends you a gift, that's something.

When everybody down to the groundskeepers and those boys in white coats remember you with trophies, that's something. When you have a father and mother who work all their lives so that you can have an education and build your body, it's a blessing.

When you have a wife who has been a tower of strength and shown more courage than you dreamed existed, that's the finest I know. So I close in saying that I might have had a bad break, but I have an awful lot to live for.

"Labor, like Israel, has many sorrows"

JOHN L. LEWIS

The Great Depression put tremendous pressure on the labor movement. With unemployment at 25 percent, business did not have to worry about finding workers and workers could not be picky about the jobs they secured. Union busting was an accepted practice among businesses and relatively easy to execute. Labor leaders such as John L. Lewis turned to radical measures. Unafraid to incur public wrath with strikes, and frustrated with the relatively docile American Federation for Labor, Lewis formed the Committee for Industrial Organization in 1935. The two organizations later merged.

Unlike Huey Long's call for an overturning of society, Lewis's demands were less confrontational, even if his tactics were not. As this September 3, 1937, speech shows, he sought a constructive role for labor in American life, one that did not threaten moneyed interests, but rather complemented it.

The United States Chamber of Commerce, the National Association of Manufacturers, and similar groups representing industry and financial interests are rendering a disservice to the American people in their attempts to frustrate the organization of labor and in their refusal to accept collective bargaining as one of our economic institutions.

These groups are encouraging a systematic organization under the sham pretext of local interests. They equip these vigilantes with tin hats, wooden clubs, gas masks, and lethal weapons and train them in the arts of brutality and oppression.

No tin hat brigade of goose-stepping vigilantes or bibble-babbling mob of blackguarding and corporation-paid scoundrels will prevent the onward march of labor, or divert its purpose to play its natural and rational part in the development of the economic, political, and social life of our nation.

Unionization, as opposed to communism, presupposes the relation of employment; it is based upon the wage system, and it recognizes fully and unreservedly the institution of private property and the right to investment profits. It is upon the fuller development of collective bargaining, the wider expansion of the labor movement, the increased influence of labor in our national councils, that the perpetuity of our democratic institutions must largely depend.

The organized workers of America, free in their industrial life, conscious partners or production, secure in their homes, and enjoying a decent standard of living, will prove the finest bulwark against the intrusion of alien doctrines of government.

Do those who hatched this foolish cry of communism in the CIO fear the increased influence of labor in our democracy? Do they fear its influence will be cast on the side of shorter hours, a better system of distributed employment, better homes for the underprivileged, Social Security for the aged, a fairer distribution of our national income? Certainly the workers that are being organized want a voice in the determination of these objectives of social justice.

Certainly labor wants a fairer share of the national income. Assuredly labor wants a larger participation in increased productive efficiency. Obviously the population is entitled to participate in the fruits of the genius of our men of achievement in the field of material sciences.

Labor has suffered just as our farm population has suffered from a viciously unequal distribution of the national income. In the exploitation of both classes of workers has been the source of panic and depression, and upon the economic welfare of both rests the best assurance of a sound and permanent prosperity.

Under the banner of the Committee for Industrial Organization, American labor is on the march. Its objectives today are those it had in the beginning: to strive for the unionization of our unorganized millions of workers for the acceptance of collective bargaining as a recognized American institution.

It seeks peace with the industrial world. It seeks cooperation and mutuality of effort with the agricultural population. It would avoid strikes. It would have its rights determined under the law by the peaceful negotiations and contract relationships that are supposed to characterize American commercial life.

Until an aroused public opinion demands that employers accept that rule, labor has no recourse but to surrender its rights or struggle for their realization with its own economic power.

Labor, like Israel, has many sorrows. Its women weep for their fallen, and they lament for the future of the children of the race. It ill behooves one who has supped at labor's table and who has been sheltered in labor's house to curse with equal fervor and fine impartiality both labor and its adversaries when they become locked in deadly embrace.

I repeat that labor seeks peace and guarantees its own loyalty, but the voice of labor, insistent upon its rights, should not be annoying to the ears of justice nor offensive to the conscience of the American people.

❧ *"Sit Down! Sit Down!"*

A HOW-TO GUIDE TO SIT-DOWN STRIKES

In the mid-1930s the sit-down strike swept the country as a tactic for labor unions. Increasingly harsh rhetoric and conflicts raised the stakes in the labor-ownership struggle that marked the decade. Between the autumn of 1936 and the spring of 1937, close to 500,000 workers participated in sit-down strikes. Instead of walking off the job, workers refused to leave their work stations until ownership met their demands.

Sit-down strikes gave workers several strategic advantages. Workers had the security of registering their protests from inside an industrial building instead of more vulnerable picket lines, making it easier to defend themselves and preventing the use of "scabs" as replacements for them at work. Symbolically, workers also made a statement of their interest in continuing to work and their desire to maintain the productive capacity of the factories. Workers often thought that they had even a greater interest in the property rights of the factory than the owners.

The following document comes from the League of Industrial Democracy publication that provides practical advice on how to hold a sit-down strike as well as the moral justification for them

When they tie the can to a union man,
Sit down! Sit down!

Whey they give him the sack, they'll take
 him back,
Sit down! Sit down!

Sit down, just take a seat,
Sit down, and rest your feet,
Sit down, you've got 'em beat
Sit down! Sit down!

A new strike technique has swept the country, arousing enthusiasm among workers, and bewilderment among employers. In industry after industry, in state after state, the workers remain at their posts but refuse to work. No longer is it possible to introduce strikebreakers, for the workers are in possession. Nor are the workers readily dispersed, for they can barricade themselves in a strong defensive position. If strikebreakers or police storm the factory gate, they are clearly responsible in the eyes of the public for whatever violence may occur. The employer cannot too easily afford to alienate public opinion, nor risk damage to his machinery. And so the workers remain in possession of the plant, in much more comfort and security than on the picket line....

Keeping Comfortable
Sit-downers have had a host of new problems to solve not the least of which have been living in factory buildings. Food, sleeping quarters, and sanitation are matters that must be properly attended to if morale is to be kept up and health maintained for long. The necessary work must be done, and facilities for recreation provided. In all of these respects our experience with sit-downs, brief though it has been, is illuminating.

With hundreds or perhaps several thousands of sit-downers in a plant, the problem of food becomes urgent. The union must assume responsibility for seeing that the workers receive three meals a day. This is a severe strain on the union treasury, but thus far adequate meals have been furnished. Indeed, in some strikes most of the sit-downers have gained weight. One of the most important committees in many sit-down strikes is the chiseling committee, which seeks donations from food merchants. It calls for resourcefulness when the committee is unable to obtain the food for the menu planned, and the cook must prepare whatever is brought back. The Midland Steel Products Company sit-downers in Detroit were aided by a daily donation of 30 gallons of milk by the milk drivers' union. Often the means furnished by the union are supplemented by food brought to individual strikers by their families or friends.

Usually the food is cooked in a nearby hall or restaurant, and brought in milk cans, kettles, or other large containers to the plant. In the case of the Wahl-Eversharp Pen Company of Chicago, police refused to allow friends of the strikers to bring food into the plant. The sit-downers then lowered a rope from an upper window to the roof of an adjoining bakery, and obtained food in this fashion. The menu of sit-downers is usually simple, but adequate. Barrels, kegs, and whatever else is suitable are used for chairs, and tables are likewise improvised. Newspapers sometimes serve as table-cloths. Liquor is strictly forbidden.

Usually the cooking is done by a committee of the strikers' wives. In large strikes, however, a professional cook may be obtained. The cook in the Flint strike, for example, was sent there to help by the Cooks' Union of Detroit. He had previously cooked for four other sit-down strikes. For the Flint strike the union installed new kitchen equipment worth more than $1,000.

"The food goes into the factories in twenty kettles of various sizes," the cook reported. "The amount of food the strikers use is immense. Five hundred pounds of meat, one thousand pounds of potatoes, three hundred loaves of bread, one hundred pounds of coffee, two hundred pounds of sugar, thirty gallons of fresh milk, four cases of evaporated milk!"

In Detroit a cooperative kitchen was established to feed 800 sit-down strikers in the Bohn Aluminum, Cadillac, and Fleetwood plants:

"The kitchen runs on efficient lines, not speed-up, in two shifts. About 50 men and women comprise the working crew; the first shift working from 7:00 until 2:00 in the afternoon, the second from 11:00 in the morning until 6:00 in the afternoon. Everyone attends the meetings held at 2:00 o'clock daily at I.A.S. Hall where the various committees make their reports. There is the kitchen committee, which takes care of preparing the food, with a chef from the Cooks' Union, Local No. 234, to supervise the preparation of it. Then there is a finance committee, with two treasurers, working in shifts, one from the Cadillac plant and one from the Bohn Aluminum plant."

Other important committees were the drivers' committee, which delivered the food, and the chiseling committee, which covered the city for donations of food or money. About two-thirds of the supplies were obtained in this fashion....

A Typical Set of Rules

Sit-downers must govern their community, and solve each problem as it arises. Fundamentally these problems are similar, though new situations will arise in each plant. The rules adopted by the sit-down strikers in the Standard Cotton products Company in Flint, Michigan, may be taken as fairly typical. With fewer than a hundred strikers, they were able to transact business in a full meeting held at 10 o'clock each morning, without the more complex and elaborate organization that a large plant would require. A strike committee of five members was placed in charge. Other officers included a chairman, a secretary, a judge, a press agent, and three clerks. There was a patrol committee of two, a food committee of two, a clean-up committee of three, and an entertainment committee of one.

Posted on the wall of the mess hall were the following rules, which were added to from time to time by majority vote:

Rules and Regulations

Rule No. 1. Any man who disturbs anyone while sleeping without good reason will have to wash the dishes and mop floor for one day.

Rule No. 2. Any man found drinking or looking for argument will wash dishes and mop floor for one day—first offense.

Rule No. 3. Every man who leaves must get a pass from the committee and check with the clerk. Passes must be shown to the doorman when going in and out, and on returning must check with the clerk. The doorman must obey these rules very strictly.

Rule No. 4. Doormen answer the phone and if the call is important he calls a committee man. No long distance calls shall be made. All local calls are allowed. No profane language used over the phone.

Rule No. 5. When photographers or outsiders

come in no one speaks to them but a committee man.

Rule No. 6. Everyone must line up single file before meals are served. Dishwashers will be appointed before each meal by the clean-up committee. Every man must serve his turn.

Rule No. 7. Anyone eating between meals must wash his own dishes.

Rule No. 8. Every man must attend meetings.

Rule No. 9. No standing on tables.

Rule No. 10. No passes will be issued after 12:00 pm—except emergency calls.

Rule No. 11. Judge's decision on all broken rules must be regarded as final.

Rule No. 12. No conversation about the strike to the management. Any information concerning the strike will be furnished by the committee.

Rule No. 13. No more than a two-hour grace period on a 20-minute leave.

Rule No. 14. No women allowed in the plant at any time.

Rule No. 15. No passes issued during meals and not until the dishes are done unless it is business.

Rule No. 16. All committees must attend meetings and report their activities.

Rule No. 17. No card playing or walking around or any disturbance during meetings....

The sit-down strike has served notice on society that mere ownership does not carry with it all possible rights with reference to a factory. Those who work in it, who make it produce with their labor and who depend upon it for their livelihood, should likewise have a voice in its control. Those who invest their lives in an industry have at least as much at stake as those who merely invest their money. The sit-down strike brings these facts forcibly to public attention. It is interesting to note that, in the sit-down strike, workers are re-establishing the control over the tools of production that they lost with the Industrial Revolution.

The ethical case for the sit-down strike has well been presented by Rabbi Edward L. Israel, former chairman of the Social Justice Commission of the Central conference of American Rabbis. The problem involved, Rabbi Israel asserts, is one of the comparative emphasis of human rights over against property rights. The entire struggle of the human race from bondage toward freedom, he points out

has been a constant battling against vested interests.

The argument that a worker has a property right on his job has thus been stated by Homer Martin, president of the automobile workers union:

"What more sacred property right is there in the world than the right of a man in his job? This property right involves the right to support his family, feed his children and keep starvation away from the door. This property right is the very foundation stone of American homes. It is the most sacred, most fundamental property right in America. It means more to the stabilization of American life, morally, socially and economically, than any other property right."

"They had no right to sit down there"

CHARLES STEWART MOTT

On the other side of the picket lines, ownership had a very different perspective on the rights of workers and the impact of strikes. General Motors shareholder, philanthropist, and three-time mayor of Flint, Michigan, Charles Stewart Mott shared his view of the sit-down strikes and President Roosevelt's New Deal program with historian Studs Terkel in 1970.

CSM: Alfred P. Sloan came to [General Motors] in 1932 and was made president. He was a master of corporate procedure. He brought order out of chaos. For every one share of stock in 1913, we had 562&! shares in 1935. We enlisted the help of the DuPont company. At one time, they held twenty-four percent of the stock. I don't know what we'd have done without them. Since then, it's gone up and up and up.

I never became involved in labor matters. Even in companies where I own all the stock, I leave those matters to those better able to handle it. I'm not the kind of person that worries, certainly not about something that's water over the dam. I get more pleasure out of the foundation business than anything I can think of.

At board meetings, labor matters were described but not discussed. We had a vice president in charge of labor relations, a very able chap.

He was in close contact with the directors of GM to see that he didn't cross them up—that he does things the way they approve of. We meet the first Monday of every month. Sometimes, he'd appear to tell us what the situation was. We'd merely approve.

I knew Frank Murphy. (Laughs) I don't like to speak ill of a dead man, but he certainly lacked an awful lot of things that might have been good. Frank was mayor of Detroit in the early Thirties. I remember him saying: "The water department of Detroit is in terrible shape. We supply water to contiguous communities, and they can't pay. Water companies are tough things…." Well, I own six or eight or ten, I guess, water companies. And they're the easiest things to run. I said to him, "If they take water and don't pay, all you have to do is apply to the courts and demand payment. You'd collect." He didn't understand…. He was governor during the sit-down strikes, and he didn't do his job. He didn't enforce the law. He kept his hands off. He didn't protect our property.

ST: You feel the National Guard should have evicted the sit-downers?

CSM: They had no right to sit-down there. They were illegally occupying it. The owners had the right to demand from the governor to get those people out. It wasn't done. The same as today.

Communities allow all this hoodlum stuff. It's an outrage. When you have people breaking into stores, and you have police and the National Guard with things loaded, and they don't stop those people—it's terrible. They should have said, "Stop that thing. Move on, or we'll shoot." And if they didn't, they should have been shot. They'd have killed a certain number of people, but it would have been a lot less than would have been killed afterwards. It's an absolute duplicate of the Thirties, with the sit-down strikes.

ST: What are your memories of Franklin D. Roosevelt?

CSM: Someone said to me: Did you see the picture on those new dimes? It's our new destroyer. It was a picture of Roosevelt. He was the great destroyer. He was the beginner of our downhill slide. Boy, what he did to this country. I don't think we'll ever get over it. Terrible.

ST: Do you remember seeing lines of unemployed men?

CSM: I recollect there were such things.

🐦 "Peaceable assembly for lawful discussion cannot be made a crime"

DE JONGE V. OREGON

Like several states in the 1930s, Oregon had a law that made it illegal to participate in meetings organized by groups that sought to overthrow the government. In 1937, Dirk De Jonge was found guilty by an Oregon court for taking part in a meeting of the Communist Party. The Supreme Court, however, reversed the decision, stating that the law represented an infringement on freedom of speech.

The decisions contrasted with Roosevelt's accusations that the Supreme Court was too conservative. Throughout Roosevelt's first two terms, the Supreme Court overturned much of the New Deal legislation saying it was unconstitutional. Infuriated, Roosevelt attempted to increase the number of justices on the court to fifteen so that he could create a majority that would rule in his favor. The effort failed.

Appellant, Dirk De Jonge, was indicted in Multnomah County, Oregon, for violation of the Criminal Syndication Law of that State. The Act…defines "criminal syndication" as the "the doctrine which advocates crime, physical violence, sabotage or any unlawful acts or methods as a means of accomplishing or effecting industrial or political change or revolution."…

The charge is that appellant assisted in the conduct of a meeting which was called under the auspices of the Communist Party, an organization advocating criminal syndicalism….

The stipulation set forth various extracts from the literature of the Communist Party to show its advocacy of criminal syndicalism. The stipulation does not disclose any activity by the defendant as a basis for his prosecution other than his participation in the meeting in question. Nor does the stipulation show that the Communist literature distributed at the meeting contained any advocacy of criminal syndicalism or of any unlawful conduct….

The broad reach of the statute as thus applied is plain. While defendant was a member of the Communist Party, that membership was not necessary to conviction on such a charge. A like fate might have attended any speaker, although not a member, who "assisted in the conduct" of the meeting. However innocuous the object of the meeting, however lawful the subjects and tenor of the addresses, however reasonable and timely the discussion, all those assisting in the conduct of the meeting would be subject to imprisonment as felons if the meeting were held by the Communist Party.... Thus if the Communist Party had called a public meeting in Portland against the tariff, or the foreign policy of the Government, or taxation, or relief, or candidacies for the offices of President, members of Congress, Governor or State legislators, every speaker who assisted in the conduct of the meeting would be equally guilty with the defendant in this case, upon the charge as here defined and sustained. The list of illustrations might be indefinitely extended to every variety of meetings under the auspices of the Communist Party although held for the discussion of political issues or to adopt protests and pass resolutions of an entirely innocent and proper character.

While the States are entitled to protect themselves from the abuse of privileges of our institutions through an attempted substitution of force and violence in the place of peaceful political action in order to effect revolutionary changes in government, none of our decisions go to the length of sustaining such curtailment of the right of free speech and assembly as the Oregon statute demands in its present application....

Freedom of speech and of the press are fundamental rights which are safeguarded by the due process clause of the Fourteenth Amendment of the Federal Constitution.... The right of peaceable assembly is a right cognate to those of free speech and free press and is equally fundamental. As this court said in United States v. Cruikshank, "The very idea of a government, republican in form, implies a right on the part of its citizens to meet peaceably for consultation in respect to public affairs and to petition for a redress of grievances." The First Amendment of the Federal Constitution expressly guarantees that right against abridgment by Congress. But explicit mention there does not argue exclusion elsewhere. For the right is one that cannot be denied without violating those fundamental principles of liberty and justice which lie at the base of all civil and political institutions—principles which the Fourteenth Amendment embodies in the general term of its due process clause.

These rights may be abused by using speech or press or assembly in order to incite violence and crime. The people through their legislatures may protect themselves against that abuse. But the legislative intervention can find constitutional justification only by dealing with the abuse. The rights themselves must not be curtailed. The greater the importance of safeguarding the community from incitement to the overthrow of our institutions by force and violence, the more imperative is the need to preserve inviolate the constitutional rights of free speech, free press and free assembly in order to maintain the opportunity for free political discussion, to the end that government may be responsive to the will of the people and that changes, if desired, may be obtained by peaceful means. Therein lies the security of the Republic, the very foundation of constitutional government.

It follows from these considerations that, consistently with the Federal Constitution, peaceable assembly for lawful discussion cannot be made a crime. The holding of meetings for peaceable political action cannot be proscribed. Those who assist in the conduct of such meetings cannot be branded as criminals on that score. The question, if the rights of free speech and peaceable assembly are to be preserved, is not as to the auspices under which the meeting is held but as to its purpose; not as to the relations of the speakers, but whether their utterances transcend the bounds of the freedom of speech which the Constitution protects. If the persons assembling have committed crimes elsewhere, if they have formed or are engaged in a conspiracy against the public peace and order, they may be prosecuted for their conspiracy or other violation of valid laws. But it is a different matter when the State, instead of prosecuting them for such offenses seizes upon mere participation in a peaceable assembly and a lawful public discussion as the basis for a criminal charge.

We hold that the Oregon statute as applied to the particular charge as defined by the state court is repugnant to the due process clause of the Fourteenth Amendment.

❧ "Pioneers in the industry"

DAVID PACKARD

In the 1930s, the foundation's of the fantastically successful "Silicon Valley" were laid as a cluster of Stanford University engineering students started to apply their education to practical industrial purposes.

David Packard was one of Engineering Professor Fred Terman's students. Initially, Packard moved to the East Coast after graduation, but soon after, Terman talked Packard into returning to California to start a company with fellow student Bill Hewlett. The two formed Hewlett-Packard, now a multibillion corporation. The garage in which they started is considered the birthplace of Silicon Valley.

Largely because of [Fred] Terman's classes, the four of us—Hewlett, [Ed] Porter, [Barney] Oliver, and I—became fast friends. It is not a coincidence that a few years later this group would become the management team of Hewlett-Packard.

Fred Terman's keen interest in radio engineering induced him to become acquainted with almost all of the pioneers in the industry, many of whom were located in the Palo Alto area. Early wireless work by Stanford graduate Cyril F. Elwell was organized into the Federal Telegraph Company at the beginning of the century. Lee De Forest invented the vacuum tube in Palo Alto in 1908, and Fritz Kolster developed the radio direction finder in the 1920s.

I remember Terman saying something like: "Well, as you can see, most of these successful radio firms were built by people without much education," adding that business opportunities were even greater for someone with a sound theoretical background in the field. That got us thinking, and in our senior year, with Terman's encouragement, Bill Hewlett, Ed Porter, Barney Oliver, and I were making tentative plans to try to do something on our own after graduation. [Two years later] I got together with Bill Hewlett, and at that time we had our first "official" business meeting. The minutes of the meeting, dated August 23, 1937, are headed "tentative organization plans and a tentative work program for a proposed business venture."

During those months Fred Terman had been thinking about how Bill and I might proceed, and in the summer of 1938 he arranged a Stanford fellowship for me. It carried a stipend of $500 a year,

but more important, it reunited me with Hewlett.

My bosses at GE gave me their blessing and an unpaid leave of absence, and in August Lu [Lucille Packard] and I drove back to California with a used Sears Roebuck drill press in the rumble seat. It would be HP's first piece of equipment....

Terman had arranged for me to do the laboratory work on the Varian research project up at Charlie Litton's place, Litton Engineering Laboratories, in Redwood City. He had also arranged for me to get credit for my work at GE so that I could get my EE degree from Stanford with just one year of residence....

Most important, Hewlett was back in town as well. During the interim, he had obtained his master's degree from MIT and upon graduation had exactly one job offer, with Jensen Speaker in Chicago. But Terman came through for him too, putting Bill together with a San Francisco doctor who was interested in developing some medical equipment.

Now that Bill and I were back together, we started putting our plans to work. Bill had found a two-story house on Addison Avenue in Palo Alto, and Lu and I rented the lower floor. Bill, who at the time was still a bachelor, lived in a little building out back. There was also a one-car garage, and that became our workshop.

That garage has been declared a California Historical Landmark. Terman used to say that he knew when HP had orders, because the cars had been moved to the driveway so Hewlett and Packard could work.

Terman became chairman of Stanford's engineering school, and eventually dean of the entire university. He continued to create close ties between the university and industry, long before schools back east accepted the notion of mixing academics with business. Many of the most successful companies of today's Silicon Valley are descendants of firms founded by Terman's proteges.

And here's an interesting footnote: Terman really wanted to live in Massachusetts. Although he was the son of a Stanford professor, he had earned his Ph.D. at MIT because, he said, "a serious young engineer had to go back east." Then a severe illness prevented him from taking a teaching position at MIT, and during a long convalescence back home, he began to teach at Stanford instead.

"The city is the great playground and the great battleground of the Nation"

REPORTS OF THE URBANISM COMMITTEE OF THE NATIONAL RESOURCES COMMITTEE

The devastating impact of the Depression on cities forced the federal government to re-examine the increasingly important role urban communities played in the United States. To that end, Congress appointed the Urbanism Committee of the National Resources Committee to explore the "New View of the City" and make recommendations on how the federal government can play a more constructive role.

The committee discovered that cities held more than half the nation's population and presented some of the most vexing problems, but also the most promising opportunities. The rapid growth of cities was shocking; in less than 150 years, the number of cities in the country had increased 150-fold.

The committee's report marked a starting point of new federal policies aimed at assisting in the improvement of urban development, supporting slum clearance programs in an organized fashion and experimenting with the creation of "greenbelt towns" on the outskirts of cities.

A New View of the City

The city has seemed at times the despair of America, but at others to be the Nation's hope, the battleground of democracy. Surely in the long run, the Nation's destiny will be profoundly affected by the cities which have two-thirds of its population and its wealth. There is liberty of developments in isolation and wide spaces, but there is also freedom in the many-sided life of the city where each may find his own kind. There is democracy in the scattered few, but there is also democracy in the thick crowd with its vital impulse and its insistent demand for a just participation in the gains of our civilization. There is fertility and creation in the rich soil of the broad countryside, but there is also fertility and creativeness in forms of industry, art, personality, emerging even from the city streets and reaching toward the sky.

The faults of our cities are not those of decadence and impending decline, but of exuberant vitality crowding its way forward under tremendous pressure—the flood rather than the drought. The city is both the great playground and the great battleground of the Nation—at once the vibrant center of a world of hectic amusement lovers and also the dusty and sometimes smoldering and reddened area of industrial conflict. It is the cities that must meander the ambiguous and shifting boundaries between recreation and vice, not only for their own citizens but for some of their visitors as well. It is the cities that must deal with the tragic border lines of order and justice in bitter industrial struggles. On these two problems alone many a "good government" has been wrecked.

Urban Trends Examined

1. There has been a distinct shift in the Nation's status from a predominantly rural to an urban people, a development so swift as to be without precedent in the history of the world. The number of cities or urban places in the United States has increased from a mere half dozen in 1790 to 3,165 in 1930. The nation's urban population has risen from only 3 percent of the total population in 1790, 7 percent in 1830, 26 percent in 1880 to 56 percent in 1930. The family has grown smaller and the older-age group larger. American cities instead of maintaining a birth rate sufficient to reproduce themselves must recruit from the country. The conditions of rural life today are therefore the preconditions of urban living tomorrow. Low standards of rural life are of concern not merely to our agricultural regions but to our cities as well and to the Nation as a whole. Unless steps are taken to avert it, farm tenancy and sharecropping, now the lot of one-half of our rural inhabitants, will set up a dependent economic class suffering from the same type of economic disfranchisement suffered by the city artisan when the factory first succeeded the household unit of production and when the machine supplanted the hand tool.

2. The unprecedented mobility arising from the harnessing of steam, electricity, and the internal-combustion engine to men and materials is responsible for this phenomenal urban development. Swifter forms of urban and interurban transportation have further led to suburban migration and caused the emergence of metropolitan districts instead of individual cities as the actual areas of urban life. In 1930 almost one-half of the Nation's population—that is, 54,753,000 persons or 45 per-

cent of the total—resided in the 96 metropolitan districts with at least 100,000 inhabitants each. These 96 metropolitan districts contained within their large central cities 37,814,000 urbanites; while 17,000,000 of our people have become suburbanites.

3. Urbanization and suburbanization have meant not only a concentration of the Nation's population, but a centralization of enterprise in the Nation's cities, metropolitan districts, urban satellites, and industrial areas. Of more than 3,000 counties of the country, the 155 which contain the larger industrial cities embraced, in the year 1929, 74 percent of all industrial wage earners, 81 percent of all salaried employees, 79 percent of all wages paid, 83 percent of all salaries paid, 65 percent of all the industrial establishments and 80 percent of the value added to manufactured products. Forty percent of all the mail in the country originates in the 12 largest metropolitan cities. The states containing the 11 largest cities in the country accounted for over half of the total wholesale trade, while the 93 cities over 100,000 reported three-fourths of the total.

4. These preponderantly urban activities vitally affect the life and livelihood of the Nation, and it is inevitable that urban institutions, associations, and instruments of social guidance should grow up in an attempt to facilitate and regulate urban life, if only to keep the seething millions from trampling one another down in the workaday urban world. Taking government alone as one of those instruments of urban society, we find that while the number of cities has doubled and the size of our urban population has trebled since 1890, the budgets and pay rolls of urban governments have increased at an even faster rate, with expenditures trebling since the year 1915. Today, urban governments, in performing the essential public services without which our cities could not continue to exist, employ 1 million persons who constitute one-third of all the public employees. They spent, in 1932, 4 billion dollars annually, which was one-third of all the governmental expenditures in the country and about one-twelfth of the total national income. In like measure the States and also the Federal Government have engaged in public activities dealing with urban problems. In Washington some 70 Federal agencies, bureaus, and divisions are now engaged in various urban services. The Federal Government has offi-

cially recognized its responsibility in the field of urban problems by causing to be made the present survey on the role of the urban community in the national economy.

🍂 *"The South represents right now the Nation's No. 1 problem"*

THE ECONOMIC CONDITIONS OF THE SOUTH

Seventy years after the Civil War, the South's economy was still woefully behind the rest of the country. Poverty, poor education, mismanagement, and widespread economic plight plagued the region. In 1938, the National Emergency Council completed *The Report on The Economic Conditions of the South* and found them badly wanting.

"It is my conviction," wrote President Roosevelt, "that the South represents right now the Nation's No. 1 economic problem." The report criticized many of the management practices employed in the South and highlighted the absence of policies designed to remedy numerous problems—needless to say, it was not very well-received by southerners.

Section 2
Soil

Nature gave the South good soil. With less than a third of the Nations' area, the South contains more than a third of the Nation's good farming acreage. It has two-thirds of all the land in America receiving a 40-inch annual rainfall or better. It has nearly half of the land on which crops can grow for 6 months without danger of frost.

This heritage has been sadly exploited. Sixty-one percent of all the Nation's land badly damaged by erosion is in the Southern States. An expanse of southern farm land as large as South Carolina has been gullied and washed away; at least 22 million acres of once fertile soil has been ruined beyond repair. Another area the size of Oklahoma and Alabama combined has been seriously damaged by erosion. In addition, the sterile sand and gravel washed off this land has covered over a fertile valley acreage equal in size to Maryland.

There are a number of reasons for this wastage:

Much of the South's land originally was so fertile that it produced crops for many years no matter how carelessly it was farmed. For generations thousands of southern farmers plowed their furrows up and down the slopes, so that each furrow served as a ditch to hasten the run-off of silt-laden water after every train. While many farmers have now learned the importance of terracing their land or plowing it on the contours, thousands still follow the destructive practices of the past.

Half of the South's farmers are tenants, many of whom have little interest in preserving soil they do not own.

The South's chief crops are cotton, tobacco, and corn; all of these are inter-tilled crops—the soil is plowed between the rows, so that it is left loose and bare of vegetation.

The top-soil washes away much more swiftly than from land planted to cover crops, such as clover, soybeans, and small grains. Moreover, cotton, tobacco, and corn leave few stalks and leaves to be plowed under in the fall; and as a result the soil constantly loses its humus and its capacity to absorb rainfall.

Even after harvest, southern land is seldom planted to cover crops which would protect it from the winter rains. This increases erosion tenfold.

Southeastern farms are the smallest in the Nation. The operating units average only 71 acres, and nearly one-fourth of them are smaller than 20 acres. A farmer with so little land is forced to plant every foot of it in cash crops; he cannot spare an acre for soil restoring crops or pasture. Under the customary tenancy system, moreover, he has every incentive to plant all his land to crops which will bring in the largest possible immediate cash return. The landlord often encourages him in this destructive practice of cash-cropping.

Training in better agricultural methods, such as planting soil-restoring crops, terracing, contour-plowing, and rotation, has been spreading, but such training is still unavailable to most southern farmers. Annually the South spends considerably more money for fertilizer than for agricultural training through its land-grant colleges, experiment stations, and extension workers.

Forests are one of the best protections against erosion. Their foliage breaks the force of the rain; their roots bind the soil so that it cannot wash away; their fallen leaves form a blanket of vegetable cover which soaks up the water and checks run-off. Yet the South has cut away a large part of its forest, leaving acres of gullied, useless soil. There

has been comparatively little effort at systematic reforestation. Overgrazing, too, has resulted in serious erosion throughout the Southwest.

There is a close relationship between this erosion and floods, which recently have been causing a loss to the Nation estimated at about $35,000,000 annually. Rainfall runs off uncovered land much more rapidly than it does from land planted to cover crops or forest. Recent studies indicate that a single acre of typical corn land lost approximately 127,000 more gallons of rainfall in a single year than a similar field planted to grass. Another experiment showed that land sodded in grass lost less than 1 percent of a heavy rain through immediate run-off, while nearby land planted to cotton lost 31 percent. In short, unprotected land not only is in danger of destruction; it also adds materially to the destructive power of the swollen streams into which it drains.

These factors—each one reinforcing all the others—are causing an unparalleled wastage of the South's most valuable asset, its soil. They are steadily cutting down its agricultural income, and steadily adding to its cost of production as compared with other areas of the world which raise the same crops.

For example, it takes quantities of fertilizer to make worn-out, eroded land produce. The South, with only one-fifth of the Nation's income, pays three-fifths of the Nation's fertilizer bill. In 1929 it bought 5 1/2 million tons of commercial fertilizer at a cost of $161,000,000. And although fertilizer performs a valuable and necessary service, it does not restore the soil. For a year or two it may nourish a crop, but the land still produces meagerly and at high cost.

Moreover, southern farmers cannot pile on fertilizer fast enough to put back the essential minerals which are washing out of their land. Each year, about 27,5000,000 tons of nitrogen and phosphorous compounds are leached out of southern soil and send down the rivers to the sea.

The South is losing more than $300,000,000 worth of fertile topsoil through erosion every year. This is not merely a loss of income—it is a loss of irreplaceable capital.

Section 7
Health
For years evidence has been piling up that food, clothing, and housing influence not only the sick-

ness rate and death rate but even the height and weight of school children. In the South, where family incomes are exceptionally low, the sickness and death rates are unusually high. Wage differentials become in fact differentials in health and life; poor health in turn, affects wages.

The low-income belt of the South is a belt of sickness, misery and unnecessary death. Its large proportion of low-income citizens are more subject to disease than the people of any similar area. The climate cannot be blamed—the South is as healthful as any section for those who have the necessary care, diet, and freedom from occupational disease.

Several years ago the United States Public Heath Service conducted syphilis-control demonstrations in selected rural areas in the South. These studies revealed a much higher ratio of syphilis among Negroes than among whites, but showed further than this higher ratio was not due to physical differences between races. It was found to be due to the greater poverty and lower living conditions of the Negroes. Similar studies of such diseases have shown that individuals health cannot be separated from the health of the community as a whole.

The presence of malaria, which infects annually more than 2,000,000 people, is estimated to have reduced the industrial output of the South one-third. One of the most striking examples of the effect of malaria on industry was revealed by the Public Health Service in studies among employees of a cotton mill in eastern North Carolina. Previous to the attempts to control malaria, the records of the mill one month showed 66 looms were idle as a result of ill-health. After completion of control work, no looms were idle for that reason. Before control work, 238,046 pounds of cloth were manufactured in one month. After completion of the work production rose to 316,804 pounds in one month—an increase of 33 1/3 percent.

In reports obtained in 1935 from 9 lumber companies, owning 14 sawmill villages in 5 southern States, there was agreement that malaria was an important and increasing problem among the employees. During the year 7.6 percent of hospital admissions, 16.4 percent of physician calls, and 19.7 percent of dispensary drugs were for malaria. The average number of days off duty per case of malaria was 9, while days in the hospital for the same cause were 5. Ten railroads in the South listed

malaria as an economic problem and a costly liability. Four utility companies had full-time mosquito-fighting crews at work during the year. The average case admitted to a company hospital lasted 3 days and the average number of days off duty because of malaria was 11. Each case of malaria was said to cost the companies $40.

It we attempt to place a monetary value on malaria by accepting the figure of $10,000 as the value of an average life and using the death rate of 3.943 for malaria reported by the census for 1936, the annual cost of deaths from this disease is $39,500,000. To this figure could be added the cost of illness, including days of work lost.

The health-protection facilities of the South are limited. For example, there are only one-third as many doctors per capita in South Carolina as there are in California. The South is deficient in hospitals and clinics, as well as in health workers. Many counties have no facilities at all.

The South has only begun to look into its pressing industrial hygiene problems, although it has 26 percent of the male mine workers in the United States and 14 percent of the male factory workers. These are the workers with which modern industrial health protection is most concerned.

The experience as to pneumonia and tuberculosis among employees of the Tennessee Coal, Iron & Railroad Co. and their dependents during the 11-year period from 1925 to 1935 gives an indication of health conditions among miners in the South. The situation generally is probably worse than shown by the figures for this company, whose workers have relatively better protection against disease. For this period the number under observation averaged slightly more than 77,000 persons. These were 3,780 cases of pneumonia, of which 739 terminated fatally. This resulted in an average frequency per 1,000 of approximately 4.9 pneumonia cases per year among surface workers, 4.7 among coal miners, and 10.6 among ore miners. The rate of 4.2 for dependents included also the pneumonia of childhood and infancy. A fatality rate of 30.7 deaths per 1,000 cases of pneumonia was found among surface workers, a rate of 26.8 among coal miners, and 24.8 among ore miners. Death from tuberculosis occurred at an annual rate of 1.467 per thousand workers among coal miners, 1.232 among ore miners and 0.566 among surface workers.

Prior to 1936 only one State in the South gave consideration to industrial hygiene. Today, with the aid of Social Security funds, seven additional States have industrial-hygiene units, and approximately 7,000,000 of the 10,000,000 gainful workers are receiving some type of industrial-hygiene service. However, these industrial-hygiene units have started their programs only recently, and it will be some time before adequate health services will be available. The funds now being spent for this activity in the eight States which have industrial-hygiene services do not meet the problem of protecting and improving the health of these workers. Approximately $100,000 is now being budgeted for this work, although it is known that the economic loss due to industrial injuries and illnesses among these workers is hundreds of millions of dollars.

Reports of one of the largest life-insurance companies show that more people in the southern area than elsewhere die without medical aid. The same company reported in a recent year a rise of 7.3 percent in the death rate in the nine South Atlantic States, though in no other region had the death rate risen above 4.8 percent, and in some sections it had declined.

The scourge of pellagra, that affects the South almost exclusively, is a disease chiefly due to inadequate diet; it responds to rather simple preventive measures, including suitable nourishing food. Even in southern cities from 60 to 88 percent of the families of low incomes are spending for food less than enough to purchase an adequate diet.

❧ *"All of us are descendents from immigrants and revolutionists"*

FRANKLIN D. ROOSEVELT

The day before President Roosevelt delivered this address to the Daughters of the American Revolution, the organization had condemned Roosevelt's New Deal legislation but commended its expansion of the navy. The DAR was a conservative lot, marked by affluence and an Anglo-Saxon heritage. Roosevelt, who shared the same heritage and income level, was considered a traitor to his class. The New Deal represented a revolutionary step to assist the poor—a group consisting mainly of minorities and recent immigrants. Resentment between classes was rampant; the rich looked down on the massses, while the poor were disgusted by the excesses of the wealthy. Here Roosevelt gently reminds his audience of their common bind with all Americans, rich or poor, immigrants or not.

I couldn't let a fifth year go by without coming to see you. I must ask you to take me just as I am, in a business suit—and I see you are still in favor of national defense—take me as I am, with no prepared remarks. You know, as a matter of fact, I would have been here to one of your conventions in prior years—one or more—but it is not the time that it takes to come before you and speak for half an hour, it is the preparation for that half hour. And I suppose that for every half-hour speech that I make before a convention or over the radio, I put in ten hours preparing it.

So I have to ask you to bear with me, to let me just come here without preparation to tell you how glad I am to avail myself of this opportunity, to tell you how proud I am, as a revolutionary descendant, to greet you.

I thought of preaching on a text, but I shall not. I shall only give you the text, and I shall not preach on it. I think I can afford to give you the text because it so happens, through no fault of my own, that I am descended from a number of people who came over in the Mayflower. More than that, every one of my ancestors on both sides—and when you go back four generations or five generations it means thirty-two or sixty-four of them— every single one of them, without exception, was in this land in 1776. And there was only one Tory among them.

The text is this: remember, remember always that all of us, and you and I especially, are descended from immigrants and revolutionists.

I am particularly glad to know that today you are making this fine appeal to the youth of America. To these rising generations, to our sons and grandsons and great-grandsons, we cannot overestimate the importance of what we are doing in this year, in our own generation, to keep alive the spirit of American democracy. The spirit of opportunity is the kind of spirit that has led us as a nation—not as a small group but as a nation—to meet the very great problems of the past.

We look for a younger generation that is going to be more American than we are. We are doing the best that we can, and yet we can do better than that, we can do more than that, by inculating in the boys and girls of this country today some of the underlying fundamentals, the reasons that brought our immigrant ancestors to this country, the reasons that impelled our revolutionary ancestors to throw off a fascist yoke.

We have a great many things to do. Among other things in this world is the need of being very, very certain, no matter what happens, that the sovereignty of the United States will never be impaired.

There have been former occasions, conventions of the Daughters of the American Revolution, when voices were raised, needed to be raised, for better national defense. This year, you are raising those same voices and I am glad of it. But I am glad also that the government of the United States can assure you today that it is taking definite, practical steps for the defense of the nation.

🍂 The Neutrality Act of 1937

CONGRESS

Although Roosevelt was growing increasingly concerned about the rise of Adolf Hitler and his Fascist Party in Germany, the Isolationist movement in the United States was a powerful counterweight to any initiative the President might take to react. Although the national economy had made some improvements during Roosevelt's first term, the economy took a new downward turn in 1937.

Domestic policy would have to remain on the forefront and Roosevelt was compelled to compromise his international tendencies to perpetuate support for the New Deal. When the Spanish Civil War erupted and the prospects of another European war were increasing, Congress passed The Neutrality Act of 1937, forbidding almost any involvement with a nation at war. Isolationists did not want to let the country fall into the same situation it did in 1917, when its business ties to the Allies helped draw the United States into World War I.

Two years after this act, when Germany invaded Poland and ignited World War II, some of the provisions were relaxed in The Neutrality Act of 1939.

Export of Arms, Ammunition, and Implements of War

Section 1. (a) Whenever the President shall find

that there exists a state of war between, or among, two or more foreign states, the President shall proclaim such fact, and it shall thereafter be unlawful to export, or attempt to export, or cause to be exported, arms, ammunition, or implements of war from any place in the United States to any belligerent state named in such proclamation, or to any neutral state for transshipment to, or for the use of, any such belligerent state.

The President shall, from time to time, by proclamation, extend such embargo upon the export of arms, ammunition, or implements of war to other states as and when they may become involved in such war.

Whenever the President shall find that a state of civil strife exists in a foreign state and that such civil strife is of a magnitude or is being conducted under such conditions that the export of arms, ammunition, or implements of war from the United States to such foreign state would threaten or endanger the peace of the United States, the President shall proclaim such fact, and it shall thereafter be unlawful to export, or attempt to export, or cause to be exported, arms, ammunition, or implements of war from any place in the United States to such foreign state, or to any neutral state for transshipment to, or for the use of, such foreign state.

The President shall, from time to time by proclamation, definitely enumerate the arms, ammunition, and implements of war, the export of which is prohibited by the section. The arms, ammunition, and implements of war so enumerated shall include these enumerated in the President's proclamation Numbered 2163, of April 10, 1936, but shall not include raw materials or any other articles or materials not of the same general character as those enumerated in the said proclamation, and in the Convention for the Supervision of the International Trade in Arms and Ammunition and in Implements of War, signed at Geneva June 17, 1925.

Whoever, in violation of any of the provisions of this Act, shall export, or attempt to export, or cause to be exported, arms, ammunition, or implements of war from the United States shall be fined not more than $10,000, or imprisoned not more than five years, or both.

In the case of the forfeiture of any arms, ammunition, or implements of war by reason of a violation of this Act such arms, ammunition, or implements of war shall be delivered to the Secretary of War for such use or disposal thereof as shall be approved by the President of the United States.

Financial Transactions

Section 3. (a) Whenever the President shall have issued a proclamation under the authority of section 1 of this Act, it shall thereafter be unlawful for any person within the United States to purchase, sell, or exchange bonds, securities, or other obligations of the government of any belligerent state or of any state wherein civil strife exists, named in such proclamation, or of any political subdivision of any such state, or of any person acting for or on behalf of the government of any such state, or of any faction or asserted government within any such state wherein civil strife exists, or of any person acting for or on behalf of any faction or asserted government within any such state wherein civil strife exists, issued after the date of such proclamation, or to make any loan or extend any credit to any such government, or person, or to solicit or receive any contribution for any such government, political subdivision, faction, asserted government, or person: Provided, That if the President shall find that such action will serve to protect the commercial or other interests of the United States or its citizens, he may, in his discretion, and to such extent and under such regulations as he may prescribe, except from the operation of this section ordinary commercial credits and short-time obligations in aid of legal transactions and of a character customarily used in normal peacetime commercial transactions. Nothing in this subsection shall be construed to prohibit the solicitation or collection of funds to be used for medical aid and assistance, or for food and clothing to relieve human suffering, when such solicitation or collection of funds is made on behalf of and for use by any person or organization which is not acting for or on behalf of any such government, political subdivision, faction, or asserted government, but all such solicitations and collections of funds shall be subject to the approval of the President and shall be made under such rules and regulations as he shall prescribe

Whoever shall violate the provisions of this section or of any regulations issued hereunder shall, upon conviction thereof, be fined not more than $50,000 or imprisoned for not more than five years, or both. Should the violation be by a corporation, organization, or association, each officer or agent thereof participating in the violation may be liable to the penalty herein prescribed.

Exceptions — American Republics

Section 4. This Act shall not apply to an American republic or republics engaged in war against a non-American state or states, provided the American republic is not cooperating with a non-American state or states in such war.

National Munitions Control Board

Section 5. (a) There is hereby established a National Munitions Control Board (hereinafter referred to as the 'Board') to carry out the provisions of this Act. The Board shall consist of the Secretary of State, who shall be chairman and executive officer of the Board, the Secretary of the Treasury, the Secretary of War, the Secretary of the Navy, and the Secretary of Commerce. Except as otherwise provided in this Act, or by other law, the administration of this Act is vested in the Department of State. The Secretary of State shall promulgate such rules and regulations with regard to the enforcement of this section as he may deem necessary to carry out its provisions. The Board shall be convened by the chairman and shall hold at least one meeting a year.

Every person who engages in the business of manufacturing, exporting or importing any of the arms, ammunition, or implements of war referred to in this Act, whether as an exporter, importer, manufacturer, or dealer, shall register with the Secretary of State his name or business name, principal place of business, and places of business in the United States, and a list of the arms, ammunition, and implements of war which he manufactures, imports or exports.

Every person required to register under this section shall notify the Secretary of State of any change in the arms, ammunition, or implements of war which he exports, imports, or manufactures;

It shall be unlawful for any person to export, or attempt to export, from the United States to any other state, any of the arms, ammunition, or implements of war referred to in this Act, or to import, or attempt to import to the United States from any other state, any of the arms, ammunition, or implements of war referred to in this Act, without first having obtained a license therefor e.

The President is hereby authorized to proclaim upon recommendation of the Board from time to time a list of articles which shall be considered arms, ammunition, and implements of war for the purposes of this section.

American Vessels Prohibited from Carrying Arms to Belligerent States

Section 6. (a) Whenever the President shall have issued a proclamation under the authority of section 1 of this Act, it shall thereafter be unlawful, until such proclamation is revoked, for any American vessel to carry any arms, ammunition, or implements of war to any belligerent state, or to any state wherein civil strife exists, named in such proclamation, or to any neutral state for transshipment to, or for the use of, any such belligerent state or any such state wherein civil strife exists.

Whoever, in violations of the provisions of this section, shall take, or attempt to take, or shall authorize, hire, or solicit another to take, any American vessel carrying such cargo out of port or from the jurisdiction of the United States shall be fined not more than $10,000, or imprisoned not more than five years, or both; and, in addition, such vessel, and her tackle, apparel, furniture, and equipment, and the arms, ammunition, and implements of war on board, shall be forfeited to the United States.

Use of American Ports as Base of Supply
Section 7. (a) Whenever, during any war in which the United States is neutral, the President, or any person thereunto authorized by him, shall have cause to believe that any vessel, domestic or foreign, whether requiring clearance or not, is about to carry out of a port of the United States, fuel, men, arms, ammunition, implements of war or other supplies to any warship, tender, or supply ship of a belligerent state, but the evidence is not deemed sufficient to justify forbidding the departure of the vessel as provided for by section 1, title V, chapter 30, of the Act approved June 15, 1917, and if, in the President's judgment, such action will serve to maintain peace between the United States and foreign states, or to protect the commercial interests of the United States and its citizens, or to promote the security of neutrality of the United States, he shall have the power and it shall be his

duty to require the owner, master, or person in command thereof, before departing from a port of the United States, to give a bond to the United States, with sufficient sureties, in such amount as he shall deem proper, conditioned that the vessel will not deliver the men, or any part of the cargo, to any warship, tender, or supply ship of a belligerent state.

If the President, or any person thereunto authorized by him, shall find that a vessel, domestic or foreign, in a port of the United States, has previously cleared from a port of the United States during such war and delivered its cargo or any part thereof to a warship, tender, or supply ship of a belligerent state, he may prohibit the departure of such vessel during the duration of the war.

Submarines and Armed Merchant Vessels

Section 8. Whenever, during any war in which the United States is neutral, the President shall find that special restrictions placed on the use of the ports and territorial waters of the United States by the submarines or armed merchant vessels of a foreign state, will serve to maintain peace between the United States and foreign states, or to protect the commercial interests of the United States and its citizens, or to promote the security of the United States, and shall make proclamation therefore, it shall thereafter be unlawful for any such submarine or armed merchant vessel to enter a port or the territorial waters of the United States or to depart therefrom, except under such conditions and subject to such limitations as the President may prescribe. Whenever, in his judgment, the conditions which have caused him to issue his proclamation have ceased to exist, he shall revoke his proclamation and the provisions of this section shall thereupon cease to apply.

Travel on Vessels of Belligerent States

Section 9. Whenever the President shall have issued a proclamation under the authority of section 1 of this Act it shall thereafter be unlawful for any citizen of the United States to travel on any vessel of the state or states named in such proclamation, except in accordance with such rules and regulations as the President shall prescribe....

Arming of American Merchant Vessels Prohibited

Section 10. Whenever the President shall have issued a proclamation under the authority of section 1, it shall thereafter be unlawful, until such proclamation is revoked, for any American vessel engaged in commerce with any belligerent state, or any state wherein civil strife exists, named in such proclamation, to be armed or to carry any armament, arms, ammunition, or implements of war, except small arms and ammunition therefor which the President may deem necessary and shall publicly designate for the preservation of discipline aboard such vessels.

"Extremely powerful bombs may thus be constructed"

ALBERT EINSTEIN

Europe was on the verge of world war in the summer of 1939. Earlier in the year, German scientists had conducted experiments on uranium splitting atoms. The announcement of the results startled the refugee community of Jewish European scientists who had been living and working in the United States, England and Sweden, including Albert Einstein. Not only were they aware of the potential of splitting atoms as a military weapon, they were alarmed that Nazi Germany might be conducting experiments to achieve that same goal.

On August 2, 1939, encouraged by his scientific colleagues, Einstein drafted a letter to President Roosevelt to alert him to these events and express the magnitude of their importance. Although Einstein did not know Roosevelt, an acquaintance of his did. Lehman Brother economist Alexander Sachs hand delivered the letter to the president on October 11, six weeks after the war had started.

The letter set in motion a series of events which led to the start of the Manhattan Project, a massive secret undertaking to produced the first atom bomb in the southwestern U.S. desert. Ironically, although German science unveiled the potential for atomic weapons, Hitler did not fully grasp the potential of splitting atoms and placed a higher priority on the development of other technologies, such as that rocketry and jets.

Sir,

Some recent work by E. Fermi and L. Szilard, which has been communicated to me in manuscript, leads me to expect that the element uranium may be turned into a new and important source of energy in the immediate future. Certain aspects of the situation which has arisen seem to call for watchfulness and, if necessary, quick action on the part of the administration. I believe, therefore, that it is my duty to bring to your attention the following facts and recommendations.

In the course of the last four months it has been made probable—through the work of Joliot in France as well as Fermi and Szilard in America—that it may become possible to set up a nuclear chain reaction in a large mass of uranium, by which vast amounts of power and large quantities of new radium-like elements would be generated. Now it appears almost certain that this could be achieved in the immediate future.

This new phenomenon would also lead to the construction of bombs, and it is conceivable—though much less certain—that extremely powerful bombs of a new type may thus be constructed. A single bomb of this type, carried by boat and exploded in a port, might very well destroy the whole port together with some of the surrounding territory. However, such bombs might very well prove to be too heavy for transportation by air.

The United States has only very poor ores of uranium in moderate quantities. There is some good ore in Canada and the former Czechoslovakia, while the most important source of uranium is Belgian Congo.

In view of this situation you may think it desirable to have some permanent contact maintained between the administration and the group of physicists working on chain reactions in America. One possible way of achieving this might be for you to entrust with this task a person who has your confidence and who could perhaps serve in an unofficial capacity. His task might comprise the following:

To approach government departments, keep them informed of the further development, and put forward recommendations for government action, giving particular attention to the problem of securing a supply of uranium ore for the United States.

To speed up the experimental work, which is at present being carried on within the limits of the budgets of university laboratories, by providing funds, if such funds be required, through his contacts with private persons who are willing to make contributions for this cause, and perhaps also by obtaining the cooperation of industrial laboratories which have the necessary equipment.

I understand that Germany has actually stopped the sale of uranium from Czechoslovakian mines which she has taken over. That she should have taken such early action might perhaps be understood on the grounds that the son of the German under-secretary of state, Von Weizsacker, is attached to the Kaiser-Wilhelm Institute in Berlin, where some of the American work on uranium is now being repeated.

❧ "I am in love with freedom"

E. B. WHITE

As World War II raged in Europe and Germany scored victory after victory, the American response was one of ambivalence. An ocean away, many people could not see how the German conquest of Europe could affect them. Others admired the efficiency and success of Nazi Germany. Although President Roosevelt feared German expansion and resented Hitler's brand of despotism, he could not convince the country to see his way.

E. B. White, the gifted writer for the *New Yorker* magazine, saw people accommodating their views to German success and scoffing at the inefficiencies of a democracy. Repulsed by it, he wrote the following column entitled "Freedom," offering an eyewitness view of American attitudes before its involvement in the war. In hindsight, White's column may seem obvious, but at the time he was stating a daring point of view.

I have often noticed on my trips up to the city that people have recut their clothes to follow the fashion. On my last trip, however, it seemed to me that people had remodeled their ideas too—taken in their convictions a little at the waist, shortened the sleeves of their resolve, and fitted themselves out in a new intellectual ensemble copied from a smart design out of the very page of history. It seemed to me they had strung along with Paris a little too long.

I confess to a disturbed stomach. I feel sick when I find anyone adjusting his mind to the new tyranny that is succeeding abroad. Because of its fundamental strictures, fascism does not seem to me to admit of any compromise or any rationalization, and I resent the patronizing air of persons who find in my plain belief in freedom a sign of immaturity. If it is boyish to believe that human beings should live free, then I'll gladly arrest my development and let the rest of the world grow up.

I shall report some of the strange remarks I heard in New York. One man told me that he thought perhaps the Nazi ideal was a sounder ideal than our constitutional system "because have you ever noticed what fine alert young faces the young German soldiers have in the newsreel?" He added: "Our American youngsters spend all their time at the movies—they're a mess." That was his summation of the case, his interpretation of the new Europe. Such a remark leaves me pale and shaken. If it represents the peak of our intelligence, then the steady march of despotism will not receive any considerable setback at our shores.

Another man informed me that our democratic notion of popular government was decadent and not worth bothering about—"because England is really rotten and the industrial towns there are a disgrace." That was the only reason he gave for the hopelessness of democracy; and he seemed mightily pleased with himself, as though he were more familiar than most with the anatomy of decadence, and had detected subtler aspects of the situation than were discernible to the rest of us.

Another man assured me that anyone who took any kind of government seriously was a gullible fool. You could be sure, he said that there is nothing but corruption "because of the way Clemenceau acted at Versailles." He said it didn't make any difference really about this war. It was just another war. Having relieved himself of this majestic bit of reasoning, he subsided.

Another individual, discovering signs of zeal creeping into my blood, berated me for having lost my detachment, my pure skeptical point of view. He announced that he wasn't going to be swept away by all this nonsense, but would prefer to remain in the role of innocent bystander, which he said was the duty of any intelligent person. (I noticed, however, that he phoned later to qualify his remarks, as though he had lost some of his innocence in the cab on the way home.)

Those are just a few samples of the sort of talk that seemed to be going round—talk that was full of defeatism and disillusion and sometimes of a too studied innocence. Men are not merely annihilating themselves at a great rate these days, but they are telling one another enormous lies, grandiose fibs. Such remarks as I heard are fearfully disturbing in their cumulative effect. They are more destructive than dive bombers and mine fields, for they challenge not merely one" immediate position but one's main defenses. They seemed to me to issue either from persons who could never really come to grips with freedom, so as to understand her, or from renegades. Where I expected to find indignation, I found paralysis, or a sort of dim acquiescence, as in a child who is dully swallowing a distasteful pill. I was advised of the growing anti-Jewish sentiment by a man who seemed to be watching the phenomenon of intolerance not through tears of shame but with a clear intellectual gaze, as through a well-ground lens.

The least a man can do at such a time is to declare himself and tell where he stands. I believe in freedom with the same burning delight, the same faith, the same intense abandon that attended its birth on this continent more than a century and a half ago. I am writing my declaration rapidly, much as though I were shaving to catch a train. Events abroad give a man a feeling of being pressed for time. Actually I do not believe I am pressed for time, and I apologize to the reader for a false impression that may be created. I just want to tell, before I get slowed down, that I am in love with freedom and that it is an affair of long standing and that it is a fine state to be in, and that I am deeply suspicious of people who are beginning to adjust to fascism and dictators merely because they are succeeding in war. From such adaptable natures a smell arises. I pinch my nose.

For as long as I can remember I have had a sense of living somewhat freely in a natural world. I don't mean I enjoyed freedom of action, but my existence seemed to have the quality of freeness. I've traveled with secret papers pertaining to a divine conspiracy. Intuitively I've always been aware of the vitally important pact that a man has with himself, to be all things to himself, and to be identified with all things, to stand self-reliant, taking advantage of his haphazard connection with a planet, riding his luck, and following his bent with the tenacity of a hound. My first and greatest love affair was with this thing we call freedom, this lady of infinite allure, this dangerous and beautiful and sublime being who restores and supplies us all.

It began with the haunting intimation (which I presume every child receives) of his mystical inner life; of God in man; of nature publishing her-self through the "I." This elusive sensation is moving and memorable. It comes early in life: a boy, we'll say, sitting on the front steps on a summer night, thinking of nothing in particular, suddenly hearing as with a new perception and as though for the first time the pulsing sound of crickets, overwhelmed with the novel sense of identification with the natural company of insects and grass and night, conscious of a faint answering cry to the universal perplexing question: "What is 'I'?" Or a little girl, returning from the grave of a pet bird and leaning with her elbows on the windowsill, inhaling the unfamiliar draught of death, suddenly seeing herself as part of the complete story. Or an older you, encountering for the first time a great teacher who by some chance word or mood awakens something in the youth beginning to breathe as an individual and conscious of strength in his vitals. I think the sensation must develop in many men as a feeling of identity with God—an eruption of the spirit caused by allergies and the sense of divine existence as distinct from mere animal existence. This is the beginning of the affair with freedom.

But a man's free condition is of two parts: the instinctive freeness he experiences as an animal dweller on a planet, and the practical liberties he enjoys as a privileged member of human society. The latter is, of the two, more generally understood, more widely admired, more violently challenged and discussed. It is the practical and apparent side of freedom. The United States, almost alone today, offers the liberties and the privileges and the tools of freedom. In this land the citizens are still invited to write their plays and books, to paint their pictures, to meet for discussion, to dissent as well as to agree, to mount soapboxes in the public square, to enjoy education in all subjects without censorship, to hold court and judge one another, to compose music, to talk politics with their neighbors without wondering whether the secret police are listening, to exchange ideas as well as goods, to kid the government when it needs kidding, and to read real news of real events instead of phony news manufactured by a paid agent of the state. This is a fact and should give every person pause.

To be free, in a planetary sense, is to feel that you belong to earth. To be free, in a social sense, is to feel at home in a democratic framework. In

Adolf Hitler, although he is a freely flowering individual, we do not detect either type of sensibility. From reading his book I gather that his feeling for the earth is not a sense of communion but a driving urge to prevail. His feeling for men is not that they co-exist, but that they are capable of being arranged and standardized by a superior intellect—that their existence suggests not a fulfillment of their personalities but a submersion of their personalities in common racial destiny. His very great absorption in the destiny of the German people somehow loses some of its effect when you discover, from his writings, in what vast contempt he holds all people. "I learned," he wrote, "…to gain an insight into the unbelievably primitive opinions and arguments of the people." To him the ordinary man is a primitive, capable only of being used and led. He speaks continually of people as sheep, halfwits, and impudent fools—the same people from whom he asks the utmost in loyalty, and to whom he promises the ultimate in prizes.

Here in America, where our society is based on belief in the individual, not contempt for him, the free principle of life has a chance of surviving. I believe that it must and will survive. To understand freedom is an accomplishment all men may acquire who set their minds in that direction; and to love freedom is a tendency many Americans are born with. To live in the same room with freedom, or in the same hemisphere, is still a profoundly shaking experience for me.

One of the earliest truths (and to him most valuable) that the author of *Mein Kampf* discovered was that it is not the written word, but the spoken word, that in heated moments moves great masses of people to noble or ignoble action. The written word, unlike the spoken word, is something every person examines privately and judges calmly by his own intellectual standards, not by what the man standing next to him thinks. "I know," wrote Hitler, "that one is able to win people far more by the spoken than by the written word…" Later he adds contemptuously: "For let it be said to all knights of the pen and to all the political dandies, especially of today: the greatest changes in this world have never yet been brought about by a goose quill! No, the pen has always been reserved to motivate these changes theoretically."

Luckily I am not out to change the world—that's being done for me, and at a great clip. But I know that the free spirit of man is persistent in nature; it recurs, and has never successfully been wiped out, by fire or flood. I set down the above remarks merely (in the words of Mr. Hitler) to motivate that spirit, theoretically. Being myself a knight of the goose quill, I am under no misapprehension about "winning people;" but I am inordinately proud these days of the quill, for it has shown itself, historically, to be the hypodermic that inoculates men and keeps germs of freedom always in circulation, so that there are individuals in every time in every land who are the carriers, the Typhoid Marys, capable of infecting others by mere contact and example. These persons are feared by every tyrant—who shows his fear by burning the books and destroying the individuals. A writer goes about his task today with the extra satisfaction that comes from knowing that he will be the first to have his head lopped off—even before the political dandies. In my own case this is a double satisfaction, I am the same as dead and would infinitely prefer to go into fascism without my head than with it, having no use for it any more and not wishing to be saddled with so heavy an encumbrance.

❧ *"This is London"*

EDWARD R. MURROW

CBS radio correspondent Edward R. Murrow brought World War II into American homes. Reporting from London during the German air raids of 1940-41, he conveyed a sense of immediacy that was new to the world. Never before could Americans, sitting comfortably at home hear live accounts of the terror of war.

By September 1940, England was alone. Germany had marched through Scandinavia, Belgium, Holland, Luxembourg and France in lightning strikes. Combining air power with tanks, Germans pulverized not just armies, but entire cities and towns. The war was brought to civilians in a way never seen before. As Hitler turned his attention to England, he launched his air force, the Luftwaffe, to try to pound the island-nation into submission or at least weaken its resolve.

But as Murrow's reports showed, if anything, the British became more resolute in their determination to fight. Evoking images of ordinary citizens carrying on in the face of pillage, King George VI offering a steadying voice of assurance, the suspense of defenseless citizens waiting for the bombs to fall and the terror of being bombed, Murrow helped Americans empathize with Britain's plight.

This is London, about ten minutes to four in the morning. Tonight's raid which started about eight is still in progress. The number of planes engaged is about the same as usual, perhaps a few more than last night. Barring lucky hits, both damage and casualties should be no greater than on previous nights. The next three hours may bring a change, but so far the raid appears to be routine, with the Germans flying perhaps a little lower than they did last night.

Often we wonder what you'd like to hear from London at four in the morning. There's seldom any spot news after midnight, so we just talk about the city and its people. Today I went to our district post office. There was a long line of people waiting for their mail. Their offices or homes had been bombed, and the mailman couldn't find them. There were no complaints. But that's not quite right. One woman said: "They've got to stop this. It can't go on." Her neighbor said: "Have you ever thought what would happen to you if we gave in?" And the lady replied, "Yes, I know, but have you seen what happened to Peter Robinson's?" Others in the queue—those who've been called by Mr. Churchill the more robust elements of the community—silenced the lady with well-modulated laughter.

To me one of the most impressive things about talking with Londoners these days is this—there's no mention of money. No one knows the dollar value of the damage done during these last sixteen days. But nobody talks about it. People who've had their homes or offices bombed will tell you about it, but they never think to tell you what the loss amounted to, whether it was so many tens or hundreds of pounds. The lead of any well-written news story dealing with fire, flood, or hurricane should tell something of the total damage done in terms of dollars, but here it's much more important that the bomb missed you; that there's still plenty of food to eat—and there is.

My own apartment is in one of the most heavily bombed areas of London, but the newspapers are on the doorstep each morning—so is the bottle of milk. When the light switch is pressed, there is light, and the gas stove still works, and they're still building that house across the street, still putting in big windowpanes. Today I saw shop-windows in Oxford Street, covered with plywood. In front of one there was a redheaded girl in a blue smock, painting a sign on the board covering the place where the window used to be. The sign read "Open as usual." A block away men were working an air hammer, breaking up huge blocks of masonry that had been blown into the streets, cracking those big lumps so that they might be carted away in trucks.

The people who have something to do with their hands are all right. Action seems to drive out fear. Those who have nothing to do would be better off outside London and there are signs that they will be encouraged to go. London comes to resemble a small town. There's something of a frontier atmosphere about the place. The other night I saw half a block evacuated. Time bombs plus incendiaries did it. In half an hour the people who had been turned out of their homes had been absorbed in nearby houses and apartments. Those who arranged for the influx of unexpected guests had, I think, been frightened when those bombs came down, but they were all right when there was something to do. Blankets to get out of closets, tea to be made, and all that sort of thing.

I've talked to firemen fighting a blaze that was being used as a beacon by German bomb aimers. They told me that the waiting about in fire stations was worst of all. They didn't mind the danger when there was something to do. Even my censor when I arrived in the studio tonight was sitting here underground composing music.

A half an hour before the King made his broadcast tonight, the air-raid alarm sounded. At that moment a man with a deep voice was telling the children of Britain by radio how the wasps build their nests. He said, "Good night, children everywhere." There was a brief prayer for the children who went down in mid-Atlantic last week. There was a hymn well sung. After that a piano playing some nursery song, I didn't know its name. There was a moment of silence. Then the words, "This is London, His Majesty, the King." The King spoke for half a minute and then the welcome sound of the "all-clear," that high, steady note of the siren, came rolling through the open window. One almost expected His Majesty to pause and let the welcome sound come out through the loudspeaker, but he probably didn't hear it since he was speaking from an air-raid shelter under Buckingham Palace. The only news in the King's speech was the announcement of two new medals, but his warning of grimmer days ahead must be taken as another indication of government policy—a warning that the full weight of German bombing is yet to be experienced.

Since the disastrous retreat from Norway, the government has been issuing few sunshine statements. Nearly every statement has been couched in subtle language, has contained a warning of worse things to come.

And now the King has added his warning to those of his ministers. He took the advice of his ministers, as he must, in speaking as he did, and his ministers judged, and rightly, that these people can stand up to that sort of warning. There has been much talk of terror bombings, but it is clear that London has not yet experienced anything like the full power of the Luftwaffe in these night raids. The atmosphere for full-scale terror bombing is not right. There is as yet no sizable portion of the population prepared to talk terms with the Nazis. You must remember that this war is being fought with political as well as military weapons. If the time comes when the Germans believe that mass night raids will break this government, then we may see German bombers quartering this night sky in an orgy of death and destruction such as no modern city has ever seen. There are no available official figures, but I have watched these planes night after night and do not believe that more than one hundred and fifty have been used in any single night. The Germans have more planes than that. Sometime they may use them. The people had to be warned about that. Therefore, the King spoke as he did.

October 10, 1940

This is London, ten minutes before five in the morning. Tonight's raid has been widespread. London is again the main target. Bombs have been reported from more than fifty districts. Raiders have been over Wales in the west, the Midlands, Liverpool, the southwest, and northeast. So far as London is concerned, the outskirts appear to have suffered the heaviest pounding. The attack has decreased in intensity since the moon faded from the sky.

All the fires were quickly brought under control. That's a common phrase in the morning communiques. I've seen how it's done; spent a night with the London fire brigade....

I must have seen well over a hundred fire bombs come down and only three small fires were started. The incendiaries aren't so bad if there is someone there to deal with them, but those oil bombs present more difficulties.

As I watched those white fires flame up and die down, watched the yellow blazes grow dull and disappear, I thought what a puny effort is this to burn a great city. Finally, we went below to a big room underground. It was quiet. Women spoke softly into telephones. There was a big map of London on the wall. Little colored pins were being moved from one point to another and every time a pin was moved it meant that fire pumps were on their way through the black streets of London to a fire. One district has asked for reinforcements from another, just as an army reinforces its front lines in the sector bearing the brunt of the attack....

We picked a fire from the map and drove to it. And the map was right. It was a small fire in a warehouse near the river. Not much of a fire; only ten pumps working on it, but still big enough to be seen from the air. The searchlights were bunched overhead and as we approached we could hear the drone of a German plane and see the burst of anti-aircraft fire directly overhead. Two pieces of shrapnel slapped down in the water and then everything was drowned in the hum of the pumps and the sound of hissing water. Those firemen in their oilskins and tin hats appeared oblivious to everything but the fire. We went to another blaze—just a small two-story house down on the East End. An incendiary had gone through the roof and the place was being gutted. A woman stood on a corner, clutching a rather dirty pillow. A policeman was trying to comfort her. And a fireman said, "You'd be surprised what strange things people pick up when they run out of a burning house."

And back at headquarters I saw a man laboriously and carefully copying names in a big ledger—the list of firemen killed in action during the last month. There were about a hundred names.

I can now appreciate what lies behind those lines in the morning communiques—all fires were quickly brought under control.

CHAPTER NINE

1941–1960

War, Prosperity and an Uneasy Peace

❧ Four Freedoms Speech

FRANKLIN D. ROOSEVELT

On January 6, 1941, Roosevelt delivered his "Four Freedoms Speech" outlining the principles for which the United States would be willing to go to war. The four freedoms he outlined were freedom of speech, freedom of worship, freedom from want, and freedom from fear. When the war broke out, painter Norman Rockwell did a series of paintings illustrating the four freedoms. The paintings went on a national tour to raise money for the war effort.

The Nation takes great satisfaction and much strength from the things which have been done to make its people conscious of their individual stake in the preservation of democratic life in America. Those things have toughened the fiber of our people, have renewed their faith and strengthened their devotion to the institutions we make ready to protect.

Certainly this is no time for any of us to stop thinking about the social and economic problems which are the root cause of the social revolution which is today a supreme factor in the world.

For there is nothing mysterious about the foundations of a healthy and strong democracy. The basic things expected by our people of their political and economic systems are simple. They are:

Equality of opportunity for youth and for others.

Jobs for those who can work.

Security for those who need it.

The ending of special privilege for the few.

The preservation of civil liberties for all.

The enjoyment of the fruits of scientific progress in a wider and constantly rising standard of living.

These are the simple, basic things that must never be lost sight of in the turmoil and unbelievable complexity of our modern world. The inner and abiding strength of our economic and political systems is dependent upon the degree to which they fulfill these expectations.

Many subjects connected with our social economy call for immediate improvement.
As examples:
We should bring more citizens under the coverage of old-age pensions and unemployment insurance.

We should widen the opportunities for adequate medical care.

We should plan a better system by which persons deserving or needing gainful employment may obtain it.

I have called for personal sacrifice. I am assured of the willingness of almost all Americans to respond to that call.

A part of the sacrifice means the payment of more money in taxes. In my Budget Message I shall recommend a greater portion of this great defense program be paid from taxation that we are paying today. No person should try, or be allowed, to get rich out of this program; and the principle of tax payments in accordance with ability to pay should be constantly before our eyes to guide our legislation.

If the Congress maintains these principles, the voters, putting patriotism ahead of pocketbooks, will give you their applause.

In the future days, which we seek to make secure, we look forward to a world founded upon four essential human freedoms.

The first is the freedom of speech and expression—everywhere in the world.

The second is the freedom of every person to worship God in his own way—everywhere in the world.

The third is freedom from want—which, translated into world terms, means economic understandings which will secure to every nation a healthy peacetime life for its inhabitants—everywhere in the world.

The fourth is freedom from fear—which, translated into world terms, means a world-wide reduction of armaments to such a point and in such a thorough fashion that no nation will be in a position to commit an act of physical aggression against any neighbor—anywhere in the world.

That is no vision of a distant millennium. It is a definite basis for a kind of world attainable in our own time and generation. That kind of world is the very antithesis of the so-called new order of tyranny which the dictators seek to create with the crash of a bomb.

To that new order we oppose the greater conception—the moral order. A good society is able to face schemes of world domination and foreign revolutions alike without fear.

Since the beginning of our American history,

we have been engaged in change—in perpetual peaceful revolution—a revolution which goes on steadily, quietly adjusting itself to changing conditions—without the concentration camp or the quick-lime in the ditch. The world order which we seek is the cooperation of free countries, working together in a friendly, civilized society.

This nation has placed its destiny in the hands and heads and hearts of its millions of free men and women; and its faith in freedom under the guidance of God. Freedom means the supremacy of human rights everywhere. Our support goes to those who struggle to gain those rights or keep them. Our strength is our unity of purpose.

To that high concept there can be no end save victory.

❧ "An Act to Promote the Defense of the United States"

THE LEND-LEASE ACT

Desperate for supplies to protect England, British Prime Minister Winston Churchill implored Roosevelt for assistance to stave off Germany's expected invasion. By early 1941, Roosevelt had no doubt that the United States needed to throw its weight behind England. Even though sympathies were starting to sway, there was still a strong isolationist sentiment.

Roosevelt had to find a way to provide supplies to Churchill and still skirt the objections of isolationists. He came up with the Lend-Lease Program. In exchange for the lease of some British islands in the Caribbean Sea, the United States provided England with ships and munitions. Technically skirting the Neutrality laws, Congress passed the Lend-Lease Act in March 1941 after a bitter debate.

Be it enacted That this Act may be cited as "An Act to Promote the Defense of the United States."

Section 3

Notwithstanding the provisions of any other law, the President may, from time to time, when he deems it in the interest of national defense, authorize the Secretary of War, the Secretary of the Navy, or the head of any other department or agency of the Government to manufacture in arsenals, factories, and shipyards under their jurisdiction, or otherwise procure, to the extent to which

funds are made available therefor, or contracts are authorized from time to time by the Congress, or both, any defense article for the government of any country whose defense the President deems vital to the defense of the United States.

To sell, transfer title to, exchange, lease, lend, or otherwise dispose of, to any such government any defense article, but no defense article not manufactured to be procured under paragraph (1) shall in any way be disposed of under this paragraph, except after consultation with the Chief of Staff of the Army or the Chief of Naval Operations of the Navy, or both. The value of defense articles disposed of in any way under authority of this paragraph, and procured from funds heretofore appropriated, shall not exceed $1,300,000,000. The value of such defense articles shall be determined by the head of the department, agency of officer as shall be designed in the manner provided in the rules and regulations issued hereunder. Defense articles procured from funds hereafter appropriated to any department or agency of the Government, other than from funds authorized to be appropriated under this Act, shall not be disposed of in any way under authority of this paragraph except to the extent hereafter authorized by the Congress in the Acts appropriating such funds or otherwise.

To test, inspect, prove, repair, outfit, recondition, or otherwise to place in good working order, to the extent to which funds are made available therefore, on contracts are authorized from time to time by the Congress, or both, any defense article for any such government, or to procure any or all such services by private contract.

To communicate to any such government any defense information, pertaining to any defense information, pertaining to any defense article furnished to such government under paragraph (2) of this subsection.

To release for export any defense article disposed of in any way under this subsection to any such government.

The terms and conditions upon which any such foreign government receives any aid authorized under subsection (a) shall be those which the President deems satisfactory, and the benefit to the United States may be payment or repayment in kind or property, or any other direct or indirect benefit which the President deems satisfactory.

After June 30, 1943, or after the passage of a

concurrent resolution by the two Houses before June 30, 1943, which declares that the powers conferred by or pursuant to subsection (a) are no longer necessary to promote the defense of the United States, neither the President nor the head of any department or agency shall exercise any of the powers conferred by or pursuant to subsection (a); except that until July 1, 1946, any of such powers may be exercised to the extent necessary to carry out a contract or agreement with such a foreign government made before July 1, 1943, or before the passage of such concurrent resolution, whichever is the earlier.

Nothing in this Act shall be construed to authorize or to permit the authorization of convoying vessels by naval vessels of the United States.

Nothing in this Act shall be construed to authorize or to permit the authorization of the entry of any American vessel into a combat area in violation of section 3 of the Neutrality Act of 1939.

Section 8

The Secretaries of War of the Navy are hereby authorized to purchase or otherwise acquire arms, ammunition, and implements of war produced within the jurisdiction of any country to which section 3 is applicable, whenever the President deems such purchase or acquisition to be necessary in the interests of the defense of the United States.

Section 9

The President may, from time to time, promulgate such rules and regulations as may be necessary and proper to carry out any of the provisions of this Act; and he may exercise any power or authority conferred on him by this Act through such department, agency, or officer as he shall direct.

"We are on the verge of war, but it is not yet too late to stay out"

CHARLES LINDBERGH

Charles Lindbergh was one of the leading voices in the isolationist "America First" movement. Lindbergh had visited Germany in the 1930s and was very impressed by Hitler, his management of Germany and the might of the Luftwaffe.

When the war broke out in Europe and some of Hitler's more brutal tactics became known, Lindbergh tempered his compliments of the Führer.

Nevertheless, he remained a stalwart isolationist. On September 1, 1941, in Des Moines, Iowa, he outlined the reasons for his position and condemned Roosevelt, the British and the Jews for attempting to lead the United States into war against Germany.

When Japan bombed Pearl Harbor three months later, Lindbergh and the isolationists dropped their objections to American involvement in the war. Lindbergh offered to join the Air Force. But Roosevelt, furious at Lindbergh for his prewar comments, refused to let him wear an American uniform. Nevertheless, Lindbergh flew extensively in the Pacific as a civilian to assist the war effort.

We can not allow the natural passions and prejudices of other peoples to lead our country to destruction.

The Roosevelt administration is the third powerful group which has been carrying this country toward war. Its members have used the war emergency to obtain a third presidential term for the first time in American history. They have used the war to add unlimited billions to a debt which was already the highest we have ever known. And they have used the war to justify the restriction of congressional power and the assumption of dictatorial procedures on the part of the president and his appointees.

The power of the Roosevelt administration depends upon the maintenance of a wartime emergency. The prestige of the Roosevelt Administration depends upon the success of Great Britain to whom the president attached his political future at a time when most people thought that England and France could easily win the war. The danger of the Roosevelt administration lies in its subterfuge while its members have promised us peace they have led us to war heedless of the platform upon which they were elected.

In selecting these three groups as the major agitators for war I have included only those whose support is essential to the war party. If any of these groups; the British, the Jewish, or the administration stops agitating for war, I believe there will be little danger of our involvement. I do not believe that any two of them are powerful enough to carry this country to war without the support of the third. And to these three, as I have said, all other groups are of secondary importance.

When hostilities commenced in Europe in 1939 it was realized by these groups that the

American people had no intention of entering the war. They knew it would be worse than useless to ask us for a declaration of war at that time. But they believed that this country could be enticed into the war in very much the same way that it was enticed into the last one.

They planned, first to prepare the United States for foreign war under the guise of American defense, second to involve us in the war, step by step without our realization, third, to create a series of incidents which would force us into the actual conflict.

These plans were of course to be covered and assisted by the full power of their propaganda. Our theaters soon became filled with plays portraying the glory of war. Newsreels lost all semblance of objectivity. Newspapers and magazines began to lose advertising if they carried anti-war articles. A smear campaign was instituted against individuals who opposed intervention. The terms fifth-columnist, traitor, Nazi, anti-Semitic were thrown ceaselessly at anyone who dared to suggest that it was not to the best interests of the United States to enter war. Men lost their jobs if they were frankly anti-war, many others dared no longer speak. Before long lecture halls that were opened to advocates of war were closed to speakers who opposed it, a fear campaign was inaugurated.

We were told that aviation, which has held the British fleet off the continent of Europe, made America more vulnerable than ever before to invasion. Propaganda was in full swing. There was no difficulty in obtaining billions of dollars for arms under the guise of defending America. Our people stood united on a program for defense.

Congress passed appropriation after appropriation for guns and planes and battleships with the approval of the overwhelming majority of our citizens. That a large portion of these appropriations was to be used to build arms for Europe, we did not learn until later. That was another step. To use a specific example, in 1939 we were told that we should increase our air corps to a total of 5,000 planes. Congress passed the necessary legislation. A few months later the administration told us that United States should have at least 50,000 planes for our national safety. But almost as soon, almost as fast as fighting planes were turned out from our factories they were sent abroad, although our own air corps was in the utmost need of new equipment.

So that today, two years after the start of war, the American army has only a few hundred thoroughly modern bombers and fighters, less in fact than Germany is able to produce in a single month.

Ever since its inception, our arms program has been laid out for the purpose of carrying on the war in Europe far more than for the purpose of building an adequate defense for America.

Only one thing holds this country from war today; that, is the rising opposition of the American people. Our system of democracy and representative government is on test today as it has never been before. We are on the verge of war in which the only victor would be chaos and frustration. We are on the verge of war for which we are still unprepared and for which no one has offered a feasible plan of victory; a war which cannot be won without sending our soldiers across an ocean to fight and to force a landing on a hostile coast against armies stronger than our own.

We are on the verge of war, but it is not yet too late to stay out. It is not yet too late to show that no amount of money, or propaganda, or patronage can force a free and independent people into war against its will.

❧ "A date which will live in infamy"

ROOSEVELT ASKS FOR WAR AGAINST JAPAN

Just before dawn on December 7, 1941, the Japanese Air Force launched a surprise attack against the United States Pacific Fleet in Pearl Harbor, Hawaii, destroying most of its battleships. Casualties totaled 2,280 killed and 1,109 wounded. Simultaneously, Japanese forces successfully attacked the Philippines, Guam, Midway, Hong Kong, the Malay Peninsula and several other military bases.

Stunned by the strike, Roosevelt asked Congress on December 8 to declare war against Japan. Congress unanimously approved the request the same day. Three days later, Germany and Italy declared war against the United States.

Yesterday, December 7, 1941—a date which will live in infamy—the United States of America was suddenly and deliberately attacked by naval and air forces of the Empire of Japan.

The United States was at peace with that nation and, at the solicitation of Japan, was still in conversation with its Government and its Emperor looking toward the maintenance of peace in the Pacific. Indeed, one hour after Japanese air squadrons had commenced bombing in Oahu, the Japanese Ambassador to the United States and his colleague delivered to the Secretary of State a formal reply to a recent American message. While this reply stated that it seemed useless to continue the existing diplomatic negotiations, it contained no threat to hint of war or armed attack.

It will be recorded that the distance of Hawaii from Japan makes it obvious that the attack was deliberately planned many days or even weeks ago. During the intervening time the Japanese Government has deliberately sought to deceive the United States by false statements and expressions of hope for continued peace.

The attack yesterday on the Hawaiian Islands has caused severe damage to American naval and military forces. Very many American lives have been lost. In addition American ships have been reported torpedoed on the high seas between San Francisco and Honolulu.

Yesterday the Japanese Government also launched an attach against Malaya. Last night Japanese forces attacked Hong Kong. Last night Japanese forces attacked Guam. Last night Japanese forces attacked the Philippine Islands. Last night the Japanese attached Wake Island. This morning the Japanese attacked Midway Island.

Japan has, therefore, undertaken a surprise offensive extending throughout the Pacific area. The facts of yesterday speak for themselves. The people of the United States have already formed their opinions and well understand the implications to the very life and safety of our nation.

As Commander-in-Chief of the Army and Navy, I have directed that all measures be taken for our defense.

Always will we remember the character of the onslaught against us.

No matter how long it may take us to overcome this premeditated invasion, the American people in their righteous might will win through to absolute victory.

I believe I interpret the will of the Congress and of the people when I assert that we will not only defend ourselves to the uttermost but will make very certain that this form of treachery shall never endanger us again.

Hostilities exist. There is no blinking at the fact that our people, our territory and our interests are in grave danger.

With confidence in our armed forces—with the unbonded, determination of our people—we will gain the inevitable triumph—so help us God.

I ask that the Congress declare that since the unprovoked and dastardly attack by Japan on Sunday, December seventh, a state of war has existed between the United States and the Japanese Empire.

✤ "Every possible protection against espionage and sabotage"

JAPANESE RELOCATION ORDER

The suddenness and sweeping nature of the Japanese attacks in the Pacific startled the United States into hasty action. Many feared that Japanese in the United States and American citizens of Japanese descent might pose a threat. On February 19, 1942, Roosevelt issued the Japanese Relocation Order allowing the military to relocate any person of Japanese origin into designated areas.

Quickly, the military set up relocation camps and rounded up 112,000 Japanese on the West Coast, about two-thirds of whom were American citizens. The action was later condemned as a flagrant and unnecessary violation of civil rights. In 1988, the government formally apologized for the action and offered $20,000 to the surviving Japanese who were interned in the camps. No camps were ever set up for Americans of Italian or German descent. Close to 25,000 Japanese-Americans fought in the U.S. military during the war.

Executive Order Authorizing the Secretary of War to Prescribe Military Areas

Whereas the successful prosecution of the war requires every possible protection against espionage and against sabotage to national-defense materials, national-defense premises, and national-defense utilities.

Now, therefore, by virtue of the authority vested in me as President of the United States, and Commander in Chief of the Army and Navy, I hereby, authorize and direct the Secretary of War, and the Military Commanders whom he may from time to time designate, whenever he or any designated Commander, deems such action necessary or desirable, to prescribe military areas in such places and of such extent as he or the appropriate Military Commander may determine, from which any or all persons may be excluded, and with respect to which, the right of any person to enter, remain in, or leave shall be subject to whatever restrictions the Secretary of War or the appropriate Military Commander may impose in his discretion. The Secretary of War is hereby authorized to provide for residents of any such area who are excluded therefrom, such transportation, food, shelter, and other accommodations as may be necessary, in the judgment of the Secretary of War or the said Military Commander, and until other arrangements are made, to accomplish the purpose of this order. The designation of military areas in any region or locality shall supersede designations or prohibited and restricted areas by the Attorney General under the Proclamations of December 7 and 8, 1941, and shall supersede the responsibility and authority of the Attorney General under the said Proclamations in respect of such prohibited and restricted areas.

I hereby further authorize and direct the Secretary of War and the said Military Commanders to take such other steps as he or the appropriate Military Commander may deem advisable to enforce compliance with the restrictions applicable to each Military area hereinabove authorized to be designated, including the use of Federal troops and other Federal Agencies, with authority to accept assistance of state and local agencies.

I hereby further authorize and direct all Executive Departments, independent establishments and other Federal Agencies, to assist the Secretary of War or the said Military Commanders in carrying out this Executive Order, including the furnishings of medical aid, hospitalization, food, clothing, transportation, use of land, shelter, and other supplies, equipment, utilities, facilities, and services.

"Even if a person had a fraction of Japanese blood in him, he must leave on demand"

MONICA SONE

Monica Sone was the daughter of two Japanese immigrants who lived in Washington State at the outbreak of the war. She and her family were forced to leave their home and live in an American relocation camp in 1942. In her 1953 autobiography, *Nisei Daughter,* she described the experience.

In February, Executive Order No. 9066 came out, authorizing the War Department to remove the Japanese from such military areas as it saw fit, aliens and citizens alike. Even if a person had a fraction of Japanese blood in him, he must leave on demand.

A pall of gloom settled upon our home. We couldn't believe that the government meant that the Japanese-Americans must go, too. We had heard the clamoring of superpatriots who insisted loudly, "Throw the whole kaboodle out. A Jap's a Jap, no matter how you slice him. You can't make an American out of little Jap Junior just by handing him an American birth certificate." But we had dismissed these remarks as just hot blasts of air from an overheated patriot. We were quite sure that our rights as American citizens would not be violated, and we would not be marched out of our homes on the same basis as enemy aliens.

In anger, Henry [her brother] and I read and reread the Executive Order. Henry crumpled the newspaper in his hand and threw it against the wall. "Doesn't my citizenship mean a single blessed thing to anyone? Why doesn't somebody make up my mind for me. First they want me in the army. Now they're going to slap an alien 4-C on me because of my ancestry. What the hell!"

Once more I felt like a despised, pathetic two-headed freak, a Japanese and an American, neither of which seemed to be doing me any good.

On the twenty-first of April, a Tuesday, the general [John DeWitt] gave us the shattering news. "All the Seattle Japanese will be moved to Payallup by May 1. Everyone must be registered Saturday and Sunday between 8 am and 5 pm. They will leave next week in three groups, on Tuesday,

Thursday and Friday."

Up to that moment, we had hoped against hope that something or someone would intervene for us. Now there was no time for moaning. A thousand and one details must be attended to in this one week of grace. Those seven days sputtered out like matches struck in the wind, as we rushed wildly about. Mother distributed sheets, pillowcases and blankets, which we stuffed into seabags. Into the two suitcases, we packed heavy winter overcoats, plenty of sweaters, woolen slacks and skirts, flannel pajamas and scarves. Personal toilet articles, one tin plate, tin cup and silverware completed our luggage. The one seabag and two suitcases apiece were going to be the backbone of our future home, and we planned it carefully.

Henry went to the Control Station to register the family. He came home with twenty tags, all numbered "10710," tags to be attached to each piece of baggage, and one to hang from our coat lapels. From then on, we were known as Family #10710.

On our last Sunday, Father and Henry moved all our furniture and household goods down to the hotel and stored them in one room. We could have put away our belongings in the government storage place or in the basement of our church, which was going to be boarded up for the duration, but we felt that our property would be safer under the watchful eyes of Sam, Peter and Joe.

Monday evening we received friends in our empty house where our voices echoed loudly and footsteps clattered woodenly on the bare floor. We sat on crates, drank bottles of Coke and talked gayly about our future pioneer life. Henry and Minnie held hands all evening in the corner of the living room. Minnie lived on the outskirts of the Japanese community and her district was to leave in the third and last group.

That night we rolled ourselves into army blankets like jelly rolls and slept on the bare floor. The next morning Henry rudely shouted us back into consciousness. "Six-thirty! Everybody wake up, today's the day!"

I screamed, "Must you sound so cheerful about it?"

"What do you expect me to do, bawl?"

On this sour note, we got up stiffly from the floor, and exercised violently to start circulation in our paralyzed backs and limbs. We jammed our blankets into the long narrow seabag, and we carefully tied the white pasteboard tag, 10710, on our coat lapels. When I went into the bathroom and looked into the mirror, tears suddenly welled in my eyes. I was crying, not because it was the last time I would be standing in a modern bathroom, but because I looked like a cross between a Japanese and a fuzzy bear. My hideous new permanent wave had been given to me by an operator who had never worked on Oriental hair before. My hair resembled scorched mattress filling, and after I had attacked it savagely with a comb and brush, I looked like a frightened mushroom. On this morning of mornings when I was depending on a respectable hairdo so I could leave town with dignity, I was faced with this horror. There was nothing to do but cover it with a scarf.

Downstairs we stood around the kitchen stove where Mother served us a quick breakfast of coffee in our tin cups, sweet rolls and boiled eggs which rolled noisily on our tin plates. Henry was delighted with the simplicity of it all. "Boy, this is going to be living, no more company manners and dainty napkins. We can eat with our bare hands. Probably taste better, too."

Mother fixed a stern eye on Henry, "Not as long as I'm around."

The front doorbell rang. It was Dunks Oshima, who had offered to take us down to Eighth and Lane in a borrowed pickup truck. Hurriedly the menfolk loaded the truck with the last few boxes of household goods which Dunks was going to take down to the hotel. He held up a gallon can of soy sauce, puzzled, "Where does this go, to the hotel, too?"

Nobody seemed to know where it had come from or where it was going, until Mother finally spoke up guiltily, "Er, it's going with me. I didn't think we'd have shoyu where we're going."

Henry looked as if he were going to explode. "But Mama, you're not supposed to have more than one seabag and two suitcases. And of all things, you want to take with you—shoyu!"

I felt mortified. "Mama, people will laugh at us. We're not going on a picnic!"

But Mother stood her ground. "Nonsense. No one will ever notice this little thing. It isn't as if I were bringing liquor!"

"Well!" I said. "If Mama's going to take her shoyu, I'm taking my radio along." I rescued my fifteen-year-old radio from the boxes which were going down to the hotel. "At least it'll keep me from talking to myself out there."

Sumi began to look thoughtful, and she rummaged among the boxes. Henry bellowed, "That's enough! Two suitcases and one seabag a person, that's final! Now let's get going before we decide to take the house along with us."

Mother personally saw to it that the can of shoyu remained with her baggage. She turned back once more to look at our brown and yellow frame house and said almost gayly, "Good-by, house."

Through the barracks, there were a medley of creaking cots, whimpering infants and explosive night coughs. Our attention was riveted on the intense little wood stove which glowed so violently I feared it would melt right down to the floor. We soon learned that this condition lasted for only a short time, after which it suddenly turned into a deep freeze. Henry and Father took turns at the stove to produce the harrowing blast which all but singed our army blankets, but did not penetrate through them. As it grew quieter in the barracks, I could hear the light patter of rain. Soon I felt the "splat! splat!" of raindrops digging holes into my face. The dampness on my pillow spread like a mortal bleeding, and I finally had to get out and haul my cot toward the center of the room. In a short while Henry was up. "I've got multiple leaks, too. Have to complain to the landlord first thing in the morning."

All through the night I heard people getting up, dragging cots around. I stared at our little window, unable to sleep. I was glad Mother had put up a makeshift curtain on the window for I noticed a powerful beam of light sweeping across it every few seconds. The lights came from high towers placed around the camp where guards with Tommy guns kept a twenty-four-hour vigil. I remembered the wire fence encircling us, and a knot of anger tightened in my breast. What was I doing behind a fence like a criminal? If there were accusations to be made, why hadn't I been give a fair trial? Maybe I wasn't considered an American anymore. My citizenship wasn't real, after all. Then what was I? I was certainly not a citizen of Japan as my parents were. On second thought, even Father and Mother were more alien residents of the United States than Japanese nationals for they had little tie with their mother country. In their twenty-five years in

America, they had worked and paid their taxes to their adopted governments as any other citizen.

Of one thing I was sure. The wire fence was real. I no longer had the right to walk out of it. It was because I had Japanese ancestors. It was also because some people had little faith in the ideas and ideals of democracy. They said that after all these were but words and could not possibly insure loyalty. New laws and camps were surer devices. I finally buried my face in my pillow to wipe out burning thoughts and snatch what sleep I could.

"Our nations shall work together in war and peace"

TEHERAN CONFERENCE

December 1, 1943

From November 28 to December 1, 1943, Roosevelt, Churchill and Soviet Union Premier Joseph Stalin met for the first time to coordinate the Allied war effort. By this time, the hour of maximum danger had passed. Soviet troops had stopped the German invasion in an incredibly brutal battle at Stalingrad and were starting, slowly, to push the invaders back. The British and Americans had expelled the Germans from North Africa, successfully invaded Italy earlier in the year, and had started to beat back the Japanese in the Pacific.

The official pronouncement at the conclusion of the meeting was deliberately vague. Other than expressing their confidence in an Allied victory and a pledge to withdraw their troops from Iran at the conclusion of the war, there was little of substance publicly announced. But behind the scenes, the three leaders were laying the groundwork for the invasion of France the following spring to create a second front against Germany.

We—the President of the United States, the Prime Minister of Great Britain, and the Premier of the Soviet Union, have met these four days past, in this, the Capital of our Ally, Iran, and have shaped and confirmed our common policy.

We express our determination that our nations shall work together in war and in the peace that will follow.

As to war—our military staffs have joined in our roundtable discussions, and we have concerted our plans for the destruction of the German forces. We have reached complete agreement as to the scope and timing of the operations to be undertaken from the east, west and south.

The common understanding which we have here reached guarantees that victory will be ours.

And as to peace—we are sure that our concord will win an enduring Peace. We recognize fully the supreme responsibility resting upon us and all the United Nations to make a peace which will command the goodwill of the overwhelming mass of the peoples of the world and banish the scourge and terror of war for many generations.

With our Diplomatic advisers we have surveyed the problems of the future. We shall seek the cooperation and active participation of all nations, large and small, whose peoples in heart and mind are dedicated, as are our own peoples, to the elimination of tyranny and slavery, oppression and intolerance. We will welcome them, and they may choose to come, into a world family of Democratic Nations.

No power on earth can prevent our destroying the German armies by land, their U Boats by sea, and their war planets from the air.

Our attack will be relentless and increasing.

Emerging from these cordial conferences we look with confidence to the day when all peoples of the world may live free lives, untouched by tyranny and according to their varying desires and their own consciences.

We came here with hope and determination. We leave here, friends in fact, in spirit and in purpose.

Roosevelt, Churchill and Stalin

Declaration of the Three Powers Regarding Iran

[This declaration was published on December 7, 1943.]
The President of the United States, the Premier of the U.S.S.R. and the Prime Minister of the United Kingdom, having consulted with each other and with the Prime Minister of Iran, desire to declare the mutual agreement of their three Governments regarding their relations with Iran.

The Governments of the United States, the U.S.S.R. and the United Kingdom recognize the assistance which Iran has given in the prosecution of the war against the common enemy, particularly by facilitating the transportation of supplies from overseas to the Soviet Union.

The three Governments realize that the war has caused special economic difficulties for Iran,

and they are agreed that they will continue to make available to the government of Iran such economic assistance as may be possible, having regard to the heavy demands made upon them by their worldwide military operations and to the worldwide shortage of transport, raw materials and supplies for civilian consumption.

With respect to the post-war period, the Governments of the United States, the U.S.S.R. and the United Kingdom are in accord with the Government of Iran that any economic problems confronting Iran at the close of hostilities should receive full consideration, along with those of other members of the United Nations, by conferences or international agencies held or created to deal with international economic matters.

The Governments of the United States, the U.S.S.R. and the United Kingdom are at one with the Government of Iran in their desire for the maintenance of the independence, sovereignty and territorial integrity of Iran. They count upon the participation of Iran, together with all other peace-loving nations, in the establishment of international peace, security and prosperity after the war, in accordance with the principles of the Atlantic Charter, to which all four Governments have subscribed.

Winston S. Churchill
Joseph V. Stalin
Franklin D. Roosevelt
Washington, March 24, 1947—The text of the military and other conclusions reached at the Teheran conference, as announced today by the State Department:

The conference:

Agreed that the partisans in Yugoslavia should be supported by supplies and equipment to the greatest possible extent, and also by Commando operations;

Agreed that, from the military point of view, it was most desirable that Turkey should come into the war on the side of the Allies before the end of the year;

Took note of Marshal Stalin's statement that if Turkey found herself at war with Germany, and as a result Bulgaria declared war on Turkey or attacked her, the Soviet Union would immediately be at war with Bulgaria. The conference further took note that this fact could be explicitly stated in the forthcoming negotiations to bring Turkey into the war;

Took note that Operation Overload [the landings in Normandy] would be launched during May, 1944, in conjunction with an operation against southern France. The latter operation would be undertaken in as great a strength as availability of landing craft permitted. The conference further took note of Marshal Stalin's statement that the Soviet forces would launch an offensive at about the same time with the object of preventing the German forces from transferring from the eastern to the western front;

Agreed that the military staffs of the three powers should henceforward keep in close touch with each other in regard to the impending operations in Europe. In particular it was agreed that a cover plan to mystify and mislead the enemy as regards these operations should be concerted between the staffs concerned.

Winston S. Churchill
Joseph V. Stalin
Franklin D. Roosevelt
Teheran, December 1, 1943

"Never have I crossed the trail of any man as beloved as Capt. Henry T. Waskow"

ERNIE PYLE

Ernie Pyle was one of the great correspondents of World War II. His accounts from the front brought home the everyday struggles of combat soldiers. He earned enormous affection from both his readers and the soldiers he covered. One of his most poignant columns was about the death of Captain Henry T. Waskow of Belton, Texas, on the Italian frontline. Pyle would be killed in the spring of 1945 in the Pacific.

At the Front Lines in Italy, January 10, 1944—In this war I have known a lot of officers who were loved and respected by the soldiers under them. But never have I crossed the trail of any man as beloved as Capt. Henry T. Waskow of Belton, Texas.

Capt. Waskow was a company commander in the 36th Division. He had led his company since long before it left the States. He was very young, only in his middle twenties, but he carried in him a sincerity and gentleness that made people want to be guided by him.

"After my own father, he came next," a sergeant told me.

"He always looked after us," a soldier said. "He'd go to bat for us every time."

"I've never known him to do anything unfair," another one said.

I was at the foot of the mule trail the night they brought Capt. Waskow's body down. The moon was nearly full at the time, and you could see far up the trail and even part way across the valley below. Soldiers made shadows in the moonlight as they walked.

Dead men had been coming down the mountain all evening, lashed onto the backs of mules. They came lying belly-down across the wooden pack-saddles, their heads hanging down on the left side of the mule, their stiffened legs sticking out awkwardly from the other side, bobbing up and down as the mule walked.

The Italian mule-skinners were afraid to walk beside dead men, so Americans had to lead the mules down that night. Even the Americans were reluctant to unlash and lift the bodies at the bottom, so an officer had to do it himself, and ask others to help.

The first one came early in the morning. They slid him down from the mule and stood him on his feet for a moment, while they got a new grip. In the half-light he might have been merely a sick man standing there, leaning on the others. Then they laid him on the ground in the shadow of the low stone wall alongside the road.

I don't know who that first one was. You feel small in the presence of dead men, and ashamed at being alive, and you don't ask silly questions.

We left him there beside the road, that first one, and we all went back into the cowshed and sat on water cans or lay on the straw, waiting for the next batch of mules.

Somebody said the dead soldier had been dead for four days, and then nobody said anything more about it. We talked soldier talk for an hour or more. The dead man lay all alone outside in the shadow of the low stone wall.

Then a soldier came into the cowshed and said there were some more bodies outside. We went out into the road. Four mules stood there, in the moonlight, in the road where the trail came down off the mountain. The soldiers who led them stood there waiting. "This one is Captain Waskow," one of them said quietly.

Two men unlashed his body from the mule and lifted it off and laid it in the shadow beside the low stone wall. Other men took the other bodies off. Finally there were five lying end to end in a long row, alongside the road. You don't cover up dead men in the combat zone. They just lie there in the shadows until somebody else comes after them.

The unburdened mules moved off to their olive orchard. The men in the road seemed reluctant to leave. They stood around, and gradually one by one I could sense them moving close to Capt. Waskow's body. Not so much to look, I think, as to say something in finality to him, and to themselves. I stood close by and I could hear.

One soldier came and looked down, and he said out loud, "God damn it." That's all he said, and then he walked away. Another one came. He said, "God damn it to hell anyway." He looked down for a few last moments, and then he turned and left.

Another man came; I think he was an officer. It was hard to tell officers from men in the half-light, for all were bearded and grimy dirty. The man looked down into the dead captain's face, and then he spoke directly to him, as though he were alive. He said: "I'm sorry, old man."

Then a soldier came and stood beside the officer, and bent over, and he too spoke to his dead captain, not in a whisper but awfully tenderly, and he said:

"I sure am sorry, sir."

Then the first man squatted down, and he reached down and took the dead hand, and he sat there for a full five minutes, holding the dead hand in his own and looking intently into the dead face, and he never uttered a sound all the time he sat there.

And finally he put the hand down, and then reached up and gently straightened the points of the captain's shirt collar, and then he sort of rearranged the tattered edges of his uniform around the wound. And then he got up and walked away down the road in the moonlight, all alone.

❧ Landing on Omaha Beach

BOB SLAUGHTER

On the morning of June 6, 1944, Allied troops landed in Normandy, France, to open a second European front against Germany. Five beachheads were established, two by American troops, two by the British and one by Canadians. While both the British and the Canadians encountered relatively light resistance, American soldiers met stiff resistance at both its landings, especially at Omaha Beach.

Soldiers from the 1st and 29th Infantry Divisions were assigned to take the beachhead along with amphibious tanks and Army Rangers. Their assignment was to secure the beachhead for demolition task forces that would clear the area of minefields. But exposed to point-blank enemy fire across the beach from a well-protected and heavily armed defense, the initial infantryman encountered a hailstorm of bullets and shrapnel. Despite the heavy casualties, the U.S. troops would take the beach, but at a brutal cost.

Bob Slaughter of the 29th Infantry Division survived the terrible battle and recalled his experience years later.

We saw the bomb explosions causing fires that illuminated clouds in the otherwise dark sky. We were twelve miles offshore as we climbed into our seat assignments on the LCAs and were lowered into the heavy sea from davits. The navy hadn't begun its firing because it was still dark. We couldn't see the armada but we knew it was there.

Prior to loading, friends said their so longs and good lucks. I remember finding Sergeant Jack Ingram, an old friend from Roanoke. He had suffered a back injury during training and I asked him how he felt. "I'm okay. Good luck, I'll see you on the beach." Another Roanoker, a neighbor and classmate, George D. Johnson, who'd joined the army with me, asked, "Are your men ready?" I couldn't imagine why he asked, but I answered yes.

Sergeant Robert Bizler of Shamokin, Pennsylvania, joked, "I'm going to land with a comb in one hand"—running his hand through his blond hair—"and a pass to Paris in the other." The feeling among most of the men was that the landing would be a "walk-in" affair but later we could expect a stiff counterattack. That didn't worry us too much, since by then tanks, heavy artillery, and air support should bolster our defense until the beachhead grew strong enough for a breakout.

All of us had a letter signed by the Supreme Commander, General Eisenhower, saying that we were about to embark upon a great crusade. A few of my cohorts autographed it and I carried it in my wallet throughout the war.

The Channel was extremely rough, and it wasn't long before we had to help the craft's pumps by bailing with our helmets. The cold spray blew in and soon we were soaking wet. I used a gas cape as shelter. Lack of oxygen under the sack brought seasickness.

As the sky lightened, the armada became visible. The smoking and burning French shoreline also became more defined. At 0600, the huge guns of the Allied navies opened up with what must have been one of the greatest artillery barrages ever. The diesels on board our craft failed to muffle the tornadic blasting. I could see the *Texas* firing broadside into the coastline. Bomm-ba-ba-boom-ba-ba-boom! Within minutes, giant swells from the recoil of those guns nearly swamped us and added to the seasickness and misery. But one could also actually see the two-thousand-pound missiles tumbling on their targets. Twin-fuselaged P-38 fighter-bombers were also overhead protecting us from the Luftwaffe and giving us a false sense of security. This should be a piece of cake.

A few thousand yards from shore we rescued three or four survivors from a craft that had been swamped and sunk. Other men were left in the water bobbing in their Mae Wests, because we did not have room for them.

About two or three hundred yards from shore we encountered artillery fire. Near misses sent water skyward and then it rained back on use. The British coxswain said he had to lower the ramp and for us to quickly disembark. Back in Weymouth these sailors had bragged they had been on several invasions and we were in capable hands. I heard Sergeant Willard Norfleet say, "These men have heavy equipment. You will take them all the way in."

The coxswain pleaded, "But we'll all be killed!" Norfleet unholstered his .45 Colt, put it to the sailor's head, and ordered "All the way in!" The craft kept going, plowing through the choppy water.

I thought, if this boat doesn't hurry and get us in, I'll die from seasickness. Thinking I was immune to this malady, I had given my puke bag to a buddy who already had filled his. Minus the paper bag, I used my steel helmet.

About 150 yards from shore, I raised my head despite the warning, "Keep your head down." I saw the boat on our right taking a terrific licking from small arms. Tracer bullets were bouncing and skipping off the ramp and sides as the enemy zeroed in on the boat which had beached a few minutes before us. Had we not delayed a few minutes to pick up the survivors of the sunken craft, we might have taken that concentration of fire.

Great plumes of water from enemy artillery and mortars sprouted close by. We knew then this was not going to be a walk-in. No one thought the enemy would give us this kind of opposition at the water's edge. We expected A and B Companies to have the beach secured by the time we landed. In reality no one had set foot in our sector. The coxswain had missed the Vierville church steeple, our point to guide on, and the tides also helped pull us two hundred yards east.

The location didn't make much difference. We could hear the "p-r-r-r-r, p-r-r-r-r" of enemy machine guns to our right, towards the west. It was obvious someone down there was catching that hell, getting chewed up where we had been supposed to come in.

The ramp went down while shells exploded on land and in the water. Unseen snipers were shooting down from the cliffs, but the most havoc came from automatic weapons. I was at the left side of the craft, about fifth from the front. Norfleet led the right side. The ramp was in the surf, and the front of the boat buckled violently up and down. Only two at a time could exit.

When my turn came, I sat on the edge of the bucking ramp, trying to time my leap on the down cycle. I sat there way too long, causing a bottleneck and endangering myself and the men to follow. But the ramp was bounding six or seven feet, and I was afraid it would slam me in the head. One man was crushed and killed instantly.

When I did get out, I was in the water. It was very difficult to shed the sixty pounds of equipment, and if one were a weak swimmer he could drown before he inflated his Mae West. Many were in the water and drowned, good swimmers or not. There were dead men floating in the water and live men acting dead, letting the tide take them in. Initially, I tried to take cover behind one of the heavy timbers and then noticed an innocent-looking Teller mine tied to the top. I crouched down to chin deep in the water as shells fell at the water's edge. Small-arms fire kicked up sand. I noticed a GI running, trying to get across the beach. He was weighed down with equipment and having difficulty moving. An enemy gunner shot him. He screamed for a medic. An aidman moved quickly to help him and he was also shot. I'll never forget seeing that medic lying next to that wounded soldier, both of them screaming. They died in minutes.

Boys were turned into men. Some would be very brave men; others would soon be dead men, but any who survived would be frightened men. Some wet their pants, others cried unashamedly. Many just had to find within themselves the strength to get the job done. Discipline and training took over.

For me, it was time to get the hell away from the killing zone and across the beach. Getting across the beach became an obsession. I told Pfc Walfred Williams, my number one gunner, to follow. He still had his fifty-one-pound machine gun tripod. He once told me he developed his strength by cradling an old iron cookstove in his arms and walking around with it, daily. I felt secure with Williams on the gun. A Chicago boy of nineteen, he was dependable and loyal. He loved the army and didn't believe a German weapon could kill him. I didn't think so either. (We were both wrong. Enemy shrapnel killed him six weeks after D-Day. Part of me would die with him.)

Our rifles were encased in a plastic bag to shield them from salt water. Before disembarking, because I wanted to be ready, I had removed the covering and fixed the bayonet. I gathered my courage and started running as fast as I could to lessen the target, but since I am six-foot-five, I presented a good one. It was a long way to go, one hundred yards or more. We were loaded with gear, our shoes full of water, our impregnated woolen clothes soaked. I tripped in a tidal pool of a few inches of water, began to stumble, and accidentally fired my rifle, barely missing my foot. But I made it to the seawall.

I was joined by Private Sal Augeri, and Private Ernest McCanless and Williams. Augeri lost the machine gun receiver in the water. We still had one box of MG ammo and the tripod. I had gotten sand in my rifle, so I don't believe we had a weapon that would fire. I felt like a naked morsel on a giant sandy platter.

I took off my assault jacket and spread out my raincoat so I could clean my rifle. It was then I saw

bullet holes in my jacket and raincoat. I lit my first cigarette; I had to rest and compose myself because I became weak in the knees.

🍂 *The G.I. Bill*

CONGRESS

Grateful for the sacrifices of American soldiers and aware of the problems returning World War I veterans faced, Congress passed the G.I. Bill in 1944 giving an extraordinary array of benefits to veterans. Education aid, housing assistance, medical care, unemployment compensation, job training and more would all be provided by the federal government when the war ended.

Officially called the Servicemen's Readjustment Act, the G.I. Bill eased the transition of returning veterans and provided an enormous boost to the post-war economy. Opportunities unimaginable to many of the 8 million service men and women prior to the war were being provided at virtually no cost.

Title I

Chapter 1: Hospitalization, Claims, and Procedures
Section 100. The Veterans' Administrations is hereby declared to be an essential war agency and entitled, second only to the War and Navy Departments, to priorities in personnel, equipment, supplies, and material under any laws, Executive orders, and regulations pertaining to priorities, and in appointments of personnel from civil-service registers the Administrator of Veterans' Affairs is hereby granted the same authority and discretion as the War and Navy Departments and the United States Public Health Service:

Provided, That the provisions of this section as to priorities for materials shall apply to any State institution to be built for the care or hospitalization of veterans....

Any person entitled to a prosthetic appliance shall be entitled, in addition, to necessary fitting and training, including institutional training, in the use of such appliance, whether in a Service or a Veterans' Administration hospital, or by outpatient treatment, including such service under contract....

Section 300. The discharge or dismissal by reason of the sentence of a general court martial of any person from the military or naval forces, or the discharge of any such person on the ground that he was a conscientious objector who refused to perform military duty or refused to wear the uniform or otherwise to comply with lawful orders of competent military authority, or as a deserter, or as an officer by the acceptance of his resignation for the good of the service, shall bar all rights of such person, based upon the period of service from which he is so discharged or dismissed, under any laws administered by the Veterans' Administration: Provided, That in the case of any such person, if it is established to the satisfaction of the Administrator that at the time of the commission of the offense such person was insane, he shall not be precluded from benefits to which he is otherwise entitled under the laws administered by the Veterans' Administration: And provided further, That this section shall not apply to any war risk, Government (converted) or national service life-insurance policy....

Title II
Section 400. (a) Subsection (f) of section 1, title 1, Public Law Numbered 2, Seventy-third Congress, added by the Act of March 24, 1943 (Public Law Numbered 16, Seventy-eighth Congress), is hereby amended to read as follows:

"(f) Any person who served in the active military or naval forces on or after September 16, 1940, and prior to the termination of hostilities in the present war, shall be entitled to vocational rehabilitation subject to the provisions and limitations of Part VII, or to education or training subject to the provisions and limitations of part VIII."

(b) Veterans Regulation Numbered 1 (a), is hereby amended by adding a new part VIII as follows:

Part VIII
"1. Any person who served in the active military or naval service on or after September 16, 1940, and prior to the termination of the present war, and who shall have been discharged or released therefrom under conditions other than dishonorable, and whose education or training was impeded, delayed, interrupted, or interfered with by reason of his entrance into the service, or who desires a refresher or retraining course, and who either shall have served ninety days or more, exclusive of any period he was assigned for a course of education or training under the Army specialized program or the Navy college training program, which course was a continuation of his civilian course and was pursued to completion, or as a cadet or midshipman at one of the

service academies, or shall have been discharged or released from active service by reason of an actual service-incurred injury or disability, shall be eligible for and entitled to receive education or training under this part: Provided, That such course shall be initiated not later than two years after either date of his discharge or the termination of the present war, whichever is the later. Provided further, That no such education or training shall be afforded beyond seven years after the termination of the present war: And provided further, That any such person who was not over 25 years of age at the time he entered the service shall be deemed to have had his education or training impeded, delayed, interrupted, or interfered with.

"2. Any such eligible person shall be entitled to education or training, or a refresher or retraining course, at an approved educational or training institution, for a period of one year (or the equivalent thereof in continuous part-time study), or for such lesser time as may be required for the course of instruction chosen by him. Upon satisfactory completion of such course of education or training, according to the regularly prescribed standards and practices of the institutions, except as a refresher or retraining course, such person shall be entitled to an additional period or periods of education or training, not to exceed the time such person was in active service on or after September 16, 1940, and before the termination of the war, exclusive of any period he was assigned for a course of education or training under the Army specialized training program or the Navy college training program, which course was a continuation of his civilian course and was pursued to completion, or as a cadet or midshipman at one of the service academies, but in no event shall the total period of education or training exceed four years: Provided, That his work continues to be satisfactory throughout the period, according to the prescribed standards and practices of the institution: Provided, however, That wherever the additional period of instruction ends during a quarter or semester and after a major part of such quarter or semester has expired, such period of instruction shall be extended to the termination of such unexpired quarter or semester.

"3. Such person shall be eligible for and entitled to such course of education or training as he may elect, and at any approved educational or training institution at which he chooses to enroll, whether or not located in the state in which he resides, which will accept or retain him as a student or trainee in any field or branch of knowledge which such institution finds him qualified to undertake or pursue: Provided, That, for reasons satisfactory to the Administrator, he may change a course of instruction: And provided further, That any such course of education or training may be discontinued at any time, if it is found by the Administrator that, according to the regularly prescribed standards and practices of the institution, the conduct or progress of such person is unsatisfactory....

"5. The Administrator shall pay to the educational or training institution, for each person enrolled in full time or part time course of education or training, the customary cost of tuition, and such laboratory, library, health, infirmary, and other similar fees as are customarily charged, and pay for books, supplies, equipment, and other necessary expenses, exclusive of board, lodging, other living expenses, and travel, as are generally required for the successful pursuit and completion of the course by other students in the institution: Provided, That in no event shall such payments, with respect to any person, exceed $500 for an ordinary school year: Provided further, That no payments shall be made to institutions, business or other establishments furnishing apprentice training on the job: And provided further, That if any such institution has no established tuition fee, or if its established tuition fee shall be found by the Administrator to be inadequate compensation to such institution for furnishing such education or training, he is authorized to provide for the payment, with respect to any such person, of such fair and reasonable compensation as will not exceed $500 for an ordinary school year.

"6. While enrolled in and pursuing a course under this part, such person, upon application to the Administrator, shall be paid a subsistence allowance of $50 per month, if without a dependent or dependents, or $75 per month, if he has a dependent or dependents, including regular holidays and leave not exceeding thirty days in a calendar year. Such person attending a course on a part-time basis, and such person receiving compensation for productive labor performed as part of their apprentice or other training on the job at institutions, business or other establishments, shall be entitled to receive such lesser sums, if any, as subsistence or dependency

allowances, as may be determined by the Administrator: Provided, That any such person eligible under this part, and within the limitations thereof, may pursue such full time or part-time course or courses as he may elect, without subsistence allowance....

"8. No department, agency, or officer of the United States in carrying out the provisions of this part, shall exercise any supervision or control, whatsoever, over any State educational agency, or State apprenticeship agency, or any educational or training institution: Provided, That nothing in this section shall be deemed to prevent any department, agency, or officer of the United States from exercising any supervision or control which such department, agency, or officer is authorized, by existing provisions of law, to exercise over any Federal educational or training institution, or to prevent the furnishing of education or training under this part in any institution over which supervision or control is exercised by such other department, agency, or officer under authority of existing provisions of law....

"11. As used in this part, the term 'educational or training institutions' shall include all public or private elementary, secondary, and other schools furnishing education for adults, business schools and colleges, scientific and technical institutions, colleges, vocational schools, junior colleges, teachers colleges, normal schools, professional schools, universities, and other educational institutions, and shall also include business or other establishments providing apprenticeship agency or State board of vocational education, or any State apprenticeship council or the Federal Apprentice Training Service established in according with Public Numbered 308, Seventy-fifth Congress, or any agency in the executive branch of the Federal Government authorized under other laws to supervise such training."...

Title III Loans for the Purchase or Construction of Homes, Farms, and Business Property
Chapter V. General Provisions for Loans
Section 500. (a) Any person who shall have served in the active military or naval service of the United States at any time on or after September 16, 1940, and prior to the termination of the present war and who shall have been discharged or released there-

from under conditions other than dishonorable after active service of ninety days or more, or by reason of an injury or disability incurred in service in line of duty, shall be eligible for the benefits of this title. Any such veteran may apply within two years after separation from the military or naval forces, or two years after termination of the war, whichever is the later date, but in no event more than five years after the termination of the war, to the Administrator of Veterans' Affairs for the guaranty by the Administrator of not to exceed 50 percent of a loan or loans for any of the purposes specified in sections 501, 502 and 503: Provided, That the aggregate amount guaranteed shall not exceed $2,000. If the Administrator finds that the veteran is eligible for the benefits of this title and that the loan applied for appears practicable, the Administrator shall guarantee the payment of the part thereof as set forth in this title....

Purchase or Construction of Homes
Section 501. (a) Any application made by a veteran under this title for the guaranty of a loan to be used in purchasing residential property or in constructing a dwelling on unimproved property owned by him to be occupied as his home may be approved by the Administrator of Veterans' Affairs if he finds that the proceeds of such loans will be used for payment for such property to be purchased or constructed by the veteran; that the contemplated terms of payment required in any mortgage to be given in part payment of the purchase price or the construction cost bear a proper relation to the veteran's present and anticipated income and expenses; and that the nature and condition of the property is such as to be suitable for dwelling purposes; and that the purchase price paid or to be paid by the veteran for such property or the construction cost, including the value of the unimproved lot, does not exceed the reasonable normal value thereof as determined by proper appraisal.

(b) Any application for the guaranty of a loan under this section for the purpose of making repairs, alteration, or improvements in, or paying delinquent indebtedness, taxes, or special assessments on, residential property owned by the veteran and used by him as his home, may be approved by the Administrator if he finds that the proceeds of such loan will be used for such purpose or purposes....

Purchase of Farms and Farm Equipment
Section 502. Any application made under this title for the guaranty of a loan to be used in purchasing any land, buildings, livestock, equipment, machinery, or implements, or in repairing, altering, or improving any buildings or equipment, to be used in farming operations conducted by the applicant, may be approved by the Administrator of Veterans' Affairs if he finds that the proceeds of such loan will be used in payment for real or personal property purchased or to be purchased by the veteran, or for repairing, altering, or improving any buildings or equipment, to be used in bona fide farming operations conducted by him; that such property will be useful in and reasonably necessary for efficiently conducting such operations; that the ability and experience of the veteran, and the nature of the proposed farming operations to be conducted by him, are such that there is a reasonable likelihood that such operations will be successful....

Title IV
Chapter VI. Employment of Veterans
Section 600, (a) In the enactment of the provisions of this title Congress declares as its intent and purpose that there shall be an effective job counseling and employment placement service for veterans, and that, to this end, policies shall be promulgated and administered, so as to provide for them the maximum of job opportunity in the field of gainful employment....

Title V
Chapter VII. Readjustment Allowances for Former Members of the Armed Forces Who Are Unemployed
Section 700. (a) Any person who shall have served in the active military or naval service of the United States at any time after September 16, 1940, and prior to the termination of the present war, and who shall have been discharged or released from active service under conditions other than dishonorable, after active service of ninety days or more, or by reason of an injury or disability incurred in service in line of duty, shall be entitled, in accordance with the provisions of this title and regulations issued by the Administrator of Veterans' Affairs pursuant thereto, to receive a readjustment allowance as provided herein for each week of unemployment, not to exceed a total of fifty-two weeks, which (1) begins after the first

Sunday of the third calendar month after the date of enactment hereof, and (2) occurs not later than two years after discharge or release or the termination of the war, whichever is the later date: Provided, That no such allowance shall be paid for any period for which he receives increased pension under part VII of Veterans Regulation 1 (a) or a subsistence allowance under part VIII of such regulation: Provided further, That no readjustment allowance shall be payable for any week commencing more than five years after the termination of hostilities in the present war....

❧ "Liberty lies in the hearts of men and women"

JUDGE LEARNED HAND

In 1944 during "I Am an American Day" Judge Learned Hand spoke on the meaning of liberty.

As a federal judge for more than twenty years, Hand would become one of the most forceful protectors of liberty in American history. At the time of the speech, however, he was articulating the central purpose of the war against totalitarian Germany. His address became known as the "Spirit of Liberty" speech.

We have gathered here to affirm a faith, a faith in a common purpose, a common conviction, a common devotion. Some of us have chosen America as the land of our adoption; the rest have come from those who did the same. For this reason we have some right to consider ourselves a picked group, a group of those who had the courage to break from the past and brave the dangers and the loneliness of a strange land. What was the object that nerved us, or those who went before us, to this choice? We sought liberty—freedom from oppression, freedom from want, freedom to be ourselves. This then we sought; this we now believe that we are by way of winning. What do we mean when we say that first of all we seek liberty? I often wonder whether we do not rest our hopes too much upon constitutions, upon laws, and upon courts. These are false hopes; believe me, these are false hopes. Liberty lies in the hearts of men and women; when it dies there, no constitution, no law, no court can save it; no constitution, no law, no court can even do much to

help it. While it lies there, it needs no constitution, no law, no court to save it. And what is this liberty which must lie in the hearts of men and women? It is not the ruthless, the unbridled will; it is not freedom to do as one likes. That is the denial of liberty, and leads straight to its overthrow. A society in which men recognize no check upon their freedom soon becomes a society where freedom is the possession of only a savage few—as we have learned to our sorrow.

What, then, is the spirit of liberty? I cannot define it; I can only tell you my own faith. The spirit of liberty is the spirit which is not too sure that it is right; the spirit of liberty is the spirit which seeks to understand the minds of other men and women; the spirit of liberty is the spirit which weighs their interest alongside its own without bias; the spirit of liberty remembers that not even a sparrow falls to earth unheeded; the spirit of liberty is the spirit of him who, near two thousand years ago, taught mankind that lesson it is has never learned, but has never quite forgotten—that there may be a kingdom where the least shall be heard and considered side-by-side with the greatest. And now in that spirit, that spirit of an American which has never been, and which may never be—nay, which never will be except as the conscience and courage of Americans create it—yet in the spirit of America which lies hidden in some form in the aspirations of us all; in the spirit of that America for which our young men are at this moment fighting and dying; in that spirit of liberty and of America so prosperous, and safe, and contented, we shall have failed to grasp its meaning, and shall have been truant to its promise, except as we strive to make it a signal, a beacon, a standard, to which the best hopes of mankind will ever turn? In confidence that you share that belief, I now ask you to raise your hands and repeat with me this pledge:

I pledge allegiance to the flag of the United States of America, and to the Republic for which it stands—one nation, indivisible, with liberty and justice for all.

"A United Nations
conference on the
proposed world
organization should be
summoned"

YALTA (CRIMEA) CONFERENCE

By February 1945, it had become clear that the Allies would win World War II. The most looming issues had become how to finish the conflict, when Germany and Japan would capitulate, what to do with the conquered and destroyed countries after the war, and how to preserve peace. Roosevelt, Churchill and Stalin met at Yalta in the Russian Crimea to ponder these questions and hammer out an agreement.

Although united in their goal of conquering Germany, friction among the three leaders was starting to grow. Conflicting interests emerged. Stalin was interested in keeping the Soviet Union's influence in Poland, which it occupied. Similarly, England hoped to maintain its position of power in Greece. The outlines of conflict in the coming Cold War were starting to form.

Nevertheless, the outcome yielded several agreements, the most promising of which was a pledge to create the United Nations along with a mutually agreed upon framework to structure it. Other results included a plan to divide Germany after the war, an agreement to prosecute war criminals, plans on how to proceed with re-establishment of Poland and Yugoslavia as sovereign nations, and a pledge from Russia to attack Japanese forces in mainland China, an event that occurred one day before Japan surrendered.

Protocol of Proceedings of Crimea Conference
The Crimea Conference of the heads of the Governments of the United States of America, the United Kingdom, and the Union of Soviet Socialist Republics, which took place from Feb. 4 to 11, came to the following conclusions:

World Organization
It was decided:
That a United Nations conference on the proposed world organization should be summoned for Wednesday, 25 April, 1945, and should be held in the United States of America

The nations to be invited to this conference should be: the United Nations as they existed on 8 Feb., 1945; and Such of the Associated Nations as have declared war on the common enemy by 1 March, 1945. (For this purpose, by the term "Associated Nations and Turkey.) When the conference on world organization is held, the delegates

of the United Kingdom and United States of America will support a proposal to admit to original membership two Soviet Socialist Republics, i.e., the Ukraine and White Russia.

That the United States Government, on behalf of the three powers, should consult the Government of China and the French Provisional Government in regard to decisions taken at present conference concerning the proposed world organization.

That the text of the invitation to be issued to all the nations which would take part in the United Nations conference should be as follows:

"The Government of the Untied States of America, on behalf of itself and of the Governments of the United Kingdom, the Union of Soviet Socialist Republics and the Republic of China and of the Provisional Government of the French Republic, invite the Government of _____ to send representatives to a conference to be held on 25 April, 1945, or soon thereafter, at San Francisco, in the United States of America, to prepare a charter for a general international organization for the maintenance of international peace and security.

"The above-named Governments suggest that the conference consider as affording a basis for such a Charter the proposals for the establishment of a general international organization which were made public last October as a result of the Dumbarton Oaks conference and which have now been supplemented by the following provisions for Section C of Chapter VI:

C. Voting
"1. Each member of the Security Council should have one vote.

"2. Decisions of the Security Council on procedural matters should be made by an affirmative vote of seven members.

"3. Decisions of the Security Council on all matters should be made by an affirmative vote of seven members, including the concurring votes of the permanent members; provided that, in decisions under Chapter VIII, Section A and under the second sentence of Paragraph 1 of Chapter VIII, Section C, a party to a dispute should abstain from voting.

"Further information as to arrangements will be transmitted subsequently.

"In the event that the Government of _____ desires in advance of the conference to present views or comments concerning the proposals, the Government of the United States of America will be pleased to transmit such views and comments to the other participating Governments."

D. Territorial Trusteeship:

It was agreed that the five nations which have permanent seats on the Security Council should consult each other prior to the United Nations conference on the question of territorial trusteeship.

The acceptance of this recommendation is subject to its being made clear that territorial trusteeship will only apply to (a) existing mandates of the League of Nations; (b) territories detached from the enemy as a result of the present war; (c) any other territory which might voluntarily be placed under trusteeship; and (d) no discussion of actual territories is contemplated at the forthcoming United Nations conference or in the preliminary consulations, and it will be a matter for subsequent agreement which territories within the above categories will be placed under trusteeship.

I. Declaration of Liberated Europe

The following declaration has been approved:

The Premier of the Union of Soviet Socialist Republics, the Prime Minister of the United Kingdom and the President of the United States of America have consulted with each other in the common interests of the peoples of their countries and those of liberated Europe. They jointly declare their mutual agreement to concert during the temporary period of instability in liberated Europe the policies of their three Governments in assisting the peoples liberated from the domination of Nazi Germany and the peoples of the former Axis satellite states of Europe to solve by democratic means their pressing political and economic problems.

The establishment of order in Europe and the rebuilding of national economic life must be achieved by processes which will enable the liberated peoples to destroy the last vestiges of nazism and fascism and to create democratic institutions of their own choice. This is a principle of the Atlantic Charter—the right of all peoples to choose the form of government under which they will live—the restoration of sovereign rights and self-government to those peoples who have been forcibly deprived of them by the aggressor nations.

To foster the conditions in which the liberated peoples may exercise these rights, the three Governments will jointly assist the people in any European liberated state or former Axis satellite state in Europe where, in their judgment conditions require, (a) to establish conditions of internal peace; (b) to carry out emergency measures for the relief of distressed peoples; (c) to form interim governmental authorities broadly representative of all democratic elements in the population and pledged to the earliest possible establishment through free elections of Governments responsive to the will of the people; and (d) to facilitate where necessary the holding of such elections.

The three Governments will consult the other United Nations and provisional authorities or other Governments in Europe when matters of direct interest to them are under consideration.

When, in the opinion of the three Governments, conditions in any European liberated state or any former Axis satellite state in Europe make such action necessary, they will immediately consult together on the measure necessary to discharge the joint responsibilities set forth in this declaration.

By this declaration we reaffirm our faith in the principles of the Atlantic Charter, our pledge in the Declaration by the United Nations and our determination to build in cooperation with other peace-loving nations world order, under law, dedicated to peace, security, freedom and general well-being of all mankind.

In issuing this declaration, the three powers express the hope that the Provisional Government of the French Republic may be associated with them in the procedure suggested.

Dismemberment of Germany

It was agreed that Article 12 (a) of the Surrender Terms for Germany should be amended to read as follows:

"The United Kingdom, The United States of America and the Union of Soviet Socialist Republics shall possess supreme authority with respect to Germany. In the exercise of such authority they will take such steps, including the complete disarmament, demilitarization and dismemberment of Germany as they deem requisite for future peace and Security."

The study of the procedure of the dismemberment of Germany was referred to a committee consisting of Mr. [Anthony] Eden [their Foreign Secretary] (chairman), Mr. [John] Winant [of the United States] and Mr. [Fedor T.] Gusev. This body would consider the desirability of associating with it a French representative.

Zone of Occupation for the French and Control Council for Germany

It was agreed that a zone in Germany, to be occupied by the French forces, should be allocated to France. This zone would be formed out of the British and American zones and its extent would be settled by the British and Americans in consultation with the French Provisional Government.

It was also agreed that the French Provisional Government should be invited to become a member of the Allied Control Council for Germany.

Reparation

The following protocol has been approved:

Protocol

On the Talks Between the Heads of Three Governments at the Crimean Conference on The Question of the German Reparations in Kind:

Germany must pay in kind for the losses caused by her to the Allied nations in course of the war. Reparations are to be received in the first instance by those countries which have borne the main burden of the war, have suffered the heaviest losses and have organized victory over the enemy.

Reparations in kind is to be exacted from Germany in three following forms:

Removals within two years from the surrender of Germany or the cessation of organized resistance from the national wealth of Germany located on the territory of Germany herself as well as outside her territory (equipment, machine tools, ships, rolling stock, German investments abroad, shares of industrial, transport, and other enterprises in Germany, etc.) these removals to be carried out chiefly for the purpose of destroying the war potential of Germany.

Annual deliveries of goods from current production for a period to be fixed.

Use of German Labor.

For the working out on the above principles of a detailed plan for exaction of reparation from Germany an Allied reparations commission will be set up in Moscow. It will consist of three representatives—one from the Union of Soviet Socialist Republics, one from the United Kingdom and one from the United States of America.

With regard to the fixing of the total sum of the reparation as well as the distrubution of it among the countries which suffered from the German aggression, the Soviet and American delegations agreed as follows:

"The Moscow reparation commission should take in its initial studies as a basis for discussion the suggestion of the Soviet Government that the total sum of the reparation in accordance with the points (a) and (b) of the Paragraph 2 should be 20 billion dollars and that 50 percent of it should go to the Union of Soviet Socialist Republics."

The British delegation was of the opinion that, pending consideration of the reparation questions by the Moscow reparation commission, no figures of reparation should be mentioned.

The Soviet-American proposal has been passed to the Moscow reparation commission as one of the proposals to be considered by the commission.

Major War Criminals

The conference agreed that the question of the major war criminals should be the subject of inquiry by the three Foreign Secretaries for report in due course after the close of the conference.

Poland

The following declaration on Poland was agreed by the conference:

"A new situation has been created in Poland as a result of her complete liberation by the Red Army. This calls for the establishment of a Polish Provisional Government which can be more broadly based than was possible before the recent liberation of the western part of Poland. The Provisional Government which is now functioning in Poland should therefore be reorganized on a broader democratic basis with the inclusion of democratic leaders from Poland itself and from Poles abroad. This new Government should then be called the Polish Provisional Government of National Unity.

"M. Molotov, Mr. Harriman and Sir A. Clark Kerr are authorized as a commission to consult in the first instance in Moscow with members of the present Provisional Government and with other Polish democratic leaders from within Poland and from abroad, with a view to the reorganization of the present Government along the above lines. This Polish Provisional Government of National Unity shall be pledged to the holding of free and unfettered elections as soon as possible on the basis of universal suffrage and secret ballot. In these elections all democratic and anti-Nazi parties shall have the right to take part and to put forward candidates.

"When a Polish Provisional Government of National Unity has been properly formed in conformity with the above, the Government of the U.S.S.R., which now maintains diplomatic relations with the present Provisional Government of Poland, and the Government of the United Kingdom and the Government of the United States of America will establish diplomatic relations with the new Polish Provisional Government of National Unity, and will exchanged Ambassadors by those reports the respective Governments will be kept informed about the situation in Poland.

"The three heads of Government consider that the eastern frontier of Poland should follow the Curzon Line with digressions from it in some regions of five to eight kilometers in favor of Poland. They recognize that Poland must receive substantial accessions of territory in the north and west. They feel that the opinion of the new Polish Provisional Government of National Unity should be sought in due course of the extent of these accessions and that the final delimitation of the western frontier of Poland should hereafter await the peace conference."

Yugoslavia
It was agreed to recommend to Marshall Tito and to Dr. [Ivan] Subasitch:

That the Tito-Subasitch agreement should immediately be put into effect and a new Government formed on the basis of the agreement.

That as soon as the new Government has been formed it should declare:

That the Anti-Fascist Assembly of the National Liberation (AVNOJ) will be extended to include members of the last Yugoslav Skupstina who have not compromised themselves by collaboration with the enemy, thus forming a body to be

known as a temporary Parliament and

That legislative acts passed by the Anti-Fascist Assembly of National Liberation (AVNOJ) will be subject to subsequent ratification by a Constituent Assembly; and that this statement should be published in the communique of the conference.

Italo-Austrian Frontier
Notes on these subjects were put in by British delegation, and the American and Soviet delegations agreed to consider them and give their views later.

Yugoslav-Bulgarian Relations
There was an exchange of views between the Foreign Secretaries on the question of the desirability of a Yugoslav-Bulgarian pact of alliance. The question at issue was whether a state under an armistice regime could be allowed to enter into a treaty with another state. Mr. Eden suggested that the Bulgarian and Yugoslav Governments should be informed that this could not be approved. Mr. Stettinius suggested that the British and American Ambassadors should discuss the matter further with Mr. Molotov in Moscow. Mr. Molotov agreed with the proposal of Mr. Stettinius.

Southeastern Europe
The British delegation put in notes for the consideration of their colleagues on the following subjects:

The Control Commission in Bulgaria.

Greek claims upon Bulgaria, more particularly with reference to reparations.

Oil equipment in Romania.

Iran

Mr. Eden, Mr. Stettinius and Mr. Molotov exchanged views on the situation in Iran. It was agreed that this matter should be pursued through the diplomatic channel.

Agreement Regarding Japan
The leaders of the three great powers—the Soviet Union, the United States of America and Great Britain—have agreed that in two or three months after Germany has surrendered and the war in Europe has terminated, the Soviet Union shall enter into the war against Japan on the side of the Allies on condition that:

The status quo in Outer Mongolia (the Mongolian People's Republic) shall be preserved;

The former rights of Russia violated by the treacherous attack of Japan in 1904 shall be restored, viz:

The southern part of Sakhalin as well as the islands adjacent to it shall be returned to the Soviet Union;

The commercial port of Dairen shall be internationalized, the pre-eminent interests of the Soviet Union in this port being safeguarded, and the lease of Port Arthur as a naval base of the U.S.S.R. restored;

The Chinese-Eastern Railroad and the South Manchurian Railroad, which provide an outlet to Dairen, shall be jointly Soviet-Chinese company, it being understood that the pre-eminent interests of the Soviet Union shall be safeguarded and that China shall retain full sovereignty in Manchuria;

The Kurile Islands shall be handed over to the Soviet Union.

It is understood that the agreement concerning Outer Mongolia and the ports and railroads referred to above will require concurrence of Generalissimo Chaing Kai-shek. The President will take measures in order to obtain this concurrence on advice from Marshal Stalin.

The heads of the three greatest powers have agreed that these claims of the Soviet Union shall be unquestionably fulfilled after Japan has been defeated.

For its part, the Soviet Union expresses its readiness to conclude with the National Government of China a pact of friendship and alliance between the U.S.S.R. and China in order to render assistance to China with its armed forces for the purpose of liberating China from the Japanese yoke.

Joseph V. Stalin
Franklin D. Roosevelt
Winston S. Churchill
February 11, 1945

❧ "I think this is the end of the war"

COLONEL PAUL W. TIBBETS, JR.

On August 6, 1945, Colonel Paul W. Tibbets, Jr., and his crew aboard the B-29 bomber the Enola Gay dropped the first atom bomb on Hiroshima. More than 60,000 people were killed instantly. Another 100,000 were injured. Many thousands of these would die painful deaths over the next few years from the effects of radiation. Four square miles of the bustling Japanese city were leveled. Three days later a second bomb was dropped on Nagasaki with similar casualties. Shortly afterwards, Japan surrendered, ending World War II.

As we approached the city, we strained our eyes to find the designated aiming point. From a distance of 10 miles, [bombardier Tom] Ferebee suddenly said, "Okay, I've got the bridge." He pointed dead ahead, where it was just becoming visible. [Navigator Dutch] Van Kirk, looking over his shoulders, agreed. "No question about it," he said, scanning an air-photo and comparing it with what he was seeing. The T-shaped bridge was easy to spot. Even though there were many other bridges in this sprawling city, there was no other bridge that even slightly resembled it.

Van Kirk's job was finished so he went back and sat down.... Now it was up to Tom and me. We were only 90 seconds from the bomb release when I turned the plane over to him on autopilot.

"It's all yours," I told him, removing my hands from the controls and sliding back a bit in a not very successful effort to relax. My eyes were fixed on the center of the city, which shimmered in the early morning sunlight.

In the buildings and on the streets there were people, of course, but from six miles up they were invisible. To the men who fly the bombers, targets are inanimate, consisting of buildings, bridges, docks, factories, railroad yards. The tragic consequences to humanity are erased from one's thoughts in wartime because war itself is a human tragedy. Of course, one hopes that civilians will have the good sense to seek protection in bomb shelters. In the case of Hiroshima, I was to learn later that Eatherly's weather plane, over the city three-quarters of an hour before our arrival, had set off air sirens but, when nothing happened, ours were ignored.

By this time, Tom Ferebee was pressing his left eye against the viewfinder of the bomb sight..."We're on target," he said, confirming that the sighting and release mechanism were synchronized, so that the drop would take place automatically at a precalculated point in our bomb run. At 17 seconds after 9:14 am, just 60 seconds before the scheduled bomb release, he flicked a toggle switch that activated a high-pitched radio tone. This tone, ominous under the circumstances, sounded in the headphones of the men aboard our plane and the two airplanes that were with us.

A moment before, [co-pilot] Bob Lewis had made this notation in his informal log of the flight: "There will be a short intermission while we bomb our target."

Exactly one minute after it began, the radio tone ceased and at the same instant there was the sound of the pneumatic bomb-bay doors opening automatically. Out tumbled "Little Boy," a mis-named package of explosive force infinitely more devastating than any bomb or cluster of bombs ever dropped before.

With the release of the bomb, the plane was instantly 9,000 pounds lighter. As a result, its nose leaped up sharply and I had to act quickly to execute the most important task of the flight: to put as much distance as possible between our plane and the point at which the bomb would explode. The 155 degree diving turn to the right, with its 60 degree bank, put a great strain on the airplane and its occupants. Bob Caron, in his tail-gunner's station, had a wild ride that he described as something like being the last man in a game of crack-the-whip.

When we completed the turn, we had lost 1,700 feet and were heading away from our target with engines at full power.... I was flying this biggest of all bombers as if it were a fighter plane.

Bob Lewis and I had slipped our dark glasses over our eyes, as I had directed the other crewmen to do, but we promptly discovered that they made it impossible to fly the plane through this difficult get-away maneuver because the instrument panel was blacked out. We pushed the glasses back on our foreheads in a what-the-hell manner, realizing that we would be flying away from the actual flash when it occurred. Ferebee, in the bombardier's position in the nose of the plane, became so fascinated with watching the bomb's free-fall that he forgot all about the glasses....

For me, struggling with the controls, the 43 seconds from bomb release to explosion passed quickly. To some in the plane, it seemed an eternity. [Lieutenant Morris] Jeppison was quoted as saying that he had counted down the seconds in his mind, apparently too fast, and had the sickening feeling that the bomb was a dud.

Whatever our individual thoughts, it was a period of suspense. I was concentrating so intently on flying the airplane that the flash did not have the impact on my consciousness that one might think, even though it did light up the interior of the plane for a long instant. There was a startling sensation other than visual, however, that I remember quite vividly to this day. My teeth told me, more emphatically than my eyes, of the Hiroshima explosion. At the moment of the blast, there was a tingling sensation in my mouth and the very definite taste of lead upon my tongue. This, I was later told by scientists, was the result of electrolysis—an interaction between the fillings in my teeth and the radioactive forces that were loosed by the bomb.

"Little Boy" exploded at the preset altitude of 1,890 feet above the ground, but Bob Caron in the tail was the only one aboard our plane to see the incredible fireball that, in its atom-splitting fury, was a boiling furnace with an inner temperature calculated to be 100 million degrees Fahrenheit.

Caron, looking directly at the flash through glasses so dense that the sun penetrated but faintly, thought for a moment that he must have been blinded. Ferebee, without glasses but facing in the opposite direction from a relatively exposed position, felt as if a giant flashbulb had gone off a few feet from his face.

I continued my course from the target, awaiting the shock wave, which required almost a minute to reach us.... We must have been 9 miles from the point of the explosion when the shock wave reached us. This was the moment for which we had been bracing ourselves. Would the plane withstand the blow? The scientists were confident that it would, yet they admitted there were some aspects of the nuclear weapon's behavior about which they were not quite certain.

Caron, the only man aboard the plane with an immediate view of the awesome havoc we had created, tried to describe it to us. Suddenly, he saw the shock wave approaching at the speed of sound—almost 1,100 feet a second. Condensing moisture from the heated air at the leading edge of the shock wave made it quite visible, just as one sees shimmering air rising from the ground on a hot, humid day.

Before Caron could warn us to brace ourselves, the wave struck the plane with violent force. Our B-29 trembled under the impact and I gripped the controls tightly to keep us in level flight.... At a news conference next day, Bob Lewis told reporters that it felt as if some giant had struck the plane with a telephone pole.

Although Caron had told of a mushroom-shaped cloud, and said that it seemed to be "coming toward us," we were not prepared for the awesome sight that met our eyes as we turned for a heading that would take us alongside the burning, devastated city.

The giant purple mushroom cloud, which the tail-gunner had described, had already risen to a height of 45,000 feet, 3 miles above our own altitude, and was still boiling upward like something terribly alive. It was a frightening sight, and even though we were several miles away, it gave the appearance of something that was about to engulf us.

Even more fearsome was the sight on the ground below. At the base of the cloud, fires were springing up everywhere amid a turbulent mass of smoke that had the appearance of bubbling hot tar. If Dante had been with us in the plane, he would have been terrified! The city we had seen so clearly in the sunlight a few minutes before was now an ugly smudge. It had completely disappeared under this awful blanket of smoke and fire.

A feeling of shock and horror swept over all of us.

"My God!" Lewis wrote as the final entry in his log.

As we viewed the awesome spectacle below, we were sobered by the knowledge that the world would never be the same. War, the scourge of the human race since time began, now held terrors beyond belief. I reflected to myself that the kind of war in which I was engaged over Europe in 1942 was now outdated.

But as I swung southward on the return flight to our base, the feeling of tenseness gave way to one of relief. Our mission, for which we had practiced diligently for so long, had been successful. All doubts about the mystery weapon had been removed.

"I think this is the end of the war," I said to Bob Lewis.

🌿 "Total victory"

HARRY S. TRUMAN

On August 15, 1945, Japan surrendered. President Harry S. Truman's announcement of Japan's sudden capitulation came as a great relief. The explosion of atomic bombs over Hiroshima and Nagasaki meant that an invasion of Japan would not be necessary. An assault on Japan's mainland would have cost the lives of tens (if not hundreds) of thousands of American soldiers.

Truman's address, however, was not exultant. A front-line soldier himself in World War I, he knew the bittersweet joys of victory, the difficulties of returning home, and the implications of atomic weapons.

I am speaking to you, the Armed Forces of the United States, as I did after V Day in Europe, at a moment of history. The war, to which we have devoted all the resources and all the energy of our country for more than three and a half years, has now produced total victory over all our enemies.

This is a time for great rejoicing and a time for solemn contemplation. With the destructive force of war removed from the world, we can now turn to the grave task of preserving the peace which you gallant men and women have won. It is a task which requires our most urgent attention. It is one in which we must collaborate with our allies and the other nations of the world. They are determined as we are that war must be abolished from the earth, if the earth, as we know it, is to remain. Civilization cannot survive another total war.

I think you know what is in the hearts of our countrymen this night. They are thousands of miles away from most of you. Yet they are close to you in deep gratitude and in a solemn sense of obligation. They remember—and I know they will never forget—those who have gone from among you, those who are maimed, those who, thank God, are still safe after years of fighting and suffering and danger.

And I know that in this hour of victory their thoughts—like yours—are with your departed Commander-inCchief, Franklin D. Roosevelt. This is the hour for which he so gallantly fought and so bravely died.

I think I know the American soldier and sailor. He does not want gratitude or sympathy. He had a job to do. He did not like it. But he did it. And how he did it!

Now, he wants to come back home and start again the life he loves—a life of peace and quiet, the life of the civilian.

But he wants to know that he can come back to a good life. He wants to know that his children will not have to go back to the life of the fox-hole and the bomber, the battleship and the submarine.

I speak in behalf of all your countrymen when I pledge to you that we shall do everything in our power to make those wishes come true.

For some of you, I am sorry to say military service must continue for a time. We must keep an occupation force in Japan, just as we are cleaning out the militarism of Germany. The United Nations are determined that never again shall either of those countries be able to attack its peaceful neighbors.

But the great majority of you will be returned to civilian life as soon as the ships and planes can get you here. The task of moving so many men and women thousands of miles to their homes is a gigantic one. It will take months to accomplish. You have my pledge that we will do everything possible to speed it up. We want you back with us to make your contribution to our country's welfare and to a new world of peace.

The high tide of victory will carry us forward to great achievements in the era which lies ahead. But we can perform them only in a world which is free from the threat of war. We depend on you, who have known war in all its horror, to keep this nation aware that only through cooperation among all nations can any nation remain wholly secure.

On this night of total victory, we salute you of the Armed Forces of the United States—wherever you may be. What a job you have done! We are all waiting for the day when you will be home with us again.

Good luck and God bless you.

❧ "We are now facing a problem more of ethics than of physics"

BERNARD BARUCH

The bombing of Hiroshima and Nagasaki ended World War II, but it unleashed the difficult problem of what to do with atomic weapons. While in the past new weapons had esca-lated man's capacity to inflict damage upon one another, nobody had invented a weapon that could wipe out humanity. Now such a weapon existed.

In 1946, President Truman appointed millionaire financier and influential advisor Bernard Baruch to present a plan to control atomic energy to the recently formed United Nations. On June 14, he delivered this speech in presenting the first proposal to oversee the disarmament of nations. The Soviet Union vetoed the plan and within a few years had developed its own atomic weaponry. The United States could no longer be so forthcoming in its offers to disarm.

We are here to make a choice between the quick and the dead.

That is our business.

Behind the black portent of the new atomic age lies a hope which, seized upon with faith, can work our salvation. If we fail, then we have damned every man to be a slave of fear. Let us not deceive ourselves, we must elect world peace or world destruction.

Science has torn from nature a secret so vast in it potentialities that our minds cower from the terror it creates. The terror is not enough to inhibit the use of the atomic bomb. The terror created by weapons has never stopped man from employing them. For each new weapon a defense has been produced, in time. But now we face a condition in which adequate defense does not exist.

Science, which gave us this dread power, shows that it can be made a giant help to humanity, but science does not show us how to prevent its baleful use. So we have been appointed to obviate that peril by finding a meeting of the minds and the hearts of our people. Only in the will of mankind lies the answer.

In this crisis we represent not only our governments but, in a larger way, we represent the peoples of the world. We must remember that the peoples do not belong to the governments, but the governments belong to the peoples. We must answer their demands; we must answer the world's longing for peace and security.

In that desire the United States shares ardently and hopefully. The search of science for the absolute weapon has reached fruition in this country. But she stands ready to proscribe and destroy this instrument—to lift its use from death to life—if the world will join in a pact to that end.

In our success lies the promise of a new life, freed from the heart-stopping fears that now beset the world. The beginning of victory for the great ideals for which millions have bled and died lies in building a workable plan. Now we approach the fulfillment of the aspirations of mankind. At the end of the road lies the fairer, better, surer life we crave and mean to have.

Only by a lasting peace are liberties and democracies strengthened and deepened. War is their enemy. And it will not do to believe that any of us can escape war's devastation. Victor, vanquished, and neutrals alike are affected physically, economically, and morally.

Against the degradation of war we can erect a safeguard. That is the guerdon for which we reach. Within the scope of the formula we outline here, there will be found, to those who seek it, the essential elements of purpose. Others will see only emptiness. Each of us carries his own mirror in which is reflected hope—or determined desperation—courage or cowardice.

There is famine throughout the world today. It starves men's bodies. But there is a greater famine—the hunger of men's spirit. That starvation can be cured by the conquest of fear, and the substitution of hope, from which springs faith—faith in each other; faith that we want to work together toward salvation; and determination that those who threaten the peace and safety shall be punished.

The peoples of these democracies gathered here have a particular concern with our answer, for their peoples hate war. They will have a heavy exaction to make of those who fail to provide an escape. They are not afraid of an internationalism that protects; they are unwilling to be fobbled off by mouthings about narrow sovereignty, which is today's phrase for yesterday's isolationism.

The basis of a sound foreign policy, in this new age, for all the nations here gathered, is that: anything that happens, no matter where or how, which menaces the peace of the world, or the economic stability, concerns each and all of us.

That, roughly, may be said to be the central theme of the United Nations. It is with that thought we gain consideration of the most important subject that can engage mankind—life itself.

Now, if ever, is the time to act for the common good. Public opinion supports a world movement toward security. If I read the signs aright, the peoples want a program, not composed merely of pious thoughts, but of enforceable sanctions—an international law with teeth in it.

We of this nation, desirous of helping to bring peace to the world and realizing the heavy obligations upon us, arising from our possession of the means for producing the bomb and from the fact that it is part of our armament, are prepared to make our full contribution toward effective control of atomic energy.

But before a country is ready to relinquish any winning weapons, it must have more than words to reassure it. It must have a guarantee of safety, not only against the offenders in the atomic area, but against the illegal users of other weapons—bacteriological, biological, gas—perhaps—why not?—against war itself.

In the elimination of war lies our solution, for only then will nations cease to compete with one another in the production and use of dread "secret" weapons which are evaluated solely by their capacity to kill. This devilish program takes us back not merely to the Dark Ages but from cosmos to chaos. If we succeed in finding a suitable way to control atomic weapons, it is reasonable to hope that we may also preclude the use of other weapons adaptable to mass destruction. When a man learns to say "A" he can, if he chooses, learn the rest of the alphabet, too.

Let this be anchored in our minds.

Peace is never long preserved by weight of metal or by an armament race. Peace can be made tranquil and secure only by understanding and agreement fortified by sanctions. We must embrace international cooperation or international disintegration.

Science has taught us how to put the atom to work. But to make it work for good instead of for evil lies in the domain dealing with the principles of human duty. We are now facing a problem more of ethics than of physics.

The solution will require apparent sacrifice in pride and in position, but better pain as the price than death as the price of war.

GEORGE KENNAN

By 1947, all pretense of cooperation between the United States and the Soviet Union had been abandoned. Their wartime alliance was over. A new "cold war" between capitalism and communism was underway on a global scale. The emergence of nuclear weapons made the stakes higher than ever.

George Kennan, a policy director in the State Department based in Moscow, was the first person to describe the nature of the simmering conflict and articulate the United States' policy against the spread of communism emanating from Moscow. He described this "containment" policy in an anonymous article published in *Foreign Affairs*. The essay provided the framework of United States policy against the Soviet Union for the next forty years. Although Kennan later would say that American policy sometimes veered from this roadmap, his prophecy of lengthy engagement and ultimate United States victory proved correct.

Of the original ideology [communism], nothing has been officially junked. Belief is maintained in the basic badness of capitalism, in the inevitability of its destruction, in the obligation of the proletariat to assist in that destruction and to take power into its own hands. But stress has come to be laid primarily on those concepts which relate most specifically to the Soviet regime itself: to its position as the sole truly Socialist regime in a dark and misguided world, and to the relationships of power within it.

The first of these concepts is that of the innate antagonism between capitalism and Socialism. We have seen how deeply that concept has become imbedded in foundations of Soviet power. It has profound implications for Russia's conduct as a member of international society. It means that there can never be on Moscow's side any sincere assumptions of a community of aims between the Soviet Union and powers which are regarded as capitalism. It must invariably be assumed in Moscow that the aims of the capitalist world are antagonistic to the Soviet regime and, therefore, to the interests of the peoples it controls. If the Soviet Government occasionally sets its signature to documents which would indicate the contrary, this is to be regarded as a tactical maneuver permissible in dealing with the enemy (who is without honor) and should be taken in the spirit of caveat emptor. Basically, the antagonism remains. It is postulated. And from it flow many of the phenomena which we find disturbing in the Kremlin's conduct of foreign policy: the secretiveness, the lack of frankness, the duplicity, the war suspiciousness, and the basic unfriendliness of purpose. These phenomena are there to stay, for the foreseeable future. There can be variations of degree and of emphasis. When there is something the Russians want from us, one of the other of these features of their policy may be thrust temporarily into the background; and when that happens there will always be Americans who will leap forward with gleeful announcements that "the Russians have changed," and some who will even try to take credit for having brought about such changes." But we should not be misled by tactical maneuvers. These characteristics of Soviet policy, like the postulate from which they flow, are basic to the internal nature of Soviet power, and will be with us, whether in the foreground or the background, until the internal nature of Soviet power is changed.

This means that we are going to continue for a long time to find the Russians difficult to deal with. It does not mean that they should be considered as embarked upon a do-or-die program to overthrow our society by a given date. The theory of the inevitability of the eventual fall of capitalism has the fortunate connotation that there is no hurry about it. The forces of progress can take their time in preparing the final coup de grace. Meanwhile, what is vital is that the "Socialist fatherland"—that oasis of power which has been already won for Socialism in the person of the Soviet Union—should be cherished and defended by all good Communists at home and abroad, its fortunes promoted, its enemies badgered and confounded. The promotion of premature, "adventuristic" revolutionary projects abroad which might embarrass Soviet power in any way would be an inexcusable, even counter-revolutionary act. The cause of Socialism is the support and promotion of Soviet power, as defined in Moscow.

This brings us to the second of the concepts important to contemporary Soviet outlook. That is the infallibility of the Kremlin. The Soviet concept of power, which permits no focal points of organization outside the Party itself, requires that the Party leadership remain in theory the sole repository of truth. For if truth were to be found elsewhere, there would be justification for its expression in organized activity. But it is precisely that which the Kremlin cannot and will not permit.

The leadership of the Communist Party is therefore always right, and has been always right ever since in 1929 Stalin formalized his personal power by announcing that decisions of the Politburo were being taken unanimously.

On the principle of infallibility there rests the iron discipline of the Communist Party. In fact, the two concepts are mutually self-supporting. Perfect discipline requires recognition of infallibility. Infallibility requires the observance of discipline. And the two together go far to determine the behaviorism of the entire Soviet apparatus of power. But their effect cannot be understood unless a third factor be taken in account: namely, the fact that the leadership is at liberty to put forward for tactical purposes any particular thesis which it finds useful to the cause at any particular moment and to require the faithful and unquestioning acceptance of that thesis by the members of the movement as a whole. This means that truth is not constant but is actually created, for all intents and purposes, by the Soviet leaders themselves. It may vary from week to week, from month to month. It is nothing absolute and immutable—nothing which flows from objective reality. It is only the most recent manifestation of the wisdom of those in whom the ultimate wisdom is supposed to reside, because they represent the logic of history. The accumulative effect of these factors is to give to the whole subordinate apparatus of Soviet power an unshakeable stubbornness and steadfastness in its orientation. This orientation can be changed at will by the Kremlin but by no other power. Once a given party line has been laid down on a given issue of current policy, the whole Soviet governmental machine, including the mechanism of diplomacy, moves inexorably along the prescribed path, like a persistent toy automobile wound up and headed in a given direction, stopping only when it meets with some unanswerable force. The individuals who are the components of this machine are unamenable to argument or reason which comes to them from outside sources. Their whole training has

taught them to mistrust and discount the glib persuasiveness of the outside world. Like the white dog before the phonograph, they hear only the "master's voice." And if they are to be called off from the purposes last dictated to them, it is the master who must call them off. Thus the foreign representative cannot hope that his words will make any impression on them. The most that he can hope is that they will be transmitted to those at the top, who are capable of changing the party line. But even those are not likely to be swayed by any normal logic in the words of the bourgeois representative. Since there can be no appeal to common purposes, there can be no appeal to common mental approaches. For this reason, facts speak louder than words to the ears of the Kremlin; and words carry the greatest weight when they have the ring of reflecting, or being backed by, facts of unchallengeable validity.

But we have seen that the Kremlin is under no ideological compulsion to accomplish its purposes in a hurry. Like the Church, it is dealing in ideological concepts which are of long-term validity, and it can afford to be patient. It has no right to risk the existing achievements of the revolution for the sake of vain baubles of the future. The very teachings of Lenin himself require great caution and flexibility in the pursuit of Communist purposes. Again, these precepts are fortified by the lessons of Russian history: of centuries of obscure battles between nomadic forces over the stretches of a vast unfortified plain. Here caution, circumspection, flexibility and deception are the valuable qualities; and their value finds natural appreciation in the Russian or the oriental mind. Thus the Kremlin has no compunction about retreating in the face of superior force. And being under the compulsion of no timetable, it does not get panicky under the necessity for such retreat. Its political action is a fluid stream which moves constantly, wherever it is permitted to move, toward a given goal. Its main concern is to make sure that it has filled every nook and cranny available to it in the basin of world power. But if it finds unassailable barriers in its path, it accepts these philosophically and accommodates itself to them. The main thing is that there should always be pressure, increasing constant pressure toward the desired goal. There is no trace of any feeling in Soviet psychology that that goal must be reached at any given time.

These considerations make Soviet diplomacy at once easier and more difficult to deal with than the diplomacy of the individual aggressive leaders like Napoleon and Hitler. On the one hand it is more sensitive to contrary force, more ready to yield on individual sectors of the diplomatic front when that force is felt to be too strong, and thus more rational in the logic and rhetoric of power. On the other hand it cannot be easily defeated or discouraged by a single victory on the part of its opponents. And the patient persistence by which it is animated means that it can be effectively countered not by sporadic acts which represent momentary whims of democratic opinion but only intelligent long-range policies on the part of Russia's adversaries—policies no less steady in their purpose, and no less variegated and resourceful in their application, than those of the Soviet Union itself.

In these circumstances it is clear that the main element of any United States policy toward the Soviet Union must be that of a long-term, patient but firm and vigilant containment of Russian expansive tendencies. It is important to note, however, that such a policy has nothing to do with outward histrionics: with threats or blustering or superfluous gestures of outward "toughness." While the Kremlin is basically flexible in its reaction to political realities, it is by no means unamenable to considerations of prestige. Like almost any other government, it can be placed by tactless and threatening gestures in a position where it cannot afford to yield even though this might be dictated by its sense of realism. The Russian leaders are keen judges of human psychology, and as such they are highly conscious that loss of temper and of self-control is never a source of strength in political affairs. They are quick to exploit such evidences of weakness. For these reasons, it is a sine qua non of successful dealing with Russia that the foreign government in question should remain at all times cool and collected and that its demands on Russian policy should be put forward in such a manner as to leave the way open for a compliance not too detrimental to Russian prestige.

In light of the above, it will be clearly seen that the Soviet pressure against the free institutions of the Western world is something that can be contained by the adroit and vigilant application of counter-force at a series of constantly shifting geographical and political points, corresponding to the shifts and maneuvers of Soviet policy, but which cannot be charmed or talked out of existence. The

Russians look forward to a duel of infinite duration, and they see that already they have scored great successes. It must be borne in mind that there was a time when the Communist Party represented far more of a minority in the sphere of Russian national life than Soviet power today represents in the world community....

The issue of Soviet-American relations is in essence a test of the over-all worth of the United States as a nation among nations. To avoid destruction the United States need only measure up to its own best traditions and prove itself worthy of preservation as a great nation.

Surely, there was never a fairer test of national quality than this. In the light of these circumstances, the thoughtful observer of Russian-American relations will find no cause for complaint in the Kremlin's challenge to American society. He will rather experience a certain gratitude to a Providence which, by providing the American people with this implacable challenge, has made their entire security as a nation dependent on their pulling themselves together and accepting the responsibilities of moral and political leadership that history plainly intended them to bear.

❧ "We find ourselves, our Nation, in a world position of vast responsibility"

THE MARSHALL PLAN

Two years after World War II ended, Europe was an economic wreck. Poverty and disease were rampant. Dislocation was still a problem. Even in England, food rations were tighter than during wartime. The Soviet Union loomed as an ominous presence eager to export its communist ideology, and doing so with force in Eastern Europe and with chicanery in Western Europe.

Fearful that continued economic desperation would foster socialist/communist sentiment, Secretary of State George C. Marshall crafted a massive economic aid program to assist European countries. He announced the "Marshall Plan" in a dry, 12-minute speech at the June 5, 1947, Harvard commencement address.

Eighteen European countries responded. Over the next five years, more than 12 billion dollars in economic aid was dispersed to Europe, helping to inject economic activity and thwart the spread of communism. Marshall won the Nobel Peace Prize in 1953.

I need not tell you gentlemen that the world situation is very serious. That must be apparent to all intelligent people. I think one difficulty is that the problem is one of such enormous complexity that the very mass of facts presented to the public by the press and radio make it exceedingly difficult for the man in the street to reach a clear appraisement of the situation. Furthermore, the people of this country are distant from the troubled areas of the earth and it is hard for them to comprehend the plight and consequent reactions of the long-suffering peoples, and the effect of those reactions on their governments in connection with our efforts to promote peace in the world.

In considering the requirements for the rehabilitation of Europe the physical loss of life, the visible destruction of cities, factories, mines, and railroads was correctly estimated, but it has become obvious during recent months that this visible destruction was probably less serious than the dislocation of the entire fabric of European economy. For the past 10 years conditions have been highly abnormal. The feverish preparation for war and the more feverish maintenance of the war effort engulfed all aspects of national economics. Machinery has fallen into disrepair or is entirely obsolete. Under the arbitrary and destructive Nazi rule, virtually every possible enterprise was geared into the German war machine. Long-standing commercial ties, private institutions, banks, insurance companies and shipping companies disappeared, through loss of capital, absorption through nationalization or by simple destruction. In many countries, confidence in the local currency has been severely shaken. The breakdowns of the business structure of Europe during the war was complete. Recovery has been seriously retarded by the fact that two years after the close of hostilities a peace settlement with Germany and Austria has not been agreed upon. But even given a more prompt solution of these difficult problems, the rehabilitation of the economic structure of Europe quite evidently will require a much longer time and greater effort than had been foreseen.

There is a phase of this matter which is both interesting and serious. The farmer has always produced the foodstuffs to exchange with the city dweller for the other necessities of life. This division of labor is the basis of modern civilization. At the present time it is threatened with breakdown. The town and city industries are not producing adequate goods to exchange with the food-producing farmer. Raw materials and fuel are in short supply. Machinery is lacking or worn out. The farmer or the peasant cannot find the goods for sale which he desires to purchase. So the sale of his farm produce for money which he cannot use seems to him an unprofitable transaction. He therefore, has withdrawn many fields from crop cultivation and is using them for grazing. He feeds more grain to stock and finds for himself and his family an ample supply of food, however short he may be on clothing and the other ordinary gadgets of civilization. Meanwhile people in the cities are short of food and fuel. So the governments are forced to use their foreign money and credits to procure these necessities abroad. This process exhausts funds which are urgently needed for reconstruction. Thus a very serious situation is rapidly developing which bodes no good for the world. The modern system of the division of labor upon which the exchange of products is based is in danger of breaking down.

The truth of the matter is that Europe's requirements for the next 3 or 4 years of foreign food and other essential products—principally from American—are so much greater than her present ability to pay that she must have substantial additional help, or face economic, social and political deterioration of a very grave character.

The remedy lies in breaking the vicious circle and restoring the confidence of the European people in the economic future of their own countries and of Europe as a whole. The manufacturer and the farmer throughout wide areas much be able and willing to exchange their products for currencies the continuing value of which is not open to question.

Aside from the demoralizing effect on the world at large and the possibilities of disturbances arising as a result of the desperation of the people concerned, the consequences to the economy of the United States should be apparent to all. It is logical that the United States should do whatever it is able to do to assist in the return of normal economic health in the world, without which there can be no political stability and no assured peace. Our policy is directed not against any country or doctrine but against hunger, poverty, desperation, and chaos. Its purpose should be the revival of a working economy in the world so as to permit the emergence of political and social conditions in which free institutions can exist. Such assistance, I am convinced, must not be on a piecemeal basis as various crises develop. Any assistance that this Government may render in the future should provide a cure rather than a mere palliative. Any government that is willing to assist in the task of recovery will find full cooperation, I am sure, on the part of the United States Government. Any government which maneuvers to block the recovery of other countries cannot expect help from us. Furthermore, governments, political parties, or groups which seek to perpetuate human misery in order to profit therefrom politically or otherwise will encounter the opposition of the United States.

It is already evident that, before the United States Government can proceed much further in its efforts to alleviate the situation and help start the European world on its way to recovery, there must be some agreement among the countries of Europe as to the requirements of the situation and the part those countries themselves will take in order to give proper effect to whatever action might be undertaken by this Government. It would be neither fitting nor efficacious for this Government to undertake to draw up unilaterally a program designed to place Europe on its feet economically. This is the business of the Europeans. The initiative, I think, must come from Europe. The role of this country should consist of friendly aid in the drafting of a European program and of later support of such a program so far as it may be practical for us to do so. The program should be a joint one, agreed to by a number, if not all European nations.

An essential part of any successful action on the part of the United States is an understanding on the part of the people of America of the character of the problem and the remedies to be applied. Political passion and prejudice should have no part. With foresight, and a willingness on the part of our people to face up to the vast responsibility which history has clearly placed upon our country, the difficulties I have outlined can and will be overcome.

"Collective defense for the preservation of peace"

THE NORTH ATLANTIC TREATY

Thwarting Soviet expansion in Europe would require more than economic nourishment from the Marshall Plan. Having muscled its way into Eastern European countries, the Soviet Army was perched at the threshold of Western Europe. Western leaders realized that they needed to form a military alliance to discourage any notions Stalin might have of invading other European countries.

In a dramatic departure from United States diplomatic history, Congress approved the North Atlantic Treaty on April 4, 1949. It was the military alliance with eleven other countries (Belgium, Canada, Denmark, England, France, Iceland, Italy, Luxembourg, the Netherlands, Norway and Portugal) that created the North Atlantic Treaty Organization (NATO).

The Parties to this Treaty reaffirm their faith in the purposes and principles of the Charter of the United Nations and their desire to live in peace with all peoples and all governments.

They are determined to safeguard the freedom, common heritage and civilization of their peoples, founded on the principles of democracy, individual liberty and the rule of law.

They seek to promote stability and well-being in the North Atlantic area.

They are resolved to unite their efforts for collective defense and for the preservation of peace and security.

They therefore agree to this North Atlantic Treaty:

Art. 1. The Parties undertake, as set forth in the Charter of the United Nations, to settle any international disputes in which they may be involved by peaceful means in such a manner that international peace and security, and justice, are not endangered, and to refrain in their international relations from the threat or use of force in any manner inconsistent with the purposes of the United Nations.

Art. 2. The Parties will contribute toward the further development of peaceful and friendly international relations by strengthening their free institutions, by bringing about a better understanding of the principles upon which these institutions are founded, and by promoting conditions of stability and well-being. They will seek to eliminate conflict in their international economic policies and will encourage economic collaboration between any or all of them.

Art. 3. In order more effectively to achieve the objectives of this Treaty, the Parties, separately and jointly, by means of continuous and effective self-help and mutual aid, will maintain and develop their individual and collective capacity to resist armed attack.

Art. 4. The Parties will consult together whenever, in the opinion of any of them, the territorial integrity, political independence or security of any of the Parties is threatened.

Art. 5. The Parties agree that an armed attack against one or more of them in Europe or North America shall be considered an attack against them all; and consequently they agree that, if such an armed attack occurs, each of them, in exercise of the right of individual or collective self-defense recognized by Article 51 of the Charter of the United Nations, will assist the Party or Parties so attacked by taking forthwith, individually and in concert with the other Parties, such action as it deems necessary, including the use of armed force, to restore and maintain the security of the North Atlantic area.

Any such armed attack and all measures taken as a result thereof shall immediately be reported to the Security Council. Such measures shall be terminated when the Security Council has taken the measures necessary to restore and maintain international peace and security.

Art. 6. For the purpose of Article 5 an armed attack on one or more of the Parties is deemed to include an armed attack on the territory of any of the Parties in Europe or North America, on the Algerian departments of France, on the occupation forces of any Party in Europe, on the islands under the jurisdiction of any Party in the North Atlantic area north of the Tropic of Cancer or on the vessels or aircraft in this area of any of the Parties.

Art. 7. This Treaty does not affect, and shall not be interpreted as affecting, in any way the rights and obligations under the Charter of the Parties which are members of the United Nations, or the primary responsibility of the Security Council for the maintenance of international peace and security.

Art. 8. Each Party declares that none of the international engagements now in force between it and any other of the Parties or any third state is in conflict with the provisions of this Treaty, and undertakes not to enter into any international engagement in conflict with this Treaty.

Art. 9. The Parties hereby establish a council, on which each of them shall be represented, to consider matters concerning the implementation of this Treaty. The council shall be so organized as to be able to meet promptly at any time. The council shall set up such subsidiary bodies as may be necessary; in particular it shall establish immediately a defense committee which shall recommend measures for the implementation of Articles 3 and 5.

Art. 10. The Parties may, by unanimous agreement, invite any other European state in a position to further the principles of this Treaty and to contribute to the security of the North Atlantic area to accede to this Treaty. Any state so invited may become a party to the Treaty by depositing its instrument of accession with the Government of the United States of America. The Government of the United States of America will inform each of the Parties of the deposit of each such instrument of accession.

Art. 11. The Treaty shall enter into force between the states which have ratified it as soon as the ratifications of the majority of the signatories, including the ratifications of Belgium, Canada, France, Luxembourg, the Netherlands, the United Kingdom and the United States, have been deposited and shall come into effect with respect to other states on the date of the deposit of their ratifications.

Art. 12. After the Treaty has been in force for ten years, or at any time thereafter, the Parties shall, if any of them so requests, consult together for the purpose of reviewing the Treaty, having regard for the factors then affecting peace and security in the North Atlantic area, including the development of universal as well as regional arrangements under the Charter of the United Nations for the maintenance of international peace of security.

Art. 13. After the Treaty has been in force for twenty years, any Party may cease to be a party one year after its notice of denunciation has been given to the Government of the United States of America, which will inform the Governments of the other parties of the deposit of each notice of denunciation.

🌿 "Trust Yourself"

DR. BENJAMIN SPOCK

When World War II ended 8 million service men and women returned to civilian life and a booming post-war economy. The combination of the war and the Depression had compelled many couples to postpone having children. That came to a quick end in 1946 when the "baby boom" began. For the next fifteen years, the numbers of American babies brought into the world was at an all-time high. This generation of Americans would come to dominate the country's demographic trends and heavily influence the nation's cultural priorities.

Dr. Benjamin Spock's *Baby and Child Care* served as the national guidebook for American parents. Published in 1945, the book offered a reassuring voice to millions of families struggling with the challenges of parenthood. The fact-filled book provided answers to the myriad questions that arise when raising children. Over the next twenty years, more than 28 million copies of the book were sold.

His message of tolerance helped supplant the highly disciplined nature of child-rearing practiced up until that point. Later, some critics blamed Spock's message of parental permissiveness as one of the causes of the undisciplined lifestyles of the young in the 1960s.

1. You know more than you think you do.

Soon you're going to have a baby. Maybe you have one already. You're happy and excited, but if you haven't had much experience, you wonder whether you are going to know how to do a good job. Lately you have been listening more carefully to your friends and relatives when they talk about bringing up a child. You've begun to read articles by experts in the magazines and newspapers. After the baby is born, the doctor and nurses will begin to give you instructions, too. Sometimes it sounds like a very complicated business. You find out all the vitamins a baby needs and all the inoculations. One mother tells you that egg should be given early because of its iron, and another says that egg should be delayed to avoid allergy. You hear that a baby is easily spoiled by being picked up too much but also that a baby must be cuddled plenty; that fairy tales make children nervous, and that fairy tales are a wholesome outlet.

Don't take too seriously all that the neighbors say. Don't be overawed by what the experts say. Don't be afraid to trust your own common sense. Bringing up your child won't be a complicated job

if you take it easy, trust your own instincts and follow the directions that your doctor gives you. We know for a fact that the natural loving care that kindly parents give their children is a hundred times more valuable than their knowing how to pin a diaper on just right or how to make a formula expertly. Everytime you pick your baby up— let's assume it's a girl—even if you do it a little awkwardly at first, everytime you change her, bathe her, feed her, smile at her, she's getting a feeling that she belongs to you and that you belong to her. Nobody else in the world, no matter how skillful, can give that to her.

It may surprise you to hear that the more people have studied different methods of bringing up children, the more they have come to the conclusion that what good mothers and fathers instinctively feel like doing for their babies is usually best, after all. Furthermore, all parents do their best job when they have natural, easy confidence in themselves. Better to make a few mistakes from being natural than to do everything letter-perfect out of a feeling of worry.

Prenatal classes for expectant mothers and fathers are provided in many communities by the Visiting Nurse Association, the Red Cross, or the city or county health department. They are very helpful in discussing the questions and problems that all expectant parents have concerning pregnancy, delivery, and care of the baby.

2. How you learn to be a parent.

Fathers and mothers don't really find out how to care for and manage children from books and lectures, though these may have value in answering specific questions and doubts. They learned the basics from the way they themselves were handled while they were children. That's what they were always practicing when they "played house" and cared for their dolls.

You'll find that you learn the rest gradually through the experience of caring for your children. It's taking care of your baby, finding out that you can feed, change, bathe, and burp successfully, and that your baby responds contentedly to your ministrations that gives you the feelings of familiarity, confidence, and love. A solid relationship and a mutual trust are established very early. Then when your baby, let's say a girl, begins to feel like a separate person with ideas and a will of her own, at about a year, you and she will have a solid basis for coping with such common problems as excessive explorativeness and negativism.

3. Don't be afraid of your baby.

You'd think from what some people say about babies demanding attention that they come into the world determined to get their parents under their thumb by hook or by crook. This isn't true. Your baby is born to be a reasonable, friendly human being.

Don't be afraid to feed her when you think she's really hungry. If you are mistaken, she'll merely refuse to take much.

Don't be afraid to love her and enjoy her. Every baby needs to be smiled at, talked to, played with, fondled—gently and lovingly—just as much as she needs vitamins and calories. That's what will make her a person who loves people and enjoys living. The baby who doesn't get any loving will grow up cold and unresponsive.

Don't be afraid to respond to other desires of hers as long as they seem sensible to you and as long as you don't become a slave to her. When she cries in the early weeks, it's because she's uncomfortable for some reason or other—maybe it's hunger or indigestion, or fatigue, or tension. The uneasy feeling you have when you hear her cry, the feeling that you want to comfort her, is meant to be part of your nature, too. Being held, rocked, or walked may be what she needs.

Spoiling doesn't come from being good to a baby in a sensible way, and it doesn't come all of a sudden. Spoiling comes on gradually when parents are too afraid to use their common sense or when they really want to be slaves and encourage their babies to become slave drivers.

Everyone wants the child to turn out to be healthy in her habits and easy to live with. But each child herself wants to eat at sensible hours and later to learn good table manners. Her bowels (as long as the movements don't become too hard) will move according to their own health pattern, which may or may not be regular; and when she's a lot older and wiser, you can show her where to sit to move them. She will develop her own pattern of sleep according to her own needs. In all these habits she will sooner or later want to fit into the family's way of doing things, with only a minimum of guidance from you.

4. Enjoy children as they are—that's how they'll grow up best.

Every baby's face is different from every other's. In the same way, every baby's pattern of development is different. One may be very advanced in her general bodily strength and coordination, an early sitter, stander, walker—a sort of infant athlete. And yet she may be slow in doing careful, skillful things with her fingers, in talking. Even babies who are athletes in rolling over, standing, and creeping may turn out to be slow to learn to walk. Babies who are advanced in their physical activities may be very slow in teething, and vice-versa. Children who turn out later to be smart in schoolwork may have been so slow in beginning to talk that their parents were afraid for a while that they were dull; and children who have just an

ordinary amount of brains are sometimes very early talkers.

I am purposely picking out examples of children with mixed rates of development to give you an idea of what a jumble of different qualities and patterns of growth each individual person is composed.

One baby is born to be big-boned and delicate. Some individuals really seem to be born to be fat. If they lose weight during an illness, they gain it back promptly afterwards. The troubles that they have in the world never take away their appetites. The opposite kind of individuals stay on the thin side, even when they have the most nourishing food to eat, even though life is running smoothly for them.

Love and enjoy your children for what they are, for what they look like, for what they do, and forget about the qualities they don't have. I don't give you this advice just for sentimental reasons. There's a very important practical point here. The children who are appreciated for what they are, even if they are homely, or clumsy, or slow, will grow up with confidence in themselves—happy. They will have a spirit that will make the best of all the capacities that they have, and of all the opportunities that come their way. They will make light of any handicaps. But children who have never been quite accepted by their parents, who have always felt that they were not quite right, will grow up lacking confidence. They'll never be able to make full use of what brains, what skills, what physical attractiveness they have. If they start life with a handicap, physical or mental, it will be multiplied tenfold by the time they are grown up.

❧ "Financing studies, research, instruction and other educational activities"

THE FULBRIGHT ACT

Millions and millions of dollars of surplus military supplies were left idle when World War II ended. Aiming to use these weapons of war to nurture peace, Senator Fulbright of Arkansas proposed using the proceeds from the sale of military supplies for educational and cultural purposes. Among other things, his legislation created the Fulbright Scholarships, allowing American students to study abroad, thus helping to strengthen United States ties to the rest of the world. The act was approved August 1, 1946.

To Amend the Surplus Property Act

of 1944

...Section 2. Section 32 (b)(2) In carrying out the provisions of this section, the Secretary of State is hereby authorized to enter into an executive agreement or agreements with any foreign government for the use or currencies, or credits for currencies, or such government acquired as a result of such surplus property disposals, for the purpose of providing, by the formation of foundations or otherwise, for (A) financing studies, research, instruction, and other educational activities of or for American citizens in schools and institutions of higher learning located in such foreign country, or of the citizens of such foreign country in American schools and institutions of higher learning located outside the continental United States, Hawaii, Alaska (including the Aleutian Islands), Puerto Rico, and the Virgin Islands, including payment for transportation, tuition, maintenance, and other expenses incident to scholastic activities; or (B) furnishing transportation for citizens of such foreign country who desire to attend American schools and institutions of higher learning in the continental United States, Hawaii, Alaska (including the Aleutian Islands), Puerto Rico and the Virgin Islands, and whose attendance will not deprive citizens of the United States
of an opportunity to attend such schools and institutions:...

Provided further, That for the purpose of selecting students and educational institutions qualified to participate in this program, and to supervise the exchange program authorized herein, the President of the United States is hereby authorized to appoint a Board of Foreign Scholarships, consisting of ten members, who shall serve without compensation, composed of representatives of cultural, educational, student and war veterans groups, and including representatives of the United States Veterans' Administration, State education institutions, and privately endowed educational institutions: And Provided further, That in the selection of American citizens for study in foreign countries under this paragraph preference shall be given to applicants who shall have served in the military or naval forces of the United States during World War I or World War II, and due consideration shall be given to applicants from all geographical areas of the United States.

❧ "There shall be equality of treatment and opportunity for all persons in the armed services"

EXECUTIVE ORDER 9981 ELIMINATES MILITARY SEGREGATION

After former slaves fought on the Union side in the Civil War, the government abolished slavery and enfranchised black men to vote. When black regiments fought heroically in World War II, the government later eliminated the substantial indignities of a segregated army. Some black soldiers were lynched. Many questioned how they would perform under the stress of combat. Despite the doubts and the scorn, thousands of black soldiers did their duty honorably.

President Truman issued the order in 1948, but it would take several years to implement. Many white military officers and men bristled at the edict and some branches of the military resisted. The onset of the Korean War in 1950, however, sped up the process of integration. By the end of the conflict, 90 percent of the military was integrated. Ultimately, the integration of the armed forces was considered a model success story in achieving the goal of a color-blind society.

Whereas it is essential that there be maintained in the armed services of the United States the highest standards of democracy, with equality of treatment and opportunity for all those who serve in the country's defense:

Now, therefore, by virtue of the authority vested in me as President of the United States, and as Commander-in-Chief of the armed services, it is hereby ordered as follows:

It is hereby declared to be the policy of the President that there shall be equality of treatment and opportunity for all persons in the armed services without regard to race, color, religion or national origin. This policy shall be put into effect as rapidly as possible, having due regard to the time required to effectuate any necessary changes without impairing efficiency or morale.

There shall be created in the National Military Establishment an advisory committee to be known as the President's Committee on Equality of Treatment and Opportunity in the Armed Services, which shall be composed of seven members to be designated by the President.

The Committee is authorized on behalf of the President to examine the rules, procedures and practices of the armed services in order to determine in what respect such rules, procedures and practices may be altered or improved with a view to carrying out the policy of this order....

All executive departments and agencies of the Federal Government are authorized and directed to cooperate with the Committee in its work....

❧ "The Six Thousand Houses That Levitt Built"

HARPER'S MAGAZINE

Owning a house has always been central to the American Dream. The G.I. Bill helped millions of young men gain the potential to afford a home of their own. Bill Levitt provided a way for them to realize it, simultaneously revolutionizing the construction industry and housing development patterns across the country.

Borrowing heavily from Henry Ford's mass-production techniques, Levitt successfully built 2,350 housing units for the Navy during World War II. Armed with this ability, he decided after the war to apply the same techniques to creating massive housing divisions at the outskirts of cities. The first one, named Levittown, was built in 1948 on Long Island outside of New York City.

It was a smashing success. Demand, pent up for almost twenty years by the Depression and World War II, was overwhelming. Levitt build 17,000 units for the first Levittown at a pace of up to thirty-six houses a day. (Prior to the war, the average contracting company built no more than five houses a year.)

Levittown and its equivalents emerged across the country. In 1955, 75 percent of the housing starts in the country were for Levittowns or similar housing subdivisions. Levitt's influence, combined with rise of automobiles, lay the groundwork for the dramatic growth of suburbs in the United States.

The following excerpt by *Harper's* writer Eric Larrabee described the conditions that made Levittown possible.

Levitt—Bill Levitt refers to the firm in the third person singular—is now at work on a 1,400-acre, 6,000-house project called "Levittown," near Hicksville, Long Island, where 4-room "bungalows" are rented, to veterans only, for 65 dollars a month. Each house comes complete with a radiant-heating, General Electric range and refrigerator, and venetian blinds. The grounds will be landscaped, all utilities will be connected, and there will be concrete roads. Levittown will be zoned as a park district, and Levitt will build one swimming pool for each thousand houses—also three shopping centers (with nearly a hundred retail units), five schools (built by the county on public contract), and six churches (plots donated by Levitt & Sons). Levittown will be finished by the end of this year. "Anyone who comes to us now," Bill Levitt said last April, "will have a house in October."

As soon as one of the first 1,800 veterans to rent a house in Levittown has been there a year, he is given an option by Levitt to buy the house for $7,990; if he does not buy, Levitt will rent for one year more. "I think they'll buy all right," he has said, with a pride anyone might reasonably take in watching well-made plans come to fruition. The veterans will be backed by GI loans and will thus require no cash, they will get back a $100 deposit from Levitt, and the carrying charges on the loan will be less than the rent they are paying—a combination difficult to resist. Some of the veteran tenants, however, feeling that the company has been trying to pressure them into a purchase, have claimed that very few of their number actually wish to buy. Levitt now proposes to continue to rent the vast majority of the houses, but at the end of two years from the completion of the project there will be nothing to prevent him from selling them at whatever price the market will bear. If he does so, his profit should be in seven figures. The 1947 price on the basic small Levitt house was $7,500 (earlier he sold 31 pilot models for $6,990, in eight hours, but is now sorry that the price was so widely publicized). Costs have risen since then and comparisons on the basis of profit per house are deceptive (according to Bill Levitt, they are no longer used in the firm), but it was estimated in 1947 that he undersold his nearer competitor by $1,500 and still made $1,000 profit on each house.

Levitt, in short, is a phenomenon. Previously the firm had built only conventional homes on Long Island's North Shore, though the various "Strathmores"—"class" developments near one of which the main office is still located—foreshadowed a larger scale operation. It was a wartime experience (Levitt did 2,350 rental units for the navy at Norfolk, Virginia) that infected them permanently with a bug for volume. They still build some houses in the higher brackets for the station-wagon trade, but it is with the mass production of a standard 4-room house that the name Levitt has become firmly associated. Bill Levitt is becoming a kind of bellwether of the building trades, and he believes that he is setting patterns which the others must eventually adopt. The housing industry, if it can properly be called an industry, has traditionally been based on limited construction by small contractors, consumer financing, and craft unions. Levitt & Sons are substituting mass construction by a single company, production financing, and either industrial unions or no unions at all.

❦ "The time has arrived for the Democratic Party to get out of the shadow of states' rights"

HUBERT HUMPHREY

In the South, the Democratic Party had dominated politics since the Reconstruction Era and had been fierce advocates of states' rights as a way to justify the constitutionality of segregationist "Jim Crow" laws. When Roosevelt emerged as the champion of the underprivileged, however, a strain was placed within the party. The Democratic Party could not simultaneously champion the rights of blacks on a national level and maintain the racist policies of the South.

In 1948, the stress of this inherent conflict was starting to erode party unity. South Carolina Senator Strom Thurmond threatened to lead a "Dixiecrat" block of Southern Democrats out of the party if a civil rights platform was adopted in the presidential platform.

With this as background, Minneapolis Mayor Hubert Humphrey emerged at the Democratic convention demanding that Democrats formally embrace civil rights. "There are those who say we are rushing this issue of civil rights. I say we are 172 years late," Humphrey proclaimed. The Democrats adopted civil rights as a plank in the platform, and the Dixiecrats bolted from the party. Humphrey, who became known as "the Happy Warrior" became a national figure and the slow erosion of Democratic dominance in the South began.

I do not believe that there can be any compromise of the guarantees of civil rights which I have mentioned.

In spite of my desire for unanimous agreement on the platform, there are some matters which I think must be stated without qualification. There can be no hedging—no watering down.

There are those who say to you—we are rushing this issue of civil rights. I say we are 172 years late.

There are those who say—this issue of civil rights is an infringement on states' rights. The time has arrived for the Democratic Party to get out of the shadow of states' rights and walk forthrightly into the bright sunshine of human rights.

People—human beings—this is the issue of the twentieth century. People—all kinds and all sorts of people—look to America for leadership, for help, for guidance.

My friends—my fellow Democrats—I ask you for a calm consideration of our historic opportunity. Let us forget the evil passions, the blindness of the past. In these times of world economic, political, and spiritual—above all, spiritual—crisis, we cannot—we must not—turn from the path so plainly before us.

The path has already led us through many valleys of the shadow of death. Now is the time to recall those who were left on that path of American freedom.

For all of us here, for the millions who have sent us, for the whole two billion members of the human family—our land is now, more than ever, the last best hope on earth. I know that we can—I know that we shall—begin here the fuller and richer realization of that hope—that promise of a land where all men are free and equal, and each man uses his freedom and equality wisely and well.

🌿 *"The Eightieth 'do-nothing' Congress"*

HARRY TRUMAN

President Truman was the common-man president. A surprise selection as vice president in the 1944 election, Truman was as startled as anyone that he found himself as president upon Roosevelt's death. For the first time since the nineteenth century, America had a president with humble origins. Having been an unsuccessful farmer and store owner himself as a young man in rural Missouri, he understood the day-to-day issues that the vast majority of citizens confronted.

The Republican nominee for president in 1948, Thomas E. Dewey, was heavily favored to win the election. Truman, however, rose to the occasion. Feisty and determined, he waged the definitive whistle-stop campaign, blasting the Republican-majority Congress as the Eightieth "do-nothing" Congress at every opportunity. Speaking off the cuff, Truman delivered 275 speeches between Labor Day and election days. This typical speech was given October 7, 1948, in Elizabeth, New Jersey. Ultimately, Truman stunned the pundits and newspapers with his victory.

You are here because you are interested in the issues of this campaign. You know, as all the citizens of this great country know, that the election is not all over but the shouting. That is what they would like to have you believe, but it isn't so—it isn't so at all. The Republicans are trying to hide the truth from you in a great many ways. They don't want you to know the truth about the issues in this campaign. The big fundamental issue in this campaign is the people against the special interests. The Democratic party stands for the people. The Republican party stands, and always has stood, for special interests. They have proved that conclusively in the record that they made in this "do-nothing" Congress.

The Republican party candidates are going around talking to you in high-sounding platitudes trying to make you believe that they themselves are the best people to run the government. Well now, you have had experience with them running the government. In 1920 to 1932, they had complete control of the government. Look what they did to it!

This country is enjoying the greatest prosperity it has ever known because we have been following for sixteen years the policies inaugurated by Franklin D. Roosevelt. Everybody benefited from these policies—labor, the farmer, businessmen, and white-collar workers.

We want to keep that prosperity. We cannot keep that if we don't lick the biggest problem facing us today, and that is high prices.

I have been trying to get the Republicans to do something about high prices and housing ever since they came to Washington. They are responsible for that situation, because they killed price control, and they killed the housing bill. That Republican Eightieth "do-nothing" Congress absolutely refused to give any relief whatever in either one of those categories.

What do you suppose the Republicans think you ought to do about high prices?

Senator Taft, one of the leaders in the Republican Congress, said, "If consumers think the price is too high today, they will wait until the price is lower. I feel that in time the law of supply and demand will bring prices into line."

There is the Republican answer to the high cost of living.

If it costs too much, just wait.

If you think fifteen cents is too much for a loaf of bread, just do without it and wait until you can afford to pay fifteen cents for it.

If you don't want to pay sixty cents a pound for hamburger, just wait.

That is what the Republican Congress thought you ought to do, and that is the same Congress that the Republican candidate for president said did a good job.

Some people say I ought not to talk so much about the Republican Eightieth "do-nothing" Congress in this campaign. I will tell you why I will talk about it. If two-thirds of the people stay at home again on election day as they did in 1946, and if we get another Republican Congress like the Eightieth Congress—the Tabers and the Tafts, the Martins and the Hallecks, would be the bosses. The same men would be the bosses the same as those who passed the Taft-Hartley Act, and passed the rich man's tax bill, and took Social Security away from a million workers.

Do you want that kind of administration? I

don't believe you do—I don't believe you do.

I don't believe you would be out here interested in listening to my outline of what the Republicans are trying to do to you if you intended to put them back in there.

When a bunch of Republican reactionaries are in control of the Congress, then the people get reactionary laws. The only way you can get the kind of government you need is by going to the polls and voting the straight Democratic ticket on November 2. Then you will get a Democratic Congress, and I will get a Congress that will work with me. Then we will get good housing at prices we can afford to pay; and repeal of that vicious Taft-Hartley Act; and more Social Security coverage; and prices that will be fair to everybody; and we can go on and keep sixty-one million people at work; we can have an income of more than $217 billion, and that income will be distributed so that the farmer, the workingman, the white-collar worker, and the businessman get their fair share of that income.

That is what I stand for.

That is what the Democratic party stands for.

Vote for that, and you will be safe.

🍀 Christmas Message

JAMES FOLSOM

White Southern governors in the 1940s were not typically known for embracing civil rights issues. Alabama Governor James Folsom defied convention in his 1949 Christmas radio address, however, questioning whether Alabama Negroes were being oppressed and denied opportunities. Citing the words of Jesus Christ, he called upon Alabama citizens to treat each other as they would have others treat them.

I am happy to have this opportunity to talk to the people of Alabama on Christmas Day. This is the greatest day, the most revered day, of our entire calendar. It is the birthday of Christ, who was the greatest humanitarian the world has ever known.

This is a day to talk about loving our neighbors, lending help to the less fortunate, and bringing joy to others by good work.

We set aside Thanksgiving Day to honor the Almighty's bountifulness to us; we celebrate the Fourth of July, which marks the freedom of our country; but on Christmas Day we pay tribute for the freedom of our souls.

It is great to live in America, with all of its plenty and bounty—yet it behooves us not to forget that we are the most blessed people on earth. And to remember that with that greatness goes a like share of responsibility.

The world looks to America today for leadership, for physical relief, for spiritual uplifting. These things we must provide if we are to retain our position of greatness. Because, like the foolish and wise virgins, those who have and use not, from their possessions shall be taken away. They will wither away because they are not used.

This nation has prospered in many and magnificent ways, and it has done so under the freedom of a democratic government, a government in which the people retain the final source of power through their exercise of the ballot.

The very foundation of democracy itself rests upon Christianity, upon the principles set forth by Christ himself. And I believe that it is no mere speculation to say that, without a government which guaranteed the freedom of religious worship, this nation would never have become the great America which it is today.

So often in our democracy we have failed to make the most of the very weapons itself—that is, providing a human, decent way of life for all of our people.

Under the extensive freedom of a democratic country, there emerges a pattern of life which creates economic barriers among the people. And as a democracy grows in years and expansiveness, there comes about a controlling minority group. That group controls because through the advantages and opportunities it obtains great portions of wealth. Wealth means power and power influence. And so often that influence becomes an evil thing, in that it is used for a few, and not for the good of all. It is for that reason that we must have laws to establish control over power and authority, control over forces which are based on self-gain and exploitation. And it is necessary that we have laws to establish a measure of assistance and help for those who are not able to grub out a meager, respectable living.

And so we founded in this country great and far-reaching welfare programs. These programs were not created, nor are they operated, as a great leveler, but rather as an obligation of a democracy to its people, in order that the unfortunate may feast on more than crumbs and clothe themselves with more than rags.

What has gone before us in the way of welfare work exemplifies rich rewards of human endeavor. But we are actually just becoming of age, just beginning to scratch the surface in fulfilling the needs which are so widespread. So long as we have a person hungry, ill clothed, or without medical aid, we can take no pride in what has been done.

It is a good Christmas to turn our thoughts to the neglected because Christmas is a time to think of others and not of ourselves. It is a time for us to ask questions of our inner self....

Our Negroes, who constitute 35 percent of our population in Alabama—are they getting 35 percent of the fair share of living? Are they getting adequate medical care to rid them of hookworms, rickets, and social diseases? Are they provided with sufficient professional training which will produce their own doctors, professors, lawyers, clergymen, scientists—men and women who can pave the way for better health, greater earning powers, and a higher standard of living for all of their people? Are the Negroes being given their share of democracy, the same opportunity of having a voice in the government under which we live?

As long as the Negroes are held down by deprivation and lack of opportunity, the other poor people will be held down alongside them.

There are others, too, who should share in our thoughts of the neglected—wounded veterans, the blind, the shut-ins, the crippled and on and on.

The job for us here in Alabama is a positive one. It is time for us to adopt a positive attitude toward our fellow man.

Let's start talking fellowship and brotherly love and doing-unto-others, and let's do more than talk about it—let's start living it.

In the past few years there has been too much negative living, too much stirring up of old hatreds, and prejudices, and false alarms. And the best way in the world to break this down is to lend our ears to the teachings of Christianity and the ways of democracy.

We must all constantly strive to put our democracy to fuller service for our people in order that all may be more richly rewarded with the fullness of the earth.

And certainly that is in keeping with the spirit of Christ, who said, "Do unto others as you would have them do unto you."

I hope the time will soon come when nations are brought together by the spirit of Christmas in much the same manner in which families join in reunion during the Holy Week.

People feel better when they gather together for the sake of love and fellowship. Their hearts are cleansed and kindled by the warm fire of eternal goodness. Nothing but good comes out of people at Christmas time—and that is how it should be at all times....

I believe that the people of all nations, the people of Alabama, the people of China, Africa, Russia, and tiny Luxembourg—I believe that all of them want to see lasting peace and goodness on this earth. And it is that great desire in the hearts of the people that gives me hope for a brighter future, a world without constant warfare, suffering, and distress.

I believe that such a goal is within our grasp—that it can become a force real and wonderful for all people, if we will set our hearts and our minds to that end....

"The attack upon Korea makes it plain that Communism will now use armed invasion"

TRUMAN ORDERS U.S. INTO THE KOREAN WAR

The United States' containment policy against Communism resulted in potential conflicts all over the world. Iran, Greece and all of Eastern Europe became potential flash points in the efforts to hold back the tide of Soviet communism. In 1949, an entire new arena of concern arose with the communist overthrow of China. Suddenly, the United States faced a growing threat of communism in Asia.

In the spring of 1950, North Korea's communist government attacked South Korea, sweeping aside all resistance. A sprinkling of American troops had been stationed in South Korea. Undermanned and under-equipped, they went into headlong retreat. The United Nations, determined not to make the same mistakes as the ill-fated League of Nations, stepped in to defend South Korea with the United States taking the lead role. China would later enter the war directly on behalf of North Korea.

More than 50,000 American soldiers died over the next three years in what became known as "The Forgotten War." An armistice was signed on July 27, 1953, dividing the country at the 38th parallel. There has never been a peace treaty. American troops continue to help South Korea protect the border from North Korea.

In Korea the Government forces, which were armed to prevent border raids and to preserve internal security, were attacked by invading forces from North Korea. The Security Council of the United Nations called upon the invading troops to cease hostilities and to withdraw to the 38th parallel. This they have not done, but on the contrary have pressed the attack. The Security Council called upon all members of the United Nations to render every assistance to the United Nations in the execution of this resolution. In these circumstances I have ordered United States air and sea forces to give the Korean Government troops cover and support.

The attack upon Korea makes it plain beyond all doubt that Communism has passed beyond the use of subversion to conquer independent nations and will now use armed invasion and war. It has defied the orders of the Security Council of the United Nations issued to preserve international peace and security. In these circumstances the occupation of Formosa by Communist forces would be a direct threat to the security of the Pacific area and to the United States forces performing their lawful and necessary functions in that area.

Accordingly I have ordered the Seventh Fleet to prevent any attack on Formosa. As a corollary of this action I am calling upon the Chinese Government of Formosa to cease all air and sea operations against the mainland. The Seventh Fleet will that this is done. The determination of the future status of Formosa must await the restoration of security in the Pacific, a peace settlement with Japan, or consideration by the United Nations.

I have also directed that United States Forces in the Philippines be strengthened and that military assistance to the Philippine Government be accelerated.

I have similarly directed acceleration in the furnishing of military assistance to the forces of France and the Associated States in Indochina and the dispatch of a military mission to provide close working relations with those forces.

I know that all members of the United Nations will consider carefully the consequences of this latest aggression in Korea in defiance of the Charter of the United Nations. A return to the rule of force in international affairs would have far reaching effects. The United States will continue to uphold the rule of law.

I have instructed Ambassador Austin, as the representative of the United States to the Security Council, to report these steps to the Council.

❧ Declaration of Conscience

MARGARET CHASE SMITH

On June 1, 1950, Maine Republican Senator Margaret Chase Smith—at the time, the only female senator—stood up on the Senate floor to disassociate herself and seven other senators from the highly charged attacks on suspected Communists by fellow Republican Senator Joseph McCarthy of Wisconsin. Despite the "Declaration of Conscience," McCarthy's denounciations would continue for four more years, unchecked by public opinion, the Republican Party and the majority of the Senate.

Mr. President, I speak as a Republican. I speak as a woman. I speak as a United States senator. I speak as an American.

The United States Senate has long enjoyed worldwide respect as the greatest deliberative body in the world. But recently that deliberative character has too often been debased to the level of a forum of hate and character assassination sheltered by the shield of congressional immunity.

It is ironical that we senators can debate in the Senate, directly or indirectly, by any form of words, impute to any American who is not a senator any conduct or motive unworthy or unbecoming an American—and without that nonsenator American having any legal redress against us—yet if we say the same thing in the Senate about our colleagues we can be stopped on the grounds of being out of order.

It is strange that we can verbally attack anyone else without restraint and with full protection, and yet we hold ourselves above the same type of criticism here on the Senate floor. Surely the United States Senate is big enough to take self-criticism and self-appraisal. Surely we should be able to take the same kind of character attacks that we "dish out" to outsiders.

I think it is high time for the United States Senate and its members to do some real soul-searching and to weigh our consciences as to the manner in which we are performing our duty to the people of America and the manner in which we are using or abusing our individual powers and privileges.

I think it is high time that we remembered that we have sworn to uphold and defend the Constitution. I think it is high time that we remembered that the Constitution, as amended, speaks not only of the freedom of speech but also of trial by jury instead of trial by accusation.

Whether it be a criminal prosecution in court or a character prosecution in the Senate, there is little practical distinction when the life of a person has been ruined.

Those of us who shout the loudest about Americanism in making character assassinations are all too frequently those who, by our own words and acts, ignore some of the basic principles of Americanism—the right to criticize; the right to hold unpopular beliefs; the right to protest; the right of independent thought.

The exercise of these rights should not cost one single American citizen his reputation or his right to a livelihood, nor should he be in danger of losing his reputation or livelihood merely because he happens to know someone who holds unpopular beliefs. Who of us does not? Other-wise none of us could call our souls our own. Otherwise thought control would have
set in.

The American people are sick and tired of being afraid to speak their minds lest they be politically smeared as Communists or Fascists by their opponents. Freedom of speech is not what it used to be in America. It has been so abused by some that it is not exercised by others.

The American people are sick and tired of seeing innocent people smeared and guilty people whitewashed. But there have been enough proved cases, such as the Amerasia case, the Hiss case, the Coplon case, the Gold case, to cause nationwide distrust and strong suspicion that there may be something to the unproved, sensational accusations.

As a Republican, I say to my colleagues on this side of the aisle that the Republican Party faces a challenge today that is not unlike the challenge it faced back in Lincoln's day. The Republican Party so successfully met that challenge that it emerged from the Civil War as the champion of a united nation—in addition to being a party which unrelentingly fought loose spending and loose programs.

Today our country is being psychologically divided by the confusion and the suspicions that are bred in the United States Senate to spread like cancerous tentacles of "know nothing, suspect everything" attitudes. Today we have a Democratic administration which has developed a mania for loose spending and loose programs. History is repeating itself—and the Republican Party again has the opportunity to emerge as the champion of unity and prudence....

Yet to displace [the Democratic administration] with a Republican regime embracing a philosophy that lacks political integrity or intellectual honesty would prove equally disastrous to the nation. The nation sorely needs a Republican victory. But I do not want to see the Republican Party ride to political victory on the Four Horsemen of Calumny—fear, ignorance, bigotry, and smear.

I doubt if the Republican Party could do so, simply because I do not believe the American people will uphold any political party that puts political exploitation above national interest. Surely we Republicans are not so desperate for victory.

I do not want to see the Republican Party that way. While it might be a fleeting victory for the Republican Party, it would be a more lasting defeat for the American people. Surely it would ultimately be suicide for the Republican Party and the two-party system that has protected our American liberties from the dictatorship of a one-party system.

As members of the minority party, we do not have the primary authority to formulate the policy of our government. But we do have the responsibility of rendering constructive criticism, of clarifying issues, of allaying fears by acting as responsible citizens.

As a woman, I wonder how the mothers, wives, sisters, and daughters feel about the way in which members of their families have been politically maligned in Senate debate—and I use the word "debate" advisedly.

As a United States senator, I am not proud of

the way in which the Senate has been made a publicity platform for irresponsible sensationalism. I am not proud of the reckless abandon in which unproved charges have been hurled from this side of the aisle. I am not proud of the obviously staged, undignified countercharges which have been attempted in retaliation from the other side of the aisle.

I do not like the way the Senate has been made a rendezvous for vilification, for selfish political gain at the sacrifice of individual reputations and national unity. I am not proud of the way we smear outsiders from the floor of the Senate and hide behind the cloak of congressional immunity and still place ourselves beyond criticism on the floor of the Senate.

As an American, I am shocked at the way Republicans and Democrats alike are playing directly into the Communist design of "confuse, divide, and conquer." As an American, I do not want a Democratic administration whitewash or coverup any more than I want a Republican smear or witch-hunt.

As an American, I condemn a Republican Fascist just as much as I condemn a Democrat Communist. I condemn a Democrat Fascist just as much as I condemn a Republican Communist. They are equally dangerous to you and me and to our country. As an American, I want to see our nation recapture the strength and unity it once had when we fought the enemy instead of ourselves.

❧ "I decline to accept the end of man"

WILLIAM FAULKNER

The great Southern writer William Faulkner won the Nobel Prize in 1950. He had written twenty novels by then, including *The Sound and the Fury* and *As I Lay Dying,* about man's capacity to prevail and rise above their circumstances. Faulkner addressed his acceptance speech to his fellow writers grappling in the anxious post-war years with the arrival of the atomic bomb.

I feel that this award was not made to me as a man, but to my work—a life's work in the agony and sweat of the human spirit, not for glory and least of all for profit, but to create out of the materials of the human spirit something which did not exist before. So this award is only mine in trust. It will not be difficult to find a dedication for the money part of it commensurate with the purpose and significance of its origin. But I would like to do the same with the acclaim too, by using this moment as a pinnacle from which I might be listened to by the young men and women already dedicated to the same anguish and travail, among whom is already that one who will some day stand where I am standing.

Our tragedy today is a general and universal physical fear so long sustained by now that we can even bear it. There are no longer problems of the spirit. There is only one question: When will I be blown up? Because of this, the young man or woman writing today has forgotten the problems of the human heart in conflict with itself which alone can make good writing because only that is worth writing about, worth the agony and the sweat.

He must learn them again. He must teach himself that the basest of all things is to be afraid: and, teaching himself that, forget it forever, leaving no room in his workshop for anything but the old verities and truths of the heart, the universal truths lacking which any story is ephemeral and doomed—love and honor and pity and pride and compassion and sacrifice. Until he does so, he labors under a curse. He writes not of love but of lust, of defeats in which nobody loses anything of value, of victories without hope and, worst of all, without pity or compassion. His griefs grieve on no universal bones, leaving no scars. He writes not of the heart but of the glands.

Until he learns these things, he will write as though he stood among and watched the end of man. I decline to accept the end of man. It is easy enough to say that man is immortal simply because he will endure: that when the last ding-dong of doom has clanged and faded from the last worthless rock hanging tideless in the last red and dying evening, that even then there will still be one more sound: that of his puny inexhaustible voice, still talking. I refuse to accept this. I believe that man will not merely endure: he will prevail. He is immortal, not because he alone among creatures has an inexhaustible sacrifice and endurance. The poet's, the writer's, duty is to write about these things. It is his privilege to help man endure by lifting his heart, by reminding him of the courage and honor and hope and pride and compassion and pity and sacrifice which have been the glory of his past. The poet's voice need not merely be the record of man, it can be one of the props, the pillars to help him endure and prevail.

❧ "City of the Big Shoulders"

CARL SANDBURG

In 1950, writer-poet Carl Sandburg won the Pulitzer Prize for his collection *Complete Poems*. Sandburg helped define how Americans think of themselves and their history. The author of a laudatory biography of Abraham Lincoln, he nurtured the image of "Honest Abe" Lincoln. His poems celebrated American vigor. "Chicago" may be his most famous poem and is typical of his work. "Freedom Is a Habit" celebrated American freedom.

Chicago
Hog Butcher for the World,
Tool Maker, Stacker of Wheat,
Player with Railroads and the Nation's Freight handler;
Stormy, husky, brawling,
City of the Big Shoulders:
They tell me you are wicked and I believe them, for I have seen your painted women under the gas lamps luring the farm boys.
And they tell me you are crooked and I answer: Yes, it is true I have seen the gunman kill and go free to kill again.
And they tell me you are brutal and my reply is: On the faces of women and children I have seen the marks of wanton hunger.
And having answered so I turn once more to those who sneer at this my city, and I give them back the sneer and say to them:
Come and show me another city with lifted head singing so proud to be alive and coarse and strong and cunning.
Flinging magnetic curses amid the toil of piling job on job, here is a tall bold slugger set vivid against the little soft cities;
Fierce as a dog with tongue lapping for action, cunning as a savage pitted against the wilderness,
Bareheaded,

Shoveling,
Wrecking,
Planning,
Building, breaking, rebuilding,
Under the smoke, dust all over his mouth, laughing with white teeth,
Under the terrible burden of destiny laughing as a young man laughs,
Laughing even as an ignorant fighter laughs who has never lost a battle,
Bragging and laughing that under his wrist is the pulse, and under his ribs the heart of the people,
Laughing!
Laughing the stormy, husky, brawling laughter of Youth, half-naked, sweating, proud to be Hog Butcher, Tool maker, Stacker of Wheat, Player with Railroads and Freight Handler of the Nation.

Freedom is a Habit
Freedom is a habit
and a coat worn
some born to wear it
some never to know it.
Freedom is cheap
or again as a garment
is so costly
men pay their lives
rather than not have it.
Freedom is baffling:
men having it often
know not they have it
till it is gone and
they no longer have it.
What does this mean?
Is it a riddle?
Yes, it is first of all
in the primers of riddles.
To be free is so-so:
you can and you can't:
walkers can have freedom
only by never walking
away their freedom
unless they overrun:
eaters have often outeaten
their freedom to eat
and drinkers overdrank
their fine drinking freedom.

"Old soldiers never die; they just fade away"

DOUGLAS MACARTHUR'S SPEECH TO CONGRESS

Douglas MacArthur is one of the commanding figures of twentieth-century American history. Having served in the Philippines at the start of the century, and distinguished himself in the trenches of World War I, MacArthur rose to great prominence in the army. He commanded the troops that attacked the "Bonus Army" of veterans in Washington, D.C., in 1932 and led the American forces in the Pacific during World War II. His "island hopping" strategy to retake the Pacific islands in the march to Japan saved thousands of American lives and his imperious, yet magnanimous style as commander of Allied forces in postwar Japan helped ease that country's transition from bitter enemy to trusted ally.

When the Korean conflict started, MacArthur defied military convention with his amphibious assault on Inchon, dramatically reversing North Korea's military advantage into a rout. But as MacArthur moved his forces into North Korea and toward China, he endangered American policy. Despite repeated orders from Truman to refrain from threatening China both with troops and in rhetoric, MacArthur persisted, finally prompted Truman to sack the immensely popular general.

MacArthur was treated as a conquering hero on his return to the United States, culminating in his April 19, 1951, address to Congress. Although the speech is best remembered for its "old soldiers never die" passage, most of the address is devoted to analyzing the dangers and opportunities of post-World War II Asia. In retrospect, his analysis provides an intriguing perspective not only on the Korean war, but also on Vietnam.

I stand on this rostrum with a sense of deep humility and great pride—humility in the wake of those great American architects of our history who have stood here before me, pride in the reflection that this forum of legislative debate represents human liberty in the purest form yet devised.

Here are centered the hopes and aspirations and faiths of the entire human race.

I do not stand here as advocate for any partisan cause, for the issues are fundamental and reach quite beyond the realm of partisan considerations. They must be resolved on the highest plane of national interest if our course is to prove sound and our future protected.

I trust, therefore, that you will do me the justice of receiving that which I have to say as solely expressing the considered viewpoint of a fellow American.

I address you with neither rancor nor bitterness in the fading twilight of life, with but one purpose in mind: to serve my country.

The issues are global, and so interlocked that to consider the problems of one sector oblivious to those of another is but to court disaster for the whole. While Asia is commonly referred to as the gateway to Europe, it is no less true that Europe is the gateway to Asia, and the broad influence of the one cannot fail to have its impact upon the other. There are those who claim our strength is inadequate to protect on both fronts, that we cannot divide our effort. I can think of no greater expression of defeatism.

If a potential enemy can divide his strength on two fronts, it is for us to counter his effort. The Communist threat is a global one. Its successful advance in one sector threatens the destruction of every other sector. You cannot appease or otherwise surrender to Communism in Asia without simultaneously undermining our efforts to halt its advance in Europe.

Beyond pointing out these general truisms, I shall confine my discussion to the general areas of Asia.

Before one may objectively assess the situation now existing there, he must comprehend something of Asia's past and the revolutionary changes which have marked her course up to the present. Long exploited by the so-called colonial powers, with little opportunity to achieve any degree of social justice, individual dignity, or a higher standard of life such as guided our own noble administration of the Philippines, the people of Asia found their opportunity in the war just past to throw off the shackles of colonialism and now see the dawn of new opportunity, and heretofore unfelt dignity, and the self-respect of political freedom.

Mustering half of the earth's population, and 60 percent of its natural resources, these peoples are rapidly consolidating a new force, both moral and material, with which to raise the living standard and erect adaptations of the design of modern progress to their own distinct cultural environments.

Whether one adheres to the concept of colonization or not, this is the direction of Asian progress and it may not be stopped. It is a corollary to the shift of the world economic frontiers as the whole epicenter of world affairs rotates back toward the area whence it started.

In this situation, it becomes vital that our own country orient its policies in consonance with this basic evolutionary condition rather than pursue a course blind to the reality that the colonial era is now past and the Asian people covert the right to shape their own free destiny. What they seek now is friendly guidance, understanding, and support, not imperious direction; the dignity of equality, not the shame of subjugation.

Their prewar standard of life, pitifully low, is infinitely lower now in the devastation left in war's wake. World ideologies play little part in Asian thinking and are little understood.

What the people strive for is the opportunity for a little more food in their stomachs, a little better clothing on their backs, a little firmer roof over their heads, and the realization of a normal nationalist urge for political freedom.

These political-social conditions have but an indirect bearing upon our own national security, but do form a backdrop to contemporary planning which must be thoughtfully considered if we are to avoid the pitfalls of unrealism.

Of more direct and immediate bearing upon our national security are the changes wrought in the strategic potential of the Pacific Ocean in the course of the postwar.

Prior thereto the western strategic frontier of the United States lay on the lateral line of the Americas, with an exposed island salient extending out through Hawaii, Midway, and Guam to the Philippines. That salient proved not an outpost of strength but an avenue of weakness along which the enemy could and did attack. The Pacific was a potential area of advance for any predatory force intent upon striking at the bordering land area.

All this was changed by our Pacific victory. Our strategic frontier then shifted to embrace the entire Pacific Ocean, which became a vast moat to protect us as long as we held it. Indeed, it acts as a protective shield for all of the Americas and all free lands of the Pacific Ocean area. We control it to the shores of Asia by a chain of islands extending in an arc from the Aleutians to the Marianas, held by us and our free allies.

From this island chain we can dominate with sea and air power every Asiatic port from Vladivostok to Singapore...and prevent any hostile movement to the Pacific.

Any predatory attack from Asia must be an amphibious effort. No amphibious force can be successful without control of the sea lanes and the air over those lanes in its avenue of advance. With naval and air supremacy and modest ground elements to defend bases, any major attack from continental Asia toward us or our friends of the Pacific would be doomed to failure.

Under such conditions, the Pacific no longer represents menacing avenues of approach for a prospective invader. It assumes, instead, the friendly aspect of a peaceful lake....

The Japanese people since the war have undergone the greatest reformation recorded in modern history. With a commendable will, eagerness to learn, and marked capacity to understand, they have from the ashes left in war's wake erected in Japan an edifice dedicated to the primacy of individual liberty and personal dignity, and in the ensuing process there has been created a truly representative government committed to the advance of political morality, freedom of economic enterprise, and social justice.

Politically, economically, and socially Japan is now abreast of many free nations of the earth and will not again fail the universal trust. That it may be counted upon to wield a profoundly beneficial influence over the course of events in Asia is attested by the magnificent manner in which the Japanese people have met the recent challenge of war, unrest, and confusion surrounding them from the outside an checked Communism within their own frontiers without the slightest slackening in their forward progress.

I sent all four of our occupation divisions to the Korean battlefront without the slightest qualms as to the effect of the resulting power vacuum upon Japan. The results fully justified my faith....

With this brief insight into the surrounding areas, I now turn to the Korean conflict.

While I was not consulted prior to the president's decision to intervene in support of the Republic of Korea, that decision, from a military standpoint, proved a sound one. As I say, a brief and sound one, as we hurled back the invader and decimated his forces. Our victory was complete, and our objectives within reach when Red China intervened with numerically superior ground forces.

This created a new war and an entirely new situation, a situation not contemplated when our forces were committed against the North Korean invaders—a situation which called for new decisions in the diplomatic sphere to permit the realistic adjustment of military strategy. Such decisions have not been forthcoming.

While no man in his right mind would advocate sending our ground forces into continental China, and such was never given a thought, the new situation did urgently demand a drastic revision of strategic planning if our political aim was to defeat this new enemy as we had defeated the old.

Apart from the military need, as I saw it, to neutralize the sanctuary protection given the enemy north of the Yalu, I felt that military necessity in the conduct of the war made necessary 1) the intensification of our economic blockade against China; 2) the imposition of a naval blockade against the China coast; 3) removal of restrictions on air reconnaissance of China's coastal areas and of China's coastal areas and of Manchuria; 4) removal of restrictions on the forces of the Republic of China on Formosa, with logistical support to contribute to their effective operation against the Chinese mainland.

For entertaining these views, all professionally designed to support our forces in Korea and to bring hostilities to an end with the least possible delay and at a saving of countless American and Allied lives, I have been severely criticized in lay circles, principally abroad, despite my understanding that from a military standpoint the above views have been fully shared by practically every military leader concerned with the Korean campaign, including our own Joint Chiefs of Staff.

I called for reinforcements, but was informed that reinforcements were not available. I made clear that if not permitted to destroy the enemy built-up bases north of the Yalu, if not permitted to utilize the friendly force of some 600,000 men on Formosa, if not permitted to blockade the China coast to prevent the Chinese Reds from getting succor from without, and if there were to be no hope of major reinforcements, the position of the command from the military standpoint forbade victory.

We could hold Korea by constant maneuver and at an approximate area where our supply-line advantages were in balance with the supply-line disadvantages of the enemy, but we could hope at best for only an indecisive campaign with its terrible and constant attrition upon our forces if the enemy utilized its full military potential.

I have constantly called for the new political decisions essential to a solution.

Efforts have been made to distort my position. It has been said in effect that I was a warmonger. Nothing could be further from the truth.

I know war as few other men now living know it, and nothing to me—nothing to me—is more revolting. I have long advocated its complete abolition, as its very destructiveness on both friend and foe has rendered it useless as a means of settling international disputes....

But once war is forced upon us, there is no other alternative than to apply every available means to bring it to a swift end. War's very object is victory, not prolonged indecision.

In war there can be no substitute for victory.

There are some who for varying reasons would appease Red China. They are blind to history's clear lesson, for history teaches with unmistakable emphasis that appeasement but begets new and bloodier war. It points to no single instance where the end has justified that means, where appeasement has led to more than a sham peace. Like blackmail, it lays the basiss for new and successively greater demands until, as in blackmail, it lays the basis for new and successively greater demands until, as in blackmail, violence becomes the only other alternative. Why, my soldiers asked of me, surrender military advantages to an enemy in the field? I could not answer.

Some may say to avoid spread of the conflict into an all-out war with China. Others, to avoid Soviet Union intervention. Neither explanation seems valid, for China is already engaging with the maximum power it can commit, and the Soviet will not necessarily mesh its actions with our moves. Like the cobra, any new enemy will more likely strike whenever it feels that the relativity in military or other potential is in its favor on a worldwide basis.

The tragedy of Korea is further heightened by the fact that its military action is confined to its territorial limits. It condemns that nation, which it is our purpose to save, to suffer the devastating impact of full naval and air bombardment while the enemy's sanctuaries are fully protected from such attack and devastation.

Of the nations of the world Korea alone, up to

now, is the sole one which has risked its all against communism. The magnificence of the courage and fortitude of the Korean people defies description. They have chosen to risk death rather than slavery. Their last words to me were "Don't scuttle the Pacific."

I have just left your fighting sons in Korea. They have met all tests there, and I can report to you without reservation that they are splendid in every way. It was my constant effort to preserve them and end this savage conflict honorably and with the least loss of time and a minimum sacrifice of life. Its growing bloodshed has caused me the deepest anguish and anxiety. Those gallant men will remain often in my thoughts and in my prayers always.

I am closing my fifty-two years of military service. When I joined the Army, even before the turn of the century, it was the fulfillment of all of my boyish hopes and dreams. The world has turned over many times since I took the oath of the plain at West Point, and the hopes and dreams have long since vanished, but I still remember the refrain of one of the most popular barrack ballads of that day which proclaimed most proudly that old soldiers never die, they just fade away. And, like the old soldier of that ballad, I now close my military career and just fade away, an old soldier who tried to do his duty as God gave him the light to see that duty. Goodbye.

"Our little girl named it Checkers…and we are going to keep it"

RICHARD M. NIXON

Richard Nixon's "Checkers Speech" was one of the most extraordinary political addresses in United States history. Nixon had been nominated as vice president on the 1952 Republican ticket under Eisenhower. As a Republican senator from California, he had made a national name for himself in his attacks on suspected Communists in government, most notably Alger Hiss. He had also gained many enemies for his hardball tactics.

In the middle of the presidential campaign, stories appeared questioning an $18,000 fund that he had. Faced with being forced off the ticket, Nixon went on national television to make his case. He bared his financial and personal history to the nation, describing his modest means and bemoaning the smear tactics that he had to endure. Most famously, he said the only questionable political gift he had received was a cocker spaniel, Checkers, that his daughters loved. He vowed he would keep Checkers "regardless of what they say about it."

The speech was unprecedented. Nixon successfully intertwined his personal life into the political fight, using television to reach a national audience. Viewers responded overwhelmingly in favor of Nixon. The address salvaged his place on the Republican ticket and set a precedent for the use of television and personal anecdotes in political campaigning for decades to come.

My fellow Americans: I come before you tonight as a candidate for the Vice Presidency and as a man whose honesty and integrity has been questioned.

Now, the usual political thing to do when charges are made against you is to either ignore them or to deny them without giving details. I believe we have had enough of that in the United States, particularly with the present Administration in Washington, D.C.

To me the office of the Vice Presidency of the United States is a great office, and I feel that the people have got to have confidence in the integrity of the men who run for that office and who might attain them.

I have a theory, too, that the best and only answer to a smear or to an honest misunderstanding of the facts is to tell the truth. And that is why I am here tonight. I want to tell you my side of the case.

I am sure that you have read the charge, and you have heard it, that I, Senator Nixon, took $18,000 from a group of my supporters.

Now, was that wrong? And let me say that it was wrong. I am saying it, incidentally, that it was wrong, not just illegal, because it isn't a question whether it was legal or illegal, that isn't enough. The question is, was it morally wrong. I say that it was morally wrong—if any of that $18,000 went to Senator Nixon, for my personal use. I say that it was morally wrong if it was secretly given and secretly handled.

And I say that it was morally wrong if any of the contributors got special favors for the contributions they made.

And now to answer those questions let me say this: Not one cent of the $18,000 or any other money of that type ever went to me for my personal use. Every penny of it was used to pay for political expenses that I did not think should be charged to the taxpayers of the United States.

It was not a secret fund. As a matter of fact, when I was on "Meet the Press"—some of you may have seen it, last Sunday—Peter Edson came up to me, after the program, and he said, "Dick, what about this fund we hear about?" and I said, "Well, there is no secret about it. Go out and see Dana Smith, who was the administrator of the fund," and I gave him his address. And I said, "You will find that the purpose of the fund simply was to defray political expenses that I did not feel should be charged to the Government."

And, third, let me point out, and I want to make this particularly clear, that no contributor to this fund, no contributor to any of my campaigns, has ever received any consideration that he would not have received as an ordinary constituent.

I just don't believe in that, and I can say that never while I have been in the Senate of the United States, as far as the people that contributed to this fund are concerned, have I made a telephone call for them to an agency, nor have I gone down to an agency on their behalf.

And the records will show that, the records which are in the hands of the Administration.

Well, then, some of you will say, and rightly, "Well, what did you use the fund for, Senator? Why did you have to have it?"

Let me tell you in just a word how a Senate office operates. First of all, the Senator gets $15,000 a year in salary. He gets enough money to pay for one trip a year, in salary. He gets enough money to pay for one trip a year, a round trip, that is, for himself and his family, between his home in Washington, D.C., and then he gets an allowance to handle the people that work in his office to handle his mail.

And the allowance for my State of California is enough to hire thirteen people. And let me say, incidentally, that this allowance is not paid to the Senator.

It is paid directly to the individuals that the Senator puts on his payroll, but all of these people and all of these allowances are for strictly official business; business, for example, when a constituent writes in and wants you to go down to the Veterans' Administration and get some information about his GI policy—items of that type, for example. But there are other expenses which are not

covered by the Government. And I think I can best discuss those expenses by asking you some questions.

Do you think that when I or any other Senator makes a political speech, has it printed, should charge for the printing of that speech and the mailing of that speech to the taxpayers?

Do you think, for example, when I or any other Senator makes a trip to his home States to make a purely political speech that the cost of that trip should be charged to the taxpayers?

Do you think when a Senator makes political broadcasts or political television broadcasts, radio or television, that the expense of those broadcasts should be charged to the taxpayers?

I know what your answer is. It is the same answer that audiences give me whenever I discuss this particular problem.

The answer is no. The taxpayers should not be required to finance items which are not official business but which are primarily political business.

Well, then the question arises, you say, "Well, how do you pay for these and how can you do it legally?" And there are several ways that it can be done, incidentally, and it is done legally in the United States Senate and in the Congress.

The first way is to be a rich man. I don't happen to be a rich man. So I couldn't use that.

Another way that is used is to put your wife on the payroll. Let me say, incidentally, that my opponent, my opposite number for the Vice Presidency of the Democratic ticket, does have his wife on his payroll and has had her on his payroll for the past ten years. Now just let me say this: That is his business, and I am not critical of him for doing that. You will have to pass judgment on that particular point, but I have never done that for this reason:

I have found that there are so many deserving stenographers and secretaries in Washington that needed the work that I just didn't feel it was right to put my wife on the payroll—my wife sitting over here.

She is a wonderful stenographer. She used to teach stenography and she used to teach shorthand in high school. That was when I met her. And I can tell you folks that she has worked many hours nights and many hours on Saturdays and Sundays in my office, and she had done a fine job, and I am proud to say tonight that in the six years I have been in the House and in the Senate of the

United States Pat Nixon has never been on the government payroll.

What are other ways that these finances can be taken care of? Some who are lawyers, and I happen to be a lawyer, continue to practice law, but I haven't been able to do that.

I am so far away from California and I have been so busy with my senatorial work that I have not engaged in any legal practice and, also, as far as law practice is concerned, it seemed to me that the relationship between an attorney and the client was so personal that you couldn't possibly represent a man as an attorney and then have an unbiased view when he presented his case to you in the event that he had one before the government.

And so I felt that the best way to handle these necessary political expenses of getting my message to the American people and the speeches I made—the speeches that I had printed for the most part concerned this one message of exposing this administration, the Communism in it, the corruption in it—the only way that I could do that was to accept the aid which people in my home State of California, who contributed to my campaign and who continued to make these contributions after I was elected, were glad to make.

And let me say I am proud of the fact that not one of them has ever asked me for a special favor. I am proud of the fact that not one of them has ever asked me to vote on a bill other than my own conscience would dictate. And I am proud of the fact that the taxpayers by subterfuge or otherwise have never paid one dime for expenses which I thought were political and should not be charged to the taxpayers.

Let me say, incidentally, that some of you may say, "Well, that is all right, Senator, that is your explanation, but have you got any proof?" and I would like to tell you this evening that just an hour ago we received an independent audit of this entire fund. I suggested to Governor Sherman Adams, who is the chief of staff of the Eisenhower campaign, that an independent audit and legal report be obtained, and I have that audit in my hand.

It is an audit made by price Waterhouse & Co. Firm, and the legal opinion by Gibson, Dunn & Crutcher, lawyers in Los Angeles, the biggest law firm, and incidentally one of the best ones in Los Angeles.

I am proud to report to you tonight that this audit and this legal opinion is being forwarded to General Eisenhower, and I would like to read to you the opinion that was prepared by Gibson, Dunn & Crutcher, based on all the pertinent laws and statutes, together with the audit report prepared by the certified public accountants.

"It is our conclusion that Senator Nixon did not obtain any financial gain from the collection and disbursement of the funds by Dana Smith; that Senator Nixon did not violate any Federal or State law by reason of the operation of the fund; and that neither the portion of the fund paid by Dana Smith directly to third persons, nor the portion paid to Senator Nixon, to reimburse him for office expenses, constituted income in a sense which was either reportable or taxable as income under income tax laws." Signed Gibson, Dunn and Crutcher, by Elmo H. Conley.

That is not Nixon speaking, but that is an independent audit which was requested because I want the American people to know all the facts and I am not afraid of having independent people go in and check the facts, and that is exactly what they did.

But then I realized that there are still some who may say, and rightly so—and let me say that I recognize that some will continue to smear, regardless of what the truth may be—but that there has been understandably, some honest misunderstanding on this matter, and there are some that will say, "Well, maybe you were able, Senator, to fake this thing. How can we believe what you say—after all, is there a possibility that maybe you got some sums in cash? Is there a possibility that you might have feathered your own next?" and so now what I am going to do—and, incidentally, this is unprecedented in the history of the American politics—I am going at this time to give to this television and radio audience a complete financial history, everything I have earned, everything I have spent, everything I own, and I want you to know the facts.

I will have to start early. I was born in 1913. Our family was one of modest circumstances, and most of my early life was spent in a store, out in East Whittier. It was a grocery store, one of those family enterprises.

The only reason we were able to make it go was because my mother and dad had five boys, and we all worked in the store. I worked my way through college and, to a great extent through law school. And then, in 1940, probably the best thing that ever happened to me happened. I married Pat, who is sitting over here.

We had rather a difficult time, after we were married, like so many of the young couples who might be listening to us. I practiced law. She continued to teach school.

Then, in 1942, I went into the service. Let me say that my service record was not a particularly unusual one. I went to the South Pacific. I guess I'm entitled to a couple of battle stars. I got a couple of letters of commendation. But I was just there when the bombs were falling. And then I returned. I returned to the United States, and in 1946, I ran for Congress. When we came out of the war, Pat and I—Pat during the war had worked as a stenographer, and in a bank, and as an economist for a government agency—and, when we came out, the total of our savings, from both my law practice, her teaching, and all the time that I was in the war, the total for that entire period was just a little less than $10,000—every cent of that, incidentally, was in government bonds—well, that's where we start, when I go into politics.

Now, whatever I earned since I went into politics—well, here it is. I jotted it down. Let me read the notes.

First of all, I have my salary as a congressman and senator.

Second, I have a received a total in this past six years of $1,600 from estates which were in my law firm at the time that I severed my connection with it. And, incidentally, as I said before, I have not engaged in any legal practice, and have not accepted any fees from business that came into the firm after I went into politics.

I have made an average of approximately $1,500 a year, from nonpolitical speaking engagements and lectures. And then, fortunately, we have inherited a little money. Pat sold her interest in her father's estate for $3,000, and I inherited $1,500 from my grandfather. We lived rather modestly.

For four years we lived in an apartment in Parkfairfax, Alexandria, Virginia. The rent was eighty dollars a month. And we saved for the time that we could buy a house. Now, that was what we took in.

What did we do with this money? What do we have today to show for it? This will surprise you, because it is so little, I suppose, as standards generally go of people in public life.

First of all, we've got a house in Washington, which cost $41,000 and on which we owe $20,000. We have a house in Whittier, California, which cost $13,000, and on which we owe $10,000. My folks are living there at the present time.

I have just $4,000 in life insurance, plus my G.I. policy, which I have never been able to convert, and which will run out in two years.

I have no life insurance whatever on Pat. I have no life insurance on our two youngsters, Patricia and Julie.

I own a 1950 Oldsmobile car. We have our furniture. We have no stocks or bonds of any type. We have no interest of any kind, direct or indirect, in any business. Now, that is what we have. What do we owe?

Well, in addition to the mortgage, the $20,000 mortgage on the house in Washington, a $10,000 one on the house in Whittier, I owe $4,500 to the Riggs Bank, in Washington, C.C., with interest at 4 percent. I owe $3,500 to may parents, and the interest on that loan, which I pay regularly, because it is a part of the savings they made through the years they were working so hard—I pay regularly 4 percent interest. And then I have a $500 loan, which I have on my life insurance.

Well, that's about it. That's what we have. And that's what we owe. It isn't very much. But Pat and I have the satisfaction that every dime that we have got is honestly ours.

I should say this, that Pat doesn't have a mink coat. But she does have a respectable Republican cloth coat, and I always tell her that she would look good in anything.

One other thing, I probably should tell you because if I don't they will probably be saying this about me, too. We did get something, a gift, after the election.

A man down in Texas heard Pat on the radio mention the fact that our two youngsters would like to have a dog, and, believe it or not, the day before we left on this campaign trip we got a message from Union Station in Baltimore, saying they had a package for us. We went down to get it. You know what it was?

It was a little cocker spaniel dog, in a crate that he had sent all the way from Texas, black and white, spotted, and our little girl, Tricia, the six-year-old, named it Checkers.

And, you know, the kids, like all kids, loved the dog, and I just want to say this, right now, that regardless of what they say about it, we are going to keep it.

It isn't easy to come before a nationwide audience to bare your life, as I have done. But I want to say some things before I conclude, that I think most of you will agree on.

Mr. Mitchell, the chairman of the Democratic National Committee, made the statement that if a man couldn't afford to be in the United States Senate, he shouldn't run for the Senate. And I just want to make my position clear.

I don't agree with Mr. Mitchell when he says that only a rich man should serve his government, in the United States or in the Congress. I don't believe that represents the thinking of the Democratic Party, and I know it doesn't represent the thinking of the Republican Party

I believe that it's fine that a man like Governor Stevenson, who inherited a fortune from his father, can run for President. But I also feel that it is essential in this country of ours that a man of modest means can also run for President, because, you know—remember Abraham Lincoln—you remember what he said, "God must have loved the common people, he made so many of them."

And now I'm going to suggest some courses of conduct.

First of all, you have read in the papers about other funds, now. Mr. Stevenson apparently had a couple. One of them in which a group of business people paid and helped to supplement the salaries of state employees. Here is where the money went directly into their pockets, and I think that what Mr. Stevenson should do should be to come before the American people, as I have, give the names of the people that contributed to that fund, give the names of the people who put this money into their pockets, at the same time that they were receiving money from their state government and see what favors, if any, they gave out for that.

I don't condemn Mr. Stevenson for what he did, but until the facts are in there is a doubt that would be raised. And as far as Mr. Sparkman is concerned, I would suggest the same thing. He's had his wife on the payroll. I don't condemn him for that, but I think that he should come before the American people and indicate what outside sources

of income he has had. I would suggest that under the circumstances both Mr. Sparkman and Mr. Stevenson should come before the American people, as I have, and make a complete financial statement as to their financial history, and if they don't it will be an admission that they have something to hide.

And I think you will agree with me—because, folks, remember, a man that's to be President of the United States, a man that is to be Vice President of the United States, must have the confidence of all the people. And that's why I'm doing what I'm doing, and that is why I suggest that Mr. Stevenson and Mr. Sparkman, if they are under attack, that should be what they are doing.

Now, let me say this: I know that this is not the last of the smears. In spite of my explanation tonight, other smears will be made. Others have been made in the past. And the purpose of the smears, I know, is this, to silence me, to make me let up.

Well, they just don't know who they are dealing with. I'm going to tell you this: I remember, in the dark days of the Hiss trial, some of the same columnists, some of the same radio commentators who are attacking me now and misrepresenting my position, were violently opposing me at the time I was after Alger Hiss. But I continued to fight, because I knew I was right, and I can say to this great television and radio audience that I have no apologies to the American people for my part in putting Alger Hiss where he is today. And as far as this is concerned, I intend to continue to fight.

Why do I feel so deeply? Why do I feel that in spite of the smears, the misunderstanding, the necessity for a man to come up here and bare his soul, as I have—why is it necessary for me to continue this fight? And I want to tell you why.

Because, you see, I love my country. And I think my country is in danger. And I think the only man that can save America at this time is the man that's running for president, on my own ticket, Dwight Eisenhower.

You say, why do I think he is in danger? And I say, look at the record. Seven years of the Truman-Acheson Administration, and what's happened? Six hundred million people lost to the Communists.

And a war in Korea in which we have lost 117,000 American casualties, and I say to all of you that a policy that results in a loss of 600 million people to the Communists and a war which costs us 117,000 American casualties isn't good enough for America, and I say that those in the State Department that made the mistakes which caused that war and which resulted in those losses should be kicked out of the State Department just as fast as we can get them out of there.

And let me say that I know Mr. Stevenson won't do that, because he defends the Truman policy, and I know that Dwight Eisenhower will do that, and that he will give America the leadership that it needs.

Take the problem of corruption. You have read about the mess in Washington. Mr. Stevenson can't clean it up because he was picked by the man, Truman under whose Administration the mess was made.

You wouldn't trust the man who made the mess to clean it up. That is Truman. And, by the same token you can't trust the man who was picked by the man who made the mess to clean it up, and that is Stevenson. And so I say, Eisenhower, who owes nothing to Truman, noting to the big-city bosses—he is the man who can clean up the mess in Washington.

Take Communism. I say that as far as that subject is concerned the danger is great to America. In the Hiss case they got the secrets which enabled them to break the American secret State Department code.

They got secrets in the atomic bomb case which enabled them to get the secret of the atomic bomb five years before they would have gotten it by their own devices. And I say that any man who called the Alger Hiss case a red herring isn't fit to be President of the United States.

I say that a man who, like Mr. Stevenson, has pooh-poohed and ridiculed the Communist threat in the United States—he said that they are phantoms among ourselves—he has accused us, that have attempted to expose the Communists, of looking for Communists in the Bureau of Fisheries and Wildlife. I say that a man who says that isn't qualified to be President of the United States.

And I say that the only man who can lead us into this fight to rid the government of both those who are communists and those who have corrupted this government is Eisenhower, because General Eisenhower, you can be sure, recognizes the prob-

lem, and knows how to handle it.

Let me say this, finally. This evening I want to read to you just briefly excerpts from a letter that I received, a letter which after all this is over no one can take away from us. It reads as follows:

"Dear Senator Nixon:

Since I am only nineteen years of age, I can't vote in this presidential election, but believe me if I could you and General Eisenhower would certainly get my vote. My husband is in the Fleet marines in Korea. He is in the front lines. And we have a two-month-old son he has never seen. And I feel confident that with great Americans like you and General Eisenhower in the White House, lonely Americans like myself will be united with their loved ones now in Korea. I only a pray to God that you won't be too late. Enclosed is a small check to help you in your campaign. Living on eighty-five dollars a month it is all I can afford at present, but let me know what else I can do."

Folks, it is a check for ten dollars, and it is one that I shall never cash. And just let me say this: We hear a lot about prosperity these days, but I say why can't we have prosperity built on peace, rather than prosperity built on war? Why can't we have prosperity and an honest government in Washington, D.C., at the same time?

Believe me, we can. And Eisenhower is the man that can lead the crusade to bring us that kind of prosperity.

And, now, finally, I know that you wonder whether or not I am going to stay on the Republican ticket or resign. Let me say this: I don't believe that I ought to quit, because I am not a quitter. And, incidentally, Pat is not a quitter. After all, her name was Patricia Ryan and she was born on St. Patrick's Day, and you know the Irish never quit.

But the decision, my friends, is not mine. I would do nothing that would harm the possibilities of Dwight Eisenhower to become President of the United States. And for that reason I am submitting to the Republican National Committee tonight through this television broadcast the decision which it is theirs to make. Let them decide whether my position on the ticket will help or hurt. And I am going to ask you to help them decide. Wire and write the Republican National Committee whether you think I should stay on or whether I should get off. And whatever their decision is, I will abide by it.

But just let me say this last word. Regardless of what happens, I am going to continue this fight. I am going to campaign up and down America until we drive the crooks and the Communists and those that defend them out of Washington, and remember, folks, Eisenhower is a great man. Folks, he is a great man, and a vote for Eisenhower is a vote for what is good for America.

🍂 "Patriotism is not the fear of something; it is the love of something"

ADLAI E. STEVENSON

Illinois Governor Adlai E. Stevenson ran as the Democratic candidate for President against Eisenhower in 1952. The Democrats were on the defensive, having been charged by McCarthy and other Republicans with having allowed Communists to infiltrate the government and for overseeing the bloody stalemate in Korea.

On August 27 at Madison Square Garden in New York City, Stevenson confronted these charges with a definition of patriotism that does not depend on the diminishment of others. Although Stevenson lost the 1952 and 1956 Presidential elections, his eloquence brought voice to the liberal community of the 1950s.

True patriotism, it seems to me, is based on tolerance and a large measure of humility.

There are men among us who use "patriotism" as a club for attacking other Americans. What can we say for the self-styled patriot who thinks that a Negro, a Jew, a Catholic, or a Japanese-American is less an American than he? That betrays the deepest article of our faith, the belief in individual liberty and equality which has always been the heart and soul of the American idea.

What can we say for the man who proclaims himself a patriot—and then for political or personal reasons attacks the patriotism of faithful public servants? I give you, as a shocking example, the attacks which have been made on the loyalty and the motives of our great wartime Chief of Staff, General Marshall.

To me this is the type of "patriotism" which is, in Dr. Johnson's phrase, "the last refuge of scoundrels."

The anatomy of patriotism is complex. But surely intolerance and public irresponsibility cannot be cloaked in the shining armor of rectitude and righteousness. Nor can the denial of the right to hold ideas that are different—the freedom of man to think as he pleases. To strike freedom of the mind with the fist of patriotism is an old and ugly subtlety....

Men who have offered their lives for their country know that patriotism is not the fear of something; it is the love of something. Patriotism with us is not the hatred of Russia; it is the love of this Republic and of the ideal of liberty of man and mind in which it was born, and to which the Republic is dedicated.

With this patriotism—patriotism in its large and wholesome meaning—Americans can master its power and turn it to the noble cause of peace. We can maintain military power without militarism; political power without oppression; and moral power without compulsion or complacency.

The road we travel is long, but at the end lies the grail of peace. And in the valley of peace we see the faint outlines of a new world, fertile and strong. It is odd that one of the keys to abundance should have been handed to civilization on a platter of destruction. But the power of the atom to work evil gives only the merest hint of its power for good.

I believe that man stands on the eve of his greatest day. I know, too, that that day is not a gift but a prize—that we shall not reach until we have won it.

🍂 "We may not now relax our guard"

DWIGHT D. EISENHOWER ANNOUNCES KOREAN ARMISTICE

Three years of bitter war in Korea ended in a stalemate. On July 26, 1953, an armistice was signed ending hostilities and setting a demilitarized zone along the 38th Parallel. Having handily won the 1952 Presidential election, Eisenhower helped forge the agreement early in his new term. He announced the agreement on a television broadcast shortly after the signing.

North and South Korea remained officially at war. To help prevent the renewal of an active conflict, the United States stationed troops in South Korea for the balance of the century.

My fellow citizens, tonight we greet, with prayers of thanksgiving, the official news that an armistice was signed almost an hour ago in Korea. It will quickly bring to an end the fighting between the United Nations forces and the Communist armies. For this nation the cost of repelling aggression has been high. In thousands of homes it has been incalculable. It has been paid in terms of tragedy.

With special feelings of sorrow—and of solemn gratitude—we think of those who were called upon to lay down their lives in that far-off land to prove once again that only courage and sacrifice can keep freedom alive upon the earth. To the widows and orphans of this war, and to those veterans who bear disabling wounds, America renews tonight her pledge of lasting devotion and care.

Our thoughts turn also to those other Americans wearied by many months of imprisonment behind the enemy lines. The swift return of all of them will bring joy to thousands of families. It will be evidence of good faith on the part of those with whom we have signed this armistice.

Soldiers, sailors, and airmen of sixteen different countries have stood as partners beside us throughout these long and bitter months. America's thanks go to each. In this struggle we have seen the United Nations meet the challenge of aggression—not with pathetic words of protest, but with deeds of decisive purpose. It is proper that we salute particularly the valorous armies of the Republic of Korea, for they have done even more than prove their right to freedom. Inspired by President Syngham Rhee, they have given an example of courage and patriotism which again demonstrates that men of the West and men of the East can fight and work and live together side by side in pursuit of a just and noble cause.

And so at long last the carnage of war is to cease and the negotiation of the conference table is to begin. On this Sabbath evening each of us devoutly prays that all nations may come to see the wisdom of composing differences in this fashion before, rather than after, there is resort to brutal and futile battle.

Now as we strive to bring about that wisdom, there is, in this moment of sober satisfaction, one thought that must discipline our emotions and steady our resolution. It is this: We have won an armistice on a single battleground—not peace in the world. We may not now relax our guard nor cease our quest.

Throughout the coming months, during the period of prisoner screening and exchange, and during the possibly longer period of the political conference which looks toward the unification of Korea, we and our United Nations allies must be vigilant against the possibility of untoward developments.

And, as we do so, we shall fervently strive to insure that this armistice will, in fact, bring free peoples one step nearer to a goal of a world of peace.

My fellow citizens, almost ninety years ago, Abraham Lincoln, at the end of the war, delivered his second inaugural address. At the end of that speech he spoke some words that I think more nearly would express the true feelings of America tonight than would any other words ever spoken or written. You recall them: "With malice toward none, with charity for all, with firmness in the right as God gives us to see the right, let us strive on to finish the work we are in…to do all which may achieve and cherish a just and lasting peace among ourselves and with all nations."

This is our resolve and our dedication.

"Have you no sense of decency, sir?"

JOSEPH WELCH, SENATOR JOSEPH MCCARTHY

After five years of using his position on the Committee of Un-American Activities to elevate his career by tearing down others, Senator Joseph McCarthy's tactics came to an abrupt end when he took on the U.S. Army. Prior to that, he and counsel Roy Cohn had investigated and destroyed the careers of hundreds of men and women in Hollywood, the State Department and other government agencies with accusations of communist activities.

In the fearful environment of the Cold War, their tactics initially enjoyed popular support. However, as McCarthy's accusations became increasingly shrill and were directed at more and more respected circles, the established political community and media began to slowly speak out against McCarthy.

In the spring of 1954, McCarthy accused the American military, including Secretary of the Army Robert T. Stevens, of hampering the investigating committee. With a national television audience watching, McCarthy squared off against Stevens' defense counsel Joseph Welch. The encounter prompted a national rejection of McCarthy. Three years after the hearing, McCarthy died of alcoholism.

WELCH: Mr. Cohn, tell me once more: Every time you learn of a Communist or a spy anywhere, is it your policy to get them out as fast as possible?

Cohn: Surely, we want them out as fast as possible, sir.

WELCH: And whenever you learn of one from now on, Mr. Cohn, I beg of you, you will tell somebody about them quickly.

COHN: Mr. Welch, with great respect, I work for the committee here. They know how we go about handling situations of Communist infiltration. If they are displeased with the speed with which I and the group of men who work with me proceed, if they are displeased with the order in which we move, I am sure they will give me appropriate instructions along those lines, and I will follow any which they give me.

WELCH: May I add a small voice, sir, and say whenever you know about a subversive or a Communist or a spy, please hurry. Will you remember those words?

MCCARTHY: Mr. Chairman, in view of that question—

MUNDT: Have you a point of order?

MCCARTHY: Not exactly, Mr. Chairman, but in view of Mr. Welch's request that the information be given once we know of anyone who might be performing any work for the Communist Party, I think we should tell him that he has in his law firm a young man named Fisher whom he recommended, incidentally, to do work on this committee, who has been for a number of years a member of an organization which was named, oh, years and years ago as a legal bulwark of the Communist Party, and organization which always swings to the defense of Communists. I certainly assume that Mr. Welch did not know of this young man at the time he recommended him as the assistant counsel for this committee, but he has such terror and such a great desire to know where anyone is located who may be serving the Communist cause, Mr. Welch, that I thought we should just call to your attention the fact that your Mr. Fisher, who is still in your law firm today, whom you asked to have down here looking over the secret and classified material, is a member of an organization, not named by me but named by various committees, named by the Attorney General, as I recall, and I think I quote this verbatim, as "the legal bulwark of the Communist Party." He belonged to that for a sizeable number of years, according to his own admission, and he belonged to it long after it had been exposed as the legal arm of the Communist Party.

Knowing that, Mr. Welch, I just felt that I had a duty to respond to your urgent request that before sundown, when we know of anyone serving the Communist cause, we let the agency know. We are now letting you know that your man did belong to this organization for either three or four years, belong to it long after he was out of law school. I have hesitated bringing that up, but I have been rather bored with your phony requests to Mr. Cohn here that he personally get every Communist out of government before sundown. Therefore, we will give you information about the young man in your own organization.

I am not asking you at this time to explain why you tried to foist him on this committee. Whether you knew he was a member of that Communist organization or not, I don't know. I assume you did not, Mr. Welch, because I get the impression that, while you are quite a good actor, you play for a laugh. I don't think you yourself would ever knowingly aid the Communist cause. I think you are unknowingly aiding it when you try to burlesque this hearing in which we are attempting to bring out the facts, however...

WELCH: Mr. Chairman, under these circumstances I must have something approaching a personal privilege.

MUNDT: You may have it, sir. It will not be taken out of your time.

WELCH: Senator McCarthy, I did not know— Senator, sometimes you say "May I have your attention?"

MCCARTHY: I am listening to you. I can listen with one ear.

WELCH: This time I want you to listen with both.

MCCARTHY: Yes.

WELCH: Senator McCarthy, I think until this moment—

MCCARTHY: Jim, will you get the news story to the effect that this man belonged to this Communist-front organization? Will you get the citations showing that this was the legal arm of the Communist Party, and the length of time that he belonged, and the fact the he was recommended by Mr. Welch? I think that should be in the record.

WELCH: You won't need anything in the record when I have finished telling you this. Until this moment, Senator, I think I never really gauged your cruelty or your recklessness. Fred Fisher is the young man who went to Harvard Law School and came into my firm and is starting what looks to be a brilliant career with us. When I decided to work for this committee I asked Jim St. Clair, who sits on my right, to be my first assistant. I said to Jim, "Pick somebody in the firm who works under you that you would like." He chose Fred Fisher and they came down on an afternoon plane. That night, when we had taken a little stab at trying to see what the case was about, Fred Fisher and Jim. St. Clair and I went to dinner together. I then said to these two young men, "Boys, I don't know anything about you except I have always liked you, but if there is anything funny in the life of either one of you that would hurt anybody in this case you speak up quick."

Fred Fisher said, "Mr. Welch, when I was in law school and for a period of months after, I belonged to the Lawyers Guild," as you have suggested, Senator. He went on to say, "I am secretary of the Young Republican League in Newton with the son of Massachusetts' Governor, and I have the respect and admiration of my community and I am sure I have the respect and admiration for the twenty-five lawyers or so in Hale and Dorr."

I said, "Fred, I just don't think I am going to ask you to work on the case. If I do, one of these days that will come out and go over national television and it will just hurt like the dickens."

So, Senator, I asked him to go back to Boston. Little did I dream you could be so reckless and so cruel as to do injury to this lad. It is true he is still with Hale and Dorr. It is, I regret to say, equally true that I fear he shall always bear a scar needlessly inflicted by you. If it were in my power to forgive you your reckless cruelty, I would do so. I like to think I am a gentleman, but your forgiveness will have to come from someone other than me.

MCCARTHY: Mr. Chairman.

MUNDT: Senator McCarthy?

MCCARTHY: May I say that Mr. Welch talks about this being cruel and reckless. He was just

baiting; he has been baiting Mr. Cohn here for hours, requesting that Mr. Cohn, before sundown, get out of any department of government anyone who is serving the Communist cause. I just give this man's record, and I want to say, Mr. Welch, that it has been labeled long before he became a member, as early as 1944—

WELCH: Senator, may we not drop this? We know he belonged to the Lawyers Guild, and Mr. Cohn nods his head at me. I did you, I think, no personal injury, Mr. Cohn.

COHN: No, sir.

WELCH: I meant to do you no personal injury, and if I did, I beg your pardon.

Let us not assassinate this lad further, Senator. You have done enough. Have you no sense of decency, sir, at long last? Have you left no sense of decency?

❧ Brown v. Board of Education: "Separate but equal has no place"

SUPREME COURT CHIEF JUSTICE EARL WARREN

Brown v. Board of Education was one of the landmark decisions of U.S. judicial history and a central pillar of the Civil Rights movement in the 1950s. Argued by the National Association for the Advancement of the Colored People counsel Thurgood Marshall, the case was one of a series of lawsuits brought to federal courts assailing the "separate but equal" doctrine established by the 1896 *Plessy v. Ferguson* decision. "That the Constitution is color-blind is our dedicated belief," Supreme Court justices determined.

Brown v. Board of Education overturned the almost universal separation of schools according to race in the South and unleashed heated passions across the country over the next twenty years. Chief Justice Earl Warren wrote the decision and secured the unanimous support of his colleagues.

These cases come to us from the state of Kansas, South Carolina, Virginia, and Delaware. They are premised on different facts and different local conditions, but a common legal question justifies their consideration together in this consolidated opinion.

In each of these cases, minors of the Negro race, through their legal representatives, seek the aid of the courts in obtaining admission to the public schools of their community on a nonsegregated basis. In each instance, they had been denied admission to schools attended by white children under laws requiring or permitting segregation according to race. This segregation was alleged to deprive the plaintiffs of the equal protection of the laws under the Fourteenth Amendment. In each of the cases other than the Delaware case, a three-judge federal District Court denied relief to the plaintiffs on the so-called "separate but equal" doctrine announced by this Court in *Plessy v. Ferguson*, 163 U.S. 537. Under that doctrine, equality of treatment is accorded when the races are provided substantially equal facilities, even though these facilities be separate. In the Delaware case, the Supreme Court of Delaware adhered to that doctrine, but ordered that the plaintiffs be admitted to the white schools because of their superiority to the Negro schools.

The plaintiffs contend that segregated public schools are not "equal" and cannot be made equal," and that hence they are deprived of the equal protection of the laws. Because of the obvious importance of the question presented, the Court took jurisdiction. Argument was heard in the 1952 term, and re-argument was heard this term on certain questions propounded by the Court.

Re-argument was largely devoted to the circumstances surrounding the adoption of the Fourteenth Amendment in 1868. It covered exhaustively consideration of the amendment in Congress, ratification by the states, then-existing practices in racial segregation, and the views of proponents and opponents of the amendment. This discussion and our own investigation convince us that, although these sources cast some light, it is not enough to resolve the problem with which we are faced. At best, they are inconclusive. The most avid proponents of the Post-War Amendments undoubtedly intended them to remove all legal distinctions among "all persons born or naturalized in the United States." Their opponents, just as certainly, were antagonistic to both the letter and the spirit of the Amendments and wished them to have the most limited effect. What others in Congress and the state legislatures had in mind cannot be determined with any degree of certainty.

An additional reason for the inconclusive nature of the Amendment's history, with respect to segregated schools, is the status of public education at that time. In the South, the movement toward free common schools, supported by general taxation, had not yet taken hold. Education of white children was largely in the hands of private groups. Education of Negroes was almost nonexistent, and practically all of the race was illiterate. In fact, any education of Negroes was forbidden by law in some states. Today, in contrast, many Negroes have achieved outstanding success in the arts and sciences as well as in the business and professional world. It is true that public education had already advanced further in the North, but the effect of the Amendment on Northern States was generally ignored in the congressional debates. Even in the North, the conditions of public education did not approximate those existing today. The curriculum was usually rudimentary; ungraded schools were common in rural areas; the school term was but three months a year in many states; and compulsory school attendance was virtually unknown. As a consequence, it is not surprising that there should be so little in the history of the Fourteenth Amendment relating to its intended effect on public education.

In the first cases in this Court construing the Fourteenth Amendment, decided shortly after its adoption, the Court interpreted it as proscribing all state-imposed discriminations against the Negro race. The doctrine of "separate but equal" did not make its appearance in this Court until 1896 in the case of *Plessy v. Ferguson*, supra, involving not education but transportation. American courts have since labored with the doctrine for over half a century. In this Court, there have been six cases involving the "separate but equal" doctrine in the field of public education. In *Cumming v. Board of Education* and *Gong Lum v. Rice*, the validity of the doctrine itself was not challenged. In more recent cases, all on the graduate school level, inequality was found in that specific benefits enjoyed by white students were denied to Negro students of the same educational qualifications. In none of these cases was it necessary to reexamine the doctrine to grant relief to the Negro plaintiff. And in *Sweatt v. Painter*, the Court expressly reserved decision on the question whether *Plessy v. Ferguson* should be held inapplicable to public education.

In the instant cases, that question is directly presented. Here unlike *Sweatt v. Painter*, there are findings below that the Negro and white schools involved have been equalized, or are being equalized, with respect to buildings, curricula, qualifications and salaries of teachers, and other "tangible" factors. Our decision, therefore, cannot turn on merely a comparison of these tangible factors in the Negro and white schools involved in each of the cases. We must look instead to the effect of segregation itself on public education.

In approaching this problem, we cannot turn the clock back to 1868 when the amendment was adopted, or even to 1896 when Plessy v. Ferguson was written. We must consider public education in the light of its full development and its present place in American life throughout the nation. Only in this way can it be determined if segregation in public schools deprives these plaintiffs of the equal protection of the laws.

Today, education is perhaps the most important function of state and local governments. Compulsory school-attendance laws and the great expenditures for education both demonstrate our recognition of the importance of education to our democratic society. It is required in the performance of our most basic public responsibilities, even service in the armed forces. It is the very foundation of good citizenship. Today it is a principal instrument in awakening the child to cultural values, in preparing him for later professional training, and in helping him to adjust normally to his environment. In these days, it is doubtful that any child may reasonably be expected to succeed in life if he is denied the opportunity of an education. Such an opportunity, where the state has undertaken to provide it, is a right which must be made available to all on equal terms.

We come then to the question presented: Does segregation of children in public schools solely on the basis of race, even though the physical facilities and other "tangible" factors may be equal, deprive the children of the minority group of equal educational opportunities? We believe that it does.

In Sweatt v. Painter, in finding that a segregated law school for Negroes could not provide them equal educational opportunities, this Court relied in large part on "those qualities which are incapable of objective measurement but which make for greatness in a law school." In McLaurin v. Oklahoma State Regents, the Court, in requiring that a Negro admitted to a white graduate school be treated like all other students, again resorted to intangible considerations: "…his ability to study, to engage in discussions and exchange views with other students, and, in general, to learn his profession." Such considerations apply with added force to children in grade and high schools. To separate them from others similar age and qualifications solely because of their race generates a feeling of inferiority as to their status in the community that may affect their hearts and minds in a way unlikely ever to be undone. The effect of this separation on their educational opportunities was well stated by a finding in the Kansas case by a court which nevertheless felt compelled to rule against the Negro plaintiffs:

"Segregation of white and colored children in public schools has a detrimental effect upon the colored children. The impact is greater when it has the sanction of the law; for the policy of separating the races is usually interpreted as denoting the inferiority of the Negro group. A sense of inferiority affects the motivation of a child to learn. Segregation with the sanction of law, therefore, has a tendency to retard the educational and mental development of Negro children and to deprive them of some of the benefits they would receive in a racially integrated school system."

Whatever may have been the extent of psychological knowledge at the time of Plessy v. Ferguson, this finding is amply supported by modern authority. Any language in Plessy v. Ferguson contrary to this finding is rejected.

We conclude that in the field of public education the doctrine of "separate but equal" has no place. Separate educational facilities are inherently unequal. Therefore, we hold that the plaintiffs and others similarly situated for whom the actions have been brought are, by reason of the segregation complained of, deprived of the equal protection of the laws guaranteed by the Fourteenth Amendment. This disposition makes unnecessary any discussion whether such segregation also violates the Due Process Clause of the Fourteenth Amendment.

Because there are class actions, because of the wide applicability of this decision, and because of the great variety of local conditions, the formulation of decrees in these cases presents problems of considerable complexity. On reargument, the consideration of appropriate relief was necessarily subordinated to the primary question—the constitutionality of segregation in public education. We have announced that such segregation is a denial of the equal protection of the laws.

Cooper v. Aaron: "Equal justice under the law is thus made a living truth"

SUPREME COURT CHIEF JUSTICE EARL WARREN

After *Brown v. Board of Education,* the Little Rock, Arkansas school board adopted a plan to desegregate the school system. Black children were assigned to attend a previously all-white high school. State and local officials violently opposed the plan, compelling President Eisenhower to send National Guard troops to escort and protect the teenage students against white mobs.

Based on the disruption of public order and the school's educational program, the school board appealed to the federal courts to suspend the desegregation plan in *Cooper v. Aaron.* The Supreme Court refused the request.

Law and order are not to be preserved by depriving the Negro children of their constitutional rights.

The controlling legal principles are plain. The command of the Fourteenth Amendment is that no "State" shall deny any person within its jurisdiction the equal protection of the laws. The prohibitions of the Fourteenth Amendment extend to all action of the State denying equal protection of the laws; whatever the agency of the State taking the action or whatever the guise in which it is taken. In short, the constitutional rights of children not to be discriminated against in school admission on grounds of race or color declared by this Court in the Brown case can neither be nullified openly and directly by the state legislators or state executives or judicial officers, nor nullified indirectly by them through evasive schemes for segregation whether attempted "ingeniously or ingenuously."...

Article vi of the Constitution makes the Constitution the "supreme Law of the Land." In 1803, Chief Justice Marshall, speaking for a unanimous Court, referring to the Constitution as "the fundamental paramount of law of the nation," declared in the notable case of Marbury v. Madison, that "It is emphatically the province and duty of the judicial department to say what the law is." This decision declared the basic principle that the federal judiciary is supreme in the exposition of the law of the Constitution, and that principle has ever since been respected by this Court and the Country as a permanent and indispensable feature of our constitutional system. It follows that the interpretation of the Fourteenth Amendment enunciated by this Court in the Brown case is the supreme law of the land, and Article vi of the Constitution makes it of binding effect on the States "any Thing in the Constitution or Laws of any State to the Contrary notwithstanding." Every state legislator and executive and judicial officer is solemnly committed by oath taken pursuant to Article vi, clause three, "to support this Constitution."

No state legislator or executive or judicial officer can war against the Constitution without violating his undertaking to support it.

It is, of course, quite true that the responsibility for public education is primarily the concern of the States, but it is equally true that such responsibilities, like all other state activity, must be exercised consistently with federal constitutional requirements as they apply to state action. The Constitution created a government dedicated to equal justice under the law. The Fourteenth Amendment embodied and emphasized that ideal. State support of segregated schools through any arrangement, management, funds, or property cannot be squared with the Amendment's command that no State shall deny to any person within its jurisdiction the equal protection of the laws. The right of a student not to be segregated on racial grounds in schools so maintained is indeed so fundamental and pervasive that it is embraced in the concept of due process of law.

The basic decision in Brown was unanimously reached by this Court only after the case had been briefed and twice argued and the issues had been given the most serious consideration. Since the first Brown opinion three new Justices have come to the Court. They are at one with the Justices still on the Court who participated in that basic decision as to its correctness, and that decision and the obedience of the States to them, according to the command of the Constitution, are indispensable for the protection of the freedoms guaranteed by our fundamental charter for all of us. Our constitutional ideal of equal justice under law is thus made a living truth.

"There are no rules for our kind of show, so we'll make up our own"

LUCILLE BALL ON "I LOVE LUCY"

Although television had been first broadcast in 1928 by a General Electric station in Schenectady, New York, it took twenty years for the new medium to develop a major audience. But once it arrived, it became a national phenomenon. One of the first great hits was "I Love Lucy," starring the husband-and-wife team of Lucille Ball and Desi Arnaz. Lucille Ball recalls the start up of the show, which remained popular with audiences almost fifty years later.

When I was going into my fourth month of pregnancy, CBS suddenly gave Desi the green light: they would finance a pilot for a domestic television show featuring the two of us as a married couple. A show that might go on the air that fall.

"You've got a month to put one together," [said agent Don Sharpe]. "They want the pilot by February fifteenth."

For ten years, Desi and I had been trying to become co-stars and parents; now our dearest goals were being realized much too fast. We suddenly felt unprepared for either and began to have second thoughts.

At that time, television was regarded as the enemy by Hollywood. So terrified was Hollywood of this medium, movie people were afraid to make even guest appearances. If I undertook a weekly television show and it flopped, I might never work in movies again.

It would mean each of us would have to give up our respective radio programs, and Desi would have to cancel all his band engagements. It was a tremendous gamble; it had to be an all-or-nothing commitment.

But this was the first real chance Desi and I would have to work together, something we'd both been longing for, for years.

We continued to wrestle with the decision, trying to look at things from every angle. Then one night Carole Lombard appeared to me in a dream. She was wearing one of those slinky bias-cut gowns of the thirties, waving a long black cigarette holder in her hand. "Go on, kid," she advised me airily. "Give it a whirl."

The next day I told Don Sharpe, "We'll do it. Desi and I want to work together more than anything else in the world."

We called my radio writers on "My Favorite Husband" and together dreamed up a set of television characters. Originally, we were Lucy and Larry Lopez; it wasn't until we started our first shows that we became the Ricardos. Desi would be a Cuban bandleader who worked in New York City; I would play a housewife with burning stage ambitions....

A week later our agent phoned to say, "Phillip Morris wants to sponsor you!" We were on our way.

However, in the next few weeks the deal twisted and changed and almost blew up. The sponsor had a second demand: they not only wanted a weekly show, they also wanted it done live in New York. In 1951, a show done live on the West Coast appeared on the East Coast in fuzzy kinescope—with the image about as sharp as a piece of cheesecloth.

We refused to move to New York. Desi suggested that we film the show, live, in front of an audience. The network people screamed. A filmed show costs twice as much as a live one. The sponsor wouldn't put up more money and neither would CBS. So Desi made a canny offer: In return for a $1,000 weekly salary cut for us, we were given complete ownership of the show; originally, CBS had owned half of it. CBS also agreed to advance the enormous sums of money needed to film production, with Desi as producer.

All Desi had ever managed was a sixteen-piece Latin band. Now he had to rent a studio and equipment and find actors, cameramen, stagehands, cutters, film editors, writers, and scripts for thirty-nine weekly shows.

When the deal was finally set, it was late March. We had to start filming by August 15 to be on the air by October. We could rehearse and film a half-hour show in a week, but cutting editing, and scoring would take another five weeks at least....

Lucy Ricardo's nutty predicaments arose from an earnest desire to please. And there was something touching about her stage ambitions. As we were discussing her with our writers, Desi spoke up. "She tries so hard, she can't dance and she can't sing, she's earnest and pathetic, Oh, I love that Lucy!" And so the title of the show was born.

I had always known that Desi was a great

showman, but many were surprised to learn he was a genius with keen instincts for comedy and plot. He has a quick, brilliant mind; he can instantly find the flaw in any story line; and he has inherent good taste and an intuitive knowledge of what will and will not play. He is a great producer, a great director. He never stays on too long or allows anybody else to.

We had the characters of Lucy and Ricky clear in our minds, Jess Oppenheimer suggested that we add another man and wife—an older couple in a lower income bracket. The writers could then pit couple against couple, and the men against the women. I had known Bill Frawley since my RKO starlet days as a great natural comic; we all agreed upon him for Fred Mertz. We then started thinking about a TV wife for Bill.

We considered a number of actresses, and then one day Desi heard about a fine actress from the Broadway stage named Vivian Vance. As far as I was concerned, it was Kismet. Viv and I were extraordinarily compatible. We both believe wholeheartedly in what we call "an enchanted sense of play," and use it liberally in our show. It's a happy frame of mind, the light touch, skipping into things instead of plodding. It's looking at things from a child's point of view and believing. The only way I can play a funny scene is to believe it. Then I can convincingly eat like a dog under the table, freeze to death beneath burning-hot klieg lights, or bake a loaf of bread ten feet long.

We had no way of knowing how comical she and Bill would be together. Vivian was actually much younger than Bill. Up until then, she'd usually been cast in glamorous "other woman" parts. But she went along gamely with Ethel Mertz's dowdy clothes, no false eyelashes or eye makeup, and hair that looked as if she had washed and set it herself. But she drew the line at padding her body to look fatter....

She and Bill scrapped a good deal, and this put a certain amount of real feeling into their stage quarrels. Bill became the hero of all the henpecked husbands. He couldn't walk down the street without some man coming up to him and saying, "Boy, Fred, you tell that Ethel off something beautiful!"

So much good luck was involved in the casting. Early in the series, our writers wanted to write a show in which the Mertzes had to sing and dance. We then learned for the first time that both

Vivian and Bill had had big musical comedy careers. Vivian had been in Skylark with Gertrude Lawrence, and Bill was a well-known vaudeville hoofer.

I had insisted upon having a studio audience; otherwise, I knew, we'd never hit the right tempo. We did the show every Thursday night in front of four hundred people, a cross-section of America. I could visualize our living and working together on the set like a stock company, then filming it like a movie, and at the same time staging it like a Broadway. "We'll have opening night every week," I chortled.

Desi's first problem was that there were no movie studies in Hollywood with accommodations for an audience. We also wanted a stage large enough to film the show in its natural sequence, with no long delays setting up stage decorations or shifting lights.

Desi hired Academy Award-winning cameraman Karl Freund, whose work I had admired at MGM, and discussed the problems with him. Karl flew to New York for a week to see how television cameras could be moved around without interfering too much with the audience's view of the action. He came back pretty unimpressed. "There are no rules for our kind of show, so we'll make up our own."

Karl Freund hit upon a revolutionary new way of filming a show with three cameras shooting the action simultaneously. One of these cameras is far back, another recording the medium shots, with a third getting the close-ups. The film editor then has three different shots of a particular bit of action. By shifting back and forth between the three, he can get more variety and flexibility than with the one-camera technique.

But moving three huge cameras about the stage between the actors and the audience called for the most complex planning.

First Desi rented an unused movie studio. By tearing down partitions, he joined two giant soundstages. This gave us enough room to build three permanent sets—the Ricardo living room, bedroom, and kitchen—and a fourth set, which was sometimes the New York nightclub where Ricky worked and sometimes an alligator farm or a vineyard in Italy or the French Alps—whatever the script called for. The roving cameras couldn't roll easily on the wooden stage, so a smooth concrete floor was laid down.

While the three rooms slowly took form before our eyes, bleachers for three hundred people were built facing them. The Los Angeles Fire and Health departments threw a mountain of red tape at us when they learned we were inviting a large weekly audience into a movie studio. Desi had to add restrooms, water fountains, and an expensive sprinkler system. Microphones were installed over the heads of the audience; we wanted our laughs live—some of the canned laughter you hear today came from our Lucy show audiences....

It took me a long time to recover physically from Lucie's birth, but I had no time to pamper myself. Six weeks after she arrived, I walked on the Lucy set to start filming the series.

Rehearsals got under way to the pounding of hammers and buzzing of saws; the set was only half-built and a whole wall of the soundstage was still missing when we started. Desi was so nervous that he memorized everybody's lines and moved his own lips as they spoke; he also kept flicking his eyes around the stage watching the progress of the three cameras. He soon got over this, but proved to be the fastest learner of dialogue.

We rehearsed the first show twelve hours a day. Then on Friday evening, August 15, 1951, the bleachers filled up by eight o'clock and Desi explained to the audience that they would be seeing a brand new kind of television show. He stepped behind the curtain and we all took our places.

Sitting in the bleachers that first night were a lot of anxious rooters: DeDe and Desi's mother, Dolores; our writers; Andrew Hickox; and a raft of Philip Morris representatives and CBS officials. To launch the series, the network had paid out $300,000. They hoped it would last long enough to pay back that advance.

We were lucky all the way. The first four shows put us among the top ten on television. Arthur Godfrey, one of the giants, preceded us and urged his watchers to stay tuned to *I Love Lucy*. Our twentieth show made us number one on the air and there we stayed for three wild, incredible years.

I Love Lucy has been called the most popular television show of all time. Such national devotion to one show can never happen again; there are too many shows, on many more channels, now. But in 1951-1952, our show changed the Monday night habits of America. Between nine and nine-thirty, taxis disappeared from the streets of New York. Marshall Fields department store in Chicago hung up a sign: "We Love Lucy too, so from now on we will be open Thursday nights instead of Monday." Telephone calls across the nation dropped sharply during that half hour, as well as the water flush rate, as whole families sat glued to their seats.

During our first season someone told Desi that our show had a hit rating of 70. He looked worried, thinking that a "grade" of 70 was barely passing. "You're kidding," he said, not realizing that a rating of 70 was indeed phenomenal.

"Half of the sexual outlet of the total male population is being secured from sources which are socially disapproved"

THE KINSEY REPORT

Like other television couples, Desi and Lucy Ricardo slept in separate beds. The gap between the American sexual behavior that society wanted to believe existed and American sexual practices as they actually existed was enormous. Alfred Kinsey helped bridge that span.

An accomplished scientist, Kinsey had been a very successful in studying nature. The Massachusetts Horticultural Society had named his book *Edible Wild Plants of North America* the most important book of the year in the early 1940s. As a teacher at Indiana University, however, students asked him about sexual matters. Alarmed by the lack of knowledge among students and the scarcity of information about the topic, he set up systematic studies of sexual practices among Americans.

In 1948, he published *Sexual Behavior in the Human Male*. Packed with charts, graphs, footnotes and statistics, the study explored the frequency and nature of sexual encounters between men of different age groups, educational backgrounds and income levels. The 800-page book tore down the myths of sexual behavior of men, revealing the existence of widespread homosexual relations and delving into matters such as extra-marital relationships, different types of sexual positions and their frequency and almost anything else pertaining to sex.

The book, which was followed by *Sexual Behavior of the Human Female* in 1953, was a sensation, selling hundreds of thousands of copies and outraging conservative leaders and churches across the nation. Kinsey had laid bare the hypocrisy of American society regarding sex and helped pave the way for the sexual revolution of the 1960s.

Marital intercourse is the one type of sexual activity which is approved by our Anglo-American mores and legal codes. For those males who are married and living with their wives, marital intercourse accounts for most of the sexual outlet; and to them, a successful adjustment means sufficiently frequent and emotionally effective intercourse with their wives. It is, in consequence, inevitable in any study of human sexual behavior that especial attention be given to the nature of marital relationships.

Sociologists and anthropologists generally consider that the family is the basis of human society, and at least some students believe that the sexual attraction between the anthropoid male and female has been fundamental to the development of the human and infra-human family. Supporting data for these opinions are adduced from a study of the anthropoid family. But whatever the phylogenetic history of the human family, the evidence is clear that the sexual factor contributes materially to its maintenance today....

Society is interested in the nature of marital intercourse because it is interested in the maintenance of the family. Society is interested in maintaining the family as a way for men and women to live together in partnerships that may make for more effective functioning than solitary living may allow. Society is interested in maintaining the family as a means of providing homes for children that result from coitus; and in Jewish and many Christian philosophies, this is made a prime end of marriage. Society is also interested in maintaining families as a means of providing a regular sexual outlet for adults, and as a means of controlling promiscuous sexual activity. While these latter interests are not so often formulated in the thinking of our culture, these functions of marriage are more evident in some primitive cultures. Whatever other interests are involved, the sexual factor is one which is of considerable concern to any group that is interested in the maintenance of the family....

Incidence and Significance

Marital intercourse is the one sort of sexual activity which involves practically 100 per cent of the eligible males in the population. There are exceedingly few who marry and then fail to have any inter-

course with their wives. Exceptions occur only among those who never live with their spouses after marriage, among those few who are physically incapable of even attempting intercourse, among a few of those who are primarily homosexual and whose wives may be similarly homosexual....

But although marital intercourse thus provides the chief source of outlet for married males, immediately from the time of onset of marriage, it falls considerably short of constituting the total outlet of those individuals. In the married population taken as a whole, it does not ordinarily provide more than 85 per cent of the total sexual outlet. The remaining orgasms of the married male are derived from masturbation, nocturnal emissions, petting and heterosexual coitus with partners other than wives, the homosexual, and especially in some Western rural areas, from intercourse with other animals....

If we note that marital intercourse does not supply the whole of the outlet of married males, it is even more important to note that it does not supply even half of the outlet of the male population taken as a whole. Only 60 per cent of the white American males are married at any particular time. Calculating from the age distribution of the total population, and from the mean frequencies of total outlet in each age group, it develops that there are, on an average, 231 orgasms per week per hundred males between adolescence and old age. Calculating the orgasms secured in marital intercourse in each male group, and correcting for the incidence of married males in the total population, there prove to be, on an average, 106 orgasms per week which are derived from coitus with spouses, per hundred males of the total population (single and married). This means that only 45.9 per cent of the total outlet of the total population is derived from marital intercourse.

Thus it will be seen that marital intercourse, although it is the most important single source of sexual outlet, does not provide even half of the total number of orgasms experienced by the males in our American population. Allowing for the socially and legally accepted 5 or 6 per cent of the outlets which is secured from nocturnal emissions, it is to be concluded that approximately half of the sexual outlet of the total male population is being secured from sources which are socially disapproved and in large part illegal and punishable under the criminal codes.

Roll Over, Beethoven

CHUCK BERRY

Unencumbered by the responsibility of the Great Depression or the terror of World War II, teenagers in the 1950s embraced a new, more carefree lifestyle than their parents. Material prosperity had eased the economic pressures of mainstream America, and leisure become more of an option. A new, high-energy brand of music emerged: it was called rock 'n roll. Derived in part from black music, rock 'n roll literally shook the nation to a "happening beat."

Chuck Berry was one of the first popular rock stars. His 1950s song "Roll Over, Beethoven," which is excerpted, below, helped drive and symbolize the rise of a new generation with new ideas of what good music is.

Well I'm a write a letter,
Gonna mail it to my local D.J.
Yes, it's a jumpin' little record
I want my jockey to play;
Roll over Beethoven,
I gotta hear it again today.

You know my temp'rature's rising
And the juke box blowin' a fuse,
My heart's beatin' rhythm
And my soul keeps a-singin' the blues;
Roll over Beethoven and tell Tchaikowsky the news.

I got the rockin' pneumonia,
I need a shot of rhythm and blues,
I caught the rollin' arthritis,
Sittin' down at a rhythm review;
Roll over Beethoven, they're rockin' in two by two.

Well, if you feel you like it,
Go get your lover,
Then reel and rock it.
Roll it over,
Then move on up just a trifle further,
Then reel and rock with another,
Roll over Beethoven, dig these rhythm and blues.

Well, early in the morning,
and I'm givin' you a warnin',
Don't you step on my blue suede shoes;
Hey, diddle diddle,
I'm a playin' my fiddle,
Ain't got nothin' to lose;
Roll over Beethoven and tell Tchaikowsky the news.

Roll over Beethoven,
Roll over Beethoven,
Roll over Beethoven,
Roll over Beethoven,
Roll over Beethoven,
And dig these rhythm and blues.

This Land Is Your Land

WOODY GUTHRIE

Raised in the rural Great Plains, Woody Guthrie wandered the country when the dust storms arrived during the Great Depression. A populist and a talented musician, Guthrie played his guitar and wrote songs on behalf of union causes and the impoverished. By 1958, when Guthrie wrote "This Land Is Your Land," he was no longer a wandering guitar player, but a nationally known folk singer. The song not only honored the nation's natural bounty, it embraced it as a resource for everybody to enjoy. "This Land Is Your Land" would become an anthem for the pending environmental movement which sought to preserve Guthrie's vision.

Words and music by Woody Guthrie. TRO © Copyright 1956 (Renewed) 1970 (Renewed) Ludlow Music, Inc., New York, New York. Used by permission.

This land is your land
This land is my land
From California to the New York island
From the redwood forest to the Gulf Stream waters;
This land was made for you and me.

As I was walking
that ribbon of highway
I saw above me
that endless skyway
I saw below me
that golden valley
This land was made for you and me.

I've roamed and rambled
and I followed my footsteps
to the sparkling sand of
her diamond deserts
And all around me
a voice was sounding
This land was made for you and me.

When the sun comes shining
and I was strolling
and the wheatfields waving
and the dust clouds rolling
As the fog was lifting
a voice was chanting
This land was made for you and me.

"Refrain from riding buses owned and operated by the city of Montgomery"

RESOLUTION OF THE CITIZENS' MASS MEETING

December 5, 1955

While riding a bus in Montgomery, Alabama, on December 1, 1955, Rosa Parks, an NAACP organizer and seamstress, refused to give up her seat for a white man who had gotten on to the bus after her. Parks was arrested for this. As in many other Southern cities, blacks in Montgomery were required to yield their seats on buses to white passengers.

The arrest set off a citywide protest against the law by the entire black community. At the Holt Street Baptist Church, a minister new to Montgomery was elected president of the newly formed Montgomery Improvement Association: twenty-six-year-old Rev. Martin Luther King, Jr.

"You know my friends there comes a time when people get tired of being trampled over by the iron feet of oppression," King told the association's mass meeting on December 5. "There comes a time my friends when people get tired of being flung across the abyss of humiliation where they experience the bleakness of nagging despair. There comes a time when people get tired of being pushed out of the glittering sunlight of life's July and left standing amidst the piercing chill of an Alpine November."

Vowing to use peaceful, Christian tactics to prevail in their desire to reverse the bus law, the meeting called for a boycott by all blacks of Montgomery buses. After an extended boycott, during which King's house was firebombed, the Supreme Court overturned Montgomery's bus law in November 1956. The boycott marked the beginning of King's remarkable career as a civil rights activist and the start of the non-violent movement against racism in the south. The text of the resolution calling for the boycott follows.

WHEREAS, there are thousands of Negroes in the city and county of Montgomery who ride busses owned and operated by the Montgomery City

Lines, Incorporated, and

WHEREAS, said citizens have been riding busses owned and operated by said company over a number of years, and

WHEREAS, said citizens, over a number of years, and on many occasions have been insulted, embarrassed and have been made to suffer great fear of bodily harm by drivers of busses owned and operated by said bus company, and

WHEREAS, the drivers of said busses have never requested a white passenger riding on any of its busses to relinquish his seat and stand so that a Negro may take his seat; however, said drivers have on many occasions too numerous to mention requested Negro passengers on said busses to relinquish their seats and stand so that white passengers may take their seats, and

WHEREAS, said citizens of Montgomery city and county pay their fares just as all other persons who are passengers on said busses, and are entitled to fair and equal treatment, and

WHEREAS, there has been any number of arrests of Negroes caused by drivers of said busses and they are constantly put in jail for refusing to give white passengers their seats and stand.

WHEREAS, in March of 1955, a committee of citizens did have a conference with one of the officials of said bus line; at which time said official arranged a meeting between attorneys representing the Negro citizens of this city and attorneys representing the Montgomery City Lines, Incorporated and the city of Montgomery, and

WHEREAS, the official of the bus line promised that as a result of the meeting between said attorneys, he would issue a statement of policy clarifying the law with reference to the seating of Negro passengers on the bus, and

WHEREAS, said attorneys did have a meeting and did discuss the matter of clarifying the law, however, the official said bus lines did not make public statements as to its policy with reference to the seating of passengers on its busses, and

WHEREAS, since that time, at least two ladies have been arrested for an alleged violation of the city segregation law with reference to bus travel, and

WHEREAS, said citizens of Montgomery city and county believe that they have been grossly mistreated as passengers on the busses owned and operated by said bus company in spite of the fact that they are in the majority with reference to the number of passengers riding on said busses.

Be it Resolved As Follows:

That the citizens of Montgomery are requesting that every citizen in Montgomery, regardless of race, color, or creed, to refrain from riding busses owned and operated in the city of Montgomery by the Montgomery City Lines, Incorporated until some arrangement has been worked out between said citizens and the Montgomery City Lines, Incorporated.

That every person owning or who has access to automobiles use their automobiles in assisting other persons to get to work without charge.

That the employers of persons whose employees live a great distance from them, as much as possible afford transportation to your own employees.

That the Negro citizens of Montgomery are ready and willing to send a delegation of citizens to the Montgomery City Lines to discuss their grievances and to work out a solution for the same.

Be it further resolved that we have not, are not, and have no intentions of using an unlawful means or any intimidation to persuade persons not to ride the Montgomery City Lines' busses.

However, we call upon your consciences, both moral and spiritual, to give your whole-hearted support to this undertaking. We believe we have [a just] complaint and we are willing to discuss this matter with the proper officials.

❧ "Through nonviolence, courage displaces fear; love transforms hate"

STUDENT NONVIOLENT COORDINATING COMMITTEE STATEMENT OF PURPOSE

The nonviolence movement spread after the success of the Montgomery bus boycott. Although the Rev. Martin Luther King, Jr., played a leading role as the founder and president of the Southern Christian Leadership Conference, he was by no means the only leader.

In the spring of 1960, 126 student delegates from the Conference met at Shaw University in Raleigh, North Carolina to form a new organization called the Student Nonviolent

Coordinating Committee. The Rev. James Lawson prepared the following statement of purpose for the committee.

The committee, which included future Georgia Congressman John Lewis, staged sit-ins at whites-only food counters, bus stations and other areas that African-Americans were not allowed to use. Students participating in the sit-in movement displayed extraordinary courage. Thousands were beaten and thrown into jails, several were killed. The violence they suffered shocked much of the nation and eventually helped compel the South to repeal its Jim Crow laws.

Carrying out the mandate of the Raleigh Conference to write a statement of purpose for the movement, the Temporary Student Nonviolent Coordinating Committee submits for careful consideration the following draft. We urge all local, state or regional groups to examine it closely. Each member of our movement must work diligently to understand the depths of nonviolence.

We affirm the philosophical or religious ideal of nonviolence as the foundation of our purpose, the pre-supposition of our faith, and the manner of our action. Nonviolence as it grows from Judaic-Christian traditions seeks a social order of justice permeated by love. Integration of human endeavor represents the crucial first step towards such a society.

Through nonviolence, courage displaces fear; love transforms hate. Acceptance dissipates prejudice; hope ends despair. Peace dominates war; faith reconciles doubt. Mutual regard cancels enmity. Justice for all overthrows injustice. The redemptive community supersedes systems of gross social immorality.

Love is the central motif of nonviolence. Love is the force by which God binds man to himself and man to man. Such love goes to the extreme; it remains loving and forgiving even in the midst of hostility. It matches the capacity of evil to inflict suffering with an even more enduring capacity to absorb evil, all the while persisting in love.

By appealing to conscience and standing on the moral nature of human existence, nonviolence nurtures the atmosphere in which reconciliation and justice become actual possibilities.

🐦 "Private foreign investments advanced to a high"

UNITED STATES FOREIGN INVESTMENT, FROM THE 1958 SURVEY OF CURRENT BUSINESS

After World War II, the United States not only increased its political, military and diplomatic presence abroad, it also greatly accelerated its economic ties. Throughout United States history, the country had been a great magnet for foreign investors in Europe. But in the twentieth century, the flow of investment reversed. From 1915 to the 1970s, instead of being a debtor nation, the United States was a creditor nation, and by the 1950s it was the largest creditor nation in the world.

Private foreign investment offered new opportunities for company profits and gave businesses greater capacity to meet domestic demand and thus keep prices down. But increased foreign investment also meant increased foreign exposure to crises abroad.

This 1958 report by the U.S. Department of Commerce describes where American companies were investing. A significant portion was going into oil exploration and extraction in the Middle East. This particular investment would help keep the price of gasoline in the United States very low for many years. But it also laid the seeds for the oil crises of the 1970s when Middle East oil was held back from the rest of the world.

In 1957, for the second successive year, private United States foreign investments were nearly $4 billion. Direct investments by United States companies in their foreign branches and subsidiaries increased more than $3 billion reaching a total book value of over $25 billion by the end of 1957.

Part of the expansion in direct investments in both 1956 and 1957 was attributable to large cash payments for newly acquired properties or oil leases, but most of the stepped-up outflow reflected continued expectations of strong long-run demand for basic materials here and abroad, coupled with a tendency to establish production facilities abroad to supply foreign markets.

Other private capital investment in 1957 totaled $1.1 billion, mainly representing purchases of foreign dollar bonds and long- and short-term bank loans....

Earnings on private foreign investments advanced to a high of $3.7 billion in 1957, nearly

$300 million more than the 1956 amount, reflecting the rapidly growing amount of capital invested. Over two-thirds of the gain was accounted for by direct investments, even though much of the investment outlay in the past 2 years has been in properties which are not yet fully productive. Interest and dividend receipts from portfolio and short-term investments rose considerably as these investments expanded.

The geographic distribution of direct investment in 1957 showed as usual a concentration in the Western hemisphere and Europe, which accounted for seven-eighths of the total...investments in less developed countries since 1950 have been largely in petroleum and mining, with the notable exception of some Latin American countries where both local and foreign capital are now developing the industrial and market potential.

Resource development with the aid of foreign capital is often the most effective initial stimulus to rising national incomes, especially since it is usually accompanied by the construction of transportation and other public utilities. In this connection, it is significant that a number of investment projects just beginning or under consideration involve large outlays for resource development in areas where private United States investment has previously not been large....

Despite recurring crises, the flow of United States direct investment capital to the Middle East area held at an annual rate of about $100 million in 1956 and 1957. There were sharp fluctuations in the flow of funds to individual parts of the area, but these often reflected temporary variations in cash positions rather than trends in fixed investment or exploration and development. The latter activity is going forward extensively, and in addition to the sums accounted for as capital expenditures, roughly $25 million was spent in essentially non-producing countries in the Middle East and North Africa in search for additional reserves.

The current rate of capital outflow to this area is less than in earlier postwar years, when production was being expanded. Crude oil produced in the Middle East by United States operators, or as their share of joint operations, fluctuated widely as a result of the Suez crisis and later developments, but averaged 2 million barrels per day in 1957, about 50 per cent of the total produced in the free world outside the Western hemisphere. Major expenditures are in prospect for the area to develop new reserves in North Africa, in offshore locations, and in Iran, and in unproven areas....

A steady rate of investment was maintained in the Far East, yielding an increase in direct investments of about $175 million for 1957. Additions to investments in Australia were about $50 million, mainly for manufacturing plants. The rise in Indonesia largely reflected petroleum activities, and in Japan the principal industry showing increases was manufacturing, with petroleum also higher than in 1956. Increases in the Philippine Republic were spread over several industries....

On an industry basis, investment in the petroleum industry dominated the growth of direct investments in 1957, increasing by $1.7 billion to a total book value of about $9 billion. Over half of the rise was in Latin America, with Venezuela far in the lead. Output by the United States companies in Venezuela reached a high of a little over 2 million barrels per day during the Suez crisis, when Middle East production was cut back, and averaged 1.9 million barrels per day in 1957, up about 9 per cent over 1956 output.

Most of the Latin American increase was financed by larger capital outflows from the United States, and reinvested earnings were also higher. Parent companies in the United States were under considerable pressure to raise the funds required for expansion in this and other areas, and placed several large security issues in the United States capital market....

❧ The Highway Act of 1958

CONGRESS

By the 1950s, the automobile had become far and away the dominant mode for transportation. The country's highway infrastructure, however, was severely lacking. At the same time, former World War II soldiers and officers recalled how wide and convenient German highways were for military purposes. Thus, with the Cold War at its height, the combined reasons of defense, a growing car-owner population and the prospect of billions of dollars in construction revenues, Congress was convinced to undertake a major reconstruction of the country's highway system.

In 1956, a new law was devised to revamp road construction aid to states. Two years later, The Highway Act of 1958 revised and codified the whole highway system. The federal government agreed to pay for half the costs of new highways, a responsibility that had previously been mainly borne by states. The two laws changed the landscape. Not only were more than 40,000 miles of highway built, but it also altered the development patterns of the country. Communities, neighborhoods and shopping centers would be come to be designed to meet the needs of the automobile. The act is excerpted below.

Chapter I, Federal Aid Highways

Section 101. Declaration of policy—(b) It is hereby declared to be in the national interest to accelerate the construction of the Federal-aid highway systems, including the National System of Interstate and Defense Highways, since many of such highways, or portions thereof, are in fact inadequate to meet the needs of local and interstate commerce, for the national and civil defense.

It is hereby declared that the prompt and early completion of the National System of Interstate and Defense Highways, so named because of its primary importance to the national defense and hereafter referred to as the "Interstate System," is essential to the national interest and is one of the most important objectives of this Act. It is the intent of Congress that the Interstate System be completed as nearly as practicable over the period of availability of the thirteen years' appropriations authorized for the purpose of expediting its construction, reconstruction, or improvement, inclusive of necessary tunnels and bridges, through the fiscal year ending June 30, 1969, under section 108 (b) of the Federal Aid highway Act of 1956, and that the entire System in all States be brought to simultaneous completion. Insofar as possible in consonance with this objective, existing highways located on an interstate route shall be used to the extent that such use is practicable, suitable, and feasible, it being the intent that local needs, to the extent practicable, suitable and feasible, shall be given equal consideration with the needs of interstate commerce....

Section 103. Federal-aid systems. (a) For the purposes of this title, the three Federal-aid systems, the primary and secondary systems, and the Interstate System, are continued pursuant to the provisions of this section.

(b) The Federal-aid primary system shall consist of an adequate system of connected main highways, selected or designated by each State through its State highway department, subject to the approval of the Secretary as provided by subsection (e) of this section. This system shall not exceed 7 per centum of the total highway mileage of such State, exclusive of mileage within national forests, Indian, or other Federal reservations and within urban areas, as shown by the records of the State highway department on November 9, 1921....

(c) The Federal-aid secondary system shall be selected by the State highway departments and the appropriate local road officials in cooperation with each other, subject to approval by the Secretary as provided in subsection (e) of this section. In making such selections, farm-to-market roads, rural mail routes, public school bus routes, local rural roads, county roads, township roads, and roads of the county road class may be included, so long as they are not on the Federal-aid primary system or on the Interstate System....

(d) The Interstate System shall be designated within the United States, including the District of Columbia, and it shall not exceed forty-one thousand miles in total extent. It shall be so located as to connect by routes, as direct as practicable, the principal metropolitan areas, cities, and industrial centers, to serve the national defense and, to the greatest extent possible, to connect at suitable border points with routes of continental importance in the Dominion of Canada and the Republic of Mexico....

Section 109. Standards. (a) The Secretary shall not approve plans and specifications for proposed projects on any Federal-aid system if they fail to provide for a facility (1) that will adequately meet the existing and probably future traffic needs and conditions in a manner conducive to safety, durability, and economy of maintenance; (2) that will be designed and constructed in accordance with standards best suited to accomplish the foregoing objectives and to conform to the particular needs of each locality.

(b) The geometric and construction standards to be adopted for the Interstate System shall be those approved by the Secretary in cooperation with the State highway departments. Such standards shall be adequate to accommodate the types and volumes of traffic forecast for the year 1975. The right-of-way width of the Interstate System shall be adequate to permit construction of projects on the Interstate System up to such standards. The Secretary shall apply such standards uniformly throughout the States....

Section 120. Federal share payable. (a) Subject to the provisions of subsection (d) of this section, the Federal share payable on account of any project, financed with primary, secondary and urban funds, on the Federal-aid primary system and the Federal-aid secondary system shall not exceed 50 per centum of the cost of construction, except that in the case of any State containing nontaxable Indian lands, individual and tribal, and public domain lands (both reserved and unreserved) exclusive of national forests and national parks and monuments, exceeding 5 per centum of the total area of all lands therein, the Federal share shall be increased by a percentage of the remaining cost equal to the percentage that the area of all such lands in such States, is of its total area...

"Three minutes and twenty seconds for each candidate"

NIXON-KENNEDY DEBATE

By 1960 television had become a part of most Americans' daily lives. Presidential candidates Richard Nixon and John F. Kennedy squared off to confront each other with Howard K. Smith as moderator. A new era in politics had arrived. Suddenly appearance and style in front of a television camera became important ingredients for political success. Although radio audiences reacted more favorably to Nixon's resonant voice, the larger television audience scored the tanned and vigorous Kennedy as the winner. After the election was over and Kennedy had won, Nixon attributed his narrow loss to his pale and sweaty appearance in the debate. Here are the closing statements to the first televised presidential debate.

SMITH: Three minutes and twenty seconds for each candidate. Vice President Nixon, will you make the first summation?

NIXON: Thank you, Mr. Smith.

Senator Kennedy, first of all I think it is well to put in perspective where we really do stand with regard to the Soviet Union in this whole matter of growth.

The Soviet Union has been moving faster than we have, but the reason for that is obvious. They start from a much lower base.

Although they have been moving faster in growth than we have, we find for example today that their total gross national product is only 44 percent of our total gross national product. That's the same percentage that it was twenty years ago; and as far as the absolute gap is concerned, we find that the United States is even further ahead than it was twenty years ago.

Is this any reason for complacency?

Not at all, because these are determined men, they are fanatical men, and we have to get the very most out of our economy.

I agree with Senator Kennedy completely on that score.

Where we disagree is in the means that we would use to get the most out of our economy.

I respectfully submit that Senator Kennedy too often would rely too much on the federal government on what it would do to solve our problems, to stimulate growth.

I believe that when we examine the Democratic platform, when we examine the proposals that I have made, that these proposals that he makes would not result in greater growth for this country than would be the case if we followed the programs that I have advocated.

There are many of the points that he has made that I would like to comment upon; the one in the field of health is worth mentioning.

Our health program, the one that Senator Javits and other Republican senators as well as I supported, is one that provides for all people over sixty-five who want health insurance—the opportunity to have it if they want it. It provides a choice of having either government insurance or private insurance, but it compels nobody to have insurance who does not want it.

His program under Social Security would require everybody who had Social Security to take government health insurance whether he wanted it or not, and it would not cover several million people who are not covered by Social Security at all.

Here is one place where I think that our program does a better job than his.

The other point that I would make is this: the downgrading of how much things cost, I think many of our people will understand better when they look at what happened when during the Truman administration, when the government was spending more than it took in.

We found savings over a lifetime eaten up by inflation. We found the people who could least afford it, people on retired incomes, people on fixed incomes, we found them unable to meet their bills at the end of the month.

It is essential that a man who is president of this country certainly stand for every program that will mean growth, and I stand for programs that mean growth and progress.

But it is also essential that he not allow a dollar spent that could be better spent by the people themselves.

SMITH: Senator Kennedy, your conclusion.

KENNEDY: The point was made by Mr. Nixon that the Soviet production is only 44 percent of ours. I must say that 44 percent in that Soviet country is causing us a good deal of trouble tonight. I want to make sure that it stays in that relationship. I don't want to see the day when it's 60 percent of ours and 70 and 75 and 80 and 90 percent of ours, with all the force and power that it could bring to bear in order to cause our destruction.

Secondly, the vice president mentioned medical care for the aged. Our program was an amendment to the Kerr bill; the Kerr bill provided assistance to all those who are not on Social Security. I think it's very clear the contrast.

In 1935 when the Social Security Act was written, 94 out of 95 republicans voted against it. Mr. Landon ran in 1936 to repeal it.

In August of 1960 when we tried to get it again, this time for medical care, we received the support of one Republican in the Senate on this occasion.

Thirdly, I think the question before the American people is, as they look at this country, and as they look at the world around them, the goals are the same for all Americans; the means are at question; the means are at issue.

If you feel that everything that is being done now is satisfactory, that the relative power and prestige and strength of the United States is increasing in relation to that of the Communists, that we are gaining more security, that we are achieving everything as a nation that we should achieve, that we are achieving a better life for our citizens and greater strength, then I agree. I think you should vote for Mr. Nixon.

But if you feel that we have to move again in

the sixties, that the function of the president is to set before the people the unfinished business of our society, as Franklin Roosevelt did in the thirties, the agenda for our people, what we must do as a society to meet our needs in this country and protect our security and help the cause of freedom—as I said at the beginning, the question before us all that faces all Republicans and all Democrats is, can freedom in the next generation conquer, or are the Communists going to be successful? That's the great issue.

And if we meet our responsibilities, I think freedom will conquer. If we fail—if we fail to move ahead, if we fail to develop sufficiently military and economic and social strength here in this country, then I think that the tide could begin to run against us, and I don't want historians ten years from now to say these were the years when the tide ran out for the United States. I want them to say these were the years when the tide came in, these were the years when the United started to move again. That's the question before the American people, and only you can decide what you want, what you want this country to be, what you want to do with the future.

I think we're ready to move. And it is that great task, if we are successful, that we will address ourselves.

"Guard against the military industrial complex"

DWIGHT EISENHOWER

Eisenhower had served in the United States army since World War I. As Commander-in-Chief of the European invasion in World War II, he oversaw the Allied defeat of Nazi Germany. In 1952, his sterling reputation as a military leader carried him to the presidency for the balance of the decade.

His military credentials as Commander-in-Chief were beyond dispute. So when he sat down to deliver his farewell address to a television audience, it came as something of a shock that he would warn the nation of the dangers of the military industrial complex that he had helped build. He described it, however, as a necessary evil. Though he did not say so explicitly, his standing as a military leader helped give him the credibility to stand up to the pressures of this new, powerful interest group.

The end of Eisenhower's term as president, not only

marked the end of the 1950s, but also the end of an era in government. A new, younger generation was rising to national power that would set a more youthful, vigorous course. His farewell address was a warning to his successors of one of the many things they would have to be wary of in the coming years.

Three days from now, after half a century in the service of our country, I shall lay down the responsibilities of office as, in traditional and solemn ceremony, the authority of the presidency is vested in my successor.

This evening I come to you with a message of leavetaking and farewell, and to share a few final thoughts with you, my countrymen.

We now stand ten years past the midpoint of a century that has witnessed four major wars among great nations. Three of these involved our own country. Despite these holocausts, America is today the strongest, the most influential, and most productive nation in the world. Understandably proud of this preeminence, we yet realize that America's leadership and prestige depend not merely upon our unmatched material progress, riches, and military strength but on how we use our power in the interests of world peace and human betterment.

Throughout America's adventure in free government our basic purposes have been to keep the peace, to foster progress in human achievement, and to enhance liberty, dignity, and integrity among people and among nations. To strive for less would be unworthy of a free and religious people. Any failure traceable to arrogance or our lack of comprehension or readiness to sacrifice would inflict upon us grievous hurt both at home and abroad....

A vital element in keeping the peace is our military establishment. Our arms must be mighty, ready for instant action, so that no potential aggressor may be tempted to risk his own destruction.

Our military organization today bears little relation to that known by any of my predecessors in peacetime, or indeed by the fighting men of World War II or Korea.

Until the latest of our world conflicts, the United States had no armaments industry. American plowshares could, with time and as required, make swords as well. But now we can no longer risk emergency improvisation of national defense; we have been compelled to create a permanent armaments industry of vast proportions. Added to this, 3.5 million men and women are directly engaged in the defense establishment. We annually spend on military security more than the net income of all United States corporations.

Now, this conjunction of an immense military establishment and a large arms industry is new in the American experience. The total influence—economic, political, even spiritual—is felt in every city, every state house, every office of the federal government. We recognize the imperative need for this development. Yet we must not fail to comprehend its grave implications. Our toil, resources, and livelihood are all involved; so is the very structure of our society.

In the councils of government, we must guard against the acquisition of unwarranted influence, whether sought or unsought, by the military industrial complex. The potential for the disastrous rise of misplaced power exists and will persist.

We must never let the weight of this combination endanger our liberties or democratic processes. We should take nothing for granted. Only an alert and knowledgeable citizenry can compel the proper meshing of the huge industrial and military machinery of defense with our peaceful methods and goals, so that security and liberty may prosper together.

Akin to and largely responsible for the sweeping changes in our industrial military posture has been the technological revolution during recent decades.

In this revolution research has become central. It also becomes more formalized, complex, and costly. A steadily increasing share is conducted for, by, or at the direction of the federal government.

Today the solitary inventor, tinkering in his shop, has been overshadowed by the task forces of scientists in laboratories and testing fields. In the same fashion, the free university, historically the fountainhead of free ideas and scientific discovery, has experienced a revolution in the conduct of research. Partly because of the huge costs involved, a government contract becomes virtually a substitute for intellectual curiosity.

For every old blackboard there are now hundreds of new electronic computers.

Another factor in maintaining balance involves the element of time. As we peer into society's future, we—you and I, and our government—must avoid the impulse to live only for today, plundering, for our own ease and convenience, the precious resources of tomorrow.

We cannot mortgage the material assets of our grandchildren without risking the loss also of their political and spiritual heritage. We want democracy to survive for all generations to come, not to become the insolvent phantom of tomorrow.

Such a confederation must be one of equals. The weakest must come to the conference table with the same confidence as do we, protected as we are by our moral, economic, and military strength. That table, though scarred by many past frustrations, cannot be abandoned for the certain agony of the battlefield.

Disarmament, with mutual honor and confidence, is a continuing imperative. Together we must learn how to compose differences—not with arms but with intellect and decent purpose. Because this need is so sharp and apparent, I confess that I lay down my official responsibilities in this field with a definite sense of disappointment. As one who has witnessed the horror and the lingering sadness of war, as one who knows that another war could utterly destroy this civilization which has been so slowly and painfully built over thousands of years, I wish I could say tonight that a lasting peace is in sight.

Happily, I can say that war has been avoided. Steady progress toward our ultimate goal has been made. But so much remains to be done. As a private citizen, I shall never cease to do what little I can to help the world advance along that road.

❧ "The trumpet summons us again"

JOHN F. KENNEDY

The election of John F. Kennedy as president launched a new era in American history; a new generation of people were shouldering the mantle of leadership. His inaugural address articulated the spirit of idealism that drove Kennedy's dream in the context of a hostile international environment. Kennedy spoke directly to the issues of the Cold War, but his words transcended that specific issue to embrace the fundamental tenets of American democracy. The speech reflected the times and helped set the course of history for the balance of the century.

We observe today not a victory of a party but a celebration of freedom—symbolizing an end as well as a beginning—signifying renewal as well as change. For I have sworn before you and Almighty God that same solemn oath our forebears prescribed nearly a century and three quarters ago.

The world is very different now. For man holds in his mortal hands that power to abolish all forms of human poverty and all forms of human life. And yet the same revolutionary beliefs for which our forebears fought are still at issue around the globe—the belief that the rights of man come not from the generosity of the state but from the hand of God.

We dare not forget today that we are the heirs of that first revolution. Let the word go forth from this time and place, to friend and foe alike, that the torch has been passed to a new generation of Americans—born in this century, tempered by war, disciplined by a hard and bitter peace, proud of our ancient heritage—and unwilling to witness or permit the slow undoing of those human rights to which this nation has always been committed, and to which we are committed today at home and around the world.

Let every nation know, whether it wishes us well or ill, that we shall pay any price, bear any burden, meet any hardship, support any friend, oppose any foe to assure the survival and success of liberty.

This much we pledge—and more.

To those allies whose cultural and spiritual origins we share, we pledge the loyalty of faithful friends. United, there is little we cannot do in a host of cooperative ventures. Divided, there is little we can do—for we dare not meet a powerful challenge at odds and split asunder.

To those new states whom we welcome to the ranks of the free, we pledge our word that one form of colonial control shall not have passed away merely to be replaced by a far more iron tyranny. We shall not always expect to find them supporting our view. But we shall always hope to find them strongly supporting their own freedom—and to remember that, in the past, those who foolishly sought power by riding the back of the tiger ended up inside.

To those people in the huts and villages of half the globe struggling to break the bonds of mass misery, we pledge our best efforts to help them help themselves, for whatever period is required—not because the Communists may be doing it, not because we seek their votes, but because it is right. If a free society cannot help the many who are poor, it cannot save the few who are rich.

To our sister republics south of our border, we offer a special pledge—to convert our good words into good deeds—in a new alliance of progress—to assist free men and free governments in casting off the chains of poverty. But this powerful revolution of hope cannot become the prey of hostile powers. Let all our neighbors know that we shall join with them to oppose aggression or subversion anywhere in the Americas. And let every other power know that this hemisphere intends to remain the master of its own house.

To that world assembly of sovereign states, the United Nations, our last best hope in an age where the instruments of war have far outpaced the instruments of peace, we renew our pledge of support—to prevent it from becoming merely a forum for invective—to strengthen its shield of the new and the weak—and to enlarge the area in which its writ may run.

Finally, to those nations who would make themselves our adversary, we offer not a pledge but a request: that both sides begin anew the quest for peace, before the dark powers of destruction unleashed by science engulf all humanity in planned or accidental self-destruction.

We dare not tempt them with weakness. For only when our arms are sufficient beyond doubt can we be certain beyond doubt that they will never be employed.

But neither can two great and powerful groups of nations take comfort from our present course—both sides overburdened by the cost of modern weapons, both rightly alarmed by the steady spread of the deadly atom, yet both racing to alter that uncertain balance of terror that stays the hand of mankind's final war.

So let us begin anew—remembering on both sides that civility is not a sign of weakness, and sincerity is always subject to proof. Let us never negotiate out of fear. But let us never fear to negotiate.

Let both sides explore what problems unite us instead of belaboring those problems which divide us. Let both sides, for the first time, formulate serious and precise proposals for the inspection and control of arms—and bring the absolute power to destroy other nations under the absolute control of all nations.

Let both sides seek to invoke the wonders of science instead of its terrors. Together let us explore the stars, conquer the deserts, eradicate disease, tap the ocean depths, and encourage the arts and commerce.

Let both sides unite to heed in all corners of the earth the command of Isaiah—to "undo the heavy burdens and to let the oppressed go free."

And if a beachhead of cooperation may push back the jungle of suspicion, let both sides join in a new endeavor—not a new balance of power, but a new world of law, where the strong are just and weak secure and the peace preserved.

All this will not be finished in the first one hundred days. Nor will it be finished in the first one thousand days, nor in the life of this administration, nor even perhaps in our lifetime on this planet. But let us begin.

In your hands, my fellow citizens, more than mine, will rest the final success or failure of our course. Since this country was founded, each generation of Americans has been summoned to give testimony to its national loyalty. The graves of young Americans who answered the call to service surround the globe.

Now the trumpet summons us again—not as a call to bear arms, though arms we need—not as a call to battle, though embattled we are—but a call to bear the burden of a long twilight struggle, year in and year out, "rejoicing in hope, patient in tribulation"—a struggle against the common enemies of man: tyranny, poverty, disease, and war itself.

Can we forge against these enemies a grand and global alliance, North and South, East and West, that can assure a more fruitful life for all mankind? Will you join in that historic effort?

In the long history of the world, only a few generations have been granted the role of defending freedom in its hour of maximum danger. I do not shrink from this responsibility—I welcome it. I do not believe that any of us would exchange places with any other people or any other generation. The energy, the faith, the devotion which we bring to this endeavor will light our country and all who serve it—and the glow from that fire can truly light the world.

And so, my fellow Americans, ask not what your country can do for you—ask what you can do for your country.

My fellow citizens of the world, ask not what America will do for you, but what together we can do for the freedom of man.

Finally, whether you are citizens of America or citizens of the world, ask of us here the same high standards of strength and sacrifice which we ask of you. With a good conscience our only sure reward, with history the final judge of our deeds, let us go forth to lead the land we love, asking His blessing and His help, but knowing that here on earth God's work must truly be our own.

❧ To Kill a Mockingbird

HARPER LEE

Harper Lee's 1960 novel *To Kill a Mockingbird* was an instant success. It won the Pulitzer Prize, sold more than 2 1/2 million copies within a year and became a staple in high school English classrooms across the country. Lee tells the story of a courageous Southern lawyer, Atticus Finch, who defies popular sentiment to represent a client in court, endangering his own elevated position in society.

At a time when the country was on the verge of tumultuous change, when love was called upon to overcome hate and when the sanctity of the individual was held above all else, *To Kill a Mockingbird* struck a chord with a nation that largely wanted to do the right thing.

Atticus paused and took out his handkerchief. Then he took off his glasses and wiped them, and we saw another "first"; we had never seen him sweat—he was one of those men whose faces never perspired, but now it was shining tan.

"One more thing, gentlemen, before I quit. Thomas Jefferson once said that all men are created equal, a phrase that the Yankees and the distaff side of the Executive branch in Washington are fond of hurling at us. There is a tendency in this year of grace, 1935, for certain people to use this phrase out of context, to satisfy all conditions. The most ridiculous example I can think of is that the people who run public education promote the stupid and idle along with the industrious—because all men are created equal, educators will gravely tell you, the children left behind suffer terrible feelings of inferiority. We know all men are not created equal in the sense that some people would have us believe—some people are smarter than others, some people have more opportunity because they're born with it, some men make more money than others, some ladies make better cakes than others—some people are born gifted beyond the normal scope of most men.

"But there is one way in this country in which all men are created equal—there is one human institution that makes a pauper the equal of a Rockefeller, the stupid man the equal of an Einstein, and the ignorant man the equal of any college president. That institution, gentleman, is a court. It can be the Supreme Court of the United States or the humblest J.P. court in the land, or this honorable court which you serve. Our courts have their faults, as does any human institution, but in this country our courts are the great levelers, and in our courts all men are created equal.

"I'm no idealist to believe firmly in the integrity of our courts and in the jury system—that is no ideal to me, it is a living, working reality. Gentlemen, a court is no better than each man of you sitting before me on this jury. A court is only as sound as its jury, and a jury is only as sound as the men who make it up. I am confident that you gentlemen will review without passion the evidence you have heard, come to a decision, and restore this defendant to his family. In the name of God, do your duty."

CHAPTER TEN

1961–1974

Dreams, Realized and Lost

❧ "When television is bad, nothing is worse"

NEWTON MINOW

Appointed as chairman of the Federal Communications Commission by President Kennedy, Newton Minow wasted little time in expressing his displeasure with the state of television. On May 9, 1961, Minow chastised the National Association of Broadcasters for the mediocrity of television, famously describing it as a "vast wasteland."

By this time, television had become part of the daily fabric of American life. Launched in the early 1940s, it took several years for television to reach a mass audience. A television was expensive to own and the size of the audience did not justify extensive programming. By the 1950s, however, television had found its way into the typical American household. As Minow states, its influence became profound, even if it was not always desirable.

Despite Minow's sharp rebuke and call to improve, his speech could have been repeated at almost any time over the next thirty-five years (with minor revisions and noting a few sterling exceptions) and still ring true.

It may come as a surprise to some of you, but I want you to know that you have my admiration and respect. Yours is a most honorable profession. Anyone who is in the broadcasting business has a tough row to hoe. You earn your bread by using public property. When you work in broadcasting, you volunteer for public service, public pressure, and public regulation. You must compete with other attractions and other investments, and the only way you can do it is to prove to us every three years that you should have been in business in the first place.

I can think of easier ways to make a living.

But I cannot think of more satisfying ways.

I admire your courage—but that doesn't mean I would make life any easier for you. Your license lets you use the public's airwaves as trustees for 180 million Americans. The public is your beneficiary. If you want to stay on as trustees, you must deliver a decent return to the public—not only to your stockholders. So, as a representative of the public, your health and your product are among my chief concerns...

I have confidence in your health.

But not in your product.

It is with this and much more in mind that I come before you today.

One editorialist in the trade press wrote that "the FCC of the New Frontier is going to be one of the toughest FCCs in the history of broadcast regulation." If he meant that we intend to enforce the law in the public interest, let me make it perfectly clear that he is right—we do.

If he meant that we intend to muzzle or censor broadcasting, he is dead wrong.

It would not surprise me if some of you had expected me to come here today and say in effect, "Clean up your own house, or the government will do it for you."

Well, in a limited sense, you would be right—I've just said it.

But I want to say to you earnestly that it is not in that spirit that I come before you today, nor is it in that spirit that I intend to serve the FCC.

I am in Washington to help broadcasting, not to harm it; to strengthen it, not to weaken it; to reward it, not to punish it; to encourage it, not threaten it; to stimulate it, not censor it.

Above all, I am here to uphold and protect the public interest.

What do we mean by "the public interest"? Some say the public interest is merely what interests the public.

I disagree.

So does your distinguished president, Governor Collins. In a recent speech he said, "Broadcasting, to serve the public interest, must have a soul and a conscience, a burning desire to excel, as well as to sell; the urge to build the character, citizenship, and intellectual stature of people, as well as to expand the gross national product.... By no means do I imply that broadcasters disregard the public interest.... But a much better job can be done, and should be done."

I could not agree more.

And I would add that in today's world, with chaos in Laos and the Congo aflame, with Communist tyranny on our Caribbean doorstep and relentless pressure on our Atlantic alliance, with social and economic problems at home of the gravest nature, yes, and with technological knowledge that makes it possible, as our president has said, not only to destroy our world but to destroy poverty around the world—in a time of peril and opportunity, the old complacent, unbalanced fare of action-adventure and situation comedies is simply not good enough.

Your industry possesses the most powerful voice

in America. It has an inescapable duty to make that voice ring with intelligence and with leadership. In a few years this exciting industry has grown from a novelty to an instrument of overwhelming impact on the American people. It should be making ready for the kind of leadership that newspapers and magazines assumed years ago, to make our people aware of their world.

Ours has been called the jet age, the atomic age, the space age. It is also, I submit, the television age. And just as history will decide whether the leaders of today's world employed the atom to destroy the world or rebuild it for mankind's benefit, so will history decide whether today's broadcaster employed their powerful voice to enrich the people or debase them....

Like everybody, I wear more than one hat. I am chairman of the FCC. I am also a television viewer and the husband and father of other television viewers. I have seen a great many television programs that seemed to me eminently worthwhile, and I am not talking about the much-bemoaned good old days of "Playhouse 90" and "Studio One."

I am talking about the past season. Some were wonderfully entertaining, such as "The Fabulous Fifties," and the "Fred Astaire Show," and the "Bing Crosby Special"; some were dramatic and moving, such as Conrad's "Victory" and "Twilight Zone"; some were marvelously informative, such as "The Nation's Future," "CBS Reports," and "The Valiant Years." I could list many more—programs that I am sure everyone here felt enriched his own life and that of his family. When television is good, nothing—not the theater, not the magazines or newspaper—nothing is better.

But when television is bad, nothing is worse. I invite you to sit down in front of your television set when your station goes on the air and stay there without a book, magazine, newspaper, profit-and-loss sheet, or rating book to distract you—and keep your eyes glued to that set until the station signs off. I can assure you that you will observe a vast wasteland.

You will see a procession of game shows, violence, audience participation shows, formula comedies about totally unbelievable families, blood and thunder, mayhem, violence, sadism, murder, western badmen, western good men, private eyes, gangsters, more violence, and cartoons. And, endlessly, commercials—many screaming, cajoling, and

offending. And most of all, boredom. True, you will see a few things you will enjoy. But they will be very, very few. And if you think I exaggerate, try it.

Is there one person in this room who claims that broadcasting can't do better?

Well, a glance at next season's proposed programming can give us little heart. Of seventy-three and a half hours of prime evening time, the networks have tentatively scheduled fifty-nine hours to categories of "action-adventure," "situation comedy, variety, quiz, and movies."

Is there one network president in this room who claims he can't do better?

Well is there at least one network president who believes that the other networks can't do better?

Gentlemen, your trust accounting with your beneficiaries is overdue.

Never have so few owed so much to so many.

Why is so much of television so bad? I have heard many answers: demands of your advertisers; competition for ever higher ratings; the need always to attract a mass audience; the high cost of television programs; the insatiable appetite for programming material—these are some of them. Unquestionably these are tough problems not susceptible to easy answers.

But I am not convinced that you have tried hard enough to solve them....

Certainly I hope you will agree that ratings should have little influence where children are concerned. The best estimates indicate that during the hours of 5 to 6 pm, 60 percent of your audience is composed of children under twelve. And most young children today, believe it or not, spend as much time watching television as they do in the schoolroom. I repeat—let that sink in—most young children today spend as much time watching television as they do in the schoolroom. It used to be said that there were three great influences on a child: home, school, and church. Today there is a fourth great influence, and you ladies and gentlemen can control it.

If parents, teachers, and ministers conducted their responsibilities by following the ratings, children would have a steady diet of ice cream, school holidays, and no Sunday school. What about your responsibilities? Is there no room on television to teach, to inform, to uplift, to stretch, to enlarge the capacities of our children? Is there no room for programs deepening their understanding of children in other lands? Is there no room for a children's news show explaining something about the world to them at their level of understanding? Is there no room for reading the great literature of the past, teaching them the great traditions of freedom? There are some fine children's shows, but they are drowned out in the massive doses of cartoons, violence, and more violence. Must these be your trademarks? Search your consciences and see if you cannot offer more to your young beneficiaries, whose future you guide so many hours each and every day....

You must reexamine some fundamentals of your industry. You must open your minds and open your hearts to the limitless horizons of tomorrow. I can suggest some words that should serve to guide you:

"Television and all who participate in it are jointly accountable to the American public for respect for the special needs of children, for community responsibility, for the advancement of education and culture, for the acceptability of the program materials chosen, for decency and decorum in production, and for propriety in advertising. This responsibility cannot be discharged by any given group of programs, but can be discharged only through the highest standards of respect for the American home, applied to every moment of every program presented by television.

"Program materials should enlarge the horizons of the viewer, provide him with wholesome entertainment, afford helpful stimulation, and remind him of the responsibilities which the citizen has toward his society."

These words are not mine. They are yours. They are taken literally from your own Television Code. They reflect the leadership and aspirations of your own great industry. I urge you to respect them as I do. And I urge you to respect the intelligence and farsighted leadership of Governor LeRoy Collins and to make this meeting a creative act. I urge you at this meeting and, after you leave, back home, at your stations and your networks, to strive ceaselessly to improve your product and to better serve your viewers, the American people.

I hope that we at the FCC will not allow ourselves to become so bogged down in the mountain of papers, hearings, memoranda, orders, and the daily routine that we close our eyes to the wider view of the public interest. And I hope that you

broadcasters will not permit yourselves to become so absorbed in the chase for ratings, sales, and profits that you lose this wider view. Now more than ever before in broadcasting history, the times demand the best of all of us.

We need imagination in programming, not sterility; creativity, not imitation; experimentation, not conformity; excellence, not mediocrity. Television is filled with creative, imaginative people. You must strive to set them free.

Television in its young life has had many hours of greatness—its "Victory at Sea," its Army-McCarthy hearings, its "Peter Pan," its "Kraft Theater," its "See It Now," its "Project 20," the World Series, its political conventions and campaigns, the Great Debates—and it has had its endless hours of mediocrity and its moments of public disgrace. There are estimates that today the average viewer spends about two hundred minutes daily with television, while the average reader spends thirty-eight minutes with magazines and forty minutes with newspapers. Television has grown faster than a teenager, and now it is time to grow up....

❧ Silent Spring

RACHEL CARSON

Rachel Carson's book *Silent Spring* awakened the nation to the dangers of pollution. A professional scientist, Carson identified man-made pesticides and other pollutants as spoiling not only the natural wilderness, but also farms and human communities. She noted the correlation of increasing cancer rates to the rise of pesticides and other chemicals. And she warned about the dangers of continuing on a path of self-destruction unless fundamental changes were made.

The book, published in 1962, helped spark a nationwide environmental movement that targeted the harmful effects of DDTs and other pesticides, the importance of protecting wildlife, and a wide range of other environmental initiatives. From the creation of Earth Day to national legislation to mitigate pollution, *Silent Spring* helped unleash a wave of reforms to make the United States a safer, cleaner place than it might otherwise be.

There was once a town in the heart of America where all life seemed to live in harmony with its surroundings. The town lay in the midst of a checkerboard of prosperous farms, with fields of grain and hillsides of orchards where, in spring, white clouds of bloom drifted above the green fields. In autumn, oak and maple and birch set up a blaze of color that flamed and flickered across a backdrop of pines. Then foxes barked in the hills and deer silently crossed the fields, half hidden in the mists of the fall mornings.

Along the roads, laurel, viburnum and alder, great ferns and wildflowers delighted the traveler's eye through much of the year. Even in winter the roadsides were places of beauty, where countless birds came to feed on the berries and on the seed heads of the dried weeds rising above the snow. The countryside was, in fact, famous for the abundance and variety of its bird life, and when the flood of migrants was pouring through in spring and fall people traveled from great distances to observe them. Others came to fish the streams, which flowed clear and cold out of the hills and contained shady pools where trout lay. So it had been from the days many years ago when the first settlers raised their houses, sank their wells, and built their barns.

Then a strange blight crept over the area and everything began to change. Some evil spell had settled on the community: mysterious maladies swept the flocks of chickens; the cattle and sheep sickened and died. Everywhere there was a shadow of death. The farmers spoke of much illness among their families. In the town the doctors had become more and more puzzled by new kinds of sickness appearing among their patients. There had been several sudden and unexplained deaths, not only among adults but even among children, who would be stricken suddenly while at play and die within a few hours.

There was a strange stillness. The birds, for example—where had they gone? Many people spoke of them, puzzled and disturbed. The feeding stations in the backyards were deserted. The few birds seen anywhere were moribund; they trembled violently and could not fly. It was a spring without voices. On the mornings that had once throbbed with the dawn chorus of robins, catbirds, doves, jays, wrens, and scores of other bird voices there was now no sound; only silence lay over the fields and woods and marsh.

On the farms the hens brooded, but no chicks hatched. The farmers complained they were unable to raise any pigs—the litters were small and the young survived only a few days. The apple trees were coming into bloom but no bees droned among the blossoms, so there was no pollination and there would be no fruit.

The roadsides, once so attractive, were now lined with browned and withered vegetation as though swept by fire. These, too, were silent, deserted by all living things. Even the streams were now lifeless. Anglers no longer visited them, for all the fish had died.

In the gutters under the eaves and between the shingles of the roofs, a white granular powder still showed a few patches; some weeks before it had fallen like snow upon the roofs and the lawns, the fields and streams.

No witchcraft, no enemy action had silenced the rebirth of new life in this stricken world. The people had done it themselves.

This town does not actually exist, but it might easily have a thousand counterparts in America or elsewhere in the world. I know of no community that has experienced all of the misfortunes I describe. Yet every one of these disasters has actually happened somewhere, and many real communities have already suffered a substantial number of them. A grim specter has crept upon us almost unnoticed, and this imagined tragedy may easily become a stark reality we all shall know.

What has already silenced the voices of spring countless towns in America? This book is an attempt to explain.

🐦 *Port Huron Statement*

STUDENTS FOR A DEMOCRATIC SOCIETY

Issued in 1962 by Students for a Democratic Society (SDS), the Port Huron Statement raised the standard for "participatory democracy." It came to represent a clarion call from the young against the older establishment. Students saw the bureaucracy of government, universities and the military as dehumanizing. They sought to change the world for the better.

"Loneliness, estrangement, isolation describe the vast distance between man and man today," the SDS wrote. "We would replace power rooted in possession, privilege, or circumstance by power and uniqueness rooted in love, reflectiveness, reason, and creativity."

But as the 1960s unfolded, disillusionment with authority heightened. Resistance to the Vietnam War increased with chants of "Make love, not war." While the initial pronouncements of the SDS were rather mild and idealistic, as the confrontations heightened, their actions become more radical. Many students became increasingly violent in their actions. The most extreme faction was the Weathermen based in Chicago.

Embracing Marxist-Leninist theory, they sought to destroy the apparatus of "Amerikan" society and eventually resorted to armed robbery, bombings, terrorism to achieve their goals.

In a participatory democracy, the political life would be based in several root principals:

That decision-making of basic social consequence be carried on by public groupings;

That politics has the function of bringing people out of isolation and into community, thus being a necessary, though not sufficient, means of finding meaningful personal life;

That the political order should serve to clarify problems in a way instrumental to their solution; it should provide outlets for the expression of personal grievance and aspiration; opposing views should be organized as to illuminate choices and facilitate attainment of goals; channels should be commonly available to relate men to knowledge and to power so that private problems—from bad recreation facilities to personal alienation—are formulated as general issues.

The economic sphere should involve incentives worthier than money or survival. It should be educative, not stultifying; creative not mechanical; self-directed, not manipulated, encouraging independence, a respect for others, a sense of dignity and a willingness to accept social responsibility, since it is this experience that has crucial influence on habits, perceptions and individual ethics;

That the economic experience is so personally decisive that the individual must share in its full determination;

That the economy itself is of such social importance that its major resources and means of production should be open to democratic participation and subject to democratic social regulation.

🍂 "The other Americans are those who live at a level of life beneath moral choice"

MICHAEL HARRINGTON

Not all Americans participated in the post-war economic boom. In 1962, Michael Harrington wrote *The Other America: Poverty in the U.S.* exploring the large pockets of American society that struggled against poverty amidst the affluence of the wealthiest country in the world.

The Other America directly impacted public policy. Its publication prompted President Kennedy to begin drafting legislation to try to remedy the problems of poverty. His proposals would become the basis of President Lyndon B. Johnson's "Great Society."

The United States in the Sixties contains an affluent society within its borders. Millions and tens of millions enjoy the highest standard of life the world has ever known. This blessing is mixed. It is built upon a peculiarly distorted economy, one that often proliferates pseudo-needs rather than satisfying human needs. For some, it has resulted in a sense of spiritual emptiness, of alienation. Yet a man would be a fool to prefer hunger to satiety, and the material gains at least open up the possibility of a rich and full existence.

At the same time, the United States contains an underdeveloped nation, a culture of poverty. Its inhabitants do not suffer the extreme privation of the peasants of Asia or the tribesmen of Africa, yet the mechanism of the misery is similar.

The new nations, however, have one advantage: poverty is so general and so extreme that it is the passion of the entire society to obliterate it. Every resource, every policy, is measured by its effect on the lowest and most impoverished. There is a gigantic mobilization of the spirit of the society: aspiration becomes a national purpose that penetrates to every village and motivates a historic transformation.

But this country seems to be caught in a paradox. Because its poverty is not so deadly, because so many are enjoying a decent standard of life, there are indifference and blindness to the plight of the poor. There are even those who deny that the culture of poverty exists. It is as if Disraeli's famous remark about the two nations of the rich and the poor had become true in a fantastic fashion. At precisely that moment in history where for the first time a people have the material ability to end poverty, they lack the will to do so. They cannot see, they cannot act. The consciences of the well-off are the victims of affluence; the lives of the poor are the victims of a physical and spiritual misery.

The problem, then, is to a great extent one of vision. The nation of the well-off must be able to see through the wall of affluence and recognize the alien citizens on the other side. And there must be vision in the sense of purpose, of aspiration: if the word does not grate upon the ears of gentle America, there must be a passion to end poverty, for nothing less than that will do.

In this summary chapter, I hope I can supply at least some of the material for such a vision. Let us try to understand the other America as a whole, to see its perspective for the future if it is left alone, to realize the responsibility and the potential for ending this nation in our midst.

But, when all is said and done, the decisive moment occurs after all the sociology and the description is in. There is really no such thing as "the material for a vision." After one reads the facts, either there are anger or shame, or there are not. And, as usual, the fate of the poor hangs upon the decision of the better-off. If this anger and shame are not forthcoming, someone can write a book about the other America a generation from now and it will be the same, or worse.

Perhaps the most important analytic point to have emerged in this description of the other America is the fact that poverty in America forms a culture, a way of life and feeling, that it makes a whole. It is crucial to generalize this idea, for it profoundly affects how one moves to destroy poverty.

The most obvious aspect of this interrelatedness is in the way in which the various subcultures of the other America feed into one another. This is clearest with the aged. There the poverty of the declining years is, for some millions of human beings, a function of the poverty of the earlier years. If there were adequate medical care for everyone in the United States, there would be less misery for old people. It is as simple as that. Or there is the relation between the poor farmers and the unskilled workers. When a man is driven off the land because of the impoverishment worked by technological progress, he leaves one part of the culture of poverty and joins another. If something were done about the low-income farmer, that would immediately tell in the statistics of urban unemployment and the economic underworld. The same is true of Negroes. Any gain for America's minorities will immediately be translated into an advance for all the unskilled workers. One cannot raise the bottom of a society without benefiting everyone above.

Indeed, there is a curious advantage in the wholeness of poverty. Since the other America forms a distinct system within the United States, effective action to any one decisive point will have a "multiplier" effect; it will ramify through the entire culture of misery and ultimately through the entire society.

Then poverty is a culture in the sense that the mechanism of impoverishment is fundamentally the same in every part of the system. The vicious circle is a basic pattern. It takes different forms for the unskilled workers, for the aged, for the Negroes, for the agricultural workers, but in each case the principle is the same. There are people in the affluent society who are poor because they are poor, and who stay poor because they are poor.

To realize this is to see that there are some tens of millions of Americans who are beyond the welfare state. Some of them are simply not covered by social legislation: they are omitted from Social Security and from minimum wage. Others are covered, but since they are so poor they do not know how to take advantage of the opportunities, or else their coverage is so inadequate as to not make a difference.

The welfare state was designed during that great burst of social creativity that took place in the 1930s. As previously noted its structure corresponds to the needs of those who played the most important role in building it: the middle third, the organized workers, the forces of urban liberalism, and so on. At the worst, there is "socialism for the rich and free enterprise for the poor," as when the huge corporation farms are the main beneficiaries of the farm program while the poor farmers get practically nothing; or when public funds are directed to aid in the construction of luxury housing while the slums are left to themselves (or become more dense as space is created for the well-off).

So there is the fundamental paradox of the welfare state: that it is not built for the desperate, but for those who are already capable of helping themselves. As long as the illusion persists that the poor are merrily free-loading on the public dole, so long will the other America continue unthreatened. The truth, it must be understood, is the exact opposite. The poor get less out of the welfare state than any group in America.

This is, of course, related to the most distinguishing mark of the other America: its common sense of hopelessness. For even when there are programs designed to help the other Americans, the poor are held back by their own pessimism.

On one level this fact has been described in this book as a matter of "aspiration." Like the Asian peasant, the impoverished American tends to see life as a fate, an endless cycle from which there is no deliverance. Lacking hope (and he is realistic to feel this way in many cases), that famous solution to all problems—let us educate the poor—becomes less and less meaningful. A person has to feel that education will do something for him if he is to gain from it. Placing a magnificent school with a fine faculty in the middle of a slum is, I suppose, better than having a run-down building staffed by incompetents. But it will not really make a difference so long as the environment of the tenement, the family, and the street counsels the children to leave as soon as they can and to disregard schooling.

On another level, the emotions of the other America are even more profoundly disturbed. Here it is not lack of aspiration and of hope; it is a matter of personal chaos. The drunkenness, the unstable marriages, the violence of the other America are not simply facts about individuals. They are the description of an entire group in the society who react this way because of the conditions under which they live.

In short, being poor is not one aspect of a person's life in this country; it is his life. Taken as a whole, poverty is a culture. Taken on the family level, it has the same quality. These are people who lack education and skill, who have bad health, poor housing, low levels of aspiration and high levels of mental distress. They are, in the language of sociology, "multiproblem" families. Each disability is the more intense because it exists within a web of disabilities. And if one problem is solved, and the others are left constant, there is little gain.

One might translate these facts into the moralistic language so dear to those who would condemn the poor for their faults. The other Americans are those who live at a level of life beneath moral choice, who are so submerged in their poverty that one cannot begin to talk about free choice. The point is not to make them wards of the state. Rather, society must help them before they can help themselves.

✺ "Ich bin ein Berliner"

JOHN F. KENNEDY

By 1963, President Kennedy had earned his stripes as a cold warrior. Having told an American television audience that he would risk war to defend Berlin and having successfully gone "eyeball to eyeball" with Soviet General Secretary Nikita Khrushchev in the Cuban missile crisis, Kennedy visited Berlin itself. The Soviets had erected a wall around West Berlin a year earlier. The barricaded city became an island of freedom, surrounded by Communist East Germany. When Kennedy spoke on June 26 the Communists had strung a red cloth across the Brandenburg Gate to prevent East Berliners from seeing the event. Evoking the spirit of freedom and democracy, Kennedy states in no uncertain terms that he and the U.S. military will share the fate of West Berlin.

I am proud to come to this city as the guest of your distinguished mayor, who has symbolized throughout the world the fighting spirit of West Berlin. And I am proud to visit the Federal Republic with your distinguished chancellor, who for so many years has committed Germany to democracy and freedom and progress, and to come here in the company of my fellow American General Clay, who has been in this city during its great moments of crisis and will come again if ever needed.

Two thousand years ago the proudest boast was Civis Romanus sum. Today, in the world of freedom, the proudest boast is Ich bin ein Berliner.

I appreciate my interpreter translating my German!

There are many people in the world who really don't understand, or say they don't, what is the great issue between the free world and the Communist world. Let them come to Berlin. There are some who say that communism is the wave of the future. Let them come to Berlin. And there are some who say in Europe and elsewhere we can work with the Communists. Let them come to Berlin. And there are even a few who say that it is true that communism is an evil system, but it permits us to make economic progress. Lass' sie nach Berlin kommen. Let them come to Berlin.

Freedom has many difficulties and democracy is not perfect, but we have never had to put a wall up to keep our people in, to prevent them from leaving us. I want to say, on behalf of my countrymen, who live many miles away on the other side of the Atlantic, who are far distant from you, that they take the greatest pride that they have been able to share with you, even from a distance, the story of the last eighteen years. I know of no town, no city, that has been besieged for eighteen years that still lives with the vitality and the force, and the hope and the determination of the city of West Berlin. While the wall is the most obvious and vivid demonstration of the failures of the Communist system, for all the world to see, we take no satisfaction in it, for it is, as your mayor has said, an offense not only against history but an offense against humanity, separating families, dividing husbands and wives and brothers and sisters, and dividing a people who wish to be joined together.

What is true of this city is true of Germany— real, lasting peace in Europe can never be assured as long as one German out of four is denied the elementary right of free men, and that is to make a free choice. In eighteen years of peace and good faith, this generation of Germans has earned the right to be free, including the right to unite their families and their nation in lasting peace, with good will to all people. You live in a defended island of freedom, but your life is part of the main. So let me ask you, as I close, lift your eyes beyond the dangers of today, to the hopes of tomorrow, beyond the freedom merely of this city of Berlin, or your country of Germany, to the advance of freedom everywhere, beyond the wall to the day of peace and justice, beyond yourselves and ourselves of all mankind.

Freedom is indivisible, and when one man is enslaved, all are not free. When all are free, then we can look forward to that day when this city will be joined as one and this country and this great continent of Europe in a peaceful and hopeful globe. When that day finally comes, as it will, the people of West Berlin can take sober satisfaction in the fact that they were on the front lines for almost two decades.

All free men, wherever they may live, are citizens of Berlin, and, therefore, as a free man, I take pride in the words, Ich bin ein Berliner.

"Hurst took his gun out again, pointed it at Lee and shot him...Hurst was acquitted"

ROBERT MOSES IN MISSISSIPPI

Of all the Southern states, Mississippi reacted to integration efforts with stiffest resistance. In the 1950s, the Rev. George Lee tried to convince blacks to register to vote. He was ambushed and killed for his efforts. Amzie Moore, a World War II veteran, was also involved with the NAACP effort to register blacks and in 1960 he invited Robert Moses, a black Harvard graduate who worked as a teacher, to organize a student campaign to start a voting rights campaign.

In the summer of 1961, Moses arrived in McComb, Mississippi, to try to accomplish that goal. As the following account by Moses shows, being thrown in jail proved to be a mild form of white retribution for encouraging blacks in registering to vote. Beatings and even murder were a common occurence. Nevertheless, Moses persisted and over the next few years, in spite of the violence, he organized several successful voter registration drives.

We planned to make another registration attempt on the 19th of August.... This was the day then that Curtis Dawson and Preacher Knox and I were to go down and try to register. This was the day that Curtis Dawson drove to Steptoe's, picked me up and drove down to Liberty and we were to meet Knox at the courthouse lawn, and instead we were to walk through the town and on the way back were accosted by Billy Jack Caston and some other boys. I was severely beaten. I remember very sharply that I didn't want to go immediately back into McComb because my shirt was very bloody and I figured that if we went back in we would probably be fighting everybody. So, instead, we went back out to Steptoe's where we washed down before we came back into McComb.

Well, that very same day, they had had the first sit-in in McComb, so when we got back everybody was excited and a mass meeting was planned for that very night. And Hollis [Watkins] and Curtis [Hayes] had sat down in the Woolworth lunch counter in McComb and the town was in a big uproar. We had a mass meeting that night and made plans for two things: One, the kids made plans to continue their sit-in activity, and two, we made plans to go back down to Liberty to try to register some more. We felt it was extremely important that we try and go back to town immediately so the people in the county wouldn't feel that we had been frightened off by the beating and before they could get a chance there to rally their forces.

Accordingly, on Tuesday, August 31, there was more activity in Liberty and McComb. In McComb, there were more sit-ins, in Liberty, another registration attempt coupled with an attempt by us to find the person who had done the beating and have his trial. Well, it turned out that we did find him, that they did have his trial, that they had a six-man Justice of the Peace jury, that in a twinkling of an eye the courthouse was packed. That is, the trial was scheduled that day and in two hours it began and in those two hours farmers came in from all parts of the county bearing their guns, sitting in the courthouse. We were advised not to sit in the courthouse except while we testified, otherwise we were in the back of the room. After we testified, the sheriff came back and told us that he didn't think it was safe for us to remain there while the jury gave its decision. Accordingly, he escorted us to the county line. We read in the papers the next day that Billy Jack Caston had been acquitted.

To top it off, the next week John Hardy was arrested and put in jail in Walthall County. He had been working there for two weeks and they had been taking people down, and finally one day he had taken some people down to the registrar's office, had walked in, they had been refused the right to register, and he had asked the registrar why. The registrar recognized him, took the gun out of his drawer and smacked John on the side of his head with the pistol. John staggered out onto the street and was walking down the street when he was accosted by the sheriff who arrested him and charged him with disturbing the peace....

A couple of days before John Hardy was arrested, we had gone back into Amite County to Liberty. This time I was not beaten, but Travis Britt was. I think that was on the 5th of September, and I stood by and watched Travis get pummeled by an old man, tall, reedy and thin, very, very, very mean with a lot of hatred in him.... At that particular occasion, Travis and I had been sitting out front of the courthouse and then decided to move around back because the people began to gather out front. Finally, everybody, about 15 people, gathered around back and began questioning Travis and myself.... They

were asking him where he was from and how come a nigger from New York City could think that he could come down and teach people down here how to register to vote and have all those problems up there in New York City, problems of white girls going with nigger boys and all such like that.... Well, that Travis Britt incident followed by the John Hardy incident in Walthall County just about cleaned us out. The farmers in both those counties were no longer willing to go down; people in Pike County and McComb were in an uproar over the sit-in demonstrations and the fact that Brenda Travis, a sixteen-year-old girl, was in jail, and for the rest of the month of September we just had a tough time. Wasn't much we could do. The kids were in jail; people were in jail on the sit-in charges, had a $5,000 bail over their heads, and the problem was to raise that money and get them out of jail, and then sit down and see if we couldn't collect the pieces together.

Well, we got through September aided in great measure by some of the lawyers from the Justice Department who finally began to come in investigating the voting complaints. They stayed in for about a two-week period and while they were there they gave a lot of support and confidence to the people of the Negro community and allowed us to go back into Walthall and Amite in the voter registration campaign and raise some hope that perhaps something would be done.

And then, finally, the boom lowered, on September 31: Herbert Lee was killed in Amite County.... The Sunday before Lee was killed, I was down at Steptoe's with John Doar from the Justice Department and he asked Steptoe was there any danger in that area, who was causing the trouble and who were the people in danger. Steptoe had told him that E.H. Hurst who lived across from him had been threatening people an that specifically he, Steptoe, Herbert Lee and George Reese were in danger of losing their lives. We went out, but didn't see Lee that afternoon. At night John Doar and the other lawyers from the Justice Department left. The following morning about 12 noon, Doc Anderson came by the Voter Registration office and said a man had been shot in Amite County.... I went down to take a look at the body and it was Herbert Lee; there was a bullet hole in the left side of his head just above his ear ....

Our first job was to try to track down those people…who had been at the shooting, who had seen the whole incident…. Essentially, the story was this: They were standing at the cotton gin early in the morning and they saw Herbert Lee drive up in this truck with a loan of cotton, E.H. Hurst following behind him in an empty truck. Hurst got out of his truck and came to the cab on the driver's side of Lee's truck and began arguing with Lee. He began gesticulating towards Lee and pulled out a gun which he had under his shirt and began threatening Lee with it. One of the people that was close by said that Hurst was telling Lee, "I'm not fooling around this time, I really mean business," and that Lee told him, "Put the gun down. I won't talk to you unless you put the gun down." Hurst put the gun back under his coat and then Lee slid out on the other side, on the offside of the cab. As he got out, Hurst ran around the front of the cab, took his gun out again, pointed it at Lee and shot him…. Hurst was acquitted. He never spent a moment in jail. In fact, the sheriff had whisked him away very shortly after the crime was committed. I remember reading very bitterly in the papers the next morning, a little short article on the front page of the McComb *Enterprise Journal*, said that the Negro had been shot in self-defense as he was trying to attack E.H. Hurst. That was it. You might have thought he had been a bum. There was no mention that Lee was a farmer, that he had a family, that he had nine kids, beautiful kids, that he had been a farmer all his life in Amite County and that he had been a very substantial citizen. It was as if he had been drunk or something and had gotten into [a] fight and gotten shot…. Now we knew in our hearts and minds that Hurst was attacking Lee because of the voter registration drive, and I suppose that we all felt guilty and felt responsible, because it's one thing to get beat up and it's another thing to be responsible, or to participate in some way in a killing.

Shortly after Lee was killed, the kids were released from jail who had been in jail for a month on the sit-in cases, including Brenda. Brenda was not allowed to go back in the school and in early October she and 115 students marched out and marched downtown. It's no doubt in my mind that part of the reason for the march, part of the reason for the willingness of so many students to do it, was the whole series of beatings culminating in the killing that had taken place in that area. Well, needless to say, the white community was completely on edge by this time. 115 students stopped in front of

the city hall to begin praying one by one, Brenda first, then Curtis, then Hollis, then Bobby Talbort and then finally all of us herded up the steps and into the city courthouse, and Bob Zellner, who was the only white participant, was attacked on the steps as he went up and then the mob outside, waiting, milling around, threatening, and inside, the police brought the people down, the white people, the so-called good citizens of the town, to come down and take a look at this Moses guy, and they would come down and stand at the front of the jail and say, "Where's Moses?" …

We were finally taken up one by one into a kind of kangaroo court which they held upstairs which was crowded with citizens from the town: the sheriff, the local county attorney, the local judges…. Well, they let all the kids who were under 18 off, and took those who were over 18 down to the county jail and we stayed in jail for several days….

🌺 "Segregation now, segregation tomorrow, segregation forever"

GEORGE WALLACE

Alabama Governor George Wallace was one of several white Southern Democratic politicians who bitterly fought against the federal government's attempts to integrate the South. In 1962, after being sworn in as governor of Alabama, Wallace openly defied the Supreme Court's orders to eliminate state segregation policies, proclaiming them to be inconsistent with Christianity and American freedom.

Wallace's forceful words and actions to support his racist position earned him a leading role in the anti-integration movement in the South that would lead to runs for the presidency in 1968 and in 1972, when he was paralyzed by a would-be assassin's bullet. Years later, Wallace apologized for his racist beliefs.

Today I have stood where Jefferson Davis stood and took an oath to my people. It is very appropriate then that from this Cradle of the Confederacy, this very heart of the great Anglo-Saxon Southland, that today we sound the drum for freedom….

Let us rise to the call of freedom-loving blood that is in us and send our answer to the tyranny that clanks its chains upon the South. In the name of the greatest people that ever trod this earth, I draw the line in the dust and toss the gauntlet before the feet of tyranny, and I say: segregation now, segregation tomorrow, segregation forever....

Government has become our God. It is a system that is the very opposite of Christ. The international racism of the liberals seeks to persecute the international white minority to the whim of the international colored so that we are footballed about according to the favor of the Afro-Asian bloc.... [If the races] amalgamate into the one unit as advocated by the Communist philosopher, then we become a mongrel unit of one under a single, all-powerful government.... We invite the Negro citizen of Alabama to work with us from his separate racial station to grow in individual freedom and enrichment....

But we warn those of any group who would follow the false doctrines of communistic amalgamation that we will not surrender our system of government, our freedom of race and religion [that] was won at a hard price; and if it requires a hard price to retain it, we are able—and quite willing—to pay it.

❧ "Daddy, why do white people treat colored people so mean?"

MARTIN LUTHER KING, JR.'S LETTER FROM A BIRMINGHAM CITY JAIL

The Rev. Martin Luther King, Jr., was arrested for participating in a civil rights march in Birmingham, Alabama, in 1963. While serving his sentence a group of liberal white clergymen in Birmingham issued a statement supporting integration but condemning the demonstrations as "extreme measures" that would "incite hatred and violence." This was King's response.

Demonstrations against racism continued while King was in jail. City police employed fire hoses, attack dogs and cattle prods to suppress the demonstrators, most of whom would not yield and many of whom ended up in jail. The conflict culminated when four black girls were killed in the bombing of a church.

The violence of the white attacks shocked the nation. This, combined with the eloquence and power of King's message, helped prompt the passage in Congress of the Civil Rights Act of 1964 and the Voting Rights Act of 1965.

I am in Birmingham because injustice is here. Just as the prophets of the eighth century B.C. left their villages and carried "thus saith the Lord" far beyond the boundaries of their home towns, and just as the Apostle Paul left his village of Tarsus and carried the gospel of Jesus Christ to the far corners of the Greco-Roman world, so am I compelled to carry the gospel of freedom beyond my own home town. Like Paul, I must constantly respond to the Macedonian call for aid.

Moreover, I am cognizant of the interrelatedness of all communities and states. I cannot sit idly by in Atlanta and not be concerned about what happens in Birmingham. Injustice anywhere is a threat to justice everywhere. We are caught in an inescapable network of mutuality, tied in a single garment of destiny. Whatever affects one directly, affects all indirectly. Never again can we afford to live with the narrow, provincial "outsider agitator" idea. Anyone who lives inside the United States can never be considered an outsider anywhere within its bounds.

You deplore the demonstration taking place in Birmingham. But your statement, I am sorry to say, fails to express a similar concern for the conditions that brought about the demonstrations.

Birmingham is probably the most thoroughly segregated city in the United States. Its ugly record of brutality is widely known. Negroes have experienced grossly unjust treatment in the courts. There have been more unsolved bombings of Negro homes and churches in Birmingham than in any other city in the nation. These are the hard, brutal facts of the case. On the basis of these conditions, Negro leaders sought to negotiate with the city fathers. But the latter consistently refused to engage in good-faith negotiation.

Then, last September, came the opportunity to talk with leaders of Birmingham's economic community. In the course of the negotiations, certain promises were made by the merchants—for example, to remove the stores' humiliating racial signs....[But a] few signs, briefly removed, returned; the others remained.

As in so many past experiences, our hopes had been blasted, and the shadow of deep disappointment settled upon us. We had no alternative except to prepare for direct action, whereby we would present our very bodies as a means of laying our case before the conscience of the local and the national community. Mindful of the difficulties involved, we decided to undertake a process of self-purification. We began a series of workshops on nonviolence, and we repeatedly asked ourselves: "Are you able to accept blows without retaliating?" "Are you able to endure the ordeal of jail?"

You may well ask: "Why direct action? Why sit-ins, marches and so forth? Isn't negotiation a better path?" You are quite right in calling for negotiation. Indeed, this is the very purpose of direct action. Nonviolent direct action seeks to create such a crisis and foster such a tension that a community which has constantly refused to negotiate is forced to confront the issue. It seeks so to dramatize the issue that it can no longer be ignored. My citing the creation of tension as part of the work of the nonviolent-resister may sound rather shocking. But I must confess that I am not afraid of the word "tension." I have earnestly opposed violent tension, but there is a type of constructive, nonviolent tension which is necessary for growth. Just as Socrates felt that it was necessary to create tension in the mind so that individuals could rise from the bondage of myths and half-truths to the unfettered realm of creative analysis and objective appraisal, so must we see the need for nonviolent gadflies to create the tension in society that will help men rise from the dark depths of prejudice and racism to the majestic heights of understanding and brotherhood.

The purpose of our direct-action program is to create a situation so crisis-packed that it will inevitably open the door to negotiation. I therefore concur with you in your call for negotiation. Too long has our beloved Southland been bogged down in a tragic effort to live in monologue rather than dialogue....

We know through painful experience that freedom is never voluntarily given by the oppressor; it must be demanded by the oppressed. Frankly, I have yet to engage in a direct-action campaign that was "well timed" in the view of those who have not suffered unduly from the disease of segregation. For years now I have heard the word "Wait!" It rings in the ear of every Negro with piercing familiarity. This "Wait" has almost always meant "Never." We must come to see, with one of our distinguished jurists, that "justice too long delayed is justice denied."

We have waited for more than 340 years for our constitutional and God-given rights. The nations of Asia and Africa are moving with jet-like speed toward gaining political independence, but we still creep at horse-and-buggy pace toward gaining a cup of coffee at a lunch counter. Perhaps it is easy for those who have never felt the stinging darts of segregation to say, "Wait." But when you have seen the vicious mobs lynch your mothers and fathers at will and drown your sisters and brothers at whim; when you see the vast majority of your twenty million Negro brothers smothering in an airtight cage of poverty in the midst of an affluent society; when you suddenly find your tongue twisted and your speech stammering as you seek to explain to your six-year-old daughter why she can't go to the public amusement park that has just been advertised on television, and see tears welling up in her eyes when she is told that Funtown is closed to colored children, and see ominous clouds of inferiority beginning to form in her little mental sky, and see her beginning to distort her personality by developing an unconscious bitterness toward white people; when you have to concoct an answer for a five-year-old son who is asking: "Daddy, why do white people treat colored people so mean?"; when you take a cross-country drive and find it necessary to sleep night after night in the uncomfortable corners of your automobile because no motel will accept you; when you are humiliated day in and day out by nagging signs reading "white" and "colored"; when your first name becomes "nigger," your middle name becomes "boy" (however old you are) and your last name becomes "John," and your wife and mother are never given the respected title "Mrs."; when you are harried by day and haunted by night by the fact that you are a Negro, living constantly at tiptoe stance, never quite knowing what to expect next, and are plagued with inner fears and outer resentments; when you are forever fighting a degenerating sense of "nobodiness"— then you will understand why we find it difficult to wait. There comes a time when the cup of endurance runs over, and men are no longer willing to be plunged into the abyss of despair. I hope, sirs, you can understand our legitimate and unavoidable impatience....

Oppressed people cannot remain oppressed forever. The yearning for freedom eventually manifests itself, and that is what has happened to the American Negro. Something within has reminded him of his birthright of freedom, and something without has reminded him that it can be gained. Consciously or unconsciously, he has been caught up by the Zeitgeist, and with his black brothers of Africa and his brown and yellow brothers of Asia, South America and the Caribbean, the United States Negro is moving with a sense of great urgency toward the promised land of racial justice. If one recognizes this vital urge that has engulfed the Negro community, one should readily understand why public demonstrations are taking place. The Negro has many pent-up resentments and latent frustrations, and he must release them. So let him march; let him make prayer pilgrimages to the city hall; let him go on freedom rides—and try to understand why he must do so. If his repressed emotions are not released in nonviolent ways, they will seek expression through violence; this is not a threat but a fact of history. So I have not said to my people: "Get rid of your discontent." Rather, I have tried to say that this normal and healthy discontent can be channeled into the creative outlet of nonviolent direct action. And now this approach is being termed extremist.

But though I was initially disappointed at being categorized as an extremist, as I continued to think about the matter I gradually gained a measure of satisfaction from the label. Was not Jesus an extremist for love: "Love your enemies, bless them that curse you, do good to them that hate you, and pray for them which despitefully use you, and persecute you." Was not Amos an extremist for justice: "Let justice roll down like waters and righteousness like an ever-flowing stream." Was not Paul an extremist for the Christian gospel: "I bear in my body the marks of the Lord Jesus." Was not Martin Luther an extremist: "Here I stand; I cannot do otherwise, so help me God." And John Bunyan: "I will stay in jail to the end of my days before I make a butchery of my conscience." And Abraham Lincoln: "This nation cannot survive half slave and half free." And Thomas Jefferson: "We hold these truths to be self-evident, that all men are created equal...." So the question is not whether we will be extremists, but what kind of extremists we will be. Will we be extremists for hate or for love? Will we be extremists for the preservation of injustice? In that dramatic scene on Calvary's hill three men were crucified. We must never forget that all three were crucified for the same crime—the crime of extremism. Two were extremists for immor-

tality, and thus fell below their environment. The other, Jesus Christ, was an extremist for love, truth and goodness, and thereby rose above his environment. Perhaps the South, the nation and the world are in dire need of creative extremists....

I have no fear about the outcome of our struggle in Birmingham, even if our motives are at present misunderstood. We will reach the goal of freedom in Birmingham and all over the nation, because the goal of America is freedom. Abused and scorned though we may be, our destiny is tied up with America's destiny. Before the pilgrims landed at Plymouth, we were here. Before the pen of Jefferson etched the majestic words of the Declaration of Independence across the pages of history, we were here. For more than two centuries our forebears labored in this country without wages; they made cotton king; they built the homes of their masters while suffering gross injustice and shameful humiliation—and yet out of a bottomless vitality they continued to thrive and develop. If the inexpressible cruelties of slavery could not stop us, the opposition we now face will surely fail. We will win our freedom because the sacred heritage of our nation and the eternal will of God are embodied in our echoing demands....

Over the past few years I have consistently preached that nonviolence demands that the means we use must be as pure as the ends we seek. I have tried to make clear that it is wrong to use immoral means to attain moral ends. But now I must affirm that it is just wrong, or perhaps even more so, to use moral means to preserve immoral ends....

I wish you had commended the Negro sit-inners and demonstrators of Birmingham for their sublime courage, their willingness to suffer and their amazing discipline in the midst of great provocation. One day the South will recognize its real heroes. They will be the James Merediths, with the noble sense of purpose that enables them to face jeering and hostile mobs, and with the agonizing loneliness that characterizes the life of the pioneer. They will be old, oppressed, battered Negro women, symbolized in a seventy-two-year-old woman in Montgomery, Alabama, who rose up with a sense of dignity and with her people decided not to ride segregated buses, and who responded with ungrammatical profundity to one who inquired about her weariness: "My feets is tired, but my soul is at rest." They will be the young high school and college students, the young ministers of the gospel and a host of their elders, courageously and nonviolently sitting in at lunch counters and willingly going to jail for conscience' sake. One day the South will know that when these disinherited children of God sat down at lunch counters, they were in reality standing up for what is best in the American dream and for the most sacred values in our Judeo-Christian heritage, thereby bringing our nation back to those great wells of democracy which were dug deep by the founding fathers in their formulation of the Constitution and the Declaration of Independence.

If I have said anything in this letter that overstates the truth and indicates an unreasonable impatience, I beg you to forgive me. If I have said anything that understates the truth and indicates my having a patience that allows me to settle for anything less than brotherhood, I beg God to forgive me.

I hope this letter finds you strong in the faith. I also hope that circumstances will soon make it possible for me to meet each of you, not as an integrationist or a civil-rights leader but as a fellow clergyman and a Christian brother. Let us all hope that the dark clouds of racial prejudice will soon pass away and the deep fog of misunderstanding will be lifted from our fear-drenched communities, and in some not too distant tomorrow the radiant stars of love and brotherhood will shine over our great nation with all their scintillating beauty.

🐦 "I Have a Dream"

MARTIN LUTHER KING, JR.

On August 23, 1963, civil rights organizers held a massive march on Washington, D.C., calling for legislative action. Martin Luther King, Jr., was the principle. Set on the steps of the Lincoln Memorial and broadcast to a television audience, the stunningly eloquent speech helped advance the cause of civil rights.

I am happy to join with you today in what will go down in history as the greatest demonstration for freedom in the history of our nation.

Fivescore years ago, a great American, in whose symbolic shadow we stand today, signed the Emancipation Proclamation. This momentous decree came as a great beacon light of hope to millions of Negro slaves who had been seared in the flames of withering injustice. It came as a joyous daybreak to end the long night of their captivity.

But one hundred years later, the Negro still is not free; one hundred years later, the life of the Negro is still sadly crippled by the manacles of segregation and the chains of discrimination; one hundred years later, the Negro lives on a lonely island of poverty in the midst of a vast ocean of material prosperity; one hundred years later, the Negro is still languished in the corners of American society and finds himself in exile in his own land.

So we've come here today to dramatize a shameful condition. In a sense we've come to our nation's capital to cash a check. When the architects of our republic wrote the magnificent words of the Constitution and the Declaration of Independence, they were signing a promissory note to which every American was to fall heir. This note was the promise that all men, yes, black men as well as white men, would be guaranteed the unalienable rights of life, liberty, and the pursuit of happiness.

It is obvious today that America has defaulted on this promissory note in so far as her citizens of color are concerned. Instead of honoring this sacred obligation, America has given the Negro people a bad check; a check which has come back marked "insufficient funds." We refuse to believe that there are insufficient funds in the great vaults of opportunity of this nation. And so we've come to cash this check, a check that will give us upon demand the riches of freedom and the security of justice.

We have also come to this hallowed spot to remind America of the fierce urgency of now. This is no time to engage in the luxury of cooling off or to take the tranquilizing drug of gradualism. Now is the time to make real the promises of democracy; now is the time to rise from the dark and desolate valley of segregation to the sunlit path of racial justice; now is the time to lift our nation from the quicksands of racial injustice to the solid rock of brotherhood; now is the time to make justice a reality for God's children. It would be fatal for the nation to overlook the urgency of the moment. This sweltering summer of the Negro's legitimate discontent will not pass until there is an invigorating autumn of freedom and equality.

Nineteen sixty-three is not an end, but a beginning. And those who hope that the Negro needed to blow off steam and will now be content, will have a rude awakening if the nation returns to business as usual.

There will be neither rest nor tranquility in America until the Negro is granted his citizenship rights. The whirlwinds of revolt will continue to shake the foundations of our nation until the bright day of justice emerges.

But there is something that I must say to my people who stand on the warm threshold which leads into the palace of justice. In the process of gaining our rightful place we must not be guilty of wrongful deeds.

Let us not seek to satisfy our thirst for freedom by drinking from the cup of bitterness and hatred. We must forever conduct our struggle on the high plane of dignity and discipline. We must not allow our creative protest to degenerate into physical violence. Again and again we must rise to the majestic heights of meeting physical force with soul force.

The marvelous new militancy which has engulfed the Negro community must not lead us to a distrust of all white people, for many of our white brothers, as evidenced by their presence here today, have come to realize that their destiny is tied up with our destiny, and they have come to realize that their freedom is inextricably bound to our freedom. This offense we share mounted to storm the battlements of injustice must be carried forth by a biracial army. We cannot walk alone.

And as we walk, we must make the pledge that we shall always march ahead. We cannot turn back. There are those who are asking the devotees of civil rights, "When will you be satisfied?" We can never be satisfied as long as the Negro is the victim of the unspeakable horrors of police brutality.

We can never be satisfied as long as our children are stripped of their selfhood and robbed of their dignity by signs stating "for whites only." We cannot be satisfied as long as a Negro in Mississippi cannot vote and a Negro in New York believes he has nothing for which to vote. No, we are not satisfied, and we will not be satisfied until justice rolls down like water and righteousness like a mighty stream.

I am not unmindful that some of you have come here out of excessive trials and tribulation. Some of you have come fresh from narrow jail cells.

Some of you have come from areas where your quest for freedom left you battered by the storms of persecution and staggered by the winds of police brutality. You have been the veterans of creative suffering. Continue to work with the faith that unearned suffering is redemptive.

Go back to Mississippi; go back to Alabama; go back to South Carolina; go back to Georgia; go back to Louisiana; go back to the slums and ghettos of the northern cities, knowing that somehow this situation can, and will be changed. Let us not wallow in the valley of despair.

So I say to you, my friends, that even though we must face the difficulties of today and tomorrow, I still have a dream. It is a dream deeply rooted in the American dream that one day this nation will rise up and live out the true meaning of its creed— we hold these truths to be self-evident, that all men are created equal.

I have a dream that one day on the red hills of Georgia, sons of former slaves and sons of former slave-owners will be able to sit down together at the table of brotherhood.

I have a dream that one day, even the state of Mississippi, a state sweltering with the heat of injustice, sweltering with the heat of oppression, will be transformed into an oasis of freedom and justice.

I have a dream my four little children will one day live in a nation where they will not be judged by the color of their skin but by the content of their character. I have a dream today!

I have a dream that one day, down in Alabama, with its vicious racists, with its governor having his lips dripping with the words of interposition and nullification, that one day, right there in Alabama, little black boys and black girls will be able to join hands with little white boys and white girls as sisters and brothers. I have a dream today!

I have a dream that one day every valley shall be exalted, every hill and mountain shall be made low, the rough places shall be made plain, and the crooked places shall be made straight and the glory of the Lord will be revealed and all flesh shall see it together.

This is our hope. This is the faith that I go back to the South with.

With this faith we will be able to hear out of the mountain of despair a stone of hope. With this faith we will be able to transform the jangling discords of our nation into a beautiful symphony of brotherhood.

With this faith we will be able to work together, to pray together, to struggle together, to go to jail together, to stand up for freedom together, knowing that we will be free one day. This will be the day when all of God's children will be able to sing with new meaning—"my country 'tis of thee; sweet land of liberty; of thee I sing; land where my fathers died, land of the pilgrim's pride; from every mountain side, let freedom ring"—and if America is to be a great nation, this must become true.

So let freedom ring from the prodigious hill-tops of New Hampshire.

Let freedom ring from the mighty mountains of New York.

Let freedom ring from the heightening Alleghenies of Pennsylvania.

Let freedom ring from the snow-capped Rockies of Colorado.

Let freedom ring from the curvaceous slopes of California.

But not only that.

Let freedom ring from Stone Mountain of Georgia.

Let freedom ring from Lookout Mountain of Tennessee.

Let freedom ring from every hill and molehill of Mississippi, from every mountainside, let freedom ring.

And when we allow freedom to ring, when we let it ring from every village and hamlet, from every state and city, we will be able to speed up that day when all of God's children—black men and white men, Jews and Gentiles, Prostestants and Catholics—will be able to join hands and to sing in the words of the old Negro spiritual, "Free at last, free at last; thank God Almighty, we are free at last."

❧ "The shots which killed President Kennedy were fired by Lee Harvey Oswald"

THE WARREN COMMISSION REPORT

On November 22, 1963, the dynamism and vitality of President Kennedy's administration came to a sudden and dramatic end. While seated in his car in a Presidential motorcade through downtown Dallas with his wife at his side, Kennedy was assassinated. Three shots rang out, killing the President, wounding Governor John Connally and shocking the country.

Police quickly arrested a suspect, Lee Harvey Oswald, who had killed a patrolman 45 minutes after the assassination and then hidden in a movie theater. While being escorted through a police station basement, Jack Ruby shot Oswald at point blank range in front of live television cameras.

The circumstances of the shooting, Oswald's shady past as a resident of the Soviet Union and dealings with Cuban dissidents, and Ruby's subsequent role, the magnitude of the assassination and the apparent shortcomings in security, prompted wide ranging speculation of a conspiracy hatched either abroad or within the United States.

President Lyndon B. Johnson, who was sworn in as President hours after Kennedy's death, called for an exhaustive investigation headed by Chief Justice Earl Warren. A team of 27 government lawyers and staffers, assisted by numerous experts, investigated the assassination. On September 24, 1964, they submitted a report to Johnson concluding that Oswald had indeed killed the President and had acted alone. Despite the findings, conspiracy theories persisted through the years that followed.

For many, the Kennedy assassination and the extraordinarily public killing of Oswald ended an era of American innocence. The increasing militancy of the Civil Rights movement, the television coverage of the Vietnam War, the widespread skepticism of military pronouncements concerning the war, student demonstrations and finally the Watergate scandal, all stood in stark contrast to the hopeful days that Kennedy came to represent.

This Commission was created to ascertain the facts relating to the preceding summary of events and to consider the important questions which they raised. The Commission has addressed itself to this task and has reached certain conclusions based on all the available evidence....

1. The shots which killed President Kennedy and wounded Governor Connally were fired from the sixth floor window at the southeast corner of the Texas School Book Depository. This determination is based upon the following:

Witnesses at the scene of the assassination saw a rifle being fired from the sixth floor window of the Depository Building, and some witnesses saw a rifle in the window immediately after the shots were fired.

The nearly whole bullet found on Governor Connally's stretcher at Parkland Memorial Hospital and the two bullet fragments found in the front seat of the Presidential limousine were fired from the 6.5-

millimeter Mannlicher-Carcano rifle found on the sixth floor of the Depository Building to the exclusion of all other weapons.

The three used cartridge cases found near the window on the sixth floor at the southeast corner of the building were fired from the same rifle which fired the above-described bullet and fragments, to the exclusion of all other weapons.

The windshield in the Presidential limousine was struck by a bullet fragment on the inside surface of the glass, but was not penetrated.

The nature of the bullet wounds suffered by President Kennedy and Governor Connally and the location of the car at the time of the shots established that the bullets were fired from above and behind the Presidential limousine, striking the President and the Governor as follows:

President Kennedy was first struck by a bullet which entered at the back of his neck and exited through the lower portion of his neck, causing a wound which would not necessarily have been lethal. The President was struck a second time by a bullet which entered the right-rear portion of his head, causing a massive and fatal wound.

Governor Connally was struck by a bullet which entered on the right side of his back and traveled downward through the right side of his chest, exiting below his right nipple. This bullet then passed through his right wrist and entered his left thigh where it caused a superficial wound.

There is no credible evidence that the shots were fired from the Triple underpass, ahead of the motorcade, or from any other location.

The weight of evidence indicates that there were three shots fired.

3. Although it is not necessary to any essential findings of the Commission to determine just which shot hit Governor Connally, there is very persuasive evidence from the experts to indicate that the same bullet which pierced the President's throat also caused Governor Connally's wounds. However, Governor Connally's testimony and certain other factors have given rise to some difference of opinion as to this probability but there is no question in the mind of any member of the Commission that all the shots which caused the President's and Governor Connally's wounds were fired from the sixth floor window of the Texas School Book Depository.

4. The shots which killed President Kennedy and wounded Governor Connally were fired by Lee Harvey Oswald. This conclusion is based upon the following:

The Mannlicher-Carcano 6.5 millimeter Italian rifle from which the shots were fired was owned by and in the possession of Oswald.

Oswald carried this rifle into the Depository building on the morning of November 22, 1963.

Oswald, at the time of the assassination, was present at the window from which the shots were fired.

Shortly after the assassination, the Mannlicher-Carcano rifle belonging to Oswald was found partially hidden between some cartons on the sixth floor and the improvised paper bag in which Oswald brought the rifle to the Depository was found close by the window from which the shots were fired.

Based on testimony of the experts and their analysis of films of the assassination, the Commission has concluded that a rifleman of Lee Harvey Oswald's capabilities could have fired the shots from the rifle used in the assassination within the elapsed time of the shooting. The Commission has concluded further that Oswald possessed the capability with a rifle which enabled him to commit the assassination.

Oswald lied to the police after his arrest concerning important substantive matters.

Oswald had attempted to kill Maj. Gen. Edwin A. Walker (Resigned, U.S. Army) on April 10, 1963, thereby demonstrating his disposition to take human life.

5. Oswald killed Dallas Police Patrolman J. D. Tippit approximately 45 minutes after the assassination. This conclusion upholds the finding that Oswald fired the shots which killed President Kennedy and wounded Governor Connally and is supported by the following:

Two eyewitnesses saw the Tippit shooting and seven eyewitnesses heard the shots and saw the gunman leave the scene with revolver in hand. These nine eyewitnesses positively identified Lee Harvey Oswald as the man they saw.

The cartridge cases found at the scene of the shooting were fired from the revolver in the possession of Oswald at the time of his arrest to the exclusion of all other weapons.

The revolver in Oswald's possession at the time of his arrest was purchased by and belonged to Oswald.

Oswald's jacket was found along the path of flight taken by the gunman as he fled from the scene of the killing.

6. Within 80 minutes of the assassination and 35 minutes of the Tippit killing Oswald resisted arrest at the theatre by attempting to shoot another police officer.

7. The commission has reached the following conclusions concerning Oswald's interrogation and detention by the Dallas police:

Except for the force required to effect his arrest, Oswald was not subjected to any physical coercion by any law enforcement officials. He was advised that he could not be compelled to give any information and that any statements made by him might be used against him in court. He was advised of his right to counsel. He was given the opportunity to obtain counsel of his own choice and was offered legal assistance by the Dallas Bar Association, which he rejected at that time.

Newspaper, radio, and television reporters were allowed uninhibited access to the area through which Oswald had to pass when he moved from his cell to the interrogation room and other sections of the building, thereby subjecting Oswald to harassment and creating chaotic conditions which were not conducive to orderly interrogation or the protection of the rights of the prisoner.

The numerous statements, sometimes erroneous, made to the press by various local law enforcement officials, during this period of confusion and disorder in the police station, would have presented serious obstacles to the obtaining of a fair trial for Oswald. To the extent that the information was erroneous or misleading, it helped create doubts, speculations, and fears in the mind of the public which might otherwise not have arisen.

8. The Commission has reached the following conclusions concerning the killing of Oswald by Jack Ruby on November 24, 1963:

Ruby entered the basement of the Dallas Police Department shortly after 11:17 am and killed Lee Harvey Oswald at 11:21 am.

Although the evidence of Ruby's means of entry is not conclusive, the weight of evidence indicates that he walked down the ramp leading from Main Street to the basement of the police department.

There is no evidence to support the rumor that Ruby may have been assisted by any members of

the Dallas Police Department in the killing of Oswald.

The Dallas Police Department's decision to transfer Oswald to the county jail in full public view was unsound. The arrangements made by the police department on Sunday morning, only a few hours before the attempted to transfer, were inadequate. Of critical importance was the fact that news media representatives and others were not excluded from the basement even after the police were notified of threats to Oswald's life. These deficiencies contributed to the death of Lee Harvey Oswald.

9. The Commission has found no evidence that either Lee Harvey Oswald or Jack Ruby was part of any conspiracy, domestic or foreign, to assassinate President Kennedy. The reasons for this conclusion are:

The Commission has found no evidence that anyone assisted Oswald in planning or carrying out the assassination. In this connection it has thoroughly investigated, among other factors, the circumstances surrounding the planning of the motorcade route through Dallas, the hiring of Oswald by the Texas School Book Depository Co. on October 15, 1963, the method by which the rifle was brought into the building, the placing of cartons of books at the window, Oswald's escape from the building, and the testimony of eyewitnesses to the shooting.

The Commission has found no evidence that Oswald was involved with any person or group in a conspiracy to assassinate the President, although it has thoroughly investigated, in addition to other possible leads, all facets of Oswald's associations, finances, and personal habits, particularly during the period following his return from the Soviet Union in June 1962.

The Commission has found no evidence to show that Oswald was employed, persuaded, or encouraged by any foreign government to assassinate President Kennedy or that he was an agent of any foreign government, although the Commission has reviewed the circumstances surrounding Oswald's defection to the Soviet Union, his life there from October of 1959 to June of 1962 so far as it can be reconstructed, his known contacts with the Fair Play for Cuba Committee, and his visits to the Cuban and Soviet Embassies in Mexico City during his trip to Mexico from September 26 to October 3, 1963, and his known contacts with the Soviet Embassy in the United States.

The Commission has explored all attempts to identify himself with various political groups, including the Communist Party, U.S.A., the Fair Play for Cuba Committee, and the Socialist Workers Party, and has been unable to find any evidence that the contacts which he initiated were related to Oswald's subsequent assassination of the President

All of the evidence before the Commission established that there was nothing to support the speculation that Oswald was an agent, employee, or informant of the FBI, the CIA, or any other agent governmental agency. It has thoroughly investigated Oswald's relationships prior to the assassination with all agencies of the U.S. Government. All contacts with Oswald by any of these agencies were made in the regular exercise of their different responsibilities.

No direct or indirect relationship between Lee Harvey Oswald and Jack Ruby has been discovered by the Commission, nor has it been able to find any credible evidence that either knew the other, although a thorough investigation was made of the many rumors and speculations of such a relationship.

The Commission has found no evidence that Jack Ruby acted with any other person in the killing of Lee Harvey Oswald.

After careful investigation the Commission has found no credible evidence either that Ruby and Officer Tippit, who was killed by Oswald, knew each other or that Oswald and Tippit knew each other.

Because of the difficulty of proving negatives to a certainty the possibility of others being involved with either Oswald or Ruby cannot be rejected categorically, but if there is any such evidence it has been beyond the reach of all the investigative agencies and resources of the United States and has not come to the attention of this Commission.

10. In its entire investigation the commission has found no evidence of conspiracy, subversion, or disloyalty to the U.S. government by any Federal, State, or local official.

11. On the basis of the evidence before the Commission it concludes that Oswald acted alone. Therefore, to determine the motives for the assassination of President Kennedy, one must look to the assassin himself. Clues to Oswald's motives can be found in his family history, his education or lack of it, his acts, his writings, and the recollections of those who had close contacts with him throughout his life. The Commission has presented this report all of the background information bearing on motivation which it could discover. Thus, others may study Lee Oswald's life and arrive at their own conclusions as to his possible motives.

The Commission could not make any definitive determination of Oswald's motives. It has endeavored to isolate factors which contributed to his character and which might have influenced his decision to assassinate President Kennedy. These factors were:

His deep-rooted resentment of all authority which was expressed in a hostility toward every society in which he lived;

His inability to enter into meaningful relationships with people, and a continuous pattern of rejecting his environment in favor of new surroundings;

His urge to try to find a place in history and despair at times over failures of his various undertakings;

His capacity for violence as evidenced by his attempt to kill general Walker;

His avowed commitment to Marxism and communism, as he understood the terms and developed his own interpretation of them; this was expressed by his antagonism toward the United States, by his defection to the Soviet Union, by his failure to be reconciled with life in the United States even after his disenchantment with the Soviet Union, and by his efforts, though frustrated, to go to Cuba.

Each of these contributed to his capacity to risk all in cruel and irresponsible actions.

12. The Commission recognizes that the varied responsibilities of the President require that he make frequent trips to all parts of the United States and abroad. Consistent with their high responsibilities Presidents can never be protected from every potential threat. The Secret Service's difficulty in meeting its protective responsibility varies with the activities and the nature of the occupant of the Office of President and his willingness to conform to plans for his safety. In appraising the performance of the Secret Service it should be understood that it has to do its work within such limitations. Nevertheless, the Commission believes that recommendations for

improvements in Presidential protection are compelled by the facts disclosed in this investigation.

The complexities of the Presidency have increased so rapidly in recent years that the Secret Service has not been able to develop or to secure adequate resources of personnel and facilities to fulfill its important assignment. This situation should be promptly remedied.

The Commission has concluded that the criteria and procedures of the Secret Service designed to identify and protect against persons considered threats to the President, were not adequate prior to the assassination.

The Protective Research Section of the Secret Service, which is responsible for its preventive work, lacked sufficient trained personnel and the mechanical and technical assistance needed to fulfill its responsibility.

Prior to the assassination the Secret Service's criteria dealt with direct threats against the President. Although the Secret Service treated the direct threats against the President adequately, it failed to recognize the necessity of identifying other potential sources of danger to his security. The Secret Service did not develop adequate and specific criteria defining those person or groups who might present a danger to the President. In effect, the Secret Service largely relied upon other Federal and State agencies to supply the information necessary for it to fulfill its preventive responsibilities, although it did ask for information about direct threats to the President.

The Commission has concluded that there was insufficient liaison and coordination of information between the Secret Service and other Federal agencies necessarily concerned with Presidential protection. Although the FBI, in the normal exercise of its responsibility, had secured considerable information about Lee Harvey Oswald, it had no official responsibility, under the Secret Service criteria existing at the time of the President's trip to Dallas, to refer to the Secret Service the information it had about Oswald. The Commission has concluded, however, that the FBI took an unduly restrictive view of its role in preventive intelligence work prior to the assassination. A more carefully coordinated treatment of the Oswald case by the FBI might well have resulted in bringing Oswald's activities to the attention of the Secret Service.

The Commission has concluded that some of the advance preparations in Dallas made by the Secret Service, such as the detailed security measures taken at Love Field and the Trade Mart, were thorough and well executed. In other respects, however, the Commission has concluded that the advance preparation for the President's trip were deficient.

Although the Secret Service is compelled to rely to a great extent on local law enforcement officials, its procedures at the time of the Dallas trip did not call for well-defined instructions as to the respective responsibilities of the police officials and others assisting in the protection of the President.

The Procedures relied upon by the Secret Service for detecting the presence of an assassin located in a building along a motorcade route were inadequate. At the time of the trip to Dallas, the Secret Service as a matter of practice did not investigate, or cause to be checked, any building located along the motorcade route to be taken by the President. The responsibility for observing windows in these buildings during the motorcade was divided between local police personnel stationed on the street to regulate crowds and Secret Service agents riding in the motorcade. Based on its investigation the Commission has concluded that these arrangements during the trip to Dallas were clearly not sufficient.

The configuration of the Presidential car and the seating arrangements of the Secret Service agents in the car did not afford the Secret Service agents the opportunity they should have had to be of immediate assistance to the President at the first sign of danger.

Within these limitations, however, the Commission finds that the agents most immediately responsible for the President's safety reacted promptly at the time the shots were fired from the Texas School Book Depository Building.

Clay comes out to meet Liston

CASSIUS CLAY

Cassius Clay burst on to the sporting scene in the early 1960s. Young, brash and black, Clay won the Olympic gold medal in boxing as an amateur and quickly made a mark as a potent professional heavyweight boxer. His rise in boxing circles coincided with the extraordinary attention he was able to cast upon himself. Boasting of exploits, often in rhyme, Clay was a different kind of athlete and a different kind of black. He did not fit the stereotype of an unassuming Negro applied to the former champion Joe Louis or the brutish, scary current heavyweight champion Sonny Liston. Clay was his own man with own opinions, unafraid to say them to a disapproving audience. He represented the newfound confidence of American blacks and the ascending spirit of youthful rebellion.

In 1964, as he started to flirt with converting to Islam, Clay was slated to fight Liston in a championship fight. The odds were 7-1 against him. Many of the boxing press corps chose to skip the fight, disgusted with Clay's antics and convinced that Clay would be demolished and. Undaunted, Clay wrote the following poem predicting his victory. True to form, Clay won. He soon converted to Islam and became Muhammad Ali. His hard-fought championship was taken away a few years later when he refused to join the Army in protest, saying "No Viet Cong ever called me 'nigger.'" Ali ultimately won back his title and became one of the most admired and recognized men in the world for his athletic and humanitarian accomplishments.

Clay comes out to meet Liston
And Liston starts to retreat.
If Liston goes back any further
He'll end up in a ringside seat.

Clay swings with a left,
Clay swings with a right,
Look at young Cassius
Carry the fight.

Liston keeps backing
But there's not enough room.
It's a matter of time.
There Clay lowers the boom.

Now Clay swings with a right,
What a beautiful swing,
And the punch raises the bear
Clear out of the ring.

Liston is still rising
And the ref wears a frown,
For he can't start counting
Till Sonny comes down.

Now Liston disappears from view.
The crowd is getting frantic,
But our radar stations have picked him up,
He's somewhere over the Atlantic.

Who would have thought

When they came to the fight
That they'd witness the launching of a human
    satellite?

Yes, the crowd did not dream
When they laid down their money
That they would see
A total eclipse of the Sonny!

The Great Society

LYNDON B. JOHNSON

Upon becoming President, Johnson pushed forward sweeping social legislation to achieve his goal of creating the "Great Society." Many of the proposals had been initiated by Kennedy. Sentiment after the assassination helped propel Congressional approval of the measures. But the legislation was more an extension of Franklin Roosevelt's New Deal. Johnson, who had grown up poor in rural Texas, looked upon Roosevelt as a hero and was determined to continue his legacy.

Johnson described his vision for the Great Society in a commencement address at the University of Michigan in May 1964.

I have come today from the turmoil of your Capitol to the tranquility of your campus to speak about the future of our country. The purpose of protecting the life of our nation and preserving the liberty of our citizens is to pursue the happiness of our people. Our success in that pursuit is the test of our success as a nation. For a century we labored to settle and to subdue a continent. For half a century, we called upon unbounded invention and untiring industry to create an order of plenty for all our people. The challenge of the next half century is whether we have the wisdom to use that wealth to enrich and elevate our national life, and to advance the quality of our American civilization.

Your imagination, your initiative, and your indignation will determine whether we build a society where progress is the servant of our needs, or a society where old values and new visions are buried under unbridled growth. For in your time we have the opportunity to move not only toward the rich society and the powerful society, but upward to the Great Society. The Great Society rests on abundance and liberty for all. It demands an end to poverty and racial injustice, to which we are totally committed in our time. But that is just the beginning.

The Great Society is a place where every child can find knowledge to enrich his mind and to enlarge his talents. It is a place where leisure is a welcome chance to build and reflect, not a feared cause of boredom and restlessness. It is a place where the city of man serves not only the needs of the body and the demands of commerce, but the desire for beauty and the hunger for community.

It is a place where man can renew contact with nature. It is a place which honors creation for its own sake and for what it adds to the understanding of the race. It is a place where men are more concerned with the quality of their goals than the quantity of their goods. But most of all, the Great Society is not a safe harbor, a resting place, a final objective, a finished work. It is a challenge constantly renewed, beckoning us toward a destiny where the meaning of our lives matches the marvelous products of our labor....

So will you join in the battle to give every citizen the full equality which God enjoins and the law requires, whatever his belief, or race, or the color of his skin? Will you join in the battle to give every citizen an escape from the crushing weight of poverty? Will you join in the battle to make it possible for all nations to live in enduring peace as neighbors and not as mortal enemies? Will you join in the battle to build the Great Society, to prove that our material progress is only the foundation on which we will build a richer life of mind and spirit?

There are timid souls who say this battle cannot be won, that we are condemned to a soulless wealth. I do not agree. We have the power to shape the civilization that we want. But we need your will, your labor, your hearts, if we are to build that kind of society.

❧ The War on Poverty

LYNDON B. JOHNSON

Central to the creation of a Great Society was Johnson's "War on Poverty." The Economic Opportunity Act of 1964 served as the pillar of this effort. Sweeping reforms were implemented allowing the government to intervene in the marketplace to foster greater economic equality. The federal government's bureaucratic structure was decentralized and numerous new programs were introduced. Several failed.

Good intentions did not always translate into sound policy. However, programs such as Head Start, free legal services and the introduction of local health clinics did make a substantive difference in the lives of millions of people.

Other features of the Great Society included civil rights legislation and the introduction of government-run medical insurance, mainly Medicare, the medical and hospital insurance plan for the elderly financed through the Social Security system.

We are citizens of the richest and most fortunate nation in the history of the world. One hundred and eighty years ago we were a small country struggling for survival on the margin of a hostile land. Today we have established a civilization of free men which spans the entire continent.

The path forward has not been an easy one. But we have never lost sight of our goal—an America in which every citizen shares all the opportunities of his society, in which every man has a chance to advance his welfare to the limit of his capacities.

We have come a long way toward this goal. We still have a long way to go. The distance which remains is the measure of the great unfinished work of our society. To finish that work I have called for a national war on poverty. Our objective: total victory. There are millions of Americans—one-fifth of our people—who have not shared in the abundance which has been granted to most of us, and on whom the gates of opportunity have been closed.

What does this poverty mean to those who endure it? It means a daily struggle to secure the necessities for even a meager existence. It means that the abundance, the comforts, the opportunities they see all around them are beyond their grasp. Worst of all, it means hopelessness for the young. The young man or woman who grows up without a decent education, in a broken home, in a hostile and squalid environment, in ill health or in the face of racial injustice—that young man or woman is often trapped in a life of poverty. He does not have the skills demanded by a complex society. He does not know how to acquire those skills. He faces a mounting sense of despair which drains initiative and ambition and energy.

Our tax cut will create millions of new jobs— new exits from poverty. But we must also strike down all the barriers which keep many from using those exits. The war on poverty is not a struggle simply to support people, to make them dependent on the generosity of others. It is a struggle to give people a chance. It is an effort to allow them to develop and use their capacities, as we have been allowed to develop and use ours, so that they can share, as others share, in the promise of this nation.

Because it is right, because it is wise, and because, for the first time in our history, it is possible to conquer poverty, I submit, for the consideration of the Congress and the country, the Economic Opportunity Act of 1964. The act does not merely expand old programs or improve what is already being done. It charts a new course. It strikes at the causes, not just the consequence of poverty. It can be a milestone in our 180-year search for a better life for our people.

This act provides five basic opportunities:

It will give almost half a million underprivileged young Americans the opportunity to develop skills, continue education, and find useful work.

It will give every American community the opportunity to develop a comprehensive plan to fight its own poverty—and help them to carry out their plans.

It will give dedicated Americans the opportunity to enlist as volunteers in the war against poverty.

It will give many workers and farmers the opportunity to break through particular barriers which bar their escape from poverty.

It will give the entire nation the opportunity for a concerted attack on poverty through the establishment, under my direction, of the Office of Economic Opportunity, a national headquarters for the war against poverty.

This is how we propose to create these opportunities. First, we will give high priority to helping young Americans who lack skills, who have not completed their education or who cannot complete it because they are too poor. The years of high school and college are the most critical stage of a young person's life. If they are not helped then, many will be condemned to a life of poverty which they, in turn, will pass on to their children.

I therefore recommend the creation of a Job Corps, a work-training program, and a work-study program. A new national Job Corps will build toward an enlistment of 100,000 young men. They will be drawn from those whose background, health, and education make them least fit for useful work.

Those who volunteer will enter more than one hundred camps and centers around the country. Half of these young men will work in the first year, on special conservation projects to give them education, useful work experience, and to enrich the natural resources of the country. Half of these young men will receive, in the first year, a blend of training, basic education, and work experience in job training centers. These are not simply camps for the underprivileged. They are new educational institutions, comparable in innovation to the land-grant colleges. Those who enter them will emerge better qualified to play a productive role in American society.

A new national work-training program operated by the Department of Labor will provide work and training for 200,000 American men and women between the ages of sixteen and twenty-one. This will be developed through state and local governments and nonprofit agencies. Hundreds of thousands of young Americans badly need the experience, the income, and the sense of purpose which useful full- or part-time work can bring. For them such work may mean the difference between finishing school or dropping out. Vital community activities from hospitals and playgrounds to libraries and settlement houses are suffering because there are not enough people to staff them. We are simply bringing these needs together.

A new national work-study program operated by the Department of Health, Education, and Welfare will provide federal funds for part-time jobs for 140,000 young Americans who do not go to college because they cannot afford it. There is no more senseless waste than the waste of the brain-power and skill of those who are kept from college by economic circumstances. Under this program they will, in a great American tradition, be able to work their way through school. They and the country will be richer for it.

Second, through a new community action program we intend to strike at poverty at its source—in the streets of our cities and on the farms of our countryside among the very young and the impoverished old. This program asks men and women throughout the country to prepare long-range plans for the attack on poverty in their own local communities. These are not plans prepared by Washington and imposed upon hundreds of different situations. They are based on the fact that local citizens best understand their own problems, and know best how to deal with those problems. These plans will be local plans striking at the many unfilled needs which underlie poverty in each community, not just one or two. Their components and emphasis will differ as needs differ. These plans will be local plans calling upon all the resources available to the community—federal and state, local and private, human and material. And when these plans are approved by the Office of Economic Opportunity, the federal government will finance up to 90 percent of the additional cost for the first two years.

Third, I ask for the authority to recruit and train skilled volunteers for the war against poverty.... If the state requests them, if the community needs and will use them, we will recruit and train them and give them a chance to serve.

Fourth, we intend to create new opportunities for certain hard-hit groups to break out of the pattern of poverty. Through a new program of loans and guarantees we can provide incentives to those who will employ the unemployed. Through programs of work and retraining for unemployed fathers and mothers we can help them support their families in dignity while preparing themselves for new work. Through funds to purchase land, organize cooperatives, and create new and adequate family farms we can help those whose life on the land has been a struggle without hope.

Fifth, I do not intend that the war against poverty become a series of uncoordinated and unrelated efforts that perish for lack of leadership and direction. Therefore this bill creates, in the Executive Office of the President, a new office of Economic Opportunity. Its director will by my personal chief of staff for the war against poverty. I intend to appoint Sargent Shriver to this post. He will be directly responsible for these new programs. He will work with and through existing agencies of the government. This program—the Economic Opportunity Act—is the foundation of the war against poverty.

And this program is much more than a beginning. Rather it is a commitment. It is a total commitment by this President, and this Congress, and this nation, to pursue victory over the most ancient of mankind's enemies. On many historic occasions the President has requested from Congress the authority to move against forces which were endangering the well-being of our country. This is such an occasion.

On similar occasions in the past we have been called upon to wage war against foreign enemies which threatened our freedom. Today we are asked to declare war on a domestic enemy which threatens the strength of our nation and the welfare of our people. If we now move forward against this enemy—if we can bring to the challenges of peace the same determination and strength which has brought us victory in war—then this day and this Congress will have won a secure and honorable place in the history of the nation, and the enduring gratitude of generations of Americans yet to come.

"Extremism in the defense of liberty is no vice"

BARRY GOLDWATER

In 1964 the conservative wing of the Republican party successfully nominated Arizona senator Barry Goldwater for president in favor of the "eastern establishment" moderates such as New York Governor Nelson Rockefeller and Pennsylvania Governor William Scranton. Attempting to buck the national trend to turn toward government and legislation to solve society's problems, Goldwater was crushed in a landslide by Lyndon B. Johnson.

Nevertheless, Goldwater's acceptance speech at the Republican convention and his subsequent campaign laid down the roots for the conservative movement that would eventually sweep Ronald Reagan into the White House in 1980.

From this moment, united and determined, we will go forward together, dedicated to the ultimate and undeniable greatness of the whole man. Together we will win.

I accept your nomination with a deep sense of humility. I accept, too, the responsibility that goes with it, and I seek your continued help and your continued guidance. My fellow Republicans, our cause is too great for any man, did he not have with him the heart and the hands of this great Republican party. And I promise you tonight that every fiber of my being is consecrated to our cause, that nothing shall be lacking from the struggle that can be brought to it by enthusiasm, by devotion, and plain hard work.

In this world no person, no party can guarantee anything, but what we can do and what we shall do is to deserve victory, and victory will be ours. The good Lord raised this mighty Republic to be a home for the brave and to flourish as the land of the free—not to stagnate in the swampland of collectivism, not to cringe before the bully of communism.

Now, my fellow Americans, the tide has been running against freedom. Our people have followed false prophets. We must, and we shall, return to proven ways—not because they are old, but because they are true.

We must, and we shall, set the tide running again in the cause of freedom. And this party, with its every action, every word, every breath, and every heartbeat, has but a single resolve, and that is freedom.

Freedom made orderly for this nation by our constitutional government. Freedom under a government limited by laws of nature and of nature's God. Freedom balanced so that liberty lacking order will not become the slavery of the prison cell; balanced so that liberty lacking order will not become the license of the mob and of the jungle.

Now, we Americans understand freedom; we have earned it, we have lived for it, and we have died for it. This nation and its people are freedom's models in a searching world. We can be freedom's missionaries in a doubting world.

But, ladies and gentlemen, first we must renew freedom's mission in our own hearts and in our own homes....

Those who seek absolute power, even though they seek it to do what they regard as good, are simply demanding the right to enforce their own version of heaven on earth, and let me remind you that they are the very ones who always create the most hellish tyranny.

Absolute power does corrupt, and those who seek it must be suspect and must be opposed. Their mistaken course stems from false notions, ladies and gentlemen, of equality. Equality, rightly understood as our founding fathers understood it, leads to liberty and to the emancipation of creative differences; wrongly understood, as it has been so tragically in our time, it leads first to conformity and then to despotism.

Fellow Republicans, it is the cause of Republicanism to resist concentration of power, private or public, which enforce such conformity and inflict such despotism.

It is the cause of Republicanism to ensure that power remains in the hands of the people—and so help us God, that is exactly what a Republican president will do with the help of a Republican Congress.

It is further the cause of Republicanism to restore a clear understanding of the tyranny of man over man in the world at large. It is our cause to dispel the foggy thinking which avoids hard decisions in the delusion that a world conflict will somehow resolve itself into a world of harmony—and this is hogwash.

It is further the cause of Republicanism to remind ourselves, and the world, that only the strong can remain free: that only the strong can keep the peace....

I can see a day when all the Americas, North and South, will be linked in a mighty system—a system in which the errors and misunderstandings of the past will be submerged one by one in a rising tide of prosperity and interdependence.

We know that the misunderstandings of centuries are not to be wiped away in a day or wiped away in an hour. But we pledge, we pledge, that human sympathy—what our neighbors to the south call an attitude of simpatico—no less than enlightened self-interest will be our guide.

And I can see this Atlantic civilization galvanizing and guiding emergent nations everywhere. Now, I know this freedom is not the fruit of every soil. I know that our own freedom was achieved through centuries of unremitting efforts by brave and wise men. And I know that the road to freedom is a long and a challenging road, and I know also that some men may walk away from it, that some men resist challenge, accepting the false security of governmental paternalism.

And I pledge that the America I envision in the years ahead will extend its hand in help in teaching and in cultivation so that all new nations will be at least as encouraged to go our way, so that they will not wander down the dark alleys of tyranny or to the dead-end streets of collectivism.

My fellow Republicans, we do no man a service by hiding freedom's light under the bushel of mistaken humility. I seek an American proud of its past, proud of its ways, proud of its dreams, and determined actively to proclaim them. But our examples to the world must, like charity, begin at home.

In our vision of a good and decent future, free and peaceful, there must be room, room for the liberation of the energy and the talent of the individual, otherwise our vision is blind at the outset.

We must assure a society here which while never abandoning the needy, or forsaking the helpless, nurtures incentives and opportunity for the creative and the productive.

We must know the whole good is the product of many single contributions. And I cherish the day when our children once again will restore as heroes the sort of men and women who, unafraid and undaunted, pursue the truth, strive to cure disease, subdue and make fruitful our natural environment, and produce the inventive engines of production—science and technology.

This nation, whose creative people have enhanced this entire span of history, should again thrive upon the greatness of all those things which we—we as individual citizens—can and should do.

During Republican years, this again will be a nation of men and women, of families proud of their role, jealous of their responsibilities, unlimited in their aspiration—a nation where all who can will be self-reliant.

We the Republicans see in our constitutional form of government the great framework which assures the orderly but dynamic fulfillment of the whole man as the great reason for instituting orderly government in the first place.

We see in private property and in economy based upon and fostering private property the one way to make government a durable ally of the whole man rather than his determined enemy. We see in the sanctity of private property the only durable foundation for constitutional government in free society.

And beyond all that we see and cherish diversity of ways, diversity of thoughts, of motives, and accomplishments. We don't seek to live anyone's life for him. We only seek to secure his rights, guarantee him opportunity, guarantee him opportunity to strive, with government performing only those needed and constitutionally sanctioned tasks which cannot otherwise be performed.

We Republicans seek a government that attends to its inherent responsibilities of maintaining a stable monetary and fiscal climate, encouraging a free and competitive economy, and enforcing law and order.

Thus do we seek inventiveness, diversity, and creative difference within a stable order, for we Republicans define government's role where needed at many, many levels—preferably, though, the one closest to the people involved: our towns and our cities, then our counties, then our states, then our regional contacts, and only then the national government.

That, let me remind you, is the land of liberty built by decentralized power. On it also we must have balance between the branches of government at every level.

Balance, diversity, creative difference—these are the elements of Republican equation. Republicans agree, Republicans agree heartily to disagree on many, many of their applications. But we have never disagreed on the basic fundamental issue of why you and I are Republicans.

This is a party—this Republican party is a party for free men. Not for blind followers and not for conformists.

Back in 1858 Abraham Lincoln said this of the Republican party—and I quote him because he probably could have said it during the last week or so. It was composed of "strained, discordant and even hostile element."

Yet all of these elements agreed on [a] paramount objective: to arrest the progress of slavery, and place it in the course of ultimate extinction.

Today, as then, but more urgently and more broadly than then, the task of preserving and enlarging freedom at home and safeguarding it from the forces of tyranny abroad is great enough to challenge all our resources and to require all our strength.

Anyone who joins us in all sincerity, we welcome. Those, those who do not care for our cause, we don't expect to enter our ranks, in any case. And let our Republicanism so focused and so dedicated not be made fuzzy and futile by unthinking and stupid labels.

I would remind you that extremism in the defense of liberty is no vice!

And let me remind you also that moderation in the pursuit of justice is no virtue!

The beauty of the very system we Republicans are pledged to restore and revitalize, the beauty of this federal system of ours, is in its reconciliation of diversity with unity. We must not see malice in honest differences of opinion, and no matter how great, so long as they are not inconsistent with the pledges we have given to each other in and through our Constitution.

Our Republican cause is not to level out the world or make its people conform in computer-regimented sameness. Our Republican cause is to free our people and light the way for liberty throughout the world. Ours is a very human cause for humane goals. This party, its good people, and its unquestionable devotion to freedom will not fulfill the purposes of this campaign which we launch here now until our cause has won the day, inspired the world, and shown the way to a tomorrow worthy of all our yesteryears.

I repeat, I accept your nomination with humbleness, with pride, and you and I are going to fight for the goodness of our land. Thank you.

🌿 "A serious threat to international peace"

GULF OF TONKIN RESOLUTION

Three months before the 1964 Presidential election, President Johnson sought approval from Congress to expand the U.S. military ability to wage war on Communist North Vietnam to prevent its war against non-Communist South Vietnam. The Gulf of Tonkin Resolution granted that authority and was based on a naval encounter between U.S. destroyers in the North Vietnamese gulf and hostile ships.

Some historians dispute the U.S. account of the incident and believe that Johnson used the encounter to bolster his anti-Communist credentials prior to the election. The Democrats, still sensitive to criticisms that they had "lost China" to the Communists did not want to be perceived as being soft on Communism. Only two members of Congress voted against the resolution.

The effect of the joint resolution, however, was to allow a much greater U.S. role in the war than was originally intended. As the war expanded, U.S. participation escalated to levels nobody had foreseen in 1964.

Resolved by the Senate and House of Representatives of the United States of America in Congress assembled.

Whereas naval units of the Communist regime in Vietnam, in violation of the Charter of the United Nations and of international law, have deliberately and repeatedly attacked United States naval vessels lawfully present in international waters, and have thereby created a serious threat to international peace; and

Whereas these attacks are part of a deliberate and systematic campaign of aggression that the Communist regime in North Vietnam has been waging against its neighbors and the nations joined with them in the collective defense of their freedom; and

Whereas the United States is assisting the peoples of Southeast Asia to protect their freedom and has no territorial, military, or political ambitions in that area, but desires only that these people should be left in peace to work out their own destinies in their own way:

Now therefore, be it resolved by the Senate and the House of Representatives of the United States of America in Congress assembled:

Section 1—The Congress approves and supports the determination of the President, as Commander in Chief, to take all necessary measures to repel any armed attack against the forces of the United States and to prevent further aggression.

Section 2—The United States regards as vital to its national interest and to world peace the maintenance of international peace and security in Southeast Asia. Consonant with the Constitution and the Charter of the United Nations and in accordance with its obligations under the Southeast Asia Collective Defense Treaty, the United States is, therefore, prepared, as the President determines, to take all necessary steps, including the use of armed force, to assist any member or protocol state of the Southeast Asia Collective Defense Treaty requesting assistance in defense of its freedom.

Section 3—This resolution shall expire when the President shall determine that the peace and security of the area is reasonably assured by international conditions created by action of the United Nations or otherwise, except that it may be terminated earlier by concurrent resolution of the Congress.

Approved August 10, 1964

"Recommendation of additional deployments to Vietnam"

ROBERT MCNAMARA

By the middle of 1965, the U.S. military needed to make a decision. Despite 75,000 troops stationed in Vietnam, the Communist forces were gaining an upper hand in South Vietnam. Secretary of Defense Robert McNamara traveled to Vietnam to review the situation and make an assessment and recommendation to President Johnson. At the time, North Vietnamese troops had stepped up their attacks and students in American college campuses were starting to protest the wrar.

Fearful of the impact of withdrawing American troops and abandoning an ally and dubious that the existing commitment would reverse the situation, McNamara called for an escalation of American troops. He warned, however, that by raising the stakes, it would become more difficult to withdraw in the future. Johnson accepted the recommendation, but limited the increase to 50,000 additional troops.

Thus, the slippery slope of escalation began its descent. Ultimately, more than 2 million American men and women would be sent to Vietnam.

SUBJECT: Recommendations of additional deployments to Vietnam

1. Introduction. Our object in Vietnam is to create conditions for a favorable outcome by demonstrating to the [Vietcong/Democratic Republic of Vietnam] that the odds are against their winning. We want to create these conditions, if possible, without causing the war to expand into one with China or the Soviet Union and in a way which preserves support of the American people and, hopefully, of our allies and friends. The following assessments...are addressed to the achievement of that object....

3. Estimate of the situation. The situation in South Vietnam is worse than a year ago (when it was worse than the year before that). After a few months of stalemate, the tempo of the war has quickened. A hard VC push is now on to dismember the nation and to maul the army. The VC main and local forces, reinforced by militia and guerrillas, have the initiative and, with large attacks (some in regimental strength), are hurting [Army of the Republic of Vietnam] forces badly.... The government is able to provide security to fewer and fewer people in less and less territory as terrorism increases. Cities and towns are being isolated as fewer and fewer roads and railroads are usable and power and communications lines are cut.

The economy is deteriorating—the war is disrupting rubber production, rice distribution, vegetable production, and the coastal fishing industry, causing the loss of jobs and income, displacement of people and frequent breakdown or suspension of vital means of transportation and communication; foreign exchange earnings have fallen; and severe inflation is threatened.

The odds are less than even that the Ky government will last out the year. Ky is "executive agent" for the directorate of generals.... His tenure depends upon unity of the armed forces behind him....

Rural reconstruction (pacification) even in the...area around Saigon is making little progress. Gains in the IV Corps are being held, but in I and II Corps and the adjacent III Corps areas it has lost ground fast since the end of the VC monsoon offensive (300,000 people have been lost to the VC and tens of thousands of refugees have poured out of these areas)....

There are no signs that we have throttled the inflow of supplies for the VC or can throttle the flow while their material needs are as low as they are: indeed, more and better weapons have been observed in VC hands, and it is probably that there has been a further buildup of North Vietnamese regular units in the I and II Corps area....

4. Options open to us. We must choose among three courses of action with respect to Vietnam, all of which involve different probabilities, outcomes and costs:

Cut our losses and withdraw under the best conditions that can be arranged—almost certainly conditions humiliating to the United States and very damaging to our future effectiveness on the world scene.

Continue at about the present level, with U.S. forces limited to say 75,000, holding on and playing for the breaks—a course of action which, because our position would grow weaker, almost certainly would confront us later with a choice between withdrawal and an emergency expansion of forces, perhaps too late to do any good.

Expand promptly and substantially the U.S. military pressure against the Vietcong in the South and maintain the military pressure against the North Vietnamese in the North while launching a vigorous effort on the political side to lay the groundwork for a favorable outcome by clarifying our objectives and establishing channels of communication. This alternative would stave off defeat in the short run and offer a good chance of producing a favorable settlement in the longer run; at the same time it would imply casualties and material and would make any later decision to withdraw even more difficult and more costly than would be the case today.

My recommendations in paragraph 5 below are based on the choice of the third alternative (Option c) as the course of action involving the best odds of the best outcome with the most acceptable cost to the United States.

5. Military recommendations. There are now 15 U.S. (and 1 Australian) combat battalions in Vietnam; they, together with other combat personnel and noncombat personnel, bring the total U.S. personnel to approximately 75,000.

I recommend the deployment of U.S. ground troops in Vietnam be increased by October to 34 maneuver battalions (or, if the Koreans fail to provide the expected 9 battalions promptly, to 43 battalions). The battalions, together with increases in helicopter lift, air squadrons, naval units, air defense combat support, and miscellaneous log support and advisory personnel in Vietnam to approximately 175,000 (200,000 if we must make up for the Korean failure). It should be understood that the deployment of more men (perhaps 100,000) may be necessary in early 1966, and that the deployment of additional forces thereafter is possible but will depend on developments.

I recommend that Congress be requested to authorize the call-up of approximately 235,000 men in the Reserve and National Guard. The call-up would be for a two-year period; but the intention would be to release them after one year, by which time they will be relieved by regular forces if conditions permitted.

I recommend that the regular armed forces be increased to approximately 375,000 men....

I recommend that a supplemental appropriate of approximately $X for FY 1966 be sought from the Congress to cover the first part of the added cost attributable to the buildup in and for the war in Vietnam. A further supplemental appropriation might be required later in the fiscal year....

7. Action against North Vietnam. We should continue the program of bombing military targets in North Vietnam. While avoiding striking population and industrial targets not closely related to the DRV's supply of war material to the VC, we should announce to Hanoi and carry out actions to destroy such supplies and interdict their flow. The number of strike sorties against North Vietnam...should increase slowly from the present level of 2,500 a month to 4,000 or more a month....

❧ Tinker v. Des Moines: "Schools may not be enclaves of totalitarianism"

SUPREME COURT JUSTICE ABE FORTAS

Mary Beth Tinker was an eighth-grade student at Warren Harding Junior High School in Des Moines, Iowa, who objected to American involvement in the Vietnam War. In December 1965, she and fellow students decided to wear black armbands to school to support a Christmas truce

Alarmed Des Moines public school principals banned students from wearing armbands. Tinker and five other students who wore armbands were suspended from school. Thirteen-year-old Tinker objected, claiming that her right to free speech was being infringed. The Supreme Court agreed. Justice Abe Fortas wrote the court's opinion in *Tinker v. Des Moines,* stating that students have a right to symbolic political expression.

...[I]n our system, undifferentiated fear or apprehension of disturbance is not enough to overcome the right of freedom of expression. Any departure from absolute regimentation may cause trouble. Any variation from the majority's opinion may inspire fear. Any word spoken, in class, in the lunchroom, or on the campus, that deviates from views of another person may start an argument or cause a disturbance. But our Constitution says we must take this risk,...and our history says that it is this sort of hazardous freedom—this kind of openness—that is the basis of our national strength and of the independence and vigor of Americans who grow up and live in this relatively permissive, often disputatious, society.

In order for the State in the person of school officials to justify prohibition of a particular expression of opinion, it must be able to show that its action was caused by something more than a mere desire to avoid the discomfort and unpleasantness that always accompany an unpopular viewpoint. Certainly where there is no finding and no showing that engaging in the forbidden conduct would "materially and substantially interfere with the requirements of appropriate discipline in the operation of the school," the prohibition cannot be sustained.

It is also relevant that the school authorities did not purport to prohibit the wearing of all symbols of political and controversial significance. The record shows that students in some of the schools wore buttons relating to national political campaigns, and some even wore the Iron Cross, traditionally a symbol of Nazism. The order prohibiting the wearing of armbands did not extend to these. Instead, a particular symbol—black armbands worn to exhibit opposition to this Nation's involvement in Vietnam—was singled out for prohibition. Clearly, the prohibition of expression of one particular opinion, at least without evidence that it is necessary to avoid material and substantial interference with schoolwork or discipline, is not constitutionally permissible.

In our system, state-operated schools may not be enclaves of totalitarianism. School officials do not possess absolute authority over their students. Students in schools as well as out of school are "persons" under our Constitution. They are possessed of fundamental rights which the State must respect, just as they themselves must respect their obligations to the State. In our system, students may not be regarded as closed-circuit recipients of only that which the State chooses to communicate. They may not be confined to the expression of those sentiments that are officially approved. In the absence of specific showing of constitutionally valid reasons to regulate their speech, students are entitled to freedom of expression of their views.

❧ The Things They Carried

TIMOTHY O'BRIEN

Defense Secretary McNamara's recommendation forever changed the lives of millions of men. One of the young soldiers who went to Vietnam was Timothy O'Brien. A combat veteran and gifted writer, he would later write several novels about the war and the American men who fought it. This is an excerpt from his book, *The Things They Carried.*

First Lieutenant Jimmy Cross carried letters from a girl named Martha, a junior at Mount Sebastian College in New Jersey. They were not love letters, but Lieutenant Cross was hoping, so he kept them folded in plastic at the bottom of his rucksack. In the late afternoon, after a day's march, he would dig his foxhole, wash his hands under a canteen, unwrap the letters, hold them with the tips of his fingers, and spend the last hour of light pretending. He would imagine romantic camping trips into the White Mountains in New Hampshire. He would sometimes taste the envelope flaps, knowing her tongue had been there. More than anything, he wanted Martha to love him as he loved her, but the letters were mostly chatty, elusive on the matter of love. She was a virgin, he was almost sure. She was an English major at Mount Sebastian, and she wrote beautifully about her professors and roommates and midterm exams, about her respect for Chaucer and her great affection for Virginia Woolf. She often quoted lines of poetry; she never mentioned the war except to say, Jimmy, take care of yourself. The letters weighed 10 ounces. They were signed Love, Martha, but Lieutenant Cross understood that Love was only a way of signing and did not mean what he sometimes pretended it meant. At dusk, he would carefully return the letters to his rucksack. Slowly, a bit distracted, he would get up and move among his men, checking the perimeter, then at full dark he would return to his hole and watch the night and wonder if Martha was a virgin.

The things they carried were largely determined by necessity. Among the necessities or near-necessities were P-38 can openers, pocket knives, heat tabs, wristwatches, dog tags, mosquito repellent, chewing gum, candy, cigarettes, salt tablets, packets of Kool-Aid, lighters, matches, sewing kits, Military Payment Certificates, C rations, and two or three canteens of water. Together, these items weighed between 15 and 20 pounds, depending upon a man's habit or rate of metabolism. Henry Dobbins, who was a big man, carried extra rations; he was especially fond of canned peaches in heavy syrup over pound cake. Dave Jensen, who practiced field hygiene, carried a toothbrush, dental floss, and several hotel-sized bars of soap he'd stolen on R&R

in Sydney, Australia. Ted Lavender, who was scared, carried tranquilizers until he was shot in the head outside the village of Than Khe in mid-April. By necessity, and because it was sop, they all carried steel helmets that weighed 5 pounds including the liner and camouflage cover. They carried the standard fatigue jackets and trousers. Very few carried underwear. On their feet they carried jungle boots—2.1 pounds—and David Jensen carried three pairs of socks and a can of Dr. Scholl's foot powder as a precaution against trench foot. Until he was shot, Ted Lavender carried six or seven ounces of premium dope, which for him was a necessity. Mitchell Sanders, the rto, carried condoms. Norman Bowker carried a diary. Rat Kiley carried comic books. Kiowa, a devout Baptist, carried an illustrated New Testament that had been presented to him by his father, who taught Sunday school in Oklahoma City, Oklahoma. As a hedge against bad times, however, Kiowa also carried his grandmother's distrust of the white man, his grandfather's old hunting hatchet. Necessity dictated. Because the land was mined and booby-trapped, it was sop for each man to carry a steel-centered, nylon-covered flask jacket, which weighed 6.7 pounds, but which on hot days seemed much heavier. Because you could die so quickly, each man carried at least one large compress bandage, usually in the helmet band for easy access. Because the nights were cold, and because the monsoons were wet, each carried a green plastic poncho that could be used as a raincoat or groundsheet or makeshift tent. With its quilted liner, the poncho weighed almost two pounds, but it was worth every ounce. In April, for instance, when Ted Lavender was shot, they used his poncho to wrap him up, then to carry him across the paddy, then to lift him into the chopper that took him away.

They were called legs or grunts.

To carry something was to hump it, as when Lieutenant Jimmy Cross humped his love for Martha up the hills and through the swamps. In its intransitive form, to hump meant to walk, or to march, but it implied burdens far beyond the intransitive.

Almost everyone humped photographs. In his wallet, Lieutenant Cross carried two photographs of Martha. The first was a Kodacolor snapshot signed Love, though he knew better. She stood against a brick wall. Her eyes were gray and neutral, her lips slightly open as she stared straight-on at the camera. At night, sometimes, Lieutenant Cross wondered who had taken the picture, because he knew she had boyfriends, because he loved her so much, and because he could see the shadow of the picture-taker spreading out against the brick wall....

🐝 "To enforce the fifteenth Amendment"

THE VOTING RIGHTS ACT OF 1965

The successful lobbying efforts of the Civil Rights movement resulted in national legislation stripping away the barriers to equal citizenship that the white South had erected after Reconstruction. One of the most important obstacles had been tests in which black citizens were denied the right to vote for failing to answer questions correctly. Using this tactic, in addition to blatant intimidation and other methods, many southern communities effectively removed blacks from the election process.

Although several laws were passed to try to reverse these tactics, literacy tests, poll taxes and other tactics were still commonly employed in the 1960s. In 1964, the 24th Amendment was ratified banning the use of poll taxes. One year later, the Voting Rights Act of 1965 closed some of the other loopholes.

An Act to enforce the fifteenth Amendment to the Constitution of the United States, and for other purposes.

Section 2. No voting qualification or prerequisite to voting, or standard, practice, or procedure shall be imposed or applied by any State or political subdivision to deny or abridge the right of any citizen of the United States to vote on account of race or color....

Section 4. (a) To assure that the right of citizens of the United States to vote is not denied or abridged on account of race or color, no citizen shall be denied the right to vote in any Federal, State, or local election because of his failure to comply with any test or device in any State with respect to which the determinations have been made under subsection (b) or in any political subdivision with respect to which such determinations have been made as a separate unit, unless the United States District Court for the District of Columbia in an action for a declaratory judgment brought by such State or subdivision against the United States has determined that no such test or device has been used during the five years preceding the filing of the action for the purpose or with the effect of denying or abridging the right to vote on account of race or color, he shall consent to the entry of such judgment.

(b) The provisions of subsection (a) shall apply in any State or in any political subdivision of a state which (1) the Attorney General determines maintained on November 1, 1964, any test or device, and with respect to which (2) the Director of the Census determines that less than 50 per centum of the persons of voting age residing therein were registered on November 1, 1964, or that less than 50 per centum of such persons voted in the presidential election of November 1964.

(c) The phrase "test or device" shall mean any requirement that a person as a prerequisite for voting or registration for voting (1) demonstrate an ability to read, write, understand, or interpret any matter, (2) demonstrate any educational achievement or his knowledge of any particular subject, (3) possess good moral character, or (4) prove his qualifications by the voucher of registered voters of members of any class.

(d) For purposes of this section no State or political subdivision shall be determined to have engaged in the use of tests or devices for the purpose or with the effect of denying or abridging the right to vote on account of race or color if (1) incidents of such use have been few in number and have been promptly and effectively corrected by the State or local action, (2) the continuing effect of such incidents have been eliminated, and (3) there is no reasonable probability of their recurrence in the future.

(2) No person who demonstrates that he has successfully completed the sixth primary grade in a public school in, or a private school accredited by, any State or territory, the District of Columbia, or the Commonwealth of Puerto Rico in which the predominant classroom was other than English, shall be denied the right to vote in any Federal, State, or local election because of his inability to read, write, understand, or interpret any matter in the English language, except that in States in which State law provides that a different level of education is presumptive of literacy, he shall demonstrate that he has successfully completed an equivalent level of education in a public school in, or a private school accredited by, any State or terri-

tory, the District of Columbia, or the Commonwealth of Puerto Rico in which the predominant classroom language was other than English.

"One of the greatest acts of industrial irresponsibility in the present century"

RAPLH NADER'S UNSAFE AT ANY SPEED

One of the driving forces of America's economic might in the post-war era was the extraordinary boom in the automobile industry. In 1965, an obscure consumer protection advocate named Ralph Nader wrote *Unsafe at Any Speed,* an indictment of the auto industry for its focus on profits rather than safety. The book prompted Congress to pass new safety regulations for cars and energized a nationwide consumer protection movement.

The Sporty Corvair: The "one-car" accident

John F. Gordon did not become president of the world's largest manufacturing company by using strong words. But on October 17, 1961, as the keynote speaker before the annual National Safety Congress, the head of General Motors was among friends—"professionals" from the National Safety Council and other organizations that make up the closely knit traffic safety establishment. Mr. Gordon saw "diversionary forces" undermining safety progress. "The traffic safety field," he declared, "has in recent years been particularly beset by self-styled experts with radical and ill-conceived proposals…The general thesis of these amateur engineers is that cars could be made virtually foolproof and crashproof, that this is the only practical route to greater safety and that federal regulations of vehicle design is needed. This thesis is, of course, wholly unrealistic. It also is a serious threat to a balanced approach to traffic safety. To begin with, it is completely unrealistic even to talk about a foolproof and crashproof car. This is true because an automobile must still be something that people will want to buy and use…We can only design into it the greatest degree of safety that is consistent with the other essential functional characteristics. Beyond that, we must depend on intelligent use.

The suggestions that we abandon hope of teaching drivers to avoid traffic accidents and concentrate on designing cars that will make collisions harmless is a perplexing combination of defeatism and wishful thinking."

Mr. Gordon finished his address, entitled "Safeguarding Safety Programs," amid enthusiastic and confirming applause. It was a rare occasion for a top auto executive to speak about vehicle safety design in any vein, even in an argumentative context of raising and demolishing straw men. The national media gave wide circulation to his criticism of "self-styled experts" and, in subsequent months, General Motors management made sure that every GM dealer received copies of the address to distribute throughout the local community.

Mrs. Rose Pierini did not read about Mr. Gordon's complaints. She was learning to adjust to the loss of her left arm which was severed two months earlier when the 1961 Chevrolet Corvair she was driving turned over on its top just beyond the San Marcos overpass on Holister Street in Santa Barbara, California. Exactly thirty-four months later, in the same city, General Motors decided to pay Mrs. Pierini $70,000 rather than continue a trial which for three days threatened to expose on the public record one of the greatest acts of industrial irresponsibility in the present century.

Mrs. Pierini's experience with a Corvair going unexpectedly and suddenly out of control was not unique. There simply are too many Corvairs with such inclinations for her case to be singular. What was distinctive about the "accident" was the attempt to find the cause of it on the basis of investigation, instead of resorting to the customary, automatic placing of blame on the driver.

As described by a California Highway Patrol officer, John Bortolozzo, who witnessed the flip-over while travelling about thirty-five miles per hours in a thirty-five mph zone in the right lane headed towards Goleta. He saw the car move towards the right side of the road near the shoulder and then "all of a sudden the vehicle made a sharp cut to the left and swerved over." Bortolozzo testified at the trial that he rushed over to the wreck and saw an arm with a wedding band and wristwatch lying on the ground. Two other men came over quickly and began to help Mrs. Pierini out of the vehicle while trying to stop the torrent of blood gushing forth from the stub of her arm. She was very calm, observed Bortolozzo, only saying

that "something went wrong with my steering."

After helping Mrs. Pierini to the ambulance, the officer made a check of the vehicle while it was on its top. He noticed that the left rear tire was deflated because of an air-out. Looking at the road, he noticed some gouge marks made by the metal rim of the left rear tire. He gave his opinion at the trial that the distinctive design features of the Corvair caused it to go out of control and flip over as had other Corvairs in accidents he had investigated. It was during the cross-examination of Officer Bortolozzo by defense lawyers that General Motors decided to settle the case.

Up to this point no engineering experts had been called to testify by plaintiff Pierini, but already the case had been going badly for General Motors. Two members of the respected California Highway Patrol had taken direct aim on the Corvair design. One of them Charles Hanna, mentioned a confidential circular put out by the highway patrol dealing with handling hazards of certain rear-engine cars, including the Corvair. Hanna, a fourteen-year veteran of the patrol who had investigated over four thousand accidents, testified that "I have had many, many chances to observe accidents involving this type of vehicle. And they all have the same type of pattern."

Mr. James A. Johnson, service manager of Washburn Chevrolet Company, where the Pierini Corvair was purchased, told the court that his company sold an accessory specially designed for the Corvair by a nearby manufacturer. Attached underneath the vehicle to each end of the lower control arms, this accessory reduced excessive caving-in, or tuck-under, of the rear wheels on cornering or other stress situations.

The dealership's proprietor, Shelton B. Washburn, confirmed that as early as 1961 General Motors provided dealers with regular production option 696, which they could sell to Corvair owners. RPO 696 included heavier suspension springs and shock absorbers, a front stabilizer bar, and rear-axle rebound straps to reduce tuck-under. This RPO was a factory installed kit and not openly advertised. It was intended to meet the demands of the most knowledgeable Corvair owners who take their cornering seriously.

Mr. Johnson, in reply to questioning by plaintiff's counsel, stated that he had been at a General Motors training center at Burbank in 1959 to receive instructions and training about the new Corvair model. There, General Motors personnel told him that the different tire pressures, front and rear, in Corvair automobiles were a critical factor in their stability. There followed these exchanges:

COUNSEL: Were you instructed by your superiors to tell members of the public that tire pressures on the Corvair were vital, important, crucial, and critical?

JOHNSON: No.

COUNSEL: Did you instruct your subordinates to tell members of the public and customers of Washburn Chevrolet that tire pressures on the Corvair were vital, important, crucial or critical?

JOHNSON: We didn't tell the public this, no.

COUNSEL: Is it true that tire pressures on a Corvair are a must: they have got to be just right for the stability of the car?

JOHNSON: Yes.

"It is hard to call the Hell's Angels anything but mutants"

HUNTER S. THOMPSON

Hunter S. Thompson helped invent a new type of journalism in the 1960s. Laced with cynicism, he cast a bitter eye on the subjects he covered, from the 1972 Presidential campaign to the American culture on display at Las Vegas. His "gonzo journalism," which was sometimes influenced by hallucinogenic drugs, represented an extremist take that many would argue offered a more truthful perspective then the more moderate and mainstream accounts.

In 1966, before Thompson's books *Fear and Loathing in Las Vegas* and *The Great White Shark Hunt* earned him a national reputation, he spent several months with the Hell's Angels motorcycle gang in California. He wrote the book *Hell's Angels* about that experience and exploring the fascination Americans have always had with the unrepentant, unfettered freedom of the renegade outlaw.

Far from being freaks, the Hell's Angels are a logical product of the culture that now claims to be shocked at their existence. The generation represented by the editors of *Time* has lived so long in a world full of Celluloid outlaws hustling toothpaste and hair oil that it is no longer capable of confronting the real thing. For twenty years they have sat with their children and watched yesterday's out-

laws raise hell with yesterday's world...and now they are bringing up children who think Jesse James is a television character. This is the generation that went to war for Mom, God and Apple Butter, the American Way of Life. When they came back, they crowned Eisenhower and then retired to the giddy comfort of their TV parlors, to cultivate the subtleties of American history as seen by Hollywood.

To them the appearance of the Hell's Angels must have seemed like a wonderful publicity stunt. In a nation of frightened dullards there is a sorry shortage of outlaws, and those few who make the grade are always welcome: Frank Sinatra, Alexander King, Elizabeth Taylor, Raoul Duke...they have that extra "something."

Charles Starkweather had something extra too, but he couldn't get an agent, and instead of taking his vitality to Hollywood, he freaked out in Wyoming and killed a dozen people for reasons he couldn't explain. So the state put him to death. There were other outlaws who missed the brass ring in the fifties. Lenny Bruce was one; he was never quite right for television. Bruce had tremendous promise until about 1961, when the people who'd been getting such a kick out of him suddenly realized he was serious. Just like Starkweather was serious...and like the Hell's Angels are serious....

Now, looking for labels, it is hard to call the Hell's Angels anything but mutants. They are urban outlaws with a rural ethic and new, improvised style of self-preservation. Their image of themselves derives mainly from Celluloid, from Western movies and two-fisted TV shows that have taught them most of what they know about the society they live in. Very few read books, and in most cases their formal education ended at fifteen or sixteen. What little they know of history has come from mass media, beginning with comics...so if they see themselves in terms of the past, it's because they can't grasp the terms of the present, much less the future. They are the sons of poor men and drifters, losers and the sons of losers. Their backgrounds are overwhelmingly ordinary. As people, they are like millions of other people. But in their collective identity they have a peculiar fascination so obvious that even the press recognized it, although not without cynicism. In its ritual flirtation with reality the press has viewed the Angels with a mixture of awe, humor and terror—justified, as always, by a slavish dedication to the public appetite, which most journalists find so puzzling and contemptible that they have long since abandoned the task of understanding it to a handful of poll-takers and "experts."

The widespread appeal of the Angels is worth pondering. Unlike most other rebels, the Angels have given up hope that the world is going to change for them. They assume, on good evidence, that the people who run the social machinery have little use for outlaw motorcyclists, and they are reconciled to being losers. But instead of losing quietly, one by one, they have banded together with a mindless kind of loyalty and moved outside the framework, for good or ill. They may not have an answer, but at least they are still on their feet. One night about halfway through one of their weekly meetings I thought of Joe Hill on his way to face a Utah firing squad and saying his final words: "Don't mourn. Organize." It is safe to say that no Hell's Angel had ever heard of Joe Hill or would know a Wobbly from a bushmaster, but there is something very similar about the attitudes. The Industrial Workers of the World had serious blueprints for society, while the Hell's Angels mean only to defy the social machinery. There is no talk among the Angels of "building a better world," yet their reactions to the world they live in are rooted in the same kind of anarchic, para-legal sense of conviction that brought the armed wrath of the Establishment down on the Wobblies. There is the same kind of suicidal loyalty, the same kinds of in-group rituals and nicknames, and above all the same feeling of constant warfare with an unjust world. The Wobblies were losers, and so are the Angels…and if every loser in this country rode a motorcycle the whole highway system would have to be modified.

There is an important difference between the words "loser" and "outlaw." One is passive and the other is active, and the main reasons the Angels are such good copy is that they are acting out the day-dreams of millions of losers who don't wear any defiant insignia and who don't know how to be outlaws. The streets of every city are thronged with men who would pay all the money they could get their hands on to be transformed—even for a day—into hairy, hard-fisted brutes who walk over cops, extort free drinks from terrified bartenders and thunder out of town on big motorcycles after raping the banker's daughter. Even people who think the

Angels should be put to sleep, find it easy to identify with them. They command a fascination, however reluctant, that borders on psychic masturbation.

The Angels don't like being called losers, but they have learned to live with it. "Yeah, I guess I am," said one. "But you're looking at one loser who's going to make a hell of a scene on the way out."

Learning From Las Vegas

ROBERT VENTURI, DENISE SCOTT BROWN AND STEVEN IZENOUR

The automobile changed the landscape of America. Communities were no longer built around the needs of pedestrians and horses, but rather cars. Towns and cities no longer needed to be compact clusters of buildings. Cars gave builders and city planners breathing space. The result was a new sprawling urban and suburban landscape. Billboards, motels designed specifically for the needs of travelers, fast-food restaurants, large signs with flashing neon to attract motorists all came to dominate roadside vistas.

And if sprawl became the distinguishing feature of American cities, then Las Vegas was the most distinctive of all. Built in the 1950s as a destination resort city for gamblers, the city in the desert of Nevada was, by the 1960s, a neon sensation marked by shining lights, night shows and a sensory free-for-all.

While the architecture and planning community generally snubbed its nose at the ticky-tack nature of Las Vegas, architects Robert Venturi, Denise Scott Brown and Steven Izenour saw Las Vegas as a distinctly American type of architecture, symbolizing the freedom of expression, boldness and daring of the American spirit. The three published the book *Learning from Las Vegas* explaining what American architecture could learn from its most vulgar city.

The Las Vegas Strip at night, like the Martorama interior, is symbolic images in dark, amorphous space; but, like the Amalienburg, it glitters rather than glows. Any sense of enclosure or direction comes from lighted signs rather than from reflected light. The source of light in the Strip is direct; the signs themselves are the source. They do not reflect the light from external, sometimes hidden, sources as is the case with most billboards and Modern architecture. The mechanical movement is greater to accommodate the greater spaces, greater speeds, and greater impacts that our technology permits and our sensibilities respond to. Also, the tempo of our economy encourages that changeable and disposable environmental decoration known as advertising art. The messages are different now, but despite the differences the methods are the same, and architecture is no longer simply the "skillful, accurate, and magnificent play of masses seen in light."

The Strip by day is a different place, no longer Byzantine. The forms of the buildings are visible but remain secondary to the signs in visual impact and symbolic content. The space of the urban sprawl is not enclosed and directed as in traditional cities. Rather, it is open and indeterminate, identified by points in space and patters on the ground; these are two-dimensional or sculptural symbols in space rather than buildings in space, complex configurations that are graphic or representational. Acting as symbols, the signs and buildings identify the space by their location and direction, and space is further defined and directed by utility poles and street and parking patterns. In residential sprawl the orientation of houses toward the street, their stylistic treatment as decorated sheds, and their landscaping and lawn fixtures—wagon wheels, mailboxes on erect chairs, colonial lamps, and segments of split-rail fence—substitute for the signs of commercial sprawl as the definers of space.

Like the complex architectural accumulations of the Roman Forum, the Strip by day reads as chaos if you perceive only its forms and exclude its symbolic content. The Forum, like the Strip, was a landscape of symbols with layers of meaning evident in the location of roads and buildings, buildings representing earlier buildings, and the sculpture piled all over. Formally the Forum was an awful mess; symbolically it was a rich mix.

The series of triumphal arches in Rome is a prototype of the billboard (mutatis mutandis for scale, speed, and content). The architectural ornament, including pilasters, pediments, and coffers, is a kind of bas-relief that makes only a gesture toward architectural form. It is as symbolic as the bas-reliefs of processions and the inscriptions that compete for the surface. Along with their function as billboards carrying messages, the triumphal arches in the Roman Forum were spatial markers channeling processional paths within a complex urban landscape. On Route 66 the billboards set in a series at a constant angle toward

the oncoming traffic, with a standard distance between themselves and from the roadside, perform a similar formal-spatial function. Often the brightest, cleanest, and best-maintained elements in industrial sprawl, the billboards both cover and beautify the landscape. Like the configurations of sepulchral monuments along the Via Appia (again mutatis mutandis for scale), they mark the way through the vast spaces beyond urban sprawl. But these spatial characteristics of form, position, and orientation are secondary to their symbolic function. Along the highway, advertising Tanya via graphics and anatomy, like advertising the victories of Constantine via inscriptions and bas-reliefs, is more important than identifying the space.

Urban Sprawl and the Megastructure

The urban manifestations of ugly and ordinary architecture and the decorated shed are closer to urban sprawl than to the megastructure. We have explained how, for us, commercial vernacular architecture was a vivid initial source for symbolism in architecture. We have described in the Las Vegas study the victory of symbols-in-space over forms-in-space in the brutal automobile landscape of great distances and high speed, where the subtleties of pure architectural space can no longer be savored. But the symbolism of urban sprawl lies also in its residential architecture, not only in the strident, roadside communications of the commercial strip (decorated shed or duck). Although the ranch house, split level or otherwise, conforms in its spatial configuration to several set patterns, it is appliqued with varied though conforming ornament, evoking combinations of Colonial, New Orleans, Regency, Western, French Provincial, Modern, and other styles. Garden apartments—especially those of the Southwest—equally are decorated sheds whose pedestrian courts, like those of motels, are separate from, but close to, the automobile.

Sprawl City's image is a result of process. In this respect it follows the canons of Modern architecture that require form to result from function, structure, and construction methods, that is, from the process of its making. But for our time the megastructure is a distortion of normal city building processes for the sake inter alia of image. Modern architects contradict themselves when they support functionalism and the megastructure. They do not recognize the image of the process city when they see it on the Strip, because it is both too familiar and too different from what they have been trained to accept.

✒ My Day: July 5, 1962

ELEANOR ROOSEVELT

Before there was feminism, there was Eleanor Roosevelt. The niece of Theodore Roosevelt and wife to Franklin D. Roosevelt, Eleanor Roosevelt directly influenced American policy. A liberal by inclination, she was widely despised by conservatives for using her position to advance her causes.

Undaunted, Eleanor Roosevelt wrote a daily column called "My Day"—not only while she was First Lady, but for many years afterward—about a wide variety of subjects. Her resolution to continue to take stands on controversial issues infuriated her critics, but made her a hero to thousands of women who admired her courage to speak her mind.

This July 5, 1962, column defends the Supreme Court's decision to not allow prayer in school. Written two years after the election of the nation's first Catholic President, the subject was intensely controversial.

The nation's governors, in their annual meeting in Hershey, Pennsylvania, had a wordy wrangle regarding the resolution to be submitted to Congress for an amendment to the First Article of the Constitution, which of course deals with freedom of religion and the separation of church and state.

All this, it seems to me, stems from a misunderstanding of what the Supreme Court ruled regarding the New York State Board of Regents—written prayer and the saying of it in the schools of the state under state direction.

The fact is that this is a prayer written and backed by the government of the state and directed to be used in the schools, and which the Supreme Court has declared unconstitutional. The prayer is innocuous, but this procedure would be an injection of state interference in religious education and religious practice.

Under our Constitution no individual can be forced by government to belong to a special religion or to conform to a special religious procedure. But any school, or any group of people, or any individual may say a prayer if he or they so wish if it is not under the order of the government or connected with government direction in any way. This seems to me very clear in the Supreme Court deci-

sion and conforms exactly, I think, with the Constitution.

It is my feeling that many of our newspapers put sensational headlines on stories pertaining to this decision, and people have suddenly—without really reading the court ruling themselves—reacted emotionally.

Someone reported to me that he had heard a man on the radio in tears saying that he never thought he would live to see the day when God would be outlawed from our schools. Another told me that a Southern woman wrote to her daughter in New England, saying she was horrified to find that the Supreme Court was controlled by the Communists and, of course, the Communists were controlled by the Eastern European Jews. Such nonsense, such ignorance is really vicious.

One hears it said, of course, that at present in the South the accusation of communisim is rather loosely bandied about and covers whatever you happen not to like. Not knowing, however, that the Jewish communities of Eastern Europe are constantly trying to get away from those Soviet-controlled countries because they do not have security or equality of opportunity makes the accusation of their influence in communism and adherence to it a show of complete ignorance of the situation as it really exists. If any people have a reason for disliking communism, it is the Jews.

When unthinking emotions are aroused, we usually find that whatever prejudices are held are channeled by the emotions into expressions that have nothing to do with reality but simply are an outlet for the prejudices.

Years ago, in the South, I can remember my husband telling me when he took to Warm Springs the first nurse who had been trained in physiotherapy and had worked for the State of New York, that he hardly dared mention the fact that she happened to be a Roman Catholic. He hoped—before anyone discovered this fact—that her kindliness of spirit, her skill and her helpfulness would have won a place among the neighbors where she was going to work.

He was right, but he could not help being amused when an old man came to see him and said: "Miss——is such a good woman. But I thought when I heard she was a Roman Catholic she ought to have horns and a tail!"

This attitude has worn off somewhat, but in

certain areas, such as where the author of the letter I have mentioned comes from, one can still find astounding beliefs about the Roman Catholics and the Jews.

There is a general lack of knowledge, too, about what communism is and how much influence it may have in our country. And the emotional reaction to a Supreme Court decision, such as we are witnessing, seems to me to be the product of an unwillingness to read with care what is actually said and an unwillingness to look at the Constitution and reread the First Amendment.

I thought the President's comment was one of the very best. The Constitution does not specify that we are not to be a religious people; it gives us the right to be religious in our own way, and it places upon us the responsibility for the observance of our religion. When the President said that he hoped this decision would make us think more of religion and our observance individually and at home, he emphasized a fact which I think it would be well for all of us to think about.

Real religion is displayed in the way we live in our day-by-day activities at home, in our own communities, and with our own families and neighbors. The Supreme Court emphasized that we must not curtail our freedom as safeguarded under the First Article of the Constitution.

❧ That Problem That Has No Name

BETTY FRIEDAN

The feminist movement of the 1960s represented perhaps the most profound changes in American society. Betty Friedan was on the forefront of women's liberation. In her groundbreaking book *The Feminine Mystique,* Friedan challenged the fallacy of universal contentment among suburban wives.

Raised in Peoria, Illinois, and a graduate of Smith College, Frieden had married and settled into her role as a wife and mother outside of New York City. In the 1950s, she occasionally wrote articles for women's magazines.

In 1957, she was asked to do a fifteenth-anniversary report on her graduating class from Smith. She went interviewing former classmates and was startled by the widespread discontent and frustration with their roles in society. Unfulfilled and isolated, the women were dissatisfied with their lives. Thinking that she had discovered a great article to write, she submitted proposals to women's magazines, all of which rejected it outright.

Furious at the response, she determined to write a book. *The Feminine Mystique* was published in 1963. It sold 3 million copies and became the defining document of the feminist movement.

The problem lay buried, unspoken, for many years in the minds of American women. It was a strange stirring, a sense of dissatisfaction, a yearning that women suffered in the middle of the twentieth century in the United States. Each suburban wife struggled with it alone. As she made the beds, shopped for groceries, matched slipcover material, ate peanut butter sandwiches with her children, chauffeured Cub Scouts and Brownies, lay beside her husband at night—she was afraid to ask even of herself the silent question—"Is this all?"

For over fifteen years there was no word of this yearning in the millions of words written about women, for women, in all the columns, books and articles by experts telling women their role was to seek fulfillment as wives and mothers. Over and over women heard in voices of tradition and of Freudian sophistication that they could desire no greater destiny than to glory in their own femininity. Experts told them how to catch a man and keep him, how to breastfeed children and handle their toilet training, how to cope with sibling rivalry and adolescent rebellion; how to buy a dishwasher, bake bread, cook gourmet snails, and build a swimming pool with their own hands; how to dress, look, and act more feminine and make marriage more exciting; how to keep their husbands from dying young and their sons from growing into delinquents. They were taught to pity the neurotic, unfeminine, unhappy women who wanted to be poets or physicists or presidents. They learned that truly feminine women do not want careers, higher education, political rights—the independence and the opportunities that the old-fashioned feminists fought for. Some women, in their forties and fifties, still remembered painfully giving up those dreams, but most of the younger women no longer even thought about them. A thousand expert voices applauded their femininity, their adjustment, their new maturity. All they had to do was devote their lives from earliest girlhood to finding a husband and bearing children.

By the end of the nineteen-fifties, the average marriage age of women in America dropped to 20, and was still dropping, into the teens. Fourteen million girls were engaged by 17. The proportion of women attending college in comparison with men dropped from 47 percent in 1920 to 35 percent in 1958. A century earlier, women had fought for higher education; now girls went to college to get a husband. By the mid-fifties, 60 percent dropped out of college to marry, or because they were afraid too much education would be a marriage bar. Colleges built dormitories for "married students," but the students were almost always the husbands. A new degree was instituted for the wives—"Ph.T." (Putting Husband Through).

The American girls began getting married in high school. And the women's magazines, deploring the unhappy statistics about these young marriages, urged that courses on marriage, and marriage counselors, be installed in the high schools. Girls started going steady at twelve and thirteen, in junior high. Manufacturers put out brassieres with false bosoms of foam rubber for little girls of ten. And an advertisement for a child's dress, sizes 3-6x, in the *New York Times* in the fall of 1960, said: "She Too Can Join the Man-Trap Set."

By the end of the fifties, the United States birthrate was overtaking India's. The birth-control movement, renamed Planned Parenthood, was asked to find a method whereby women who had been advised that a third or fourth baby would be born dead or defective might have it anyhow. Statisticians were especially astounded at the fantastic increase in the number of babies among college women. Where once they had two children, now they had four, five, six. Women who had once wanted careers were now making careers out of having babies. So rejoiced *Life* magazine in a 1956 paean to the movement of American women back to the home.

In a New York hospital, a woman had a nervous breakdown when she found she could not breastfeed her baby. In other hospitals, women dying of cancer refused a drug which research had proved might save their lives: its side effects were said to be unfeminine. "If I have only one life, let me live it as a blonde," a larger-than-life-sized picture of a pretty, vacuous woman proclaimed from a newspaper, magazine, and drugstore ads. And across America, three out of every ten women dyed their hair blonde. They ate a chalk called Metrecal, instead of food, to shrink to the size of the thin young models. Department-store buyers reported that American women, since 1939, had become

three and four sizes smaller. "Women are out to fit the clothes, instead of vice-versa," one buyer said.

Interior decorators were designing kitchens with mosaic murals and original paintings, for kitchens were once again the center of women's lives. Home sewing became a million-dollar industry. Many women no longer left their homes, except to shop, chauffeur their children, or attend a social engagement with their husbands. Girls were growing up in America without ever having jobs outside the home. In the late fifties, a sociological phenomenon was suddenly remarked: a third of American women now worked, but most were no longer young and a very few were pursuing careers. They were married women who held part-time jobs, selling or secretarial, to put their husbands through school, their sons through college, or to help pay the mortgage. Or they were widows supporting families. Fewer and fewer women were entering professional work. The shortages in the nursing, social work, and teaching professions caused crises in almost every American city. Concerned over the Soviet Union's lead in the space rate, scientists noted that America's greatest source of unused brainpower was women. But girls would not study physics: it was "unfeminine." A girl refused a science fellowship at Johns Hopkins to take a job in a real-estate office. All she wanted, she said, was what every other American girl wanted—to get married, have four children and live in a nice house in a nice suburb.

The suburban housewife—she was the dream image of the young American women and the envy, it was said, of women all over the world. The American housewife—freed by science and labor-saving appliances from the drudgery, the dangers of childbirth and the illnesses of her grandmother. She was healthy, beautiful, educated, concerned only about her husband, her children, her home. She had found true feminine fulfillment. As a housewife and mother, she was respected as a full and equal partner to man in his world. She was free to choose automobiles, clothes, appliances, supermarkets; she had everything that women everywhere dreamed of.

In the fifteen years after World War II, this mystique of feminine fulfillment became the cherished and self-perpetuating core of contemporary American culture. Millions of women lived their lives in the image of those pretty pictures of the

American suburban housewife, kissing their husbands goodbye in front of the picture window, depositing their stationwagonsful of children at school, and smiling as they ran the new electric waxer over the spotless kitchen floor. They baked their own bread, sewed their own and their children's clothes, kept their new washing machines and dryers running all day. They changed the sheets on the beds twice a week instead of once, took the rug-hooking class in adult education, and pitied their poor frustrated mothers, who had dreamed of having a career. Their only dream was to be perfect wives and mothers; their highest ambition to have five children and a beautiful house, their only fight to get and keep their husbands. They had no thought for the unfeminine problems of the world outside the home; they wanted the men to make the major decisions. They gloried in their role as women, and wrote proudly on the census blank: "Occupation: housewife."

For over fifteen years, the words written for women, and the words women used when they talked to each other, while their husbands sat on the other side of the room and talked shop or politics or septic tanks, were about problems with children, or how to keep their husbands, happy, or improve their children's school, or cook chicken or make slipcovers. Nobody argued whether women were inferior or superior to men; they were simply different. Words like "emancipation" and "career" sounded strange and embarrassing; no one had used them for years. When a Frenchwoman named Simone de Beauvoir wrote a book called *The Second Sex*, an American critic commented that she obviously "didn't know what life was all about," and besides, she was talking about French women. The "women problem" in American no longer existed.

If a woman had a problem in the 1950's and 1960's, she knew that something must be wrong with her marriage, or with herself. Other women were satisfied with their lives, she thought. What kind of a woman was she if she did not feel this mysterious fulfillment waxing the kitchen floor? She was so ashamed to admit her dissatisfaction that she never knew how many other women shared it. If she tried to tell her husband, he didn't understand what she was talking about. She did not really understand it herself. For over fifteen years women in America found it harder to talk about this problem than about sex. Even the psychoanalysts had no name for it. When a woman went to a psychiatrist for help, as many women did, she would say, "I'm so ashamed," or "I must be hopelessly neurotic." "I don't know what's wrong with women today," a suburban psychiatrist said uneasily. "I only know something is wrong because most of my patients happen to be women. And their problem isn't sexual." Most women with this problem did not go to see a psychoanalyst, however, "There's nothing wrong really," they kept telling themselves. "There isn't any problem."

But on April morning in 1959, I heard a mother of four, having coffee with four other mothers in a suburban development fifteen miles from New York, say in a tone of quiet desperation, "the problem." And the others knew, without words, that she was not talking about a problem with her husband, or her children, or her home. Suddenly they realized they all shared the same problem, the problem that has no name. They began, hesitantly, to talk about it. Later, after they picked up their children at nursery school and taken them home to nap, two of the women cried, in sheer relief, just to know they were not alone.

"Hippity-hop, I'm a Bunny"

GLORIA STEINEM

Hugh Hefner introduced *Playboy* magazine, featuring photographs of partially (and later completely) nude women, in 1953. It was an instant success. Hefner soon expanded his operations to include Playboy Clubs in which scantily clad waitresses, called Playboy Bunnies, served patrons.

In 1963, Gloria Steinem took a job as a Playboy bunny for a magazine article she planned to write. The article "I Was a Playboy Bunny" caused an instant sensation, and not necessarily positive for Steinem, who was subsequently harassed for writing the piece. Nonetheless, Steinem's account represented one of the first successful attempts by women to express the frustration and humiliation of their diminished position in society.

Twenty years after her experience, Steinem wrote that the experience made her "realize that all women are Bunnies. Since feminism, I've finally stopped regretting that I wrote this article."

I undertook a reporting assignment armed with a large diary and this ad:

"GIRLS:
Do Playboy Club Bunnies Really
Have Glamorous Jobs,
Meet Celebrities, And
Make Top Money?

Yes, it's true! Attractive young girls can now earn $200-$300 a week at the fabulous New York Playboy Club, enjoy the glamorous and exciting aura of show business, and have the opportunity to travel to other Playboy Clubs throughout the world. Whether serving drinks, snapping pictures, or greeting guests at the door, the Playboy Club is the stage—the Bunnies are the stars.

The charm and beauty of our Bunnies has been extolled in Time, Newsweek, and Pageant, and Ed Sullivan has called The Playboy Club '...the greatest new show biz gimmick.' And the Playboy Club is now the busiest spot in New York.

If you are pretty and personable, between 21 and 24, married or single, you probably qualify. No experience necessary.

Apply in person at SPECIAL INTERVIEWS being held Saturday and Sunday, January 26-27, 10 am-3 pm. Please bring a swimsuit and leotards.

THE PLAYBOY CLUB
5 East 59th Street"

Thursday, January 24th, 1963

I've decided to call myself Marie Catherine Ochs. It is, may my ancestors forgive me, a family name. I have some claim to it, and I'm well versed in its European origins. Besides, it sounds much too square to be phony.

Friday 25th

I've spent the entire afternoon making up a background for Marie. She shares my apartment, my phone, and my measurements. Though younger than I by four years (I was beyond the Bunny age limit), Marie celebrates the same birthday and went to the same high school and college. But she wasn't a slave to academics—not Marie. After one year she left me plodding along the path to a B.A. and boarded a tourist flight to Europe. She had no money, but short periods as a waitress in London, a hostess-dancer in Paris, and a secretary in Geneva were enough to sustain her between beachcombing and other escapades. Last year, she came back to New York and worked briefly as a secretary. Three mutual friends have agreed to give her strong per-

sonal recommendations. To know her is to love her.

Tomorrow is the day. Marie makes her first trip out of this notebook and into the world. I'm off to buy her a leotard....

Wednesday 30th

I arrived at the club promptly at 6:30, and business appeared to be booming. Customers were lined up in the snow to get in, and several passersby were standing outside with their faces pressed to the glass. The elevator boy, a Valentino-handsome Puerto Rican, cheerfully jammed me in his car with two uniformed black porters, five middle-aged male customers, two costumed Bunnies, and a stout matron in a mink coat. We stopped at the sixth floor. "Is this where I get out?" said the matron.

"Sure, darling," drawled the elevator boy, "if you want to be a Bunny." Laughter.

I looked around me. Dim lights and soft carpets had given way to unpainted cement blocks and hanging light bulbs. There was a door marked UNNIES; I could see the outlines where the B had been. A sign, hand-written on a piece of torn cardboard, was taped underneath: KNOCK!! Come on, guys. Please cooperate?!! I walked through the door and into a bright, crowded hallway.

Two girls brushed past me. One was wearing nothing but bikini-style panties; the other had on long black tights of fine mesh, and lavender satin heels. They both rushed to a small wardrobe room on my right, yelled out their names, collected costumes, and rushed back. I asked the wardrobe mistress for Miss Burgess. "Honey, we just gave her a going-away present." Four more girls bounced up to ask for costumes, collars, cuffs and tails. They had on tights and high heels but nothing from the waist up. One stopped to study a bulletin-board list titled "Bunny of the Week."

I retreated to the other end of the tiny hall. I opened into a large dressing room filled with metal lockers and long rows of dressing tables. Personal notes were taped to the mirrors ("Anybody want to work B Level Saturday night?" and "I'm having a swingin' party Wednesday at Washington Square Village, all Bunnies welcome..."). Cosmetics were strewn along the counters, and three girls sat in a row applying false eyelashes with the concentration of yogis. It looked like a cartoon of a chorus girls' dressing room.

A girl with very red hair, very red skin, and a

black satin Bunny costume turned her back to me and waited. I understood that I was supposed to zip her up, a task that took several minutes of pulling and tugging. She was a big girl and looked a little tough, but her voice when she thanked me was tiny and babylike. Judy Holliday could not have done better. I asked her about Miss Burgess. "Yeah, she's in that office," said Baby Voice, gesturing toward a wooden door with a glass peephole in it, "but Sheralee's the new Bunny Mother." Through the glass, I could see two girls, a blonde and a brunette. Both appeared to be in their early twenties and nothing like the matronly woman pictured in the brochure. Baby Voice tugged and pulled some more. "This isn't my costume," she explained, "that's why it's hard to get the crotch up." She walked away, snapping her fingers and humming softly.

The brunette came out of the office and introduced herself to me as Bunny Mother Sheralee. I told her I had mistaken her for a Bunny. "I worked as a Bunny when the club opened last month," she said, "but now I've replaced Miss Burgess." She nodded toward the blond who was trying on a three-piece beige suit that I took to be her going-away present. "You'll have to wait a while honey," said Sheralee. I sat down.

By 7:00 I had watched three girls tease their hair into cotton-candy shapes and four more stuff their bosoms with Kleenex. By 7:15 I had talked to two other prospective Bunnies, one a dancer, the other a part-time model from Texas. At 7:30, I witnessed the major crises of a Bunny who had sent her costume to the cleaners with her engagement ring pinned inside. At 7:40, Miss Shay came up to the office and said, "There's no one left but Marie." By 8:00, I was sure that she was waiting for the manager of the club to come tell me that my real identity had been uncovered. By 8:15, when I was finally called in, I was nervous beyond all proportion.

I waited while Sheralee looked over my application. "You don't look twenty-four," she said. Well, that's that, I thought. "You look much younger." I smiled in disbelief. She took several Polaroid pictures of me. "For the record," she explained. I offered her the personal history I had so mistakenly fabricated and typed, but she gave it back with hardly a glance. "We don't like our girls to have any background," she said firmly. "We just

want you to fit the Bunny image." She directed me to the costume room.

I asked if I should put on my leotard.

"Don't bother with that," said Sheralee. "We just want to see that Bunny image."

The wardrobe mistress told me to take off my clothes and began to search for an old Bunny costume in my size. A girl rushed in with her costume in her hand, calling for the wardrobe mistress as a wounded soldier might yell, "Medic! I've broken my zipper," she wailed, "I sneezed!"

"That's the third time this week," said the wardrobe mistress sternly. "It's a regular epidemic." The girl apologized, found another costume, and left.

I asked if a sneeze could really break a costume.

"Sure" she said. "Girls with colds usually have to be replaced."

She gave me a bright blue satin. It was so tight that the zipper caught my skin as she fastened the back. She told me to inhale as she zipped again, this time without mishap, and stood back to look at me critically. The bottom was cut up so high that it left my hip bones exposed as well as a good five inches of untanned derriere. The boning in the waist would have made Scarlet O'Hara blanch, and the entire construction tended to push all available flesh up to the bosom. I was sure it would be perilous to bend over. "Not too bad," said the wardrobe mistress, and began to stuff an entire plastic dry-cleaning bag into the top of my costume. A blue satin band with matching Bunny ears attached was fitted around my head like an enlarged bicycle clip, and a grapefruit-sized hemisphere of white fluff was attached to hooks at the costume's rear-most point. "Okay, baby," she said, "put on your high heels and go show Sheralee." I looked in the mirror. The Bunny image looked back.

"Oh, you look sweet," said Sheralee. "Stand against the wall and smile pretty for the birdie." She took several more Polaroid shots.

The baby-voiced redhead came in to say she still hadn't found a costume to fit. A tiny blond in lavender satin took off her tail and perched on the desk. "Look," she said, "I don't mind the demerits—okay, I got five demerits—but don't I get points for working overtime?"

Sheralee looked harassed and turned to Miss Burgess. "The new kids think the girls from Chicago get special treatment, and the old kids won't train the new ones."

"I'll train the little buggers," said Baby Voice. "Just get me a costume."

I got dressed and waited. And listened:

"…he gave me thirty bucks, and I only got him cigarettes."

"Bend over, honey, and get yourself into it."

"I don't know, he makes Milk of Magnesia or something."

"You know people commit suicide with those plastic bags?"

"Then this schmuck orders a Lace Curtain. Whoever heard of a Lace Curtain?"

"I told him our tails were asbestos, so he tried to burn it to find out."

"Last week I netted thirty buck in tips. Big deal."

Sheralee called me back into the office. "So you want to be a Bunny," she said.

"Oh yes, very much," I said.

"Well…" —she paused significantly—"we want you to be!" I was startled. No more interviews? No investigation? "Come in tomorrow at three. We'll fit your costume and have you sign everything." I smiled and felt foolishly elated.

Down the stairs and up Fifth Avenue. Hippity-hop, I'm a Bunny!…

Evening, Tuesday 5th

The Bunny Room was chaotic. I was pushed and tugged and zipped into my electric-blue costume by the wardrobe mistress, but this time she allowed me to stuff my own bosom, and I was able to get away with only half a dry cleaner's bag. I added the tiny collar with clip on bow tie and the starched cuffs with Playboy cuff links. My nameplate was centered in a ribbon rosette like those won in horse shows, and pinned just above my bare right hipbone. A major policy change, I was told, had just shifted name tags from left hip to right. The wardrobe mistress also gave me a Bunny jacket: it was a below-zero night, and I was to stand by the front door. The jacket turned out to be a brief shrug of imitation white fur that covered the shoulders but left the bosom carefully bare.

I went in to be inspected by Bunny Mother Sheralee. "You look sweet", she said, and advised that I keep any money I had with me in my costume. "Two more girls have had things stolen from their lockers." She said, and added that I should be sure and tell the lobby director the exact amount of money I had with me. "Otherwise they may think you stole tips." Table Bunnies, she explained, were allowed to keep any tips they might receive in cash (though the club did take up to 50 percent of all their charge tips), but hat-check Bunnies could keep no tips at all. Instead, they were paid a flat twelve dollars for eight hours. I told her that twelve dollars a day seemed a good deal less than the salary of two to three hundred dollars mentioned in the advertisement. "Well, you won't work hat check all the time, sweetie." She said. "When you start working as a table Bunny, you'll see how it all averages out."

I took a last look at myself in the mirror. A creature with three-quarter inch eyelashes, blue satin ears, and an overflowing bosom looked back. I asked Sheralee if we had to stuff ourselves so much. "Of course you do," she said. "Practically all the girls just stuff and stuff. That's the way Bunnies are supposed to look."

The elevator opened on the mezzanine, and I made my professional debut in the Playboy Club. It was crowded, noisy and very dark. A group of men with organizational name tags on their lapels stood nearby. "Here's my Bunny honey now," said one, and flung his arm around my shoulders as if we were fellow halfbacks leaving the field.

"Please, sir," I said, and uttered the ritual sentence we had learned from the Bunny Father lecture: "You are not allowed to touch the Bunnies." His companions laughed and laughed. "Boy oh boy, guess she told you!" said one, and tweaked my tail as I walked away.

The programmed phrases of the Bunny bible echoing in my mind, I climbed down the carpeted spiral stairs between the mezzanine ("Living Room Piano Bar, buffet dinner now being served") and the lobby ("Check your coats; immediate seating in the Playmate Bar"), separated from the street by only a two-story sheet of glass. The alternative was a broad staircase in the back of the lobby, but that, too, could be seen from the street. All of us, customers and Bunnies alike, were a living window display. I reported to the lobby director. "Hello, Bunny Marie," he said. "How's things?" I told him that I had fifteen dollars in my costume. "I'll remember," he said. I had a quick and humiliating vision of all the hat-check Bunnies lined up for inspection.

There was a four-deep crowd of impatient men surrounding the Hat Check Room. The head hat-check Bunny, a little blonde who had been imported from Chicago to straighten out the system, told me to take their tickets and call the numbers out to two "hang boys" behind the counter. "I'll give you my number if you give me yours," said a balding man, and turned to the crowd for appreciation....

Friday 22nd

...It was four in the morning. I went to the Bunny Room and took off my costume. A pretty blonde was putting chairs together to sleep on. She had promised to take another girl's lunch shift after her regular eight hours in the Playmate Bar, and there wasn't time to go home in between. I asked why she did it.

"Well," she said, "the money's not too bad. Last week I made two hundred dollars."

At last I had found a girl who made at least the low end of the promised salary—but only by working round the clock.

In Sheralee's office, pinned to the bulletin board, was a list of cities next in line for Playboy Clubs (Pittsburgh, Boston, Dallas, and Washington D.C.) and a yellow printed sheet titled WHAT IS A BUNNY?

"A Bunny," began the text, "like the Playboy Playmate, is...beautiful, desirable.... We'll do everything in our power to make you—the Bunny—the most envied girl in America, working in the most exciting and glamorous setting in the world."

I turned in my costume for the last time. "So long, honey," said the blonde. "See you in the funnies."

❧ "We hereby constitute ourselves as the National Organization for Women"

THE NATIONAL ORGANIZATION FOR WOMEN

In June 1966, Betty Friedan and other activists sharply criticized the Equal Employment Opportunity Commission for its lack of zeal in enforcing the sex-discrimination clause of the Civil Rights Act of 1964. Rebuffed in their attempts to stimulate action, Friedan and twenty-seven other women decided to form their own organization to advocate for women's rights.

At its founding conference in 1966 in Washington, D.C., the National Organization for Women issued its statement of purpose emphasizing job opportunities. One year later, the agenda had broadened to include sweeping reforms of a wide spectrum of issues. It adopted a Bill of Rights articulating eight demands ranging from the need for child-care centers to the legalization of abortion.

NOW quickly became the leading and largest organization in the feminist movement. Thirty years after issuing the statements, many of the demands have been widely accepted.

Statement of Purpose

We, men and women who hereby constitute ourselves as the National Organization for Women, believe that the time has come for a new movement toward true equality for all women in America, and toward a fully equal partnership of the sexes, as part of the world-wide revolution of human rights now taking place within and beyond our national borders....

We reject the current assumption that a man must carry the sole burden of supporting himself, his wife, and family, and that a woman is automatically entitled to lifelong support by a man upon her marriage, or that marriage, home and family are primarily women's world and responsibility—hers, to dominate—his, to support. We believe that a true partnership between the sexes demands a different concept of marriage, an equitable sharing of the responsibilities of home and children and of the economic burdens of their support....

In the interests of the human dignity of women, we will protest, and endeavor to change, the false image of women now prevalent in the mass media, and in the texts, ceremonies, laws, and practices of the major social institutions. Such images perpetuate contempt for women by society and by women for themselves....we believe that women will do most to create a new image of women by acting now, and by speaking out in behalf of their own equality, freedom, and human dignity—not in pleas for special privilege, nor in enmity toward men, who are also victims of the current, half-equality between the sexes—but in an active, self-respecting partnership with men.

NOW Bill of Rights

Equal Rights Constitutional Amendment
    Enforce Laws Banning Sex Discrimination in

Employment
      Maternity Leave Rights in Employment and in
Social Security Benefits
      Tax Deduction for Home and Child Care
Expenses for Working Parents
      Child Day Care Centers
      Equal and Unsegregated Education
      Equal Job Training Opportunities and
Allowances for Women in Poverty
      The Right of Women to Control Their
Reproductive Lives

We Demand:
      That the U.S. Congress immediately pass the
Equal Rights Amendment to the Constitution to
provide that "Equality of rights under the law shall
not be denied or abridged by the United States or by
any state on account of sex," and such then be immediately ratified by the several states.
      That equal employment opportunity be guar-
anteed to all women, as well as men, by insisting
that the Equal Employment Opportunity
Commission enforces the prohibitions against racial
discrimination.
      That women be protected by law to ensure
their rights to return to their jobs within a reasonable time after childbirth without loss of seniority
or other accrued benefits, and be paid maternity
leave as a form of social security and/or employee
benefit.
      Immediate revision of tax laws to permit the
deduction of home and child-care expenses for
working parents.
      That child-care facilities be established by law
on the same basis as parks, libraries, and public
schools, adequate to the needs of children from the
pre-school years through adolescence, as a community resource to be used by all citizens from all
income levels.
      That the right of women to be educated to
their full potential equally with men be secured by
federal and state legislation, eliminating all discrimination and segregation by sex, written and
unwritten, at all levels of education, including colleges, graduate and professional schools, loans and
fellowships, and federal and state training programs
such as the Job Corps.
      The right of women in poverty to secure job
training, housing, and family allowances on equal
terms with men, but without prejudice to a parent's

right to remain at home to care for his or her children; revision of welfare legislation and poverty
programs which deny women dignity, privacy, and
self-respect.
      The right of women to control their own
reproductive lives by removing from the penal code
laws limiting access to contraceptive information
and devices, and by repealing penal laws governing
abortion.

✒ *Miranda v. Arizona: "The right to remain silent"*

SUPREME COURT JUSTICE EARL WARREN

The Supreme Court ruled in 1966 that anyone arrested and
charged with a crime must be notified of his or her rights,
thus assuring citizens of their Fifth and Sixth Amendment
rights. The decision came out of the court case *Miranda v.
Arizona* in which Ernest Miranda was arrested for the 1963
kidnapping and rape of young woman in Phoenix, Arizona.
      Miranda was convicted and sentenced to 20 years in jail
based on a confession he made to police after a two-hour
interrogation. He was not offered the opportunity to consult a
lawyer. The Supreme Court determined that Miranda's Fifth
Amendment right against self-incrimination was denied, as
was the Sixth Amendment guarantee of assistance of counsel. A retrial was ordered. Again, Miranda was found guilty
and sentenced to 20 years in prison.

The cases before us raise questions which go to the
roots of our concepts of American criminal jurispru-
dence: the restraints society must observe consistent
with the Federal Constitution in persecuting individuals for crime. More specifically, we deal with
the admissability of statements obtained from an
individual who is subjected to custodial police interrogation and the necessity for procedures which
assure that the individual is accorded his privilege
under the Fifth Amendment to the Constitution
not to be compelled to incriminate himself....
      It is obvious that [the police] interrogation
environment is created for no purpose other than
to subjugate the individual to the will of his exam-
iner. This atmosphere carries its own badge of
intimidation. To be sure, this is not physical intimidation, but it is equally destructive to human digni-

ty. The current practice of incommunicado interrogation is at odds with one of our Nation's most cherished principles—that the individual may not be compelled to incriminate himself. Unless adequate protective devices are employed to dispel the compulsion inherent in custodial surroundings, no statement obtained from the defendant can truly be the product of his free choice....

At the outset, if a person in custody is to be subjected to interrogation, he must first be informed in clear and unequivocal terms that he has the right to remain silent....

In order fully to apprise a person interrogated of the extent of his rights under this [judicial] system then, it is necessary to warn him not only that he has the right to consult with an attorney, but also that if he is indigent a lawyer will be appointed to represent him....

To summarize, we hold that when an individual is taken into custody or otherwise deprived of his freedom by the authorities in any significant way and is subjected to questioning, the privilege against self-incrimination is jeopardized. Procedural safeguards must be employed to protect the privilege, and unless other fully effective means are adopted to notify the person of his right of silence and to assure that the exercise of the right will be scrupulously honored, the following measures are required. He must be warned prior to any questioning that he has the right to remain silent, that anything he says can be used against him in a court of law, that he has the right to the presence of an attorney, and that if he cannot afford an attorney one will be appointed for him prior to any questioning if he so desires. Opportunity to exercise these rights must be afforded to him throughout the interrogation. After such warnings have been given, and such opportunity afforded him, the individual may knowingly and intelligently waive these rights and agree to answer questions or make a statement. But unless and until such warnings and waiver are demonstrated by the prosecution at trial, no evidence obtained as a result of interrogation can be used against him.

🐝 "Dissent is the great problem of America today"

DANIEL J. BOORSTIN

Daniel J. Boorstin is one of the leading historians and scholars of the late twentieth century. The winner of the Pulitzer Prize and librarian of Congress, he has been a keen commentator on American history and contemporary trends. Among other things, he originated the term "pseudo-event" to describe the tendency among American politicians and media to celebrate celebrity and not substance.

On October 13, 1967, he addressed the managing editors of the Associated Press in Chicago. Civil rights, Vietnam, the counter-culture and a wide variety of other movements were dividing the country into different camps. With that as a backdrop, Boorstin identified the deterioration of disagreement into dissent as a self-fulfilling recipe for division. He explored the role of the ascending media in that cycle of division. And though the crises of the 1960s quieted with time, the media's role in accentuating the differences has only grown with time.

This afternoon I would like to talk briefly about the problems we share, we historians and newspapermen, and that we all share as Americans.

About sixty years ago Mark Twain, who was an expert on such matters, said there are only two forces that carry light to all corners of the globe, the sun in the heaven and the Associated Press. This is, of course, not the only view of your role. Another newspaperman once said it's the duty of a newspaper to comfort the afflicted and afflict the comfortable.

If there ever was a time when the light and the comfort which you can give us was needed, it's today. And I would like to focus on one problem.

It seems to me that dissent is the great problem of America today. It overshadows all others. It's a symptom, an expression, a consequence, and a cause of all others.

I say dissent and not disagreement. And it is the distinction between dissent and disagreement which I really want to make. Disagreement produces debate, but dissent produces dissension. "Dissent," which comes from the Latin, means originally to feel apart from others.

People who disagree have an argument, but people who dissent have a quarrel. People may disagree but may both count themselves in the majority, but a person who dissents is by definition in a minority. A liberal society thrives on disagreement but is killed by dissension. Disagreement is the lifeblood of democracy; dissension is its cancer.

A debate is an orderly exploration of a common problem that presupposes that the debaters are worried by the same question. It brings to life new facts and new arguments which make possible a better solution. But dissension means discord. As the dictionary tells us, dissension is marked by a break in friendly relations. It is an expression not of a common concern but of hostile feelings. And this distinction is crucial.

Disagreement is specific and programmatic; dissent is formless and unfocused. Disagreement is concerned with policy; dissenters are concerned with identity, which usually means themselves. Disagreers ask, What about the war in Vietnam? Dissenters ask, What about me? Disagreers seek solutions to common problems; dissenters seek power for themselves.

The spirit of dissent stalks our land. It seeks the dignity and privilege of disagreement, but is entitled to neither. All over the country on more and more subjects, we hear more and more people quarreling and fewer and fewer people debating. How has this happened? What can and should we do about it?…

The profession which you gentlemen represent together with the American standard of living leads us also towards the exaggeration of the importance of dissent in our society. Since dissent is more dramatic and more newsworthy than agreement, media inevitably multiply and emphasize dissent. It is an easier job to make a news story of men who are fighting with one another than it is to describe their peaceful living together.

All this has been reinforced by certain obvious developments in the history of the newspaper and the other media within the last half century or so— the increasingly frequent and repetitious news reporting. The movement from the weekly newspaper to the daily newspaper to several editions a day, the rise of radio reporting of news every hour on the hour with news breaks in between, all require that there be changes to report. There are increasingly voluminous spaces both of time and of print which have to be filled.

And all these reports become more and more inescapable from the attention of the average citizen. In the bar, on the beach, in the automobile, the transistor radio reminds us of the headaches of our society. Moreover, the increasing vividness of reports also tempts us to depict objects and people in motion, changing, disputing. The opportunity to show people in motion, changing, disputing. The opportunity to show people in motion and to show them vividly had its beginning, of course, in the rise of photography and Mathew Brady's pioneer work in the Civil War and then more recently with the growth of the motion picture and television. All this tempts us to get a dramatic shot of a policeman striking a rioter or vice versa. We now have tape recorders on the scene to which people can express their complaints about anything.

Moreover, the rise of opinion is a new category. The growth of opinion polling has led to the very concept of "opinion" as something people can learn about. There was a time when information about the world was divided into the category of fact or the category of idea. But more recently, especially with the growth of market research in this century, people now must have opinions. They are led to believe by the publication of opinion polls that their opinion—whether it be on the subject of miniskirts or marijuana or foreign policy—is something that separates them from others. Moreover, if they have no opinion, even that now puts them in a dissenting category….

Moreover, the very character of American history has accentuated our tendency to dissent. We are an immigrant society. We are made up of many different groups who came here and who felt separate from one another, who were separated not so much by doctrine or belief as by the minutiae of daily life. By language, religious practices, cuisine, and even manners. Until the 1930s and 1940s, the predominant aim of those who were most concerned with the problem of immigration was to restrict immigration or to assimilate those immigrants who were admitted. To "Americanize the immigrant"—this was the motto of those who were most concerned with this question.

But in the last few decades we have had a movement from "assimilation" to "integration." And this is an important distinction. In about the 1930s Louis Adamic began writing, and, in his book *A Nation of Nations* in 1945 he began an emphasis which has often been repeated. It was no longer the right of the immigrant to be

Americanized, to be assimilated; it was now the right of the immigrant to remain different. The ideal ceased to be that of fitting into the total society and instead became the right to retain your differences....

I find in this world today, in this country a growing belief in the intrinsic virtue of dissent. It's worth noting that some of the greatest American champions of the right to disagree to express disagreement—Thomas Jefferson, Oliver Wendell Holmes, Jr., William James, John Dewey, and others—were also great believers in the duty of the community to peacefully be governed by the will of the majority. But more recently dissent itself has been made into a virtue. Dissent for dissent's sake....

Professional dissenters do not, cannot seek to assimilate their program or ideals into American culture. Their main object is to preserve their separate identity as a dissenting minority. They're not interested in the freedom of anybody else. The motto of this group might be an emendation of the old maxim of Voltaire which I'm sure you've all heard. But nowadays people would say, "I do not agree with a word you say. And I will defend to the death my right to say so."

Once upon a time our intellectuals competed for their claim to be spokesmen of the community. Now the time has almost arrived when the easiest way to insult an intellectual is to tell him that you or most other people agree with him. The way to menace him is to put him in the majority, for the majority must run things and must have a program, and dissent needs no program.

Dissent, then, has tended to become the conformity of our most educated classes. In many circles to be an outspoken conformist, that is, to say that the prevailing ways of the community are not "evil," requires more courage than to run with the dissenting pack.

The conformity of nonconformity, the conformity of dissent produces little that is fruitful in its conclusions and very little effective discussion or internal debate. For the simple reason that it does not involve anybody in attacking or defending the program. Programs, after all, are the signs of "the establishment."...

The affirmations of differentness and feeling apart cannot hold a society together. In fact, these tend to destroy the institutions which make fertile disagreement possible, and fertile institutions decent. A sniper's bullet is an eloquent expression of dissent, of feeling apart. It doesn't express disagreement. It is formless, inarticulate, unproductive. A society of disagreers is a free and fertile and productive society. A society of dissenters is a chaos leading only to dissension.

Now I would like in conclusion to suggest that we are led to a paradox. A paradox that must be solved. A free and literate society with a high standard of living and increasingly varied media, one that reaches more and more people more and more of the time—such a society finds it always easier to dramatize its dissent rather than disagreement. It finds it harder and harder to discover, much less to dramatize, its agreement on anything. This ends then in some questions which I will pose to you gentlemen to which I hope you may have answers. At least they seem to me to be crucial ones.

First, is it possible to produce interesting newspapers that will sell but which do not dramatize or capitalize on or catalyze dissent and dissension, the feeling of apartness in the community? Is it possible to produce interesting newspapers that will sell but which do not yield to the temptation to create and nourish new dissent by stirring people to feel apart in new ways?

Second, is it possible at the same time to find new ways of interesting people in disagreement in specific items and problems and programs and specific evils?

Finally, is it possible for our newspapers—without becoming Pollyanas or chauvinists or superpatriots or Good Humor salesmen—to find new ways of expressing and affirming, dramatizing, and illuminating what people agree upon?

This is your challenge. The future of American society in no small measure depends on whether and how you answer it.

"We will protect ourselves...by whatever means necessary"

BLACK PANTHER PARTY PLATFORM

The Black Panther Party was the most well-known militant black political organization to emerge from the increasingly politicized Black Power movement of the 1960s. Aiming to elevate conditions for black Americans, the Black Panthers engaged in both community-building enterprises and vigorous advocacy efforts. Most of the public focus centered on its more radical, and later illegal, activities which eventually undermined the organization.

This October 1966 manifesto reflected the increasing frustration of black Americans at the lack of progress in overcoming racial prejudice, despite the progress being made in the courtroom and with the civil rights reforms. Using the words of the Declaration of Independence, the party tried to demonstrate the hypocrisy of American democracy.

1. We want freedom. We want power to determine the destiny of our Black Community.

We believe that black people will not be free until we are able to determine our destiny.

2. We want full employment for our people.

We believe that the federal government is responsible and obligated to give every man employment or a guaranteed income. We believe that if the white American businessman will not give full employment, then the means of production should be taken from the businessmen and placed in the community so that the people of the community can organize and employ all of its people and give a high standard of living.

3. We want an end to the robbery by the white man of our Black Community.

We believe that this racist government has robbed us and now we are demanding the overdue debt of forty acres and two mules. Forty acres and two mules was promised 100 years ago as restitution for slave labor and mass murder of black people. We will accept the payment in currency which will be distributed to our many communities. The Germans are now aiding the Jews in Israel for the genocide of Jewish people. The Germans murdered six million Jews. The American racist has taken part in the slaughter of over fifty million black people; therefore, we feel that this is a modest demand that we make.

4. We want decent housing, fit for shelter of human beings.

We believe that if the white landlords will not give decent housing to our black community, then the housing and the land should be made into cooperatives so that our community, with government aid, can build and make decent housing for its people.

5. We want education for our people that exposes the true nature of this decadent American society. We want education that teaches us our true history and our role in the present-day society.

We believe in an educational system that will give to our people a knowledge of self. If a man does not have knowledge of himself and his position in society and the world, then he has little chance to relate to anything else.

6. We want all black men to be exempt from military service.

We believe that Black people should not be forced to fight in the military service to defend a racist government that does not protect us. We will not fight and kill other people of color in the world who, like black people, are being victimized by the white racist government of America. We will protect ourselves from the force and violence of the racist police and the racist military, by whatever means necessary.

7. We want an immediate end to POLICE BRUTALITY and MURDER of black people

We believe we can end police brutality in our black community by organizing black self-defense groups that are dedicated to defending our black community from racist police oppression and brutality. The Second Amendment to the Constitution of the United States gives a right to bear arms. We therefore believe that all black people should arm themselves for self-defense.

8. We want freedom for all black men held in federal, state, county and city prisons and jails.

We believe that all black people should be released from the many jails and prisons because they have not received a fair and impartial trial.

9. We want all black people when brought to trial to be tried in court by a jury of their peer group or people from their black communities, as defined by the Constitution of the United States.

We believe that the courts should follow the United States Constitution so that black people will receive fair trials. The 14th Amendment of the

U.S. Constitution gives a man a right to be tried by his peer group. A peer is a person from a similar economic, social, religious, geographical, environmental, historical and racial background. To do this the court will be forced to select a jury from the black community from which the black defendant came. We have been, and are being tried by all-white juries that have no understanding of the "average reasoning man" of the black community.

10. We want land, bread, housing, education, clothing, justice and peace. And as our major political objective, a United Nations-supervised plebiscite to be held throughout the black colony in which only black colonial subjects will be allowed to participate for the purpose of determining the will of black people as to their national destiny.

When, in the course of human events, it becomes necessary for one people to dissolve the political bands which have connected them with another, and to assume, among the powers of the earth, the separate and equal stations to which the laws of nature and nature's God entitle them, a decent respect to the opinions of mankind requires that they should declare the causes which impel them to the separation.

We hold these truths to be self-evident, that all men are created equal; that they are endowed by their Creator with certain unalienable rights; that among these are the life, liberty, and the pursuit of happiness. That, to secure these rights, governments are instituted among men, deriving their just powers from the consent of the governed; that, whenever any form of government becomes destructive of these ends, it is the right of the people to alter or to abolish it, and to institute a new government, laying its foundation on such principles, and organizing its powers in such form, as to them shall seem most likely to effect their safety and happiness. Prudence, indeed, will dictate that governments long established should not be changed for light and transient causes; and, accordingly, all experience hath shown, that mankind are more disposed to suffer, while evils are sufferable, than to right themselves by abolishing the forms to which they are accustomed. But, when a long train of abuses and usurpations, pursuing invariably the same object, evinces a design to reduce them under absolute despotism, it is their right, it is their duty, to throw off such govern-

ment, and to provide new guards for their future security.

🌿 "What is the spirit of 1967?"

EUGENE MCCARTHY

By 1967 criticism of the Vietnam War was mounting. No politician with national standing, however, had taken a stand against American involvement in the Southeast Asian conflict. But on December 2, 1967, Wisconsin Democratic Senator Eugene McCarthy spoke out against the war at the Conference of Concerned Democrats meeting in Chicago.

His speech and his subsequent decision to run against President Lyndon B. Johnson for the Democratic presidential nomination set in motion a sequence of events that raised the political stakes of the war. When McCarthy did far better than expected in Democratic primaries, Johnson announced his decision to not run for re-election. Robert F. Kennedy and Hubert Humphrey entered the race, casting McCarthy to the political sidelines.

In 1952, in this city of Chicago, the Democratic Party nominated as its candidate for the presidency Adlai Stevenson.

His promise to his party and to the people of the country then was that he would talk sense to them....

Under the presidency of John F. Kennedy his ideas were revived in new language and in a new spirit. To the clear sound of the horn was added the beat of a steady and certain drum.

John Kennedy set free the spirit of America. The honest optimism was released. Quiet courage and civility became the mark of American government, and new programs of promise and of dedication were presented: the Peace Corps, the Alliance for Progress, the promise of equal rights for all Americans—and not just the promise but the beginning of the achievements of that promise.

All the world looked to the United States with new hope, for here was youth and confidence and an openness to the future. Here was a country not being held by the dead hand of the past, nor frightened by the violent hand of the future which was grasping at the world.

This was the spirit of 1963.

What is the spirit of 1967? What is the mood of America and of the world toward America today?

It is a joyless spirit—a mood of frustration, of anxiety, of uncertainty.

In place of the enthusiasm of the Peace Corps among the young people of America, we have protests and demonstrations.

In place of the enthusiasm of the Alliance for Progress, we have distrust and disappointment.

Instead of the language of promise and of hope, we have in politics today a new vocabulary in which the critical word is "war": war on poverty, war on ignorance, war on crime, war on pollution. None of these problems can be solved by war but only by persistent, dedicated, and thoughtful attention.

But we do have one war which is properly called a war—the war in Vietnam, which is central to all of the problems of America.

A war of questionable legality and questionable constitutionality.

A war which is diplomatically indefensible; the first war in this century in which the United States, which at its founding made an appeal to the decent opinion of mankind in the Declaration of Independence, finds itself without the support of the decent opinion of mankind.

A war which cannot be defended in the context of the judgment of history. It is being presented in the context of an historical era which is past. Munich appears to be the starting point of history for the secretary of state and for those who attempt to support his policies. What is necessary is a realization that the United States is a part of the movement of history itself; that it cannot stand apart, attempting to control the world by imposing covenants and treaties and by violent military intervention; that our role is not to police the planet but to use military strength with restraints and within limits, while at the same time we make available to the world the great power of our economy, of our knowledge, and of our good will.

A war which is not defensible even in military terms, which runs contrary to the advice of our greatest generals—Eisenhower, Ridgway, Bradley, and MacArthur—all of whom admonished us against becoming involved in a land war in Asia. Events have proved them right, as estimate after estimate as the time of success and the military commitment necessary to success has had to be revised—always upward: more troops, more

extensive bombing, a widening and intensification of the war. Extension and intensification of the war. Extension and intensification have been the rule, and projection after projection of success have been proved wrong.

With the escalation of our military commitment has come a parallel of overleaping of objectives: from protecting South Vietnam, to nation building in South Vietnam, to protecting all of Southeast Asia, and ultimately to suggesting that the safety and security of the United States itself is at stake.

Finally, it is a war which is morally wrong. The most recent statement of objectives cannot be accepted as an honest judgment as to why we are in Vietnam. It has become increasingly difficult to justify the methods we are using as we have moved from limited targets and somewhat restricted weapons to greater variety and more destructive instruments of war, and also have extended the area of operations almost to the heart of North Vietnam.

Even assuming that both objectives and methods can be defended, the war cannot stand the test of proportion and prudent judgment. It is no longer possible to prove that the good that may come with what is called victory, or projected as victory, is proportionate to the loss of life and property to other disorders that follow from this war....

Beyond all these considerations, two further judgments must be passed: a judgment of individual conscience, and another in the broader context of history itself.

The problem of individual conscience is, I think, set most clearly before us in the words of Charles Peguy in writing about the Dreyfus case: "a single injustice, a single crime, a single illegality, if it is officially recorded...will bring about the loss of one's honor, the dishonor of a whole people."

And the broader historical judgment as suggested by Arnold Toynbee in his comments on Rome's war with Carthage: "Nemesis is a potent goddess.... War posthumously avenges the dead on the survivors, and the vanquished on the victors. The nemesis of war is intrinsic. It did not need the invention of the atomic weapon to make this apparent. It was illustrated more than two thousand years before our time, by Hannibal's legacy to Rome." Hannibal gained a "posthumous victory over Rome. Although he failed to defeat the great nation militarily because of the magnitude of her military manpower and solidity of the structure of the Roman commonwealth, he did succeed in inflicting grievous wounds on the commonwealth's body social and economic. They were so grievous that they festered into the revolution that was precipitated by Tiberius Gracchus and that did not cease till it was arrested by Augustus a hundred years later…This revolution," Toynbee said, "was the nemesis of Rome's superficially triumphant career of military conquest," and ended, of course, the Republic and substituted for it the spirit of the dictators and of the Caesars.

Those of us who are gathered here tonight are not advocating peace at any price. We are willing to pay a high price for peace—for an honorable, rational, and political solution to this war, a solution which will enhance our world position, which will permit us to give the necessary attention to our other commitments abroad, both military and non-military, and leave us with both human and physical resources and with moral energy to deal effectively with the pressing domestic problems of the United States itself.

I see little evidence that the administration has set any limits on the price which it will pay for a military victory which becomes less and less sure and more hollow and empty in promise.

The scriptural promise of the good life is one in which the old men see the visions and the young men dream dreams. In the context of this war and all of its implications, the young men of America do not dream dreams, but many live in the nightmare of moral anxiety, of concern and great apprehension; and the old men, instead of visions which they can offer to the young, are projecting, in the language of the secretary of state, a specter of one billion Chinese threatening the peace and safety of the world—a frightening and intimidating future.

The message from the administration today is a message of apprehension, a message of fear, yes—even a message of fear.

This is not the real spirit of America. I do not believe that it is. This is a time to test the mood and spirit:

To offer in place of doubt—trust.

In place of expediency—right judgment.

In place of ghettos, let us have neighborhoods and communities.

In place of incredibility—integrity.

In place of murmuring, let us have clear speech; let us again hear America singing.

In place of disunity, let us have dedication of purpose.

In place of near despair, let us have hope.

This is the promise of greatness, which was seated for us by Adlai Stevenson and which was brought to form and positive action in the words and actions of John Kennedy.

Let us pick up again these lost strands and weave them again into the fabric of America.

Let us sort out the music from the sounds and again respond to the trumpet and the steady drum.

"What we need in the United States is not violence or lawlessness but love and wisdom, and compassion"

ROBERT F. KENNEDY ANNOUNCES THE DEATH OF MARTIN LUTHER KING, JR.

On April 4, 1968, the Rev. Martin Luther King, Jr., was assassinated by James Earl Ray—a white man. That same evening Robert F. Kennedy was scheduled to speak to a Cleveland audience in a black neighborhood. Kennedy delivered the news of King's death to the crowd.

The brother of the assassinated president, Robert Kennedy spoke, without notes, of his own sadness over King's death as well the anguish and hopes for the country. Unlike other cities where black neighborhoods erupted in riots, Cleveland did not. Two months later Kennedy, too, would be assassinated in a California hotel.

I have bad news for you, for all of our fellow citizens, and people who love peace all over the world, and that is that Martin Luther King was shot and killed tonight.

Martin Luther King dedicated his life to love and to justice for his fellow human beings, and he died because of that effort.

In this difficult day, in this difficult time for the United States, it is perhaps well to ask what kind of nation we are and what direction we want to move in. For those of you who are black—considering the evidence there evidently is that there were white people who were responsible—you can be filled with bitterness, with hatred, and a desire for revenge. We can move in that direction as a country, in great polarization—black people amongst black, white people amongst white, filled with hatred toward one another.

Or we can make an effort, as Martin Luther King did, to understand and to comprehend, and to replace that violence, that stain of bloodshed that has spread across our land, with an effort to understand with compassion and love.

For those of you who are black and are tempted to be filled with hatred and distrust at the injustice of such an act, against all white people, I can only say that I feel in my own heart the same kind of feeling. I had a member of my family killed, but he was killed by a white man. But we have to make an effort in the United States, we have to make an effort to understand, to go beyond these rather difficult times.

My favorite poet was Aeschylus. He wrote, "In our sleep, pain which cannot forget falls drop by drop upon the heart until, in our own despair, against our will, comes wisdom through the awful grace of God."

What we need in the United States is not division; what we need in the United States is not hatred; what we need in the United States is not violence or lawlessness but love and wisdom, and compassion toward one another, and a feeling of justice towards those who still suffer within our country, whether they be white or they be black.

So I shall ask you tonight to return home, to say a prayer for the family of Martin Luther King, that's true, but more importantly to say a prayer for our own country, which all of us love—a prayer for understanding and that compassion of which I spoke.

We can do well in this country. We will have difficult times. We've had difficult times in the past. We will have difficult times in the future. It is not the end of violence; it is not the end of lawlessness; it is not the end of disorder.

But the vast majority of white people and the vast majority of black people in this country want to live together, want to improve the quality of our life, and want justice for all human beings who abide in our land.

Let us dedicate ourselves to what the Greeks wrote so many years ago: to tame the savageness of man, to make gentle the life of this world.

Let us dedicate ourselves to that, and say a prayer for all our country and for our people.

❧ "Mostly women and children were killed"

THE PEERS REPORT: THE MY LAI MASSACRE

By the beginning of 1968, the war in Vietnam was in full force. The Viet Cong launched the Tet Offensive in February against the United States and South Vietnam. Although the Viet Cong lost an enormous number of guerrillas in the campaign and it was considered by many to be a military defeat, it was a political victory. The fierceness of the attack and ability of the Viet Cong to assault allegedly secure bases stunned Americans who had been led to believe that the war was under control. Anti-war protests at home escalated. Meanwhile, the war proceeded in Vietnam with a newfound ferocity. American troops slogged on in the jungles and paddies.

In March, a company of American soldiers, "Charlie Company," or C/1-20, led by Captain Ernest Medina and Lieutenant William Calley, Jr., was ordered to take a small coastal hamlet called My Lai that was suspected of being a Viet Cong base. The veteran unit had been in the area before and had suffered casualties. Bent on revenge, the company massacred as many as 400 old men, women and children.

Army officials attempted to suppress the incident, which had been reported by a helicopter pilot, Hugh Thompson, who witnessed the shooting while flying directly overhead and rescued some of villagers. Eventually, *New York Times* reporter Seymour Hersh broke the story in the newspaper. Lieutenant General William R. Peers headed an army investigation into the incident. It resulted in the conviction of Calley for 22 murders. Although Calley was sentenced to life in prison, President Nixon commuted it to house arrest.

The My Lai Massacre shocked the nation and brought the anti-war movement into a heightened pitch. The incident also helped formulate an unfortunate stereotype of Vietnam veterans as cold-blooded killers that would linger for many years.

During the period 16-19 March 1968, a tactical operation was conducted into Son My village, Son Tinh District, Quang Ngai Province, Republic of Vietnam, by Task Force (TF) barker, a battalion-size unit of the Americal Division.

TF Barker was an interim organization of the 11th Brigade, created to fill a tactical void resulting from the withdrawal of a Republic of Korea Marine Brigade from the Quang Ngai area. The Task Force was composed of a rifle company from each of the 11th Brigade's three organic infantry battalions—A/3-1 Inf, B/4-3 Inf, C/1-20 Inf. The commander was LTC Frank A. Barker (now deceased).

The plans of the operation were never reduced to writing, but it was reportedly aimed at destroying the 48th VC Local Force (LF) Battalion, thought to be located in Son My Village, which also served as a VC staging and logistical support base. On two previous operations in the area, units of TF Barker had received casualties from enemy fire, mines and booby-traps and not been able to close effectively with the enemy.

On 15 March 1968, the new 11th Brigade commander, COL Oran K. Henderson, visited the TF Barker command post at Landing Zone (LZ) Dottie and talked to the assembled staff and commanders. He urged them to press forward aggressively and eliminate the 48th LF Battalion. Following these remarks, LTC Barker and his staff gave an intelligence briefing and issued an operations order. The company commanders were told that most of the population of Son My were "VC or VC sympathizers" and were advised that most of the civilian inhabitants would be away from Son My and on their way to market by 0700 hours. The operation was to commence at 0725 hours on 16 March 1968 with a short artillery preparation, following which C/1-20 Inf was to combat assault into an LZ immediately west of My Lai and then sweep east through the subhamlet. Following C company's landing, B/4-3 Inf was to reinforce C/1-20 Inf, or to conduct a second combat assault to the east of My Lai into an LZ south of the subhamlet of My Lai or "Pinkville." A/3-1 Inf was to move from its field location to blocking positions north of Son My.

During or subsequent to the briefing, LTC Barker ordered the commanders of C/1-20 Inf, and possibly B/4-3 inf, to burn the houses, kill the livestock, destroy foodstuffs, and perhaps to close the wells. No instructions were issued as to the safeguarding of noncombatants found there.

During a subsequent briefing by CPT Medina to his men, LTC Barker's orders were embellished, a revenge element was added, and the men of C/1-20 Inf were given to understand that only the enemy would be present in My Lai on 16 March and that the enemy was to be destroyed. In CPT Michles' briefing to his platoon leaders, mention was also apparently made of the burning of dwellings.

On the morning of 16 March 1968, the operation began as planned. A/3-1 Inf was reported in blocking positions at 0725 hours. At about that same time the artillery preparation and fires of the supporting helicopter gunship were placed on the C/1-20 Inf LZ and a part of My Lai. LTC Barker controlled the artillery preparation and combat assault from his helicopter. COL Henderson and his command group also arrived overhead at approximately this time.

By 0750 hours all elements of C/1-20 Inf were on the ground. Before entering My Lai, they killed several Vietnamese fleeing the area in the rice paddies around the subhamlet and along Route 521 to the south of the subhamlet. No resistance was encountered at this time or later in the day.

The infantry assault on My Lai began a few minutes before 0800 hours. During the 1st Platoon's movement through the southern half of the subhamlet, its members were involved in widespread killing of Vietnamese inhabitants (comprised almost exclusively of old men, women, and children) and also in property destruction. Most of the inhabitants who were not killed immediately were rounded up into two groups. The first group, consisting of about 70-80 Vietnamese, was taken to a large ditch east of My Lai and later shot. A second group, consisting of 20-50 Vietnamese, was taken south of the hamlet and shot there on a trail. Similar killings of smaller groups took place within the subhamlet.

Members of the 2d Platoon killed at least 60-70 men, women, and children, as they swept through the northern half of My Lai and through Binh Tay, a small subhamlet about 400 meters north of My Lai. They also committed several rapes.

The 3d Platoon, having secured the LZ, followed behind the 1st and 2d and burned and destroyed what remained of the houses in My Lai and killed most of the remaining livestock. Its members also rounded up and killed a group of 7-12 women and children.

There was considerable testimony that orders to stop the killing were issued two or three times during the morning. The 2d Platoon received such an order around 0920 hours and promptly complied. The 1st Platoon continued its killings until perhaps 1030 hours, when the order was repeated. By this time the 1st Platoon had completed its sweep through the subhamlet.

By the time C/1-20 Inf departed My Lai in the early afternoon, moving to the northeast for link-up with B/4-3 Inf, its members had killed at least 175-200 Vietnamese men, women, and children. The evidence indicates that only three or four were confirmed as Viet Cong, although there were undoubtedly several unarmed VC (men, women, and children) among them and many more active supporters and sympathizers. One man from the company was reported wounded from the accidental discharge of his weapon.

Since C Company had encountered no enemy opposition, B/4-3 Inf was air-landed in its LZ between 0815 and 0830 hours, following a short artillery preparation. Little if any resistance was encountered, although the 2d Platoon suffered 1 [Killed in Action] and 7 [Wounded in Action] from mines and/or boobytraps. The 1st Platoon moved eastward separately from the rest of B Company to cross and secure a bridge over the Song My Khe (My Khe River). After crossing the bridge and approaching the outskirts of the subhamlet of My Khe, elements of the platoon opened fire on the subhamlet with an M-60 machinegun and M-16 rifles. The fire continued for approximately five minutes, during which time some inhabitants of My Khe, mostly women and children, were killed. The lead elements of the platoon then entered the subhamlet, firing into the houses and throwing demolitions into shelters. Many noncombatants apparently were killed in the process.

It is believed that only ten men in B/4-3 Inf directly participated in the killings and destruction in My Khe; two of these are dead and the remaining eight have either refused to testify or claim no recollection of the event. As a result, it has not been possible to reconstruct the events with certainty. It appears, however, that the number of noncombatants killed by B/4-3 Inf on 16 March 1968 may have been as high as 90. The company reported a total of 38 VC [Killed in Action] on 16 March, but it is likely that few if any were Viet Cong.

On the evening of 16 March 1968, after C/1-20 Inf and B/4-3 Inf had linked up in a night defensive position, a Viet Cong suspect was apparently tortured and maimed by a U.S. officer. He was subsequently killed along with some additional suspects by Vietnamese National police in the presence of U.S. personnel.

During the period 17-19 March 1968 both C/1-20 Inf and B/4-3 Inf were involved in additional burning and destruction of dwellings, and in the mistreatment of Vietnamese detainees.

❧ "The largest antiwar action this country has ever seen"

MARCH ON WASHINGTON

American involvement in the Vietnam War had prompted anti-war protests starting in 1965. But as American participation escalated and as the number of soldiers being killed mounted, so too did the clamor to end the war. Television coverage of combat, increasingly skeptical news accounts and the objections of young Americans compelled to serve in the draft all heightened the stakes. The Vietnam War became a highly divisive and emotional issue, pitting family members, generations and different segments of society against each other.

Scores of anti-war organizations sprang up across the country. In November 1969 a massive "March on Washington" was staged to protest the war. An estimated 500,000 people participated in the protest, which did include some violent incidents. The following comes from a pamphlet "March Against Death—A Vietnam Memorial" that was used in the planning of the event.

The New Mobilization Committee to End the War in Vietnam is calling the American people to Washington, D.C., to March Against Death in Vietnam, and to demonstrate for life; for an immediate and unconditional withdrawal of all U.S. troops from Vietnam; for self-determination for Vietnam and black America; for an end to poverty and racism.

The Fall Offensive of the New Mobilization incorporates a variety of anti-war activities taking place all over the United States. It will culminate with the massing of many thousands of people in Washington, D.C., for the March Against Death (November 13-15) and finally end on Nov. 15 with a mass march and rally—the most significant and possibly the largest antiwar action this country has ever seen.

March Against Death
At midnight, Nov. 13, the first of fifty state delegations totaling 43,000-45,000 persons will begin walk-

ing from Arlington National Cemetery in a solemn single-file procession past the White House to the steps of the Capitol. There will be at least as many people in each state delegation as the number of slaughtered G.I.s from the state; there will be additional people representing the cities and towns of Vietnam that have been destroyed. The marchers will all be wearing placards with the name of either a dead G.I. or a Vietnamese city or town, and as he passes the White House, each person will call out the name on his placard.

The March Against Death will conclude thirty-six hours later with a memorial service at the Capitol steps on the morning of Nov. 15, preceding the mass march and rally. The placards deposited on the Capital steps will later be taken by representative parents of dead G.I.s, antiwar veterans and G.I. groups, clergy and Congressmen to the White House as part of the mass march and rally.

Organizing the Project

The principal resources lending strength to the March Against Death are organizations which have sponsored readings of the names of the war dead in various parts of the country: A Quaker Action Group, American Friends Service Committee, SANE, War Resisters League, Women Strike for Peace, Women's International League for Peace and Freedom, Fellowship of Reconciliation, the Resistance, Resist, Clergy and Laymen Concerned About Vietnam, and others, combined with newer groups such as the Vietnam Moratorium, veterans and G.I. groups, the next of kin of G.I.s who have been killed in Vietnam, and others that will join in.

Individual sponsors of the November actions of the New Mobilization Committee to End the War in Vietnam include: the Rev. William Sloan Coffin, Jr., Dave Dellinger, Douglas Dowd, Donald Kalish, Mrs. Martin Luther King, Jr., Sid Lens, Stewart Meacham, Sid Peck, Dr. Benjamin Spock, Cora Weiss.

What You Can Do

Contact the new Mobilization Washington Action Office, 1029 Vermont Ave., N.W., Washington, D.C. 2005 (phone: 202-737-8600) for the name and address of the March Against Death committee which is organizing in your area.

If your area has not yet had a meeting to mobilize for the March Against Death as part of its Fall Offensive to end the war, contact the Washington Action Office for speakers and literature.

Plan local and statewide activities focusing attention on the human and political toll of Vietnam. Reading the names of the war dead from your area and local death marches are possible activities.

Write your Congressmen to ask if they will participate in the March Against Death. Send the Washington office a copy of your letter. If they will not, ask how many more deaths it will take before they will publicly call for U.S. withdrawal from Vietnam.

The Washington Action office for the March Against Death has leaflets for distribution and buttons and posters for sale. It is suggested that local organizing committees sell these materials as part of their own fund-raising campaign and arrange that a percentage of the profits be contributed to the New Mobilization Committee to End the War in Vietnam. Quantity price list available on request.

Individual contributions are, of course, especially welcome.

❧ "The Best Story Ever Written"

SESAME STREET

In 1968, the Children's Television Workshop in New York City changed children's television. Prior to *Sesame Street,* children's television consisted of either pure entertainment or pure education. Rarely, did the two concepts intersect. But *Sesame Street* introduced a new way to entertain and educate children at the same time.

Employing Muppet™! puppets developed by Jim Henson, a cast of human characters and entertaining skits, *Sesame Street* captivated children (and their parents) and taught some of the basics of early education. The show not only was enormously popular in its own right, but it also changed the way many children s television programming was done.

Two of the most popular characters in the show were the Muppets™! Ernie and Bert. Their delightful relationship both provided direct instruction and served as a model of how two characters with some peculiar eccentricities can get along. The following Bert-and-Ernie skit, *Ernie's Short Story: The Best Story Ever Written,* is an example of the way *Sesame Street* could bring life to the ABCs of education.

ERNIE: (Dramatically): A-B-C-D-E-F-G. Now comes the sad part, Bert. (Sadly) H-I-J-K-L-M-N-O-P. (Sniffle)

BERT: That's the alphabet, Ernie.

ERNIE: (Getting his composure) Just a second, Bert. Now comes the action part.

BERT: 'Course.

ERNIE: (Excitedly) Q-R-S-T-U-V! Now comes the big finish! W-X-Y...(Long pause)

BERT: Well?

ERNIE: Well what, Bert?

BERT: Well finish it!

ERNIE: What? And tell you how the story ends? Then you won't read it yourself, Bert!

✒ "In a hierarchy, each employee tends to rise to his level of incompetence"

THE PETER PRINICPLE

Laurence Peter was a college professor in California who realized after working thirty years in a variety of bureaucracies that something was amiss. Capable writers were being promoted to become inept editors. Effective teachers were elevated out of the classroom to become incompetent supervisors. Gifted political campaigners could not meet the basic qualifications of the office to which they had been elected.

Peter developed the Peter Principle, an elaborate theory that spoofed the foibles of the modern corporation and the inherently American belief in merit-based advancement. Despite good intentions, this tendency had resulted in society-wide ineptitude. "We have come to expect incompetence as a necessary feature of civilization," he wrote. "We may be irked but we are no longer amazed when automobile makers take back thousands of new cars for repairs, when law reforms fail to check crime, when moon rockets can't get off the ground, when widely used medicines are found to be poisons, when universities must teach freshmen to read, or when a 100-ton airliner is brought down by a duck."

In 1969, his book *The Peter Principle: Why Things Always Go Wrong* was published. It was an instant success, selling more than 200,000 copies in its first year. The book had hit a national chord by skewering the age of business conglomerates and growing government bureaucracies. This excerpt is from a *Los Angeles Times Magazine* article, the subject of which eventually became the book.

In a hierarchy, each employee tends to rise to his level of incompetence: Every post tends to be occu-pied by an employee incompetent to execute its duties.

The Principle applies to all levels in the educational hierarchy. Competent teachers become incompetent principals; competent principals become incompetent superintendents. Frequently the very characteristics that were responsible for the promotion were the source of incompetence at the new level.

The career of Dr. Cy Softleigh, a competent psychiatrist in the state mental hospital, illustrates this well.

Softleigh was an effective psychotherapist. His pleasant confident manner, his readiness to listen long and say little, his soft voice, his steadfast avoidance of preaching or dogmatism, all con-tributed to his success. He accepted a promotion to the post of hospital supervisor.

Now frequently he has to speak at public meet-ings or address medical groups. He speaks now as he spoke then—softly, mildly, briefly and without authority. In short, he is incompetent as a public speaker and a failure as a promoter of his depart-ment. He does not qualify for further promotion, and will remain in the post where he is now inef-fective.

Another typical example is Grant Swinger, an official at Deeprest City Welfare Department who showed outstanding ability to procure money from government and charitable foundations. When the war on poverty was declared, Swinger was appoint-ed director of the city's Anti-Disadvantagement Program, on the assumption that the man who best understood the mighty could best help the weak. At the time of writing, Swinger is still raising money to complete an office block to house him-self, his advisory council and his staff. His next pro-ject will be to obtain a grant for a survey of the needs and desires of the disadvantaged.

Ronald Reagan could read a script and was therefore competent as an actor. He could also read a political speech and so was qualified as a political campaigner. A competent campaigner, he was elected and immediately achieved his level when he took the oath of office before Brown's term expired. California had two governors for three days. When questioned, Reagan said he did not know what he was doing at the time. He had not read what he had signed. He thought he had taken a loyalty oath. Governor Reagan stood with his right hand raised going through this ritual with as much understanding as Actor Reagan had when he stood before a television prompter.

History tells us of many celebrated examples. Macbeth, a competent general, was an incompetent king. Socrates, a successful teacher, was an incompetent defense attorney.

The Peter Principle operates everywhere. Manufacturers include lengthy instructions regarding anticipated breakdowns during the warranty period; modern laundries destroy shirt buttons; once-flourishing businesses go bankrupt; high schools graduate illiterates; computers bungle everything from school timetables to printing pay checks. Such mishaps occur because every day more and more people are arriving at their levels of incompetence.

At this point I must emphasize that the Principle operates at all levels of a hierarchy. I have found some misconceptions on this point. Some critics have mistakenly seen my work as placing in the hands of the lowly and unfair means of belittling their superiors. This is not so. The lowest rank of every hierarchy must contain its proportion of incompetents like Miss Ditto. True, some competent people are being added at this level through recruitment, but they are being rapidly drawn off by promotion. Only the incompetent remain.

❧ "We demand to be busted by policewomen only"

NO MORE MISS AMERICA!

By the end of the 1960s the feminist movement had become increasingly outspoken in its beliefs. Central to their argument against society was the effects of gender stereotyping. Society's response to women based on their appearance and "feminine" qualities was sharply condemned as being patronizing and as a way to subjugate women.

The annual Miss America Pageant in Atlantic City epitomized everything the feminist movement objected to in chauvinistic American society. In 1968, the feminist group New York Radical Women launched a militant protest against the event. Bearing "freedom ashcans" in which to dump various symbols of the oppression of women, New York Radical Women were barred from the convention hall, but staged a protest outside. The demonstration, however, attracted national media attention and elevated the cause of radical feminism. Protestors distributed the following handout stating their position to the media and spectators on the Atlantic City boardwalk.

On September 7 in Atlantic City, the Annual Miss America Pageant will again crown "your ideal." But this year, reality will liberate the contest auction-block in the guise of "genyoine" de-pasticized, breathing women. Women's Liberation Groups, black women, high-school and college women, women's peace groups, women's welfare and social-work groups, women's job-equality groups, pro-birth control and pro-abortion groups—women of every political persuasion—all are invited to join us in a day-long boardwalk-theater event, starting at 1:00 pm on the Boardwalk in front of Atlantic City's Convention Hall. We will protest the image of Miss America, an image that oppresses women in every area in which it purports to represent us. There will be: Picket Lines; Guerrilla Theater; Leafleting; Lobbying Visits to the contestants urging our sisters to reject the Pageant Farce and join us; a huge Freedom Trash Can (into which we will throw bras, girdles, curlers, false eyelashes, wigs, and representative issues of *Cosmopolitan*, *Ladies' Home Journal*, *Family Circle*, etc.—bring any such woman-garbage you have around the house); we will also announce a Boycott of all those commercial products related to the pageant, and the day will end with a Women's Liberation rally at midnight when Miss America is crowned on live television. Lots of other surprises are being planned (come and add your own!) but we do not plan heavy disruptive tactics and so do not expect a bad police scene. It should be a groovy day on the Boardwalk in the sun with our sisters. In case of arrests, however, we plan to reject all male authority and demand to be busted by policewomen only. (In Atlantic City, women cops are not permitted to make arrests—dig that!)

Male chauvinist-reactionaries on this issue had best stay away, nor are male liberals welcome in the demonstrations. But sympathetic men can donate money as well as cars and drivers.

Male reporters will be refused interviews. We reject patronizing reportage. Only newswomen will be recognized.

We Protest:

The Degrading Mindless-Boob-Girlie Symbol.
The Pageant contestants epitomize the roles we are all forced to play as women. The parade down the

runway blares at the metaphor of the 4-H Club county fair, where the nervous animals are judged for teeth, fleece, etc. and where the best "specimen" gets the blue ribbon. So are women in our society forced daily to compete for male approval, enslaved by ludicrous "beauty" standards we ourselves are conditioned to take seriously.

Racism with Roses. Since its inception in 1921, the pageant has not had one Black finalist, and this has not been for a lack of test-case contestants. There has never been a Puerto Rican, Alaskan, Hawaiian, or Mexican-American winner. Nor has there ever been a true Miss America—an American Indian.

Miss America as a Military Death Mascot. The highlight of her reign each year is a cheerleader-tour of American troops abroad—last year she went to Vietnam to pep-talk our husbands, fathers, sons and boyfriends into dying and killing with a better spirit. She personifies the "unstained patriotic womanhood our boys are fighting for." The Living Bra and the Dead Soldier. We refuse to be used as Mascots for Murder.

The Consumer Con-Game. Miss America is a walking commercial for the Pageant's sponsors. Wind her up and she plugs your product on promotion tours and TV—all in an "honest, objective" endorsement. What a shill.

Competition Rigged and Unrigged. We deplore the encouragement of an American myth that oppresses men as well as women: the win-or-you're-worthless competitive disease. The "beauty contest" creates only one winner to be "used" and forty-nine losers who are "useless."

The Woman as Pop Culture Obsolescent Theme. Spindle, mutilate, and then discard tomorrow. What is so ignored as last year's Miss America? This only reflects the gospel of our society, according to Saint Male: women must be young, juicy, malleable—hence age discrimination and the cult of youth. And we women are brainwashed into believing this ourselves!

The Unbeatable Madonna-Whore Combination. Miss America and *Playboy*'s centerfold are sisters over the skin. To win approval, we must be both sexy and wholesome, delicate but able to cope, demure yet titillatingly bitchy. Deviation of any sort brings, we are told, disaster. "You won't get a man!!"

The Irrelevant Crown on the Throne of Mediocrity. Miss America represents what women are supposed to be: unoffensive, bland, apolitical. If you are tall, short, over or under what weight The Man prescribes you should be, forget it. Personality, articulateness, intelligence, commitment—unwise. Conformity is the key to the crown—and, by extension, to success in our society.

Miss America as Dream Equivalent To—? In this reputedly democratic society, where every little boy supposedly can grow up to be president, what can every little girl hope to grow to be? Miss America. That's where it's at. Real power to control our own lives is restricted to men, while women get patronizing pseudo-power, an ermine cloak, and a bunch of flowers; men are judged by their actions, women by their appearance.

Miss America as Big Sister Watching You. The Pageant exercises Thought Control, attempts to sear the Image onto our minds, to further make women oppressed and men oppressors; to enslave us all the more in high-heeled, low-status roles; to inculcate false values in young girls; to use women as beasts of buying; to seduce us to prostitute ourselves before our own oppression.

NO MORE MISS AMERICA

❧ "I am strong, I am invincible, I am woman"

HELEN REDDY

Having rejected the "Establishment's" perception of women as servants to men, a new emphasis was placed by women on creating a new definition. Singer Helen Reddy's "I Am Woman" helped create a new sense of inner strength to enter into new arenas of accomplishment, formerly shut out to women.

I am woman, Hear me roar
in numbers too big to ignore
and I know too much to go back to pretend
'cause I've heard it all before
and I've been down on the floor,
no one's ever gonna keep me down again.
Oh, Yes, I am wise but it's wisdom born of pain.
Yes, I paid the price but look how much I've
gained.
If I have to I can do anything.
I am strong,

I am invincible,
I am woman.

You can bend but never break me
'cause it only serves to make me
more determined to achieve my final goal.
And I come back even stronger,
not a novice any longer,
'cause you've deepened the conviction in my soul.
Oh, woman!
I am woman!
I am woman!

I am woman, watch me grow
see me standing toe to toe
as I spread my lovin' arms across the land.
But I'm still an embryo
with a long, long way to go
until I make my brother understand.
Oh, woman!
I am woman!
I am woman!

The Right Stuff

TOM WOLFE

Throughout the 1960s the United States worked feverishly to build a rocket that would take man to the moon. No effort would be spared in this "race to the moon" against the Soviet Union, which had succeeded in sending the first man into space. A national campaign to improve math and sciences studies was implemented in schools across the country.

The focal point of attention, however, was the NASA Space Program in southern Florida featuring a collection of hot-shot fighter pilots who were the nation's first astronauts. Infusing his non-fiction writing with novel-like style and drama in the emeriging New Journalism style, writer Tom Wolfe wrote the book *The Right Stuff* about the men and their ethos that represented the United States venture into the last frontier of space. This excerpt is about Chuck Yeager, who—although he was not actually a pilot—served as the ideal for the modern American frontiersmen.

Anyone who travels very much on airlines in the United States soon gets to know the voice of the airline pilot...coming over the intercom...with a particular drawl, a particular folksiness, a particular down-home calmness that is so exaggerated it begins to parody itself (nevertheless!—it's reassuring)...the voice that tells you, as the airliner is caught in thunderheads and goes bolting up and down a thousand feet at a single gulp, to check your seat belts because "it might get a little choppy"...the voice tells you (on a flight from Phoenix preparing for its final approach into Kennedy Airport, New York, just after dawn): "Now, folks, uh...this is the captain...ummmm...We've got a little ol' red light up here on the control panel that's tryin' to tell us the landin' gears're not...uh...lockin' into position when we lower 'em...Now...I don't believe that little ol' red light knows what it's talkin' about—I believe it's that little ol' red light that iddn' workin' right"...faint chuckle, long pause, as if to say, I'm not even sure all this is really worth going into—still, it may amuse you..."But...I guess to play it by the rules, we oughta humor that little ol' light...so we're gonna take her down to about, oh, two or three hundred feet over the runway at Kennedy, and the folks down there on the ground are gonna see if they caint give us a visual inspection of those ol' landin' gears"—with which he is obviously on intimate ol'-buddy terms, as with every other working part of this mighty ship—"and if I'm right...they're gonna tell us everything is copacetic all the way aroun' an' we'll jes take her on in"...and, after a couple of low passes over the field, the voice returns: "Well folks, those folks down there on the ground—it must be too early for 'em or somethin'—I 'spect they still got sleepers in their eyes...'cause they say they caint tell if those ol' landin' gears are all the way down or not....But, you know, up here in the cockpit we're convinced they're all the way down, so we're jes gonna take her on in...And oh"...(I almost forgot)..."while we take a little swing out over the ocean an' empty some of that surplus fuel we're not gonna be needin' anymore—that's what you might be seein' comin' out of the wings—our lovely little ladies...if they'll be so kind...they're gonna go up and down the aisles and show you how we do what we call 'assumin' the position'" another faint chuckle (We do this so often, and it's so much fun, we even have a funny little name for it)...and the stewardesses, a bit grimmer, by the looks of them, than that voice, start telling the passengers to take their glasses off and take the ballpoint pens out of their pockets, and they show them the position, with the head lowered...while down on the field at Kennedy the little yellow emergency trucks start roaring across the field—and even though in your pounding heart and your sweating palms and your boiling brainpan you know this is a critical moment in your life, you still can't quite bring yourself to believe it, because if it were…how could the captain, the man who knows the actual situation most intimately…how could he keep drawlin' and chucklin' and driftin' and lollygaggin' in that particular voice of his—

Well!—who doesn't know that voice! And who can forget it!—even after he is proved right and the emergency is over.

That particular voice may sound vaguely Southern or Southwestern, but it is specifically Appalachian in origin. It originated in the mountains of West Virginia, in the coal country, in Lincoln County, so far up in the hollows that as the saying went, "they had to pipe in daylight." In the late 1940s and early 1950s this up-hollow voice drifted down from on high, from over the high desert of California, down, down, down from the upper reaches of the Brotherhood into all phases of American aviation. It was amazing. It was Pygmalion in reverse. Military pilots and then, soon, airline pilots, pilots from Maine and Massachusetts and the Dakotas and Oregon and everywhere else, began to talk in that polker-hollow West Virginia drawl, or as close to it as they could bend their native accents. It was the drawl of the most righteous of all the possessors of the right stuff: Chuck Yeager.

❦ "One small step for man, one giant leap for mankind"

NEIL ARMSTRONG LANDS ON THE MOON

On July 20, 1969, United States astronauts Neil Armstrong and Buzz Aldrin landed on the moon. America had won the race. This is the transcript of Armstrong's and Aldrin's conversation with NASA officials in Houston, as Armstrong prepares to step on to the moon's surface. Armstrong reported later that he had misspoken—his original intention had been to say "one small step for a man, one giant leap for mankind."

ARMSTRONG: Everything is go here. We're just waiting for the cabin pressure to be equal, to be low enough pressure to open the hatch, it's about .1 on our gauge now.

HOUSTON: Neil this is Houston, over.

ARMSTRONG: Go ahead Houston.

HOUSTON: Roger, we're showing a relatively static pressure on your cabin, do you think you can open the hatch at this pressure, about .12 psi?

ARMSTRONG: We're gonna try it

HOUSTON: Roger….

ARMSTRONG: Ok, Houston, I'm on the porch.

HOUSTON: Roger, Neil. Columbia, Columbia, this is Houston 1 minute 30 seconds till all systems go, over.

ARMSTRONG: Houston, this is Neil, radio check.

HOUSTON: Neil this is Houston, loud and clear, break, break, Buzz this is Houston, radio check and verify TV circuit breaker in.

ALDRIN: Roger, TV circuit breaker's in.

HOUSTON: Roger. And, we're getting a picture on the TV.

ARMSTRONG: I'm, at the foot of the ladder. The LAM foot pads are only, depressed in the surface about 1 or 2 inches. Although the surface appears to be, very, very fine grained as you get close to it. It's almost like a powder down there. It's very fine. Ok, I'm gonna step off the LAM now.

That's one small step for man, one giant leap for mankind.

Buzz, the surface is fine and powdery, I can, I can pick it up loosely with my toe. It does adhere in fine layers, ahh like powdered charcoal to the spool and insides of my boot. I only go in a small fraction of an inch, maybe an eighth of an inch. But, I can see the footprints of my boot from the treads in the fine sandy particles.

HOUSTON: Neil, this is Houston, we're copying.

❦ "Hey, we're going to change everything"

DAVID CROSBY RECALLS WOODSTOCK

The culmination of the counterculture that marked the 1960s occurred at an obscure dairy farm owned by Max Yasgur in

Bethel, New York. Rock 'n roll promoters Michael Lang and Artie Kornfield wanted to start a recording studio in Woodstock, New York, and decided to launch the effort with a music festival August 15 to 19, 1969. Concerned that the crowds would be too large for Woodstock, they relocated the event to Yasgur's farm.

They planned to attract 25,000 people for the multi-band event and hoped for 75,000. Some of the brightest pop stars of the era appeared, including Joan Baez, Arlo Guthrie, Janis Joplin, The Who, Grateful Dead, Santana and Jimi Hendrix. By the end of the wild three-day event, more than 400,000 people had participated in the rain-soaked, drug-ingesting, skinny-dipping, lovemaking rock n' roll extravaganza.

We were just starting our first tour as Crosby, Stills, Nash, and Young. We had played the previous night in Chicago Auditorium Theater, two shows. That was our first show anywhere—ever—with Joni Mitchell opening. Joni wanted to come but was supposed to do "The Dick Cavett Show" the next night or the night after. And by the time we were ready to go here, her manager told her, "Hey, look, you can't go. You might not be able to get back out."

We hired a plane somewhere, probably Long Island, and flew out to where the helicopters were picking people up and taking them out to the site. I don't know where that was. I don't remember much about it. At the time I was high as a kite. We got in the helicopter and flew out to it and by this time I was realizing that it was way more than anybody had realized was going to happen.

We flew in. I think Nash told me that his helicopter lost its tail rudder and auto-rotated down the last twenty feet and scared him to death. I got in easy as pie and slogged through the mud. If there is an overriding impression of Woodstock, it's mud. There was a ton of mud everywhere, all the time. And after that it was a blur. I can remember flashes. I remember a tent. I remember that Christine, my girlfriend, was very unhappy that she had dressed up pretty to come because we were in a field of deep mud and a tent. At one point, I think I went to a motel. They got me a motel. I'm not sure how they did that because the roads were impassable in all directions all the time.

Part of my haziness about it is due to the fact that this was when I first encountered a kind of pot that I've since come to call Pullover Pot. It was Colombian Gold, little tiny budlets of gold Colombian pot; it still had that fresh-turned dirt furrow smell. But if you smoked it—I remember

smoking it for the first time in Florida, and I was driving someplace and I smoked it and I pulled over and listened to the radio for a while because I couldn't remember where I was going. And some friends of mine, a guy named Rocky and another guy named Big John, had brought a bunch of this stuff up and they were just giving it to their favorite people. And so I was in a ripe old state wandering around there. A lot of people were on psychedelics. I didn't take psychedelics to play; I couldn't. If you take it and try to play, the guitar gets three feet thick and the strings turn to rubber and it just doesn't work.

I remember images. I remember we didn't just stay backstage. I snuck out and I wandered around; nobody really knew who anybody was. I remember being out at dusk and seeing this state trooper carrying a little girl who had just cut her foot. A pretty little girl. She had stepped on a piece of glass in the mud and he was carrying her back to his car. He carried her back, put her in the seat, got something wrapped around her foot and it was soaked with blood. And watched about the nearest twenty or thirty hippies push this police car out of the mud. And I thought to myself, "Hmmm, something other than the usual is going on here."

Because there was no animosity. There was a feeling going on with everybody at that point. We felt very encouraged by seeing each other. Everybody was thrilled that there were so many of us. We thought, "Hey, we're going to change everything. We're going to stop the war tomorrow." Well, it didn't work out that way. But at that point we were all thrilled with the idea that our values were triumphant someplace in the world. That, at least for this one small space of time in this one little town in New York, the hippie ethic was the ruling way to do. And it felt great. I can't say that it would have solved all the world's problems if it had spread and taken over everywhere. I don't even know if it would work. But I know that for that weekend for that town in New York, it was great. It felt great. It felt wonderful. There wasn't any of the classic "I don't want to get involved." If somebody had a problem, you tried to help them. If you had a sandwich and somebody was hungry, you'd tear it in half. That was how everybody was doing it right then.

🌱 "To you, the great silent majority of Americans, I ask for your support"

RICHARD NIXON

Almost a year after being sworn in as president, Richard Nixon told the nation his plan for the gradual withdrawal of combat troops from Vietnam in a November 3, 1969, television address. At the time, the country was sharply divided. The antiwar movement was growing and protesters had organized a massive march on Washington. More than 35,000 Americans had been killed in Vietnam and there did not appear to be a resolution in sight.

In his lengthy speech, Nixon outlined the historic reasons for the war, the course of U. S. involvement in the conflict, and his own actions since taking office. Without giving details, he vowed to gradually withdraw U.S. combat troops to be replaced by South Vietnamese soldiers, while simultaneously pressing negotiations for an honorable peace.

Nixon turned to the "silent majority" that he believed endorsed the goals of the war, for support in his decision to prolong the conflict. It ended up taking three full years for the U.S. to remove its military presence from Vietnam. Almost 20,000 more soldiers were killed during that time. Shortly after pulling the last soldiers out of Southeast Asia, Nixon won the 1972 election in a landslide against the anti-war Democratic candidate George McGovern.

…We have faced other crises in our history and have become stronger by rejecting the easy way out and taking the right way in meeting our challenges. Our greatness as a nation has been our capacity to do what had to be done when we knew our course was right.

I recognize that some of my fellow citizens disagree with the plan for peace I have chosen. Honest and patriotic Americans have reached different conclusions as to how peace should be achieved.

In San Francisco a few weeks ago, I saw demonstrators carrying signs reading, "Lose in Vietnam, bring the boys home."

Well, one of the strengths of our free society is that any American has a right to reach that conclusion and to advocate that point of view. But as president of the United States, I would be untrue to my oath of office if I allowed the policy of this nation to be dictated by the minority who hold that point of view and who try to impose it on the nation by mounting demonstrations in the street.

For almost two hundred years, the policy of this nation has been made under our Constitution by those leaders in the Congress and the White House elected by all of the people. If a vocal minority, however fervent its cause, prevails over reason and the will of the majority, this nation has no future as a free society.

And now I would like to address a word, if I may, to the young people of this nation who are particularly concerned, and I understand why they are concerned, about this war. I respect your idealism. I share your concern for peace. I want peace as much as you do.

There are powerful reasons I want to end this war. This week I will have to sign eighty-three letters to mothers, fathers, wives, and loved ones of men who have given their lives for America in Vietnam. It is very little satisfaction to me that this is only one-third as many letters as I signed the first week in office. There is nothing I want more than to see the day come when I do not have to write any of these letters.

I want to end the war to save the lives of those brave young men in Vietnam. But I want to end it in a way which will increase the chance that their younger brothers and their sons will not have to fight in some future Vietnam someplace in the world. And I want to end the war for another reason. I want to end it so that the energy and dedication of you, our young people now too often directed into bitter hatred against those responsible for the war, can be turned to the great challenges of peace, a better life for all Americans, a better life for all people on this earth.

I have chosen this plan for peace. I believe it will succeed.

If it does succeed, what the critics say now won't matter. If it does not succeed, anything I say then won't matter.

I know it may not be fashionable to speak of patriotism or national destiny these days. But I feel it is appropriate to do so on occasion.

Two hundred years ago this nation was weak and poor. But even then, America was the hope of millions in the world. Today we have become the strongest and richest nation in the world. And the wheel of destiny has turned so that any hope the world has for the survival of peace and freedom will be determined by whether the American people have the moral stamina and the courage to meet the challenge of free world leadership.

Let historians not record that when America was the most powerful nation in the world we passed on the other side of the road and allowed the last hopes for peace and freedom of millions of people to be suffocated by the forces of totalitarianism.

And so tonight—to you, the great silent majority of my fellow Americans—I ask for your support.

I pledged in my campaign for the presidency to end the war in a way that we could win the peace. I have initiated a plan of action which will enable me to keep that pledge.

The more support I can have from the American people, the sooner that pledge can be redeemed; for the more divided we are at home, the less likely the enemy is to negotiate at Paris.

Let us be united for peace. Let us also be united against defeat. Because let us understand: North Vietnam cannot defeat or humiliate the United States. Only Americans can do that.

Fifty years ago, in this room and at this very desk, President Woodrow Wilson spoke words which caught the imagination of a war-weary world. He said, "This is the war to end wars." His dream for peace after World War I was shattered on the hard realities of great power politics, and Woodrow Wilson died a broken man.

Tonight I do not tell you that the war in Vietnam is the war to end wars. But I do say this: I have initiated a plan which will end this war in a way that will bring us closer to that goal to which Woodrow Wilson and every American president in our history has been dedicated—the goal of a just and lasting peace.

As president I hold the responsibility for choosing the best path to that goal and then leading the nation along it.

I pledge to you tonight that I shall meet this responsibility with all of the strength and wisdom I can command in accordance with your hopes, mindful of your concerns, sustained by your prayers.

Thank you and good night.

The New York Times v. United States: "The newspapers nobly did precisely that which the Founders hoped and trusted they would do"

SUPREME COURT JUSTICE HUGO BLACK

The New York Times started on June 13, 1971, to publish "The Pentagon Papers," a series of damaging internal documents provided by Pentagon analyst Daniel Ellsberg that showed the military's own misgivings about the Vietnam War and the unlikely prospects for victory. The Nixon administration went to court to bar the further publication of the documents, a portion of which *The Washington Post* also published.

In *New York Times v. United States,* Solicitor General Erwin Griswold argued that the publication of the papers would affect the nation's security. In an opinion written by Justice Hugo Black, the Supreme Court rejected the argument.

Our Government was launched in 1789 with the adoption of the Constitution. The Bill of Rights, including the First Amendment, followed in 1791. Now, for the first time in the 182 years since the founding of the Republic, the federal courts are asked to hold that the First Amendment does not mean what it says, but rather means that the Government can halt the publication of current news of vital importance to the people of the country.

The Bill of Rights changed the original Constitution into a new charter under which no branch of government could abridge the people's freedoms of press, speech, religion, and assembly. Yet the Solicitor General argues and some members of the Court appear to agree that the general powers of the Government adopted in the original Constitution should be interpreted to limit and restrict the specific and emphatic guarantees of the Bill of Rights adopted later. I can imagine no greater perversion of history. Madison and the other Framers of the First Amendment, able men that they were, wrote in language they earnestly believed could never be misunderstood: "Congress shall make no law…abridging the freedom…of the press." Both history and language of the First

Amendment support the view that the press must be left free to publish news, whatever the source, without censorship, injunctions, or prior restraints."

In the First Amendment the Founding Fathers gave the free press the protection it must have to fulfill its essential role in our democracy. The press was to serve the governed, not the governors. The Government's power to censor the press was abolished so that the press would remain forever free to censure the Government. The press was protected so that it could bare the secrets of government and inform the people. Only a free and unrestrained press can effectively expose deception in government. And paramount among the responsibilities of a free press is the duty to prevent any part of the government from deceiving the people and sending them off to distant lands to die of foreign fevers and foreign shot and shell. In my view, far from deserving condemnation for their courageous reporting, *The New York Times*, *The Washington Post*, and other newspapers should be commended for serving the purpose that the Founding Fathers saw so clearly. In revealing the workings of government that led to the Vietnam War, the newspapers nobly did precisely that which the Founders hoped and trusted they would do.

"The condition of the Indian people ranks at the bottom"

RICHARD NIXON

Just as the United States was turning it attention to the discriminations against blacks, women and other minorities during the 1960s, so too did the nation re-examine its policies toward Native Americans.

The government's legacy in its treatment of Native Americans was dismal. Having waged war against Indians for centuries, the government relocated tribes into reservations on some of the bleakest land in the country and instituted policies designed to obliterate Native American culture. Corruption marred the implementation of even the most well-meaning policies instituted in various reform efforts.

Hoping to reverse this dismal relationship, President Nixon proposed a series of sweeping reforms in 1970 designed to create a new, more amenable relationship between the government and the tribes. The move instituted a series of far-reaching legislative reforms and judicial decisions that started to reverse the plight of Native Americans.

The first Americans—the Indians—are the most deprived and most isolated minority group in our nation. On virtually every scale of measurement—employment, income, education, health—the condition of the Indian people ranks at the bottom.

This condition is the heritage of centuries of injustice. From the time of their first contact with European settlers, the American Indians have been oppressed and brutalized, deprived of their ancestral lands and denied the opportunity to control their own destiny. Even the Federal programs which are intended to meet their needs have frequently proven to be ineffective and demeaning.

But the story of the Indian in America is something more than the record of the white man's frequent aggression, broken agreements, intermittent remorse and prolonged failure. It is a record also of endurance, of survival, of adaptation and creativity in the face of overwhelming obstacles. It is a record of enormous contributions to this country—to its art and culture, to its strength and spirit, to its sense of history and its sense of purpose.

It is long past time that the Indian policies of the Federal government began to recognize and build upon the capacities and insights of the Indian people. Both as a matter of justice and as a matter of enlightened social policy, we must begin to act on the basis of what the Indians themselves have long been telling us. The time has come to break decisively with the past and to create the conditions for a new era in which the Indian future is determined by Indian acts and Indian decisions.

The first and most basic question that must be answered with respect to Indian policy concerns the historic and legal relationship between the Federal government and Indian communities. In the past, this relationship has oscillated between two equally harsh and unacceptable extremes.

On the one hand, it has—at various times during previous Administrations—been the stated policy objective of both the Executive and legislative branches of the Federal government eventually to terminate the trusteeship relationship between the Federal government and the Indian people. As recently as August of 1953, in House Concurrent Resolution 108, the Congress declared that termination was the long-range goal of its Indian policies. This would mean that Indian tribes would eventually lose any special standing they had under Federal law: the tax exempt status of their lands would be discontinued; Federal responsibility for their economic and social well-being would be repudiated; and the tribes themselves would be effectively dismantled. Tribal property would be divided among individual members who would then be assimilated into the society at large.

This policy of forced termination is wrong, in my judgment, for a number of reasons. First, the premises on which it rests are wrong. Termination implies that the Federal government has taken on a trusteeship responsibility for Indian communities as an act of generosity toward a disadvantaged people and that it can therefore discontinue this responsibility on a unilateral basis whenever it sees fit. But the unique status of Indian tribes does not rest on any premise such as this. The special relationship between Indians and the Federal government is the result instead of solemn obligations which have been entered into by the United States Government. Down the through the years, through written treaties and through formal and informal agreements, our government has made specific commitments to the Indian people. For their part, the Indians have surrendered claims to vast tracts of land and have accepted life on government reservations. In exchange, the government has agreed to provide community services such as health, education and public safety, services which would presumably allow Indian communities to enjoy a standard of living comparable to that of other Americans.

This goal, of course, has never been achieved. But the special relationship between the Indian tribes and the Federal government which arises from these agreements continues to carry immense moral and legal force. To terminate this relationship would be no more appropriate than to terminate the citizenship rights of any other American.

The second reason for rejecting forced termination is that the practical results have been clearly harmful in the few instances in which termination actually has been tried. The removal of Federal trusteeship responsibility has produced considerable disorientation among the affected Indians and has left them unable to relate to a myriad of Federal, State and local assistance efforts. Their economic and social condition has often been worse after termination than it was before.

The third argument I would make against forced termination concerns the effect it has had upon the overwhelming majority of tribes which still enjoy a special relationship with the Federal government. The very threat that this relationship may someday be ended has created a great deal of apprehension among Indian groups and this apprehension, in turn, has had a blighting effect on tribal progress. Any step that might result in greater social, economic, or political autonomy is regarded with suspicion by many Indians who fear that it will only bring them closer to the day when the Federal government will disavow its responsibility and cut them adrift.

In short, the fear of one extreme policy, forced termination, has often worked to produce the opposite extreme: excessive dependence on the Federal government. In many cases this dependence is so great that the Indian community is almost entirely run by outsiders who are responsible and responsive to Federal officials in Washington D.C., rather than to the communities they are supposed to be serving. This is the second of the two harsh approaches which have long plagued our Indian policies....

I believe that both of these policy extremes are wrong. Federal termination errs in one direction, Federal paternalism errs in the other. Only by clearly rejecting both of these extremes can we achieve a policy which truly serves the best interests of the Indian people. Self-determination among the Indian people can and must be encouraged without the threat of eventual termination. In my view, in fact, that is the only way that self-determination can effectively be fostered.

This, then, must be the goal of any new national policy toward the Indian people; to strengthen the Indian's sense of community. We must assure the Indian that he can assume control of his own life without being separated involuntarily from the tribal group. And we must make it clear that Indians can become independent of Federal control without being cut off from Federal concern and Federal support. My specific recommendations to the Congress are designed to carry out this policy.

Because termination is morally and legally unacceptable, because it produces bad practical results, and because the mere threat of termination tends to discourage greater self-sufficiency among Indian groups, I am asking the Congress to pass a new Concurrent Resolution which would expressly renounce, repudiate and repeal the termination policy as expressed in house Concurrent Resolution 108 of the 83rd Congress. This resolution would explicitly affirm the integrity and right to continued existence of all Indian tribes and Alaska native governments, recognizing that cultural pluralism is a source of national strength. It would assure these groups that the United States Government would continue to carry out its treaty and trusteeship obligations to them as long as the groups themselves believed that such a policy was necessary or desirable. It would guarantee that whenever Indian groups decided to assume control or responsibility for government service programs, they could do so and still receive adequate Federal financial support. In short, such a resolution would reaffirm for the Legislative branch—as I hereby affirm for the Executive branch—that the historic relationship between the Federal government and the Indian communities cannot be abridged without the consent of the Indians.

Even as we reject the goal of forced termination, so must we reject the suffocating pattern of paternalism. But how can we best do this? There is no reason why Indian communities should be deprived of the privilege of self-determination merely because they receive monetary support from the Federal government. Nor should they lose Federal money because they reject Federal control....

It should be up to the Indian tribe to determine whether it is willing and able to assume administrative responsibility for a service program which is presently administered by a Federal agency. To this end, I am proposing legislation which would empower a tribe or group of tribes or any other Indian community to take over the control or operation of Federally-funded and administered programs in the Department of Interior and the Department of Health, Education and Welfare whenever the tribal council or comparable community government group voted to do so....

Under the proposed legislation, Indian control of Indian programs would always be a wholly voluntary matter. It would be possible for an Indian group to select that program or that specified portion of a program that it wants to run without assuming responsibility for other components. The "right of retrocession" would also be guaranteed; this means that if the local community elected to administer a program and then later decided to give it back to the Federal government it would always be able to do so.

Appropriate technical assistance to help local organizations successfully operate these programs would be provided by the Federal government.... The legislation I propose would include appropriate protections against any action which endangered the rights, the health, the safety or the welfare of individuals. It would also contain accountability procedures to guard against gross negligence or mismanagement of Federal funds....

One of the saddest aspects of Indian life in the United States is the low quality of Indian education. Drop-out rates for Indians are twice the national average and the average educational level for all Indians under Federal supervision is less than six school years. Again, at least a part of the problem stems from the fact that the Federal government is trying to do for Indians what many Indians could do better for themselves....

Consistent with our policy that the Indian community should have the right to take over the control and operation of federally funded programs, we believe every Indian community wishing to do so should be able to control its own Indian schools. This control would be exercised by school boards selected by Indians and functioning much like other school boards throughout the nation....

We must also take specific action to benefit Indian children in public schools.

Economic deprivation is among the most serious of Indian problems. Unemployment among Indians is ten times the national average; the unemployment rate runs as high as 80 percent on some of the poorest reservations. Eighty percent of reservation Indians have an income which falls below the poverty line; the average annual income for such families is only $1,500....

I also urge that legislation be enacted which would permit any tribe which chooses to do so to enter into leases of its land for up to 99 years. Indian people now own over 50 million acres of land that are held in trust by the Federal government. In order to compete in attracting investment capital for commercial, industrial and recreational development of these lands, it is essential that the tribes be able to offer long-term leases. Long-term leasing is preferable to selling such property since it enables tribes to preserve the trust ownership of their reservation homelands....

Despite significant improvements in the past decade and a half, the health of Indian people still lags twenty to twenty-five years behind that of the general population. The average age at death among Indians is forty-four years, about one-third less than the national average. Infant mortality is nearly 50 percent higher for Indians and Alaska natives than for the population at large; the tuberculosis rate is eight times as high and the suicide rate is twice that of the general population. Many infectious diseases such as trachoma and dysentery that have all but disappeared among other Americans continue to afflict the Indian people.

This Administration is determined that the health status of the first Americans will be improved. In order to initiate expanded efforts in this area, I will request the allocation of an additional $10 million for Indian health programs for the current fiscal year.

Indian health programs will be most effective if more Indians are involved in running them. Yet— almost unbelievably we are presently able to identify in this country only thirty physicians and fewer than four hundred nurses of Indian descent. To meet this situation, we will expand our efforts to train Indians for health careers....

The United States Government acts as a legal trustee for the land and water rights of American Indians. These rights are often of critical economic importance to the Indian people; frequently they are also the subject of extensive legal dispute. In many of these legal confrontations, the Federal government is faced with an inherent conflict of interest. The Secretary of the Interior and the Attorney General must at the same time advance both the national interest in the use of land and water rights and the private interests of Indians in land which the government holds as trustee....

I am calling on the Congress to establish an Indian Trust Counsel Authority to assure independent legal representation for the Indians' natural resource rights. At least two of the board members would be Indian....

To help guide the implementation of a new national policy concerning American Indians, I am recommending to the Congress the establishment of a new position in the Department of the Interior—Assistant Secretary for Indian and Territorial Affairs....

🌿 "Go ahead and make your stand at Wounded Knee"

MARY CROW DOG

Despite Nixon's intentions at reforming Native American policy, Congress did not pass all of the necessary enabling legislation and there were problems in the implementation of effective reform. Indian activists grew impatient, denouncing some of their tribal leaders as "Uncle Tomahawks." Several urban Native Americans founded the American Indian Movement (AIM) to advance "Red Power."

Reversing the American stereotype of the cowboy-Indian conflict, the activism helped Americans see Native Americans as the victims rather than the villains of westward expansion. In 1972, AIM and other activitists occupied and ransacked the Indian Bureau in Washington, D.C. In February 1973, another AIM-led group seized the village of Wounded Knee, South Dakota, and declared an "Independent Sioux Nation." They held the village—the site of a brutal massacre of about 300 Native American women, children and elderly 80 years earlier—for 71 days, causing significant destruction in the process. Mary Crow Dog wrote about her role in the 1973 seige in her autobiography *Lakota Woman*.

The Oglala elders thought that we all had been wasting our time and energies in Rapid City and Custer when the knife was at our throats at home. And so, finally and inevitably, our caravan started rolling toward Pine Ridge. [Tribal president Dicky] Wilson was expecting us. His heavily armed goons had been reinforced by a number of rednecks with Remingtons and Winchesters on gun racks behind their driver's seats, eager to bag themselves an Injun. The marshals and FBI had come too, with some thirty armored cars equipped with machine guns and rocket launchers. These were called APCs, Armored Personnel Carriers. The tribal office had been sandbagged and a machine gun installed on its roof. The Indians called it "Fort Wilson." Our movements were kept under observation and reported several times a day. Still we came on.

To tell the truth, I had not joined the caravan with the notion that I would perform what some people later called "that great symbolic act." I did not even know that we would wind up a Wounded Knee. Nobody did....

There was still no definite plan for what to do. We had all assumed that we would go to Pine Ridge town, the administrative center of the reservation, the seat of Wilson's and the government's power. We had always thought that the fate of the Oglalas would be settled there. But as the talks progressed it became clear that nobody wanted us to storm Pine Ridge, garrisoned as it was by the goons, the marshals, and the FBI. We did not want to be slaughtered. There had been too many massacred Indians already in our history. But if not Pine Ridge, then what? As I remember, it was the older women like Ellen Moves Camp and Gladys Bissonette who first pronounced the magic words "Wounded Knee," who said, "Go ahead and make your stand at Wounded Knee. If you men won't do it, you can stay here and talk for all eternity and we women will do it."

When I heard the words "Wounded Knee" I became very, very serious. Wounded Knee—Canpke Opi in our language—has a special meaning for our people. There is the long ditch into which the frozen bodies of almost three hundred of our people, mostly women and children, were thrown like so much cordwood. And the bodies are still there in their mass grave, unmarked except for a cement border. Next to the ditch, on a hill, stands the white painted Catholic church, gleaming in the sunlight, the monument of an alien faith imposed upon the landscape. And below it flows Cankpe Opi Wakpala, the creek along which the women and children were hunted down like animals by Custer's old Seventh, out to avenge themselves for their defeat by butchering the helpless ones. That happened long ago, but no Sioux ever forgot it.

Wounded Knee is part of our family's history. Leonard's great-grandfather, the first Crow Dog, had been one of the leaders of the Ghost Dancers. He and his group had held out in the icy ravines of the Badlands all winter, but when the soldiers came in force to kill all the Ghost Dancers he had surrendered his band to avoid having his people killed. Old accounts describe how Crow Dog simply sat down between the rows of soldiers on one side, and the Indians on the other, all ready and eager to start shooting. He had covered himself with a blanket and was just sitting there. Nobody knew what to make of it. The leaders on both sides were so puzzled that they just did not get around to opening fire. They went to Crow Dog, lifted the blanket, and asked him what he meant to do. He told them that sitting there with the blanket over him was the only thing he could think of to make all the hotheads, white and red, curious enough to forget fighting. Then he persuaded his people to lay down their

arms. Thus he saved his people just a few miles away from where Big Foot and his band were massacred. And old Uncle Dick Fool Bull, a relative of both the Crow Dogs and my own family, often described to me how he himself heard the rifle and cannon shots that mowed our people down when he was a little boy camping only two miles away. He had seen the bodies, too, and described to me how he had found a body of a dead baby girl with an American flag beaded on her tiny bonnet.

Before we set out for Wounded Knee, Leonard and Wallace Black Elk prayed for all of us with their pipe. I counted some fifty cars full of people. We went right through Pine Ridge. The half-bloods and goons, the marshals and the government snipers on their rooftop, were watching us, expecting us to stop and start a confrontation, but our caravan drove right by them, leaving them wondering. From Pine Ridge it was only eighteen miles more to our destination. Leonard was in the first car and I was way in the back.

Finally, on February 27, 1973, we stood on the hill where the fate of the old Sioux Nation, Sitting Bull's and Crazy Horse's nation, had been decided, and where we, ourselves, came face to face with our fate. We stood silently, some of us wrapped in our blankets, separated by our personal thoughts and feelings and yet united, shivering a little with excitement and the chill of a fading winter. You can almost hear our heartbeats.

It was not cold on this next-to-last day of February—not for a South Dakota February anyway. Most of us had not even bothered to wear gloves. I could feel a light wind stirring my hair, blowing it gently about my face. There were a few snowflakes in the air. We all felt the presence of the spirits of those lying close by in the long ditch, wondering whether we were about to join them, wondering when the marshals would arrive. We knew that we could not have to wait long for them to make their appearance.

Suddenly the spell was broken. Everybody got busy. The men were digging trenches and making bunkers, putting up low walls of cinder blocks, establishing a last-resort defense perimeter around the Sacred Heart Church. Those few who had weapons were checking them, mostly small-bore .22s and old hunting rifles. We had only one automatic weapon, an AK-47 that one Oklahoma boy had brought back from Vietnam as a souvenir.

Altogether we had twenty-six firearms—not much compared to what the other side would bring up against us. None of us had any illusions that we could take over Wounded Knee unopposed. Our message to the government was: "Come and discuss our demands or kills us!" Somebody called someone on the outside from a telephone inside the trading post. I could hear him yelling proudly again and again, "We hold the Knee!"

The occupiers were besieged by federal marshals until May 8, when AIM surrendered after securing a promise that the complaints would be investigated. Two Indians and one marshal were killed during the fighting.

❧ *"To protect and enhance the quality of the Nation's air resources"*

THE CLEAN AIR ACT OF 1970

Aroused to action by public concern, Congress passed the Clean Air Act of 1970 making states responsible for the emission of pollutants within their boundaries. The legislation marked a major step in the nation's imposing controls on the rising levels of smog, acid rain, and other impacts of air pollution.

However, the act set the framework for years of regional disputes over the creation of pollution that drifted on to other states, principally from the Midwest to the East in the form of acid rain. New legislation approved in 1990 set stricter federal standards to impose controls on chemical contamination and strengthened federal authority to implement environmental improvements.

The Congress finds—

that the predominant part of the Nation's population is located in its rapidly expanding metropolitan and other urban areas, which generally cross the boundary lines of local jurisdictions and often extend into two or more States;

that the growth in the amount and complexity of air pollution brought about by urbanization, industrial development, and the increasing use of motor vehicles, has resulted in mounting dangers to the public health and welfare, including injury to agricultural crops and livestock, damage to and the deterioration of property, and hazards to air and ground transportation;

that air pollution prevention (that is, the

reduction or elimination, through any measures, of the amount of pollutants produced or created at the source) and air pollution control at its source is the primary responsibility of States and local governments; and

that Federal financial assistance and leadership is essential for the development of cooperative Federal, State, regional, and local programs to prevent and control air pollution.

(b) Declaration.

The purposes of this subchapter are—

to protect and enhance the quality of the Nation's air resources so as to promote the public health and welfare and the productive capacity of its population;

to initiate and accelerate a national research and development program to achieve the prevention and control of air pollution;

to provide technical and financial assistance to State and local governments in connection with the development and execution of their air pollution prevention and control programs; and

to encourage and assist the development and operation of regional air pollution prevention and control programs.

(c) Pollution prevention

A primary goal of this chapter is to encourage and otherwise promote reasonable Federal, State, and local governmental actions, consistent with the provisions of this chapter, for pollution prevention.

❧ *"No person in the United States shall, on the basis of sex, be excluded from… any education program"*

TITLE IX

In 1972, Congress passed Title IX, prohibiting sex discrimination in schools that receive public funding. The impact was felt across the country, particularly in athletic programs which were required to devote the same resources to girls' athletics as they were to boys' programs.

Twenty-five years after the enactment of Title IX, girls' sports—which had previously been almost unheard of—

have become enormously popular and have led to the start of several professional women's sports leagues, including basketball and soccer.

Title IX - Prohibition of Sex Discrimination

Sec. 901(a) No person in the United States shall, on the basis of sex, be excluded from participation in, be denied the benefits of, or be subjected to discrimination under any education program or activity receiving Federal financial assistance, except that:

in regard to admissions to educational institutions, this section shall apply only to institutions of vocational education, professional education, and graduate higher education, and to public institutions of undergraduate higher education:

in regard to admissions to educational institutions, this section shall not apply (a) for one year from the date of enactment of this Act, nor for six years after such date in the case of an educational institution which has begun the process of changing from being an institution which admits only students of one sex to being an institution which admits students of both sexes, but only if it is carrying out a plan for such a change which is approved by the Commissioner of Education or (B) for seven years from the date an educational institution begins the process of changing from being an institution which admits students of both sexes, but only if it is carrying out a plan for such a change which is approved by the Commissioner of Education, whichever is the later;

this section shall not apply to an educational institution which is controlled by a religious organization if the application of this subsection would not be consistent with the religious tenets of such organization;

this section shall not apply to an educational institution whose primary purpose is the training of individuals for the military services of the United States, or the merchant marine; and

in regard to admissions this section shall not apply to any public institution of undergraduate higher education which is an institution that traditionally and continually from its establishment has had a policy of admitting only students of one sex.

(b) Nothing contained in subsection (a) of this section shall be interpreted to require any educational institution to grant preferential or disparate treatment to the members of one sex on account of an imbalance which may exist with respect to the total number or percentage of persons of that sex participating in or receiving the benefits of any federally supported program or activity, in comparison with the total number or percentage of persons of that sex in any community, State, section, or other area: Provided, that this subsection shall not be construed to prevent the consideration in any hearing or proceeding under this title of statistical evidence tending to show that such an imbalance exists with respect to the participation in, or receipt of the benefits of, any such program or activity by the members of one sex.

(c) For purposes of this title an educational institution means any public or private preschool, elementary or secondary school, or any institution of vocational, professional, or higher education, except that in the case of an educational institution composed of more than one school, college, or department which are administratively separate units, such term means each such school, college, or departments.

Roe v. Wade: "Personal privacy includes the abortion decision"

SUPREME COURT JUSTICE HARRY A. BLACKMUN

Perhaps the most controversial Supreme Court decision in the last thirty years, *Roe v. Wade* determined that a citizen's right to personal liberty allows a woman to decide whether to bear a child. The 1973 decision written by Justice Harry A. Blackmun prohibits states from regulating that choice during the first trimester of a woman's pregnancy, but allows for certain regulations thereafter.

The case pitted "Jane Roe," who was later revealed to be Norma McCorvey, against Dallas (Texas) County District Attorney Henry Wade, who was enforcing the state law prohibiting abortion as a criminal offense. The majority (7-2) found in favor of Roe. Although the decision was widely hailed in some circles, it galvanized the "right to life" movement, which has remained a vocal and powerful constituency in American politics.

This Texas federal appeal and its Georgia companion, *Doe v. Bolton*, post, p. 179, present constitutional challenges to state criminal abortion legislation. The Texas statutes under attack here are typical of those that have been in effect in many States for approximately a century. The Georgia statutes, in contrast, have a modern cast and are a legislative product that, to an extent at least, obviously reflects the influences of recent attitudinal change, of advancing medical knowledge and techniques, and of new thinking about an old issue.

We forthwith acknowledge our awareness of the sensitive and emotional nature of the abortion controversy, of the vigorous opposing views, even among physicians, and of the deep and seemingly absolute convictions that the subject inspires. One's philosophy, one's experiences, one's exposure to the raw edges of human existence, one's religious training, one's attitudes toward life and family and their values, and the moral standards one established and seeks to observe, are all likely to influence and to color one's thinking and conclusions about abortion.

In addition, population growth, pollution, poverty, and racial overtones tend to complicate and not to simplify the problem.

Our task, of course, is to resolve the issue by constitutional measurement, free of emotion and of predilection.

II

Jane Roe, a single woman who was residing in Dallas County, Texas, instituted this federal action in March 1970 against the District Attorney of the county. She sought a declaratory judgment that the Texas criminal abortion statutes were unconstitutional on their face, and an injunction restraining the defendant from enforcing the statutes.

Roe alleged that she was unmarried and pregnant; that she wished to terminate her pregnancy by an abortion "performed by a competent, licensed physician, under safe, clinical conditions"; that she was unable to get a "legal" abortion in Texas because her life did not appear to be threatened by the continuation of her pregnancy; and that she could not afford to travel to another jurisdiction in order to secure a legal abortion under safe conditions. She claimed that the Texas statutes were unconstitutionally vague and that they abridged her right of personal privacy, protected by the First, Fourth, Fifth, Ninth and Fourteenth Amendments. By an amendment to her complaint Roe purported to sue "on behalf of

herself and all other women" similarly situated....

I. Ancient attitudes. These are not capable of precise determination. We are told that at the time of the Persian Empire abortifications were known and that criminal abortions were severely punished. We are also told, however, that abortion was practiced in Greek times as well as in the Roman Era, and that "it was resorted to without scruple." The Ephesian, Soranos, often described as the greatest of the ancient gynecologists, appears to have been generally opposed to Rome's prevailing free-abortion practices. He found it necessary to think first of the life of the mother, and he resorted to abortion when, upon this standard, he felt the procedure advisable. Greek and Roman law afforded little protection to the unborn. If abortion was prosecuted in some places, it seems to have been based on a concept of a violation of the father's right to his offspring. Ancient religion did not bar abortion.... This right of privacy, whether it be founded in the Fourteenth Amendment's concept of personal liberty and restrictions upon state action, as we feel it is, or, as the District Court determined, in the Ninth Amendment's reservation of rights to the people, is broad enough to encompass a woman's decision whether or not terminate her pregnancy. The detriment that the State would impose upon the pregnant woman by denying this choice altogether is apparent. Specific and direct harm medically diagnosable even in early pregnancy may be involved. Maternity, or additional offspring, may force upon the woman a distressful life and future. Psychological harm may be imminent. Mental and physical health may be taxed by child care. There is also the distress, for all concerned, associated with the unwanted child, and there is the problem of bringing a child into a family already unable, psychologically and otherwise, to care for it. In other cases, as in this one, the additional difficulties and continuing stigma of unwed motherhood may be involved. All these are factors the woman and her responsible physician necessarily will consider in consultation.

On the basis of elements such as these, appellant and some amici argue that the woman's right is absolute and that she is entitled to terminate her pregnancy at whatever time, in whatever way, and for whatever reason she alone chooses. With this we do not agree. Appellant's arguments that Texas either has no valid interest at all in regulating the abortion decision, or no interest strong enough to support any limitation upon the woman's sole determination, are unpersuasive. The Court's decisions recognizing a right of privacy also acknowledge that some state regulation in areas protected by that right is appropriate. As noted above, a State may properly assert important interests in safe-guarding health, in maintaining medical standards, and in protecting potential life. At some point in pregnancy, these respective interests become sufficiently compelling to sustain regulation of the factors that govern the abortion decision. The privacy right involved, therefore, cannot be to be absolute. In fact, it is not clear to us that the claim asserted by some amici that one has an unlimited right to do with one's body as one pleases bears a close relationship to the right of privacy previously articulated in the Court's decisions. The Court has refused to recognize an unlimited right of this kind in the past. *Jacobson v. Massachusetts,* 197 U. S. II (1905) (vaccination); *Buck v. Bell,* 274 U.S. 200 (1927) (sterilization).

We, therefore, conclude that the right of personal privacy includes the abortion decision, but that this right is not unqualified and must be considered against important state interests in regulation.

We note that those federal and state courts that have recently considered abortion law challenges have reached the same conclusion. A majority, in addition to the District Court in the present case, have held state laws unconstitutional, at least in part, because of vagueness or because of overbreadth and abridgement of rights.... In a recent development, generally opposed by the commentators, some States permit the parents of a stillborn child to maintain an action for wrongful death because of prenatal injuries. Such an action, however, would appear to be one to vindicate the parents' interest and is thus consistent with the view that the fetus, at most, represents only the potentiality of life. Similarly, unborn children have been recognized as acquiring rights or interests by way of inheritance or other devolution of property, and have been represented by guardians ad litem. Perfection of the interests involved, again, has generally been contingent upon live birth. In short, the unborn have never been recognized in the law as persons in the whole sense.

X

In view of all this, we do not agree that, by adopting one theory of life, Texas may override the rights of the pregnant woman that are at stake. We repeat, however, that the State does have an important and legitimate interest in preserving and protecting the health of the pregnant woman, whether she be a resident of the State or a nonresident who seeks medical consultation and treatment there, and that it has still another important and legitimate interest in protecting the potentiality of human life. These interests are separate and distinct. Each grows in substantiality as the woman approaches term and, at a point during pregnancy, each becomes "compelling."

With respect to the State's important and legitimate interest in the health of the mother, the "compelling" point, in light of present medical knowledge, is at approximately the end of the first trimester. This is so because the now-established medical fact, referred to above at 149, that until the end of the first trimester mortality in abortion may be less than mortality in normal childbirth. It follows that, from and after this point, a State may regulate the abortion procedure to the extent that the regulation reasonably relates to the preservation and protection of maternal health. Examples of permissible state regulation in this area are requirements as to the qualification of the person who is to perform the abortion; as to the licensure of that person; as to the facility in which the procedure is to be performed, that is, whether it must be a hospital or may be a clinic or some other place of less-than-hospital status; as to the licensing of the facility; and the like.

This means, on the other hand, that, for the period of pregnancy prior to this "compelling" point, the attending physician, in consultation with his patient, is free to determine, without regulation by the State, that, in his medical judgment, the patient's pregnancy should be terminated. If that decision is reached, the judgment may be effectuated by an abortion free of interference by the State.

With respect to the State's important and legitimate interest in potential life, the "compelling" point is viability. This is so because the fetus then presumably has the capability of meaningful life outside the mother's womb. State regulation protective of fetal life after viability thus has both logical and biological justifications. If the State is interested in protecting fetal life after viability, it may go so far as to proscribe abortion during that period, except when it is necessary to preserve the life of health of the mother.

Measured against these standards, Art. 1196 of the Texas penal Code, in restricting legal abortions to those "procured or attempted by medical advice for the purpose of saving the life of the mother," sweeps too broadly. The statute makes no distinction between abortions performed early in pregnancy and those performed later, and it limits to a single reason, "saving" the mother's life, the legal justification for the procedure. That statute, therefore, cannot survive the constitutional attack made upon it here.

This conclusion makes it unnecessary for us to consider the additional challenge to the Texan statute asserted on grounds of vagueness. See *United States v. Vuirth*, 402 U. S., at 67-72.

XI

To summarize and to repeat:

1. A state criminal abortion statute of the criminality only a life-saving procedure on behalf of the mother, without regard to pregnancy stage and without recognition of the other interests involved, is violative of the Due Process Clause of the Fourteenth Amendment.

For the state prior to approximately the end of the first trimester, the abortion decision and its effectuation must be left to the medical judgment of the pregnant woman's attending physician.

For the stage subsequent to approximately the end of the first trimester, the State, in promoting its interest in the health of the mother, may, if it chooses, regulate the abortion procedure in ways that are reasonably related to maternal health.

For the stage subsequent to viability, the State in promoting its interest in the potentiality of human life may, if it chooses, regulate, and even proscribe, abortion except where it is necessary, in appropriate medical judgment, for the preservation of the life or health of the mother.

2. The State may define the term "physician," as it had been employed in the preceding paragraphs of this Part XI of this opinion, to mean only a physician currently licensed by the State, and may proscribe any abortion by a person who is not a physician as so defined.

In *Doe v. Bolton*, past, p. 179, procedural requirement contained in one of the modern abortion statutes are considered. That opinion and this one, of course, are to be read together.

This holding, we feel, is consistent with the relative weights of the respective interests involved, with the lessons and examples of medical and legal history, with the lenity of the common law, and with the demands of the profound problems of the present day. The decision leaves the State free to place increasing restrictions on abortion as the period of pregnancy lengthens, so long as those restrictions are tailored to the recognized state interests. The decision vindicates the right of the physician to administer medical treatment according to his professional judgment up to the points where important state interests provide compelling justifications for intervention. Up to those points, the abortion decision in all its aspects is inherently, and primarily, a medical decision, and basic responsibility for it must rest with the physician. If an individual practitioner abuses the privilege of exercising proper medical judgment, the usual remedies, judicial and intra-professional, are available.

XII

Our conclusion that Art. 1196 is unconstitutional means, of course, that the Texas abortion statutes, as a unit, must fall. The exception of Art. 1196 cannot be struck down separately, for then the State would be left with a statute proscribing all abortion procedures no matter how medically urgent the case.

Although the District Court granted appellant Roe declaratory relief, it stopped short of issuing an injunction against enforcement of the Texas statutes. The Court has recognized that different considerations enter into a federal court's decision as to declaratory relief, on the other. *Zwickler v. Koota*, 389 U. S. 241, 252-255 (1967); *Dombrowski v. Pfister*, 380 U. S. 479 (1965). We are not dealing with a statute that, on its face, appears to abridge free expression, an area of particular concern under Dombrowski and refined in *Younger v. Harris*, 401 U. S., at 50.

We find it unnecessary to decide whether the District Court erred in withholding injunctive relief, for we assume the Texas prosecutorial authorities will give full credence to this decision that the present criminal abortion statutes of that State are unconstitutional.

"The President shall consult with Congress"

THE WAR POWERS RESOLUTION

In the wake of the Vietnam War, Congress sought a greater role in the President's capacity to use military forces abroad. Starting in 1970, Congress introduced legislation requiring the President to gain Congressional approval for introducing armed forces into potentially hostile situations. President Nixon fought the measure, saying it would erode his Constitutional authority and limit the President's ability to act swiftly in international conflicts. In 1973, Congress passed the War Powers Resolution. Nixon vetoed the legislation, but Congress overrode the veto. The resolution later influenced the use of military, or decision not to use military, in Nicaragua and Panama in the 1980s, and Iraq, Somalia and Bosnia in the 1990s.

Section 1. This joint resolution may be cited as the "War Powers Resolution."

Section 2. (a) It is the purpose of this joint resolution to fulfill the intent of the framers of the Constitution of the United States and insure that the collective judgment of both the Congress and the President will apply to the introduction of United States Armed Forces into hostilities, or into situations where imminent involvement in hostilities is clearly indicated by the circumstances, and to the continued use of such forces in hostilities or in such situations,

(b) Under article 1, section 8, of the Constitution, it specifically provided that the Congress shall have the power to make all laws necessary and proper for carrying into execution, not only its own powers but also all other powers vested by the Constitution in the government of the United States, or in any department or officer thereof.

(c) The constitutional power of the President as Commander-in-Chief to introduce United States Armed Forces into hostilities, or into situations where imminent involvement in hostilities is clearly indicated by the circumstances, are exercised only pursuant to (1) a declaration of war, (2) specific statutory authorization, or (3) a national emergency created by attack upon the United States, its territories or possessions, or its armed forces.

Section 3. The President in every possible instance shall consult with Congress before introducing United States Armed Forces into hostilities or into a situation where imminent involvement in hostilities is clearly indicated by the circumstances, and after every such introduction shall consult regularly with the Congress until United States Armed Forces are no longer engaged in hostilities or have been removed from such situations.

Section 4. (a) In the absence of a declaration of war, in any case in which United States Armed Forces are introduced—

into hostilities or into situations where imminent involvement in hostilities is clearly indicated by the circumstances;

into the territory, airspace or waters of a foreign nation, while equipped for combat, except for deployments which relate solely to supply, replacement, repair, or training of such forces; or

in numbers which substantially enlarge United States Armed Forces equipped for combat already located in a foreign nation; the President shall submit within 48 hours to the Speaker of the House of Representatives and to the President pro tempore of the Senate a report, in writing, setting forth—

the circumstances necessitating the introduction of United States Armed forces;

the constitutional and legislative authority under which such introduction took place; and

the estimated scope and duration of the hostilities or involvement.

The President shall provide such other information as the Congress may request in the fulfillment of its constitutional responsibilities with respect to committing the Nation to war and to the use of United States Armed Forces abroad.

Whenever United States Armed Forces are introduced into hostilities or into any situation described in subsection (a) of this section, the President shall, so long as such armed to (a) Each report submitted pursuant to section 4(a)(1) shall be transmitted to the Speaker of the House of Representatives and to the President pro tempore of the Senate on the same calendar day. Each report so transmitted shall be referred to the Committee on Foreign Affairs of the House of Representatives and to the Committee on Foreign

Relations of the Senate for appropriate action. If, when the report is transmitted, the Congress has adjourned sine die or has adjourned in excess of three calendar days, the Speaker of the House of Representatives and the President pro tempore of the Senate, if they deem it advisable (or if petitioned by at least 30 percent of the membership of their respective Houses) shall jointly request the president to convene Congress in order that it may consider the report and take appropriate action pursuant to this section.

(b) Within sixty calendar days after a report is submitted or is required to be submitted pursuant to section 4(a)(1), whichever is earlier, the President shall terminate any use of United States Armed Forces with respect to which such report was submitted (or required to be submitted), unless the Congress (1) has declared war or has enacted specific authorization for such use of United States Armed Forces, (2) has extended by law such sixty-day period, or (3) is physically unable to meet as a result of an armed attack upon the United States. Such sixty-day period shall be extended for not more than an additional thirty days if the President determines and certifies to the congress in writing that unavoidable military necessity respecting the safety of the United States Armed forces requires the continued use of such armed forces in the course of bringing about a prompt removal of such forces.

Notwithstanding subsection (b), at any time that United States Armed Forces are engaged in hostilities outside the territory of the United States, its possessions and territories without a declaration of war or specific statutory authorization, such forces shall be removed by the President if the Congress so directs by concurrent resolution.

♉ "Richard M. Nixon warrants impeachment and trial, and removal from office"

ARTICLES OF IMPEACHMENT, ISSUED BY THE HOUSE JUDICIARY COMMITTEE

On the night of June 17, 1972, police arrested five men for burglarizing the Democratic National Committee's office in the Watergate building in Washington, D.C. Although the burglars gave false names, it came out that one of the burglars, James McCord, was Chief of Security for the Committee to Re-elect the President. Thus, the Watergate scandal began.

Doggedly pursued by *Washington Post* reporters Bob Woodward and Carl Bernstein, the Watergate investigations revealed widespread abuses of power by the Nixon Administration. Among the items that caused a public outcry were Nixon's Enemies List, his "dirty tricks" campaign to undermine the credibility of Senator Edmund Muskie, hush money to participants in the Watergate break-in and blatant attempts by Nixon and his top aides to coverup the affair.

Special prosecutors and a Congressional committee investigated Nixon, revealing signs of personal corruption by Nixon himself. In 1970, he paid $792 in federal income taxes and $878 in 1971. Federal money had been used for the renovation of his homes in San Clemente, California and Key Biscayne, Florida. In July 1974, the House Judiciary Committee voted three articles of impeachment, charging Nixon with obstruction of justice, abuse of presidential power, and unconstitutionally defying subpoenas from Congress.

Article I

In his conduct of the office of President of the United States, Richard M. Nixon, in violation of his constitutional oath faithfully to execute the office of President of the United States...and in violation of his constitutional duty to take care that the laws be faithfully executed, has prevented, obstructed, and impeded the administration of justice....Richard M. Nixon, using the powers of his high office, engaged personally and through his subordinates and agents in a course of conduct or plan designed to delay, impede, and obstruct the investigation of such unlawful entry; to cover up, conceal and protect those responsible; and to conceal the existence and scope of other unlawful covert activities....In all of this, Richard M. Nixon has acted in a manner contrary to his trust as president and subversive of constitutional government, to the great prejudice of the cause of law and justice and to manifest injury of the people of the United States.

Wherefore Richard M. Nixon, by such conduct, warrants impeachment and trial, and removal from office.

Article II

Using the powers of the office of President of the United States, Richard M. Nixon...has repeatedly engaged in conduct violating the constitutional rights of citizens, impairing the due and proper administration of justice in the conduct of lawful inquiries, or contravening the laws governing agencies of the executive branch....

Wherefore, Richard M. Nixon, by such conduct, warrants impeachment and trial, and removal from office.

Article III
In his conduct of the office of President of the United States, Richard M. Nixon...has failed without lawful cause or excuse to produce papers and things, as directed by duly authorized subpoenas...and willfully disobeyed such subpoenas...thereby assuming for himself functions and judgments necessary to the exercise of the sole power of impeachment vested by the Constitution in the House of Representatives....

Wherefore, Richard M. Nixon, by such conduct, warrants impeachment and trial, and removal from office.

"My faith in the Constitution is whole"

BARBARA JORDON

Texas Congresswoman Barbara Jordan sat on the House Judiciary Committee that considered the impeachment of President Nixon for his role in the Watergate scandal. A lawyer, and the first black woman to be elected to the Texas State Senate, Jordan delivered an opening statement that gripped the nation, comparing the actions of the Nixon administration with the quoted aspirations of the Constitution's authors.

Mr. Chairman, I join my colleague Mr. Rangel in thanking you for giving the junior members the glorious opportunity of sharing the pain of this inquiry. Mr. Chairman, you are a strong man, and it has not been easy but we have tried as best we can to give you as much assistance as possible.

Earlier today we heard the beginning of the Preamble to the Constitution of the United States, "We, the people." It is a very eloquent beginning. But when that document was completed, on the seventeenth of September in 1787, I was not included in that "We, the people." I felt somehow for many years that George Washington and Alexander Hamilton just left me out by mistake.

But through the process of amendment, interpretation, and court decision I have finally been included in "We, the people."

Today, I am an inquisitor. I believe hyperbole would not be fictional and would not overstate the solemness that I feel right now. My faith in the Constitution is whole, it is complete, it is total. I am not going to sit here and be an idle spectator to the diminution, the subversion, the destruction of the Constitution.

"Who can so properly be the inquisitors for the nation as the representatives of the nation themselves?" [Federalist Papers, No. 65] The subject of its jurisdiction are those offenses which proceed from the misconduct of public men. That is what we are talking about. In other words, the jurisdiction comes from the abuse of violation of some public trust. It is wrong, I suggest, it is a misreading of the Constitution for any member here to assert that for a member to vote for an article of impeachment means that that member must be convinced that the president should be removed from office. That Constitution doesn't say that. The powers relating to impeachment are an essential check in the hands of this body, the legislature, against and upon the encroachment of the executive. In establishing the division between the two branches of the legislature, the House and the Senate, assigning to the one the right to accuse and to the other the right to judge, the framers of this Constitution were very astute. They did not make the accusers and the judges the same person.

We know the nature of impeachment. We have been talking about it awhile now. "It is chiefly designed for the president and his high ministers" to somehow be called into account. It is designed to "bridle" the executive if he engages in excesses. "It is designed as a method of national inquest into the conduct of public men." [Federalist Papers, No. 65] The framers confined in the Congress the power if need be, to remove the president in order to strike a delicate balance between a president swollen with power and grown tyrannical, and preservation of the independence of the executive. The nature of impeachment is a narrowly channeled exception to the separation-of-powers maxim; the federal convention of 1787 said that. It limited impeachment to high crimes and misdemeanors and discounted and opposed the term "maladministration." It is to be used only for "great misdemeanors," so it was said in the North Carolina ratification convention. And in the Virginia ratification convention: "We do not trust our liberty to a particular branch. We need on one branch to check the other."

The North Carolina ratification convention: "No one need be afraid that officers who commit oppression will pass with immunity."

"Prosecutions of impeachments will seldom fail to agitate the passion of the whole community," said Hamilton in the Federalist Papers, number 65. "And to divide it into parties more or less friendly or inimical to the accused." I do not mean political parties in that sense.

The drawing of political lines goes to the motivation behind impeachment; but impeachment must proceed within the confines of the constitutional term "high crimes and misdemeanors."

Of the impeachment process, it was Woodrow Wilson who said that "nothing short of the grossest offenses against the plain law of the land will suffice to give them speed and effectiveness. Indignation so great as to overgrow party interest may secure a conviction; but nothing else can."

Common sense would be revolted if we engaged upon this process for petty reasons. Congress has a lot to do. Appropriations, tax reform, health insurance, campaign finance reform, housing, environmental protection, energy sufficiency, mass transportation. Pettiness cannot be allowed to stand in the face of such overwhelming problems. So today we are not being petty. We are trying to be big because the task we have before us is a big one.

This morning, in a discussion of the evidence, we were told that the evidence which purports to support the allegations of misuse of the CIA by the president is thin. We are told that that evidence is insufficient. What that recital of evidence this morning did not include is what the president did know on June 23, 1972. The president did know that is was republican money, that it was money from the Committee for the Re-Election of the President, which was founded in the possession of one of the burglars arrested on June 17.

What the president did know on June 23 was the prior activities of E. Howard Hunt, which included his participation in the break-in of Daniel Ellsberg's psychiatrist, which included Howard Hunt's participation in the Dita Beard ITT affair, which included Howard Hunt's fabrication of fables

designed to discredit the Kennedy administration.

We were further cautioned today that perhaps these proceedings ought to be delayed because certainly there would be new evidence forthcoming from the president of the United States. There has not even been an obfuscated indication that this committee would receive any additional materials from the president. The committee subpoena is outstanding, and if the president wants to supply that material, the committee sits here.

The fact is that yesterday, the American people waited with great anxiety for eight hours, not knowing whether their president would obey an order of the Supreme Court of the United States.

At this point I would like to juxtapose a few of the impeachment criteria with some of the president's actions.

Impeachment criteria: James Madison, from the Virginia ratification convention. "The president be connected in any suspicious manner with any person and there be grounds to believe that he will shelter him, he may be impeached."

We have heard time and time again that the evidence reflects payment to the defendants of money. The president had knowledge that these funds were being paid and that these were funds collected for the 1972 presidential campaign.

We know that the president met with Mr. Henry Petersen twenty-seven times to discuss matters related to Watergate and immediately thereafter met with the very persons who were implicated with the information Mr. Petersen was receiving and transmitting to the president. The words are "if the president be connected in any suspicious manner with any person and there be grounds to believe that he will shelter that person, he may be impeached."

Justice Story: "Impeachment is intended for occasional and extraordinary cases where a superior power acting for the whole people is put into operation to protect their rights and rescue their liberties from violations."

We know about the Huston plan. We know about the break-in of the psychiatrist's office. We know that there was absolute complete direction in August 1971 when the president instructed Ehrlichman to "do whatever is necessary." This instruction led to a surreptitious entry into Dr. Fielding's office.

"Protect their right." "Rescue their liberties from violation."

The South Carolina ratification convention impeachment criteria: those are impeachable "who behave amiss or betray their public trust."

Beginning shortly after the Watergate break-in and continuing to the present time, the president has engaged in a series of public statements and actions designed to thwart the lawful investigation by government prosecutors. Moreover, the president has made public announcements and assertions bearing on the Watergate case which the evidence will show he know to be false.

These assertions, false assertions, impeachable, those who misbehave. Those who "behave amiss or betray their public trust."

James Madison again at the Constitutional Convention: "A president is impeachable if he attempts to subvert the Constitution."

The Constitution charges the president with the task of taking care that the laws by faithfully executed, and yet the president has counseled his aides to commit perjury, willfully disregarded the secrecy of grand jury proceedings, concealed surreptitious entry, attempted to compromise a federal judge while publicly displaying his cooperation with the process of criminal justice.

"A president is impeachable if he attempts to subvert the Constitution."

If the impeachment provision in the Constitution of the United States will not reach the offenses charged here, then perhaps the eighteenth-century Constitution should be abandoned to a twentieth-century paper shredder. Has the president committed offenses and planned and directed and acquiesced in a course of conduct which the Constitution will not tolerate? That is the question. We know that. We know the question. We should now forthwith proceed to answer the question. It is reason, and not passion, which must guide our deliberations, guide our debate, and guide our decision.

❧ Letter of Resignation

RICHARD NIXON

On August 9, 1974, Richard Nixon made history as the first president to resign from office. When it became obvious that Congress would impeach him over Watergate, Nixon decided to submit his resignation to Secretary of State Henry Kissinger.

For the next 25 years, Nixon struggled to cleanse his place in history, writing books, commenting on foreign affairs, and advising some of his successors. Nixon's presidency was marked with some significant accomplishments. These included establishing the Environmental Protection Agency and the Occupational Safety and Health Administration, ending the war in Vietnam, initiating diplomatic relations with China and Russia, expanding the federal food stamp program, indexing Social Security payments and many other measures.

Nevertheless, Nixon's presidency will forever be remembered for its premature termination. Ultimately, Watergate resulted in a wave of reform measures designed to prevent the abuses of office laid bare by the scandal. Campaign finance reforms, public disclosures of finances and the introduction of the independent prosecutor's office all came about because of Watergate.

Dear Mr. Secretary,

I hereby resign the Office of President of the United States.

Sincerely,

Richard Nixon

❧ "Our long national nightmare is over"

GERALD FORD

Gerald Ford was the first and only president to reach that office without being elected. When Spiro Agnew resigned as vice president in late 1973 Nixon selected Ford, who was serving as Speaker of the House of Representatives, to be his vice president. When Nixon resigned from office on August 9, 1974, Ford stepped up to take his place.

Intending to ease concerns at home and abroad over this unprecedented event, Ford assured the nation of his modest ambitions to continue the country's course in a steady fashion. Several months after he delivered this speech, he would pardon Nixon, unleashing a heap of criticism and accusations that a deal was made. When the 1976 election arrived, Ford lost in a closer than expected race to Jimmy Carter. Many attribute his loss to the decision to pardon Nixon.

The oath that I have taken is the same oath that was taken by George Washington and by every president under the Constitution. But I assume the presidency under extraordinary circumstances never before experienced by Americans. This is an hour of history that troubles our minds and hurts our hearts.

Therefore, I feel it is my first duty to make an unprecedented compact with my countrymen. Not an inaugural address, not a fireside chat, not a campaign speech—just a little straight talk among friends. And I intend it to be the first of many.

I am acutely aware that you have not elected me as your president by your ballots, and so I ask you to confirm me as your president with your prayers. And I hope that such prayers will also be the first of many.

If you have not chosen me by secret ballot, neither have I gained office by any secret promises. I have not campaigned either for the presidency or the vice-presidency. I have not subscribed to any partisan platform. I am indebted to no man, and only to one woman—my dear wife—as I begin this very difficult job.

I have not sought this enormous responsibility, but I will not shirk it. Those who nominated and confirmed me as vice president were my friends and are my friends. They were of both parties, elected by all the people and acting under the Constitution in their name. It is only fitting then that I should pledge to them and to you that I will be the president of all the people.

Thomas Jefferson said the people are the only sure reliance for the preservation of our liberty. And down the years, Abraham Lincoln renewed this American article of faith, asking "Is there any better way or equal hope in the world?"

I intend, on Monday next, to request of the speaker of the House of Representatives and the president pro tempore of the Senate the privilege of appearing before the Congress to share with my former colleagues and with you, the American people, my views on the priority business of the nation and to solicit your views and their views. And may I say to the Speaker and the others, if I could meet with you right after these remarks, I would appreciate it.

Even though this is late in an election year, there is no way we can go forward except together and no way anybody can win except by serving the people's urgent needs. We cannot stand still or slip backwards. We must go forward now together.

To the peoples and governments of all friendly nations, and I hope that could encompass the whole world, I pledge an uninterrupted and sincere search for peace. America will remain strong and united, but its strength will remain dedicated to the safety and sanity of the entire family of man, as well as to our own precious freedom.

I believe the truth is the glue that holds gov-

ernment together, not only our government but civilization itself. That bond, though strained, is unbroken at home and abroad.

In all my public and private acts as your president, I expect to follow my instincts of openness and candor with full confidence that honesty is always the best policy in the end.

My fellow Americans, our long national nightmare is over.

Our Constitution works; our great Republic is a government of laws and not of men. Here the people rule. But there is a greater power, by whatever name we honor him, who ordains not only righteousness but love, not only justice but mercy.

As we bind up the internal wounds of Watergate, more painful and more poisonous than those of foreign wars, let us restore the golden rule to our political process, and let brotherly love purge our hearts of suspicion and of hate.

In the beginning, I asked you to pray for me. Before closing, I ask again for your prayers, for Richard Nixon and for his family. May our former president, who brought peace to millions, find it for himself. May God bless and comfort his wonderful wife and daughters, whose love and loyalty will forever be a shining legacy to all who bear the lonely burdens of the White House.

I can only guess at those burdens, although I have witnessed at close hand the tragedies that befell three presidents and the lesser trials of others.

With all the strength and all the good sense I have gained from life, with all the confidence my family, my friends, and my dedicated staff impart to me, and with the good will of countless Americans I have encountered in recent visits to forty states, I now solemnly reaffirm my promise I made to you last December 6: to uphold the Constitution, to do what is right as God gives me to see the right, and to do the very best I can for America.

God helping me, I will not let you down.
Thank you.

❧ "I Am Somebody"

THE REV. JESSE JACKSON

By the 1970s, the Civil Rights movement had become fragmented. The assassination of Martin Luther King, Jr., the divisions within the movement itself and simply the exhaustion of carrying on the struggle, had all contributed to a waning of energy. In addition, the issues had changed. Having successfully won victories in their battle for equality in the legislatures and the court rooms, the next—and in many ways more difficult—phase was to actualize King's dream.

Rev. Jesse Jackson, a close associate of King's, focused his efforts in the 1970s toward building a greater sense of self-esteem, particularly among black youths, so they would have the confidence to exercise their newfound rights. He attempted to make his effort national in scope and incorporated people of all color, including whites, to form the Rainbow Coalition, an organization dedicated to fostering racial harmony in civic, social and political arenas. Eventually, Jackson would be the first black man to make a serious run for the Presidency. One effective tool he used in accomplishing his goal was to have his audiences recite his refrain: "I Am Somebody."

I am somebody
I am somebody
I may be poor
But I am somebody
I may be young
But I am somebody
I may be on welfare
But I am somebody
I may be small
But I am somebody
I may make a mistake
But I am somebody
My clothes are different
My face is different
My hair is different
But I am somebody
I am black, brown, white
I speak a different language
But I must be respected, protected, never
    rejected
I am God's child
I am somebody

❧ "What we need is a neighborhood where people can walk to work, raise their kids, enjoy life"

HARVEY MILK

Harvey Milk, the first openly homosexual candidate to win a seat on the San Francisco Board of Supervisors, was one of the most articulate public commentators on the flip side of American progress.

Cities, once vital centers of American vigor, were being sapped of their energy as the more affluent residents fled to the suburbs. Television was replacing social contact with neighbors. The nationalization of entertainment, advertising, politics and culture was creating an increasingly homogenized society.

In this 1977 speech shortly after being elected supervisor, Milk elaborated on the ubiquitous signs of modern decline, particularly in the cities, and sought answers on how to revitalize cities and neighborhoods. Milk, however, would be assassinated a year later, along with Mayor George Moscone, by a former supervisor.

Let's make no mistake about this: The American Dream starts with the neighborhoods. If we wish to rebuild our cities, we must first rebuild our neighborhoods. And to do that, we must understand that the quality of life is more important than the standard of living. To sit on the front steps—whether it's a veranda in a small town or a concrete stoop in a big city—and talk to our neighborhoods is infinitely more important than to huddle on the living-room lounger and watch a make-believe world in not-quite living color.

Progress is not America's only business—and certainly not its most important. Isn't it strange that as technology advances, the quality of life so frequently declines? Oh, washing the dishes is easier. Dinner itself is easier—just heat and serve, though it might be more nourishing if we ate the ads and threw the food away. And we no longer fear spots on our glassware when the guests come over. But then, of course, the guests don't come, because our friends are too afraid to come to our house and it's not safe to go to theirs.

And I hardly need to tell you that in that 19- or 24-inch view of the world, cleanliness has long since eclipsed godliness. See we'll all smell, look and actually be laboratory clean, as sterile on the inside as on the out. The perfect consumer, surrounded by the latest appliances. The perfect audience, with a ringside seat to almost any event in the world, without smell, without taste, without feel—alone and unhappy in the vast wasteland of our living rooms. I think that what we actually need, of course, is a little more dirt on the seat of our pants as we sit on the front stoop and talk to our neighbors once again, enjoying the type of summer day where the smell of garlic travels slightly faster than the speed of sound.

There's something missing in the sanitized lives we lead. Something that our leaders in Washington can never supply by simple edict, something that the commercials on television never advertise because nobody's yet found a way to bottle it or box it or can it. What's missing is the touch, the warmth, the meaning of life. A four-color spread in *Time* is no substitute for it. Neither is a 30-second commercial or a reassuring Washington press conference.

I spent many years on both Wall Street and Montgomery Street and I fully understand the debt and responsibility major corporations owe their shareholders. I also fully understand the urban battlefields of New York and Cleveland and Detroit. I see the faces of the unemployed—and of the unemployable—of the city. I've seen the faces in Chinatown, Hunters Point, the Mission and the Tenderloin…and I don't like what I see.

Oddly, I'm also reminded of the most successful slogan a business ever coined: The customer is always right.

What's been forgotten is that those people of the Tenderloin and Hunters Point, those people in the streets, are the customers, certainly potential ones, and they must be treated as such. Government cannot ignore them and neither can business ignore them. What sense is there in making products if the would-be customer can't afford them? It's not alone a question of price, it's a question of ability to pay. For a man with no money, 99 cents reduced from $1.29 is still a fortune.

American business must realize that while the shareholders always come first, the care and feeding of their customers is a close second. They have a debt and a responsibility to that customer and the city in which he or she lives, the cities in which the business itself lives or in which it grew up. To throw away a senior citizen after they've nursed you through childhood is wrong. To treat a city as disposable once your business has prospered is equally wrong and even more short-sighted.

Unfortunately for those who would like to flee them, the problems of the cities don't stop at the city limits. There are no moats around our cities that keep the problems in. What happens in New York or San Francisco will eventually happen in San Jose. It's just a matter of time. And like the flu, it usually gets worse the further it travels. Our cities must not be abandoned. They're worth fighting for,

not just by those who live in them, but by industry, commerce, unions, everyone. Not alone because they represent the past, but because they also represent the future. Your children will live there and hopefully, so will your grandchildren. For all practical purposes, the eastern corridor from Boston to Newark will be one vast strip city. So will the area from Milwaukee to Gary, Indiana. In California, it will be that fertile crescent of asphalt and neon that stretches from Santa Barbara to San Diego. Will urban blight travel the arteries of the freeways? Of course it will—unless we stop it.

So the challenge of the 80s will be to awaken the consciousness of industry and commerce to the part they must play in saving the cities which nourished them. Every company realizes it must constantly invest in its own physical plant to remain healthy and grow. Well, the cities are a part of that plant and the people who live in them are part of the cities. They're all connected; what affects one affects the others.

In short, the cheapest place to manufacture a product may not be the cheapest at all if it results in throwing your customers out of work. There's no sense in making television sets in Japan if the customers in the United States haven't the money to buy them. Industry must actively seek to employ those without work, to train those who have no skills. "Labor intensive" is not a dirty word, not every job is done better by machine. It has become the job of industry not only to create the product, but also to create the customer.

Costly? I don't think so. It's far less expensive than the problem of fully loaded docks and no customers. And there are additional returns: lower rates of crime, smaller welfare loads. And having your friends and neighbors sitting on that well-polished front stoop….

Many companies feel that helping the city is a form of charity. I think it is more accurate to consider it a part of the cost of doing business, that it should be entered on the books as amortizing the future. I would like to see business and industry consider it as such, because I think there's more creativity, more competence perhaps, in business than there is in government. I think that business could turn the south of market Area not only into an industrial park but a neighborhood as well. To coin a pun, too many of our cities have a complex, in fact, too many complexes. We don't need another concrete jungle that dies the moment you turn off the lights in the evening. What we need is a neighborhood where people can walk to work, raise their kids, enjoy life.

The cities will be saved. The cities will be governed. But they won't be run from three thousand miles away in Washington, they won't be run from the statehouse, and most of all, they won't be run by the carpetbaggers who have fled to the suburbs. You can't run a city by people who don't live there, any more than you can have an effective police force made up of people who don't live there. In either case, what you've got is an occupying army.

The cities will not be saved by the people who feel condemned to live in them, who can hardly wait to move to Marin or San Jose—or Evanston or Westchester. The cities will be saved by the people who like it here. The people who prefer the neighborhood stores to the shopping mall, who go to the plays and eat in the restaurants and go to the discos and worry about the education the kids are getting even if they have no kids of their own.

That's not just the city of the future; it's the city of today. It means new directions, new alliances, new solutions for ancient problems. The typical American family with two cars and 2.2 kids doesn't live here anymore. It hasn't for years. The demographics are different now and we all know it. The city is a city of singles and young marrieds, the city of the retired and the poor, a city of many colors who speak in many tongues.

The city will run itself, it will create its own solution. District elections was not the end. It was just the beginning. We'll solve our problems—with your help. I don't deny that. But you also need us. We're your customers. We're your future.

I'm riding into that future and frankly I don't know if I'm wearing the fabled helm of Mambrino on my head or if I'm wearing a barber's basin. I guess we wear what we want to wear and we fight what we want to fight. Maybe I see dragons where there are only windmills. But something tells me the dragons are for real and if I shatter a lance or two on a whirling blade, maybe I'll catch a dragon in the bargain.

Yesterday, my esteemed colleague on the Board said we cannot live on hope alone. I know that, but I strongly feel the important thing is not that we cannot live on hope alone, but that life is not worth living without it. If the story of Don Quixote means anything, it means that the spirit of life is just as important as its substance. What others may see as a barber's basin, you and I know is that glittering, legendary helmet.

Born to Run

BRUCE SPRINGSTEEN

Bruce Springsteen emerged as one of America's best songwriters and most popular rock stars in the early 1970s. His lyrics about the gritty, wild times of youth in an era of suburbs and consumerism resonated with Americans still yearning for a wide-open sense of freedom.

In the days we sweat it out in the streets of a runaway American dream
At night we ride through mansions of glory in suicide machines
Sprung from cages out on Highway 9
Chrome wheeled, fuel injected
And steppin' out over the line
Baby this town rips the bones from your back
It's a death trap, it's a suicide rap
We gotta get out while we're young
'Cause tramps like us, baby we were born to run
Wendy, let me in, I wanna be your friend
I want to guard your dreams and visions
Just wrap your legs round these velvet rims
And strap your hands across my engines
Together we could break this trap
We'll run till we drop, baby we'll never go back
Will you walk with me out on the wire
'Cause baby I'm just a scared and lonely rider
But I gotta know how it feels
I want to know if your love is wild
Girl I want to know if love is real
Beyond the Palace hemi-powered drones scream down the boulevard
The girls comb their hair in rear-view mirrors
And the boys try to look so hard
The amusement park rises bold and stark
Kids are huddled on the beach in a mist
I wanna die with you out on the streets tonight
In an everlasting kiss
The highways jammed with broken heroes
On a last chance power drive

Everybody's out on the run tonight
But there's no place left to hide
Together, Wendy, we can live with the sadness
I'll love you with all the madness in my soul
Someday girl, I don't know when, we're gonna get
    to that place
Where we really want to go
And we'll walk in the sun
But till then tramps like us
Baby we were born to run

CHAPTER ELEVEN

1975–1999

Modern Times

🍂 "City people don't think anything important happens in a place like Dime Box"

WILLIAM LEAST HEAT MOON

William Least Heat Moon's book *Blue Highways: A Journey Into America,* **about his journey traveling the back roads of the United States, celebrated small-town communities as the foundation of traditional American values. In the wake of the anger and self-flagellation of the 1960s, he helped Americans see again what was good—and sometimes humorous— about the nation and its people.**

Dime Box, Texas, is not the funniest town in America. Traditionally, that honor belongs to Intercourse, Pennsylvania. I prefer Scratch Ankle, Alabama, Gnawbone, Indiana, or even Humptulips, Washington. Nevertheless, Dime Box, as a name, caught my ear, so that's where I headed the next morning out of College Station.

In the humid night, the inside windows had dripped like cavern walls: Along State 21, I opened up and let warm air blow out the damp. West of the Brazos, the land unfolded even farther to the blue sky. Now the horizon wasn't ten or fifteen miles away, it was thirty or forty. On telephone wires sat scissor-tailed flycatchers, their oddly long tails hanging under them like stilts. Roadside wild-flowers—bluebonnets, purple winecups, evening primroses, and more—were abundant as crops, and where wide reaches of bluebonnets (once called buffalo clover, wolf flower, and, by the Spanish, "the rabbit") covered the slopes, their scent filled the highway. To all the land was an intense clarity as the little things gave off light.

Across the Yegua River a sign pointed south to Dime Box. Over broad hills, over the green expansion spreading under cedars and live oaks, on into a valley where I found Dime Box, essentially a three-street town. Vegetable gardens and flowerbeds lay to the side, behind, and in front of the houses. Perpendicular to the highway, two streets ran east and west: one of worn brick buildings facing the South Pacific tracks, the other a double row of false-front stores and wooden sidewalks. Disregarding a jarring new bank, Dime Box could have been an M-G-M backlot set for a Western.

You can't walk down a board sidewalk without clomping, so I clomped down to Ovcarik's Cafe and through the screendoor, which banged shut as they always do. An aroma of ham and beans. Four calendars. From long cords three naked bulbs burned, and still the place was dim. Everthing was wood except a heating stove and the Coca-Cola cooler. Near the door, a sign tacked above the flyswatter and next to the machete explained the ten-year prison term for carrying a weapon into premises where liquor is served.

At the counter I drank a Royal Crown; the waitress dropped my quarter into the cash register, a King Edward cigarbox. Forks and knives clinked on plates behind a partition in the rear. It was too much. I ordered a dinner.

She set down a long plate of ham, beans, beets, and brown gravy. I seasoned everything with hot peppers in vinegar. From the partition came a thump-thump like an empty beer bottle rapping on a table. The waitress pulled two Lone Stars from the faded cooler, foam trickling over her fingers as she carried them back. In all the time I was there, I heard a voice from the rear only once: "I'm tellin' you, he can flat out throw that ball."

A man came from the kitchen, sat beside me, and began dropping toothpicks through the small openings of Tabasco sauce bottles used as dispensers. Down the counter, a fellow with tarnished eyes said, "Is it Tuesday?" The waitress nodded, and everything fell quiet again but the clinking of forks. After a while, a single thump, and she carried back a Lone Star. The screendoor opened: a woman, old and tall, stepped into the dimness cane first, thwacking it to and fro. Loudly she croaked, "Cain't see, damn it!"

A middle-aged woman said, "Straight on, Mother. It isn't that dark." She helped the crone sit at one of the tables. They ordered the meal.

"Ain't no use," the waitress said. "Just sold the last plate to him."

Him was me. They turned and looked. "Let's go, Mother." The tall woman rose, breaking wind as she did. "Easy, Mother."

"You don't feed me proper!" she croaked and thwacked out the door.

The man with the Tabasco bottles said to no one in particular, "Don't believe the old gal needed any beans."

Again a long quiet. Then the one who

had ascertained the day said to the waitress, "Saw a cat runned over on the highway. Was it yourn?"

She shifted the toothpick with her tongue. "What color?" He couldn't remember. "Lost me an orange cat. Ain't seen Peewee in a week."

"I got me too many cats," he said. "I'll pay anybody a quarter each to kill my spares."

That stirred a conversation on methods of putting away kittens, and that led to methods of killing fire ants. The man beside me put down a toothpick bottle. It had taken some time to fill. He said, "I got the best way to kill far ants, and it ain't by diggin' or poison." No one paid attention. Finally he muttered, "Pour gasoline on the hive." No one said anything.

"Do you light it?" I asked.

"Light what?"

"The gasoline."

"Hell no, you don't light it." He held out a big, gullied palm and pointed to a tiny lump. "Got nipped there last year by a far ant. If you don't pick the poison out, it leaves a knot for two or three years."

The other man talked of an uncle who once kept sugar ants in his pantry and fed them molasses. "When they fattened up, he put them on a butter sandwich. Butter kept them from runnin' off the bread." The place was so quiet you could almost hear the heat on the tin roof. If anyone was listening to him, I couldn't tell. "Claimed molasses gave them ants real flavor," he said.

Thump-thump. The woman turned from the small window, her eyes vacant, and went to the cooler for two more bottles of Lone Star.

I walked to the post office for stamps. The postmistress explained the town name. A century ago the custom was to drop a letter and ten cents for postage into the pickup box. That was in Old Dime Box up on the San Antonio road, now Texas 21. "What happened to Old Dime Box?"

"A couple houses there yet," she said, "but the railroad came through in nineteen thirteen, three miles south, so they moved the town to the tracks—to here. Now the train's about gone. Some freights, but that's it."

"I see Czech names on stores."

"We're between Giddings and Caldwell. Giddings is mostly German and Caldwell's mostly Czech. We're close to fifty-fifty. Whites, that is. A third of Dime Box is black people."

"How do the different groups get along?"

"Pretty well. We had a to-do in the sixties over integration, but it was mostly between white groups arguing about who had the right to run the schools. Some parents bussed kids away for a spell, but that was just anger."

"Bussing in Dime Box?"

"City people don't think anything important happens in a place like Dime Box. And usually it doesn't, unless you call conflict important. Or love or babies or dying."

🍂 "Government is not the solution to our problem; government is the problem"

RONALD REAGAN

Fifteen years after Lyndon Johnson's Great Society program, which introduced social programs to help bring greater economic equality to the country, President Ronald Reagan proclaimed in his inaugural address that the time had come to pull back governmental programs. Reagan vowed to tame double-digit inflation that had eroded the nation's economy by cutting back government spending and lowering "punishing" tax rates.

Reagan's election marked the beginning of a new, more conservative era in American politics. One where business interests would take precedent over social engineering. Despite the overarching goal of trying to cut the federal deficit, the national government debt would increase almost four-fold under Reagan's and Republican successor George Bush's watch. In part, this was because of Reagan's determination to bolster the military budget and face down, at last, the Soviet threat.

To a few of us here today this is a solemn and most momentous occasion, and yet in the history of our nation it is a commonplace occurrence. The orderly transfer of authority as called for in the Constitution routinely takes place, as it has for almost two centuries, and few of us stop to think how unique we really are. In the eyes of many in the world, this every-four-year-ceremony we accept as normal is nothing less than a miracle.

The business of our nation goes forward. These United States are confronted with an economic affliction of great proportions. We suffer from the longest and one of the worst sustained inflations in our national history. It distorts our economic decisions, penalizes thrift, and crushes the struggling young and fixed-income elderly alike. It threatens to shatter the lives of millions of our people.

Idle industries have cast workers into unemployment, human misery, and personal indignity. Those who do work are denied a fair return for their labor by a tax system which penalizes successful achievement and keeps us from maintaining full productivity.

But great as our tax burden is, it has not kept pace with public spending. For decades we have piled deficit upon deficit, mortgaging our future and our children's future for the temporary convenience of the present. To continue this long trend is to guarantee tremendous social, cultural, political, and economic upheavals.

You and I, as individuals, can, by borrowing, live beyond our means, but for only a limited period of time. Why, then, should we think that collectively, as a nation, we're not bound by that same limitation? We must act today in order to preserve tomorrow. And let there be no misunderstanding: we are going to begin to act, beginning today.

The economic ills we suffer have come upon us over several decades. They will not go away in days, weeks, or months, but they will go away. They will go away because we as Americans have the capacity now, as we've had in the past, to do whatever needs to be done to preserve this last and greatest bastion of freedom.

In this present crisis, government is not the solution to our problem; government is the problem. From time to time we've been tempted to believe that society has become too complex to be managed by self-rule, that government by an elite group is superior to government for, by and of the people. Well, if no one among us is capable of governing himself, then who among us has the capacity to govern someone else? All of us together, in and out of government, must bear the burden. The solutions we seek must be equitable, with no one group singled out to pay a higher price.

We hear much of special interest groups. Well, our concern must be for a special interest group that has been too long neglected. It knows no sectional boundaries or ethnic and racial divisions, and it crosses political party lines. It is made up of men and women who raise our food, patrol our streets, man our mines and factories, teach our children, keep our homes, and heal us when we're sick—professionals, industrialists, shopkeepers, clerks, cabbies, and truck-drivers. They are, in short, "We the people," this breed called Americans.

Well, this administration's objective will be a healthy, vigorous, growing economy that provides equal opportunities for all Americans, with no barriers born of bigotry or discrimination. Putting America back to work means putting all Americans back to work. Ending inflation means freeing all Americans from the terror of runaway living costs. All must share in the productive work of this "new beginning," and all must share in the bounty of a revived economy. With the idealism and fair play which are the core of our system and our strength, we can have a strong and prosperous America, at peace with itself and the world.

So, let us take inventory. We are a nation that has a government—not the other way around. And this makes us special among the nations of the earth. Our government has no power except that granted it by the people. It is time to check and reverse the growth of government, which shows signs of having grown beyond the consent of the governed.

It is my intention to curb the size and influence of the federal establishment and to demand recognition of the distinction between the powers granted to the federal government and those reserved to the states or to the people. All of us need to be reminded that the federal government did not create the states; the states created the federal government....

We have every right to dream heroic dreams. Those who say that we're in a time when there are not heroes, they just don't know where to look. You can see heroes every day going in and out of factory gates. Others, a handful in number, produce enough food to feed all of us and then the world beyond. You meet heroes across a counter, and they're on both sides of that counter. There are entrepreneurs with faith in themselves and faith in an idea who create new jobs, new wealth, and opportunity. They're individuals and families whose taxes support the government and whose voluntary gifts support church, charity, culture, art, and education. Their patriotism is quiet, but deep. Their values sustain our national life....

Directly in front of me, the monument to a monumental man, George Washington, father of our country—a man of humility who came to greatness reluctantly. He led America out of revolutionary victory into infant nationhood. Off to one side, the stately memorial to Thomas Jefferson. The Declaration of Independence flames with his eloquence. And then, beyond the Reflecting Pool, the dignified columns of the Lincoln Memorial. Whoever would understand in his heart the meaning of America will find it in the life of Abraham Lincoln.

Beyond those monuments to heroism is the Potomac River, and on the far shore the sloping hills of Arlington National Cemetery, with its row upon row of simple white markers bearing crosses or stars of David. They add up to only a tiny fraction of the price that has been paid for our freedom.

Each one of those markers is a monument to the kind of hero I spoke of earlier. Their lives ended in places called Belleau Wood, the Argonne, Omaha Beach, Salerno, and halfway around the world on Guadalcanal, Tarawa, Pork Chop Hill, the Chosin Reservoir, and in a hundred rice paddies and jungles of a place called Vietnam.

Under one such marker lies a young man, Martin Treptow, who left his job in a small town barbershop in 1917 to go to France with the famed Rainbow Division. There, on the western front, he was killed trying to carry a message between battalions under heavy artillery fire.

We're told that on his body was found a diary. On the flyleaf under the heading "My Pledge" he had written these words: "America must win this war. Therefore I will work, I will save, I will sacrifice, I will endure, I will fight cheerfully and do my utmost, as if the issue of the whole struggle depended on me alone."

The crisis we are facing today does not require of us the kind of sacrifice that Martin Treptow and so many thousands of others were called upon to make. It does require, however, our best effort and our willingness to believe in ourselves and to believe in our capacity to perform great deeds, to believe that together with God's help we can and will resolve the problems which now confront us.

And after all, why shouldn't we believe that? We are Americans.

God bless you, and thank you.

❧ "Shy Rights: Why Not Pretty Soon?"

GARRISON KEILLOR

By the early 1980s, advocacy for minority rights had made great gains. But in many cases the stridency had faded. Also, a counter-reaction was starting to take shape, particularly with the election of Reagan as president. The term "political correctness" came into use describing—sometimes in mocking terms—the "right" way to describe a person, group or event. Even those likely to support a constant vigilance in being sensitive to others sometimes grew exasperated at the perceived need to be strictly appropriate in their use of language.

Humorist Garrison Keillor wrote the following article gently spoofing the growth of splinter advocacy groups. Keillor would become one of America's most popular humorists over the next several years with his weekly public radio show featuring stories of the fictional Lake Wobegon.

Recently I read about a group of fat people who had organized to fight discrimination against themselves. They said that society oppresses the overweight by being thinner than them and that the term "overweight" itself is oppressive because it implies a "right" weight that the fatso has failed to make. Only weightists use such terms, they said; they demanded to be called "total" people and to be thought of in terms of wholeness; and they referred to thin people as being "not all there."

Don't get me wrong. This is fine with me. If, to quote the article if I may, "Fat Leaders Demand Expanded Rights Act, Claim Broad Base of Support," I have no objections to it whatsoever. I feel that it is their right to speak up and I admire them for doing so, though of course this is only my own opinion. I could be wrong.

Nevertheless, after reading the article, I wrote a letter to President Jimmy Carter demanding that his administration take action to end discrimination against shy persons sometime in the very near future. I pointed out three target areas—laws, school, and attitudes—where shy rights maybe could be safeguarded. I tried not to be pushy but I laid it on the line. "Mr. President," I concluded, "you'll probably kill me for saying this but compared to what you've done for other groups, we shys have settled for 'peanuts.' As you may know, we are not ones to make threats, but it is clear to me that if we don't get some action on this, it could be a darned quiet summer. It is up to you, Mr. President. Whatever you decide will be okay by me. Yours very cordially."

I never got around to mailing the letter, but evidently word got around in the shy community that I had written it, and I've noticed that most shy persons are not speaking to me these days. I guess they think the letter went too far. Probably they felt that making demands is a betrayal of the shy movement (or "gesture," as many shys call it) and an insult to shy pride and that it risks the loss of some of the gains we have already made, such as social security and library cards.

Perhaps they are right. I don't claim to have all the answers. I just feel that we ought to begin, at least, to think about some demands that we might make if, for example, we had to someday. That's all. I'm not saying we should make fools of ourselves, for heaven's sake!

Shut Up (A Slogan)

Sometimes I feel that maybe we shy persons have borne our terrible burden for far too long now. Labeled by society as "wimps," "dorks," "creeps," and "sissies," stereotyped as Milquetoasts and Water Mittys, and tagged as potential psychopaths ("He kept pretty much to himself," every psychopath's landlady is quoted as saying after the arrest, and for weeks thereafter every shy person is treated like a leper), we shys are desperately misunderstood on every hand. Because we don't "talk out" our feelings, it is assumed that we don't have any. It is assumed that we never exclaim, retort, or cry out, though naturally we do on occasions when it seems called for.

Would any dare say to a woman or a Third World person, "Oh, don't be a woman! Oh, don't be so third!"? And yet people make bold with us whenever they please and put an arm around us and tell us not to be shy.

Hundreds of thousands of our shy brothers and sisters (and "cousins twice-removed," as militant shys refer to each other) are victimized every year by self-help programs that promise to "cure" shyness through hand-buzzer treatments, shout training, spicy diets, silence-aversion therapy, and every other gimmick in the book. Many of them claim to have "overcome" their shyness, but the sad fact is that they are afraid to say otherwise.

To us in the shy movement, however, shyness is not a disability or disease to be "overcome." It is simply the way we are. And in our own quiet way, we

are secretly proud of it. It isn't something we shout about at public rallies and marches. It is Shy Pride. And while we don't have a Shy Pride Week, we do have many private moments when we keep our thoughts to ourselves, such as "Shy is nice," "Walk short," "Be proud—shut up," and "Shy is beautiful, for the most part." These are some that I thought up myself. Perhaps other shy persons have some of their own, I don't know.

A "Number One" Disgrace

Discrimination against shy is our country's number one disgrace in my own personal opinion. Millions of men and women are denied equal employment, educational and recreational opportunities, and rewarding personal relationships simply because of their shyness. These injustices are nearly impossible to identify, not only because of the shy person will not speak up when discriminated against, but also because the shy person almost always anticipates being denied these rights and doesn't ask for them in the first place. (In fact, most shys will politely decline a right when it is offered to them.)

Most shy lawyers agree that shys can never obtain justice under our current adversary system of law. The Sixth Amendment, for example, which gives the accused the right to confront his accusers, is anti-shy on the face of it. It effectively denies shy persons the right to accuse anyone of anything.

One solution might be to shift the burden of proof to the defendant in case the plaintiff chooses to remain silent. Or we could create a special second-class citizenship that would take away some rights, such as free speech, bearing arms, and running for public office, in exchange for some other rights that we need more. In any case, we need some sort of fairly totally new concept of law if we shys are ever going to enjoy equality, if indeed that is the sort of thing we could ever enjoy.

A Million-Dollar Ripoff

Every year, shy persons lose millions of dollars in the form of overcharges that aren't questioned, shoddy products never returned to stores, refunds never asked for, and bad food in restaurants that we eat anyway, not to mention all the money we lose and are too shy to claim when somebody else finds it.

A few months ago, a shy friend of mine whom I will call Duke Hand (not his real name) stood at a supermarket checkout counter and watched the cashier ring up thirty fifteen-cent Peanut Dream candy bars and a $3.75 *Playhouse* for $18.25. He gave her a twenty-dollar bill and thanked her for his change, but as reached for his purchases, she said, "Hold on. There's something wrong here."

"No, really, it's O.K.," he said.

"Let me see that cash register slip," she said.

"No, really, thanks anyway," he whispered. Out of the corner of his eye, he could see that he had attracted attention. Other shoppers in the vicinity had sensed that something was up, perhaps an attempted price-tag switch or insufficient identification, and were looking his way. "It's not for me," he pleaded. "I'm only buying this for a friend."

Nevertheless, he had to stand there in mute agony while she counted all of the Peanut Dreams and refigured the total and the correct change. (In fairness to her, it should be pointed out that Duke, while eventually passing on each copy of *Playhouse* to a friend, first reads it himself.)

Perhaps one solution might be for clerks and other business personnel to try to be a little bit more careful about this sort of thing in the first place. O.K.?

How About Shy History?

To many of us shys, myself included, the worst tragedy is the oppression of shy children in the schools, and while we don't presume to tell educators how to do their work, work that they have been specially trained to do, we do feel that schools must begin immediately to develop programs of shy history, or at the very least to give it a little consideration.

History books are blatantly prejudiced against shyness and shy personhood. They devote chapter after chapter to the accomplishments of famous persons and quote them at great length, and say nothing at all, or very little, about countless others who had very little to say, who never sought fame, and whose names are lost to history.

Where in the history books do we find mention of The Lady in Black, Kilroy, The Unknown Soldier, The Forgotten Man, The Little Guy, not to mention America's many noted recluses?

Where, for example, can we find a single paragraph on America's hundreds of scale models, those brave men of average height whose job it was to pose behind immense objects such as pyramids and dynamos so as to indicate scale in drawings and photographs? The only credit that scale models ever received was a line in the caption—"For an idea of its size, note man (arrow, at left)." And yet, without them, such inventions as the dirigible, the steam shovel, and the swing-span bridge would have looked like mere toys, and natural wonders such as Old Faithful, the Grand Canyon, and the giant sequoia would have been dismissed as hoaxes. It was truly a thankless job.

Shys on "Strike"

The scale models themselves never wanted any thanks. All they wanted was a rope or device of some type to keep them from falling off tall structures, plus a tent to rest in between drawings, and in 1906, after one model was carried away by a tidal wave that he had been hired to pose in front of, they formed a union and went on strike.

Briefly, the scale models were joined by a contingent of shy artists' models who had posed for what they thought was going to be a small monument showing the Battle of Bull Run only to discover that it was actually a large bas-relief entitled "The Bathers" and who sat down on the job, bringing the work to a halt. While the artists' models quickly won a new contract and went back to work (on a non-representational basis), the scale models' strike was never settled.

True to their nature, the scale models did not picket the work sites or negotiate with their employers. They simply stood quietly a short distance away and, when asked about their demands, pointed to the next man. A year later, when the union attempted to take a vote on the old contract, it found that most of the scale models had moved away and left no forwarding addresses.

It was the last attempt by shy persons to organize themselves anywhere in the country.

Now Is the Time, We Think

Now is probably as good a time as any for this country to face up to its shameful treatment of the shy and to do something, almost anything, about it. On the other hand, maybe it would be better to wait for a while and see what happens. All I know is that it isn't easy trying to write a manifesto for a bunch of people who dare not speak their names. And that the shy movement is being inverted by a tiny handful of shy militants who do not speak for the majority of shy persons, nor even very often for themselves. This secret cadre, whose members are not known even to each other, advocate doing "less than nothing." They believe in tokenism, and the smaller the token the better. They seek only to promote more self-consciousness: that ultimate shyness that shy mystics call "the fear of fear itself." What is even more terrifying is the ultimate goal of this radical wing: They believe that they shall inherit the earth, and they will not stop until they do. Believe me, we moderates have our faces to the wall.

Perhaps you are saying, "What can I do? I share your concern at the plight of the shy and wholeheartedly endorse your two- (or three-) point program for shy equality. I pledge myself to work vigorously for its adoption. My check for ($10 $25 $50 $100 $——) is enclosed. In addition, I agree to (circulate petitions, hold fund-raising party in my home, write to congressman and senator, serve on local committee, write letters to newspaper, hand out literature door-to-door during National Friends of the Shy Drive)."

Just remember: You said it, not me.

✺ "We have been committing an act of unthinking unilateral educational disarmament"

A NATION AT RISK

The National Commission on Excellence in Education released a report in April 1983 condemning American educational standards. *A Nation At Risk: The Imperative for Educational Reform* damned American educational standards as inadequate for the times and significantly behind the standards of other countries.

At a time when the United States was the reigning superpower of the industrialized West, the report startled the country out of any sense of self-satisfaction of its internal strength. Indeed, the report invoked war-like terms in describing the country's deteriorating educational status. *A Nation At Risk* pointed out that other countries—Japan, for example (a former enemy in World War II)—were outstripping the United States in educational and industrial abilities, even Third World South Korea compared favorably to the United States.

The report made dozens of recommendations to reverse the trend, acted as a catalyst for widespread reforms across the country and provided the baseline information for an ongoing debate on how to best resolve the inadequacies of the country's educational system.

Our Nation is at risk. Our once unchallenged preeminence in commerce, industry, science, and technological innovation is being overtaken by competitors throughout the world. This report is concerned with only one of the many causes and dimensions of the problem, but it is the one that undergirds American prosperity, security, civility. We report to the American people that while we can take justifiable pride in what our schools and colleges have historically accomplished and contributed to the United States and the well-being of its people, the educational foundations of our society are presently being eroded by a rising tide of mediocrity that threatens our very future as a Nation and a people. What was unimaginable a generation ago has begun to occur—others are matching and surpassing our educational attainments.

If an unfriendly foreign power had attempted to impose on America the mediocre educational performance that exists today, we might well have viewed it as an act of war. As it stands, we have allowed this to happen to ourselves. We have even squandered the gains in student achievement made in the wake of the Sputnik challenge. Moreover, we have dismantled the essential support systems which helped make those gains possible. We have, in effect, been committing an act of unthinking, unilateral educational disarmament.

Our society and its educational institutions seem to have lost sight of the basic purposes of schooling, and of the high expectations and disciplined effort needed to attain them. This report, the result of 18 months of study, seeks to generate reform of our educational system in fundamental ways and to renew the Nation's commitment to schools and colleges of high quality throughout the length and breadth of our land.

That we have compromised this commitment is, upon reflection, hardly surprising, given the multitude of often conflicting demands we have placed on our Nation's schools and colleges. They are routinely called on to provide solutions to personal, social, and political problems that the home and other institutions either will not or cannot resolve. We must understand that these demands on our schools and colleges often exact an educational cost as well as a financial one.

On the occasion of the Commission's first meeting, President Reagan noted the central importance of education in American life when he said: "Certainly there are few areas of American life as important to our society, to our people, and to our families as our schools and colleges." This report, therefore, is as much an open letter to the American people as it is a report to the Secretary of Education. We are confident that the American people, properly informed, will do what is right for their children and for the generations to come.

History is not kind to idlers. The time is long past when America's destiny was assured simply by an abundance of natural resources and inexhaustible human enthusiasm, and by our relative isolation from the malignant problems of older civilizations. The world is indeed one global village. We live among determined, well-educated, and strongly motivated competitors. We compete with them for international standing and markets, not only with products but also with the ideas of our laboratories and neighborhood workshops. America's position in the world may once have been reasonably secure with only a few exceptionally well-trained men and women. It is no longer....

Our concern, however, goes well beyond matters such as industry and commerce. It also includes the intellectual, moral, and spiritual strengths of our people which knit together the fabric of our society. The people of the United States need to know that individuals in our society who do not possess the levels of skill, literacy, and training essential to this new era will be effectively disenfranchised, not simply from the material rewards that accompany competent performance, but also from the chance to participate fully in our national life. A high level of shared education is essential to a free, democratic society and to the fostering of a common culture, especially in a country that prides itself on pluralism and individual freedom....

The educational dimensions of the risk before us have been amply documented in testimony received by the Commission. For example:

- International comparisons of student achievement, completed a decade ago, reveal that on 19 academic tests American students were never

first or second and, in comparison with other industrialized nations, were last seven times.

- Some 23 million American adults are functionally illiterate by the simplest tests of everyday reading, writing and comprehension.
- About 13 percent of all 17-year-olds in the United States can be considered functionally illiterate. Functional illiteracy among minority youth may run as high as 40 percent.
- Average achievement of high school students on most standardized tests is now lower than 26 years ago when Sputnik was launched.
- Over half the population of gifted students do not match their tested ability with comparable achievement in school.
- The College Board's Scholastic Aptitude Tests (SAT) demonstrate a virtually unbroken decline from 1963 to 1980. Average verbal scores fell over 50 points and average mathematics scores dropped nearly 40 points.
- College Board achievement tests also reveal consistent declines in recent years in such subjects as physics and English.
- Both the number and proportion of students demonstrating superior achievement on the SATs (i.e., those with scores of 650 or higher) have also dramatically declined.
- Many 17-year-olds do not possess the "higher order" intellectual skills we should expect of them. Nearly 40 percent cannot draw inferences from written materials; only one-fifth can write a persuasive essay; and only one-third can solve mathematics problems requiring several steps.
- There was a steady decline in science achievement scores of U.S. 17-year-olds as measured by national assessments of science in 1969, 1973, and 1977.
- Between 1975 and 1980, remedial mathematics courses in public 4-year colleges increased by 72 percent and now constitute one-quarter of all mathematics courses taught in those institutions.
- Average tested achievement of students graduating from college is also lower.

Business and military leaders complain that they are required to spend millions of dollars on costly remedial education and training programs in such basic skills as reading, writing, spelling and computation. The Department of Navy, for example, reported to the Commission that one-quarter of its recent recruits cannot read at the ninth grade level, the minimum needed simply to understand written safety instructions. Without remedial work they cannot even begin, much less complete, the sophisticated training essential in much of the modern military.

❧ *"The deterioration of what was once a vibrant and viable community"*

CONFRONTING RACIAL ISOLATION IN MIAMI

In May 1980, blacks in Miami erupted in riot when an all-white jury acquitted four white police officers in the killing of a black man, Arthur McDuffie, who had been beaten to death while under police custody. The U.S. Commission on Civil Rights conducted hearings on the riots and prepared the following report.

For a new generation of blacks, the civil rights gains were perceived a hoax. Programs designed to help them work their way out of economic hardship were floundering, and the justice system seemed to be stacked against blacks. Programs, such as busing to foster integration in schools and urban renewal campaigns to improve housing, destroyed previously tight neighborhoods.

Miami was just an example of the problem—across the country, black communities were struggling.

The black community in Miami is characterized chiefly by its isolation from the city as a whole. Blacks are in the city, but in a crucial sense, they are not part of Miami. They are not politically and economically powerful sectors that control community resources and make community policies. Their concerns have not been a priority for the city, the county, or for the private sector. Their frustration fed the violence that recently erupted in the wake of what was viewed as yet another in a long line of abuses suffered at the hands of an unresponsive and uncaring officialdom.

The isolation of Miami's black community results from a series of events that have contributed to the deterioration of what was once a vibrant and viable community. What Miami needs is a recognition of the causes for the alienation that has over-

taken the black community and a commitment by responsible leaders at all levels in both the public and private sectors to provide the leadership and resources and exert the effort to turn this situation around.

One of the events that precipitated the isolation was the physical destruction of a large portion of the black community by the municipal government. Under the urban renewal program, the city tore down a massive amount of low-cost housing, forcing large numbers of blacks to leave their traditional neighborhoods and move into other areas that could not accommodate them. New units of low-cost housing were never built to replace all that had been demolished. In a city with a vacancy rate of less than one percent, the remaining low-cost housing has become severely deteriorated and overcrowded. The consequences are isolated and disparate ghettos.

Neither the children who are transported to schools outside of these communities nor those who remain in neighborhood schools receive, in many respects, an education that addresses their needs. The city has not allocated enough resources and effort to provide adequate vocational-technical programs and well-trained guidance counselors or to address the myriad other needs of students from low-income families. When children exhibit inappropriate behavior, Dade County's school system often responds by shunting them into programs that do not respond to their needs rather than intervening with effective counseling. The public school system has many capable black employees, but they are concentrated in the elementary schools and low-level administrative posts. This practice not only undermines these employees' upward mobility but also deprives young blacks of positive role models, compounding the youths' sense of isolation within the schools.

Blacks are isolated in Miami's economy, as well. Although the local economy continues to grow at a rate higher than that for the Nation as a whole, there are few black entrepreneurs, and the black unemployment rate remains high. Stymied by their own lack of capital and their inability to obtain capital from commercial lenders, would-be black businesspeople fall through the cracks of unimaginative and nonaccommodating programs of the State, local and Federal government. Blacks with the education and the talent to succeed in business often leave Miami for other parts of the country that appear to offer more opportunities for blacks. Those who remain and try to establish businesses in Miami run into many obstacles, such as insurance redlining, that increase the likelihood of failure.

Federal programs established to help the disadvantaged businessperson, including the Small Business Administration, have helped some persons. The fact remains, however, that in Miami, black entrepreneurs are receiving a disproportionately small number of the loans the Small Business Administration provides for disadvantaged businesspersons. Witnesses before this Commission questioned the degree to which other federally-funded economic development programs are benefiting blacks. Although it is clear programs like urban redevelopment are providing some assistance to some disadvantaged persons, federally-funded programs in Miami have not improved the quality of life within the black community as much as anticipated. Blacks continue to be largely excluded from many economic opportunities in Miami.

Blacks in Miami have limited employment opportunities. A few Federal agencies, such as the U.S. Postal Service and the Veterans Administration Medical Center, have significant numbers of black employees. But most Federal agencies in the city employ few blacks. Local public and private sector employers have a dismal record with regard to hiring blacks. Some employers go so far as to recruit workers from other States rather than provide on-the-job training to unskilled workers in Miami.

Compounding this situation is the fact that justice in Miami is administered in a way that excludes blacks and appears incapable of condemning official violence against them. Black complaints of police violence are common in the city. The incident that took the life of Mr. McDuffie was one of many confrontations between black residents and the system that is supposed to protect all of Miami's inhabitants. The underlying causes range from employment practices to inadequate police training and evaluation. The department screens applicants for the police force with an allegedly biased test. Dade County has established an Independent Review Panel to investigate complaints against the police, but the Panel lacks resources and has no subpoena power. A Governor's Commission found that local police

internal review procedures were totally unsatisfactory.

The proportion of the youth in the Miami juvenile justice system who are black is more than three times as great as in Dade County population. Counseling for such youth is inadequate, in part, because the system employs counselors who meet minimal educational and experience requirements. Services for rehabilitating juveniles are grossly inadequate.

Many of Miami's problems have answers—more and better-qualified teachers and counselors, better selection and training of police officers, rehabilitation of housing and so on. But remedial steps cost money. The housing situation is a good example of the cost-benefit approach that appears to have taken hold in Miami. Because it is a seller's market, landlords can rent or sell any housing they choose to make available, no matter how deteriorated. As a result, they do not appear to view rehabilitating housing as being to their advantage. In the rare instances when they are brought before municipal authorities for violation of housing ordinances, landlords generally find it cheaper to pay the fine than to make the repairs. The question is whether one approach is indeed "cheaper" than another when the trade-off involves human suffering and frustration.

As indicated throughout the report, Miami suffers the range of urban problems that seem endemic to all major American cities today. The vast majority of the black community, regardless of economic status, feels powerless and frustrated. It is possible to identify and perhaps to ameliorate some of the sources of tension, but any long-term solution requires a coordinated attack on the underlying causes of racial isolation and exclusion.

Other reports, including those by the Kerner Commission and by this Commission, have indicated many specific remedial steps that officials at each level of government could take in areas such as education, employment and housing. To the extent that Miami has implemented any of these recommendations, however, it has not been a comprehensive effort. Consequently, racial isolation and exclusion have intensified.

A major question facing Miami is whether local leaders will see it in their community's interest to take the coordinated long-term concrete action that is necessary to turn Miami around.

Other riots have occurred without generating such a commitment.

Many black Miamians are contributing to the progress of their communities and the city as a whole. Black support for a rapid transit system in a 1978 referendum made the project possible. The black Miami-Dade Chamber of Commerce, albeit with limited success, has coordinated efforts with the Greater Miami Chamber of Commerce in two projects designed to increase the number of black businesses in Dade County. But the black community in Miami has neither the size nor wealth that commands political power and accountability in Miami. Acting alone, it cannot control or improve the circumstances in which they live.

It is important to identify sectors of the community that have both the political influence and economic capacity to address problems of such magnitude. According to Miami's Mayor, the city suffers a power vacuum:

"Nobody runs Miami...[T]here is no automobile industry; there is no steel industry; there is no tobacco industry; there is no company that permeates, that dominates. So we don't really have the typical power structure that you have in some American cities. In addition to which, unlike Atlanta and other cities that have deep roots, you don't have a social structure. Nobody has really been here for more than 50 years...[E]verybody here came from somewhere else. Very few native Miamians are more than 30 years old...Then who are the wealthy people? Who are the money interests here? For the most part, absentee corporations where the management is in New York. So, therefore, when you get to the Chamber of Commerce, what you see, with all due respect, are a bunch of lawyers that represent interests and corporations. They do a nice job, but this is not Atlanta...[where] you can get together a dozen people and something will happen. That cannot happen in Miami."

Miami may not have the same power structure as some other American cities, but there is leadership in both the private and public sector that can get things done. Private sector involvement will be crucial to any successful remedial effort and is becoming increasingly important as Federal financial aid to cities is being cut back. The idea of organized private sector involvement is not new. "Metropolitan affairs non-profit corporations" (MANSc) and "community" foundations have improved the quality of urban life in a number of cities, including Detroit, Philadelphia, Pittsburgh and Atlanta. These organizations, however, tend to limit their activities or developing downtown areas to sponsoring cultural affairs.

In Miami, one project that reflects private sector leadership is the New World Center development. Working with community groups to rejuvenate the downtown area, the private sector put together a commercial package supplemented by Federal monies. Although this project emphasized physical construction, the elements of commitment, coordination, and monitoring are apparent.

The same groups, individuals, and units of government that worked together to rebuild downtown Miami can—if they want community's participation in all aspects of growth and progress in Dade County. The knowledge and skills are available; the question is one of commitment. This report unmistakably demonstrates that without such a commitment, conditions will worsen, isolation will increase and violence will recur.

🐦 Growing Up Puerto Rican in New York

MARIA DIAZ

More than two and a half million Puerto Ricans live in the United States, with about half in New York City. Although the Caribbean island is a territory of the United States, the treatment that Puerto Ricans have received in America is similar to that of previous waves of immigrants.

Maria Diaz was a young Puerto Rican woman who, after becoming pregnant as a teenager, went into a training program and then college to elevate her position. At the time of this interview, which was conducted for the U.S. Department of Labor report called *Pride Against Prejudice,* she was contemplating going to law school. She describes some of the challenges of growing up in New York City and the ambiguities of being a minority in the United States.

Welfare was our means of livelihood from when I was eight years old until I got married. The welfare case worker was around, the investigators, the social workers, all kinds of people would come around the house to ask questions of my mother. Only once in a while would they ask me something. I didn't resent it because I knew that it was going to help us, that we were going to get money, that they would ask questions about the bed, do you need another bed? I remember things like that. At that point they were helpful. They would, at that time, practically give you a full household of things. You would get money for utensils, for laundry, and for other things.

We felt dependent upon them, of course. But it was worse if we didn't have it. My mother was very bitter about it, she resented it. And that was basically why there was a lot of bickering between my mother and father. She nearly killed him one day. She picked up a can of beer and threw it at him, hit him on the head and knocked him out cold, and she had to call the police and everything, and she thought she had killed him. She had reached the end of her rope. She couldn't stand it any more because he had bought beer. "Where the hell did you get money to buy beer, and meanwhile we are starving and waiting on welfare to feed us and you're bringing in beer!"

How did this affect my school? I really don't know. I remember having to tell the teachers that I would be absent on a particular day because I had to go on with my mother to the Welfare Department. And I did feel that the teachers treated us differently. They would require certain things to be brought to school, like Scotch tape or colored chalk or crayons, stuff that I couldn't afford, so the teacher would say, "Well, you can't participate in this group that is going to do this special activity because you don't have the material." My mother was very good about trips, but she couldn't give us money to buy things. She couldn't give us money to buy cards and stuff at the museums, so I remember having one teacher who bought stuff for me. She took us down to the Stock Exchange and to another place where there was a statue of Washington. Anyway I remember the teacher buying me some cards and a little pin because I started to cry. I want one, and I couldn't have it, and she said, "Don't worry, Honey, I'll get one for you." And she did.

School was pretty good up until the eighth grade. Trouble really started in the seventh grade. I started to hang around with my "peers" as they call them, and started to drink wine, and I did all kinds of weird things at that age and in that grade. Of course, the students that were older were friends who lived in the same neighborhood. And since I associated all the time with older children, I got introduced to everything that they knew and were

doing. And by the eighth grade I was a full-fledged wino, as they say.

I remember seeing older teenagers or men— I'm not sure which—shooting up in a building where my aunt lived. That was a terrifying experience for me. I just stood on the stairway and screamed. I knew it was not a good thing to do 'cause I had heard my father talking about it. He was totally opposed to drugs. That experience of the drugs was unbelievable. It was so gruesome. I think because of that experience—it stayed with me—I never experimented with hard drugs. But nevertheless, the wine thing had developed, and a lot of kids were doing it.

I had tasted wine at home from my father's wine bottle. And during that time I was smoking. I've been smoking since I was eleven. I was hanging around with boys, too. It was thrilling. It was doing things behind people's backs. But, looking back in retrospect, it was awful because I could've been doing so many other things.

Where did the wine come from? The children would buy the wine for 50 cents a bottle—35 cents. They would go into the stores themselves and buy it. Usually we got ninth graders to go. Not only did they look older, they were older. Some of the ninth graders were seventeen. They were left back so many times. We were exposed to much older children on our grade level than would be the case in most schools. One of the problems was that if you came from Puerto Rico, and you didn't know how to speak English, even if you were seventeen, you would go into the seventh grade. They would just dump these boys into the slowest section of the grade. So we knew that those were the "dumb" kids.

They weren't dumb, but we thought they were dumb because they didn't know how to speak English. I knew how to speak English because I had been in the school system since kindergarten and because my father spoke English at home. There were children eleven years old mixed with those who were seventeen years old. I think the older children, if you can call a person seventeen years old a child, deliberately took pleasure in corrupting the younger ones. That happened to me and to a lot of other younger kids. They were simply preying on us. They would be fascinated to see an eleven or twelve-year-old kid drunk.

And then you become their tool. This was the

kind of thing that happened and continued, and then luckily we moved from that neighborhood. I went into another school where I did not know too many people. So in the ninth grade it was different. And I had good grades in the ninth grade.

I left school in the ninth grade. I had graduated. I went to graduation and that was it. I didn't want to leave school. I was prepared to go back to school in September, but when I went to Mabel Dean Bacon the first week of school, they wouldn't take me because I was pregnant. And I was only fourteen. They didn't tell me to come back after the baby was born. All they said, was, "We can't accept you here if you're pregnant. Sorry, you have to get your mother to come in and sign a discharge." And that was that. I stayed home. After that, I had the baby, and then I stayed home for about another four or five months.

And then I went to Seward Park High School. I decided I was going to go back to school. I wasn't going to stay around and do nothing. My mother was going to help with the baby, and so I went to register at Seward Park High School, and I was accepted although I was married, and they knew about the baby. I had a French teacher who thought it was just marvelous that she could call me "Madame" in the class instead of "Mademoiselle." She was just fascinated with that, and it was a wonderful experience. But then during the latter part of the semester the baby started to get sick, and I was missing a lot of classes. It was too much to do both, so I never finished.

I have noticed that a number of people have a sense of "we" and "they". And when I ask "Who do you mean by 'they'?", sometimes they say the establishment, or white America. I, too, have that sense of the "we" and the "they", but I think I can delineate exactly who the "they" and the "we" are. The "they" are usually those people who succumb to the bureaucratic structure, procedure, mentality. Those are the "they"—where there is a traditional point of view. They could be anybody, black, white, green, purple, Puerto Rican, anybody. If that mentality is the rule of the day, those are the "they's". And the "we's" are the other people who have no power to buck the "they's" but constantly try amongst themselves to do whatever they can for each other and buck the system from underneath. My answer is very different from many of my friends. To many of them, "they" are simply white Americans, the "we" are all

the rest. I account for the differences in our views partly because of character.

At this point, I have to talk about the Puerto Ricans, because I do know something about my own culture. Part of the problem has been that many Puerto Ricans have always identified themselves with whoever has been ruling them. Spain was the mother country and some people had a ritualistic feeling about Spain. Anything that Spain did was right. Other Puerto Ricans would question this, but they would have to go along with it anyway because they had no power. In spite of that long experience of loyalty to Spain and to Spanish culture, we Puerto Ricans finally developed a culture of our own. We stem out of the Spanish culture, we stem out of the Indian culture, and the Black culture. It's a very cohesive feeling.

If anyone asks me my nationality, I say Puerto Rico. I had no reason to say it otherwise and I don't feel I should say it otherwise. It used to be the census taker would ask you, "Are you black or white?" There was no other category. A lot of Puerto Ricans don't like to be defined as black. But then again, for purposes of getting grants and monies, they can't be defined as white either. We should be defined as Puerto Ricans or coffee-colored or something like that. The truth is that the Puerto Rican population comes in all shades, colors.

My emerging sense of career is not an absolutely clear-cut thing, but there are some specific influences aside from my own personality which account for this emerging sense of career, my willingness to put a lot of time in education. The kinds of things I see happening between groups of people have helped me decide what I want to do. It is the question of getting people together and getting them to unite on something. Some of my friends say that it must be discouraging to have to deal with so much conflict and antagonism but it's not discouraging at all. It's frustrating because you can't get people to see the issues right away. We can't get them to understand the purpose behind what we are saying to what we are trying to accomplish in any given situation. But then again, you know, I am gaining confidence and feel that I can continue because certain things to make sense to me no matter how much people refuse to understand that close themselves off. Eventually there will come a time when they will have no choice but to begin to understand.

I think you can do something for people by being a voice for a more decent community and society.

❧ A Tale of Two Cities

MARIO CUOMO

New York Governor Mario Cuomo soared into national prominence when he delivered the nominating speech for presidential candidate Walter Mondale at the 1984 Democratic Convention. Invoking stark images, Cuomo's stirring oratory articulated the aggravation of those left behind in the booming 1980s. Mondale would lose by a significant margin to Reagan in the fall election.

Ten days ago, President Reagan admitted that although some people in this country seemed to be doing well nowadays, others were unhappy, and even worried, about themselves, their families, and their futures. The president said he didn't understand that fear. He said, "Why, this country is a shining city on a hill." The president is right. In many ways we are "a shining city on a hill." But the hard truth is that not everyone is sharing in this city's splendor and glory.

A shining city is perhaps all the president sees from the portico of the White House and the veranda of his ranch, where everyone seems to be doing well. But there's another part of the city, the part where some people can't pay their mortgages and most young people can't afford one, where students can't afford the education they need and middle-class parents watch dreams they hold for their children evaporate.

In this part of the city there are more poor than ever, more families in trouble. More and more people who need help but who can't find it. Even worse: there are elderly people who tremble in the basements of the houses there. There are people who sleep in the city's streets, in the gutter, where the glitter doesn't show. There are ghettos where thousands of young people, without an education or a job, give their lives away to drug dealers every day. There is despair, Mr. President, in faces you never see, in places you never visit in your shining city.

In fact, Mr. President, this nation is more a "Tale of Two Cities" than it is a "Shining City on a Hill." Maybe if you visited more places, Mr. President, you'd understand.

Maybe if you went to Appalachia where some people still live in sheds and to Lackawanna where thousands of unemployed steel workers wonder why we subsidized foreign steel while we surrender their dignity to unemployment and to welfare checks; maybe if you stepped into a shelter in Chicago and talked with some of the homeless there; maybe, Mr. President, if you asked a woman who'd been denied the help she needs to feed her children because you say we need the money to give a tax break to a millionaire or to build a missile we can't even afford to use—maybe then you'd understand. Maybe, Mr. President. But I'm afraid not. Because the truth is, this is how we were warned it would be.

President Reagan told us from the beginning that he believed in a kind of social Darwinism. Survival of the fittest. Government can't do everything, we were told. So it should settle for taking care of the strong and hope that economic ambition and charity will do the rest. Make the rich richer and what falls from their table will be enough for the middle class and those trying to make it into the middle class.

The Republicans called it trickle-down when Hoover tried it. Now they call it supply side. It is the same shining city for those relative few who are lucky enough to live in its good neighborhoods. But for the people who are excluded—locked out—all they can do is to stare from a distance at that city's glimmering towers.

It's an old story. As old as our history.

The difference between Democrats and Republicans has always been measured in courage and confidence. The Republicans believe the wagon train will not make it to the frontier unless some of our old, some of our young, and some of our weak are left behind by the side of the trail. The strong will inherit the land!

We Democrats believe that we can make it all the way with the whole family intact. We have. More than once. Ever since Franklin Roosevelt lifted himself from his wheelchair to lift this nation from its knees. Wagon train after wagon train. To new frontiers of education, housing, peace. The whole family aboard. Constantly reaching out to extend and enlarge that family. Lifting them up into the wagon on the way. Blacks and Hispanics, people of every ethnic group, and Native

Americans—all those struggling to build their families claim some share of America....

We speak for the minorities who have not yet entered the mainstream: for ethnics who want to add their culture to the mosaic that is America; for women indignant that we refuse to etch into our governmental commandments the simple rule "thou shalt not sin against inequality," a commandment so obvious that it can be spelled in three letters: E.R.A; for young people demanding an education and a future, for senior citizens terrorized by the idea that their only security, their Social Security, is being threatened; for millions of reasoning people fighting to preserve our very existence from a macho intransigence that refuses to make intelligent attempts to discuss the possibility of nuclear holocaust with our enemy. Refusing because they believe we can pile missiles so high that they will pierce the clouds and the sight of them will frighten our enemies into submission.

We're proud of this diversity. Grateful we don't have to manufacture its appearance the way the Republicans will next month in Dallas, by propping up mannequin delegates on the convention floor.

But we pay a price for it. The different people we represent have many points of view. Sometimes they compete and then we have debates, even arguments. That's what our primaries were....

Inflation is down since 1980. But not because of the supply-side miracle promised by the president. Inflation was reduced the old-fashioned way, with a recession, the worst since 1932. More than 55,000 bankruptcies. Two years of massive unemployment. Two hundred thousand farmers and ranchers forced off the land. More homeless than at any time since the Great Depression. More hungry, more poor—mostly women—and a nearly $200 billion deficit threatening our future....

And what about foreign policy? They said they would make us and the whole world safer. They say they have. By creating the largest defense budget in history, one even they now admit is excessive, they failed to discuss peace with our enemies. By the loss of 279 young Americans in Lebanon in pursuit of a plan and a policy no one can find or describe. We give monies to Latin American governments that murder nuns, and then lie about it. We have been less than zealous in our support of the only real friend we have in the Middle East, the one democracy there, our flesh-and-blood ally, the state of Israel.

Our policy drifts with no real direction, other than a hysterical commitment to an arms race that leads nowhere, if we're lucky. If we're not—could lead us to bankruptcy or war....

How high will we pile the missiles? How much deeper will be the gulf between us and our enemies? Will we make meaner the spirit of our people?

This election will measure the record of the past four years. But more than that, it will answer the question of what kind of people we want to be.

We Democrats still have a dream. We still believe in this nation's future. And this is our answer, our credo: We believe in only the government we need, but we insist on all the government we need.

We believe in a government characterized by fairness and reasonableness, a reasonableness that goes beyond labels, that doesn't distort or promise to do what it knows it can't do. A government strong enough to use the words "love" and "compassion" and smart enough to convert our noblest aspirations....

We believe, as Democrats, that a society as blessed as ours, the most affluent democracy in world's history, that can spend trillions on instruments of destruction, ought to be able to help the middle class in its struggle, ought to be able to find work for all who can do it, room at the table, shelter for the homeless, care for the elderly and infirm, hope for the destitute.

We proclaim as loudly as we can the utter insanity of nuclear proliferation and the need for a nuclear freeze, if only to affirm the simple truth that peace is better than war because life is better than death.

We believe in firm but fair law and order, in the union movement, in privacy for people, openness by government, civil rights, and human rights....

That struggle to live with dignity is the real story of the shining city. It's a story I didn't read in a book or learn in a classroom. I saw it and lived it. Like many of you.

I watched a small man with thick calluses on both hands work fifteen and sixteen hours a day. I saw him once literally bleed from the bottoms of his feet, a man who came here uneducated, alone, unable to speak the language, who taught me all I needed to know about faith and hard work by the simple eloquence of his example. I learned about our kind of democracy from my father. I learned about our obligation to each other from him and from my mother. They asked only for a chance to work and to make the world better for their children and to be protected in those moments when they would not be able to protect themselves. This nation and its government did that for them.

And on January 20, 1985, it will happen again. Only on a much grander scale. We will have a new president of the United States, a Democrat born not to the blood of kings but to the blood of immigrants and pioneers.

We will have America's first woman vice president, the child of immigrants, a New Yorker, opening with one magnificent stroke a whole new frontier for the United States.

It will happen, if we make it happen.

I ask you, ladies and gentlemen, brothers and sisters—for the good of us all, for the love of this great nation, for the family of America, for the love of God. Please make this nation remember how futures are built.

❧ Texas v. Johnson: "We do not consecrate the flag by punishing its desecration"

SUPREME COURT JUSTICE WILLIAM J. BRENNAN, JR.

To the chants of fellow protestors outside the 1984 Republican National Convention in Dallas, Gregory Lee Johnson burned an American flag to express his disgust at President Reagan's policies. Texas authorities charged him with "desecration of a venerated object" and sentenced Johnson to a year in prison.

Johnson appealed on the grounds that the decision was an infringement of his civil rights. Five years later, by 5-4 vote, the Supreme Court agreed and overturned the conviction in *Texas v. Johnson.* In 1990, the Supreme Court also overturned a law passed by Congress to punish flag burners.

After publicly burning an American flag as a means of political protest, Gregory Lee Johnson was convicted of desecrating a flag in violation of Texas law. This case presents the question whether his

conviction is consistent with the First Amendment. We hold that it is not.

While the Republican National Convention was taking place in Dallas in 1984, respondent Johnson participated in a political demonstration dubbed the "Republican War Chest Tour." As explained in literature distributed by the demonstrators and in speeches made by the respondent, the purpose of this event was to protest the policies of the Reagan administration and of certain Dallas-based corporations. The demonstrators marched through the Dallas streets, chanting political slogans and stopping at several corporate locations to stage "die-ins" intended to dramatize the consequences of nuclear war. On several occasions they spray-painted the walls of buildings and overturned potted plants, but Johnson himself took no part in such activities. He did, however, accept an American flag handed to him by a fellow protestor who had taken it from a flag pole outside one of the targeted buildings.

The demonstration ended in front of Dallas City Hall, where Johnson unfurled the American flag, doused it with kerosene, and set it on fire. While the flag burned, the protestors chanted, "America, the red, white, and blue, we spit on you." After the demonstrators dispersed, a witness to the flag burning collected the flag's remains and buried them in his backyard. No one was physically injured or threatened with injury, though several witnesses testified that they had been seriously offended by the flag burning.

Of the approximately one hundred demonstrators, Johnson alone was charged with a crime. The only criminal offense with which he was charged was the desecration of a venerated object in violation of Texas Penal Code Ann. 42.09(a)(3)(1989). After a trial he was convicted, sentenced to one year in prison, and fined two thousand dollars.

The State of Texas conceded for purposes of its oral argument in this case that Johnson's conduct was expressive conduct….Johnson burned an American flag as part—indeed, as the culmination—of a political demonstration that coincided with the convening of the Republican Party and its renomination of Ronald Reagan for President. The expressive, overtly political nature of this conduct was both intentional and overwhelmingly apparent. At his trial, Johnson explained his reasons for burning the flag as follows: "The American Flag was burned as Ronald Reagan was being renominated as President. And a more powerful statement of symbolic speech, whether you agree with it or not, couldn't have been made at that time. It's quite a juxtaposition. We had new patriotism and no patriotism."…In these circumstances, Johnson's burning of the flag was conduct "sufficiently imbued with elements of communication…to implicate the First Amendment."

…The State offers two separate interests to justify this conviction: preventing breaches of peace, and preserving the flag as a symbol of nationhood and national unity. We hold that the first interest is not implicated on this record and that the second is related to the suppression of expression.

Texas claims that its interest in preventing breaches of the peace justifies Johnson's conviction for flag desecration. However, no disturbance of the peace actually occurred or threatened to occur because of Johnson's burning of the flag. Although the State stresses the disruptive behavior of the protestors during their march toward City Hall,…it admits that "no actual breach of the peace occurred at the time of the flag burning or in response to the flag burning."…The State's emphasis on the protestors' disorderly actions prior to arriving at City Hall is not only somewhat surprising, given that no charges were brought on the basis of this conduct, but it also fails to show that a disturbance of the peace was a likely reaction to Johnson's conduct. The only evidence offered by the State at trial to show the reaction to Johnson's actions was the testimony of several persons who had been seriously offended by the flag burning.

The State's position, therefore, amounts to a claim that an audience that takes serious offense at particular expression is necessarily likely to disturb peace and that the expression may be prohibited on this basis. Our precedents do not countenance such a presumption. On the contrary, they recognize that a principal "function of free speech under our system of government is to invite dispute. It may indeed best serve its high purpose when it induces a condition of unrest, creates dissatisfaction with conditions as they are, or even stirs people to anger." Terminiello v. Chicago (1949).

Texas' focus on the precise nature of Johnson's expression, moreover, misses the point of our prior decisions: their enduring lesson, that the

Government may not prohibit expression simply because it disagrees with its message, is not dependent on the particular mode in which one chooses to express an idea. If we were to hold that a State may forbid flag burning wherever it is likely to endanger the flag's symbolic role, but allow it wherever burning a flag promotes that role—as where, for example, a person ceremoniously burns a dirty flag—we would be saying that when it comes to impairing the flag's physical integrity, the flag itself may be used as a symbol—as a substitute for the written or spoken word or a "short cut from mind to mind"—only in one direction. We would be permitting a State to "prescribe what shall be orthodox" by saying that one may burn the flag to convey one's attitude toward it and its referents only if one does not endanger the flag's representation of nationhood and national unity.

…It is not the State's ends, but its means, to which we object. It cannot be gainsaid that there is a special place reserved for the flag in this Nation, and thus we do not doubt that the Government has a legitimate interest in making efforts to "preserve the national flag as an unalloyed symbol of our country."…We reject the suggestion, urged at oral argument by counsel for Johnson, that the Government lacks "any state interest whatsoever" in regulating the manner in which the flag may be displayed.

To say that the Government has an interest in encouraging proper treatment of the flag, however, is not to say that it may criminally punish a person for burning a flag as a means of political protest. "National unity as an end which officials may foster by persuasion and example is not in question. The problem is whether under our Constitution compulsion as here employed is a permissible means for its achievement."…

The way to preserve the flag's special role is not to punish those who feel differently about these matters. It is to persuade them that they are wrong.…And, precisely because it is our flag that is involved, one's response to the flag burner may exploit the uniquely persuasive power of the flag itself. We can imagine no more appropriate response to burning a flag than waving one's own, no better way to counter a flag burner's message than by saluting the flag that burns, no surer means of preserving the dignity even of the flag that burned than by—as one witness here did—according its remains a respectful burial. We do not consecrate the flag by punishing its desecration, for in doing so we dilute the freedom that this cherished emblem represents.

Johnson was convicted for engaging in expressive conduct. The State's interest in preventing breaches of the peace does not support his conviction because Johnson's conduct did not threaten to disturb the peace. Nor does the State's interest in preserving the flag as a symbol of nationhood and national unity justify his criminal conviction for engaging in political expression.

❧ *"The aggressive impulses of an evil empire"*

RONALD REAGAN

Speaking before the National Association of Evangelists in March 1983, President Ronald Reagan invoked biblical terms in his condemnation of the Soviet Union, describing it as the "evil empire." The speech on the sources of evil in the modern world describes the moral authority which Reagan drew from to wage an escalating arms race against the Soviet Union to win the Cold War. Like Reagan himself, however, the speech was roundly criticized by the liberal community. Noted historian Henry Steele Commager described it as the worst speech ever given by a president.

During my first press conference as president, in answer to a direct question, I pointed out that as good Marxist-Leninists, the Soviet leaders have openly and publicly declared that the only morality they recognize is that which will further their cause, which is world revolution.

I think I should point out I was only quoting Lenin, their guiding spirit, who said in 1920 that they repudiate all morality that proceeds from supernatural ideas or ideas that are outside class conceptions; morality is entirely subordinate to the interests of class war; and everything is moral that is necessary for the annihilation of the old exploiting social order and for uniting the proletariat.

I think the refusal of many influential people to accept this elementary fact of Soviet doctrine illustrates a historical reluctance to see totalitarian powers for what they are. We saw this phenomenon in the 1930s; we see it too often today. This does not

mean we should isolate ourselves and refuse to seek an understanding with them....

Let us pray for the salvation of all those who live in totalitarian darkness, pray they will discover the joy of knowing God.

But until they do, let us be aware that while they preach the supremacy of the state, declare it omnipotence over individual man, and predict its eventual domination of all peoples of the earth—they are the focus of evil in the modern world.

It was C. S. Lewis who, in his unforgettable *Screwtape Letters*, wrote, "The greatest evil is not now done in those sordid 'dens of crime' that Dickens loved to paint. It is not done even in concentration camps and labor camps. In those we see its final result. But it is conceived and ordered (moved, seconded, carried, and minuted) in clear, carpeted, warmed, and well-lighted offices, by quiet men with white collars and cut fingernails and smooth shaven cheeks who do not need to raise their voice."

Because these "quiet men" do not "raise their voices," because they sometimes speak in soothing tones of brotherhood and peace, because, like other dictators before them, they are always making "their final territorial demand," some would have us accept them at their word and accommodate ourselves to their aggressive impulses.

But, if history teaches anything, it teaches: simple-minded appeasement and wishful thinking about our adversaries is folly—it means that betrayal of our past, the squandering of our freedom.

So I urge you to speak out against those who would place the United States in a position of military and moral inferiority. You know, I have always believed that old Screwtape reserves his best efforts for those of you in the church.

So in your discussions of the nuclear freeze proposals, I urge you to beware the temptation of pride—the temptation blithely to declare yourselves above it all and label both sides equally at fault, to ignore the facts of history and the aggressive impulses of an evil empire, to simply call the arms race a giant misunderstanding and thereby remove yourself from the struggle between right and wrong, good and evil.

I ask you to resist the attempts of those who would have you withhold your support for this administration's efforts to keep America strong and free, while we negotiate real and verifiable reductions in the world's nuclear arsenals and one day, with God's help, their total elimination.

While America's military strength is important, let me add here that I have always maintained that the struggle now going on for the world will never be decided by bombs or rockets, by armies or military might.

The real crisis we face today is a spiritual one; at root, it is a test of moral will and faith.

Whittaker Chambers, the man whose own religious conversion made him a "witness" to one of the terrible traumas of our age, the Hiss-Chambers case, wrote that the crisis of the Western world exists to the degree in which the West is indifferent to God, the degree to which it collaborates in communism's attempt to make man stand alone without God.

For Marxism-Leninism is actually the second-oldest faith, he said, first proclaimed in the Garden of Eden with the words of temptation "Ye shall be as gods." The western world can answer this challenge, he wrote, "but only provided that its faith in God and the freedom he enjoins is as great as communism's faith in man."

I believe we shall rise to this challenge; I believe that communism is another sad, bizarre chapter in human history whose last pages even now are being written. I believe this because the source of our strength in the quest for human freedom is not material but spiritual, and, because it knows no limitation, it must terrify and ultimately triumph over those who would enslave their fellow man.

For, in the words of Isaiah, "He giveth power to the faint; and to them that have no might he increased strength. But they that wait upon the Lord shall renew their strength; they shall mount up with wings as eagles; they shall run, and not be weary."

❧ *Liar's Poker*

MICHAEL LEWIS

To many, the 1980s in America was the decade of greed. Conspicuous consumption and the accumulation of wealth were in vogue. No place symbolized that spirit more than Wall Street. Fifty years after the Great Crash and the Depression had humbled the alleged glories of investment banking, high finance once again held a lofty, if ambiguous,

status. The spirit of unrepentant capitalism was captured in fiction with Oliver Stone's movie *Wall Street*—in which the statement "Greed is good" was made famous—and the biting satire of Tom Wolfe's *Bonfire of the Vanities*. As a young Salomon Brothers investment banker turned book author, Michael Lewis described the life of a young Wall Street trainee and ethics of the vaunted trading floor in his first-person account *Liar's Poker*.

More different types of people succeeded on the trading floor than I initially supposed. Some of the men who spoke to us were truly awful human beings. They sacked others to promote themselves. They harassed women. They humiliated trainees. They didn't have customers. They had victims. Others were naturally extremely admirable characters. They inspired those around them. They treated their customers almost fairly. They were kind to trainees. The point is not that a Big Swinging Dick was intrinsically evil. The point is that it didn't matter one bit whether he was good or evil as long as he continued to swing that big bat of his. Bad guys did not suffer their comeuppance in Act V on the forty-first floor. They flourished (though whether they succeeded because they were bad people, whether there was something about the business that naturally favored them over the virtuous are separate questions). Goodness was not taken into account on the trading floor. It was neither rewarded nor punished. It just was. Or it wasn't.

Because the forty-first floor was the chosen home of the firm's most ambitious people, and because there were no rules governing the pursuit of profit and glory, the men who worked there, including the more bloodthirsty, had a hunted look about them. The place was governed by the simple understanding that the unbridled pursuit of perceived self-interest was healthy. Eat or be eaten. The men of 41 worked with one eye cast over their shoulders to see whether someone was trying to do them in, for there was no telling what manner of man had levered himself to the rung below you and was now hungry for your job. The range of acceptable behavior within Salomon Brothers was wide indeed. It said something about the ability of the free marketplace to mold people's behavior into a socially acceptable pattern. For this was capitalism at its most raw, and it was self-destructive.

As a Salomon Brothers trainee, of course, you didn't worry too much about ethics. You were just trying to stay alive. You felt flattered to be on the same team with the people who kicked everyone's ass all the time. Like a kid mysteriously befriended by the schoolyard bully, you tended to overlook the flaws of bond people in exchange for their protection. I sat wide-eyed when these people came to speak to us and observed a behavioral smorgasbord the likes of which I had never seen before encountered, except in fiction. As a student you had to start from the premise that each of these characters was immensely successful, then try to figure out why. And so it was, in this frame of mind, that I first watched the Human Piranha in action.

The Human Pirhana came to tell us about government bonds, though he was so knowledgeable about the handling of money that he could have spoken about whatever he wished. He was the only bond salesman who made traders nervous, because he generally knew their job better than they did, and if they screwed up by giving him a wrong price, he usually made a point of humiliating them on the hoot and holler. It gave other salespeople great satisfaction to see him do this.

The Human Pirhana was short and square, like the hooker on a rugby team. The most unusual thing about him was the frozen expression on his face. His dark eyes, black holes really, rarely moved. And when they did, they moved slowly, like a periscope. His mouth never seemed to alter shape; rather it expanded and contracted proportionally when he spoke. And out of that mouth came a steady stream of bottom-line analysis and profanity.

The Pirhana, that day, began by devouring the government of France. The French government had issued a bond known as the Giscard (yes, the one described by Tom Wolfe in *Bonfire of the Vanities*. Wolfe learned of the Giscard from a Salomon trader; in fact, to research his fictional bond salesman, Wolfe had come to 41 and sat spitting distance from the Human Piranha). The Pirhana was troubled by the Giscard, so dubbed because it was the brainchild of the government of Valery Giscard d'Estang. The French had raised about a billion dollars in 1978 with the bond. That wasn't the problem. The problem was that the bond was, under certain conditions, exchangeable into gold at thirty-two dollars an ounce—i.e., the holder of, say, thirty-two million dollars of the bonds, rather than accept cash, could demand one million ounces of gold.

"The fuckin' frogs are getting their faces ripped off," said the Pirhana, meaning that the French were losing a lot of money on the bond issue now that the bond had indeed become convertible and the price of gold was five hundred dollars an ounce. The stupidity of the fuckin' frogs disgusted the Pirhana. He associated it with their habit of quitting work at 5:00 pm. The European work ethic was his bete noire, though he put it differently. He had once derided a simpering group of Salomon's Englishmen and Continental Europeans who had complained of being overworked by calling them "Eurofaggots."

Once he'd finished with France, he whipped out charts to show the way a government bond arbitrage trade worked. As he spoke, the people in the front row grew nervous, and the people in the back row began to giggle, and the people in the front row grew more nervous still, fearing that the people in the back row would cause the Pirhana to feed on us all. The Pirhana didn't talk like a person. He said things like, "If you fuckin' buy this bond in a fuckin' trade, you're fucking fucked." And "If you don't pay fuckin' attention to the fuckin' two-year, you get your fuckin' face ripped off." Noun, verb, adjective. Fucker, fuck, fucking. No part of speech was spared. His world was filled with copulating inanimate objects and people getting their faces ripped off. And he said it so often, like a nervous tick, that each time he said it again, the back row giggled. The Human Pirhana, a Harvard graduate, thought nothing of it. He was always like this.

✤ "Microsoft will probably turn out to be the initial public offering of the year"

THE WALL STREET JOURNAL

Buried in the inside pages of the March 14, 1986, *The Wall Street Journal* was a short article describing the success of the initial public stock offering for a new, growing company in Redmond, Washington called Microsoft. The value of the offering totaled less than $75 million. Within twelve years Microsoft would be the second highest valued public company in America, approaching $200 billion.

Not only did the company revolutionize the use of personal computers across the United States and the world with its operating system and ubiquitous software programs, it made a lot of people who owned Microsoft stock very rich. The chairman of Microsoft, Bill Gates, would become the richest man in the United States. Ironically, future Microsoft competitor, Sun Microsytems Inc. had its initial public offering a week earlier, and was something of a disappointment.

"Microsoft Public Offering is Grabbed Up As Company's Stock Promptly Spurts $7"

Microsoft Corp. completed a splashy initial public stock offering as bullish investors bid up the price of the computer software powerhouse to $28 a share, $7 above the offering price.

Several dozen electronics companies are believed to be contemplating going public later this year, and the Microsoft offering was widely regarded as an important bellweather for such offerings.

"Microsoft will probably turn out to be the IPO of the year," said Mark Boyer, the portfolio manager of Fidelity Investments' technology fund. "Right now there appears to be a window and everybody's trying to get through it at once—so far it's working."

Underwriters Goldman, Sachs & Co. and Alex, Brown & Sons were unusually aggressive about managing the Microsoft offering. Yesterday's offering price of $21 was $2 more than the offer prospectus had anticipated, and even that original price represented a fat premium over Microsoft's public rivals. Even so, Microsoft's first trade in the over-the-counter market yesterday occurred at $25, a 19% premium to the offering price.

Microsoft, based in Redmond, Wash., also amended its offering plan to add 295,000 shares to the 2.8 million shares it planned to offer.

Microsoft's allure to investors lay partly in its particularly strong financial record. Its 1985 earnings of $31.2 million amounted to 19% of revenue, a higher profit margin than either of its two chief public rivals: Lotus Development Corp. and Ashton-Tate.

Microsoft also benefited from several popular public offerings by high-technology companies, analysts said.

For instance, Oracle Systems Corp., a Belmont, Calif., software concern, offered 2.1 million shares Wednesday at $15 a share and the price rocketed to $20.75 by day's end. Two weeks ago, Alex, Brown, which has grabbed the lion's share of recent technology stock underwritings, went public itself at $23 a share and has since been trading between $27 and $29.

Well-regarded technology concerns expected to make public offerings soon include minicomputer makers Convex Computer Corp., Alhant Computer Systems Corp. and Cypress Semiconductor Corp.

"There's so much hot money out there that as soon as you have two days in a row where people make 30% on the opening price, you're off to the races," said Michael Murphy, editor of the California Technology Stock Letter.

One smaller company, Sungard Data Systems Inc., a Wayne, Pa., computer-service concern, also picked yesterday to make an initial public offering and met with more modest success than Microsoft. Sungard offered 2.3 million shares at $11 each and the stock finished the day's over-the-counter trading at $12, although it had traded earlier at $12.50.

Not all the recent high-tech issues have been well-received, however. Sun Microsystems Inc.'s initial offering last week stirred up memories of past high-tech offering frenzies that went sour. Sun's shares were offered at $16 each, but the engineering-workstation maker's stock quickly slipped and lately has been trading in the $14 to $15 range.

❧ "I came to tell the truth, the good, the bad, and the ugly"

IRAN-CONTRA HEARINGS

In the summer of 1987, Congress held the Iran-Contra hearings to investigate the illegal sale of U.S. weapons to Iran by the Reagan Administration as a way to finance Contra rebels in Nicaragua. Incredibly, Congress had made both actions illegal. Trade—of any kind—with Iran was against the law for all U.S. companies. In addition, Congress had refused to finance the activities of the Contra rebels against the Communist Sandinista government in Nicaragua.

The Reagan Administration, however, was determined to assist the Contras (whom Reagan referred to as "freedom fighters" similar to the original patriots of the American Revolution). In an elaborate scheme to thwart Congress, government officials arranged for the sale of weapons to Iran and then funneled the proceeds to Contra rebels.

When news of the escapade was made public (initially by a Lebanese newspaper), investigations were launched by

Congress and Special Prosecutor Lawrence Walsh. Congressional hearings were held in the summer of 1987. Central to the controversy was Colonel Oliver North who had arranged many of the activities. In compelling testimony that transfixed the nation, North detailed the events but disavowed any knowledge of the President's participation.

JOHN W. NIELDS, JR.: It was not true the United States government had no communication with Mr. Hasenfus' airplane that went down in Nicaragua?

OIVER NORTH: No, it was not true. I had an indirect connection at flight, and many others I would point out.

NIELDS: In certain communist countries, the governments activities are kept secret from the people, but that is not the way we do things in America, is it?

NORTH: Counsel, I would like to go back to what I said just a few minutes ago.

I think it is very important for the American people to understand that this is a dangerous world, we live at risk and that this Nation is at risk in a dangerous world, and that they ought not be led to believe as a consequence of these hearings that this nation cannot or should not conduct covert operations.

By their very nature, covert operations or special activities are a lie. There is great deceit, deception practiced in the conduct of covert operations.

They are in essence a lie.

We make every effort to deceive the enemy as to our intent, our conduct, and to deny the association of the United States with those activities.

The intelligence committees hold hearings on all kinds of these activities conducted by our intelligence services. The American people ought not be led to believe by the way you are asking that question that we intentionally deceived the American people or had that intent to begin with.

The effort to conduct these covert operations was made in such a way that our adversaries would not have knowledge of them or that we could deny American association with them or the association of this Government with those activities.

And that is not wrong.

NIELDS: The American people were told by this Government that our Government had nothing to do with the Hasenfus airplane, and that was false, and it is a principal purpose of these hearings to replace secrecy and deception with disclosure and

truth, and that is one of the reasons we have called you here, sir.

And one question the American people would like to know the answer to is what did the President know about the diversion of the proceeds of Iranian arms sales to the contras.

Can you tell us what you knew about that, sir?

NORTH: You just took a long leap from Mr. Hasenfus' airplane.

As I told this committee several days ago, and if you will indulge me, Counsel, in a brief summary of what I said, I never personally discussed the use of the residuals or profits from the sale of United States weapons to Iran for the purpose of supporting the Nicaraguan resistance with the President.

I never raised it with him and he never raised it with me during my tenure at the National Security Council staff. Throughout the conduct of my entire tenure at the National Security Council, I assumed that the President was aware of what I was doing and had, through, my superiors, approved it.

I sought approval of my superiors for every one of my actions, and it is well documented.

I assumed when I had approval to proceed from either Judge [William P.] Clark, [Robert C.] Bud McFarlane, or [Rear] Admiral [John M.] Poindexter [each has served as national security adviser], that they had, indeed solicited and obtained the approval of the President.

To my recollection, Admiral Poindexter never told me that he met with the president on the issue of using residuals from the Iranian sales to support the Nicaraguan resistance or that he discussed the residuals or profits with the President, or that he got the president's specific approval, nor did he tell me that the President had approved such a transaction.

But again, I wish to reiterate that throughout, I believe that the President had indeed authorized such activity. No other person with whom I was in contact during my tenure at the White House told me that he or she ever discussed the issue of the residuals or profits with the President.

In late November, two other things occurred which relate to the issue.

On or about Friday, November 21, I asked Admiral Poindexter directly, "Does the President know?" He told me he did not.

And on November 25, the day I was reassigned

back to the United States Marine Corps for service, the President of the United States called me. In the course of that call, the President said to me, words to the effect that, "I just didn't know."

Those are the facts as I know them, Mr. Nields. I was glad that when you introduced this, you said that you wanted to hear the truth. I came to tell the truth, the good, the bad, and the ugly.

I am here to tell it all—pleasant and unpleasant—and I am here to accept responsibility for that which I did.

I will not accept responsibility for that which I did not do.

"We came home from this summit with everything we'd hoped to accomplish"

RONALD REAGAN

By 1987 it had become clear that the United States was on the verge of winning the Cold War. With its economy bankrupt and its ideology discredited, the Soviet Union was starting to dismantle its communist system. Soviet Premier Mikhail Gorbachev in 1986 had proposed reducing nuclear weapons by 50 percent and was starting to institute new measures allowing freedom of speech.

Reagan visited Gorbachev in 1987 to discuss the details of starting to dismantle their respective nuclear arsenals, which could destroy the world many, many times over. Upon returning, Reagan told a news conference that the meeting had been a success and that he had asked Gorbachev to tear down the Berlin Wall. Two years later, he did.

You've been hearing and reading reports that nothing was really accomplished at the summit and the United States in particular came home empty-handed. Well this was my seventh summit and the seventh time I've heard that same chorus.

You know, it might be appropriate, a noted bullfighter wrote a poem, a few lines of which do seem appropriate. "The bull fight critics ranked in rows, fill the enormous plaza full, but only one is there who really knows and he's the one who fights the bull."

The truth is we came home from this summit with everything we'd hoped to accomplish. And tonight I want to report to you on decisions made

there that directly effect you and your children's economic future.

I also have a special message, one that's about our own economy, about actions that could jeopardize the kind of progress we made toward economic health last week in Venice. As well as the prosperity that during the last six years all of us here in America have worked so hard to achieve.

But before beginning, I must make a personal note about something we saw on the last day of our journey, when we stopped in Berlin to help celebrate the anniversary of that noble city.

I know that over the years many of you have seen the pictures and news clips of the wall that divides Berlin. But believe me, no American who sees first hand the concrete and mortar, the guard posts, the machine gun towers, the dog runs, and the barbed wire can ever again take for granted his or her freedom or the precious gift that is America.

That gift of freedom is actually the birth right of all humanity. And that's why, as I stood there, I urged the Soviet leader, Mr. Gorbachev, to send a new signal of openness to the world, by tearing down that wall.

"It is grievously hurtful when vilification becomes an accepted form of political debate"

JIM WRIGHT

Texas Democrat James Wright was first elected to Congress in 1954. He rose through the ranks of his party to become Speaker of the House in 1989, only to fall from grace two years later in the wake of an ethics scandal. Upstart Republican Congressman Newt Gingrich railed against Wright for lapses in ethical standards and called for his resignation. The Ethics Committee cited 69 possible violations including taking inappropriate gifts and improperly raising money through the mass sales of a book he wrote.

Forced to resign his seat, Wright defended himself and warned Congress of the dangers of feeding off of each other's weaknesses for partisan purposes. While one could easily question the motivation behind his statements, the assessment proved to be telling for the way Congress would conduct its affairs in the coming decade.

It is intolerably hurtful to our government that qualified members of the executive and legislative branches are resigning because of the ambiguities and the confusion surrounding the ethics laws and because of their own consequent vulnerability to personal attack. That's a shame. It's happening.

And it is grievously hurtful to our society when vilification becomes a full-time occupation, when members of each party become self-appointed vigilantes carrying out personal vendettas against members of the other party. In God's name, that's not what this institution is supposed to be all about.

When vengeance becomes more desirable than vindication, harsh personal attacks on one another's motives, one another's character, drown out the quiet logic of serious debate on important issues, things that we ought to be involved ourselves in. Surely, that's unworthy of our institution, unworthy of our American political process.

All of us in both political parties must resolve to bring this period of mindless cannibalism to an end. There's been enough of it.

I pray to God that we will do that, and restore the spirit that always existed in this House. When I first came here all those years ago, in 1995, this was a place where a man's word was his bond, and his honor and the truth of what he said to were assumed—you didn't have to prove it....

I don't want to be a party to tearing up the institution; I love it. Tell you the truth, this year it has been very difficult for me to offer the kind of moral leadership that the organization needs, because every time I've tried to talk about the needs of the country, about the needs for affordable homes—Jack Kemp's idea and the idea developing here.

Every time I've tried to talk about the need for a minimum wage, tried to talk about the need for day care centers, embracing ideas on both sides of the aisle, the media have not been interest in that. They wanted to about petty personal finances.

You need—you need somebody else, someone to give you that back. We'll have the caucus on Tuesday. And then I will offer to resign from the House sometime before the end of June. Let that be a total payment for the anger and hostility we feel toward each other. Let's try not to get even with each other. Republicans, please don't get it in your heads you need to get somebody else because of John Tower. Democrats, please don't feel that you need to get somebody on the other side because of me. We ought

to be more mature than that.

Let's restore to this institution the rightful priorities of what's good for this country, and let's all work together to try to achieve them. The nation has important business, and it can't afford these distractions, and that's why I offer to resign.

I've enjoyed these years in Congress. I am grateful for all of you who have taught me things and been patient with me. Horace Greeley had a quote that Harry Truman used to like—and fame is a vapor, popularity an accident, riches take wings, those who cheer today may curse tomorrow, only one thing endures: character.

I'm not a bitter man—I'm not going to be. I'm a lucky man. God has given me the privilege of serving in this, the greatest institution on earth, for a great many years. And I'm grateful to the people of my district in Texas, I'm grateful to you, my colleagues, all of you.

God bless this institution. God bless the United States.

❧ "He is not an artist, he is a jerk"

JESSE HELMS

Contemporary art has held a controversial place in America for most of the twentieth century, particularly after World War II with the rise of Expressionism in New York City. Jackson Pollock's splattered paint, however, represented a uniquely American art form with a worldwide impact.

Often incomprehensible and seemingly simple to conceive to the layman's eye, contemporary artists have often been the subject of popular mockery. Undaunted, contemporary artists continued to push the envelope of artistic images, sometimes simply as a form of self-expression and sometimes as a way to provoke social commentary. While on the one hand they can be seen to represent an extreme of the American idea of free speech, their critics often belittle their work as self-referential or offensive.

In 1989, the schism between contemporary artists and the general public reached a high-water mark with North Carolina Senator Jesse Helms' condemnation of Andres Serrano's "Piss Christ" that had received a National Endowment for the Arts subsidy. Outraged by the government's endorsement of the image, he helped insert a restriction on future NEA expenditures prohibiting contributions for art that may be considered obscene. Helms' remarks on the floor of the Senate and the artist's response follow.

Mr. President,...I do not know Mr. Andres Serrano,

and I hope I never meet him because he is not an artist, he is a jerk.

Let us examine exactly what this bird did to get the American taxpayer to subsidize his $15,000 award through the so-called National Endowment for the Arts. Let me first say that if the Endowment has no better judgment than this, it ought to be abolished and all funds returned to the taxpayer.

What this Serrano fellow did to create this blasphemy was to fill a bottle with his own urine and then he stuck a crucifix—the Lord Jesus Christ on a cross—down in the urine, set the bottle on a table and took a picture of it.

For that, the National Endowment for the Arts contributed to a $15,000 award to honor him as an artist.

I say again, Mr. President, he is not an artist. He is a jerk. He is taunting a large segment of the American people, just as others are, about their Christian faith. I resent it, and I do not hesitate to say so.

I am not going to call the name that he applied to this work of art. In naming it he sought to create indignation, and let there be no question that he succeeded in that regard.

It is all right for him to be a jerk but let him be a jerk on his own time and with his own resources. Do not dishonor the Lord. Again, I resent it and I think the vast majority of our American people resent the National Endowment for the Arts spending the taxpayers' money to honor this individual.

The Federal program which honored Mr. Serrano, called the Awards in Visual Arts, is supported by the National Endowment for the Arts and administered by the Southeastern Center for Contemporary Arts. They call it SECCA and I am sorry to say it is in my home state.

After Mr. Serrano's selection, this deplorable photograph and some of his other works were exhibited in several cities around the country with the approval and the support of the National Endowment.

Horsefeathers. If we have sunk so low in this country as to tolerate and condone this sort of thing, then we have become a part of it.

The question is obvious. On what conceivable basis does anybody who would engage in such blasphemy and insensitivity toward the religious community deserve to be honored? The answer to that is that he does not. He deserves to be rebuked and

ignored because he is not an artist. Anybody who would do such a despicable thing—and get a tax-subsidized award of $15,000 for it—well, it tells you something about the state of this government and the way it spends our hard-earned tax dollars.

So no wonder all of the people calling my office are indignant. The Constitution may prevent the government from prohibiting Mr. Serrano's—laughably, I will describe it—"artistic expression." But the Constitution certainly does not require the American taxpayers or the federal government to fund, promote, honor, approve, or condone it.

Mr. President, the National Endowment's procedures for selecting artists and works of art deserving of taxpayer support are badly, badly flawed if this is an example of the kind of programs they fund with taxpayers' money.

I have sent word to the Endowment that I want them to review their funding criteria to ensure abuses such as this never happen again. The preliminary report we got from one person with whom we talked was sort of "Down, boy, we know what we are doing."

Well, they do not know what they are doing. By promoting, approving, and funding Mr. Serrano's sacrilege, the National Endowment for the Arts has insulted the very precepts on which this country was founded. I say again, that as an American and as a taxpayer, I resent it.

❧ "In a free society ideas, even difficult ones, are not dangerous"

ANDRES SERRANO

Letter to the National Endowment for the Arts
I am concerned over recent events regarding the misrepresentation of my work in Congress and consequent treatment in the media. The cavalier and blasphemous intentions ascribed to me on the Congressional floor bear little resemblance to reality. I am disturbed that the rush to judgment by certain members of Congress has been particularly swift and vindictive.

I am appalled by the claim of "anti-Christian

bigotry" that has been attributed to my picture, "Piss Christ." The photograph, and the title itself, are ambiguously provocative but certainly not blasphemous. Over the years, I have addressed religion regularly in my art. My Catholic upbringing informs this work which helps me to redefine and personalize my relationship with God. My use of such bodily fluids as blood and urine in this context is parallel to Catholicism's obsession with "the body and blood of Christ." It is precisely in the exploration and juxtaposition of these symbols from which Christianity draws its strength. The photograph in question, like all my work, has multiple meanings and can be interpreted in various ways. So let us suppose that the picture is meant as a criticism of the billion dollar Christ-for-profit industry and the commercialization of spiritual values that permeates our society. That it is a condemnation of those who abuse the teachings of Christ for their own ignoble ends. Is the subject of religion so inviolate that it is not open to discussion? I think not.

In writing the majority opinion in the flag burning case, Justice William J. Brennan concluded, "We never before have held that the government may insure that a symbol be used to express one view of that symbol or it's referents.... to conclude that the government may permit designated symbols to be used to communicate only a limited set of messages would be to enter into territory having no discernible or defensible boundaries."

Artists often depend on the manipulation of symbols to present ideas and associations not always apparent in such symbols. If all such ideas and associations were evident there would be little need for artists to give expression to them. In short, there would be no need to make art.

Do we condemn the use of a swastika in a work of art that does not unequivocally denounce Nazism as anti-Semitic? Not when the artist is Jewish. Do we denounce as racist a painting or photograph that is demeaning to African-Americans? Not if the artist is black. When art is decontextualised, however, it can pose a problem and create misunderstanding.

Debate and discussion are at the heart of our democracy. In a free society ideas, even difficult ones, are not dangerous. The only danger lies in repressing them.

❧ A bird's-eye view of American plutographics in the 1980s

KEVIN PHILLIPS

The 1980s witnessed an explosion of wealth. Similar to the 1920s, fortunes were made on Wall Street and in commerce. "Supply-side" economic policies implemented by the Reagan Administration justified the rapid emergence of overnight millionaires with notions such as the "trickle down theory" in which all sectors of society would benefit as the nation's overall prosperity grew.

By the end of the decade, however, it had become clear that this is not what was happening. In fact, it was a Republican analyst, Kevin Phillips, who dispelled the myth of "a rising tide lifting all ships" in his 1990 book *The Politics of Rich and Poor*. Phillips explored the widening "cleavage between rich and poor" and its implications. Despite the almost universal disgust with the bipolarization of wealth in the United States, the trend continued through the 1990s.

It is not enough to describe the United States as the world's richest nation between 1945 and 1989. The distribution of its wealth conveys a more provocative message. By several measurements, the United States in the late twentieth century led all other major industrial countries in the gap dividing the upper fifth of the population from the lower— in the disparity between top and bottom.... [A]mong major Western nations, the United States has displayed one of the sharpest cleavages between rich and poor. Opportunity has counted for more than equality, and in the 1980s, opportunity took on a new boldness and dimension.

By the middle of Reagan's term, official data had begun to show that America's broadly defined "rich"—the top half of 1 percent of the U.S. population—had never been richer. Federal policy favored the accumulation of wealth and rewarded financial assets, and the concentration of income that began in the mid-1970s was accelerating. In 1988, approximately 1.3 million individual Americans were millionaires by assets, up from 574,000 in 1980, 180,000 in 1972, 90,000 in 1964, and just 27,000 in 1953. Even adjusted for inflation, the number of millionaires had doubled between the late seventies and the late eighties. Meanwhile, the number of billionaires, according to *Forbes* magazine, went from a handful in 1981 to 26 in 1986 and 49 in 1987. As of late 1988, *Forbes* put that year's number of billionaires at 52, and *Fortune*'s September assessment hung the billion-dollar label on 51 American families.... No parallel upsurge of riches has been seen since the late nineteenth century, the era of Vanderbilts, Morgans and Rockefellers.

And it was equally conspicuous. Rising luxury consumption and social ambition prompted *New York* magazine to observe that for the third time in one hundred twenty-five years "a confluence of economic conditions has created arrivistes in such great numbers and with such immense wealth that they formed a critical mass and created a whole new social order with its own new rules of acceptable behavior." The 1980s were of a magnitude comparable with that of the post-civil War period and the 1920s, and "each of these watershed eras for New York came at a time when the need to raise capital thrust finance to the front of the national agenda and Wall Street to the center of public attention. And each era created a new class of wealthy who had so much money, so much power and so much momentum that they more or less displaced the older Establishment...."

Incomes and wealth were concentrating for several reasons. Global and national economic restructuring—the late twentieth century's worldwide revolution in trade, technology and finance—provided the underlying context. Commercial chaos is brutally Darwinian; it favors skills, enterprise and imagination. A second circumstance was that wages—the principal source of middle- and lower-class dollars—had stagnated through 1986 even while disinflation, deregulation and commercial opportunity were escalating the return on capital. Most of the Reagan decade, to put it mildly, was a heyday for unearned income as rents, dividends, capital gains and interest gained relative to wages and salaries as a source of wealth and increasing economic inequality. By 1983, as the bull market that had begun in August 1982 kept soaring, *Fortune* magazine profiled its biggest winners: Each of fifty-three stockholders had already made profits of over $100 million! One, David Packard, cofounder of Hewlett-Packard Inc., found himself richer on paper by $1.2 billion. Nine others gained over $300 million. More and bigger gains would follow in the mid-1980s, augmented by reduced tax rates on these swollen unearned incomes. In the wake of the 1978 capital gains tax reductions and the sweeping 1981 rate cuts, the effective overall, combined federal tax rate paid by the top 1 percent dropped from 30.9 percent in 1977 to 23.1 percent in 1984. No other grouped gained nearly so much.

Wealth data, of course, always display more concentration than income statistics. Upper-income taxpayers do a lopsided share of the accumulating...by the Joint Economic Committee's revised measurement, America's top 420,000 households alone accounted for 26.9 percent of U.S. family net worth—in essence, 26.9 percent of the nation's wealth. The top 10 percent of households, meanwhile, controlled approximately 68 percent. Accumulation and concentration would be simultaneous hallmarks of the 1980s.

On the income side of the ledger, the results, while less skewed, were striking enough. Here, too, the decade's biggest advances were scored by those already doing well—the business owners, investors, financiers and service-industry professionals. "The economy," said Stanford University professor Robert Hall, "has shifted in the direction of a meritocracy," and there was no mistaking how the smart, the well-educated and the highly motivated commanded a large share of the gain.... Between 1980 and 1988, the income share taken by the upper 20 percent of Americans rose from 41.6 percent to 44 percent, the highest ratio since the Census Bureau began its official measurements in 1949. Parenthetically, the share of the top 1 percent climbed from 9 percent to over 11 percent during the same period, suggesting that this particularly affluent subgroup took the overwhelming share of the top quintile's advance. Concentration like this is rare....

Ohioans Ross LaRoe and John Charles Pool put one set of comparative 1977-87 income trends in simple language for Middle America. Using data from the nonpartisan Congressional Budget Office, they wrote that "since 1977, the average after-tax income family income of the lowest 10 percent, in current dollars, fell from $3,528 to $3,157. That's a 10 percent drop. During the same period, the average family income of the top 10 percent increased from $70,459 to $89,783—up 24.4 percent. The incomes of the top 1 percent, which were 'only' $174,498 in 1977, are up to $303,900—

a whopping 74.2 percent increase over the decade."

...Although distributional ratios had not quite returned to the 1920s levels, favorable economic circumstances and federal policies had created an extraordinary pyramid of affluence—a record number of billionaires, three thousand to four thousand families worth over $50 million, almost one hundred thousand families each worth over $10 million and at least one and a quarter million households with a net worth exceeding $1 million.

The caveat was that if two to three million Americans were in clover—and another thirty to thirty-five million were justifiably pleased with their circumstances in the late 1980s—a larger number were facing deteriorating personal or family incomes or a vague but troubling sense of harder times ahead.

🐝 "A mandate for the elimination of discrimination against people with disabilities"

THE AMERICANS WITH DISABILITIES ACT

Responding to the needs of the blind, deaf, wheelchair-bound and others with disabilities, Congress passed The Americans with Disabilities Act in 1990. The legislation introduced sweeping changes to the way buildings are constructed and products are presented to the public to ensure that the disabled are not excluded. Ramps and lifts were installed for access to buildings, audio systems and signers were made available for the deaf and braille markings were placed on products ranging from glass bottles to elevator buttons. Senator Bob Dole of Kansas, who was permanently injured as a foot soldier in World War II, actively promoted the legislation.

Section 2. Findings and Purposes

Findings. The Congress finds that—

some 43,000,000 Americans have one or more physical or mental disabilities, and this number is increasing as the population as a whole is growing older;

historically, society has tended to isolate and segregate individuals with disabilities, and despite some improvements, such forms of discrimination against individuals with disabilities continues to be a serious and pervasive social problem;

discrimination against individuals with disabilities persists in such critical areas as employment, housing, public accommodations, education, transportation, communication, recreation, institutionalization, health services, voting, and access to public services;

unlike individuals who have experienced discrimination on the basis of race, color, sex, national origin, religion, or age, individuals who have experienced discrimination on the basis of disability have often had no legal recourse to redress such discrimination;

individuals with disabilities continually encounter various forms of discrimination, including outright intentional exclusion, the discriminatory effects of architectural, transportation, and communication barriers, overprotective rules and policies, failure to make modifications to existing facilities and practices, exclusionary qualification standards and criteria, segregation, and relegation to lesser services, programs, activities, benefits, jobs, or other opportunities;

census data, national polls, and other studies have documented that people with disabilities, as a group, occupy an inferior status in our society, and are severely disadvantaged socially, vocationally, economically, and educationally;

individuals with disabilities are a discrete and insular minority who have been faced with restrictions and limitations, subjected to a history of purposeful unequal treatment, and relegated to a position of political powerlessness in our society, based on characteristics that are beyond the control of such individuals and resulting from stereotypic assumptions not truly indicative of the individual ability of such individuals to participate in, and contribute to, society;

the Nation's proper goals regarding individuals with disabilities are to assure equality of opportunity, full participation, independent living, and economic self-sufficiency for such individuals; and

the continuing existence of unfair and unnecessary discrimination and prejudice denies people with disabilities the opportunity to compete on an equal basis and to pursue those opportunities for which our free society is justifiably famous, and costs the United States billions of dollars in unnecessary expenses resulting from dependency and nonproductivity.

Purpose. It is the purpose of this Act—

to provide a clear and comprehensive national mandate for the elimination of discrimination against individuals with disabilities;

to provide clear, strong, consistent, enforceable standards addressing discrimination against individuals with disabilities;

to ensure that the Federal Government plays a central role in enforcing the standards established in this Act on behalf of individuals with disabilities; and

to invoke the sweep of congressional authority, including the power to enforce the fourteenth amendment and to regulate commerce, in order to address the major areas of discrimination faced day-to-day by people with disabilities.

As used in this Act:

Auxiliary aids and services. The term "auxiliary aids and services" includes—

qualified interpreters or other effective methods of making aurally delivered materials available to individuals with hearing impairments;

qualified readers, taped texts, or other effective methods of making visually delivered materials available to individuals with visual impairments;

acquisition or modification of equipment or devices; and

other similar services and actions.

Disability. The term "disability" means, with respect to an individual—

a physical or mental impairment that substantially limits one or more of the major life activities of such individual;

a record of such an impairment; or

being regarded as having such an impairment.

State. The term "State" means each of the several States, the District of Columbia, the Commonwealth of Puerto Rico, Guam, American Samoa, the Virgin Islands, the Trust Territory of the Pacific Islands, and the Commonwealth of the Northern Mariana Islands.

In General. The term "employer" means a person engaged in an industry affecting commerce who has 15 or more employees for each working day in each of 20 or more calendar weeks in the current or preceding calendar year, and any agent of such person, except that, for two years following the effective date of this title, an employer means a person engaged in an industry affecting commerce who has

25 or more employees for each working day in each of 20 or more calendar years.

Exceptions. The term "employer" does not include—

the United States, a corporation wholly owned by the government of the United States, or an Indian tribe; or

a bona fide private membership club (other than a labor organization) that is exempt from taxation under section 501(c) of the Internal Revenue Code of 1986....

(8) Qualified individual with disability. The term "qualified individual with a disability" means an individual with a disability who, with or without reasonable accommodation, can perform the essential functions of the employment position that such individual holds or desires. For the purposes of this title, consideration shall be given to the employer's judgment as to what functions of a job are essential, and if an employer has prepared a written description before advertising or interviewing applications for the job, this description shall be considered evidence of the essential functions of the job.

Reasonable Accommodation. The term "reasonable accommodation" may include—

making existing facilities used by employees readily accessible to and usable by individuals with disabilities; and

job restructuring, part-time, or modified work schedules, reassignment to a vacant position, acquisition or modification of equipment or devices, appropriate adjustment or modifications of examinations, training materials or policies, the provision of qualified readers or interpreters, and other similar accommodations for individuals with disabilities.

Undue hardship.

In General. The term "undue hardship" means an action requiring significant difficulty or expense, when considered in light of factors set forth in subparagraph (B).

Factors to be considered. In determining whether an accommodation would impose an undue hardship on a covered entity, factors to be considered include

the nature and cost of the accommodation under this Act;

the overall financial resources of the facility or facilities involved in the provision of the reasonable accommodation; the number of persons employed at such facility; the effect on expenses and resources, or the impact otherwise of such accommodation upon the operation of the facility;

the overall financial resources of the covered entity; the overall size of the business of a covered entity with respect to the number of its employees; the number, type, and location of its facilities; and

the type of operation or operations of the covered entity, including the composition, structure, and functions of the workforce of such entity; the geographic separateness, administrative, or fiscal relationship of the facility or facilities in question to the covered entity....

🦉 "A significant prison term is required to deter others"

KIMBA WOOD SENTENCES MICHAEL MILKEN

Michael R. Milken exemplified the values that characterized the 1980s: the "decade of excess." The powerful financier from the investment bank Drexel Burnham Lambert started the "junk bond" (or more politely, high-yield) market, making a fortune in the meantime for himself and Drexel. But Milken's pursuit of wealth went beyond the bounds of law.

Federal prosecutors began to unwind a scandal of white-collar crime based on insider information starting in 1986. By 1990, Milken had been ensnared in the investigation and was tried for his transgressions. Federal District Judge Kimba M. Wood oversaw the case and on November 21, 1990, sentenced him to ten years of prison and three years of probation with community service. She left open the option of a lighter sentence depending on Milken's cooperation with prosecutors. She noted that Milken could apply his considerable talents to community service in a very productive way.

Wood's expectations were realized. Having cooperated in further investigations from jail as a model inmate, Milken's sentence was ultimately reduced. Out of jail, he oversaw major initiatives on behalf of education and cancer research. Milken's investment bank, Drexel, went out of business. The junk bond market, after a period of diminished activity, rebounded and flourished throughout most of the 1990s.

Because of the extraordinary interest that has been expressed in this case and the fact that many letters to the court reflect misconceptions about what it is that Michael Milken is being punished for, I

believe that I should briefly attempt to dispel those misconceptions, many of which were alluded to by Mr. Liman.

The letters reflect a perception that we as a society must find those responsible for the alleged abuses of the 1980's, economic harm caused savings and loan associations, takeover targets and those allegedly injured by the issuance of junk bonds as well as by insider trading and other alleged abuses, and punish these criminals in proportion to the losses believed to have been suffered. These writers ask for a verdict on a decade of greed.

While I sympathize with the anxiety expressed in these letters, the suppositions upon which these views are based cannot enter into sentencing defendant on the six counts of wrongdoing to which he plead guilty....

It is important to note as well that although many of those who wrote to the court believe that defendant should be treated harshly because they believe that he is the one responsible for the massive job josses and the financial failure of savings and loans associations, the Government did not charge him with responsibility here for those losses. For the Government to prove such charges would have required the government to try to isolate the effect of defendant's actions from all of the other forces acting in the marketplace.

For similar reasons the court cannot take into account the claims of those who urge leniency for defendant because he allegedly created jobs and business opportunities or drew capital to its most productive uses. Determinations such as these would require information not before the court and would, for example, require the court to speculate on how defendant's clients would have invested their money absent his advice, and what effect those actions would have on job creation or loss, business opportunities and productivity.

I note that these letters also reflect a legitimate public concern that everyone, no matter how rich or powerful, obey the law...and that our financial markets in which so many people who are not rich invest their savings be free of secret manipulation. This is a concern fairly to be considered by the court.

I will turn now to the conduct for which defendant is being sentenced.

You are being sentenced for six counts of criminal activity spanning approximately three years in participation with several other people involving several different transactions that violated securities laws, tax laws and other laws.

You have attempted to mitigate these crimes by claiming they represented no more than overzealous service to your clients, that they involved mere technicalities, and that they did not represent the core of how you did business.

I will speak to these points briefly before moving to the factors influencing sentencing.

To the extent that your crimes benefited your clients, that is, of course, no excuse for violating the law. In addition, there is no escaping the fact that your crimes also benefited you, not necessarily by lining your pockets directly and immediately, but by increasing your clients loyalty to you, hence, increasing your edge over competitors and increasing the likelihood that your clients would pay for your services in the future.

It has also been argued that your violations were technical ones to be distinguished from accumulating profits through insider trading and that your conduct is not really criminal or that it is only barely criminal.

It was suggested that if you were truly disposed to criminal conduct, you could have made much more money by committing more blatant crimes such as repeatedly misusing insider information.

These arguments fail to take into account the fact that you may have committed only subtle crimes because you were not disposed to any criminal behavior but because you were willing to commit only crimes that were unlikely to be detected.

We see often in this court individuals who would be unwilling to rob a bank, but who readily cash Social Security checks that are not theirs when checks come to them in the mail because they are not likely to be caught doing so.

Your crimes show a pattern of skirting the law, stepping just over to the wrong side of the law in an apparent effort to get some of the benefits from violating the law without running a substantial risk of being caught....

Your attorneys also argue that most of your business was conducted lawfully and that you would have prospered even absent the unlawful practices you admitted.

The evidence before the court on this point is sparse and equivocal. I do not know, for example, whether some of your biggest clients would have made their funds available without the benefits fund managers personally received from Drexel. Statements to the contrary made by fund managers...were unpersuasive, given their self-serving nature....

Let me turn then to the purposes of sentencing and their application here. As was pointed out, purposes are generally thought to be individual deterrence, general deterrence, punishment of just deserts, retribution and rehabilitation.

Taking them one by one, deterring you as an individual from breaking the law again has already been furthered in part by your being barred from ever again working in the securities industry, by your $200 million fine, by the 4400 million restitution fund that you have funded and by the fact that you face numerous civil lawsuit that could result in your paying more than $400 million that you have already paid to the restitution fund....

I have given considerable thought to whether a sentence of lengthy community service would be an adequate penalty here. It would have the advantage of permitting you to work productively with others which I believe you could do well rather than having you warehoused in a prison. Nevertheless, I believe that a prison term is required for the purposes of general deterrence; that is, the need to deter others from violating the law and the possibility that the sentence given in one case will prevent others from violating law.

Prison is viewed as one of the most powerful deterrents to the financial community. This view is reflected in the legislatively mandated sentencing guidelines which punish white-collar crimes with more prison time than was common before their adoption, and I have looked to those guidelines for some guidance in connection with this sentencing.

When a man of your power in the financial world, at the head of the most important department of one of the most important investment banking houses in this country, repeatedly conspires to violate, and violates securities and tax laws in order to achieve more power and wealth for himself and his wealthy clients, and commits financial crimes that are particularly hard to detect, a significant prison term is required in order to deter others.

This kind of misuse of your leadership position and enlisting employees who you supervised to assist you in violating the law are serious crimes warranting serious punishment and the discomfort and opprobrium of being removed from society....

I have taken into account that long before your current legal problems you took a significant amount of your own personal time to serve the community by working with disadvantaged children rather, for example, than using all of your personal time to acquire possessions. You also successfully encouraged your colleagues at work to do the same.

I have also taken into account the emotional support that you have provided to your family, neighbors, co-workers and competitors who found you to be forthright, honorable and honest in your dealings with them over the years.

On the other side of the scale, I must also take into account that you were head of your department and you used others in your department to effect unlawful schemes. By your example, you communicated that cutting legal and ethical corners is, at times, acceptable.

You also committed crimes that are hard to detect, and crimes that are hard to detect warrant greater punishment in order to be effective in deterring others from committing them....

As I mentioned earlier, I have no way to evaluate now the value of any cooperation you may offer the Government in the future. I have never given a defendant credit for cooperation without knowing the extent of the cooperation and without knowing how useful the information was to the Government; and I will not deviate from that practice now.

If you cooperate, and if the Government moves for a reduction in your sentence based on your cooperation, the court can adjust your sentence accordingly....

Mr. Milken, please rise.

You are unquestionably a man of talent and industry and you have consistently shown a dedication to those less fortunate than you. It is my hope that the rest of your life will fulfill the promise shown early in your career.

However, for the reasons stated earlier, I sentence you to a total of ten years in prison, consisting of two years each on counts two through six to be served consecutively, and I also sentence you to three years of probation on count one. A special condition of your probation is that you serve full-time community service, 1,800 hours per year for each of the three years, in a program to be determined by the court. I also impose the mandatory statutory assessment of $50 on each count for a total
of $300.

I advise you that you have the right to appeal this sentence.

You may be seated at this point.

❧ "Saddam Hussein started this cruel war against Kuwait"

GEORGE BUSH

In the summer of 1990, Iraq invaded Kuwait, taking over the country's substantial oil reserves and posing an ominous threat to neighboring oil-rich Saudi Arabia. Determined to stop Iraq President Saddam Hussein's apparent territorial ambitions, President George Bush and the international community demanded that Hussein withdraw from Kuwait. Hussein refused.

After securing permission to use military action and building a substantial international military force on the Kuwait border, Bush announced on January 16, 1991, that the United States and a coalition of 28 other countries was commencing air strikes against Iraqi forces. Five weeks later, on February 24, ground forces invaded Kuwait and southern Iraq, wiping out minimal resistance from demoralized and shellshocked Iraqi troops. Bush announced a ceasefire on February 27.

Just two hours ago Allied air forces began an attack on military targets in Iraq and Kuwait. These attacks continue as I speak, ground forces are not engaged. This conflict started August second when the dictator of Iraq invaded a small and helpless neighbor. Kuwait, a member of the Arab League and a member of the United Nations, was crushed, its people brutalized.

Five months ago, Saddam Hussein started this cruel war against Kuwait, tonight the battle has been joined.

This military action, taken in accord with United Nations resolutions and with the consent of the United States Congress follows months of constant and virtually endless diplomatic activity on the part of the United Nations, the United States and many, many other countries. Arab leaders sought what became known as an Arab solution. Only to conclude that Saddam Hussein was unwilling to leave Kuwait.

Others traveled to Baghdad in a variety of efforts to restore peace and justice. Our Secretary of State, James Baker, held an historic meeting in Geneva, only to be totally rebuffed. This past weekend, in a last ditch effort, the Secretary General of the United Nations went to the Middle East with peace in his heart, his second such mission. And he came back from Baghdad with no progress at all in getting Saddam Hussein to withdraw from Kuwait.

Now, the twenty-eight countries with forces in the Gulf area have exhausted all reasonable efforts to reach a peaceful resolution, have no choice but to drive Saddam from Kuwait with force, and we will not fail. As I repot to you, air attacks are under way against military targets in Iraq.

We are determined to knock out Saddam Hussein's nuclear bomb potential. We will also destroy his chemical weapons facilities. Much of Saddam's artillery and tanks will be destroyed. Our operations are designed to best protect the lives of all the coalition forces by targeting Saddam's vast military arsenal. Initial reports from General Schwarzkopf are that our operations are proceeding according to plan.

Our objectives are clear, Saddam Hussein's forces will leave Kuwait. The legitimate government of Kuwait will be restored to its rightful place. And Kuwait will once again be free.

Iraq will eventually comply with all relevant United Nations resolutions and then, when peace is restored, it is our hope, that Iraq will live as a peaceful and cooperative member of the family of nations. Thus enhancing the security and stability of the Gulf.

Some may ask, "Why act now? Why not wait?" The answer is clear. The world could wait no longer.

Sanctions, though having some effect, showed no signs of accomplishing their objective. Sanctions were tried for well over five months, and we and our allies concluded that sanctions alone would not force Saddam form Kuwait.

While the world waited Saddam Hussein systematically raped, pillaged and plundered a tiny nation. No threat to his own, he subjected the people of Kuwait to unspeakable atrocities. And among those maimed and murdered, innocent children.

While the world waited, Saddam sought to add to the chemical weapons arsenal he now possesses, an infinitely more dangerous weapon of mass destruction, a nuclear weapon. And while the world waited, while the world talked peace and withdrawal Saddam Hussein dug in and moved massive forces into Kuwait.

While the world waited, while Saddam stalled, more damage was being done to the fragile economies of the third world, the emerging democracies of Eastern Europe, to the entire world, including to our own economy.

The United States, together with the United Nations exhausted every means at our disposal to bring this crisis to a peaceful end. However, Saddam clearly felt that by stalling and threatening and defying the United Nations he could weaken the forces arrayed against him.

While the world waited, Saddam Hussein met every overture of peace with open contempt.

While the world prayed for peace, Saddam prepared for war. I had hoped that when the United States Congress, in historic debate, took its resolute action, Saddam would realize he could not prevail and would move out of Kuwait in accord with the United Nation resolutions. He did not do that. Instead, he remained intransigent, certain that time was on his side.

Saddam was warned over and over again to comply with the will of the United Nations, leave Kuwait or be driven out. Saddam has arrogantly rejected all warnings, instead he tried to make this a dispute between Iraq and the United States of America, well he failed.

Tonight, twenty-eight nations, countries from five continents, Europe and Asia, Africa and the Arab league have forces in the gulf area standing shoulder to shoulder against Saddam Hussein.

These countries had hoped the use of force could be avoided, regrettably we now believe that only force will make him leave.

🐦 "I had spent my whole life building a dream that was destroyed in one night"

SUN SOON KIM RECALLS LOS ANGELES RIOTS

On April 29, 1992, in Los Angeles, an all-white jury acquitted four white policemen for the brutal beating of Rodney King, a black man. The verdict came despite a widely broadcast video-tape of the event showing the police beating an apparently prostrate King. Los Angeles erupted in a race riot that left 52 people dead and caused up to $1 billion in property damage.

Much of the looting and destruction was aimed at Korean merchants who had set up shops in Los Angeles neighborhoods. After a lifetime of work, Sun Soon Kim owned a complex of stores that was destroyed in the riot. She told Berkeley University student Samantha M. Lee about her experience.

After five years at a dead end job of long hours and no opportunity of upward advancement, I decided that I needed a change. With the little money that Dae and I were able to save up, I decided that I was going to open my own shop. I had to think about this long and hard before I made any drastic decisions. It was not an individual decision—it required the opinion of the whole family. I was not doing this for myself; I was doing this for the family. But there were many factors involved, such as the location, the language barrier, what kind of business, and the risk factor. Operating a small business was risky, and with the little capital that was saved, I wanted the highest percentage of success. I heard Koreans talking about the formation of a small Korean community in Los Angeles. I decided to check it out. Around the same time I was thinking about the business, I found out that my cousin was moving to Los Angeles. I couldn't believe how perfect the time was. Finally, things were starting to look better.

With many discussions, my cousin and I decided we were going to be small business owners. She had brought her three kids here to obtain a better education, while her husband stayed in Korea to oversee and run his company. Together, my cousin and I bought a little shopping center that housed five stores with our life savings. She took three of them because she put in more money than I did, and I took the other two. Between the two of us, we had a market, Korean pastry shop, electronics store, clothing store, and beauty salon.

The location was great, right on Olympic Boulevard in the heart of the Korean community. Being in the Korean community really helped in that it eliminated the language barrier and cultural differences. We also received a lot of support from Korean customers, as well as other ethnic groups. Everything was going great except for the kids. They were running around with the wrong crowd. I discovered that Koreatown was no place to raise kids but a great place to do business. Too many bad influences such as drugs, smoking, alcohol, gangs, and nightclubs, but not enough families. My kids were too young and very impressionable, and I did not want them living at the store either. It seemed so unhealthy, and I did not want them to become business owners like me. I wanted them to get a good education and good paying jobs. Business was picking up and doing well, so once Sammie graduated from the eighth grade, I decided that it was time to move back to the Bay Area. The schools were good, we were near family again, and the kids would be away from all the bad influences of Koreatown.

With my cousin watching over my two stores and sending me the profits, I was able to purchase a bigger house in the Hayward hills. This purchase made me proud because the bigger house represented our economic stability, financial growth, and our achievements in America. We came with nothing except the clothes on our backs and a couple of suitcases and now we had a house. Finally, I was slowly inching toward the "American Dream" that hard work reaps success. With the steady flow of money coming in, I purchased a small cookie shop in Larkspur in Marin County. All the money that I made was for the kids. Buy the kids whatever they wanted—they were good kids and they deserved it. They were making me proud—they were doing well in school and Paul played the violin for the youth orchestra. For the next few years, life flew by without any problems. I thought I had finally reached the "American Dream."

Then an event happened in 1992 that will forever be in my memory. That was the Los Angeles riot. I had no idea that something like this was about to happen. I guess even having a prior warning would not have helped. How do you deal with something like this? Since I wasn't living in Koreatown I had no idea how much tension was out there. I would hear stories of racial incidents here and there, like the Latasha Harlins incident (a black teenager shot by a Korean shopkeeper in Los Angeles in 1991). But in reality, I had no idea how bad it was or that it was going to explode like it did.

This portion of my life, I just want to forget, like it never happened. I try to make it disappear, but it always finds it way back to me, forever haunting me. No one understands the feelings I have about this, and words probably could not accurately convey what I want to say. The impact of the riot on Korean merchants runs deeper than imagined. The theorists and scholars really can't explain the impact of the riots. How can they, when they weren't even there to experience it?

What do I remember about that day? Much of it is a blur since I've tried to forget about it. I remember coming home from work in the evening and seeing my kids running out to greet me all excited flustered. They dragged me upstairs and planted me in front of the television. The images that I saw on all the channels were of people looting, Koreans with guns, and Korean businesses in smoke and on fire. It took a couple of minutes for the images to settle, and when I realized that this was happening for real and that it was going on in Koreatown, I rushed over to the telephone to call my cousin. I tried calling her house and our five stores.

Since no one was responding, I began to panic. I was so worried that I frantically called the airlines hoping to get a flight out, but none of the airlines were flying into Los Angeles. I wanted to fly out there as soon as possible. The children wanted to go with me, but I said no after seeing the images on television, but they insisted, so I booked four seats to Los Angeles for the next day. I spent most of the evening frantically calling Los Angeles. None of the people I knew were home or answering. I needed to know what was going on. I needed answers. I could see businesses that I used to shop at being burned down or looted. I made the kids watch the television in hopes that they would be able to get a glimpse of my shopping center.

What was going on? The images on television were so incoherent, almost like a dream. Was this for real? That night was the longest and darkest night I ever experienced in my life. It was not the anticipation that was killing me, but the not knowing was. The family and I took the first flight to Los Angeles. I did not know what to expect. Koreatown was blocked off, but no one was going to stop me from going to my stores.

Koreatown looked like it went to war. I guess if I was ever in a war, I know what the end results would look like. I could still see smoke rising from buildings, and Korean merchants trying to salvage any remains of a dream. Since cars couldn't drive through, we parked our car and started to walk. I couldn't believe what I was seeing—like something from the movies. I felt like I was on the movie screen walking through the war zone, and people in the movie theater were watching this.

Words cannot describe the emotions that I was feeling, or the sights that I saw. A block or two before we reached my stores, my cousin ran out to stop me. She was crying and trying to hold me back from seeing the stores. I had to see them. I wanted to see with my own eyes that everything I saw on television the night before was real. My cousin and my husband were trying to hold my back. No one was going to stop me from seeing my stores. I kicked and fought and finally pried myself free and ran and ran. I ran without looking back. I did not care, I just wanted to see. I honestly wasn't prepared for what I was about to see.

In front of me was the remaining rubble of the stores that I had poured my money, sweat, and time into. Everything I had worked so hard to build was crumbled in front of me. I had spent my whole life building a dream that was destroyed in one night. Knowing that I had built this for the kids' future and my future was unbearable. Now we had no future. This realization broke me. I crumbled in the midst of anguish and pain. I cried and wailed tears not for myself, but for all the other merchants whose dreams had also crumbled. I sobbed for myself, my children, my cousin, and fellow immigrants. When my stores were destroyed, a part of me was destroyed. I died, not physically but emotionally. I don't remember much. I think I was just going through the motion of things.

I don't remember leaving Los Angeles. I don't even recall coming home. I know that I was in shock for awhile. I did not talk to anyone, just walked around in a daze and went through the motions of living. Two months after the riots, I knew my kids were worried about me and my physical and mental health. I had a dream one afternoon. In my dream a lion was chasing me. I ran and ran, but the lion caught me and laid on me, suffocating me in its chest. I struggled for awhile, but then I decided that it was pointless. I was going to let this lion suffocate me. But the thought of my kids without a mother and struggling without me gave me the strength and courage I needed; I was going to beat it. At that point I fought and fought. I finally got the lion off of me, and I ran and ran without looking back. I was scared that if I looked back, the lion would catch me again, and I would indeed suffocate to death. The lion to me represented the Los Angeles riots, and when the riots exploded, my version of the "American Dream" was destroyed. Even though a part of me died that day, I decided that it was not going to kill me. I was going to fight and fight hard for what I believed in. I was not going to let the riots beat me. I may have, but now I was fighting back.

It's been five years since the riots. There have been some significant changes in my life. Six months after the riots, I suffered a major heart attack where I could not be on my feet longer than a couple of hours a day. I had to sell my cookie shop in Larkspur, but with that money, my husband decided that he wanted to open his own small business. Both of my kids are in college now and are struggling with the financial changes in our household. But they are doing well in school and making me proud. The riots had been a big impact on my life, but I still do not understand why it happened. I still have questions that can't be answered, but now I'm not searching anymore. I'm letting the past go and trying to go on with my life.

❧ The Farm

WENDELL BERRY

In an era of globalization, consumerism and mass media, Kentucky farmer Wendell Berry's poetry speaks to the dignity of the individual and the importance of his place in the world. Written in 1991, Berry's The Farm contemplates a person's role in life, work and the obligation to others and nature.

Go by the narrow road

Along the creek, a burrow
Under shadowy trees
Such as a mouse makes through
Tall grass, so that you may
Forget the wide road you
Have left behind, and all
That it had led to. Or,
Best, walk up through the woods,
Around the valley rim,
And down to where the trees
Give way to cleared hillside,
So that you reach the place
Out of the trees' remembrance
Of their kind; seasonal
And timeless, they stand in
Uncounted time, and you
Have passed among them, small
As a mouse at a feast,
Unnoticed at the feet
Of all those mighty guests.
Come on a clear June morning
As the fog lifts, trees drip,
And birds make everywhere
Uninterrupted song.

However you may come,
You'll see it suddenly
Lie open to the light
Amid the woods: a farm
Little enough to see
Or call across-cornfield,
Hayfield, and pasture, clear
As if remembered, dreamed
And yearned for long ago,
Neat as a blossom now
When all its fields are mowed
And dew is fresh upon it,
Bird music all around.
That is the vision, seen
As on a Sabbath walk:
The possibility
Of human life whose terms
Are Heaven's and this earth's.

Stay years if you would know
The work and thought, the pleasure
And grief, the feat, by which
This vision lives. In fall
Or winter you should plow
A patch of bottomland

For corn; the freezes then
Will work the heavy clods.
When it's too wet to plow,
Go to the woods to fell
Trees for next winter's fuel.
Take the inferior trees
And not all from one place,
So that the woods will yield
Without diminishment.
Then trim and rick the logs;
And when you drag them out
From woods to rick, use horses
Whose hooves are kinder to
The ground than wheels. In spring
The traces of your work
Will be invisible....

But don't neglect your garden.
Household economy
Makes family and land
An independent state.
Never buy at a store
What you can grow or find
At home—this is the rule
Of liberty, also
Of neighborhood. (And be
Faithful to local merchants
Too. Never buy far off
What you can buy near home.)
As early as you can,
Plant peas, onions, and greens,
Potatoes, radishes,
Cabbage and cauliflower,
Lettuce, carrots, and beets—
Things that will stand the frost.
Then as the weather warms
Plant squashes, corn, and beans,
Okra, tomatoes, herbs,
Flowers—some for yourself
And some to give away.
In the cornfield plant pole beans,
Pumpkins, and winter squash;
Thus by diversity
You can enlarge the yield.

You have good grass and hay,
So keep a cow or two.
Milk made from your own grass
Is cheap and sweet. A cow
To milk's a good excuse

To bring you home from places
You do not want to be.
Fatten the annual calf
For slaughter. Keep a pig
To rescue scraps, skimmed milk,
And other surpluses.
Keep hens who will make eggs
And meat of offal, insects,
A little of your corn.
Eat these good beasts that eat
What you can't eat. Be thankful
To them and to the plants,
To your small, fertile homeland,
To topsoil, light and rain
That daily give you life.

Be thankful and repay
Growth with good work and care.
Work done in gratitude,
Kindly, and well, is prayer.
You did not make yourself,
Yet you must keep yourself
By use of other lives.
No gratitude atones
For bad use or too much.

This is not work for hire.
By this expenditure
You make yourself a place;
You make yourself a way
For love to reach the ground.
In its ambition and
Its greed, its violence,
The world is turned against
This possibility,
And yet the world survives
By the survival of
This kindly working love....

And so you make the farm,
And so you disappear
Into your days, your days
Into the ground. Before
You start each day, the place
Is as it is, and at
The day's end, it is as
It is, a little changed
By work, but still itself,
Having included you
And everything you've done.

And it is who you are,
And you are what it is.
You will work many days
No one will ever see;
Their record is the place.
This way you come to know
That something moves in time
That time does not contain.
For by this timely work
You keep yourself alive
As you came into time,
And as you'll leave: God's dust,
God's breath, a little Light....

Loving you has taught me the infinite
longing of the self to be given away
and the great difficulty of that entire
giving, for in love to give is to receive
and there is yet more to give;
and others have been born of our giving
to whom the self, greatened by gifts,
must be given, and by that giving
be increased, until, self-burdened,
the self, staggering upward in years,
in fear, hope, love, and sorrow,
imagines, rising like a moon,
a pale moon risen in daylight
over the dark woods, the Self
whose gift we and all others are,
the self that is by definition given.

🍃 "Human rights for all people"

MADELEINE ALBRIGHT'S REMARKS TO THE FOURTH WORLD CONFERENCE ON WOMEN

Appointed as United States Representative to the United Nations by President Bill Clinton, Madeleine Albright's successful tenure stood as a testament to the success of the feminist movement in the United States. In 1994, Albright traveled to the Fourth World Conference on Women in Beijing to address the conference in an effort to make the issue of women's rights a global movement and reaffirm the ongoing measures taking place in the United States. In 1997, Albright was appointed Secretary of State. She is the first woman to hold the position.

We have come here from all over the world to

carry forward an age-old struggle: The pursuit of economic and social progress for all people, based on respect for the dignity and value of each. We are here to promote and protect human rights and to stress that women's rights are neither separable nor different from those of men. We are here to stop sexual crimes and other violence against women; to protect refugees, so many of whom are women; and to end the despicable notion—in this era of conflicts—that rape is just another tactic of war.

We are here to empower women by enlarging their role in making economic and political decisions, an idea some find radical, but which my government believes is essential to economic and social progress around the world; because no country can develop if half its human resources are devalued or repressed.

We are here because we want to strengthen families—the heart and soul of any society. We believe that girls must be valued to the same degree as boys. We believe, with Pope John Paul ii, in the "equality of spouses with respect to family rights." We think women and men should be able to make informed judgments as they plan their families, and we want to see forces that weaken families— including pornography, domestic violence, and the sexual exploitation of children—condemned and curtailed.

Finally, we have come to this conference to assure for women equal access to education and health care, to help women protect against infection by HIV, to recognize the special needs and strengths of women with disabilities, and to attack the root causes of poverty in which so many women, children, and men are entrapped.

We have come to Beijing to make further progress toward each of these goals. But real progress will depend not on what we say here, but on what we do after we leave here. The Fourth World Conference on Women is not about conversations; it is about commitments.

For decades, my nation has led efforts to promote equal rights for women. Women in their varied roles—as mothers, farm laborers, factory workers, organizers, and community leaders—helped build America. My government is based on principles that recognize the right of every person to equal rights and equal opportunity. Our laws forbid discrimination on the basis of sex, and we work hard to enforce those laws. A rich network of non-governmental organizations has blossomed within our borders, reaching out to women and girls from all segments of society—educating, counseling, and advocating change.

The United States is a leader, but leaders cannot stand still. Barriers to the equal participation of women persist in my country. The Clinton Administration is determined to bring those barriers down. Today, in the spirit of this conference and in the knowledge that concrete steps to advance the status of women are required in every nation, I am pleased to announce the new commitments my government will undertake.

First, President Clinton will establish a White House Council on Women to plan for the effective implementation within the United States of the Platform for Action. That council will build on the commitments made today and will work every day with the non-governmental community.

Second, in accordance with recently approved law, the Department of Justice will launch a six-year, $1.6 billion initiative to fight domestic violence and other crimes against women. Funds will be used for specialized police and prosecution units and to train police, prosecutors, and judicial personnel.

Third, our Department of Health and Human Services will lead a comprehensive assault on threats to the health and security of women—promoting healthy behavior, increasing awareness about aids, discouraging the use of cigarettes, and striving to win the battle against breast cancer. As Mrs. Clinton made clear yesterday, the United States remains firmly committed to the reproductive health rights gains made in Cairo.

Fourth, our Department of Labor will conduct a grassroots campaign to improve work conditions for women in the workplace. The campaign will work with employers to develop more equitable pay and promotion policies, and to help employees balance the twin responsibilities of family and work.

Fifth, our Department of the Treasury will take new steps to promote access to financial credit for women. Outstanding U.S. micro-enterprise lending organizations will be honored through special Presidential awards, and we will improve coordination of federal efforts to encourage growth in this field of central importance to the economic empowerment of women.

Sixth, the Agency for International Development will continue to lead in promoting and recognizing the vital role of women in development. Today, we announce important initiatives to increase women's participation in political processes and to promote the enforcement of women's legal rights.

There is a seventh and final commitment my country is making today. We, the people and Government of the United States of America, will continue to speak out openly and without hesitation on behalf of the human rights of all people.

❧ Contract with America

NEWT GINGRICH, DICK ARMEY AND THE HOUSE REPUBLICANS

Under the leadership of Georgia Congressman Newt Gingrich, the Republican Party in 1994 decided to nationalize the Congressional elections. In an unprecedented move, Gingrich prepared a ten-point program that he pledged a Republican Congress would implement if elected. The House of Representatives had been Democratic for more than forty years.

More than three hundred Republican members of Congress and Congressional candidates signed the Contract with America, which was subsequently published in TV Guide.

The tactic worked. For the first time since the 1950s, the Republicans held a majority in Congress. Gingrich, who had a reputation for contentiousness, was elected Speaker of the House. Four years later, however, Republican members of Congress had grown exasperated by his confrontational (and unsuccessful) tactics and deposed him as Speaker when the Republicans nearly lost their majority in the 1998 election. The erosion of the majority occurred despite a year-long sex scandal that had plagued President Clinton.

As Republican members of the House of Representatives and citizens seeking to join that body, we propose not just to change its policies, but even more important to restore the bonds of trust between the people and their elected representatives.

That is why, in this era of official evasion and posturing, we offer instead a detailed agenda for national renewal, a written commitment with no fine print.

This year's election offers the chance, after four decades of one-party control, to bring to the House a new majority that will transform the way Congress works. That historic change would be the end of government that is too big, too intrusive, and too easy with the public's money. It can be the beginning of a Congress that respects the values and shares the faith of the American family.

Like Lincoln, our first Republican President, we intend to act with firmness in the right, as God gives us to see the right. To restore accountability to Congress. To end its cycle of scandal and disgrace. To make us all proud again of the way free people govern themselves.

On the first day of the 104th Congress, the new Republican majority will immediately pass the following major reforms, aimed at restoring the faith and trust of the American people in their government:

FIRST, require all laws that apply to the rest of the country also apply equally to the Congress;

SECOND, select a major, independent auditing firm to conduct a comprehensive audit of Congress for waste, fraud, or abuse;

THIRD, cut the number of House committees, and cut committee staff by one-third;

FOURTH, limit the terms of all committee chairs;

FIFTH; ban the casting of proxy votes in committee;

SIXTH, require committee meetings to be open to the public;

SEVENTH, require a three-fifths majority to vote to pass a tax increase;

EIGHTH, guarantee an honest accounting of our Federal Budget by implementing zero based budgeting...

Thereafter, within the first 100 days of the 104th Congress, we shall bring to the House floor the following bills, each to be given full and open debate, each to be given a clear and fair vote and each to be immediately available this day for public inspection and scrutiny:

The Fiscal Responsibility Act
A balanced budget/tax limitation amendment and a legislative line-item veto to restore fiscal responsibility to an out-of-control Congress, requiring it to live under the same budget constraints as families and businesses.

The Taking Back Our Streets Act

An anti-crime package including stronger truth-in-sentencing, "good faith" exclusionary rule exemptions, effective death-penalty provisions, and cuts in social spending from this summer's "crime" bill to fund prison construction and additional law enforcement to keep people secure in their neighborhoods and kids safe in their schools.

The Personal Responsibility Act
Discourage illegitimacy and teen pregnancy by prohibiting welfare to minor mothers and denying increased AFDC for additional children while on welfare, cut spending for welfare programs, and enact a tough two-years-and-out provision with work requirements to promote individual responsibility.

The Family Reinforcement Act
Child support enforcement, tax incentives for adoption, strengthening rights of parents in their children's education, stronger child pornography laws, and an elderly dependent-care tax credit to reinforce the central role of families in American society.

The American Dream Restoration Act
A $500-per-child tax credit; begin repeal of the marriage tax penalty, and creation of American Dream Savings Accounts to provide middle class tax relief.

The National Security Restoration Act
No U.S. troops under U.N. command and restoration of the essential parts of our national-security funding to strengthen our national defense and maintain our credibility around the world.

The Senior Citizens Fairness Act
Raise the Social Security earnings limit which currently forces seniors out of the work force, repeal the 1993 tax hikes on Social Security benefits and provide tax incentives for private long-term care insurance to let older Americans keep more of what they have earned over the years.

The Job Creation and Wage Enhancement Act
Small-business incentives, capital-gains cut and indexation, neutral-cost recovery, risk assessment/cost-benefit analysis, strengthening the Regularity Flexibility Act and unfunded mandate

reform to create jobs and raise worker wages.

The Common Sense Legal Reform Act
"Loser pays" laws, reasonable limits on punitive damages, and reform of product-liability laws to stem the endless tide of litigation.

The Citizen Legislature Act
A first-ever vote on term limits to replace career politicians with citizen legislators.

Further, we will instruct the House Budget Committee to report to the floor, and we will work to enact additional budget savings beyond the budget cuts specifically included in the legislation described above, to ensure that the Federal budget deficit will be less than it would have been without the enactment of these bills.

Respecting the judgment of our fellow citizens as we seek their mandate for reform, we hereby pledge our names to this Contract with America.

"I call it a fundamental break in the history of technology"

GEORGE GILDER

By the middle of the 1990s a new medium was emerging, connecting individuals across the globe via their personal computers. The Internet, originally an obscure governmental communications systems aimed at keeping defense engineers connected to each other, had grown into a national phenomenon.

Although computer users initially could only communicate conveniently with text messages, the development of the "World Wide Web" made computer telecommunications a far more viable and attractive means of communication. George Gilder, a supply-side economist and prophet of the emergence of the Internet, wrote about the rise of this new technology for *Forbes* magazine in 1995.

What will it take to launch a new Bill Gates—an Archimedean man who sharply shifts the center of the sphere, alters the axis of technology and economy, and builds a new business empire on new foundations? Who can inherit the imperial throne in the microcosm and telecosm currently held by the Redmond Rockefeller?

I will open the envelope in a minute. But first I want to tell you about a new software program

called Netscape Navigator Personal Edition. I brought it back from Silicon Valley in late June and put the package next to my PC. The PC was proudly running a beta version of Windows 95. I had presented Windows 95 with great fanfare to my 11-year-old son Richard as his route to the most thrilling new frontiers of the computer world. Multitasking, 32-bit operation, flat memory! Object linking and embedding! "Information at your fingertips!" But, all in all, he preferred his Mac Quadra 840AV or even Windows 3.1. They don't crash so often, he explained. I live out in the boondocks of western Massachusetts where there are no convenient full-service connections to the Internet. So I was much less excited about Netscape than I was about Windows 95. I hoped Windows 95 would put me on line through the Microsoft Network system. Some 10 minutes later, though, Richard wanted to know my credit car number so I could choose an Internet service provider. A couple of minutes after that, linked through internetMCI's 800 number, Richard was on the World Wide Web, using the InfoSeek service to examine my chapters from Telecosm on line, searching the secrets of Sim City 2000 at Maxis, exchanging messages with Microsoft Flight Simulator buffs, and exploring Disney. As far as I know, he is still there.

The next thing I knew, my brother Walter came by. He worked for a computer company, New World Technologies in Ashland, Mass., that builds customized Pentium machines and delivers them to value-added resellers within 48 hours. Walter wanted the Netscape program. He took it back to my parents' farm down the road and booted it up on a four-megabyte 386SX Dynatech previously used to map the pedigrees of a flock of Romney sheep. Soon he was on the Web scouting out the competition from Dell and Micron and showing off the Gilder Web page. This intrigued my 77-year-old mother, who had scarcely even noticed a computer before. I don't know how it happened, but before the night was out, she too was on the Web, exploring catalogs of British colleges for her namesake granddaughter who was soon to leave for London.

Now let me tell you about my introduction to Java, a new programming language that menaces Microsoft's software supremacy. I encountered Java in early June at a Sun Microsystems conference at the Westin St. Francis Hotel in downtown San

Francisco. For a speech I was to give, I had planned to use a multimedia presentation, complete with Macro-Mind Director images and QuickTime video that I had contrived with an expensive professional some months earlier. The complexities of Director prompted me to convert the program to Astound. However, it required an external disk drive and ran erratically with the eight megabytes of RAM on my PowerBook. I decided to speak nakedly from notes on the coming technologies of sand and glass and air.

Following me immediately to the stage was Sun's amiable chief scientist, John Gage. He decided to illustrate his speech entirely from the World Wide Web. He began with a handsome page, contrived minutes before, giving an account of my speech, headlined: "Gilder Addresses Sun, Tells of Technologies of Opaque Silicon and Transparent Silicon." Then he moved to the Gilder Telecosm archives run by Gordon Jacobson of Portman Communications at a Web site of the University of Pennsylvania's engineering school. Gage illustrated his talk with real-time reports on traffic conditions in San Diego (where I was about to go), weather conditions in Florida as a hurricane loomed, and developments on Wall Street as IBM bid for Lotus. He showed the Nasdaq ticker running across the screen. He showed animations of relevant charts, cute little Java gymnasts cartwheeling across the screen, three-dimensional interactive molecular models and an overflowing coffee cup, entitled "HotJava."

None of his information and images used a desktop presentation program, whether from MacroMind or from Microsoft. None of them used a database engine, whether SQL or Oracular. Indeed, except for the Gilder speech report, none were created beforehand. Incurring no memory or disk drive problems, Gage summoned all the illustrations to his PowerBook directly from the Internet. The animations employed a new computer language, Java, written for the Web by the venerable Sun programmer James Gosling. Java allows transmission of executable programs to any computer connected to the Net to be interpreted and played safely and securely in real time.

Clifford Stoll, calls it "Silicon snake oil." But I call it a fundamental break in the history of technology. It is the software complement of the hollowing out of the computer described in Forbes ASAP ("The

Bandwidth Tidal Wave," December 5, 1994). Almost overnight, the CPU and its software have become peripheral; the network, central. I had been working on a presentation on my desktop computer, using an array of presentation software. But Gage improvised a more impressive and animated presentation without using any desktop presentation programs at all. The World Wide Web and the Java language were enough. Restricted to the files of my computer, I struggled with storage problems and incompatible research formats, while he used the storage capacity and information resources of more than five million host computers on the Net....

So, open the envelope.

Let's find a new Bill Gates. Start by adding 100 pounds of extra heft, half a foot of height and two further years of schooling, then make him $12.9 billion hungrier. Give him a gargantuan appetite for pizza and Oreos, Bach, newsprint, algorithms, ideas, John Barth, Nabokov, images, Unix code, bandwidth. Give him a nearly unspellable Scandinavian name—Marc Andreessen.

Put him to work for $6.85 per hour at Illinois's National Center for Supercomputing Applications (NCSA) writing 3D visualization code on a Silicon Graphics Indy for a Thinking Machine C-5 or a Cray YMP16. Surround him on all sides by the most advanced computers and software in the world, under the leadership of cybernetic visionary Larry Smarr. What will happen next? "Boredom," Andreessen replies. Supercomputers, already at the end of their tether, turned out to be "underwhelming Unix machines."

Then, for a further image of the end of the world, take him in the fall of 1990 off to Austin, Tex., for two semesters at IBM. "They were going to take over the 3D graphics market, they were going to win the Malcolm Baldridge Award, they were going to blow Silicon Graphics [the regnant Silicon Valley 3D workstation company] off the map, all in six months." Andreessen began by doing performance analysis and moved on to work on the operating system kernel. In mid-1991, after constant delays, the company was finally ready to ship a world-beating 3D engine. But the new IBM machine turned out to be four times slower at seven times the price of the equivalent Silicon Graphics hardware that IBM had bundled a year and a half earlier with its RS6000 RISC (reduced instruction set computing) workstation. Austin IBM returned to the drawing board and Andreessen returned to Illinois to get his degree.

In both commercial and academic settings, Andreessen thus had the good fortune of working at the very heart of the old order of computing in its climactic phase. As Andreessen saw it, little of long-term interest was going on at either establishment. But both did command one huge and felicitous resource, vastly underused, and that was the Internet. "Designed for all the wrong reasons—to link some 2,000 scientists to a tiny number of supercomputers," it had exploded into a global ganglion thronged by millions of people and machines.

Many people saw the Internet as throbbing with hype and seething with problems—Clifford Stoll's book, *Silicon Snake Oil*, catalogs many: the lack of security, substance, reliability, bandwidth, easy access, the presence of porn, fraud, frivolity and freaks guarantees, so he says, that no serious business can depend on it for critical functions. But to Andreessen the problems of the Internet are only the other side of its incredible virtues.

"By usual standards," says Andreessen, "the Internet was far from perfect. But the Internet finds its own perfection—in the millions of people that are able to use it and the hundreds of thousands who can provide services for it." To Andreessen, all the problems signaled that he was at the center of the sphere, gazing in wild surmise at "a giant hole in the middle of the world"—the supreme opportunity of the age.

Andreessen saw that, for all its potential, there was a monstrous incongruity at the heart of the Internet. Its access software was at least 10 years behind. "PC Windows had penetrated all the desktops, the Mac was a huge success, and point-and-click interfaces had become part of everyday life. But to use the Net you still had to understand Unix. You had to type FTP [file transfer protocol] commands by hand and you had to be able to do addressmapping in your head between IP addresses and host names and you had to know where all the FTP archives were, you had to understand IRC [Internet relay chat] protocols, you had to know how to use this particular news reader and that particular Unix shell prompt, and you pretty much had to know Unix itself to get anything done. And the current users had little interest in making it easier. In fact, there was a definite element of not wanting to make it easier, of actually wanting to keep the riffraff out."...

[The] real opportunity was to open the Internet to the world and the world to the Internet, and that would require more than a facility for cruising through textual materials. After all, the bulk of human bandwidth is in a person's eyes and ears. For absorbing text, as Robert Lucky, author of *Silicon Dreams*, has pointed out, the speed limit is only some 55 bits per second.

To burst open the Internet would require reaching out to the riffraff who travel through pictures and sounds at megahertz speeds. To critics of a more vulgar Net, such as Stoll, more riffraff sending a callipygian naked-lady bitmaps and voluminous digital ululations from the Grateful Dead and QuickTime first-step baby videos traipsing down the lines and wriggling through the routers would soon cause a gigantic crash. Even some of Andreessen's main allies at the NCSA shared some of these fears. At CERN, Berners-Lee opposed images and video on these grounds. The technologists all held a narrowband view of the world, imagining bandwidth as an essentially scarce resource to be carefully husbanded by responsible citizens of the cybersphere.

So Tim Berners-Lee alone could not burst open the Internet pinata and give it to the world. As Richard Wiggins, author of *Internet for Everyone: A Guide for Users and Providers*, observes, "During 1992 and early 1993, graphical Gopher clients for the Macintosh and Windows evolved, and it appeared that Gopher would outstrip the fledgling Web." It was the ultimate broadband booster, Marc Andreessen, working with NCSA colleague Eric Bina, who ignited the Web rocket. One late December night in 1992 at the Espresso Royale cafe in Champaign-Urbana, Andreessen looked his friend Eric Bina in the eye and said: "Let's go for it."

Every Gates has to have his Paul Allen (or Jobs, his Steve Wozniak). Andreessen's is Bina—short and wiry where Andreessen is ursine, cautious where he is cosmic, focused where he is expansive, apprehensive where he is evangelical, bitwise where he is prodigal with bandwidth, ready to stay home and write the code where Andreessen is moving on to conquer the globe. Wildly contrasting but completely trusting and complementary, these two—in an inspired siege of marathon code-wreaking between January and March 1993—made Mosaic happen. A rich image-based program for accessing the World Wide Web and other parts of the Internet, Mosaic requires no more knowledge of its internal mechanics than is needed by the user of the steering wheel of a car. With a mere 9,000 lines of code (compared to Windows 95's 11 million lines, including 3 million lines of MSN code), Mosaic would become the most rapidly propagated software program ever written.

Andreessen could defy all the fears of an Internet image crash because he lived in a world of bandwidth abundance and fiber galore. He fully grasped the law of the telecosm. Every new host computer added to the Net would not only use the Net; it would also be a new resource for it, providing a new route for the bits and new room to store them. Every new flood of megabyte bitmaps would make the Net more interesting, useful and attractive, and increase the pressure for backbones running at gigabits per second and above. The Internet must be adapted to people with eyes and ears. They won't abuse it, he assured Bina without a smile. After all, he knew he would have to rely on Bina for much of the graphics coding.

"I was right," Bina says now. "People abused it horribly. People would scan in a page of PostScript text in a bitmap, taking over a megabyte to display a page that would take maybe 1,000 bytes of text. But Marc was also right. As a result of the glitz and glitter, thousands of people wasted time to put in pretty pictures and valuable information on the Web, and millions of people use it."…

In the end, they had created an entirely new interface for the Internet and new communications software to render it crisply accessible—a look and feel that almost immediately struck everyone who used it as an amazing breakthrough. In February 1995, Bob Metcalfe wrote a column in *InfoWorld* predicting that Web browsers would become, in effect, the dominant operating system for the next era.

Browsers are now ubiquitous. Every major company and many minor ones are building them. Some eight million people use them. IBM, AT&T, Novell, Microsoft, NetCom, Sun, Silicon Graphics, America Online, Net-Manage, Quarterdeck, Quadralay, Apple, SPRYNET, CompuServe, Frontier Technologies, Delphi, MCI, Wollongong, even the Spyglass spinoff from the NCSA—you name it—all these companies are building, licensing, enhancing or bundling a browser. Many of these ventures, led by Quarterdeck's smart hotlists and "drag-and-drop" ease of use, have outpaced Mosaic and prompted a

leapfrogging contest of can-you-top-this.

That is what happens when an entrepreneur performs a truly revolutionary act, supplies the smallest missing factor, as Peter Drucker puts it, that can transform a jumble of elements into a working system—the minimal mutation that provokes a new paradigm. In 1977, the relevant jumble was small computers, microprocessors and assembly language programming. Bill Gates and Paul Allen supplied the key increment: software tools and the Basic language for the embryonic personal computer. In 1993, Andreessen and Bina set out to supply the minimal increment to convert the entire Net, with its then one to two million linked computers (today it's an estimated seven million computers) and immense information resources, into a domain as readily accessible to an 11-year-old as a hard drive or CD-ROM on a Mac or Windows PC.

As a result, the same forces of exploding bandwidth, the same laws of the telecosm that are wreaking revolution in hardware, hollowing out the computer—rendering the CPU peripheral and the network central—are also transforming software. All forms of desktop software—operating systems, applications and utilities—are becoming similarly peripheral. The ever-growing gigapedal resources of the Internet will always dwarf any powers and functions that can be distilled on a desktop or mobilized on the backplane of a supercomputer.

"William Jefferson Clinton is acquitted"

SUPREME COURT CHIEF JUSTICE WILLIAM REHNQUIST

On December 19, 1998, the House of Representatives passed two articles of impeachment against President Bill Clinton on charges related to an adulterous affair he had with White House intern Monica Lewisnky. The impeachment articles—two of which had been rejected by the House—came about after an extended investigation by Special Prosecutor Kenneth Starr. Although Starr had initially been asked to investigate possible wrongdoing over a failed real estate deal while Clinton had been governor of Arkansas in the early 1980s, he had expanded the scope of his investigation, leading to highly charged accusations of Republican partisanship.

After a three-week Senate trial presided over by Supreme Court Chief Justice William Rehnquist, the Senate voted February 12 on the articles of impeachment. Requiring a two-thirds majority for approval, both failed. The following is the text of the articles, followed by Rehnquist's announcement of the results of each vote.

Resolved, That William Jefferson Clinton, President of the United States, is impeached for high crimes and misdemeanors and that the following articles of impeachment be exhibited to the United States Senate:

Articles of impeachment exhibited by the House of Representatives of the United States of America in the name of itself and of the people of the United States of America, against William Jefferson Clinton, President of the United States of America, in maintenance and support of its impeachment against him for high crimes and misdemeanors.

Article I

In his conduct while President of the United States, William Jefferson Clinton, in violation of his constitutional oath faithfully to execute the office of President of the United States and, to the best of his ability, preserve, protect and defend the Constitution of the United States, and in violation of his constitutional duty to take care that the laws be faithfully executed, has willfully corrupted and manipulated the judicial process of the United States for his personal gain and exoneration, impeding the administration of justice, in that:

On August 17, 1998, William Jefferson Clinton swore to tell the truth, the whole truth and nothing but the truth before a Federal grand jury of the United States. Contrary to that oath, William Jefferson Clinton willfully provided perjurious, false and misleading testimony to the grand jury concerning one or more of the following: (1) the nature and details of his relationship with a subordinate Government employee; (2) prior perjurious, false and misleading testimony he gave in a Federal civil rights action brought against him; (3) prior false and misleading statements he allowed his attorney to make to a Federal judge in that civil rights action; and (4) his corrupt efforts to influence the testimony of witnesses and to impede the discovery of evidence in that civil rights action.

In doing this, William Jefferson Clinton has undermined the integrity of his office, has brought disrepute on the Presidency, has betrayed his trust as President and has acted in a manner subversive of the rule of law and justice, to the manifest injury of the people of the United States.

Wherefore, William Jefferson Clinton, by such conduct, warrants impeachment and trial, and removal from office and disqualification to hold and enjoy any office of honor, trust or profit under the United States.

CHIEF JUSTICE WILLIAM REHQUIST: "On this article of impeachment, 45 Senators having pronounced William Jefferson Clinton, President of the United States, guilty as charged, 55 Senators having pronounced him not guilty, two-thirds of the Senators present not having pronounced him guilty, the Senate adjudges that the respondent, William Jefferson Clinton, President of the United States, is not guilty as charged in the first article of impeachment."

Article III

In his conduct while President of the United States, William Jefferson Clinton, in violation of his constitutional oath faithfully to execute the office of President of the United States and, to the best of his ability, preserve, protect and defend the Constitution of the United States, and in violation of his constitutional duty to take care that the laws be faithfully executed, has prevented, obstructed and impeded the administration of justice, and has to that end engaged personally, and through his subordinates and agents, in a course of conduct or scheme designed to delay, impede, cover up and conceal the existence of evidence and testimony related to a Federal civil rights action brought against him in a duly instituted judicial proceeding.

The means used to implement this course of conduct or scheme included one or more of the following acts:

(1) On or about December 17, 1997, William Jefferson Clinton corruptly encouraged a witness in a Federal civil rights action brought against him to execute a sworn affidavit in that proceeding that he knew to be perjurious, false and misleading.

(2) On or about December 17, 1997, William Jefferson Clinton corruptly encouraged a witness in a Federal civil rights action brought against him to give perjurious, false and misleading testimony if

and when called to testify personally in that proceeding.

(3) On or about December 28, 1997, William Jefferson Clinton corruptly engaged in, encouraged or supported a scheme to conceal evidence that had been subpoenaed in a Federal civil rights action brought against him.

(4) Beginning on or about December 7, 1997, and continuing through and including January 14, 1998, William Jefferson Clinton intensified and succeeded in an effort to secure job assistance to a witness in a Federal civil rights action brought against him in order to corruptly prevent the truthful testimony of that witness in that proceeding at a time when the truthful testimony of that witness would have been harmful to him.

(5) On January 17, 1998, at his deposition in a Federal civil rights action brought against him, William Jefferson Clinton corruptly allowed his attorney to make false and misleading statements to a Federal judge characterizing an affidavit, in order to prevent questioning deemed relevant by the judge. Such false and misleading statements were subsequently acknowledged by his attorney in a communication to that judge.

(6) On or about January 18 and January 20-21, 1998, William Jefferson Clinton related a false and misleading account of events relevant to a Federal civil rights action brought against him to a potential witness in that proceeding, in order to corruptly influence the testimony of that witness.

(7) On or about January 21, 23 and 26, 1998, William Jefferson Clinton made false and misleading statements to potential witnesses in a Federal grand jury proceeding in order to corruptly influence the testimony of those witnesses. The false and misleading statements made by William

Jefferson Clinton were repeated by the witnesses to the grand jury, causing the grand jury to receive false and misleading information.

In all of this, William Jefferson Clinton has undermined the integrity of his office, has brought disrepute on the Presidency, has betrayed his trust as President and has acted in a manner subversive of the rule of law and justice, to the manifest injury of the people of the United States.

Wherefore, William Jefferson Clinton, by such conduct, warrants impeachment and trial, and removal from office and disqualification to hold and enjoy any office of honor, trust or profit under the United States.

CHIEF JUSTICE REHQUIST: "On this article of impeachment, 50 Senators having pronounced William Jefferson Clinton, President of the United States, guilty as charged, 50 Senators having pronounced him not guilty, two-thirds of the Senators present not having pronounced him guilty, the Senate adjudges that the respondent, William Jefferson Clinton, President of the United States, is not guilty as charged in the second article of impeachment.

The Chair directs judgment to be entered in accordance with the judgment of the Senate as follows:

The Senate, having tried William Jefferson Clinton, President of the United States, upon two articles of impeachment exhibited against him by the House of Representatives, and two-thirds of the Senators present not having found him guilty of the charges contained therein: it is, therefore, ordered and adjudged that the said William Jefferson Clinton be, and he is hereby, acquitted of the charges in this said article.

Index

Ashbridge, Elizabeth, 97-100

Ashley River, 67

Asia, post-WWII analysis of, 686-689

Assembly line, 520

Astronauts, 779

Astronomy, 227

Athletic programs, 789

Atlanta Constitution, 437

Atlantic Monthly, 373, 385

Atlantic Ocean, 402, 534

Atom bomb, development of, 635-636; dropping of, 663-665

Atomic energy, control of, 666-667

Attorney General, 181

Auditorium Building, Chicago, 485

Aute, 31

Author of Her Book, 60

Autobiography of Malcolm X, 562-563

Automobile industry, 751-753

Automobiles, 520, 710, 751-753, 754

Avarice, 242, 824-825

Avary, Myrta Lockett, 384-385

Aviation, 573-576, 576

Aztecs, 33

B

Baby and Child Care, 674-676

"Baby boom", 674

"Back to Africa" movement, 562, 563

Bailey, Frederick. *See* Douglass, Frederick

Balance of power, 171

Ball, Lucille, 702-704

Baltimore Sun, 568

Baltimore, Lord, 53

Baltimore, Maryland, 211

Bancroft, 245-247

Bank of England, 521

Bank of North America, 134, 190

Banking, 134, 190, 237-239, 254, 255, 521

Banks, Joseph, 151

Banks, Nathaniel, General, 371

Baptist Church, 50

Barbe-Marbois, Marquis de, 151

Barlow, Joel, 186

Bartholdi, Frédéric Auguste, 432

Baruch, Bernard, 666-667

Baseball, 276-277, 514, 619

Bates, Edwin, 381-382

Bates, Katharine Lee, 473

Battin, William, 72

Battle Hymn of the Republic, 366-367

Battle of Bloody Marsh, 81

Battle of Fort Wagner, 364

Battle of Horseshoe Bend, 215

Battle of the Thames, 215

Battle of Tippecanoe, 215

Battle of Yellow Tavern, 371

Bayard, James, 200

Beauregard, General, 348

Beecher, Catherine, 229-230

Bell, Alexander Graham, 416

Bell Labs, 576-577

Bell Systems, 444

Bell Telephone Company, 416

Bellamy, Edward, 449

Benefits to veterans, 588, 654-658

Benjamin, Judah, 379-380

Bering, Vitus, 76

Bering Straits, 76

Berlin, 726-727

Berlin Wall, 828

Bernstein, Carl, 795

Berry, Chuck, 706

Lands, 383

Burr, Aaron, 197, 209-210; Trial, 209

Bush, George, President, 837-838

Business, 581-584, ethics, 824-825; government control, 593; government intervention in, 581-584, 741, 807-809; merit-based advancement, 776-777; protection of, 570-572; recovery measures, 593-596

Byrd, William, 75

C

C. S. A. *See* Confederate States of America

Cabeza de Vaca, Alver Nunez, 30

Cabinet officers, 397

Calamity Jane, 428-431

Calhoun, John C., 210, 254-256, 303-305

California Gold Rush, 309

California Red Flag Law, 548

California, 36, 241, 250-252, 301, 411, 517, 626; migration to, 607-608

Call of the Wild, 497

Calley, Jr., William, Lieutenant, 772

Calvert Family, 53

Calvinism, 79

Campbell, Helen, 471-473

Cane Ridge, KY., 206

Cannary, Martha. *See* Calamity Jane

Cannassatego, Chief, 80

Capahowosick, 41

Cape Horn, 250

Capitalism, 824-825

Capone, Al, 550

Caribbean Islands, 30

Carnegie, Andrew, 451

Carnegie Steel Company, 452

Carpenter, Helen, 319-320

"Carpetbaggers", 386, 416

Carrier, Willis, H., 598-599

Cars. *See* Automobiles

Carson, Christopher "Kit", 241-242, 319

Carson, Rachel, 722-723

Cartwright, Alexander, 276-277

Carver, John, 43, 46

Catholics, discrimination against, 244-245

Cavelier, Robert, Sieur de la Salle, 61

Cayugas, 29

Censure, 255

Central America, 356

Central Pacific Railroad, 402

Central Park, New York, 404

Century of Dishonor, 425

Cevola, 34

Chamberlain, Daniel H., Governor, 416, 417

Champlain, Samuel de, 41

Charles I, King, 91

Charles II, King, 60

Charleston, South Carolina, 86, 348, 363

Charlestown, Massachusetts, 120

"Charlie Company" (C/1-20), 772

Charlotte Temple, 187

Charter of Freedoms and Exemptions to Patroons, 48-49

Checkers (cocker spaniel), 692-693

"Checkers" speech, 689-695

Cherokee Nation, 28-29, 220, 256; Creation myth, 28-29

Chesapeake and Ohio Railroad, 403

Chester, 137

Chestnut, Mary, 340, 380-381

Cheyenne Indians, 374-375, 413, 425

"Chicago (poem)", 685

Chicago, Illinois, 485; 685; Great Fire, 485

Child rearing, 674-676

G

G.I. Bill, 654-658

Galloway, Joseph, 116

Galunlati, 28

Gamio, Manuel, 506

Gandhi, 286

Gangsters, 550, 586

Garcia, Jesús, 506-508

Garfield, James, President, 431; assassination of, 431

Garland, Hamlin, 413

Garrick Theater, Chicago, 485

Garrison, William Lloyd, 233-234, 257, 417

Garvey, Marcus, 562, 563

Gates, William (Bill), 826

Gay, Edwin W. 580-581

Gehrig, Lou, 619

Gender stereotyping, 777-778

General Electric, 444

Geographical Reader for the Dixie Children, 353

George III, King, 110, 114, 116, 137, 150

Georgia, 80, 83, 84, 116, 233; Trustees of, 83

Germantown, 62

Germany, 235, 244, 533, 534-542; division of, 660-661; Nazi, 573, 639, 644

Gettysburg, Pennsylvania, 361-362, 363, 366; Address, 366; Battle of, 361-362, 363, 366, 372

Ghost Dance, 461

Gilbert, Humphry, Sir, 37

"Gilded Age", 448

Gildner, George, 846-849

Gingrich, Newt, 828, 844-846

Girl Scouts, 517

"Give me liberty or give me death", 117-119

Give My Regards to Broadway, 537

God Save the King, 237

Gold Rush, 309, 413

Gold standard, 483

Goldwater, Barry, 743-746

Gompers, Samuel, 458-460

Gone with the Wind (movie), 566

"Gonzo journalism", 753

Gooding, James Henry, Corporal, 364-366

Gorbachev, Mikhail, 828

Gorney, Jay, 585

Grace, James W., Captain, 364-366

Grady, Henry W., 437-440

Graham, Benjamin, 602-604

Grand Banks, Newfoundland, 518

Grand Canyon, 513

Grant, Ulysses S., President, 371, 372-373, 375, 377-378, 416-417, 423

Grapes of Wrath, 607-608

Grasse, Comte de, 145

Gray, Daniel, 155

Gray, Thomas, 235-236

Great Awakening, 78, 79; Second, 206

Great Britain, 210, 282, 533, 638-640

"Great Compromiser". *See* Clay, Henry

Great Depression. *See* Depressions (1929)

"Great Migration", 533

Greed. *See* Avarice

Greeley, Horace, 358-359

Greene, J. W., 309

Grimké, Angelina, 257-259

Griswold, Erwin, Solicitor General, 783

Groves, George, 576-578

Grundy, Felix, 210-211

Guam, 490

Gulf of Tonkin Resolution, 746

Gunboat diplomacy, 504

Guthrie, Woody, 586, 706-707

74-76, 80-82, 92-96, 122-123, 156, 204, 208, 210, 220-222, 241, 401, 402, 409, 413, 425, 443, 468; 596-598; 784-787, 787-789; massacres of, 374, 461; religion, 208, 461; relocation of, 256-257, 313, 422

Nature, 233, 315, 513

Navy, American, 144

Navy, British, 144, 210

Neal, Joseph, 66

Negroes, 58, 83, 84, 85, 87, 90

Neighborhoods, 800-802

Neihardt, John G. 596

Neuces River, 284

Neutrality, 632-635, 636,

Neutrality Act of 1937, 632-635

Nevada, 370-371

New Bedford Mercury, 364-366

New Colossus, 432

"New Deal", 589, 591, 593-596

New England, 233

New England Primer (1690), 64

New Harmony, Indiana, 228, 264

New Harmony Gazette, 236-237

New Jersey, 128-129, 154; Constitution, 128-129

New Journalism, 779

New Mexico, 92

New Netherlands, 48, 53

New Orleans Tribune, 390-391

New Orleans, Battle of, 213, 215-216

New York, 77, 129, 145, 147, 154, 169, 171, 235; Assembly, 116

New York City, 90, 169, 226, 448, 471, 509; Draft riots in, 363; Lower East Side, 457

New York Daily Times, 307-308

New York Evening Post, 242, 509

New York Knickerbockers (Baseball team), 276

New York Nine (Baseball team), 276

New York Radical Women, 777

New York Times v. United States, 783-784

New York Times, 783

New York Tribune, 358, 457

New York Weekly Journal, 77

New York Yankees, 619

Newport, Rhode Island, 50, 448

News correspondents, 638-640, 651-652

Newspapers. *See* Press

Nez Perce Indians, 204, 422

Nicaragua, 826; military intervention in, 570-572

Nields, Jr., John W., 826-828

Nigeria, 87

Nisei Daughter, 647-649

Nixon, Richard M. President, 689-695, 711-713, 782-783, 784-787; articles of impeachment, 795-796; letter of resignation, 798

Nixon-Kennedy Debate, 711-713

Nobel Prize, 451

Nobel Prize speech (1950), 684-685

Non-Intercourse Act, 210

Nonviolence, 708, 730-733

North American Review, 452

North Atlantic Treaty, 672-674

North Atlantic Treaty Organization (NATO), 672-674

North Carolina, 105-107, 159; Assembly, 111

North Star, 289

North, Oliver, Colonel, 826-828

Northwest Ordinance, 156-159

Norway, 235

Norworth, Jack, 514

Notes on Virginia, 151-152

Noyes, John, 298-299

Nuclear reactions, 635-636

War of 1812, 171, 208, 210-212, 213, 215, 220

"War on Poverty", 741-743

War Powers Resolution, 794-795

"War to end all wars", 540

Warner Brothers, 576

Warren Commission Report, 735-739

Warren, Earl, Supreme Court Justice, 698-700, 701

Warren, Joseph, 119, 120

Warren, Mary, 66

Washington, Booker T., 479481

Washington, George, President, 107-109, 116, 121-122, 129, 142, 148-150, 159, 166, 174-175, 180-181, 187, 190, 191-195, 197, 208; Farewell Address, 191-195; Inaugural Address, First, 180-181; *Great Rule*, 191

Washington, Martha, 121

Washington (District of Columbus), 433; encampment by veterans, 588

Washington Post, 783

Waskow, Henry T., Captain, 651-652

Watergate, 795

Watson, Thomas, 416

Wayland Seminary, 479

"We the people", 159

Wealth, 242-244, 254, 277, 309, 445, 448, 449, 452, 521, 580-581; 831-833, 835; redistribution of, 608-610

Weaver, Robert, 466

Webster, Daniel, Senator, 237-239, 305-307, 314

Welch, Joseph, Senator, 696-698

Werowocomoco, 40

West Orange, New Jersey, 444

West, The, 227, 241, 256, 270, 281, 284-286, 320, 411, 423, 468

Western Federation of Miners, 526

Western Front, 538

Western Hemisphere, 223

Wheelwright, Mr., 51

"When in the course of human events", 129

Whiskey Rebellion, 187-188

White House, 213, 532

White supremacy, 560-562

White, E. B., 636-638

White, Elihah, 319

Whitman, Walt, 367-370, 423-425

Whitney, Eli, 444

Whittier, John Greenleaf, 312

Wigglesworth, Michael, 55

Wild West Show, 401

Willard, Emma, 229

Williams College, 245

Williams, Abigail, 66

Williams, Roger, 49-50

Williamsburg, Virginia, 117

Wilson, James, 159, 167-169, 399

Wilson, Woodrow, President, 483, 516, 521, 524, 528-529, 532, 533-537, 540, 546

Winslow, Governor, 50

Winthrop, John, Governor, 47, 50-52

Wirt, William, 117

Witchcraft, 64-67

Wives, 43

Wolfe, Tom, 779-780

Woman Suffrage Association, 410

Woman Suffrage Convention (1868), 391

Woman's Peace Party, 451

Women, 132, 184-185, 229; 576; higher education for, 229; rights, 228, 258, 295-297, 297, 391; status of, 757-759, 759-763, 763-764, 777-778, 778-779, 843-844; suffrage, 295, 428, 518, 532; 556; workers, 280

Women and the New Race, 556-558